THE ANCIENT ISRAELITE WORLD

This volume presents a collection of studies by international experts on various aspects of ancient Israel's society, economy, religion, language, culture, and history, synthesizing archaeological remains and integrating them with discussions of ancient Near Eastern and biblical texts.

Driven by theoretically and methodologically informed discussions of the archaeology of the Iron Age Levant, the 47 chapters in *The Ancient Israelite World* provide foundational, accessible, and detailed studies in their respective topics. The volume considers the history of interpretation of ancient Israel, studies on various aspects of ancient Israel's society and history, and avenues for present and future approaches to the ancient Israelite world. Accompanied by over 150 maps and figures, it allows the reader to gain an understanding of key issues that archaeologists, historians, and biblical scholars have faced and are currently facing as they attempt to better understand ancient Israelite society.

The Ancient Israelite World is an essential reference work for students and scholars of ancient Israel and its history, culture, and society, whether they are historians, archaeologists, or biblical scholars.

Kyle H. Keimer is an Honorary Senior Research Fellow in the Archaeology, History, and Language of Ancient Israel at Macquarie University, Australia. He co-edited *Registers and Modes of Communication in the Ancient Near East: Getting the Message Across* and is co-editing *"See the Whole Land is Before You": New Directions in the Historical Geography of the Ancient Near East*. His research focuses on integrating the archaeology of ancient Israel and the biblical texts. He also co-directed excavations at Khirbet el-Ra'i, Israel.

George A. Pierce is Associate Professor of Ancient Scripture at Brigham Young University, USA. He recently co-edited *"To Explore the Land of Canaan:" Studies in Honor of Jeffrey R. Chadwick*. His research interests include environmental reconstruction, regional settlement patterns, and digital application in archaeology. He is the supervisor of the GIS team for the Tel Shimron excavations, Israel.

THE ROUTLEDGE WORLDS

THE TOKUGAWA WORLD
Edited by Gary P. Leupp and De-min Tao

THE INUIT WORLD
Edited by Pamela Stern

THE ARTHURIAN WORLD
Edited by Miriam Edlich-Muth, Renée Ward, and Victoria Coldham-Fussell

THE MONGOL WORLD
Edited by Timothy May and Michael Hope

THE SÁMI WORLD
Edited by Sanna Valkonen, Áile Aikio, Saara Alakorva, and Sigga-Marja Magga

THE WORLD OF THE ANCIENT SILK ROAD
Edited by Xinru Liu with the assistance of Pia Brancaccio

THE WORLD OF THE BAHÁ'Í FAITH
Edited By Robert H. Stockman

THE QUAKER WORLD
Edited by C. Wess Daniels and Rhiannon Grant

THE ANCIENT ISRAELITE WORLD
Edited by Kyle H. Keimer and George A. Pierce

https://www.routledge.com/Routledge-Worlds/book-series/WORLDS

THE ANCIENT ISRAELITE WORLD

Edited by Kyle H. Keimer and George A. Pierce

LONDON AND NEW YORK

Cover image: Zev Radovan, BibleLandPictures.com

First published 2023
by Routledge
4 Park Square, Milton Park, Abingdon, Oxon OX14 4RN

and by Routledge
605 Third Avenue, New York, NY 10158

Routledge is an imprint of the Taylor & Francis Group, an informa business

© 2023 selection and editorial matter, Kyle H. Keimer and George A. Pierce; individual chapters, the contributors

The right of Kyle H. Keimer and George A. Pierce to be identified as the author of the editorial material, and of the authors for their individual chapters, has been asserted in accordance with sections 77 and 78 of the Copyright, Designs and Patents Act 1988.

All rights reserved. No part of this book may be reprinted or reproduced or utilised in any form or by any electronic, mechanical, or other means, now known or hereafter invented, including photocopying and recording, or in any information storage or retrieval system, without permission in writing from the publishers.

Trademark notice: Product or corporate names may be trademarks or registered trademarks, and are used only for identification and explanation without intent to infringe.

British Library Cataloguing-in-Publication Data
A catalogue record for this book is available from the British Library

Library of Congress Cataloging-in-Publication Data
Names: Keimer, Kyle H., editor. | Pierce, George A., editor.
Title: The ancient Israelite world / edited by Kyle H. Keimer and George A. Pierce.
Description: Abingdon, Oxon; New York, NY: Routledge, 2023. | Series: Routledge worlds | Includes bibliographical references and index. |
Identifiers: LCCN 2022021077 (print) | LCCN 2022021078 (ebook) | ISBN 9780367406844 (hardback) | ISBN 9781032349732 (paperback) | ISBN 9780367815691 (ebook)
Subjects: CYAC: Palestine-Civilivation. | Jews-History-To 70 A.D.
Classification: LCC DS121.3 .A53 2023 (print) | LCC DS121.3 (ebook) | DDC 933/.4-dc23/eng/20220511
LC record available at https://lccn.loc.gov/2022021077
LC ebook record available at https://lccn.loc.gov/2022021078

ISBN: 978-0-367-40684-4 (hbk)
ISBN: 978-1-032-34973-2 (pbk)
ISBN: 978-0-367-81569-1 (ebk)

DOI: 10.4324/9780367815691

Typeset in Bembo
by codeMantra

To Elizabeth, Cayley, Annabelle, and Hannah. I love you guys in a circle. *KHK*

To Krystal, Victoria, and Geo. I love you guys four-square. *GAP*

CONTENTS

List of figures xii
List of tables xix
List of contributors xx
Abbreviations xxv
Preface xxx

1 An Introduction to the Ancient Israelite World: The State of the Field and Future Directions 1
  Kyle H. Keimer and George A. Pierce

PART I
Backgrounds and Methodological Considerations 13

2 The Historical Geography of Ancient Israel: The Amalekite Spoil List (1 Sam 30:27–31) as a Case Study 15
  Chris McKinny

3 Competing Chronologies, Competing Histories: Ancient Israel and the Chronology of the Southern Levant ca. 1200–587 BCE 34
  Koert van Bekkum

4 The Historian and the Assemblage: On the Interpretation of Texts and Artifacts for the History of Ancient Israel 54
  Daniel Pioske

5 Between the Biblical Story and History: Writing an Archaeological History of Ancient Israel 67
  Avraham Faust

Contents

6	Texts, Archaeology, and Ethnicity: Identifying Ancient Israel *William G. Dever*	83

PART II
Material Culture   **99**

7	A Technological and Sociological Perspective on Ancient Israelite Pottery *Nava Panitz-Cohen*	101
8	Domestic Architecture, the Household, and Daily Life in Iron Age Israel *Jeffrey R. Zorn*	119
9	Monuments, Monumental Architecture, and Monumentality in Ancient Israel *Kyle H. Keimer*	142
10	Stone Volutes: United by a Common Motif not by a Common Function *Norma Franklin*	156
11	From Urban Centers into Mounds of Ruins: The Destruction of Cities during the Iron Age *Igor Kreimerman*	175
12	Regional Continuity and Change in Ancient Israel: An Analysis of Iron Age Settlement Patterns and Systems *George A. Pierce*	189

PART III
Society and Economy   **207**

13	Ancient Israel's Social Structure(s) *Gunnar Lehmann*	209
14	Tribal Kingdoms and the Tribal Element in Southern Levantine Iron Age Polities *Øystein S. LaBianca and Jeffrey P. Hudon*	224
15	Israel's Political and Administrative Structures in the Pre-Monarchic and Monarchic Periods *Zachary Thomas*	236

Contents

16 The Judahite Economy in First Temple Times: Remodeling the House of David—A Case Study from Tell en-Naṣbeh ... 251
Aaron Brody

17 The Socioeconomics of Food and Feasting in Pre-Exilic Israel and Judah ... 263
Rebekah Welton

18 Gender in Ancient Israel ... 277
Jennie Ebeling

19 Children in Ancient Israel ... 291
Kristine Henriksen Garroway

20 Social Issues in the Establishment of Biblical Law in the Iron Age ... 305
Eckart Otto

21 Warfare and Intelligence Gathering in Ancient Israel ... 317
Charlie Trimm

PART IV
Language ... **333**

22 Literacy and Scribalism in Israel during the Iron Age (ca. 1200/1150–586 BCE) ... 335
Matthieu Richelle

23 More than the Sum of Their Parts: Multimodality and the Study of Iron Age Inscriptions ... 348
Alice Mandell

24 Socio-political Gleanings from Northwest Semitic Paleography: The Inscriptions from Tel Reḥov, as a Test Case ... 363
Nathaniel E. Greene

25 Language in Israel and Judah: A Sociolinguistic Reappraisal ... 384
Timothy Hogue

26 The Composition of the Hebrew Bible: Process in the Production of Israelite Literature ... 404
Joel S. Baden

PART V
Religion   **419**

27 Religion in the House in Ancient Israel   421
   Jeremy D. Smoak

28 Visual Culture and Religion in Ancient Israel and Judah   434
   Christoph Uehlinger

29 The Archaeology of Israelite Cult: Yahwisms across Space and Time   464
   George A. Pierce and Kyle H. Keimer

30 The Role of Ritual in Biblical Narrative   480
   Dan Belnap

31 Israelite Prophecy from Its Origins to the Exile   494
   Shawn Zelig Aster

32 Death and Afterlife   505
   Christopher B. Hays

PART VI
Israel Among the Nations   **521**

33 Amorites and Canaanites: Memory, Tradition, and Legacy in Ancient Israel and Judah   523
   Aaron A. Burke

34 New Kingdom Egypt and Early Israel: Entangled Identities   537
   Aaron A. Burke

35 Philistines and Israelites/Judahites: Antagonism and Interaction   549
   Aren M. Maeir

36 Early Interactions between the Arameans and Israelites   565
   Scott W. Booth

37 Phoenicians and Ancient Israel   582
   Ilan Sharon

38 Ammonites in the World of Israel   600
   Randall W. Younker

39	The Invention of Ancient Moab *Benjamin W. Porter*	619
40	Edom and Southern Jordan in the Iron Age *Juan Manuel Tebes*	639
41	Egypt and the Levant in the Third Intermediate Period (Iron IB–IIIA): Fragmentation, Foreignness, and Fungibility *Krystal V. L. Pierce*	658
42	Reconstructing the Kushite Royal House: The Chronology of Egypt's 25th Dynasty and Its Relation to Judah *Jeremy Pope*	675
43	Israel and Assyria, Judah and Assyria *Ido Koch*	693
44	Babylon and Israel: Cultural Contact and Cultural Impact *Laurie E. Pearce*	713

PART VII
The Legacy and Future of Ancient Israel — 729

45	The Future of Studying Ancient Israel: Insights from the Archaeological Sciences with a Focus on Food and Society *Lidar Sapir-Hen*	731
46	Cyber-Archaeology and the Study of Ancient Edom and Israel *Matthew D. Howland and Thomas E. Levy*	741
47	Israel, Ancient and Modern: Representations and Misrepresentations of the Past in Dialogue with the Present *Rachel Hallote*	756

Index — 777

FIGURES

1.1	Map of the ancient Near East (map by George A. Pierce)	4
1.2	Map of ancient Israel (map by George A. Pierce)	5
2.1	Map of sites mentioned in 1 Sam 30:27–31	16
6.1	Pillar-base figurine, Lachish III. Accession no.: 34.126.53. Gift of Harris D., and H. Dunscombe Colt, 1934. The Metropolitan Museum of Art	88
6.2	8th cent. BCE Judahite shekel weights (Kletter 1999: figure 6; used with permission)	88
6.3	12th cent. BCE storage jar, Shiloh V (Gitin 2015: Pl. 1–1.15:4; used with permission)	89
6.4	The Royal Steward inscription (Barkay 1992: figure 9.49; used with permission)	90
6.5	An Israelite pillar-courtyard house (drawn by Giselle Hasel; Author's copyright)	91
7.1	Philistine pottery (courtesy of Aren M. Maeir, Tel Safi-Gath Excavations)	102
7.2	Open cooking pot sequence from the Late Bronze Age to Iron Age IIB (courtesy of Amihai Mazar, Tel Batash, and Tel Rehov Excavations)	110
7.3	Iron Age I pottery types that do not continue to Iron IIA (courtesy of Amihai Mazar, Tel Beth Shean, and Tel Rehov Excavations)	111
7.4	A selection of Iron Age IIA–B pottery types (courtesy of Amihai Mazar, Tel Batash, and Tel Rehov Excavations)	112
7.5	Iron II *lmlk* and Hippo jars (courtesy of Amihai Mazar, Tel Batash, and Tel Rehov Excavations)	113
7.6	Pottery vessels of standardized shape and size, mass-produced in Iron II (courtesy of Amihai Mazar, Tel Batash, and Tel Rehov Excavations)	113
7.7	Negebite vessels and their wheel-made counterparts; 1–2: cooking vessels; 3–4: jugs (Negebite vessels: Photo by Mariana Salzberger, courtesy of the Israel Antiquities Authority; wheel-made vessels: courtesy Amihai Mazar, Tel Rehov Excavations)	114
8.1	View of central-western section of the plan in Figure 8.7, showing typical 3RH and 4RHs, looking north. Top arrow shows stairs leading down into 160.07. Lower arrow marks the opening of Cistern 368 intended to collect water runoff from the street. Fieldstone pillars and interstitial rubble masonry are also visible. Badè Museum Photograph 1299	121

8.2	Rough fieldstone pillars in Room 361 (front) and monolithic pillars in Room 341 (back), looking north (not on the plan in Figure 8.7). Note also the large stone grinding/pounding mortar to the lower left. Walls are of field stones held in place by mud mortar. The pillars in Room 341 rest on a foundation wall and the spaces between the pillars in Room 361 are filled with sections of a rubble wall. Badè Museum Photograph 916	122
8.3	Pillar wall with intact lintels between Room 390 and Room 389 in Building 141.03, looking north. Clearance below lintels is about 1.10m high. Badè Museum Photograph A1165	122
8.4	Stairway leading down from Street 514 into Room 594 of Building 159.01, separated from Room 592 (right) by a row of fieldstone pillars with interstitial sections of rubble wall, looking northeast. Badè Museum Photograph 1292	123
8.5	The lower part of an oven built up of clay and broken potsherds, located in Street 514, looking south. Behind the oven is an olive press reused in a later wall (see caption Figure 8.8). Badè Museum Photograph 1428	124
8.6	4RH 110.01 of Stratum 2 (Neo-Babylonian–Persian periods), located just inside the outer two-chamber gate; indicates that this house type continued in use beyond the destruction of Jerusalem in 586 BCE. Access into the core part of the building was through the central Room 379 and access into all rooms on the ground floor was from Room 379. The western annex (Room 400 et al) seems to have been entered separately from the main part of the building. The stairs in Room 400 indicate the presence of at least a partial second story or useable roof area. The highest elevation on any of the monolithic stone pillars (black squares) is 777.78 and the floor seems to be ca. 776.20, indicating a minimum ceiling height of ca. 1.6m. Scale 1:125. Badè Museum Photograph A922. Plan adapted from Plans 93 and 110 in Badè Museum	127
8.7	Schematic plan of the western side of Tell en-Naṣbeh showing partial reconstruction of house plans and road layout. The olive presses in 142.02 and 142.06 were found reused in later nearby walls; a crushing basin was found in 142.02, so the location of a companion piece there seems reasonable; the second press is tentatively assigned to 142.06 because of its open plan, similar to 142.02. Scale 1:666.67 (the odd scale and orientation off of true north were dictated by the small page size). Plan adapted from Plans 141, 142, 143, 158, 159, 160, 176, and 177 in Badè Museum	130
8.8	The covered mouth of Cistern 363 in Room 617 in Building 141.06, looking north. The drain channel fed water to the cistern from the street just beyond the crouching figure. Badè Museum Photograph 1433	131
8.9	Olive press (left) and crushing basin (right) in Room 662 in Building 125.04, looking north. Badè Museum Photograph 1471	139
9.1	The Stepped Stone Structure in the City of David, Jerusalem	148
9.2	The Cultic precinct at Tel Dan	149
10.1	Map of sites with stone volutes (Map by George A. Pierce)	157
10.2	(a) Right hand door jamb slab, Tomb 5, Tamassos (height ca. 170 cm, width ca. 78 cm, depth ca. 10–18 cm) (Photo by the author). (b) Left-hand door jamb slab, Tomb 12, Tamassos (height ca. 175 cm, width 100 cm, depth 10–18 cm) (Photo by the author)	158

10.3	(a) A probable pillar base, Megiddo. M4 (M5339) with plain sides while the somewhat half circle visible was carved into the top of the stone volute (length 244 cm, height 57 cm, depth 57 cm). On site at Tel Megiddo; photo by the author. (b) A probable pillar base, Megiddo. M5 (M5340) the ca. half circle is visible carved into the top rear half of the stone volute (length 244 cm, height 57 cm, depth 56 cm). On display in the Rockefeller Museum, Jerusalem; photo by the author. (c) A probable pillar base, Megiddo. M5 (M5340) the volute motif carved on the front of the stone volute (Photo by the author)	160
10.4	A large fragment of a double-sided stone volute, Megiddo M10/M12 (length, if complete, approx. 110 cm, height 60 cm, depth 28 cm; weight less than ½ ton when complete). The stone volute is shown on the grounds of Tel Megiddo before it was relocated to the visitor's center (Photo by the author)	161
10.5	A possible stone balustrade with a volute motif on the exterior face, Jerusalem J1. Visible along the full length of the top of the stone volute and adjacent to the carved face is a carved 14 cm wide strip with two rectangular dowel holes (length 130 cm, height 60 cm, depth 43 cm; weight approx. ¾ ton) (Photos by the author)	165
12.1	Total number of sites per period, Chalcolithic through Persian periods (Zertal 2004: 601–03)	197
12.2	Map of Middle Bronze II sites (Map by the author)	198
12.3	Map of Late Bronze I sites (Map by the author)	198
12.4	Map of Late Bronze IIA sites (Map by the author)	199
12.5	Map of Late Bronze IIB sites (Map by the author)	199
12.6	Map of Iron Age I sites (Map by the author)	200
12.7	Map of Iron Age II sites (Map by the author)	201
12.8	Map of Iron Age III sites (Map by the author)	201
16.1	LMLK jar, with all four handles stamped; Tell en-Naṣbeh. Image courtesy of the Badè Museum, Pacific School of Religion	253
16.2	The settlement wall at Tell en-Naṣbeh. Image courtesy of the Badè Museum, Pacific School of Religion	254
16.3	The Ja'azaniah seal (right) and its impression (left) from Tell en-Naṣbeh. Image courtesy of the Badè Museum, Pacific School of Religion	255
16.4	Architectural plan of southeastern squares at Tell en-Naṣbeh, featuring stone-lined pits with no associated architecture, unpublished. Image courtesy of the Badè Museum, Pacific School of Religion	255
16.5	Two bronze bangles from Tell en-Naṣbeh, C-shaped (left) and O-shaped (right). Image courtesy of the Badè Museum, Pacific School of Religion, based on original images by Alon Friedman	256
16.6	Two examples of Ammonite Painted Wares from Tell en-Naṣbeh. Image courtesy of the Badè Museum, Pacific School of Religion, based on original images by Rebecca Hisiger and Aaron Brody	257
16.7	Two examples of Ammonite Black Wares from Tell en-Naṣbeh. Image courtesy of the Badè Museum, Pacific School of Religion, based on original images by Rebecca Hisiger and Aaron Brody	257
18.1	Judahites being deported following the capture of Lachish. Museum no.: 124907 © The Trustees of the British Museum	287

Figures

19.1 Faience feeding cup for infants. Accession no.: 44.4.4, Rogers Fund, 1944, The Metropolitan Museum of Art — 297
19.2 Clay feeding bowl for infants. Accession no.: 09.180.768c, Rogers Fund, 1909, The Metropolitan Museum of Art — 297
21.1 Egyptian horseman. Drawing on limestone from Thebes in the Egyptian Museum. Photograph by Charlie Trimm — 319
21.2 Relief of Ramses II at the Ramesseum showing the beating of Hittite scouts. Line drawing from James Henry Breasted, *Battle of Kadesh* (Chicago: The University of Chicago Press, 1903), pl. 1 — 320
23.1 Photo of the stone basin from Kuntillet 'Ajrud, with a line drawing of its incised rim (courtesy of the Israel Exploration Society) — 353
24.1 Reading: 'ayin-[yod?] (Ink on pottery. Stratum VI. Courtesy of Amihai Mazar) — 367
24.2 Reading: mt'| (Incised after firing. Stratum VI. Coutresy of Amihai Mazar) — 367
24.3 Reḥov 2. Incised after firing. Stratum VI. Courtesy of Amihai Mazar — 368
24.4 Reading: l (Incised after firing. Stratum VI. Courtesy of Amihai Mazar) — 369
24.5 Reading: ln[ḥ?]/[m?] (Incised after firing. Stratum VI. Courtesy of Amihai Mazar) — 369
24.6 Reading: lnmš (Incised before firing. Stratum V. Courtesy of Amihai Mazar) — 370
24.7 Reading: lšq[y?]nmš (Incised after firing. Stratum IV. Courtesy of Amihai Mazar) — 370
24.8 Reading: 'lṣd[q]šhly (Incised before firing. Stratum IV. Courtesy of Amihai Mazar) — 372
24.9 Reading: m['...]' (Incised after firing. Stratum IV. Courtesy of Amihai Mazar) — 373
24.10 Reading: [l'l]yš' (Ink on pottery. Stratum IV. Courtesy of Amihai Mazar) — 373
24.11 Reading: b (Incised before firing. Stratum IV. Courtesy of Amihai Mazar) — 374
24.12 Reading: [š] (Incised before firing. Stratum IV. Courtesy of Amihai Mazar) — 375
24.13 Cursive Developments within the Old Hebrew Script — 377
25.1 The Gezer Calendar — 388
25.2 Drawing of Khirbet Qeiyafa Inscription. Courtesy of Brian Donnely-Lewis — 389
25.3 Tel Dan Stele. Photo by Gary Todd — 390
25.4 Fragmentary stele from Samaria. Photo by Gary Todd — 392
25.5 Arad letter, 6th century BCE. Photo by Gary Todd — 395
25.6 Siloam Tunnel Inscription (replica in the Israel Museum). Photo by Gary Todd — 397
25.7 Bar-Rakib's Sam'alian Inscription (KAI 215) — 398
25.8 The Shebna (or Royal Steward) Inscription, 7th century BC. Museum no.: 125205 © The Trustees of the British Museum — 399
28.1 Two bronze plaques (mirrors?) from Tel Dan, Structure B south of main city gate, Iron Age IIB, late 9th or 8th cent.: (a) Plaque A, diameter 8.7 cm (Biran 1999: 53, Figure 12); (b) Plaque B, 9 x 7.6 cm (ibid.: 54, Figure 14; courtesy Nelson Glueck School of Biblical Archaeology, Jerusalem) — 439
28.2 Bronze statuette of a Zebu bull, H 12.4 x L 17.5 cm; from Dhahrat et-Tawileh "Bull site," an open-air sanctuary in the Dothan region; Iron Age I, 12th cent. (Mazar 1982: 30, Figure 2A–B; courtesy Amihai Mazar, Jerusalem) — 440
28.3 Basalt stela, H 115 cm, from the city gate complex at et-Tell ("Bethsaida"); Iron Age IIB, 8th cent. (Bernett and Keel 1998: 96, Figure 1d; drawing Bethsaida Excavations Project, courtesy Orbis Biblicus et Orientalis) — 441
28.4 (a) Cosmetic spoon made of ivory, H 14 cm, from Hazor, Area A, Building 241/1, Str. VI, 8th cent. (Keel and Uehlinger 1998: 200, Figure 214). (b) Fan handle made of bone, H 18 cm, from Hazor, Area A, Building 48, Str. VI, 8th cent. (Keel and Uehlinger 1998: 196, Figure 210). (c) Ivory pyxis,

	H 7.2 cm, from Hazor, Area B close to citadel, Str. VA, late 8th cent. (Keel and Uehlinger 1998: 238, Figure 234a)	443
28.5	Terracotta shrine model, H 20.8 cm, from a pit in Building 149B at Tell el-Far'ah (North), Str. VIIB, Iron Age IIB, mid-9th to 8th cent. (Muller 2002: II 147, Figure 143 e, f)	446
28.6	Terracotta offering stand, H 53.7 cm, from Taanach, Area SW 2–8, Iron Age IIA, late 10th/early 9th cent. (Keel and Uehlinger 1998: 159, Figure 184; drawing Gisela Tambour)	447
28.7	(a) Statues of Levantine deities, arguably the gods of king Hanun of Gaza, carried away as booty by Assyrian soldiers; Nimrud/Kalhu, Central Palace of Tiglathpileser III, ca. 830 BCE (Uehlinger 2002: 124, Figure 5). (b) Statues of Levantine deities carried away by Assyrian soldiers, arguably from Ashkelon; Nineveh, Southwest Palace of Sennacherib, ca. 700 BCE (Uehlinger 1997: 126, Figure 46)	448
28.8	Fragmentary ivory statuette made from the lower canine of a hippopotamus, H 8.5 cm, showing a seated, probably royal figure; Tel Reḥov, Area C, Str. C-1a (= IV), Iron Age IIA, late 9th cent. (Mazar 2022: 511, Figure 32.1; courtesy Amihai Mazar, Jerusalem)	450
28.9	(a–b) Two Judahite pillar figurines, one with molded (Lachish), the other with pinched-nose head (Beersheba), the latter with remains of paint; Iron Age IIB, late 8th century (Schroer 2018: Figures 1544 and 1545). (c) Stamp seal ("scaraboid") from Lachish, unstratified, probably 7th century (Keel and Uehlinger 1998: 330, Figure 323)	451
28.10	(a) Wall painting from Kuntillet ʿAjrud, entrance area, showing a seated royal figure holding a lotus flower (H 32 cm); Iron Age II B, ca. 800 (Meshel et al. 2012: 191, Figure 6.39). (b–c) Various ink drawings and inscriptions sketched on two pithoi from Kuntillet ʿAjrud: Pithos A from the so-called bench room in the inner gate area, Pithos B from close by in the inner courtyard; Iron Age II B, ca. 800 (Meshel et al. 2012: 87, Figure 5.24 and 92, Figure 5.35; drawings reproduced courtesy Ze'ev Meshel, Tel Aviv)	453
28.11	(a–e) Anthropomorphic, male divine figure(s) on a bull as represented on various locally produced stamp seals (a scarab, a conoid, and scaraboids) from (a) Jericho (CSSL no. 60), (b) Gibeon (CSSL no. 20), (c-d) Samaria (CSSL nos. 8, 49) and (e) Lachish (CSSL no. 127); Iron Age I-IIB, 10th to 9th cent. (Courtesy stamp seals from the southern Levant project)	456
28.12	(a–d) Solar symbolism on Israelite and Judahite scarabs, scaraboids and bullae dated to the mid- to late 8th century: (a) Samaria (CSSL no. 6); (b) Shechem (CSSL no. 7); (c) Lachish (L='ḤMLK SMK, CSSL no. 209); (d) Jerusalem (L=ḤZQYHW·'ḤZ·M LK·YHD[H]; CSSL no. 495a) (courtesy Stamp Seals from the Southern Levant Project). (e–f) Solar symbolism on seal impressions made with LMLK (royal) stamps on the handles of jars used by Judahite officials to collect taxes for the Assyrian administration, late 8th cent.: (e) flying scarab, (f) winged sun disc (courtesy Ido Koch, Tel Aviv)	457
28.13	Anepigraphic side of bifacial Judahite seal L= 'LŠMʿ BN GDLYHW (7th century BCE), bought in Jerusalem at the turn of the 20th cent. CE (Keel and Uehlinger 1998: 308, Figure 306a)	458

Figures

28.14	Terracotta group showing a standing, beardless figure flanked by quadrupeds (lions?) next to a seated, bearded figure; the undefined feature to the right could represent a standing stone. The special (sacred) character of the composition is suggested by the conspicuous elevation on four legs (Uehlinger 1997: 150, Figure 61; courtesy Orbis Biblicus et Orientalis)	460
29.1	Map of cultic sites mentioned in the chapter	468
33.1	Middle Bronze Age temples in the Levant (after Burke 2021: figure 5:10)	532
35.1	Myc IIIC (Philistine 1/Monochrome) Deep Bowl from Tell es-Safi/Gath	550
35.2	Bichrome (Philistine 2) Decorated Kraters from Tell es-Safi/Gath	551
35.3	Late Philistine Decorated Ware from Tell es-Safi/Gath	552
35.4	Jar from the Jerusalem Area with a Judahite Inscription, found in the Iron IIA temple in Area D West in the lower city of Tell es-Safi/Gath	553
35.5	Selection of Iron IB–IIA Philistine Cooking Jugs from Tell es-Safi/Gath	554
35.6	Two-horned stone altar found in the Iron IIA temple in Area D West in the lower city of Tell es-Safi/Gath	555
35.7	Phallic-shaped cultic vessels from cultic corners in Iron IIA Area A, in the upper city of Tell es-Safi/Gath	558
35.8	View of Iron IB and Iron IIA fortifications and gate in Area D East in the lower city of Tell es-Safi/Gath	560
36.1	Map of sites mentioned in the chapter	566
37.1	Phoenician bichrome pottery (courtesy of the Tel Dor Excavation Project)	591
37.2	Phoenician silver bowl (8th c.; Walters Art Museum)	595
38.1	Map of sites in Ammon (map by George A. Pierce)	602
38.2	Tripartite building, Jalul	603
38.3	Iron II settlements in Ammonite territory	604
38.4	Ammonite statue with royal diadem	605
38.5	Anthropoid Ammonite coffins	608
38.6	Amman Citadel inscription	610
38.7	Baalis seal impression	611
38.8	Four-room pillared building at Jalul	613
39.1	Map of settlements in west-central Jordan (map by George A. Pierce)	620
39.2	The Wadi al-Mujib, known as the Arnon in the Hebrew Bible, looking west from Lahun, as a winter rainstorm approaches (Image: B. Porter, March 2002)	621
39.3	Early Iron Age Lahun, looking south (Image: Lehun © Aerial Photographic Archive for Archaeology in the Middle East. APAAME_19980520_DLK-0035. Photograph: David L. Kennedy)	623
39.4	The Mesha Stele. The light gray stone is the original preserved portions. The black stone is a cast reconstructed from a frieze of now-missing portions. Original photo by Élisée Reclus (1830–1905), now in the Louvre (AP 5066)	624
39.5	The 'Ataruz temple complex with the late-ninth and eighth-century architecture shaded in dark gray (Image courtesy of Chang-Ho C. Ji)	625
39.6	The Iron Age monumental Building L at Dhiban (Image courtesy of B. Routledge)	626
39.7	Basalt orthostat with carved relief scene of lion's hindquarters and tail. The orthostat is today displayed at the entrance to the Karak Archaeological Museum in Jordan (Image: B. Porter)	627

39.8	Mudayna on the Wadi al-Thamad, looking east. (Khirbat al-Mudayna eth-Thamad © Aerial Photographic Archive for Archaeology in the Middle East. APAAME_20191029_RHB-0053. Photograph: Robert Bewley)	631
39.9	Mudaybi'. Some Iron Age features are obscured by later features built during the Middle and Late Islamic Periods. Mudeibi (Miller #435) © Aerial Photographic Archive for Archaeology in the Middle East. APAAME_20191024_DS-0327. Photograph by Dana Salameen	632
39.10	A modern fabrication of the Mesha Inscription installed in King Hussein's Gardens in 'Amman, Jordan (Image courtesy of E. Corbett)	634
40.1	Map of sites in Edom (map by George A. Pierce)	640
40.2	Bing Map satellite view of Khirbet en-Nahas, with excavation areas. © 2021 Microsoft	643
40.3	Khirbet en-Nahas, Area M slag mound (now infilled) and building	644
40.4	Khirbet en-Nahas, Area A fortress gatehouse looking to the northeast	644
40.5	Wadi Fidan 40, Iron Age graves	645
40.6	Bing Map satellite view of Busayra, with excavation areas. © 2021 Microsoft	648
40.7	Busayra, archaeological remains. Wikimedia image	649
40.8	Umm el-Biyara, Iron Age domestic structures	650
40.9	Reconstruction of the open-air shrine of 'En Hazeva	654
41.1	Reliefs showing Sheshonq I and the "conquered" cities of Judah, Karnak Temple (photo by George A. Pierce)	663
41.2	Detail of the Judahite city names, Karnak Temple (photo by George A. Pierce)	663
41.3	Victory Stela of Piankhy, Napata, Nubia	666
42.1	Map of northeast Africa and the southern Levant during the first millennium BCE. Courtesy of the University of Wisconsin-Madison Cartography Laboratory	676
43.1	Stamp seals and sealings depicting lunar imagery: 1. Tell Keisan (after Keel 2017: 589 No. 14); 2. Tel Gezer (after Keel 2013: 167 No. 3); 3. Tell Jemmeh (after Keel 2013: 23 No. 49); 4. Jerusalem (after Keel 2017: 323 No. 100); 5. Tawilan (after Eggler and Keel 2006: 447 No. 2)	705
43.2	Main types of rosette seal impressions on jar handles	706
44.1	Ariḥ family tree	717
47.1	Proposed borders of 1947 Partition Plan as reflecting densest areas of early 19th century Jewish settlements (following Ben-Bassat 2009: 45). Hatched gray: area designated for a Jewish state; dark gray: area designated for Arab state; circles: densest Jewish settlement areas	763
47.2	Map of the 1947 Partition Plan with "biblical" borders of Iron Age Israel and Judah overlaid on top. Note that the potential Arab state's borders—dark gray—included the main areas of the ancient kingdoms	765
47.3	Map showing the West Bank with "biblical" borders of Iron Age kingdoms of Israel and Judah overlaid on top. Note that all the land of the West Bank falls within the territories of the ancient kingdoms	766

TABLES

1.1	Various chronological schemes proposed for the Iron Age	7
2.1	Site identifications for 1 Sam 30:27–31	18
3.1	Neo-Assyrian references to Israel, Judah, and/or kings of those kingdoms	40
3.2	Comparative chronologies proposed for the kings of Israel and Judah	42
3.3	Chronologically significant events mentioned both in biblical texts and extra-biblical sources	42
3.4	Options for recounting 480 years between the construction of Solomon's Temple and the Exodus	46
6.1	Ethnic traits by category	86
6.2	Ethnic traits as derived from biblical texts and material remains	86
9.1	Select sites in Israel/Judah with a representative list of their monumental architecture	147
11.1	Destruction evidence at eight key archaeological sites across Israel, arranged from north to south	177
29.1	Open-air cultic places/landscapes	469
29.2	Selected examples of cultic structures	470
29.3	Selected examples of cultic spaces within buildings	471
29.4	Selected categories of objects with cultic functions	472
29.5	Locations and orientations of select cultic structures	473

CONTRIBUTORS

Shawn Zelig Aster is an Associate Professor in the Martin (Szusz) Department of Land of Israel Studies and Archaeology at Bar-Ilan University, where he also teaches in the Zalman Shamir Bible Department. He is the author of *Reflections of Empire in Isaiah 1–39: Responses to Assyrian Ideology* (SBL, 2017).

Joel S. Baden is Professor of Divinity and of Religious Studies at Yale University. He is the author of *J, E, and the Redaction of the Pentateuch* (Mohr Siebeck, 2009) and *The Composition of the Pentateuch: Renewing the Documentary Hypothesis* (Yale University Press, 2012).

Koert van Bekkum is Professor of Old Testament at the Evangelische Theologische Faculteit, Leuven. He also teaches at Theologische Universiteit Kampen|Utrecht. His research mainly concentrates on historical, literary, and theological aspects of Genesis to 2 Kings.

Dan Belnap is Professor of Ancient Scripture at Brigham Young University. He is the author of *Filets of Fatling and Goblets of Gold: The Use of Meal Events in the Ritual Imagery in the Ugaritic Mythological and Ritual Text*s (Gorgias Press, 2008).

Scott Booth is Provost and Associate Professor of Old Testament at Pillar Seminary. He specializes in Hebrew Bible and the ancient Near East during the Early Iron Age and is on staff at the Abel-Beth Maacah excavations.

Aaron Brody is the Robert and Kathryn Riddell Professor of Bible and Archaeology and Director of the Badè Museum at Pacific School of Religion in Berkeley, California. His recent publications have focused on material household religion, metallurgy, and interregional trade.

Aaron A. Burke is Professor of Near Eastern Archaeology and Kershaw Chair of Ancient Eastern Mediterranean Studies in the Department of Near Eastern Languages & Cultures at UCLA. He is the author of several volumes on Jaffa, as well as *The Amorites and the Bronze Age Near East* (Cambridge, 2021).

Contributors

William G. Dever is Professor Emeritus of Near Eastern Archaeology and Anthropology at the University of Arizona. He was formerly Director of the Hebrew Union College in Jerusalem, and then the W. F. Albright Institute of Archaeology. He is the author of 30 books and several hundred articles and book chapters.

Jennie Ebeling is Associate Professor of Archaeology in the Department of Archaeology at the University of Evansville. She co-directed the Jezreel Expedition in Israel with Norma Franklin and is the author of *Women's Lives in Biblical Times* (T&T Clark, 2010).

Avraham (Avi) Faust is Professor of Archaeology at the Department of General History, Bar-Ilan University. He has authored *The Neo-Assyrian Empire in the Southwest: Imperial Domination and Its Consequences* (Oxford, 2021), among other books and numerous articles.

Norma Franklin is a research fellow at The Zinman Institute of Archaeology of the University of Haifa and an associate fellow of the W. F. Albright Institute for Archaeological Research. She has authored numerous publications, including "The Assyrian Stylized Tree: A Date Palm Plantation and Aššurnaṣirpal II's Stemma," in *Ash-sharq* 5 (2021).

Kristine Henriksen Garroway is visiting Assistant Professor of Hebrew Bible at Hebrew Union College, Los Angeles. She is the author of *Growing Up in Ancient Israel: Children in Material Culture and Biblical Texts* (SBL, 2018).

Nathaniel E. Greene is Lecturer in Old Testament/Hebrew Bible in the School of Divinity, History, Philosophy, and Art History at the University of Aberdeen. His research interests include epigraphy and palaeography of the Levantine Iron Age, the Deuteronomistic History, and archaic state formation.

Rachel Hallote is an archaeologist and Professor of History at Purchase College, State University of New York. She is the author of several books and numerous articles about the history of the discipline of "biblical archaeology."

Christopher B. Hays is D. Wilson Moore Professor of Ancient Near Eastern Studies at Fuller Theological Seminary and Research Associate of the Department of Old Testament Studies at the University of Pretoria, South Africa. He is the author of *The Origins of Isaiah 24–27: Josiah's Festival Scroll for the Fall of Assyria* (Cambridge, 2019), among other books.

Timothy Hogue is Assistant Professor of Ancient West Asian History at the University of Tsukuba. His publications focus on social scientific approaches to the Hebrew Bible and the material culture of the ancient Levant.

Matthew D. Howland is a Postdoctoral Fellow in the J. M. Alkow Department of Archaeology and Ancient Near Eastern Cultures at Tel Aviv University. He specializes in the use of image-based modeling for the collection, analysis, and dissemination of three-dimensional and spatial datasets.

Jeffrey P. Hudon is a staff archaeologist, research associate, and adjunct professor at Andrews University as well as the administrative assistant for the Horn Archaeological Museum. His recent publications include a chapter in the edited volume *What Difference Does Time Make* (eds. J. Scurlock and R. H. Beal, 2019).

Contributors

Kyle H. Keimer was a Senior Lecturer in the Archaeology, History, and Language of Ancient Israel at Macquarie University. He has published articles on the early Israelite monarchy, ancient Near Eastern warfare, and the historical geography of the Bible.

Ido Koch is a Senior Lecturer at the Jakob M. Alkow Department of Archaeology and Ancient Near Eastern Cultures, Tel Aviv University. He is co-director of the Israeli–American archeological project at Tel Hadid and co-director of the Swiss–Israeli project "Stamp-Seals from the Southern Levant."

Igor Kreimerman is a Senior Lecturer in Archaeology at the Institute of Archaeology, the Hebrew University of Jerusalem. His research combines the use of geoarchaeology, experimental archaeology, and traditional archaeological methods for the study of formation processes, especially construction and destruction, in the Bronze and Iron Age Levant.

Øystein S. LaBianca is Senior Research Professor of Anthropology and Associate Director of the Institute of Archaeology at Andrews University. He is also senior director of the Hisban Cultural Heritage Project, which carries out archaeological excavations and community archaeology initiatives at Tall Hisban (biblical Heshbon) in Jordan.

Gunnar Lehmann is the Head of the Department of Bible, Archaeology, and Ancient Near Eastern Studies, Ben-Gurion University. The author of several volumes and numerous articles, he has also co-directed excavations most recently at Qubur al-Walaydah and Tell Keisan.

Thomas E. Levy is Distinguished Professor and holds the Norma Kershaw Chair in the Archaeology of Ancient Israel and Neighboring Lands at the University of California, San Diego. He is co-director of the Scripps Center for Marine Archaeology (SCMA) and director of the Center for Cyber-Archaeology at the Qualcomm Institute.

Alice Mandell is the Albright Chair of Biblical and Ancient Near Eastern Studies at Johns Hopkins University. She is currently completing her book, *Cuneiform Culture and the Ancestors of Hebrew*, which explores scribal practices in Canaan, with a focus on the Canaanite Amarna Letters.

Aren M. Maeir is Professor of Archaeology and Head of the Institute of Archaeology at the Martin (Szusz) Department of Land of Israel Studies and Archaeology at Bar-Ilan University. He recently edited (with Joe Uziel) *Tell es-Safi/Gath II: Excavations and Studies* (Zaphon, 2020).

Chris McKinny is a Research Fellow at Gesher Media, a faculty member at Jerusalem University College, and a senior staff member at the Tel Burna Archaeological Project. He is the author of *My People as Your People: A Textual and Archaeological Analysis of the Reign of Jehoshaphat* (Peter Lang, 2016).

Eckart Otto is Professor Emeritus at the Ludwig Maximilians-Universität in Munich, an Honorary Professor at the University of Pretoria, an Honorary Member of the Old Testament Society of Southern Africa, and Ordinary Member of the European Academy of Sciences and Arts.

Contributors

Nava Panitz-Cohen is a Research Fellow at the Institute of Archaeology at the Hebrew University of Jerusalem, Israel. She is the co-director of the Tel Abel-Beth Maacah excavations with Dr. Naama Yahalom-Mack and Dr. Robert Mullins, and is the editor of the Qedem Monograph series.

Laurie E. Pearce is a Lecturer in Akkadian in the Department of Middle Eastern Languages and Cultures at the University of California, Berkeley. Together with Cornelia Wunsch, she published *Documents of Judean Exiles and West Semites in Babylonia in the Collection of David Sofer* (CDL Press, 2016).

George A. Pierce is Associate Professor of Ancient Scripture at Brigham Young University. He co-edited (with Aren M. Maier) *To Explore the Land of Canaan*, a festschrift for Jeffery R. Chadwick (de Gruyter, 2021) and has published articles on GIS analyses of Jaffa and Ashkelon and their hinterlands and spatial analyses of Philistine and Israelite household compounds.

Krystal V. L. Pierce is Assistant Professor of Ancient Scripture at Brigham Young University. She co-edited *Excavations at the Seila Pyramid and Fag el-Gamous Cemetery* (Brill, 2020) and has authored studies on Jaffa and its Egyptian/-izing pottery.

Daniel Pioske is Assistant Professor of Biblical Studies at St. Thomas University, Minnesota. He is the author of several articles and multiple books, including *Memory in a Time of Prose: Studies in Epistemology, Hebrew Scribalism, and the Biblical Past* (Oxford, 2018). His forthcoming book, *The Bible Among the Ruins*, will appear with Cambridge University Press.

Jeremy Pope is an Associate Professor in the Department of History at the College of William & Mary, where he is also a Faculty Affiliate in Classical Studies. He is the author of *The Double Kingdom under Taharqo: Studies in the History of Kush and Egypt c. 690-664 BC* (Brill, 2014).

Benjamin W. Porter is Associate Professor of Middle Eastern Archaeology at the University of California, Berkeley. He is also a curator at, and a former director of, the Phoebe A. Hearst Museum of Anthropology. He is the author of *Complex Communities: The Archaeology of Early Iron Age West-Central Jordan* (University of Arizona, 2013).

Matthieu Richelle is Professor of Old Testament at the Université catholique de Louvain. He has taught North-West Semitic epigraphy for years at the EPHE-Sorbonne and published extensively in this field as well as on textual criticism of the Hebrew Bible.

Lidar Sapir-Hen is a Senior Lecturer in the Department of Archaeology and Ancient Near Eastern Cultures and Curator of Archaeozoological Collections of the Steinhardt Museum of Natural History, Tel Aviv University. She is currently involved with several excavations dating from the early Neolithic to Late Antiquity.

Ilan Sharon is Professor Emeritus at the Institute of Archaeology, the Hebrew University. He is co-director of the excavations at Tel Dor and has published extensively on those excavations, the chronology of the Iron Age, and the Phoenicians.

Contributors

Jeremy D. Smoak is a Senior Lecturer in Hebrew Bible at UCLA. He is the author of *The Priestly Blessing in Inscription and Scripture: The Early History of Numbers 6:24–26* (Oxford, 2016). His current research projects include a co-authored book on tomb inscriptions in ancient Judah and a monograph on Solomon's temple.

Juan Manuel Tebes is the Director of the Centro de Estudios de Historia del Antiguo Oriente at the Universidad Católica Argentina and a researcher at the Instituto de Investigaciones de la Facultad de Ciencias Sociales – CONICET.

Zachary Thomas is a Postdoctoral Fellow at the Sonia and Marco Nadler Institute of Archaeology, Tel Aviv University, Israel. His forthcoming book on the patrimonial kingdom of David and Solomon will be published by SBL Press.

Charlie Trimm is Associate Professor of Old Testament at Talbot School of Theology, Biola University. He is the author of *The Destruction of the Canaanites: God, Genocide, and Biblical Interpretation* and *Fighting for the King and the Gods: A Survey of Warfare in the Ancient Near East*.

Christoph Uehlinger is Professor of History of Religions/Comparative Religion at the Department of Religious Studies of the University of Zurich. He is the senior editor of Orbis Biblicus et Orientalis and Orbis Biblicus et Orientalis Series Archaeologica.

Rebekah Welton is a Lecturer in Hebrew Bible at the University of Exeter. She is the author of *'He is a Glutton and a Drunkard': Deviant Consumption in the Hebrew Bible* (Brill, 2020) and has also published on animals in the Israelite household, the expression "a land flowing with milk and honey," and deviant consumption.

Randall W. Younker is Professor of Archaeology and History of Antiquity and Director of the Institute of Archaeology at Andrews University. Currently, he is senior director for excavations at Tell Jalul, part of the Madaba Plains Project, and Senior Co-director of the San Miceli excavation in Sicily.

Jeffrey R. Zorn is an Adjunct Associate in the Department of Near Eastern Studies at Cornell University. His scholarly interests focus on the analysis and publication of the excavations of Tell en-Naṣbeh (1926–1935) and Area G at Tel Dor (1986–2004), among other topics.

ABBREVIATIONS

AABNER	*Advances in Ancient, Biblical, and Near Eastern Research*
AAP	*Advances in Archaeological Practice*
AAS	*Archaeological and Anthropological Sciences*
AASOR	*Annual of the American Schools of Oriental Research*
ABD	*Anchor Bible Dictionary*. Edited by David Noel Freedman. 6 vols. New York: Doubleday, 1992
ABR	*Australian Biblical Review*
ADAJ	*Annual of the Department of Antiquities of Jordan*
ADOG	*Abhandlungen der Deutschen Orientgesellschaft*
ADPV	*Abhandlungen des Deutschen Palästina-Vereins*
AEL	*Ancient Egyptian Literature*. Miriam Lichtheim. 3 vols. Berkeley: University of California Press, 1971-1980
AeL	*Ägypten und Levante*
AfO	*Archiv für Orientforschung*
AJA	*American Journal of Archaeology*
AJSR	*Association for Jewish Studies Review*
AmAnth	*American Anthropologist*
AmerAnt	*American Antiquity*
AMT	*Archaeological Method and Theory*
ANET	*Ancient Near Eastern Texts Relating to the Old Testament*. Edited by James B. Pritchard. 3rd ed. Princeton: Princeton University Press, 1969
AntOr	*Antiguo Oriente*
AoF	*Altorientalische Forschungen*
APAAA	*Archaeological Papers of the American Anthropological Association*
ARA	*Annual Review of Anthropology*
ARAM	*ARAM Society for Syro-Mesopotamian Studies*
ARC	*Archaeological Review from Cambridge*
ARE	*Ancient Records of Egypt*. James Henry Breasted. 4 vols. Chicago: University of Chicago Press, 1906
ARES	*Annual Review of Ecology and Systematics*
AUSS	*Andrews University Seminary Studies*

Abbreviations

BA	*Biblical Archaeologist*
BAAL	*Bulletin d'Archéologie et d'Architecture Libanaise*
BAR	*Biblical Archaeology Review*
BASOR	*Bulletin of the American Schools of Oriental Research*
BBSt	*Babylonian Boundary Stones and Memorial Tablets in The British Museum.* Edited by L. W. King. London: Trustees of The British Museum, 1912
BEBP	*Baker Encyclopedia of Bible Places.* Edited by John J. Bimson. Grand Rapids: Baker, 1995
BIFAO	*Bulletin de l'Institut français d'archéologie orientale*
BN	*Biblische Notizen*
B&R	*Body and Religion*
BRPBI	*Brill Research Perspectives in Biblical Interpretation*
BSOAS	*Bulletin of the School of Oriental and African Studies*
BT	*The Bible Translator*
CAD	Chicago Assyrian Dictionary
CAJ	*Cambridge Archaeological Journal*
Camb	*Inschriften von Cambyses, König von Babylon (529–521 v. Chr.).* Babylonische Texte 8–9. J. N. Strassmaier. Leipzig: Pfeiffer, 1890
CHLI	*Corpus of Hieroglyphic Luwian Inscriptions. Volume I: Inscriptions of the Iron Age. Part 1: Text. Introduction, Karatepe, Karkamiš, Tell Ahmar, Maraş, Malatya, Commagene.* Hawkins, John David. Berlin: de Gruyter, 2000
COS	*The Context of Scripture.* Edited by W. W. Hallo and K. L. Younger Jr. 4 vols. Leiden: Brill, 1997–2003; 2017 (K. L. Younger, Jr. (ed.))
CurBR	*Currents in Biblical Research*
CurBS	*Currents in Research: Biblical Studies*
DDD	*Dictionary of Demons and Deities in the Bible.* Edited by Karel van der Toorn, Bob Becking, and Pieter W. van der Horst. Leiden: Brill, 1995. 2nd rev. ed. Grand Rapids: Eerdmans, 1999
DamM	*Damaszener Mitteilungen*
DNWSI	*Dictionary of Northwest Semitic Inscriptions.* Jacob Hoftijzer and Karen Jongeling. 2 vols. Leiden: Brill, 1995
EA	*The Amarna Letters.* William L. Moran. Baltimore: Johns Hopkins University Press, 1992
EAEHL	*Encyclopedia of Archaeological Excavations in the Holy Land.* Edited by Michael Avi-Yonah. 4 vols. Jerusalem: Israel Exploration Society and Massada Press, 1975-1978
EBR	*Encyclopedia of the Bible and its Reception.* Edited by Hans-Josef Klauck et al. Berlin: de Gruyter, 2009–
EI	*Eretz-Israel*
EnvPD	*Environment and Planning D: Society and Space*
ESV	English Standard Version
GM	*Göttinger Miszellen*
GTJ	*Grace Theological Journal*
HA/ESI	*Hadashot Arkheologiyot: Excavations and Surveys in Israel*
HBAI	*Hebrew Bible and Ancient Israel*
HR	History of Religions
HTR	Harvard Theological Review
HUCA	*Hebrew Union College Annual*

Abbreviations

IEJ	Israel Exploration Journal
IJDC	International Journal of Digital Curation
IJHA	International Journal of Historical Archaeology
IJNA	The International Journal of Nautical Archaeology
IJSDIR	International Journal of Spatial Data Infrastructures Research
IJO	International Journal of Osteoarchaeology
ISPRSA	The ISPRS Annals of the Photogrammetry, Remote Sensing and Spatial Information Sciences
ISV	International Standard Version
JAA	Journal of Anthropological Archaeology
JACF	Journal of the Ancient Chronology Forum
JACiv	Journal of Ancient Civilizations
JAEI	Journal of Ancient Egyptian Interconnections
JAMT	Journal of Archaeological Method and Theory
JANEH	Journal of Ancient Near Eastern History
JANER	Journal of Ancient Near Eastern Religions
JAOS	Journal of the American Oriental Society
JAR	Journal of Archaeological Research
JARCE	Journal of the American Research Center in Egypt
JAS	Journal of Archaeological Science
JASR	Journal of Archaeological Science: Reports
JBL	Journal of Biblical Literature
JCAA	Journal of Computer Applications in Archaeology
JCH	Journal of Cultural Heritage
JCS	Journal of Cuneiform Studies
JEH	Journal of Egyptian History
JEOL	Journal of the Ancient Near Eastern Society, "Ex Orient Lux"/ Jaarbericht van het Vooraziatisch-egyptisch genootschap "Ex Oriente Lux"
JES	Journal of Eurasian Studies
JEth	Journal of Ethnobiology
JEMAHS	Journal of Eastern Mediterranean Archaeology & Heritage Studies
JETS	Journal of the Evangelical Theological Society
JESHO	Journal of the Economic and Social History of the Orient
JFA	Journal of Field Archaeology
JHS	Journal of Hebrew Scriptures
JJAR	Jerusalem Journal of Archaeology
JLE	Journal of Landscape Ecology
JLS	Journal of Lithic Studies
JMA	Journal of Mediterranean Archaeology
JMC	Journal of Material Culture
JNES	Journal of Near Eastern Studies
JNSL	Journal of Northwest Semitic Languages
JPOS	Journal of the Palestine Oriental Society
JPS	Jewish Publication Society Tanakh (Hebrew Bible)
JSOT	Journal for the Study of the Old Testament
JSSEA	Journal of the Society for the Study of Egyptian Antiquities
JTS	Journal of Theological Studies
JWP	Journal of World Prehistory

Abbreviations

KAI	*Kanaanäische Und Aramäische Inschriften. Band 1. 5., erweiterte und überarbeitete Auflage.* H. Donner and W. Röllig. Wiesbaden: Harrassowitz Verlag, 2002.
KJV	King James Version
KUSATU	*Kleine Untersuchungen zur Sprache des Alten Testaments und seiner Umwelt*
LH	Laws of Hammurabi
MAA	*Mediterranean Archaeology and Archaeometry*
MR	*Material Religion*
MTC	*Manuscript and Text Cultures*
MTSR	*Method & Theory in the Study of Religion*
NABU	*Nouvelles Assyriologiques Brève at Utilitaires*
NASB	New American Standard Version
Nbk	*Inschriften von Nabuchodonosor, König von Babylon (604–561 v. Chr.)* Babylonische Texte 8–9. J. N. Strassmaier. Leipzig: Pfeiffer, 1889
NEA	*Near Eastern Archaeology*
NEAEHL	*The New Encyclopedia of Archaeological Excavations in the Holy Land.* Edited by Ephraim Stern. 5 vols. Jerusalem: Israel Exploration Society, 1993-2008
NGSBA	*Nelson Glueck School of Biblical Archaeology, Archaeology Journal*
NIDB	*New Interpreter's Dictionary of the Bible.* Edited by Katharine Doob Sakenfeld. 5 vols. Nashville: Abingdon, 2006–2009
NLT	New Living Translation
NSAJR	*New Studies in the Archaeology of Jerusalem and its Region*
OBBS	*Oxford Bibliographies in Biblical Studies*
OEAE	*The Oxford Encyclopedia of Ancient Egypt.* Edited by Donald B. Redford. 3 vols. Oxford: Oxford University Press, 2001
OEANE	*The Oxford Encyclopedia of Archaeology in the Near East.* Edited by Eric M. Meyers. 5 vols. New York: Oxford University Press, 1997
OHO	*Oxford Handbooks Online*
OJA	*Oxford Journal of Archaeology*
Or	*Orientalia*
OTS	*Old Testament Studies*
PEQ	*Palestine Exploration Quarterly*
PIHANS	*Publications de l'Institut historique-archéologique néerlandais de Stamboul*
PNAS	*Proceedings of the National Academy of Sciences*
PPGEE	*Progress in Physical Geography: Earth and Environment*
PPP	*Palaeogeography, Palaeoclimatology, Palaeoecology*
QSR	*Quaternary Science Reviews*
RA	*Revue d'assyriologie et d'archéologie orientale*
RAr	*Revue archéologique*
RB	*Revue Biblique*
RIMA	Royal Inscriptions of Mesopotamia Assyrian Periods
RIMA II	*Assyrian Rulers of the Early First Millennium BC (1114-859 BC).* The Royal Inscriptions of Mesopotamia, Assyrian Periods, Volume 2. A. Kirk Grayson. Toronto: University of Toronto, 1991
RIMA III	*Assyrian Rulers of the Early First Millennium BC II (858-745 BC).* The Royal Inscriptions of Mesopotamia, Assyrian Periods, Volume 3. A. Kirk Grayson. Toronto: University of Toronto, 1996
RINAP	Royal Inscriptions from the Neo-Assyrian Period
RS	Ras Shamra Texts

RSAR	*Religion and Society: Advances in Research*
SAA	State Archives of Assyria
Sem	*Semitica*
SHAJ	*Studies in the History and Archaeology of Jordan*
SJA	*Southwestern Journal of Anthropology*
SJOT	*Scandinavian Journal of the Old Testament*
SR	Scientific Reports
SRT	Studies in Reformed Theology
TA	Tel Aviv
TAPA	*Transactions of the American Philological Association*
TopoiSupp	*Topoi Supplement*
TRE	*Theologische Realenzyklopädie*. Edited by Gerhard Krause and Gerhard Müller. Berlin: de Gruyter, 1977–
TynBul	*Tyndale Bulletin*
UF	*Ugarit-Forschungen*
VT	*Vetus Testamentum*
VAR	Virtual Archaeology Review
WA	World Archaeology
WdO	*Die Welt des Orients*
WTJ	Westminster Theological Journal
ZA	*Zeitschrift für Assyriologie*
ZABR	*Zeitschrift für Altorientalische und Biblische Rechtsgeschichte*
ZÄS	*Zeitschrift für ägyptische Sprache und Altertumskunde*
ZAW	*Zeitschrift für alttestamentliche Wissenschaft*
ZDPV	*Zeitschrift des Deutschen Palästina-Verein*

PREFACE

This volume was conceived in 2017, but several obligations meant that it did not progress in earnest until 2019. Little would I know that within a year the world would be changed by the COVID-19 pandemic. The loss of millions of lives worldwide and the attempts to curb the spread of the virus created an unprecedented realignment of priorities for many people. Within academia, libraries shut down, international travel for research stopped, and a new online approach to teaching had to be learned by many of us. Fortunately, several publishers made digital copies of their works available so that researchers could continue some semblance of their work. Nevertheless, the world changed. Academia changed. And we are just now settling into a new normal in a COVID world.

In 2020, I asked George to co-edit this volume with me. That was one of my best decisions on this project. The volume had been progressing slowly before that point, but once he was on-board, the pace of the project quickened. It has been a pleasure working together, something that has led to several lengthy discussions about the archaeology of ancient Israel, where it is now and where it might (or perhaps, ought to, in our opinion) go. Working with George has allowed us to move this project to completion even with the added weight each of us bore academically because of the pandemic. For his tireless efforts on this project, I thank him. I also thank the contributors, many of whom had personal experiences with COVID. Without their hard work, this volume would not exist.

Alameda, CA
1 April 2022
Kyle H. Keimer

When Kyle asked me to help co-edit this volume, I was equally thrilled and apprehensive. Thrilled because I wholly wanted to support Kyle as the subject matter is dear to both of our hearts; apprehensive because I knew the effort that editing a volume like this one entails. As we threw ourselves into the work, the challenges of COVID, academic jobs, and family and personal situations reminded us of what was truly important in life. I have been rewarded with many conversations about the archaeology of ancient Israel and biblical studies, plans for new research and publications (both solo and with Kyle), increased knowledge from each contributors' chapter, and new and renewed acquaintances in the field. I cannot thank Kyle enough for including me in this project. To each of our contributors, who all endured e-mails, phone calls, cajoling, editing, and various odd requests, I humbly thank you all as well. Heather Randall and the team at BYU Faculty Publishing Service helped immensely in copy-editing this hefty tome. Kyle and I would also like to thank our contacts at Routledge, Amy Davis-Poynter, Marcia Adams, and Elizabeth Risch, for all their assistance and patience.

Vineyard, UT
1 April 2022
George A. Pierce

1
AN INTRODUCTION TO THE ANCIENT ISRAELITE WORLD
The State of the Field and Future Directions

Kyle H. Keimer and George A. Pierce

Introduction

For over two centuries, there has been academic investigation into the lands stretching from Egypt and the eastern Mediterranean littoral (the "Levant") to as far away as modern-day Iran. The classical definition of this broad region is the "Near East," a term that is recognized for its Euro-centric and colonialist foundation. Nevertheless, it is an engrained term that encapsulates the cultures of Egypt, the Levant, Anatolia, Mesopotamia, and Persia. It is within this broader context that ancient Israel existed for nearly 700 years, from the late second millennium BCE to the mid-first millennium BCE, as an entity of various compositions before undergoing major transformations following the Assyrian conquest of the northern kingdom of Israel in the 8th century BCE and the Babylonian conquest of the kingdom of Judah in the 6th century.

The legacy left by ancient Israel was built upon, grew, and was interpreted and reinterpreted throughout the second half of the first millennium and the beginning of the first millennium CE. On the one hand, there is a historical legacy that can be investigated, and on the other, there has been (and continues to be) a living tradition of what it meant/means to be "Israel." Much of this historical legacy has become ingrained in the foundation of modern Western thought, religion, and lived experience as a result of the enduring nature of Judaism's holy writ, the Bible. Perhaps this is one of the reasons that ancient Israel is such a topic of interest for scholars and the general public alike. The lure of ancient Israel is clear from the numerous television shows on various aspects of its culture and the Bible, the immense interest in joining an archaeological excavation in biblical lands, and the various news articles, blogs, podcasts, and educational resources on archaeological discoveries and ancient Israel that appear every day. The chance to connect to the past and to learn about ancient Israel and the Bible is desired more than ever. As such, this volume provides numerous studies on various aspects of ancient Israel's existence.

Scope of This Volume

Archaeology and anthropology are at the heart of this volume. This is not to say that the biblical texts are avoided; they are not. However, for textual issues and historical reconstructions

DOI: 10.4324/9780367815691-1

based on the biblical texts, *The Biblical World* (Routledge 2021 [2nd ed.]) already exists. Instead, this volume was conceived as one in which ancient and biblical Israel was illuminated through the material culture, set within a broader interdisciplinary and theoretically explicit framework.

When such a framework is utilized, discussions between a perceived "ancient Israel"— the Israel informed from archaeology—and a "biblical Israel"—the often fabricated and/or idealized version of ancient Israel of the Hebrew Bible—come into focus. Indeed, textual studies that debate the difference between biblical and ancient Israel seldom draw from the immense body of archaeological material, anthropological archaeology, sociology, political studies, or other fields. The result is a portrait where Israel is framed as an idealized and, at times, ahistorical entity. The biblical texts themselves are understood to have undergone multiple (late) redactions, to the point that reality has been blurred or lost. To be sure, the biblical texts were redacted at various times. Yet a nuanced understanding of the material remains tells us that the picture just described is not so monolithic. Many biblical texts remember early traditions and/or early details even if they underwent later redaction or literary composition. In fact, as many of the chapters in this volume illustrate, the contexts out of which so many biblical stories emerge fit pre-7th-century BCE contexts and comport nicely with extra-biblical sources, inscriptional evidence, and the archaeological remains. Each of these corpora must be interpreted, as must the biblical text, and there is no singular interpretational framework that is appropriate.

Ancient Israel

To frame this entire volume we must ask, what is "ancient Israel?" In this volume, the term "ancient Israel" refers to the people identified as "Israel" either as a native term or one utilized by outsiders. Significantly, those who fall under this term vary over the course of time. The first external mention of the name "Israel" is the Merenptah stele from ca. 1207 BCE. It appears again in Shalmaneser III's Kurkh Monolith, the Tel Dan Inscription, and the Mesha Stele (all three of these sources are from the 9th century BCE). Most references to "Israel," however, occur in the Hebrew Bible where the term refers variously to an individual, a coalition of tribes, two different kingdoms (the northern kingdom of Israel and the southern kingdom of Judah),[1] a collective people who worship the god YHWH, and a geographic territory. Some of the uses of the term occur after the destruction of the two kingdoms, in which case there is an ideological hearkening back to a perceived period of unity.[2] The destructions of the kingdom of Israel in 722 BCE and then the kingdom of Judah in 587 BCE mark two turning points. The first saw the deportation of Israelite tribes to various parts of the Assyrian empire where over time they acculturated. Some from Israel fled to Judah and presumably brought various oral and/or written traditions that were combined with Judahite traditions into a national narrative now known as the Hebrew Bible (Schniedewind 2004: 64–90). The second turning point saw the deportation of many Judahites to various locations in the Neo-Babylonian empire.

Significantly, in contrast to the Israelite deportees, these Judahite deportees retained their distinct identity, even using their exile as a means by which to solidify such an identity. Thus, it is unsurprising that the Judahite perspective is more prominent in the biblical texts and ultimately becomes the foundation for later writings between 587 BCE and 70 CE. Prior to 587 BCE (or 722 BCE for the north), there was a national temple for YHWH in Jerusalem, and then shrines in Dan and Bethel; a royal line that stretched back for hundreds of years in Judah (and which was understood to be inviolable) and multiple royal lines in Israel; and a discreet geographic range controlled by people who understood themselves to be "Israel." After 587 BCE, each of these features ended. The power structure, religious framework, and economic system were reconfigured. A new, second temple was erected, but influences from the Babylonian and Persian worlds, including the implementation of Aramaic as the lingua franca, brought new terms of identification and association. The province of Yehud, which was the heart of the preceding kingdom of Judah, gave birth to the term "Jew," and the religion practiced by the Jews was "Judaism" as opposed to Yahwism (even if various elements of praxis had continuity).

As the post-587 BCE existence and experience of "Israel" was very different from that which came before, we use the dates of ca. 1200 to 587/6 BCE as our chronological scope in this volume. The exception is Pearce's article on Babylon, which covers the integral transitionary period of the 6th (and 5th) century. The scope of this volume is tantamount to what many refer to as the "First Temple Period"—named after the temple to YHWH that the biblical record ascribes to king Solomon in the 10th century BCE. Conceptualized biblically, this volume covers the pre-monarchic period of the emergence and settlement of Israel, the United Monarchy, and the divided monarchies of Israel and Judah. According to archaeological parlance, this is the Iron Ages I and II (see Table 1.1 for variations in the archaeological phasing).

While a volume that focuses on ancient Israel for this historical scope could stand alone, we felt that a broader perspective provides added context by which the history of ancient Israel must be understood. It is one thing to reconstruct and detail various aspects of ancient Israel's history, but an essential part of the story is how ancient Israel has been studied by modern scholars and where studies on ancient Israel are going. As such we have divided the volume into three main sections. The first covers the history of studying ancient Israel, chronological and historical considerations, and introduces the historical geography of the Bible—the main field by which we gain access to the events of antiquity because the landscape today is largely the same as it was in antiquity (Part I). The second section encompasses social, economic, religious, and ideological elements of ancient Israel's world (Parts II–VI). Finally, the third provides studies that illuminate the modern study of ancient Israel, with a bent on where the field is now moving (Part VII).

The Geographic Setting

The territory considered to be "Israel" is fluid. According to the biblical texts, the god YHWH promised to give land to the descendants of a man named Abram/Abraham. Within these texts, however, there are multiple versions of the extent of the land. Numbers 34:1–15 extends it from the Brook of Egypt (most likely the Wadi el-'Arish today) in the south to Mt. Hor and Lebo-Hamath in the north (approximately parallel to the Litanni River basin today?; cf. Num 13:21), while Gen 15:18 envisions the region from the Euphrates to the Brook of Egypt (cf. 1 Kgs 5:1 [4:21]), and 2 Sam 24:2 refers to the region from Dan to Beersheba (cf., again, 1 Kings 5:1 [4:21]). The eastern boundary is the Great Rift Valley from the Sea of Galilee/Kinneret, down the Jordan Valley, to the Dead/Salt Sea.

For most of its history, Israel (broadly defined) appears to have controlled most of the territory from Dan to Beersheba (if the material culture is any indication of political control, which it may or may not be); this is the typical picture gleaned from the biblical texts. Similar boundaries are adduced from the archaeology; however, the modern political boundaries of Lebanon, Syria, Jordan, Israel, and the Palestinian Territories have influenced our conception of ancient boundaries. Excavations are prolific within the modern state of Israel and to a lesser degree in Jordan but have been limited in the West Bank since 1967 and are nearly non-existent for southwestern Syria and southern Lebanon due to military conflicts and political/religious differences. The result is a heavy bias that allows for great understanding in some regions and very opaque understanding in others. Despite clear connections in the material culture between regions, the nature of the connections is not always possible to reconstruct. It has been easier to become compartmentalized: there is an archaeology of Israel, an archaeology of Jordan, an archaeology of the Palestinian Territories, and too seldom are the results broadly conveyed across the modern borders.

Although this situation is not ideal, the fact that the biblical texts provide some credence for an "Israel" from Dan to Beersheba means that it is not without precedence. As such, this geographic scope is adopted as the broad parameter for this volume. Of course, the articles in Part VI consider the archaeology and history of the territories surrounding this region, and as such allow for as comprehensive a picture as possible within the constraints of the modern political situation in the Near East. In fact, the authors of the articles in Part VI were asked to be very explicit about the ancient cultural, political, economic, etc. connections between ancient Israel and its various neighbors. The results, as can be seen, show the variegated ways in which ancient Israel existed with, among, and in conflict with its neighbors (Figures 1.1 and 1.2).

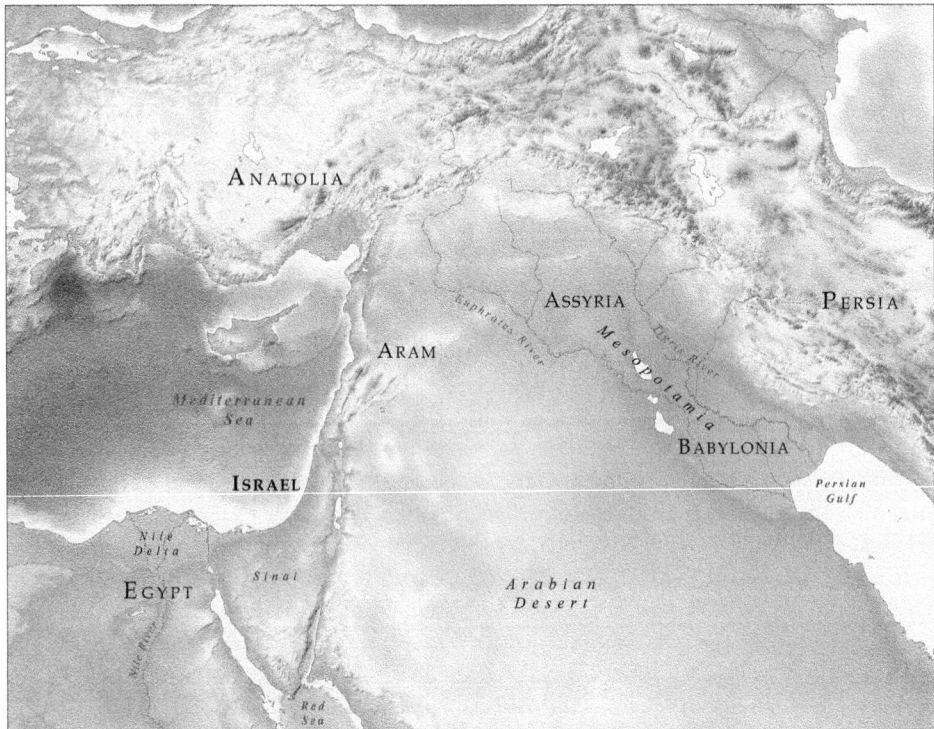

Figure 1.1 Map of the ancient Near East (map by George A. Pierce)

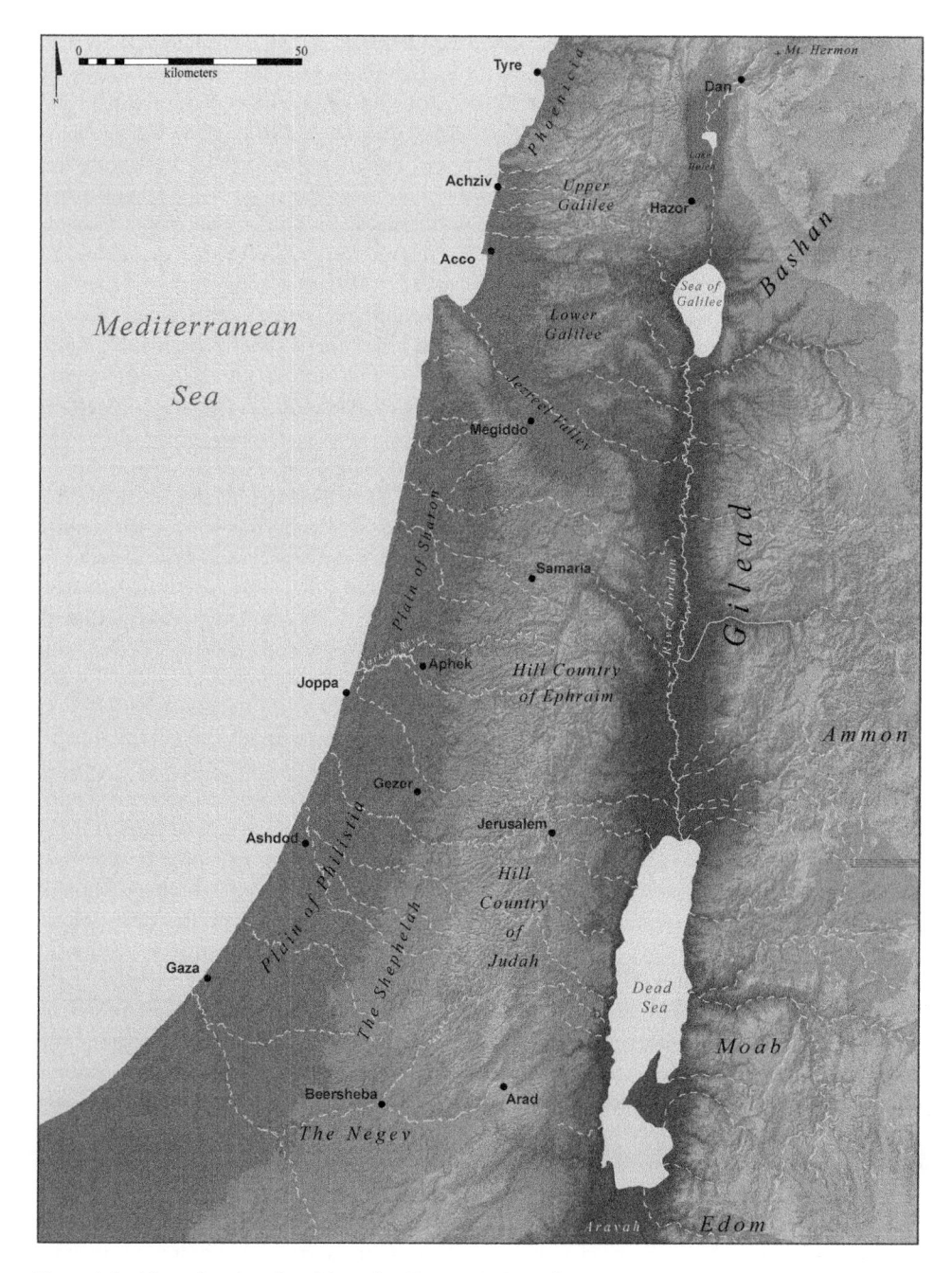

Figure 1.2 Map of ancient Israel (map by George A. Pierce)

Competing Chronologies

Early archaeological research focused on the chronology of the ancient Near East and ancient Israel, in particular. This was a result of not only the nature of the archaeological materials but was also a response to European biblical criticism in the 18th and 19th centuries CE.

The events of the Bible, it was thought, could be identified in the archaeological record, dated, and evaluated for historicity. Thus, with Petrie's development of seriation dating in the late 19th century, it became possible to chart the evolution of material culture in antiquity. Thomsen's (1836) three-age system (e.g., Stone, Bronze, and Iron Ages) was adopted, albeit with an added ethno-cultural system of nomenclature imposed (e.g., the Canaanite, Israelite, Hellenistic, Roman, Byzantine, and Arab periods [Silberman 1993: ix]) and work began to provide refined calendrical dates for these epochs and any sub-periods within them. In the early 20th century, several syntheses of the ceramic material provided chronological frameworks from the growing number of excavations in Palestine (Vincent 1923; Duncan 1930; Sellers and Albright 1931; Albright 1932; Wright 1937), and such frameworks increased over the course of the 20th century (Aharoni and Amiran 1958; Wright 1961; Amiran 1970; *EAEHL* 1973–78; Ben-Tor 1992). Each new framework sought to incorporate the ever-growing amount of archaeological material, but each was also informed to a certain degree by the biblical text.

In 1996, Israel Finkelstein proposed the "Low Chronology," which argued for the lowering in date of strata ascribed to the 10th century BCE. Such strata, he argued, should be dated to the 9th century. This revolutionary chronological scheme was more controversial than previous schemes because it called into question the way the archaeology connected to the historical events depicted in the Hebrew Bible. While still adhered to by some, ultimately, Herzog and Singer-Avitz (2004) and then Mazar (2005) arrived at alternate (but very similar) chronologies that today are the most widely accepted even as further refinements are being proposed (e.g., Garfinkel 2011; Katz and Faust 2014).[3] Thus, even after over 130 years of work on the chronology of the archaeology of ancient Israel, there is no consensus on the phasing and nomenclature of the Iron Age, even as greater refinement is being achieved (Table 1.1).

One issue that has been both a blessing and curse for the establishment of a unified chronology of ancient Israel is the biblical text itself. While it contains mention of various historical events that can be dated externally, there are far more events whose dates are unspecified and/or ambiguous as the text records them. Archaeologists have attempted to wed the events of the Bible to the archaeological record for as long as the latter has been known. Some have done it very explicitly, others with greater nuance and caution. For early "biblical" archaeologists, faith could be bolstered by having "proof" of the historicity of biblical events resulting from archaeological endeavors. Additionally, archaeology, more specifically epigraphic discoveries, could provide an explanation or reconstruction of biblical history.

One reason there have been so many chronologies proposed for the archaeology of ancient Israel is that there have been numerous views of how that archaeology relates to specific biblical periods and/or characters. To be sure, each chronological scheme has cited specific changes in the material culture to justify the divisions of the Iron Age, but historical events (often political changes recorded in the Bible) have always played an explanatory role as well.

Within this volume, we have not imposed a specific chronological framework for the contributors to follow. Most adhere to what has become known as the "Modified Conventional Chronology," though some champion the "Low Chronology." As a guiding principle, we have worked with contributors to make their chosen chronology clear for the reader. This was the most favorable approach because, if history has anything to teach us, it is that our modern chronologies, created for heuristic purposes, are anachronistic to ancient Israel and should be fluid. Even though we have a more refined chronology than ever before, we have not yet reached a level of accuracy that removes all ambiguity in the dating of archaeological materials and historical events.[4] Nor have we reached a consensus on how the two should be related.

Table 1.1 Various chronological schemes proposed for the Iron Age

	Albright (1932); Sellers and Albright (1931)	Aharoni and Amiran (1958)	Amiran (1970)	EAEHL (1975-78); NEAEHL (1993-2008)	Ben-Tor (1992)	Low Chronology (1996-)	Modified Conventional Chronology (2005-)	Various (Herzog and Singer-Avitz 2004; 2006; Garfinkel 2011; Faust and Katz 2014)
1200	c.1235 Early Iron I(a) —1150	Israelite I	I	Ia	I	LB III —1130	Ia —1140	LB III / Iron Ia —1140
1100	Early Iron I(b)			Ib		I	Ib	Ib
1000	Early Iron I(c) —925/900	Israelite II	IIa	IIa —925	IIa	—920/900 IIa	—980 IIa	—980 Transitional I/IIa Early IIa —880
900	Early Iron II —840		IIb	IIb —720	IIb	IIb —760	—840/830 IIb	—840/800 Transitional IIa/b Late IIa IIb
800		Israelite III	IIc	IIc —586	IIIa	IIc	—732/701 IIIa (IIc)	—732/701 IIc
700	Early Iron III —587				IIIb		IIIb —605/586 520	—605/586
600								
500								

The Study of Ancient Israel

Critical scholarship of the Bible began in the 18th century, intensified in the 19th, and became pluriform in the 20th and 21st centuries. Historical approaches, which once dominated the study of ancient Israel, are now but one way to evaluate the textual evidence (see the articles in Part VI of *The Biblical World*). While historical critical approaches within the field of biblical studies may not be as dominant as they once were, there are many reasons to revitalize such approaches. Foremost is because the amount of archaeological material that has been and is being uncovered in Israel and Jordan is immense. We have moved into a period of recognizing that new data is available, new questions can be asked, and novel (re-)interpretations of the archaeological and textual materials are possible and are providing fruitful advances in understanding ancient Israel.

Still, we have enormous holes in our data. Whether these are due to our past and current methods of collection, because we simply do not know how to assess them materially, or because certain behaviors and beliefs do not leave archaeological imprints, we must recognize that we are attempting to reconstruct ancient Israelite society with incomplete data. This means that our picture is always in motion as more and more excavations take place and provide us with additional material by which to refine our focus.

Therefore, useful and relevant theories and informed methodological approaches are of great benefit. Theories allow us to extrapolate and generalize processes for which we have varying degrees of attestable evidence. Applying theory is part and parcel of a coherent methodology as it requires that we think about the evidence, how to collect it, why it might be useful, etc. This volume seeks to draw upon relevant theories even as it will become clear that such theories are variant depending on the aspect of ancient Israel under investigation. We asked each contributor to approach their topics with an eye toward theory and explicit methodology for articulating and interpreting the archaeological and textual remains.

A framework that draws upon relevant theory and details explicit methodology (and/or which details past forms/applications of such) allows the processes by which we investigate ancient Israel to be clearer, and hopefully to withstand idiosyncratic or comprehensive refashioning of ancient Israel's history based on new discoveries. It is our hope that there will be long-standing value to the articles in this volume even if some of the specifics need to be adjusted due to discoveries after its publication.

One thing that is clear is that our understanding and interpretation of ancient Israel has and will continue to evolve, which means, even more so, that we need to understand Israel on its own terms and within its own contexts. Ancient Near Eastern parallels provide fruitful fodder, as do ethnographic studies, but none replicate exactly the Israelite reality. Generalizations are good and provide a broad framework within which to work, but we must also establish the micro-structure of this framework one piece at a time because there are clear variations among individual ancient Near Eastern cultures and between these cultures, both synchronically and diachronically. Moreover, even when there are solid parallels that shed additional light, we must be cognizant of the difference in scale between ancient Israel and some of its Near Eastern neighbors. Even though structures and/or institutions may have similarities, the actual operation, and process by which these elements operated can vary.

Rationale for This Volume

The pace at which excavations are taking place makes the production of a traditional archaeological history difficult. Constant new data means not only that there is more material to synthesize, but that the quantity of data is beyond a single individual to handle. Gone are the days of Albright, Anson Rainey, and others, who operated equally competently in the archaeology, texts, and languages of the ancient Near East (and the modern Middle East). Now, we work more collaboratively to allow for the greatest depth of specialization as we craft our generalizations. It is in this vein that this volume was envisioned.

Thematic topics were chosen, and the explicit call for conceptualizing the various topics via relevant theories and methodologies was meant to mitigate against the constant increase in available data, as already mentioned. Good theory and methodology provide the framework for interpreting the archaeological and textual sources, and regardless of the quantity of these sources, a solid grounding in theory with an explicit method means that even as the constituent parts move and various elements of our interpretation need updating, the way in which big picture understanding is done is clearly laid out in the chapters in this volume.

Some of the specific topics arose from the recognition that not everything shows up in the archaeological record, and not everything from the archaeological record shows up in the text. Adding complexity is the fact that we often have both visible and invisible actors. The former are those individuals who start trends observable in the material culture but who remain nameless and identity-less from a historical perspective (e.g., the potter who decided to apply red slip to vessels). The latter entail those whom we know about from texts but who leave no individualized archaeological record (e.g., individual kings or others of sociopolitical influence).

Further complexity comes when we problematize the old view, as perhaps most explicitly presented by Kathleen Kenyon in her *Amorites and Canaanites* (1966), that cultural continuity (and discontinuity) can be captured in the archaeological materials and serves to help identify cultural interaction, memorialization, and enculturation. These topics are at the fore of recent studies on ancient Israel, and it is worth considering that we need to be viewing ancient Israel as both disjunctive as a people group, but also as the product of cultural continuity that went largely uninterrupted throughout the Middle and Late Bronze Ages and is ultimately an amalgam of Amorite and Egyptian culture. There are few clear lines.

Overall, we have attempted to create a coherent narrative for this volume that contextualizes ancient Israel in history, both ancient—when there was a culture known as "Israel"—and modern—when modern Western nations were re-awakened to their pre-Classical roots and sought to explore and understand biblical Israel and its neighbors. Even so, we have allowed individual contributors to have their own voice and to express how they interpret the archaeological, textual, and/or iconographic evidence. The multiplicity of views that come through in this volume, even while hopefully coherent overall (and despite inevitable overlap with certain topics), reflects the challenge that lies before us as we attempt to better understand ancient Israel; biblical texts and archaeological remains must be interpreted, and interpretations vary. We stand too far removed temporally and culturally—and some of us, spatially—to assume that face-value readings of the text or functional interpretations of the archaeology are accurate or even the best and/or only way to view our corpora.

Many of the contributors to this volume question traditional interpretations and/or utilize different interpretive frameworks for their topics. Some are senior scholars who provide syntheses born out of years of working with the material culture and texts. Others are junior scholars who bring with them broader interdisciplinary approaches to studying the past. Many of the chapters utilize case studies to highlight the applicability of various theoretical frameworks and/or to problematize past approaches to a given topic. Similarly, many of the chapters offer syntheses that are but the beginning stages of larger projects that will lead to further changes in the way we understand and interpret ancient Israel.

While we have attempted to identify several important topics and/or themes in the study of ancient Israel, those included here are by no means comprehensive. In fact, several additional chapters were envisioned, but for one reason or another did not make it into the final volume. At the same time, the reader will notice three chapters on Egypt in Part VI. We considered it important that Egypt factor so heavily because there is a growing amount of research on Egyptian-Israelite connections. The traditional understanding that Israel is best understood through a Mesopotamian lens, while not entirely devoid of merit, is but one of the lenses through which Israel should be viewed. According to the biblical text, Israel at one point or another in its history came out of both Mesopotamia and Egypt. Archaeologically, the influence of both broader cultures is present in Israelite material culture, and textually/conceptually, the Israelite worldview also expresses ideas native to these regions. In the end, this volume offers a profound number of studies on topics not traditionally dealt with in other volumes on ancient Israel, and we believe that it will be a useful resource for furthering research on ancient Israel.

Notes

1 Even during the so-called "United Monarchy" of Saul and then David and Solomon, the terms "Israel" and "Judah" appear to mark the existence of two discreet entities that pay allegiance to a single monarch (Keimer 2021).
2 For a detailed discussion of "Israel" in this and subsequent periods, see Staples 2021.
3 For a detailed discussion of the various chronological schemes up to the time of its publication, see Mazar 2005.
4 In recent years, the field of archaeomagnetism has developed and appears to have the potential to refine our ability to date the archaeological record beyond that of radiocarbon dating.

Bibliography

Aharoni, Yohanan and Ruth Amiran. 1958. "A New Scheme for the Sub-Division of the Iron Age in Palestine." *IEJ* 8: 171–84.
Albright, William Foxwell. 1932. "The Excavation of Tell Beit Mirsim, Vol. I: The Pottery of the First Three Campaigns." *AASOR* 12: xiii–xxi, 1–165.
Amiran, Ruth. 1970. *Ancient Pottery of the Holy Land*. Jerusalem: Rutgers University Press.
Ben-Tor, Amnon, ed. 1992. *The Archaeology of Ancient Israel*. New Haven: Yale University Press.
Duncan, J. Garrow. 1930. *Corpus of Dated Palestinian Pottery*. London: British School of Archaeology in Egypt.
Finkelstein, Israel. 1996. "The Archaeology of the United Monarchy: An Alternative View." *Levant* 28: 177–87.
Garfinkel, Yosef. 2011. "The Davidic Kingdom in Light of the Finds at Khirbet Qeiyafa." *City of David Studies of Ancient Jerusalem* 6: 13*–35* (English), 31–51 (Hebrew).
Herzog, Ze'ev and Lily Singer-Avitz. 2004. "Redefining the Centre: The Emergence of State in Judah." *TA* 31: 209–44.
Katz, Hayah, and Avraham Faust. 2014. "The Chronology of the Iron Age IIA in Judah in the Light of Tel 'Eton Tomb C3 and Other Assemblages." *BASOR* 371: 103–27.
Keimer, Kyle H. 2021. "Evaluating the 'United Monarchy' of Israel: Unity and Identity in Text and Archaeology." *JJAR* 1: 68–101.
Kenyon, Kathleen M. 1966. *Amorites and Canaanites*. London: Oxford University Press.
Mazar, Amihai. 2005. "The Debate over the Chronology of the Iron Age in the Southern Levant." Pages 15–30 in *The Bible and Radiocarbon Dating: Archaeology, Text and Science*. Edited by Thomas E. Levy and Thomas Higham. London: Equinox.
Schniedewind, William M. 2004. *How the Bible became a Book: the Textualization of Ancient Israel*. Cambridge: Cambridge University Press.

Sellers, Ovid R., and William F. Albright. 1931. "The First Campaign of Excavation at Beth-Zur." *BASOR* 43: 2–13.

Silberman, Neil Asher. 1993. "Introduction to the English Edition." Pages ix–x in *NEAEHL* 1.

Staples, Jason A. 2021. *The Idea of Israel in Second Temple Judaism: A New Theory of People, Exile, and Israelite Identity*. Cambridge: Cambridge University Press.

Thomsen, Christian Jürgensen. 1836. *Ledetraad til Nordisk Oldkyndighed*. Kjöbenhavn: S. L. Møllers.

Vincent, Louis-Hugues. 1923. *Classification des Céramiques Antiques: Céramique de la Palestine*. Paris: Union académique internationale.

Wright, G. Ernest. 1937. *The Pottery of Palestine from the Earliest Times to the End of the Early Bronze Age*. New Haven: American Schools of Oriental Research.

———. 1961. "Archaeology of Palestine." Pages 73–112 in *The Bible and the Ancient Near East: Essays in Honor of W.F. Albright*. Edited by G. Ernest Wright. repr. Winona Lake: Eisenbrauns, 1979.

PART I

Backgrounds and Methodological Considerations

2
THE HISTORICAL GEOGRAPHY OF ANCIENT ISRAEL

The Amalekite Spoil List (1 Sam 30:27–31) as a Case Study

Chris McKinny

Introduction

From the opening chapters of Genesis to the conclusion of the Writings, the Hebrew Bible is intrinsically connected to physical geographical space. Whether it be the ordering of the biblical world's "sons" into regions (Gen 10) or anticipating the return of an ascended prophet to the Jordan River (Mal 4:5; cf. 2 Kgs 2:9–12), the authors and editors of the Hebrew Bible consistently placed past, present, future, and metaphorical events in the known space in which they found themselves. Therefore, an understanding of the geography of the biblical world is foundational to any study of the ancient Israelite world. This assertion is not a new development, as ancient Jewish (e.g., Josephus) and Christian (e.g., Eusebius) writers attempted to identify biblical places and nations with contemporary towns and/or peoples from their own era. Historical geography as outlined and defined by Rainey and Notley (2006: 9–24) combines the disciplines of physical geography, historical philology, toponymy,[1] and archaeology to answer historical and geographical questions related to ancient Israel. In this chapter, we will engage each of these sub-disciplines through the case study of the list of towns that received spoil taken from the Amalekites by David (1 Sam 30:27–31).

Assessing the Amalekite Spoil List in 1 Samuel 30:27–31

First Samuel 30:27–31 is a list of Judahite towns in the southern Shephelah and Negev that received spoil from David following his attack on the Amalekites. The immediate context of the list is David's recovery of lost possessions and persons from the Amalekite raid at Ziklag (1 Sam 30:1–26). Yet it seems likely that this list also refers to David's practice of raiding the territory of the Geshurites, the Girzites, and the Amalekites to send spoil both to the Judahite tribal leaders and their rival, Achish king of Gath (1 Sam 27:8–12). According to this passage, David's raids took place in the Negev of Judah, the Negev of the Jerahmeelites, and the Negev of the Kenites. We can also point out that the Amalekites made a counter-raid against the Negev of the Cherethites (1 Sam 30:14), which is likely in the western Negev basin in the vicinity of Gerar and Ziklag, and against the Negev of Caleb (perhaps identical with the Negev of Judah), which should probably be located in the transition between the southern hill country and northern Negev (1 Sam 30:14; see Figure 2.1).

Figure 2.1 Map of sites mentioned in 1 Sam 30:27–31

The list of towns in 1 Samuel 30:27–31 seems to encompass all these sub-regions of the Negev save perhaps the Negev of the Cherethites; it reads (in the MT and with v. 26 included):

> When David came to Ziklag, he sent part of the spoil to his friends, the elders of Judah, saying, "Here is a present for you from the spoil of the enemies of the LORD"; it was for those in Bethel, in Ramoth of the Negeb, in Jattir, in Aroer, in Siphmoth, in Eshtemoa, in Racal, in the towns of the Jerahmeelites, in the towns of the Kenites, in Hormah, in Bor-ashan, in Athach, in Hebron, all the places where David and his men had roamed.

Scholars have noted the textual difficulty with the list as the Hebrew and various Greek versions of 1 Samuel 30:27–31 differ in the number and spelling of the place names (e.g., Auld 2012: 344–45; Dietrich 2019; McCarter 1980: 436; Na'aman 2010: 178–79 [with earlier literature]; Smith 1899: 250–51; Tsumura 2007: 646–48). Rainey (Rainey and Notley 2006: 150) described the various issues as follows:

> The list of the towns that received this largess is a contribution to the historical geography of the Negeb and the southern Judean hill country. The Hebrew and Greek lists are not always compatible and the textual solutions are not always transparent.

The above statement defines the problem I address in this paper. Specifically, I will attempt to reconstruct the original list of 1 Samuel 30:27–31 using a cross-disciplinary approach that will incorporate the following lines of evidence:

1   by employing textual criticism of the various manuscript versions in the MT, LXX, and 4QSAM[a] (see Table 2.1). The spelling, order, and (even) the presence of biblical place names may vary across manuscripts. Particularly in lists of biblical toponyms, textual criticism should be used as a first step for establishing the textual dataset for comparison with subsequent lines of inquiry.

2. by comparing the list to related biblical texts (e.g., Josh 15:20–62). Comparing a specific toponym in a regional list (or in the narrative) to other biblical texts is perhaps the most important element for establishing the plausibility of a textual critical reconstruction, as well as suggesting a candidate for site identification. In other words, if a toponym is mentioned in multiple biblical sources it makes it much easier to establish the very existence of a biblical town, as well as argue for its presence in a given text.

3. by analyzing extra-biblical, contemporary documents where relevant (e.g., the Arad Ostraca). Like the previous point, extra-biblical documents sometimes refer to toponyms that appear in the biblical text. Where it occurs, this information is chronologically diagnostic, as there is usually clear indications of the period of composition of the document (e.g., the Arad Ostraca were written between the 8th and early 6th centuries BCE). Thus, toponyms in extra-biblical sources provide more straightforward evidence for contemporary realia than biblical topographic texts, as the dates of composition of the latter are debated. The main limitation is that there are so few texts that contain relevant toponyms, although these texts sometimes refer to additional place names not mentioned in the biblical text (e.g., Beth-haRapid in Lachish Letter No. 4).

4. by re-examining late Antique and early modern locational evidence to aid in locating biblical toponyms. There are many sources for place names of Palestine (c. 4th century to early 20th century CE) that vary in their scope, language, and relation to biblical place names. In many ways, Eusebius' *Onomasticon*, as well as the maps, travelogues, and surveys of 19th- and early 20th-century explorers of Palestine (e.g., Edward Robinson, the Survey of Western Palestine), represent primary sources for the historical geographer. These sources have been underutilized by modern scholarship, but the increasing amount of digitized (and freely available) early maps, surveys, and travelogues make this a rich dataset for scholars to utilize in historical geography. Assuming that a ruin is within the correct geographical area, the presence of a similar Arabic toponym to a biblical toponym should be considered the most important evidence for suggesting the identification of a ruin with a biblical place name.

5. by utilizing up-to-date archaeological research and data to assist in identifying biblical place names with archaeological ruins and to help determine the historical setting of the list.[2] Archaeological excavations and surveys provide an ever-growing and improving dataset to compare with the above-mentioned lines of evidence. Excavations can often determine the periods of occupation at a site, as well as establish the nature of that occupation across the various periods. For example, consider Lachish strata VII–II. The site was occupied from the Late Bronze through the Iron IIC (i.e., contemporary with Israel/Judah's presence in Canaan) with a gap during the Iron I and a Judahite administration center from the late 10th century BCE to the early 6th century BCE (cf. Josh 12:11; Isa 36:2, 8; Jer 34:7; Mic 1:13 – Garfinkel, Hasel, and Klingbeil 2021). Surface surveys are also vital for gauging the presence and nature of occupation at a site (through the collection, dating, and calculation of pottery sherds), and, accordingly, its suitability as a candidate for a biblical toponym. On the other hand, archaeological surveys can sometimes provide incomplete information about a site as there are many factors involved that might create an incomplete or distorted picture of the occupation of a given site (see, e.g., Dagan 2009; Garfinkel and Ganor 2010). Finally, considering recent persuasive arguments by Ben-Yosef (2019) regarding the so-called "architectural bias" in biblical archaeology, it is worth noting that the lack thereof of archaeological remains does not automatically rule out a site identification. Ben-Yosef has shown that the Edomites of the 11th through 9th centuries BCE were nomadic, possessed a

Chris McKinny

Table 2.1 Site identifications for 1 Sam 30:27–31

English	MT	LXX[A]	LXX[B]	4QSAM[a]	Variants	Reconstruction options	References	ID (A)	ID (B)
Bethel	בית־אל	Βαιθηλ	Βαιθσουρ	–	βιθλ(εε)μ	Bethel/Bethuel (Beth-zur?)	Josh 15:30; 19:4; 1 Chr 4:30 (Bethuel/Chesil); Josh 15:58; 1 Chr 2:45; 2 Chr 11:7; Neh 3:16 (Beth-zur)	Tell es-Saqati? (Bethuel/Chesil)	Khirbet eṭ-Ṭubeiqa (Beth-zur)
Ramoth of the Negev	ברמות־נגב	Ραμαθ νοτου	Ραμα νοτου	–	–	Ramoth of the Negev	Josh 15:29; 19:3, 8; 1 Chr 4:33; Arad Ostraca no. 24	Tell Milḥ?	–
Jattir	יתר	Ειεθερ	Γεθθορ	–	Ιεθερ	Jattir	Josh 15:48; 21:14; 1 Sam 30:27; 1 Chr 6:57	Khirbet Attir	–
Aroer	ערער	Αροηρ	Αροηρ	–	Αρικαιν	Aroer	Josh 15:22 (Adadah = Aroer)	Khirbet ʿArʿarah/Tell Esdar	–
–	–	–	Αμμαδει	–	–	Amad? (doublet for Aroer?)	–	–	–
Siphmoth	שפמות	Σαφαμως	Σαφει	–	Σεφεινμοθ	Siphmoth	Otherwise unknown	Khirbet as-Sufei?	–
Eshtemoa	אשתמע	Εσθεμα	Εσθειε	אשתמע	Νοθομ	Eshtemoa	Josh 15:50; 21:14; 1 Chr 4:17, 19; 6:57	es-Semūʿ	–
–	–	–	Γεθ	–	–	Gibeah?	Josh 15:57 (Gibeah)	Khirbet el-Qaryatein?	–
–	–	Κειμαθ	Κιναν	–	Κιναν	Kain (Kinah?)	Josh 15:57 (Kain); Josh 15:22; cf. Judg 1:16 (Kinah)	Khirbet Bani Dar (Kain)	Khirbet Ghazzeh? (Kinah)

English	Hebrew	Greek	Greek	Hebrew	Greek	Identification	References	Site	Alt.
–	–	–	Σαφέκ	–	–	Ziph?	e.g., 1 Sam 23:14–15, 24; 26:2	Tell Zîf	–
–	–	–	Θειμάθ	–	–	Timnah?	Josh 15:57; (cf. LXXB Josh 19:40)	Khirbet umm el-Asfâ?	–
Racal	רָכָל	Ραχηλ	Καρμήλῳ	–	–	Carmel	e.g., Josh 15:55; 1 Sam 15:12; 25:2	Khirbet el-Kirmil	–
Towns of the Jerahmeelites	עָרֵי הַיְּרַחְמְאֵלִי	πόλεσιν τοῦ Ιεραμηλει	πόλεσιν τοῦ Ιεραηλ	–	–	Towns of the Jerahmeelites	1 Sam 27:10; 1 Chr 2:9, 25–27; 2:33, 42	Vicinity of Ruḥama	–
Towns of the Kenites	עָרֵי הַקֵּינִי	πόλεσιν τοῦ Κειναιου	πόλεσιν τοῦ Κενεζει	עָרֵי הַקֵּנִי	–	Towns of the Kenites (Kenizzites?)	1 Sam 27:10 (LXX = Kenizzites); e.g., Gen 15:19; Num 32:12; Josh 14:6, 14	Central and Eastern Beersheba Basin	–
Hormah	חָרְמָה	Ραμμα	Ιερεμουθ	–	–	Hormah (Jarmuth?)	Num 14:45; 21:3; Deut 1:44; Josh 12:14; 15:30; 19:4; Judg 1:17; 1 Sam. 30:30; 1 Chr 4:30	Khirbet Meshash?	Khirbet Yarmûk
Bor-ashan	בּוֹר־עָשָׁן	Βορασαν	Βηρσαβεε	–	–	Beersheba (Bor-ashan?)	Josh 15:42; 19:7; 1 Chr 4:32; cf. 1 Chr 6:59	Bir es-Sebaʿ	Tell Judeideh?
Athach	עָתָךְ	Αθαγ	Νοό	–	ΑθαΧ, ΝαγεΒ	Arad (Ether?)	Josh 15:42; 19:7; 1 Chr 4:32	Tell Arad?	Khirbet el-ʿĀter?
Hebron	חֶבְרוֹן	Χεβρών	Χεβρών	חֶבְרוֹן	–	Hebron	e.g., Josh 15:42	Tell er-Rumeida	–

sophisticated, hierarchical "kingdom" based on copper mining and production, and left virtually no architectural remains as they lived in tents. This paradigm-shifting argument has wide implications for academic discussions regarding the relationship between archaeology, the biblical text, and historical reconstruction. For our purposes, Ben-Yosef's (2019) arguments are particularly relevant as 1 Sam 30:27–31 refers to settlements in regions where nomadic populations resided throughout the Iron Age (e.g., the Kenites – Josh 15:22; Judg 1:16, see below).

Site Identifications of the Amalekite Spoil List

Bethel of the Northern Negev or Beth-zur of the Northern Judean Hills

There is a textual critical issue with the first town in the spoil list. The MT and LXX[A] support the reading "Bethel," which is reflected in most translations. However, LXX[B] has Baithsour (Βαιθσουρ), which would point to Beth-zur of the northern Judean Hills (Josh 15:58; 1 Chr 2:45; 2 Chr 11:7; Neh 3:16). Given the fact that towns from the Shephelah, Negev, and Judean hill country appear in the list, either Bethel (of the Negev) or Beth-zur (Khirbet eṭ-Ṭubeiqa) are possible reconstructions, although Beth-zur would be the most northern town in the list.

If the first town in the list should be understood as "Bethel," it clearly cannot be the famous Bethel (Beitin) of the central hills (e.g., Gen 12:8), but it could be the same town as Bethuel/Bethul of the Negev (Josh. 15:30;[3] 19:4; 1 Chr. 4:30)[4] (see Albright 1924: 150). While the exact identification of this town remains uncertain (see e.g., Abel 1938: 51, 283 who suggested Khirbet er-Ras),[5] Na'aman (1980: 147) connected Bethel with Tell umm Butein. This very probable suggestion is based on the observed phenomenon of ancient place names being preserved until modern times in the Arabic names of ruins, villages, and other topographic features (as pioneered in Robinson and Smith 1841). Na'aman (2010: 180–81) later suggested that Bethel[6] should be identified with Tell es-Seba'/Tel Beersheba.[7] As we will see below, it is possible that Beersheba appears toward the end of the list.

Ramoth of the Negev

Ramoth of the Negev is the second town in the spoil list. Besides the Amalekite spoil list, "Ramah of the Negev" appears alongside "Baalath-beer" as a boundary marker limiting the territory of Simeon in Joshua 19:8 (cf. 1 Chr 4:33). Ramah of the Negev and Baalath-beer should be interpreted as being in apposition to one another as they are not demarcated by a *waw* [cf. also LXX[A]'s eos BaalethBerramoth (ἕως Βααλεθβηρραμωθ)]. Therefore, Joshua 19:8 can be translated as "as far as Baalath-beer, *that is* Ramoth (or Ramah) of the Negev." This interpretation also explains the absence of Ramoth of the Negev from the Negev District of Joshua 15:21–33, which has "Baalah" instead of Baalath-beer (Josh 15:29; cf. Balah in Josh 19:3 and Baalath in 1 Kgs 9:18; 2 Chr 8:6).[8]

The appearance of Ramoth of the Negev in Arad Ostraca no. 24 (lines 12–20) adds the extra-biblical dimension to the historical geographical discussion of the site. The town appears in connection with Judahite troop movements against the Edomites in the last days of the Judahite kingdom (Aharoni, Naveh, and Rainey 1981: 46–49; Ahituv 2008: 128–30). This text indicates that Ramoth of the Negev should be located in proximity to Arad. Accordingly, several scholars have connected the site with Tell Gharrah (i.e., Tel ʿIra; Na'aman 1980; Lemaire 1988; Rainey and Notley 2006: 159). Tell Gharrah was occupied in the Late Iron IIA and Iron IIB (Stratum VIII) before the large Iron IIC fortress (Stratum VII) was constructed (Beit-Arieh 1999: 170; see also Herzog and Singer-Avitz 2004: 228–29). The identification of Ramah of the Negev with Tell Gharrah (e.g., Rainey and Notley 2006: 266) is possible given the elevation of Tell Gharrah and the general geographical setting, however, I suggest that Tell Gharrah may be tentatively identified with Jagur (Josh 15:21). Jagur appears alongside Arad (i.e., MT's Eder), Kinah (Khirbet Ghazzeh, see below), and Aroer (i.e., MT's Adadah) in the Negev district (Josh 15:21–22). Van de Velde's map gives the alternate name of "Jurrah" for Tell Gharrah (1858), which bears a close resemblance to Jagur, as Arabic *jīm* is comparable to Hebrew *gimel* (cf. Gedor to Jedur – Josh 15:58).

If, as we have suggested, Baalath-beer and Ramoth of the Negev[9] are alternate names for the same site, then we can add Ramoth of the Negev to Kochavi's (1993) suggestion to identify Tell Milḥ (Tel Malḥata)[10] with Baalath-beer/Baalath (Josh 19:8; 1 Kgs 9:18). Tell Milḥ is one of the most important Iron Age settlements in the Beersheba Basin covering an area of 18 dunams on a small hill above several springs. The site was apparently only fortified in either the 10th or 9th century BCE (see, e.g., Beit-Arieh, Freud, and Tal 2015: 739; see discussion in McKinny forthcoming b). However, it stands to reason that the vicinity of Tell Milḥ with its important springs remained an important strategic center even during periods that are largely absent in the Beersheba Basin's archaeological record – the Late Bronze and Iron I periods. This is a good example of recognizing the importance of land resources for nomadic groups, who leave minimal archaeological footprints (see above, Ben-Yosef 2019). This is also supported by the presence of nearby Tel Masos (Hormah?), which was occupied during these earlier periods.

Jattir

Jattir (e.g., Josh 21:14) has been universally identified with Khirbet 'Attir in the southern Judean Hills since Robinson's original suggestion (1841: 194). In addition to the suitable Arabic name, Eusebius[11] described Jattir as a very large Christian village located in the interior of Daroma (beside Malatha) that was located some 20 milestones from Eleutheropolis (*Onom.* 433; 543; 569). These details accord well with Khirbet 'Attir.

While the identification of Jattir with Khirbet 'Attir comports nicely with the toponymic and philological data, our archaeological knowledge of the site has changed dramatically in the last few decades – illustrating the dynamic nature of archaeological data. Excavations were carried out at Khirbet 'Attir from 1995–1999 by H. Eshel, J. Magness, and E. Shenhav (2000, 2008). The focus of the excavation was on the southern spur of the site where a Byzantine church was excavated (Eshel, Magness, and Shenhav 2008: 2070). Iron Age IIC and Persian remains were found in Area B (eastern slope of the hill) mostly in fills with no remains preceding the 7th century BCE, and some Chalcolithic and Early Bronze sherds were uncovered in caves filled during the Byzantine period (Eshel, Magness, and Shenhav 2008: 2070). Ofer's survey of the site revealed remains from the Iron IIA (early and late), Iron IIB, and Iron IIC over an area of 15 dunams, in addition to the remains that were excavated at the site (1993b: site 1). Significantly, the more recent survey of Khirbet 'Attir also revealed remains from the Middle Bronze, Late Bronze, and Iron I (Baumgarten and Silberklang 2015: sites 153 and 165) – periods that were not present in preceding surveys or in excavations. This new archeological data seems to indicate that Jattir was one of the more significant towns in the Judean hill country, which would make it a logical recipient of spoil from Amalek.

Aroer

Aroer's appearance in the Amalek spoil list (1 Sam 30:28) is the only unambiguous reference to the town in the biblical text, although most scholars emend the MT/LXX's "Adadah" of Joshua 15:22 to Aroer attributing the error to a transmutation of both instances of *resh* (ר) to *dalet* (ד) (e.g., Aharoni 1979: 117; Simons 1959: 145). Robinson's (1841: 2.162) original suggestion to identify the site with Khirbet ʿArʿarah in the southern part of the central Beersheba Basin is widely agreed upon.

Despite this, Biran and Cohen's excavations of Khirbet ʿArʿarah (Tel ʿAroʿer) revealed a large fortress (five acres) dateable to the Iron IIB-C (Biran 1993; Biran and Cohen 1981; Thareani-Sussely 2011). On account of this, some scholars suggest that the Aroer of 1 Samuel 30:28 should be located 1.5 km north of Khirbet ʿArʿarah at Tell Esdar, which has revealed remains from the Iron I and early Iron IIA (Biran and Cohen 1981; Eldar-Nir 2015: site 12; Kallai 1986: 117; Kochavi 1992: 609).[12] The movement of a site's name from one location to another nearby location is a regular phenomenon in the southern Levant. Here, again, it is worth pointing out that the name of a location may be in place before architectural structures (which appear in the archaeological record) were constructed, and remembered long after those structures were abandoned.

Siphmoth

Siphmoth only appears in 1 Samuel 30:28 and its spelling is well-attested across the different manuscript traditions except for LXX^B's slightly corrupt Σαφει. Unfortunately, it remains completely unknown (Na'aman 2010: 180). Some suggest a connection with Zabdi the Shiphmite (Kotter 1992: 6.51), who the Chronicler states oversaw David's wine cellars along with "Shimei the Ramathite" who was over the vineyards (1 Chr 27:27). This connection is plausible although by no means certain. It is also unclear if Siphmoth should be affiliated with either the preceding Negev towns of Bethel (if it is not Beth-zur) and Ramoth of the Negev, or if it should be geographically associated with the subsequent Eshtemoa of the southern Hebron hills.[13] If it is the latter, then one possibility for Siphmoth is Hurrabat as-Sufei – a site located to the south of Eshtemoa bearing a very similar name to Siphmoth. To my knowledge, this site has not been surveyed (cf. Ofer 1993b), and it is presently located within the southern part of the village of es-Samuʿ. A few kilometers to the south of Hurrabat as-Sufei, the new survey of the region revealed Iron Age (with no sub-periods given) remains at Khirbet el-Kharabah and Khirbet al-Lasifar. These ruins are both just northeast of Upper Anim (Khirbet Ghuwein et-Foqa) and are referred to as "a large ruin on a hilltop (c. 200 × 300 m)" and occupied during the Iron Age and Byzantine periods (Baumgarten and Silberklang 2015: sites 81 and 84, cf. site 126).

Eshtemoa

Eshtemoa[14] (or Eshtemoh – Josh 15:50; cf. also Josh 21:42; 1 Chr 6:57) has been universally identified with es-Samuʿ since Robinson's initial suggestion (1841: 3.626–627).[15] The site has been examined several times revealing remains from the Chalcolithic, Early Bronze I, Iron Age I, early Iron IIA (10 dunams), late Iron IIA (25 dunams), Iron IIB (20 dunams), and Iron IIC (10 dunams), and Roman-Byzantine periods (Kochavi 1972: site 233; Ofer 1993b: site 25). Es-Samuʿ has also undergone several excavations, most of which were related to the Byzantine synagogue that was later turned into a mosque (Yeivin 1990, 2004). Of special note is an Iron IIB[16] silver hoard of five jugs and weighing 26 kg that was found beneath the floors of the synagogue (Eshel et al. 2019; Kletter and Brand 1998; Yeivin 2004).

LXX[B] Additional Toponyms? Gibeah, Kain, Ziph, and Timnah (cf. Josh 15:55–57)

Codex Vaticanus includes four additional toponyms in 1 Samuel 30:28a that are not found in the MT, LXX[A], or 4QSAM[a]. These include the following: Γὲθ, Κειμάθ, Σαφέκ, and Θειμάθ. In addition, the apparatuses in Swete and Rahlfs list the notable variant of Κιναν for Κειμάθ (Rahlfs 1979: 568; Swete 1887: 608–09). Several scholars suggest that these are doublets for other names in the list (e.g., McCarter 1980: 434; Na'aman 2010: 179). It should be noted that a similar loss of place names from a list occurs in LXX[B] in Joshua 15:59a, which includes the well-known places of Bethlehem, Tekoa, Etam, and others (McKinny 2017: 270–78; Rainey and Notley 2006: 20). While it is possible that some or all of the names are doublets, it is also possible that LXX[B] retains a list of toponyms that was simply lost in later transmission, as is clearly the case in Joshua 15:59a.

Following this line of thought, two of the names in 1 Samuel 30:28a may be plausibly reconstructed as Kain (Κειμάθ/Κιναν)[17] and Timnah (Θειμάθ) of the Maon District of the southern hill country (Josh 15:55–57). Kain has been identified with Khirbet Bani Darr. The nearby sheikh's tomb "en-Nebi Yaqin" probably preserves the name of Kinah (Conder and Kitchener 1883: 312; Aharoni 1979: 355), and Khirbet Bani Darr itself has abundant Iron IIA–C remains over an area of 35 dunams (Kochavi 1972: site 162; Ofer 1993a: site 171). The identification of Timnah of Joshua 15:57 is less certain. I have argued elsewhere that it may be plausibly identified with Khirbet umm el-Asfa, which is near Wadi et-Tebban – an Arabic toponym that could preserve "Timnah" (McKinny 2017: 260–63).[18] Khirbet umm el-Asfa has Iron IIA–C remains over an area of 12 dunams (Ofer 1993b: site 96).

The other two names – Γὲθ and Σαφέκ – are difficult to reconstruct. Γὲθ certainly cannot be "Gath" of the Philistines (Tell es-Safi) as David is said to have sent the spoil to the "elders of Judah" (1 Sam 30:26). It is also less likely that it refers to one of the other Gaths of the Shephelah,[19] as most of the towns in this list are in the Negev and southern Hebron hills (see discussion in McKinny 2018). Adopting the geographical approach that we have suggested above, it is possible that Γὲθ and Σαφέκ represent corrupted spellings of Gibeah and Ziph of the Maon District (Josh 15:55–57). Here, it should be noted that these towns are in the same district as the subsequent "Carmel" (Josh 15:55; 1 Sam 30:29), which we will discuss below. Gibeah of the hill country (cf. also Gibeon of Josh 10:41)[20] is possibly located at Khirbet el-Qaryatein on the southeastern slopes of the Judean Hills (Levin 2003: 202). Surveys and excavations at the site revealed remains from the Middle Bronze II (including fortifications), Iron II (no sub-periods), Roman, and Byzantine periods (Kallai 1986: 378, n. 97 – unpublished Aharoni survey; Derfler 2003; Derfler and Govrin 1993). Additional corroboration of this suggestion may be found in the nearby site of "Jembeh" on the Van de Velde map (1858), which could preserve a corrupted form of the name "Gibeah."

Ziph has long been associated with Tell Zif south of Hebron,[21] which preserves the name (Robinson and Smith 1841: 2.193–200). Archeological investigations at Tell Zif revealed remains from the early Iron IIA–IIC over an area of c. 13 dunams (Baruch 1997; Kochavi 1972: site 178, 179, 189; Ofer 1993b: site 147, 148, 135). If Σαφέκ represents Ziph, it is interesting to consider what Ziph's potential inclusion in the list of spoil to the elders of Judah might mean considering the Ziphites' earlier hostility toward David (1 Sam 23:14–15; 26:1–2) in favor of Saul. If Ziph was in the original spoil list, perhaps the author of Samuel was indicating that even Ziph had been reconciled to his rule. Some commentators also connect the Ziphites loyalty to Saul to references mentioning Saul setting up a monument at Carmel (1 Sam 15:12) and Nabal of Carmel's hostility toward David (1 Sam 25) (see e.g., Miller and Hayes 2006: 165–66). Obviously, we cannot be too certain about these tentative suggestions.

Carmel

The next place name in the list is "Racal," which is present in the MT, LXX[A], and as variants in the LXX tradition (Rahlfs 1979: 568; Swete 1887: 608–09). Nevertheless, most commentators reconstruct the town name as "Carmel" in light of the reading of Καρμήλῳ in LXX[B] and the lack of a town named "Racal" in the Bible or other sources (e.g., McCarter 1980: 436; Na'aman 2010: 179; Rainey and Notley 2006: 150). Khirbet el-Kirmil clearly preserves the name of Carmel (Robinson and Smith 1841: 2.193–200), and surveys at the site revealed remains from the Iron IIA-C over an area of 7 dunams (Batz 2007; Kochavi 1972: sites 222 and 223; Ofer 1993b: sites 72, 73, and T14).

Carmel appears several times in Samuel in connection with Saul, Nabal, and Abigal – who became David's wife (1 Sam 15:12; 25:2, 5, 7, 40; 27:3; 30:5; 2 Sam 2:2; 3:3). Notably, Hezro, one of David's "mighty men," also hailed from Carmel (2 Sam 23:35). As I have argued elsewhere, the historical geography of the "mighty men" list (Sam 23:8–39; 1 Chr 11:10–47) may provide important details related to the geopolitics of the early monarchy. In my view, the geographical distribution of this list may indicate "powerbases" of Davidic support in southern Ephraim, Benjamin, the vicinity of Bethlehem, and the vicinity of Hebron (McKinny forthcoming c). This may also be represented in the spoil list, which includes the southern highland towns of Jattir, Eshtemoa, Carmel, and Hebron, as well as possibly Beth-zur, Gibeah, Kinah, Ziph, and Timnah. This also aligns well with the initial support for David at Hebron (2 Sam 2:1–2), as well as Hebron later becoming the center of Absalom's revolt that was also aided and abetted by Ahithophel – who hailed from the nearby town of Gilo(h)[22] (2 Sam 15:7–12; cf. Josh 15:51).

The "Cities" of the Jerahmeelites

The next two entries in the list refer to two ethnic groups in the Negev – the Jerahmeelites and the Kenites (or Kenizzites). The "cities" should be understood as the desert settlements of these semi-nomadic entities and not distinct towns of the Negev. The Jerahmeelites appear across the various manuscript traditions in 1 Sam 30:29. Their appearance here and in David's feint to Achish in 1 Sam 27:10 indicates that they were already (or were to be) affiliated with Judah (Dietrich 2007: 197; Rainey and Notley 2006: 149). This passage identifies the Geshurites, the Girzites, and the Amalekites as the targets of David's raids (1 Sam 27:9). These were common enemies to Gath and Judah that were situated throughout the Negev alongside groups affiliated with the Judahites, which included the Jerahmeelites and Kenites (1 Sam 27:10). These latter groups were depicted as being part of the clan-based nexus of Israel, and David allowed Achish to believe that he was attacking his own people (1 Sam 27:11). Instead, David both defeated Israel's enemies while also sending spoil from his raids to various towns in the southern hill country of Judah and the Negev (1 Sam 30:28–31).

At this point, we should make a brief comment on the locations of the different "Negevs" in Samuel. The "Negevs" of the Cherethites, Judah, and the Calebites (1 Sam 30:14), as well as the locations of the Negev of the Jerahmeelites and the Negev of the Kenites (1 Sam

27:10; 30:29) can be localized to different regions of the Beersheba Basin and northern Negev Highlands (see Rainey and Notley 2006: 148). The Jerahmeelites are often connected with the region of Bir Ruḥama (modern Yeroham)[23] due to the similarity of Jerahmeel and Ruḥama (Aharoni 1958: 29). This clan is also usually connected with Arad Beth-Yeroham in the Shishak list – a toponym that occurs immediately after Arad Rabbah, the latter of which is probably to be identified with Tell ʿArad (Nos. 107–12; see Rainey and Notley 2006: 187). The Negev of Caleb (1 Sam 30:14) can be associated with the northernmost part of the Negev on account of the various biblical traditions related to Caleb in the region south of Debir (e.g., Josh 14; 15:13–19; Judg 1:11–15, 19–20). The Negev of Judah (1 Sam 27:10) could be associated with the vicinity of Beersheba, although it may an alternate term for the same region as the Negev of Caleb. The location of the Negev of the Kenites is well-established in the eastern Beersheba Basin near Arad since Judges 1:16 indicates that the Kenites settled near Arad (Naʾaman 1980). The Cherethites (and the Pelethites) are clearly associated with the Philistines.[24] In light of this, it seems likely that the Negev of the Cherethites was in the western Negev probably along Nahal Gerar (Aharoni 1958: 28–30; Naʾaman 1980: 137).

The "Cities" of the Kenites or Kenizzites

The textual critical evidence is divided on whether the next name should be understood as the "Kenites" (MT and LXX^A) or the "Kenizzites" (LXX^B and 4QSAM^a). The Kenites are more well-known[25] and were clearly associated with the eastern Negev and the town of Arad (Tell ʿArad). These two entities appear together in Genesis 15:19–21. It is possible this list is arranged from south to north[26] with the Kenites, the Kenizzites, and the Kadmonites representing desert peoples of the south; the Hittites representing a southern hill country people in the vicinity of Hebron (e.g., Gen 23); the Perizzites representing a central/northern hill country people (Gen 13:7; 34:30 – Bethel and Shechem); and the Rephaim referring to those living in northern Transjordan (cf. Gen 14:5). The Kenizzites may be associated with Kenaz who was a "son" of Eliphaz and a tribe of Edom (Gen 36:15). Caleb and Othniel were also apparently connected with the Kenizzites (Num 32:12; Josh 14:6; 15:17), as well as the northern Negev (Judg 1:15; 1 Sam 30:14). The "Kenizzites" (LXX^B – Κενεζι) instead of the "Kenites" (MT – קֵינִי)[27] also appears in 1 Sam 27:10 in the LXX, which led McCarter (1980: 413–14, 434) to favor Kenizzite in 1 Sam 27:10; 30:29. However, the reference to the Kenites in connection with Saul's attack on the Amalekites in 1 Samuel 15:6 would seem to favor the "Kenites" reading for the later passages (Naʾaman 2010: 179; Rainey and Notley 2006: 150). In 1 Samuel 15, the Kenites were spared from being attacked by Saul due to their assistance of Israel during the wilderness wanderings, which points back to Numbers 10:29–32.[28]

According to Judges 1:16, the Kenites "went up with the people of Judah from the city of palms[29] into the wilderness of Judah, which lies in the Negev near Arad, and they went and settled with the people." The Kenites are also referred to in "Kinah" a town of the Negev District (Josh 15:22; cf. *Onom.* 903) that also occurs on Arad Ostracon no. 24 (see above; Aharoni, Naveh, and Rainey 1981; cf. Ahituv 2008: 126–33). The connection between the territory east of Arad and the Kenites is strengthened by the existence of Wadi el-Qeini. Since most scholars equate Kinah with the Kenite clan,[30] the likely toponymic connection between Wadi el-Qeini[31] and Kinah led several scholars to suggest a connection between Khirbet Ghazzeh (Horvat ʿUza) and the town of Kinah (e.g., Aharoni 1958: 35 before changing his mind to Khirbet Ṭaiyib, see Aharoni 1979: 406, 438; Naʾaman 2005: 162 with earlier literature). The fortress at Khirbet Ghazzeh dates to the Iron IIC and the excavator understood that the fortress was controlled by Judah and Jerusalem (Beit-Arieh 2007). The fortress at Khirbet Ghazzeh (and the nearby fort at Horvat Radum) seem to clearly date to the 7th century BCE. However, it is worth noting that Aharoni found pottery from the Iron IIA and Iron IIB on the slopes of the wadi near the site (see discussion in Beit-Arieh and Cresson 2007: 1), which could indicate earlier activity at or near the site. In any case, two details should be born in mind. First, Beit-Arieh's (2011: sites 10, 21, and 25) survey of the vicinity revealed several sites that he generally dated to the Iron Age or Iron II. Second, we have noted above the importance of avoiding the "architectural bias" (Ben-Yosef 2019) for historical reconstruction. In this case, when the group (i.e., the Kenites) in question is a nomadic tribe within a relatively sparsely inhabited region (i.e., the Negev), it is even more important to highlight the role that archaeologically-invisible nomadic populations played in the Iron Age. In addition, it is also possible that some of the so-called Iron I/II "Negev Fortresses" (Cohen and Cohen-Amin 2004) could be related to the Kenite (or Kenizzite) and Jerahmeelite settlements, which seem to date mostly to the 11th and 10th centuries BCE (Boaretto, Finkelstein, and Shahack-Gross 2010).

Hormah

The suggestion to identify the enigmatic Hormah[32] with Tel Masos (Khirbet Meshash) remains the best option (Aharoni 1979: 216–17), at least with the settlement listed in the town lists (Josh 12:14; 15:30; 19:4; 1 Sam 30:30; 1 Chr 4:30; cf. also Judg 1:17). This location also fits with the general vicinity of the Jerahmeelites and Kenites in the southern and eastern Negev.[33]

Tel Masos is a significant site in the central Beersheba Basin located to the west of Tel Malḥata and Tel ʿIra. Tel Masos consists of three distinct settlements including the main settlement which was inhabited during the Chalcolithic period, the Late Bronze IIB, and the Iron I; a Syrian Nestorian monastery built over an Iron IIC fortress; and a Middle Bronze II "enclosure" of 20 dunams (Kempinski 1993).

We will focus our discussion on the main settlement. Late Bronze IIB sherds were found in the earliest stratum (III) of the site. These, along with the presence of a scarab from the reign of Seti II (c. 1200 BCE) establish the reality of a 13th century BCE settlement at Tel Masos (Kempinski 1993). Tel Masos was apparently the only town inhabited in the Beersheba Basin during the 13th–11th centuries BCE. According to the excavators, Strata III–I are related to the end of the 13th–11th centuries BCE/Iron I when a large settlement consisting of four-room houses was built (Kempinski 1993: 986). Following their reconstruction, Tel Masos was abandoned c. 1000 BCE.

Herzog and Singer-Avitz re-examined the pottery from Tel Masos and dated Stratum III to the end of the Late Bronze/Iron I (presumably the 13th–11th centuries BCE) and Strata II–I to the early Iron IIA (10th century BCE), the latter of which they equate to Arad XII which was apparently destroyed by Shishak (Herzog and Singer-Avitz 2004: 221–22). If such a reconstruction can be sustained, then it is possible that Tel Masos was in fact destroyed or abandoned in relation to Shishak's campaign. If so, it is tempting to relate Tel Masos to both Hormah, which became the new name for Zephath (Judg 1:17) and the "cities" of the king of Arad (Num 21:3), and Arad Beth-Yeroham on the Shishak list. In addition, this would also fit with the sending of spoil to Hormah in connection with David (1 Sam 30:30). Obviously, we cannot be certain of this reconstruction, but it fits the textual evidence and available archaeological details.

Bor-ashan and Athach = Beersheba and Arad?

Bor-ashan and Athach are among the most difficult toponyms in this list. The MT and LXX[A] agree on the spelling of Bor-ashan, but LXX[B] reads "Βηρσάβεε" (i.e., Beersheba) instead. While it cannot be considered certain, the LXX[B] reading seems preferable due to the lack of the important and oft-mentioned Negev town (e.g., 1 Sam 3:20; 8:2; 2 Sam 3:10; 17:11; 24:2, 7, 15) elsewhere in a list of towns related to the Negev.[34] Gophna and Yisrael's limited exposure of Bir es-Sebaʿ revealed Iron IIA remains under Byzantine floors, but remains were found from all periods of the Iron Age over an area of 100 dunams in surveys of the site (Cohen, Landes, and Gophna 1968: 130; Gophna and Yisraeli 1973: 115–18; Manor 1992: 642).[35]

Athach (עֲתָךְ) – the next name in the list – could be an error for Ether (עֶתֶר) with the final *kaf* (ך) of Athach perhaps relating to an original *resh* (ר). Since Ashan and Ether appear as towns together in the Simeonite town list (Josh 19:7; cf. 1 Chr 4:32) and in the Libnah district (Josh 15:42), it is possible that 1 Samuel 30:30 is another example of this pair of towns appearing together in the Hebrew Bible.[36] Since it has long been suggested that Ether of Joshua 15:42 and 19:7 should be connected with Khirbet ʿAter (Rainey 1983: 11) – an Iron II fortified ruin[37] between Tel Burna (Libnah) and Mareshah – it is tempting to connect "Bor-ashan and Athach (Ether?)" with the Ashan and Ether of the Libnah District (Josh 15:42; 19:7). However, like the possibility of Jarmuth's inclusion above, this reconstruction is less likely because the rest of the list is located in the Negev and southern highlands. The otherwise unknown "Athach" could be a corruption of "Arad" (עֲרָד),[38] which, like Beersheba, is noticeably absent from this list of prominent southern towns. Accordingly, I would like to raise the possibility that Beersheba (Bir es-Sebaʿ) and Arad (Tell ʿArad) was the original reading for these two toponyms. The appearance of Arad in the city list of Shishak (i.e., 925 BCE), as well as the archaeology of the earliest level of the Iron Age site (Stratum XII) indicate that Arad had an Iron IIA occupation (Herzog 2002: 27–49).

Hebron

Hebron is among the most mentioned towns in the biblical text and is universally identified with Tell er-Rumeida. Recent excavations by Ben-Shlomo and re-assessments of Hammond's 1960s excavation by Chadwick have added considerably to our knowledge of ancient Hebron. Hebron was extensively occupied and heavily fortified during the Early, Middle, and Late Bronze Ages, and remained a large Iron Age site from the Iron I through the late Iron II (Chadwick 1992; Eisenberg and Ben-Shlomo 2017; Garfinkel, Kreimerman, and Hasel 2019).

Conclusion

In this paper, we have discussed the historical geography of the towns of Judah that David sent spoil to following his defeat of the Amalekites (1 Sam 30:27–31). The towns were located in the Beersheba Basin and (perhaps) the Negev Highlands (Bethel, Ramoth of the Negev, Aroer, settlements of the Jerahmeelites and Kenites, Hormah, Beersheba? [i.e., Bor-ashan], and Arad? [i.e., Athach]) with other sites in the southern hill country of Judah (Jattir, Siphmoth?, Eshtemoa, Gibeah?, Kain?, Ziph?, Timnah?, Carmel, and Hebron; see Table 2.1).

There is nothing in the list (1 Sam 30:27–31) that demands that it be dated to the 8th century BCE (pre-Sennacherib campaign) as argued by Na'aman (2010: 182). I have rejected some of his identifications on historical geographical grounds (e.g., Bethel with Tell es-Sebaʻ, Hormah with Tel Halif, and Bor-ashan with Athach). I also question his overall argument to date this list to the 8th century BCE based on the fact that each of the sites "prospered in the second half of the 8th century BCE (Na'aman 2010: 181)," which he uses to date the composition of the "History of David's Rise" (i.e., 1 Sam 16–2 Sam 5) to the 8th century BCE (see studies in Bezzel and Kratz 2021).

Considering Na'aman's arguments, it is worth examining the chronological details that emerge from our list of suggested identifications. Tell es-Saqati (Bethel?) has only been surveyed, but revealed an Iron II (general) occupation. The identification of Ramah of the Negev remains debated, but if Tell el-Milḥ was the site then it was clearly one of the most important Iron IIA settlements in the Beersheba Basin. A recent survey at Jattir (Khirbet ʻAttir) revealed remains from the Iron I and Early Iron IIA (see above) in addition to later periods. Aroer (Khirbet ʻArʻarah) was only occupied during the Iron IIB-C, but the nearby site Tell Esdar was inhabited during the Iron I and Iron IIA. The location of Siphmoth cannot be identified with certainty, and my suggestions are (sites in the vicinity of Khirbet es-Sufei) are only generally dated to the Iron II. Eshtemoa (es-Semûʻ) was occupied in the Iron I and Early Iron IIA, as well as throughout the period

I put forth the possibility of connecting the additional toponyms of 1 Samuel 30:28a (LXX[B]) with the following towns from the Maon District (Josh 15:55–75): Gibeah (Khirbet el-Qaryatein?), Kain (Khirbet Bani Dar), Ziph (Tell Zîf), Timnah (Khirbet umm el-Asfa?). Along with Carmel (i.e., Racal; Khirbet el-Kirmil), each of these sites (besides Khirbet el-Qaryatein where no sub-periods were given) showed occupation ranging from the Iron IIA-C. The settlements of the Jerahmeelites and the Kenites (or Kennizites) can be generally localized to the area of Bir Ruḥama and the eastern Beersheba Basin, but the semi-nomadic nature of these groups should also be considered. It is also theoretically possible to connect these groups (especially the Jerahmeelites) with the Iron I/II Negev Fortresses, which stretched into the northern Negev Highlands. Tel Masos (Hormah?) was the main Late Bronze (only), Iron I, and early Iron IIA site in the Beersheba Basin. The archaeology of Beersheba (i.e., Bor-ashan; Bir es-Sebaʻ) is not as well-established as its sister site of Tell es-Sebaʻ (i.e., Sheba – Josh 15:26; 19:2), however, it is clear that the site was occupied in the Iron IIA-C. My suggestion to emend Athach to Arad is not certain, but neither are any other suggested identifications for Athach. Arad was occupied in the early Iron IIA. Finally, Hebron (Tell er-Rumeida) has extensive Iron I and Iron II remains (Chadwick personal communication, and see above).

In sum, a historical geographical analysis – one that identifies sites through analysis of toponyms, philological considerations, archaeology, and geographical context – of the Amalek spoil town list (1 Sam 30:27–31) allows for the possibility that the list reflects the period in which it purportedly reflects – i.e., the very late 11th or early 10th century BCE. We cannot prove with certainty that the list ultimately dates to this period, as most of the towns were also occupied in later phases of the Iron II. Nevertheless, the dispatching of spoil by a semi-nomadic outlaw and aspiring chieftain (i.e., David) taken from an enemy nomad (i.e., Amalek) to parts of his potential "kingdom" (consisting of both semi-nomadic, as well as sedentary sites) fits much better in the Iron I/II than in the Iron IIB when Judah reached its political apogee.

Notes

1 Toponymy is the study of place names. Biblical place names were often retained until the modern era in the Arabic toponyms of late Ottoman Palestine. With regard to historical geography, the study of place names from 19th century Palestine is crucial for establishing biblical site identifications and useful for understanding the culture of ancient Canaan and Israel.

2   Regarding this last point, I will also interact with Na'aman's (2010) reconstruction of the list, his suggested site identifications, and his contention that it reflects the 8th century BCE.
3   It seems clear that Chesil (כְּסִיל; Χασιλ) of Joshua 15:30 is a corruption for Bethul/Bethuel, as LXX[B] has Βαιθηλ.
4   Eusebius (2005) listed the towns separately (*Onom.* 243; 749; 951), but does not suggest a contemporary town or ruin.
5   Some scholars tentatively suggest Khirbet el-Qaryatein (Boling and Wright 1982: 383; Simons 1959: 145).
6   See also Na'aman's (2010: 181) note about the possibility that no. 130 of the Shishak list may be hypothetically reconstructed as "Bethel."
7   His latter conclusion is based on his desire to date the entire list to the years before Sennacherib's campaign in 701 BCE during which Tell es-Seba' was destroyed (Na'aman 2010: 183). Leaving the question of the date of the list aside, Na'aman's conclusion that Bethel of 1 Sam 30:27 should be related to Beersheba is unwarranted for several reasons. First, as he previously argued (Na'aman 1980: 146), Tell es-Seba' should be connected with the town of Sheba (Josh 19:2; cf. Josh 15:26 – probably a corrupt form of "Shema") – a nearby and related town to Beersheba (Bir es-Seba'). In my view, this suggestion is very important, as despite its common association with Tell es-Seba' (aka Tel Beersheva) biblical Beersheba was likely located at Bir es-Seba' near the traditional "well of Abraham" and Nahal Beersheba. Surveys and salvage excavations in the vicinity confirm that there was an important settlement from the Iron IIA-B (as well as occupation from the Iron IIC) in this vicinity (Panitz-Cohen 2005; Shemesh 2018a: sites 246–47, 253, 279, 284–85; see also discussion in Shemesh 2018b). The area of this settlement is west and north of the traditional "well of Abraham" in modern Beersheba. Second, suggesting that Tell es-Seba' was known as "Bethel" due to the presence of its famous (dismantled) altar is a very weak argument. For example, we have no idea if Beersheba itself (Bir es-Seba') also had a cultic compound (e.g., Amos 5:5) similar to the dismantled one at Tell es-Seba' and the decommissioned one at Arad (see e.g., Herzog 2001, 2010). Third, as noted above, the connection with Tell umm Butein seems probable, and, in my opinion, the nearby Iron Age ruin of Tell es-Saqaṭi (Govrin 2002: site 3), would seem to be good a candidate for identifying Bethel/Bethuel/Bethul. Aharoni identified this site (aka Tel Shoqet) with Beth-pelet (Aharoni and Avi-Yonah 2002: map 94; cf. Boling and Wright 1982: 382; Rainey and Notley 2006: 12, 149, 296), but this seems less likely,
8   Interestingly, names with the theophoric element of Baal were often given variant names that included non-Baal elements. This seems clear with Kiriath-jearim with its variant names related to "Baal." Baalath-beer/Ramah of the Negev may be another example of this. For a discussion of this development see Levin 2017.
9   After finding Iron Age occupation at Khirbet Ghazzeh (Horḅat ʿUza), Aharoni (1970: 22–24) suggested identifying the site with Ramah of the Negev.
10 See also the suggestion to connect Tell Milḥ with Moladah (Jericke 1997: 211–12; Na'aman 2010: 181), which is normally identified with the nearby site of Khirbet Waten.
11 Who also confused it with Ether of the Simeonite list (Josh 19:7, i.e., Khirbet ʿAter near Beit Jibrin, see below) (*Onom.* 433). The confusion of Jattir and Ether, is also depicted on the Medeba Map (Avi-Yonah 1954: 72–73; Donner 1992: 72).
12 Αμμαδει of Vaticanus is otherwise unknown and could be a doublet for the preceding Aroer.
13 If it is the former, then possibly Khirbet es-Sufi (along Wadi Abu Isder located west of Beer-sheba) is a possibility for Siphmoth. Iron Age remains were surveyed in the vicinity (Shemesh 2018b: site 240).
14 Eshtemoa is one of three extant toponyms in 4QSAM[a] (Parry 1999: 68).
15 Eusebius (2005) indicates that Eshtemoa was a "very large village" or "village" in Daroma near Anaea (i.e., Anim) (*Onom* 85; 429; 448).
16 The initial suggestion by Yeivin (1987) – that the horde should be dated to the Iron IIA and, in some way, related to the spoil sent by David to Eshtemoa and/or the Levitical towns – has been abandoned due to the fact that the jugs in which the silver hoard was found are well-dated to the Iron IIB (Eshel et al. 2018).
17 Kinah (Josh 15:22) of the Negev is also a possibility, see discussion below.
18 E.g., biblical Timnah is located at Tell el-Baṭâshī, but the later settlement is located at Khirbet Tibne (2 km south), which preserves the name.
19 Although it could theoretically be related to Moresheth-gath (Mic 1:1, 14). For the identification of this site with Khirbet Beit ʿAlam near Mareshah, see McKinny forthcoming a.

20 Eusebius indicates that there were two sites in the east of Daroma named Gabaa and Gabatha (*Onom.* 335), which could relate to the Gibeah mentioned in Josh 15:57 and the Gibeon in Josh 10:41.
21 Eusebius (2005) located it eight miles south of Hebron in Daroma and in the territory of Eleutheropolis (*Onom.* 464). For a discussion of this, see Notley and Safrai 2005: xvii, 89.
22 In my opinion, this town is to be located at edh-Dhahiriya near Khirbet Kefr Jul, which may preserve the name "Giloh" (McKinny 2017: 239–40).
23 Surveys revealed Iron Age remains (usually without sub-periods) at several sites in the vicinity of Bir Ruḥama (13 sites in Nahal Revivim map – Baumgarten and Eldar-Nir 2014; Eldar-Nir and Daninoo 2014: nine sites in Map of Masaf Negev; eight Iron Age sites in Yeruham Ridge map – west of Dimona – Eldar-Nir and Traubman 2015; Nahlieli and Veinberger 2015: site 37 in Map of Yeruham).
24 Prophetic texts indicate that the Cherethites were situated on the coastal plain (e.g., Ezek 25:16; Zeph 2:5). The Cherethites may also have been connected with the island of Crete based on the similar spelling between their names, although Crete is known as Caphtor in the Bible (e.g., Gen 10:14; Deut 2:23; Jer 47:4; Amos 9:7). Regardless of the dating of the text and traditions in Samuel regarding the Cherethites (see, e.g., Finkelstein 2002; Maeir 2012: 61–62), the Cherethites were certainly associated with the Philistines and were located in the Negev.
25 Gen 15:19; Num 24:21; Judg 1:16; 4:11, 17; 5:24; 1 Sam 15:6; 27:10; 30:29; 1 Chr 2:55.
26 The "Amorites" (e.g., Gen 15:16) and "Canaanites" (e.g., Gen 10:19) are general terms that refer to the entire region while the "Jebusites" are associated with both Jerusalem (e.g., Josh 15:8) and perhaps also the vicinity of Hazor (Josh 11:3).
27 Some LXX manuscripts of 1 Samuel 27:10 support the "Kenite" reading (Rahlfs 1979: 558).
28 Kallai suggested that the LXX[B] reading of 1 Samuel 30:27 may contain the name "Kinah" (Κειμαθ) in the additional toponyms of Vaticanus described above (Kallai 1986: 352). This is possible, but, in my view, it is more likely that this should be connected with Kain of the hill country (Josh 15:57) – if, in fact, these additional toponyms reflect an ancient tradition (see discussion above).
29 Either related to Jericho (Deut 34:3; Judg 3:13; 2 Chr 28:15) or Tamar ('Ain Ḥuṣb), which means "palm tree."
30 For a detailed discussion of scholarship related to the Kenites see Halpern (1992: 18–22).
31 Using similar logic Abel also suggested nearby Khirbet Samra as a possibility (1938: 417–18).
32 Ιερεμουθ of LXX[B] could relate to Jarmuth (Khirbet el-Yarmuk) of the central Shephelah (Josh 10:3, 5, 23; 12:11; 15:35; 21:29; Neh 11:29), but the geographical context points to the Negev and/or southern Shephelah.
33 Na'aman's suggestion of Tel Halif cannot be sustained (1980: 139–140, 2010: 180), as this site should be identified with En-rimmon (Josh 15:32; 19:7; 1 Chr 4:32; Neh 11:29). Tel Halif is near the Byzantine ruin of Khirbet umm er Rumanim, which preserves "Rimmon" yet does not have pre-Hellenistic remains (see Borowski 1988; McKinny 2017: 108).
34 On the other hand, it is possible that the reading "Beer-sheba" – the most commonly mentioned place name in the Negev – is a later (Greek) textual error or emendation for Bor-ashan. If so, Bor-ashan is probably a distinct site from Ashan (Tell Judeidah?) of Joshua 15:42; 19:7; 1 Chr 4:32 (McKinny 2017: 109–10, 210–14).
35 Near the traditional location of "Abraham's well" there is a small tell that is probably the same as SWP's "Khurbet el Wutn." Numerous salvage excavations in the vicinity of the junction of modern Hebron and Elat streets in Beersheba have yielded Iron II remains (see Shemesh 2018b, 2018a).
36 See Na'aman for the view that the original name in each of these instances was Athach instead of Ether (Na'aman 2010: 179). Na'aman (2010: 180) follows Jericke (1997: 324, 327) in identifying Athach with Tell 'Aitun and Kallai (1986: 357) in identifying Bor-ashan with Tell Beit Mirsim. While these identifications are possible, in my opinion, Tell 'Aitun should be associated with Etam of the Simeonite town list (1 Chr 4:32) and Tell Beit Mirsim may possibly be connected with Tochen of that same list.
37 Based on the current survey undertaken by Shai, Tavger, and McKinny.
38 The same logic for Ether would apply to Arad, as the final *kaf* (ך) could be easily mistaken for a *dalet* (ד). The second radical (ת vs. ר) is not as straightforward.

Bibliography

Abel, Felix-Marie. 1938. *Geographic de la Palestine*. Paris: Librairie Lecoffre.
Aharoni, Yohanan. 1958. "The Negeb of Judah." *IEJ* 8: 26–38.
———. 1970. "Three Hebrew Ostraca from Arad." *BASOR* 197: 16–42.
———. 1979. *The Land of the Bible: A Historical Geography*. Philadelphia: Westminster Press.
Aharoni, Yohanan, and Michael Avi-Yonah. 2002. *The Carta Bible Atlas*. 3rd ed. Jerusalem: Carta.
Aharoni, Yohanan, Joseph Naveh, and Anson F. Rainey. 1981. *Arad Inscriptions*. Jerusalem: Israel Exploration Society.
Ahituv, Shmuel. 2008. *Echoes from the Past: Hebrew and Cognate Inscriptions from the Biblical Period*. Jerusalem: Carta.
Albright, William F. 1924. "Egypt and the Early History of the Negeb." *JPOS* 4: 131–61.
Auld, A. G. 2012. *I & II Samuel: A Commentary*. Louisville: Presbyterian Publishing.
Avi-Yonah, M. 1954. *The Madaba Mosaic Map: With Introduction and Commentary*. Jerusalem: Israel Exploration Society.
Baruch, Y. 1997. "Winepresses, Caves and Tombs Near Tel Zif." *'Atiqot* 32: 43*.
Batz, S. 2007. "The Tumuli Distribution in Southern Mt. Hebron." *The Frontier and the Desert in the Land of Israel* 2: 15–38.
Baumgarten, Y., and I. Eldar-Nir. 2014. *Map of Nahal Revivim*. Jerusalem: Israel Antiquities Authority.
Baumgarten, Y., and H. Silberklang. 2015. *Map of Yattir*. Jerusalem: Israel Antiquities Authority.
Beit-Arieh, I. 1999. "Stratigraphy and Historical Background." Pages 170–80 in *Tel 'Ira: A Stronghold in the Biblical Negev*. Edited by I. Beit-Arieh. Tel Aviv: Tel Aviv University.
———. 2007. *Horvat 'Uza and Horvat Radum*. Tel Aviv: Tel Aviv University.
———. 2011. *Map of Horvat 'Uza*. Jerusalem: Israel Antiquities Authority.
Beit-Arieh, I., and B. C. Cresson. 2007. "Introduction." Pages 1–12 in *Horvat 'Uza and Horvat Radum*. Edited by I. Beit-Arieh. Tel Aviv: Tel Aviv University.
Beit-Arieh, I., L. Freud, and O. Tal. 2015. "Summary: Tel Malḥata—from the Middle Bronze Age to the Byzantine Period." Pages 739–44 in *Tel Malhata: A Central City in the Biblical Negev*. Edited by I. Beth-Arieh and L. Freud. Winona Lake: Eisenbrauns.
Ben-Yosef, E. 2019. "The Architectural Bias in Current Biblical Archaeology." *VT* 69: 361–87.
Bezzel, H., and R. G. Kratz, eds. 2021. *David in the Desert*. Berlin: de Gruyter.
Biran, Avraham. 1993. "Aroer (in Judea)." Pages 89–92 in *NEAEHL* 1.
Biran, Avraham, and Rudolph Cohen. 1981. "Aroer in the Negev." *EI* 15: 250–73.
Boaretto, Elisabetta, Israel Finkelstein, and Ruth Shahack-Gross. 2010. "Radiocarbon Results from the Iron IIA Site of Atar Haroa in the Negev Highlands and Their Archaeological and Historical Implications." *Radiocarbon* 52: 1–12.
Boling, R. G., and G. E. Wright. 1982. *Joshua*. New York: Doubleday.
Borowski, Oded. 1988. "The Biblical Identity of Tel Halif." *BA* 51: 21–27.
Chadwick, Jeffrey R. 1992. "The Archaeology of Biblical Hebron in the Bronze and Iron Ages: An Examination of the Discoveries of the American Expedition to Hebron." PhD diss., University of Utah.
Cohen, R., and R. Cohen-Amin. 2004. *Ancient Settlement of the Central Negev. Volume II. The Iron Age and the Persian Period*. Jerusalem: Israel Antiquities Authority (Hebrew).
Cohen, R., G. M. Landes, and R. Gophna. 1968. "Notes and News." *IEJ* 18: 130–34.
Conder, C. R., and H. H. Kitchener. 1883. *Memoirs of the Topography, Orography, Hydrography, and Archaeology—Judea*. London: Palestine Exploration Fund.
Dagan, Y. 2009. "Khirbet Qeiyafa in the Judean Shephelah: Some Considerations." *TA* 36: 68–81.
Derfler, S. L. 2003. "The Byzantine Church at Tel Kerioth and Religious Iconoclasm in the 8th Century." *Aram Periodical* 15: 39–47.
Derfler, S. L., and Y. Govrin. 1993. "Tel Kerioth, 1992." *IEJ* 43: 263–67.
Dietrich, W. 2007. *The Early Monarchy in Israel: The Tenth Century B.C.E.* Atlanta: Society of Biblical Literature.
———. 2019. *1 Samuel 27–2 Samuel 8*. Neukirchen-Vluyn: Neukirchener Verlag.
Donner, H. 1992. *The Mosaic Map of Madaba: An Introductory Guide*. Netherlands: Peeters.
Eisenberg, E., and D. Ben-Shlomo. 2017. *The Tel Ḥevron 2014 Excavations: Final Report*. Ariel: Ariel University Press.

Eldar-Nir, I. 2015. *Map of Khirbet 'Aroer.* Jerusalem: Israel Antiquities Authority.
Eldar-Nir, I., and D. Daninoo. 2014. *Map of Masaf Negev.* Jerusalem: Israel Antiquities Authority.
Eldar-Nir, I., and D. Traubman. 2015. *Map of Yeruham Ridge.* Jerusalem: Israel Antiquities Authority.
Eshel, H., J. Magness, and E. Shenhav. 2000. "Khirbet Yattir, 1995–1999: Preliminary Report." *IEJ* 50: 153–68.
———. 2008. "Yattir, Khirbet." Pages 2069–70 in *NEAEHL* 5.
Eshel, T., N. Yahalom-Mack, S. Shalev, et al. 2018. "Four Iron Age Silver Hoards from Southern Phoenicia: From Bundles to Hacksilber." *BASOR* 379: 197–228.
Eshel, T., Y. Erel, N. Yahalom-Mack, et al. 2019. "Lead Isotopes in Silver Reveal Earliest Phoenician Quest for Metals in the West Mediterranean." *PNAS* 116: 6007–12.
Finkelstein, Israel. 2002. "The Philistines in the Bible: A Late-Monarchic Perspective." *JSOT* 27: 131–67.
Garfinkel, Yossi, and Saar Ganor. 2010. "Khirbet Qeiyafa in Survey and in Excavations: A Response to Y. Dagan." *TA* 37: 67–78.
Garfinkel, Yossi, M. G. Hasel, M. G. Klingbeil. 2021. "The Canaanite and Judean Cities of Lachish, Israel: Preliminary Report of the Fourth Expedition, 2013–2017." *AJA* 125: 419–59.
Garfinkel, Y., I. Kreimerman, and M. G. Hasel. 2019. "First Impression on the Urban Layout of the Last Canaanite City of Lachish: A View from the Northeast Corner of the Site." Pages 122–35 in *The Late Bronze and Early Iron Ages of Southern Canaan.* Edited by Aren M. Maeir, Itzick Shai, and Chris McKinny. Berlin: de Gruyter.
Gophna, R., and Y. Yisraeli. 1973. "Soundings at Beer Sheba (Bir es-Seba')." Pages 115–18 in *Beer-sheba I: Excavations at Tel Beer-sheba 1969–71 Seasons.* Edited by Y. Aharoni. Tel Aviv: Tel Aviv University.
Govrin, Y. 2002. *Map of Nahal Yattir.* Jerusalem: Israel Antiquities Authority.
Halpern, B. 1992. "Kenites." Pages 18–22 in *ABD* 4.
Herzog, Z. 2001. "The Date of the Temple at Arad." Pages 156–78 in *Studies in the Archaeology of the Iron Age in Israel and Jordan.* Edited by A. Mazar. Sheffield: Sheffield Academic Press.
———. 2002. "The Fortress Mound at Tel Arad an Interim Report." *TA* 29: 3–109.
———. 2010. "Perspectives on Southern Israel's Cult Centralization: Arad and Beer-scheba." Pages 169–200 in *One God—One Cult—One Nation: Archaeological and Biblical Perspectives.* Edited by Reinhard G. Kratz et al. Berlin: de Gruyter.
Herzog, Z., and L. Singer-Avitz. 2004. "Redefining the Centre: The Emergence of State in Judah." *TA* 31: 209–44.
Jericke, D. 1997. *Die Landnahme im Negev. Protoisraelitische Gruppen im Süden Palästinas: Eine Archäologische und Exegetische Studie.* Wiesbaden: Harrassowitz.
Kallai, Z. 1986. *Historical Geography of the Bible: The Tribal Territories of Israel.* Jerusalem: Magnes Press.
Kempinski, A. 1993. "Masos, Tel." Pages 986–89 in *NEAEHL* 3.
Kletter, R., and E. Brand. 1998. "A New Look at the Iron Age Silver Hoard from Eshtemoa." *ZDPV* 114: 139–54.
Kochavi, M. 1972. "The Land of Judah." Pages 19–89 in *Judaea, Samaria and the Golan: Archaeological Survey 1967–1968.* Edited by M. Kochavi. Jerusalem: Archaeological Survey of Israel and Carta.
———. 1992. "Tel Esdar." Page 609 in *ABD* 2.
———. 1993. "Malhata, Tel." Pages 934–36 in *NEAEHL* 3.
Kotter, W. R. 1992. "Siphmoth." Page 51 in *ABD* 6.
Lemaire, A. 1988. "Recherches Actuelles Sur Les Sceaux Nord-Ouest Semitiques." *VT* 38: 220–30.
Levin, Y. 2003. "'From Goshen to Gibeon' (Joshua 10:41): The Southern Frontier of the Early Monarchy." *Maarav* 10: 195–220.
———. 2017. "Baal Worship in Early Israel: An Onomastic View in Light of the 'Eshba'al' Inscription from Khirbet Qeiyafa." *Maarav* 21: 203–22.
Maeir, Aren M. 2012. "The Tell es-Safi/Gath Archaeological Project 1996–2010: Introduction, Overview and Synopsis of Results." Pages 1–88 in *Tell es-Safi/Gath I: Report on the 1996–2005 Seasons.* Edited by A. M. Maeir. Wiesbaden: Harrassowitz.
Manor, Dale W. 1992. "Beer-sheba." Pages 641–45 in *ABD* 1.
McCarter, P. Kyle. 1980. *1 Samuel.* New York: Doubleday.
McKinny, C. 2017. "A Historical Geography of the Administrative Division of Judah: The Town Lists of Judah and Benjamin in Joshua 15:21–62 and 18:21–28." PhD diss., Bar Ilan University.

———. 2018. "Pressing On: Identifying the "Other" Gath and Its Implications for Understanding the Border between the Kingdoms of Israel and Judah." Pages 577–94 in *Tell It in Gath: Studies in Honor of Aren Maeir on the Occasion of His Sixtieth Birthday.* Edited by I. Shai et al. Wiesbaden: Ugarit-Verlag.

———. forthcoming a. "Following the Fathers: Identifying Moresheth-gath, the Hometown of Micah the Prophet." In *Lexham Geographic Commentary—Prophetic and Poetic Texts.* Edited by B. J. Beitzel. Bellingham: Lexham Press.

———. forthcoming b. "Going for Gold… but Bringing Home Bronze: Jerusalem's Role in the Arabah Copper Industry and the Biblical Account of Solomon (1 Kgs 9:26–28; 10:11; 11:15)." In *Lexham Geographic Commentary—Prophetic and Poetic Texts.* Edited by B. J. Beitzel. Bellingham: Lexham Press.

———. forthcoming c. "Warriors or Patrimonial Elites? A Historical Geographical Assessment of David's 'Mighty Men' (2 Sam 23:8–39; 1 Chr 11:10–47)." In *Lexham Geographic Commentary—Prophetic and Poetic Texts.* Edited by B. J. Beitzel. Bellingham: Lexham Press.

Miller, J. M., and J. H. Hayes. 2006. *A History of Ancient Israel and Judah.* 2nd ed. Louisville: Westminster John Knox Press.

Na'aman, N. 1980. "The Inheritance of the Sons of Simeon." *ZDPV* 96: 136–52.

———. 2005. *Ancient Israel and Its Neighbors: Interaction and Counteraction: Collected Essays.* Winona Lake: Eisenbrauns.

———. 2010. "The Date of the List of Towns That Received the Spoil of Amalek (1 Sam 30:26–31)." *TA* 37: 175–87.

Nahlieli, D. M., and M. Veinberger. 2015. *Map of Yeruham.* Jerusalem: Israel Antiquities Authority.

Notley, R. Steven, and Z. Safrai, eds. 2005. *Eusebius, Onomasticon: The Place Names of Divine Scripture: Including the Latin Edition of Jerome.* Leiden: Brill.

Ofer, A. 1993a. "Hebron." Pages 606–09 in *NEAEHL* 1.

———. 1993b. "The Highland of Judah during the Biblical Period." PhD diss., Tel Aviv University.

Panitz-Cohen, N. 2005. "A Salvage Excavation in the New Market in Beer-Sheba: New Light on Iron Age IIB Occupation at Beer-Sheba." *IEJ* 55: 143–55.

Parry, D. W. 1999. "4QSAMa (4Q51): A Preliminary Edition of 1 Samuel 25:3–31:4." Pages 58–71 in *The Provo International Conference on the Dead Sea Scrolls.* Edited by Donald Parry and Eugene Ulrich. Leiden: Brill.

Rahlfs, A., ed. 1979. *Septuaginta.* Stuttgart: Deutsche Bibelgesellschaft.

Rainey, Anson F. 1983. "The Biblical Shephelah of Judah." *BASOR* 251: 1–22.

Rainey, Anson F., and R. Steven Notley. 2006. *The Sacred Bridge: Carta's Atlas of the Biblical World.* Jerusalem: Carta.

Robinson, E., and E. Smith. 1841. *Biblical Researches in Palestine.* Boston: Crocker & Brewster.

Shemesh, N. 2018a. *Map of Beersheva East.* Jerusalem: Israel Antiquities Authority.

———. 2018b. *Map of Beersheva West.* Jerusalem: Israel Antiquities Authority.

Simons, J. J. 1959. *The Geographical and Topographical Texts of the Old Testament.* Leiden: Brill.

Smith, H. P. 1899. *Samuel I and II.* Edinburgh: A&C Black.

Swete, H. B., ed. 1887. *The Old Testament in Greek According to the Septuagint: Volume 1: Genesis–IV Kings.* Republished in 2010. Cambridge: Cambridge University Press.

Thareani-Sussely, Y., ed. 2011. *Tel Aroer: The Iron Age Caravan Town and the Hellenistic-Early Roman Settlement.* Jerusalem: Eisenbrauns.

Tsumura, D. T. 2007. *The First Book of Samuel.* Grand Rapids: Eerdmans.

van de Velde, C. W. M. 1858. *Map of the Holy Land.* Gotha: Justus Perthes.

Yeivin, Z. 1987. "The Mysterious Silver Hoard from Eshtemoa." *BAR* 13: 38–44.

———. 1990. "The Silver Hoard from Eshtemo'a." *'Atiqot* 10: 15*.

———. 2004. "The Synagogue at Eshtemoa' in Light of the 1969 Excavations." *'Atiqot* 48: 59*–98*, 155–58.

3
COMPETING CHRONOLOGIES, COMPETING HISTORIES

Ancient Israel and the Chronology of the Southern Levant ca. 1200–587 BCE

Koert van Bekkum

Introduction – Chronology as Creating History

In recent historical research, the south-western part of the fertile crescent of Western Asia has been variously named Palestine, Israel, Syria-Palestine, and the Southern Levant. Naming the land is also interpreting and constructing its reality. Accordingly, using a name for an archaeological site in modern Syria, Lebanon, Jordan, Israel, or the Palestinian territories unavoidably is also to enter an area of ideological and political tensions.

In a comparable way, defining a time period is to organize and classify the past, to value what has happened, and to create history "as the intellectual form in which a civilization renders account to itself of its past" (Huizinga 1936). In the Ancient Near East and Egypt, the treatment of historical subjects and the explication of historical interest most often focused on royal figures and what they accomplished and symbolized. The Sumerian King List (ca. 2000–1700 BCE), for instance, presents a flexible, partly fictitious, partly historical list of ancient Mesopotamian kings, their cities, and their amazing number of regnal years to legitimize the dynasty of Isin. At the same time, the text highlights that rulers are a different kind of people being connected to a deep, mythological past (Glassner 2004: 55–70, 117–26; Michalowski 2019). The ancient Israelite description of earliest human history in Genesis 1–11 seems to draw on this genre in its lists from Adam to Abraham (Gen 5 and 11). The biblical chapters do not legitimize dynastic dominion, but rather emphasize that every human being is created in the image of God. Yet, in being a counterpart of traditional king lists, this depiction also starts with agriculture, cities, and an enumeration of major figures.

This does not imply that the ancients were unaware of preceding phases of history, such as a period of hunters and gatherers.[1] The lists merely reflect a particular focus communicating messages regarding religion and politics and internal and external relations. Most king lists only mention successive single rulers of a given period because each of their main characters is supposed to represent his own era. Accordingly, only specific circumstances led to the rare practice of a synchronistic chronographic description of contemporary rulers. The primary example of this is the Synchronistic King List in the form of a chronicle of Assyrian and Babylonian kings (ca. 640 BCE) composed by Neo-Assyrian scribes to cover a period of more than 1,000 years in support of Ashurbanipal's Babylonian policy (Chen 2020).

The Babylonian Chronicles (6th–4th centuries BCE) from Borsippa and Babylon in part even include the early kings mentioned in the Sumerian King List. Yet, they serve dissimilar purposes, such as to reveal Marduk's ancient power or to underline how the well-being of the land was ensured by royal patronage of the temples (Glassner 2004: 263–92; Waerzeggers 2012). A third example is presented in the biblical book of Kings, which describes the synchronisms between the kings of Israel and Judah (see Kings and Their Regnal Years below). With this synchronistic information, most likely obtained from annalistic accounts – called "the book of the chronicles of the kings of Judah" and "the book of the chronicles of Israel" – the scribes underlined the original unity of both kingdoms and their relation to YHWH (Galil 1996: 10–11).

Yet it is important to realize that this view of the past is an exception. Normally, each king represented his own single era, while rivals were only mentioned as being conquered. For more than a millennium, until its end in 612 BCE, Assyria had a practice of associating successive years with the names, the eponyms, of the *līmu*, the high official who led that year's New Year festival (Yamada 2018). From the second half of the 8th until the 1st century BCE, the Babylonians recorded ominous phenomena in astronomical diaries. Yet a historical continuous counting of years did not occur due to traditional royal ideology. This only changed in 312 BCE, when the Seleucid rulers associated their era with the notion in Hellenistic royal ideology of an everlasting Golden Age and a re-beginning of history (Strootman 2015). From this moment on, historiographers had the option of developing a universal dating system, although it is at the same time clear that counting years is not a neutral affair.

Also in the present era, the dating system and periodization of the history of the Southern Levant reflect the perspective of the historian. The use of BCE/CE instead of the BC/AD system is more neutral from a religious point of view but still takes the Gregorian calendar as its point of departure, thus underlining the special place of ancient Israel in the development of Western civilization. The diverse positions regarding the Iron Age chronology in the Southern Levant cannot be reduced to political, religious, or cultural factors, but some choices do have a specific background. It is no coincidence, for instance, that the debate on the so-called high and low chronology of the Iron Age IIA in the Southern Levant started in Israel in the context of the political discussion following the Oslo I Accord of 1993 between the government of Israel and the Palestine Liberation Organization, and of the celebration of 3,000 years of Jerusalem. The question had become urgent whether modern Israel should identify itself with Jerusalem and the ancient Israelite kingdom of David and Solomon or with the mixture of Israelite and Canaanite traditions as attested in Samaria, the capital of king Omri (Mondot 2006; Noort 2004).

As a result, chronology and periodization are important means in the historiography of ancient Israel, both in the past and the present. On the one hand, the creation of an absolute chronology of the Southern Levant is an indispensable means of doing justice to the available textual and artifactual data and to the diverse perspectives on what has happened. On the other hand, competing chronologies also reflect competing histories. Accordingly, this article provides an overview of the various chronologies proposed for the history of ancient Israel and an evaluation of the assumptions and methodological considerations in the creation of a chronological scheme, and the diverse historical portraits because of the adopted chronology. The next section first offers a sketch of the general framework of the Late Bronze and Iron Age chronology in the Southern Levant. Then, the possibilities and challenges in creating such a chronology are laid out in more detail, first regarding the 9th–6th centuries and then regarding the 12th–9th centuries BCE. Finally, the conclusion pays attention to the diverse scenarios that can be related to the chronological schemes.

Chronological Framework of Egypt and the Ancient Near East

Once continuous counting and a universal chronology had become an option in the Seleucid period, a variety of scholars from the Hellenistic and Greco-Roman world, including the 3rd century BCE Babylonian and Egyptian priests Berossos and Manetho, and the 1st century CE Jewish historian Flavius Josephus, offered writings reconstructing history from their perspective. The influence of the Hellenistic chronographs can also be felt in the changes in the numbers in the Septuagint version of the book of Genesis. Noah and the Flood, for instance, is dated much earlier, because it seemed impossible that it took place during the reign of great Pharaohs and Mesopotamian kings (Laato 2015: 107–10). Until deep into the early modern period, the records and reconstructions of ancient and biblical sources were used to develop chronologies of world history. As a result, it was, for instance, determined that the history of Egypt counted 30 dynasties and that the temple of Solomon had been built during the 10th century BCE.

Since the 19th century CE, this situation drastically improved with the exploration of Egypt and the Near East, the decipherment of hieroglyphs and cuneiform, and because of the discovery of countless monuments, inscriptions, tablets, and iconographic sources. A whole network of king lists with numbers of regnal years, years named after an important event, building inscriptions, eponym lists, genealogies, annals, and chronicles help in establishing a relative chronology when they contain synchronisms of names and events. One of the most important examples connecting the relative chronologies of Mesopotamia with that of Egypt is the conquest of Egypt by the abovementioned Assyrian king Ashurbanipal and the installation of pharaoh Psamtik I as his vassal. Additionally, it was discovered that the solar eclipse noted during the eponymate of Būr-Saggilê in Assyria could be equated with the one that by astronomical calculation should have occurred on June 15, 763 BCE (Rawlinson 1867). It not only became clear that the Assyrian eponym list offered the opportunity to create an Assyro-Babylonian chronological backbone starting with the first regnal year of Adad-nirari II in 910/911 BCE, but also that the Assyrian conquest of Egypt took place in 664 BCE. Consequently, many historical dates for neighboring areas, such as Elam, Syria, Anatolia, Israel and Judah, Cyprus, the Aegean, and Nubia can be determined. As a result, the margin in a large part of the chronology of the first millennium BCE regards only months, a year, or a few years.

Due to a lack of internal and external political control by Egypt and Mesopotamia and the collapse of the Hittite empire, the data from the 11th to the first half of the 9th century BCE are less certain. Yet a network of synchronisms and astronomical data again result in a robust chronology for the period of the Egyptian New Kingdom, from the 16th to the early 11th century BCE, which can be connected to the other members of the "great power club" of the Late Bronze Age, which together constituted the flourishing international economic network of that time: the Hittite kingdom, Mitanni, Assyria, and Babylon. Although there has been some debate on how the calculated series of solar eclipses is to be applied to the available information, the so-called low Egyptian chronology is now generally considered to be the best option (Bietak and Höflmayer 2007; Kitchen 2013). Yet the precise years of some of the pharaohs within this framework are still unclear. New excavations at the tomb of Horemheb, for instance, seem to have settled the complicated discussion about the length of his reign at the end of the 14th century BCE (van Dijk 2008). It is undecided, however, how this affects Babylonian and Hittite chronology and whether this implies a higher year for the enthronement of Ramses II than the well-known 1279 BCE (Devecchi and Miller 2011: 158–68). So, the chronological uncertainty in this historical period remains about a decade.

In addition to this, technical tools are increasingly used to test traditional chronological schemes. In Anatolia, a dendrochronological sequence is available, and it is something that can be used as a calibration and check of radiocarbon dating. In Egypt, radiocarbon dating of samples from funerary contexts by Bronk Ramsey's Oxford-based project has confirmed the region's current chronological framework (Bronk Ramsey et al. 2010; Bronk Ramsey 2013; Höflmayer 2016). Most recently, archaeomagnetic dating, which measures magnetic voltage built up in ceramic remains from a specific moment in time, is being refined to be added to archaeologists' toolboxes (Stillinger 2016; Vaknin et al. 2020).

By themselves, these methods do not provide completely independent results. Besides inevitable margins of uncertainty, the methods can only be applied with help of so-called prior information obtained from traditional chronological observations, such as archaeological stratigraphy. In addition, the context of the samples must be considered. Accordingly, methods based on science can only be used as elements in a comprehensive approach integrating all available data. Such a multidisciplinary system of checks and balances also prevents the chronological framework from becoming the product of circular reasoning (Höflmayer 2016; Stillinger et al. 2018).

A small group of scholars, mainly connected to the study group "Bronze to Iron Age Chronology of the Ancient Near East" (BICANE), disagrees with the established chronological framework of Egypt and the Ancient Near East. Inspired by earlier publications about the so-called "centuries of darkness" (James et al. 1991) and pointing at weaknesses and unexplained elements in the existing chronological framework (in particular, the Third Intermediate Period in Egypt), they propose a revision of the absolute chronology of the Mediterranean and Western Asia by lowering the chronology of the Late Bronze and Iron Ages ca. 200 years. The focus of the group has been on Egypt and biblical chronology (e.g., James and Van der Veen 2015; Wallenfels 2019), while more recent work also concentrates on the Iron IIB period of the Southern Levant (Van der Veen 2020). Although most scholars regard the criticism of weak elements of the traditional chronology as valuable, the drastic down-dating of Egyptian New Kingdom dynasties is generally rejected. This is based on the confirmation of Egyptian chronology in the Oxford project. Lowering the dates also creates problems in Hittite chronology and complicates the Assyrian history before the conquest of 664 BCE (Kitchen 2009: xlii–xlvi). Moreover, archaeological strata in the Southern Levant traditionally reflecting the 13th to 7th centuries BCE would contain only the remains of the 11th to early 6th century BCE (cf. Wallenfels 2019: 497), thereby destroying firm archaeological anchors such as Hazael's destruction of Gath and Sennacherib's conquest of Lachish.

This argument brings to the issue of the relation between the absolute chronology of the ancient Near East and the material remains that were uncovered by archaeological excavations in the Southern Levant. There has been a growing awareness that ancient Near Eastern texts, including battle reports and annalistic accounts, cannot be read as straightforward historical descriptions, but need to be appreciated for their own ideological perspectives and literary qualities (Younger 1990). In general, it is also hard to relate destruction layers from the Southern Levant to concrete events (Fiaccavento 2014). Yet, the second period of Assyria's expansion, which led to its zenith in power (745–626 BCE), is most important in this regard. The campaigns of Tiglath-Pileser III in 734 through Galilee and Philistia to Egypt and in 732 against Damascus, the conquest of Samaria by his son Shalmaneser V in 721, activities of Sargon II, and the campaign of Sennacherib in 701 to the rebellious kings in the west not only brought the kingdoms of Aram and Israel to an end. They also resulted in a significant number of destructions and abandonments of cities and villages, a restructuring of society with the creation of the Assyrian provinces of Magidu, Samarina, and Ašdudu, and in new impulses for the remaining vassal state in the south, the kingdom of Judah (Faust 2015; Hasegawa, Levin, and Radner 2018; Kalimi 2014; Younger 2018). Although it is not always possible to determine who destroyed what, the devastating results of the late-8th century BCE Assyrian campaigns can be observed at dozens of sites, thus creating a firm anchor connecting the relative chronology of archaeological remains to the absolute chronology of history, with the Assyrian arrows and siege ramp from 701 BCE marking the end of Tel Lachish, Stratum III as its crown witnesses (Faust 2015: 767–74; Franklin 2018; Tappy 2018; Ussishkin 2014).

More complicated, however, is the picture on the other side of the chronological spectrum, that is, from the 15th–12th century BCE Egyptian New Kingdom involvement in the Southern Levant. Textual and iconographic remains from annals, reliefs, and the Amarna Letters abundantly make it clear that New Kingdom pharaohs campaigned in Asia and that the kings of the palatial cities in Canaan functioned as vassals. Egyptian estates and fortresses in, for instance, Gaza, Jaffa, Aphek, and Beth Shean embodied this dominion, while a whole range of Egyptian and Egyptianizing material remains reflect a lively exchange of goods. Yet this does not always result in clear dates. In the past, scholars generally assumed that destructions at the end of the Late Bronze Age were caused by the Egyptian campaigns, the conquests as described in the book of Joshua, and by the Philistines who were supposed to have arrived in the coastal plain after the battle of Ramses III with the Sea Peoples as depicted on Ramses III's temple at Medinet Habu. More detailed analyses, however, have made it clear that this was not based on a careful interpretation of the textual and iconographical records and a reconstruction of the archaeological remains on their own terms. According to both the texts and archaeology, most cities plundered by the Egyptians suffered only minor structural damage (Hasel 1998). Migration and colonization are complicated phenomena and the arrival of groups related to the Sea Peoples is merely to be seen as a process (Kahn 2011, 2016; Killebrew and Lehmann 2013; Maeir 2020: 16–21; Yasur-Landau 2010). In addition, an appreciation of the literary and religious encoding of the later description of Israel's settlement in Canaan in biblical texts, also in relation to archaeology, leads to the conclusion that they contain rather moderate historical claims of a process from conquest to coexistence, with some violent moments in the beginning resulting in a cultural and religious mixed multitude (van Bekkum 2011).

The end of the Late Bronze Age was a process caused by multiple factors stretching out over more than a century, which occurred in some regions much later than in others. There is general agreement that Tel Hazor came to an end in the mid-13th century BCE. New excavations at Tel Abel Maacah confirm that thereafter, the geopolitical balance shifted, and the area of the Upper Galilee and the northern Jordan Valley became a buffer zone (David 2016; Yahalom-Mack, Panitz-Cohen, and Mullins 2018). Yet the Canaanite palatial city of Tel Lachish in the Shephelah and those of Tell Keisan, Tel Yoqneam, Tel Megiddo, Khirbet Belamah and Tell Taanach in the Jezreel Valley remained in function deep into the 12th century BCE (Taha and van der Kooij 1999; 2007; van Bekkum 2011: 471–93). This mixed picture is confirmed by an analysis from the perspective of interregional trade, which also shows that it depends on the definition whether it is possible to speak of a "collapse" of Late Bronze society (Millek 2020).

These conclusions can only be drawn because there are some firm chronological anchors (cf. van Bekkum 2011: 437–49). The end of Late Bronze Lachish and Megiddo at ca. 1150 and 1130 are more or less certain because of the cache of bronze objects with a cartouche of Ramses III and the base of a statue of Ramses VI (Ussishkin 1985, 1995). Excavations have also secured the relations between Tel Beth Shean, Level IX, and the Amarna period, while the later layers of the Ramesside period can be assured by the find of a Year 18 stela of Ramses II and radiocarbon measurements (Mazar 2011a). Nearby Canaanite Tel Rehov thrived during this period under the protection of the Beth Shean garrison and continued to do so without Beth Shean into the Iron Age I (Mazar and Davidovich 2019). Because of a scribal workshop on the second floor with a letter from Ugarit, the destruction of the Egyptian estate at Tel Aphek in the Sharon can be dated to ca. 1230 BCE (Gadot and Yadin 2009: 583–86). The city of Tel Gezer, Stratum XV, seems to be the one that was robbed and partly destroyed by Merenptah's forces in 1207 BCE as indicated in the famous "Israel" stela (Hasel 1998: 184–88, cf. Abbas 2020; Kahn 2012). The next stratum at Gezer also came to a violent end, while in Stratum XIII the first "Philistine" painted wares occur, which help in dating the related strata in Tel Ashdod and Tel Miqne (Ekron) and the beginnings of the Philistine settlement in Tel Qasile (Stager 1995: 342, 345–48). Recent exploration, including radiocarbon analysis, of the Late Bronze – Iron Age transition at Tel es-Safi/Gath, Tel Burna, Tel Azekah, and Tel ʿEton in the Shephelah shed further light on the complex nature of the processes and mechanisms that occurred during the transition (Faust and Katz 2015; Maeir, Shai, and McKinny 2019).

As a result, the absolute chronology of the Late Bronze and Iron Age Southern Levant is determined by chronological anchors from both the late 8th and the 14th–12th centuries BCE. The period in between is less defined, yet the following sections will show that it is possible to come to reasonable conclusions, also regarding this period.

Kings and Their Regnal Years (Iron Age IIB Chronology)

The next step is to inspect how the non-biblical and biblical indicators regarding the history of ancient Israel fit into this general framework. As indicated above, doing justice to the three kinds of available sources – ancient Near Eastern texts and iconography, material remains, and biblical texts – is not an easy task. One of the reasons for this is that the main biblical source for this period, the Primary History (Genesis to 2 Kings), is not a "found", but a "transmitted" text, while it is also contested to what extent its biblical books were written before the Babylonian exile and reflect historical memories.[2]

This also affects the study of chronology. By means of chronological indicators, the Primary History divides the (pre-)history of Israel into four periods. The "contemporary" history of the kings of Israel and Judah is part of the period from the building of the temple until its destruction (1 Kgs 12 – 2 Kgs 25). Its "pre-history" of Israel's formation as a people in the exodus, at the mountain of Sinai, and in the fulfillment of the promise of the land is told with the help of lists, legal material, and stories and framed in a plot from the exodus to the building of the temple (Exod 1 – 1 Kgs 11). This is preceded by the "family history" of the patriarchs shaped with help of genealogical lists, (oral) traditions, and the narrative about Joseph in Egypt (Gen 12–50). Finally, the beginnings of everything and their relation to Israel are constituted by a "proto-historical narrative" from creation to Israel's ancestor Abram with help of a genealogical scheme and ancient Near Eastern mythological language (Gen 1–11). Two so-called *Distanzangaben*, that is, the remark that the Israelites were in Egypt for 430 years (Exod 12:40, cf. Gen 15:13, 16) and the notion that there were 480 years between the exodus and the building of the temple in Solomon's fourth year (1 Kgs 6:1), keep these periods together (cf. Machinist 2019: 217–18).

From the ancient versions, Josephus, and rabbinic interpretation until present times, there has been much speculation to what extent this periodization reflects a common idea about Israel's history.[3] Yet these numbers primarily need to be interpreted in their own literary context, then related to other parts of the Primary History, and only then to their historical background. When this very last step is taken, connections between the biblical chronological data and the ancient Near Eastern chronological network appear for kings from Israel and Judah who are mentioned in the Neo-Assyrian and Babylonian inscriptions and annalistic texts.

In Table 3.1, years in bold and italics denote regnal years explicitly mentioned in records, which accordingly can be firmly established. Other years are to a high degree of certainty calculated with help of synchronisms with other Mesopotamian sources (cf. Galil 1996: 156–58; Kuan 1995; Laato 2015: 63–70).

The overview illustrates that the precise dates of some of the events that happened during the first millennium BCE are still disputed. An example is the question of how to interpret the claim of two Assyrian kings to have conquered Samaria (cf. Becking 2021: 50–65). At the same time, there is an impressive amount of information available and the order and dates of the kings of Israel and Judah in the book of Kings strikingly parallel the inscriptions. Biblical and non-biblical information regarding other Syrian and southern Levantine kings also fits this framework, such as the 9th century kings Hazael of Damascus and Mesha of Moab. Hence, since the 1920s scholars not only assume that the synchronic tradition of Israelite and Judean kings in the book of Kings is reliable but also undergird this with detailed analyses.[4] Yet offering a precise absolute chronology of the ca. 120 numerological indications is still complicated, also because of four specific problems related to the data themselves (Laato 2015: 13–24; Weingart 2020: 25–31).

First, there is the textual critical problem that many variations occur in the transmission of the biblical text, in particular, the early translations. Most scholars interpret them as attempts to improve the Hebrew original and to solve chronological issues. Accordingly, most scholars stick to the Masoretic text as the *lectio difficilior*. Second, due to Mesopotamian

Table 3.1 Neo-Assyrian references to Israel, Judah, and/or kings of those kingdoms

853	Shalmaneser III battles at Qarqar against a Syrian coalition, including Ahab of Israel (Kurkh Monolith)
841	Shalmaneser III receives tribute from Jehu of bit Ḫumri (Black Obelisk)
802/796	Adad-nirari III receives tribute from Jehoash of Israel (Rimah Stela)
740/738	Tiglath-Pileser III receives tribute from Menahem of Israel (Iran Stela, cf. 2 Kgs 15:19–20)
734–732	Tiglath-Pileser III receives tribute from Ahaz of Judah and conquers Galilee and Transjordan (Summary Inscription 7, cf. 2 Kgs 16:6–9)
733–731	Tiglath-Pileser III mentions the death of Pekah and the enthronement and tribute by Hoshea (Summary Inscriptions 4, 9, and 13, cf. 2 Kgs 15:30)
722–720	Shalmaneser V's and Sargon II's conquest of Samaria and deportation of its inhabitants (Sargon II Display Inscriptions, Nimrud Prism, and Assur-Charter; Babylonian Chronicle I, cf. 2 Kgs 17:5–6; 18:9–12)
701	Sennacherib's conquest of Lachish and attack on Hezekiah of Judah in Jerusalem (Taylor Prism; Bull Inscription; Nebi Yebus Slab, cf. 2 Kgs 18–19)
ca. 676	Esarhaddon is provided forced laborers by Manasseh of Judah for rebuilding Nineveh (Esarhaddon Prism B)
667	Ashurbanipal receives tribute from Manasseh of Judah for his campaign against Egypt (Rassam Cylinder; Ashurbanipal Cylinder C)
597	Nebuchadnezzar II conquers Jerusalem on 2 Adar/16 March and installs a new king (Jerusalem Chronicle, cf. 2 Kgs 24:10–17)

influences, the traditional use of the calendar in which the new year started in autumn with the month Tishri (as in the Gezer Calendar), at some moment in history shifted to a start in spring, that is, in the month Nisan. Although it is likely that this happened during the reign of Josiah, it is not always clear what system is assumed in each biblical text under discussion. Third, like in the ancient Near Eastern context, regnal years are counted by calendric years. Yet it depends on the period and region whether the remaining months of the calendric year of enthronement are actually counted as the first year. Most scholars agree that there are indications of a change in the use of the system in Israel at the end of the 9th century BCE, while Judah was more consistent. Yet, there is disagreement about the question of which of the two was used in each of the three cases, the accession or the non-accession-year-system. Therefore, other scholars take just one system as a point of departure in their chronological reconstructions and try to be open to the possibility of applying the other system. A fourth factor is the existence of coregencies, for instance by Jotham, who governed Judah on behalf of his father Uzziah because of his illness (2 Kgs 15:5). Most likely, these years of coregency were in the end counted as full regnal years, just as happened elsewhere in the ancient Near East. Assuming attestations of coregencies in the book of Kings is a formidable instrument in solving chronological problems but applying it too often without explicit indications in the text weakens the solutions significantly.

The combination of the striking synchronisms with the non-biblical texts and the particularities of the chronological issues of the synchronic tradition in the book of Kings strongly suggest that these data are not artificial, but the outcome of a serious, successful effort of the scribes to create a chronological framework with help of archival data. As a result, it can be safely concluded that the biblical chronological data for the "contemporary" history of the kings of Israel and Judah, that is, from the accession of Rehoboam and Jeroboam I to the destruction of Samaria and Jerusalem, can indeed be used for the reconstruction of an absolute chronological framework based on precise regnal years. There is even reason to assume that the synchronistic presentation of the kings of Israel and Judah predates the 7th and 6th century Assyrian Synchronistic King List and Babylonian Chronicles and finds its origin in 9th century BCE discussions regarding the relationship between the northern and southern kingdoms (Weingart 2020: 171–74, 200–04). From a modern historical perspective, it is impossible to calculate all numbers with certainty, but many of them between ca. 930 BCE and 587 BCE can be.

Table 3.2 offers a simplified overview of three reconstructions, with overlapping reigns and coregencies displayed in italics (Galil 1996: 147; Laato 2015: 112–13; Thiele 1983: 217).

Secured dates in these reconstructions also make it possible to date other events depicted in biblical and non-biblical iconographic and textual representations. The examples in Table 3.3 can be mentioned.

It is often stated that Jerusalem fell in 586 BCE because according to 2 Kgs 25:8 and Jer 52:12 the city was captured in Nebuchadnezzar's 19th year. Yet a detailed review of all the evidence – including Jer 52:29, which mentions a deportation of Jerusalem's inhabitants in Nebuchadnezzar's 18th year – results in the observation that the years of the Babylonian king are counted in different ways. As a result, the city actually fell in the fourth month (Tammuz), that is, in July 587 BCE (Young 2004; Young 2012: 18–21). There is also agreement on the year of Josiah's death and on the uncertainty regarding the precise dates of the events as described in the Tel Dan and Mesha Stela. Much more contested, however, is the historical context of the Asiatic campaign by pharaoh Shoshenq I, which is related to the hot debate concerning the beginning of the Iron Age IIA territorial kingdoms in the Southern Levant.

Table 3.2 Comparative chronologies proposed for the kings of Israel and Judah

Kings of Israel	Thiele	Galil	Laato	Kings of Judah	Thiele	Galil	Laato
Jeroboam I	930–910	930–909	930–909	Rehoboam	931–913	931–914	930–914
Nadab	910–909	909–908	909–908	Abijah	913–911	914–911	913–910
Baasha	909–886	908–885	908–885	Asa	911–870	911–870	910–870
Elah	886–885	885–884	885–884	Jehosaphat	*872*–848	870–845	870–847
Zimri	885	884	884	Jehoram	*853*–841	*853*–843	847–846
Tibni	885–880	884–880		Ahaziah	841	843–842	846
Omri	885–874	*884*–873	884–873	Athaliah	841–835	842–835	845–840
Ahab	874–853	873–852	873–852	Joash	835–796	842–802	840–801
Ahaziah	853–852	852–851	852–851	Amaziah	796–767	*805*–776	*805*–786
Joram	852–841	851–842	851–845	Uzziah	*792*–740	788–736	786–735
Jehu	841–814	842–815	845–818	Jotham	*750*–732	758–742	*750*–735
Jehoahaz	814–798	*819*–804	818–802	Ahaz	*735*–716	*742*–726	735–716
Jehoash	798–782	*805*–790	802–787	Hezekiah	716–687	726–697	715–697
Jeroboam II	782–753	790–750	787–747	Manasseh	*697*–643	697–642	697–643
Zechariah	753–752	750–749	747–746	Amon	643–641	642–640	643–641
Shallum	752	749	746	Josiah	641–609	640–609	641–609
Menahem	752–742	749–738	746–737	Jehoahaz	609	609	609
Pekaiah	742–740	738–739	737–735	Jehoiakim	609–598	609–598	609–598
Pekah	752–732	*750*–732	735–732	Jehoiachin	598–597	598–597	598–597
Hoshea	732–723	732–722	732–723	Zedekiah	597–586	597–586	597–586

Table 3.3 Chronologically significant events mentioned both in biblical texts and extra-biblical sources

925	Shoshenq I's Asiatic campaign (Topographical list at Karnak; Shoshenq Megiddo Fragment, cf. 1 Kgs 14:25)
852/841	Hazael of Damascus against "[Ahaz]yahu" of Israel and "[Jeho]ram" of Judah (Tel Dan Stela, cf. 2 Kgs 8:28–29; 10:32)
850/841	Mesha defeats the house of Omri (Mesha Stele, cf. 2 Kgs 3)
609	Josiah of Judah dies in the battle of Megiddo against pharaoh Necho II (Babylonian Chronicle, cf. 2 Kgs 23:29–30)
589–587	Siege and fall of Jerusalem (Ezek 24:1; 2 Kgs 25:2, 8; Jer 39:2; 52:12, 29)

Tribes and the Rise of the Territorial Kingdoms (Iron Age I–IIA Chronology)

Due to the so-called 'Great Power Eclipse,' the geopolitical context of the Iron I – Iron IIA Southern Levant is mostly elucidated by studying the 11th–9th-century history of the Neo-Hittite kingdoms (Emanuel 2015; Galil 2014; Harrison 2021; Younger 2016). Archaeologically, the more southern areas experienced a major transformation in their general social structure, that is, they went from areas dominated by villages and tribal structures to lands defined by more hierarchy, administrative towns, and centralization, with the Iron II territorial kingdoms of Israel and Judah, Edom, Ammon, and Moab as its result. The questions, then, are when and how this transition took place.

Regarding the 'when' of the rise of the kingdom(s) of ancient Israel it is to be noted that between the late 1950s and mid-1980s, the six-chamber gates excavated at Tel Hazor, Tel Megiddo, Tel Gezer, and remains from the City of David in Jerusalem were interpreted as the archaeological substantiation of the so-called 'Golden Age' of David and Solomon. Despite some doubts, destruction layers at the beginning and middle of the Iron IIA were connected to the conquests of David and to Shoshenq I's/Shishak's Asiatic campaign against Rehoboam (1 Kgs 14:25), while the development of administrative buildings in provincial towns and Phoenician influences in the architecture were interpreted as reflecting building activities by King Solomon (e.g., Holladay 1995).[5]

A real shift in academic debate, however, occurred in 1996 with a proposal by Israel Finkelstein, who concluded that the lowering of the destruction of Late Bronze Tel Lachish to 1130 BCE had the Philistines arriving much later than previously assumed, and that the date of the beginning of the Iron Age IIA had to be lowered from 1000 to ca. 920 BCE. In his view, the traditional consensus simply took uncertain biblical texts of a much later date as a point of departure and failed to interpret the material remains on their own terms. He considered the 10th century BCE to be a "dark age." Writing commenced in the 9th century, but at that time was still sporadic and did not include complex texts. Finkelstein suggested that until the very beginning of the 9th century the Southern Levant was not governed by kings, but by tribal chiefs, warlords, and local rulers. In addition, both the most important building activities of the Iron IIA and the relations with Phoenicia would suggest that the first state formation did not take place in the southern, but in the northern hills. In his view, the first real territorial kingdom of the Southern Levant was that of Omri of Samaria (ca. 882–871 BCE, cf. 1 Kgs 16:23–28), while Judah and Jerusalem came later and only started to thrive after the Assyrian destruction of the northern kingdom (Finkelstein 1996, 2013a and 2013b). By referring to the Israelite king Omri and his supposed "Omride architecture" Finkelstein betrayed that his "alternative view" also used a biblical Archimedean point in reorganizing the material, that is, 1 Kgs 16. Still, his proposal instigated a fierce debate, which not only related to the issues concerning chronology and state formation in the Southern Levant, but also to the identity of modern Israel.[6]

The main discussion took place between defendants of the new Low Chronology and a Modified Conventional Chronology. They agreed that David and Shoshenq I indeed had too easily been used in interpreting and dating the Iron IIA material remains. A new, more independent archaeological basis for the period between the Egyptian New Kingdom's involvement in the Southern Levant and the Assyrian conquests had to be found. Further, it turned out to be important to reckon with cultural and ideological contrasts in the material culture and with regional differences in the spread of new ceramic forms and decoration. The presence of 22nd and 23rd dynasty Egyptian seal amulets in Iron IIA Levantine strata could function as a possible *terminus a quo* in dating them (Münger 2003). In addition, old and new excavations indicate that already in the 10th and 9th century BCE there was some impressive architecture in Jerusalem (Gadot and Uziel 2017; Mazar 2009 and 2011). New epigraphic finds underlined that the level of literacy in the Iron I–IIA should not be underestimated.[7] Finally, extensive research into the 11th to 9th century BCE copper mines in Faynan and Timna revolutionized the understanding of nomadic societies as such, and of the early nomadic kingdom of Edom and its relation to Israel (Ben-Yosef 2019, 2020, cf. Finkelstein 2020; see also Tebes, this volume).

As a result, it has become highly unlikely that Shoshenq I sustained his claims on the former Egyptian Province in Asia through the severe destruction of cities and villages (Finkelstein and Piazetsky 2006: 57–58). Yet the complete demolition of a whole city, that of Gath during a campaign by the Aramean king Hazael (ca. 835–832 BCE, cf. 2 Kgs 12:18), has been firmly established by the major archaeological excavations at Tell es-Safi/Gath (Maeir 2012: 43–49). The end of this Philistine kingdom changed the socioeconomic structure of the region significantly (Ben-Yosef and Sergi 2018). Accordingly, this destruction is now generally acknowledged as a better chronological anchor in the period under discussion. It might even be used as the boundary between the Iron IIA and Iron IIB periods. The starting date of the Iron IIA, however, is still disputed, although radiocarbon analysis, mainly in combination with other means, has turned out to be helpful in narrowing the gap between the Modified Conventional and the Low Chronology.[8] Hence, the beginning of the Iron Age IIA is now estimated at ca. 980 BCE or 950 BCE (Mazar 2011b).

Despite this partial consensus, the revised chronological framework is used to tell remarkably diverse narratives about the earliest Iron IIA kingdoms. Did everything start in the north with Omri (Finkelstein 2019)? Was Tel es-Safi/Gath the center of the most important polity in the region until its destruction, so that Judah could only thrive after Hazael had destroyed Gath, Judah's enemy in the west (Maeir et al 2013)? Have new excavations elucidated how Judah already had become a kingdom at the end of the 11th century BCE, which developed into a united kingdom shortly thereafter (Garfinkel 2021)? Or do these solutions fail to acknowledge the nomadic origin of the kingdom of Judah because they all suffer from an architectural bias (Ben-Yosef 2021)? These views diverge because there is a dissimilarity between the socio-archaeological and anthropological models that are used as heuristic devices in historical reconstructions. Much depends on how one defines political control (Hays 2015; Keimer 2020; van Bekkum 2014: 226–36), and to what extent an indigenous understanding of socio-political structures is used in drawing a picture of the early Israelite monarchy, that is, of the kings Saul, David, and Solomon (Keimer and Thomas 2022). Yet these names reveal that biblical texts also play a significant part, whether they are to be interpreted as religious or as political communication (van Bekkum 2017: 169–75).

This also affects the understanding of biblical chronology before Rehoboam and Jeroboam, in particular the notion in 1 Kgs 6:1 that the building of the temple took place in the fourth year of the reign of King Solomon and 480 years after Israel's exodus from Egypt. Taking the established number of 930 BCE for the end of Solomon's reign as a point of departure, some scholars use this indication to date the exodus at 1446 BCE (e.g., Merrill 2008: 83–92; Stripling 2021). Others argue that this verse is not to be understood in a historical way, but that the number is part of the Deuteronomistic chronology and only indicates that there were 12 generations between the exodus from Egypt and Solomon's temple, which would also be supported by the Levitical genealogies in 1 Chron 6 (e.g., Laato 2015: 98–105). Be that as it may, from a historical perspective, it is unavoidable to ask how this chronology relates to history. For, on the one hand, there is hardly any precise southern Levantine historical information available for the period under discussion. On the other hand, however, David is mentioned as the founder of a dynasty in the 9th century BCE Tel Dan Stela and possibly also in the last lines of the Mesha Stela (cf. Lemaire 2021; Suriano 2007), while Israel is attested as a people, possibly even as being sedentary and active in agriculture, in the Merenptah Stela from the late 13th century BCE (Hasel 2008, cf. Kahn 2012; Abbas 2020). In addition, it is to be noted that in Egypt and Assyria, *Distanzangaben* relating a monument or temple to its origin in the past were often based on other chronological data, but at the same time cannot always be used to calculate the actual date of construction and sometimes also had a symbolic meaning (Hoffmeier 2007: 238–39; Mahieu 2021, Pruzsinszky 2005). Accordingly, there is reason to ask how the biblical text itself presents the chronology from the exodus to the building of the temple as indicated in Exod 16:35 and the 480 years of 1 Kgs 6:1.[9]

From a literary perspective, it is striking how often the chronological notes in the Masoretic text between Exod 16:35 and 1 Kgs 6:1 combine two elements: (a sum of) "forty years" and "rest."[10] The frequent attestations of "forty" and of numbers related to that figure make it unlikely that the remark concerning the 480 years in 1 Kgs 6:1 is a late insertion (thus Li 2019). Already early in the scholarly discussion of the number 40, it was also observed that this number symbolizes the time in which a responsible group of people is punished and dies, which is longer than a generation.[11] Within this framework, the number sometimes also represents a time of testing Israel's loyalty and a time of grace, because Israel did not lack anything in the desert.[12] These notions of obedience and disobedience, punishment and protection also resonate in the use of the number and in the part or sum of it in Judges and Samuel.[13] An interesting parallel of the number 40 as a symbol for divine punishment is found in the Mesa Stela: Kemosh was angry with his country and, therefore, Moab was suppressed by Omri and his son for 40 years. Historically, this regards the period of the Israelite subjugation of Moab by Omri and Ahab between ca. 880 and 850 BCE (Lemaire 2021: 22, 32–36).

The second element, that of "rest" from battle and conflict,[14] not only denotes the result of liberation by YHWH but also the goal of conquering the promised land.[15] After the conquest, all enemies are defeated and the land can be inherited because God has fulfilled all the promises (Josh 11:23; 21:44; 22:4; 23:1). However, after Joshua's death, rest and unrest constantly alternate until YHWH brings peace and rest through the election of David and his dynasty (2 Sam 7). Only in this way, the goal of the exodus is achieved, and the temple of YHWH can be built. In this light, it is worth exploring how the numbers indeed add up to the *Distanzangabe* of 480 years, the number mentioned in 1 Kgs 6:1–2, which possibly alludes to the genre of, or is derived from a temple dedication inscription (Hurvitz 1992: 226–33). If all figures from Exod 16 to 1 Kgs 6 are taken into account, without ruling out some of them because of literary-critical considerations, and assuming that overlaps are explicitly mentioned in the text (e.g. Judg 10:7) and periods of leadership without chronological indications should not be counted, there are at least two options for arriving at 480 years (see Table 3.4). In this way a chronology of disobedience and grace is created, that is, 12 times 40 years (cf. Noth 1943: 21–5).

The remaining three years in the first reconstruction might be related to the period in the wilderness after Kadesh Barnea, which is sometimes not counted as 38, but as 40 years (Num 14:33–34; Josh 14:7, 10), to the succession of Ish-Bosheth by David, and to the antedating of Solomon's years which can be inferred from the exact dates given for the construction of the temple (1 Kgs 6:1, 37–38, cf. Thiele 1983: 51–52). The second possibility only needs Solomon's antedating to add up to an exact number of 480 years.

Without chronological notices, the theological periodization is attested in Ps 78, 132, and Ps 114:1–2 "When Israel came out of Egypt (...), Judah became God's sanctuary" (cf. 1 Kgs 8:21, 51; 9:9). This chronological *Gerüst* in the Primary History from the exodus to the building of the temple also explains the solid attestation in the Masoretic tradition of the strange number of two regnal years for Saul in 1 Sam 13:1 (Gilmour and Young 2013). The 300 years of Judg 11:36 do not seem to be part of it, because this remark is not made by the narrator or editor, but by Jephthah, for whom exaggerating is clearly part of his negotiation tactics with the Ammonites: Israel never made any mistake, always respected the borders of Edom, Moab and Ammon, never had any problems with Balak, only conquered

Table 3.4[a] Options for recounting 480 years between the construction of Solomon's Temple and the Exodus

2nd year	Exod 40:17; Num 1:1; 9:1; 10:11 – into the desert	2	2
38 years	Deut 1:3 – into the desert from Kadesh	40	40
40 years	Num 33:38, cf. Exod 7:7; 16:35; Num 14:33–34; Deut 2:7, 14; 8:2–4; 29:4; 31:1; 34:7; Josh 5:6; 14:10 – into the desert	40	40
45 years	Josh 14:10, cf. 14:7 – since Israel was in the desert	45	45
110 years	Josh 24:29; Judg 2:8 – death of Joshua	70[b]	
8 years	Judg 3:8 – oppression by Cushan-Rishathaim	78	53
40 years	Judg 3:11 – Othniel	118	93
18 years	Judg 3:14 – oppression by Moab	136	111
80 years	Judg 3:30 – Ehud	216	191
20 years	Judg 4:3 – oppression by Jabin	236	211
40 years	Judg 5:31 – Debora	276	251
7 years	Judg 6:1 – oppression by Midianites	283	258
40 years	Judg 8:28 – Gideon	323	298
3 years	Judg 9:22 – Abimelech	326	301
23 years	Judg 10:2 – Tolah	349	324
22 years	Judg 10:3 – Jair	371*~	346
18 years[c]	Judg 10:8 – oppression by Philistines and Ammonites	389	364*
6 years	Judg 12:7 – Jephthah	395	370
7 years	Judg 12:9 – Ibzan	402	377
10 years	Judg 12:10 – Elon	412	387
8 years	Judg 12:14 – Abdon	420	395~
40 years	Judg 13:1 – oppression by Philistines	411*	435
20 years	Judg 15:20; 16:31 – Samson	391~	384*/415~
40 years	1 Sam 4:18 – Eli	411*	415~
20 years	1 Sam 7:2 – Ark in Kiriath Jearim	431	435
2 years	1 Sam 13:1 – Saul	433	437
2 years[d]	2 Sam 2:10 – Ish-Bosheth	435	439
7 years	2 Sam 2:11 – David in Hebron	440	444
40 years	2 Sam 5:4–5; 1 Kgs 2:11 – David in Hebron and Jerusalem	473	477
4 years	1 Kgs 6:1 – Solomon	477	481

a Both calculations take their point of departure in the observation that many texts present the exodus as a clear point of departure (Exod 40:17; Num 1:1; 9:1; 10:11; 33:38; Deut 1:3; 1 Kgs 6:1)

b The first possibility counts the references to Joshua's age – 85 in Josh 14:10, and 110 in Josh. 29:24/Judg 2:8 – as a number, that is, as 25, as the difference between 85 and 110. The second possibility, that of Noth, assumes that not mentioning Joshua's time as Israel's leader implies that his years should not be counted and that the double reference to the Philistine oppression is to be added together. For options based on redaction-historical considerations, see Focken (2014: 223–26); Laato (2015: 100–05).

c Possible overlaps are created by mentioning the oppression by the Philistines and Ammonites together (Judg 10:7) and by the options of placing Samson, Eli, or Samuel during the 40 years of Philistine oppression (Judg 13:1; 15:20; 1 Sam. 4:18; 7:15).

d Ish-Bosheth's reign likely overlaps with part of David's reign in Hebron.

the area north of the Arnon in response to an attack by Sihon, and has been living there three centuries already (van Bekkum 2018: 62–63).

When this literary appreciation of the chronological indications from Exod 16 to 1 Kgs 6 is compared to the chronology of the kings of Israel and Judah in 1 Kgs 12 – 2 Kgs 25 and to historical information, several observations can be made. Both systems make use of well-known ancient Near Eastern chronographic practices. But while the first combines the counting of regnal years with a precise synchronistic system underlining Israel's unity, the second utilizes years to highlight symbolic numbers and to present a *Distanzangabe* pointing at Israel's exodus from Egypt as the ultimate foundation of the temple. The latter framework also reflects chronographic interest and antiquarian intent. Yet the omission of the years of leadership of important figures such as Joshua and Samuel and the use of the number 40 indicate that it refers to history in a more symbolic way. Therefore, a concrete use of dates in historical reconstruction before the 10th century BCE is not to be preferred, for the main emphasis in the framework is theological. It is not easy to answer the question of why the transfer from a "pre-historical" to a "historical" period occurs at the end of the reign of Solomon. Yet it might be no coincidence that the precise chronology goes back to the advanced royal administration of late Iron IIA to Iron IIC, while the more symbolic framework relates to the more fragmented historical picture of Iron I and early Iron IIA. The fact that *Distanzangaben* are often based on other chronological information and the use of chronological symbolism in the Mesha Stela is helpful in this regard. This shows that it is likely that the chronological framework aimed at the building of the temple indeed presupposes pieces of information available through the Iron I scribal activity of the Late Bronze southern scribal tradition which finally became part of the administration of the Iron II kings (cf. Pioske 2013). Another reason for the scribes to use a poetically functioning chronology for David and Solomon could be that they serve as paradigmatic kings in the portrayal of the triad of deity, king, and nation in the book of Kings. Be that as it may, whenever the textual chronological framework from the Exodus to the building of the temple was created, it typically reflects the historical horizon and literary imagination of the Iron Age scribes.

As a result, according to the testimony of biblical chronology, the tribes of Israel were in the land when Merneptah's generals campaigned through the region in 1207 BCE. Moreover, in the light of the texts and even without making use of historical information from the Southern Levant in the Amarna period or from Egypt, it is a matter of open debate when and how the exodus and settlement took place (cf. Janzen 2021; Levy, Schneider, and Propp 2015; van Bekkum 2011).

Conclusion – Chronologies, Histories, and Scenarios

If chronology is the backbone of history, modern historians are not the first who offer a historical perspective on ancient Israel and try to understand the continuity and change of its past. Over the last two centuries, an enormous amount of information, knowledge, and methods have become available which contribute to the understanding of not only ancient Israel itself but also of the ways chronographic interest took form and antiquarian intent was translated into periodization and the counting of years. The vast knowledge of the Ancient Near East and Egypt during the Late Bronze and Iron Ages and the further establishment of their chronology offer a framework for the reconstruction of the history and archaeology of the Southern Levant.

From a chronological perspective, this results in rather precise dates for the history of ancient Israel during the Iron Age IIA–B period, that is, from the second half of the 10th century BCE to the destruction of Jerusalem in July 587. Strikingly, historians, both in the past and the present, have much more difficulty in reconstructing the previous centuries. Despite diverse kinds of information and, today, of sophisticated tools, due to a lack of precise data the choice of a certain kind of periodization influences the chronological reconstruction significantly. Moreover, the competing chronologies also reflect competing histories, which in their turn are rooted in diverse political and religious perspectives and worldviews. For the history of ancient Israel as a discipline, this is not a disadvantage. It only shows that in reconstructing the past and in trying to do justice to the available textual and iconographical sources and material remains, more scenarios are possible than is often assumed. At the same time, the picture becomes more precise, progress is made, and inevitable facts are being established. The past matters, and thus do the years and eras.

Notes

1 See the remarks preceding a king list regarding the inhabitants of the steppe before "the canal was dug" in a newly reconstructed Sumerian flood story from Old Babylonian Ur (Peterson 2016).
2 For literary and historical reasons, the Primary History as a whole is a better point of departure for diachronic analysis and chronological indications than the Pentateuch and the Former Prophets, or the Tetrateuch and the Deuteronomistic History (cf. Van Bekkum 2021: 8–9, 28–37).
3 One proposal, possibly also attested in the Septuagint and the Samaritan Pentateuch, is that the 430 years of Exod 12:40 highlight that Israel's sojourn in Egypt was exactly twice as long as that of the patriarchs in Canaan. Others assume that the number is part of a chronological system assigning 1,200 years from the birth of Abraham to the construction of Solomon's temple, or that it mirrors the length of the total of regnal years of the kings of Judah. Regarding the 480 years between the exodus and the building of the first temple, it is proposed that this is the same as the period between the dedication of the first and the second temple, or that it reflects 12 generations. For a discussion and literature, see, e.g., Bailey 1996; Galil 2010; Hughes 1990.
4 For the history of research, see Galil 1996: 1–10; Laato 2015: 5–13; and Weingart 2020: 2–12.
5 The archaeological part of this section is an updated version of van Bekkum 2017: 163–67.
6 For a summary and analysis, see Faust 2021, cf. section 1; Finkelstein, Mazar, and Schmidt 2007.
7 For new inscriptions from Tell Zayit, Khirbet Qeiyafa, Tel Beth Shemesh, Tell es-Safi, Tel Rehov, and Khirbet al-Raʿi, see Eshel and Levin 2015; McCarter, Bunimovitz, and Lederman 2011; Misgav, Garfinkel, and Ganor 2009: 243–58; Rollston et al. 2021; Tappy and McCarter 2008. For a broader perspective, see Richelle 2016.
8 Asscher et al. 2015; Ben-Yosef et al. 2012; Boaretto et al. 2018; Katz and Faust 2014; Toffolo et al. 2014.
9 For the history of research, see Focken 2014: 21–30; Li 2019. The interpretation of the 480 years as 12 generations was offered by Bertheau, Nöldeke, Wellhausen, Rowley, and Cogan. Harrison also connected it to the 12 tribes (Li 2019: 38, 43–44).
10 As indicated above, the often-deviating numbers in the Septuagint are to be studied by paying attention to the context of the translators, who had to rethink biblical chronological indications in the light of the continuous counting of years that had become an option in historiography since the Seleucids.
11 Exod 16:35; Num 14:33–34; 32:13; 33:38; Josh 5:6; 14:7, 10; see De Koning 1940: 29–30; Noth 1943: 21.
12 Deut 1:3; 2:7; 8:2–4; 29:4.
13 Judg 3:8, 11, 14, 30; 4:3; 5:31; 6:1; 8:28; 9:22; 10:2; 10:3; 10:8; 12:7; 12:9; 12:10; 12:14; 13:1; 15:20; 16:31; 1 Sam 4:18; 7:2; 13:1; 2 Sam 2:10; 2:11; 5:4–5, cf. 1 Kgs 2:11; 1 Kgs 6:1.
14 *šqṭ* –Josh. 14:15; Judg 3:11, 30; 5:31; 8:28, cf. Josh 11:23; Judg 18:7, 27; and *nwḥ* – Josh 1:13–15; 21:44; 23:1; 2 Sam. 7:1, 11; 1 Kgs 5:4, cf. Deut 12:9–10; 1 Kgs 8:1, 56.
15 Exod 23:20, Deut 3:20; 25:19; Josh 1:13–15; 21:44; 23:1.

Bibliography

Abbas, M. R. 2020. "The Canaanite and Nubian Wars of Merenptah: Some Historical Notes." *Égypte Nilotique et Méditerranéenne* 13: 133–49.

Asscher, Y., et al. 2015. "Absolute Dating of the Late Bronze to Iron Age Transition and the Appearance of the Philistine Culture in Qubur el-Walaydah, Southern Levant." *Radiocarbon* 57: 77–97.

Bailey, L. R. 1996. "Biblical Math as *Heilsgeschichte*?" Pages 84–102 in *A Gift of God in Due Season: Essays on Scripture and Community in Honor of James A. Sanders*. Edited by R. D. Weis and D. M. Carr. Sheffield: Sheffield Academic Press.

Becking, B. E. J. H. 2021. *Israel's Past Seen from the Present: Studies on History and Religion in Ancient Israel and Judah*. Berlin: De Gruyter.

Ben-Yosef, E. 2019. "The Architectural Bias in Current Biblical Archaeology." *VT* 69: 361–87.

———. 2020. "And Yet, a Nomadic Error: A Reply to Israel Finkelstein." *AntOr* 18: 33–60.

———. 2021. "Rethinking the Social Complexity of Early Iron Age Nomads." *JJAR* 1: 154–78.

Ben-Yosef, E., et al. 2012. "A New Chronological Framework for Iron Age Copper Production at Timna (Israel)." *BASOR* 367: 31–71.

Ben-Yosef. E., and O. Sergi. 2018. "The Destruction of Gath by Hazael and the Arabah Copper Industry: A Reassessment." Pages 461–80 in *Studies in the History and Archaeology of Israel: Essays in Honor of Aren M. Maeir on the Occasion of his Sixtieth Birthday*. Edited by I. Shai et al. Münster: Zaphon.

Bietak, M., and F. Höflmayer. 2007. "Introduction: High or Low Chronology." Pages 13–23 in *The Synchronization of Civilizations in the Eastern Mediterranean in the Second Millennium B.C.* Edited by M. Bietak and E. Czerny. Wien: Verlag der Österreichische Akademie der Wissenschaften.

Boaretto, E., et al. 2018. "The Chronology of the Late Bronze—Iron Age Transition in the Southern Levant." *Radiocarbon* 60: 1–11.

Bronk Ramsey, C. 2013. "Using Radiocarbon Evidence in Egyptian Chronological Research." Pages 29–39 in *Radiocarbon and the Chronologies of Ancient Egypt*. Edited by A. J. Shortland et al. London: Oxbow Books.

Bronk Ramsey, C., et al. 2010. "Radiocarbon-Based Chronology for Dynastic Egypt." *Science* 328: 1554–57.

Chen, F. 2020. *Study on the Synchronistic King List from Ashur*. CM 51. Leiden: Brill.

David, A. 2016. "A *Mnḫprrʿ* Scarab from Tel Abel Beth Maacah." *JAEI* 9: 1–13.

de Koning, J. 1940. *Studiën over de El-Amarnabrieven en het Oude Testament*. Delft: W. D. Meinema.

Devecchi, E., and J. L. Miller. 2011. "Hittite-Egyptian Synchronisms and Their Consequences for Ancient Near Eastern Chronology." Pages 139–76 in *Egypt and the Near East—the Crossroads*. Edited by J. Mynářová. Prague: Charles University.

Emanuel, J. P. 2015. "King Taita and His 'Palistin': Philistine State of Neo-Hittite Kingdom?" *AntOr* 13: 11–40.

Eshel, E., and Y. Levin. eds. 2015. *"See, I Will Bring a Scroll Recounting What Befell Me" (Ps 40:8): Epigraphy and Daily Life from the Bible to the Talmud*. Göttingen: Vandenhoeck & Ruprecht.

Faust, A. 2015. "Settlement, Economy, and Demography under Assyrian Rule in the West: The Territories of the Former Kingdom of Israel as a Test Case." *JAOS* 135: 765–89.

———. 2021. "The 'United Monarchy' on the Ground: The Disruptive Character of the Iron Age I–II Transition and the Nature of Political Transformations." *JJAR* 1: 15–67.

Faust, A., and H. Katz. 2015. "A Canaanite Town, a Judahite Center, and a Persian Period Fort: Excavating Over Two Thousand Years of History at Tel 'Eton." *NEA* 78: 88–102.

Fiaccavento, C. 2014. "Destructions as Historical Markers Towards the End of the 2nd and during the 1st Millennium BC in the Southern Levant." Pages 205–59 in *Overcoming Catastrophes: Essays on Disastrous Agents Characterization and Resilience Strategies in Pre-Classical Southern Levant*. Edited by L. Nigro. Rome: La Sapienza.

Finkelstein, I. 1996. "The Archaeology of the United Monarchy: An Alternative View." *Levant* 28: 177–87.

———. 2013a. *The Forgotten Kingdom. The Archaeology and History of Northern Israel*. Atlanta: SBL.

———. 2013b. "Geographical and Historical Realities behind the Earliest Layer in the David Stories." *SJOT* 27: 131–50.

———. 2019. "First Israel, Core Israel, United (Northern) Israel." *NEA* 82: 8–15.

———. 2020. "The Arabah Copper Polity and the Rise of Iron Age Edom: A Bias in Biblical Archaeology?" *AntOr* 18: 11–32.
Finkelstein, I., A. Mazar, and B. Schmidt. 2007. *The Quest for the Historical Israel: Debating Archaeology and the History of Early Israel*. Atlanta: SBL.
Finkelstein, I., and E. Piasetzky, E. 2006. "The Iron I–IIA in the Highlands and Beyond: ^{14}C Anchors, Pottery Phases and The Shoshenq I Campaign." *Levant* 38: 45–61.
Focken, F. -E. 2014. *Zwischen Landnahme und Königtum. Literarkritische und Redaktionsgeschichtliche Untersuchungen zum Anfang und Ende der Deuteronomistischen Richtererzählungen*. Göttingen: Vandenhoeck & Ruprecht.
Franklin, N. 2018. "Megiddo and Jezreel Reflected in the Dying Embers of the Northern Kingdom of Israel." Pages 189–208 in *The Last Days of the Kingdom of Israel*. Edited by S. Hasegawa, C. Levin, and K. Radner. Berlin: de Gruyter.
Gadot, T., and J. Uziel. 2017. "The Monumentality of Iron Age Jerusalem Prior to the 8th Century BCE." *TA* 44: 123–40.
Gadot, Y., and E. Yadin. 2009. *Aphek-Antipatris II: The Remains on the Acropolis*. Tel Aviv: Emery and Yass Publications.
Galil, G. 1996. *The Chronology of the Kings of Israel and Judah*. Leiden: Brill.
———. 2010. "Dates and Calendars in Kings." Pages 427–44 in *The Books of Kings: Sources, Composition, Historiography and Reception*. Edited by A. Lemaire and B. Halpern. Leiden: Brill.
———. 2014. "A Concise History of Palistin/Patin/Unqi/ʿmq in the 11th–9th Centuries BC." *Semitica* 56: 75–104.
Garfinkel, Y. 2021. "The 10th Century BCE in Judah: Archaeology and the Biblical Tradition." *JJAR* 1: 126–54.
Gilmour, R., and I. Young. 2013. "Saul's Two Year Reign in 1 Samuel 13:1." *VT* 63: 150–54.
Glassner, J. -J. 2004. *Mesopotamian Chronicles*. Edited by B. R. Foster. Atlanta: SBL.
Harrison, T. P. 2021. "The Iron Age I-II Transition in the Northern Levant: An Emerging Consensus?" *JJAR* 1: 325–51.
Hasegawa, S., C. Levin, and K. Radner, eds. 2018. *Last Days of the Kingdom of Israel*. Berlin: De Gruyter.
Hasel, M. G. 1998. *Domination and Resistance: Egyptian Military Activity in the Southern Levant, 1300-1185 BC*. Leiden: Brill.
———. 2008. "Merneptah's Reference to Israel: Critical Issues for the Origin of Israel. Pages 47–59 in *Critical Issues in Early Israelite History*. Edited by R. S. Hess. Winona Lake: Eisenbrauns.
Hays, C. B. 2015. "Biblical Claims About Solomon's Kingdom in Light of Egyptian 'Three-Zone' Ideology of Territory." Pages 503–15 in *Israel's Exodus in Transdisciplinary Perspective*. Edited by Levy et al. New York: Springer.
Hoffmeier, J. K. 2007. "What Is the Biblical Date for the Exodus? A Response to Bryant Wood." *JETS* 50: 225–47.
Höflmayer, F. 2016. "Radiocarbon Dating and Egyptian Chronology: From the 'Curve of Knowns' to Bayesian Modelling." *OHO*. doi:10.1093/oxfordhb/9780199935413.013.64.
Holladay, J. S. 1995. "The Kingdoms of Israel and Judah: Political and Economic Centralization in the Iron IIA–B" (ca. 1000–757 BCE)." Pages 368–98 in *The Archaeology of Society in the Holy Land*. Edited by T. E. Levy. New York: Facts on File.
Hughes, J. 1990. *Secrets of the Times: Myth and History in Biblical Chronology*. Sheffield: Sheffield Academic Press.
Huizinga, Johan. 1936. *In the Shadow of Tomorrow*. New York: W.W. Norton.
Hurvitz, A. 1992. *I Have Built You an Exalted House: Temple Building in Light of Mesopotamian and Northwest Semitic Writings*. Sheffield: Sheffield Academic Press.
James, P., and P. G. van der Veen, eds. 2015. *Solomon and Shishak: Current Perspectives from Archaeology, Epigraphy, History and Chronology*. Oxford: Archaeopress.
James, P., et al. 1991. *Centuries of Darkness: A Challenge to the Conventional Chronology of Old World Archaeology*. London: Jonathan Cape.
Janzen, M. D., ed. 2021. *Five Views on the Exodus: Historicity, Chronology, and Theological Implications*. Grand Rapids: Zondervan.
Kahn, D. 2011. "The Campaign of Ramesses III against Philistia." *JAEI* 3–4: 1–11.
———. 2012. "A Geo-Political and Historical Perspective of Merneptah's Policy in Canaan." Pages 255–68 in *The Ancient Near East in the 12th-10th Centuries BCE: Culture and History*. Edited by G. Galil et al. Münster: Ugarit Verlag.

———. 2016. "The Historical Background of a Topographical List of Ramesses III." Pages 161–68 in *Rich and Great: Studies in Honour of Anthony J. Spalinger on the Occasion of His 70th Feast of Thoth*. Edited by R. Landgráfová and J. Mináři. Prague: Charles University.

Kalimi, I., ed. 2014. *Sennacherib at the Gates of Jerusalem*. Leiden: Brill.

Katz, H., and A. Faust. 2014. "The Chronology of the Iron Age IIA in Judah in the Light of Tel 'Eiton Tomb C3 and Other Assemblages." *BASOR* 371: 103–27.

Keimer, K. H. 2020. "The Historical Geography of 1 Kings 9:11–14." *PEQ* 152: 186–206.

Keimer, K. H., and Z. Thomas. 2020-2021 [2022]. "Etic and Emic Expressions of Power in Ancient Israel: Recalibrating a Discussion." *JEOL* 48.

Killebrew, A. E., and G. Lehmann, eds. 2013. *The Philistines and Other "Sea Peoples" in Text and Archaeology*. Atlanta: SBL.

Kitchen, K. A. 2009. *The Third Intermediate Period in Egypt, 1100–650 B.C.* Warminster: Arin & Phillips.

———. 2013. "Establishing Chronology in Pharaonic Egypt and the Ancient Near East: Interlocking Textual Sources Relating to c. 1600–664 BC." Pages 1–18 in *Radiocarbon and the Chronologies of Ancient Egypt*. Edited by A. J. Shortland et al. London: Oxbow Books.

Kuan, J. K. -J. 1995. *Neo-Assyrian Historical Inscriptions and Syria-Palestine*. Hong Kong: Alliance Bible Seminary.

Laato, A. 2015. *Guide to Biblical Chronology*. Sheffield: Sheffield Phoenix Press.

Lemaire, A. 2021. "The Mesha Stela: Revisited Texts and Interpretation." Pages 20–39 in *Epigraphy, Iconography, and the Bible*. Edited by M. Lubetski and E. Lubestki. Sheffield: Sheffield Phoenix Press.

Levy, T. E., T. Schneider, and W. H. C. Propp, eds. 2015. *Israel's Exodus in Transdisciplinary Perspective. Text, Archaeology, Culture, and Geoscience*. New York: Springer.

Li, X. 2019. "A Purely Symbolic Theory on the Chronology of 1 Kings 6:1." *ABR* 67: 3–47.

Machinist, P. 2019. "Periodization in Biblical Historiography. The Domestication of Stranger Kings: Making History by List in Ancient Mesopotamia." Pages 215–37 in *Historical Consciousness and the Use of the Past in the Ancient World*. Edited by J. Baines et al. Sheffield/Bristol: Equinox.

Maeir, A. M. 2020. "Introduction and Overview." Pages 3–52 in *Tell es-Safi/Gath II: Excavations and Studies*. Edited by A. M. Maeir and J. Uziel. Münster: Zaphon.

Maeir, A. M., ed. 2012. *Tell es-Safi/Gath I: The 1996–2005 Seasons. Vol. 1. Text*. Wiesbaden: Harrassowitz.

Maeir, A. M., et al. 2013. "On the Constitution and Transformation of Philistine Identity". *OJA* 32: 1–38.

Maeir, A. M., I. Shai, and C. McKinny, eds. 2019. *The Late Bronze and Early Iron Ages of Southern Canaan*. Berlin: De Gruyter.

Mahieu, B. 2021. "The Assyrian *Distanzangaben* in Relation to the Regnal Years Recorded in the Assyrian King List." *Iraq* 83: 67–85.

Mazar, A. 2011a. "The Egyptian Garrison Town at Beth-Shean." Pages 155–89 in *Egypt, Canaan, and Israel: History, Imperialism, Ideology and Literature*. Edited by S. Bar, D. Kahn, and J. J. Shirly. Leiden: Brill.

———. 2011b. "The Iron Age Chronology Debate: Is the Gap Narrowing? Another Viewpoint." *NEA* 74: 105–11.

Mazar, A., and U. Davidovich. 2019. "Canaanite Reḥob: Tel Rehov in the Late Bronze Age." *BASOR* 381: 163–91.

Mazar, E. 2009. *The Palace of King David: Excavations at the Summit of the City of David. Preliminary Report of Seasons 2005–2007*. Jerusalem: Shoham Academic Research and Publication.

———. 2011. *Discovering the Solomonic Wall in Jerusalem: A Remarkable Archaeological Adventure*. Jerusalem: Shoham Academic Research and Publication.

McCarter, K. P., S. Bunimovitz, and Z. Lederman. 2011. "An Archaic Baal Inscription from Tel Beth-Shemesh." *TA* 38: 179–93.

Merrill, E. H. 2008. *Kingdom of Priests: A History of the Old Testament*. Grand Rapids: Baker Academic.

Michalowski, P. 2019. "The Domestication of Stranger Kings: Making History by List in Ancient Mesopotamia." Pages 15–38 in *Historical Consciousness and the Use of the Past in the Ancient World*. Edited by J. Baines et al. Sheffield: Equinox.

Millek, J. M. 2020. *Exchange, Destruction, and a Transitioning Society: Interregional Exchange in the Southern Levant from the Late Bronze Age to the Iron I*. Tübingen: Universität Tübingen.

Misgav, H., Y. Garfinkel, and S. Ganor. 2009. Pages 243–57 in *Khirbet Qeiyafa, Vol. 1: Excavation Report 2007–2008*. Edited by Y. Garfinkel and S. Ganor. Jerusalem: Israel Exploration Society.

Mondot, J. -F. 2006. *Une Bible pour deux mémoires. Archéologiques israéliens et palestiniens.* Paris: Stock.

Münger, S. 2003. "Egyptian Stamp-Seal Amulets and Their Implications for the Chronology of the Early Iron Age." *TA* 30: 66–82.

Noort, E. 2004. "Reconstructie van de geschiedenis van Israël. De casus van de 'High or Low Chronology' in de koningstijd." *NTT* 58: 309–22.

Noth, M. 1943. *Überlieferungsgeschichtliche Studien. Die sammelnden und bearbeitenden Geschichtswerke im Alten Testament.* Halle an der Saale: Niemeyer.

Peterson, J. 2016. "The Divine Appointment of the First Antediluvian King: Newly Recovered Content from the Ur Version of the Sumerian Flood Story." *JCS* 70: 37–51.

Pioske, D. D. 2013. "The Scribe of David: A Portrait of a Life." *Maarav* 20: 163–88.

Pruzsinszky, R. 2005. "Zum Verständnis der Assyrischen Distanzangaben: Beiträge zur Assyrischen Chronologie." *SAA* 14: 23–31.

Rawlinson, H. C. 1867. "The Assyrian Canon Verified by the Record of a Solar Eclipse, B.C. 763." *The Athenæum* 2064: 660–61.

Richelle, M. 2016. "Elusive Scrolls: Could Any Hebrew Literature Have Been Written Prior to the Eighth Century BCE?" *VT* 66: 1–39.

Rollston, C., et al. 2021. "The Jerubbaʿal Inscription from Khirbet al-Raʿi: A Proto-Canaanite (Early Alphabetic) Inscription." *IJAR* 2: 1–15.

Stager, L. E. 1995. "The Impact of the Sea Peoples in Canaan (1185–1050 BCE)." Pages 332–48 in *The Archaeology of Society in the Holy Land.* Edited by T. E. Levy. Leicester: Leicester University.

Stillinger, M. D. 2016. "Archaeomagnetism as a Complementary Dating Technique to Address the Iron Age Chronology Debate in the Southern Levant." *NEA* 79: 90–106.

Stillinger, M. D., et al. 2018. "A Rejoinder on the Value of Archaeomagnetic Dating Integrative Methodology Is the Key to Addressing Levantine Iron Age Chronology." *NEA* 81: 141–44.

Stripling, S. 2021. "The Fifteenth-Century (Early-Date) Exodus View." Pages 25–52 in *Five Views on the Exodus: Historicity, Chronology, and Theological Implications.* Edited by Mark D. Janzen. Grand Rapids: Zondervan.

Strootman, R. 2015. "Seleucid Era." *Encyclopædia Iranica.* Online: www.iranicaonline.org/articles/seleucid-era.

Suriano, M. 2007. "The Apology of Hazael: A Literary and Historical Analysis of the Tel Dan Inscription." *JNES* 66: 163–76.

Taha, H., and G. van der Kooij. 1999. "Les Fouilles de Khirbet Belameh." *L'Archéologie Palestinnienne. Dossiers d'Archéologie* 240: 138–45.

———. 2007. *The Water Tunnel System at Khirbet Balʿama.* Ramallah: Palestinian Antiquities.

Tappy, R. E. 2018. "The Annals of Sargon II and the Archaeology of Samaria: Rhetorical Claims, Empirical Evidence." Pages 147–88 in *The Last Days of the Kingdom of Israel.* Edited by S. Hasegawa, C. Levin, and K. Radner. Berlin: de Gruyter.

Tappy, R. E., and P. K. McCarter, eds. 2008. *Literate Culture and Tenth-Century Canaan: The Tel Zayit Abecedary in Context.* Winona Lake: Eisenbrauns.

Thiele, E. R. 1983. *The Mysterious Numbers of the Hebrew Kings.* Grand Rapids: Zondervan.

Toffolo, M. B. et al. 2014. "Absolute Chronology of Megiddo, Israel, in the Late Bronze and Iron Ages: High Resolution Radiocarbon Dating." *Radiocarbon* 56: 21–44.

Ussishkin, D. 1985. "Level VII at Tel Lachish and the End of the Late Bronze Age in Canaan." Pages 213–30 in *Palestine in the Bronze and Iron Ages.* Edited by J. N. Tubb. London: Routledge.

———. 1995. "The Destruction of Megiddo at the End of the Late Bronze Age and Its Historical Significance." *TA* 22: 240–67.

———. 2014. "Sennacherib's Campaign to Judah: The Archaeological Perspective with an Emphasis on Lachish and Jerusalem." Pages 75–104 in *Sennacherib at the Gates of Jerusalem: Story, History, and Historiography.* Edited by Isaac Kalimi and Seth Richardson. Leiden: Brill.

Vaknin, Y., et al. 2020. "The Earth's Magnetic Field in Jerusalem During the Babylonian Destruction: A Unique Reference for Field Behavior and an Anchor for Archaeomagnetic Dating." *PLOS One* 15: doi.org/10.1371/journal.pone.0237029.

van Bekkum, K. 2011. *From Conquest to Coexistence: Ideology and Antiquarian Intent in the Historiography of Israel's Settlement in Canaan.* Leiden: Brill.

———. 2014. "'The Situation Is More Complicated:' Archaeology and Text in the Historical Reconstruction of the Iron Age IIA Southern Levant." Pages 215–44 in *Exploring the Narrative. Jerusalem and Jordan in the Bronze and Iron Ages: Papers in Honour of Margreet Steiner.* Edited by E. J. van der Steen et al. London: Bloomsbury.

———. 2017. "'How the Mighty Have Fallen:' Sola Scriptura and the Historical Debate on David as a Southern Levantine Warlord." Pages 159–82 in *Sola Scriptura: Biblical and Theological Perspectives on Scripture, Authority, and Hermeneutics.* Edited by Hans Burger, Arnold Huijgen, and Eric Peels. Leiden: Brill.

———. 2018. "'Let YHWH, the Judge, Decide.' Literary, Historical and Theological Aspects of the Jephthah Narrative." Pages 61–69 in *Reading and Listening: Meeting One God in Many Texts. Festschrift for Eric Peels on the Occasion of His 25th Jubilee as Professor of Old Testament Studies.* Edited by Jaap Dekker and Gert Kwakkel. Bergambacht: Uitgeverij 2VM.

———. 2021. *"But As for Me and My House, We Will Serve YHWH:" Joshua 24 and Christian Theology in a Context of Religious Plurality.* Leuven: ETF Leuven.

van der Veen, P. G. 2020. *Dating the Iron IIB Archaeological Horizon in Israel and Judah: A Reinvestigation of "Neo-Assyrian (Period)" Sillilographic and Ceramic Chronological Markers from the 8th and 7th Centuries B.C.* Münster: Zaphon.

van Dijk, J. 2008. "New Evidence on the Length of the Reign of Horemheb." *JARCE* 44: 193–200.

Waerzeggers, C. 2012. "The Babylonian Chronicles: Classification and Provenance." *JNES* 71: 285–98.

Wallenfels, R. 2019. "Shishak and Shoshenq: A Disambiguation." *JAOS* 139: 487–500.

Weingart, K. 2020. *Gezählte Geschichte: Systematik, Quellen und Entwicklung der synchronistischen Chronologie in den Königebüchern.* Tübingen: Mohr Siebeck.

Yahalom-Mack, N., N. Panitz-Cohen, and R. Mullins. 2018. "From a Fortified Canaanite City to 'a City and Mother' in Israel: Five Seasons of Excavation at Tel Abel Beth Maacah." *NEA* 81: 145–56.

Yamada, S. 2018. "Neo-Assyrian Eponym Lists and Eponym Chronicles: Contents, Stylistic Variants and Their Historical-Ideological Background." Pages 75–96 in *Conceptualizing Past, Present and Future.* Edited by S. Fink and R. Rollinger. Münster: Ugarit-Verlag.

Yasur-Landau, A. 2010. *The Philistines and Aegean Migration at the End of the Late Bronze Age.* Cambridge: Cambridge University Press.

Young, R. A. 2012. *Hezekiah in History and Tradition.* Leiden: Brill.

Young, R. C. 2004. When Did Jerusalem Fall? *JETS* 47: 21–38.

Younger, K. L. 1990. *Ancient Conquest Accounts: A Study in Ancient Near Eastern and Biblical History Writing.* Sheffield: JSOT Press.

———. 2016. *A Political History of the Arameans: From Their Origins to the End of Their Polities.* Atlanta: SBL.

———. 2018. "Assyria's Expansion West of the Euphrates (ca. 870-701 BCE)." Pages 17–33 in *Archaeology and History of Eighth-Century Judah.* Edited by Z. I. Farber and J. L. Wright. Atlanta: SBL.

4
THE HISTORIAN AND THE ASSEMBLAGE

On the Interpretation of Texts and Artifacts for the History of Ancient Israel

Daniel Pioske

We now stand a century removed from that morning of 17 March 1922, when W.F. Albright (1922) arrived at the site of Tell el-Ful, just north of Jerusalem, with $1000 in hand to oversee his first excavation. The centenary of Albright's initial foray into what he would term "biblical archaeology" offers an occasion to reflect on where we are 100 years hence, inheritors of what has become the most intensely excavated landscape on earth and the question of how these remains relate to a historical period and people long viewed through the lens of the biblical writings. Indeed, in contrast to the "six baskets full of potsherds and other small objects" that Albright (1922: 7) reports from the first day of his dig, what makes our moment distinct is the sheer amount of archaeological data that we now possess 100 years later, extracted from entire precincts of ancient Levantine cities and large-scale regional surveys in ways unimaginable to Albright or his contemporaries.

Amid the growing accumulation of material finds from the southern Levant, a host of important studies have reflected on the relationship between these artifacts and the texts we possess from antiquity for how we understand the history of ancient Israel.[1] But what is often absent from these discussions is a more rigorous engagement with the philosophical underpinnings of the interpretive methods we employ. As Albright (1969: 6) noted, "we all, of course, have presuppositions of a philosophical order"—we all hold to certain philosophical commitments that motivate our historical undertakings, determining what questions we ask of the data before us and, consequently, what conclusions we draw. Yet it remains the case that few historians or archaeologists of ancient Israel have occupied themselves with the vibrant discussions of interpretive theory that have occupied other historical fields.[2] One result has been scholarly arguments about the history of ancient Israel that, to paraphrase J. Sasson's (1981: 3–24) review of these efforts some decades ago, can generate more heat than light because the working presuppositions of those involved are not clearly articulated.

The intent of what follows is to attend to a particular line of interpretive theory for how we might conceive of the relationship between texts and artifacts for the history of Israel's ancient past. Many paths could be taken, but the one pursued here is compelled by a hermeneutic that resists the desire to ground its convictions by way of an appeal to specific warrants, archaeological or textual, that are presumed to secure the historical interpretations we put forward. Instead, the interpretive framework advocated for in this study is one that contends with indeterminacy and multiplicity, an approach that is sensitive to the fragmented character of the evidence we possess from ancient Israel but also the limits involved in the interpretive process itself as it pertains to representing a historical past that is always absent, always elusive, ever beyond our powers of restoration.[3]

To do so, this study begins by developing a way of thinking about historical interpretation that is indebted to the idea of an assemblage, a framework developed initially in Gilles Deleuze and Félix Guattari's *A Thousand Plateaus* (1987). In part, the advantage of this approach is the familiarity of its leading concept to archaeologists and historians accustomed to the practices of excavation. Yet what is also attractive about this framework is its capacity to encompass distinct and even discordant types of traces without according precedence to any one form. The second movement of this study illustrates how this interpretive approach unfolds via a case study of the history of Jerusalem's status in the centuries between Abdi-Heba and David's rule (ca. 1300–1000 BCE).

The Assemblage

What complicates the historical study of ancient Israel are the particular constraints imposed by the evidence available. The "revolution" (Miller 1987: 62) anticipated through the recovery of an archive of texts on par with those unearthed at Ugarit or Nineveh, for example, has not yet been realized for the Israelite or Judahite kingdoms of the Iron Age (ca. 1000–586 BCE), much less for the more depressed communities that took hold in the region during the Persian Period (515–330 BCE). Absent a large cache of contemporaneous documents from these eras, the Hebrew Bible remains the most detailed and substantial written source for the southern Levant's ancient history.

But it is also a difficult source. In part, our historical readings of these texts are hampered by their richly curated quality, documents formed through a series of scribal revisions and reshaped by later writers over many generations in such a way that we do not have access to their original appearance (Carr 2011; Kratz 2005). What also obscures the claims of these writings is that they are voiced by nameless storytellers and bards, scribes whose anonymity makes our attempt to tether their texts to a specific time and place a nearly impossible task (Breed 2014: 75–92; Weitzman 2016: 67–83). Theories abound, of course, about the date and setting of particular biblical passages, but even the best among them cannot attain the precision of how the classical historian locates Xenophon's *Hellenica* or Diodorus' *Library*. Instead, what we find in the Hebrew Bible are ancient documents crafted by writers who have largely disappeared into the textual worlds they devised, with the information drawn on for the stories they told and the reasons for writing them down resisting our best efforts to identify them by way of approaches that would wrest their authors from the pasts they portray.

The archaeological evidence from the southern Levant is not without its own difficulties. Long subsisting under the impress of the various empires that fought to control it, the region's terrain has been subject to a volatile history that has transformed its landscape. This was particularly so during Roman rule of the territory when its engineers often cleared sites down to the bedrock to build, thereby removing the ruins of earlier settlements that preceded them. Regarding Jerusalem, for example, which witnessed heavy Roman involvement, large swaths of the most ancient areas of the city were cleared of remains from the communities that existed before Roman governance (Keel 2007: 75–79; Mazar 2006: 255–72; Pioske 2015: 186–90). The hilly topography of the highland region where important biblical sites were once located has also occasioned problems related to erosion and resettlement. At Shiloh (Khirbet Seilun), to cite one instance, the most elevated area of the mound where a possible sanctuary once stood, remembered in the Hebrew Bible as a meaningful precursor to the Jerusalem temple, has produced few archaeological remains because most were lost through the vicissitudes of weather and further occupancy (Finkelstein, Bunimovitz, and Lederman 1993: 7–8, 374–89). Thus, the question of whether a sacred enclosure once existed at the location in the early Iron Age period remains, archaeologically, largely unanswerable.

Such issues remind us of certain problems involved when reconstructing the history of ancient Israel, problems of absence and erasures that are only compounded as we attempt to draw on what has survived from antiquity within both the written and material records for the histories we write.[4] The prevailing response to these difficulties for the history of ancient Israel can be described as an "Archimedean" approach to historical interpretation. On this view, either the biblical writings or archaeological remains are used as a fixed framework on which the historian's inquiries are founded, employed as the final arbiter by which the historical value of other forms of evidence can be assessed. What is sought through this approach are more certain forms of knowledge, then, that could anchor historical investigations otherwise adrift, whether such moorings were established by way of the supposed realism or authenticity of biblical storytelling (Von Rad 1964), to cite one example, or the presumed directness and transparency of archaeological evidence, as another (Dever 2017: 16; Finkelstein 2010). From either perspective, the ambition is to locate a more stable historical vantage point among the evidence we study, a *Punctum Archimedis* that would help secure the historical interpretations we put forward amid the uncertainties involved in reconstructing an ancient past.

The Archimedean quest has a lengthy legacy (Rorty 1979), manifesting itself among historians in their search for objective knowledge untainted by our handling of it, a more scientific or quantitative basis for our historical methods, or in the specter of the Word that has haunted even the most rigorously secular approaches. It has also proven illusory (Gadamer 2006: 267–304; Ricoeur 2004: 261–92; Rorty 1979: 315–94). What has become apparent, that is, is that we cannot escape ourselves in the interpretive process, that our historical perspectives are embodied and contextualized in such a way that no vantage point offers us the possibility of perceiving the past unencumbered by our involvements in what insights are achieved. As F. Nietzsche (1994: 87) underscored long ago, ours is a perspectival knowing, beholden to the position we happen to occupy.

What this means is that no form of historical evidence is less laden by our interpretations of it than others; no remnant from antiquity, written or material, is more transparent and capable of securing our historical propositions in the face of more opaque phenomena. Rather, whether we approach archaeological remains or ancient texts, we are confronted by the entanglements of interpretation "all the way down," as Rorty observes (1991: 100). We are awash in a sea of contingencies—historical, social, and cultural, amid many others—that in every moment saturate and condition the meanings we draw out from the evidence before us. Any visions of the past apart from our mediations of it are, in the end, illusory; they are the *fata morgana* of shipwrecked souls.

For the history of ancient Israel, what is required then is a framework supple enough to accommodate the contingent and unsettled interpretive processes by which this history must develop. To this end, what is advocated here is an approach guided by the notion of an assemblage (cf. Pioske 2019: 19–25). At the outset, what is expedient about an interpretive framework modeled on an assemblage is that it establishes interpretive relationships without fixed foundations, bereft of any form of evidence that is, *prima facie*, of more fundamental historical importance, more secure in what it signifies, than other types. An archaeological assemblage is a clear instance of this phenomenon. For what we find within an area of excavation is an array of distinct materials, ranging from ceramics to faunal remains to, when fortunate, brief epigraphic notations, whose historical significance cannot be established in advance of their recovery or apart from the broader assemblage in which they are located. Instead, what makes the items within an assemblage historically meaningful are their associations with other elements in which they are situated, relationships that cannot be predetermined but are dependent on what happens to appear within the assemblage itself when it is uncovered. No one artifact within an assemblage is of any more consequence than another, accordingly, nor can any one item be interpreted separately from the context of the other materials in which it comes to light. Each component within an assemblage is bound to all others for the interpretation of its specific historical meaning. The *in-situ* artifact, as has long been recognized, is of far more historical value than those items found on the antiquities market precisely because it was recovered within an assemblage of other artifacts that help to determine its meaning.

It is through the familiar image of the archaeological assemblage that the outline of a different interpretive approach than that of the Archimedean method can thus be discerned. For our interests, what is distinctive about an assemblage is the heterogeneous character of the components that comprise it, a mass of entities of "very different regimes of signs," as Deleuze and Guattari (1987: 21) put it, which have no necessary relationships between one another aside from being located within a particular aggregation. But it is this feature of an assemblage, what Deleuze and Guattari term an *agencement*, or an active process of arranging together, that accords this framework its particular interpretive possibilities (Buchanan 2015; Nail 2017). That is, what an assemblage affords is the prospect of diverse components to be grouped within it regardless of their underlying nature or essence. What this means for our purposes is that both the referential claims of ancient texts and the iconic or indexical significance of artifacts can be brought together within a single interpretive framework without situating them in a hierarchical pattern of significance.

A key feature of an assemblage within Deleuze and Guattari's (1987: 7–12) work, in fact, is that of heterogeneity and multiplicity. In contrast to the more recent trend of writing "archaeological" or "biblical" histories of ancient Israel limited to a more uniform collection of evidence, this emphasis on variegated components within an assemblage provides the possibility of exploring the interpretive relationships between diverse forms. Distinct entities within a historical assemblage—the homes of border communities occupying liminal spaces between rival groups, a collection of loom weights on the floor of a structure, a story of deception and loss (Judg 16:13–14)—can be interpreted together, on this view, despite their dissimilar modes of signification. Historical interpretation guided by the notion of an assemblage resists ideas of epistemic precedence because it resists foundations. Instead, this framework prizes "equally the vase and the poem, the graves and the funeral orations made over them," as Martin (2008: 321) describes this aim in his own reflection on method.

How the elements of an assemblage arrange together is what Deleuze and Guattari (1987: 9–11, 310–50) describe as an assemblage's "territory."[5] But this idea of territory is always dynamic and elastic, responsive to new movements and entities that may comprise it. Within an archaeological assemblage, for example, new insights are continually realized when further areas of a dig are exposed or deeper strata unearthed, thus preventing any finalized or "overcoded" (Deleuze and Guattari 1987: 9) interpretations of the history of a site from being put forward. For the historian's assemblage, the process of territorialization is necessarily wed to the depositional and referential features of the historical traces we study, where spatial and chronological territories appear by virtue of the timeframe and places to which our artifacts and texts attest. The past worlds described in ancient writings and evidenced by artifacts are those territories defined, in other words, in time and space (see note 7, below).

But it is the way elements relate within an assemblage that matters most for our interpretive interests. The first feature to emphasize is our involvement in the assemblages that become known. An archaeological assemblage is dependent, to return to our example, on the decisions made by those archaeologists who select a site to dig and the practices they employ to excavate it. Deleuze and Guattari (1987: 111–48) contend that all assemblages arise through specific judgments and inclinations; they are "passional," the outcome of our subjective modes of selection and desires. An assemblage is meaningless unless we interact with it, this is to say, whereby we constitute and draw out connections through it by way of our focus on specific associations and arrangements over others. An assemblage of textual and artifactual evidence pertaining to an ancient site such as Jerusalem appears to us, to draw near to a tautology, only because we decide to look for it.

Yet within the assemblages that we effect, it is the emergent associations that guide our interpretive activities. In a manner distinct from the Archimedean perspective, led by the model of the jigsaw puzzle spread out before us whose pieces must fit together or be set aside (Deleuze and Guattari 1994: 23), the components within an assemblage rarely attain elegant couplings between them. Instead, the dominant image that opens *A Thousand Plateaus* is that of the rhizome (Deleuze and Guattari 1987: 1–25), its mass of shoots spawning nodules and accretions rather than direct lines of correspondence. But for historians of antiquity whose evidence is always fragmented and partial, clear convergences between textual and artifactual data points are rather limited. What an assemblage provides, then, is a different frame of reference for how we might conceive of the interpretive relationships among the evidence we possess from antiquity, one that foregoes the pursuit of straightforward correlations. Instead, what appears within an assemblage is a density (or absence) of associations between the claims of texts and the artifacts known to us, formations forged through processes of triangulation where a certain mass of affiliations coagulate among the assemblage before us, and, in other regions, empty expanses obtain.

The benefit of this approach for the histories we write of ancient Israel is that it solicits associations between texts and artifacts without privileging either, attuned to the flows and oscillations of various types of evidence from antiquity rather than attending, in theory or practice, to one form. In resisting the foundationalist desires of the Archimedean perspective, a further advantage of this interpretive framework is that it is sensitive to the character of historical representation itself, a representation that cannot be securely anchored for the simple reason that our object of study no longer exists. Historians are more conjurers than cartographers, evoking something absent through our writings rather than sketching a figure that is present before our eyes (Ricoeur 1988: 153). Our attention is therefore drawn to those "apparitions" summoned, as M. de Certeau (1973: 11) remarks in his study of historiography, "on the basis of definitively silent imprints" (cf. Ricoeur 2004: 366) that appear within the assemblage of evidence we possess.

The question this approach raises is its application. In the following, the intent is to draw on this interpretive framework to inquire into an enigmatic historical period frequently overlooked regarding Jerusalem's ancient history.[6] This study centers on Jerusalem's status during the centuries between two rulers named within texts from antiquity: that of Abdi-Heba (ca. 14th century BCE), an Egyptian vassal and local ruler of Jerusalem referred to within the Amarna Letters (EA 285–290), and David (ca. 10th century BCE), subjugator of Jerusalem according to the Books of Samuel and Chronicles (2 Sam 5:6–9; 1 Chr 11:4–9).

Assemblages and Silent Imprints: Jerusalem, ca. 1300–1000 BCE

Jerusalem is one of the most intensely studied locations on earth, the *axis mundi* on which history itself turned according to medieval thinkers, and yet "we know very little" of the location, Na'aman writes (2014: 489), during the centuries that preceded the time in which the biblical scribes claimed that David established it as his ruling center (ca. 1000 BCE). In part, our understanding of the site's history during these closing moments of the Late Bronze Age (ca. 1300–1200/1130 BCE) and the span of the Iron I period (ca. 1200/1130–980 BCE) is hampered by the fact that the Hebrew Bible rarely refers to Jerusalem before the story of David's acquisition of it (2 Sam 5:6–9). In texts prior to this story, Jerusalem appears only once in a cryptic allusion to the king of "Salem" in Gen 14:18 and in a dozen passages within the Books of Joshua and Judges focused predominantly on boundaries and identity, offering little on the character of the city itself apart from the name of a ruler (Adonizedek) and its populace (Jebusites). But what also complicates our historical investigations into these centuries is the paucity of archaeological evidence from the settlement. In contrast to the Middle Bronze Age (ca. 1950–1550 BCE) and especially the late Iron Age (ca. 830–586 BCE), the material culture recovered from the intervening centuries of Jerusalem's existence is quite meager (Keel 2007: 101–32; Uziel, Baruch, and Szanton 2019).

Such circumstances provide a constructive case study for how an interpretive framework modeled on an assemblage might unfold. For what is lacking during these centuries of Jerusalem's existence is an appreciable quantity of archaeological remains or textual references by which to reconstruct the history of the settlement on their basis alone, or, further, that would offer the possibility of locating numerous convergences between them. Instead, an approach to the history of the location during this period must proceed more indirectly, being solicitous of those associations that appear among the assemblage of written and material traces that have endured.

The first point to be made is that our current evidence consolidates around Jerusalem being inhabited in the span from 1300 BCE to 1000 BCE. This may appear as a rather trivial detail. But during an era in which several locations in the southern Levant were abandoned and/or destroyed (e.g., Hazor, Megiddo, Beth-Shean, Lachish), it is significant that we possess evidence that Jerusalem was less affected by the broader forces of disruption that swept through the region at this time. Rather than turmoil, a sense of continuity is expressed within Jerusalem's material culture across these centuries, its remains indicating the presence of a community that lived at the site throughout both the Late Bronze Age and Iron I eras (Cahill 2003: 27–54; De Groot and Bernick-Greenberg 2012: 149–54; Keel 2007: 122–29; Shiloh 1984: 26–27; Steiner 2001: 24–41). The biblical writings, though vague, nevertheless also convey the impression that Jerusalem was occupied in the centuries before David acquired it (i.e., Josh 10; 2 Sam 5).[7]

What such evidence provides is the occasion to inquire more deeply into the history of those communities who lived in Jerusalem during these centuries. Indications of continuous occupation at the site during this era offer the opportunity, furthermore, of triangulating what we know about Jerusalem at the time of Abdi-Heba with that of the settlement during David's reign, thereby allowing us to draw out some insights into the character of the site between these eras. Given the absence of an occupational gap in Jerusalem's settlement history or other evidence that would suggest substantial cultural or demographic upheaval, the Jerusalem of the 14th century BCE likely held much in common with that of the 10th century BCE site that followed it, with the intervening centuries being marked by continuity instead of disruption.

In the time of Abdi-Heba, what we know is that Jerusalem was a modest stronghold outpost controlled by Egypt. Some archaeological remains descend from this era (Cahill 2003: 27–33; De Groot and Bernick-Greenberg 2012: 149–50), including a collection of LBA pottery recovered from different areas of the site, the walls of a few isolated structures and their associated floors, and items from tombs found in the area of the Dominus Flevit Church and Nahlat Ahim quarter (Barkay 1996: 34; Cahill 2003: 26; Maeir 2017: 70; Steiner 2001: 29, 36). At a minimum, then, the archaeological record attests to Jerusalem being settled at the time by a population whose material traces, however faint, have persisted.

But other insights into the location are provided among the written references to it in the Amarna Letters (EA). Within this corpus, we come across six letters sent out from Jerusalem to a nameless pharaoh (EA 285–290), including brief descriptions of the status of Jerusalem under Abdi-Heba's rule (Na'aman 2011). The existence of these documents demonstrates the administrative nature of Jerusalem in the 14th century BCE, written, as they are, by a local scribe who was stationed at the site.[8] Though we do not know the scribe's name, we can ascertain certain historical details surrounding this individual by virtue of the script and language the scribe used, both of which were notable for their "northern" features in comparison to other letters from this corpus written from additional locations (e.g., Gath, Gezer, Shechem) in the southern Levant (Moran 1975). For such reasons, Moran concludes that the scribe who composed the Jerusalem letters was not native to the city, but was brought there, perhaps by Abdi-Heba himself, after being trained in regions to the far north somewhere in Syria (Moran 1975: 156; cf. Na'aman 2011: 36).

Though the Amarna Letters span a period of perhaps three decades that end around 1334/32 BCE with the inception of Tutankhamun's reign, the scribe that wrote these letters on behalf of Abdi-Heba was not the last that worked from Jerusalem. Recent archaeological evidence from the location has shown that other scribes were also present within its precincts. In 2010 and 2013, fragments of two different cuneiform tablets were recovered from the Ophel area of Jerusalem (Mazar et al. 2010; Mazar et al. 2014), the first dated to the general period of Abdi-Heba and the second to a somewhat later, Ramesside period (13th–12th centuries BCE). In addition, an alphabetic inscription was recovered from the same excavation site in 2012, stemming from either the Iron I or early Iron IIA period (Mazar, Ben-Shlomo, and Ahituv 2013). So it is, then, that we find an accumulation of scribal activity at Jerusalem produced by a "contingent of scribes," as Rollston (2010: 20) describes them, from the period of Abdi-Heba and after, epigraphic evidence that then finds associations with those references to David's scribe listed among the king's officials (2 Sam 8:16–18; 2 Sam 20:23–26) who would have resided in Jerusalem in the 10th century BCE (Pioske 2013).

The administrative character of Jerusalem suggested by these vestiges of scribalism is further reinforced by other concentrations of textual and artifactual evidence. The Amarna Letters are again of consequence, providing descriptions of an Egyptian garrison of 50 soldiers (EA 289: 42–44) stationed at the settlement during the time of Abdi-Heba (EA 285–87). On the surface, what this means is that Late Bronze Age Jerusalem had the infrastructure to house and supply this contingent alongside its residents. But tensions between the garrison and Abdi-Heba, culminating in the eventual transfer of these soldiers to Gaza, also reveal details pertaining to a large public building in Jerusalem that Abdi-Heba sought to seize from this security force (EA 285: 23–25). Though architectural remains from LBA Jerusalem are scanty, this structure would have stood within the old Middle Bronze Age fortification system that had enclosed the settlement (Maeir 2017). The extent of these MBA fortifications and the duration of their use is still much debated (De Groot and Bernick-Greenberg 2012: 148–54; Uziel, Baruch, and Szanton 2019: 179–80), but what can be said is that elements of the Middle Bronze Age city wall, 3m thick in certain segments and composed of massive cyclopean stones, would have been a striking feature of Jerusalem's landscape during the time of Abdi-Heba and in the centuries after. To these structures can be added a cultic site of some type that would have also been present in Jerusalem at this time, likely connected to the city's namesake, the sun deity Shalem (Keel 2007: 110–28), though traces of this Canaanite sanctuary have long been lost (Barkay 1996).

Economically, archaeological finds from Jerusalem indicate that the location was involved in international trade in the final stages of the Late Bronze Age, evidenced by Cypriot and Mycenaean pottery (Uziel, Baruch, and Szanton 2019: 172), as well as remains of Nile perch and saltwater fish from abroad (Van Neer et al. 2004). Within the Amarna Letters, we also come across two references to caravans of tribute sent out from Jerusalem to Egypt (EA 287–288), offering insights into what Jerusalem was able to deliver to the Egyptian king. Comprised of slaves, prisoners, and silver, the quantity of items sent from Jerusalem is "the most valuable," Na'aman (2011: 39) comments, of any tribute recorded from central and southern Canaan during this timeframe. How Jerusalem was able to amass these resources is still difficult to ascertain, but the location's assets likely flowed from the "lands" that Jerusalem controlled within its highland environs (EA 287: 63), including agricultural tracts, small villages, and pastoral populations that would have supplied it with commodities (Benz 2016: 81–110). Thus, alongside Abdi-Heba's scribe and, likely, Abdi-Heba himself, whose familiarity with the pharaoh expressed in his letters suggests that he likely spent his youth in Egypt (Na'aman 2011: 36), the Jerusalem of the Late Bronze era emerges as a site that encompassed a diverse, international collection of individuals and goods.

Abdi-Heba was not the last Egyptian vassal who governed from Jerusalem. Of the others who ruled on behalf of this empire in the 13th and 12th centuries BCE, however, no trace remains. As with Abdi-Heba, these local leaders from Jerusalem would have likely jostled with other rulers of nearby city-states to the west for territory and influence, such as those stationed at Gezer and Gath (EA 287: 4–31), in addition to being forced to contend with the unruly non-sedentary populations around Jerusalem that Abdi-Heba vividly describes (EA 286: 55–56). But around 1130 BCE Egyptian control of Canaan comes to an end. Jerusalem was no doubt affected by these broader developments, both economically and in terms of its governance, throughout the decades of the early and mid-12th century BCE. Yet unlike the important centers at Lachish to its southwest or Shechem to its north, Jerusalem somehow escapes destruction at this time. Instead, with the advent of the Iron Age I in the last decades of this century, our written and material evidence suggests continuity and even renewal at the site.

The most significant archaeological find from the 11th century BC settlement is also the most controversial. Situated along the eastern slope of what is now the City of David and adjacent to the Kidron Valley, a monumental support structure was built into this area of the site to stabilize it for further building projects positioned above (Cahill 2003: 33–54; Shiloh 1984: 16–17; Steiner 2001: 28–50). Disagreements about the dating of this "Stepped Stone Structure" and its various components have persisted over the previous decades due in large measure to its complex composition and the nature of the material finds recovered from its fill. Nevertheless, there is an emerging sense that elements of this support system were initially built in the Iron I period in a time that likely preceded David (Cahill 2003: 34–42; Faust 2010; Keel 2017: 57–58; Mazar 2010; Pioske 2015: 225–27; Sergi 2017; Steiner 2001: 28–41). What has further advanced this interpretation is the recent unearthing of a large building above the Stepped Stone Structure that was bonded to it, some features of which also likely date to the 11th century BCE (Faust 2010: 118–23; Mazar 2009: 56–63;

Mazar 2010: 40–46; Uziel, Baruch, and Szanton 2019: 172). In the era after the Egyptian withdrawal from the region, it appears that certain precincts of Jerusalem came to be refurbished, with a series of monumental building projects undertaken within the settlement during a century in which few public works of any scale were attempted or attained in the central highlands.

No inscriptions or other texts from the period relate to us the identity of those who accomplished these building projects in Jerusalem. Other archaeological remains from the Iron I era are, like the Late Bronze Age, sparse and comprised mostly of scattered pottery and the fragments of a few buildings that can be connected to the local Canaanite population that resided at the location. But what coalesces around these material finds are biblical references to Jerusalem that claim it was inhabited at this time by a community identified as "Jebusite" (Na'aman 2014). Appearing in no other ancient Near Eastern text outside of the Hebrew Bible, some have argued that the name of this group was a concocted appellation rendered by scribes much later to artificially differentiate Israelite groups from Canaanite ones in a more distant past (Hübner 2002). But given the traces of occupation we possess for the Jerusalem of this era, the strong biblical memories of a Jebusite population in Jerusalem across several biblical books are, at the very least, suggestive. This is particularly so considering the repeated assertions that those of a Jebusite background continued to live in Jerusalem long after David acquired it (Judg 1:21; 1 Kgs 9:20; Zech 9:7), a claim that would be rather mystifying if it were simply contrived. The lack of details surrounding the fate of the Jebusites in the aftermath of David's takeover of Jerusalem (2 Sam 5:6–9), furthermore, intimate the sense that this local population may have continued to reside in Jerusalem during the Davidic period and after (Na'aman 2014: 489) without being eliminated or relocated.

It is this late Iron I/early Iron II Jebusite settlement of the late 11th/early 10th century BCE that the biblical writers claim David obtained. The details of how David subdued Jerusalem are mostly absent from the story told of the settlement's conquest in the Book of Samuel or its later retelling in Chronicles, both reports stating only that David resided, after its takeover, in the "fortress" of Zion (2 Sam 5:9//1 Chr 11:4). What David would have secured is better known through the evidence reviewed above. From the perspective of this assemblage, it appears that the Jerusalem of the late 11th/early 10th century BCE was a stronghold site that had been a local ruling center in the highland region for many centuries prior. The remains of what were already ancient fortifications that enclosed the site and the ruins of previous structures from former occupants would have been scattered throughout the highland settlement of this time. In addition to these older vestiges of previous inhabitants, the presence of the Stepped Stone Structure, components of which were constructed by the local Canaanite population and built alongside, or above, more venerable structures used by Middle and Late Bronze Age residents of the site, positioned Jerusalem as one of the most strategic highland centers of its era in the southern Levant. Jerusalem had long attracted ambitious and opportunistic local leaders such as the biblical figure of David, in this light, by virtue of its defensive infrastructure and ideological potential (Pioske 2015: 216–59).

When we step back from this particular assemblage, what appears are certain concentrations of evidence, written and material, that pertain to key features of the site during the period between 1300 BCE and 1000 BCE. Among these are the outlines of a location whose natural and built environment was exploited by local leaders for centuries before a David would have ruled, making this figure simply one in a lengthy succession of individuals who drew on Jerusalem's stronghold position to govern the difficult terrain and restive populations that surrounded it. When walking the paths of this highland site our attention would have been drawn to the old, dilapidated MBA fortifications that circumscribed the location and to the terraces and fields situated among the valleys that surrounded it. We would be made aware of remnants of Egyptian structures and monuments scattered throughout the location (Barkay 1996), and within the confines of the settlement, we would encounter a large public building or buildings that would have been situated above the area of the Gihon Spring, structures that were reinforced, sometime in the 11th century BCE, by an impressive support system. It is perhaps this complex that the biblical writers refer to as the "Fortress of Zion" (2 Sam 5:7), a pre-Davidic edifice, according to these writings, that resided alongside other Canaanite buildings and homes at a site that for centuries had been named "the foundation of (the deity) Shalem," twin sibling of the Dawn until a new dispensation would take hold at Jerusalem in the Iron Age IIA.

Conclusion

There are other ways to tell the story of Jerusalem's history from 1300 to 1000 BCE, including bypassing this period altogether in favor of attending to other eras with more robust archaeological and written remains. However, what this case study on Jerusalem has sought to provide is a brief illustration of how an interpretive framework informed by the workings of an assemblage would unfold. Foregoing the desire to accord certain forms of evidence more historical weight in the pursuit of firmer epistemological foundations that, in the end, are illusory, this framework instead contends with the indeterminacies and ambiguities that emerge when reconstructing an ancient past. To do so, this interpretive approach seeks out those associations, some faint, others more vivid, that emerge between the writings and artifacts that pertain to certain ancient locations and times. In the case of Jerusalem, the hope is that new evidence will emerge in the future that will occasion new formations and a greater density of data within the assemblage of evidence that we possess. Until then, this approach beckons us to gather and examine whatever traces may be connected to this location in the present, to endeavor to represent what is absent, making "a place for the dead" in the histories we recount (de Certeau 1988: 100). "How, indeed," Ricoeur (2004: 264) writes, "could one ignore the simple fact that in history one is concerned with practically nothing but the dead of other times?"

Notes

1 For more recent studies that stem from different methodological perspectives, see Ahlström 1991: 116–41; Bloch-Smith 2016: 13–27; Bunimovitz and Faust 2010: 43–54; Dever 2000: 91–116; Finkelstein 2010: 1–8; Frendo 2011; Frevel 1989: 35–89; Halpern 1997: 311–41; Miller 1987: 51–62; Na'aman 2010: 165–83; Niemann 2001: 79–121; Pioske 2019: 1–25; Rainey 2001: 40–49; Richelle 2018. For studies on the relationship between texts and artifacts from those outside the discipline of ancient Israelite history, see especially Martin 2008; Moreland 2001; Vermeule 1996; Wolf 2009.
2 For important exceptions, see, for example, Moore 2006; Schloen 2001; Wilson 2018: 1–69.
3 So Ricoeur (2004: 280) summarizes his theory of historical representation: "We can say this: the historian's representation is indeed a present image of an absent thing." For important remarks on absence and death for the historian's work, see de Certeau 1988: 99–102.
4 For a broader perspective on more general issues pertaining to how the non-written remains unearthed by archaeologists relate to the claims made within ancient texts, see the opening chapter of Andrén 1998: 1–8 and Laurence 2004: 99–113.
5 For Deleuze and Guattari (1987: 87), such territories can be described as consisting of both word and things: "An assemblage of enunciation," they write, for example, "does not speak 'of' things; it speaks *on the same level as* states of things and states of content."

6 In Bieberstein's (2017) recent history of Jerusalem and Keel's (2017) condensed history of an original two-volume work, these centuries of Jerusalem's existence, for example, are both effectively passed over in silence.
7 An immediate objection to the historical character of these biblical references is that they were written down long after the events to which they allude. There is near consensus that Joshua 10, for example, was written in the 7th century BCE at the earliest, if not the later exilic or post-exilic periods—some 500 years after the account it reports (Dozeman 2015: 5–31). 2 Sam 5 is likely an earlier account than that of Joshua 10, but still not contemporaneous with the early 10th century BCE events it portrays (Dietrich 2019: 456–502). But within an interpretive framework modeled on an assemblage, the dating of when certain texts were composed is less significant than the associations that appear between what these written references claim and what has survived in the archaeological record. This is to say that even late texts can, at moments, retain information from previous periods in time, while texts written closer to the period that they depict can be erroneous or intentionally deceive (Pioske 2015: 26–30). What matters more for a historical assemblage, in the end, are the constellations of textual references and artifacts that appear among the traces we possess.
8 On the local provenance of these letters, see Goren, Finkelstein, and Na'aman 2004.

Bibliography

Ahlström, Gösta. 1991. "The Role of Archaeological and Literary Remains in Reconstructing Israel's History." Pages 116–41 in *The Fabric of History: Text, Artifact and Israel's Past*. Edited by D. Vikander. Sheffield: Sheffield Academic Press.
Albright, William Foxwell. 1922. "Preliminary Reports on Tell el-Full," *BASOR* 6: 7–8.
———. 1969. "The Impact of Archaeology on Biblical Research—1966." Pages 1–14 in *New Directions in Biblical Archaeology*. Edited by D. Freedman and J. Greenfield. Garden City: Doubleday.
Andrén, Anders. 1998. *Between Artifacts and Texts: Historical Archaeology in Global Perspective*. New York: Plenum Press.
Barkay, Gabriel. 1996. "A Late Bronze Age Temple in Jerusalem?" *IEJ* 46: 23–43.
Benz, Brendon. 2016. *The Land Before the Kingdom of Israel: A History of the Southern Levant and the People Who Populated it*. Winona Lake: Eisenbrauns.
Bieberstein, Klaus. 2017. *A Brief History of Jerusalem: From Its Earliest Settlement to Its Destruction in 70 AD*. Wiesbaden: Harrassowitz.
Bloch-Smith, Elizabeth. 2016. "Archaeology: What It Can Teach Us." Pages 13–27 in *The Wiley-Blackwell Companion to Ancient Israel*. Edited by S. Niditch. Malden: John Wiley & Sons.
Breed, Brennan. 2014. *Nomadic Text: A Theory of Biblical Reception History*. Bloomington: Indiana University Press.
Buchanan, Ian. 2015. "Assemblage Theory and Its Discontents." *Deleuze Studies* 9: 382–92.
Bunimovitz, Shlomo, and Avraham Faust. 2010. "Re-Constructing Biblical Archaeology: Toward an Integration of Archaeology and the Bible." Pages 43–54 in *Historical Biblical Archaeology and the Future: The New Pragmatism*. Edited by T. E. Levy. London: Routledge.
Cahill, Jane. 2003. "Jerusalem at the Time of the United Monarchy. The Archaeological Evidence." Pages 13–80 in *Jerusalem in Bible and Archaeology. The First Temple Period*. Edited by A. Vaughn and A. Killebrew. Atlanta: SBL.
Carr, David. 2011. *The Formation of the Hebrew Bible: A New Reconstruction*. New York: Oxford University Press.
de Certeau, Michel. 1973. *L'Absent de l'histoire*. Paris: Mame.
———. 1988. *The Writing of History*. New York: Columbia University Press.
De Groot, Alon, and Hannah Bernick-Greenberg. 2012. *Excavations at the City of David 1978–1985, Directed by Yigal Shiloh. Vol. VIIB: Area E: The Finds*. Jerusalem: Hebrew University Press.
Deleuze, Gilles, and Félix Guattari. 1987. *A Thousand Plateaus: Capitalism and Schizophrenia.*. Minneapolis: University of Minnesota Press.
———. 1994. *What Is Philosophy?* London. Verso.
Dever, William G. 2000. "Biblical and Syro-Palestinian Archaeology: A State-of-the-Art Assessment at the Turn of the Millennium." *Currents in Research: Biblical Studies* 8: 91–116
———. 2017. *Beyond the Texts: An Archaeological Portrait of Ancient Israel and Judah*. Atlanta: SBL.
Dietrich, Walter. 2019. *Samuel*. Teilband 3. 1 Sam 27–2 Sam 8. Göttingen: Vandenhoek & Ruprecht.

Dozeman, Thomas. 2015. *Joshua 1–12*. New Haven, CT: Yale University Press.
Faust, Avraham. 2010. "The Large Stone Structure in the City of David: A Reexamination." *ZDPV* 126: 116–31.
Finkelstein, Israel. 2010. "Archaeology as a High Court in Ancient Israelite History: A Reply to Nadav Na'aman." *JHS* 10: 1–8.
Finkelstein, Israel, Shlomo Bunimovitz, and Zvi Lederman. 1993. *Shiloh: The Archaeology of a Biblical Site*. Tel Aviv: Tel Aviv University Press.
Frendo, Anthony. 2011. *Pre-Exilic Israel, the Hebrew Bible, and Archaeology: Integrating Text and Artefact*. New York: T&T Clark.
Frevel, Christian. 1989. "'Dies ist der Ort, von dem geschrieben steht …' Zum Verhältnis von Bibelwissenschaft und Palästinaarchäologie." *BN* 47: 35–89.
Gadamer, Hans-Georg. 2006. *Truth and Method*. Translated by J. Weinsheimer and D. Marshall. 2nd ed. New York: Continuum.
Goren, Yuval, Israel Finkelstein, and Nadav Na'aman. 2004. *Inscribed in Clay: Provenance Studies of the Amarna Letters and Other Ancient Near Eastern Texts*. Tel Aviv: Institute of Archaeology, Tel Aviv Univeristy.
Halpern, Baruch. 1997. "Text and Artifact: Two Monologues?" Pages 311–41 in *The Archaeology of Ancient Israel: Constructing the Past, Interpreting the Present*. Edited by N. Silberman and D. Small. Sheffield: Sheffield Academic Press.
Hübner, Ulrich. 2002. "Jerusalem und die Jebusiter." Pages 31–42 in *Kein Land für sich allein. Studien zum Kulturkontakt in Kanaan, Israel/Palästina und Ebirnâri für Manfred Weippert zum 65. Geburtstag*. Edited by U. Hübner and E. Knauf. Göttingen: Vandenhoek & Ruprecht.
Keel, Othmar. 2007, *Die Geschichte Jerusalems und die Entstehung des Monotheismus*. Volume I. Göttingen: Vandenhoek & Ruprecht.
———. 2017. *Jerusalem and the One God: A Religious History*. Edited by B. Strawn. Minneapolis: Fortress Press.
Kratz, Reinhard. 2005. *The Composition of the Narrative Books of the Old Testament*. Translated by J. Bowden. London: T&T Clark.
Laurence, Ray. 2004. "The Uneasy Dialogue Between Ancient History and Archaeology." Pages 99–113 in *Archaeology and Ancient History: Breaking Down the Boundaries*. Edited by E. Sauer. London: Routledge.
Maeir, Aren M. 2017. "Assessing Jerusalem in the Middle Bronze Age: A 2017 Perspective." Pages 64–74 in *New Studies in the Archaeology of Jerusalem and its Region 11*. Edited by Y. Gadot, Y. Zelinger, K. Cytryn-Silverman, and J. Uziel. Jerusalem: Israel Antiquities Authority.
Martin, Richard. 2008. "Words Alone Are Certain Good(s): Philology and Greek Material Culture." *TAPA (1974–2014)* 138: 313–49.
Mazar, Amihai. 2006. "Jerusalem in the 10th Century B.C.E: The Glass Half-Full." Pages 255–72 in *Essays on Ancient Israel in Its Near Eastern Context: A Tribute to Nadav Na'aman*. Edited by Y. Amit et al. Winona Lake, IN: Eisenbrauns.
———. 2010. "Archaeology and the Biblical Narrative: The Case of the United Monarchy." Pages 29–58 in *One God–One Cult–One Nation: Archaeological and Biblical Perspectives*. Edited by R. Kratz and H. Spieckermann. Berlin: de Gruyter.
Mazar, Eilat. 2009. *The Palace of King David: Excavations at the Summit of the City of David. Preliminary Report of Seasons 2005–2007*. Jerusalem: Shoham.
Mazar, Eilat, David Ben-Shlomo, and Shmuel Ahituv. 2013. "An Inscribed Pithos from the Ophel, Jerusalem." *IEJ* 63: 39–49.
Mazar, Eilat, Wayne Horowitz, Takayoshi Oshima, and Yuval Goren. 2010. "A Cuneiform Tablet from the Ophel in Jerusalem." *IEJ* 60: 4–21.
———. 2014. "Jerusalem 2: A Fragment of a Cuneiform Tablet from the Ophel Excavations." *IEJ* 64: 129–39.Miller, Max. 1987. "Old Testament History and Archaeology." *BA* 49: 51–62.
Moore, Megan Bishop. 2006. *Philosophy and Practice in Writing a History of Ancient Israel*. New York: T&T Clark.
Moran, William. 1975. "The Syrian Scribe of the Jerusalem Amarna Letters." Pages 146–66 in *Unity and Diversity. Essays in the History, Literature and Religion of the Ancient Near East*. Edited by H. Goedicke and J. J. M. Roberts. Baltimore: Johns Hopkins University Press.
Moreland, John. 2001. *Archaeology and Texts*. London: Duckworth.Na'aman, Nadav. 2010. "Does Archaeology Really Deserve the Status of 'High Court' in Biblical Historical Research?" Pages 165–83 in *Between Evidence and Ideology*. Edited by B. Becking and L. Grabbe. Leiden: Brill.

———. 2011. "Jerusalem in the Amarna Period." Pages 31–48 in *Jérusalem Anitque et Médiévale: Mélanges en l'honneur d'Ernest-Marie Laperrousaz*. Edited by C. Arnould-Béhar and A. Lemaire. Paris: Peeters.

———. 2014. "Jebusites and Jabeshites in the Saul and David Story-Cycles." *Biblica* 95: 481–97.

Nail, Thomas. 2017. "What Is an Assemblage?" *Substance* 46: 21–37.

Niemann, Hermann Michael. 2001. "Von oberflächen, schichten und strukturen. Was leistet die Archäologie für die erforschung der geschichte israels und judas?" Pages 79–121 in *Steine—Bilder—Texte. Historische Evidenz außerbiblischer und biblischer Quellen*. Edited by C. Hardmeier. Leipzig: Evangelische Verlagsastalt.

Nietzsche, Friedrich. 1994 [1887]. *On the Genealogy of Morality*. Edited by K. Ansell-Pearson. Translated by C. Diethe. Cambridge: Cambridge University Press.

Pioske, Daniel. 2013. "The Scribe of David: A Portrait of a Life." *Maarav* 20: 163–88.

———. 2015. *David's Jerusalem: Between Memory and History*. New York: Routledge.

———. 2019. "The 'High Court' of Ancient Israel's Past: Archaeology, Texts, and the Question of Priority." *Journal of Hebrew Scripture* 19: 1–25.

Rainey, Anson. 2001. "Stones for Bread: Archaeology Versus History." *NEA* 64: 40–49.

Richelle, Mathieu. 2018. *The Bible and Archaeology*. Peabody, MA: Hendrickson.

Ricoeur, Paul. 1988. *Time and Narrative*. Vol. III. Translated by K. Blamey and D. Pellauer. Chicago: University of Chicago Press.

———. 2004. *Memory, History, Forgetting*. Translated by K. Blamey and D. Pellauer. Chicago: University of Chicago Press.

Rollston, Christopher. 2010. "A Fragmentary Cuneiform Tablet from the Ophel (Jerusalem): Methodological Musings about the Proposed Genre and Sitz im Leben." *Antiguo Oriente* 8: 11–21.

Rorty, Richard. 1979. *Philosophy and the Mirror of Nature*. Princeton: Princeton University Press.

———. 1991. *Objectivity, Relativism, Truth*. Cambridge: Cambridge University Press.

Sasson, Jack. 1981. "On Choosing Models for Recreating Israelite Pre-Monarchic History." *JSOT* 21: 3–24.

Schloen, J. David. 2001. *House of the Father as Fact and Symbol: Patrimonialism in Ugarit and the Ancient Near East*. Winona Lake: Eisenbrauns.

Sergi, Omer. 2017. "The Emergence of Judah as a Political Entity between Jerusalem and Benjamin." *ZDPV* 133: 1–23.

Shiloh, Yigal. 1984. *Excavations at the City of David, I. 1978–1982. Interim Report of the First Five Seasons*. Jerusalem: Hebrew University Press.

Steiner, Margreet. 2001. *Excavations by Kathleen M. Kenyon in Jerusalem 1961–1967, III. The Settlement in the Bronze and Iron Ages*. London: Oxford University Press.

Uziel, Joe, Yuval Baruch, and Nahshon Szanton. 2019. "Jerusalem in the Late Bronze Age—The Glass Half Full." Pages 171–84 in *The Late Bronze and Early Iron Ages of Southern Canaan*. Edited by A. M. Maeir et al. Berlin: De Gruyter.

Van Neer Wim, Omri Lernau, Renée Friedman, Gregory Mumford, Jeroen Poblóme, and Marc Waelkens. 2004. "Fish Remains from Archaeological Sites as Indicators of Former Trade Connections in the Eastern Mediterranean." *Paléorient* 30: 101–48.

Vermeule, Emily. 1996. "Archaeology and Philology: The Dirt and the Word." *TAPA* 126: 1–10.

Von Rad, Gerhard. 1964 [1944]. "The Beginnings of Historical Writing in Ancient Israel." Pages 166–204 in *The Problem of the Hexateuch and Other Essays*. Translated by E. W. Dicken. London: SCM Press.

Weitzman, Steven. 2016. "Text and Context in Biblical Studies: A Brief History of a Troubled Relationship." Pages 67–83 in *The Wiley Blackwell Companion to Ancient Israel*. Edited by S. Niditch. London: John Wiley & Sons.

Wilson, Ian D. 2018. "History and the Hebrew Bible: Culture, Narrative, and Memory." *BRPBI* 3: 1–69.

Wolf, Alex. 2009. "A Dialogue of the Deaf and the Dumb: Archaeology, History and Philology." Pages 10–23 in *Approaching Interdisciplinarity: Archaeology, History and the Study of Early Medieval Britain, c.400–1100*. Edited by Z. L. Devlin and C. Holas-Clark. Oxford: Archaeopress.

5
BETWEEN THE BIBLICAL STORY AND HISTORY

Writing an Archaeological History of Ancient Israel

Avraham Faust

Introduction

Until about 25 years ago, the history of ancient Israel was largely based on a critical reading of the biblical narrative. Although parts of the narrative were agreed to be non-historical, and some were disputed, the major components of the story—from the tribal social organization of the period of the Judges onward—were seen as mostly historical. The minimalists challenge of the 1990s and the subsequent debates had a major impact on the discipline, and altered the discourse, leading to the separation of the literary, biblical Israel, from the historical Israel. At the heart of this development is the relationship between the biblical text and the archaeological record, and in particular, the degree of historicity contained in the former and the way in which the latter mirrors specific sociocultural realities.

The present chapter will not only provide a synthesis of this debate, but it will provide evidence for the historicity or non-historicity of specific biblical "histories." The first part of the paper will outline the development of scholarship, and how the distinction between "biblical Israel" and "historical Israel" came into being. This will be followed by an examination of the historical epochs that are currently debated, including a review of the implications of these developments on the growing role of archaeology in reconstructing Israel's history. The main part of the article will briefly review the history of ancient Israel as it stands today—what is regarded as historical, what is viewed as ahistorical, and what is debated—and will offer outlines of this history. The final part of the chapter will offer new directions for biblical archaeology and new ways to integrate texts and artifacts in reconstructing the history of ancient Israel in its broadest sense.

Between Biblical Israel and Historical Israel: History of 20th-Century Research

The Bible as (Mostly) History

Until the late 20th century, biblical Israel and historical Israel were viewed as (largely) one and the same. The reconstructed history of Israel was based, although critically (by each period's standards), on the biblical narrative.

DOI: 10.4324/9780367815691-6

This history began, if we ignore the elements that were always regarded as mythical, with the stories about the Patriarchs, which were a sort of prequel or family history covering three or four generations. The main body of history began in the sojourn in Egypt, continued in the Exodus, the conquest, the life in the land before the monarchy, and the processes leading to its foundation, culminating in the story of the monarchy, its expansion, division, and describing the separate existence of Israel and Judah until their destruction by Assyria and Babylonia (respectively), and the exile of much of their population. The end of this history was in the period of return, or restoration, and the (re)erection of the temple in Jerusalem under Persian hegemony.

History Questioned: The Conquest

This basic outline was viewed as historical, despite various corrections and adjustments. The first large-scale challenge to a main component in this historical outline came with Albrecht Alt's questioning of Joshua's conquest.[1] Alt's doubts were based on (1) inner contradictions within the biblical texts regarding the question of whether some sites or even regions were conquered (as explicitly described in Josh 1–12; 21:41) or not (as mentioned, for example, in Josh 13:1–6; 23:4 and Judg 1:27–36, and as implied by many descriptions in the book of Judges), and (2) the understanding, based on Egyptian texts, that the regions the Israelites actually conquered were sparsely settled by Canaanites in the first place, whereas the regions they appeared not to have conquered were those where Canaanites lived. Since the conquest description is regarded as late (today it is considered part of the Deuteronomistic history, commonly considered to be written toward the end of the Iron Age), Alt concluded that it is not historical, and in reality, the Israelite settlement was a gradual and mostly peaceful process, in which semi-nomadic groups settled in the sparsely settled parts of Canaan. Only in the late 7th century BCE, hundreds of years after the events described, was a coherent narrative description of a unified conquest written, based on a combination of stories that passed through the generations (some historical and some not). Alt's reconstruction, which came to be known as "the peaceful infiltration" model, met with fierce opposition. The most vociferous was William F. Albright, who supported the historicity of the core narrative of the book of Joshua, in what came to be known as the "unified military conquest" model.

Albright introduced archaeology into the debate, encouraging excavations in key sites to show that the Israelites indeed destroyed the major Canaanite sites at the end of the Late Bronze Age. Both scholars had many followers, and for a few decades, these two schools divided the scholarly community—Martin Noth and Yohanan Aharoni can be counted as leading voices in the first school, and John Bright, G. Ernest Wright, and Yigael Yadin in the second. Given the nature of the debate, archaeology came to be very prominent, and many excavations and extensive surveys were carried out in an attempt to prove one of the models.

Since the 1960s additional explanations were offered, including the "social revolution," the "evolution," and the "cyclic settlement" models. By the early 1990s, there were at least five schools competing for hegemony. The accumulating evidence led many scholars to abandon the unified conquest model. Not only did the general argument raised by Alt, based on textual evidence, resonate with the majority, but the accumulating archaeological evidence seemed to discredit the Albrightian school; many sites were not destroyed at the end of the Late Bronze Age, and a few did not even exist. Those that were destroyed, moreover, were not devastated at the same time—at least a century separates the destruction of Hazor and Lachish, hardly within what can be considered a single campaign. Thus, while not all the details are agreed upon even today (it is important to emphasize that the origin of the settlers is still debated), there is a broad agreement that the settlement process was mostly peaceful.

Questioning the Patriarchal (Ancestral) Age

Questioning the conquest, however, was only the beginning. In the 1970s, the historicity of the Patriarchs also came under heavy criticism. Until then, the broad outlines of the story were generally accepted as historical, although scholars debated what was the exact background to the stories; based on possible historical parallels to details, names, places, etc., views ranged from the Intermediate Bronze Age (then called Middle Bronze I), through the Middle and (early) Late Bronze Ages, and even to the Iron Age I. The works of van Setters (1975) and Thompson (1974), however, questioned these parallels, and especially their attribution to these specific periods. These publications were influential, and while not accepted by all, many scholars today (perhaps most) do not view the Patriarchal age as historic. Some, however, point to various details that could not have been written after the fact, and therefore still place the stories in the Bronze Age (e.g., Kitchen 2003), and many others take a cautious approach.

It should be noted that in contrast to most other parts of Israel's history, the limited scope of the Patriarchal activities—telling the story of individuals and small families—means that the role of archaeology in the debate is relatively limited, supplying information regarding the possible (or impossible) cultural background to the stories, and informing biblical scholars on the reliability of the Bible at large and hence influencing scholars' overall judgment on the plausibility of the stories being historical in the first place.

Doubting the Israelites and Questioning the "United Monarchy": Biblical Minimalism and Its Aftermath

Thus, toward the end of the 20th century, most of Israel's "pre-" and "proto-history", i.e., events taking place before the Israelites were finally settled in Canaan, was doubted. The reality in the settlement period (i.e., the period of the Judges), and mainly from the establishment of the monarchy onward, however, was still seen as historical.

This too changed in the 1990s, with the sudden emergence of the so-called minimalist school. The term refers to a small group of scholars who, simplistically put, claimed that the Bible was a literary creation, written hundreds of years after the events it (supposedly) described, and cannot be used as a source of information about the Iron Age. Members of this school suggested that earlier "histories" of Israel were simply a retelling of the Bible and are a modern construct—a "monster"—which they attempt to deconstruct (see, e.g., Davies 1992; Lemche 1998). A distinction emerged between "biblical Israel," i.e., the literary creation, and "historical Israel" as confirmed (mostly) by archaeology. While not convincing many, the minimalists completely altered the discourse, most noticeably on two issues which had been taken for granted previously, but which became topics of dispute: (1) identifying the Iron Age I highland population as Israelite; and, (2) the existence of the "united monarchy" (i.e., the kingdoms of Saul, David, and Solomon, which "united" the various highland groups).[2]

Although some of their criticisms of past research were well-founded, most of the minimalists' claims about past realities were not based on archaeological data, nor on any new insights into the texts, but on stripping the latter of any historical value. The minimalists' contribution was to a large extent based on assumptions and assertions that did not rely on data and did not stem from such. Hence, notwithstanding the minimalists' great impact on the discourse, it did not win over many converts, and the school remained very small. The challenges they set were met by many works. The use of the term "Israelites" in the Iron I was justified not only on the basis of the relevant archaeological data but also by reference to Israelites as a group of people in an Egyptian text from the late 13th century BCE (e.g., Bloch-Smith 2003; Dever 2003; Faust 2006; Hawkins 2013; and many others).[3] Their assertions regarding the lack of evidence for the "united monarchy" were also widely discredited (e.g., Dever 2001; Halpern 2001 Na'aman 1996).

There is, however, another twist to this tale.

Iron Age Low Chronology and the Narrowing Consensus

In the mid-1990s, within the new intellectual climate, Finkelstein (1996, 1998) suggested lowering the Iron Age chronology. The bottom line of the complex argument was that strata traditionally dated to the 10th century, and attributed to David and\or Solomon, should be dated to the 9th century, and attributed to the Omrides. The "real" 10th-century remains were those that were traditionally dated to the 11th century, and these were usually rather poor, especially in the territories of the new monarchy. As Finkelstein (1996: 185) noted, "accepting the Low Chronology means stripping the United Monarchy of monumental buildings." Unlike the minimalists' assertions, however, the low chronology was based on data and argumentations that could be, and also were, debated (for early responses, see, e.g., Ben-Tor and Ben-Ami 1998; Bunimovitz and Faust 2001; Mazar 1997).

The re-dating of what was viewed by most as the archaeological correlates for the "united monarchy" fitted nicely with the new skeptical approaches that became prevalent in biblical studies. This led to scrutinizing the archaeological evidence, resulting in additional doubts. Scholars[4] noted, for example, (1) the lack of any remains (even sherds) from the 10th century BCE in Jerusalem, the supposed capital of David's (and Solomon's) empire, (2) the lack of evidence for international trade at the time, including significant Phoenician trade, and\or (3) any contact with Arabia (Sheba), (4) the lack of any 10th-century finds from Edom, supposedly conquered by David (2 Sam 8:13–14; 1 Kgs 11:15–16), and more. The evidence, it was understood, pointed to the existence of all these in the late Iron Age, when (1) Jerusalem was a mega-city for the first time in its history, (2) international trade reached an unprecedented peak as the Phoenicians reached the Atlantic ocean, (3) trade with south Arabia was identified archaeologically, as was (4) a kingdom founded in Edom. Some scholars therefore came to the conclusion that the biblical description of the "united monarchy" must be a late Iron Age creation, which projected the era's realities into the distant past, to the time of the legendary founder of the Davidic dynasty, in order to justify contemporaneous political and religious claims (e.g., the highly influential, even if controversial, works of Finkelstein and Silberman 2001, 2006).

Despite its huge impact, most archaeologists and many biblical scholars rejected this skeptical approach, either because they rejected the low chronology and its tenants (e.g., Garfinkel et al. 2019; Mazar 2011),[5] or because they did find many correlates between substantial parts of the biblical story and the 10th-century reality, and even various descriptions and details that could not have been written later (see for example Faust 2015; Mazar 2010). The historicity of the "united monarchy" is still at the center of a heated debate, to which we shall later return.

While the historicity of the "united monarchy" is debated, even those who questioned its existence (with the exception of "hard-core" biblical minimalists) agree that from the 9th century BCE onward the Bible is sitting pretty well with other lines of evidence. As Herzog (1999) concluded his popular article that sparked a public debate in Israel:

> The historical existence of the kingdoms of Israel and Judah can be… identified since the 9th century. Relative to other peoples who are part of the western culture this is quite an early time, and this is perhaps a partial comfort for these who need it.[6]

The Study of Biblical Israel at the Beginning of the Third Millennium and the (Growing) Role of Archaeology

One consequence of the debate over the historicity of the Bible—and from the ensuing changes in the nature of the evidence and argumentations—is that archaeology became the main source of information in the deliberations. From a handmaiden of biblical studies, archaeology is now in the driver's seat. Two different reasons, or processes, led to this change:

1. The increased doubts over the historicity of large parts of the biblical texts mean that they cannot be brought as evidence in the debate against their historicity unless they are supported by extra-biblical evidence. Given the extreme rarity of textual sources before the 9th and mostly 8th centuries, this means recourse to archaeology.
2. The archaeology of the Land of Israel supplies scholars with an unparalleled wealth of archaeological data, which is far more detailed than that of any other part of the world, with hundreds of planned excavations, thousands of salvage excavations, and extensive surveys (cf. Faust and Safrai 2005, 2015, 2022).

Subsequently, the debate relies more and more on archaeological evidence. The end result is that the traditional "history" of the biblical period is to a large extent "dead."[7] Naturally, this opens the way to new and promising directions, like social and cultural history, for which archaeology is most suited (more than to political history, which has stood at the heart of the discourse in biblical archaeology, in sharp contrast to most other brands of archaeology where sociocultural questions are the bread and butter of the discipline). Although such directions were developing in the 1980s in both biblical studies and biblical archaeology, these were to a large extent abandoned following the re-emergent debate about the historicity of the Bible in the 1990s, and the ensuing minimalist debate.

I will return to these promising new avenues below, but as the debates (re)focused on the historicity of the biblical narrative, it is time to see where we stand today on these issues.

The History of Israel: What Is Left?

So, what about the biblical history of Israel?

The Patriarchs and Matriarchs

Many today discredit the biblical ancestors of Israel as real figures and their background as grounded within the culture of the Bronze Age, while others strongly advocate for the historicity of this background or are undecided (for various views, see Dever 2001; Kitchen 2003; Thompson 1974; van Setters 1975). The ephemeral nature of the stories, referring to a small family, enables scholars to leave the question open, and the period is often simply left out of histories of ancient Israel. Notably, as already hinted above, the current debate about the ancestral period focuses on the (possible) background to the stories, as archaeology cannot directly locate individuals.

The Exodus and the Conquest

While there is a broad agreement that Joshua's conquest is ahistorical, it is interesting to note that most scholars agree that there was an "Exodus group" (even if small) that left Egypt and joined the Israelites in the highlands, becoming part of Israel and contributing the Exodus narrative to its collective memory (e.g., Bietak 2003; Halpern 1992). This view, however, is not shared by all, and some scholars deny any historicity to the narratives (e.g., Finkelstein and Silberman 2001: 61–63; for the different views, see also various papers in Levy, Schneider, and Propp 2015). Among those who see some historical kernel, moreover, there is disagreement about when the core event take place, the majority placing it in the 13th century (e.g., Bietak 2003), at the time of Ramses II, while a smaller group strongly advocate for the 12th century (e.g., Halpern 1992), at the time of Ramses III. A few advocate for an even earlier date, but this is based on an attempt to fit the evidence into a tenuous biblical chronology (e.g., Bimson 1981).

The Emergence of Israel

As to the beginning of Israel, most scholars—but again not all—think that Israel as a distinct group indeed began in the Iron I, in the Cisjordanian highlands (e.g., Bloch-Smith 2003; Faust 2006, 2016; Hawkins 2013). In this context, it is worth mentioning the hundreds of small villages (the "settlement sites") that were established at this time and received much scholarly attention during the 20th century. It seems difficult not to see a connection between these sites and biblical references to the "simple," rural reality in the "period of the judges."

We have seen that there is an agreement that the conquest did not take place in the manner described in the book of Joshua (chapters 1–12) and that the process of settlement was mostly peaceful. Most also agree that the settled groups eventually coalesced into what the Bible views as "Israel," but there is a debate about when this identity became widespread. It is clear, however, that this was a long process, continuing well into the Iron II. While it is clear that there was a group by the name "Israel" already in the late 13th century, as an Egyptian Pharaoh of this era (Merenptah) boasts a victory over them, some suggested that not all the settlers were necessarily members of this group and prefer to speak about "proto-Israelites" in an Iron I context.

The sources of the settling population, moreover, are also debated, and the only agreement is that they were varied. According to many, the first group included semi-nomads (*Shasu* groups) accompanied by a few para-social elements (like the *'Apiru*), but this is not accepted by all. Still, it is clear that from an early stage, other groups joined in, including sedentary Canaanites, as well as the above-described (small) "exodus group." According to this scenario, the Egyptian pressure over Canaan that intensified toward the end of the Late Bronze Age (late 13th and 12th centuries) was responsible for the initial settlement of groups that were pushed aside by the imperial grip over the lowlands, leading the settlers to define themselves in contrast to the Egyptian imperial system and its Canaanite collaborators. Despite various changes, this identity remained a major one for the highland settlers, and the Philistine pressure of the 11th century led the people to (re)stress it (Faust 2006, 2016, and references there).

The "United Monarchy"

The "United Monarchy," as noted, is at the center of a heated debate. While all agree that the current form of the biblical narratives contains later additions and exaggerations, many biblical scholars (especially Europeans) and a small group of archaeologists, go further and vehemently negate the existence of such a kingdom, while many others identify a historical core to the stories. Supporters of the historicity of the kingdoms of David and Solomon bring various archaeological, and to an extent historical, evidence to support their position.

First, we should note that the main reasons raised in the mid- to late 1990s for denying any historical background to the "United Monarchy" have not stood the test of time. Referring to the examples mentioned earlier, it is clear today that (1) 10th-century sherds were found in every excavation area in the City of David, including on the lower eastern slopes, and it appears that the hill was fully settled at the time. Moreover, it appears that there were also a few public structures that functioned at this time, including the Large Stone Structure (although not in its original function) and those on the Ophel (e.g., Faust 2017). As for (2) international trade, it is clear today that the Phoenician westward expansion started in the 10th century, and that the Atlantic was reached in the 9th century at the latest (e.g., Gonzales de Canales, Serrano, and Llompart 2006; López Castro et al. 2016). And (3) there were even contacts with the Indian ocean at the time (Gilboa and Namdar 2015), hence some knowledge of Arabia is likely. As for (4) Edom, recent discoveries revealed beyond any doubt that during the 10th century, activity in the copper mines of Feinan (and Timna) reached an unparalleled peak (e.g., Ben-Yosef, Langgut, and Sapir-Hen 2017; Levy, Ben-Yosef, and Najjar 2018; Levy, Najjar, and Ben-Yosef 2014; Sapir-Hen and Ben-Yosef 2014). Additionally, recent archaeological discoveries have added even more flesh to the archaeological skeletons of the 10th century, supporting social or political complexity at the time (e.g., Ben-Yosef, Langgut, and Sapir-Hen 2017; Faust and Sapir 2018; Garfinkel, Ganor, and Hasel 2018; Levy, Najjar, and Ben-Yosef 2014; and Tebes, this volume).

Second, a broad examination of the vast data at our disposal indicates that complex processes were taking place in the 10th century BCE, and it appears that the transition from the Iron I to the Iron II was accompanied by deep crisis, including significant changes in settlement patterns, abandonment of large parts of the rural sector (first in the highlands, and later in other parts of the country), destruction of many urban centers in the lowlands, as well as drastic changes in many aspects of material culture, like the disappearance of regional ceramic traditions (like the collared rim jars in the highlands, and the Aegean-inspired Philistine pottery in the southern coastal plain), the enlargement of the ceramic repertoire in the highlands, massive adoption of slip and burnish, and more. Among the changes, one should stress the cessation in the use of temples in a number of lowland sites, destroyed in the early 10th century and then rebuilt without temples (e.g., Megiddo, Tel Qasile, and probably also Beth Shean, and more), and the formalization of the four-room (longitudinal four-spaces) house plan, and the widespread usage of a formalized plan of the structures in the 10th century (Faust 2021, and references).

Third, already in the late 1990s, there were scholars who rejected the skeptical approach to the highland polity of David and Solomon because of various biblical traditions, which could not have been written in the late Iron Age (e.g., Halpern 2001: 57–72, 224–26). These included the central role of Gath in these stories, or the importance of Shiloh (see even Finkelstein 2007: 18). To these elements, one today can add many others, like the memory that the Philistines were once circumcised (Faust 2015), Solomon's sale of land to Hiram (Keimer 2020), the identification of Toi (as Taita) in north Syria (Galil 2014; Steitler 2010), and more.

The Divided Monarchy and Later

When one moves beyond the time of David and Solomon, there seems to be a growing consensus that the Bible can serve as a historical source, even if partial and biased, and from the 9th century onward, practically all archaeologists agree that the biblical narratives contain a growing body of historical data. And even if this is accompanied by heated debates about many details, like the reality under Neo-Babylonian rule (Barstad 1996; Faust 2012a; Lipschits 2005), the larger outlines of the biblical narrative seem to reflect history.

Thus, we hear throughout the book of Kings and the prophetic books about Israel's wars with the Arameans, the importance of Tyre in maritime trade, the existence of Philistine city-states and the kingdoms of Ammon, Moab and Edom, the Assyrian conquest of the northern kingdom and its hegemonic control of the south, the collapse of this empire and the rise of Babylonia, which subsequently destroyed Judah, and later a return of people and the erection of the Second Temple, and more. Interestingly, not only is the arrival of the Assyrians in the 730s reflected in the Bible, but the fact that the Assyrians are not mentioned in any historical narrative pertaining to an earlier epoch seems to give historical credence to the stories of these earlier epochs; had these stories been written (or even heavily edited) much after the fact, one would expect to see references to this empire creeping into the "earlier" contexts. Thus, the broad history outlined by the biblical texts is apparently correct, as are, in many cases, even the details supplied.

Archaeology and the Bible: Toward a New Synthesis?

While the biblical narrative is clearly problematic as a historical source, using other sources, when available, especially the vast archaeological data at our disposal, can help us in reconstructing the "big" historical questions that stand at the base of the current debates. Often, archaeology paints a bigger picture into which the textual information is embedded, and which in practice then "decides" the historicity of the narrative. This, of course, is a reversal of the traditional role, as the texts now complement a reconstruction informed by archaeology. This role reversal, however, opens the way to a much broader discussion, addressing far larger sets of questions, expanding not only our understanding of Iron Age history, society, and practice, but also enabling new insights into the texts themselves from a different and fresh perspective, bringing new meaning to biblical archaeology as a discipline.

Many studies on the intersection between the Bible and archaeology are devoted to Israel's "big" history, for example: did the conquest or the Exodus take place, and is there any proof of the historicity of various biblical narratives? Biblical archaeology, the discipline that evolved from the marriage of biblical studies and archaeology, developed in the shadow of the texts as a direct attempt to tackle the traditional questions using new (at the time) methods. Consequently, it focused on issues of political history or topics directly related to biblical texts, answering questions that stemmed from these texts (see Bunimovitz and Faust 2010).

As interesting and important as these questions are—and most of this paper is devoted to them, acknowledging their significance—they seem to ignore the main potential of archaeology.

Since biblical archaeology evolved as a handmaiden of biblical studies, it developed in a completely different way than most other branches of archaeology, which are more anthropological in orientation. It did not systematically address social and anthropological issues. Despite the large database available, these topics were relegated to the margins of this sub-field.

This is an unfortunate situation since archaeology is much better equipped to deal with these questions than with identifying short-term events that correspond with biblical descriptions. Even worse is that the archaeology of ancient Israel has the largest archaeological dataset in the world (e.g., Faust and Safrai 2005, 2015, 2022, and references), but it is not used in a way that makes it useful for archaeologists working in other sub-disciplines.

Toward a New Biblical Archaeology

Elsewhere, Bunimovitz and I (2010) suggested that current attitudes are not only problematic from an archaeological perspective, ignoring the full potential of the discipline, but ironically also limit our ability to properly use the biblical sources. Subsequently, we have suggested a new way to revitalize biblical archaeology, which will greatly expand the realm of the field, moving it in new directions and embracing new questions, while at the same time shedding new light and bringing new insights into the old questions.

We suggest a reconstruction of biblical archaeology founded on a different integration between archaeology and the Bible. On the one hand, we called for an archaeological agenda that places cultural and social issues at the center of the discussion—and which is not dictated by the biblical text—hence expanding our research questions. On the other hand, integrating the Bible as a cultural document in the quest to answer these questions will restore the biblical text to its central place within the discourse and will also shed new light on these very texts while raising new questions concerning them.

As noted, the archaeology of the Land of Israel in general, and that of the biblical period in particular, has produced a rich and detailed database, originating from thousands of (planned and salvage) excavations and extensive surveys, that has not been fully used yet, especially regarding social and cultural questions. Progress in world archaeology in the last decades has enriched the discipline with a plethora of theoretical and practical approaches and immensely enlarged the range of issues dealt with by archaeologists as well as the ways to tackle them, like social organization, political structures, spatial analysis, gender, social stratification, ideology, the senses, etc. (see, e.g., Hamilakis 2013; Hodder 2012; Hodder and Hutson 2003; Renfrew and Bahn 2016). A thorough restudy of the rich Iron Age archaeological database at our disposal will undoubtedly reveal various behavioral patterns that demand explanation. It should be emphasized that no such patterns could have been discerned in the past, since the research perceptions and questions were different, focusing on the political history and on questions arising from the texts (even if to disprove them, see Finkelstein and Silberman 2001, whose entire agenda is biblical, even if the conclusions are quite negative).

Bunimovitz and I suggested initiating research by identifying patterns in the vast archaeological record and explaining these patterns via comprehensive reference to the cultural context in which they were embedded, using all sources of information, including textual. Despite the problems involved in using the Bible as a historical source, there is no doubt that it is a cultural document which incorporates contemporary, Iron Age "layers" and can provide valuable information about Iron Age society. The incidental information contained in the Bible, just like the language of the people, provides insights into the social and spiritual world in which the authors created their material culture, and is less influenced by the biases described earlier in this paper. As Murray (1998, xxxi) wrote (in a different context):

> It does not matter whether the stories… are true… And even a forgery is an important piece of evidence for the period that perpetrated it… This principle of unconscious revelation through representation… is one of the most powerful tools in the modern historian's study of mentalities.

And in King and Stager's (2001: 7) words:

> (F)or our purposes, then, it matters little whether the biblical accounts are "true" in the positivistic sense of some historians and biblical scholars... The stories must have passed some test of verisimilitude, that is, having the appearance of being true or real. In this sense, the biblical accounts, and many other ancient accounts, however self-serving and tendentious, become grist for the cultural historian's mill.

Both the biblical text and a period's material culture are cultural products of the very same society. Both words and artifacts open a door into the cognitive world of the people who created them; they represent worldviews, cosmology, spatial perception, ideology, symbolism, etc. The present approach,

> places texts and maps in the same role as anthropological descriptions or natural scientific laws.... Unlike these sources, as products of the society under study, they enable us to give *interpretation from within* that society. That is, they may enable us to give the same interpretation to archaeological material as people from within that society would have given.
>
> (Dark 1995: 57; italics in the original)

A few studies demonstrate the new approach presented here, along with its potential (see also Faust 2012b, 2019).

Archaeology, Texts, Language, and Israelite Cosmology

The phenomenon of directing Iron Age buildings and settlements in ancient Israel to the east, and avoiding the west, went unnoticed by previous scholarship (Faust 2001). Because this tendency is not mentioned in the text, it was not looked for in the past and was revealed only by a scrutiny of the archaeological data.

The tendency to direct doorways of structures to the east and avoid the west influenced not only dwellings but also city gates, and it appears to have had an impact on Iron Age urban planning (e.g., Faust 2001, 2002, and this has been corroborated by dozens of houses published since). An examination of various climatic and functional considerations does not explain the phenomenon. Many ethnographic studies, however, have demonstrated the strong influence that cosmological principles can have on the planning of buildings and settlements (e.g., Oliver 1987; Steadman 2015; Waterson 1997). And in many cases, the east is preferred (Frazer 1968: 47; Parker Pearson and Richards 1994: 15). In the case of the ancient Israelites, however, we have additional information. The common Biblical Hebrew word for east is *qedem/qedma* (forward), while the west is *ahora* (backward; Drinkard 1992a, 1992b). Moreover, additional words for those directions indicate that the east had a good connotation while the west had a bad one. The common word for "west" in Biblical Hebrew is *yam*, literary "Sea," which is the most conspicuous element in this direction. But the word *yam*, besides designating a large body of water and westerly orientation, had some other meanings as well, and in many cases, it represents the forces of chaos, sometimes personified in the *Leviathan* or other legendary creatures (Lewis 1993: 335; see also Keel 1978: 23, 35, 49, 50, 55, 73–75; Stoltz 1995: 1397–98).

The matching of the archaeological pattern, human tendency to prefer the east, and the evidence that the Israelites not only oriented themselves to the east but had even attributed positive and negative meaning to the various directions, seem to be sufficient to conclude that the Israelites viewed the east as a hospitable place (and the west as an inhospitable one), and this is the reason for the eastward orientation of structures and settlements. Still, the available evidence allows us to go one step further. Ezekiel 40–48 describes the temple in Jerusalem. The description is not historical, and, at best, contains some historical elements, but this is irrelevant for the present discussion. According to this description, the Temple courts had three gates each, the main one in the east, and two others in the south and north. It is striking that no entrance is described in the west. More important is the description of the eastern gates. This is the main gate through which Ezekiel enters the temple (40: 4, ff.). Later, however, the eastern gate is described as closed, since this is the gate through which God is entering the Temple (44: 2; see also 43: 1–4; and chapter 46). The matching of the description with the archaeological data—where east is preferred, and west is avoided—is therefore complete.

Thus, an archaeological pattern, along with language and texts (which are used as a substitute for human informants about cognition), seems to give an important insight into some of the cosmological principles of the ancient Israelites. This is because both the texts and the archaeological finds are cultural products reflecting the perception and beliefs of the society that produced them. Notably, the entire discussion, including the biblical one, stemmed from an archaeological agenda, which in turn shed new light on the texts themselves.

The Longitudinal Four-Space (Four-Room) House and the Israelite Mind

Another example is the longitudinal four-spaces (LFS) (better known as the four-room) house. This house is the dominant type of domestic building in ancient Israel from the beginning of the Iron Age until the Babylonian Exile, and numerous studies have been devoted to its origins and the ethnic identity of its inhabitants (e.g., Holladay 1997; Netzer 1992; Shiloh 1970, 1973). The high popularity of the LFS house was explained as either expressing its close relation with the Israelites and/or its functional suitability to the needs of the Iron Age peasants, regardless of their ethnicity. Neither of these explanations, however, seem to account for the synchronic and diachronic dominance of the LFS house as a preferable architectural type in all levels of Iron Age settlement (from cities to hamlets and farmsteads), in different geographical and ecological niches, for almost 600 years(!). Moreover, the plan served as a template not only for domestic, but also for public buildings, and even for the late Iron Age Judahite tombs (e.g., Barkay 1999). The fact that the house disappeared in the 6th century seems also to refute any "functional" explanation, as no changes in peasant life and no architectural or agricultural inventions were made then. We have therefore suggested that an adequate explanation for the unique phenomenon must relate to the ideological/cognitive realm (Faust and Bunimovitz 2003, 2014).

Developing in the Iron Age I to fill the functional needs of the hill zone settlers, the building was adopted in the process of ethnic negotiation and boundary construction which accompanied the Israelite ethnogenesis and crystallized in the 10th century BCE as part of the renegotiation of this identity (Faust 2021). Some of its architectural characteristics (few of them revealed by access analysis) reflect Israelite values and practices: e.g., egalitarian ethos, purity practices, privacy, and cosmology. These are reflected in the spatial syntax of the house, as well as in the biblical text (Faust and Katz 2017). Moreover, because the Israelites were preoccupied with order (Douglas 1966), once this kind of house became typical, it eventually became the appropriate and "right" one. It is thus the dialectic between function, process, and mind that created the 'Israelite House' which, once crystallized, lived for hundreds of years before disappearing following the destruction of the kingdoms of Israel and Judah, when its creators and maintainers lost coherence and were dispersed.

Whether all the explanations raised by us for the specific plan of the LFS house and its popularity will prove to be correct is irrelevant now. We should stress that the entire discussion and all lines of reasoning stemmed from an archaeological agenda. Even the discussion of purity laws and their relevance to the Israelite household had developed to explain an archaeological pattern (Faust and Katz 2017), but this has clear implications even on the dating of the biblical texts (cf. Faust 2019).

A Fresh Restart? Anthropological Biblical Archaeology and its Potential Contribution to Biblical Studies and Biblical History

The approach proposed here has significant implications not only for broadening research possibilities and in bringing biblical archaeology closer to other branches of archaeology, but also to the discipline of biblical studies, as it will expand our understanding of the texts and add new questions and new dimensions to the study of the Bible itself (as in the study of orientations and their meanings, and for dating various biblical passages). Furthermore, this approach will shed new light even on the broad, historical questions on which (or for which) the sub-discipline of biblical archaeology was founded.

One example exemplifies the potential of the new, or anthropological biblical archaeology: the debate over the "united monarchy." Studies on this entity had always focused on looking for clear markers for a large kingdom, like a large capital or impressive buildings (Finkelstein 1996, 1998; Finkelstein and Silberman 2001, 2006; Mazar 1997; Yadin 1958; and many others). More subtle mechanisms were rarely considered. Within the scope of this article, I would just like to draw attention to the *potential* of anthropological approaches by referring to the Aztec empire. Michael E. Smith and Frances Berdan (1992: 353) opened their article on "Archaeology and the Aztec Empire," with the following statement:

> The relative invisibility of the Aztec empire in archaeological terms has long been noted by scholars.

Not only did this "invisibility" not lead them to suggest that the Aztec empire did not exist, but Smith and Berdan (1992: 357, 363) raised a number of potential indications for identifying the empire, for example, a decline in the standards of living in villages in territories that were supposed to have been annexed (since they will now pay more taxes). Whether this is applicable to the "United Monarchy" is irrelevant—what is important is that identifying an empire can involve studying villages and analyzing standards of living. These are questions that are usually ignored in biblical archaeology, as they are supposedly not interesting enough in a field that is looking for "big" issues like king David. But addressing these "uninteresting" issues can solve the "interesting" questions better than looking for king Solomon's graffiti.

Summary

Using the Bible as the main, sometimes only source of information, early histories of Israel were a (critical) paraphrase of the biblical story. As the reliability of the texts eroded, these histories began to be questioned. Serious doubts on the historicity of a main component of biblical history were initially raised regarding the Israelite conquest, and later also about the ancestors (the Patriarchs), the Exodus, and more recently also about the Israelite identity of the highland settlers and the existence of the "United Monarchy." The skeptical approaches peaked in the 1990s, with the emergence of the minimalist school which attempted to deny the Bible any relevance for the study of the Iron Age, but this extreme approach was rejected by mainstream scholarship. A major outcome of these debates, however, was placing archaeology in the driver's seat and putting biblical studies in a subsidiary position in historical reconstructions.

The historicity of Israel's ancestors is still debated. Given the nature of the narratives there is little that can be directly examined archaeologically, and although most scholars agree that the present form of the story is very late, whether there is any historical background to the stories is still questioned. While there seems to be some indication that an "Exodus group," even if small, arrived in Canaan, there is a wide consensus that the conquest is not historical. Once we move to the reality of life in Canaan, it seems to me that the Bible contains at least some genuine memories. Thus, that the hub of Israelite (or proto-Israelite) settlement was in the highlands is clearly corroborated by archaeology, and so are, in my view, the circumstances surrounding the group's ethnogenesis. And despite the heated debates, it appears that many of the circumstances that gave rise to the monarchy are also in line with the biblical tradition. Whether a "united monarchy" existed is still debated, but it seems to me that there is growing evidence that supports the existence of such a polity. Moving to the time of the two kingdoms, it appears that the biblical story has much to contribute to the study of ancient Israel. From the 9th century onward, there seems to be an agreement that the main historical narratives of the Bible—even if biased and partial—are largely based on actual events, which are corroborated by external sources.

It appears, however, that beyond supplying direct answers to the "big" historical questions of biblical history, we can now move forward and develop new approaches, which will raise new questions, not derived from the texts, but whose tackling will require the use of all the available information, including these very texts, which will themselves be read from a different perspective, and through new glasses. This "new biblical archaeology" (or "anthropological biblical archaeology") will not only bring a new meaning into the dated and out-of-fashion biblical archaeology and will greatly expand the issues we are dealing with, but will also enable us to bring new, broader, and better answers to the "big" historical question, which stood at the heart of the discipline since its inception.

Notes

1 For a summary of the debate until the 1980s, see Finkelstein 1988 and references.
2 The term is a scholarly construct, and for various reasons is used here in quotation mark (see also Faust 2021).
3 Many simply refer to the bulk of the highland settlers as Israelites, while others, following Dever, prefer to talk about proto-Israelites.
4 Naturally, many of the archaeological arguments were raised by archaeologist (but not all) and were then used also by biblical scholars. See for example various papers in Handy 1997, as well as Ussishkin 1998; Finkelstein and Silberman 2001, 2006; and more.
5 Note that Finkelstein himself took a large step "backward," and now dates not only the transition to the Iron IIA, but even to the late Iron IIA, to the 10th century (e.g., Finkelstein and Piasetzky 2011: 51; Kleiman et al. 2019: 534–35).
6 This is my translation from the closing words of the original, Hebrew version of the article. In the English translation of the paper this last statement is missing.
7 This can be seen, for example, in the rarity of large-scale "histories" of ancient Israel, which were popular until about 20 years ago. A rare, recent attempt at such a large-scale history was, ironically, carried out by an archaeologist (Dever 2017).

Bibliography

Barkay, G. 1999. "Burial Caves and Dwellings in Judah during Iron Age II: Sociological Aspects." Pages 96–102 in *Material Culture, Society and Ideology, New Directions in the Archaeology of the Land of Israel*. Edited by A. Faust and A. Maeir. Ramat Gan: Bar-Ilan University (Hebrew).

Barstad, H. M. 1996. *The Myth of the Empty Land*. Oslo: Scandinavian University Press.

Ben-Tor, A., and D. Ben-Ami. 1998. "Hazor and the Archaeology of the Tenth Century B.C.E." *IEJ* 48: 1–37.

Ben-Yosef, E., D. Langgut, and L. Sapir-Hen. 2017. "Beyond Smelting: New Insights on Iron Age (10th c. BCE) Metalworkers Community from Excavations at a Gatehouse and Associated Livestock Pens in Timna, Israel." *JAS Reports* 11: 411–26.

Bietak, M. 2003. "Israelites Found in Egypt: Four-Room House Identified in Medinat Habu." *BAR* 29: 41–49, 82–83.

Bimson, J. J. 1981. *Redating the Exodus and Conquest*. Sheffield: Almond Press.

Bloch-Smith, E. 2003. "Israelite Ethnicity in Iron I: Archaeology Preserves What Is Remembered and What Is Forgotten in Israel's History." *JBL* 122: 401–25.

Bunimovitz, S., and A. Faust. 2001. "Chronological Separation, Geographical Segregation or Ethnic Demarcation? Ethnography and the Iron Age Low Chronology." *BASOR* 322: 1–10.

———. 2010. "Re-Constructing Biblical Archaeology: Toward an Integration of Archaeology and the Bible." Pages 43–54 in *Historical Biblical Archaeology and the Future—The New Pragmatism*. Edited by T. E. Levy. London: Equinox.

Dark, K. 1995. *Theoretical Archaeology*. London: Duckworth.

Davies, P. R. 1992. *In Search of "Ancient Israel."* Sheffield: Sheffield Academic Press.

Dever, W. G. 2001. *What Did the Biblical Writers Know, and When Did They Know It?* Grand Rapids: Eerdmans.

———. 2003. *Who Were the Early Israelites, and Where Did They Come From?* Grand Rapids: Eerdmans.

———. 2017. *Beyond the Texts: An Archaeological Portrait of Ancient Israel and Judah*. Atlanta: SBL.

Douglas, M. 1966. *Purity and Danger: An Analysis of the Concept of Pollution and Taboo*. London: Routledge.

Drinkard, J. F. 1992a. "Direction and Orientation." Page 204 in *ABD* 1.

———. 1992b. "East." Page 248 in *ABD* 1.

Faust, A. 2001. "Doorway Orientation, Settlement Planning and Cosmology in Ancient Israel during Iron Age II." *OJA* 20: 129–55.

———. 2002. "Accessibility, Defense, and Town Planning in Iron Age Israel." *TA* 29: 297–317.

———. 2006. *Israel's Ethnogenesis: Settlement, Interaction, Expansion and Resistance*. London: Equinox.

———. 2012a. *Judah in the Neo-Babylonian Period: The Archaeology of Desolation*. Atlanta: SBL.

———. 2012b. *The Archaeology of Israelite Society in Iron Age II*. Translated by R. Ludlum. Winona Lake: Eisenbrauns.

———. 2015. "The Bible, Archaeology, and the Practice of Circumcision in Israelite and Philistine Societies." *JBL* 134: 273–90.

———. 2016. "The Emergence of Israel and Theories of Ethnogenesis." Pages 155–73 in *Blackwell Companion to Ancient Israel*. Edited by S. Niditch. Oxford: Blackwell.

———. 2017. "Jebus, the City of David, and Jerusalem: Jerusalem from the Iron I to the Neo-Babylonian Period." Pages 35–72 in *Jerusalem: From Its Beginning to the Ottoman Conquest*. Edited by A. Faust, J. Schwartz, and E. Baruch. Ramat Gan: Ingeborg Renner Center for Jerusalem Studies (Hebrew).

———. 2019. "The World of P: The Material Realm of Priestly Writings." *VT* 69: 173–218.

———. 2021. "The 'United Monarchy' on the Ground: The Disruptive Character of the Iron I-II Transition and the Nature of Political Transformations." *JJAR* 1: 15–67.

Faust, A., and S. Bunimovitz. 2003. "The Four Room House: Embodying Israelite Society." *NEA* 66: 22–31.

———. 2014. "The House and the World: The Israelite House as a Microcosm." Pages 143–64 in *Family and Household Religion: Toward a Synthesis of Old Testament Studies, Archaeology, Epigraphy, and Cultural Studies*. Edited by R. Albertz, B. A. Nakhai, S. M. Olyan, and R. Schmitt. Winona Lake: Eisenbrauns.

Faust, A., and H. Katz. 2017. "The Archaeology of Purity and Impurity: A Case-Study from Tel 'Eton, Israel." *CAJ* 27: 1–27.

Faust, A., and Z. Safrai. 2005. "Salvage Excavations as a Source for Reconstructing Settlement History in Ancient Israel." *PEQ* 137: 139–58.

———. 2015. *The Settlement History of Ancient Israel: A Quantitative Analysis.* Ramat Gan: Rennert Center for Jerusalem Studies, Bar-Ilan University (Hebrew).

———. 2022. "Toward a Quantitative History of Ancient Israel: Burials as a Test-Case." *JAA* 65, article 101374.

Faust, A., and Y. Sapir. 2018. "The 'Governor's Residency' at Tel 'Eton, The United Monarchy, and the Impact of the 'Old House Effect' on Large-Scale Archaeological Reconstructions." *Radiocarbon* 60: 801–20.

Finkelstein, I. 1988. *The Archaeology of the Period of Settlement and Judges.* Jerusalem: Israel Exploration Society.

———. 1996. "The Archaeology of the United Monarchy: An Alternative View." *Levant* 28: 177–87.

———. 1998. "Bible Archaeology or the Archaeology of the Palestine in the Iron Age? A Rejoinder." *Levant* 30: 167–74.

———. 2007. "Digging for the Truth: Archaeology and the Bible." Pages 9–20 in *The Quest for Historical Israel: Debating Archaeology and the History of Early Israel.* Edited by B. B. Schmidt. Atlanta: SBL.

Finkelstein, I., and E. Piasetzky. 2011. "The Iron Age Chronology Debate: Is the Gap Narrowing?" *NEA* 74: 50–53.

Finkelstein, I., and N. Silberman. 2001. *The Bible Unearthed: Archaeology's New Vision of Ancient Israel and Its Sacred Texts.* New York: Touchstone.

———. 2006. *David and Solomon: In Search of the Bible's Sacred Kings and the Roots of the Western Tradition.* New York: Free Press.

Frazer, D. 1968. *Village Planning in the Primitive World.* London: Studia Vista.

Galil, G. 2014. "A Concise History of Palistin/Patin /Unqi/'mq in the 11th–9th Centuries BC." *Semitica* 56: 75–104.

Garfinkel, Y., S. Ganor, and M. Hasel. 2018. *In the Footsteps of King David: Revelations from an Ancient Biblical City.* London: Thames and Hudson.

Garfinkel, Y., M. G. Hasel, M. G. Klingbeil, H. G. Kang, G. Choi, S. -Y. Chang, S. Hong, S. Ganor, I. Kreimerman, and C. Bronk Ramsey. 2019. "Lachish Fortifications and State Formation in the Biblical Kingdom of Judah in Light of Radiometric Datings." *Radiocarbon* 61: 1–18.

Gilboa, A., and D. Namdar. 2015. "On the Beginning of South Asian Spice Trade with the Mediterranean: A Review." *Radiocarbon* 57: 265–83.

Gonzales de Canales, F., L. Serrano, and J. Llompart. 2006. "The Pre-Colonial Phoenician Emporium of Huelva ca 900–770 BC." *BABesch* 81: 13–29.

Halpern, B. 1992. "The Exodus from Egypt: Myth or Reality?" Pages 86–113 in *The Rise of Ancient Israel.* Edited by H. Shanks et al. Washington DC: Biblical Archaeology Society.

———. 2001. *David's Secret Demons: Messiah, Murderer, Traitor, King.* Grand Rapids: Eerdmans.

Hamilakis, Y. 2013. *Archaeology and the Senses: Human Experience, Memory, and Affect.* New York: Cambridge University Press.

Handy, L. K., ed. 1997. *The Age of Solomon: Scholarship at the Turn of the Millennium.* Leiden: Brill.

Hawkins, R. 2013. *How Israel Became a People.* Nashville: Abingdon Press.

Herzog, Z. 1999. "The Bible—No Evidence on the Ground." *Haaretz*, October 29 (Hebrew).

Hodder, I. 2012. *Entangled: An Archaeology of the Relationships Between Humans and Things.* Chichester: Wiley-Blackwell.

Hodder, I., and S. Hutson. 2003. *Reading the Past.* 3rd ed. Cambridge: Cambridge University Press.

Holladay, J. S. 1997. "Four Room House." Pages 337–41 in vol. 2 of *OEANE*.

Keel, O. 1978. *Symbols of the Biblical World: Ancient Near-Eastern Iconography and the Book of Psalms.* New York: Seabury Press.

Keimer, K. H. 2020. "The Historical Geography of 1 Kings 9:11–14." *PEQ* 152: 186–206.

King, P. J., and L. E. Stager. 2001. *Life in Biblical Israel.* Louisville: Westminster John Knox Press.

Kitchen, K. A. 2003. *On the Reliability of the Old Testament.* Grand Rapids: Eerdmans.

Kleiman, A., A. Fantalkin, H. Mommsen, and I. Finkelstein. 2019. "The Date and Origin of the Black-on-Red Ware: The View from Megiddo." *AJA* 123: 531–55.

Lemche, N. P. 1998. *Prelude to Israel's Past: Background and Beginnings of Israelite History and Identity.* Peabody: Hendrickson.

Levy, Thomas E., E. Ben-Yosef, and M. Najjar. 2018. "Intensive Surveys, Large-Scale Excavation Strategies and Iron Age Industrial Metallurgy in Faynan, Jordan: Fairy Tales Don't Come

True." Pages 245–58 in *Mining for Ancient Copper: Essays in Memory of Beno Rothenberg.* Edited by E. Ben-Yosef. Winona Lake: Eisenbrauns.

Levy, Thomas E., M. Najjar, and E. Ben-Yosef. 2014. "Conclusions." Pages 977–1001 in *New Insights into the Iron Age Archaeology of Edom, Southern Jordan—Surveys, Excavations and Research from the Edom Lowlands Regional Archaeology Project.* Edited by T. E. Levy, M. Najjar, and E. Ben-Yosef. Los Angeles: UCLA.

Levy, Thomas E., Thomas Schneider, and William H. C. Propp, eds. 2015. *Israel's Exodus in a Transdisciplinary Perspective: Text, Archaeology, Culture, and Geoscience.* New York: Springer.

Lewis, T. J. "Israel, Religion of." 1993. Pages 332–36 in *The Oxford Companion to the Bible.* Edited by B. M. Metzger and M. D. Coogan. Oxford: Oxford University Press.

Lipschits, O. 2005. *The Fall and Rise of Jerusalem: Judah Under Babylonian Rule.* Winona Lake: Eisenbrauns.

López Castro, J. L., A. Ferjaou, A. Mederos Martín, V. Martínez Hahnmüller, and I. B. Jerbania. 2016. "La Colonización Fenicia Inicial en el Mediterráneo Central: Nuevas Excavaciones Arqueológicas en Utica (Túnez)." *Trabajos de Prehistoria* 73: 68–89.

Mazar, A. 1997. "Iron Age Chronology: A Reply to I. Finkelstein." *Levant* 29: 157–67.

———. 2010. "Archaeology and the Biblical Narrative: The Case of the United Monarchy. Pages 29–58 in *One God—One Cult—One Nation. Archaeological and Biblical Perspectives.* Edited by R. G. Kratz and H. Spieckermann. Berlin: de Gruyter.

———. 2011. "The Iron Age Chronology Debate: Is the Gap Narrowing? Another Viewpoint." *NEA* 74: 105–11.

Murray, O. "Introduction." 1998. Pages xi–xliv in *The Greeks and Greek Civilization.* Edited by J. Burckhardt. New York: St. Martin's Press.

Na'aman, N. 1996. "The Contribution of the Amarna Letters to the Debate on Jerusalem's Political Position in the Tenth Century BCE." *BASOR* 304: 17–27.

Netzer, E. 1992. "Domestic Architecture in the Iron Age." Pages 193–201 in *The Architecture of Ancient Israel from the Prehistoric to the Persian Period.* Edited by A. Kempinski and R. Reich. Jerusalem: Israel Exploration Society.

Oliver, P. 1987. *Dwellings, the House Across the World.* Oxford: Phaidon Press.

Parker Pearson, M., and C. Richards. 1994. "Ordering the World: Perceptions of Architecture, Space and Time." Pages 1–37 in *Architecture and Order, Approaches to Social Space.* Edited by M. Parker Pearson and C. Richards. London: Routledge.

Renfrew, C., and P. Bahn. 2016. *Archaeology: Theories, Methods and Practice.* London: Thames and Hudson.

Sapir-Hen, L., and E. Ben-Yosef. 2014. "The Socioeconomic Status of Iron Age Metalworkers: Animal Economy in the 'Slaves' Hill,' Timna, Israel." *Antiquity* 88: 775–90.

Shiloh, Y. 1970. "The Four Room House, Its Situation and Function in the Israelite City." *IEJ* 20: 180–90.

———. 1973. "The Four Room House—the Israelite Type-House?" *EI* 11: 277–85 (Hebrew).

Smith, M. E., and F. F. Berdan. 1992. "Archaeology and the Aztec Empire." *WA* 23: 353–67.

Steadman, S. R. 2015. *Archaeology of Domestic Architecture and the Human Use of Space.* Walnut Creek: Left Coast Press.

Steitler, C. 2010. "The Biblical Toi of Ḥamath and the Late Hittite State 'P/Walas(a)tin.'" *BN* 146: 81–99.

Stoltz, F. 1995. "Sea." Pages 1390–402 in *DDD.*

Thompson, T. L. 1974. *The Historicity of the Patriarchal Narratives: The Quest for Historical Abraham.* Berlin: de Gruyter.

Ussishkin, D. 1998. "Jerusalem in the Period of David and Solomon: The Archaeological Evidence." Pages 57–58 in *New Studies on Jerusalem, Vol. 4.* Edited by A. Faust and E. Baruch. Ramat Gan: Bar-Ilan University (Hebrew).

van Setters, J. 1975. *Abraham in History and Tradition.* New Haven: Yale University Press.

Waterson, R. 1997. *The Living House, An Anthropology of Architecture in South-East Asia.* Singapore: Thames and Hudson.

Yadin, Y. 1958. "Solomon's City Wall and Gate at Gezer." *IEJ* 8: 80–86.

6
TEXTS, ARCHAEOLOGY, AND ETHNICITY
Identifying Ancient Israel

William G. Dever

Introduction

Characterizing any people or nation in comparative and cross-cultural studies requires analyzing their "ethnicity," i.e., their self-understanding, particularly regarding their neighbors. Ethnicity is important beyond the challenge of defining it. It *matters*—in the lives of ordinary people, in the history of nations. One has only to look at American history, from the introduction of slavery 350 years ago, to the Civil War, to the present. The history of America, as well as the future of much of the world, lies in trying to resolve ethnic conflicts. In this case, we will focus on ancient Israel and Judah in the Iron Age, ca. 1200–600 BCE, looking at both textual and archaeological data.[1]

Defining Terms

The concept of ethnicity has come to be a major issue in many fields, from politics and public affairs to more theoretical and anthropological discussions. Because the discussion is so controversial and often polemical, we must attempt to clarify the issue by defining some basic terms.

"*Race.*" Ethnic conflicts are often described in terms of "racism." But anthropologists have long abandoned the concept of race. There are no such things as "white," "black," or "Jewish" human races. Since the emergence of modern humans some 70,000–100,000 years ago, we all belong biologically to a single race, *homo sapiens sapiens*. The diversity among various groups of people is due mostly to cultural differences, not to genetics.

"*Ethnicity.*" This is a notoriously difficult term. Definitions vary widely, but for our purposes here the following will suffice.[2] Ethnicity (Gk. *ethnos,* "people") is the way in which a particular society defines itself in terms of a common and distinctive cultural heritage. It may have, but does not require, a concept of real or imaginary common ancestry and usually a territorial homeland. Ethnicity is partly ideologically and socially constructed, and it is therefore dynamic, subject to negotiation, with shifting boundaries *vis-à-vis* other groups. "Ethnicity" may be an abstract concept, but the national and personal identity that it subsumes is real. Ethnicity is complex; but nevertheless, it has an ontology, is heritable, and can be empirically defined in terms of characteristic traits. Ethnicity is not, however, about race, population, civilization, or nationhood. Ultimately, ethnicity is a function of culture in the broadest sense.[3]

"*Culture.*" By culture, we mean a pattern of collective adaptation to the natural and social environment that provides a set of core values for a community; shapes individual and group identity; governs thought and behavior; and is transmittable. Culture is usually defined as the result of both biological and ideational factors. It is thus both objective (nature) and subjective (nurture). Culture is all about who people are, what they typically do, and what others think they are. Like its product, ethnicity, it is all about a sense of "peoplehood" in a particular time, place, and context. That sense of peoplehood, however, may not be homogeneous.[4]

A Brief History of Scholarship on Ethnicity

Neither biblical scholars nor archaeologists had traditionally paid much specific attention to the concept of ethnicity, despite some general theoretical literature. That was presumably because they were confident that they *knew* who the ancient Israelites were. By the early 1990s, however, postmodernism's radical skepticism precipitated the "literary turn" in biblical studies, i.e., a turn away from positivist historiography.[5] Thus scholars in both fields now began to pay attention to the fundamental concept of ethnicity, but mainly to question it.

For instance, biblicists like Lemche (1991: 151) asserted that "the Canaanites did not know themselves that they were Canaanites." Whitelam (1996: 228) declared that "it is no longer possible to distinguish an 'Israelite' material culture from an indigenous material culture in terms of the archaeological data." Thompson (1999: 234; cf. 1997: 175, the latter specifically questioning archaeology) went as far as to declare that "ethnicity is an interpretive fiction… ethnicity is hardly a common aspect of human existence at this very early period" (i.e., in ancient Israel).

The revisionist argument was already evident in Davies's 1992 manifesto, *In Search of "Ancient Israel."* Davies distinguished three Israels: (1) "biblical Israel," a fictitious construct of the biblical writers in the Persian period; (2) "ancient Israel," an artificial construct of later and modern Jewish and Christian scholars; and (3) a "historical Israel," which might be presumed to have existed in the Iron Age, but about which we can say little or nothing since sources are inadequate.

Among archaeologists working in Israel, one may note the more measured skepticism of Finkelstein's (1988; cf. 1996) pioneering work and of Herzog and Bar-Yosef (2002) and Kletter (2006). Ethnicity was recognized as a reality, but there were doubts about identifying it based on material culture remains (and the biblical texts were virtually ignored). It is worth noting that the discussion was now becoming more polemic, more identified with politics and nationalism—in this case, Zionism.

Both biblicists and archaeologists were borrowing, even if unwittingly, from the anthropological literature of the time, synthesized in Sian Jones's *The Archaeology of Ethnicity: Constructing Identities in the Past and Present* (1997). The key concept is "constructing." Ethnicity is an ideological phenomenon; it is scarcely reflected in real life, i.e., in material culture.

A few mainstream and evangelical biblical scholars began to address the issue of ethnicity in the 1990s, like Ahlström (1993), Brett (1996), Edelman (1996), and Sparks (1998). Not directly influenced by postmodernism, like the biblical revisionists cited above, they were cautiously optimistic about identifying ancient Israelite ethnicity. But they scarcely acknowledged the potential of archaeological data.[6]

All along, some archaeologists had been more optimistic about employing the mounting material culture data to characterize ancient Israelite ethnicity, however modest. Specifically challenging radical postmodernist scholars (the European "revisionists" above), Dever (1992; see also 1995a; 1995b; 1998) began in 1992 to employ archaeological "trait-lists" to distinguish Iron Age Israel from her neighbors.[7]

Other archaeologists, however, contested these early programmatic efforts. Not until somewhat later did archaeologists produce full-scale ethnic portraits of ancient Israel, like those of Dever himself (2003; cf. 2017); Killebrew (2005); and Faust (2006; cf. 2012b).[8]

There the matter seemed to rest. A way forward would depend on (1) a more appropriate methodology; and (2) a productive dialogue between specialists dealing with both our sources: texts and artifacts.

Methodological Considerations

For many years, the controversy about ethnicity revolved mainly around the efficacy of "trait-lists," going back to the anthropologist and ethnographer Fredrik Barth's seminal work *Ethnic Groups and Boundaries: The Social Organization of Culture Difference* (1969).

Barth had identified an ethnic group as a population who:

1. are largely biologically self-perpetuating;
2. share a fundamental, recognizable, relatively uniform set of cultural values, including language, realized in cultural forms;
3. constitute a partly independent "interaction sphere;"
4. have a membership that defines itself, as well as being defined by others, as a category distinct from other categories of the same order;
5. perpetuate their self-identity both by developing rules for maintaining ethnic boundaries as well as for participating in inter-ethnic social encounters.[9]

Dever had employed Barth's (1969) trait list as early as 1995, but colleagues castigated him for "misinterpreting" Barth. They insisted that Barth had not endorsed such trait lists. But he had, noting only that such lists have some limitations, due to the complexity of specific ethnic identities.[10] Again, polemics, often political in nature, obscured the issue of methodology.

This may be the place to challenge some common notions about ethnicity.

1. Critics declare that ethnicity is (only) a "construct." Of course, it is: so is every human claim to knowledge, to an apprehension of some external reality. The fact that ethnicity is "constructed" does not mean that it is unreal. On the contrary, ethnicity as an ideal does exist as culture. Additionally, some aspects of ethnicity are not constructed at all; they are inherent in being human (below).
2. Another objection to trying to define ethnicity is that it is "fluid" and "dynamic." That is simply to say that it is characteristically, fundamentally human, so all definitions are provisional.
3. Ethnicity is also said to be "negotiated." Again, that is banal. Every aspect of human nature and behavior is negotiated, from the moment an infant grasps for its mother's breast. Early Israelite ethnicity was crystallized by conflicts with the continuing Canaanite presence in the land, especially by competition with incoming "Sea Peoples," Philistines, and others.
4. Finally, ethnic boundaries are said to be "porous." Again, all cultural (if not geographical) boundaries are permeable, so many societies are porous.

Despite some skepticism about ethnicity—deriving largely from postmodernist aversions to all "metanarratives"—characterizing an entity requires distinguishing its essential characteristics, i.e., traits. However, as several scholars have noted, ethnic traits can be divided into "primordial" and "instrumental" categories, i.e., biologically and culturally derived characteristics.[11] Some traits are indeed "constructed," and therefore subject to choice and changes, and thus difficult to define. But other traits are ingrained in the accidents of birth, and in our DNA.

It may be helpful at this point to enumerate some ethnic traits by category, some objective, others ideational (Table 6.1).

Table 6.1 Ethnic traits by category

Primordial	Instrumental
Place of birth	Family, social class
DNA (gender, body type, IQ, etc.)	Later nurture
Citizenship	Education
Native language	Wider cultural experience
Initial social class	Mature selfhood
Early upbringing	Vocation
	Worldview
About these, the individual has no choice, so they are not "constructs"	With maturity, there are many choices, alternatives.

Who Is an "Israelite"?

If the distinctions just articulated have any validity, how might they apply to defining ethnicity in ancient Israel? Again, a chart may be helpful, but this time categorizing ethnic traits as those derived from the biblical texts, and those based on material culture remains (Table 6.2).

Table 6.2 Ethnic traits as derived from biblical texts and material remains

The biblical ideal	Possible archaeological correlates
Descendants of Abraham	Territorial borders, Cisjordan settlement patterns, mostly rural.
Heirs of "Promised Land," Canaan	
Not "Canaanites," or foreigners	Hebrew language, names
Adherents of Mosaic Yahwism	Houses, furnishings
Keepers of Mosaic law: circumcision, Sabbath, Kashrut, all 613 commandments.	Family structure, patrimonial "Domestic Mode of Production"
Native speakers of Hebrew	diet
Curators of a "simpler culture"	dress
Identifying as the chosen people and citizens of a state	Pottery, other industries
	Art and aesthetics
	Burials
	Cult

While these trait lists might facilitate defining ethnicity, several caveats are necessary—especially with the biblical ideal. These traits are problematic for many reasons (see especially Faust 2020).

1. These traits are all generalizations about the Israelite people as a whole; there were obviously many individual exceptions. For instance, we know that many people were not exclusively Yahwists, did not keep all the Mosaic laws, and may not even have been natives.
2. These lists of the biblical writers, all male, are elitist and highly selective, hardly representative of the masses. This is "the literary Israel": it reflects religious and theological orthodoxy.
3. Many of these traits are imaginative, mostly fictitious aspects of Israel's "foundation myths." They really are constructs.
4. Some of these traits, even if applicable to ancient Israel, are not unique to that people, so are not definitive.
5. Nearly all reflect the realities of the later era of Israel's history, in the 8th–6th centuries BCE, the time when the biblical texts were written and edited. They may be of relatively little value in defining earlier Israel (much less for post-exilic Judaism).
6. Above all, this biblical portrayal of ancient Israelite ethnicity is the *ideal,* never fully realized at any time in the Iron Age. It is the "all Israel" of the biblical writers themselves, Judahites, southerners. Even the Hebrew language in the Divided Monarchy reflects ethnic diversity. Much of the national epic is written in the southern dialect, in contrast to what some Hebraists call the "Israelian" dialect.[12] As archeology shows dramatically, "real-life" Israel was often very different, and much more varied.

Because of such inherent limitations in trait lists, Barth's caution should be taken seriously. And to be fair, some of the revisionist critics noted above may have a point.

While various ethnic markers do appear to have some validity, they remain problematic in some cases. For instance, extensively excavated sites like Rehov IV on the Aramean border, Dor and Tell Qasile X on the coast, and Tel Batash (Timna) IV on the Philistine border are difficult to classify, particularly in the 10th century BCE Are they "Aramean," "Philistine," "Phoenician," or "Israelite?"[13]

Ethnic boundaries are often said to be fluctuating and porous. Yet in several cases, Israelite and Judahite borders can be fixed with some certainty by mapping the distribution of representative artifacts. In the 10th century BCE, the border with Philistia can be fixed by lining up strata at putative Israelite and Philistine sites, analyzing disturbances and destruction layers, then noting how subsequent strata change. The wars of David were apparently successful; in the aftermath, the border with Philistia remained fixed for four more centuries, evident in material culture remains.[14]

Another case is instructive. If we plot distribution maps of the 8th–7th centuries BCE, artifacts like typical Judahite pillar-base figurines and shekel weights, we can establish a clear and lasting border by the 8th–7th centuries BCE (Figures 6.1 and 6.2). These items are indeed ethnic markers: they simply do not appear in Philistia (or for that matter in the northern kingdom of Israel).[15]

A comparison of three 12th–11th century BCE sites is pertinent: Gezer XIII–XI; Ekron, VII–V; and 'Izbet Sartah III–II. These sites lie in the same ecological niche, and they are *ca.*11–25 km apart (one can see Gezer from Ekron). Yet based on material culture, Gezer is clearly in the continuing Late Bronze urban Canaanite tradition. Ekron is a newly established settlement with well documented Philistine ("Sea Peoples") material culture, featuring Aegean-style *megara*, hearths, and Mycenaean IIIC1b pottery. 'Izbet Sartah is like typical Israelite villages elsewhere, with pillar-courtyard houses, silos, and collared rim storage jars (Figure 6.3).

Figure 6.1 Pillar-base figurine, Lachish III. Accession no.: 34.126.53. Gift of Harris D., and H. Dunscombe Colt, 1934. The Metropolitan Museum of Art

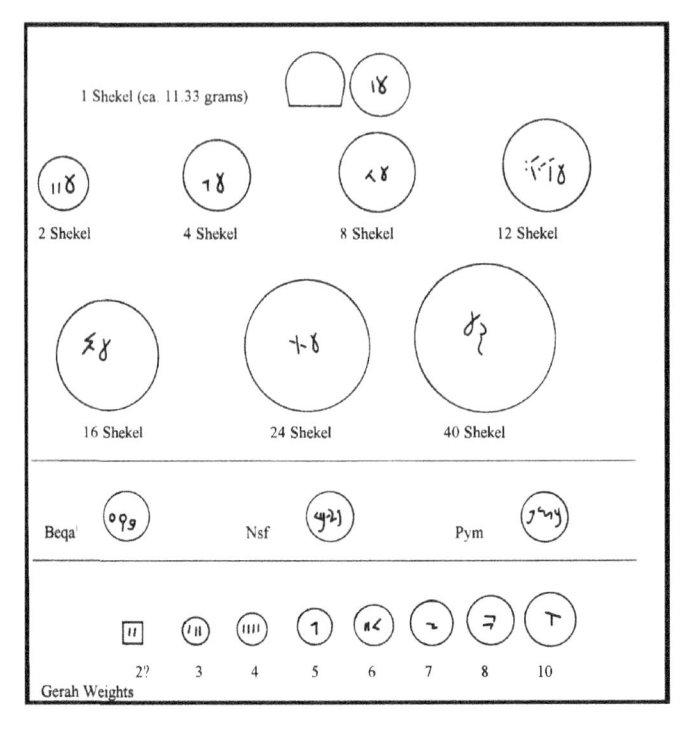

Figure 6.2 8th cent. BCE Judahite shekel weights (Kletter 1999: figure 6; used with permission)

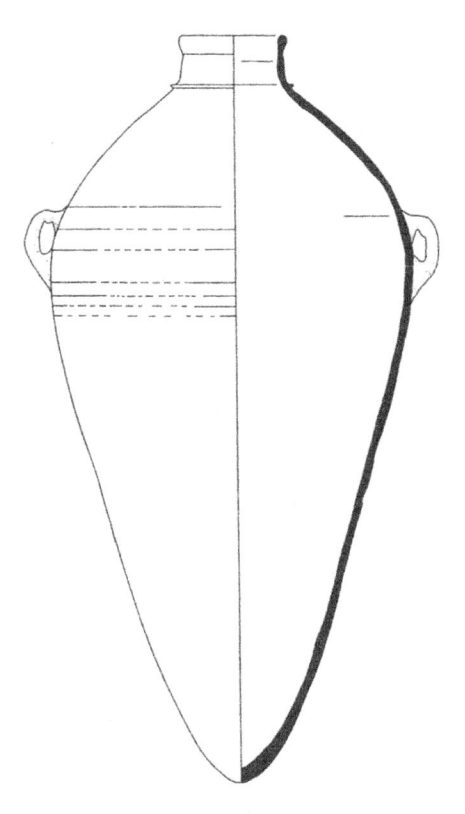

Figure 6.3 12th cent. BCE storage jar, Shiloh V (Gitin 2015: Pl. 1–1.15:4; used with permission)

Here ethnic labels for some sites would seem to be legitimate. Yet the population may have been mixed, since the concepts of "ethnicity" was still in flux this early. The story of Samson and Delilah fits perfectly with such permeable borders in Iron I. Nevertheless, ethnicity does exist, as both objective fact and as a social construct or concept. And it can be described with some confidence if we have sufficient and appropriate evidence.

Two Sources for Distinguishing Ancient Israelite Ethnicity

As historians we possess only two sources for comprehending ancient Israelites' ethnicity: (1) the biblical texts and (2) archaeological data (including extra-biblical textual discoveries). The severe limitations of the textual data—the Hebrew Bible, in the form in which we have it—have already been noted and are widely recognized. Nevertheless, most biblicists dealing with ethnicity have proceeded as though that were the only evidence that we have. They have either ignored the archaeological data or dismissed it by failing to understand what modern archaeology is and what it does.

One of the few full-scale treatments by biblicists is Sparks's *Ethnicity and Identity in Ancient Israel: Prolegomena to the study of Ethnic Sentiments and Their Expression in the Hebrew Bible* (1998). Yet, only at the outset does Sparks even mention archaeology, and then only to assert that it is irrelevant. He states that archaeologists are unable to distinguish Israelite from Canaanite pottery, and that in any case, pottery reflects culture, not ethnicity. Sparks (1998: 9) states further that "the evidence derived from the [archaeological] sources has failed to provide any clear distinction between a supposed Israelite material culture and competing cultures that might be identified with other ethnic groups."[16]

The failure of some biblicists to contribute much that is useful to the discussion of ethnicity is that while they are increasingly skeptical about their source, they dismiss the alternate source of archaeology because they simply do not understand the *meaning of things*. They are logocentric, obsessed with texts—with a history of the literature—rather than a "real-life" history of ancient Israel and the Israelite people. That leaves archaeology as now our primary source.[17]

Assessing the Archaeological Data for Ancient Israelite Ethnicity: Some Case Studies

It is the archaeological data that are now primary, providing an independent witness to supplement, correct, and possibly corroborate the biblical narratives.

The essential point in archaeological research is that "artifacts are material correlates"—the embodiments—of human thought and behavior. Artifacts are thus reliable clues to *culture*, by which ethnic identity, both individual and collective, is formed, reshaped, and maintained.[18]

Nearly all of the archaeologically attested traits or material correlates of ethnicity could be documented in depth, but that is beyond our purview here. For instance, the shifting borders of ancient Israel in all periods can now be mapped in some detail (above). Studies

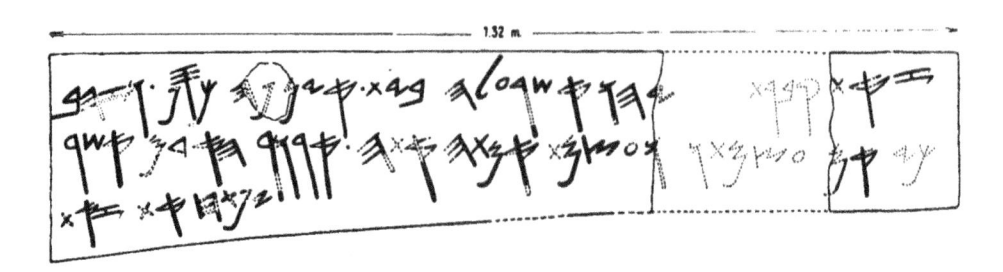

Figure 6.4 The Royal Steward inscription (Barkay 1992: figure 9.49; used with permission)

of changing settlement types and patterns help to define the socio-economic and political organization, family structure, and thus culture, ethnicity, and identity.

Other ethnic traits that are easily illuminated by the archaeological data would include distinctive ceramic repertoires; a diet largely excluding pork consumption; Hebrew language in ostraca and personal names found nowhere else in the southern Levant (Figure 6.4); a distinctive cult of Yahweh (even if not exclusively monotheistic); unique bench-tombs and ancestral burials; female figurines (above) and balance weights that fix ethnic boundaries (especially in Judah); a "culture of simplicity"; and state-level citizenship.[19]

Some presumable ethnic traits, however, cannot always be archaeologically verified, such as birth and DNA (although we have growing evidence); dress (but see the Lachish relief); or many rituals like circumcision and other rites of passage. Additionally, several archaeologically attested cultural and ethnic traits are not unique to ancient Israel but appear in similar guise in the cultures of her close neighbors—the "others" with whom ethnicity is always negotiated.[20]

Some of the most productive data on ethnicity come from very recent "household archaeology" and its emphasis on ancient Israelite family structure—the essence of its society. In particular, the excavation of private houses and their furnishings illuminates Israelite family life and highlights the role of women, half the population (Figure 6.5).

Because ethnicity is a dynamic concept, describing ancient Israelite ethnicity entails distinguishing the Iron Age I settlement horizon from the Iron Age II monarchical period. For the former, the principal issue is how the Israelite people emerged in Canaan, i.e., how and why Israel differed. Here the basic studies are those of Dever (2003), Killebrew (2005), and Faust (2006). In the typical pattern of hill country villages, new distinctive pillar-courtyard houses, with a mix of collared rim storage jars and transitional Late Bronze/ Iron I Canaanite style pottery, appear to be reliable ethnic markers. This agrarian society can be contrasted with a complex of continuing Canaanite urban sites and Philistine enclaves in other regions.

It is this "Israel" (the "Proto-Israelites" of Dever and others) that is envisioned in the contemporary Victory Stele of Merenptah, dated *ca.* 1210 BCE. The cultural values are those of an isolated rural society.[21] For example, as in many rural societies, the earliest Israelites were

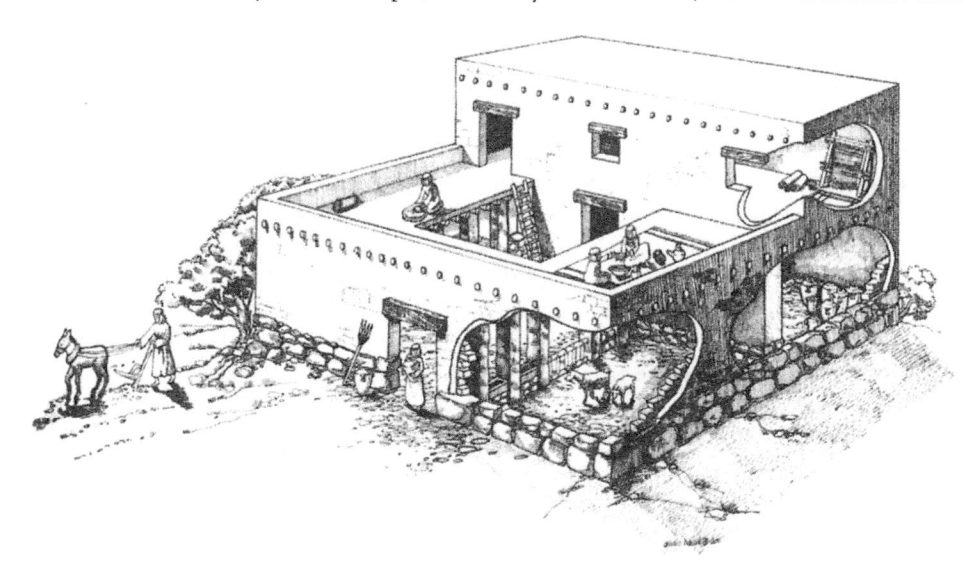

Figure 6.5 An Israelite pillar-courtyard house (drawn by Giselle Hasel; Author's copyright)

individualistic and egalitarian. In a less stratified society, social cohesion could be maintained by a sort of instinctive self-identity. Nevertheless, the biblical portrait of tribal conflicts in the period of the judges should be noted (even if "the Twelve Tribes" is partly fictional).

From the 10th century BCE on (Iron Age II), Israel can be recognized as a state.; in the 9th–early 6th century BCE a divided monarchy of Israel in the north and Judah in the south with its capital in Jerusalem. A 10th century BCE Judahite state assumes a capital, an administrative center, obviously in Jerusalem. Revisionists like Finkelstein and others assert that we have no archaeological evidence, that the whole of Judah was sparsely populated, and that Jerusalem was a tiny village.

The fact is that we have reasonably good evidence for Jerusalem as a 10th century BCE capital (Pioske 2015; and see Pioske this volume). This would include the Bronze Age monumental water system that was no doubt still in operation in the Iron IIA, the large stepped-stone structure (the biblical *millo*, or filling), the smaller stepped-stone structure, which is perhaps "David's citadel," and the early phase of private houses on the eastern slopes of the Ophel. Additionally, almost every detail of the plan and furnishings of the Temple can now be illuminated archaeologically. The published pottery from Str. 14 includes the hand-burnished bowls and cooking pots that derive from contexts radiocarbon dated to the 10th century BCE. As for population, reliable estimates show that Jerusalem could easily have had a population of 1,000 or more, a true urban site by any criteria for the time. And of course, the later Tel Dan stele refers to "the dynasty of David" and mentions kings of both Israel and Judah whose names are known from the Hebrew Bible.[22]

Now the distinguishing features of the Israelite state are walled urban centers, centralized administration, monumental architecture and other feats of engineering, standardized industries, international trade, social stratification, an increasingly literate society, and substantial population growth. Here several recent studies document these changes (Dever 2017; Faust 2012b). Beginning in the Iron IIA, we have a national homeland with well-defined defensible borders and a citizenry with a sense of destiny in the larger world, perhaps first in Judah but soon following in the north.

With increased social stratification, more multi-ethnic class and individual identities emerged. We see a royal family and their entourage, administrative officials, landed gentry, scribes, the military, urban elites, a priestly caste, and local practitioners. There would have been the bourgeoise: merchants and entrepreneurs; artisans and craftsmen; rural property owners. The proletariat would have included: villagers and farmers; indentured servants; slaves; resident aliens (*gerîm*); pastoralists and nomads; "Nazarites" and other dissidents; outcasts of all sorts. All these folk were "Israelites" collectively, but with varied *personal* senses of identity (cf. Keimer 2021). Of course, the north very soon took a different path to statehood, with a new capital at Samaria, and no doubt a growing sense of a northern and more cosmopolitan ethos. That ideology is clearly reflected in the Hebrew Bible and its polemics.

Despite the evolution of Israelite society over several centuries, there are many aspects of continuity between the Iron Age I and Iron Age II. In particular, the ubiquitous pillar-courtyard houses remain in use, and pottery shows a marked continuity. However, the political division of the country can now be seen in several elements, namely: a few pottery styles (e.g., Samaria Ware, Hippo jars, (pre-)*lmlk* jars); artifacts like female figurines and scale-weights; burial customs; and Hebrew dialects. Practically, it is possible to test whether or not material culture can be used to identify ethnicity by selecting several regions east and west of the Jordan and then assembling: (1) a corpus of representative pottery; (2) a group of inscriptions; (3) plans of house-types; and (4) artistic and iconographic objects.

Once the material culture is assembled, a group of knowledgeable archaeologists who together are experts on the whole region determine if these material elements can be associated with any particular geographic region. If groupings appear and are consistent, it must be asked if those groupings reflect a people, that is, a distinct ethnic group? Most mainstream archaeologists would answer "Yes," even if there is some overlap. Those who are hesitant are working with an overly rigid and negative theory about ethnicity. A radical few would be simply spoilers asserting that the notion that ethnicity is a "modern construct" defies reason.

What we have, based on material culture alone, embodies a "core" of social values that provided the cohesion essential to a people's continuing sense of themselves. When that core can be tied to an ancestral homeland, we have a definition of ethnicity beyond a reasonable doubt. Despite some changes, an overall concept of "Israelite" identity is reflected in the material culture—especially when compared with now well-known material culture as evidence of ethnic Egyptians, Philistines, Phoenicians, Arameans, Ammonites, Moabites, Edomites, and other peoples of the Iron Age (above) in the eastern Mediterranean world (below). If we can confidently identify these ethnic groups—as nearly all mainstream scholars do—why not the ancient Israelites?[23]

Future Research

In assessing our two sources for defining ethnicity in ancient Israel, it has become obvious that henceforth the archaeological data will be primary. Yet some dialogue with biblical studies, while rare to date, could be helpful in arriving at a working definition, which is clearly possible.

That raises a perennial question: could we define "ethnicity," Israelite or otherwise, *without* texts? The answer is that we could, but without the complete context, and perhaps without a specific label. That is, we could characterize a particular culture with some confidence as "A," then compare it with culture "B." In short, had the Hebrew Bible never been written, we could still characterize the ethnic entity in question here generally.

Fortunately, we do have a reliable ethnic label in the well-known Victory Stele of Merenptah, securely dated to ca. 1210 BCE (above). This text mentions "the Israelite people," a plural gentilic with the determinative sign for a loosely affiliated group rather than a nation-state. This most likely refers to the complex of late 13th/early 12th century BCE villages in the Central Hill Country, of which the Egyptian intelligence was well informed (see Trimm, this volume).[24]

Despite some optimism, we must guard against reading modern notions of ethnicity back into ancient Israel. For instance, many individuals today can change their identity almost completely. They can adopt other cultures and nationalities, learn other languages, or even become multi-ethnic. Few individuals had such options in the remote past. The essentials—birth, homeland, and native language—were immutable. Secondary traits could rarely be changed to any significant degree. There was much less individual variety and much more homogeneity. Nevertheless, we know that the population of Israel included people of foreign extraction ("Uriah the Hittite"); slaves; captives taken in battle; and *gerîm* or "resident aliens." Then there is the biblical epithet "the people of the land" (*'am hā-āretz*). Who are they? Even with texts, we cannot be sure.

Recent discussions of Israelite ethnicity have once again raised the question of whether an ethnically defined Israel was unique, as once thought (for example, Wright 1950). In the light of recent archaeological evidence, the answer is that Israel was different in some respects, but certainly not unique. It shared numerous cultural affinities with other Iron Age polities, especially in Transjordan.

If ancient Israel was not then unique, why is distinguishing its culture so important? The best answer may be that its moral and ethical values are part of the Western Cultural Tradition, to which much of the modern world is still heir.[25] Even if some aspects are "foundation myths," no people can survive without some such myths. Archaeology allows narratives about Israelite peoplehood in the biblical texts to be examined and appropriated critically. Then, using archaeology as separate and often supplementary data, we can further specify what ordinary people—not the state—thought and did as Israelites.

The entity known as Israel came to an end with the destruction of the northern kingdom in the late 8th century BCE and the fall of Jerusalem in the south in the early 6th century BCE. When some of the captives who were taken to Babylon or their descendants returned to Judah in the late 6th century BCE, they could no longer think of themselves as "Israelites." They were now their successors, living in the Persian province of Yehud—known henceforth as Jews, and identifying with nascent Judaism.

Now there was no national homeland, not even a common ancestry, as Jews intermarried with Samaritans and other foreigners brought in by conquering powers (see Faust 2012a). The books of Ezra and Nehemiah vividly portray their ongoing ethnic conflicts. But the Jewish *community* survived in Judah and in the diaspora—a testimony to the enduring power of the concept of ethnicity.

Notes

1 This essay covers only ancient Israel in the Iron Age ca. 1200–600 BCE, not post-exilic Judaism. We use the term "Israel" for both the northern kingdom of that name and the southern kingdom of Judah, just as the biblical writers often do. To save cumbersome citations, reference will often be made to Dever 2017, where one will find full discussions and copious references.
2 On "ethnicity" as difficult to define, see Killebrew 2005: 9, 10 and references there. For general orientation, see Emberling 1997; Eriksen 1991; Glazer and Moynihan 1995; McGuire 1982; Riggs 1985; Thompson 1989.
3 Here we argue that the concepts of ethnicity and culture are very similar and interrelated, although culture is broader. For contrary views, see Noll 2002: 162; Sparks 1998: 4.
4 See further Geertz 1973 and Shennan 1989, the latter with specific reference to archaeology. On evidence, see further below, Emberling 1997 and McGuire 1982.
5 Biblicists' skepticism about their sources is clearly influenced by postmodern epistemology. On the "literary turn," see further Dever 2017, especially pp. 23–58 and references there.
6 Davies (1992: 24, n. 4) cites the vast archaeological data we now have in only one footnote referring to Mazar (1990)—but only to dismiss it as irrelevant to his *Persian period* Israel. Dever 1992 and 1995a; 1995b were early responses to Davies (Dever 2001: 294). It is not surprising that some theorists, influenced by postmodernist preoccupation with power, see ethnicity as originating in "oppressive social contexts."
7 Despite calls for a dialogue between biblicists and archaeologists for 50 years, little progress has been made, in my judgment. Over-specialized, we simply talk past each other (Dever 2001: 78–81). Dever 2017 is among the few works that attempt a full-scale reconciliation of our two sources for history-writing.
8 See Finkelstein 1996, Herzog and Bar-Yosef 2002, and Kletter 2006. But other mainstream scholars like Stager (1998) and Mazar (1990: 353, cited as definitive in Sparks 1998: 9) remained more sanguine; the latter observed that defining ethnicity is difficult, but he did not think it impossible.
9 Barth (1969) adds, however, that citing single traits may be misleading, especially if they are not unique.
10 See Kletter 2006, who misconstrued Dever's views.
11 See Sparks 1998: 19–21 and Killebrew 2005: 9, 10. The primordial designation relies partly on "essentialism," now widely criticized. However, biology *is* destiny to a significant degree. Here we combine the two approaches.

12 Regarding the "languaging" of ancient Israel and Judah, see the chapter by Hogue, this volume.
13 Tel Reḥov lacks the typical Israelite pillar-courtyard houses and has a few Aramaic ostraca. Tell Qasīle, while in Philistia, exhibits typical Israelite red-slipped and burnished pottery. Tell Batash also has similar pottery, but otherwise seems to have a mixed material culture. It may have become "Israelite" with the Judahite territorial expansion in the 10th century, as nearby Beth-shemesh and Gezer did (Faust 2021). See further below on flexible boundaries.
14 See Dever 2017: 325–29.
15 See Kletter 1999; 2006.
16 Sparks (1998) illustrates how many biblicists ignore or misrepresent the archaeological data—not just the revisionists noted above. A recent handbook (Moore and Kelle 2011) shows how the problem persists. Occasional archaeological data are cited, but often naively. On the lack of dialogue, see n7 above.
17 Although "the meaning of things" is now a major thrust in worldwide archaeology (Olsen 2010), some archaeologists have not caught on. For instance, Sergi (2019: 42, citing Finkelstein 1996) asserts that the archaeological data may only reflect "the subsistence economy and the social mode of life… not ethnic identity": But "mode of life"—how people habitually live and think—is precisely what "ethnicity" *is*. This is what the eminent sociologist Bordieu (1977) calls *habitus*. On "history from things," see further Dever 2017: 8–36. Dever (2017) utilized the notion of Hodder (1986) that things can be *read* just as texts. The assertion of biblicists like Sparks (1998: 4) that ancient Israelites would not have viewed pottery as having anything to do with their ethnicity is astonishing. What people make and do is the material expression of who they think they are—ethnicity.
18 See note 16 above. There is some debate about how culture and ethnicity may be related, and which is primary (Sparks 1998: 18–19).
19 Full treatment with references will be found in Faust 2012b; 2020 and Dever 2012; 2017. On pig consumption, see Sapir-Hen 2019; Faust 2020. Other "Israelite" ethnic traits are difficult to quantify, like four-room houses and collared rim storage jars. But the point is that the few exceptions prove the general rule. These traits only *dominate* at sites that are clearly Israelite on other criteria (Faust 2006: 11–20, 33–70).
20 The literature is vast; but see Yasur-Landau, Ebeling, and Mazar 2011 and Albertz et al. 2014, with copious references.
21 For the significance of the Merenptah Stele, see Dever 2017: 191–94 and references. For contrast with the Iron II period, see summaries in Faust 2012b and Dever 2012; 2017.
22 On Jerusalem, see further Dever 2017: 276–83.
23 House style is particularly significant; see Faust 2012b: 213–29; 2016; 2020; Dever 2012: 142–69; 2017: 170–72, all with full references. Faust has emphasized the ethnic notions of "simplicity," "egalitarianism," and "purity." See Dever 2012 on "agrarian" models, although these are admittedly not unique to ancient Israel.
24 Regarding biblical peoples and ethnicity, or group affiliation, see Younger 2017 on Aramean city-states; on Phoenicia, Elayi 2018; Killebrew 2005 and Killebrew and Lehman 2013 for Philistia. On Transjordan, see Bienkowski 1992 and MacDonald, Adams, and Bienkowski 2001. On Egypt, see Killebrew 2005.
25 For a comprehensive defense of the Western cultural tradition—but only for its best features—see Dever 2001 or Pinker 2019 for a broader secular approach.

Bibliography

Albertz, Rainer et al., eds. 2014. *Family and Household Religion: Toward a Synthesis of Old Testament Studies, Archaeology, Epigraphy, and Cultural Studies.* Winona Lake: Eisenbrauns.
Ahlström, Gösta W. 1993. *The History of Ancient Palestine from the Paleolithic Period to Alexander's Conquest.* Sheffield: Sheffield Academic Press.
Barkay, Gabriel. 1992. "The Iron Age II–III." Pages 302–73 in *The Archaeology of Ancient Israel.* Edited by Amnon Ben-Tor. New Haven: Yale University Press.
Barth, Fredrik, ed. 1969. *Ethnic Groups and Boundaries: The Social Organization of Culture Difference.* Boston: Little Brown & Company.
Bienkowski, Piotr. 1992. *Early Edom and Moab: The Beginning of the Iron Age in Southern Jordan.* Sheffield: Collins.
Bordieu, Pierre. 1977. *Outline of a Theory of Practice.* Cambridge: Cambridge University Press.

Brett, M.G., ed. 1996. *Ethnicity and the Bible*. Leiden: Brill.
Davies, Philip R. 1992. *In Search of "Ancient Israel": A Study in Biblical Origins*. Sheffield: Sheffield Academic Press.
Dever, William G. 1992. "How to Tell a Canaanite from an Israelite." Pages 27–56 in *The Rise of Ancient Israel*. Edited by Hershel Shanks. Washington, DC: Biblical Archaeology Society.
———. 1995a. "Ceramics, Ethnicity, and the Question of Israel's Origins." *BA* 58: 200–13.
———. 1995b. "'Will the Real Israel Please Stand Up?' Part I. Archaeology and Israelite Historiography." *BASOR* 29: 61–80.
———. 1998. "Archaeology, Ideology, and the Quest for 'Ancient' or 'Biblical Israel.'" *NEA* 61: 39–52.
———. 2001. *What Did the Biblical Writers Know and When Did They Know It? What Archaeology Can Tell Us about the Reality of Ancient Israel*. Grand Rapids: Eerdmans.
———. 2003. *Who Were the Early Israelites and Where Did They Come From?* Grand Rapids: Eerdmans.
———. 2012. *The Lives of Ordinary People in Ancient Israel: Where Archaeology and the Bible Intersect*. Grand Rapids: Eerdmans.
———. 2017. *Beyond the Texts: An Archaeological Portrait of Ancient Israel and Judah*. Atlanta: SBL.
Edelman, Diana V. 1996. "Ethnicity and Early Israel." Pages 25–56 in *Ethnicity and the Bible*. Edited by. M. G. Brett. Leiden: Brill.
Elayi, Josette. 2018. *The History of Phoenicia*. Atlanta: Lockwood Press.
Emberling, G. 1997. "Ethnicity in Complex Societies: Archaeological Perspectives." *JAR* 5: 229–34.
Eriksen, Thomas H. 1991. "The Cultural Contexts of Ethnic Difference." *Man* 26: 127–44.
Faust, Avraham. 2006. *Israel's Ethnogenesis: Settlement, Interaction, Expansion and Resistance*. London: Equinox.
———. 2012a. *Judah in the Neo-Babylonian Period: The Archaeology of Desolation*. Atlanta: SBL.
———. 2012b. *The Archaeology of Israelite Society in Iron Age II*. Winona Lake: Eisenbrauns.
———. 2020. "An All-Israelite Identity: Historical Reality or Biblical Myth?" Pages 169–92 in *The Wide Lens in Archaeology: Honoring Brian Hesse's Contributions to Archaeology*. Edited by J. Lev-Tov, P. Hesse and A. Gilbert. Atlanta: Lockwood.
———. 2021. "Between the Highland Polity and Philistia: The United Monarchy and the Resettlement of the Shephelah in the Iron Age IIA, with a Special Focus on Tel 'Eton and Khirbet Qeiyafa." *BASOR* 383: 115–36.
Finkelstein, Israel. 1988. *The Archaeology of the Israelite Settlement*. Jerusalem: Israel Exploration Society.
———. 1996. "Ethnicity and the Origin of the Iron I Settlers in the Highlands of Canaan: Can the Real Israel Stand Up?" *BA* 59: 198–212.
Geertz, Clifford. 1973. *The Interpretation of Culture: Selected Essays by Clifford Geertz*. New York: Basic Books.
Gitin, Seymour, ed. 2015. *The Ancient Pottery of Israel and its Neighbors from the Iron Age Through the Hellenistic Period*. 2 Vols. Jerusalem: Israel Exploration Society.
Glazer, Nathan and Daniel P. Moynihan, eds. 1995. *Ethnicity: Theory and Practice*. Cambridge: Harvard University Press.
Herzog, Z., and O. Bar-Yosef. 2002. "Different Views on Ethnicity in the Archaeology of the Negev." Pages 151–81 in *Aharon Kempinski Memorial Volume: Studies in Archaeology and Related Disciplines*. Edited by E. Oren and S. Ahituv. Beersheba: Ben Gurion University Press.
Hodder, Ian. 1986. *Reading the Past: Current Approaches to Interpretation*. Cambridge: Cambridge University Press.
Jones, Siân. 1997. *The Archaeology of Ethnicity: Constructing Identities in the Past and Present*. London: Routledge.
Keimer, Kyle H. 2021. "Evaluating the 'United Monarchy' of Israel: Unity and Identity in Text and Archaeology." *JJAR* 1: 68–101.
Killebrew, Ann E. 2005. *Biblical Peoples and Ethnicity: An Archaeological Study of Egyptians, Canaanites, Philistines, and Early Israel*. Atlanta: SBL.
Killebrew, Ann E., and Gunnar Lehmann, eds. 2013. *The Philistines and Other "Sea Peoples" in Text and Archaeology*. Atlanta: SBL.
Kletter, Raz. 1999. "Pots and Polities: Material Remains in Late Iron Age Judah in Relation to Its Political Borders." *BASOR* 314: 19–54.
———. 2006. "Can a Proto-Israelite Please Stand Up? Notes on the Ethnicity of Iron Age Israel." Pages 537–86 in *"I Will Speak the Riddles of Ancient Times": Archaeological and Historical Studies in*

Honor of Amihai Mazar on the Occasion of His Sixtieth Birthday, 2 vols. Edited by A. M. Maeir and P. de Mirosohedji. Winona Lake: Eisenbrauns.

Lemche, Niels P. 1991. *The Canaanites and Their Land: The Tradition of the Canaanites.* Sheffield: Sheffield Academic Press.

Mazar, Amihai. 1990. *Archaeology of the Land of the Bible. 10,000–586 BCE.* New York: Doubleday.

MacDonald, Burton, M. Adams, B. Russell, and P. Bienkowski, eds. 2001. *The Archaeology of Jordan.* Sheffield: Sheffield Academic Press.

McGuire, R. H. 1982. "The Study of Ethnicity in Historical Archaeology." *JAA* 1: 159–78.

Moore, Megan B., and Brad K. Kelle, eds. 2011. *Biblical History and Israel's Past: The Changing Study of the Bible and History.* Grand Rapids: Eerdmans.

Noll, K. L. 2002. *Canaan and Israel in Antiquity: An Introduction.* BS 83. Sheffield: Sheffield Academic Press.

Olsen, Bjørnar. 2010. *In Defense of Things: Archaeology and the Ontology of Objects.* Archeology in Society Series. New York: AltaMira Press.

Pinker, S. 2019. *Enlightenment Now: The Case for Reason, Science, Humanism, and Progress.* New York: Penguin Books.

Pioske, D. 2015. *David's Jerusalem: Between Memory and History.* New York: Routledge

Riggs, F. W. 1985. *Ethnicity: Concepts and Terms Used in Ethnicity Research.* Honolulu: COCTA.

Sapir-Hen, Lidar. 2019. "Food, Pork Consumption, and Identity in Ancient Israel." *NEA* 82: 276–79.

Sergi, Omer. 2019. "The Fundamentals of Israelite Ethnicity in the Central Canaanite Highland in the Iron Age I–IIA." *NEA* 82: 42–51.

Shennan, J. S., ed. 1989. *Archaeological Approaches to Cultural Identity.* London: Hyman.

Sparks, Kenton L. 1998. *Ethnicity and Identity in Ancient Israel: Prolegomena to the Study of Ethnic Sentiments and Their Expression in the Hebrew Bible.* Winona Lake: Eisenbrauns.

Stager, Lawrence, E. 1998. "Forging an Identity: The Emergence of Ancient Israel." Pages 123–76 in *The Oxford Encyclopedia of the Biblical World.* Edited by M. D. Coogan. Oxford: Oxford University Press.

Thompson, Richard A. 1989. *Theories of Ethnicity: A Critical Appraisal.* New York: Greenwood.

Thompson, Thomas L. 1997. "Defining History and Ethnicity in the Southern Levant." Pages 166–87 in *Can a "History of Israel" Be Written?* Edited by L. L. Grabbe. Sheffield: Sheffield Academic Press.

———. 1999. *The Mythic Past: Biblical Archaeology and the Myth of Israel.* New York: Basic Books.

Whitelam, Keith W. 1996. *The Invention of Ancient Israel: The Silencing of Palestinian History.* New York: Routledge.

Wright, G. Ernest. 1950. *The Old Testament Against Its Environment.* London: SCM Press.

Yasur-Landau, Asaf, Jennie R. Ebeling, and Laura B. Mazow, eds. 2011. *Household Archaeology in Ancient Israel and Beyond.* Leiden: Brill.

Younger, K. Lawson, Jr. 2017. *A Political History of the Arameans: From Their Origins to the End of Their Polities.* Atlanta: SBL.

PART II

Material Culture

7
A TECHNOLOGICAL AND SOCIOLOGICAL PERSPECTIVE ON ANCIENT ISRAELITE POTTERY

Nava Panitz-Cohen

Introduction

Pottery is both the bane and the blessing of archaeologists. On the one hand, as the typically most abundant material culture dataset recovered in many historical-period excavations, it can be daunting and difficult to process. On the other hand, this very trait, along with its omnipresence in every type of archaeological context, allows pottery to provide a critical and virtually unmatched window into numerous aspects of ancient life, including, first and foremost, chronology (mainly relative, on both the micro and macro levels), as well as regional affiliation (political boundaries, cultural identity) and economic organization (subsistence, production, trade). Foodways, burial customs, and building function are additional parameters that can be inferred. Beyond these relatively tangible characteristics, pottery can also serve as the material correlate of more-elusive features of ancient life that are generally less recognizable in the archaeological record, including status, social complexity, gender relations, behavior, ideology, and religious beliefs (*inter alia*, Rice 2015: 335ff; Roux 2011, 2019: 283–315; Skibo 1999; Sinopoli 1992; van der Leeuw and Pritchard 1984; Wright 1991). Achieving these more-subtle understandings requires methods borrowed from related disciplines, including, *inter alia*, middle-range theories, sociological models, ethno-archaeological analogies, experimental reconstruction, and the application of analytic scientific methods (e.g., Costin 2000; Longacre 1991; Pollard and Bray 2007; Schiffer 1976; Tite 2017). All of these are tools that enable the pottery "to talk" and to serve as a proxy for a wide variety of issues that are of great archaeological, historical, and human interest. More than any other artifact category, pottery engages in the interface of how humans interact with their environment and with each other.

This chapter seeks to highlight methodological approaches for a more nuanced analysis of the Iron Age pottery of ancient Israel that address, but also go beyond historical and chronological reconstruction, and can enlighten our understanding of social, political, and ideological aspects of the ancient Israelite world. The abundance and wide variety of archaeological ceramic data from the Iron Age that are available in Israel today provide a sound jumping board for the application of these theories and methods to the particular historical and geo-political setting of ancient Israel, providing an enriched understanding of the socio-cultural processes that characterized it, particularly when evaluated in context and in relation to other material culture datasets.

Ceramic Research Methodologies in Brief

The toolbox of the archaeologist studying pottery has developed in concurrence with the three major theoretical trends in archaeology—culture history, processualism, and post-processualism (Dessel and Joffe 2000; Rice 1984: 245). The study of pottery has been an integral part of archaeology as a modern, scientific discipline since the second half of the 19th century (Renfrew and Bahn 2000: 34) and has undergone several stages (although not entirely sequential and certainly not mutually exclusive), as follows:

1 *Descriptive-classificatory*: Pottery is a means of identifying a culture or people and establishing a chronology and inter-regional and ethnic connections. Viewing pottery this way falls within the culture-historical approach, wherein a culture's artifacts can be described and classified into an order that is chronologically (and hence, historically) and regionally significant, based on typological and stratigraphical criteria. The description is often correlated with a particular national or ethnic group and/or historical event that can be defined in time and space, such as migration or conquest; as such, the term "pots equal people" has been coined. Typology, seriation, and sequence dating are the methods most used in this approach, as well as direct historical, ethnological comparisons.

In the study of the pottery of ancient Israel, there was an additional dimension that was not part of culture-historical oriented ceramic analysis in New World and European archaeology, namely, the Old Testament text which provided the absolute chronology, as well as the explanatory framework for much of the historical events and cultural phenomena under discussion. One of the most familiar examples of such ceramic analysis is that of the Philistines, a national/ethnic group mentioned in the Bible, whose archaeological fingerprint was first proposed by MacKenzie (Dothan 1982: 24) in the form of an Aegean-style pottery he identified at Beth Shemesh in 1909. This pottery was subsequently adopted as a direct litmus test for Philistines wherever it was found (Figure 7.1).

Figure 7.1 Philistine pottery (courtesy of Aren M. Maeir, Tel Safi-Gath Excavations)

Examples of the "pots equal people"/typological approach in the study of ancient Israelite pottery abound and, in fact, continue to comprise an analytic framework for not a small portion of current ceramic research; this approach comprises the basis for much of the way the chronological framework is determined.[1]

2   *Explanatory/empirical*: Rising from the understanding that it is not enough to classify vessels, and that context and function need to be explained, this approach views pottery as an integral part of social and economic organization ("ceramic sociology": i.e., kinship patterns in the learning and transmission of the craft, the role of style in social interaction, production organization; e.g., Arnold 1988; DeBoer 1991; Lechtman 1977; Plog 1980; Rice 2015: 388–410), and as playing a critical role in subsistence and adaptation to the environment ("ceramic ecology"; i.e., procurement of raw materials, environmental effects, use-function, development of foodways, etc.; Kolb 1988, 1989; Matson 1965). As such, the term "pots as tools" was coined (Braun 1983). This category reflects the rise of Processualism or New Archaeology beginning in the 1960s that emphasized the cross-cultural universalism of cultural processes. The specific historical or ethnic frameworks that so interested the culture-historians studying ancient Israel, specifically those that involved the biblical text, were no longer a viable or dominant factor. Within this theoretical framework came the use of statistical quantification and natural science methods such as provenance studies (Quinn 2013; Shepard 1995; Waksman 2017) and radiocarbon dating (Taylor and Bar-Yosef 2014), as well as the application of indirect ethno-archaeological analogy to ceramic study, with an emphasis on production organization and craft specialization (Costin 1991; Longacre 1991; Rice 1984, 2015: 350–62).

It can be said that while New World and European archaeology embraced these research goals and methods early on, such an approach came of age only at a later stage in the interpretation of the pottery of ancient Israel, partly due to the centrality of the historical biblical narrative to archaeological research, as noted above. It was (is) manifested via a range of studies using scientific methods, such as radiocarbon dating, provenance (*inter alia*, Neutron Activation Analysis and petrography), residue analysis and three-dimensional scanning (Karasik and Smilansky 2008), as well as an emphasis on ceramic technology. More than any of the Processual-oriented methods, it was radiocarbon dating that advanced ceramic research, as it exempted pottery from its traditional (and still important) task as the chronological indicator. Provenance studies grounded and expanded knowledge of inter-regional relations, distribution/trade, and settlement patterns.

Processual-influenced studies of ancient Israelite pottery shifted the focus from one-on-one ethnic identification toward a more socio-cultural-oriented understanding.[2] To name but a few of these studies: (1) differences between the pottery in the rural hill country and the urban valleys in Iron Age I were explained by adaptive environmental and economic factors rather than the presence of different ethnic groups such as Canaanites or Israelites; (2) the disappearance of painted pottery at the end of the second millennium BCE was the suggested result of technological rather than ethnic or historical reasons (Franken and London 1995); (3) collared-rim pithoi, which were considered the *fossil directeur* of the early Israelites, were redefined as reflecting marital patterns joining hill-country women with men from the valley city of Megiddo in late Iron Age I (Esse 1992); (4) Philistine pottery was disassociated from its putative ethnic affiliation and instead, an attempt was made to relate its production and distribution to social and economic regional dynamics, i.e., its role as a prestige ware of its time (Bunimovitz 1990).

3   *Interpretive/contextual*: This approach claims that pottery comprises a symbol of behavior, values, and beliefs just as much as it signifies an ethnic group or is a pot in which to cook

and can be used to infer and interpret these more abstract aspects of culture, mainly from a socio-technological perspective (Roux 2019; Skibo and Schiffer 1995). As such, this may be termed "pots as symbols." This approach finds its theoretical underpinnings in post-processualist archaeology beginning in the 1990s. The methodologies of pottery studies in this paradigm are diverse and heterogeneous and, in fact, many are gleaned from the previous two categories, with an added emphasis on the social sciences, particularly behavioral, cognitive, and gendered models, emphasizing the power of individual choice (agency; Hodder 1986: 25), the impact of personal experience (habitus; Dobres and Hoffman 1994: 217–18), and a socio-cultural perspective on technology. The potter and his/her choices and social environment, just as much as the consumer, play a vital role in interpreting ancient pottery according to this approach. Interestingly, this approach advocates a return to particular historical events, as well as ethnicity, as a valid interpretive context, thus reducing the centrality of the cross-cultural component that characterized the Processualists.

This theoretical paradigm combines different approaches and models, so that it is more difficult to define pottery studies that strictly conform to this approach. Examples of such a strain of research in Iron Age pottery include: (1) Faust's (2000) attempt to explain the inception of red slip and hand burnished pottery in Iron Age IIA as symbolizing changing gender and power relations within the extended family as a result of macro-political change on the state level, with the establishment of the monarchy; (2) Bunimovitz and Faust's (2001) study that viewed the selective distribution of Iron Age IA Philistine Monochrome pottery not as the result of chronological or historical factors (e.g., Finkelstein 2018), but as a result of the manipulation of symbolic social and ethnic boundaries, following ethno-archaeological studies of similar situations; (3) viewing the avoidance of painted pottery among the Israelites as opposed to decorative traditions of contemporary Philistines, Phoenicians, Cypriots, and Edomites as a deliberate means of ethnic identity negotiation (Faust 2013); (4) conceptualizing the mixed pottery assemblage of Tell Qasile in the late Iron Age I not as a duality of Philistines versus Canaanites, but rather as "situational and contextual patterns of behavior of one and the same community" (Lehmann 2021: 281); (5) the appropriation of the typical Canaanite-Israelite chalice shape, considered a ritual vessel in those spheres, into the late Philistine ceramic repertoire and the attendant symbolic role it played in the formation of Philistine social boundaries and group identity in the later Iron Age (Gadot et al. 2014).

Concepts in Ceramic Analysis

This brief review and the selected examples from the Iron Age show how the pottery analyst has a very extensive department store where she or he can shop for theoretical models and methods with which to achieve nuanced insights into ancient Israelite life via the ceramic dataset. I will now discuss a selection of the concepts and methods that archaeologists use for this purpose, taken from all three of the theoretical paradigms presented above (and combinations thereof), and look at certain pottery groups of Iron Age Israel against this multifarious conceptual background.

Ceramic Technology and the Organization of Pottery Production

Among the analytic concepts that emerged from the processual paradigm, and that were embellished and adapted in the ensuing post-processual approach to ceramics, one of the most powerful is the understanding that technology is not merely a technical way to solve a problem usually related to subsistence and adaptation to one's environment, but also represents a deep-seated expression of a social group's identity and cultural choices (Roux 2019). This is because learning and practicing a craft, in our case ceramics, from the stage of procuring raw materials via (especially) the formation and firing techniques, and the emergence of the final product, are transmitted from generation to generation mainly within the confines of the social group (usually kin-related) and thus, come to embody that group (Dobres and Hoffman 1994; Gosselain 1998; Roux 2019: 4–6, 276–78, 294–316; Sillar 1997). These technical skills and motor-habit patterns become emblematic of the producing group whose social, cultural, ethnic, and sometimes also political identity and behavior are, for the most part, constant and conservative and quite resistant to change (Roux 2017). In this way, a deep-seated understanding of ancient ceramic technology opens an important window into social group identity, behavior, and beliefs (Bijker, Hughes, and Pinch 2012).

This approach greatly broadened the concept of style that was originally applied mainly to the decoration or shape of a pot to include all stages of its manufacture (the "*chaîne opératoire*"; Roux 2017, 2019: 283–315).[3] This "technological style" (Lechtman 1977) defines the entire range of elements that constitute technological behavior as style-bearing factors since each variable entails a choice on the part of the makers that is culturally conditioned (Schiffer 1999: 10–12; van der Leeuw 1991: 23–24). In fact, it is these choices that are the source of artifact variability that allow for typological (and other) classification. Notably, pottery technology sometimes even has a non-functional or non-efficient dimension, solely because the "way of doing" represents social identity (Lemonnier 1993: 5).

Having established that pottery production takes place within a social, cultural, and ideological context, understanding the way it is organized plays a vital role in ceramic analysis from a sociological perspective, alongside its significance for economic insights (Costin 1991; Duistermaat 2017). The ability to infer the level and mode of production, as briefly outlined below, has the potential to demonstrate the socio-economic status, as well as gender and social relations and other behavioral patterns, of the people behind the (making of the) pots. This inference can be achieved by three main methods: examining the end products for technological clues, tracing regional and inter-regional distribution patterns, and perceptions from pertinent ethno-archaeological data.

The traditional model, based on cross-cultural, ethno-archaeological observations, contends that there are three basic levels of production that range from simple (individual household production) to more complex (household or cottage industry) to hierarchal-complex (industry/factory; Costin 1991; Rice 2015: 350–62; Sinopoli 1992: 98–102). This linear progression was understood to reflect the rising complexity of the pottery-producing, and in turn, consuming society (Earle 2002: 130–31). Accompanying these evolutionary stages are notions of increasing scale and intensity of production, types of specialization, and shifting gender patterns. Simply put, the mode of production on the household level entails hand-making, lack of production paraphernalia such as a wheel or kiln, conducted in the house exclusively by non-specialist women making a small output of non-standardized pottery, with no profit. The household industry entails mostly specialist women working part- or (rarely) full-time, with hand-making and occasionally with a wheel and kiln, within the household compound, and producing surplus that yields a small profit margin; men can be potters but mostly participate in auxiliary production tasks, as well as in distribution. The industrial mode entails only men, working full-time with fast wheels and firing in kilns, mass-producing substantial amounts of standardized pottery for a high-profit margin, and operating an efficient distribution mechanism.

The type and intensity of production are also assessed according to the social and economic association of the producers, who are designated as "attached" or "independent specialists" (Earle 2002: 128–30; Rice 2015: 357–58). Attached specialists work under the control or sponsorship of some authority/institution, such as elites, priests, governors, etc., that manipulate production and demand (Costin 1996; Sillar 1997). Individual specialists produce a wider range of products for general consumers, operating without specific directives or intervention, other than local preferences and needs, although taxation and tribute demands may affect their scale of production (Sherratt and Sherratt 2001).[4]

While this evolutionary model reflects pottery production modes in their social and economic context and is grounded in cross-cultural, ethno-archaeological observations, clearly the situation is much more complex, non-linear, and multi-variable, certainly so in the archaeological record. It must be kept in mind that the identification of the level of production and type of specialization (in and of itself a complicated task) does not necessarily reflect a strict, one-on-one correlation to social complexity, gender roles, and/or economic feasibility; other aspects need to be factored in, such as environment, historical events, technological developments, innovative individuals, itinerant potters, personal agency and choice, and more. The many aberrations from this basic model reflect the intense dynamics involved in pottery production, which can be compounded when making the leap from ethno-archaeological data to archaeological ceramics, and when assessing the data in their diachronic and synchronic contexts (Duistermaat 2017: 116–17; 135–36).[5]

Despite these caveats, concepts related to the organization of production in the broad sense, at the interface between the technical and the socio-economic, are an essential tool for gaining meaningful sociological insights and are obtainable when a large and well-stratified/contextualized ceramic corpus is available for analysis. For the pottery of the ancient Israelite world, such analyses are conducted on the village, city, and state level, within the context of the historical framework of the United Monarchy, and the trajectories of the Israelite and Judahite kingdoms (see below).

Pottery Consumption, Distribution, Recycling, and Discard

To round out this very brief review of how ceramics can be studied from a sociological perspective to gain insights into ancient Israelite life, are some of the more tangible, behavior-oriented aspects; these include consumption and distribution, as well as recycling and discard. While reflecting economic and political behavior and interactions, in fact, the way pots were used and exchanged also bear a socio-cultural, as well as a symbolic component; such actions were certainly motivated by practicality and profits but took place within the sphere of human behavior and group identities and as such, have sociological value for the study of the ancient Israelite world.

Consumption

Vessel use-function is one of the most-direct parameters in the study of pottery as, most often, form follows function. Study of vessel function goes beyond assessing the compatibility of shape, technology, and use, and includes analytic methods such as residue analysis and experimental archaeology (Barnard and Eerkins 2017). The definition of use-function enhances our ability to recreate building functions, household, and gender-related activity areas, cultic and burial practices and beliefs, and economic ties (e.g., Arnold 2008; Rice 1996; Skibo 2013; Skibo and Schiffer 1995; Yasur-Landau, Ebeling and Mazow 2011). Joining use-function is the spatial distribution of the pottery vessels in their context, which has high potential for determining both its use and significance (Panitz-Cohen 2020a). Yet, it should be kept in mind that the situation is more nuanced than assuming a simple, one-on-one relationship between form and function, as a wealth of options are possible and evidenced in the archaeological record. For example, while one would expect a storeroom to contain many storage jars and pithoi, buildings that are consensually identified as storerooms in Iron IIB at Beersheba contained cooking pots and serving vessels that contradict the storage function (Aharoni 1973: 15). The deposition of vessels in burials represents a re-contextualization and discontinuation of their original function, and vessels that have functions in households (e.g., bowls for serving) take on different tasks in ritual contexts (e.g., bowls as offerings and the Iron IIB favissa at Yavneh; Panitz-Cohen 2010). The evidence is often multi-vocal, as seen in a very rich, mixed-function pottery assemblage recovered from unique architectural contexts at Tel Reḥov in the late Iron IIA, indicating a multi-operational use of this quarter involving concurrent industrial, commercial, and ritual activities, as well as feasting and conspicuous consumption (Panitz-Cohen 2020b).

Distribution and Exchange

Pottery distribution involves the socio-economic and political arrangements involved in circulating the products, as opposed to the mechanics of manufacturing a pot. The distribution of pottery has a reciprocal influence on manufacturing decisions, including stylistic and functional considerations, as well as scale and intensity (Bey and Pool 1992; Duistermaat 2017: 115; Earle 2002: 162–80; Kramer 1997; Rice 2015: 186–204). Trade of pottery can be broadly divided into two main categories: simple utilitarian wares that are exchanged, if at all, on a local level, and prestige ware, which often is imported. These comprise different targets and market mechanisms; the local market or exchange system is a place/situation where social interaction of exchanging goods and reciprocal barter is dominant, while long(er)-distance trade in more prestigious wares is conducted as a formal process based on supply and demand and profit maximization, involving intermediaries and agents (Rice 2015: 186–93). There are intermediate exchange circumstances as well, such as vessels involved in the payment of tithes and taxes, and formal or informal gift-giving. In traditional societies such as ancient Israel, social mechanisms also probably played a role in the distribution of pottery, for example, via dowries or gift exchange within kinship groups (e.g., Longacre 1991; Kramer 1997).

In the study of ancient Israelite pottery, provenance studies are at the base of our ability to trace the circulation of pottery from its place of manufacture to its place of use, within the confines of the Israelite and Judahite kingdoms during the Iron II. Knowing the path and mechanisms of distribution provides information not only about the economic aspect of trade networks, but also their socio-cultural connotations (e.g., Earle 2002: 235–49). For example, the local production of Phoenician Bichrome vessels (whose main production center was the Lebanese coast) at Megiddo in the Jezreel Valley in late Iron I and early Iron IIA possibly comprised an attempt of locals to imitate Phoenician trade patterns in this peripheral region, as well as to emulate the prestige associated with such vessels as imports (Arie, Buzaglo, and Goren 2013: 562–63). The regional restriction of certain storage jar types, such as the Hippo jars in Israel and the *lmlk* jars in Judah in the Iron II was an economically motived, administrative decision, but also reflected the deliberate maintenance of the group/national identity of existing political borders (see also below).

It is also important to note that distribution patterns of commercial storage jars, such as Phoenician torpedo jars (e.g., Waiman-Barack 2016), and small vessels earmarked for importation (e.g., Cypriot wares [Gilboa 2015] and small Phoenician flasks containing cinnamon

[Namdar et al. 2013]), have a different significance than those of other types of usually locally made vessels, for example, cooking pots (e.g., Shai, Ben-Shlomo, and Maeir 2012); the latter have socio-cultural implications for the movement of people and ideas (such as cuisine), in addition to commodities and economic ties.

The Last Chapter: Discard and Recycling

To end the cycle that began with production and continued with distribution, the closing chapter in the "biography" of the pottery vessel (e.g., Deal and Hagstrum 1995; Holtorf 2000) deals with its discard, and possible recycling or secondary use. This can range from deposition in a tomb, to dumping in a refuse pile, to grinding the sherds to create temper for pottery making (grog; Rice 2015: 82). These actions, while technical, are culturally embedded and time-sensitive, so that their identification and understanding can shed light on various parameters of ancient life, such as burial customs, economic arrangements, and technical knowledge (e.g., Senior 1995).

Ceramic Continuity and Change

Finally, an important angle to the sociological analysis of ancient pottery is understanding the mechanisms of ceramic continuity and change, which emphasizes the diachronic dimension, but also reflects the social context. Classifying and quantifying ceramic types, identifying the *chaîne opératoire*, the levels of production, the degree and kind of specialization, and the cultural mores and ideologies accompanying the technology, along with distribution and consumption patterns, are imperative components of the holistic ceramic analysis propounded here. These are, however, for the most part, static conditions, so that familiarity with the underpinnings of the ways that pottery changes (or does not) is crucial for rounding out the dynamic, contextual picture; moreover, this is the very platform for chronological determinations, when the (gradual or punctuated) appearance and disappearance of ceramic types identified in strata comprise the basis for dating in most archaeological excavations. Describing the pottery of the early and late Iron Age as different needs to be explained and contextualized, both historically and socially.

As a traditional craft that is pervasive and deeply rooted in the subsistence and culture of a society, ceramics tend to be conservative and resistant to change. Thus, it is the change more than the continuity that demands explanation. Various models seek to explain ceramic change, including diffusionist theories wherein change results from the movement of people, commodities, or ideas (Hodder 1978). Evolutionary models of ceramic change underscore the idea that the more-adaptive cultural and technological traits will survive over time, while others will stagnate, with change being a unilinear and progressive trajectory from simple to complex, always striving for improvement (Carneiro 2003). A systems theory explanation views pottery as part of the sub-systems of environment and technology (ceramic production), economy and politics (ceramic distribution), and ideology or beliefs (ceramic use). In this way, pottery is one of the most intertwined components of the social system and virtually any change in one or more of the sub-systems can generate (morphological, technological, and/or[?] stylistic) change in pottery (Arnold 1988).

Iron Age Pottery of Ancient Israel: Trajectories and Patterns

The Iron Age pottery of ancient Israel is, on the one hand, deeply rooted in the local, long-lived Canaanite tradition while, on the other hand, the vessels and their mode of manufacture and decoration demonstrate innovative characteristics that are partly the result of local developments and partly the product of external influences, be they anthropomorphic or technical, or both. The breakdown of the Mediterranean trade system at the end of the Late Bronze Age resulted in major economic, demographic, and social changes, yet did not signal the termination of all inter-regional connections but rather, evoked a qualitative shift in their nature during the early Iron Age, and a change in balance between the local and the 'global' (Sherratt 1998). The migration of people from the Mediterranean basin, alongside changing settlement patterns in regions such as the Central Hill Country and the Negev resulting from the ad hoc movement of local people, as well as state-controlled initiatives (in the latter part of Iron II), impacted ceramic production and trade, as well as use. In the Iron Age I, when production and long-distance trade were no longer the exclusive domain of the city-state elites and the Egyptian overlords, new technological and entrepreneurial initiatives became possible, as did political self-determination and cultural interactions. The role of the Phoenicians[6] in the development of Iron Age pottery was particularly significant, as they were agents of both commercial endeavors and material-cultural dissemination, including a robust ceramic tradition that was widely traded and imitated.[7] The formation of territorial states in the region—Israel, Judah, Edom, Moab, Ammon—impacted the way pottery was made, decorated, used and traded and, in many ways, reflected the cultural and political interaction, or borders, between these polities over time.

One cannot talk of "the Iron Age pottery of ancient Israel" as a monolithic entity. In fact, one of the outstanding features of this corpus is the increased degree of regionality and fractionality as opposed to the previous Late Bronze Age, when the ceramic tradition was relatively uniform, both on a typological and a technological basis.[8] The establishment of the territorial states of Israel and Judah and the demarcation of borders, both real and perceived, permanent and temporary, are processes that resulted in the accelerated development of local/regional production and technical traditions, as well as shifts in the level of production from household industry to factory industry, especially seen in the pottery of the 9th to 7th centuries BCE. In fact, it is more the exception than the rule when we witness pottery forms and decoration that are shared throughout the country, considering the well-defined regional (often ethnically identified) groups, including Philistine, Phoenician, Israelite, and Judahite, as well as Transjordanian traditions, such as Edomite and Ammonite (Ben-Shlomo et al. 2008; Gitin 2015). Some ceramic traditions were shared over broad regions and time spans such as red slip and burnish, black juglets, Assyrian-shaped bowls and bottles, Iron I and Iron IIA cooking pots, while others were mutually exclusive and competitive (e.g., Hippo jars, *lmlk* jars and cooking pots in the Iron IIB–IIC).

When overviewing Iron Age pottery on a diachronic basis, there is a clear divide between Iron I and Iron IIA, although the changes did not necessarily take place at exactly the same time and there are regional expressions to them; moreover, a few vessel shapes and technologies continued almost unchanged until late Iron IIA, such as open carinated cooking pots whose long-lived conservativism reflects deep-seated culinary practices that did not change (Figure 7.2; Panitz-Cohen 2020a: 251, 2021). For example, the inception of red slip and hand burnish, a hallmark of Iron IIA, is detected at northern sites at a somewhat later stage than in the south. Iron I fossil types, such as the pithos, the carinated handled krater, small hemispherical bowls, and strainer jugs (Figure 7.3), as well as formation techniques of wheel-coiling and production mainly conducted in localized household workshops, make way for new morphological and technical traditions, such as the increased use of the potters' wheel, higher firing temperatures, and new shapes, such as carinated bowls, narrow-necked jugs,

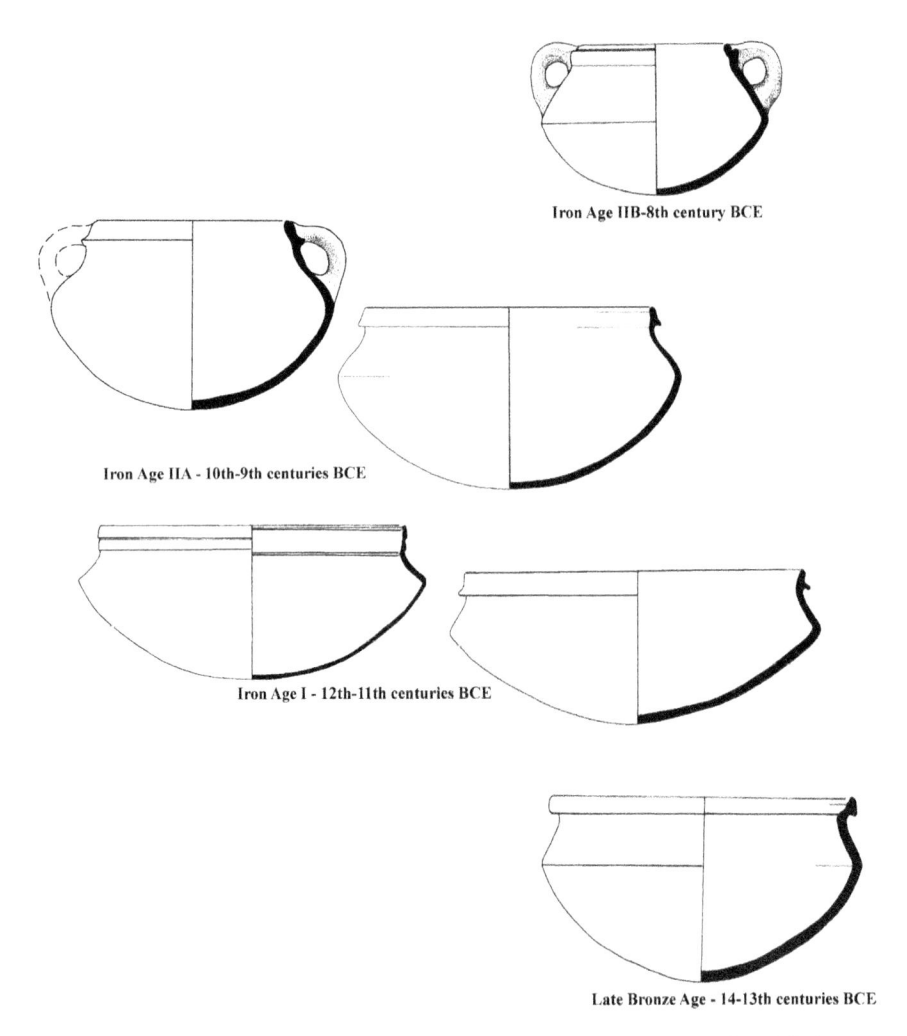

Figure 7.2 Open cooking pot sequence from the Late Bronze Age to Iron Age IIB (courtesy of Amihai Mazar, Tel Batash, and Tel Rehov Excavations)

sack-shaped and torpedo storage jars, black juglets, and cooking jugs (Cohen-Weinberger and Panitz-Cohen 2014; Figure 7.4).

Production became increasingly specialized during the course of Iron Age II, seen in certain standardized shapes manufactured in centralized workshops on a largely industrial and mass-produced scale; in some cases, we can identify attached specialization, for example, Hippo storage jars in the north and *lmlk* storage jars in the south (Figure 7.5), each part of an official administrative-economic system operating under the auspices of the Israelite and Judahite states, respectively (Karasik, Harush and Smilanksy 2020; Kleiman 2017). Decanters and hole mouth jars (in both the north and south) and the so-called "Judean bowls" in the south in Iron IIB are additional examples of centralized, standardized, and specialized mass-production, although most likely not under state control, but economically regulated due to contents and consumption patterns.

Viewing the social and cultural context of pottery production and consumption in ancient Israel, it is important to keep in mind that the economic base of Israelite and Judahite

A Thorough Perspective on Ancient Israelite Pottery

Collared-rim pithos

Hemispherical bowl

Carinated krater

Strainer jug

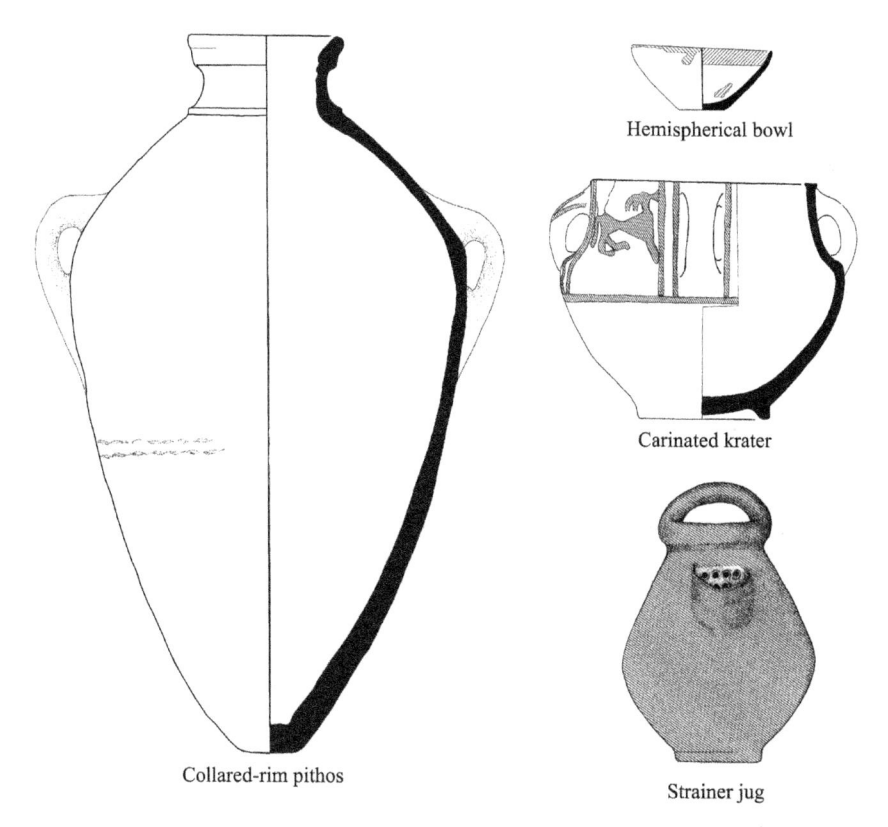

Figure 7.3 Iron Age I pottery types that do not continue to Iron IIA (courtesy of Amihai Mazar, Tel Beth Shean, and Tel Rehov Excavations)

society comprised mainly small agricultural villages and farmsteads, rather than urban centers, so that we can surmise that most production took place within kinship-based groups on a household workshop level, and was intertwined with other means of subsistence, especially agriculture (Arnold 1988; Faust 2000). This level of production bespeaks the involvement of local women in the process, comprising an economic sphere of empowerment for the Israelite woman (London 2008; Skibo and Schiffer 1995).

The pottery forms and techniques that are found throughout the country (albeit with certain typological and technological differences), such as decanters, black juglets, lamps, and most cooking pot shapes (the latter mainly in early Iron II; Figure 7.6), reflect the kin-based affinity of the population whose pre-state social basis continued to exist alongside the crystallization of formal political borders. Pottery-producing groups and their inherent technical and cultural traditions remained the same, transmitted from generation to generation, regardless of the formalities and demands of Israelite or Judahite kingdoms' control. Alongside this, economic and political forces, such as Phoenician-led trade, Assyrian involvement, and state intervention, either for taxation or in times of crisis (e.g., the standardized Hippo jars in Israel, and the centralized, controlled production of *lmlk* jars in Judah in preparation for the Assyrian attack; Karasik, Harush and Smilansky 2020; Panitz-Cohen 2020b), were the agents of concurrent industrial formalized production.

A consummate example of this interplay of mutual influence alongside exclusivity in ceramic traditions can be seen in the Iron IIA-B ceramic assemblage termed "Negebite" ware.

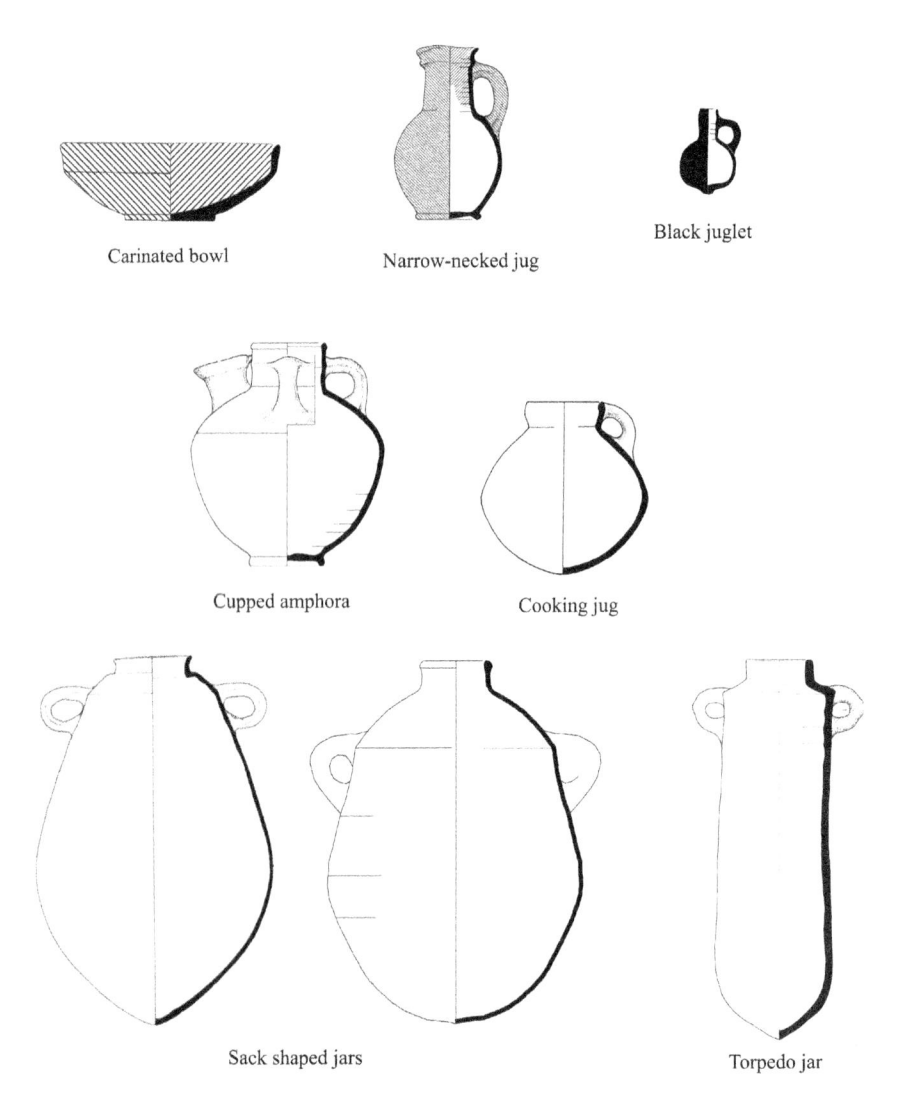

Figure 7.4 A selection of Iron Age IIA–B pottery types (courtesy of Amihai Mazar, Tel Batash, and Tel Rehov Excavations)

This was a simple, even crude, hand-made, low-fired production line, found throughout Judah but mainly in the south, that co-existed with the household industry and specialized mass-production modes typical of this period, representing multiple, simultaneous levels of production (Figure 7.7). Often, the very same shapes were produced, ruling out function as the guiding principle for this technology. Clay sources were also generally shared with the wheel-made wares (Freud 2014; Tebes 2006). The vast difference between these modes of production, sometimes even found together in the same room, reflect diverse groups with varying socio-economic and perhaps ethnic identities, be they sedentary and pastoralist, local and immigrant, wealthy and destitute, or elite and commoner. This case well reflects the multi-vocal character of Iron Age pottery and how understanding factors of technology and style in a specific historical and geographical context contribute an important dimension to our understanding of the ancient Israelite world.

Lamelech jar   **Hippo jar**

Figure 7.5 Iron II *lmlk* and Hippo jars (courtesy of Amihai Mazar, Tel Batash, and Tel Rehov Excavations)

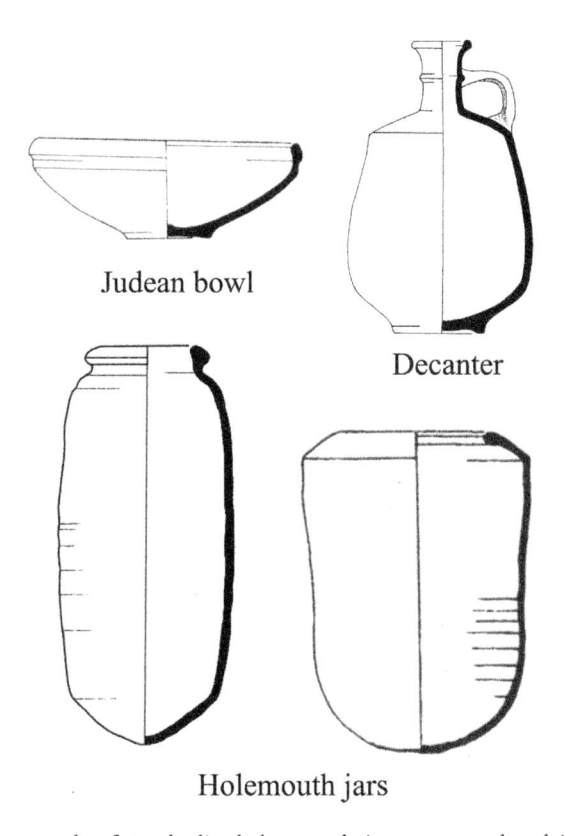

Judean bowl

Decanter

Holemouth jars

Figure 7.6 Pottery vessels of standardized shape and size, mass-produced in Iron II (courtesy of Amihai Mazar, Tel Batash, and Tel Rehov Excavations)

Figure 7.7 Negebite vessels and their wheel-made counterparts; 1–2: cooking vessels; 3–4: jugs (Negebite vessels: Photo by Mariana Salzberger, courtesy of the Israel Antiquities Authority; wheel-made vessels: courtesy Amihai Mazar, Tel Rehov Excavations)

Notes

1 For a detailed review, see London (1983: 6–36), and for a recent typological-regional treatment, see Gitin (2015).
2 For a review of such studies in the pottery of ancient Israel until the 1980s, see London 1983: 37–58.
3 The definition of *chaîne opératoire* is "a series of operations that transform raw material into a finished product, whether it is a consumer object or a tool (Creswell 1976: 13).
4 Other types of specialization related to pottery production have been defined, including site, resource, and community specialization (Kramer 1997; Rice 2015: 357–61; Schortman and Urban 2004; Sillar 1997).
5 Duistermaat (2017: 124–35) defined this situation as "entanglement" and proposes a much more multi-variate approach to the assessment of the organization of pottery production.
6 Although we cannot speak of the Phoenicians as an organic national entity, being composed of various city-states and identified mostly externally (Sader 2019), their ceramics, in fact, demonstrate a relatively homogeneous and well-defined corpus.
7 Among the various Phoenician ceramic groups, the Bichrome and Late Philistine Decorated Ware traditions that began in late Iron I and early Iron IIA, should be especially noted as having impacted Iron Age Israelite pottery shapes, technology, and decoration.
8 Interestingly, this uniformity stands out especially against the background of the geo-political picture painted by the Amarna letters, with clearly defined borders and often hostile relations between Canaanite city-states (Panitz-Cohen 2014: 552).

Bibliography

Aharoni, Yohanan. 1973. *Beer-sheba I: Excavations at Tel Beer-sheba*. Tel Aviv: Institute of Archaeology, Tel Aviv University.

Arie, E., E. Buzaglo, and Y. Goren. 2006. "Petrographic Analysis of Iron I Pottery." Pages 558–67 in *Megiddo IV: The 1998–2002 Seasons*. Edited by I. Finkelstein, D. Ussishkin, and B. Halpern. Tel Aviv: Institute of Archaeology, Tel Aviv University.

Arnold, Dean. 1988. *Ceramic Theory and Cultural Process*. Cambridge: Cambridge University Press.

———. 2008. *Social Change and the Evolution of Ceramic Production and Distribution in a Maya Community*. Boulder: University Press of Colorado.

Barnard, H., and J. W. Eerkends. 2017. "Assessing Vessel Function by Organic Residue Analysis." Pages 625–50 in *The Oxford Handbook of Archaeological Ceramic Analysis*. Edited by A. M. W. Hunt. Oxford: Oxford University Press.

Ben-Shlomo, David, Itzick Shai, Alexander Zuckerman, and Aren M. Maeir. 2008. "Cooking Identities: Aegean-Style Cooking Jugs and Cultural Interaction in Iron Age Philistia and Neighboring Regions." *AJA* 112: 225–46.

Bey, G. J., and C. A. Pool. 1992. *Ceramic Production and Distribution: An Integrated Approach*. Boulder: Westview Press.

Bijker, W. E., T. P. Huges, and T. Pinch, eds. 2012. *The Social Construction of Technological Systems. New Directions in the Sociology and History of Technology*. Cambridge: Massachusetts Institute of Technology.

Braun, David. 1983. "Pots as Tools." Pages 107–34 in *Archaeological Hammers and Theories*. Edited by J. A. Moore and A. S. Keene. New York: Academic Press.

Bunimovitz, Shlomo. 1990. "Problems in the 'Ethnic' Identification of the Philistine Culture." *TA* 15–16: 68–76.

Bunimovitz, Shlomo, and Avraham Faust. 2001. "Chronological Separation, Geographical Segregation or Ethnic Demarcation? Ethnography and the Iron Age Low Chronology." *BASOR* 322: 1–10.

Carneiro, R. L. 2003. *Evolutionism in Cultural Anthropology. A Critical History*. Colorado: Westview Press.

Cohen-Weinberger, Anat, and Nava Panitz-Cohen. 2014. "The Black Juglets." Pages 403–14 in *Khirbet Qeiyafa, Vol 2. Excavation Report 2009–2013. Stratigraphy and Architecture (Areas B, C, D, E)*. Edited by Yossi Garfinkel, Saar Ganor and Michael G. Hasel. Jerusalem: Israel Exploration Society, the Hebrew University of Jerusalem.

Costin, C. L. 1991. "Craft Specialization: Issues in Defining, Documenting and Explaining the Organization of Production." Pages 1–56 in *Archaeological Method and Theory, Volume 3*. Edited by M. B. Schiffer. Tucson: University of Arizona Press: Tucson.

———. 1996. "Craft Production and Mobilization Strategies in the Inka Empire." Pages 211–25 in *Craft Specialization and Social Evolution: In Memory of V. Gordon Childe*. Edited by B. Wailes. Philadelphia: University of Pennsylvania.

———. 2000. "The Use of Ethnoarchaeology for the Archaeological Study of Ceramic Production." *JAMT* 7: 377–403.

Creswell, R. 1976. "Techniques et Culture, Les Bases D'un Programme De Travail." *Techniques et Culture* 1: 7–59.

Deal, M., and M. B. Hagstrum. 1995. "Ceramic Reuse Behavior Among the Maya and Wanka: Implications for Archaeology." Pages 111–25 in *Expanding Archaeology*. Edited by J. M. Skibo, W. H. Walker and A. E. Nielson. Salt Lake City: University of Utah Press.

DeBoer, W. R. 1991. "The Decorative Burden: Design, Medium, and Change." Pages 144–61 in *Ceramic Ethnoarchaeology*. Edited by W. A. Longacre. Tucson: University of Arizona Press.

Dessel, J. P., and A. H. Joffe. 2000. "Alternative Approaches to Early Bronze Age Pottery." Pages 31–58 in *Ceramics and Change in the Early Bronze Age of the Southern Levant*. Edited by G. Philip and D. Baird. Sheffield: Sheffield Academic Press.

Dobres, M. A., and C. R. Hoffman. 1994. "Social Agency and the Dynamics of Prehistoric Technology." *JAMT* 1: 211–58.

Dothan, Trude. 1982. *The Philistines and Their Material Culture*. New Haven: Yale University Press.

Duistermaat, K. 2017. "The Organization of Production: Towards a Relational Approach." Pages 162–80 in *The Oxford Handbook of Archaeological Ceramic Analysis*. Edited by A. M. W. Hunt. Oxford: Oxford University Press.

Earle, Timothy K. 2002. *Bronze Age Economics*. Cambridge, MA: Westview Press.

Esse, D. L. 1992. "The Collared Pithos at Megiddo: Ceramic Distribution and Ethnicity." *JNES* 51: 81–103.

Faust, A. 2000. "The Rural Community in Ancient Israel during Iron Age II." *BASOR* 317: 17–39.

———. 2013. "Simplicity: Pottery and Ethnic Negotiations in Early Israel." *Ars Judaica* 9: 7–18.

Finkelstein, Israel. 2018. "Philistine Chronology: An Update." *IEJ* 68: 221–31.

Franken, H. J., and Gloria London. 1995. "Why Painted Pottery Disappeared at the End of the Second Millennium BCE." *BA* 58: 214–22.

Freud, Liora. 2014. "Local Production of Edomite Cooking Pots in the Beersheba Valley." Pages 283–306 in *Unearthing the Wilderness: Studies on the History and Archaeology of the Negev and Edom in the Iron Age*. Edited by Juan Manuel Tebes. Leuven: Peeters.

Gadot, Y., I. Finkelstein, M. Iserlis, A. M. Maeir, P. Nahshoni, and D. Namdar. 2014. "Tracking Down Cult: Production, Function and Content of Chalices in Iron Age Philistia." *TA* 41: 55–76.

Gilboa, Ayelet. 2015. "Iron Age I–II: Cypriot Imports and Local Imitations." Pages 483–508 in *The Ancient Pottery of Israel and Its Neighbors from the Iron Age through the Hellenistic Period*. Edited by S. Gitin. Jerusalem: Israel Exploration Society.

Gitin, S., ed. 2015. *The Ancient Pottery of Israel and Its Neighbors from the Iron Age through the Hellenistic Period*. 2 Vols. Jerusalem: Israel Exploration Society.

Gosselain, O. P. 1998. "Social and Technical Identity in a Clay Crystal Ball." Pages 78–106 in *The Archaeology of Social Boundaries*. Edited by M. T. Stark. Washington, DC: Smithsonian Institution Press.

Hodder, Ian. 1978. "Simple Correlations Between Material Culture and Society: A Review." Pages 3–24 in *The Spatial Organization of Culture*. Edited by Ian Hodder. Pittsburgh: University of Pittsburgh Press.

———. 1986. *Reading the Past: Current Approaches to Interpretation in Archaeology*. Cambridge: Cambridge University Press.

Holtorf, C. 2000. "Notes on the Life History of a Pot Sherd." *JMC* 7: 49–71.

Karasik, A., and U. Smilansky. 2008. "3D Scanning Technology as a Standard Archaeological Tool for Pottery Analysis: Practice and Theory." *JAS* 35: 1148–68.

Karasik. A., O. Harush, and U. Smilansky. 2020. "The Morphology of Iron Age Storage Jars and Its Relation to the Handbreadth Measure (Biblical Tefach)." *BASOR* 384: 183–90.

Kleiman, A. 2017. "A North Israelite Royal Administrative System and its Impact on Late-Monarchic Judah." *HBAI* 6: 354–71.

Kolb, C. C. 1988. *Ceramic Ecology Revisited 1987. The Technology and Socioeconomics of Pottery*. Oxford: Archaeopress.

———. 1989. *Ceramic Ecology, 1988. Current Research on Ceramic Materials*. Oxford: Archaeopress.

Kramer, C. 1997. *Pottery in Rajasthan: Ethnoarchaeology in Two Indian Cities*. Washington, DC: Smithsonian Institution Press.

Lechtman, H. 1977. "Style in Technology – Some Early Thoughts." Pages 3–20 in *Material Culture. Styles, Organization and Dynamics of Technology*. Edited by H. Lechtman and R. Merrill. St. Paul: West Publishing.

Lehmann, Gunnar. 2021. "The Emergence of Early Phoenicia." *JJAR* 1: 272–324.

Lemonnier, P. 1993. *Technological Choices: Transformation in Material Cultures since the Neolithic*. London: Routledge.

London, Gloria A. 1983. *Ceramic Analysis in Israel: The Past One Hundred Years*. Tucson: University of Arizona.

———. 2008. "Fe(male) Potters as the Personification of Individuals, Places, and Things as Known from Ethnoarchaeological Studies." Pages 155–80 in *The World of Women in the Ancient and Classical Near East*. Edited by B. Alpert Nakhai. Newcastle: Cambridge Scholars Publishing.

Longacre, W. A. ed. 1991. *Ceramic Ethnoarchaeology*. Tucson: University of Arizona Press.

Matson, F. R. 1965. *Ceramics and Man*. Chicago: Aldine.

Namdar, D., A. Gilboa, R. Neumann, I. Finkelstein, and S. Weiner. 2013. "Cinnamaldehyde in Early Iron Age Phoenician Flasks Raises Possibility of Levantine Trade with Southeast Asia." *MAA* 13: 1–19.

Panitz-Cohen, N. 2010. "The Pottery Assemblage." Pages 110–45 in *Yavneh I: The Excavation of the 'Temple Hill' Repository Pit and the Cult Stands*. Edited by R. Kletter, I. Ziffer and W. Zwickel. Göttingen: Academic Press Fribourg.

———. 2014. "The Southern Levant (Cisjordan) during the Late Bronze Age." Pages 541–60 in *The Oxford Handbook of the Archaeology of the Levant, c.8000–332 BCE*. Edited by M. Steiner and A. E. Killebrew. Oxford: Oxford University Press.

———. 2020a. "Iron Age IIA Local Pottery." Pages 109–266 in *Tel Rehov. A Bronze and Iron Age City in the Beth-Shean Valley. Volume IV: Pottery Studies, Inscriptions and Figurative Art*. Edited by Amihai

Mazar and Nava Panitz-Cohen. Jerusalem: Institute of Archaeology, the Hebrew University of Jerusalem.

———. 2020b. "Spatial Distribution of Finds in Stratum IV Buildings in Area C." Pages 355–406 in *Tel Reḥov. A Bronze and Iron Age City in the Beth-Shean Valley. Volume V: Various Objects and Natural Science Studies*. Edited by Amihai Mazar and Nava Panitz-Cohen. Jerusalem: Institute of Archaeology, the Hebrew University of Jerusalem.

———. 2021. "Ceramics in the Iron Age." Pages 197–214 in *The T&T Clark Handbook of Food in the Hebrew Bible and Ancient Israel*. Edited by Janling Fu, Cynthia Shafer-Elliot and Carol Meyers. London: T&T Clark/Bloomsbury.

Plog, S. 1980. *Stylistic Variation in Prehistoric Ceramics*. London: Cambridge University Press.

Pollard, A. M., and P. Bray. 2007. "A Bicycle Made for Two? The Integration of Scientific Techniques into Archaeological Interpretation." *ARA* 36: 245–59.

Quinn, P. S. 2013. *Ceramic Petrography: The Interpretation of Archaeological Pottery and Related Artefacts in Thin Section*. Oxford: Archaeopress.

Renfrew, Colin, and Paul Bahn. 2000. *Archaeology. Theory, Methods, Practice*. London: Thames and Hudson.

Rice, Prudence M. 1984. "Overview and Prospect." Pages 245–55 in *Pots and Potters: Current Approaches in Ceramic Archaeology*. Edited by Prudence M. Rice. Los Angeles: Institute of Archaeology, University of California Los Angeles.

———. 1996. "Ceramic Analysis: Function, Style and Origins." *JAR* 4: 133–63.

———. 2015. *Pottery Analysis. A Sourcebook*. Chicago: Chicago University Press.

Roux, V. 2011. "Anthropological Interpretation of Ceramic Assemblages: Foundations and Implementations of Technological Analysis." Pages 80–88 in *Archaeological Ceramics: A Review of Current Research*. Edited by S. Scarcella. Oxford: Archaeopress.

———. 2017. "Ceramic Manufacture: The Chaîne Opératoire Approach." Pages 101–13 in The *Oxford Handbook of Archaeological Ceramic Analysis*. Edited by A. M. W. Hunt. Oxford: Oxford University Press.

———. 2019. *Ceramics and Society*. New York: Springer.

Sader, Helene. 2019. *The History and Archaeology of Phoenicia*. Atlanta: SBL Press.

Schiffer, M. B. 1976. *Behavioral Archaeology*. New York: Academic Press.

———. 1999. *The Material Life of Human Beings*. London and New York Routledge.

Schortman, E. M., and P. A. Urban. 2004. "Modeling the Roles of Craft Production in Ancient Political Economies." *JAR* 12: 185–226.

Senior, L. M. 1995. "The Estimation of Prehistoric Values. Cracked Pot Ideas in Archaeology." Pages 92–110 in *Expanding Archaeology*. Edited by J. M. Skibo, W. H. Walker and A. E. Nielsen. Salt Lake City: University of Utah Press.

Shai, Itzick, David Ben-Shlomo, and Aren M. Maeir. 2012. "Late Iron Age Judean Cooking Pots with Impressed Handles: A New Class of Stamped Impressions from the Kingdom of Judah," Pages 225–44 in *'Go Out and Study the Land' (Judges 18:2), Archaeological, Historical and Textual Studies in Honor of Hanan Eshel*. Edited by A. M. Maeir, J. Magness and L. H. Schiffman. Leiden: Brill.

Shepard, A. 1995. *Ceramics for the Archaeologist*. Ann Arbor: Braun-Brumfield.

Sherratt, A., and S. Sherratt. 2001. "Technological Change in the East Mediterranean Bronze Age." Pages 15–38 in *The Social Context of Technological Change, Egypt, and the Near East, 1650-1550 B.C.* Edited by A. J. Shortland. Oxford: Oxbow Books.

Sherratt, S. 1998. "Sea Peoples" and the Economic Structure of the Late Second Millennium in the Eastern Mediterranean." Pages 292–313 in *Mediterranean Peoples in Transition. Thirteenth to Tenth Centuries BCE. In Honor of Professor Trude Dothan*. Edited by S. Gitin, A. Mazar and E. Stern. Jerusalem: Israel Exploration Society.

Sillar, B. 1997. "Reputable Pots and Disreputable Potters: Individual and Community Choice in Individual and Community Choice in Present-day Pottery Production and Exchange in the Andes." Pages 1–20. in *Not So Much a Pot, More a Way of Life*. Edited by C. G. Cumberpatch and P. W. Blinkhorn. Oxford: Oxbow Books.

Sinopoli, C. M. 1992. *Approaches to Archaeological Ceramics*. New York: Plenum Press.

Skibo, J. M. 1999. "Pottery and People." Pages 1–8 in *Pottery and People. A Dynamic Interaction*. Edited by J. M. Skibo and G. M. Feinman. Salt Lake City: University of Utah Press.

———. 2013. *Understanding Pottery Function*. New York: Springer.

Skibo, J. M., and M. B. Schiffer. 1995. "The Clay Cooking Pot. An Exploration of Women's Technology." Pages 80–91 in *Expanding Archaeology*. Edited by J. M. Skibo, W. H. Walker and N. E. Nielsen. Salt Lake City: University of Utah Press.

Taylor, R. E., and O. Bar-Yosef. 2014. *Radiocarbon Dating, An Archaeological Perspective*. New York: Routledge.

Tebes, Juan Manuel. 2006. "Iron Age "Negevite" Pottery." *AntOr* 4: 9–117.

Tite, M. S. 2017. "History of Scientific Research." Pages 8–15 in *The Oxford Handbook of Archaeological Ceramic Analysis*. Edited by A. M. W. Hunt. Oxford: Oxford University Press.

van der Leeuw, S. E. 1991. "Variation, Variability, and Explanation in Pottery Studies." Pages 11–39 in *Ceramic Ethnoarchaeology*. Edited by W. A. Longacre. Tucson: University of Arizona Press.

van der Leeuw, S. E., and A. C. Pritchard. eds. 1984. *The Many Dimensions of Pottery. Ceramics in Archaeology and Anthropology*. Amsterdam: University of Amsterdam.

Waiman-Barak, P. 2016. "Circulation of Early Iron Age Goods. Phoenician and Egyptian Ceramics in the Early Iron Age – An Optical Mineralogy Perspective." Ph.D. diss., University of Haifa.

Waksman, Y. 2017. "Provenance Studies: Productions and Compositional Groups." Pages 148–61 in *The Oxford Handbook of Archaeological Ceramic Analysis*. Edited by A. M. W. Hunt. Oxford: Oxford University Press.

Wright, R. P. 1991. "Women's Labor and Pottery Production in Prehistory." Pages 194–223 in *Engendering Archaeology. Women and Prehistory*. Edited by J. M. Gero and M. W. Conkey. Oxford: Basil Blackwell.

Yasur-Landau, A., J. R. Ebeling, and L. B. Mazow, eds. 2011. *Household Archaeology in Ancient Israel and Beyond*. Leiden: Brill.

8
DOMESTIC ARCHITECTURE, THE HOUSEHOLD, AND DAILY LIFE IN IRON AGE ISRAEL[1]

Jeffrey R. Zorn

Introduction

The household was the basic social, economic, political, educational, ritual, and judicial unit in the ancient southern Levant, including Israel, and consisted of a dwelling and its associated objects and installations, its inhabitants (primarily, but not entirely, family members) and their activities (Brody 2011: 239; Oksuz, Hardin and Wilson 2019: 219; Pierce 2021: 259; see also Lehmann and Garroway, both this volume). It also included possessions such as animals, agricultural and grazing land, and possibly a tomb. A house was constructed according to the mental template of its builders as a place of shelter, as a private and not a public space, and once occupied the house also shaped the experiences of those who inhabited it. The house was the physical representation of its inhabitants (Meyers 2012: 225–26). This essay examines the types of dwellings used by average (i.e., non-elite) Israelites of the Iron Age (most of the ancient population), the households which occupied them, and aspects of the daily activities associated with them.

Methods and Limitations

Data on domestic architecture and daily life in ancient Israel come from four main sources: biblical texts, archaeology, ethnographic parallels, and ancient art (Hardin 2012: 521–24). Each of these has inherent strengths and weaknesses. Biblical texts mention many aspects of daily life, which are often useful in describing certain practices (e.g., the song of the vineyard in Isa 5). However, the biblical texts often reflect elite male interests, and where other characters or aspects of culture are portrayed, it is through that cultural lens. For example, storage pits, common in and around Iron Age houses are not at all mentioned in the texts, though the crops (mainly grain) that were most likely stored in them appear often. The texts also mention a variety of construction materials, techniques, and furnishings, but often these are for elite homes, the royal palace, or the temple in Jerusalem, and not the dwellings of common Israelites (e.g., Jer 22:13–15).

Archaeological data does not suffer from the biases of the biblical writers and so has the potential to provide direct data on the lives of typical Israelite families. Yet, archaeological data has its own limits. The best data comes from completely excavated buildings which suffered catastrophic destructions leaving objects of daily use where they were last used, and with walls preserved high enough to show the place of doorways. However, the same destruction that creates and seals such an in situ deposit can also destroy ephemeral objects, such as those made of wood, cloth, or reeds. Even materials which survive such a destruction may not survive centuries in the ground (e.g., various metals). There is no guarantee that an archaeologist will find and be able to completely excavate each room of such a dwelling. In addition, the great majority of buildings did not come to cataclysmic ends and so in situ deposits across all the rooms of a dwelling are relatively rare. Moreover, portable materials may not be recovered in the contexts in which they were used, but in areas where they were stored or left by ancient looters. At times houses were abandoned and the occupants took whatever they could move with them, leaving little for the archaeologist. The ancients also periodically cleaned their dwellings. In such cases only the detritus crushed into floors is found, which may give an idea of the life history of a space, but not its final use. Even if an archaeologist finds and completely excavates a house with in situ deposits there is no certainty that it will be properly and fully recorded, interpreted, or ever published.

Archaeological materials must be interpreted, and this is usually done via comparisons to living cultures which seem similar to the past culture being studied. Ethnographic/ethnoarchaeological inference helps scholars bridge the gap from the modern post-industrial world to the pre-modern rural/agricultural peasant society of ancient Israel. Ethnographic comparisons may suggest ways to explain how and why buildings or objects were used. However, such comparisons cannot be definitive and have their own limitations. Such inference works best when the cultures compared share many obvious traits and where there seem to be direct associations between the compared aspects. However, not all past behaviors necessarily have modern correlates; in some areas and times certain practices may have been common, but not so in others. In addition, ethnoarchaeologists can have their own biases, and, for example, may not report on aspects of a society that may be important to other scholars, or they may only be able to examine the studied culture at certain times of the year and not others. Their informants may not be truthful or willing to discuss certain aspects of their society. Besides using living cultures, analogies can sometimes be drawn from the material remains and texts of cultures that were neighbors of ancient Israel or which were in some ways similar.

Aspects of daily life can also appear in ancient art and iconography. However, other than stamps, seals, and figurines Israel has not produced much that is helpful in this regard. Mesopotamia and especially Egypt do provide welcome data that is chronologically and geographically close to Israel, but it must be used with caution. Not only are these different cultures, but the art reflects the interests of the elites who commissioned it and often only portrays some, and not all aspects of a process.

Building Materials

Because the central hill country of the southern Levant, formed primarily of various types of limestone, was the heartland of ancient Israel it is not surprising that most Israelite domestic architecture made much use of limestone fieldstones. Basalt occurs around the Sea of Galilee and was sometimes used for architecture, though it was probably most commonly used to produce grinding stones used in grain preparation. Load-bearing stone walls were usually constructed in foundation trenches, though sometimes partition and non-load-bearing walls were constructed on a building's floor. Ideally, builders tried to base their walls on bedrock, though on a deep tell site with centuries of accumulated debris they would have to settle on a firm debris layer. Sometimes the stubs of old walls were built on and reused in a new structure. The foundations could be the same width as the wall, or wider, depending on the soil. Fieldstones were usually laid in rough courses. Sometimes the walls were a single relatively large stone wide, but often they were built from two rows of smaller stones, flat faces toward the exterior of the wall, with the core between

Figure 8.1 View of central-western section of the plan in Figure 8.7, showing typical 3RH and 4RHs, looking north. Top arrow shows stairs leading down into 160.07. Lower arrow marks the opening of Cistern 368 intended to collect water runoff from the street. Fieldstone pillars and interstitial rubble masonry are also visible. Badè Museum Photograph 1299

rows filled with even smaller stones and debris. These stone courses were leveled and held in place by mud mortar and smaller chinking stones (Figure 8.1). Often there was no difference between foundation courses and those above floor level. True ashlar construction of square-cut stones was reserved for elite structures, but stones of near ashlar quality were sometimes used in domestic contexts, mostly at points that required special reinforcing, such as corners, points where walls met, and doorways. Stone pillars could be single monolithic ashlars or stacked flat fieldstones (Figure 8.2). Pillars built up of field stones would become increasingly unstable the taller they became, which might have influenced acceptable door and ceiling heights. Rough ashlars could also be used as lintels for spanning short distances, such as the gaps between pillars (Figure 8.3). Thresholds into houses were usually slightly raised stones and served as a barrier to street runoff. Stones were also used for stairs, either leading down into a house or up to a second story (Figure 8.4). Stone stairs were, however, not common and access to a second story or roof was often likely gained via a wooden ladder. Cobble-size stones were sometimes used to pave certain rooms, though most floors were tamped dirt, or sometimes the bedrock on which the house was built (Braemer 1982: 114–22; 125–29, 133–36 Hirschfeld 1995: 245; King and Stager 2001: 21–23; Netzer 1992b: 17–22, 26; Reich 1992: 1–5, 9–16).

Clay, besides serving as a mortar, was used for mold-made, sun-dried mudbricks, piled or rammed wall construction, wall plaster, roofing, and various installations (e.g., ovens and bins; Figure 8.5). The clay was often mixed with chopped straw as a binding agent (Exod 5:7–18). Mudbrick walls were usually constructed on fieldstone socles at least several courses high to keep the bricks away from surface moisture. Mudbricks might also be used for pillars. Mud plaster on walls (Lev 14:41–45) and roofs, sometimes whitewashed (Ezek 13:10–18), was vital for preserving the underlying stones, bricks, and timbers from erosion and decay and needed annual renewal. A stone roller was used to compress the mud plaster on the roof. Whitewashed mud plaster might also reflect sunlight, helping to keep interiors cooler during the summer (Braemer 1982: 122–24, 129; Holladay 1992: 309, 1997: 340; King and Stager 2001: 28; Netzer 1992b: 20, 23–25; Reich 1992: 5–7).

Wood (e.g., terebinth, acacia, tamarisk, sycamore, oak, pine) was used for a variety of purposes including doors (also doorjambs and probably lintels), roof beams, pillars (set on stone

Figure 8.2 Rough fieldstone pillars in Room 361 (front) and monolithic pillars in Room 341 (back), looking north (not on the plan in Figure 8.7). Note also the large stone grinding/pounding mortar to the lower left. Walls are of field stones held in place by mud mortar. The pillars in Room 341 rest on a foundation wall and the spaces between the pillars in Room 361 are filled with sections of a rubble wall. Badè Museum Photograph 916

Figure 8.3 Pillar wall with intact lintels between Room 390 and Room 389 in Building 141.03, looking north. Clearance below lintels is about 1.10m high. Badè Museum Photograph A1165

Figure 8.4 Stairway leading down from Street 514 into Room 594 of Building 159.01, separated from Room 592 (right) by a row of fieldstone pillars with interstitial sections of rubble wall, looking northeast. Badè Museum Photograph 1292

bases or a stone floor), for the construction of temporary structures/booths (e.g., Neh 8:14–17; Isa 1:8; Job 27:18) and possibly for features like cages/coups. Larger timbers necessary to span wide rooms were harder to acquire, so rooms tended to be narrow, ca. 2.0–2.5m typically. The available wood beams had to support not only the heavy mud roof but also any objects stored on the roof and any people present there. It is sometimes suggested that relatively wide rooms were open courtyards because of problems in securing strong enough timbers that were also long enough to span such spaces. The roof timbers, which were integrated into the tops of the walls, helped reinforce and brace the upper courses, keeping them from collapsing if the roof was maintained. Such cross timbers also allowed relatively thin walls to support a second story. As noted, access to upper parts of houses was often likely by a wooden ladder (Braemer 1982: 110–11, 129; King and Stager 2001: 23–27; Netzer 1992b: 23–25; Reich 1992: 7–8, 12–14).

While stones, earth, and wood were the primary construction materials, other resources were used as well. Reeds and/or brush were used as a layer between the beams and mud in a roof and possibly for other installations. Lime plaster might be used for floors or to coat the inside of a cistern (Braemer 1982: 137; Netzer 1992b: 23–24; Reich 1992: 9, 16).

Certain aspects of Israelite house construction, however, remain largely undetectable because they are not mentioned in texts and do not typically survive archaeologically. For example, because doors and their frames were likely wood and so do not survive it is uncertain how they were hinged, or if and how a door could be locked. It is also unknown if interior entryways between rooms ever had doors or cloth partitions/hangings (Braemer 1982: 132–33).

When a building or settlement was destroyed in whole or in part (e.g., by war, earthquake, or accident) and rebuilt, the earlier remains were simply leveled off to allow for new construction. This resulted in the raising of floors and surfaces in the area. Stones might be robbed out for new walls and the resulting robber trenches backfilled. Sometimes a building or part of a building would reach the end of its useful life and be intentionally torn down, or abandoned, and salvageable materials (e.g., wooden roof beams and doors) would be recovered and reused (Netzer 1992b: 27).

Figure 8.5 The lower part of an oven built up of clay and broken potsherds, located in Street 514, looking south. Behind the oven is an olive press reused in a later wall (see caption Figure 8.8). Badè Museum Photograph 1428

In all, the building materials and techniques employed in Israelite houses were simple and ready at hand, and house construction was likely a household matter (perhaps with guidance from those in the kin group with the most experience in such matters), though where neighboring buildings shared walls decisions and work were likely shared across extended families. Also, while some tasks, such as gathering stones over an extended period might be done by an individual, other tasks, such as putting up a roof, could be done more efficiently by a larger group from an extended family.

The combination of stones, mudbricks, mortar, and cross timbers created structures that were quite durable if they were maintained, though they were susceptible to earthquake damage. However, just because materials were simple and accessible, and construction knowledge was a traditional skill, does not mean that the construction of an Israelite dwelling was a quick and simple task. Construction of such blocks of houses required a vast amount of resources and coordination of effort. Rough estimates involving such a two-story house suggest that construction required several hundred tons of stone, over 100 tons of mudbrick (this does not include mud used as mortar or plaster), tens of tons of timber, and unquantified amounts of other materials such as brush, reeds, straw, lime, etc. Collecting all the materials (including any quarrying, shaping of timbers, and the making of bricks) and then building a house could take months of human and animal labor, which was time potentially lost to subsistence tasks since construction would have to take place during fair weather, which was also when harvesting and much agricultural processing took place (Clark 2003: 37–42). However, certain materials, like straw, would have been abundant after threshing and winnowing and some materials could be salvaged for reuse in new construction. At some hill country sites, rock-cut storage pits and cisterns are found in and around houses, and the hewing of such underground features, done in advance of house construction, required significant additional labor and planning (though the work may also have provided additional building stone). Some degree of planning was also required to create the narrow roads that wound through a walled settlement. The plumb line was known (Amos 7:7–8) and Ezekiel mentions the use of a standard-length measuring reed in his vision of a rebuilt temple (40:3). House walls were usually built in relatively straight lines and to a uniform thickness, suggesting the use of the builder's line (Netzer 1992b: 21–22). However, corners rarely meet at a 90° angle, suggesting that devices like the builders' triangle were not used. Not insisting on strict orthogonality allowed houses to better fit the local topography (e.g., the town wall and the street might follow the natural contour lines of the hill).

Floors were rarely level, often sloping upwards toward the adjacent walls. In some cases, this was intentional to prevent water from concentrating in the critical interface between floor and wall; in other cases, it was probably unintended. Structures on tells are often built on meters of debris, much of it organic, which loses about 90% of its volume in the first decades after deposition (Shahack-Gross et al. 2005: 1427, 1430). The surface of a tell was in constant subsidence at different rates due to how much organic debris vs. consolidated deposits there was underground. This is not necessarily a deficiency. The main need for flat floors is to stabilize furniture. If there is little or none (see below) this is obviated. On the other hand, since most ceramic containers had round or pointed bases, they can be more securely placed in small hollows in the floor or between protrusions.

House Contents

Texts occasionally mention various kinds of household furniture, such as tables, chairs, beds, and couches but often in contexts that suggest homes of the well-to-do or royalty (Amos 6:4;

2 Kgs 4:8–10). It is unclear what furniture, if any, would have been found in a typical house. Most likely Israelites sat and slept on their floors. It is unknown if rugs were in use. Bedding was likely bundled up and stashed away against walls when not in use (Dever 2012: 174–76). Most of the contents of a typical Israelite dwelling were likely various kinds of containers such as ceramics, baskets, and sacks used primarily for food storage, along with various implements required for preparing and serving/consuming food and drink, looms, and farm equipment (e.g., plows) along with permanent or semi-permanent installations such as ovens and querns.

House Forms
Basic Types

While houses are mentioned often in the Bible, their forms and the arrangement and functions of their rooms are not described. Archaeology provides most of the data on Israelite houses. The most well-known and ubiquitous house types found in the Iron Age southern Levant, especially within the area of ancient Israel, are the Four-Room House (4RH) and the Three-Room House (3RH) of which several hundred examples are known (Braemer 1982; Holladay 1997: 337; Shiloh 1987: 3–4). The basic spatial divisions of the 4RH are even replicated in a type of Judahite tomb that becomes especially common in the 8th century (Faust and Bunimovitz 2008: 150). The 4RH and 3RH are roughly rectangular structures in which a broad back room is fronted by three or two elongated front spaces of roughly equal length (King and Stager 2001: 28–29). Any of these rooms may be divided into smaller spaces by cross walls which may be added or removed according to the needs of the occupants. Often, though not always, the walls between the central long room and one or both side rooms are constructed in whole or in part of a row of pillars, spaced about one meter apart and constructed on fieldstone foundations that run the length of the pillar wall. Sometimes the space between pillars is filled by a section of rubble wall or a trough for use as a manger (Stager 1985: 14). The side rooms are often paved, at least in part, with stone cobbles, while the central room and back room are often of stamped earth. Sometimes an extra side room is added to one or two sides of the core structure. In addition, there may be an extra unit of rooms and/or a broad open courtyard attached to the front or side of such a building. Occasionally there may be an extra back room. Israelite 4RH/3RH were small. Individual rooms were typically in the range of 6–8m long by 1.5–3.0m wide for side rooms and 2.5–4.0m for main rooms. Ground floor plans indicate that the footprints of most urban houses were in the range of 50–75m^2, with only a few dwellings reaching a size of around 120m^2, and those predominantly in the rural sector (Faust 1999). As discussed below, the usually relatively small size of these buildings affects debates involving the presence of open courtyards and second stories (Netzer 1992b: 24–25; Schloen 2001: Tables 5, 7, and 9).

Often the entrance to these buildings is in the central room of a 4RH or one of the long rooms of a 3RH, which is often the wider of the long rooms. Doorways were typically 0.60–1.10m wide. Access to the other rooms is usually from this main, wider space. Some rooms had no doorways and would have to have been entered from above. Ground floor heights were likely in the range of 1.6–2.0m (e.g., the house in Figure 8.6), but apparently, not all rooms had ceilings of such a height as demonstrated, for example, by the low in situ stone lintels found in one house at Tell en-Naṣbeh (Figure 8.3; Braemer 1982: 128; Holladay 1997: 338; Stager 1985: 11). Possibly such a low space was used for penning animals, or perhaps the ancient Israelites had different standards for acceptable door heights. It is uncertain how common windows were in typical Iron Age houses. In crowded urban settings, adjacent houses often shared walls or were built so close to each other that windows had no

A Look at the Daily Life in Iron Age Israel

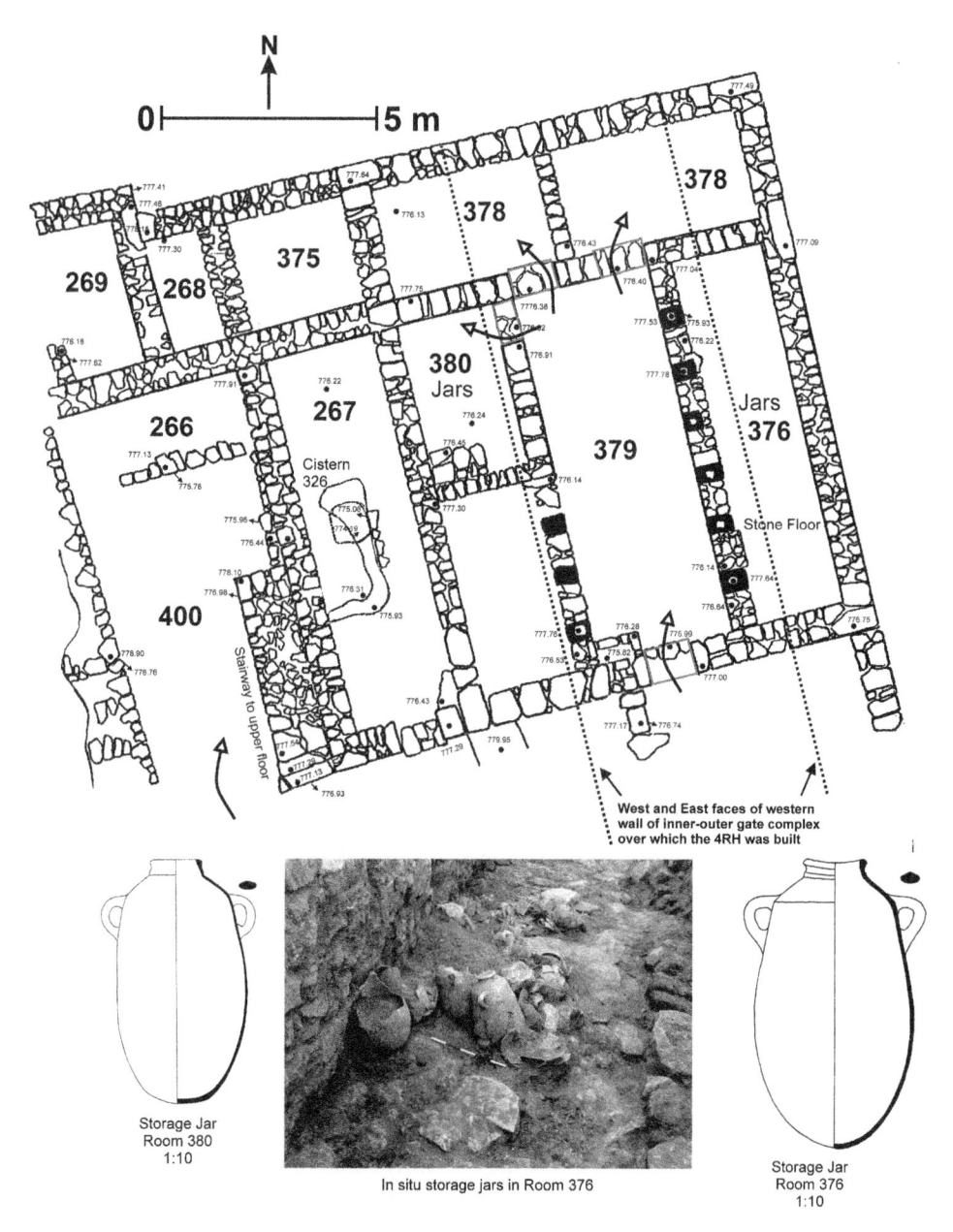

Figure 8.6   4RH 110.01 of Stratum 2 (Neo-Babylonian–Persian periods), located just inside the outer two-chamber gate; indicates that this house type continued in use beyond the destruction of Jerusalem in 586 BCE. Access into the core part of the building was through the central Room 379 and access into all rooms on the ground floor was from Room 379. The western annex (Room 400 et al) seems to have been entered separately from the main part of the building. The stairs in Room 400 indicate the presence of at least a partial second story or useable roof area. The highest elevation on any of the monolithic stone pillars (black squares) is 777.78 and the floor seems to be ca. 776.20, indicating a minimum ceiling height of ca. 1.6m. Scale 1:125. Badè Museum Photograph A922. Plan adapted from Plans 93 and 110 in Badè Museum

use. Moreover, house walls are generally not preserved high enough to provide evidence of window openings. For security, privacy, and temperature control any windows were likely narrow. Houses along the periphery of a site could have outward-oriented back rooms arranged in a band as a kind of casemate-like wall or houses could be integrated into an actual casemate fortification (Braemer 1982: 130–32, 143–45; Hardin 2010: 160).

Houses of these types are found in large urban sites, smaller towns and villages, and scattered homesteads. While the 4RH and 3RH are very common, they are not the only house types found at likely Israelite sites. There are Two-Room structures and multi-chamber buildings that bear no resemblance to the 4RH or 3RH. Especially large and fine urban versions of the 4RH, often set off by themselves, even functioned as the dwellings of high officials (Holladay 1992: 316; Shiloh 1970: 183–88).

Space needs varied over a household's lifecycle. Houses served the needs of their inhabitants, and their plans could be relatively easily modified depending on those needs. Neighborhoods were defined more by social/kin relationships than by architecture (Schloen 2001: 110). As a result, house boundaries were fluid. Houses could expand or contract to mirror the growth or shrinkage of a household by adding or subtracting rooms, especially in cases where related households spread across several contiguous houses. An entire room in a neighboring house could be added by blocking all doorways from that room into the neighboring structure and opening an entrance to the room in the wall between the two houses. Because of the organic expansion and contraction of households and the houses they occupied, the houses themselves were likely grouped along family/lineage lines along narrow streets and even blind alleys, and not according to a formal urban plan.

Origins and Distribution

As with most archaeological origins, the origins of the 4RH/3RH are uncertain and there is no scholarly consensus (Bunimovitz and Faust 2003: 411; Fritz 2007, 116–17; Stager 1985: 17). Some have suggested that the plan developed from the tent structures of presumed nomadic Israelite forebearers (Shiloh 1987: 6–7). This is based on ethnographic parallels to nomadic tents functioning as a broad room with a stone-built courtyard in front. Others suggest that the plan evolved from pillared houses of the Late Bronze Age, best exemplified at Tel Batash (Finkelstein 1988: 244–58; Holladay 1997: 337). The evidence to support either theory is scanty. Others have even argued that this house plan emerged congruent with the Israelites themselves, and has no forerunners (Holladay 1992: 310–11).

Because houses of this type are found predominantly in areas associated with the Israelites, many scholars link the origin of the 4RH/3RH to the Israelites and some see these structures as a type of *fossile directeur* that helps identify sites as Israelite, even suggesting a special connection to the Israelite mindset and way of life (Bunimovitz and Faust 2003; Faust and Bunimovitz 2014). However, an increasing number of such houses have been found beyond Israelite territory, such as at Philistine Tell Qasile and at Tell es-Sa'idiyeh and Tell Umayri in Jordan. Either 4RHs and 3RHs were known and used to some extent by Israel's neighbors, or the existence of these houses outside of core Israelite territory indicate the presence of Israelites in those areas (Holladay 1992: 310). What is reasonably clear is that buildings of this type begin to appear in the 12th century (Netzer 1992a: 193–95; Shiloh 1987: 6), become increasingly common thereafter, and at least some houses of this type continued in use from the Babylonian Period well into the Persian Period, as for example at Tell en-Naṣbeh (Figure 8.6).

Nature of the House
Function

Houses reflect the ever-changing lifecycles of their households which grow and contract over time. The Israelite house had to provide space for living/sleeping quarters, work/cooking space, and areas for various kinds of storage, such as food and drink in jars, pits, baskets, sacks and cisterns, fuel for cooking (brush and dung; Ezek 4:15), chaff and straw, animals, and items like bedding, clothing, tools, and so on (Holladay 2009: 65). Food stores were especially important because the threat of drought necessitated keeping multi-year reserves on hand whenever possible. The house also functioned as a locus of hospitality, where strangers were transformed, for at least a while, into members of the household. Not surprisingly, data related to the ground floor is best attested. Roof or second-story activities can only be surmised when it is possible to identify deposits on top of collapsed ceilings (Herr 2009: 196; Meyers 2002a: 286). Most ground floor space was devoted to storage, food preparation and cooking, weaving, penning of animals, and certain aspects of cult. However, room functions likely shifted seasonally, and even over the course of a day, depending, for example, on the weather, lighting, and the timing of tasks. A single cookie-cutter approach will not work, and it must be acknowledged that despite many similarities, each house and household will present distinct aspects (Holladay 1997: 337–40; 2009: 65–68).

Issues

There are two key interrelated issues that frame debates about the nature and functions of Israelite domestic architecture manifested in the 4RH/3RH, which in turn affect the understanding of other aspects of Israelite society. First is the existence/nature of second stories, and the second is whether Iron Age houses had open courtyards or were completely roofed over. These two issues, along with problems estimating the amount of living space required per person, for example, impact efforts to establish population estimates for individual dwellings, settlements, and entire regions.

Second Stories

Several texts indicate that the flat roofs of Israelite houses were used for various purposes, such as sleeping (1 Sam 9:25–26), drying agricultural products (Judg 2:6), and even cultic activities (Jer 19:13, 32:29; Zeph 1.5; Hardin 2010: 176–77). House roofs were supposed to have parapets for safety reasons (Deut 22:8); such parapets would also have caused water to accumulate on the roof and possibly this water was diverted to a cistern by a drainpipe/gutter (Braemer 1982: 137; Stager 1985: Figure 8). Texts also occasionally mention rooms on a second story (2 Kgs 4:10). However, the texts do not give any indication of how common such rooms were or much about activities above the ground floor. Because no Iron Age houses have survived above their roof levels it can be difficult to determine if a house had a built-up second story, or the amount of potentially useable roof space. Sometimes stairs are found that indicate access to an upper (or lower) story. In Tell en-Naṣbeh Stratum 3 the lower floors of houses along the downhill side of the ring road were entered via stairs leading down from the road, indicating that the roof was at approximately street level (see Figures 8.1, 8.4, and 8.7). Occasionally it is possible to isolate in situ items on a lower floor from those that collapsed from a second story (Herr 2009: 194, 196). Thick, substantial walls might also indicate the presence of a second story over part of a house. On the other hand, thin walls

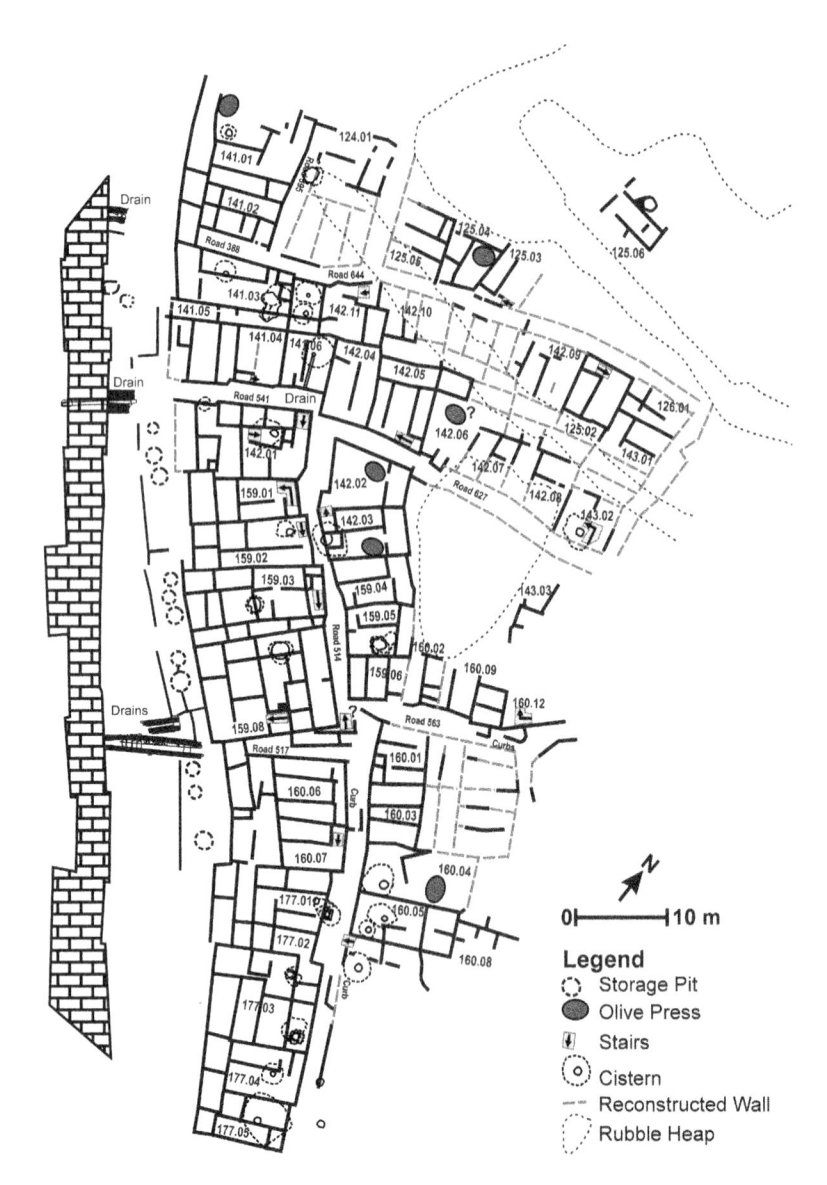

Figure 8.7 Schematic plan of the western side of Tell en-Naṣbeh showing partial reconstruction of house plans and road layout. The olive presses in 142.02 and 142.06 were found reused in later nearby walls; a crushing basin was found in 142.02, so the location of a companion piece there seems reasonable; the second press is tentatively assigned to 142.06 because of its open plan, similar to 142.02. Scale 1:666.67 (the odd scale and orientation off of true north were dictated by the small page size). Plan adapted from Plans 141, 142, 143, 158, 159, 160, 176, and 177 in Badè Museum

are not necessarily evidence against a second story. Sometimes houses are very small, and if the ground floor space was taken up with spatially demanding activities such as bulk storage, animal pens, and cooking there may not have been any choice but to use a second story for other necessary purposes, even if the walls do not seem sturdy enough (Brody 2011: 241–42;

Figure 8.8 The covered mouth of Cistern 363 in Room 617 in Building 141.06, looking north. The drain channel fed water to the cistern from the street just beyond the crouching figure. Badè Museum Photograph 1433

but see Netzer 1992b: 21). Ethnographically, second stories are attested across the Near East and are usually the household's living/sleeping spaces in summer. They are also attested as areas for drying crops (Josh 2:6). Travel between houses could also be done across rooftops (Dever 2012: 178; Holladay 1997: 340; Kramer 1982: 88). It is likely then that most houses had at least partial second stories and the debate then is more over how extensive they were (Netzer 1992a: 196–97).

Courtyards

Closely related to the issue of the presence and nature of the second story of Israelite houses is the debate over whether these houses possessed open courtyards (Oksuz, Hardin, and Wilson 2019: 237–38). In the past, it was often suggested that the widest long room of a 3RH, or the central room of a 4RH, functioned as an open courtyard, though this is less commonly accepted at present. Various arguments can be offered on both sides of the debate (Dever 2012: 151–54).

Those who argue for an open courtyard note several factors. In a crowded, densely packed settlement of narrow streets and blind alleys houses with no courtyard would have had poor lighting and ventilation, making interior conditions unpleasant (Fritz 2007: 114–16; Schloen 2001: 109). Many of the rooms suggested as courtyards possess ovens or a hearth. If they were roofed spaces, they would have often been filled with smoke from dung-fueled fires. In the summer, such cooking activities, coupled with the lack of ventilation, would have led to uncomfortable heat buildup. It may be noted that many Iron Age houses have cisterns, which were likely fed from roof runoff most likely directed into a courtyard or from adjacent streets (see Figures 8.1 and 8.8; Dever 2012: 152–53 n. 16; as were wells in courtyards at Ugarit, Schloen 2001: 320).

There are several arguments against the existence of open courtyards (Braemer 1982: 153; Holladay 2009: 70; Netzer 1992a: 196–97; Stager 1985: 15–16). An open courtyard would be unusable during inclement weather. A courtyard in, for example, a 3RH would severely limit the amount of available roofed living and storage space and the available roofed space might then not support estimated sizes for typical families. An open central courtyard in a 4RH could potentially cause problems in moving from the left to right wings of the house if the rest of the second story was built up. In some instances (e.g. Shechem; Holladay 1992: 316) what appears to be a roof was found over a space which might be expected to have served as a courtyard.

In this debate, however, it should be noted that courtyard houses have a long history in the ancient Near East and the Mediterranean world, even in areas with more severe weather than Israel, including the northern Levant, stretching from at least the Bronze Age to the modern era. For example, at Ugarit, most of the houses seem to have had at least one courtyard to provide light and ventilation (Schloen 2001: 109). Ethnographic studies indicate that open courtyards in pre-modern parts of the Middle East had a variety of functions. They provided a place for cooking during the summer that did not trap heat inside the house that could stay shady for much of the day, even in the summer. They were also the site of wells and coops. They were used for temporary storage, weaving, shearing, milking and milk processing, and cooking and baking in ovens (Kramer 1982: 91, 108–09). Similar observations have been made regarding traditional Palestinian dwellings where courtyards were used for food preparation and eating, sleeping, laundry, seasonal crafts, meeting space, storage, and as the location of cisterns (Amiry and Tamari 1989: 17; Canaan 1933: 22–25; Hirschfeld 1995: 272–74, 279, 290).

The available data suggests the possibility of a middle course in these two debates, especially when Israelite family structure is also considered (mentioned below; see also Lehmann, this volume). That is, not every Israelite house had to fit a single template. Some dwellings may have had an internal courtyard, others not. Some may have had a complete second story, while others may have had partial second stories, or only had a roof surface. These differences might be explained by the presence of extended families occupying their own contiguous blocks of houses. Under favorable conditions, the female members of such related households may have gathered in the open internal courtyard of one of their houses for some activity (Meyers 2002b: 23–25). For example, the women of an extended family might gather to grind grain and bake bread in a shared oven in one house's courtyard in good weather (which would also save on fuel), but in rainy or snowy conditions they may have gathered to use an oven in one of the completely roofed dwellings. This would help explain why ovens and hearths, while common, are not found in every house. Indeed, sometimes they are found in streets outside a house (Figure 8.5). Such considerations may have also determined where women gathered to weave. Similarly, not every dwelling would need a complete second story. For example, a section of open roof would be useful for drying crops, so, perhaps the members of a related set of households reserved the roof of one of their dwellings for such a purpose, while another building had a complete second story, while a third contained an open courtyard. At Tell en-Naṣbeh not every house had a cistern, which is perhaps explainable if cisterns were shared across an extended-family in several dwellings (Figure 8.7). Such cisterns would likely be located in the houses with courtyards. Ethnoarchaeological data may tend to support this middle course since not all such houses studied have complete second stories; one study noted that only half the houses had a second story (Kramer 1982: 134).

Stables

It has been suggested that some side rooms, especially those with stone floors and troughs between pillars were animal stables. Stone floors would better support the weight of animals and would make it easier to muck out straw and filth. Such stables would protect animals in winter and their body heat would help warm the home. However, some houses do not have any stone paving at all, and some rooms with stone paving seem to have been used for storage (Figure 8.6; Holladay 1997: 339; Stager 1985: 12–15). These are additional indicators that one model does not fit all the data and that rooms may change purpose depending on family needs.

Sanitation

Little is known about how Israelites disposed of human waste. Only a few toilets with cesspits have been found in Jerusalem and Lachish (King and Stager 2001: 71–75). During the day, probably most men relieved themselves in the fields, though not always (e.g., 1 Sam. 25:22). How human wastes were dealt with inside settlements is less clear. Apparently, human excrement, probably combined with straw, could be used as a fuel for cooking fires (Ezek 4:12). It is unknown whether other excrement was left in the streets and partially washed away during rain, or perhaps was left in ruined parts of buildings, or if it was collected and dumped outside the settlement (Dever 2012: 185). Biblical texts do not mention chamber pots, though such were known in Roman Palestine (Hirschfeld 1995: 277). Cisterns were likely breeding grounds for mosquitoes and thus vectors for disease. Some cisterns, linked to streets, may have been contaminated by human and animal waste.

House Orientation

Another issue involves whether Israelites favored a specific orientation for their houses. Some (Faust and Bunimovitz 2003: 29, 2014: 154–55) have argued that Israelite houses tended to face toward the east because of Yahweh's association with the sun. However, other factors are just as likely to be involved. For example, in tightly clustered hilltop settlements house orientation likely depended on the slope, the presence of pre-existing structures, and where alleys were located since houses had to front on to those (e.g., Figure 8.7 in which it is clear that no preference for orientation is apparent). An eastern facing might also be connected to the angle of sunlight and shade at different times of the year and how those affected household activities.

Meaning of House Size and Quality

Possibly significant differences in building size, quality of construction materials and techniques, and the nature of small finds correlate with greater wealth and/or prestige and reflect the dynamics of kin groups expanding and contracting through marriage, adoption, and taking on clients/dependents (Faust and Bunimovitz 2014: 149–50; Routledge 2009: 53–60). The better houses might be inhabited by the leading families, who governed related households of the patronymic associations clustered around them in nearby and adjoining buildings (Schloen 2001: 150–51). The basic 3RH/4RH plan is, however, common across sites, and both come in a range of different sizes indicating that house type itself was not a status marker (Holladay 1992: 316–17).

Purity

Some (Faust and Bunimovitz 2003: 29) have argued that Israelite houses were designed to allow women to remain hidden for reasons of impurity, but others contend that the texts containing these laws originate from late sources and were not operative in the Iron Age (Meyers 2009: 36, n.1).

Inhabitants and Demography

Family Structure and Family Size

As in most societies, the family was the most basic Israelite social unit, and the needs of the family are reflected in the form and contents of the Israelite house. Moreover, such families were enmeshed in broader social networks across their settlement, and beyond (Meyers 1997: 36–38). They were also dynamic and fluid. Families went through lifecycles of expansion and contraction as members were born, aged, died, or left/joined the family in some other way (e.g., marriage, adoption), which is also reflected in changes in their houses.

The smallest Israelite social unit was the nuclear family, consisting of a conjugal couple and their children. However, these nuclear families also typically belonged to larger kinship networks consisting of the oldest living male and his wife/wives, his adult sons and their wives and children, unmarried daughters, and perhaps other dependent members of the broader kin group (widows, orphans), as well as dependent individuals not directly part of the kin group; such as servants and slaves, hired workers, guests/visitors (e.g., the story of Micah in Judg 17; Pierce 2021: 260). The family members, their dwelling(s) and belongings (including land), and their activities made up the household. Such households were what the biblical texts call a *bêt-'āb*. These were largely self-sufficient economic units based on reciprocity, producing enough for their own purposes, with some set aside in storage and some left over for barter. The extended-family was the biblical ideal, but due to high mortality rates individual nuclear-families were likely as common if not more common. Multiple households were tied together into larger kin-based networks which the biblical writers generally call a *mišpāḥā*, best rendered in English as "patronymic association," "lineage," or less adequately as "clan" and likely often inhabiting contiguous blocks of houses in a settlement (Hardin 2010: 177–85). Above this level was the even looser association called a *šēbeṭ* or *maṭṭeh* rendered as "tribe" which, while still expressed in terms of kinship (even if fictive), is often based more on the geographical area inhabited (Dever 2012: 157–58; King and Stager 2001: 35–40). In such a society, the interests of the individual were subordinated to the needs of the family (see Lehmann, this volume).

Because of uncertainties over whether Israelite 4RH/3RH possessed open courtyards, over the extent of roofed first and second stories, and over the amount of roofed space required by people in traditional societies there is equal uncertainty over the nature (nuclear or extended) and size of the families which occupied these dwellings. A 3RH with a ground floor plan of 51m^2 and all three rooms of equal size could be occupied by very different numbers of people, and therefore types of families, depending on the assumptions made. If one assumes 10m^2 of roofed/person, a completely roofed over, single-story house of this size could accommodate five people. If one room were an open courtyard, the available roofed space would be 34m^2, enough for three people. If there were a complete roofed second story (doubling the ground floor space), there would be 102m², enough for ten people, while with an open courtyard there would be 68m², or enough for about seven people. In other words, the same basic floor plan could accommodate anywhere from 3 to 10 people at 10m²/person. If one assumes a need for less roofed space per person, for example, 8m², then the same structure could accommodate from 4 to 12/13 people. With a smaller estimate, the example dwelling would seem more suitable for a nuclear-family, while the larger estimate might favor an extended-family. A larger 4RH of 80m², following the above parameters of rooms of equal size on the first and second story and 10m² of roofed space could accommodate from five inhabitants (one floor with open courtyard) to as many as 16 (two stories, completely roofed; Holladay 1992: 312; Pierce 2021: 259–60; Schloen 2001: 168; 174–75).

Given these uncertainties, it is not surprising that there is disagreement over the nature of the households that inhabited such dwellings. Some scholars (e.g., Stager 1985: 18–23) believe that typical Israelite houses were occupied by nuclear-family households of typically 3–7 individuals, and that a larger extended-family of 10–30 people was clustered together in a neighborhood consisting of several adjoining houses. Other scholars (Schloen 2001: 126, 148 n. 21, 167–69) argue that around one-third of dwellings were occupied by extended-family households, though because of high birth and high mortality rates, these would have been on the small side (family size average seven and household size ten) and about two-thirds were occupied by nuclear-family households (family size average about 3.5 and households about five). Because of deaths resulting from multiple childbirths, women typically did not live much beyond 30 and men not beyond 40 (Dever 2012: 201; Meyers 1997: 18; Schloen 2001: 123). For this reason, three-generation households would be rarer than those of two generations. Under both the above scenarios, the various extended families, found either in individual houses or spread across several houses, were then part of larger patronymic associations.

Some scholars note differences in average house sizes between urban (smaller) and rural (larger) contexts and argue that the larger rural dwellings housed larger extended families and that the smaller urban dwellings housed smaller nuclear families (Faust and Bunimovitz 2003: 25–27, 2014: 147–49). Others explain the dichotomy in urban vs. rural house sizes in terms of the nature of the settlement (Schloen 2001: 140–41). Houses in unfortified villages and homesteads tended to be large because more space was available, whereas houses in fortified urban centers tended to be smaller due to the necessity of crowding as many people as possible inside the fortifications. The types and sizes of families remained the same in the two contexts, but each individual had more room in the non-urban setting.

Israelite Settlements

Most Israelites lived in villages and towns of half a hectare to 3–4 hectares in size located on the top of a hill (see also G. Pierce, this volume). In the Iron Age I, these were mostly unfortified, or semi-fortified, with outward-facing backrooms of houses on the periphery of the settlement serving as a sort of casemate-like wall, while in the Iron Age II many were fortified with large, solid walls. Some Israelites also lived in scattered open homesteads. Only a few sites were much larger. Even the largest of Israelite settlements were small compared to cities in neighboring Mesopotamia and Egypt. For much of the Iron Age, Jerusalem was only 16 hectares, and only swelled to about 57 by the end of that period (by comparison, Nineveh was 750 hectares). Lachish, Judah's second-largest settlement was only about 8 hectares. Unfortified settlements tend to have no obvious plan, whereas fortified sites often follow a ring road plan (Figure 8.7 shows part of the ring road plan with crossroads at Tell en-Naṣbeh). In such a plan, a band of 4RH/3RH, with backrooms faced outward, ranged around the periphery of the site following the natural contours of the hill and fronted inward onto a road running around the site, with or without interruptions. Another band of houses fronted the same road on the opposite side of the road. Additional roads would run across the center of the site and there could be more roads depending on the size and layout of the settlement. Walled Iron Age towns were crowded. Areas around gates were likely the main open spaces where significant numbers of people could gather (Herzog 1992: 258–63; Shiloh 1978: 36–46, 1987: 8–11).

Estimating the population of ancient settlements is notoriously difficult and dependent on various assumptions. Such estimates are usually based on population density coefficients applied to the presumed built-up area of the settlement. Often these are based on the estimated number of houses found in each area at a site and then extrapolated across the entire site. Yet estimates of the number of inhabitants per dwelling vary widely, which leads to wide variances in site-wide estimates (Dever 2012: 71–72, 151, 156). Another important factor is the nature of the settlement itself. A densely crowded, fortified rural settlement (e.g., Tell en-Naṣbeh) would have had more inhabitants per hectare than a regional center with more space devoted to public architecture (e.g., Lachish or Megiddo) or than a small unwalled village (e.g., Khirbet er-Rasm). Coefficients have therefore ranged from about 200/hectare up to 500/hectare (Schloen 2001: 165–82).

Depending on assumed population densities, the smaller settlements and homesteads probably had populations of around 50–150, with larger towns up to a thousand, and regional centers up to a few thousand (Dever 2012: 48–49). The smaller sites were likely occupied by a single patronymic association, and the larger towns by several such associations, probably living in adjoining houses clustered into neighborhoods. Based on evaluations of architectural and artifactual remains there was not a great deal of social stratification in these towns and villages. More such social variation would have been present in regional and national centers such as Lachish and Jerusalem.

Daily Life

Agriculture and Food

In pre-industrial societies, most people were agriculturalists of one sort or another. Israel was no different. Agricultural practices and products are mentioned repeatedly in the Hebrew Bible as aspects of daily life and are also used as metaphors. Most people, whether they lived in a village or a city, were farmers and pastoralists. Indeed, even government officials and many craft specialists likely spent some time in agricultural pursuits. Israel's cultic calendar was aligned with major agricultural events (e.g., Deut 16:1–16; King and Stager 2001: 353–54). Food was available seasonally and needed to be stored for future use. In ancient Israel most families likely had a diversified subsistence base that relied, depending on location, on some combination of grains (mainly wheat and barley), olives (as oil), and grapes, known as the "Mediterranean triad." Most of the caloric values came from grains and legumes (providing a protein supplement since meat was reserved for special feasts) (see Welton, this volume).

The variety of food strategies exploited was necessary to mitigate the droughts, locust invasions, and famines that were endemic to the region. Planting, tending, harvesting, processing food, maintaining buildings and equipment, and a myriad of other tasks consumed the time of Israelite families which had to be self-sufficient, at least on the patronymic association level. Some of these activities, such as harvesting, required intense, sustained labor by all members of the family in a narrow window of time. Storage media included mainly ceramic containers, storage pits, above-ground silos or bins, baskets, and sacks. Because agriculture was the key to survival for most Israelites, the inalienability of land and rules of inheritance, usually through the male line, appear in various contexts in the biblical texts (e.g., Num 27:1–11; Num 36; Meyers 1997: 19–21).

Room and Space Functions

Archaeological research of well-excavated and well-published individual houses, combined with ethnographic studies, have provided welcome data that allows for a better understanding of how the rooms in Israelite houses may have functioned.[2] These studies also suggest that rooms may have had multiple functions depending on the season, or even the time of day, and that room functions changed with the lifecycle of the occupants of the house. Some factors were more permanent, such as the size of a room, or the presence of heavy or unmovable installations/objects (e.g., an oven or oil press), though the size of a room could be altered, and a heavy stone object could be moved if needed. A room reserved for a widowed mother or used for penning animals could be repurposed for additional storage after the mother's death or if the herd decreased in size. On the other hand, some objects and activities could be more easily shifted around a dwelling. So, a room might be used for weaving at one point in the day, but for cultic activity, food preparation, etc. at some other point; a single space could potentially be used simultaneously for several activities (Hardin 2010: 142–43, 147, 155–60). However, it is important to remember that because a paved side room of one studied house in its final period of use may have been used, for example, as a stable does not mean that all paved side rooms in ancient Israel always had this function. Additionally, it is likely that related households shared resources and activity spaces, and so not every house had to contain the same features as its neighbors. Several hill country sites contain olive press installations scattered across the settlement (Schloen 2001: 138; Figures 8.7 and 8.9). However, not every house had its own press. Most likely a single olive press served the needs of several households belonging to a patronymic association. Olive pressing was a seasonal activity, but the bulky, heavy presses were not easily moved. To what purposes were these spaces adapted after the pressing was complete? Thus, the archaeological remains found in a single dwelling (an oven, olive press, clusters of loom weights, cistern, etc.) may indicate activities beyond the household level that incorporated a larger kinship unit (Holladay 1992: 315–16).

Even with these caveats, a few generalizations may be made. Cisterns and storage pits clearly belong to the ground floor. In addition, due to weight considerations, much of the ground floor space of any house would have been taken up with storage. This would include penning areas for the household's animals, space for bulk food storage, and tools. It has been estimated that in a society heavily dependent on grain for basic subsistence around 150–250kg of wheat/barley per person would be required annually (Schloen 2001: 144–45). One estimate (Holladay 1992: 314) suggests that around 90 *lmlk* type jars, occupying an area of ca. 23m^2 (or less, if stacked) would be required simply to store a typical family's total grain requirements (including amounts set aside for seed, longer-term storage, taxation, and accounting for waste, and so on) and not including space requirements for other typical food stocks such as oil, wine, and legumes. This also does not include space that would have been used for storing other bulky materials like dung and brush. Heavy stone implements such as mortars, grinding stones, and olive presses were also likely on the ground floor, though occasionally querns are found in roof collapse. Cooking in an oven would have been done on the ground floor. Small objects, used on an ad hoc basis (ceramics such as cooking pots, bowls, etc., tools/agricultural implements) may have been stored when and where space was available. At least one living/sleeping space per house would be needed, more if a house were occupied by more than a single nuclear family. Probably such living spaces were on the second floor to escape summer heat. Open roof spaces could be used for sleeping in the summer and for drying crops. Some activities were more portable and could be practiced anywhere. For example, spinning thread and weaving cloth could be done on the ground floor in the vicinity of the oven, but could also be done on the second story.

Education

The knowledge necessary for survival in a world of dry farming and herding was passed on in the home. This included not only how to raise, process, and store food, but also knowledge of the environment around the settlement. Skills involving house construction and maintenance were acquired in the family. Professions were largely hereditary, so any skills, such as potting, were passed on through the family. Family and kin-network traditions were learned in the family as well as whatever was known of national history. Religious beliefs, proper ways to foster ties to the god of the family, wisdom traditions, poetry and mythology and attendant rituals were also part of the education provided by the family. Parents also exercised considerable judicial authority (King and Stager 2001: 45–46, Meyers 1997: 30–32).

Gender and Social Roles

Many household tasks were divided along gender lines. Male roles tended to be seasonal and punctuated (clearing land, building terraces, house construction, hewing tombs and cisterns, plowing, sowing, threshing, winnowing) and usually away from the house, while female roles were more daily and continuous throughout the year (food production, spinning and weaving, basketry, gathering/producing fuel, procuring water, washing, bearing and raising children) and more centered in the home. Space was also gendered. Some spaces were more used by women, others more by men. Even when space use overlapped/was shared, how the space was viewed likely differed. However, men's and women's efforts had to be integrated. If men did not clear and plow the land, there was no grain for women to grind and turn into bread. Moreover, children would have worked as soon as they were able and for as long as they could. Of course, there were parts of the year when time was of the essence, such as during harvests, when all family members who could participate did so. Yet even in these joint efforts, gender roles were in play such as men cutting the grain and women collecting and binding it into sheaves (Ruth 2; Meyers 1997: 24–27, 2002b: 18; King and Stager 2001: 146–58).

Because the house was the focus primarily of female activities many of the objects and installations found in houses provide more data on the roles of Israelite women, rather than men. In fact, it is possible to say that more is now known archaeologically about the daily activities of Israelite women than of men (see Ebeling, this volume).

The activities carried out by men and women were part of social processes that helped create/shape identities and communal bonds. Each group had its own social networks that arose from associated communal tasks. So, groups of women gathered to share in tasks such as food production and weaving. Men might have to gather for larger tasks such as terrace and house construction. Moreover, male networks could be strengthened through work for the state in corvee work gangs and military service, tasks often far from home but probably organized along kin lines.

Figure 8.9 Olive press (left) and crushing basin (right) in Room 662 in Building 125.04, looking north. Badè Museum Photograph 1471

Notes

1 All illustrations used in this article are used by permission of the Badè Museum, Pacific School of Religion.
2 The field of household archaeology as applied to the area of ancient Israel and its neighbors has burgeoned considerably in the last two decades. Some of the many recent examples and discussions, and additional references, can be found in Gadot and Yasur-Landau (2006), Hardin (2010), Herr (2009), and especially in Yasur-Landau et al. (2011).

Bibliography

Amiry, Suad, and Vera Tamari. 1989. *The Palestinian Village Home*. London: British Museum Press.
Braemer, Frank. 1982. *L'architecture domestique du Levant à l'âge du Fer*. Paris: Éditions Recherche sur les civilisations.
Brody, Aaron J. 2011. "The Archaeology of the Extended Family: A Household Compound from Iron II Tell en-Naṣbeh." Pages 237–54 in *Household Archaeology in Ancient Israel and Beyond*. Edited by Assaf Yasur-Landau et al. Leiden: Brill.
Bunimovitz, Shlomo, and Avraham Faust. 2003. "Building Identity: The Four-Room House and the Israelite Mind." Pages 411–23 in *Symbiosis, Symbolism, and the Power of the Past: Canaan, Ancient Israel, and Their Neighbors from the Late Bronze Age through Roman Palaestina*. Edited by W. G. Dever and S. Gitin. Winona Lake: Eisenbrauns.
Canaan, Taufik. 1933. *The Palestinian Arab House: Its Architecture and Folklore*. Jerusalem: Syrian Orphanage Press.
Clark, Douglas R. 2003. "Bricks, Sweat and Tears: The Human Investment in Constructing a 'Four-room' house." *NEA* 66: 34–43.
Dever, William, G. 2012. *The Lives of Ordinary People in Ancient Israel: When Archaeology and the Bible Intersect*. Grand Rapids: Eerdmans.
Faust, Avraham. 1999. "Differences in Family Structure Between Cities and Villages in Iron Age II." *TA* 26: 233–52.
Faust, Avraham, and Shlomo Bunimovitz. 2003. "The Four Room House: Embodying Iron Age Israelite Society." *NEA* 66: 22–31.
———. 2008. "The Judahite Rock-Cut Tomb: Family Response at a Time of Change." *IEJ* 58: 150–70.
———. 2014. "The House and the World: The Israelite House as a Microcosm." Pages 143–164 in *Family and Household Religion: Toward a Synthesis of Old Testament Studies, Archaeology, Epigraphy, and Cultural Studies*. Edited by Rainer Albertz et al. Winona Lake: Eisenbrauns.
Finkelstein, Israel. 1988. *The Archaeology of the Israelite Settlement*. Jerusalem: Israel Exploration Society.
Fritz, Volkmar. 2007. "On the Construction of the Four-Room House." Pages 114–18 in *"Up to the Gates of Ekron": Essays on the Archaeology and History of the Eastern Mediterranean in Honor of Seymour Gitin*. Edited by Sidnie W. Crawford et al. Jerusalem: W.F. Albright Institute of Archaeological Research and Israel Exploration Society.
Gadot, Yuval, and Assaf Yasur-Landau. 2006. "Beyond Finds: Reconstructing Life in the Courtyard Building of Level K-4." Pages 583–600 in *Megiddo IV: The 1998–2002 Seasons*. Edited by Israel Finkelstein et al. Tel Aviv: Emery and Claire-Yass Publications in Archaeology, Institute of Archaeology, Tel Aviv University.
Hardin, James W. 2010. *Lahav II: Households and the Use of Domestic Space at Iron II Tell Halif: An Archaeology of Destruction*. Winona Lake: Eisenbrauns.
———. 2012. "Household Archaeology in the Southern Levant: An Example from Iron Age Tell Halif." Pages 519–56 in *New Perspectives on Household Archaeology*. Edited by Bradley J. Parker, and Catherine P. Foster. Winona Lake: Eisenbrauns.
Herr, Larry G. 2009. "The House of the Father at Iron I Tall Al-'Umayri, Jordan." Pages 191–98 in *Exploring the Longue Durée: Essays in Honor of Lawrence E. Stager*. Edited by J. David Schloen. Winona Lake: Eisenbrauns.
Herzog, Zeev. 1992. "Settlement and Fortification Planning in the Iron Age." Pages 231–74 in *The Architecture of Ancient Israel from the Prehistoric to the Persian Period*. Edited by Aharon Kempinski and Ronny Reich. Jerusalem: Israel Exploration Society.

Hirschfeld, Yizhar. 1995. *The Palestinian Dwelling in the Roman–Byzantine Period*. Jerusalem: Franciscan Printing Press.

Holladay, John S. Jr. 1992. "House, Israelite." *ABD* 3: 308–18.

———. 1997. "Four-Room House." *OEANE* 2: 337–42.

———. 2009. "'Home Economics 1407' and the Israelite Family and Their Neighbors: An Anthropological/Archaeological Exploration." Pp. 61–88 in *The Family in Life and in Death: The Family in Ancient Israel: Sociological and Archaeological Perspectives*. Edited by Patricia Dutcher-Walls. New York: T&T Clark International.

King, Philip J., and Lawrence E. Stager. 2001. *Life in Biblical Israel*. Louisville: Westminster John Knox Press.

Kramer, Carol. 1982. *Village Ethnoarchaeology: Rural Iran in Archaeological Perspective*. New York: Academic Press.

Meyers, Carol. 1997. "The Family in Early Israel." Pages 1–47 in *Families in Ancient Israel*. Edited by Leo G. Perdue et al. Louisville: Westminster John Knox Press.

———. 2002a. "From Household to House of Yahweh: Women's Religious Culture in Ancient Israel." Pages 277–303 in *Congress Volume Basel 2001*. Edited by André Lemaire. Leiden and Boston: Brill.

———. 2002b. "Having Their Space and Eating There Too: Bread Production and Female Power in Ancient Israelite Households." *Nashim: A Journal of Jewish Women's Studies & Gender Issues* 5: 14–44.

———. 2009. "In the Household and Beyond: The Social World of Israelite Women." *Studia Theologica - Nordic Journal of Theology* 63: 19–41.

———. 2012. "Feast Days and Food Ways: Religious Dimensions of Household Life." Pages 225–50 in *Family and Household Religion: Toward a Synthesis of Old Testament Studies, Archaeology, Epigraphy, and Cultural Studies*. Edited by Rainer Albertz et al. Winona Lake: Eisenbrauns.

Netzer, Ehud. 1992a. "Domestic Architecture in the Iron Age." Pages 193–201 in *The Architecture of Ancient Israel from the Prehistoric to the Persian Period*. Edited by Aharon Kempinski and Ronny Reich. Jerusalem: Israel Exploration Society.

———. 1992b. "Massive Structures: Processes in Construction and Deterioration." Pages 17–27 in *The Architecture of Ancient Israel from the Prehistoric to the Persian Period*. Edited by Aharon Kempinski and Ronny Reich. Jerusalem: Israel Exploration Society.

Oksuz, Latif, James W. Hardin, and Jared Wilson. 2019. "The K8 House: A New Domestic Space from the Iron Age II at Tell Halif, Israel." *PEQ* 151: 218–44

Pierce, George A. 2021. "The 'Four-Room-House' Complex at Tell Dothan, Area A: An Analysis of Function, Demography, and Cultural Identity." Pages 249–65 in *To Explore the Land of Canaan: Studies in Biblical Archaeology in Honor of Jeffrey R. Chadwick*. Edited by Aren M. Maeir and George A. Pierce. Berlin: de Gruyter.

Reich, Ronny. 1992. "Building Material and Architectural Elements in Ancient Israel." Pages 1–16 in *The Architecture of Ancient Israel from the Prehistoric to the Persian Period*. Edited by Aharon Kempinski and Ronny Reich. Jerusalem: Israel Exploration Society.

Routledge, Bruce. 2009. "Average Families? House Size Variability in the Southern Levantine Iron Age." Pages 42–60 in *The Family in Life and in Death: The Family in Ancient Israel: Sociological and Archaeological Perspectives*. Edited by Patricia Dutcher-Walls. New York: T&T Clark.

Schloen, J. David. 2001. *The House of the Father as Fact and Symbol: Patrimonialism in Ugarit and the Ancient Near East*. Winona Lake: Eisenbrauns.

Shahack-Gross, Ruth, Rosa-Maria Albert, Ayelet Gilboa, Orna Nagar-Hilman, Ilan Sharon, and Steve Weiner. 2005. "Geoarchaeology in an Urban Context: The Uses of Space in a Phoenician Monumental Building at Tel Dor (Israel)." *JAS* 32: 1417–31.

Shiloh, Yigal. 1970. "The Four-Room House: Its Situation and Function in the Israelite City." *IEJ* 20: 180–90.

———. 1978. "Elements in the Development of Town Planning in the Israelite City." *IEJ* 28: 36–51.

———. 1987. "The Casemate Wall, the Four Room House, and Early Planning in the Israelite City." *BASOR* 268: 3–15.

Stager, Lawrence E. 1985. "The Archaeology of the Family in Ancient Israel." *BASOR* 260: 1–35.

Yasur-Landau, Assaf, Jennie R. Ebeling and Laura B. Mazow, eds. 2011. *Household Archaeology in Ancient Israel and Beyond*. Leiden: Brill.

9
MONUMENTS, MONUMENTAL ARCHITECTURE, AND MONUMENTALITY IN ANCIENT ISRAEL

Kyle H. Keimer

Introduction

Since the days of Morgan (1881), it has been recognized that architecture—the human-built environment—reflects social relations within and among cultures; all architecture is a cultural product (cf. Love 2013). Specific architectural designs reflect the compromise between needs and costs and are unique to specific contexts (Abrams 1989; McGuire and Schiffer 1983). In ancient Israel, specific architectural forms have been identified and associated with the Israelites—the four-room house in particular—and have been part of the larger discussion of how to identify a group's material expression of cohesion and identity. Aside from a few studies (Faust 2005, 2017; Faust and Bunimovitz 2003), however, most studies on architecture, "monumental" or domestic, have not integrated the essential social element in the discussion. Instead, architecture and what makes a building monumental have been summarized, described functionally, and tied to sociopolitical complexity in ways that assume evolutionary social forms that are anachronistic and/or problematic in their specific application to ancient Israel and other ancient Near Eastern cultures.

Ancient Israel's social structure was tribal. According to the biblical texts, from the late 11th century BC until the 6th century BC, these tribes organized as one or more kingdoms wherein individuals from one or more tribes were elevated to the position of king. This reality is important to understand as part of any discussion about monuments, monumental structures, and the concept of monumentality. As Love (2013: 751) notes, "social conditions have equal, if not greater, influence on the material outcome than do the type, availability or abundance of raw materials." This goes for the selection of the type of material being used, the form of structure/monument being built, and the place within the hearts and minds of the people taking in the finished product.

Monumental architecture traditionally has been contrasted to domestic architecture; the former is for administrative and/or communal purposes and is built by the governing authority, while the latter is for familial/individual purposes and is built by individual families/clans. Similarly, monumental structures are perceived as larger in size than domestic structures. Thus, the difference between monumental and domestic architecture is an issue of both size and function.[1] While this distinction has merits, it implies that we know what was significant for ancient populations and how something of significance should appear materially. Though this may be possible, it is by no means equivocal; we are not always able to identify or articulate what ancient peoples thought was significant or how they reified materially those items, ideas, and/or symbols, particularly if we are lacking texts from that people group. Our values cannot be imposed upon those of antiquity uncritically or even potentially categorically. Moreover, the idea that large buildings mean coherent and/or centralized political rule is an equation that must be evaluated. If we want to discuss monuments, the monumental, and monumentality (3M) in ancient Israel, then we need to begin by defining what we mean by these terms. To do this, we draw upon relevant theoretical discussion before turning to a chronological appraisal of 3M in ancient Israel.

Defining Terms: Monuments, Monumental, and Monumentality

The term "monumental" is ubiquitous in the literature on ancient Israel, but it is seldom defined. In fact, it has been used rather fluidly to refer to large structures and/or structures that imply political presence or development. Trigger (1990: 119) defined monumental architecture as a building whose "scale and elaboration exceed the requirements of any practical functions that a building is intended to perform." This implies that there are elites and non-elites, the former wielding enough influence and/or power over the latter that the latter do the formers' bidding. But, in the ancient Near East, patrimonialism reigned as a social construct (Schloen 2001). The separation between elite and non-elite was not always as marked as is assumed. When one's social world is structured on the family, the main power dynamic is always dyadic and relational, and less so quantifiable in terms of wealth possession or other types of physical capital. Additionally, more recent studies on 3M have articulated how the term "monumental" needs to be applied to contexts in addition to the realm of architecture. Objects, ideas, and even places can be considered monumental. Thus, something can be defined as monumental if it stands out because of its execution, meaning, and/or impact on viewers (Hogue 2021: 2; Pauketat 2014; Smoak and Mandell 2019: 310). To determine whether something should be defined as monumental requires considering not only its tangible aspects but also its symbolic or ideological aspects as well. The latter lead us into the cognitive realm and are essential for defining our other terms: monument and monumentality.

Osborne (2014: 3) defines and distinguishes a "monument" from "monumentality," likening the two terms to art historians' form and meaning, respectively. Further, monuments are things-that-do; they memorialize, which both draws people to the past and prompts them to interpret the present. There is thus a relational aspect to monuments even though they (can) stay the same physically; how they are understood and what they stand for changes over time—sometimes rapidly (Osborne 2017: 88). In Osborne's words (2014: 10), monuments:

> activate social memory...perhaps more obvious manifestations of the materialization of memory are those monuments, especially memorial sculptures, that are created with the explicit goal of reminding people about significant places, events, or people.

In this regard, monuments can also materialize ideology (DeMarrais et al. 1996; Glatz 2009: 136). An object's (or building's) monumentality, therefore, is "an artefact's potential to anchor conceptual integration networks from which social structures emerge" (Hogue 2021: 1).

In both definitions, what constitutes a "monument" and what makes something "monumental" are culturally and historically defined (cf. Wu 1995: 4; Jackson and Wright 2014: 117). Within a given context, monuments are both constitutive and causal of community-level imagination as Hogue argues (2021: 5). A monument becomes monumental when its monumentality is accepted by a given social network. The larger the network, the greater a monument's monumental stature becomes, and its monumentality is actualized. For example, the Ark of the Covenant can be considered a monument. This object was small in size but created a conceptual network wherein YHWH was understood to be present and associated with the people utilizing the Ark. Its monumentality grew over the generations as its use in military and ritual situations affirmed YHWH's presence with Israel. The place the Ark held in the collective imagination by the time David brought it to Jerusalem made David's action monumental and set the tone for later biblical authors' understanding of YHWH's selection of Jerusalem for residence.

Additionally, standing stones (*mazzebot*) are monuments; their erection can be a monumental act; and their monumentality is established through their ability to remind people of specific events and to serve as conceptual markers for group identity (e.g., Gen 28:18–22; 35:20; Josh 4:2–8, 20–24). Equally monumental are auditory monuments such as David's lament for Saul and Jonathan, as van Bekkum (2017: 174) notes.

With our definitions for our 3M in place, one thing that must be stated is that there is a false connection between monumentality and centralized political control. The reality is more often the opposite; when a polity is weakly organized, monumentality becomes a way of projecting authority and maintaining a situation (Erasmus 1965: 278; Kaplan 1963; Marcus 2003). Additionally, monumental construction readily appears in societies that are not centralized or in which there is no centralizing government. More accurately, we can say that monumentality can be associated with central places, with the recognition that what makes a place "central" is contingent upon any number of variables (ideological, economic, social, political, etc.). Underlying everything, however, is an evolving or living network of social relations where integrative and agreeable outcomes must be established between two or more parties for monumentality to become possible.

While monumental projects can be the result of forced labor at the behest of a ruling elite, they can also be the result of community pride and honor (Cowgill 1964: 154). Ancient Israel, as with most of the cultures in the ancient Near East, utilized honor and shame for productivity, social normalization, and prestige gathering. Tribes and/or clans could be motivated to participate in the production of monumental projects through affective elements in addition to displays of power. Such monumental projects could also be for economic, social, or ritual purposes to the exclusion of political reasons (e.g., the establishment of the Tabernacle at Shiloh).

Thus, tribal-level social organization can result in monumental buildings—i.e., buildings that stand out due to their meaning, impact on viewers, and/or their execution.[2] To be sure, the latter does/can include the scale of a building and can refer to the building's overall size and/or to the size of the constructional elements of which it is comprised. Establishing a given building's monumental stature requires a case-by-case evaluation based on its context within a given site and/or across a given geographical realm. At the same time, the use of particular materials can also capture the imagination of a conceptual integration network and further an ideology: the use of basalt for monumental inscriptions (cf. Keimer 2015); lapis lazuli for (heirloom) seals; cedar wood for buildings.

Before continuing, it is important to clarify the concept of the "palace" as this term is often qualified by the concept of being "monumental." Reich (1992: 202) defines palaces as:

> buildings which served as royal residences of the monarch, members of his family and his household staff, and functioned as centers of administration due to the offices of the

ruler and the court officials located in them. Also defined as palaces are official buildings which served as residences and offices of high officials, local rulers, governors of districts and towns, etc.

He goes on to say that:

> there is little difficulty in distinguishing between palaces and ordinary private houses. This is easily done on the basis of architectural differences, such as the size of the building and its location in the most desirable area of the city, the limited number of palaces in a city in comparison with ordinary houses, the extensive use of rare and costly building materials in palaces, and the types of small finds recovered from the buildings which attest to the owner's superior rank. The palace also generally contained an audience or throne room in which the monarch received his subjects and functionaries. Special annexes—treasure houses, archives, etc.—were sometimes also included in the palaces.

It is the multiplicity of categories that Reich outlines that makes his definition commendable. It is not just the size of the building or of the stones making the building—though these are certainly valid considerations—but it is the small finds, type of construction materials, location within a given site, and the presence of unique rooms all viewed together that suggest a building's monumental status. Of course, we must offer a couple of caveats to Reich's definition: (1) it does assume the presence of a royal component in a society, and, by extension negates the possibility of non-monarchic or local, non-/sub-monarchic power players from having palaces, something that is problematic considering archaeological evidence from across the Near East (Fleming 2012); (2) some of the aspects mentioned are only preserved in destruction layers at best, meaning that some tell-tale elements of monumental stature are archaeological happenstance. Not to mention, unless texts are found, the identification of specific rooms or buildings as treasure houses, archives, or having other functions is reliant upon the remaining archaeological materials and the archaeologists' interpretation.

The Iron Age I

We transition now to look at both the archaeological and textual evidence for 3M in ancient Israel. We do not see monumental stones—stones requiring either specialized knowledge for fashioning them into specific shapes and/or that require more than two to three people to move—utilized in "Israelite" construction for most of the Iron I. Such stonework only begins to appear toward the end of this period, in the late 11th or early 10th century. Monumental buildings, however, appear already in the mid-Iron I.

Archaeology

Israelite 3M in the Iron I is difficult to establish. Outside of the Central Hill Country, wherein sites are typically referred to as "Israelite," it is difficult to establish whether any sites in the Shephelah, valleys, and/or Galilee should be considered "Israelite." Large buildings that stand out in comparison to surrounding structures are clearly present in this period, but the best examples come from sites not typically identified as Israelite in the Iron Age I (e.g., Building 2072 at Megiddo, Str. VIA;[3] Building 350 at Ekron, Str. V; the Area D Building at Kh. er-Ra'i, Str. IX). Perhaps Shechem's *migdol* temple fell into Israelite hands, but this depends on how one interprets the Abimelech narratives in Judg 9 (cf. Stager 1999).

One exception is the large structure on Mt. Ebal, which has been identified as Joshua's altar, mentioned in Josh 8:30 (Zertal 1986). Not everyone agrees on this specific interpretation, but regardless this structure is large and unique and may have served as a central site for cultic or other activities in the region. Another is the open-air shrine known as the "Bull Site," located northeast of Shechem. This site was poorly preserved and built of fieldstones in a circular pattern (Mazar 1982). More substantial is the tower at Giloh (Building 105).[4]

Text

According to the books of Judges and 1–2 Samuel, which purport to describe the Iron Age I period (12th through early 10th centuries), there are some structures that we could consider to be monumental. The Tabernacle and the Ark of the Covenant are the main ones described in the text, though neither remains archaeologically. Both find their origins in New Kingdom Egypt, which provides the best, if not only parallels, and highlight an Israelite worldview as developed out of an Egyptian context (cf. Falk 2020). Reference is also made to the Temple of Baal/El Berit (Judg 9:4, 46) and a city gate (Judg 9:35, 40, 44) at Shechem; the towers (*migdalim*) of Shechem (Judg 9:46, 49), Peniel (Judg 8:9, 17), and Thebez (Judg 9: 51–52); Gaza's city gates (Judg 16:2) and Temple of Dagan (Judg 16:26–30); and the House of Micah (a temple complex? Judg 18:2–3). There are also implied and explicit references to city walls in the books of Joshua and Judges. These features, which are attested archaeologically at several sites are what led ten of the 12 spies to doubt Israel's ability to enter Canaan.

Joshua 4:2–8, 20–24 recounts how Joshua set up 12 stones taken from the Jordan River. An accompanying rationale is provided: so that when future generations ask about the meaning of the stones, an opportunity is provided for the Israelites to recount how YHWH is mighty, as evidenced by his separation of the waters of the Reed Sea and the Jordan River. In this instance, a physical monument leads to the remembrance of Israel's "monumental" God. In fact, in early Israel, it appears that oral stories, such as this, and/or songs achieved monumental status (e.g., the Passover; Exod 15; Judg 5) and created the foundation for later religious expression.

Meaning

In both the archaeological record and biblical sources, monumental structures are largely cultic in nature in the Iron I. This belies the fact that monumentality is derived from the religious sphere and not the political in this period. The uniting element of cult—even if such cult was manifest in various material ways instead of one uniform way—allowed pan-tribal affiliations to develop and cohere even as they evolved (see Pierce and Keimer, this volume).

The Iron Age II

Archaeology

Early Iron IIA[5]

The early Iron IIA (10th century) attests to numerous monumental structures. Free-standing city walls with large, well-built gates appear (see Table 9.1). The earliest Israelite site with

Table 9.1 Select sites in Israel/Judah with a representative list of their monumental architecture

Site (N-S)	Iron I	Early Iron IIA	Late Iron IIA	Iron IIB	Iron IIC
Dan		City gate; fortifications; cultic compound	City gate; fortifications; cultic compound	City gate; fortifications; cultic compound	
Hazor		Casemate wall; city gate	Solid city wall	Pillared building; water system	
H. Tevet					
Beth Shean		Administrative compound (Buildings A–C)	Administrative compound		
Megiddo		Building 1723; Palace 6000; casemate wall; city gate	Building 338; water system; solid wall; city gate; pillared buildings	Pillared buildings; city gate; solid wall	
Jezreel			Administrative compound		
Samaria			Administrative compound; palace; water system(?); fortifications		
Kh. Marjameh				Tower; city wall	
Tell en-Nasbeh				Massive grain storage	
Gezer		Palace 10,000; casemate wall; city gate	City wall; city gate		
Tel Motza			Cultic building	Cultic building; massive grain storage	
Jerusalem	SSS, LSS	SSS, LSS, Far House; administrative building; the straight wall; Temple		Broad wall; Silwan tombs	Manasseh wall
Kh. Qeiyafa		Area A building; casemate wall; city gates			
Ramat Rahel				Administrative complex	Administrative complex

these features is Kh. Qeiyafa where "proto-ashlars" (i.e., roughly rectangular hewn stones) first appear and were used in the city gates (Keimer 2014).[6] Such hewn stones improve in quality over the course of the Iron IIA. By the mid- to late 10th century, similar fortifications and stones appear at Megiddo (Str. VB-VA/IVB), Hazor (X–IX), Gezer (VIII), and then even later at Lachish (IV) where Podium A was also constructed. This latter feature is understood to be the foundation for a Judahite palace from the very end of the 10th or early 9th century. Additional buildings that are monumental in size or that are built of larger stones were erected at Megiddo (Building 1723, Palace 6000) and Gezer (Palace 10,000), while tri-partite/pillared buildings appear at Tell el-Hesi (x3), Tel Malhata, Tel Hadar, Tell Abu Hawam, Qasile, Beth Shemesh, and Tel Masos in this period.[7]

Large buildings and a wall made of large stones have been found in Jerusalem and dated to the 10th century (Mazar 2015: 459–74). Similarly, the Stepped Stone Structure (SSS; Figure 9.1) and Large Stone Structure (LSS) atop it are constructed no later than the beginning of this period (Cahill 2003).

Some early rock-cut tombs appear at this time (Eton Tomb), but these only become more prominent from the later 9th century onward. These tombs are massive undertakings, often including multiple *arcosolia* and, by the 8th century at the latest, repositories for the collection of bones. Suriano (2018) has made the case that such tombs are physical manifestations of Israel's/Judah's understanding of the Yahwistic covenant of land. These tombs represent Israel's connection to the land and to earlier generations. Given the widespread use of these tombs by the end of the Iron Age, we should conceive of them as monuments expressing a collective narrative; one that binds the present with the past.

Cultic architecture is most magnificently displayed at Tel Dan, where a cultic building (temple), altar, and surrounding courtyards were excavated (Figure 9.2; Biran 2008: 32–49). A convincing case has been made that the Northern Kingdom's other main shrine at Bethel was located just northeast of the settlement on a high hill (Tavger 2015).

Figure 9.1 The Stepped Stone Structure in the City of David, Jerusalem

Figure 9.2 The Cultic precinct at Tel Dan

Late Iron IIA

Monumental structures for defensive or administrative purposes continue to appear in the 9th century BCE. In fact, such structures outnumber those that have been excavated from the 10th century (see Figure 9.1). Tripartite/pillared buildings are also far more common. Ashlar masonry becomes more refined, and we even see the adoption of the Phoenician technique of header-stretcher construction (e.g., at Samaria). Stone volute capitals also presumably appear in this period, though none have been found in their primary context (see Franklin this volume).

It is at this time (late 10th/early 9th century) that the cultic structure at Tel Motza appears to have been founded. Though fragmentary, several cultic vessels and some architectural similarities with the description of Solomon's temple in Jerusalem (1 Kgs 6–7) have led to its identification as a temple.

Iron IIB-C

Similar monumental military and administrative buildings persist through the late Iron Age, but toward the end of the 8th century BCE, new monumental phenomena appear: free-standing rock-cut tombs in Jerusalem (Silwan); rock-cut family tombs throughout Judah (though see above); and now a limited number of Assyrian buildings in what was the northern Kingdom of Israel and in the Coastal Plain (see Faust 2021: 152–59). Rectilinear fortresses, which first appear in the late Iron IIA only in Judah (e.g., Arad XI), become more numerous as control over trade through the Arabah and Negev became more contentious between Judah and Edom (Keimer forthcoming).

The impetus for the change in burial practices in Judah is unclear but there is a corresponding shift in iconography in Judah that embraces Egyptian(-izing) motifs that were not as common in the Iron IIA.

In addition to the Motza cultic structure, which continues into the 8th century before being renovated in the 7th (Str. IV; Greenhut 2009), a temple is built at Arad (Str. X–IX). Based on the presence of altar horns at Beersheba, presumably there was a cultic structure there as well, but because the horns were found reused, nothing can be postulated about such a structure.

Other monumental construction projects include public silos (Megiddo Str IVA; Str. II; Tell en-Nasbeh [see Zorn 2022]; Beth Shemesh II) and public water systems (Megiddo; Hazor; Ibleam; Beersheba; Jerusalem; Gibeon; Hebron [text reference and later pool]; Tell es-Sa'idiyeh; Gezer [Macalister reservoir?]; Arad [citadel reservoir]; Kadesh Barnea).

The monumental structures erected by the Neo-Assyrian Empire served a propagandistic purpose. These structures were surprisingly limited, but they were situated at strategic locations and often were prominent landmarks (e.g., at Megiddo and Ad Halom, near Ashdod).

Text

The most significant monumental structure recorded in the biblical text is Solomon's temple, a structure for which there are no archaeological remains. This temple is the cultic core of Israel's and then divided Judah's existence. In the north, Jeroboam's cultic compounds at Dan and Bethel have been identified. Aside from such temples/shrines, the biblical texts tell us that several high places existed throughout much of the Iron Age—until the cultic reforms of Hezekiah in the late 8th century.

The Hebrew Bible also records several different administrative and/or economic buildings that are clearly monumental in their own way. David's *bet hammelek* (house of the king; cf. 2 Chr 25:24) was built using expensive, imported cedar wood and "cut stones" (*even kir*; 2 Sam 5:11; 7:2; 1 Chr 17:1; 2 Chr 2:2). Conceptually, the house of the king is related to other terms for "palace" utilized in Hebrew: *armon, hekhal*. Later, Solomon's palace (1 Kgs 7:1–12) and the "house of the forest of Lebanon" (1 Kgs 7:2–6) were also exorbitantly constructed. Three chapters are dedicated to describing the effort of building YHWH's temple in Jerusalem (1 Kgs 6–8).

We read of *mishkenot* "storehouses" (2 Chr 32:28) and *otsarot* "treasuries" (2 Chr 32:27), the latter of which have been identified with the magazines north of the palace at Lachish (IV), with pillarless halls adjoining buildings at Hazor (VIII–VII), long narrow rooms in the Ostraca House at Samaria, the large hall of Megiddo Building 1482 (VA–IVB), and long room 401 (IVA) (Herzog 1992: 228–229).

The text also records a number of monuments that appear to have expressed monumentality for the author(s) of the biblical text and/or their audiences: Saul's *yad* (1 Sam 15:12), which connects the idea of a marker and the idea of political power; Absalom's *yad*, meant to remind people of him since he had no sons (2 Sam 18:18; see also Isa 56:5); the erection of *mazzebot* and/or altars by several individuals; the Passover and Exodus events, which play a major role in the prophetic tradition (see Aster this volume for more on the prophetic tradition); Nehustan, which took on a cultic role of its own over the course of the Iron Age; Ahab's house of ivory (1 Kgs 22:39; cf. Amos 3:15; 6:4); the golden calves at Dan and Bethel (and in the Exodus); Shebna's tomb in Jerusalem (possibly equated with the tomb of the royal steward in Silwan); and, the Jerusalem Temple itself as the representation of YHWH's presence among Israel (this includes the Tabernacle also).

Meaning

We see large structures built at some point in the early Iron IIA (generally the mid- to late-10th century). These appear at Hazor (city wall, city gate, the presumed "palace" in Area B),

Gezer (city wall, city gate, Palace 10,000), and Megiddo (city wall, city gate, Palace 6000). In each of these instances, these features are rebuilt (in the case of fortifications) and/or built over (in the case of Gezer Palace 10,000 and Megiddo Palace 6000 and Building 1723) in the late Iron IIA (9th century). One way to understand this is that these monumental markers were tied to one political structure and were then de-established in favor of new structures built by a new political structure. One could argue that there is a conscious attempt to replace markers of Judahite control in the north, under Solomon, with markers of more localized control under Jeroboam and/or his successors, the general outline of which is presented in the biblical texts.[8]

Kaplan (1963) already noted that public works are typically built as "accretions over long periods of time" rather than all at once (cf. Pauketat 2000). Whether we are looking at the archaeology or the textual references, monumental structures appear in times of uncertainty or transition. Examples include the transition from Megiddo VA–IVB to IVA, Gezer VIII to VII, and Hazor X–IX to VIII. In each instance the buildings that represented southern, Solomonic control were built over with new buildings representing northern Israelite control. Hazor doubled in size, Megiddo became a "stable city," and Gezer became a border site.

Not only do we see a re-purposing (i.e., "destruction") of buildings 1723 and Palace 6000 at Megiddo from VA–IVB to IVA, but also building 1482 is diminished in size. If, as Herzog proposes (1992: 229), this building housed both a treasury and scribes' chambers, then the omission of the treasury part of the building and part of the scribes' chambers in Str. IVA would indicate that other sites may have adopted those functions (e.g., Samaria and/or Jezreel, or even Tirzah or Tel Rehov). Megiddo in the days of Solomon was a strategic site, but during the period of the divided northern kingdom, its value differed from what it had been earlier.

We need to consider that "monumental" architecture in the 10th century and then again in the northern kingdom in the 9th century is due more to the unstable political situation than it is a marker of actual political stability or development (cf. Marcus 2003). The north, which saw a change of dynasties multiple times was always being re-set politically; each new dynasty needed to exert its authority. This is best exemplified by the fact that the capital of the northern Kingdom of Israel moved three times (Shechem to Penuel to Tirzah to Samaria); each move coinciding with a coup and the establishment of a new line of kings. In the south, this was not necessary as power was firmly ensconced in the Davidic line, but we may have evidence of a similar struggle in the reign of Rehoboam. The list of sites fortified by him in 2 Chr 11:5–12 has occasioned much debate but certainly makes sense considering the present discussion. Rehoboam fortified sites both on the borders of Judah and in its interior to protect against external threat(s) *and* internal rebellion. He had already lost the allegiance of the northern tribes and was on the brink of losing the support of his own tribe as well; his situation was precarious, and he needed a display that highlighted Judahite unity. Thus, the presence of monumental architecture is not necessarily a mark of power and state formation, but a marker of political instability and attempts to display power that was weakly founded (cf. Finkelstein 2000: 132; Williamson 1996).

Focus of the Monumental in Construction and Destruction

Monumental structures and/or objects were those that played a communicative role in the psyche of their ancient Israelite/Judahite audiences. As such there were certain buildings/objects that people granted greater significance. In both the archaeological record and the biblical texts, those objects that established the most extensive conceptual integration networks were cultic and/or political by function; the realms of religion and governance were ubiquitous in the ancient Near East even as they took various forms. They were also the elements of society that carried with them the most authority. It is no wonder that temples and palaces were monumental (physically and/or symbolically)—they played central roles for *numerous* households, clans, lineages, and/or tribes, not just a few. They reached the greatest audience, conceptually.

The centrality of these structures not only played a (positive) role among natives of the culture but also served as lightning rods for making religio-political statements via conquest and destruction of other cultures. Repeatedly, temples and palaces were invaders' targets and served as visual fodder for spreading the (royal) ideology of the invaders. The destruction or conquest of these structures provided the greatest medium for advertising a change in authority. In times of political change, it is such buildings/objects that new powers sought to establish, adopt, adapt, or destroy. Examples from ancient Israel include Jehu's decommissioning of the Ba'al Temple at Shechem (2 Kgs 10:18–28); the decommissioning of the Lachish gate shrine; the destruction of Canaanite Hazor's administrative and cultic buildings and paraphernalia (e.g., Areas A and C in particular).

In the vein of the current discussion, the idea of conspicuous consumption needs to be addressed. While there is no one-size-fits-all in the ancient Near East, those in power, and those who have an established power, do not appear to build monumental works just to show off. Manzo (2017) argues that in ancient Nubia monumental architecture served as the location at which social relationships were enacted through public activity. Within Israel/Judah, the so-called "lateral-access podium" structures were similar locales that enacted both the interaction and separation of governmental entities with/from locals (Sharon and Zarzecki-Peleg 2006).

In the case of the Neo-Assyrian Empire, which was the most powerful of its time, monumental structures similarly served a purpose more than just aggrandizing the ruler. This was true in the heart of the empire at the various capital cities (palaces served real functions as the nexuses of socioeconomic, political, and ideological expression and operation), and on the periphery where monumental structures, albeit conscripted in overall size, were erected. Podium structures appeared in the southern Levant, but these were typically single buildings or a small cluster of buildings. Such was all that was needed to control the local population; major construction projects were unnecessary because everyone knew how powerful the Assyrian Empire was.

Conclusions

We come back to Osborne's statement that, "perhaps more obvious manifestations of the materialization of memory are those monuments, especially memorial sculptures, that are created with the explicit goal of reminding people about significant places, events, or people" (Osborne 2014: 10). There is a shift from the early Iron Age to the later Iron Age. In the early Iron Age, "monuments" were songs and poems, occasional monuments, and cultic structures. In the late Iron Age, cultic structures continue in greater number and administrative/political structures appear in earnest. Overall, structures express monumentality the most in ancient Israel. This is the portrait we have from the biblical texts and the archaeological record.

Occasionally, objects express monumentality—the Ark of the Covenant, Nehushtan, Goliath's sword—but these have not been preserved for us, and there is ambiguity when ascribing monumentality to most archaeological remains in Israel. Many items certainly were monumental, but the fluidity in cultic assemblages and other material remains coupled with the lack of any certain remembrance in the biblical text means we must be cautious when attempting to ascribe monumentality to such items.

Buildings and objects both need to be understood for their functional and symbolic meanings. Structures are needed for protection and shelter, administration, and cultic praxis. Various objects develop to make living life possible. But, in all instances, ancient Israel (as any other culture) ascribed meaning to its physical realia. The concepts of the monument and monumentality extend from their shared experience and imagination and must be considered if we are to appreciate that which was meaningful and valuable to the ancient Israelites. When this is done, it allows for an added level of interpretation to be applied to the archaeology of ancient Israel and the biblical texts.

Notes

1. These distinctions are implicit in Kempinski and Reich's classic volume on architecture in ancient Israel (1992). The use of the term "public" instead of "monumental" attests to a clear awareness of the problem of the latter term, but still assumes that both size and function are what determine a building's publicness. More recent studies have highlighted how the delineation between public and private is not always clear in the ancient Near East (e.g., Garfinkle 2008, 2013; Schloen 2001).
2. We see evidence of tribal cooperation and/or tribal/clan-level exploitation in the biblical text in general (e.g., Judg 5; 1 Kgs 4), though there are no mentions of construction projects in early (pre-monarchic through the reign of Saul) Israel. Such references appear during the monarchic period and even the post-exilic period (e.g., Neh 4).
3. Harrison (2004: 106–108) notes the various features in Str. VI that suggest cultural mixing; there are Canaanite, Philistine, and Israelite elements present.
4. Hawkins (2012: 113–16) makes a strong case that Building 105 at Giloh, and the Mt. Ebal structure served similar cultic purposes (see Pierce and Keimer, this volume).
5. For the early Iron Age, the Modified Conventional Chronology is used.
6. Kh. Qeiyafa spans the late 11th to early 10th centuries BCE. As such it can be considered an Iron Age I- or IIA-period site. It is a transitionary site archaeologically, one that continues some Iron I material culture traditions but has greater affinity with later Iron IIA materials; for this reason, it is put at this point in this discussion.
7. The earliest examples of this type of building come from Tell Hadar, Tel Masos (Building 1039), and Tell el-Hesi, and may have been erected as early as the late 11th century.
8. Regardless of how one dates Strata VB and VA–IVB at Megiddo, there is a clear change in the nature of the site between Str VI and VB, and between Str VB and VA–IVB. If Str VA–IVB is not founded until the late 10th/early 9th century, then the changes at the site could be associated with one of the first kings of the northern kingdom of Israel, or perhaps the Omride dynasty. The change between Str VA–IVB and Str IVA may then be associated with the overthrow of the Omride dynasty by Jehu, and Str VB could be the settlement "built" by Solomon. Of course, 1 Kgs 9 does not clarify what Solomon actually built at Megiddo; there is no reason to doubt Judahite control over the site regardless of the architectural remains because the connection between the monumental structures of Str VA–IVB and Solomon have been made by modern archaeologists and are not an explicit ancient claim (Keimer and Thomas 2022).

Bibliography

Abrams, Elliot M. 1989. "Architecture and Energy: An Evolutionary Perspective." *AMT* 1: 47–87.

Biran, Avraham. 2008. "A Chronicle of the Excavations 1966–1992." Pages 9–63 in *Dan I: A Chronicle of the Excavations, the Pottery Neolithic, the Early Bronze Age and the Middle Bronze Age Tombs*. Edited by Avraham Biran, David Ilan, and Raphael Greenberg. Jerusalem: Hebrew Union College – Jewish Institute of Religion.

Cahill, Jane M. 2003. "Jerusalem at the Time of the United Monarchy: The Archaeological Evidence." Pages 13–80 in *Jerusalem in Bible and Archaeology: The First Temple Period*. Edited by Andrew G. Vaughn and Ann E. Killebrew. Atlanta: SBL.

Cowgill, George L. 1964. "The End of Classic Maya Culture: A Review of Recent Evidence." *SJA* 20: 145–59.
DeMarrais, Elizabeth, Luis Jaime Castillo, and Timothy Earle. 1996. "Ideology, Materialization, and Power Strategies." *Current Anthropology* 37: 15–31.
Erasmus, Charles J. 1965. "Monument Building: Some Field Experiments." *SJA* 21: 277–301.
Falk, David. 2020. *The Ark of the Covenant in Its Egyptian Context: An Illustrated Journey*. Peabody: Hendrickson Publishing.
Faust, Avraham. 2005. "The Israelite Village: Cultural Conservatism and Technological Innovation." *TA* 32: 204–19.
———. 2017. "The Bounded Landscape: Archaeology, Language, Text, and the Israelite Perception of Space." *JMA* 30: 3–32.
———. 2021. *The Neo-Assyrian Empire in the Southwest: Imperial Domination and Its Consequences*. Oxford: Oxford University Press.
Faust, Avraham, and Shlomo Bunimovitz. 2003. "The Four Room House: Embodying Iron Age Israelite Society." *NEA* 66: 22–31.
Finkelstein, Israel. 2000. "Omride Architecture." *ZDPV* 116: 114–38.
Fleming, Daniel E. 2012. "Textual Evidence for a Palace at Late Bronze Emar." Pages 101–09 in *Organization, Representation, and Symbols of Power in the Ancient Near East: Proceedings of the 54th Rencontre Assyriologique Internationale at Würzburg, 20–25 July 2008*. Edited by Gernot Wilhelm. Winona Lake: Eisenbrauns.
Garfinkle, Steven J. 2008. "Was the Ur III State Bureaucratic? Patrimonialism and Bureaucracy in the Ur III Period." Pages 55–61 in *The Growth of an Early State in Mesopotamia: Studies in Ur III Administration*. Edited by Steven J Garfinkle and J. Cale Johnson. Madrid: Consejo Superior de Investigaciones Científicas.
———. 2013. "The Third Dynasty of Ur and the Limits of State Power in Early Mesopotamia." Pages 153–67 in *From the 21st Century B.C. to the 21st Century A.D.: Proceedings of the International Conference on Sumerian Studies Held in Madrid 22–24 July 2010*. Edited by Steven J. Garfinkle and Manuel Molina. Winona Lake: Eisenbrauns.
Glatz, Claudia. 2009. "Empire as Network: Spheres of Material Interaction in Late Bronze Age Anatolia." *JAA* 28: 127–41.
Greenhut, Zvi. 2009. "The Excavations: Stratigraphy and Architecture." Pages 9–60 in *Salvage Excavations at Tel Moza: The Bronze and Iron Age Settlements and Late Occupations*. By Zvi Greenhut and Alon de Groot. Jerusalem: Israel Antiquities Authority.
Harrison, Timothy P. 2004 *Megiddo 3: Final Report on the Stratum VI Excavations*. Chicago: Oriental Institute.
Hawkins, Ralph K. 2012. *The Iron Age I Structure on Mt. Ebal: Excavation and Interpretation*. Winona Lake: Eisenbrauns.
Herzog, Ze'ev. 1992. "Administrative Structures in the Iron Age." Pages 223–30 in *The Architecture of Ancient Israel*. Edited by Aharon Kempinski and Ronny Reich. Jerusalem: Israel Exploration Society.
Hogue, Timothy. 2021. "Thinking Through Monuments: Levantine Monuments as Technologies of Community-Scale Motivated Social Cognition." *CAJ* 31: 401–17.
Jackson, Sarah E., and Joshua Wright. 2014. "The Work of Monuments: Reflections on Spatial, Temporal and Social Orientations in Mongolia and the Maya Lowlands." *CAJ* 24: 117–40.
Kaplan, David. 1963. "Men, Monuments, and Political Systems." *SJA* 19: 397–410.
Keimer, Kyle H. 2014. "Iron Age Stone Quarries." Pages 333–45 in *Khirbet Qeiyafa Vol. 2: Excavation Report 2009–2013: Stratigraphy and Architecture (Areas B, C, D, E)*. By Yosef Garfinkel, Saar Ganor, and Michael G. Hasel. Jerusalem: Israel Exploration Society.
———. 2015. "The Impact of Ductus on Script Form and Development in Monumental Northwest Semitic Inscriptions." *UF* 46: 189–212.
———. forthcoming. "Geographical Factors in the Defense of the Kingdoms of Judah and Israel." *"See the Whole Land Is Before You": New Directions in the Historical Geography of the Ancient Near East*. Edited by Chris McKinny et al. Berlin: De Gruyter.
Keimer, Kyle H., and Zachary Thomas. 2020-2021 [2022]. "Etic and Emic Expressions of Power in Ancient Israel: Recalibrating a Discussion." *JEOL* 48.
Kempinski, Aharon, and Ronny Reich. 1992. "Preface." Pages xi-xii in *The Architecture of Ancient Israel: From the Prehistoric to the Persian Periods*. Edited by Aharon Kempinski and Ronny Reich. Jerusalem: Israel Exploration Society.

Love, Serena. 2013. "Architecture as Material Culture: Building Form and Materiality in the Pre-Pottery Neolithic of Anatolia and Levant." *JAA* 32: 746–58.

Manzo, Andrea. 2017. "Architecture, Power, and Communication: Case Studies from Ancient Nubia." *African Archaeological Review* 34: 121–43.

Marcus, Joyce. 2003. "Monumentality in Archaic States: Lessons Learned from Large-Scale Excavations of the Past." Pages 115–34 in *Theory and Practice in Mediterranean Archaeology: Old World and New World Perspectives*. Edited by John K. Papadopoulos and Richard M. Leventhal. Los Angeles: Cotsen Institute of Archaeology.

Mazar, Amihai. 1982 "The "Bull Site": An Iron Age I Open Cult Place." *BASOR* 247: 27–42.

Mazar, Eilat. 2015. "The Solomonic (Early Iron Age IIA) Royal Quarter of the Ophel." Pages 459–74 in *The Ophel Excavations to the South of the Temple Mount, 2009–2013: Final Reports Volume I*. By Eilat Mazar. Jerusalem: Shoham.

McGuire, Randall H., and Michael B. Schiffer. 1983. "A Theory of Architectural Design." *JAA* 2: 277–303.

Morgan, Lewis Henry. 1881. *Houses and House-Life among the American Aborigines*. Washington: Government Printing Office.

Osborne, James F. 2014. "Monuments and Monumentality." Pages 1–19 in *Approaching Monumentality in Archaeology*. Edited by James F. Osborne. Albany: State University of New York Press.

———. 2017. "Monuments of the Hittite and Neo-Assyrian Empires During the Late Bronze and Iron Ages." Pages 87–105 in *Mercury's Wings: Exploring Modes of Communication in the Ancient World*. Edited by F. S. Naiden and Richard J. A. Talbert. New York: Oxford University Press.

Pauketat, T. R. 2000. "The Tragedy of the Commoners." Pages 113–29 in *Agency in Archaeology*. Edited by M.-A. Dobres and J. Robb. London and New York: Routledge.

———. 2014. "From Memorials to Imaginaries in Monumentality of Ancient North America." Pages 431–46 in *Approaching Monumentality in Archaeology*. Edited by James F. Osborne. Albany: State University of New York Press.

Reich, Ronny. 1992. "Palaces and Residences in the Iron Age." Pages 202–22 in *The Architecture of Ancient Israel: From the Prehistoric to the Persian Periods*. Edited by Aharon Kempinski and Ronny Reich. Jerusalem: Israel Exploration Society.

Schloen, J. David. 2001. *The House of the Father as Fact and Symbol: Patrimonialism in Ugarit and the Ancient Near East*. Winona Lake: Eisenbrauns.

Sharon, Ilan, and Anabel Zarzecki-Peleg. 2006. "Podium Structures with Lateral Access: Authority Ploys in Royal Architecture in the Iron Age Levant." Pages 145–67 in *Confronting the Past: Archaeological and Historical Essays on Ancient Israel in Honor of William G. Dever*. Edited by Seymour Gitin et al. Winona Lake: Eisenbrauns.

Smoak, Jeremy D., and Alice Mandell. 2019. "Texts in the City: Monumental Inscriptions in Jerusalem's Urban Landscape." Pages 309–43 in *Size Matters – Understanding Monumentality Across Ancient Civilizations*. Edited by Federico Buccellati et al. Bielefeld: Transcript Verlag.

Stager, Lawrence E. 1999. "The Fortress-Temple at Shechem and the 'House of El, Lord of the Covenant.'" Pages 228–49 in *Realia Dei: Essays in Archaeology and Biblical Interpretation in Honor of Edward F. Campbell, Jr. at His Retirement*. Edited by Prescott H. Williams Jr. and Theodore Hiebert. Atlanta: Scholars Press.

Suriano, Matthew. 2018. *A History of Death in the Hebrew Bible*. New York: Oxford University Press.

Tavger, Aharon. 2015. "E.P. 914 East of Beitin and the Location of the Ancient Cult Site of Bethel." *In the Highland's Depth* 5: 49–69.

Trigger, Bruce G. 1990. "Monumental Architecture: A Thermodynamic Explanation of Symbolic Behaviour." *WA* 22: 119–32.

van Bekkum, Koert. 2017. "'How the Mighty Have Fallen.' Sola Scriptura and the Historical Debate on David as a Southern Levantine Warlord." Pages 159–82 in *Sola Scriptura: Biblical and Theological Perspectives on Scripture, Authority, and Hermeneutics*. Edited by Hans Burger et al. Leiden: Brill.

Williamson, H. G. M. 1996. "Tel Jezreel and the Dynasty of Omri." *PEQ* 128: 41–51.

Wu, H. 1995. *Monumentality in Early Chinese Art and Architecture*. Stanford: Stanford University Press.

Zertal, Adam. 1986. "An Early Iron Age Cultic Site on Mount Ebal: Excavation Seasons 1982–1987: Preliminary Report." *TA* 13: 105–65.

Zorn, Jeffrey R. 2022. "Standing on Hole-y Ground: The Storage Pits at Tell En-Naṣbeh and the Role of the State." Pages 337–74 in *Material, Method, and Meaning: Papers in Eastern Mediterranean Archaeology in Honor of Ilan Sharon*. Edited by Uri Davidovich et al. Münster: Zaphon.

10
STONE VOLUTES
United by a Common Motif not by a Common Function

Norma Franklin

Stone Volutes and the Volute Motif

Over 55 stone volutes (stone blocks with a volute motif carved on one, or both, faces) have been discovered to date at 16 sites in present-day Israel, Jordan, and Syria (Figure 10.1). The first stone volute was excavated at Megiddo in 1903 by Schumacher. Its carved volute motif was thought to belong to the Ionic order, giving rise to the appellation "Proto-Ionic" or "Proto-Aeolic." Similar volute motifs were already known from Ohnefalsch-Richter's 1889 excavation of two underground burial chambers (Tombs 5 and 12) from the Cypriot necropolis at Tamassos (1896: 10–34). There, the entrances to both tombs were flanked by large stone slabs carved to represent pilasters crowned with a volute motif. The tombs are now dated to the Cypro-Archaic II period (600–480 BCE), and their carved stone decoration is recognized as imitating earlier wood-built tombs (Buchholz, Matthäus, and Walcher 2002: 221, 224–25, 230; Walcher 2005; 2007; Matthäus 2007: 216). Unfortunately, neither Schumacher nor those who came after him, realized that the volute motifs at Tamassos were carved on large stone slabs that served as revetments to hold back the surrounding earth—that is, they were not individual stone volutes. (Figure 10.2A and B). This mistake gave rise to the erroneous idea that all stone volutes were structural capitals.

Stone Volutes from the Northern Kingdom of Israel

Megiddo[1]

The site of Megiddo is unique; not only was the first stone volute found there, but it also has the largest number found at any one site. An in-depth analysis of the volutes' findspots can help provide a date for the initial use of stone volutes as well as help disprove the misconception that they were structural capitals.

The first stone volute (M1)[2] found by Schumacher was in secondary use as a building block in a large Stratum II Assyrian building known as the Fortress. The stone volute's findspot is marked as Wall E at Corner F of Schumacher's Grid Square R30 (1908: Tafel xxxv), later known as Grid Square P13 on the excavation grid of the Oriental Institute of the University of Chicago (OI).

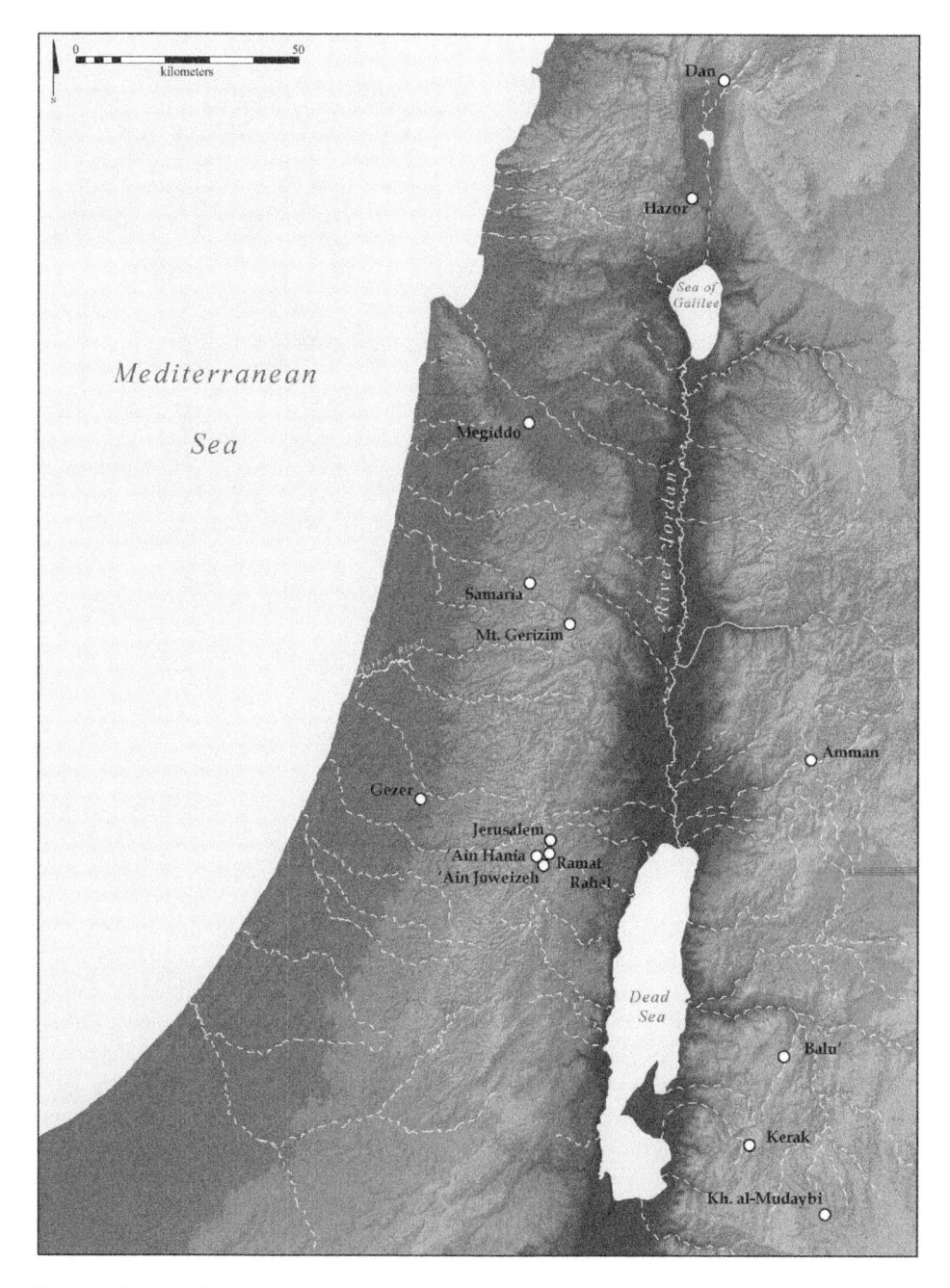

Figure 10.1 Map of sites with stone volutes (Map by George A. Pierce)

The second stone volute (M3)[3] was discovered in secondary use in another wall of the Fortress (Grid Square O12). Its exact location is noted on the OI's plan of the Fortress (Lamon and Shipton: 1939: 83–84, figure 95).

The third stone volute (M2)[4] was found in Grid Square Q13, buried below the purposely laid deep constructional Stratum IV fill that marks the demise of Stratum V (Franklin 2017: 90,

Figure 10.2 (a) Right hand door jamb slab, Tomb 5, Tamassos (height ca. 170 cm, width ca. 78 cm, depth ca. 10–18 cm) (Photo by the author). (b) Left-hand door jamb slab, Tomb 12, Tamassos (height ca. 175 cm, width 100 cm, depth 10–18 cm) (Photo by the author)

note 13). It was uncovered with two ceramic cult stands[5] and was near three stone altars[6] (Fisher 1929: 68–71, figures 46–48, 50; 141). However, a rather general findspot was also provided for these artifacts "south of the long storeroom," that is, in Rooms 6 and 7 of Building 10 in Stratum V (Fisher 1929: 66, figure 44; Lamon and Shipton 1939: figures 6, 10, 11; 55, figure 67; 141).

A fourth stone volute (M8)[7] and the fragment of a fifth (M6)[8] were also discovered in the immediate vicinity of M2, but no exact location was provided. A sixth, much smaller stone volute (M11)[9] was found just south of Locus 2050 in Grid Square O14 and is attributed to Stratum VB (Lamon and Shipton 1939: 160, figure 406 [Stratum VB in Area BB]). This brought the number of stone volutes to six, and all were discovered within a defined area of ca. 75 by 25 m.

There is also a seventh stone volute (M7),[10] which probably came from the same area. Purchased in 1932 by the Rockefeller Archaeological Museum, its provenance was simply given as "Megiddo." It is identical to the first stone volute (M1) discovered by Schumacher in the Fortress. For ca. 20 years following Schumacher's excavation, the area of the Fortress was left uncovered and exposed, resulting in local villagers plundering the exposed masonry for use as building material[11] (Fisher 1929: 18; Lamon and Shipton 1939: 56). Therefore, it is highly probable that M7 was illicitly taken from the area of the Fortress following its excavation and later sold to the museum once its value was recognized.

Schumacher proposed that M1 had served as a structural capital, and the OI adopted that idea. Fisher[12] suggested that the stone volutes had once adorned a temple to Astarte, the remains of which he had identified as sandwiched between the Fortress and an earlier "Hebrew structure." Fisher, believing the stone volutes to be a Cypriot influence, attributed them and his Astarte temple to ca. 800–600 BCE (1929: 71–72, figures 50, 51; 74; Lamon and Shipton

1939: 56–57, n. 48). However, when excavation continued under the direction of Fisher's successor, Guy in 1927, there was no evidence for the existence of an Astarte temple, and the "Hebrew structure" was revealed to be a building with ashlar foundations, which became known as Building 338 of Stratum IV.

Prior to the publication of the final excavation report (Lamon and Shipton 1939), May, the expedition's epigrapher, published his own analysis regarding the stone volutes (1935). While May returned to Fisher's original idea regarding the existence of a temple, he thought that Building 338 itself was the temple (May 1935: 4). In order to reinforce his theory, May simply reallocated the pottery cult stands and the three stone altars to Building 338, even though these artifacts were all attributed to Stratum V (Lamon and Shipton 1939: 55 n. 37 *contra* May 1935: 12–17).

In 1933, the architect Concannon was commissioned to produce a plan and two illustrations showing the presumed location of the stone volutes in Building 338 (May 1935: pls. V, VI). Lamon and Shipton, the authors of *Megiddo I*, were conscious that May had perpetrated a stratigraphic error and tried to rectify matters in their publication (Cline 2020: 211, 214–15). This they did tactfully (perhaps too much so?), stressing that no cultic objects should be associated with Building 338, and the building was clearly part of the Stratum IV stable city (Lamon and Shipton 1939: 44, 49, 58–59). However, somewhat strangely, they republished May's illustrations of Building 338, with a few lines of text regarding the "glaring errors" (Lamon and Shipton 1939: 56–57, figure 68). To this day, the "glaring errors" have been consistently ignored, and the fiction that the stone volutes originated in Building 338 has continued.[13]

To summarize, Building 338 is securely attributed to Stratum IV (Kleiman, Kaplan, and Finkelstein 2016). Four stone volutes were discovered buried in the pre-Stratum IV fill—that is, in Stratum V, south of Building 338; two stone volutes were reused as building blocks in Stratum II, and a near-identical stone volute was purchased. Therefore, it is possible to attribute the seven stone volutes (M1, M2, M3/M9, M6, M7, M8, and M11) to Stratum V and the 9th century BCE.

The excavations at Megiddo also yielded two large stone volutes (M4 and M5, respectively).[14] M4 was found immediately west of the rim of Silo 1414 in Grid Square P9, and M5 was found ca. 20 m further southwest in Grid Square Q9, incorporated into a Stratum III wall in Locus 1565. The two stone volutes are a matching pair, the only difference being that M5 has a volute motif carved on one face, while M4, with the exception of its sides being slightly carved, is otherwise plain.

Their original location is unknown; however, the OI (continuing to follow the line set by the Tamassos examples) proposed that they originally flanked Gate 1567 of Stratum IV in Grid Square Q10 (Lamon and Shipton 1939: 12–16, figures 17, 18). While the built-up foundations of Gate 1567 were of ashlar masonry, the superstructure itself would have been made of mudbrick, making the use of these stone volutes, as suggested by the OI, unrealistic (Franklin 2011: 108). Ussishkin proposed an alternative location: the entrance to the Stratum V Palace 1723 (1970a: 213–15; 2018: 348–51, figures 16, 17). Once again, only the lower courses of the palace were built of ashlar masonry, and the upper courses were of mudbrick. An important point, apparently not considered by either the OI or Ussishkin, is that each stone volute weighs approximately two tons! Therefore, it should be obvious that these massive stone elements could not have been placed on top of a mudbrick wall, and there is no evidence for full-height ashlar-built walls or stone pilasters that could have carried their excessive weight.

Figure 10.3 (a) A probable pillar base, Megiddo. M4 (M5339) with plain sides while the somewhat half circle visible was carved into the top of the stone volute (length 244 cm, height 57 cm, depth 57 cm). On site at Tel Megiddo; photo by the author. (b) A probable pillar base, Megiddo. M5 (M5340) the ca. half circle is visible carved into the top rear half of the stone volute (length 244 cm, height 57 cm, depth 56 cm). On display in the Rockefeller Museum, Jerusalem; photo by the author. (c) A probable pillar base, Megiddo. M5 (M5340) the volute motif carved on the front of the stone volute (Photo by the author)

There are, however, other important clues regarding their original placement. As noted by Lamon and Shipton (1939: 15) and remarked on by Shiloh (1979: 3) and Ussishkin (1970a: 215), each stone volute has a semi-circular depression on its upper surface. If the two stone volutes are placed back-to-back (with the carved face of M5 exposed) the two semi-circles form a complete circle (Lamon and Shipton 1939: figure 17; Franklin 2011: 136–37, figure 4). In addition, there are three pairs of mortices or dowel holes, some 7 to 10 cm deep, located equidistant from each semicircle: two sets on M4 and one set on M5. The circular depression is then immediately recognizable as a guide to position a wooden column with tenons, and the mortices would have aided in holding such a wooden column securely in place (see Wright 2005: 59; Figure 10.3A– C). In short, the weight and dimension of these two massive stone volutes negate their use as capitals. Instead, when placed back-to-back, they form one architectural element: a stone base with a volute motif[15] for a wooden column (Franklin 2011: 137). A parallel to such an arrangement is depicted on the 9th century BCE Šamaš Tablet (*BBSt* 36) from the temple of Šamaš in Sippar.[16] The tablet shows a palm-tree pole resting on a volute-motif base, presumably of stone, and crowned with a volute-motif capital, presumably of wood, and nearby is another volute-motif base supporting a sun disk (Ornan 2005: 63–65, 241, figure 65).

Therefore, it appears that Megiddo stone volutes M4 and M5 may have supported such a cultic palm-tree pole that may have been capped by a wooden volute-motif capital. Usually, such wooden palm-tree poles or wooden capitals do not survive in the archaeological record (see Kletter 2015: 58). Yet, excavations at Khorsabad discovered the remains of two wooden poles covered in thin metal sheeting to imitate the imbrications of a palm trunk, one was placed to the right of the entrance to the Sîn Temple, and the other to the right of the entrance to the Šamaš Temple (Loud 1936: 90, figure 99; 97–98; 104–7).

A double-faced stone volute M12 was discovered reused as a building block in Room 1,051 of the Stratum III Assyrian Building 1052 in Grid Square L7 (Lamon and Shipton 1939: 55 n. 37, figure 89). The northern half of Room 1051[17] was later removed as Loci 2100 and 2102 to reveal the Stratum V Building 2081, which was identified as a cultic space

Figure 10.4 A large fragment of a double-sided stone volute, Megiddo M10/M12 (length, if complete, approx. 110 cm, height 60 cm, depth 28 cm; weight less than ½ ton when complete). The stone volute is shown on the grounds of Tel Megiddo before it was relocated to the visitor's center (Photo by the author)

due to the pottery stands and stone altars found *in situ* (Loud 1948: 43–46, figures 99–103; Ussishkin 2018: 380, figure 17:20). Unfortunately, M12 was not given a registration number, nor was it photographed; in addition, there is no information regarding what happened to it post-excavation. It does appear that undocumented M12 was confused with another double-faced stone volute (M10) that had no registration number and no recorded findspot (see Shiloh 1976: 67–69, figure 1, pl. 1). In 1952, a stone volute, apparently M10/M12, was brought down from an unspecified location on the tell, (Figure 10.4) and today it is on display at the Megiddo visitor center.[18] Finally, in 1973, Shiloh identified the fragment of another extremely large stone volute (M13) (1976: 68–69, pl. 2); however, its current location is unknown.

The 11 Megiddo stone volutes[19] were found either in secondary use as a building material in Strata II and III or buried in the Stratum IV fill laid down over Stratum V, the layer in which they originated in the 9th century BCE. It is important to note none was in use as a stone volute nor as a building material in Stratum IV during the 8th century BCE. Thus, all the stone volutes from Megiddo appear to belong to Stratum V in the 9th century BCE.

Samaria

In the 1930s, the Joint Expedition to Samaria-Sebaste discovered six stone volutes, three complete and three fragmented, in two distinct groups on the northeast and southeast corners of the acropolis, ca.100 m apart. They were all in secondary, or perhaps even tertiary use. The three complete stone volutes (S1, S2, S3) were used as building blocks in the foundations of a Roman-period building, the fragment of a fourth (S4) was reused in an apparent Persian-period wall, and the fragments of two others (S5, S6) were found near one of the Hellenistic towers (Crowfoot, Kenyon, and Sukenik 1942: 14–16, figure 6, plates vii/1, xxx, xxix, xxxvii/1/2).

While all the stone volutes were found reused in Persian- and Roman-period remains, they were attributed to the Omride dynasty of the 9th century BCE in Building Period I by the excavators. They proposed that the original location of the Samaria stone volutes was in an unexcavated area of ca. 100 m and situated between the findspots (Crowfoot, Kenyon, and Sukenik 1942: 14). In 1932, a fanciful illustration was produced by the expedition's architect Pinkerfeld depicting the stone volutes' crowning pilasters that were attached to a full-height ashlar-built wall (Crowfoot, Kenyon, and Sukenik 1942: 15, figure 7). However, there is no known building or any other archaeological evidence to support such a reconstruction. Another stone volute fragment (S7) was later discovered by Shiloh reused in the *cavea* of the Roman theater (1979: 8).

Hazor

Two stone volutes were found in Yadin's excavations of Hazor, apparently in secondary use in Grid Squares F9 and F10 of Area B. According to Yadin, they were in secondary use as windbreakers for an oven in Enclosure 3264 of Stratum VII. However, Shochat and Gilboa wrote, "[t]he renowned dismantling and re-use of the two proto-Aeolic capitals as windbreakers for a *tannur* [oven] in enclosure 3264 was attributed by Yadin to Stratum VII without any apparent reason" (2019: 372, n. 11). In fact, the only certainty is that the two stone volutes had to have been buried before Building 3148a of Stratum VA sealed their findspot (see Yadin et al. 1989: 108–09, plan xxiv).[20]

Stone volute H1 was carved on one face, while stone volute H2 was bifacial; otherwise, they are identical. Yadin continued the idea, based on the Tamassos tombs, that the stone volutes must have originally flanked an entrance to a monumental building. The only building in the vicinity was Citadel 3090 of Stratum VIII (Yadin et al. 1989: 90–94, plan xx, including section A–A on pp. 93–94). Nonetheless, it cannot be stressed enough that there is no evidence to support that the stone volutes originated in Stratum VIII or flanked the gateway of any building.

While the Stratum VIII city was originally attributed to the 9th century BCE building projects of the Omride dynasty (Yadin et al. 1960: 36–37), this date has recently been challenged, with the beginning of the Stratum VIII city reallocated to 830/800 BCE (Shochat and Gilboa 2019: 368, table 2). That is, the multi-phased Strata VIII–V city of Hazor and the Stratum IV city of Megiddo, both date to ca. the 8th century BCE and are more or less contemporary (Shochat and Gilboa 2019: 377). In addition, Finkelstein notes, while quoting Yadin (1972: 14), that although Citadel 3090 was never removed, there was enough evidence to indicate that in Hazor Stratum X–IX, now dated to the early 9th century BCE by him, there was an earlier monumental building with which the stone volutes should be associated (1999: 60–61, 67, n. 21; 2000: 239, 242).

Gezer

The fragment of another stone volute (G1) was revealed in debris dumped into the so-called Great Maccabean Reservoir during Macalister's excavation of the site (1904: 11). The fragment was only recognized as a stone volute by Brandl 80 years after its excavation (1984: 173–76). It was presumably left on site and has not been seen in over a century.

Dan

In 1984, the first Tel Dan stone volute (D1 [registration no. 18351]) was discovered in Area B and was reused as a regular building block in Wall 6033 of the southwest chamber of the Upper Gate, which was tentatively dated to the Hellenistic period (Biran 1985: 86; 1994: 253, ill. 209b; Biran, Ilan, and Greenberg 1996: 25). In 1994, three stone volute fragments were found in Area A, Locus 5133 in secondary or tertiary use as regular building blocks in the foundation courses of a poorly constructed Hellenistic wall that was built across the earlier Iron Age plaza. Two of the stone volute fragments (registration nos. 15736/1, 15736/2) were restored to form a complete volute (D2), with the third fragment remaining solitary as D3 (registration no. 15738) (Biran 1994: 241; Biran, Ilan, and Greenberg 1996: 17).

Despite the lack of archaeological evidence, the stone volutes were attributed to an 8th century BCE gate structure. Recently, the excavators acknowledged that the stone volutes could have originated in the late 10th–9th-century levels that have yet to be fully exposed, laying below the 8th-century BCE Lower and Upper Gate areas (Ilan, pers. comm.).

Samaria: Mount Gerizim[21]

The excavation of a large Samaritan temple precinct and adjacent structures on Mount Gerizim was conducted by Magen from 1983 to 2003. He discerned two phases, the earliest dating to the 5th century BCE Persian period, and the latest dating to the early 2nd century Hellenistic period (Magen 2007: 158, 191). Two nearly complete stone volutes and the fragment of a third were found. MG1 (registration no. 10025), MG2 (registration no. 10540), and the fragment MG3 were all roughly refashioned, apparently for secondary use, and found in debris near the bottom of a monumental Hellenistic-period stairway that led up to the Samaritan summit temple. They are only carved on one face and are extremely thin, measuring 21 cm thick, relative to their size (see Arie 2021: 46★ figure 5, 48★ figure 7). Their dimensions preclude them from having been load-bearing structural components, and their relatively small bases also prevent them from having been freestanding elements.

MG 1–3 were initially attributed to the Iron Age (ca. 9th–8th centuries BCE), as this was the (then) accepted date for all other known stone volutes. To reconcile the fact that Mount Gerizim was not settled in the 9th–8th centuries BCE, it was proposed that the stone volutes had originally stood in a temple or monumental building in Iron Age Shechem and were only relocated to Mount Gerizim during the Persian period (Stern and Magen 2002: 55–56; Lipschits 2011: 207); this, however, is untenable. First, a 7th century BCE date for the construction of the first temple was proposed by Arie based on his reevaluation of the pottery and existing architecture. Also, under Arie's supervision, the two near-complete stone volutes (MG1, MG2) were restored in the laboratory of The Israel Museum (Arie 2021: 39★–63★, figures 3–8). Their reconstruction highlights the difference between them and other examples from Israel—they are unique. Second, one of their distinctive features is that their volutes protrude beyond their narrow bases, making them in-effect hanging volutes. Hanging stone volutes are not known prior to the 7th or 6th century BCE. They are found on the pilaster reliefs from the Tamassos tombs, and on the even later 3rd century BCE orthostats from Umm el-Amed in Lebanon (Kahwagi-Janho 2014: 98–100, figures 2, 3; 103).

Therefore, the question must be asked: Does Arie's recognition of the existence of 7th century pottery prove that the earliest temple and stone volutes date to the 7th century BCE? Or does the pottery point to a pre-temple use of the site, making both the temple and the stone volutes attributable to the 5th century BCE? Whichever scenario is correct does not diminish the fact that the Mount Gerizim stone volutes[22] are a much later development and cannot be included in the corpus of the 9th century northern Israelite stone volutes.

Stone Volutes from the Kingdom of Judah

Jerusalem: City of David

The first Judahite stone volute (J1) was discovered broken in half at the base of the City of David's east scarp with debris dating from the 5th to 3rd centuries BCE (Kenyon 1963: 16); its original location is unknown. The usual volute motif has the distinctive addition of two oculi located on either side of the apex of the central triangle.[23] A clue to its function is provided by a narrow, carved strip, 14 cm wide, along its upper surface, a "ribbon," adjacent to the stone volute's decorated face, and two dowel holes, ca. 35 cm from either end (Shiloh 1979: 11). This stone volute is also relatively narrow, measuring 130 cm long, and 60 cm high, but only 43 cm wide. These narrow dimensions together with the marks along its upper surface may signify that it was an elaborate stone balustrade (Franklin 2011: 137–38), similar to the balustrade with volute motifs depicted on the "false windows" at Tamassos (Walcher 2005: 78–83; Figure 10.5A and B).

In the Givati Parking Lot excavation, a fragment of a smaller stone volute (J2) was found in mixed debris dating from the Iron Age II to the Hellenistic period. The excavators

Figure 10.5a and b A possible stone balustrade with a volute motif on the exterior face, Jerusalem J1. Visible along the full length of the top of the stone volute and adjacent to the carved face is a carved 14 cm wide strip with two rectangular dowel holes (length 130 cm, height 60 cm, depth 43 cm; weight approx. ¾ ton) (Photos by the author)

postulated that when whole, the stone volute was located at the entrance of an Iron Age II building (Ben-Ami and Tchekhanovets 2015: 67–71, figures 1B, 2A, 2B). However, once again, there is no archaeological evidence to support such a reconstruction.

The 2012 excavations conducted by Eilat Mazar south of the Temple Mount revealed a small fragment of a stone volute (J3) in Herodian-period debris. Unfortunately, the fragment was too small to provide any more information (Karlin and Mazar 2015: 549–52, figure III.4.1).

The original location and date of all the City of David stone volutes[24] are unknown.

Ramat Rahel

Aharoni initiated excavations in 1954 and discovered four complete stone volutes (RR1, RR2, RR8, RR10) and nine fragments (RR3, RR4, RR5,[25] RR6, RR7, RR9) (1956: 141, 151, pls. 22A, 23A, 22B, 27; 1961: 103, figure 6; 1965: 19; Lipschits and Ras 2016: 535–42, table 35.1, figure 35.1–7; Shiloh 1979: 15, table 2). Three more fragments were found during the renewed excavations at Ramat Rahel (Lipschits 2011: 209–10, figure 3); however, many of the fragments are small, so it is unclear how many stone volutes are represented.

It has been proposed that the stone volutes originated in Building Phase I, dating to the late 8th or early 7th century BCE (Lipschits et al. 2011: 20). While there is still uncertainty regarding their initial use in either Building Phase I or II, the deep central groove running from the front to back, cut midway into the upper surface of each stone volute, is thought to be a later modification (Lipschits et al. 2011: 20). The latest use for the Ramat Rahel stone volutes appears to be during the Persian period, as many were found in debris associated with the dismantled and robbed-out structures in Building Phase III (Lipschits, Gadot, and Oeming 2020: 477–83). If the stone volutes were in use during the Persian period, it is probable that the deep central groove was added then, implying that the stone volutes originated in Building Phase II, no later than 630 BCE (Lipschits, Gadot, and Oeming 2020: 481).

Armon Hanatziv

Three well-preserved stone volutes and approximately nine fragments of much smaller, unique stone volutes were excavated at Armon Hanatziv in 2019–2020 (Billig, Froid, and Bocher 2021: 77). The three complete stone volutes (AH1–AH3) are similar in style to the other stone volutes from Judah. However, these stone volutes have an elaborately carved abacus, and the central triangle is slightly convex, plus they were to be viewed in the round as they are carved on all four sides. In addition, the workmanship is extremely fine, and they are considerably smaller than any of the other stone volutes (Billig, Froid, and Bocher 2021: 88–89, figures 9, 10). Although the site was not well preserved and lacked clear stratigraphy, the stone volutes were attributed to the earliest building phase, dated to the mid-7th century BCE based on associated pottery (Billig, Froid, and Bocher 2021: 79; 86–88, figure 8; 94).

Stone volutes AH1 and AH2 were found placed together in a stone-cut niche (Locus 24). They appear to have been deliberately buried, possibly to preserve them from misuse (Billig, Froid, and Bocher 2021: 80, figure 2; 88; 97). The third stone volute (AH3) lay a few meters away from the first two, on a plaster-covered bedrock surface (Locus 26) (Billig, Froid, and Bocher 2021: 80, figure 2; 88–89, figure 10).

The approximately nine fragments of miniature stone volutes were discovered in debris in two rock-cut trenches (Loci 22, 23) that were cut across the site ca. seven meters north of AH1–AH3. These volutes were originally ca. 10–14 cm high and are comprised of only a central triangle and two side volutes, with the central triangle projecting above the volutes (Billig, Froid, and Bocher 2021: 91–94, figure 12). Also found were an unspecified number of balustrade fragments; together with the miniature stone volute fragments, they have been reconstructed as a stone window balustrade based on the "woman at a window" ivory plaques (Billig, Froid, and Bocher 2021: 92–94, figures 13, 14). However, the only known examples of window balustrades with stone volutes are the false windows from Cypriot tombs,[26] the most famous being the two false windows from Tomb 5 at Tamassos (Walcher 2005: 78–83, figures 1–6).

'Ain Joweizeh (Walajeh)

In the 1980s, a volute motif (AJ1) carved on a large stone slab was discovered, located at one end of a 233 m long spring tunnel at 'Ain Joweizeh (Marcus and Ben-Yosef 1984). It is lodged at the base of a 5.76 m deep shaft at the junction of Segment 33 and Segment 34 (Ein Mor and Ron 2016: 131–32, figure 3). Volute motif AJ1 is not a stand-alone stone volute; it is a large stone slab weighing ca 5.3 tons with a volute motif carved on its upper section (Ein Mor and Ron 2016: 137–41, figures 8–10). It closely resembles the volute motifs carved at the entrances to Tamassos tombs 5 and 12 (Franklin 2011: 132, figure 1) and shares similarities with the 3rd century BCE orthostats from Umm el-Amed in Lebanon (Kahwagi-Janho 2014: 98–100, figures 2, 3). Its original location is unknown; however, based on comparisons, it cannot be earlier than the 6th century BCE, perhaps even dating as late as the 3rd century BCE.

'Ein Hania

A fragment of a stone volute (EH1) was discovered embedded in a later wall near the spring of 'Ein Hania[27] (Baruch pers. comm.). There is no further information available at the time of this publication.

Stone Volutes from the Kingdom of Ammon

The Amman Citadel

To date, the only Ammonite examples are from the Citadel of Amman. The halves of two stone volutes were found in different locations on the citadel. The first was a squat bifacial stone volute (A1), discovered in 1993; the second (A2) is similar to the first, but its volute motif is slightly different—that is, the two stone volutes are not a pair (Najjar 1999: 109). Both most closely resemble the stone volutes from the northern Kingdom of Israel.

Stone Volutes from the Kingdom of Moab

In the Kingdom of Moab, seven stone volutes, or fragments of stone volutes, have been found at four sites. All of these examples most closely resemble the stone volutes from the Kingdom of Judah.

Khirbat al-Mudaybi

Four stone volutes (Md1–4) were documented during regional surveys (Glueck 1933: 13, figure 2; 1934: 67–68, figure 26; Negueruela 1982: 395, figure 1). A fifth (Md5) was found in excavations conducted by the Karak Resources Project, and a sixth (Md6)[28] has been reported.

The only stone volute whose original location is known is Md5. It was found lying carved side down, on top of rock tumble and other debris that was more or less level with the modern surface (Andrews et al. 2002: 135). The debris was part of the collapsed superstructure of the site's gatehouse; it appears that Md5 was once attached to one of the gate's protruding piers, but it had toppled over when the gatehouse's superstructure collapsed (Karak Resources Project n.d.). Unfortunately, the excavators did not realize that the Megiddo, Samaria, and Hazor reconstructions were not based on any sound archaeological evidence; thus, they reconstructed the stone volutes as structural capitals that supported a flat roof over the gatehouse. Such a reconstruction is untenable, given that the gatehouse's superstructure most likely would have been a vaulted arch built of mudbrick. In addition, the stone volutes were narrow with a width of just ca. 47 cm, a height of ca. 93 cm, and ca. 186 cm in length (Drinkard 1997: 249–50), rendering them unsuitable for use as structural capitals. However, their location at the narrowest part of the gate, vulnerable to passing traffic, shows that these stone volutes functioned as orthostats, protecting the mudbrick superstructure of the gate (Franklin 2011: 135–36; see also Wright 2005: 58).

The volute motif carved on these stone volutes is distinctive: for example, the base of the central triangle extends the full length of the stone volute, and two oculi are carved on either side of the triangle's apex, akin to the stone volutes from Judah. Khirbat al-Mudaybi was originally built as a small fort, and the stone volutes are attributed to this earliest phase. Although a firm date cannot be established, they are attributed to ca. 7th century BCE (Pace 2015: 280).

'Ain Sara

In 1983, a large, apparently well-preserved limestone stone volute (AS1) was discovered built into a modern wall in the garden of a restaurant at 'Ain Sara, near Kerak. It is very similar to the Khirbat al-Mudaybi stone volutes but much smaller. 'Ain Sara is known for its medieval remains; however, there is evidence for earlier occupation levels now destroyed by building work (Donner and Knauf 1986: 266–77, esp. Abb. 116).

Kerak

In 2006, a small fragment of a stone volute (K1) was recognized at the castle of Kerak in secondary use within a cistern shaft from the Ayyubid and Mamluk periods (Hübner 2012: 19–22, esp. Abb 2, 3).

Balu'

In 2008, an unusual basalt fragment of a stone volute (B1) was excavated by the Balu'a Regional Archaeological Project. It was found reused as part of a Nabatean-period altar, but it clearly came from the large Iron Age site of el-Bālūʻ dated to the 8th–7th centuries BCE based on associated pottery (Tyson and Ninow 2019: 158–67, Tafel 22).

Stone Volutes from Turkey and Cyprus: A Comparison

Turkey

In the Carian region of Turkey, ten stone volutes are documented (Baran 2019: 235).[29] None is thought to have been a structural component to support a roof or entryway.

Cyprus

In Cyprus, there are ca. 81 stone volutes classified as stele crowns, which are votive capitals attributed to the 7th–5th centuries BCE, and none served as structural capitals (Baran 2013: 56; Walcher 2009: 45–64). In Tombs 5 and 12 at Tamassos, there are two pairs of reliefs imitating pilasters with volute-motif crowns that are attributed to the Cypro-Archaic II (ca. 600–480 BCE; Buchholz, Matthäus, and Walcher 2002: 230; see Figures 1A and 1B, above).

The Role of Stone Volutes

Previous studies have concentrated on the presumed architectural role of stone volutes as structural capitals that support a flat roof (see Mazar 2009 and Billig, Froid, and Bocher 2021: 90, figure 11), capitals crowning pilasters that were integrated into the framework of a wall (see Lamon and Shipton 1939: 57, figure 68; Crowfoot, Kenyon, and Sukenik 1942: 15, figure 7; and Yadin et al. 1989: 91, plan XX, section A–A), or door lintels (Lipschits et al. 2020: 464, figure 18.4). Such reconstructions are based on the Tamassos tombs, which postdate Levantine examples by ca. 300 years. As noted by Katz—based on her study of shrine models—stone volutes do not have an architectural function as structural capitals (2016: 112). It is, in fact, to Iron Age orthostats that we should turn to find the likely function of many Levantine stone volutes.[30]

In monumental mudbrick buildings,[31] stone orthostats—sometimes plain, sometimes sculpted—were used to protect the lower mudbrick courses (Wright 2000: 4/45). In the 10th and 9th centuries BCE, Syro-Anatolian orthostats—often decorated—were placed in public locations, such as city and citadel gates, and in the approach to palaces and temples[32] (Harmanşah 2013: 136). Most of these decorated orthostats are now displayed in museums around the world. Unfortunately, to facilitate transportation, they were reduced in depth: for example, the Zincirli orthostats, originally ca. 1 m thick, were shaved to 15 cm thin slabs (Tamur 2017: 27, figures 5, 6, 8; 40). These decorated orthostats—some of basalt, some of limestone—were originally solid stone blocks not relatively thin reliefs. As such, stone orthostats and stone volutes had a similar depth relative to their height and length.

The earliest example of an orthostat decorated with a volute motif is from the 'Ain Dara' Temple in present-day northwest Syria (Abu Assaf 1990). Originally constructed ca. 1250–1100 BCE (Novák 2012: 50), it continued in use until ca. 740 BCE (Yalçin 2020: 134). The temple was built of limestone, but all the decorated reliefs were of basalt (Novák 2012: 47, figure 4; 50). During the last phase of the temple (ca. 900 BCE), an ambulatory was added that circled the building (Yalçin 2020: 145). Within it, there is a large basalt orthostat (Relief F15) featuring a carved volute motif (AD1). This orthostat served as a stabilizing element, a revetment, and its undecorated back once integrated into the central midpoint of the ambulatory's mudbrick wall.

Stone orthostats are usually the only surviving evidence of decorative stonework in the ancient Near East until the end of the 7th century BCE when changes in building techniques enabled decorative stonework to be placed higher in structures (Yalçin 2020: 144). That is, prior to the 7th century BCE stone volutes could not have served as structural capitals in structures built using mudbrick and wood due to their size and weight.

Conclusion

Stone volutes had a variety of roles; some were orthostats, placed to protect significant buildings, such as Md1-Md6 protecting the gate passage at Khirbat al-Mudaybi in Moab. Others may have served as balustrades: for example, J1 in the City of David, Jerusalem. At Megiddo, the six near-identical stone volutes (M1, M2, M3/9, M6, M7, M8) appear to have been associated with a 9th century BCE cultic building, while the two large stone volutes (M4, M5) together served as a base for a wooden cultic pillar. Stone volutes H1 and H2 from Hazor and M10/12 from Megiddo may have also had a connection to cultic sites. The three finely carved small stone volutes from Armon Hanatziv (AH1–AH3) may have been non-structural votive capitals or stele crowns. Interestingly, those same capitals were well preserved because they were buried, possibly for their protection or to prevent misuse (Ussishkin 1970b), or conversely, to obliterate their memory (*damnatio memoriae*; Herrmann 2019: 399–405). It is the volute *motif* that unites the stone volutes, not their architectural placement. They had a variety of functions, but not one of the approximately 55 stone volutes from ancient Israel or Judah served as a structural capital.

Notes

1 For an analysis of the stratigraphy and the terminology used in this article see Franklin 2006 in general and Tables 1 and 2 (2006: 96, 103) and Franklin 2017.
2 This chapter will use Shiloh's (1979) numbering system and extend the numbering system to the stone volutes discovered thereafter. Each will be discussed within the order they were found at each site.

3 Shiloh does not seem to have personally seen this stone volute, and there is no registration number or museum display number associated with it. It appears that Shiloh's M3 and M9 are the same stone volute. If so, then M3/M9 is on display at the Rockefeller Archaeological Museum (IDA 36.2189) in Jerusalem. Ussishkin (1989: 160) noted that Shiloh had duplicated the M3 stone volute but that Shiloh mistakenly thought it was an M3 and M8 being the same.
4 Volute M2 (registration no. 3657; no. A13394) is on display at the Oriental Institute Museum.
5 The pottery stands are registration nos. 2985, 2986.
6 The stone altars (registration nos. 2982, 2983, 2984) were found in Grid Square R12 (Lamon and Shipton 1939: 148), immediately south of the ceramic cult stands discovered in Grid Square Q13.
7 Volute M8 (IDA 36.2190) is on display at the Hecht Museum at the University of Haifa.
8 Volute fragment M6 (IDA 36.2191) is not on display.
9 The miniature stone volute M11 (registration no. A340) is on display at the Oriental Institute Museum, has the same design but is much smaller, and has painted decoration (Loud 1948: pl. 270/1 [registration nos. A18359, C8859]).
10 Volute M7 (IDA 32.2845) is on display at the Museum of the Bible in Washington, D.C.
11 The village was Lajjun, only 1 km south of Megiddo. Local villagers were employed as unskilled labor by both expeditions.
12 Fisher served as the first field director of the OI excavations from September 1925 to May 1927; for the identity and tenure of the OI expeditions' members, see Cline 2020.
13 *Contra* Shiloh 1979: 4–6, table 1; Kendirci 2012:10, 21–23, 48–53; and Ussishkin 1989: 160; 2018: 367. Interestingly, May's theory regarding cult may well be relevant once Building 338 is removed from the equation. The stone volutes, cult stands, and stone altars all date to the 9th century BCE and were found within a relatively small area. Furthermore, recent excavations conducted nearby by the Megiddo Expedition of Tel Aviv University have revealed a 9th century BCE cultic area in Area Q, Level Q5, which is in the OI's Grid Square R11 (Kleiman et al. 2017: 24–52) and close to the findspot of the cultic items excavated by the OI.
14 These volutes are registered as nos. M5339 and M5340.
15 Unfortunately, these two stone volutes are not displayed together; thus, this function is not immediately obvious. M4 was left on site and is located on the left of the path that leads to Silo 1414. M5 is displayed at the rear of the central court in the right-hand arcade of the Rockefeller Archaeological Museum in Jerusalem.
16 For a zoomable, high-resolution image: https://www.britishmuseum.org/collection/object/W_1881-0428-34-a.
17 The southern half of Grid Square L7 was left untouched by the OI team but was eventually excavated by the Tel Aviv University excavation team in 1994 and 1996 as Grid Squares W, Y, Z.41/42 of Level H-1 (Finkelstein, Ussishkin, and Halpern 2000: 154–55, figures 7.16, 7.18).
18 Shiloh (1976: 67–68, figure 1, pl. 1; 1979: 12, n. 18) reported a conversation that he had with a member of the Israel National Parks Authority: In 1952, an Englishman, whom Shiloh presumed to be P. L. O. Guy, brought the stone volute down from the tell. However, it is unlikely to have been Guy as he was already terminally ill with cancer, passing away in December 1952. The person who was involved in moving the stone volute was probably Harry Parker, a British member of the archaeological team who continued to supervise activities concerning Megiddo on behalf of the OI until 1954. In 1952, Parker is known to have supervised the removal of certain stone items and their eventual shipment to Masonic lodges in the United States (Cline 2020: 293, n. 13). This scenario is a better match for the story related to Shiloh in the 1970s. Furthermore, the removal of items from the tell would have been supervised by the Israeli Department of Antiquities rather than the Israel National Parks, as Megiddo was only declared a national park in 1966.
19 M1, M2, M3/M9, M4, M5, M6, M7, M8, M10/12, M11, and M13.
20 Kleiman (2021: 1–17) discussed the context and burial of the stone volutes, but he did not query Yadin's reconstruction.
21 Mount Gerizim has been considered here as part of the geographical region of Samaria; however, unlike the other northern kingdom of Israel sites, Mount Gerizim was not settled prior to the fall of Israel in 720 BCE.
22 The closest examples to the Mount Gerizim stone volutes are from the region of ancient Caria, e.g., four stone volutes from two temples in Alâzeytin, and one from each of the following sites Sazköy, Pedasa, Euromos, and Datça. While their dates are uncertain, it may be as early as the 7th century BCE (Baran 2013: 55, 57–58, figures 2–10; 2019: 234, 241–42; Betancourt dates the Alâzeytin

examples to the second half of the 6th century BCE [1977: 55, see figures 16–19 and pls. 29–35]). Other stone volutes with similar features are from temples on the island of Lesbos: three from Klopedi (Betancourt 1977: figure 41, pl. 49) and one each from Mytilene and Eressos (Betancourt 1977: figure 43, pls. 50, 51). North of Lesbos, on the mainland, the temple in Neandria yielded three stone volutes (Betancourt 1977: see figures 25, 26, pl. 41); their original placement is unknown.

23 This addition was also found on the other Judahite, and Moabite examples.
24 There is a possibility of another, now lost, stone volute (J4) discovered by Parker in 1909–1911 (Gibson: forthcoming).
25 RR5 is unique, as it is a small bifacial stone volute (Lipschits and Ras 2016: 535–36, table 35.1. no 5, figure 35.2/1).
26 Similar false windows with stone volutes were reported at Kouklia-*Palaepaphos*, Kourion, and Ktima (Walcher 2005: 80–82).
27 It is possible that EH1 and AJ1 from 'Ain Joweizeh may originally have come from the same—still unknown—building, as the two springs are ca. 500 m from each other. For the location, see Ein Mor and Ron 2016: 129, figure 1.
28 The sixth stone volute has not yet been published (see Bean 2018).
29 In particular, Sazköy and Alazeytin (Baran 2013: 54; 62–64, figures 2–6; 65, figures 7–10); see also n. 21 above.
30 Admittedly, the architectural significance of orthostats in the Iron Age is rarely studied (Harmanşah 2013: 160) because there is often no indication that a stone block, carved or plain, was used as an orthostat unless it is found *in situ*.
31 Unbaked mudbrick was the primary building material until the advent of stone construction technology in the 6th century BCE.
32 The Assyrians also adopted the use of orthostats from northern Syria (Aro 2009: 13). However, the Assyrian orthostats or reliefs were carved from gypsum which is not suitable for exterior use unless protected with varnish or paint (Harmanşah 2013: 164–65).

Bibliography

Abu Assaf, Ali. 1990. *Der Temple von 'Ain Dārā*. Mainz: Philipp von Zabern.
Aharoni, Yohanan. 1956. Excavations at Ramat Raḥel, 1954: Preliminary Report. *IEJ* 6: 102–11, 137–57.
———. 1961. Excavations at Ramat Rahel. *BA* 24 (4): 97–118.
———. 1965. The Citadel of Ramat Rahel. *Archaeology* 18: 15–25.
Andrews, Stephen J., David R. Berge, John I. Lawlor, and Gerald L. Mattingly. 2002. The Karak Resources Project 1999: Excavations at Khirbat al-Muḍaybiʻ. *ADAJ* 46: 125–40.
Arie, Eran. 2021. Revisiting Mount Gerizim: The Foundation of the Sacred Precinct and the Proto-Ionic Capitals. *New Studies in the Archaeology of Jerusalem and Its Region* 14: 39*–63*.
Aro, Sanna. 2009. The Origins of the Artistic Interactions between the Assyrian Empire and North Syria Revisited. Pages 9–17 in *Of God(s), Trees, Kings, and Scholars: Neo-Assyrian and Related Studies in Honour of Simo Parpola*. Edited by Mikko Luukko, Saana Svärd and Raija Mattila. Helsinki: Finnish Oriental Society.
Baran, Abdulkadir. 2013. A New Aeolic Style Pilaster Capital from Karia. Pages 53–66 in *A Festschrift for Orhan Bingöl on the Occasion of His 67th Birthday*. Edited by Görkem Kökdemir. Ankara: Bilgin Kültür Sanat Yayıncılık.
———. 2019. The Role of the Carians in the Development of Greek Architecture. Pages 233–44 in *Listening to the Stones: Essays on the Architecture and Function in Ancient Greek Sanctuaries in Honour of Richard Alan Tomlinson*. Edited by Elena C. Partida and Barbara Schmidt-Dounas. Oxford: Archaeopress.
Bean, Adam L. 2018. "Sculpted Stones and Inscribed Sherds: Contextualizing Artifacts from Khirbat al-Mudaybiʻ." Paper presented at the ASOR Annual Meeting, Denver, CO, November 17.
Ben-Ami, Doron, and Yana Tchekhanovets. 2015. A New Fragment of Proto-Aeolic Capital from Jerusalem. *TA* 42: 67–71.
Betancourt, Philip P. 1977. *The Aeolic Style in Architecture: A Survey of Its Development in Palestine, the Halikarnassos Peninsula, and Greece, 1000–500 B.C.* Princeton: Princeton University Press.
Billig, Yaacov, Liora Froid, and Efrat Bocher. 2021. A Royal Mansion from the First Temple Period at Armon Ha-Naẓiv. *New Studies in the Archaeology of Jerusalem and Its Region* 14: 77–100 (Hebrew).
Biran, Avraham. 1985. Notes and News: Tel Dan, 1984. *IEJ* 35: 186–89.

———. 1994. *Biblical Dan*. Jerusalem: Israel Exploration Society; Hebrew Union College.
Biran, Avraham, David Ilan, and Raphael Greenberg. 1996. *Dan I: A Chronicle of the Excavations, the Pottery Neolithic, the Early Bronze Age and the Middle Bronze Age Tombs*. Jerusalem: Nelson Glueck School of Biblical Archaeology, Hebrew Union College-Jewish Institute of Religion.
Brandl, Baruch. 1984. A Proto-Aeolic Capital from Gezer. *IEJ* 34: 173–76.
Buchholz, Hans-Günter, Hartmut Matthäus, and Katja Walcher. 2002. The Royal Tombs of Tamassos: State of Research and Perspectives. *Cahiers du Centre d'Études Chypriotes* 32: 219–42.
Cline, E. H. 2020. *Digging Up Armageddon: The Search for the Lost City of Solomon*. Princeton: Princeton University Press.
Crowfoot, J. W., Kathleen M. Kenyon, and E. L. Sukenik. 1942. *The Buildings at Samaria*. Samaria-Sebaste: Reports of the Work of the Joint Expedition in 1931–1933 and of the British Expedition in 1935 1. London: Palestine Exploration Fund.
Donner, Herbert, and Ernst Axel Knauf. 1986. Ġawr aṣ-Ṣâfī/Wâdi al-Karak. *AfO* 33: 266–67.
Drinkard Jr., Joel E. 1997. New Volute Capital Discovered. *BA* 60: 249–50.
Ein Mor, Daniel, and Zvi Ron. 2016. 'Ain Joweizeh: An Iron Age Royal Rock-Cut Spring System in the Naḥal Refa'im Valley, near Jerusalem. *TA* 43: 127–46.
Finkelstein, Israel. 1999. Hazor and the North in the Iron Age: A Low Chronology Perspective. *BASOR* 314: 55–70.
———. 2000. Hazor XII–XI with an Addendum on Ben-Tor's Dating of Hazor X–VII. *TA* 27: 231–47.
Finkelstein, Israel, David Ussishkin, and Baruch Halpern, eds. 2000. *Megiddo III: The 1992–1996 Seasons*. Tel Aviv: Institute of Archaeology, Tel Aviv University.
Fisher, Clarence S. 1929. *The Excavation of Armageddon*. OIC 4. Chicago: University of Chicago Press.
Franklin, Norma. 2006. Revealing Stratum V at Megiddo. *BASOR* 342: 95–111.
———. 2011. From Megiddo to Tamassos and Back: Putting the "Proto-Ionic Capital" in Its Place. Pages 129–40 in *The Fire Signals of Lachish: Studies in the Archaeology and History of Israel in the Late Bronze Age, Iron Age, and Persian Period in Honor of David Ussishkin*. Edited by Israel Finkelstein and Nadav Na'aman. Winona Lake: Eisenbrauns.
———. 2017. Entering the Arena: The Megiddo Stables Reconsidered. Pages 87–101 in *Rethinking Israel: Studies in the History and Archaeology of Ancient Israel in Honor of Israel Finkelstein*. Edited by Oded Lipschits, Yuval Gadot and Matthew Adams. Winona Lake: Eisenbrauns.
Gibson, Shimon. forthcoming. "An Iron Age Toilet Seat (see 'Throne of Solomon') from Captain Montague Brownlee Parker's 1909–11 Excavations in Jerusalem."
Glueck, Nelson. 1933. Further Explorations in Eastern Palestine. *BASOR* 51: 9–18.
———. 1934. Exploration in Eastern Palestine I. *AASOR* 14: 1–113.
Guy, P. L. O. 1931. *New Light from Armageddon: Second Provisional Report (1927–29) on the Excavations at Megiddo in Palestine*. Chicago: University of Chicago Press.
Harmanşah, Ömür. 2013. *Cities and the Shaping of Memory in the Ancient Near East*. Cambridge: Cambridge University Press.
Herrmann, Virginia R. 2019. The Reuse of Orthostats and Manipulation of Memory in the Iron Age Syro-Hittite Kingdoms. *Sem* 61: 399–439.
Hübner, Ulrich. 2012. Ein moabitisches Kapitell-Fragment aus Kerak (Jordanien). *Natur und Mensch: Jahresmitteilungen der Naturhistorischen Gesellschaft Nürnberg* 2012: 19–22.
Kahwagi-Janho, Hany. 2014. Les chapiteaux à volutes verticales du Liban. *Chronos* 29: 95–125.
Karak Resources Project. n.d. The Volute Capitals of Mudaybiʻ. https://www.karakresourcesproject.org/volute-capitals-of-mudaybi (accessed February 12, 2022).
Karlin, Margo, and Eilat Mazar. 2015. A Proto-Aeolic Capital from the Ophel. Pages 549–52 in *The Ophel Excavations to the South of the Temple Mount, 2009–2013: Final Reports, Vol. 1*. By Eilat Mazar. Jerusalem: Shoham.
Katz, Haya. 2016. *Portable Shrine Models*. Oxford: British Archaeological Reports.
Kendirci, Recep. 2012. Iron Age Aeolic Style Capitals in the Israel and Palestine Area. MA thesis, Uppsala University, Uppsala, Sweden.
Kenyon, Kathleen M. 1963. Excavations in Jerusalem, 1962. *PEQ* 95: 7–21.
Kleiman, Assaf. 2021. The Cultural Biography of Two Volute Capitals at Iron Age Hazor. *PEQ*. doi: 10.1080/00310328.2021.1951987.
Kleiman, Assaf, Adam Kaplan, and Israel Finkelstein. 2016. Building 338 at Megiddo: New Evidence from the Field. *IEJ* 66: 161–76.
Kleiman, Assaf, Margaret E. Cohen, Erin Hall, Robert S. Homsher, and Israel Finkelstein. 2017. Cult Activity at Megiddo in the Iron Age: New Evidence and a Long-Term Perspective. *ZDPV* 133: 24–52.

Kletter, Raz. 2015. Shrine Models and Volute Capitals. Pages 55–64 in *Yavneh II: The 'Temple Hill' Repository Pit; Fire Pans, Kernos, Naos, Painted Stands, 'Plain' Pottery, Cypriot Pottery, Inscribed Bowl, Dog Bones, Stone Fragments, and Other Studies*. By in Raz Kletter, Irit Ziffer, and Wolfgang Zwickel. Fribourg: Academic; Göttingen: Vandenhoeck & Ruprecht.

Lamon, Robert S., and Geoffrey M. Shipton. 1939. *Megiddo I: Seasons of 1925–34, Strata I-V*. Chicago: University of Chicago Press.

Loud, Gordon. 1936. *Khorsabad*, Part I: *Excavations in the Palace and at a City Gate*. Chicago: University of Chicago Press.

———. 1948. *Megiddo II: Seasons of 1935–39*. Chicago: University of Chicago Press.

Lipschits, Oded. 2011. The Origin and Date of the Volute Capitals from the Levant. Pages 203–25 in *The Fire Signals of Lachish: Studies in the Archaeology and History of Israel in the Late Bronze Age, Iron Age, and Persian Period in Honor of David Ussishkin*. Edited by Israel Finkelstein and Nadav Na'aman. Winona Lake: Eisenbrauns.

Lipschits, Oded, Yuval Gadot, Benjamin Arubas, and Manfred Oeming. 2011. Palace and Village, Paradise and Oblivion: Unravelling the Riddles of Ramat Raḥel. *NEA* 74: 1–49.

Lipschits, Oded, Yuval Gadot, and Manfred Oeming. 2020. Strategic Location and Natural Surroundings. Pages 3–7 in *Ramat Raḥel IV: The Renewed Excavations by the Tel Aviv-Heidelberg Expedition (2005–2010): Stratigraphy and Architecture*. By Oded Lipschits, Manfred Oeming, and Yuval Gadot. Tel Aviv: Tel Aviv University.

Lipschits, Oded, and Keren Ras. 2016. Iron II Architectural Elements. Pages 535–52 in *Ramat Raḥel III: Final Publication of Yohanan Aharoni's Excavations (1954, 1959–1962), Vol. 2*. By Oded Lipschits, Yuval Gadot and Liora Freud. Tel Aviv: Tel Aviv University.

Macalister, R. A. S. 1904. Sixth Quarterly Report on the Excavations of Gezeh. *PEQ* 36: 9–26.

Magen, Yitzhak. 2007. The Dating of the First Phase of the Samaritan Temple on Mount Gerizim in Light of the Archaeological Evidence. Pages 157–211 in *Judah and the Judeans in the Fourth Century B.C.E.* Edited by Oded Lipschits, Gary N. Knoppers and Rainer Albertz. Winona Lake: Eisenbrauns.

Marcus, M., and S. Ben-Yosef. 1984. 'Ain Joweizeh—The Longest Spring Tunnel in the Judean Hills. *Niqrot Zurim* 8: 6–54 (Hebrew).

Matthäus, Hartmut. 2007. The Royal Tombs of Tamassos: Burial Gifts, Funeral Architecture and Ideology. *Cahiers du Centre d'Études Chypriotes* 37: 211–30.

May, Herbert G. 1935. *Material Remains of the Megiddo Cult*. Chicago: University of Chicago Press.

Mazar, Eilat. 2009. *The Palace of King David: Excavations at the Summit of the City of David; Preliminary Report of Seasons 2005–2007*. Jerusalem: Shoham.

Najjar, Mohammed. 1999. "Ammonite" Monumental Architecture. Pages 103–12 in *Ancient Ammon*. Edited by Burton Macdonald and Randall W. Younker. Leiden: Brill.

Negueruela, Ivan. 1982. The Proto-Aeolic Capitals from Mudeibi'a, in Moab. *ADAJ* 26: 395–401.

Novák, Mirko. 2012. Temple of 'Ain Dāra in the Context of Imperial and Neo-Hittite Architecture and Art. Pages 41–54 in *Temple Building and Temple Cult: Architecture and Cultic Paraphernalia of Temples in the Levant (2.-1. Mill. B.C.E.); Proceedings of a Conference on the Occasion of the 50th Anniversary of the Institute of Biblical Archaeology at the University of Tübingen (28–30 May 2010)*. Edited by Jens Kamlah in cooperation with Henrike Michelau. Wiesbaden: Harrassowitz.

Ohnefalsch-Richter, Max. 1896. Graeco-Phoenician Architecture in Cyprus: With Special Reference to the Origin and Development of the Ionic Volute. *Journal of the Royal Institute of British Architects* 3: 109–34.

Ornan, Tallay. 2005. *The Triumph of the Symbol: Pictorial Representation of Deities in Mesopotamia and the Biblical Image Ban*. Fribourg: Academic; Göttingen: Vandenhoeck & Ruprecht.

Pace, James H. 2015. The Origin and Purpose of Khirbat al-Mudaybi'. *Review & Expositor* 112: 280–87.

Schumacher, Gottlieb. 1908. *Tell el-Mutesellim: Report of the Excavations Conducted from 1903 to 1905 with the Support of His Majesty the German Emperor and the Deutsche Orient-Gesellschaft from the Deutscher Verein zur Erforschung Palästinas, Vol. 1: Reports of Finds*. Leipzig: Rudolf Haupt.

Shiloh, Yigal. 1976. New Proto-Aeolic Capitals Found in Israel. *BASOR* 222: 67–77.

———. 1979. *The Proto-Aeolic Capital and Israelite Ashlar Masonry*. Jerusalem: Institute of Archaeology, The Hebrew University of Jerusalem.

Shochat, Harel, and Ayelet Gilboa. 2019. Elusive Destructions: Reconsidering the Hazor Iron Age II Sequence and Its Chronological and Historical Implications. *Levant* 50: 363–86.

Stern, Ephraim, and Yitzhak Magen. 2002. Archaeological Evidence for the First Stage of the Samaritan Temple on Mount Gerizim. *IEJ* 52: 49–57.

Tamur, Erhan. 2017. Style, Ethnicity and the Archaeology of the Aramaeans: The Problem of Ethnic Markers in the Art of the Syro-Anatolian Region in the Iron Age. *Forum Kritische Archäologie* 6: 1–72.

Tyson, Craig W., and Friedbert Ninow. 2019. A Basalt Volute Capital Fragment from *el-Bālū'*, Jordan. *ZDPV* 135: 158–67.

Ussishkin, David. 1970a. On the Original Position of Two Proto-Ionic Capitals at Megiddo. *IEJ* 20: 213–15.

———. 1970b. The Syro-Hittite Ritual Burial of Monuments. *JNES* 29: 124–28.

———. 1989. Schumacher's Shrine in Building 338 at Megiddo. *IEJ* 39: 149–72.

———. 2018. *Megiddo-Armageddon: The Story of the Canaanite and Israel City*. Jerusalem: Israel Exploration Society; Biblical Archaeology Society.

Walcher, Katja. 2005. Royal Tomb 5 of Tamassos: An Analysis of Its Decoration with Regard to Religious or Representative Prototypes. Pages 77–89 in *Cyprus: Religion and Society from the Late Bronze Age to the End of the Archaic Period; Proceedings of an International Symposium on Cypriote Archaeology, Erlangen, 23–24 July 2004*. Edited by Vassos Karageorghis, Hartmut Matthäus, and Sabine Rogge. Möhnesee: Bibliopolis.

———. 2007. Die Architektur und Bauornamentik der Königsgräber von Tamassos. Pages 65–88 in *Begegnungen: Materielle Kulturen auf Zypern bis in die römische Zeit*. Edited by Sabine Rogge. Münster: Waxmann.

———. 2009. *Die Architektur und Bauornamentik der archaischen Königsgräber von Tamassos auf Zypern*. Rahden, Westf.: Marie Leidorf.

Wright, George R. H. 2000. *Ancient Building Technology, Vol. 1: Historical Background*. Leiden: Brill.

———. 2005. *Ancient Building Technology, Vol. 2: Materials*. Leiden: Brill.

Yadin, Yigael. 1972. *Hazor: The Head of All Those Kingdoms (Joshua 11:10)*. London: Oxford University Press.

Yadin, Yigael, Yohanan Aharoni, Ruth Amiran, Amnon Ben-Tor, Moshe Dothan, Trude Dothan, Immanual Dunayevsky, Shulamit Geva, and Ephraim Stern. 1989. *Hazor III–IV: An Account of the Third and Fourth Seasons of Excavation, 1957–1958, Vol. 2: Text*. Jerusalem: Israel Exploration Society.

Yadin, Yigael, Yohanan Aharoni, Ruth Amiran, Trude Dothan, Immanuel Dunayevsky, and Jean Perrot. 1960. *Hazor II: An Account of the Second Season of Excavations, 1956*. Jerusalem: Israel Exploration Society.

Yalçin, Serdar. 2020. Orientalizing Architecture: Prinias, 'Ain Dārā and Hittite Echoes in Greek Architectural Sculpture. *Studi Micenei ed Egeo-Anatolici* 6: 133–45.

11
FROM URBAN CENTERS INTO MOUNDS OF RUINS
The Destruction of Cities during the Iron Age

Igor Kreimerman

Introduction

Destruction events—such as the burning of Lachish by Sennacherib, the destruction of Jerusalem by Nebuchadnezzar II, or natural disasters, such as the reported earthquake in the Book of Amos (1:1)—are among the most prominent events described in the Hebrew Bible and contemporary sources. Therefore, they are pivotal to historical reconstructions, chronological studies, and attempts to bridge archaeological and historical sources.

This chapter focuses on such destruction events themselves, outlining their importance to the societies of the Southern Levant during the Iron Age. Literary and archaeological sources complement the study of destruction; textual sources supply information about destruction events, their causes, and how these events were perceived. But, most extant sources are royal inscriptions written to convey a message using formulaic language and hyperbole; consequently, these texts cannot be taken at face value (Younger 1990; Baker 2014; Bachvarova 2016). Furthermore, such texts mainly represent the views and actions of rulers of large cities, kingdoms, and empires; thus, they rarely depict the views and considerations that motivated the actions of smaller cities and nomadic groups. Finally, although extensive textual evidence is available for some events, others lack written sources. Archaeology supplies a wealth of data on the material aspect of destruction, facilitating the reconstruction of activities undertaken immediately before it occurred (Driessen and Macdonald 1997; Zuckerman 2007; Matthiae 2009; Driessen 2013) and, for example, how a fire progressed during the event. At the same time, archaeological evidence about the cause and identity of a destructive agent is often lacking, and the interpretation of existing data is rarely straightforward. Furthermore, excavations normally reveal a small part of a settlement; thus, complex reconstructions based on limited evidence are needed.

To facilitate an archaeological discussion of destruction, a *destruction layer* must first be properly defined. Earlier I suggested—following Finkelstein (2009: 113) with adjustments—that a *destruction layer* is an archaeological layer that fulfills at least one of the following two criteria (Kreimerman 2017a: 176):

1 It contains abundant archaeological finds and especially *de facto refuse* (Schiffer 1972, 1987; LaMotta and Schiffer 1999) on many—though not necessarily all—of its floor

levels. Cases in which items are discarded in rubbish pits, favissae, or burials should be excluded.

2   It contains evidence of conflagration—such as ash, charcoal, burnt bricks, or calcified stones—outside of cooking or industrial areas.

This definition is inclusive. Alongside layers featuring evidence of destruction throughout an entire site, it also includes layers showing localized destruction. Thus, while some site areas may show evidence of a fire or restorable pottery (or both), others may not show such evidence.

The vast majority of destruction layers in the Iron Age Southern Levant can be attributed to six chronological horizons. The first two occurred in Iron Age I, while the latter four took place in Iron Age II. The first destruction horizon is dated to Iron Age Ia (the mid-12th century BCE). Evidence of this first horizon has been found in many of the major Canaanite cities (Kreimerman 2017a). Evidence of the next massive horizon has mainly been found in northern valleys and dated to Iron Age Ib (Finkelstein 2002; Fiaccavento 2014).

Although a few destruction events took place in early Iron Age IIa (Garfinkel, Kreimerman, and Zilberg 2016: 94–96; Mazar 2020), the first significant wave of destruction has been dated no earlier than late Iron Age IIa, during the mid-to late 9th century BCE. These destruction events are commonly associated with the Aramean military campaigns (Galil 2000; Maeir 2004; Na'aman 2013; Kleiman 2016; Mazar 2016). The next two waves of destruction are related to the Assyrian military campaigns—especially those of Tiglath Pileser III and Sennacherib (Dever 2007; Faust 2008; Bagg 2013; Arav 2014). Destruction layers' attribution to these campaigns, and the campaigns of Sargon II and Shalmaneser V, is based mainly on historical considerations. After almost a century without destruction, destruction events attributed, on chronological grounds, to the late 7th to early 6th centuries BCE took place. Clearly, these destruction events are not contemporary; however, establishing each destruction layer's exact date is normally difficult. Scholars use historical considerations to attribute these layers to the various Babylonian campaigns, although some prefer to assign them to local struggles—for instance, the struggles between Judah and the Edomites (Kletter 2003; Koch and Lipschits 2013; Thareani 2014).

Partial destructions throughout Israel have been associated with the earthquake mentioned with respect to Uzziah's reign (Amos 1:1; Zech 14:5; Yadin 1972: 113, 179–82; Dever 1992; Ussishkin 2004a: 83; Maeir 2012: 49–50). The evidence cited to support this association comprises mainly collapsed or cracked walls, which are not unique to earthquakes. Furthermore, an earthquake that could have hit such an extensive area, such that Hazor in the north and Lachish to the south were both destroyed, had to have been very strong and, therefore, left evidence of much more severe damage (Ambraseys 2005: 330–32). Finally, no proof suggests that all of these destruction events occurred simultaneously. They could have happened over several decades and resulted from unrelated events.

The interpretation of the six outlined destruction horizons is mainly based on the extent of literary evidence. Due to the scarcity of historical sources in the Iron Age I, various theories have been put forward to interpret these two horizons. Explanations range from societal crises (Zuckerman 2007; Cline 2014) to earthquakes (Lamon and Shipton 1939; Nur 2008; Cline 2011), accidents (Millek 2017), and warfare—between different states during their formation (Yadin 1970; Ussishkin 1995; Harrison 2004; Finkelstein 2013; Kreimerman 2017a, 2020) or nearby independent cities (Knauf 2000). In contrast, during the Iron Age II, for which written sources sketch a historical outline, one main cause of destruction was repeated across all four destruction horizons: inter-state (or empire-state) warfare.

Several studies have suggested possible different extents of destruction, resulting from the different processes sites have undergone (e.g., Driessen and Macdonald 1997; Panitz-Cohen 2006; Finkelstein 2009; Matthiae 2009; Kreimerman 2017a). This is also clearly shown in Table 11.1; while, in some cases, destruction was thorough, encompassing an entire site, in other cases, evidence of destruction appeared only in specific areas within a settlement.

The distinction between *thorough* and *partial* destruction is important for several reasons (Kreimerman 2020). The most significant difference for this chapter's purposes is intentionality. The causes of partial destruction, especially when evidence is found in a single building, are difficult to determine based on excavation reports, which contain only general data about the locations of fire indicators and the distribution of finds. In such cases, destruction may have resulted from an accidental fire, earthquake, or conflict. Causes are clearer when destruction is confined to structures of a particular type, such as public or religious buildings. In such cases, evidence of fire in separate structures points to separate fires in those buildings. Accordingly, if these fires occurred simultaneously, then it is most likely that those buildings were chosen for burning and thus this destruction was intentional. The case is even more apparent when an entire settlement has been burnt. Because ancient structures were generally built to be fire-resistant (Gordon 1953; Kreimerman and Shahack-Gross 2019), a fire would not expand easily from one structure to another. Therefore, before fire could burn down an entire settlement, most structures would have had to be ignited separately. So, when relatively large parts of a site have been excavated and evidence of fire has been reported in all areas, the apparent destruction was likely intentional.

Table 11.1 Destruction evidence at eight key archaeological sites across Israel, arranged from north to south

Site	Iron age Ia	Iron age Ib	Iron age IIa	Iron age IIb	Iron age IIc
Hazor	–	–	Stratum IX (partial)	Stratum VI (partial), Stratum Va	–
Megiddo	Stratum VIIa (partial destruction)	<u>Stratum VIa</u>	Va–IVb?	IVa?	–
Reḥov	–	Stratum VII (localized in part of D-4a)	Stratum V (partial destruction), <u>Stratum IV</u>	Stratum IIIa	–
Jerusalem	–	–	–	–	<u>586 BCE</u>
Ashdod	–	Stratum XII (rapid abandonment)	Stratum X (partial), Stratum IX (by city gate)	Stratum VIII (partial)	–
Ashkelon	–	–	–	–	<u>Stratum XII</u>
Lachish	<u>Level VI</u>	Occupation gap	Level V?, Level IVa?	<u>Level III</u>	<u>Level II</u>
Tell Beit Mirsim	–	–	Stratum B3?	<u>Stratum A2</u>	–

Underline indicates that such evidence encompasses an entire site. – Indicates a lack of destruction (not an occupation gap).

A proper review of the various facets of destruction by fire requires an examination using four timescales: (1) pre-destruction; (2) during the destruction; (3) after the destruction in the short and medium terms; and (4) the destruction's long-term impact.

Pre-Destruction

The destruction of cities was relatively rare in the Iron Age (Table 11.1). For instance, Lachish features three clear destruction layers: Levels VI, III, and II. Additionally, partial destruction might be evident in Levels IV and V, though such evidence is not universally agreed upon (Ussishkin 2004a: 76–78, 82–83). At Megiddo, Stratum VI was violently destroyed and, possibly, strata VIIA, Va-IVb and IVa were partially destroyed (Finkelstein 2009). At Hazor, Stratum Va was destroyed, and strata IX and VI may have been partially destroyed.

Table 11.1 covers a timespan of roughly 600 years. No site shows more than five destruction layers, even if partial destruction is included. Therefore, destruction seems to have been very uncommon, rarely occurring more than once in a century. Some sites, such as Jerusalem and Ashkelon, were destroyed only once in the discussed timeframe. The infrequency of destruction is best explained by economic considerations. City construction was a large-scale project that required hundreds of workers, considerable resources, and the sophisticated organization and manipulation of the workforce (Trigger 1990; Maran et al. 2006; Keimer, Kreimerman, and Garfinkel 2015; Brysbaert 2018). Cities were the center of residents' life. Each resident's social status, property, and domicile were fixed to their city. Consequently, a city's destruction was undesirable for residents.

For city rulers, whether in power for decades or having newly conquered a city, a city was a major asset. After all, cities were the centers of economic mechanisms that had developed over decades, and they allowed rulers to efficiently exploit the land and its resources and profit from taxes. For these reasons, in times of war, city destruction was undesirable for both residents and prospective conquerors.

While texts do not always explicitly describe cities' exact fates after a conquest, often not mentioning whether a city was destroyed, they clarify in some cases that conquest did not lead to destruction (e.g., 2 Sam 5: 6–9; RIMA 3: A.0.102.1: 15–18; Güterbock 1956: 92–93; Charpin and Ziegler 2003: 242–45). The correlation between historical sources and archaeological studies has revealed additional examples. For instance, after the Assyrian conquest, Samaria and Megiddo seem to have not been destroyed (Tappy 2007; Finkelstein 2009). Also, few destruction layers—if any—seem attributable to the campaign of Shoshenq I (Ussishkin 1990; Finkelstein and Piasetzky 2009).

When a city was destroyed, this damage did not occur immediately after the city's conquest, as explicit textual references demonstrate (2 Kgs 25: 1–10; Jer 52: 4–14; Rutz and Michalowski 2016). In other cases, evidence confirms actions undertaken in conquered cities, such as looting or even a conqueror using buildings in subdued cities (RIMA 3, 17:5; Charpin 1995). Other actions might be inferred even if they are rarely mentioned; conquered cities normally contained granaries with supplies crucial to armies far from home. While the fates of destroyed cities' inhabitants in the pre-imperial period are unknown, evidence confirms that during the Assyrian and Babylonian campaigns, such inhabitants were mostly exiled (Oded 1979; Na'aman 1993; Trimm 2017: 317–46; Thareani 2019). Moving considerable quantities of people definitely required extensive preparations, including allocating new lands to transfer exiles into and arranging their logistical needs along the way (Oded 1979). Consequently, the inhabitants of the conquered cities likely continued to reside in their homes for a while before their exile, just as the speech of the Rabshakeh suggests

(2 Kgs 18: 31–32). Archaeologically, the period between conquest and destruction is demonstrated through the absence of arrowheads and skeletons in most destruction layers. Although an army could not conceivably omit archers when attacking and conquering a city—and indeed, in some cases, numerous arrowheads have been found in destruction debris, such as at Lachish III, Beersheba II, and Jerusalem (Gottlieb 2004, 2016; Vejil and Mazar 2015)—for the most part, arrowheads are absent from destruction layers, even those clearly attributed to military campaigns, such as Lachish II, Tel Batash II or Tel 'Ira VII (Kreimerman 2016). This absence suggests that some cities capitulated to avoid battle. Consequently, someone had to have decided to burn them down. Skeletons are also absent from most destruction layers, including at Lachish III, Beersheba II, and Jerusalem, where battle evidence is extensive. This lack of skeletons is due to cities having probably been cleansed of corpses for hygiene reasons so that the conquering army could exploit the captured cities (Kreimerman 2017b).

During Destruction

Fire has profoundly affected the vast majority of materials found in a typical ancient Near Eastern city. Most organic materials—including various types of food, clothing, furniture, and beams—are likely to have been charred or turned to ash (Braadbaart and Poole 2008). Fire also considerably changes the physical and mineralogical properties of mud bricks (Forget et al. 2015), and under some conditions, they might crack or fall apart. Finally, under certain fire conditions, stones might calcify (Regev et al. 2010). Thus, aside from storage vessels themselves, the vast majority of materials stored in houses and construction materials become unusable after fire exposure. As a result, a city's reconstruction would require considerable energy, comparable to the effort required to build an entirely new settlement.

To understand destruction's impact in the context of warfare, as with any other sort of violence, the perspectives of the victim, the perpetrator, and the witness should be reviewed (Krohn-Hansen 1994; Osterholtz 2012). While the victim and perpetrator's perspectives have received much scholarly attention in research in relation to destruction, a spectator's perspective has generally been overlooked, and it requires further research.

The visual impact of a fire that lasted for several hours or even a few days would have been imposing. Fire transforms individually identifiable buildings into a mass of burnt bricks and charcoal. The transformative effect of violence is known to be especially imposing (Pauketat 2009; Osterholtz 2012: 131–35; Harmanşah 2015). While city construction transformed disparate people into a consolidated group with a distinct joint identity (Brysbaert 2018), the burning of a city symbolized the severing of such connections between people and the land. The sight of such razing must have immediately changed former residents' mental map of their city (Hitchcock 2013). Furthermore, for both a site's residents and residents of neighboring cities who could have seen such a spectacle of burning from afar, the sight would have represented the attackers' ultimate superiority over the destroyed city. This superiority entailed not only military might but also ideological and religious dominance, as the destruction of a city and—usually—its temples probably suggested that the gods had left the city, allowing it to be destroyed (Dobbs-Allsopp 1993; Fried 2003; Jacobs 2016). Therefore, unsurprisingly, city destruction—especially when intended to prevent future habitation—was often ritualistic. Generally, such rituals are similar in Hittite, Mesopotamian, and Assyrian texts and in the Hebrew Bible (Gevirtz 1963; Stern 1991; Roszkowska-Mutschler 1992; Del Monte 2005; Wright 2015; Kreimerman and Segev 2019).

Anthropological studies have stressed that a credible threat of violence could achieve control as powerfully as actual violence (Krohn-Hansen 1994; Parsons 2007). Indeed, both royal inscriptions and visual depictions of war are well known to have been used as propaganda intended to deter rival parties from conflict (Younger 1990; Levtow 2014). This forms a background for demoralizing efforts during sieges, best known from the Assyrian military campaigns, including speeches by messengers before city gates, cutting down fruit trees, and torturing captives (Hasel 2005; Lewis 2008; Eph'al 2013: 53–54; Lamb 2014; Siddal 2019: 43–44). Similarly, witnessing the burning of a neighboring city could lead another threatened city's residents to conclude that resistance would be futile (Saggs 1963), especially when the burning city was larger and better fortified or more symbolically important than the besieged city that had not yet surrendered. Despite such considerations, psychological warfare cannot be argued as the *primary* goal of city destruction, mainly because evidence shows delays between conquest and destruction, as well as destruction itself—alongside residents' exile—occurring sometimes only after a campaign had concluded.

The Afterlife of Destroyed Mounds

Greenberg (2016) has correctly stressed that many ruined cities become material, strategic, and symbolic resources and thus take on new roles in the settlement landscape. When the destruction of a city was partial in nature and concentrated around its fortifications or in buildings of specific types—such as religious or public buildings—reconstruction has usually followed (Kreimerman 2017a; 2020). However, the reconstruction of cities immediately after thorough destruction was rather rare, happening mainly when the conqueror could not exert control over the conquered area (Kreimerman 2021). Destroyed sites were clearly favorable locations for habitation. First, most Iron Age cities were positioned on top of tells that were inhabited for centuries due to their proximity to major roads, sources of water, fertile fields, and other economic resources. Also, some building materials from destroyed cities, such as quarried stone, could be reutilized. In addition, the reconstruction of a city, and particularly of the temples within, was of theological importance and was considered to be a favorable action (Fried 2003; Harmanşah 2013; Davis 2019).

Ruined cities commonly became foci for the activity of squatters, who used the material assets of the mounds. The extent of squatters' activity changed from site to site, as exemplified by the outcome of Sennacherib's campaign. After the destruction of Level III at Lachish, one of the inner-gate chambers was reused, probably for domestic activities (Ussishkin 2004b: 652). Ussishkin has identified several walls, floors, and installations at the passage of the outer gate, suggesting that they were built to block the progress of the Assyrian attack (Ussishkin 2004c: 553–54). Nevertheless, these rather thin walls built on top of Level III floors, some of which form corners with others, were built of mudbricks that do not show evidence of exposure to fire in contrast to other Level III features in their vicinity. One feature, Locus 4961, is a circular installation partially blocking the entrance to the outer gate courtyard and clearly could not have been present during the regular activity of the gate (Ussishkin 2004c: 554). Therefore, these features are likely to represent ephemeral structures built after the city was destroyed (Ussishkin 2004c: 553–54).

Even with this new interpretation, the extent of activity at Lachish is limited to the gate area and is of domestic nature. Thus, a question arises regarding the identity of its new occupants. On the one hand, the pottery of the post–Level III phase is indistinguishable from the pottery found in the destruction debris of Level III (Ussishkin 2004b: 652). Consequently, while it is problematic to equate pots with people, it might be assumed that the occupants were, broadly speaking, Judean. Yet, it is unclear if these were the former inhabitants of Lachish who returned to the site. A return of the city's residents could be expected to be accompanied by reclamation of objects from the destruction debris and by reconstruction or re-inhabitation of their own structures. Yet, despite extensive excavations around the site, no reconstructed domestic structures have been found, and no reclamation processes could be attested (Tufnell 1953; Aharoni 1975; Ussishkin 2004d; Garfinkel et al. 2021).

At other sites that were destroyed in Sennacherib's campaign, there is different evidence. Tell Beit Mirsim poses a difficult case, as there seem to be two subphases in the last Iron Age Stratum to Stratum A2 in several places. Y. and M. Aharoni suggest dubbing the most recent phase Stratum A3 (Aharoni and Aharoni 1976). This phase is characterized by the construction of several buildings around the site. These buildings were relatively large and built of massive stones, which were probably removed from the ruined city wall, leaving the settlement unfortified (Albright 1943: 44–45, 66; Blakely and Hardin 2002: 14–24). The dating of this stratum has been debated, with suggestions spanning from the late 6th century BCE to the idea that Strata A2 and A3 were destroyed in two different Assyrian campaigns (Albright 1943; Aharoni and Aharoni 1976; Blakely and Hardin 2002). The most plausible explanation, however, is that Stratum A2 was destroyed within Sennacherib's campaign, whereas Stratum A3 was the result of relatively extensive squatters' activity (Finkelstein and Na'aman 2004). For our discussion, it is noteworthy that while the energy input at Tell Beit Mirsim was much more extensive than at Lachish, at this site also the newly constructed buildings do not show close familiarity with the destroyed city. Not a single building of the previous phase was reconstructed. Similar evidence is found at Beersheba, where Stratum I includes the construction of new buildings on top of the ruins, following a different plan than the destroyed city of Stratum II (Herzog 2016: 233–40). At both Tell Beit Mirsim and Beersheba, the pottery of the destroyed layer and the squatters' phase is indistinguishable.

This situation is markedly different from that of Tell Halif. After the destruction of the fortified settlement of Stratum VIB, some of the domestic structures were cleared and reoccupied, and new installations were built within them (Blakely and Hardin 2002: 24; Hardin 2010: 93, 111; Cole 2015: 33–36). In this case, it seems that the inhabitants were familiar with the destroyed settlement; that they had fled the city of Stratum VIB and returned to the site cannot be ruled out.

Finally, the case of Beth-Shemesh must be considered. Following the destruction of the Iron Age IIB city on the tell, the mound was not reoccupied in a later period, except for the water system that continued to function (Bunimovitz and Lederman 2003, 2016). Sometime during the 7th century BCE, a large unfortified settlement was constructed adjacent to the mound. Its material culture indicates that this was most probably a Judean town (Hadad, Ben-Ari, and De Groot 2020). Clearly, it would have been more beneficial to construct 7th-century BCE Beth-Shemesh on top of the destroyed city so that it enjoyed a prominent position on top of the mound, which would bestow at least some protection and allow easier access to the still-functioning water system. It therefore seems that the choice not to build the city at this site was intentional, perhaps resulting from the political situation in which the Assyrians wanted to avoid another rebellion by Judah and thus preventing large-scale construction on top of the destroyed mounds.

As the case of Sennacherib's campaign suggests, the level of activity within ruined cities varied based on the resources that the city provided, squatters' familiarity with the ruined cities, and the political situation.

Long-Term Impact of Destruction

Cities that were able to escape destruction by a large force, such as Jerusalem in Sennacherib's campaign, gained a prominent status, and it seems that on the eve of Nebuchadnezzar II's campaign, the prevalent view in Judean society was that Jerusalem would never fall (Lipschits 2005: 70–74), although of course some people, including Jeremiah, had a different view (Malamat 1975: 137–38). The ultimate destruction of Jerusalem in 586 BCE became a central event in the formation of Judaism, as it had to be explained and justified from a theological point. This destruction is lamented until today, hundreds of years after the actual event. Indeed, the commemoration of destroyed cities as part of rituals hundreds of years after they occurred, and even after the cities have been rebuilt is a well-known phenomenon. In some cases, the depicted destructions did not reflect historical destruction events but instead reflected the rise in the importance of the "destroyed" cities to a status that facilitated their inclusion in the rituals (Michalowski 1983: 242–43; Gabbay 2014: 158–68).

Mounds of destroyed sites continued to play a symbolic role for many years after their destruction (Jones and Russell 2012; Paz 2015; Greenberg 2016; Van Dyke 2019; Maran 2020). Biblical Hebrew and other Near Eastern languages contain a specific word, *tell* (תל), that refers to an artificial mound created by ruins (Deut 13:17; Josh 8:28; Jer 49:2) and which is distinct from natural mounds (Wright 1939). It is acknowledged in the Hebrew Bible that some cities were built on such mounds (Josh 11:13; Jer 30:18).

A noteworthy phenomenon is the avoidance of resettling destroyed sites. It is possible that evidence for this pattern appears already in the Intermediate Bronze Age when people avoided settling on top of abandoned Early Bronze Age mounds (Mazar 2006). If so, this suggests that the abandoned mounds had taken on a new, although marginalized, role in the cognitive maps of the people of the Intermediate Bronze Age, who surely acknowledged their existence (Paz 2015). Regrettably, this exact cognitive role cannot be reconstructed, especially due to the absence of written sources from the period. As mentioned above, we know of a Near Eastern tradition, which appears also in the Hebrew Bible, of a ritual destruction followed by a ban (חרם) (e.g., Num 21: 1–3; Duet 13: 13–18; 20: 15–18; Josh 6: 16–26) on the inhabitation of the decimated site (Gevirtz 1963; Stern 1991; Roszkowska-Mutschler 1992; Del Monte 2005; Kreimerman and Segev 2019). It seems that some of these stories in the Hebrew Bible describing the decimation of cities and subsequent ban on their habitation were written centuries after the supposed events. When examined both literarily and archaeologically, it becomes clear that the described events—such as the destruction of Jericho, 'Ai, and Hazor, did not necessarily happen. Instead, the stories are of an etiological nature and reflect a re-interpretation of existing monuments in the landscape (Alt 1953: 176–92; Coogan 1990).

As artificial mounds in the landscape were sometimes identified in ancient times as representing destroyed cities, it is of no surprise that the ruins themselves became symbols and foci of cults decades after the destruction. Thus, these remains might help trace the above-mentioned etiological stories. The best examples of this trait come from Hazor (Zuckerman 2011). The highest point of the acropolis of the Late Bronze Age city had been dominated by a ceremonial precinct. When an Iron Age I settlement was constructed on top of the ruins, no structures were built on top of Building 7050, the main building of the Ceremonial Precinct. The same tradition of avoiding construction on top of the main building was followed throughout the Iron Age, until in Stratum V, dated to the mid- to late 8th century BCE, a wall was built around the core of the building, probably to demarcate the area where construction was forbidden (Sandhaus 2013: 115–17). In other places during the Iron Age

I, standing stones were built into Late Bronze Age destruction debris, suggesting that ruin cults were practiced (Ben-Ami 2006; Zuckerman 2011). Zuckerman (2011: 393) has suggested that leaving a mound of ruins in the middle of the site and at the cult places built into the ruins reflects the new inhabitants' rediscovery and appropriation of the remains.

The Iron Age I inhabitants, followed by those of the Iron Age II, must have reinterpreted the remains in a process that ultimately led to the formulation of the Biblical conquest narrative. Similar evidence of cultic activities or depositions of items within the ruins have been reported from Iron Age Ia Lachish (Weissbein et al. 2020: 23), Iron Age Ib Tel Kinrot (Münger, Zangenberg, and Pakkala 2011: 77–78), Iron Age IB or early Iron Age IIA Megiddo (Kleiman et al. 2017: 26), and Iron Age I–II Tell el-Burak (Kamlah, Sader, and Schmitt 2016). While the evidence from Hazor, especially the mound of ruins left in the middle of the site, is clear, the mere presence of cultic installations on top of ruins in other cases does not in itself show that the ruins were the foci of cultic activities. The most similar cases to Hazor, where ruins occupied a prominent position in the urban landscape of a city and were shaped intentionally into a tumulus-like mound within a city centuries after the destruction, are found in the Aegean (Prent 2003; Maran 2016, 2020).

Finally, of course, mounds of ruins have become foci of archaeological work, taking place hundreds and thousands of years after the cities were decimated (Greenberg 2016). The excavation of the destroyed sites brings new reinterpretations of the remains (Driessen 2013), an example of which could be seen in this very contribution. This topic is beyond the scope of this essay.

References

Aharoni, Miriam and Yohanan Aharoni. 1976. "The Stratification of Judahite Sites in the 8th and 7th Centuries B.C.E." *BASOR* 224: 73–90.

Aharoni, Yohanan. 1975. *Investigations at Lachish: The Sanctuary and the Residency (Lachish V)*. Tel Aviv: Institute of Archaeology, Tel Aviv University.

Albright, William F. 1943. *The Excavation of Tell Beit Mirsim III: The Iron Age*. AASOR 21–22.

Alt, Albrecht. 1953. *Kleine Schriften Zur Geschichte Des Volkes Israel, I*. München: C.H. Beck.

Ambraseys, Nicholas. 2005. "Historical Earthquakes in Jerusalem: A Methodological Discussion." *Journal of Seismology* 9: 329–40.

Arav, Rami. 2014. "A Chronicle of Inevitable Destruction: Stages in the Conquest and Destruction of Bethsaida by Tiglath Pileser III." Pages 2–25 in *Bethsaida in Archaeology, History and Ancient Culture*. Edited by Harold J. Ellens. Newcastle upon Tyne: Cambridge Scholars Publishing.

Bachvarova, Mary R. 2016. "The Destroyed City in Ancient 'World History': From Agade to Troy." Pages 36–78 in *The Fall of Cities in the Mediterranean: Commemoration in Literature, Folk Song, and Liturgy*. Edited by Mary R. Bachvarova, Dorota Dutsch, and Ann Suter. Cambridge: Cambridge University Press.

Bagg, Ariel M. 2013. "Palestine Under Assyrian Rule: A New Look at the Assyrian Imperial Policy in the West." *JAOS* 133: 119–44.

Baker, Heather D. 2014. "I Burnt, Razed (and) Destroyed Those Cities: The Assyrian Accounts of Deliberate Architectural Destruction." Pages 45–57 in *Architecture and Armed Conflict: The Politics of Destruction*. Edited by JoeAnne M. Mancini and Keith Bersnahan. London: Routledge.

Ben-Ami, Doron. 2006. "Early Iron Age Cult Places: New Evidence from Tel Hazor." *TA* 33: 121–33.

Blakely, Jeffrey A., and James W. Hardin. 2002. "Southwestern Judah in the Late Eighth Century B.C.E." *BASOR* 326: 11–64.

Braadbaart, Freek and Imogen Poole. 2008. "Morphological, Chemical and Physical Changes During Charcoalification of Wood and Its Relevance to Archaeological Contexts." *JAS* 35: 2434–45.

Brysbaert, Ann. 2018. "Constructing Monuments, Perceiving Monumentality: Introduction." Pages 21–47 in *Constructing Monuments, Perceiving Monumentality & the Economics of Building*. Edited by Ann Brysbaert, Victor Klinkenberg, Anna Gutiérrez Garcia, and Irene Vikatou. Leiden: Sidestone.

Bunimovitz, Shlomo and Zvi Lederman. 2003. "The Final Destruction of Beth Shemesh and the Pax Assyriaca in the Judean Shephelah." *TA* 30: 3–26.

———. 2016. "'Your Country Is Desolate, Your Cities Are Burned with Fire:' The Death of a Judahite Border Town Level 2: Iron IIB ca. 790–701 BCE." Pages 419–69 in *Tel Beth-Shemesh: A Border Community in Judah: Renewed Excavations 1990–2000: The Iron Age*. Edited by Shlomo Bunimovitz and Zvi Lederman. Winona Lake: Eisenbrauns.

Charpin, Dominique. 1995. "La Fin Des Archives Dans le Palais De Mari." *RA* 89: 29–40.

Charpin, Dominique, and Nele Ziegler. 2003. *Mari et Le Proche-Orient à l'Époque Amorrite. Essai d'Histoire Politique*. Paris: SPEOA.

Cline, Eric H. 2011. "'Whole Lotta Shakin' Going On: The Possible Destruction by Earthquake of Stratum VIA at Megiddo." Pages 55–70 in *The Fire Signals of Lachish: Studies in the Archaeology and History of Israel in the Late Bronze Age, Iron Age, and Persian Period in Honor of David Ussishkin*. Edited by Israel Finkelstein and Nadav Na'aman. Winona Lake: Eisenbrauns.

———. 2014. *1177 B.C.: The Year Civilization Collapsed*. Princeton: Princeton University Press.

Cole, Dan P. 2015. *Lahav V: The Iron, Persian, and Hellenistic Occupation within the Walls at Tell Halif, Excavations in Field II: 1977–1980*. Winona Lake: Eisenbrauns.

Coogan, Michael D. 1990. "Archaeology and Biblical Studies: The Book of Joshua." Pages 19–32 in *The Hebrew Bible and Its Interpreters*. Edited by William H. Propp, Baruch Halpern, and David N. Freedman. Winona Lake: Eisenbrauns.

Davis, andrew R. 2019. *Reconstructing the Temple: The Royal Rhetoric of Temple Renovation in the Ancient Near East and Israel*. Oxford: Oxford University Press.

Del Monte, Giuseppe F. 2005. "The Hittite Ḥerem." Pages 21–45 in *Memoriae Igor M Diakonoff*. Edited by Leonid E. Kogan, Natalia Koslova, Sergey Loesov and Serguei Tishchenko. Winona Lake: Eisenbrauns.

Dever, William G. 1992. "A Case-Study in Biblical Archaeology: The Earthquake of ca. 760 BCE." *EI* 23: 27*–35*.

———. 2007. "Archaeology and the Fall of the Northern Kingdom: What Really Happened?" Pages 78–92 in *"Up to the Gates of Ekron": Essays on Archaeology and History of the Eastern Mediterranean in Honor of Seymour Gitin*. Edited by S. White Crawford, Amnon Ben-Tor, J. P. Dessel, William G. Dever, Amihai Mazar, and Joseph Aviram. Jerusalem: Israel Exploration Society.

Dobbs-Allsopp, F. W. 1993. *Weep, O Daughter of Zion: A Study of the City-Lament Genre in the Hebrew Bible*. Rome: Pontifical Institute.

Driessen, Jan. 2013. "Time Capsules? Destructions as Archaeological Phenomena." Pages 5–22 in *Destruction. Archaeological, Philological and Historical Perspectives*. Edited by Jan Driessen. Louvain-la-Neuve: Presses Universitaires de Louvain.

Driessen, Jan, and Colin F. Macdonald. 1997. *The Troubled Island: Minoan Crete Before and After the Santorini Eruption*. Liege: Université de Liège.

Eph'al, Israel. 2013. *The City Besieged: Siege and Its Manifestations in the Ancient Near East*. Jerusalem: Magness.

Faust, Avraham. 2008. "Settlement and Demography in Seventh-Century Judah and the Extent and Intensity of Sennacherib's Campaign." *PEQ* 140: 168–94.

Fiaccavento, Chiara. 2014. "Destructions as Historical Markers Towards the End of the 2nd and During the 1st Millenium BC in Southern Levant." Pages 205–59 in *Overcoming Catastrophes: Essays on Disastrous Agent Characterization and Resilence Strategies in Pre-Classical Southern Levant*. Edited by Lorenzo Nigro. Rome: La Sapienza Expedition to Palestine & Jordan.

Finkelstein, Israel. 2002. "The Campaign of Shoshenq I to Palestine: A Guide to the 10th Century BCE Polity." *ZDPV* 118: 109–35.

———. 2009. "Destructions: Megiddo as a Case Study." Pages 113–26 in *Exploring the Longue Durée: Essays in Honor of Lawrence E. Stager*. Edited by David J. Schloen. Winona Lake: Eisenbrauns.

———. 2013. *The Forgotten Kingdom: The Archaeology and History of Northern Israel*. Atlanta: SBL.

Finkelstein, Israel and Nadav Na'aman. 2004. "The Judahite Shephelah in the Late 8th and Early 7th Centuries BCE." *TA* 31: 60–79.

Finkelstein, Israel and Eli Piasetzky. 2009. "Radiocarbon-Dated Destruction Layers: A Skeleton for Iron Age Chronology in the Levant." *OJA* 28: 255–74.

Forget, Mathilde C. L., Lior Regev, David E. Friesem,, and Ruth Shahack-Gross. 2015. "Physical and Mineralogical Properties of Experimentally Heated Chaff-Tempered Mud Bricks: Implications for

Reconstruction of Environmental Factors Influencing the Appearance of Mud Bricks in Archaeological Conflagration Events." *JASR* 2: 80–93.
Fried, Lisbeth S. 2003. "The Land Lay Desolate: Conquest and Restoration in the Ancient Near East." Pages 21–54 in *Judah and the Judeans in the Neo-Babylonian Period*. Edited by Oded Lipschits and Joseph Blenkinsopp. Winona Lake: Eisenbrauns.
Gabbay, Uri. 2014. *No Pacifying the Hearts of the Gods: Sumerian Emesal Prayers of the First Millennium BC*. Wiesbaden: Harrassowitz.
Galil, Gershon. 2000. "The Boundaries of Aram Damascus in the 9th–8th Centuries BCE." Pages 35–41 in *Studies in Historical Geography & Biblical Historiography*. Edited by Gershon Galil and Moshe Weinfeld. Leiden: Brill.
Garfinkel, Yosef, et al. 2021. "The Canaanite and Judean Cities of Lachish, Israel: Preliminary Report of the Fourth Expedition, 2013–2017." *AJA* 125: 419–59.
Garfinkel, Yosef, Igor Kreimerman, and Peter Zilberg. 2016. *Debating Khirbet Qeiyafa: A Fortified City in Judah from the Time of King David*. Jerusalem: Israel Exploration Society.
Gevirtz, Stanley. 1963. "Jericho and Shechem: A Religio-Literary Aspect of City Destruction." *VT* 13: 52–62.
Gordon, D H. 1953. "Fire and the Sword: The Technique of Destruction." *Antiquity* 27(107): 149–52.
Gottlieb, Yulia. 2004. "The Arrowheads and Selected Objects of the Siege Battle." Pages 1907–69 in *The Renewed Archaeological Excavations at Lachish (1973–1994)*. By David Ussishkin. Tel Aviv: Sonia and Marco Nadler Institute of Archaeology, Tel Aviv University.
———. 2016. "Beer-Sheba Under Attack: A Study of Arrowheads and the Story of the Destruction of the Iron Age Settlement." Pages 1192–1228 in *Beer-Sheba III: The Early Iron IIA Enclosed Settlement and the Late Iron IIA–IIB Cities*. By Zeev Herzog and Lily Singer-Avitz. Tel Aviv: Institute of Archaeology, Tel Aviv University.
Greenberg, Raphael. 2016. "The Afterlife of Tells." Pages 337–43 in *Proceedings of the 2nd International Congress on the Archaeology of the Ancient Near East, Vol 1*. Edited by Ingolf Thuesen. Winona Lake: Eisenbrauns.
Güterbock, Hans G. 1956. "The Deeds of Suppiluliuma as Told by His Son, Mursili II." *JCS* 10: 41–68, 75–98, 107–30.
Hadad, Eli, Nathan Ben-Ari, and Alon De Groot. 2020. "A Century Old Enigma: The Seventh-Century BCE Settlement at Tel Beth Shemesh (East)." *IEJ* 70: 173–88.
Hardin, James W. 2010. *Lahav II: Households and the Use of Domestic Space at Iron II Tell Halif: An Archaeology of Destruction*. Winona Lake: Eisenbrauns.
Harmanşah, Ömür. 2013. *Cities and the Shaping of Memory in the Ancient Near East*. Cambridge: Cambridge University Press.
———. 2015. "ISIS, Heritage, and the Spectacles of Destruction in the Global Media." *NEA* 78: 170–77.
Harrison, Timothy P. 2004. *Megiddo 3: Final Report on the Stratum VI Excavations*. Chicago: Oriental Institute.
Hasel, Michael G. 2005. *Military Practice and Polemic: Israel's Laws of Warfare in Near Eastern Perspective*. Berrien Springs: Andrews University Press.
Herzog, Zeev. 2016. "The Eastern Quarter." Pages 119–241 in *Beer-Sheba III: The Early Iron IIA Enclosed Settlement and the Late Iron IIA–IIB Cities*. Edited by Zeev Herzog and Lily Singer-Avitz. Tel Aviv: Institute of Archaeology, Tel Aviv University.
Hitchcock, Louise A. 2013. "Destruction and Identity: Trauma, Migration, and Performativity in the Late Bronze Age Mediterranean." Pages 203–20 in *Destruction. Archaeological, Philological and Historical Perspectives*. Edited by Jan Driessen. Louvain-la-Neuve: Presses Universitaires de Louvain.
Jacobs, John. 2016. "The City Lament in the Ancient Near East." Pages 13–35 in *The Fall of Cities in the Mediterranean: Commemoration in Literature, Folk Song, and Liturgy*. Edited by Mary R. Bachvarova, Dorota Dutsch, and Ann Suter. Cambridge: Cambridge University Press.
Jones, Siân, and Lynette Russell. 2012. "Archaeology, Memory and Oral Tradition: An Introduction." *IJHA* 16: 267–83.
Kamlah, Jens, Hélène Sader, and Aaron Schmitt. 2016. "A Cultic Installation with a Standing Stone from the Phoenician Settlement at Tell El-Burak." *Berytus* 55: 135–68.
Keimer, Kyle H., Igor Kreimerman, and Yosef Garfinkel. 2015. "From Quarry to Completion: Ḥirbet Qēyafa as a Case Study in the Building of Ancient Near Eastern Settlements." *ZDPV* 131: 109–28.

Kleiman, Assaf. 2016. "The Damascene Subjugation of the Southern Levant as a Gradual Process (ca. 842–800 BCE)." Pages 57–76 in *In Search of Aram and Israel: Politics, Culture and Identity*. Edited by Omer Sergi, Manfred Oeming, and Izaak J. de Hulster. Tübingen: Mohr Siebeck.

Kleiman, Assaf, et al. 2017. "Cult Activity at Megiddo in the Iron Age: New Evidence and a Long-Term Perspective." *ZDPV* 133: 24–52.

Kletter, Raz. 2003. "Iron Age Hoards of Precious Metals in Palestine: An 'Underground Economy'?" *Levant* 35: 139–52.

Knauf, Ernst A. 2000. "Who Destroyed Megiddo VIA?" *BN* 103: 30–35.

Koch, Ido and Oded Lipschits. 2013. "The Rosette Stamped Jar Handle System and the Kingdom of Judah at the End of the First Temple Period." *ZDPV* 129: 55–78.

Kreimerman, Igor. 2016. "Siege Warfare, Conflict and Destruction: How Are They Related?" Pages 229–45 in *From Sha'ar Hagolan to Shaaraim: Essays in Honor of Prof. Yosef Garfinkel*. Edited by Saar Ganor, Igor Kreimerman, Katharina Streit, and Madeleine Mumcuoglu. Jerusalem: Israel Exploration Society.

———2017a. "A Typology for Destruction Layers: The Late Bronze Age Southern Levant as a Case Study." Pages 173–203 in *Crsis to Collapse: The Archaeology of Social Breakdown*. Edited by Tim F. Cunningham and Jan Driessen. Louvain-la-Neuve: Presses Universitaires de Louvain.

———. 2017b. "Skeletons in Bronze and Iron Age Destruction Contexts in the Southern Levant: What Do They Mean?" *West & East* 2: 13–30.

———. 2020. "Why Were Cities Destroyed in Times of War? A View from the Southern Levant in the Third and Second Millennia BCE." Pages 345–83 in *Societies at War (Melammu Symposia 10)*. Edited by Kai Ruffing, Kerstin Droß-Krüpe, Sebastian Fink, and Robert Rollinger. Vienna: Österreichische Akademie der Wissenschaften.

———. 2021. "After the Flames Died Down: Defeat, Destruction, and Forced Abandonment in the Bronze and Iron Age Levant." Pages 229–60 in *Culture of Defeat: Submission in Written Sources and the Archaeological Record*. Edited by Katharina Streit and Marianne Grohmann. Atlanta: Gorgias.

Kreimerman, Igor, and Yair Segev. 2019. "'Burn the Town with Fire…and It Shall Remain an Everlasting Ruin Never to Be Rebuilt' (Deut. 13:17): On The Complete Destruction of Cities and Its Relation to the Biblical and Ex-Biblical Ḥerem." Pages 209–28 in *NSAJR 13*. Edited by Orit Peleg-Barkat, Yehiel Zelinger, Joe Uziel, and Yuval Gadot. Jerusalem: Hebrew University, Institute of Archaeology.

Kreimerman, Igor and Ruth Shahack-Gross. 2019. "Understanding Conflagration of One-Story Mud-Brick Structures: An Experimental Approach." *AAS* 11.6: 2911–28.

Krohn-Hansen, Christian. 1994. "The Anthropology of Violent Interaction." *JAR* 50: 367–81.

Lamb, D T. 2014. "'I Will Strike You Down and Cut off Your Head' (1 Sam 17:46): Trash Talking, Derogatory Rhetoric, and Psychological Warfare in Ancient Israel." Pages 111–30 in *Warfare, Ritual, and Symbol in Biblical and Modern Contexts*. Edited by Brad E. Kelle, Frank R. Ames and Jacob L. Wright. Atlanta, GA: SBL.

Lamon, Robert S., and Geoffrey M. Shipton. 1939. *Megiddo I: Strata I–V*. Chicago: Oriental Institute.

LaMotta, Vincent M., and Michael B. Schiffer. 1999. "Formation Process of House Floor Assemblages." Pages 19–29 in *The Archaeology of Household Activities*. Edited by Penelope M. Allison. New York: Routledge.

Levtow, Nathaniel B. 2014. "Monumental Inscriptions and the Ritual Representation of War." Pages 25–46 in *Warfare, Ritual, and Symbol in Biblical and Modern Contexts*. Edited by Brad E. Kelle, Frank R. Ames and Jacob L. Wright. Atlanta: SBL.

Lewis, Theodore J. 2008. "'You Have Heard What the Kings of Assyria Have Done' Disarmament Passages Vis-à-Vis Assyrian Rhetoric of Intimidation." Pages 75–100 in *Isaiah's Vision of Peace in Biblical and Modern International Relations*. Edited by Raymond Cohen and Raymond Westbrook. New York: Palgrave Macmillan.

Lipschits, Oded. 2005. *The Fall and Rise of Jerusalem: Judah under Babylonian Rule*. Winona Lake: Eisenbrauns.

Maeir, Aren M. 2004. "The Historical Background and Dating of Amos VI 2: An Archaeological Perspective from Tell Eṣ-Ṣâfī/Gath." *VT* 54: 319–34.

———. 2012. "The Tell Es-Safi/Gath Archaeological Project 1996–2010: Introduction, Overview and Synopsis of Results." Pages 1–88 in *Tell Es-Safi/Gath I: The 1996–2005 Seasons*. Edited by Aren M. Maeir. Wiesbaden: Harrassowitz.

Malamat, Abraham. 1975. "The Twilight of Judah: The Egyptian-Babylonian Maelstorm." Pages 123–43 in *Congress Volume Edinburgh 1974*. Edited by John A. Emerton. Leiden: Brill.

Maran, Joseph. 2016. "The Persistence of Place and Memory: The Case of the Early Helladic Rundbau and the Mycenaean Palatial Megara of Tiryns." Pages 153–73 in *Von Baden bis Troia: Ressourcennuntzung, Metallurgie und Wissentransfer*. Edited by Martin Bartelheim, Barbara Horejs, and Raiko Krauss. Rahden: Marie Leidorf.

———. 2020. "The Presence of the Past: Ruin Mounds and Social Memory in Bronze and Early Iron Age Israel and Greece." Pages 177–98 in *Nomads of the Mediterranean: Trade and Contact in the Bronze and Iron Ages*. Edited by Ayelet Gilboa and Assaf Yasur-Landau. Leiden: Brill.

Maran, Joseph, Carsten Juwig, Hermann Schwengel, and Ulrich Thaler. 2006. *Constructing Power: Architecture, Ideology and Social Practice*. Hamburg: Lit Verlag.

Matthiae, Paolo. 2009. "Crisis and Collapse: Similarity and Diversity in the Three Destructions of Ebla from EB IVA to MB II." *Scienza dell' Antichità* 15: 43–83.

Mazar, Amihai. 2006. "Tel Beth-Shean and the Fate of Mounds in the Intermediate Bronze Age." Pages 105–18 in *Confronting the Past: Archaeological and Historical Essays on Ancient Israel in Honor of William G. Dever*. Edited by Sy Gitin, J. Edward Wright, and J. P. Dessel. Winona Lake: Eisenbrauns.

———. 2016. "Culture, Identity and Politics Relating to Tel Reḥov in the 10th–9th Centuries BCE." Pages 89–119 in *In Search of Aram and Israel: Politics, Culture and Identity*. Edited by Omer Sergi, Manfred Oeming, and Izaak J de Hulster. Tübingen: Mohr Siebeck.

———. 2020. "The Tel Reḥov Excavations: Overview and Synthesis." Pages 69–140 in *Tel Reḥov: A Bronze and Iron Age City in the Beth-Shean Valley, Volume I: Introduction, Synthesis and Excavations on the Upper Mound*. Edited by Amihai Mazar and Nava Panitz-Cohen. Jerusalem: Hebrew University, Institute of Archaeology.

Michalowski, Piotr. 1983. "History as Charter Some Observations on the Sumerian King List." *JAOS* 103: 237–48.

Millek, Jesse M. 2017. "Sea Peoples, Philistines, and the Destruction of Cities: A Critical Examination of Destruction Layers 'Caused' by the 'Sea Peoples.'" Pages 113–40 in *"Sea Peoples" Up-to-Date: New Research on Transformations in the Eastern Mediterranean in the 13th–11th Centuries BCE*. Edited by Peter M. Fischer and Teresa Bürge. Vienna: Österreichische Akademie der Wissenschaften.

Münger, Stefan, Jürgen Zangenberg, and Juha Pakkala. 2011. "Kinneret: An Urban Center at the Crossroads, Excavations on Iron IB Tel Kinrot at the Lake of Galilee." *NEA* 74: 68–90.

Na'aman, Nadav. 1993. "Population Changes in Palestine Following Assyrian Deportations." *TA* 20: 104–24.

———. 2013. "The Kingdom of Judah in the 9th Century BCE: Text Analysis versus Archaeological Research." *TA* 40: 247–276.

Nur, Amos. 2008. *Apocalypse: Earthquakes, Archaeology, and the Wrath of God*. Princeton: Princeton University Press.

Oded, Bustenai. 1979. *Mass Deportations and Deportees in the Neo-Assyrian Empire*. Wiesbaden: Reichert.

Osterholtz, Anna J. 2012. "Hobbling and Torture as Performative Violence: An Example from the Prehistoric Southwest." *Kiva* 78: 123–44.

Panitz-Cohen, Nava. 2006. "Distribution of Finds, Activity Areas and Population Estimates." Pages 173–94 in *Timnah (Tel Batash) III: The Finds from the Second Millennium BCE*. Edited by Nava Panitz-Cohen and Amihai Mazar. Jerusalem: Hebrew University, Institute of Archaeology.

Parsons, Kenneth A. 2007. "Structural Violence and Power." *Peace Review* 19: 173–81.

Pauketat, Timothy R. 2009. "Wars, Rumors of Wars, and the Production of Violence." Pages 245–61 in *Warfare in Cultural Context: Practice, Agency, and the Archaeology of Violence*. Edited by Axel E. Nielsen and William H. Walker. Tucson: University of Arizona Press.

Paz, Sarit. 2015. "(In)Visible Cities: The Abandoned Early Bronze Age Tells in the Landscape of the Intermediate Bronze Age Southern Levant." *ARC* 30: 28–36.

Prent, Mieke. 2003. "Glories of the Past in the Past: Ritual Activities at Palatial Ruins in Early Iron Age Crete." Pages 81–103 in *Archaeologies of Memory*. Edited by Ruth M. Van Dyke and Susan E. Alcock. Malden: Blackwell.

Regev, Lior, Kirstin M. Poduska, Lia Addadi, Steve Weiner, and Elisabetta Boaretto. 2010. "Distinguishing Between Calcites Formed by Different Mechanisms Using Infrared Spectrometry: Archaeological Applications." *JAS* 37: 3022–29.

Roszkowska-Mutschler, Hanna. 1992. "'...And on Its Site I Sowed Cress...': Some Remarks on the Execration of Defeated Enemy Cities by the Hittite Kings." *JACiv* 7: 1–12.

Rutz, Matthew and Piotr Michalowski. 2016. "The Flooding of Ešnunna, the Fall of Mari: Hammurabi's Deeds in Babylonian Literature and History." *JCS* 68: 15–43.

Saggs, Henry W. F. 1963. "Assyrian Warfare in the Sargonid Period." *Iraq* 25: 145–54.

Sandhaus, Débora. 2013. "Hazor in the Ninth and Eighth Centuries B.C.E." *NEA* 76: 110–17.

Schiffer, Michael B. 1972. "Archaeological Context and Systemic Context." *AmerAnt* 37: 156–65.

———. 1987. *Formation Processes of the Archaeological Record.* Albuquerque: University of New Mexico Press.

Siddal, Luis R. 2019. "The Nature of Siege Warfare in the Neo-Assyrian Period." Pages 35–52 in *Brill's Companion to Sieges in the Ancient Mediterranean.* Edited by Jeremy Armstrong and Matthew Trundle. Leiden: Brill.

Stern, Philip D. 1991. *The Biblical Ḥerem: A Window on Israel's Religious Experience.* Atlanta: Scholars.

Tappy, Ron. 2007. "The Final Years of Israelite Samaria: Toward a Dialogue between Texts and Archaeology." Pages 258–79 in *"Up to the Gates of Ekron": Essays on Archaeology and History of the Eastern Mediterranean in Honor of Seymour Gitin.* Edited by S White Crawford, Amnon Ben-Tor, J. P. Dessel, William G. Dever, Amihai Mazar, and Joseph Aviram. Jerusalem: Israel Exploration Society.

Thareani, Yifat. 2014. "The Self-Destruction of Diversity: A Tale of the Last Days in Judah's Negev Towns." *AntOr* 12: 185–224.

———. 2019. "From Expelled Refugee to Imperial Envoy: Assyria's Deportation Policy in Light of the Archaeological Evidence from Tel Dan." *JAA* 54: 218–34.

Trigger, Bruce G. 1990. "Monumental Architecture: A Thermodynamic Explanation of Symbolic Behaviour." *WA* 22: 119–32.

Trimm, Charlie. 2017. *Fighting for the King and the Gods: A Survey of Warfare in the Ancient Near East.* Atlanta: SBL.

Tufnell, Olga. 1953. *Lachish III (Tell Ed-Duweir): The Iron Age.* London: Oxford University Press.

Ussishkin, David. 1990. "Notes on Megiddo, Gezer, Ashdod, and Tel Batash in the Tenth to Ninth Centuries B. C." *BASOR* 277/278: 71–91.

———. 1995. "The Destruction of Megiddo at the End of the Late Bronze Age and Its Historical Significance." *TA* 22.2: 240–67.

———. 2004a. "A Synopsis of the Stratigraphical, Chronological and Historical Issues." Pages 50–119 in Ussishkin 2004d.

———. 2004b. "Area GE: The Inner City-Gate." Pages 624–89 in Ussishkin 2004d

———. 2004c. "Area GW: The Outer City-Gate." Pages 535–623 in Ussishkin 2004d

———. 2004d. *The Renewed Archaeological Excavations at Lachish (1973–1994).* Tel Aviv: Institute of Archaeology, Tel Aviv University.

Van Dyke, Ruth M. 2019. "Archaeology and Social Memory." *ARA* 48: 207–25.

Vejil, Victor, and Eilat Mazar. 2015. "Arrowheads." Pages 469–485 in *The Summit of the City of David Excavations 2005–2008, Final Reports Volume I: Area G,*. Edited by Eilat Mazar. Jerusalem: Shoham.

Weissbein, Itamar, et al. 2020. "The Level VI North-East Temple at Tel Lachish." *Levant* 51: 76–104.

Wright, G. Ernest. 1939. "Cities Standing on Their Tells." *BA* 2: 11–12.

Wright, Jacob L. 2015. "Urbicide: The Ritualized Killing of Cities in the Ancient Near East." Pages 147–66 in *Ritual Violence in the Hebrew Bible.* Edited by Saul M. Olyan. Oxford: Oxford University Press.

Yadin, Yigael. 1970. "Megiddo of the Kings of Israel." *BA* 33: 65–96.

———. 1972. *Hazor: The Head of All Those Kingdoms (Joshua 11:10).* London: Oxford University Press.

Younger, K. Lawson, Jr. 1990. *Ancient Conquest Accounts: A Study in Ancient Near Eastern and Biblical History Writing.* Sheffield: Sheffield Academic Press.

Zuckerman, Sharon. 2007. "Anatomy of a Destruction: Crisis Architecture, Termination Rituals and the Fall of Canaanite Hazor." *JMA* 20: 3–32.

———. 2011. "Ruin Cults at Iron Age I Hazor." Pages 387–94 in *The Fire Signals of Lachish: Studies in the Archaeology and History of Israel in the Late Bronze Age, Iron Age, and Persian Period in Honor of David Ussishkin.* Edited by Israel Finkelstein and Nadav Na'aman. Winona Lake: Eisenbrauns.

12
REGIONAL CONTINUITY AND CHANGE IN ANCIENT ISRAEL

An Analysis of Iron Age Settlement Patterns and Systems

George A. Pierce

No man is an island, entire of itself; every man is a piece of the continent, a part of the main.
—*John Donne, Meditation XVII, Devotions upon Emergent Occasions (1959 [1624]: 108)*

Introduction

John Donne's observation on the human condition of not existing in isolation but rather being connected to each other rings equally true for archaeological sites. Archaeological sites, for the most part, do not exist in isolation. No site is an island (even island sites); sites are situated within regions, however defined, and interact with other sites and their natural environment. The necessity of regional syntheses for archaeology cannot be overstated. Such studies help to determine relationships between people, land, and resources (Renfrew and Bahn 1999: 74). They also serve to increase awareness of regional diversity and complexity of adaptations as well as the rate of change (Trigger 1989: 286). Regional analysis can be a tool for studying settlement mechanisms (Finkelstein and Lederman 1997: 1), informing the archaeologist of non-habitation sites such as artifact scatters, field boundaries, and even isolated agricultural installations that give evidence of human interaction with the surrounding landscape. Even the "empty space" between sites attests to land use, or lack thereof, and contributes to the knowledge of a region as much as a major site (Smith and Parsons 1989: 179). Such studies provide means of comparison to other regions or periods (Kowalewski 2008: 248). Spatial analyses on a regional scale place archaeological sites within a broader context, elucidate their function within a settlement system and, when examined diachronically, can assess the changes in regional settlement patterns and systems as the site expanded or contracted over time.

For the ancient Israelite world, regional syntheses are requisite to evaluate persistent broad questions of chronology, culture history, social and political organization, and commercial associations. Such a regional focus for the Iron Age southern Levant stimulates queries about the Sea Peoples and Philistine migration, the Israelite emergence and settlement, or Canaanite perseverance (Faust 2006; Shavit 2008; Faust and Katz 2011). Discussions of kingship, state formation, and imperial control in the Iron Age II (Finkelstein 1999, 2003) require regional perspectives. The common thread throughout regional settlement studies and underscoring these overarching research topics in the archaeology of ancient Israel recalls Donne's expression of connection and emphasizes the notion that rarely would a site exist in isolation.

Fundamentally, archaeology examines connections and identity, two facets of the human experience scalable from the individual level, how one sees oneself (identity) and how one exercises agency to interact with others (connections), to the regional and supra-regional levels with collective identities of a people group and connections realized through cultural, political, or economic bonds. The two concepts are neither mutually dependent nor exclusive. A region could be connected to another economically yet have no cohesive political or cultural identity between the regions, and the same situation could be extended to settlements within a region or groups or individuals within a site. Recognition of the connections between the inhabitants within a region as reflected in settlement patterns and systems and the linkages between the region to other regions are paramount for understanding such associations in ancient Israel and the wider Near East in the Iron Age.

This chapter will discuss the scalability of spatial analyses, assess the value of analyzing settlement patterns and systems on a regional level, and present a case study examining the continuity and changes in settlement patterns and systems in the northern hill country of Manasseh in the Iron Age. Admittedly, these are biases in this research due to the focus on ancient Israel in the Iron Age within narrow geographic parameters rather than a broader *longue durée* perspective. Also, it must be noted that ancient settlement patterns lacked uniformity because not all settlements were active at the same time. Rather than being lights on a board that are on all at the same time, settlements are more akin to traffic lights that alternate between green, yellow, and red, or more aptly, like a holiday light string in which certain bulbs are illuminated then fade as others grow brighter and then fade in cycles. We are also biased by quantitative data constituting the database from which our maps of Iron Age settlements of the southern Levant are derived and limited by published excavation, survey, and salvage archaeology data. Despite these hindrances, the analysis of settlement patterns and systems helps us to answer questions about ancient behavior; that is, what can we determine and accept to be orderly for ancient Israel once the settlements are mapped and typologies hypothesized (Haggett, Cliff, and Frey 1977: 1).[1]

The Scalability of Regional Spatial Analysis

Spatial analysis of settlements within a region is scalable on three levels: *microscale* (individual structures), *mesoscale* (intra-settlement patterns), and *macroscale* (regional settlement distributions), or simply, habitation, community, and society (Trigger 1968: 55, 73). On a microscale, buildings can reflect the technical skill of construction as well as various facets of individuals and their social organization and hierarchy such as wealth, rank, family structure, social and political institutions, craft specialization, cult ideology and praxis, and personal preferences for style and fashion. The layout and contents of an individual structure may indicate the function of the building or the class of its inhabitant. Further, a dwelling may reveal familial organization (see Zorn, this volume). The subsistence regime of the household determines a structure's portability (i.e., whether a family lives in a portable construction like a tent or in a permanent habitation), and buildings are constructed using the materials of the environment to mitigate the same environment's effects (Trigger 1968: 56–57).

Considerations of the mesoscale involve the community layout (Trigger 1968: 60–66). The location, size, and stability of a community are limited by environment and subsistence technology, which includes not only the production of food but also storage, processing, and transportation of food (and water in some cases). Specialized site functions such as forts, garrisons, watchtowers, or outposts suggest the complexity of political organization together with the communal need for control or defense. Assuming that a settlement is composed of one or more communities, the community pattern may correspond to social, ethnic, or occupational groups. The physical layout of the settlement may reflect familial or kinship relations. Intra-site patterns within settlements in complex societies may also exhibit configurations of buildings determined by religious or ethnic affiliation or cosmologic ideology, while the location of such sites may be determined less by subsistence strategies than commercial interests. Concerning site function and specialization, Trigger notes that an investigation of commerce and production at the site level, which should include a determination of imported versus locally produced goods together with locations of workshops in relation to habitation, is necessary for estimations of site size and social complexity (1968: 64). The presence or absence of trade goods may reveal the integration of the community into the regional or supra-regional economy or indicate a settlement's self-reliance (Trigger 1967: 152).

The basic unit of society in ancient Israel was the "house of the father" (*bet 'av*; see Zorn and Lehmann, both in this volume), which was likely expressed as not only a house but a house compound that was likely part of a household cluster linked by common descent, whether real or fictive.[2] As such, the house can form its own unit of analysis on a micro or mesolevel to assess variation between households on a site or regional basis. Elements of house construction such as foundations, floors, walls, roofs, doors, and overall dimensions may also evince cultural or regional homogeneity or disparity. Activity areas provide the opportunity to consider household organization and deposition of artifacts or botanical or faunal remains and gendered areas (Laugier and Pierce 2020). On a household level, spatial analysis would include the features of a household or household cluster such as the house itself and courtyard area in which tasks such as cutting or scraping, sewing and basketry, production or modification of tools, and food preparation and consumption would occur, together with any associated pits, which provide information about storage, reuse, or disposal. Certain household activities may be considered universal regardless of the region and may be reflected in the archaeology of a farmstead, village, or urban dwelling such as the procurement, preparation, and storage of food consumed daily, spinning and weaving fabrics, and tool preparation and maintenance. Activities signaling specialization may include the production of chipped stone, ground stone, or bone tools, intensified fabric production, ornament manufacture, or specialized food production (oil, wine, lentils, fruits, honey, etc.).

Zonal or regional settlement patterns on a macroscale are influenced by the same considerations affecting the mesoscale (Trigger 1968: 66–70). In particular, the area's ecology and the ability of a population to exploit natural resources such as soil types, water sources, or fauna as well as the ability to mitigate harsher environs greatly determines the density and distribution of settlements (Trigger 1967: 152). Economic factors such as trade, including resource exploitation or craft production, political organization, warfare and security concerns, and religious ideologies all factor into the regional settlement pattern. Spaces between settled areas, a "no man's land" of sorts, should be noted and settlement boundaries analyzed for indicators of competing groups such as fortifications or other visible signs of aggression or defense. Trigger (1968: 70) also states that migration and population change due to disease or economic reasons are additional dynamic factors that shape the overall regional pattern.

On a regional level, the scalability of analysis permits the investigation of "nested" categories from the household level to the region. For example, consideration may be given to activity areas (equal to a feature) and include non-portable facilities like hearths, storage pits, grinding installations, ovens or other cooking facilities or work areas composed of several of these features together such as a grinding area adjacent to an oven (Pierce 2021a and sources there). The next level would be the house itself as part of a household cluster (all the features associated with the same household) or a household group that shared common features such as storage pits, water, presses for oil or wine, and burial facilities (Schloen 2001: 165–83). Following this, areas of a site could be compared or contrasted. Finally, all the sites in a discrete region could be examined in relation to each other and to other regions, in which analyses specifically focused on particular aspects of society or culture could be conducted (e.g., regional networks of exchange in relation to cult and ritual paraphernalia; see Pierce and Keimer, this volume). In most regions of ancient Israel, and the wider southern Levant, that exhibit some level of homogeneity, the key is to look for diversity or variations in the pattern of settlement to determine the distinct aspects of the communities being studied.

Landscape as Palimpsest

For regions like ancient Israel that were almost continually inhabited by successive groups for millennia, "landscape as palimpsest" is a fundamental concept for the area of interest. Crawford (1953: 51) developed the analogy with a palimpsest:

> A document that has been written on and erased over and over again; and it is the business of the field archaeologist to decipher it… whereas the vellum document was seldom wiped clean more than once or twice, the land has been subjected to continual change throughout the ages.

Landscape as palimpsest can be conceived as the "progressive superposition of one landscape on another and sometimes the selective removal of parts of the earlier landscapes by later landscapes" (Wilkinson 2003: 7). While the temporal differences are often critical for understanding the various forces impacting the landscape in successive periods, the continuity within the landscape is partially represented by the notion of persistent places that are "repeatedly used during long-term occupation of the region", even though the use may be episodic. The signature landscape resulting from the settlement patterns and land use of one period may continue in later periods or may be changed entirely depending on the organization and exploitation strategy used by later inhabitants. For example, whereas the Bronze Age in the southern Levant was marked by a landscape of tells, the signature landscape for the Iron Age was one of dispersal and growth in the rural sector (Wilkinson 2003: 130). This rural expansion comprised episodic settlement between 1000 and 600 BCE into what would have been considered "marginal" land during the Bronze Age. Assyrian royal initiatives such as the resettlement of conquered peoples and/or more stable environmental conditions served as catalysts for this shift in settlement patterns (see Koch, this volume). Additionally, an economic impetus such as the Phoenician demand for the by-products of cash crops like grapes and olives encourage settlement especially in areas with access via trade routes to coastal centers (Lehmann 2001: 94). Farms likely engaged in all four sectors of the agricultural economy, namely, wine and viticulture, olives and oil extraction, cereals, and animal husbandry (Dar 1986: 253). Olives were probably grown in the closest zone of cultivation to the main building(s) while cereals were grown further away based on the location of threshing surfaces on or near second- and third-quality soils. Iron Age farmstead features include rural trackways, field towers, wine and oil presses, cisterns (usually rock-hewn), and agricultural terraces and field boundary walls, all of which were antecedents of the "Roman landscape mosaic" into which all the elements coalesced (Wilkinson 2003: 135–37).

The multi-period, although likely not continual, utilization of the farmstead land, associated structures, and installations from the Iron Age through the Roman-Byzantine era attest to the temporal durability of such feature types as well as the continuity of farming practices in antiquity (Finkelstein 1978, 1981). Each successive land tenant had to contend with not only the physical landscape as a palimpsest with the persistence of features and installations hewn into the landscape but also with the cognitive elements within a dynamic landscape that is brimming with memory and meaning.

Site Hierarchies and Typologies

Analysis of settlement patterns should begin with the formulation of a site typology, that is, "a classification that reflects the difference in size, function, features, and other attributes of sites dating to the same period" (Flannery 1976: 163). Significant information about settlement systems often derives from regional survey and may produce relatively objective site types such as regional and secondary centers,[3] villages, hamlets, farmsteads, campsites, or other categories with implicit administrative hierarchies. Also, it should be acknowledged that some sites will also include intramural burials, or a cemetery situated nearby, but individual burial sites or cemeteries may be discovered in isolation without an associated settlement and deserve a separate category apart from habitation sites. An additional category of "site with pottery only" (e.g., a surveyed pottery scatter or pottery found during excavation without associated features) accounts for sites without visible architecture or other features.

Often, site typologies as determined by investigators result in a site-size driven scale to avoid interpretation of site function. However, the site-size approach is difficult to implement since the areas reported for many surveyed sites, if at all, are often estimates.[4] Further, while the surface pottery may indicate many periods of occupation, the extent and nature of activities at a surveyed site are not always evident without excavation. Given the fragmentary nature of most salvage operations, estimates of site size are often lacking in preliminary reports. Salvage excavations are also conducted in places that are completely altered by development; often, there are no traces of archaeological materials left once the development project is completed. Settlement typology based on size alone not only neglects the function of a site and its associated artifacts but is problematic due to its reliance on data from surveys, rescue archaeology, and sites and monuments registries that may delineate a protective boundary around a site without noting the site's actual size.

Ancient textual sources of site typologies and hierarchies express the organization and types of settlements that were most important within their cultural sphere. The array of site types within Old Babylonian terminology and Ugaritic administrative texts evinces the awareness of distinctive settlement hierarchies within ancient cognition ranging from fortified towns and their various components to unfortified towns, villages, and specialized sites such as watchtowers or agricultural estates (Burke 2008: 103–22).

Terminology for settlements in the Amarna letters also reveals ancient concepts of site hierarchies. In EA 137, Rib-Hadda of Byblos appealed for help from the Egyptian king, asking either to be restored to the throne of Byblos or to be allowed to settle in what the letter denotes as *ālāni pu-ru-zi*. The noun *pu-ru-zi*, likely a Canaanite loanword since it is absent in other cuneiform texts, distinguishes this type of settlement from the general term *ālu*, or "city," that could be used to refer to the spectrum of Bronze and Iron Age site types (see CAD A/1: 379–88). Na'aman (2005: 283) posits that *pu-ru-zi* is related to the Hebrew root *prz* employed in several biblical passages and translated as "unwalled villages." The category of "unwalled villages" in the Amarna letters and the Hebrew Bible likely included villages, hamlets, agricultural estates, and farmsteads and were located on the periphery of the territories of fortified cities.

Frick's work on the concept and meaning of *'îr*, commonly translated as "city" in the Hebrew Bible, also details the nouns used to describe other settlement types in the Hebrew Bible (1977: 42–61). The term *'îr* (pl. *'ārîm*) is used 1,090 times in the Hebrew Bible and was understood as a walled place of refuge. His examination of the semantic range of *'îr* resulted in the following meanings:

> (1) A fortified structure for defensive purposes; (2) A walled, permanent settlement; (3) A quarter within such a settlement, especially the citadel containing the temple or temples and the administrative quarters; and (4) In a more comprehensive political and economic sense, the city includes the citadel, the fixed settlement, and is the center of and marketplace for the surrounding secondary settlements of a less permanent nature.
>
> *(Frick 1977: 39)*

The Hebrew Bible uses multiple terms to denote features of a city's defenses such as *migdāl*, *bîrâ*, and *ṣerîaḥ*. The most common, *migdāl*, or "tower," is used to connote a stand-alone structure, usually to form a line of defense, or a nucleated settlement around a fortified tower. Frick (1977: 47) posits that cities germinated from a *migdāl* and its associated settlement, and this would accord well with archaeological findings of towers at Iron I and II habitation sites (Mazar 1990: 92 and see below). Types of cities denoted in the Hebrew Bible include store cities, chariot cities, cities of defense, royal cities, cities of refuge, and Levitical cities (Frick 1977: 136–42).

While the semantic range of *'îr* encapsulates any place of human dwelling with some defensive works, the biblical authors used several terms for unwalled and/or impermanent habitation sites from which the lower tiers of an Iron Age settlement hierarchy can be derived. The noun *ḥāṣēr* (pl. *ḥāṣērîm*), possibly derived from a root meaning either "to encompass, surround" or "to be present, settle, or dwell," refers to unwalled villages, and Lev 25:31 states their apposition to walled cities: "But houses in villages that have no walls around them shall be classed as open country...." The settlement narratives in Joshua also communicate the relationship between walled and unwalled secondary settlements with the phrases "cities and their villages" (literally "and her daughters;" see Josh 19:6–23, 17:11). A similar phrase expressed in the Hebrew Bible, "the city and its towns," seems to be used in contexts of conquest and recognizes the parent-child relationship between larger centers and surrounding villages, typically as a named urban center (Num 21:25, 32:42; Josh 15:45, 47; Judg 1:27; Jer 49:2). Other infrequent terms used to denote smaller or impermanent settlements include: *ḥawwōt yā'îr*, small villages in Gilead conquered by the tribe of Manasseh (Num 32:41); *nāweh* (cf. Akkadian *nawûm*), likely pastoral encampments and associated animal enclosures; and *kāpār*, possibly a loanword from Akkadian or Aramaic, contrasted with fortified cities and translated as "unwalled villages" (1 Sam 6:18; Frick 1977: 55–61).

Although ancient sources communicate great insight and cultural details necessary for analyzing ancient settlement systems, it is difficult to typologize all the different types of sites in Iron Age Israel and Judah due to the limits of excavation and survey data. Regardless, typologies should strive to recognize the dichotomy between the fortified urban centers and rural unfortified sites as well as the social complexity and political authority needed to construct fortifications and maintain monumental architecture or cultic complexes.

Why Settlement Patterns and Systems Matter

Definitions for settlement "pattern" and "system" emphasize the relationships between people and the site and the sites within a pattern to each other, somewhat transcending the social vs. ecological divide. Settlement *patterns* are "the regularities formed by the distributions of multiple places where people lived or carried out activities, including regularities in the relations of these places and activities to each other and to other features of the environment" (Kowalewski 2008: 226–27). Patterns reveal choices made to establish areas of occupation ranging from single farmsteads (and their associated elements such as watchtowers, presses, caves used for storage, or field boundaries) to urban centers with dozens of households, monumental architecture (see Keimer this volume), and some sort of defensive works. Often these choices are constrained by four factors affecting the placement of settlements across the globe, namely, access to arable land, a source of water, defensibility, and proximity to networks of trade and communication (Pierce 2021b: 22).

Yet the patterns, often represented as simple markers on a map, are only part of the story. Settlement *systems* are the natural or cultural processes behind the patterns, or how these factors interact with each other to produce the resulting settlement pattern (Kowalewski 2008: 226). Simply, the system is the "set of 'rules' that generated the pattern" (Flannery 1976: 162). While the pattern may intimate choices made about the location of a particular site, that site was also part of a system – how the sites functioned within a region, whether as an individual farmstead or a central palace, attracting goods and services and functioning as a market center or a gateway to other regions (see Pierce and Master 2015 or Pierce 2015 for a discussion of the ports of Ashkelon and Jaffa as regional maritime gateways).[5] Thus, establishing the pattern of sites in an area of interest based on relative chronology is only one step, albeit an important one, in understanding the settlement system and the society of those inhabiting that region.

Since patterns reflect the environment, technology, and various institutions of social interaction and control, the resulting pattern may be a compromise between competing determinants and be unique to a particular region or cultural group (Willey 1953: 1; Trigger 1968: 53). With increasing cultural complexity, a tendency exists for aggregation of settlements into an urban environment that provides a range of specialized facilities such as cultic centers, warehouses, palaces or administrative buildings, artisan workshops, and defensive works, yet the pattern of such complex societies may differ between groups. For example, the pattern in a river-oriented locale such as Egypt will not be the same as the pattern in the riverine environment of Mesopotamia (Trigger 1968: 72–74). Regardless of the form(s) or complexity of the settlement systems, "identification of successive spatial systems is, in effect, necessary to write the history of a regional society" (Leveau 1999: 187).

For ancient Israel, a comprehensive regional analysis should search for the distinctive aspects of the ancient Israelite culture and society while attempting to acknowledge continuity and changes occurring regionally and diachronically. The initial goal should be to determine universal activities per level of analysis (household to region) and then assess variation between households at a site, sites within a region, and regions compared to other regions (e.g., the hill country versus Shephelah). Universal household activities are those that would be performed by every house, regardless of any specialization, preserved in the archaeological record as the artifacts and activity areas associated with those activities. Such universal activities would include primarily food procurement, preparation, and storage and would be reflected in grinding stones, storage pits, storage jars and cooking pots/jugs, faunal and botanical remains, and ash or charcoal deposits. Once the universal household activities are determined, then variation can be determined between households as well as possible household specializations, regional specializations, and other unique elements preserved in the archaeological record. Variations could include differences between households in food preparation areas or distinctions in botanical or faunal remains, which may indicate discrepancies in socio-economic status, food procurement activities, or availability of foodstuffs. Distinctions in site locations and types may also highlight the social, cultural, political, or economic processes affecting society during a particular chronological period.

Case Study: Continuity and Change in the Land of Manasseh

To illustrate the endurance of the settlement patterns of Iron Age Israel and the settlement systems adapted to various pressures resulting in variations, a regional analysis (on a macroscale) of the northern hill country of Manasseh serves as a case study. This region stretching from the Dothan Valley in the north to Samaria in the south and nearly 30 km wide, designated the Shechem syncline, was intensively surveyed as part of the Manasseh Hill Country Survey, a project lasting 23 years and producing five volumes of data (Zertal 2004: 1–4), from which the data for this case study was drawn. Additionally, several sites within the area have been excavated and published, permitting analyses on the micro- and mesoscales.[6]

The land of Manasseh sits at a lower elevation than the hill country territories of Ephraim, Benjamin, and Judah to the south. While the hills of Ephraim rise to heights of 915 m above sea level, Manasseh varies from 60 m above sea level in the valleys to 760 m above sea level on its highest peaks. Despite the number and height of Manasseh's hills, these rises are separated by valleys affording relatively easy travel and areas for agriculture and pastoralism. This fact, combined with road junctions at strategic locations, prompted Aharoni (1962: 27) to assert that urbanization likely developed earlier here than in the region of Ephraim and persisted in a *longue durée* perspective. The region has numerous springs and is traversed by several wadis. Zertal (2004: 14) noted that all the landforms (mountains, internal valleys, river valleys, and desert fringe) except for "seashore" could be found within the territory of Manasseh.

The typology and hierarchy used in the current study and illustrated on the maps accompanying the discussion of settlement patterns from the MB II to Iron III below follow the typology and chronology of Zertal (2004: 18–19, 45–69).[7]

- Habitation sites-sites with evidence of human habitation and/or building activity, with or without defensive works
  - City (*'îr* and its associated synonyms discussed above): any dwelling place, with or without defensive works but likely a regional center with a densely built environment (greater than 1 ha)
  - Village (*ḥāṣēr, kāpār, ḥawwōt*): an unwalled, possibly semi-permanent, settlement (less than 1 ha)
  - Small (less than 0.5 ha), hamlet or isolated residence, farmsteads
  - Impermanent encampments or enclosures (*nāweh*)
- Specialized sites (determined by presumed use)
  - Forts
  - Camp[8]
  - Burial locations (cemeteries or tombs)
- Scatters (only pottery present; unknown use)

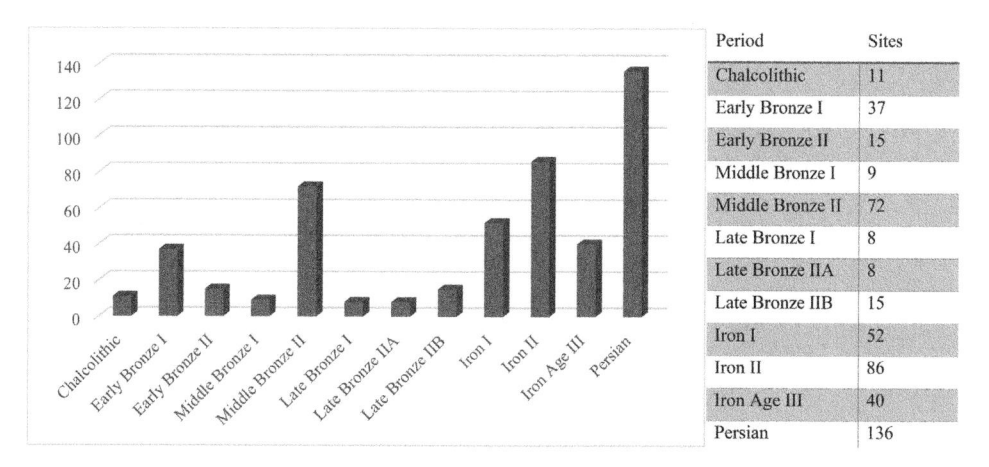

Period	Sites
Chalcolithic	11
Early Bronze I	37
Early Bronze II	15
Middle Bronze I	9
Middle Bronze II	72
Late Bronze I	8
Late Bronze IIA	8
Late Bronze IIB	15
Iron I	52
Iron II	86
Iron Age III	40
Persian	136

Figure 12.1 Total number of sites per period, Chalcolithic through Persian periods (Zertal 2004: 601–03)

The total number of settlements varies by period, surging and shrinking as observed throughout the southern Levant in the proto-historical and historical periods (Figure 12.1). Following a decrease in settlements from the Early Bronze Age II into the Middle Bronze Age I (Early Bronze IV or Intermediate Bronze Age) to only nine sites in the area of interest, a resurgence of settlement in the MB II can be observed. The Late Bronze Age witnessed another drop in number of sites in the LB I and IIA with the sites nearly doubling in number in the LB IIB. Another increase in the total number of sites in the area can be observed in Iron Age I with growth in Iron Age II. In Iron Age III, the number of sites dropped, but another massive growth in settlement numbers occurred in the Persian period.[9]

The total number of archaeological sites per period provides a generalized picture of the ebb and flow of settlement in the northern hills of Manasseh in the Bronze and Iron Ages (Figures 12.2–12.8).[10] As stated above, recognizing the continuity and change between periods lends insight into not only the pattern (i.e., where the sites are located) but also the settlement system (why the sites are located where they are and how they interacted with other sites). While the total number of sites in the region increased from MB I to MB II, signaling a change in the pattern, seven of the nine MB I sites continued into MB II (Figure 12.2).

The number of settlements declined in the LB as observed elsewhere in Canaan, the eight sites dated to the LB I were continuations of MB II settlements (Figure 12.3). Although the total number of sites is the same between LB I and LB IIA (n=8 for both), no LB IIA pottery was found at some sites (e.g., el-Qitneh, Khirbet Qumy, or Khirbet Shreim), possibly indicating that those sites fell into disuse, while other sites appear to have been resettled at sites occupied during the MB II (Khirbet en-Najjar) or newly founded (Ras el-'Ain; Figure 12.4).[11] In the LB IIB, six sites persisted from the preceding LB IIA, and eight sites were resettled at sites occupied during the MB (Figure 12.5). One surveyed site, Dhahrat et-Tawileh (the "Bull Site"), appears to be newly founded in this period given the presence of some LB IIB forms, but overall, most of the ceramics and their parallels to Giloh and Taanach led the excavator to date the site to the early Iron Age I (Mazar 1982: 36; see also Pierce and Keimer, this volume).

As expected, the Iron Age settlement patterns show some continuity with the patterns of previous periods with notable diachronic changes. Ceramics dated to the Iron Age I, the

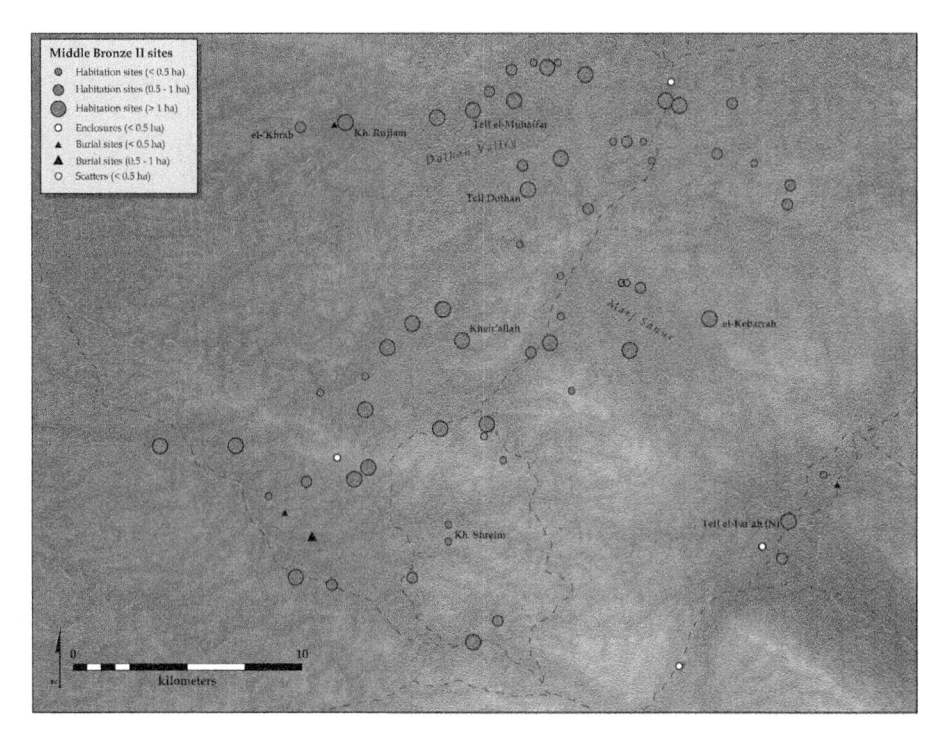

Figure 12.2 Map of Middle Bronze II sites (Map by the author)

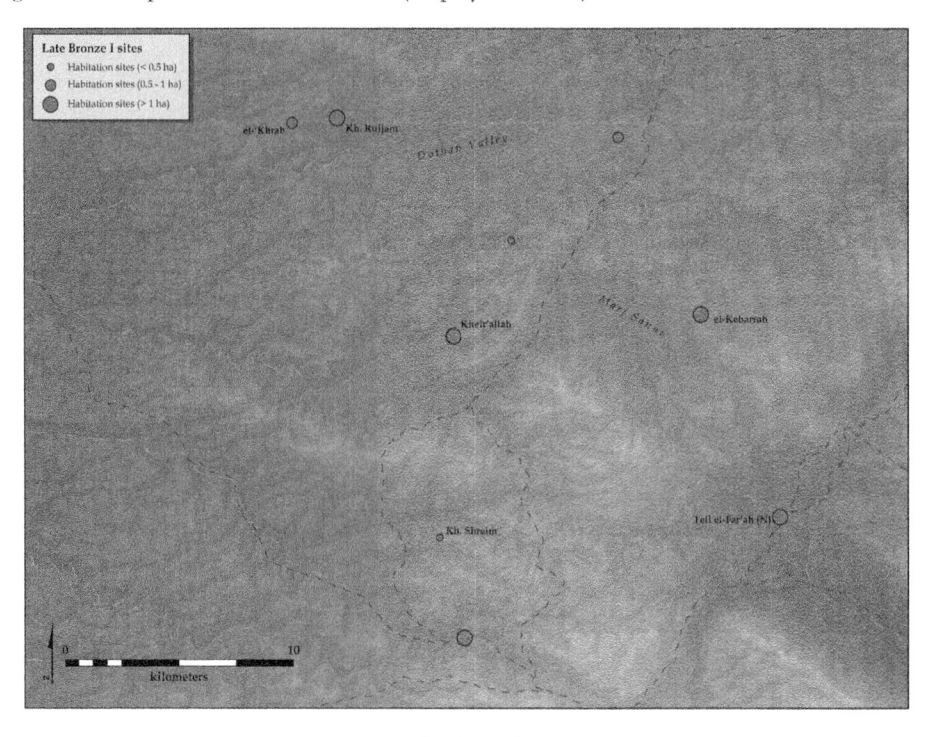

Figure 12.3 Map of Late Bronze I sites (Map by the author)

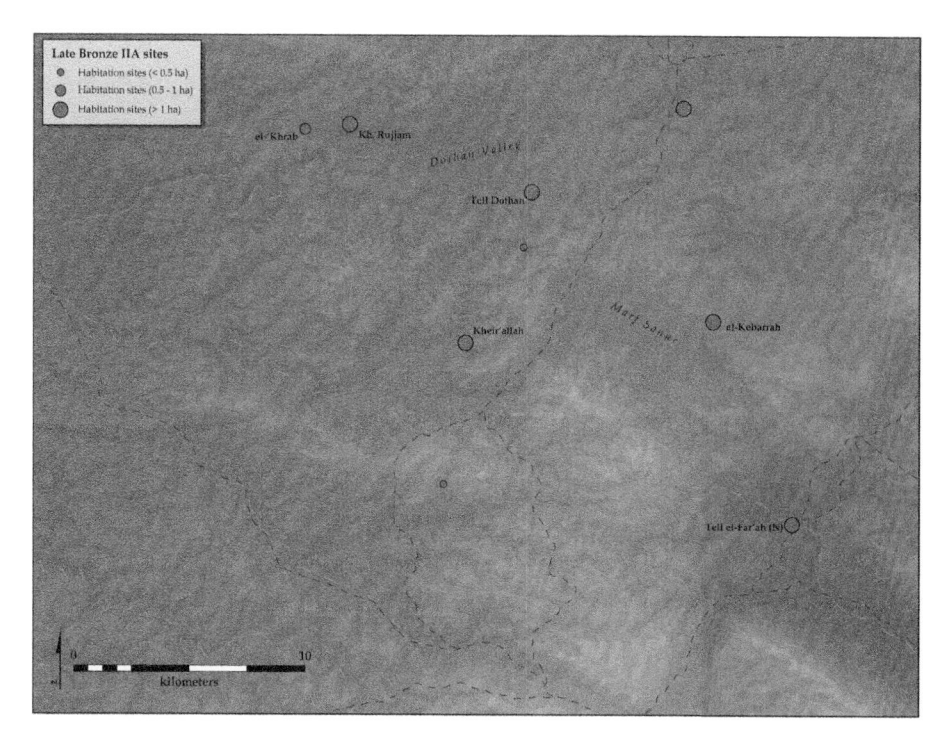

Regional Continuity and Change in Ancient Israel

Figure 12.4 Map of Late Bronze IIA sites (Map by the author)

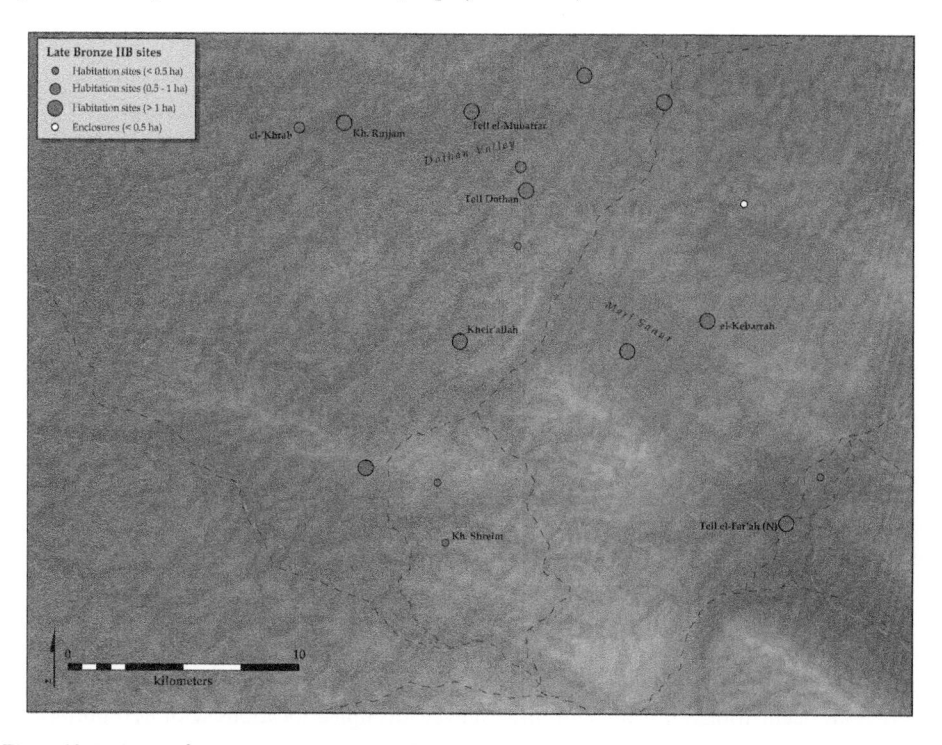

Figure 12.5 Map of Late Bronze IIB sites (Map by the author)

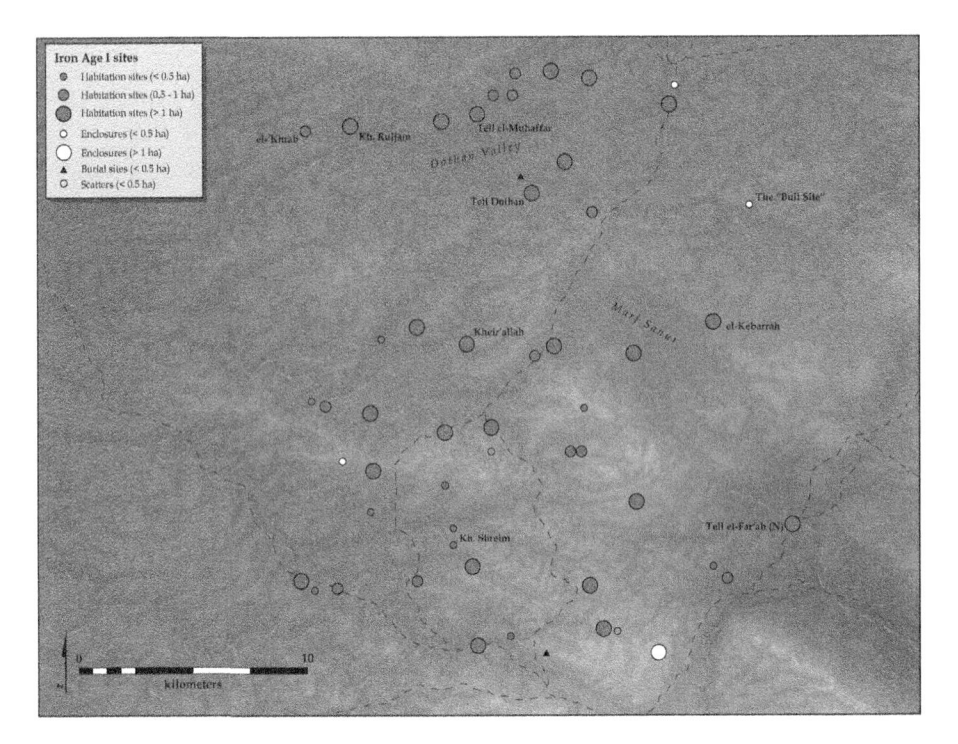

Figure 12.6 Map of Iron Age I sites (Map by the author)

period associated with the emergence and settlement of ancient Israel, appear at 52 sites, ten of which appear to continue from the LB IIB or have some pottery forms that can be dated to that period (Figure 12.6). Eight sites were founded at places previously occupied in the LB I or IIA, with 31 sites overall re-occupying places with MB II material culture. Twenty-one sites were newly founded in Iron I. In this period associated with Israel's emergence and settlement in the hill country, we can observe that although the number of sites increases from the preceding LB IIB, the pattern of where sites were located followed that of the MB and LB; that is, sites were located in the hills just on the edge of the internal valleys, close to routes running through the region.

In Iron II, the settlement pattern again expands to 86 sites in total with 37 sites continuing from Iron I and another 37 sites being newly founded in that period (Figure 12.7).[12] Fifteen Iron I sites showed no evidence of continuation into Iron II and were either abandoned or destroyed. Sites dated to this period included not only the expected habitation sites, both walled and unwalled, but also a large regional center, the capital of the northern kingdom of Israel at Samaria, as well as forts and a large cemetery (Khallet el-Butmeh; Zertal 2004: 433). Although a nearest-neighbor analysis indicates that the sites are not clustered around the capital, a pattern of sites in a semi-circular pattern radiating out from Samaria along the trackways at distances of 5, 10, and 20 km can be observed.[13]

An expected decrease in the overall number of sites occurred following the Assyrian conquest in the 8th century BCE (Figure 12.8). Pottery dated to Iron III was collected at 40 sites; 23 of which were occupied in the preceding period, 14 were established in Iron III with no previous occupational history, and three sites re-occupied locations with MB pottery or architecture. Some types of sites persisted such as the forts near Samaria, which functioned as an Assyrian administrative center.

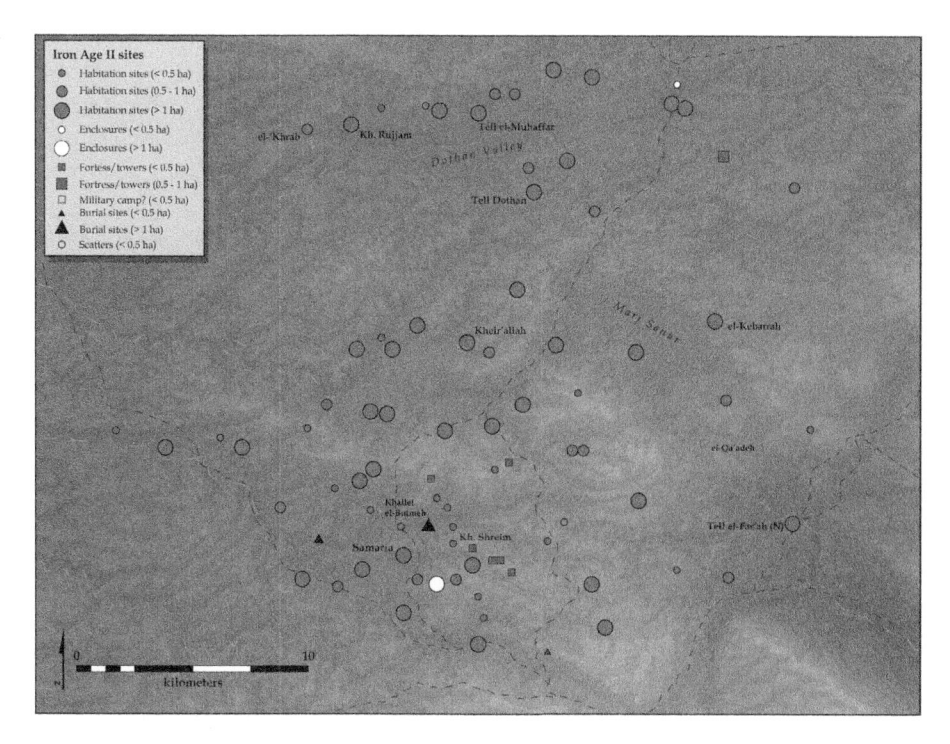

Figure 12.7 Map of Iron Age II sites (Map by the author)

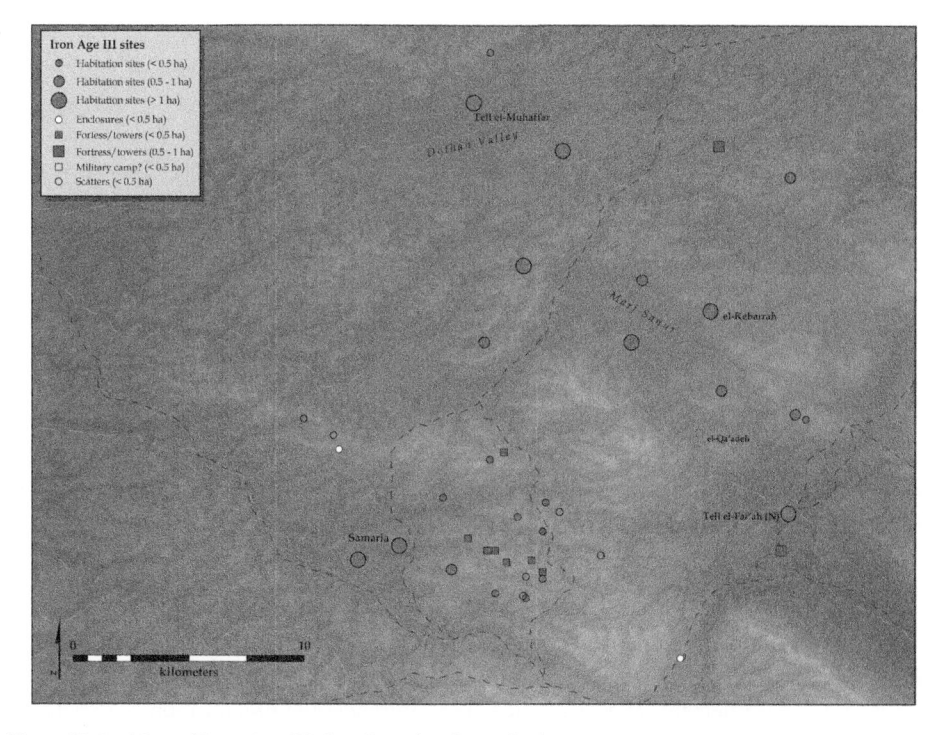

Figure 12.8 Map of Iron Age III sites (Map by the author)

The sites with the longest continual occupational histories from the MB to Iron III are Tell el-Muhaffar, el-'Khrab, Khirbet Rujjam, el-Kebbarah, Kheir'allah, and Khirbet Shreim. As the Iron Age progressed, this number decreased in the Iron II with only Tell el-Muhaffar and el-Kebbarah having any Iron III forms. Their longevity illustrates the persistence of settlement patterns and systems in the southern Levant despite the march of time and changes in cultures, societies, or political hegemony.

The archaeologically visible settlement patterns imposed on the landscape of the northern hills of Manasseh reflect conscious choices made by their inhabitants regarding the availability of natural resources, safety, and proximity to pathways. Whether established at previously occupied MB or LB locales or newly founded, Iron Age sites were established in the hills and along the fringes of the valleys to preserve as much arable land as possible with wells being dug at the base of hills or tels to be able to reach the water table. Sites in the Dothan Valley were mainly established along the northern edge, suggesting that the east-west trade route ran along the northern edge of the valley (Pierce 2005: 19). Similarly, the sites of Khirbet Keibar and el-Kebarrah, two of the longest-lived sites in the region flanked the Marj Sanur, providing gravitational points for trackways that skirted those meadowlands. Embedded within the patterns are hierarchies of sites intimating how the settlement system may have functioned with villages and farmsteads connected to larger, more established centers. Forts in the Iron II and III provided security for Samaria and guarded approaches to the region but could not withstand the Assyrian campaigns that may have been conducted from camps such as the one at el-Qa'adeh.

Illustrating the concept of "landscape as palimpsest," the settlement patterns in northern Manasseh exhibited a certain amount of continuity in location and changes in clustering and dispersal throughout the periods addressed by this study, yet the pull of central places with political control such as Shechem, Tirzah (Tell el-Far'ah [N]), and Samaria, as well as economic opportunities afforded by the trade networks that crossed the region, remained constant throughout the Iron Age, influencing the settlement system. The intense settlement throughout the region in the Iron I and II and decrease in the Iron III following the Assyrian campaigns signal a change in settlement patterns from somewhat "static" in the Bronze and early Iron Ages to "dynamic" in the Iron II from the 9th century and in subsequent periods. Similar to other regions' settlement patterns post-721 BCE (Pierce 2015: 184–86, 191–92), smaller farmsteads and enclosures focused on agricultural output were established in the hills east of Samaria while the rest of the region appears to be devoid of such sites.

Conclusion

Trigger's (1967: 158) observation that "What is important is that Settlement Archaeology forces us to think through problems from a new angle – that of social relations" should influence our consideration of the connectivity of Israelite (and Judahite) sites to each other and Israel's situation in the wider Mediterranean world. Since regional studies should consider the physical environment as well as cultural influences on the landscape and the effects of those processes (Verhagen 2018: 14–15), analyses of patterns and systems can integrate seemingly divergent approaches to the cultural landscape by adopting both a processual stance focused on settlement patterns, land use, environment, and subsistence as well as the post-processual viewpoint that includes subjective elements such as cognition and perception. Ultimately, the consequences of human actions within the settlement system result in spatial patterns of settlement, and such landscapes can reflect the organization of society or communicate cultural values (Johnson 2005: 118; Federov 2013: 208).

The product of either diverse approaches or a more rigid settlement systems paradigm should include a holistic view of the region that includes all aspects of environment and culture to reconstruct the past landscape in which ancient Israel acted. The threads of landscape as palimpsest, the cognition and perception of the environment as reflected in the settlement pattern, and the economies of settlement and human activities that were subject to ecology, subsistence requirements, commerce, and politics can be woven together. While a complete picture of Iron Age Israel and Judah may never be ascertained, several components of their settlement histories can be discovered and can be one of many justifiable interpretations of the ancient Israelite world.

Notes

1 Such approaches are mostly "normative" in that each artifact or feature (or site) manifests the shared ideas, values, and beliefs of the community that created, used, or inhabited them, respectively.
2 Household, or rather "houseful," is here defined as a group of people co-residing and interacting with one another, not necessarily related by biological kinship (Laslett 1983: 514; Pierce 2021a: 259).
3 Within these two categories, there may be an "segregated elite district" with a residential component likely located in a topographically prominent area of the site (an acropolis) with ceremonial-civic architecture such as a palace or temple complex (e.g., Jerusalem or Hazor) or in cases without a residential aspect, an isolated ceremonial-civic precinct.
4 Survey work conducted at previously surveyed MB sites in the western Galilee employed GPS equipment to record the extent of artifact scatters, visible architectural remains, or presently buried features affecting the shape of the site (e.g., terraces or fortifications), resulting in the correction of past site size estimates (Yasur-Landau, Cline, and Pierce 2008: 63).
5 A good example of the difference between pattern and system would be that discussing where settlements are located describes the pattern, while assessing the distance between settlements or determining shared resources (or some similar analysis) would likely reflect the "rules" of the settlement system within a given cultural group.
6 Among others, these sites include Samaria (Reisner, Fisher, and Lyon 1924; Crowfoot and Crowfoot 1938; Crowfoot, Kenyon, and Sukenik 1942; Crowfoot, Crowfoot, and Kenyon 1957), Tell Dothan (Cooley and Pratico 1995; Master et al. 2005), Dhahrat et-Tawileh (the "Bull Site"; Mazar 1982), and Khirbet Belameh (Taha and van der Kooij 1999).
7 Zertal (2004: 45–69) dated the sites using collected pottery to the following periods: MB II (2000–1550 BCE), LB (1550–1200 BCE), Iron I (1200–1000 BCE), Iron II (1000–721 BCE), and Iron III (721–535 BCE). No distinction was made for sub-periods or centuries in the Iron II, nor was any sub-periodization proffered in the discussion of settlement patterns diachronically.
8 Based on survey and excavation, Zertal (2004: 343–46) suggested that el-Qa'adeh (Site 154) was an Assyrian military camp.
9 The overall number of sites would continue to grow in the Hellenistic, Roman, and Byzantine periods (Monson 2005: 9–11).
10 Sites are represented on the maps in this chapter by graduated symbols by area (hectares) as determined by the surveyor (Zertal 2004). Sites shown with larger symbols with longer occupational histories may not have been that size throughout their use. Conversely, short-lived sites only extant periodically are more likely to have their size correctly estimated. Established trackways mapped by for the SWP (and marked in places as "Roman road") are shown in dashed lines.
11 Although Free, the excavator of Dothan, (1954: 14, 1955: 8, 1956: 45) and Zertal (2004: 150) mention LB II pottery, and Tomb 1 had five levels dating from LB IIA to Iron I, no "substantial ceramic assemblage or coherent architecture on the tell" could be determined, leaving the possibilities of either an unrecognized strata of occupation or the Iron I residents retaining LB II pottery as heirlooms (Master et al. 2005: 65). The percentage of LB IIA (15%) and LB IIB (15%) pottery compared to Iron I forms (70%) at Ras el-'Ain, together with the paucity of extant architecture, suggests that situation like Tell Dothan was also in effect at Ras el-'Ain and warrants further consideration of the presence of heirlooms and the persistence and longevity of LB forms in the early Iron Age.

12 Twelve sites were settled at places previously occupied in the MB or LB.
13 A similar network of sites can be observed 5km distant from Tell el-Farʻah (N).

Bibliography

Aharoni, Yohanan. 1962. *The Land of Israel in Biblical Times: A Historical Geography.* Jerusalem: Bialik Institute.

Burke, Aaron A. 2008. *"Walled Up to Heaven": The Evolution of Middle Bronze Age Fortification Strategies in the Levant.* Winona Lake: Eisenbrauns.

Cooley, Robert E., and Gary D. Pratico. 1995. "Dothan: The Western Cemetery, with Comments on Joseph Free's Excavations, 1953 to 164." Pages 147–90 in *Preliminary Excavation Reports: Sardis, Bir Umm Fawakhir, Tell el-Umeiri, The Combined Caesarea Excavations, and Tell Dothan.* Edited by William G. Dever. Ann Arbor: ASOR.

Crawford, O. G. S. 1953. *Archaeology in the Field.* London: Phoenix House.

Crowfoot, J. W., and G. M. Crowfoot. 1938. *Samaria-Sebaste II: Early Ivories from Samaria.* London: PEF.

Crowfoot, J. W., G. M. Crowfoot, and K. M. Kenyon. 1957. *Samaria-Sebaste III: The Objects from Samaria.* London: PEF.

Crowfoot, J. W., K. M. Kenyon, and E. L. Sukenik. 1942. *Samaria Sebaste I: The Buildings at Samaria.* London: PEF.

Dar, Shimon. 1986. *Landscape and Pattern: An Archaeological Survey of Samaria, 800 BCE–636 CE.* Oxford: British Archaeological Reports.

Donne, John. 1959. *Devotions Upon Emergent Occasions.* London: Thomas Iones, 1624. Repr., Ann Arbor: The University of Michigan Press,

Faust, Avraham. 2006. *Israel's Ethnogenesis: Settlement, Interaction, Expansion, and Resistance.* London: Equinox.

Faust, Avraham, and Haya Katz. 2011. "Philistines, Israelites and Canaanites in the Southern Trough Valley during the Iron Age I." *AeL* 21: 231–47.

Federov, Roman. 2013. "Genesis of the Cultural Landscape of Urals and Siberia." *JES* 4: 207–16.

Finkelstein, Israel. 1978. "Rural Settlements in the Foothills and in the Yarkon Basin in the Israelite–Hellenistic Periods." MA thesis, Tel Aviv University. (Hebrew)

———. 1981. "Israelite and Hellenistic Farms in the Foothills and in the Yarqon Basin." *EI* 15: 331–48, 86*.

———. 1999. "State Formation in Israel and Judah: A Contrast in Context, A Contrast in Trajectory." *NEA* 62: 35–52.

———. 2003. "City-States to States: Polity Dynamics in the 10th-9th Centuries BCE." Pages 75–83 in *Symbiosis, Symbolism and the Power of the Past.* Edited by W. G. Dever and S. Gitin. Winona Lake: Eisenbrauns.

Finkelstein, Israel, and Zvi Lederman. 1997. "Introduction." Pages 1–8 in *Highlands of Many Cultures: The Southern Samaria Survey. The Sites: Volume 1.* Edited by I. Finkelstein and Z. Lederman. Tel Aviv: Emery and Claire Yass Publications in Archaeology, Tel Aviv University.

Flannery, Kent V. 1976. "Evolution of Complex Settlement Systems." Pages 162–73 in *The Early Mesoamerican Village.* Edited by Kent V. Flannery. San Diego: Academic Press.

Free, Joseph P. 1954. "The Second Season at Dothan." *BASOR* 135: 14–20.

———. 1955. "The Third Season at Dothan." *BASOR* 139: 3–9.

———. 1956. "The Excavation of Dothan." *BA* 19: 43–48.

Frick, Frank S. 1977. *The City in Ancient Israel.* Missoula: Scholars Press.

Haggett, Peter, andrew Cliff, and Allan Frey. 1977. *Locational Analysis in Human Geography.* London: Edward Arnold.

Johnson, Matthew. 2005. "Thinking about Landscape." Pages 116–19 in *Archaeology: The Key Concepts.* Edited by Colin Renfrew and Paul Bahn. New York: Routledge.

Kowalewski, S. A. 2008. "Regional Settlement Pattern Studies." *JAR* 16: 225–85.

Laslett, Peter. 1983. "Family and Household as Work Group and Kin Group: Areas of Traditional Europe Compared." Pages 513–63 in *Family Forms in Historic Europe.* Edited by R. Wall, J. Robin and P. Laslett. Cambridge: Cambridge University Press.

Laugier, Elise J., and George A. Pierce. 2020. "Spatial Analysis." Pages 839–53 in *Ashkelon 7: The Iron Age I*. Edited by Lawrence E. Stager, Daniel M. Master and Adam J. Aja. University Park: Eisenbrauns.

Lehmann, Gunnar. 2001. "Phoenicians in Western Galilee: First Results of an Archaeological Survey in the Hinterland of Akko." Pages 65–112 in *Studies in the Archaeology of the Iron Age in Israel and Jordan*. Edited by A. Mazar. Sheffield: Sheffield Academic Press.

Leveau, P. 1999. "The Integration of Archaeological, Historical and Paleoenvironmental Data at the Regional Scale: The Vallée de Baux, Southern France." Pages 181–91 in *Environmental Reconstruction in Mediterranean Landscape Archaeology*. Edited by P. Leveau, F. Trément, K. Walsh, and G. Barker. Oxford: Oxbow Books.

Master, Daniel M., John M. Monson, Egon H. E. Lass, and George A. Pierce, eds. 2005. *Dothan I: Remains from the Tell (1953–1964)*. Winona Lake: Eisenbrauns.

Mazar, Amihai. 1982. "The 'Bull Site': An Iron Age I Open Cult Place." *BASOR* 247: 27–42.

———. 1990. "Iron Age I and II Towers at Giloh and the Israelite Settlement." *IEJ* 40: 77–101.

Monson, John M. 2005. "Regional Settlement: Dothan in the Northern Arena." Pages 7–14 in *Dothan I: Remains from the Tell (1953–1964)*. Edited by Daniel M. Master et al. Winona Lake: Eisenbrauns.

Moran, William L. 1992. *The Amarna Letters*. Baltimore: Johns Hopkins University Press.

Na'aman, Nadav. 2005. "Amarna *ālāni pu-ru-zi* (EA 137) and Biblical *'ry hprzy/hprzwt* ('Rural Settlements')." Pages 284–88 in *Canaan in the Second Millennium BCE: Collected Essays, Volume 2*. Winona Lake: Eisenbrauns.

Pierce, George A. 2005. "GIS Studies of Tell Dothan and the Dothan Valley." Pages 15–20 in *Dothan I: Remains from the Tell (1953–1964)*. Edited by Daniel M. Master et al. Winona Lake: Eisenbrauns.

———. 2015. "'The Territory Facing Jaffa': Cultural Landscapes of a Mediterranean Port and its Hinterland (ca. 2000–539 BCE)." PhD diss., University of California, Los Angeles.

———. 2021a. "The 'Four-Room House' Complex at Tell Dothan, Area A: An Analysis of Function, Demography, and Cultural Identity." Pages 249–65 in *"To Explore the Land of Canaan": Studies in Biblical Archaeology in Honor of Jeffrey R. Chadwick on the Occasion of his 66th Birthday*. Edited by. Aren M. Maeir and George A. Pierce. Berlin: de Gruyter.

———. 2021b. "Environmental and Socio-economic Context: Environmental Features." Pages 17–35 in *T&T Clark Handbook of Food in the Hebrew Bible and Ancient Israel*. Edited by Janling Fu, Cynthia Shafer-Elliott, and Carol Meyers. London: T&T Clark/Bloomsbury.

Pierce, George A., and Daniel M. Master. 2015. "Ashkelon as Maritime Gateway and Central Place." Pages 109–23 in *Ashkelon 5: The Land Behind Ashkelon*. Edited by Jacob Huster. Winona Lake: Eisenbrauns.

Reisner, George A., et al. 1924. *Harvard Excavations at Samaria, 1908–1910*. Cambridge: Harvard University Press.

Renfrew, Colin, and Paul Bahn. 1999. *Archaeology: Theories, Methods, and Practice*. London: Thames and Hudson.

Schloen, J. David. 2001. *The House of the Father as Fact and Symbol: Patrimonialism in Ugarit and the Ancient Near East*. Winona Lake: Eisenbrauns.

Shavit, Alon. 2008. "Settlement Patterns of Philistine City-States." Pages 135–64 in *Bene Israel: Studies in the Archaeology of Israel and the Levant During the Bronze and Iron Ages in Honour of Israel Finkelstein*. Edited by A. Fantalkin and A. Yasur-Landau. Leiden: Brill.

Smith, K. P., and J. R. Parsons. 1989. "Regional Archaeological Research in Iceland: Potential and Possibilities." Pages 179–202 in *The Anthropology of Iceland*. Edited by E. P. Durrenburger and G. Pálsson. Iowa City: University of Iowa Press.

Taha, H., and G. van der Kooij. 1999. "Les Fouilles de Khirbet Belameh." *L'Archéologie Palestinnienne. Dossiers d'Archéologie* 240: 138–45.

Trigger, Bruce G. 1967. "Settlement Archaeology-Its Goals and Promise." *AmerAnt* 32: 149–60.

———. 1968. "The Determinants of Settlement Patterns." Pages 42–53 in *Settlement Archaeology*. Edited by K.C. Chang. Palo Alto: National Press.

———. 1989. *A History of Archaeological Thought*. Cambridge: Cambridge University Press.

Verhagen, Philip. 2018. "Spatial Analysis in Archaeology: Moving into New Territories." Pages 11–25 in *Digital Geoarchaeology*. Edited by C. Siart et al. Cham: Springer.

Wilkinson, Tony J. 2003. *Archaeological Landscapes of the Near East*. Tucson: The University of Arizona Press.

Willey, G. R. 1953. *Prehistoric Settlement Patterns in the Virú Valley, Peru*. Washington, D.C.: Smithsonian Institution.
Yasur-Landau, Assaf, Eric H. Cline, and George A. Pierce. 2005. "Middle Bronze Age Settlement Patterns in the Western Galilee, Israel." *JFA* 33: 59–83.
Zertal, Adam. 2004. *The Manasseh Hill Country Survey. Volume 1: The Shechem Syncline*. Leiden: Brill.

PART III

Society and Economy

13
ANCIENT ISRAEL'S SOCIAL STRUCTURE(S)

Gunnar Lehmann

In the social sciences, the notion of *social structure* refers to the patterns through which a society organizes itself. These patterns include the social relationships of its members and the social and physical characteristics of its communities. In ancient societies of the Bronze and Iron Ages, social relationships structured and constrained behavior across all spheres of life legitimating specific cultural and social arrangements such as kinship, gender roles, division of labor, and other institutional practices including aspects of social inequality and ranking in hierarchical structures.

Social structures are, however, not simply determinations of social behavior in the past. Rather, the notion of social structure is related to agency as in Giddens' theory of structuration and Bourdieu's theory of practice (Bourdieu 1977; Giddens 1993). While social structures may limit or determine human behavior, agency emphasizes the capacity of individuals to act independently and to make their own choices. Giddens and Bourdieu argue that structure and agency are essentially a duality and do not represent a dichotomy. Social structures provide sets of rules that enable individuals to perform within a society. In following and considering such rules, actors make their personal choices, ultimately reproducing these very structures. Social structures in this sense are thus embedded in agency rather than simply determining individual behavior. Although this chapter will focus on the contribution of archaeology in the understanding of the social structures of ancient Israel, it also draws on biblical sources, ancient epigraphy, and anthropological comparisons with other societies of different periods.

Previous studies which explored the social structure of ancient Israel include de Vaux's study of social institutions (1965), Lemche's (1985) analysis of early Israel, and Vanderhooft's (1990) investigation into kinship organization. Other notable studies are Matthews and Benjamin's (1993) *Social World of Ancient Israel*, Reviv's (1993) *Society in the Kingdoms of Israel and Judah*, and Bendor's (1996) examination of family structures. Norman Gottwald's (1979) *Tribes of Yahweh* was a milestone in the research on the ancient Israelite society. Most of these and other studies, which we cannot mention in more detail here for lack of space, [1] based their studies on an analysis of ancient textual evidence. Only a few scholars focused primarily on the archaeological record, such as Bunimovitz (1993, 1994), Faust (2006, 2012), Maeir (Hitchcock and Maeir 2013; Maeir and Shai 2016), and Stager (1985).

Discussing the social structure of ancient Israel implies an understanding of who the ancient Israelites were. Here is not the place to discuss this question in full. Sufficient to note that the emergence of early Israel is not an archaeological fact, its earliest awareness took the form of narratives and textual traditions. Archaeologists can only try to correlate their data with what was possibly the historical background of this tradition. "Israel" is mentioned already at the very end of the 13th century BCE as the name of a group of people in the Merenptah stela (Weingart 2014: 4–5). In biblical sources, "Israel" appears either as a region which is distinguished from Judah to its south (1 Sam 15:52, 10:20) or as the community of worshippers of the "god of Israel." Over time, the notion "Israel" had different meanings in various historical contexts. The collective identity of "ancient Israel" emerged through their social practices in specific locations and historical situations. Their emerging ethnicity was only one form of social identity not easily studied with archaeological methods. Ethnicity is not something that one "has," but something that one "does" (Jenkins 2008: 5) in a dynamic process with constant changes, interactions, and often blurred boundaries with changing identities in various contexts (Maeir 2021). In this chapter, the notion of "ancient Israel" was not the historical result of a unilineal evolution. There was never one "ancient Israel," but several ever-changing social identities with that name which emerged from complex processes of social, economic, and cultural interactions in specific historical situations.

The Social Structure in the Textual Tradition

Studying the social structure of "ancient Israel" poses, thus, a challenge. The biblical traditions specify tribal structures of the society preceding the rise of the state. They refer to the social structure in a somewhat schematic and superficial portrayal as for example in the census reports of Numbers 26. In Joshua 7:16–18, the society is hierarchically broken down from the largest unit, the *shebet* (שבט), typically rendered "tribe," down to the *mishpaha* (משפחה) translated as "clan" or "lineage" and to the *bet-ab* (בית-אב) which is the "extended family" (Andersen 1969; Bendor 1996). These notions are difficult to translate to modern anthropological terms and their meaning is not always clearly distinguished from one another in the biblical text (Gottwald 1979; Lemche 1985). It is unclear whether they in fact represent the reality of the social organization during the early Iron Age or whether they were projected back into a distant past by later writers of the monarchic and postexilic periods. The kinship organization in ancient Israel is associated with a sedentary society and there is no evidence of survival from an earlier nomadic stage (McNutt 1999: 86).

The Bet-Ab

The *bet-ab* was the smallest unit of social organization constituting the primary and most extensive social structure (Dutcher-Walls 2009: 10; Faust 2012: 11). This basic social structure of kinship is the main component of Bronze and Iron Age societies. It is the common main social element in early states *and* in tribal societies. At this level, cooperation and social interaction are most intense (Sahlins 1968: 16). The *bet-ab* in the biblical traditions is a flexible patrimonial system that forms the nucleus of historical sedentary and non-sedentary societies in the Levant.

As in modern western societies, some of the most important decisions for the community were made in the family. However, unlike modern western families, the individual had only limited autonomy in determining her/his future life. The extended family determined marriage partners, work roles, and residence locality.

Members of the *bet-ab* lived together; they owned and shared property and land as their most important means of production. In theory, all land was divinely owned and inherited by families (Bendor 1996: 144, cf. 1 Sam. 26:19, 2 Sam. 14:16, 20:19, and 21:3.7). It was possibly not owned by individuals but belonged to the entire *bet-ab* (Bendor 1996: 39). Ownership issues between landholders are addressed in the biblical verse "Do not remove your neighbor's landmark" (Deut 19:14; compare Deut 27:17), and some aspects of land ownership were regulated by the *mishpaha*, an alliance of *batei-ab*. Comparably, Dresch (1989: 276–86) points out that in rural Yemenite highland communities arable land is privately held by extended or joint families (*el-beit*), which form the primary units of production and consumption (see also Mundy 1995: 62–80).

The expression *bet-ab* underlines the patriarchal, patrilinear and patrilocal character of the Israelite family. The Israelite genealogies include usually only males and women appear in these traditions only as an exception. The patriarch had absolute authority over the entire family, which was not mediated by any laws outside of the family. Within the *bet-ab* three to four generations resided as is implied by several biblical references (Lev 18:7–16; Num 14:18; Deut 5:8; Gen 7:1, 7 and 4:8–26).

The *bet-ab* consists of individual households (i.e., extended families) or nuclear families (Dutcher-Walls 2009: 2–10; Faust 2012: 11). The Hebrew term *bayit* (בית) "house" is vague and can refer to both the nuclear family (Geus 1976; Halpern 1991) and the extended family (Hopkins 1985; Reviv 1993). Lack of an unambiguous term/notion for the nuclear family may imply that there was traditionally no legitimate identity and community without an association to a *bet-ab*. The present consensus among scholars considers the *bet-ab* and not the nuclear family the basic social unit (Bendor 1996: 121–23; Holladay 1995: 386–87; Lang 1985: 85, 97).

The Mishpaha

The *bet-ab* was not isolated but was associated with a larger social structure, the *mishpaha* (Faust 2012: 10). The extended families comprising small-scale, politically autonomous communities were integrated regionally into their *mishpaha* through trade, ritual, and shifting alliances that were regularly negotiated. The *mishpaha* provided nubile partners for endogamous marriages to preserve the system of land tenure (cf. Num 36:1–12). It also regulated legal matters on a mutually accepted and authorized level of communal consensus. The manpower to defend the land owned by the extended families was recruited by the *mishpaha*.

There is a debate whether land was owned by the *mishpaha* (Faust 2012: 10) or by the *bet-ab* with the *mishpaha* only being responsible for redeeming lands and similar ownership disputes (see Num 27:4, 11 or Ruth 4:3–6; Hopkins 1985: 258). In my view, the *mishpaha* was the result of marriage alliances, which the *batei-ab* had to form with other extended families since none of the small *batei-ab* was able to establish a self-sufficient endogamous community all by itself (Lehmann 2004). Exogamous marriages meant associating with other neighboring kinship groups, which carried the danger that the ancestral inheritance became accessible to these neighbors. To be able to marry neighboring kinship groups and yet protect their ancestral inheritance, the extended families had to establish complex marriage alliances that seem to correspond to the *mishpahot* (lineages) of the Bible.

The *batei-ab* and their *mishpaha* did not aspire to create state-like institutions and avoided centralizing political power in their communities. Instead, political and ritual authority was hold by elders of the *batei-ab* who were recognized by the entire *mishpaha* (1 Sam 30:27–31; 1 Kgs 20). Their collective leadership operated at the level of the *mishpahah* (Faust 2012: 12).

The Shevet (Tribe)

The term *shevet* constitutes the largest social unit in the ancient Israelite society as it appears in Josh 7:16–18 (Gottwald 1999: 245–56; Lemche 1985: 274–85). An alternative Hebrew word for "tribe" is *matteh* (מטה). The *shevet* represents an alliance of *mishpahot* who reside in a territorial unit. The biblical tradition constructed the tribes in genealogical lists with an assumed patrilinear descent (Gen 49; Num 1 and 26; Deut 33; 1 Sam 10:20–21). The genealogies are essentially political constructions and relate to landscapes and settlements inhabited by kinship groups. The kinship relations are often fictive, and genealogies can be modified according to political circumstances and needs. Thus, they could include or exclude relevant kinship groups and their mythological ancestors. The *shevet* was an alliance of solidarity and a legal community, closely connected to a territory that the tribe was to defend (Judg 6–8 and 20). It was, however, impossible to compel individual kinship groups to participate in such a common military contingent (Judg 12:2 and 21:9).

Was Israel a Tribal Society?

There is no standardized definition for what a "tribe" is, and many anthropologists consider the term too ambiguous to be useful.[2] "Tribal societies" are social networks defining themselves in terms of kinship and sharing a common territory. These groups are integrated by cross-cutting genealogies and are "lacking class structure or full-time segmental specialization. They are nonhierarchical in the sense that decision-making occurs primarily through consensus rather than through the full-time exercise of power by formal sanctified authorities" (Braun and Plog 1982: 504; Eickelman 1981: 91). An archaeological perspective of tribal social trajectories suggests that sedentary tribes were not a marginal phenomenon, but a dominant social form in the human past (Parkinson 2002: 9).

Service imagined "tribes" as an evolutionary stage of a stateless, non-centralized political formation without hierarchy (Service 1962) and as predecessors of states (Sahlins 1968). Essential aspects of a strict "neo-evolutionary" approach with sequences from bands to tribes to chiefdoms to states have been criticized for neglecting the complexities inherent in the evolvement of social systems (Yoffee 2004). The Bronze Age societies of the Levant, especially in the southern Levant, did not develop in the form of a simple evolutionary "stepladder" of stages (Yoffee 1995: 545–47). Rather, they are characterized by repeated cycles of growth and crises during which urban societies converted to rural ones and back to urban, from state to stateless formations and back to states. Moreover, social groups conforming to tribes, chiefdoms and early states appear to have coexisted contemporarily side-by-side, at times replacing a "more advanced" developed stage with its evolutionary predecessor.

Tribes in this approach are fundamentally a category of political organization. Politically they do not function upon distinct, centralized political institutions, but develop out of the ongoing social life of kin-based groups (Winthrop 1991: 307). Thus, tribal societies develop political integration "bottom-up" from small kinship groups and through negotiations and consensus among peers rather than impersonal centralized political or legal institutions. They reside within their territory (Marx 1977) and their members are linked by extended kinship ties, ritual obligations, and mutual responsibility for the resolution of disputes (Marx 1977; Winthrop 1991: 307).

- In early states and chiefdoms, the extended families are assembled in a hierarchical system with mechanisms of "top-down" control. Early states and chiefdoms were usually

- ruled by monarchs. They exert and create hierarchical power structures through networks and communication with a low level of formal, non-bureaucratic institutions.
- In contrast, tribal groups strive for political independence. The extended families rule themselves through elders and the authority of charismatic kinship leaders. Their power throughout the lineage and outside of their own extended families is limited. Factual or assumed kinship is one of the most important characteristics of legitimate power in tribal groups.

Land ownership and self-defense are central aspects of tribal societies (Carapico 1998: 68). Anthropological research in sedentary tribal mountain societies such as in Afghanistan, Yemen, or the Berber (Amazigh) of North Africa, demonstrates that tribal alliances are essentially opposed to any government from outside their kin and wary of any domination by people that do not belong to their extended family or lineage (Noelle-Karimi 1997: 125ff; Roberts 2014; Weir 2007). The main reason is that the tribal groups want to protect their land, the main source of survival and their most important means of production. Thus, one of the most essential foundations of tribal societies is the control over their agricultural land, which is considered their ancestral inheritance (Ugaritic *nhlt*, Hebrew נהלה).

The absence of any hierarchy of rights to land, which is essential for the royal ideology of the city-state, is one of the basic characteristics of the tribal societies (Relaki and Catapoti 2013: 13–14). In the Hebrew Bible, the land is the deity's creation and his property (Ps 24:1, 95:4f.) and the land is given by the deity exclusively to those who will cultivate it as their ancestral inheritance. There is no mention of any royal rights in this context. Biblical law determined that land should remain in the family to which it had been apportioned and could not be sold permanently outside of it (Westbrook 1991).

Within Israelite society, the land was owned by the *bet-ab*, while the *mishpaha* was primarily protective and restorative for the constituent households.[3] Notably, landholding of most of the traditional rural communities of the Near East is "not organized into larger genealogical units, that is to say 'tribes'" (Routledge 2004: 117).

The Hebrew term *shevet* designates a social integration above the level of the *mishpaha*. Some scholars regard the *shevet* as an authentic and powerful tribal corporation in pre-monarchic times. On the contrary, I am arguing that the *shevet* was in fact an elusive and largely imaginary association even in the pre-monarchic period (Geus 1976: 156; Lemche 1996: 117). At best, the *shevet* represented short-lived and fragile tribal alliances. Ethnographic and historical comparisons suggest that tribal federations at the level of the *shevet* were bonded by traditions of consensus, but, with their lack of concentration of authority, they were always fragile and had to face persistent processes of fragmentation.

Routledge interprets the so-called classic characteristics of Near Eastern "tribal" societies as cultural resources that could be combined and articulated in a variety of ways.

> In particular, (1) segmentation as a mode of identification; (2) domestic autonomy, especially as embodied in the house as both a structure and a metaphor; and (3) genealogy as an idiom for representing extrahousehold relations are all well recognized as key resources for constituting identity under the rubric of 'tribalism'.
>
> (Routledge 2004: 92)

Due to the constant states of flux of boundaries of tribal social trajectories (Parkinson 2002: 9), the *shevet* was in terms of practical social impact on ordinary life the least significant of the circles of kinship within tribal alliances (Wright 1992). Rather than an efficient corporation of government, the *shevet* appears to have been mainly a geographical unit (Geus 1976: 144–45; Reviv 1993: 55–59; Zobel 2004: 306).

Textual analyses identified those biblical passages that present Israel as a politically significant alliance of twelve tribes as later constructions with no bearing on the beginning of the settlement process in the highlands (Schorn 1997: 52–53). Similar approaches to a "tribal" past are known from ancient Greece where the construction, if not invention, of "archaic" tribal structures in Attica, seems to be a comparable later pursuit of the 6th century BCE (Bourriot 1976; Roussel 1976).

In fact, the Israelite tribes remain somewhat elusive in the biblical traditions. Their territory is never exactly defined,[4] no tribal leaders are mentioned in specific political contexts as decision makers and the political and economic impact of tribes in historical situations is unclear. The entire notion of the concept and the social composition of the tribe appears to be vague.

Tribal elders had apparently little leadership function within the *shevet*, whereas there was a strong patrimonial leadership of elders within the subdivisions of the *mishpaha* and *bet-ab* (Lemche 1985: 274–80). Charismatic and patrimonial authority may have emerged in the realm of the *shevet*; however, efficient political leadership was exercised only within the *mishpahot* with limited political influence beyond these kinship bonds.

> Integration and cooperation are typically strongest at the lowest level of the nuclear or extended family, weaker in higher levels of organization, and weakest at the level of 'nation' or tribal confederacy (if one exists). The smaller units in a tribal system (for example, clans or lineages) rarely unite with each other politically. When they do, it is normally because of some threat or crisis that requires it. In between times of threat, some sense of solidarity and unity and loose bonding are maintained through economic and religious ties (for example, trade and ritual). A sense of unity is further supported by genealogical myths of common descent, fictitious kinship links by means of mythical or assumed ancestry.
>
> *(McNutt 1999: 84; see also Schäfer-Lichtenberg 1983: 287–89)*

Comparing the kinship structure of the Hebrew Bible with sedentary tribal societies in the Middle East and North Africa[5] suggests identifying the biblical *mishpaha*, and not the *shevet*, as the ancient equivalent for the "tribe" (modern Arab *qabile*). Although the Hebrew Bible is often ambiguous in the use of *shevet* and *mishpaha*, it seems that the *shevet* neither functioned as an autonomous legal entity nor as a cultic community (Zobel 2004: 307).

It is unlikely that the fragmented kinship groups in the early Iron Age central highlands acted as a "national" unit with a sense of "ethnic consciousness." Rather, the politics and the economies of the fragmented kinship groups were primal, pursued regarding varying local interests. Identities of kinship groups in stateless societies usually evolved in a bottom-up approach emphasizing their local and diverging interests. Numerous historical examples from comparable societies in Yemen, Afghanistan, and North Africa[6] demonstrate that local lineages follow above all particularistic interests that override any wider "ethnic consciousness" (Parkinson 2002: 8). This implies that there was no powerful "national" association of Israelite tribes before the forceful domination of the local lineages, according to the biblical narrative, by the early tribal monarchies of the 10th and 9th centuries BCE.

In what sense, then, was ancient Israel tribal? During the early Iron Age, the societies inhabiting the central highlands were constituted of local kinship groups. The lineages and clans did not freely unite in a common state or kingdom but kept a certain distance from one another. These groups were "tribal" in the sense that their social structure was constructed bottom-up avoiding political integration above the level of the *mishpaha*/lineage. Yet, ancient Israel was not "tribal" in the sense that tribes would have formed a unified political body with a centralized concentration of authority. Ancient Israelite tribes remained elusive associations beyond shaping territorial and symbolical identities.

Social Structure and Archaeology in a Long-Term Perspective

In search of the ancient Israelite society, or rather societies, the approach followed here regards individuals rather than social entities as meaningful agents. This is to avoid a top-down approach, in which entire ethnic entities are regarded as the main agents ("Canaanites", "Philistines", "Israelites", etc.) in shaping the behavior of humans in the past. In contrast, this chapter emphasizes the diversity of ancient societies and communities in a bottom-up approach. I am arguing that social identity in ancient Israel was foremost formed in small communal bodies such as kinship groups and segmented social organizations. Anthropological and historical studies demonstrate that the integration of such segmented groups into larger territorial coherences was often a slow and reversible process.

Late Bronze Age Beginnings

Ancient Israel is deeply rooted in the social world of the Late Bronze Age (LB). The settlement pattern suggests that the societies in the LB highlands were most possibly organized in regional kinship groups. Evidence for this is the dispersed and sparse LB settlement in the highlands, especially in the south. The northern parts of the highland around Dothan, Shechem, and Tell el-Far'ah (North) were – relatively – more densely inhabited and may very well represent what Merenptah knew as "Israel" since there was simply no other highland region with a comparable settlement density during this period (see G. Pierce, this volume). The low LB population density in the central hill country is the result of an abandonment of the region at the end of the Middle Bronze Age.

A few tombs with rich grave goods such as very large numbers of ceramics and metal artifacts appear to be chiefdom burials. Such burials were excavated at Tell Dothan, Khirbet 'Ara, and Khirbet Jedur (Ben-Arieh 1981; Cooley and Pratico 1995; Gadot et al. 2014). A similar chiefdom stronghold in the south with fortifications and a cemetery was Khirbet er-Rabud (Kochavi 1973–74).

Finkelstein (1988– 94) and Bunimovitz (1994) explained – each with a different view of the circumstances – the lack of populations as cyclic processes of sedentarization and nomadization. They assume that non-sedentary groups inhabited the highlands during the LB and began settling down in the transition to the Iron Age. According to Finkelstein, these non-sedentary groups merged with others who originated from a local sedentary background in the lowlands and moved to the highlands. Finkelstein called this social blend "Israelites" since they eventually formed the population of the Northern Kingdom of Israel. Currently, there is not sufficient evidence to prove this hypothesis (Faust 2006: 176–87).

In contrast, there are doubts whether ancient Israel ever had a nomadic past (Bendor 1996: 217, 262–63; Dever 1993). True nomads need sedentary populations. They are not autarkic and cannot provide for themselves all requirements (Khazanov 1994). As a result, nomadic populations are significantly smaller than the sedentary population they need for their economy (Ibn Khaldun 1967: 122). These basic principles of nomadism do not support the hypothesis of ancient Israelite nomadism.

Moreover, the question of nomadic origins of early Israel easily falls into the trap of modern dichotomous concepts, which ignore the multifaceted realities of the past. Ancient societies may very well have been able to apply different modes of subsistence in a flexible and suitable way, breaking through such modern dichotomies as nomadism and sedentarism (Marfoe 1979). The kinship groups of early Israel were certainly not Bedouin, yet a versatility of agricultural and pastoral practices (not nomadism) may well have characterized their economy of poverty and opportunity.

LB texts also mention the 'Apiru or Habiru as a significant social phenomenon that was associated with the highlands (Lemche 1985; Loretz 1984; Na'aman 1986; Weippert 1971). The notion 'Apiru/Habiru is vague and its meaning most certainly changed over time. The earliest meaning designates social outcasts and people, which could neither be controlled by the Egyptians nor by the local rulers. The notion may very well be associated with the later word for "Hebrews", but the exact development of the meaning and the social realities it represents remains uncertain. Notably, there is no explicit archaeological evidence for the 'Apiru during the LB.

Iron Age I

Unfortunately, the chronology of the transition from the LB to the Iron I is somewhat confusing. There is a consensus that this transition took place in the 12th century BCE. Yet there are several notions for this one period. Archaeologists at Tel Aviv call this period "LB III", while at the Hebrew University it is known as "Iron IA". Recently it was suggested to call this period "Late Bronze Age-Iron Age I Transition" (Faust and Katz 2019). The differences are only of semantic character. Confusing for the non-archaeologists is the fact that all scholars refer to the same period with the same material culture yet create three different periodizations from ca. 1200 to 1130 BCE. In this chapter, we chose to call this period LB III because the local pottery is overwhelmingly of LB character. In archaeological surveys, sites dating to the 12th century BCE were usually recorded as LB sites.

The implication of this is that there are only relatively few sites in the central highlands, which were safely dated specifically to the 12th century BCE. Unfortunately, there are additional problems with the precise dating of the highland sites. One of the most important indications of a settlement during this period are storage jars called collared rim storage jars. However, these jars commenced already during the 13th century BCE (Artzy 1994). Chronologically, sites with collared rim storage jars may have been founded as early as the 13th century BCE and could have continued all through the Iron I. A more precise chronological dating is only possible with the more distinct cooking pot typology. Dating the sites of the Israelite/Proto-Israelite settlement in this way suggests that the major settlement move occurred only during the Iron I, after ca. 1130 BCE. To conclude, the highlands were sparsely inhabited during the LB. A settlement process which is usually associated with the Israelite or Proto-Israelite settlement began as early as the late 13th century BCE. During the first half of the 12th century BCE until ca. 1130 BCE, this settlement did not expand substantially. A dramatic increase in sites set in only in the second half of the 12th century BCE and developed during the 11th century BCE into a dense settlement pattern of very small rural hamlets with few larger villages or "village towns."

The increase of settlements and the growth of population size within such a short period implies that this settlement process was not natural or gradual; it must have been connected with migrations. This raises the question of which historical events and processes in the late 12th century BCE triggered the migration into the central hill country. Many LB sites in the coastal plain and in the highlands were abandoned in this period during the transition from the LB to the Iron Age. Notably, new Iron I sites were founded in many cases immediately next to abandoned LB sites. This indicates profound changes in the population and their traditional pattern of landownership.

The combination of abandonment and new nearby settlements is especially evident in the highlands around Khirbet er-Rabud, Khirbet Jedur, Jerusalem, Shechem and Tell el-Far'ah (North). Notably, it is less evident around Tell Dothan although there are a few abandoned villages. Settlement in the Tell Dothan valley continued in most cases from the LB through the Iron I. As already noted, these settlements could very well have related to the "Israel" of Merenptah.

This settlement pattern which emerged in the central hill country during the late 12th and 11th centuries BCE was a rural landscape of very small villages with only a few houses. Within these villages, there was little differentiation in the architecture with no large-size structures such as elaborated fortifications, palaces, temples, large-scale storage facilities, or administrative buildings. Some hamlets arranged houses and fences contiguously on the village perimeter. This form of village was not well suited for defense and was more probably constructed to keep the livestock safe within the compound.

I assume that the entire population of a typical Iron I hamlet comprised one extended family and not a *mishpaha*. According to my calculations, the population of such hamlets must have been in most cases less than 200 inhabitants (for a similar estimate of the total population of a hamlet, see Schloen 2001: 154–55). The extended family constituted the living world of the people in the central hill country, the early "Israelites." The extended family was the basic economic unit of the Iron I settlements. This small community was an intimate world of a few people who interacted with each other every day over their entire lives. Only on a few occasions people travelled to perform rituals and economic exchanges with other members of the *mishpaha*, the lineage. On such occasions, the extended families married their children within the *mishpaha*, since their own communities in the hamlets could not provide marriage partners for all the young people (Lehmann 2004). Marrying within the *mishpaha* secured the patrimony, the *nahalah*, and produced consanguinity throughout the villages of the lineage (Stager 1988: 222).

As demonstrated above, the rural societies of *mishpahot* during the Iron I were not firmly integrated into tribes, which were ruled by powerful leaders in a strict top-down hierarchy. The tribal system as it appears in the biblical tradition did not emerge from within the ancient Israelite societies. I am arguing that it appeared as a royal construction with the aim to govern the various kinship groups of the 9th and 8th centuries BCE dispersed in the kingdom.

Sedentary tribal mountain societies such as in Afghanistan, Yemen, or the Berber (Amazigh) of North Africa provide a more convincing model for the tribal societies of the central hill country. These societies are essentially opposed to any government from outside their kin and distrust powerful people who do not belong to their extended family or lineage (Noelle-Karimi 1997: 125ff; Roberts 2014; Weir 2007). Land ownership and self-defense are central aspects for these communities (Carapico 1998: 68).

As in these anthropological comparisons, the extended families of ancient Israel guarded their local autonomy and their patrimony against attempts to dominate them from outside their families. The tribe (*shevet*) was a politically weak association of lineages in a territory defined by the patrimonies of the lineages and extended families. During the early Iron Age, the tribe mainly served as a framework for mediation and negotiations among the kinship groups. True political power lay with the extended families and their lineages. A council of elders (*zeqenim*) provided leadership bottom-up from within the families and the lineage. This collective leadership was legitimized by its ancestry and recognized through its charismatic reputation. As in modern tribal societies, the support of the lineage could be withdrawn and revoked if the community felt misrepresented by a leader.

Iron Age IIA–B

The world of autonomous and endogamous village alliances, which occupied the central hill country as small interacting groups during the Iron I, ended in the transition from the Iron I to the Iron IIA. As Faust pointed out, a significant number of settlements were abandoned in the late Iron I in the transition to Iron IIA (Faust 2003, 2021). With some modifications of Faust's suggestions and with some of the critique regarding his hypotheses in mind (Finkelstein 2003), one can explain the social and political developments alternatively.

The fundamental political changes at the end of the Iron I led to an abandonment of settlements in various regions of the Southern Levant for different reasons and various political developments. In the central hill country, warlords representing powerful clans fought over the domination of the previously autonomous kinship groups and their villages. In changing alliances, charismatic leaders like Saul, David, Solomon, and others reshaped the political and social realities eventually subduing the clans.

Throughout the Iron IIA–B, most Israelite settlements in the highlands remained rural and non-urban. In the transition from the Iron I to Iron IIA, some villages were abandoned, while others were fortified. The population of abandoned villages seemed to have moved to neighboring, often fortified sites of their *mishpaha*, enlarging them in a process like the "synoecism" of late 8th century BCE Greece (Morris 2006; Snodgrass 2006). The essential point is the rural character of most of these fortified villages and the fact that they remained rural settlements in this process of growth.

It is unclear who initiated the fortifications in the transition from the Iron I to IIA. Although it is possible that warlords built some of these walls around the villages, it is also viable that local kinship groups constructed them in a communal effort. The fortifications were simple; a belt of houses around the site perimeter created casemate-like fortifications at sites like Khirbet Dawwara (Finkelstein 1990), Tell en-Nasbeh (Finkelstein 2012), Tell Dothan (Master et al. 2005: Fig. 10.4), Shechem (Campbell and Wright 2002: 1:248, Fig. 232), et-Tell (Ai) and Gibeon (Finkelstein and Fantalkin 2012: 53). At Jerusalem (Reich and Uziel, personal communication) and Hebron (Chadwick 2005: 25–33), there are indications for a re-use of MB fortifications during the early Iron Age. Similar fortified rural sites are Khirbet Qeiyafa, Tell Beit Mirsim, and more sites in the Shephelah (Lehmann and Niemann 2014) with further fortified rural sites in Moab (Routledge 2004) and the Negev highlands (Cohen and Cohen-Amin 2004).

As a result of these processes, the Iron IIA–B rural settlement in the central hill country was now characterized by larger settlements. These were, however, in my view in most cases corporate communities and not cities (Chesson and Philip 2003). Despite considerable political changes in the Iron II, there is a consensus that the fundamental kinship structure of *batei-av* and *mishpahot* was preserved throughout the Iron Age (Faust 2012: 265; Lemos 2016; Schloen 2001; Stager 2003: 70–71). The larger settlements reached a size of 3–6 hectares which corresponds with a population of about 600–1200 inhabitants.[7] Notably, this is the size range of an endogamous group, and the larger villages were now probably inhabited by an entire *mishpaha* (Lehmann 2004).

Excavations at these large villages demonstrate that there was little differentiation in the architecture within the community. There were no monumental structures such as elaborated fortifications, palaces, temples, large-scale storage facilities, or administrative buildings except for a wall and a gate. There were larger residences in the form of four-room houses, yet these were possibly inhabited by clan leaders. They resemble large rural structures of aristocrats in Proto-Geometric and Geometric Greece which also have a communal cultic function (Mazarakis Ainian 1997). This may be an indication that cultic rituals in these communities were decentralized, focusing on the clan and the veneration of the ancestors – and less concerned with the official state religion (Albertz and Schmitt 2012).

During the 8th century BCE, social change challenged the conservative tribal society of the central hill country. A new type of rural settlement broke the hereditary order of traditional settlement pattern. These settlements seem to be fortresses and most of them were found in the kingdom of Judah. They do, however, also occur in the northern kingdom of Israel (Faust 2012: 178–89). Some of these are true fortresses of the royal government and represent a novelty. Never was the monarchy so visibly represented in the rural countryside. Many of these sites date to the 7th century BCE, the period of empires, which challenged the ancient traditions in Israel, yet some sites such as Khirbet Abu et-Twein could date to the 8th century BCE to the period of the monarchies preceding the Assyrian empire. Sites like Abu et-Twein were more probably rather estates than only fortresses (Faust 2012: 180ff). Since these estates have nothing in common with the traditional kinship settlement, they may represent royal loans (Faust 2012: 22; Noth 1927: 215). These representatives of the monarchy in the countryside may be among those people who the prophets Amos, Isaiah, Micah, and Jeremiah denounced for their luxurious lifestyle and their oppression of the poor.[8] In fact, this new elite posed a challenge to the traditional tribal customs of landownership and may have even taken possession of clan lands. Such socio-economic changes eventually led to the demise of the traditional social structures discussed here.

Notes

1 See Brenner-Idan 2015; Crouch 2014; Im 2010; Kessler 2008; Maeir and Shai 2016; McNutt 1999; Miller 2005; Nam 2012; Perdue 1997; Perdue et al. 1997; Porter 2013; Simkins and Cook 1999; Smith 2009; Vincent 2013.
2 See Fried 1967; Hayden 1995; Helm 1968; Parkinson 2002.
3 For the various views see for example Bendor 1996: 82–86; Gottwald 1999: 257–67; Wright 1992: 761–69.
4 The sources of the book of Joshua are too late and do not provide reliable historical evidence for this discussion.
5 Eickelman1981: 85–104; Hart 2000; Weir 2007.
6 See Glatzer 2002; Hart 2000;Weir 2007. Compare the traditional Bedouin saying: "I, against my brothers. I and my brothers against my cousins. I and my brothers and my cousins against the world." Note that the "world" boundary begins just beyond the own lineage.
7 Applying an average estimate of 150 to 300 persons per hectare (Broshi and Finkelstein 1992; Chamberlain 2006: 126–28; Schloen 2001: 165–83; Zorn 1994).
8 de Vaux 1965: 72–73; Faust 2012: 265; Houston 2004; Perdue 1997: 209–10; Reviv 1993: 45, 64.

Bibliography

Albertz, Rainer, and Rüdiger Schmitt. 2012. *Family and Household Religion in Ancient Israel and the Levant*. Winona Lake: Eisenbrauns.
Andersen, Francis I. 1969. "Israelite Kinship Terminology and Social Structure." *BT* 20: 29–39.

Artzy, Michal. 1994. "Incense, Camels and Collared Rim Jars: Desert Trade Routes and Maritime Outlets in the 2nd Millennium B.C." *OJA* 13: 121–47.

Ben-Arieh, Sarah. 1981. "A Late Bronze Age Tomb at Tell Jedur." *EI* 15: 115–28.

Bendor, Shunya. 1996. *The Social Structure of Ancient Israel: The Institution of the Family (beit 'ab) from the Settlement to the End of the Monarchy.* Jerusalem: Simor.

Bourdieu, Pierre. 1977. *Outline of a Theory of Practice.* Cambridge, MA: Cambridge University Press.

Bourriot, Félix. 1976. *Recherches Sur la Nature Du Genos: Étude D'histoire Sociale Athénienne: Périodes Archaïque Et Classique.* Lille: Champion.

Braun, David P., and Stephen Plog. 1982. "Evolution of 'Tribal' Social Networks: Theory and Prehistoric North American Evidence." *AA* 47: 504–25.

Brenner-Idan, Athalya. 2015. *The Israelite Woman: Social Role and Literary Type in Biblical Narrative.* London: Bloomsbury.

Broshi, Magen and Israel Finkelstein. 1992. "The Population of Palestine in Iron Age II." *BASOR* 287: 47–60.

Bunimovitz, Shlomo. 1993. "The Study of Complex Societies: The Material Culture of Late Bronze Age Canaan as a Case Study." Pages 443–51 in *Biblical Archaeology Today, 1990: Proceedings of the Second International Congress on Biblical Archaeology, Jerusalem, June–July 1990.* Edited by Joseph Aviram, Avraham Biran and Alan Paris-Shadur. Jerusalem: Israel Exploration Society.

———. 1994. "Socio-Political Transformations in the Central Hill Country in the Late Bronze-Iron I Transition." Pages 179–202 in *From Nomadism to Monarchy: Archaeological and Historical Aspects of Early Israel.* Edited by I. Finkelstein and N. Na'aman. Jerusalem: Israel Exploration Society.

Campbell, Edward F., and George R. H. Wright. 2002. *Shechem III: The Stratigraphy and Architecture of Shechem/Tell Balatah.* Boston: American Schools of Oriental Research.

Carapico, Sheila. 1998. *Civil Society in Yemen: The Political Economy of Activism in Modern Arabia.* Cambridge: Cambridge University Press.

Chadwick, Jeffrey R. 2005. "Discovering Hebron: The City of the Patriarchs Slowly Yields Its Secrets." *BAR* 31: 25–33.

Chamberlain, andrew T. 2006. *Demography in Archaeology.* Cambridge: Cambridge University Press.

Chesson, Meredith S., and Graham Philip. 2003. "Tales of the City? 'Urbanism' in the Early Bronze Age Levant from Mediterranean and Levantine Perspectives." *JMA* 16: 3–16.

Cohen, Rudolph, and Rivka Cohen-Amin. 2004. *Ancient Settlement of the Central Negev: Volume 2. The Iron Age and the Persian Period.* Jerusalem: Israel Antiquities Authority.

Cooley, Robert E., and Gary D. Pratico. 1995. "Tell Dothan: The Western Cemetery, with Comments on Joseph Free's Excavations, 1953–1964." Pages 147–90 in *Preliminary Excavation Reports: Sardis, Bir Umm Fawakhir, Tell el-'Umeiri, the Combined Caesarea Expeditions, and Tell Dothan.* Edited by William G. Dever. Ann Arbor: American Schools of Oriental Research.

Crouch, Carly L. 2014. *The Making of Israel: Cultural Diversity in the Southern Levant and the Formation of Ethnic Identity in Deuteronomy.* Leiden: Brill.

De Vaux, Roland. 1965. *Ancient Israel: 1. Social Institutions.* New York: McGraw-Hill.

Dever, William G. 1993. "Cultural Continuity, Ethnicity in the Archaeological Record, and the Question of Israelite Origins." *EI* 24: 22*–33*.

Dresch, Paul. 1989. *Tribes, Government and History in Yemen.* Oxford: Clarendon Press.

Dutcher-Walls, Patricia. 2009. "The Clarity of Double Vision: Seeing the Family in Sociological and Archaeological Perspective." Pages 1–15 in *The Family in Life and in Death: The Family in Ancient Israel: Sociological and Archaeological Perspectives.* Edited by Patricia Dutcher-Walls. London: T & T Clark International.

Eickelman, Dale F. 1981. *The Middle East: An Anthropological Approach.* Englewood Cliffs: Prentice Hall.

Faust, Avraham. 2003. "Abandonment, Urbanization, Resettlement and the Formation of the Israelite State." *NEA* 66: 147–61.

———. 2006. *Israel's Ethnogenesis: Settlement, Interaction, Expansion and Resistance.* London: Equinox.

———. 2012. *The Archaeology of Israelite Society in Iron Age II.* Winona Lake: Eisenbrauns.

———. 2021. "The 'United Monarchy' on the Ground: The Disruptive Character of the Iron Age I-II Transition and the Nature of Political Transformations." *JJAR* 1: 15–67.

Faust, Avraham, and Hayah Katz, eds. 2019. *Archaeology of the Land of Israel: From the Neolithic to Alexander the Great, Volume 2.* Raanana: Open University of Israel.

Finkelstein, Israel. 1988. *The Archaeology of the Israelite Settlement.* Jerusalem: Israel Exploration Society.

———. 1990. "Excavations at Khirbet Ed-Dawwara: An Iron Age Site Northeast of Jerusalem." *TA* 17: 163–208.

———. 1994. "The Emergence of Israel: A Phase in the Cyclic History of Canaan in the 3rd and 2nd Millennia BCE." Pages 150–78 in *From Nomadism to Monarchy: Archaeological and Historical Aspects of Early Israel*. Edited by I. Finkelstein and N. Na'aman. Jerusalem: Israel Exploration Society.

———. 2003. "(De)Formation of the Israelite State: A Rejoinder on Methodology." *NEA* 66: 202–08.

———. 2012. "The Great Wall of Tell en-Nasbeh (Mizpah): The First Fortifications in Judah, and 1 Kings 15:16–22." *VT* 62: 14–28.

Finkelstein, Israel and Alexander Fantalkin. 2012. "Khirbet Qeiyafa: An Unsensational Archaeological and Historical Interpretation." *TA* 39: 38–63.

Fried, Morton H. 1967. *The Evolution of Political Society: An Essay in Political Anthropology*. New York: Random House.

Gadot, Yuval, David Ilan, Yotam Tepper, and Eli Yannai, eds. 2014. *The Bronze Age Cemetery at 'Ara*. Tel Aviv: Sonia and Marco Nadler Institute of Archaeology, Tel Aviv University.

Geus, Cornelius H. J. de. 1976. *The Tribes of Israel: An Investigation Into Some of the Presuppositions of Martin Noth's Amphictyony Hypothesis*. Assen: van Gorcum.

Giddens, Anthony. 1993. *New Rules of Sociological Method: A Positive Critique of Interpretative Sociologies*. Malden: Polity Press.

Glatzer, Bernt. 2002. "The Pashtun Tribal System." Pages 265–82 in *Concept of Tribal Society*. Edited by G. Pfeffer and D. K. Behera. New Delhi: Concept.

Gottwald, Norman K. 1979. *The Tribes of Yahweh: A Sociology of the Religion of Liberated Israel, 1250–1050 BCE*. Maryknoll: Orbis Books.

———. 1999. *The Tribes of Yahweh: A Sociology of the Religion of Liberated Israel, 1250-1050 BCE*. Sheffield: Sheffield Academic Press.

Halpern, Baruch. 1991. "Jerusalem and the Lineages in the Seventh Century BCE: Kinship and the Rise of Individual Moral Liability." Pages 11–107 in *Law and Ideology in Monarchic Israel*. Edited by Baruch Halpern and Deborah W. Hobson. Sheffield: Sheffield Academic Press.

Hart, David M. 2000. *Tribe and Society in Rural Morocco*. Portland: Frank Cass.

Hayden, Brian. 1995. "Pathways to Power: Principles for Creating Socioeconomic Inequalities." Pages 15–86 in *Foundations of Social Inequality*. Edited by T. Douglas Price and Gary M. Feinman. New York: Plenum Press.

Helm, June, ed. 1968. *Essays on the Problem of Tribe. Proceedings of the American Ethnological Society*. Seattle: University of Washington Press.

Hitchcock, Louise A., and Aren M. Maeir. 2013. "Beyond Creolization and Hybridity: Entangled and Transcultural Identities in Philistia." *ARC* 28: 51–74.

Holladay, John S. 1995. "The Kingdoms of Israel and Judah: Political and Economic Centralization in the Iron Age II A-B (ca. 1000–750 BCE)." Pages 368–98 in *Archaeology of Society in the Holy Land*. Edited by Thomas E. Levy. London: Leicester University Press.

Hopkins, David C. 1985. *The Highlands of Canaan: Agricultural Life in the Early Iron Age*. Decatur: Almond Press.

Houston, Walter J. 2004. "Was There a Social Crisis in the Eighth Century?" Pages 130–49 in *In Search of Pre-Exilic Israel: Proceedings of the Oxford Old Testament Seminar*. Edited by John Day. London: T&T Clark.

Ibn Khaldun, Abdurahman. 1967. *The Muqaddimah: An Introduction to History*. Translated by F. Rosenthal and edited by N. J. Dawood. Princeton: Princeton University Press.

Im, Pong Dae. 2010. "Social Identity in Early Israel: An Archaeological and Textual Study of Social Behaviors and Group Identity among Highland Villagers in Iron Age I Palestine." PhD diss., Graduate Theological Union.

Jenkins, Richard. 2008. *Social Identity*. London: Routledge.

Kessler, Rainer. 2008. *The Social History of Ancient Israel: An Introduction*. Minneapolis: Fortress Press.

Khazanov, Anatoly M. 1994. *Nomads in the Outside World*. Madison: University of Wisconsin Press.

Kochavi, Moshe. 1973. "Khirbet Rabud—Ancient Debir." Pages 49–75 in *Excavations and Studies: Essays in Honour of Professor Shemuel Yeivin*. Edited by Yohanan Aharoni. Tel Aviv: Institute of Archaeology, Tel Aviv University.

———. 1974. "Khirbet Rabud = Debir." *TA* 1: 2–33.

Lang, Bernhard. 1985. "The Social Organization of Peasant Poverty in Biblical Israel." Pages 83–99 in *Anthropological Approaches to the Old Testament*. Edited by Bernhard Lang. Philadelphia: Fortress Press.

Lehmann, Gunnar. 2004. "Reconstructing the Social Landscape of Early Israel: Marriage Alliances in a Rural Context." *TA* 31: 141–93.

Lehmann, Gunnar and Hermann Michael Niemann. 2014. "When Did the Shephelah Become Judahite?" *TA* 41: 77–94.

Lemche, Niels Peter. 1985. *Early Israel: Anthropological and Historical Studies on the Israelite Society before the Monarchy.* Leiden: Brill.

———. 1996. "From Patronage Society to Patronage Society." Pages 106–20 in *The Origins of the Ancient Israelite States*. Edited by V. Fritz and P. R. Davies. Sheffield: Sheffield Academic Press.

Lemos, Tracy M. 2016. "Kinship, Community, and Society." Pages 379–95 in *The Wiley Blackwell Companion to Ancient Israel*. Edited by Susan Niditch. Oxford: John Wiley & Sons.

Loretz, Oswald. 1984. *Habiru-Hebräer: Eine Sozio-Linguistische Studie Über die Herkunft des Gentiliziums 'ibri Vom Appelativum habiru*. Berlin: Mann.

Maeir, Aren M. 2021. "On Defining Israel: Or, Let's Do the Kulturkreislehre again!" *HBAI* 10: 106–48.

Maeir, Aren M., and Itzhaq Shai. 2016. "Reassessing the Character of the Judahite Kingdom: Archaeological Evidence for Non-Centralized, Kinship-Based Components." Pages 323–40 in *From Sha'ar Hagolan to Shaaraim: Essays in Honor of Prof. Yosef Garfinkel*. Edited by Saar Ganor et al. Jerusalem: Israel Exploration Society.

Marfoe, Leon. 1979. "The Integrative Transformation: Patterns of Socio-Political Organization in Southern Syria." *BASOR* 234: 1–42.

Marx, Emanuel. 1977. "The Tribe as a Unit of Subsistence: Nomadic Pastoralism in the Middle East." *AmAnth* 79: 343–63.

Master, Daniel M., John H. Monson, Egon H. E. Lass, and George A. Pierce, eds. 2005. *Dothan I: Remains from the Tell (1953–1964)*. Winona Lake: Eisenbrauns.

Matthews, Victor H., and Don C. Benjamin. 1993. *Social World of Ancient Israel, 1250–587 BCE*. Peabody: Hendrickson.

Mazarakis Ainian, Alexander. 1997. *From Rulers' Dwellings to Temples: Architecture, Religion and Society in Early Iron Age Greece (1100–700 BC)*. Jonsered: Paul Åström.

McNutt, Paula M. 1999. *Reconstructing the Society of Ancient Israel*. Louisville: Westminster John Knox Press.

Miller, Robert D. 2005. *Chieftains of the Highland Clans: A History of Israel in the Twelfth and Eleventh Centuries BC*. Grand Rapids: Eerdmans.

Morris, Ian. 2006. "The Growth of Greek Cities in the First Millennium BC." Pages 27–51 in *Urbanism in the Preindustrial World: Cross-Cultural Approaches*. Edited by Glenn Reed Storey. Tuscaloosa: University of Alabama Press.

Mundy, Martha. 1995. *Domestic Government: Kinship, Community and Polity in North Yemen*. London: I. B. Tauris.

Na'aman, Nadav. 1986. "Habiru and Hebrews: The Transfer of a Social Term to the Literary Sphere." *JNES* 45: 271–88.

Nam, Roger S. 2012. *Portrayals of Economic Exchange in the Book of Kings*. Leiden: Brill.

Noelle-Karimi, Christine. 1997. *State and Tribe in Nineteenth-Century Afghanistan: The Reign of Amir Dost Muhammad Khan (1826–1863)*. London: Curzon.

Noth, Martin. 1927. "Das Krongut der israelitischen Könige und Seine Verwaltung." *ZDPV* 50: 211–44.

Parkinson, William A. 2002. "Introduction: Archaeology and Tribal Societies." Pages 1–12 in *The Archaeology of Tribal Societies*. Edited by William A. Parkinson. Ann Arbor: International Monographs in Prehistory.

Perdue, Leo G. 1997. "The Israelite and Early Jewish Family." Pages 163–220 in *Families in Ancient Israel*. Edited by L. G. Perdue et al. Louisville: Westminster John Knox.

Perdue, Leo G., Joseph Blenkinsopp, John J. Collins, and Carol Meyers, eds. 1997. *Families in Ancient Israel*. Westminster: John Knox Press.

Porter, Benjamin W. 2013. *Complex Communities: The Archaeology of Early Iron Age West-Central Jordan*. Tucson: University of Arizona Press.

Relaki, Maria, and Despina Catapoti, eds. 2013. *An Archaeology of Land Ownership*. Hoboken: Taylor and Francis.

Reviv, Hanoch. 1993. *Society in the Kingdoms of Israel and Judah*. Jerusalem: Bialik Institute (Hebrew).

Roberts, Hugh. 2014. *Berber Government: The Kabyle Polity in Pre-Colonial Algeria*. London: Tauris.

Roussel, Denis. 1976. *Tribu et Cité: Études Sur Les Groupes Sociaux Dans Les Cités Grecques Aux Époques Archaïque at Classique.* Paris: Annales Littéraires de l'Université de Besançon.

Routledge, Bruce E. 2004. *Moab in the Iron Age: Hegemony, Polity, Archaeology.* Philadelphia: University of Pennsylvania Press.

Sahlins, Marshall D. 1968. *Tribesmen.* Englewood Cliffs: Prentice-Hall.

Schäfer-Lichtenberg, Christa. 1983. *Stadt und Eidgenossenschaft im Alten Testament: Eine Auseinandersetzung mit Max Webers Studie 'Das antike Judentum.'* Berlin: de Gruyter.

Schloen, J. David. 2001. *The House of the Father as Fact and Symbol: Patrimonialism in Ugarit and the Ancient Near East.* Winona Lake: Eisenbrauns.

Schorn, Ulrike. 1997. *Ruben und das System der Zwölf Stämme Israels: Redaktionsgeschichtliche Untersuchungen zur Bedeutung des Erstgeborenen Jakobs.* Berlin: de Gruyter.

Service, E. R. 1962. *Primitive Social Organization.* New York: Random House.

Simkins, Ronald A., and Stephen L. Cook, eds. 1999. *The Social World of the Hebrew Bible: Twenty-Five Years of the Social Sciences in the Academy.* Atlanta: SBL.

Smith, Neil G. 2009. "Social Boundaries and State Formation in Ancient Edom: A Comparative Ceramic Approach." PhD diss., University of California San Diego.

Snodgrass, Anthony M. 2006. *Archaeology and the Emergence of Greece: Collected Papers on Early Greece and Related Topics (1965–2002).* Edinburgh: Edinburgh University Press.

Stager, Lawrence E. 1985. "The Archaeology of the Family in Ancient Israel." *BASOR* 260: 1–35.

⸻. 1988. "Archaeology, Ecology, and Social History: Background Themes to the Song of Deborah." Pages 221–34 in *Congress Volume: Jerusalem, 1986.* Edited by John A. Emerton. Leiden: Brill.

⸻. 2003. "The Patrimonial Kingdom of Solomon." Pages 63–74 in *Symbiosis, Symbolism, and the Power of the Past: Canaan, Ancient Israel, and their Neighbors from the Late Bronze Age Through Roman Palaestina.* Edited by William G. Dever and Seymour Gitin. Winona Lake: Eisenbrauns.

Vanderhooft, David S. 1990. "Kinship Organization in Ancient Israel." MA thesis, York University.

Vincent, Matthew L. 2013. "Tribes and the Formation of Social Inequality: A Case Study from Central Jordan." MA thesis, University of California San Diego.

Weingart, Kirstin. 2014. *Stämmevolk - Staatsvolk - Gottesvolk? Studien zur Verwendung des Israel-Namens im Alten Testament.* Tübingen: Mohr Siebeck.

Weippert, Manfred. 1971. *The Settlement of the Israelite Tribes in Palestine: A Critical Survey of Recent Scholarly Debate.* Naperville: Allenson.

Weir, Shelagh. 2007. *A Tribal Order: Politics and Law in the Mountains of Yemen.* Austin: University of Texas Press.

Westbrook, Raymond. 1991. *Property and the Family in Biblical Law.* Sheffield: Sheffield Academic Press.

Winthrop, Robert H. 1991. "Tribe." Pages 307–12 in *Dictionary of Concepts in Cultural Anthropology.* Edited by Robert H. Winthrop. New York: Greenwood Press.

Wright, Chistopher J. H. 1992. "Family." Pages 761–69 in vol. 2 of *ABD.* Edited by D. N. Freedman. 6 vols. New York: Doubleday.

Yoffee, Norman. 1995. "Conclusion: A Mass in Celebration of the Conference." Pages 542–48, 603–04 in *Archaeology of Society in the Holy Land.* Edited by Thomas E. Levy. London: Leicester University Press.

⸻. 2004. *Myths of the Archaic State: Evolution of the Earliest Cities, States and Civilizations.* Cambridge: Cambridge University Press.

Zobel, Hans-Jürgen. 2004. "Šebet." Pages 302–11 in *Theological Dictionary of the Old Testament.* Edited by G. Johannes Botterweck, Helmer Ringgren, and Heinz-Josef Fabry. Grand Rapids: Eerdmans.

Zorn, Jeffrey R. 1994. "Estimating the Population Size of Ancient Settlements: Methods, Problems, Solutions, and a Case Study." *BASOR* 295: 31–48.

14
TRIBAL KINGDOMS AND THE TRIBAL ELEMENT IN SOUTHERN LEVANTINE IRON AGE POLITIES

Øystein S. LaBianca and Jeffrey P. Hudon

Introduction

To what extent did tribal sentiments of belonging, loyalty and duty impact and shape the social life and political order of the Israelites and their neighbors, the Ammonites, Moabites and Edomites, during the Iron Age? This is an old question that recent research by numerous ANE scholars has again brought to the fore (Bienkowski and van der Steen 2001; Joffe 2002; LaBianca 1999; LaBianca and Younker 1995). A major reason for this renewed interest is the growing infusion into biblical studies of social science perspectives and research findings that are opening new windows on efforts to comprehend and describe the social world in which the various writings that make up the Hebrew Bible came into being. Was this a world in which top-down systems of administration by imperial and monarchical bureaucrats prevailed—as was more often than not the case in ancient Egypt and Mesopotamia—or was it a bottom-up world in which agency and autonomy at the local level was sustained by notions of belonging, loyalty and duty that undergird social order in kin-based or tribally organized societies? Or was it perhaps a world in which these contrasting systems of social organization were blended in some way—with some periods trending toward a top-down order and other periods trending bottom-up? As a way forward with these questions, we set the stage by considering certain theoretical and definitional issues that we believe to be helpful for framing the topic at hand, starting with introducing global history and the notion of a Levantine Cultural Paradigm. These set the stage for a more detailed discussion of tribalism and the emergence of secondary states during the Iron Age in the Southern Levant. We conclude by offering a brief survey of tribalism and the tribal element as these are reflected in the nomenclature and stories of the Hebrew Bible.

Global History

The dawn of our global age has necessitated a new approach to history writing, namely global history. Global history draws its inspiration from our planet as seen from space—a pale blue dot (Sagan 1990) on which all of humanity's history has unfolded—along with that of all other living things and that of the planet itself, our common earth home. What animates this new approach to history writing is the urgent need for a vision of the past that overcomes the many built-in biases that permeate much traditional history writing, including biases arising from the research agendas championed by specific period-focused disciplines, denominational allegiances, national aspirations, and last but not least, ethnocentric notions of the superiority of Western civilization (orientalism) and culture (Belich et al. 2016; Crossley 2008; Geyer and Bright 1995). While still very much an emerging new field of historical inquiry, certain salient features of the approach include a deep-time perspective; embrace of *la longue durée* or long-term history, a focus on particular world regions (notably the role of seas and oceans), the interactions between these, and last but not least, an eye to uncovering the manner and extent of humanity's journey to our present age on the verge of climate catastrophe due to humans overwhelming the very forces of nature (Schäfer 2004; Sommer 2014; Steffen, Crutzen, and McNeill 2007).

An early example of history writing from the perspective of global history—and one that is close to home for those of us working in the Eastern Mediterranean lands, is *The Corrupting Sea: A Study of Mediterranean History* by Nicholas Purcell and Peregrine Horden (2000). In this influential study, the unit of analysis is an entire world region, in this case the circum-Mediterranean world, and the goal is to understand the workings of this entire region through the lens of thalassology—the study of how the affordances provided by oceans and seas have impacted and been exploited by humans and their institutions. Through this lens they posit a core characteristic of this Mediterranean world, which is the opposite of that of their muse, Fernand Braudel (1966, 1995). While for the latter, the Mediterranean world was seen as unitary, for Purcell and Horden, it is fragmentary in terms of environmental affordances and risks. The new insight they bring to their analysis, however, is how this region-wide fragmentation is overcome by connectivity that is modified over time and space by cycles of intensification and abatement in the extent to which particular localities participate in this region-wide web of connections. While case studies of particular events and places highlighted in the volume reflect the author's background as classicists, the temporal scope of their inquiry is multi-millennial. The work also devotes more attention to the challenges of daily existence—the food system—than it does to highlighting the cultural programs and predations of imperial rulers and their agents, in this way anchoring drivers of cultural change and progress predominantly in the agency role of ordinary people. Though the authors prefer thick description to making claims about a world region that could be assailed as essentialist, the wide interest in the work stems, in our opinion, from its opening a new way forward for the study of history that moves beyond the traditional focus on civilizations, empires or nations. There is also no denying that Purcell and Horden's (2000) "connectivity that overcomes fragmentation" trope approaches what we here would consider to be a key characteristic of a Mediterranean cultural paradigm.

A Levantine Cultural Paradigm

If in *The Corrupting Sea* we may discern a glimpse of a Mediterranean cultural paradigm, is it also possible to distinguish a cultural paradigm for one of its most storied sub-regions, the Southern Levant, herewith defined as the region of today's Israel, Jordan, and the Palestinian Authority territories? We believe so, and as we explain further below, what sets this paradigm apart is the extent to which it is anchored in a bottom-up vision of social order in which the tribal element plays a central role. But first, and as an aid to this task, we offer the following definition of the paradigm concept as utilized in this application: Cultural paradigms are the bundle of artifacts, ideologies, institutions, habits and practices that facilitate identity formation and path-dependent, accumulative cultural production and adaptation to changing environmental and socio-political conditions over the long term by the population of a particular world region. Noteworthy about this definition is its inclusion of the words "path-dependent, accumulative, and long-term." The point here is that cultural paradigms represent an unfolding constant (oxymoron intended) that both enfolds and transcends the agency role of particular rulers, social or religious movements, states, empires or civilizations. They represent, as it were, the guard rails that shape the accumulative unfolding of various cultural products, institutions, and practices in a given region over multiple centuries and millennia. It is this deep-time dimension of the cultural paradigm notion that makes it an apt heuristic construct for uncovering and describing accumulative cultural production over time in particular world regions—in our case here, the Southern Levant.

Tribalism and the Tribal Element

As already indicated, what sets the Levantine cultural paradigm apart is its bottom-up character where personal agency and collective action are concerned—what Hodder (2012) described as "the experience of individual action in creating a life story" and what Chapman (2000) described as "resistance or challenge to system-wide power structures through direct or indirect individual or collective action" (see Dobres and Robb 2000:9). In several recent publications, Stordalen and LaBianca (2021) have posited possible reasons for the crystallization and persistence of this bottom-up character of the social order in the Southern Levant (see also LaBianca 2009). Among these is what in the title of this chapter is referred to as the tribal element.

The mere mention of terms that include the word "tribe" (tribal, tribalism, tribalistic) is, of course, problematic both in academic and popular discourse, as they are laden with a wide range of connotations and meanings. Especially in the sub-Saharan African context, the term has significant pejorative connotations (Atanda 1972; Beattie 1971; Daniels 1971; Gulliver 2013). The situation is, however, somewhat less problematic for the Middle Eastern context, including the Southern Levant, where academic research and discourse continue to probe the meanings and connotations of the term (James 2006; Layne 1989a, 1994; Marx 1967, 1977; Salzman 1979; Shryock 1997, 2004; Shryock and Smail 2011). In this context, definitions of tribe range from the "tribe as a unit of subsistence" (Marx 1977; Salzman 1979) to the tribe as "a dialogic process" (Layne 1989a). For our purposes here, we shall define tribalism as a supple ideology of collective identity and belonging typically serving the livelihood and security needs of households expressed in terms of various notions of kin-based connections, solidarity, loyalty, duty, rights, and obligations.

Traditionally, tribes are averse to subjugation by an aggrandizing individual or elite group of any kind, not the least to becoming the subjects of a sovereign or centralized government. We need look no further than the Hebrew Bible for a great illustration of this, namely 1 Sam. 8:10–18, where Samuel is told by Yahweh how to answer the people of Israel who were asking him for a king. Though the historical and narrative context of this passage continues to be a source of study and debate among scholars (Hwang 2011), it's anti-monarchical tone and message is what is of interest here, and it is hard to deny:

> Samuel told all the words of the Lord to the people who were asking him for a king. He said, "This is what the king who will reign over you will claim as his rights: He will take your sons and make them serve with his chariots and horses, and they will run in front of his chariots. Some he will assign to be commanders of thousands and commanders of fifties, and others to plow his ground and reap his harvest, and still others to

make weapons of war and equipment for his chariots. He will take your daughters to be perfumers and cooks and bakers. He will take the best of your fields and vineyards and olive groves and give them to his attendants. He will take a tenth of your grain and of your vintage and give it to his officials and attendants. Your male and female servants and the best of your cattle and donkeys he will take for his own use. He will take a tenth of your flocks, and you yourselves will become his slaves. When that day comes, you will cry out for relief from the king you have chosen, but the Lord will not answer you in that day."

Over the past few decades, a great deal of research on tribes and the ideology of tribalism has been carried out in the Palestinian territories and Jordan that adds further insight into drivers that influence attitudes toward centralized governments among tribes. Of particular interest is Khawalde and Rabinowitz's (2002) study of how tribes evaluate each other's standing or status by ranking them on an emic scale of nobility. Thus the measure of a tribe's nobility is determined by the nobility of its lineage and its standing as an independent, self-governed polity (Khawalde and Rabinowitz 2002; Shryock 1997). Typically, tribes that can migrate with their camels and horses deep into the Eastern desert are regarded as being nobler than the less mobile agro-pastoralists whose movements are limited to seasonal shifts between adjacent lowlands and highlands. Typically, the latter provide cereal grains for the former, who in turn provide "protection" for the latter who also are regarded as less noble due to their limited mobility and servile status (LaBianca 1990; Lancaster and Lancaster 1986).

The bottom-up nature of tribal society is also reflected in flexible systems of alliances referred to by anthropologists as segmentary lineage (Sahlins 1961; Salzman 1978; Smith 1956). This refers to arrangements that enable tribal segments to coalesce under a single, unified alliance for purposes of predatory expansion or defense against a common enemy, but then return to the status quo—which is the more or less autonomous local tribal segment—when the animating joint undertaking has been accomplished. The segmentary lineage phenomenon has been studied extensively in the sub-Saharan African context but is well known also among tribal groups in the lands of the Mediterranean and the Middle East, including the Southern Levant (Lancaster 1997; Lancaster and Lancaster 1986; Layne 1989b, 1994; Marx 1977).

When considering the tribal element in the Southern Levant, it is important to emphasize the extent to which the ideology of kin-based solidarity and cooperation also prevails in villages and towns; tribes are not all nomadic. They may be semi-nomadic or permanently settled. Furthermore, the extent to which tribes are predominantly settled or nomadic may change over time and within particular regions (Antoun 1968; LaBianca 1990; Rjoub and Mahmoud 2012; Walker 2014). Important to note in this connection is the role of environmental factors in ensuring the persistence of tribalism and tribal ideology. In this regard, the Southern Levantine situation is quite different from that of the situation in Egypt or Mesopotamia. As we have discussed in much greater length elsewhere (Stordalen and LaBianca 2021), the varied topography of the region produces risks and affordances that in turn have led to the persistence of highly localized production regimes. This situation has tended to hamper the establishment of centralized administrations in the region even as it has provided fertile territory for a wide variety of symbiotic relationships to develop between herdsmen, semi-nomadic, and settled farmers. It also accounts for the persistence and influence of tribal sentiments and ideologies across the rural population of the Southern Levant.

To these drivers of a bottom-up social order in the Southern Levant must be added a bundle of related practices that add further understanding to why the tribal element has such deep roots in the lives of both urban and rural populations of the Southern Levant. What this bundle of practices has in common is that they are well suited to local ownership and control. LaBianca has reported on these elsewhere, where I have referred to them as either "little traditions" or "indigenous hardiness structures" (La Bianca 1997, 2007). They include: (1) local-level water management, or the practice of relying on natural springs, human-made cisterns, and hillside terracing for water to meet household and farming needs; (2) fluid shared commons involving pastures and croplands being held in common by different families as members of a particular tribal segment or village; (3) agropastoralism, or the practice of combining crop cultivation with animal husbandry and being able to shift back and forth between these as risk and opportunity dictates; (4) residential flexibility by means of which families can shift the location of their production activities from houses to caves or tents, depending on work that is best for their particular mode of production; (5) hospitality as a means of transmitting vital information within a tribal community and between members of a tribe and outsiders; (6) honor and shame whereby tribes have been able to police themselves without actually having to rely on a paid constabulary or a codified system of civil and/or criminal law; and finally, and as already extensively discussed, (7) tribalism—the flexible polity involving strong, in-group loyalty based on variously fluid notions of identity, common lineal descent, and cooperation.

What is noteworthy about all of these strategies is their resilience and durability—largely due to the fact that they were owned, so to speak, by the local population, not by outsiders. They are, one might say, legacy possessions essential to survival underneath the comings and goings of dynastic and imperial influences. They attest to the existence of a locally owned bundle of risk-abatement strategies that go back to prehistoric times. While this particular cluster of practices represents neither an exhaustive nor an exclusive bundle of local survival strategies, they provide a window on the reproductive processes of valorized cultural practices and traditions that have persisted throughout generations, centuries, and millennia. Despite multiple millennia of imperial domination and predation, the region of the Southern Levant has thus proven to be extremely resistant to top-down domination and control.

Endemic Polycentrism and the Emergence of Secondary States in the Southern Levant

It is in light of this inextinguishable nature of tribal sentiments and ideologies in the Southern Levant that the emergence of centralized states in the region must be examined. Here tribes and tribalism have held sway for millennia, having outlasted the rise and fall of a long succession of centralized administrations—whether indigenous or foreign in nature. For this reason, the band-tribe-chiefdom-state model of societal evolution (Service 1975, 1988) adopted for understanding the rise of Iron Age kingdoms in this region by some biblical scholars (Frick 1985, 1999) is simply not applicable (LaBianca and Younker 1995).

An alternative to this model is the endemic polycentrism hypothesis (LaBianca 2009). Drawing on the research of Jan Assmann (1996) regarding the social organization of pharaonic Egypt, this hypothesis posits that polycentrism is an even more powerful force in the Levant than it was in Egypt. In Assmann's Egypt, coercive, unicentric forces tended to prevail over polycentric ones, the latter breaking through only when the former crumbled (1996: 84). By contrast, in the Southern Levant, the opposite was the case, with polycentrism being more the norm than the exception. Here political power has tended to be concentrated in the hands of non-state actors: local strongmen, warlords, tribal chieftains, and village elders. Thus, despite reverberating with the hegemonic and often predatory actions and legacies of imperial world-making projects, the Southern Levant has rarely been truly tamed by any one imperial power except, perhaps, the Romans. Indeed, one of the most enduring attributes of the Levantine cultural paradigm is this polycentric inertia—its ability to go on producing multiple local cultural worlds beneath the ruptures and hierarchies introduced by imperial world makers in the region.

To account for this resistance to hierarchical organization, we would highlight four salient characteristics of the Southern Levant. First are its natural endowments (especially its great elevational and topographical variability) which have made parts of the region difficult to dominate by foreign invaders. Unlike the situation in the civilizational epicenters of the Fertile Crescent, where agriculture depended primarily on river-basin irrigation agriculture, agriculture in the Southern Levant has mostly depended on local-level collection and storage of rainwater using hillside terraces, diversion dams, reservoirs, and cisterns. Second is the region's geographic position astride an intercontinental land bridge linking the continents of Africa, Europe, and Asia. Having served since prehistoric times as a vital corridor of communication, migration, and trade, the Southern Levant has long been a coveted piece of real estate over which rival dynasties in Egypt, Mesopotamia, Anatolia, Greece, Rome, and Western Europe have sought to exert control and domination. Third is the region's proximity to the Arabian steppe. This steppe has served not only as the desert headquarters of long-distance caravan trade but also as a wellspring of Bedouin culture and aspirations. Since earliest antiquity, Bedouin tribes from the Arabian steppe have infiltrated the fertile highlands of both Transjordan and Cis-Jordan, replenishing its population while emboldening it in its resistance to foreign domination and control. And fourth is the Mediterranean Sea (Braudel 1966, 1995; Purcell and Horden 2000), which connects the Southern Levant to ports of call around the Mediterranean and beyond. Coastal cities, such as Tyre, Sidon, Ashkelon, and Caesarea, are harbors through which trade goods could be channeled from inland cities and towns to distant ports of call and vice versa. At various points in time, this same coastline also served as a point of access to the region by seafaring invaders such as the Philistines, Greeks, Romans, and Crusaders.

The fate of efforts to build centripetal and hierarchical polities in the Southern Levant is reflected in its archaeological record. When compared to the birthplaces of pristine civilizations such as Egypt and Mesopotamia, the Southern Levant is notable for its far less impressive archaeological traces of centralized government power. Remains of monumental buildings, archives yielding inscriptions, or statues containing royal propaganda begin to appear in the region nearly two millennia after their appearance in Egypt and Mesopotamia. By comparison, their scale is modest at best when they finally do appear at the end of the second millennium BC. Not surprisingly, archaeologists have had a hard time locating traces of the Israelite monarchy under David and Solomon in the archaeological record. The same can be said for the kingdoms of Ammon, Moab, and Edom—Israel's neighbors on the other side of the Jordan River. In none of the so-called "capitals" of the Iron Age kingdoms of Transjordan (Rabbath-Ammon, Dhiban, and Busayra) are there true traces of centralized government power; their monarchies and any centralizing tendencies were short-lived and did not last beyond the Neo-Babylonian period. In a region where polycentricity has been the norm since early antiquity, it is fortunate for archaeologists that they have other traces to rely on than monumental buildings or inscriptions—neither has much chance of appearing where the apparatus of a strong centralized state was never successfully installed.

Iron Age Tribal Kingdoms in the Southern Levant

To the extent that political power was centralized in the hands of local rulers of some sort, it would have been in the hands of what we have referred to elsewhere as local "tribal kings" (LaBianca 1999; LaBianca and Younker 1995). Thus, in the case of the Iron Age kingdoms of ancient Ammon, Edom, Israel, and Moab the sentiments of tribalism and local social structure were not extinguished. Instead, they persisted even as a thin veneer of royal bureaucracy was superimposed on top of this fundamental social structure (LaBianca 1999). Elsewhere LaBianca has posited the following ten salient features of tribal kingdoms: (1) tribal social structure was intimately linked to the way people obtained food; (2) land- and range-tied agricultural regimes co-existed; (3) tribal affiliations were based on generative genealogies, i.e. genealogies allowing for the manipulation of claimed ancestors; (4) pre-monarchical tribal social structure was not extinguished by the rise of kings; (5) the emergence of supra-tribal polities did not produce dimorphic social structures similar to those in Egypt and Mesopotamia; (6) tribal hinterlands were administered from fortified towns; (7) most people lived in the rural hinterland beyond the towns; (8) power within the tribal kingdoms was heterarchical rather than hierarchical. It was counterpoised between different political centers, each of which had different resources available to it; (9) territorial boundaries between different heterarchical authorities overlapped; and (10) the coalescence of tribes into tribal kingdoms occurred in three phases corresponding roughly to Iron I, Iron IIA, and Iron IIB.

Recent research on the rise of state-level polities in the Southern Levant has, for the most part, built on the tribal kingdom model (Bienkowski and van der Steen 2001; Hawkins 2013; Petter 2018; Thomas 2021b). The question this research is seeking to answer is what were the factors that gave rise to these kingdoms. To this question, some emphasize external forces, examples of which would be the hegemonic order hypothesis (Routledge 2000, 2004, 2013) and the Neo-Assyrian hypothesis (Burnett 2016; Finkelstein and Lipschits 2011). Others emphasize agency at the local level (Porter 2013; Stordalen and LaBianca 2021). Thanks to these and other related studies, a body of theory is now available to guide future research into questions about the role of tribes and tribalism in the evolution of centralized states in the Iron Age Southern Levant. Where archaeology can contribute is helping to generate data to test these various theories regarding the nature and agency behind state formation in the Iron Age Southern Levant.

Tribalism in the Hebrew Bible

The concept and practice of tribalism are deeply rooted in the Hebrew Bible and are apparent both in the tribal confederacy that became the Kingdom of Israel, and also in the various peoples inhabiting the surrounding regions. Many of these kin-based tribes had family ties to Israel, such as the Kenites (e.g., Num 10:29; Jdg 4:17), while others maintained a generally hostile relationship. The tribal territories listed in the book of Joshua share certain similarities to designated tribal allotments in Palestine and Transjordan during the Islamic and Ottoman periods (Rainey and Notley 2014: 179–85; van der Steen 2004: 252–310, 2013), but also represent tribal societies that persisted, if not flourished in demarcated regions during every historical epoch.

Intertribal conflicts and coalitions of clans into tribes usually have a territorial component. Additional details concerning many of these groups often remained unrecorded or unacknowledged by the geopolitical rulers of their time. As LaBianca (2009) and Thomas (2021a; see also Thomas, this volume) have noted, the Southern Levant displays an extensive history of *polycentrism*; that is, multiple and dispersed centers of largely autonomous political and/or social power that often co-exist in the same territories and share power with singular sovereign polities. Indeed, these central authorities themselves may arise to stabilize disputes as well as to grant or confirm tribal ownership over specific areas (Rainey and Notley 2014: 151), most notably in Transjordan (e.g., LaBianca and Younker 1995). Tribal allotments, or more specifically, family or clan-based land inheritances are vital components of tribal identity, as particularly well illustrated by the Naboth affair (1 Kgs 16), but also spoken about by the various prophetic voices that condemned the rulers and elites of Samaria and Jerusalem throughout the monarchic period.

The Song of Deborah (Judg 5) preserves an early (usually dated between the 12th and 9th centuries BCE) poem that reveals the often complex and problematic intertribal relationships that often plagued Israel (Stager 1989). While ultimately victorious in battle, Deborah's attempts to unite the tribal clans under her charismatic leadership against a common (and particularly ominous) threat posed by Jabin of Hazor and his powerful Canaanite army were only partially successful. Some of the tribal groups, for varied reasons that the song eloquently elucidates (and in turn ridicules), failed to heed Deborah's call to arms.

A series of terms attested in the Hebrew Bible define Israelite tribal structure, demonstrating that kin-based (family/extended family/clan) relationships lie at its most fundamental levels. This hierarchy of polycentric power appears in the archaeology of Israelite settlements beginning in the early 12th century BCE (Stager 1985: 17–23; Thomas 2021a). In fact, the powerful pull of tribalism lies behind the entire span of the centralized monarchy and proved a constant threat to destabilize and fracture it. The cautionary response Samuel shares with those desiring the establishment of kingship is not only an appeal to maintain a largely idealized theocracy, but its detailed warnings also clearly reveal a desire to preserve a tribal based confederacy (1 Sam 8). Only political leaders exhibiting and flexing a strong arm coupled with possessing an intimate knowledge of each tribe and clan and possessing the diplomatic acumen necessary to sustain peaceful intertribal relations as well as maintain loyalty to the king and royal court succeeded in uniting the tribes and forging them into a nation. Even a charismatic figure like David, which the Hebrew Bible depicts as a popular and strong leader, only maintained a tenuous hold over the tribes (Keimer 2021). Ironically, many of the tribal elders who traveled to Hebron to offer David their loyalty if he assumed kingship over all Israel at the beginning of his reign (2 Sam 5:1–3; 1 Chr 11:1–3), later, with Absalom's enticement, conspired in the same city to overthrow David (2 Sam 15:10). After Absalom's coup failed, these tribal leaders still argued among themselves concerning renewing loyalty to David (2 Sam 19:9–10).

Nevertheless, individual tribes remembered and honored acts of royal assistance and favors. For example, when the Ammonite king Nahash oppressed the inhabitants of Jabesh Gilead, Saul quickly raised an army, crossed over into Transjordan, and rescued the city from an Ammonite siege (1 Sam 11). Consequently, these Jabesh Gileadites recompensed their liberation much later, when they recovered the mutilated bodies of Saul and his sons from Beth Shan's wall (1 Sam 31:11–13; 1 Chr 10:11–12).

The enormously burdensome physical and financial obligations placed upon the tribes by David's son and successor King Solomon in order to maintain his lavish court and extensive bureaucracy (Fox 2000; Rainey 1970; Rainey and Notley 2014: 174–79) sowed the seeds of rebellion. Upon Rehoboam's accession to the throne after Solomon's death, a serious internal crisis threatened his sovereignty. Exhausted and spent after fulfilling Solomon's taxes and demands, the northern tribes demanded a relaxation of taxes and other obligations.

Rehoboam's coronation assembly took place not in Jerusalem, but at Shechem, an old tribal meeting center in the territory of Manasseh. Representatives from all the northern tribes attended, seeking to address their demands. They officially presented their case to Rehoboam, stating that "your father put a heavy yoke on us, but now lighten the harsh labor and the heavy yoke he put on us, and we will serve you" (1 Kgs 12:4 NIV//2 Chr 10:4). However, Rehoboam foolishly rejected their calls for governmental relief, as shown in his scornful reply: "My father made your yoke heavy; I will make it even heavier. My father scourged you with whips; I will scourge you with scorpions" (1 Kgs 12:14//2 Chr 10:14). The narrative continues, stating that: "When all Israel saw that the king refused to listen to them, they answered the king: 'What share do we have in David, what part in Jesse's son? To your tents, Israel! Look after your own house, David!'" (2 Kgs 12:16//2 Chr 10:16). Revealing the long-term tension existing between the tribe of Judah and the northern tribes, this convocation arguably provides a superb example of the deep-seated power and long-lasting presence of tribalism in ancient Israel, perhaps dating back to the warfare between the Davidic and Saulide coalitions as well as Judah's privileged position in the Davidic royal court. More pointedly, the Shechem debacle became a critical and disastrous juncture in the history of the Israelite monarchy. Even when local or regional polities split or failed militarily against a more powerful adversary, tribal groups persisted, and/or new families arose endowed with capable strong men that founded new tribal groups.

A Hypothesis for Further Research

Viewed over the long term and in the wider geographical context of the lands of ancient Israel and their neighbors, the image of the seesaw comes to mind to understand the polycentric social order of the region. During certain periods a particular polity (say that of Judah or that of the Ammonites) coalesces in a top-down direction—but, typically, it fails to endure over the long term and ends up returning to its baseline order grounded in kin-based solitaries and practices. Over time and space, there is thus a seesaw of rise and collapse of centralized state projects in the region. Based on arguments forwarded in an earlier article (LaBianca and Younker 1995), we might thus posit, based on differences in environmental affordances and the strength of the tribal element in each, that the Edomite kingdom would be more deeply grounded in tribal sentiments and practices, than would be Moab, and even less so Ammon, Israel, and Judah respectively. We offer this as a possible hypothesis for advancing further research on tribalism and the nature of state-level organization during the Iron Age in the Eastern Mediterranean.

Bibliography

Antoun, Richard T. 1968. "On the Modesty of Women in Arab Muslim Villages: A Study in the Accommodation of Traditions." *AmAnth* 70: 671–97.

Assmann, Jan. 1996. *The Mind of Egypt: History and Meaning in the Time of the Pharaohs*. New York: Henry Holt & Co.

Atanda, J. A. 1972. "Review of P. H. Gulliver, Tradition and Transition in East Africa: Studies of the Tribal Element in the Modern Era." *Economic Development and Cultural Change* 21: 200–02.

Beattie, John. 1971. "Review of P. H. Gulliver, Tradition and Transition in East Africa: Studies of the Tribal Element in the Modern Era." *BSOAS* 34: 190–92.

Belich, James, John Darwin, Margret Frenz, and Chris Wickham. 2016. *The Prospect of Global History*. Oxford: Oxford University Press.

Bienkowski, Piotr, and Eveline van der Steen. 2001. "Tribes, Trade, and Towns: A New Framework for the Late Iron Age in Southern Jordan and the Negev." *BASOR* 323: 21–47.

Braudel, F. 1966. *La Méditerranée et Le Monde Méditerranéen à L'époque de Philippe II, Vol. 2*. Paris: Armand Colin.

———. 1995. *The Mediterranean and the Mediterranean World in the Age of Philip II*. Berkeley: University of California Press.

Burnett, Joel S. 2016. "Transjordan: The Ammonites, Moabites, and Edomites." Pages 309–53 in *The World Around the Old Testament: The People and Places of the Ancient Near East*. Grand Rapids: Baker Academic.

Chapman, John. 2000. "Tension at Funerals: Social Practices and the Subversion of Community Structure in Later Hungarian Prehistory." Pages 169–95 in *Agency in Archaeology*. Edited by Marcia-Anne Dobres and John E. Robb. London: Routledge.

Crossley, Pamela Kyle. 2008. *What Is Global History*. Malden: Polity Press.

Daniels, Robert E. 1971. "Review of P. H. Gulliver, Tradition and Transition in East Africa: Studies of the Tribal Element in the Modern Era." *AmAnth* 73: 378–80.

Dobres, Marcia-Anne, and John E. Robb. 2000. "Agency in Archaeology: Paradigm or Platitude?" Pages 3–18 in *Agency in Archaeology*. Edited by Marcia-Anne Dobres and John E. Robb. London: Routledge.

Finkelstein, Israel and Oded Lipschits. 2011. "The Genesis of Moab: A Proposal." *Levant* 43: 139–52.

Fox, Nili S. 2000. *In the Service of the King: Officialdom in Ancient Israel and Judah*. Cincinnati: Hebrew Union College Press.

Frick, Frank S. 1985. *The Formation of the State in Ancient Israel: A Survey of Models and Theories*. Sheffield: Almond Press.

Frick, Frank S. 1999. "Response: Reconstructing Ancient Israel's Social World." *Semeia* 87: 233.

Geyer, Michael, and Charles Bright. 1995. "World History in a Global Age." *American Historical Review* 100: 1034–60.

Gulliver, P. H. 2013. *Tradition and Transition in East Africa: Studies of the Tribal Factor in the Modern Era*. New York: Routledge.

Hawkins, Ralph K. 2013. *How Israel Became a People*. Nashville: Abingdon Press.

Hodder, Ian. 2012. *Entangled: An Archaeology of the Relationships between Humans and Things*. Hoboken: Wiley & Sons.

Hwang, Jerry. 2011. "Yahweh's Poetic Mishpat in Israel's Kingship: A Reassessement of 1 Samuel 8–12." *WTJ* 73: 341–61.

James, Paul. 2006. *Globalism, Nationalism, Tribalism: Bringing Theory Back In*. Newbury Park: Pine Forge Press.

Joffe, Alexander H. 2002. "The Rise of Secondary States in the Iron Age Levant." *JESHO* 45: 425–67.

Keimer, Kyle H. 2021. "Evaluating the 'United Monarchy' of Israel: Unity and Identity in Text and Archaeology." *JJAR* 1: 67–100.

Khawalde, Sliman, and Dan Rabinowitz. 2002. "Race from the Bottom of the Tribe That Never Was: Segmentary Narratives Amongst the Ghawarna of Galilee." *JAR* 5: 225–43.

LaBianca, Oystein S. 1990. *Hesban 1. Sedentarization and Nomadization: Food System Cycles at Hesban and Vicinity in Transjordan*. Berrien Springs: Andrews University Press.

———. 1997. "Indigenous Hardiness Structures and State Formation in Jordan." Pages 143–57 in *Ethnic Encounters and Cultural Change*. Edited by M. Sabour and K. S. Vikør. London: C. Hurst & Co.

———. 1999. "Salient Features of Iron Age Tribal Kingdoms." *Ancient Ammon* 17: 19.

———. 2007. "Great and Little Traditions: A Framework for Studying Cultural Interaction through the Ages in Jordan." *SHAJ* IX: 275–89.

———. 2009. "The Poly-Centric Nature of Social Order in the Middle East: Preliminary Reflections from Anthropological Archaeology." Pages 1–5 in *Studies on Iron Age Moab and Neighbouring Areas in Honour of Michele Daviau*. Leuven: Peeters.

LaBianca, Oystein S., and Randall W. Younker. 1995. "The Kingdoms of Ammon, Moab and Edom: The Archaeology of Society in Late Bronze." Pages 399–415 in *The Archaeology of Society in the Holy Land*. Edited by T. E. Levy. London: Equinox.

Lancaster, William. 1997. *The Rwala Bedouin Today*. Long Grove: Waveland Press.

Lancaster, William, and Fidelity Lancaster. 1986. "The Concept of Territory Among the Rwala Bedouin." *Nomadic Peoples* 20: 41–48.

Layne, Linda L. 1989a. "The Dialogics of Tribal Self-Representation in Jordan." *American Ethnologist* 16: 24–39.

———. 1989b. "The Dialogics of Tribal Self-Representation in Jordan." *American Ethnologist* 16: 24–39. Online: doi.org/10.1525/ae.1989.16.1.02a00020.

———. 1994. *Home and Homeland: The Dialogics of Tribal and National Identities in Jordan*. Princeton: Princeton University Press.

Marx, Emanuel. 1967. *Bedouin of the Negev*. Manchester: Manchester University Press.

———. 1977. "The Tribe as a Unit of Subsistence: Nomadic Pastoralism in the Middle East." *AmAnth* 79: 343–63.

Petter, Thomas D. 2018. "Tribes and Nomads in the Iron Age Levant." Pages 391–95 in *Behind the Scenes of the Old Testament: Cultural, Social, and Historical Contexts*. Edited by Jonathan S. Greer, John W. Hilber, and John H. Walton. Grand Rapids: Baker Academic.

Porter, Benjamin W. 2013. *Complex Communities: The Archaeology of Early Iron Age West-Central Jordan*. Tucson: University of Arizona Press.

Purcell, N., and Peregrine Horden. 2000. *The Corrupting Sea: A Study of Mediterranean History*. Oxford: Blackwell.

Rainey, Anson F. 1970. "Compulsory Labour Gangs in Ancient Israel." *IEJ* 20: 191–202.

Rainey, Anson F., and R. Steven Notley. 2014. *The Sacred Bridge: Carta's Atlas of the Biblical World*. Jerusalem: Carta.

Rjoub, Abdelmajeed and Abdelaziz Mahmoud. 2012. "The Emergence of Agro-Pastoral Villages in Jordan Hamamet al-Olaimat Village as a Case Study." *Journal of Human Ecology* 38: 231–43.

Routledge, Bruce. 2000. "The Politics of Mesha: Segmented Identities and State Formation in Iron Age Moab." *JESHO* 43: 221–56.

———. 2004. *Moab in the Iron Age: Hegemony, Polity, Archaeology*. Philadelphia: University of Pennsylvania Press.

———. 2013. *Archaeology and State Theory: Subjects and Objects of Power*. London: A&C Black.

Sagan, Carl. 1990. *A Blue Pale Dot*. New York: Random House.

Sahlins, Marshall D. 1961. "The Segmentary Lineage: An Organization of Predatory Expansion." *AmAnth* 63: 322–45.

Salzman, Philip Carl. 1978. "Does Complementary Opposition Exist?" *AmAnth* 80: 53–70.

———. 1979. "Tribal Organization and Subsistence: A Response to Emanuel Marx." *AmAnth* 81: 121–24.

Schäfer, Wolf. 2004. "Global History and the Present Time." Pages 103–25 in *Wiring Prometheus: Globalisation, History and Technology*. Edited by Peter Lyth and Helmuth Trischler. Aarhus: Aarhus University Press.

Service, Elman R. 1975. *Origins of the State and Civilization: The Process of Cultural Evolution*. New York: Norton & Comp.

———. 1988. "General/Theoretical Anthropology: The Evolution of Human Societies: From Foraging Group to Agrarian State. Allen W. Johnson and Timothy Earle." *AmAnth* 90: 992–93.

Shryock, andrew. 1997. *Nationalism and the Genealogical Imagination: Oral History and Textual Authority in Tribal Jordan*. Berkeley: University of California Press.

———. 2004. "The New Jordanian Hospitality: House, Host, and Guest in the Culture of Public Display." *Comparative Studies in Society and History* 46: 35–62.

Shryock, andrew, and Daniel Lord Smail. 2011. *Deep History: The Architecture of Past and Present*. Berkeley: University of California Press.

Smith, M. G. 1956. "On Segmentary Lineage Systems." *Journal of the Royal Anthropological Institute of Great Britain and Ireland* 86: 39–80.

Sommer, Michael. 2014. "OIKOYMENH: Longue Durée Perspectives on Ancient Mediterranean 'Globality.'" Pages 175–97 in *Globalisation and the Roman World: World History, Connectivity and Material Culture*. Edited by Martin Pitts and Miguel John Versluys. Cambridge: Cambridge University Press.

Stager, Lawrence E. 1985. "The Archaeology of the Family in Ancient Israel." *BASOR* 260: 1–35.

———. 1989. "The Song of Deborah. Why Some Tribes Answered the Call and Others Did Not." *BAR* 15: 50–64.

Steffen, Will, Paul J. Crutzen, and John R. McNeill. 2007. "The Anthropocene: Are Humans Now Overwhelming the Great Forces of Nature?" *AMBIO: A Journal of the Human Environment* 36: 614–21.

Stordalen, Terje, and Øystein S. LaBianca. 2021. "A New Format for Writing the History of the Levant. Introduction to the Volume." Pages 1–17 in *Levantine Entanglements: Local Dynamics of Globalization in a Contested Region*. Edited by T. Stordalen and Ø. S. LaBianca. Sheffield: Equinox.

Thomas, Zachary. 2021a. "Polycentrism and the Terminology of Polity in Early Israel." *Bible Lands E-Review* S2. Online: biblelandsreview.files.wordpress.com/2019/02/thomas-blmj-polycentrism.pdf.

Thomas, Zachary. 2021b. "On the Archaeology of 10th Century BCE Israel and the Idea of the 'State.'" *PEQ* 153: 244–57.

van der Steen, E. J. 2004. *Tribes and Territories in Transition: The Central East Jordan Valley in the Late Bronze Age and Early Iron Age: A Study of the Sources*. Leuven: Peeters.

———. 2013. *Near Eastern Tribal Societies during the Nineteenth Century: Economy, Society and Politics between Tent and Town*. Sheffield: Equinox.

Walker, Bethany. 2014. "Planned Villages and Rural Resilience on the Mamluk Frontier: A Preliminary Report on the 2013 Excavation Season at Tall Hisban." Pages 157–92 in *History and Society during the Mamluk Period (1250–1517)*. Edited by Stephan Conermann. Bonn: University of Bonn.

15
ISRAEL'S POLITICAL AND ADMINISTRATIVE STRUCTURES IN THE PRE-MONARCHIC AND MONARCHIC PERIODS

Zachary Thomas

Introduction

Many readers of the Hebrew Bible might be puzzled over the title of this chapter; certainly, Israel had a political and administrative structure during the monarchic period, but what about the pre-monarchic period? Even as a loose and disharmonious group of tribes under one overarching social identity, early Israel does indeed appear as a political entity within the biblical text. It is important to begin here because Israel's fundamental nature as a union of tribes will continue to define it even into the monarchic period. The adoption of kingship in Israel marks not so much a change in Israel's underlying political structure as it does a shift in where power within that structure lay and what that power would be used for. How the kings of Israel and Judah enacted their duties as defenders of their land, shepherds of their people, and servants of their patron god involved them both passively and actively in the lives and labors of their subjects.

Israel's identity and unity were rooted in its self-conception as one extended family of families, demonstrated foremost by the fact that its name is literally that of its ancestor and the father of the ancestors of the tribes that composed it (Genesis 35). As a social and political entity, Israel had a segmentary structure made up of patriarchal households, clans of multiple households that claimed common descent, and tribes made up of clans that likewise claimed common descent from an ancestral figure for whom the tribe was named (Josh 7:14–18; Stager 1985). It is important to note that in the Hebrew Bible the latter are referred to as either a שבט and מטה, terms typically translated as "tribe," but also as a בית "house," as in the בית יהודה "House of Judah" or בית בנימן "House of Benjamin." Likewise, a kingdom and dynasty can also be referred to as a בית, as in the בית דוד "House of David," which also appears on the fragmentary late 9th century BCE inscription found at Tel Dan in northern Israel (COS 2.39).

Israel was not unique in the ancient Near East in having a segmentary structure made up of social units that were conceived as types of an extended family. Yet, this has not often influenced how scholars, particularly archaeologists, have reconstructed and characterized ancient Israel's social and political structure (see discussion in Keimer and Thomas 2022). This can largely be put down to the dominance of neo-evolutionist theory in Levantine archaeological scholarship. Neo-evolutionism views kinship-based social systems like the "tribe" as a fundamentally primitive stage in a society's development, rather than just as one form among many that a society may take. This view of the tribe is often contrasted with that of the "state," the apex of social and political development in neo-evolutionist thinking, in which kinship structures are overridden by more rational and institutional forms of governance, with the state's sovereignty and right to the exercise of force claimed within a given territory and run by an elite group separate from any kinship structure (Service 1971; Flannery 1972; Joffe 2018).

More recently, some scholars of the ancient Near East have turned away from the preconceptions of neo-evolutionist theory and have instead placed the emic, household-based conception of socio-political structure at the core of how they understand entities like Israel as historical and archaeological subjects. Through this approach, Near Eastern kingdoms of the Bronze and Iron Age such as Israel and Judah can be characterized as "patrimonial," one of the ideal types of political society developed by the German sociologist Max Weber (1978; Master 2001; Schloen 2001; Stager 2003). A patrimonial kingdom was understood by its constituents as one great household that encompassed and bound together multiple subsidiary households. The king sat in the position of the ultimate *paterfamilias* at the head of this household and was thus the highest figure of authority to his people, though his position was legitimated by his own status as the direct earthly servant of the patron deity (YHWH in Israel's case), the true cosmic monarch (2 Sam 7:14, 24–25).[1] The king governed his kingdom as a household so that his position of authority over his court (consisting of his direct family and patrimonial retainers) and the leadership of the tribes was conceived as literally that of a father and master over his sons and servants, who themselves would be in the father/master position within their own household units.

The basic patrimonial framework described formed the basis for the kingdom's internal politics and how administration was enacted. This did not produce a single, rigid kind of patrimonial society across the entire ancient Near East, as multiple factors including local traditions, geography, and simply the contingent nature of human social relationships could affect political dynamics in any particular place. For example, Israel is a good example of just how significant the traditional role of the tribes continued to be even after ceding ultimate authority to a king; the political volition that they continued to exercise would play the deciding role in the split of Israel's first kingdom into two (1 Kgs 12). Ultimately this makes the kingdoms of ancient Israel and Judah fundamentally different kinds of polities than the true "state" (Thomas 2021).

Sources

The evidence for Israel's political and administrative structures can be divided into two basic types: textual, consisting of the Hebrew Bible and Iron Age inscriptions from the southern Levant,[2] and the archaeological record of Israel (and Judah) during the Iron Age I-II periods. Textual and archaeological evidence from other places in the ancient Near East can also be used for comparative purposes. In studying a subject like political and administrative structures, both textual and archaeological evidence should be used together as much as possible, not only because they complement each other but also because they can address each other's limitations (see Pioske, this volume).

The internal politics and ongoing administration of Israel and Judah were subjects largely below the horizon of attention and importance for the biblical authors, with certain exceptions. Our best biblical evidence is concentrated in the narratives of pre-monarchic Israel, the beginning of the monarchy under Samuel and Saul and then its consolidation under David and Solomon in the books of Judges, 1–2 Samuel and 1 Kings. A general picture of pre-monarchic Israel's loose organization appears in Judges, while certain sections in Samuel-Kings (e.g. 1 Sam 8: 11–18, 1 Kings 4) relate directly to the administration of the kingdom. Outside of the Hebrew Bible, the corpus of inscriptions from the time of the early monarchy (10th–9th centuries BCE, Iron Age IIA) is quite limited, although it grows significantly in the time of the late monarchy (8th–early 6th centuries, Iron Age IIB–C). In both periods, seals and the clay bullae impressed with these seals that were used to enclose documents written on papyrus or vellum, materials which typically do not survive in the climate of the Levant, have been recovered from archaeological excavations. This is a good indication that much, if not most written artefacts produced in ancient Israel are now lost to us.

Archaeological evidence of political structure and administration is more difficult because it does not transmit information and meaning in the same way a text does. Even with a sound interpretative framework like patrimonialism, archaeological evidence is often ambiguous or can be interpreted in multiple ways. Nonetheless, archaeological evidence can demonstrate how the nature of politics and administration described in texts played out "on the ground." Additionally, the archaeological record is not a complete or unbiased reflection of the cultural world that created it. Our evidence is heavily biased toward the settled part of the population of both Israel and its neighbors, while the mobile part, those who practiced forms of pastoral nomadism, are much more difficult to detect archaeologically. Archaeologists and historians of ancient Israel have long assumed (under the influence of neo-evolutionist theory) that Israel's development into a more complex society and a monarchic state went together with the transition of the population from nomadic to settled. However, it is now clear from the limited instances where nomads are archaeologically visible that they would have remained part of the population at least during the 12th–9th centuries BCE (Ben-Yosef 2019, forthcoming).

Tribal Politics in the Pre-Monarchic Period

The book of Judges and the opening chapters of 1 Samuel narrate the relationships and conflicts both external and internecine of a group of tribes under the loose identity of "Israel." Whereas these books take their inherent connection for granted, the narratives of Jacob-Israel and his family in the book of Genesis provide an explicit basis for the descent of the tribes from each of the sons of this ancestral figure (Fleming 2012: 72; Gen 35:22–26). The familiar schema of Israel's tribal makeup found there is that of the "Twelve Tribes" (grouping Ephraim and Manasseh together under their father Joseph; see Kallai 1997).[3]

However, there are instances in Judges that seem to indicate a somewhat different tribal makeup from this classic 12-tribe system, namely the poem in Judg 5:2–31. Most of the 12 tribes appear in the poem but Judah, Manasseh, Gad, Levi, and Simeon do not, while some other entities, Machir, Gilead, and Meroz, are invoked for either joining or not joining the other Israelites in battle. Meroz is mentioned nowhere else so it is unclear what sort of entity it was, but Machir and Gilead appear as a son and grandson respectively of Manasseh and as fathers of their own clans in Numbers (26:29). Additionally, the muster of the בני ישראל "sons of Israel" against the Benjaminites in Jdg 20:1 is said to include the ארץ הגלעד "land of Gilead." If Machir and Gilead are being treated as tribes here (though the word does not occur in these texts) it may indicate an older idea of Israel's tribal makeup (Smith 2014: 240), but their appearance and the absence of some tribes, particularly Judah and Simeon, may be related more to the poetic nature of Judges 5 or the historical circumstances behind it (Schloen 1993).

From an ethnographic perspective, historical Near Eastern tribes and tribal confederations changed and evolved over their long-term histories (van der Steen 2013), so some measure of change in the status of kinship groups and the tribal makeup of Israel over its history is quite conceivable. Yet the notion that "Israel" as a collective identity for these tribes was externally recognizable is evident from the earliest certain appearance of the name in an extrabiblical source, on an inscription of the 19th Dynasty pharaoh Merneptah dating to the end of the 13th century BCE (COS 2.6).

Archaeologically speaking, the pre-monarchic Israel of Judges and 1 Samuel can be associated with the many small sites dating to the Iron Age I (12th–11th centuries BCE) found mostly in archaeological surveys dotting the Central Hill Country and hills of the Galilee, only a small percentage of which have been excavated. It should be borne in mind therefore that it is possible, even likely, that these surveyed sites include both sedentary settlements and places used by nomadic Israelites. Archaeology can certainly tell us much about the character of these early Israelite communities and how their material culture may have played a role in forming Israelite identity (Faust 2006), but less so in terms of if and how they were associated politically. Analyses of the Iron Age I Israelite settlements as a chiefdom-level society, the stage of neo-evolutionism between the tribe and state, have been offered but have not gained wide acceptance (Miller 2005; Ilan 2018: 296–97). Rather, we need to turn to the biblical text and comparative Near Eastern material to look at this question.

The biblical description of Israel's pre-monarchic tribal organization indicates that normative positions of leadership were held by those with traditional seniority within the tribal family, specifically the זקנים "elders," meaning the male heads of the tribe's constituent clans. Elders made decisions for their tribe and the gathered elders of the tribes of Israel could make decisions for Israel as a collective, as they did in electing David as king (2 Sam 5:3). The book of Judges collects narratives of a series of figures who provide temporary, charismatic leadership in Israel, though not in actions that necessarily involve all of the tribes, as in Judges 4–5 above and in the case of Gideon's leadership in a conflict against the Midianites (Judg 6:35, 7:24). The usual translations of the Hebrew word that describes these figures, שופט, as "judge" does not properly represent the meaning of the lexeme, which has a more general meaning of ruling or governing, rather than a specifically judicial sense (Ishida 1973).

How then to characterize pre-monarchic Israel's political nature as portrayed in the Hebrew Bible? A fitting characterization would need to explain the dynamics of "Israel" as a unifying political identity but one *without* an established succession of single leadership and *with* the autonomy of the individual tribes to participate in the political actions of this "Israel." Martin Noth (1969: 85–97) proposed that the 12 tribes constituted an amphictyony, a primarily cultic league of tribes dedicated to the Ark of the Covenant as the central shrine of their deity YHWH. Noth borrowed the idea of the amphictyony from the Greek world, where the main example is the amphictyony of Greek city-states dedicated to the upkeep of the major shrine at Delphi.[4] Although it is undeniable that YHWH and his cult were central to the biblical authors' understanding of what constituted Israel's common identity, Noth's hypothesis did not meet with lasting acceptance (de Geus 1976), and does not provide a very satisfactory explanation for the inter-tribal politics portrayed in Judges and 1 Samuel.

Comparative examples more appropriate to early Israel's immediate context can be sought within the ancient Levant itself during the Late Bronze Age (c. mid-16th–early 12th century BCE). Whatever its exact origins, Israel already existed in the Central Hill Country of Canaan by the end of this period (see above). We have an invaluable window onto the nature of political structures in Canaan in this period through the Amarna letters, the archive of correspondence from Canaanite vassals to their overlords, the 18th Dynasty pharaohs Amenhotep III and Amenhotep IV/Akhenaton (Rainey 2015).

While many of the Levantine polities under Egypt's overlordship were centralized around a single settlement and ruled by a single paramount individual, there were also instances of polities allying together as a collective, under an overarching political identity but with collective decision-making. Such an arrangement allowed several otherwise independent polities to co-operate in their mutual self-defense (or aggression) or even for more mundane purposes, such as the production of an agricultural surplus that each of the polities was liable to deliver to the pharaoh and his officials. At the same time, the autonomy of each polity meant that it could choose whether or not to participate in the collective activities of the land. As a political collectivity of autonomous tribes, holding the same overarching identity but not always working in concert, pre-monarchic Israel as described in Judges and 1 Samuel would appear to have taken the same political form as these multi-polity decentralized lands (Benz 2016).

Both these singular and collective polities are referred to in the Amarna letters using the Akkadian term *mātu* or Sumerian equivalent KUR, terms that are typically translated as "land." It seems that the Hebrew term ארץ "land" is sometimes used in the social and political designation, as we have seen in Judg 20:1. Likewise, when 2 Sam 5 refers to David and his men going to "Jerusalem and the Jebusites, inhabitants of the land (ארץ)," this likely refers to the same "land of Jerusalem" that appears in the Amarna letters (Benz 2016; Thomas 2019). The Hebrew term עיר also seems to have constituted a recognizable social unit, seen most explicitly when Absalom asks those who have come to Jerusalem to identify themselves by their עיר and they respond by naming their tribe. Though this term is usually translated as "city" or "town," it may have in some cases referred even to a mobile tent-dwelling community. An עיר may have constated a group of clans in the same settlement or camp under the leadership of clan elders or "lords" (בעלים) as can be seen in cases such as Shechem (Judges 9), Jabesh-Gilead (1 Samuel 11) and Keilah (1 Samuel 23; Thomas forthcoming).

The Early Monarchic Period and the Impact of Kingship

The request of the elders of the Israelite tribes in 1 Sam 8:5–9 for the prophet Samuel to appoint them a מלך "king" like that of their neighboring peoples, followed by YHWH's apoplexy over their rejection of the sufficiency of his divine kingship, is unique as an origin for kingship in the ancient Near East. Apart from this though, Israelite kingship did have the same primary characteristics of kingship among Israel's neighbors. As the sovereign individual endorsed by the national god, the king had an important role in practically every aspect of the life of his realm, including its martial defense and expansion, foreign relations, administration, and economy. The king was the highest judicial authority in the land and had an important role in cultic affairs as the anointed representative and servant of a patron deity (Jones 2012; Knapp 2017). As the case of Israel's first king Saul demonstrates, the legitimacy of the king's position could be called into question if he was not seen to act faithfully to his divine patron and he could fall out of favor (1 Sam 15, 28:17–19).

As discussed above, the king's position was as the father of one great household that incorporated other households, and David's appointment as king by the discretion of the people and elders of the tribes (2 Sam 2:4, 5:3) indicates the degree to which he remained answerable to the lineage groups that made up his realm. However, as in other ancient Near Eastern monarchies the customary ways that the kings of Israel and Judah exercised control over the resources of their realm (economic and human) and how they deployed them for their own ends counterweighed and even conflicted with the autonomy of the tribal leadership.

Royal Service

In his response to the elders (1 Sam 8:11–18), the prophet Samuel directly described what the impact of kingship would be on the life of the people of Israel. What he described is a "royal service system," a system of obligations that the people owed to the king within their subordinate patrimonial position. It was through the royal service system that the king could insert himself and administer his control, weather actively or passively, into the internal economic affairs of his realm. Royal service systems in the patrimonial kingdoms of the ancient Near East were systems of redistribution, through which the king accrued physical and human resources from the households within his kingdom and then redistributed them back to finance the kinds of things kings were expected to do. As ancient Israel had an agricultural economy, meaning that subsistence agriculture was the dominant household activity, agricultural produce—mostly in grain—was the main way for a household to fulfill its obligation. In lieu of this, payment could also be made in valuable commodities or craft products that the household could produce. The other important way in which the obligation was fulfilled was through service in different kinds of labor, such as in the military or on a royal building project, or by using craft skills to produce items directly for the king's household. The agricultural produce the king extracted would allow him to provide rations for those whose service took them away from the agricultural demands of their household (Schloen 2001; see also Earle 2002).

The royal service obligation a person and their household owed was typically attached to their use of agricultural land, the king being the supreme landowner in the kingdom, even over land over which clans had a longstanding claim.[5] Assyrian documents reveal that the king granted land with attached service obligations (Postgate 1971), and though no such document survives from ancient Israel, Samuel referred directly to the fact that the king would seize agricultural land to give to his עבדים "servants" (v. 14). At the same time, Samuel also stated directly that "you [household patriarchs] will be his servants" (v. 17), that is to say that the benefits and impositions of service to the king applied to all.

The description that Samuel gave to the elders covers many of the types of obligations that a king would impose through a royal service system, and in many of its details, it matches those found in other patrimonial kingdoms of the ancient Near East, such as the Late Bronze Age Syrian kingdom of Ugarit (Thomas forthcoming).[6] This includes the basic task of farming the king's own estate (v. 12) and the king's מלאכה "work" (v. 16), which likely refers to all royal projects requiring manual labor for which *corvée* labor (Hebrew מס/סבל) was drafted from among the population.[7] The king took daughters from among Israel's households to serve as flavorers, cooks, and bakers (v. 13) in order to be able to put on lavish feasts for himself, his court, and the elders of the tribes. In patrimonial kingdoms, this was a good way to ensure the continued loyalty and sense of solidarity between the king and his subordinates, and was one way for the king to literally give back some of the agricultural produce he had extracted from his people (MacDonald 2008: 142–64).

The military side of royal service features quite prominently in Samuel's words (vv. 11–12). The main way for the king to ensure that he had the soldiers to carry out a campaign or to garrison forts that defended the kingdom from attack was through service obligations fulfilled by heads of households and their sons or servants. For instance, while David's father Jesse was too old to participate in war, his three eldest sons served in Saul's army, facing Goliath and the Philistines across of Elah Valley (1 Sam 17:12–13). Military service is one of the few forms of royal service that we can say anything about archaeologically, at least in a direct sense, as when we can find the remains of military infrastructure. The site of Khirbet Qeiyafa, which is perched on a ridge overlooking the Elah Valley where David's confrontation with Goliath took place, is a good, relevant example.

The whole site, which was occupied briefly in the late 11th/early 10th centuries BCE, appears to have been a fortress built as one singular project from the outside in, rather than having been built up over time. Each dwelling appears to have been supplied with its own vessels and tools for food preparation, indicating that the occupants of these dwellings were not part of extended families (a בית אב or clan). There are no facilities for storing agricultural produce or cisterns for water at the site and no clearly agricultural tools, though several knives and some possible sword blades were found. The fort's foodstuffs were provided externally and shipped there in a large number of ceramic jars. Jars found throughout the site had thumb impressions on their handles, which likely served to mark jars that contained taxes to the king that he used to support men posted temporarily to the fort, similar to the later *LMLK* system discussed below (Garfinkel and Ganor 2009; Garfinkel et al. 2014; Keimer, Kreimerman, and Garfinkel 2015; Kang and Garfinkel 2018). Two inscriptions found at the site may also be associated with the administration of the fort, though neither is clear or well-preserved enough to say with any certainty. Some have read the longer of the two, an ostracon, as a list of names, perhaps those men assigned to the fort (Misgav, Garfinkel, and Ganor 2009; Garfinkel et al. 2015; and Richelle 2015). All this considered, Khirbet Qeiyafa can be interpreted as a patrimonial fort garrisoned by men from different tribes or clans fulfilling their royal service obligations and supplied by the king with agricultural produce taken as taxes from his subjects (Thomas forthcoming).

The Royal Court

Central to the king's political and administrative hold over his kingdom was his court, really his own immediate household made up of retainers who had a familial or close personal relationship with the king. As patrimonial retainers, they did not occupy offices *per se*, with a defined purview and necessary technical skills. Positions and responsibilities were granted by the king to those he knew and trusted, and their exact duties were probably flexible to a degree (Schloen 2001). The king relied upon these individuals and their loyalty, and as such the court of David was made up of many individuals who had a familial relationship with him or a relationship that went back to David's time before his ascent to kingship. Such personal connections would continue to characterize Solomon's court. These are the only two reigns for which we have much biblical evidence about the composition of the royal court, primarily from the lists of their retainers that appear in 2 Sam 8, 20, and 1 Kgs 4. For later kingdoms of Israel and Judah, members of the royal court and their titles occasionally show up in the biblical narratives and are also represented by seals and bullae from the late 8th century BCE (Fox 2000).

Martial roles figure quite prominently in David's court, starting with David's cousin Joab who is in charge of the צבאה "army" (2 Sam 8:16; 20:23), which was mostly made up of men mustered for duty from among the tribes (King and Stager 2001: 240–41). David also had forces attached to his household directly, a force of Cherethites and Pelethites under his valiant fellow Judahite Benaiah (2 Sam 8:18; 20:23) and a force of Gittites, that is men hailing from Philistine Gath, under Ittai (2 Sam 15:18–22). These groups of soldiers, who can be considered David's elite force, would have joined David when he was in the service of the king of Gath.

Several priests appear in both David and Solomon's courts, foremost among them the two senior priests Zadok and Abiathar, the latter who had fled Saul's wrath to join with David and his company as David rose to kingship (1 Sam 22:21–23). Zadok's son Azariah also appears to have taken over his father's position (1 Kgs 4:2). Note also that David's court prophet Nathan shares the same name as one of David's sons (2 Sam 5:14) and the father of two of Solomon's courtiers (1 Kgs 4:5); they are likely the same individual. The place of the priesthood within the king's court reinforces other indications that the House of David wanted to closely associate itself with Israel's patron deity YHWH and even control cultic practice and worship of YHWH. David first has the Ark of the Covenant brought to his new capital Jerusalem (2 Samuel 6) and Solomon then builds the Temple, YHWH's permanent earthly abode, adjacent to his palace (1 Kings 6–8; Stager 2003; Uziel and Shai 2007). The Temple and priests were not independent but essentially a branch of the royal household, and the king had ultimate control over the Temple treasury and tithes it received (Master 2014).

The only position in the court that can be associated with a technical skill is that of the scribe, as literacy was not a widespread skill in ancient Israel, though it became more so later (see below). David had only one scribe, and his sons inherited their father's role in Solomon's court. David and Solomon's scribes would have been responsible for the Book of the Acts of Solomon (1 Kgs 11:41), which would have been a chronicle of the king's reign, and for diplomatic correspondence between David, Solomon, and other kings. Royal and Temple records that later survived to be incorporated into biblical books, like the list of Solomon's administrative divisions and the list of tribal allotments in Joshua would also have been produced and kept by the scribes. We have no hard evidence for the degree to which these scribes were involved in the administration of the kingdom through formal land grants and documents that kept track of royal service obligations, taxation and distributions from royal stores, but there is enough epigraphic evidence from Iron Age I–IIA in places throughout the kingdom to suggest as much (see Tappy and McCarter 2008; Hardin, Rollston, and Blakely 2014; Rollston 2017).

Three other individuals and their titles can be linked to administration. The title of Jehosaphat son of Ahilud, מזכיר, is difficult to interpret but can perhaps be translated as "herald." Based on the functions of other royal heralds in the ancient Near East, part of his responsibilities may have been calling out the king's subjects for royal service. There is also Ahishar who is "over the house," meaning that he administered the king's royal household and tended to those within it, seeing to the king's table and his royal estates. Similar positions in the royal household are also known throughout the ancient Near East and Egypt (Fox 2000: 81–96, 110–21).

Two of Solomon's courtiers were central to the system of royal service and redistribution that supplied the necessary resources and labor for the royal court, the military infrastructure, and royal building projects. Azariah son of Nathan was in charge of the נְצָבִים (*niṣābim*), the 12 officials posted in various parts of the kingdom (see below), while Adoniram was "over the מס," that is the *corvée* labor. First Kgs 5:16 and 9:23 mention שרי הנצבים, officers who were subordinate to the *niṣābim* (Fox 2000: 146–47) in charge of the מלאכה, which likely means a project of the king involving manual labor. Jeroboam's position in charge of the *corvée* labor of the House of Joseph (the tribes of Ephraim and Manasseh) would have been as one of these officers, under the נצב in charge of the administrative division in Mount Ephraim. Adoniram then would appear to have been in charge of administering and mustering out the *corvée* labor, while the individual *niṣābim* and their subordinates were responsible for the work carried out.

Solomon's Administrative Divisions

First Kings 4 provides a list of 12 officials who carry the title נצב, literally "one who is stationed" that Solomon had throughout his realm, each of whom was responsible for provisioning the king's household for one month of the year (v. 7), though we can take the term בית "household" here to potentially cover any who were reliant on the king as they were undertaking their service obligations, such as on Solomon's building projects (1 Kgs 9:15–19). This is often referred to as a list of territorial "districts," though the text never uses such a term. The description of exactly what constitutes the remit of each of these officials varies throughout the list, but they largely follow either the existing Israelite tribal system or areas of old Canaanite communities that had at some point been incorporated into the kingdom. A system in which each official is defined by social units of the kingdom (rather than a defined territory) fits the patrimonial structure of Solomon's kingdom, and would also have made more sense if part of the population was nomadic, as nomadic groups will be found in different locations depending on the time of year. Some of the officials had an existing familial connection to the court, such as Baana son of David's advisor Hishai the Archite (2 Sam 15:37). Two of them, the son of Abinadab and Ahimaaz (vv. 11, 17), had married daughters of Solomon. In every respect, the system of divisions is a typical patrimonial administrative structure (Stager 2003; Thomas forthcoming).

Developments in the Late Monarchic Period

The biblical text offers much less information regarding political and administrative structures in the separate kingdoms of Judah and Israel than it does for the United Monarchy. Archaeological evidence for the day-to-day administration in Judah does increase significantly from the Iron Age IIB period (primarily the late 8th century BCE), though what this says about an overall change in the political structure of the kingdom is open to interpretation. We have no reason to think that the kingdoms of Israel and Judah did not remain fundamentally patrimonial until their respective terminations in the late 8th and early 6th centuries BCE respectively (Maeir and Shai 2016). The best evidence of this is the early 8th century ostraca (inscribed potsherds) found at the northern kingdom's capital Samaria. These ostraca record the transport of wine and oil to persons in Samaria, and along with the receiver they name the sender, the shipment's origin, or both in some cases. Among those named origins are several clans of the tribe of Manasseh named in the books of Numbers and Joshua. This indicates that tax and tithe in the northern kingdom of Israel continued to be levied according to kin groups and that the agricultural goods collected were redistributed by the king and his court, though exactly how the system (if there was one) represented by the Samaria ostraca remains debated, partly because the ostraca as a corpus of documents are inconsistent in their details.[8]

No similar corpus has yet been found in Judah (but see below) though it is widely accepted that the lists of groups of towns allotted to the tribes of Judah, Benjamin and Dan (prior to the latter's northward migration) given in Joshua 15, 18–19 actually reflect the administrative division of the kingdom of Judah. Albrecht Alt, who first suggested dating these lists to the time of the Divided Monarchy, considered the text to present 12 administrative divisions, with the two groups of towns in Benjamin overlapping two of those in Judah. He therefore suggested quite sensibly they were intended to fulfill the same purpose as Solomon's 12 administrative divisions, for taxation by one division per month of the year (Alt 1953 [1925]: 276–88). There are several difficulties in analyzing these lists as subsequent scholarship has pointed out, including how many divisions are counted, how to account for some missing towns, and differences between the Hebrew and Greek texts of Joshua (i.e. Aharoni 1979: 347–56; Kallai 1986; Na'aman 1991). The recent comprehensive study by McKinny (2016) has reinforced a date in the Iron Age II for the compilation of these lists, even as far back as the 9th century in their earliest form.

If Alt (1953) was basically correct that the groups of towns given in the allotments of the southern tribes represent the kingdom of Judah's administrative divisions, his view that they continued the same administrative rationale as those of the days of Solomon can only be an inference; neither the biblical text nor any inscription from the Iron Age II refers to this system. The kingdom of Judah generally seems to have remained decentralized, tribe- and clan-based even in the 8th and 7th centuries BCE when epigraphic evidence for royal administrative efforts increases. Governance at the local level may have been centered on residences like that from the 8th century at Tel Eton, which was well-built and contained clay bullae that had been affixed to papyrus documents, and the (re)fortification of sites like Lachish would be a royal project financed through redistributed agricultural surpluses and royal service (Faust and Katz 2015: 93–94; Maeir and Shai 2016: 328; cf. Schloen 2016).[9] Part of the Judahite population conceivably remained pastoral-nomadic even late into the kingdom's history, but its relationship with the administration of settled areas of the kingdom remains difficult to adduce from the evidence.

The Growth of Written Administration in Judah

During the 8th and 7th centuries BCE (Iron Age IIB–C), the kingdom of Judah experienced a significant growth in literacy, indicated *inter alia* by many archaeological finds related to the administrative use of writing, many more than in the Iron Age I–IIA. The consistency and clarity of Hebrew inscriptions from this period are indicative of an established curriculum throughout the kingdom for educating scribes, though literacy also extended to others within the royal court, military, and administration. The corpus of evidence related to administration includes letters inscribed on potsherds (ostraca), jars stamped with an inscription on their handles, and the seals or bullae of individuals who held a general title such as עבד המלך "servant of the king" or more specific title indicating a role such as אשר על הבית "who is over the house [royal household]" (Rollston 2010; Schniedewind 2013: 99–125). The king had also had a seal of his own, as evidenced by a bulla of King Hezekiah's seal (Mazar 2015).

The most frequent type of administrative inscription from late monarchic Judah are the *LMLK* jars, a specific and standardized type of four-handled storage jar impressed on the handle with the word למלך, which translates literally as "to the king," indicating some form of royal prerogative over the agricultural products that were placed in the jars. These jars are found in 8th and some 7th century BCE (Iron Age IIB and IIC) levels throughout the kingdom of Judah (Lipschits 2021). The word למלך is typically accompanied by various combinations of different forms of either a winged scarab or winged sun disk emblem and one of four geographical names located in Judah above or below the emblem: Hebron, Socoh, Ziph, and the enigmatic ממשת "MMST."[10] Numerous *LMLK* jar handles are also stamped with the seal of a personal name and sometimes their title, and sometimes circles have been incised onto the handle after the jar has been fired. Petrographic analysis of the clay from which the jars themselves were made indicates that they were produced, perhaps in an industrial fashion, in the Shephelah.[11]

The distribution of *LMLK* jars has long been associated with the Assyrian campaign against Judah in 701 BCE, particularly where they are found in levels destroyed in that campaign, most famously Lachish Stratum III. As such, the *LMLK* phenomenon is widely associated with the reign of Hezekiah and the intensification of royal control during his reign, which reached into the economic, military, and cultic spheres of the kingdom. Different proposals exist for the *raison d'être* of the administrative system behind the LMLK jars: it was borne out of Hezekiah's need to gather stocks of food for his soldiers and fortified cities in preparation for rebellion against Assyria at the end of the 8th century (Na'aman 1986; Keimer 2011); or it was related to Judah's vassaldom to Assyria, as a system by which Hezekiah could respond to the economic pressure of his tributary obligations. The continuation of this system after Hezekiah's revolt failed to throw off Assyrian hegemony would account for those *LMLK* jars that appear in the 7th century (Lipschits, Sergi, and Koch 2010).

At some point during the 7th century, the *LMLK* jars were replaced by a new type of storage jar impressed with a rosette-shaped stamp, without any writing. These presumably continued the same system of centralized, royally mandated collection of agricultural produce from landowners and/or royal estates as that of the *LMLK* jars, and were also produced in the Shephelah (Koch and Lipschits 2013).

This brings us to the difficult question of how to relate these practices to the kingdom's political and administrative structure. We can reasonably associate the practice of the *LMLK* and rosette-stamped jars with the collection of taxes from landowners that was part of the overall redistributive royal service system. Yet the elements of the *LMLK* jars, their singular jar form, and their stamps, clearly constitute a new practice in how this was achieved, opening up the possibility for the different explanations as to what prompted this.

Going any further beyond this is severely hampered by the fact that the meaning and significance of the elements of these practices and what they indicate about the system in which they functioned is elusive. This is particularly the case for the various and inconsistent elements of the *LMLK* jars (private stamps, incised circles, and so on). The four place names that appear on the *LMLK* seals are a particular problem, not least of all because "MMST" is not a place known from either the Hebrew Bible or any other text, as well as the fact that there is no discernable pattern to where seals with each particular placename appear. Hebron, Socoh, Ziph, and "MMST" could have been the location of the production of the jars, the royal estates, or perhaps storage facilities where the jars were distributed for filling, where they were received, and/or from whence supplies were redistributed as needed. If they had any relationship to the postulated administrative districts of Judah discussed above, it is uncertain (see McKinny 2016: 42–46 with previous literature).

More likely, the filled jars were distributed to fortified places that protected routes into the heartland of Judah, such as the important southern fortress of Arad. A small number of *LMLK* and rosette-stamped jar handles were found in the Iron Age IIB–C levels of the fortress, and letters on ostraca found there, apparently to the commander of the fortress in the last days of the kingdom of Judah, refer to provisions that are to be given to what may have been Greek mercenary troops. Shorter dockets on ostraca also list names and food provisions for individuals stationed at the fort (Aharoni 1981; Vaughn 1999: 192).

Conclusion

In ancient Israel social structure dictated political and administrative structure, and socially Israel was always characterized by kinship and the household, which operated at both local and super-local levels. Israel began as an identity to which several independent tribal groups belonged and under which they could co-operate. Though the tribes remained fundamental to the patrimonial, household-based structure of Israel and Judah in the monarchic period, kings gradually accrued more power to themselves through the administration of their realms' human and economic resources. This is most visible in the *LMLK* jar system of 8th–7th century Judah, but although this system seems to have relied on local social units, it also appears to have centralized resources to the control of the king on a new scale.

Notes

1 For patrimonialism in other ancient Near Eastern kingdoms in addition to Schloen's (2001) foundational study focusing on Ugarit and some other kingdoms, see Lehner 2000; Garfinkle 2008; Bilgin 2018.
2 Though 1-2 Chronicles gives details relating to the administration of David and Solomon's kingdom not found in Samuel and Kings, they are generally accepted to be a product of the books of Chronicles' context of composition in the exilic/post-exilic period and not useful for a historical reconstruction.
3 It matters little how historical we should assess the biblical idea of Israel's collective identity being rooted in a common ancestry to be, as even fictional kinship ties were understood as no less real and legitimate in the ancient Near Eastern social context (Petter 2018).
4 On the Delphic amphictyony, see Constantakopoulou 2015.
5 We can also suggest that the king's tithe of sheep flocks (v. 17) would allow the king to extract from both sedentary and mobile Israelites, though this is not to say that mobile households and clans could not also own land, which was not unusual.
6 See Mendelsohn 1956; Rainey 1975; Master 2014.
7 This much is certainly clear from the use and context of the term as it appears in 1 Kgs 5:16.
8 For some important studies on the Samaria ostraca see (Aharoni 1979: 356–568; Schloen 2001: 155–65; Niemann 2008; Nam 2012; Suriano 2016).
9 The complex of buildings on and around the podium at the center of Iron Age II Lachish are likely to have served an administrative and military function and would have provided some of the best evidence for this had the buildings and their contents been better preserved (see Ussishkin 1993).
10 Though sometimes the impression contains these other elements but does not actually include למלך itself.
11 Much has been written about the *LMLK* jar phenomenon, the following publications and their bibliographies should be consulted: Lemaire 1981; Vaughn 1999; Fox 2000; Lipschits, Sergi, and Koch 2011; Na'aman 2016.

Bibliography

Aharoni, Yohanan. 1979. *The Land of the Bible: A Historical Geography*. Rev. ed. Philadelphia: Westminster Press.
———. 1981. *Arad Inscriptions*. Jerusalem: Israel Exploration Society.
Alt, Albrecht. 1953. *Kleine Schriften Zur Geschichte Des Volkes Israel*. Band 2. Munich: C. H. Beck.
Ben-Yosef, Erez. 2019. "The 'Architectural Bias' in Current Biblical Archaeology." *VT* 69: 361–87.
———. Forthcoming. "A False Contrast? On the Possibility of an Early Iron Age Nomadic Monarchy in the Arabah (Early Edom) and Its Implications to the Study of Ancient Israel." Pages 15–16 in *"The Archaeology of the Settlement Period" Thirty Years Later. Proceedings of The Annual Aharoni Symposium of the Institute of Archaeology of Tel Aviv University, March 2017*. Edited by Ido Koch et al. Tel Aviv: Tel Aviv University.
Benz, Brendon. 2016. *The Land Before the Kingdom of Israel*. Winona Lake: Eisenbrauns.

Bilgin, Tayfun. 2018. *Officials and Administration in the Hittite World*. Berlin: de Gruyter.
Constantakopoulou, Christy. 2015. "Regional Religious Groups, Amphictionies, and Other Leagues." Pages 273–90 in *The Oxford Handbook of Ancient Greek Religion*. Edited by Esther Eidinow and Julia Kindt. Oxford: Oxford University Press.
de Geus, C. H. J. 1976. *The Tribes of Israel*. Assen: Van Gorcum.
Earle, Timothy K. 2002. *Bronze Age Economics*. Boulder: Westview.
Faust, Avraham. 2006. *Israel's Ethnogenesis*. London: Equinox.
Faust, Avraham and Hayah Katz. 2015. "A Canaanite Town, a Judahite Center, and a Period Period Fort: Excavating Over Two Thousand Years of History at Tel 'Eton." *NEA* 78: 88–102.
Flannery, Kent V. 1972. "The Cultural Evolution of Civilizations." *ARES* 3: 399–426.
Fleming, Daniel. 2012. *The Legacy of Israel in Judah's Bible*. New York: Cambridge University Press.
Fox, Nili Sacher. 2000. *In the Service of the King*. Cincinnati: Hebrew Union College Press.
Garfinkel, Yosef, and Saar Ganor, eds. 2009. *Khirbet Qeiyafa Vol. 1: Excavation Report 2007–2008*. Jerusalem: Israel Exploration Society.
Garfinkel, Yosef, Saar Ganor, Michael G. Hasel, and Martin G. Klingbeil, eds. 2014. *Khirbet Qeiyafa Vol. 2: Excavation Report 2009–2013—Stratigraphy and Architecture (Areas B, C, D, E)*. Jerusalem: Israel Exploration Society.
Garfinkel, Yosef, Mitka Golub, Haggai Misgav, and Saar Ganor. 2015. "The 'Išba'al Inscription from Khirbet Qeiyafa." *BASOR* 373: 217–33.
Garfinkle, Steven J. 2008. "Was the Ur III State Bureaucratic? Patrimonialism and Bureaucracy in the Ur III Period." Pages 55–61 in *The Growth of an Early State in Mesopotamia: Studies in Ur III Administration*. Edited by Steven J. Garfinkle and J. Cale Johnson. Madrid: Consejo Superior de Investigaciones Científicas.
Hardin, James W., Christopher A. Rollston, and Jeffrey A. Blakely. 2014. "Iron Age Bullae from Officialdom's Periphery: Khirbet Summeily in Broader Context." *NEA* 77: 299–301.
Ilan, David. 2018. "The 'Conquest' of the Highlands in the Iron Age I." Pages 283–309 in *The Social Archaeology of the Levant*. Edited by Assur Yasur-Landau et al. Cambridge: Cambridge University Press.
Ishida, Tomoo. 1973. "The Leaders of the Tribal Leagues «Israel» in the Pre-Monarchic Period." *RB* 80: 514–30.
Joffe, Alexander H. 2018. "Defining the State." Pages 3–23 in *Enemies and Friends of the State: Ancient Prophecy in Context*. Edited by Christopher A. Rollston. University Park: Eisenbrauns.
Jones, Philip. 2012. "Kingship, Ancient Near East." *The Encyclopedia of Ancient History* 7: https://doi.org/10.1002/9781444338386.wbeah01115.
Kallai, Zachariah. 1986. *Historical Geography of the Bible: The Tribal Territories of Israel*. Jerusalem: Magnes Press.
Kallai, Zachariah. 1997. "The Twelve-Tribe Systems of Israel." *VT* 47: 53–90.
Kang, Hoo-Goo, and Yosef Garfinkel. 2018. *Khirbet Qeiyafa Volume 6. Excavation Report 2007–2013: The Iron Age Pottery*. Jerusalem: Israel Exploration Society.
Keimer, Kyle. 2011. "The Socioeconomic Impact of Hezekiah's Preparations for Rebellion." PhD diss., University of California, Los Angeles.
Keimer, Kyle, Igor Kreimerman, and Yosef Garfinkel. 2015. "From Quarry to Completion: Hirbet Qeyafa as a Case Study in the Building of Ancient Near Eastern Settlements." *ZDPV* 131: 109–28.
Keimer, Kyle H., and Zachary Thomas. 2020-2021 [2022]. "Etic and Emic Expressions of Power in Ancient Israel: Recalibrating a Discussion." *JEOL* 48: 69–92.
King, Philip J., and Lawrence Stager. 2001. *Life in Biblical Israel*. Louisville: Westminster John Knox.
Knapp, andrew. 2017. "King Kingship I. Ancient Near East." *EBR* 15: 217–22.
Koch, Ido and Oded Lipschits. 2013. "The Rosette Stamped Jar Handle System and the Kingdom of Judah at the End of the First Temple Period." *ZDPV* 129: 55–78.
Lehner, Mark. 2000. "Fractal House of Pharaoh: Ancient Egypt as a Complex Adaptive System, a Trial Formulation." Pages 275–353 in *Dynamics in Human and Primate Societies*. Edited by Timothy A. Kohler and George Gumerman. New York: Oxford University Press.
Lemaire, andré. 1981. "Classification Des Estampilles Royales Judéennes." *EI* 15: 54–60.
Lipschits, Oded. 2021. *Age of Empires: The History and Administration of Judah in the 8th-2nd Centuries BCE in Light of the Storage-Jar Stamp Impressions*. University Park and Tel Aviv: Eisenbrauns and Tel Aviv University.

Lipschits, Oded, Omer Sergi, and Ido Koch. 2010. "Royal Judahite Jar Handles: Reconsidering the Chronology of the Lmlk Stamp Impressions." *TA* 37: 3–32.

———. 2011. "Judahite Stamped and Incised Jar Handles: A Tool for Studying the History of Late Monarchic Judah." *TA* 38: 5–41.

MacDonald, Nathan. 2008. *Not Bread Alone: The Uses of Food in the Old Testament.* Oxford: Oxford University Press.

Maeir, Aren M,. and Itzhaq Shai. 2016. "Reassessing the Character of the Judahite Kingdom: Archaeological Evidence for Non-Centralized, Kinship-Based Components." Pages 323–40 in *From Sha'ar Hagolan to Shaaraim: Essays in Honor of Prof. Yosef Garfinkel.* Edited by Saar Ganor et al. Jerusalem: Israel Exploration Society.

Master, Daniel M. 2001. "State Formation Theory and the Kingdom of Ancient Israel." *JNES* 60: 117–31.

———. 2014. "Economy and Exchange in the Iron Age Kingdoms of the Southern Levant." *BASOR* 372: 81–97.

Mazar, Eilat. 2015. "A Seal Impression of King Hezekiah from the Ophel Excavations." Pages 629–40 in *The Ophel Excavations to the South of the Temple Mount, 2009–2013.* Edited by Eilat Mazar. Jerusalem: Shoham.

McKinny, Christopher. 2016. "A Historical Geography of the Administrative Division of Judah: The Town Lists of Judah and Benjamin in Joshua 15:21–62 and 18:21–28." PhD dissertation. Bar Ilan University.

Mendelsohn, Isaac. 1956. "Samuel's Denunciation of Kingship in the Light of the Akkadian Documents from Ugarit." *BASOR* 143: 17–22.

Miller, Robert D. II. 2005. *Chieftains of the Highland Clans.* Grand Rapids: Eerdmans.

Misgav, Haggai, Yosef Garfinkel, and Saar Ganor. 2009. "The Ostracon." Pages 243–57 in *Khirbet Qeiyafa Vol. 1: Excavation Report 2007–2008.* Edited by Yosef Garfinkel and Saar Ganor. Jerusalem: Israel Exploration Society.

Na'aman, Nadav. 1986. "Hezekiah's Fortified Cities and the 'LMLK' Stamps." *BASOR* 261: 5–21.

———. 1991. "The Kingdom of Judah Under Josiah." *TA* 18: 3–71.

———. 2016. "The Lmlk Seal Impressions Reconsidered." *TA* 43: 111–25.

Nam, Roger S. 2012. "Power Relations in the Samaria Ostraca." *PEQ* 144: 155–63.

Niemann, Hermann Michael. 2008. "A New Look at the Samaria Ostraca: The King-Clan Relationship." *TA* 35: 249–66.

Noth, Martin. 1960. *The History of Israel.* 2nd English ed. London: Adam & Charles Black.

Petter, Thomas D. 2018. "Tribes and Nomads in the Iron Age Levant." Pages 391–95 in *Behind the Scenes of the Old Testament.* Edited by Jonathan S. Greer et al. Grand Rapids: Baker Academic.

Postgate, Nicholas. 1971. "Land Tenure in the Middle Assyrian Period: A Reconstruction." *BSOAS* 34: 496–520.

Rainey, Anson F. 1975. "Institutions: Family, Civil, and Military." Pages 71–107 in *Ras Shamra Parallels vol. II.* Edited by Loren S. Fisher. Rome: Pontificium Institutum Biblicum.

———. 2015. *The El-Amarna Correspondence.* Leiden: Brill.

Richelle, Matthieu. 2015. "Quelques Nouvelles Lectures Sur l'ostracon de Khirbet Qeiyafa." *Sem* 57: 147–62.

Rollston, Christopher A. 2010. *Writing and Literacy in the World of Ancient Israel.* Atlanta: SBL.

———. 2017. "Epigraphic Evidence from Jerusalem and Its Environs at the Dawn of Biblical History: Methodologies and a Long Durèe Perspective." Pages *7–*20 in *NSAJR, Vol. XI.* Edited by Yuval Gadot et al. Jerusalem: Hebrew University of Jerusalem/Israel Antiquities Authority/Tel Aviv University.

Schloen, J. David. 2001. *The House of the Father as Fact and Symbol: Patrimonialism in Ugarit and the Ancient Near East.* Winona Lake: Eisenbrauns.

———. 2016. "Economy and Society in Iron Age Israel and Judah." Pages 433–53 in *The Wiley Blackwell Companion to Ancient Israel.* Edited by Susan Niditch. Hoboken: Wiley-Blackwell.

———. 1993. "Caravans, Kenites, and Casus Belli: Enmity and Alliance in the Song of Deborah." *CBQ* 55:18–38.

Schniedewind, William M. 2013. *A Social History of Hebrew.* New Haven: Yale University Press.

Service, Elman R. 1971. *Primitive Social Organization.* 2nd ed. New York: Random House.

Smith, Mark S. 2014. *Poetic Heroes.* Grand Rapids: Eerdmans.

Stager, Lawrence E. 1985. "The Archaeology of the Family in Ancient Israel." *BASOR* 260:1–35.

———. 2003. "The Patrimonial Kingdom of Solomon." Pages 63–74 in *Symbiosis, Symbolism, and the Power of the Past: Canaan, Ancient Israel, and Their Neighbors from the Late Bronze Age through Roman Palaestina*. Edited by Willam G. Dever and Seymour Gitin. Winona Lake: Eisenbrauns.

Suriano, Matthew J. 2016. "Wine Shipments to Samaria from Royal Vineyards." *TA* 43:99–110.

Tappy, Ron E., and P. Kyle McCarter, eds. 2008. *Literate Culture and Tenth-Century Canaan: The Tel Zayit Abecedary in Context*. Winona Lake: Eisenbrauns.

Thomas, Zachary. 2019. "Polycentrism and the Terminology of Polity in Early Israel." *Bible Lands E-Review* S2: 1–14.

———. 2021. "On the Archaeology of 10th Century BCE Israel and the Idea of the 'State.'" *PEQ* 153: 244–257.

———. Forthcoming. *This House That I Have Built: The Patrimonial Kingdom of David and Solomon*. Atlanta: SBL.

Ussishkin, David. 1993. "Lachish." *NEAEHL* 3: 897–911.

Uziel, Joe, and Itzhaq Shai. 2007. "Iron Age Jerusalem: Temple-Palace, Capital City." *JAOS* 127: 161–70.

van der Steen, Eveline J. 2013. *Near Eastern Tribal Societies in the Nineteenth Century*. Sheffield: Equinox.

Vaughn, andrew G. 1999. *Theology, History, and Archaeology in the Chronicler's Account of Hezekiah*. Atlanta: Scholar's Press.

Weber, Max. 1978. *Economy and Society: An Outline of Interpretative Sociology*. Edited by G. Roth and C. Wittich. Berkeley: University of California Press.

16

THE JUDAHITE ECONOMY IN FIRST TEMPLE TIMES

Remodeling the House of David—A Case Study from Tell en-Naṣbeh

Aaron Brody

The economy in the era of the First Temple Period is an enormous, yet under-studied topic. As many text scholars have noted, there is frustratingly little economic evidence in our main textual sources for the lengthy period that spans the traditional times of the United and Divided Monarchies (Boer 2015; Chaney 2017; Miller, Ben Zvi, and Knoppers 2015; Nam 2012). Neither the limited epigraphic finds from the 10th–early 6th centuries BCE nor the curated anthology of texts eventually canonized in the Hebrew Bible, or *Tanakh,* are particularly replete with economic data. The corpus preserved in the Hebrew Bible pertaining to the First Temple Period is rather large, yet tends not to be focused on economic matters, except for the occasional passage relating how they impacted or were shaped by the royalty, royal administration, bureaucracy, and other elites. There are also occasional critiques of the excess of this royal system or the wealthy sprinkled throughout the prophetic books dated to, or alluding to, the 8th–6th centuries BCE (Chaney 2017).

The Temple in Jerusalem itself played its own role in the storage and distribution of wealth for the dynastic polity (Stevens 2006), the Judean patrimonial kingdom or House of David. Presumably, there were parallel functions at the state-sponsored temples in the Northern Kingdom as well such as those at Bethel and Dan and the temple of Baal at Samaria (2 Kgs 10). We must acknowledge, however, that the royal and elite portions of ancient Israelite and Judahite society likely made up less than 10–15% of the population (Chaney 2017). Thus, our textual sources only poorly represent, or provide very little information on the economies of the vast majority of the peoples in these ancient kingdoms. We must turn to other sources to help fill in this huge information gap. To represent the remaining 85–90% of the population and their economies we must rely on archaeology, interrogating the material remains from non-elite contexts to begin to fill this void. Given the fragmentary nature of both the archaeological and textual evidence, we should frame and interpret these data through the use of economic, anthropological, and archaeological theories that allow us to make better sense of elements of the economies of the past (Boer 2015; Bauer and Agbe-Davies 2010; Chaney 2017; Feinman 2017; Heijmans 2021; Hirth 2020; Katz 2008; Master 2014; Miller, Ben Zvi, and Knoppers 2015; Moreno Garcia 2021; Nam 2012; Nyman, Fogle, and Beaudry 2019; Sasson 2014; Skinner 2001; Stark and Garraty 2010).

Accordingly, I will offer insights into the economy of Judah based on my archaeological analysis of a prominent village or town site, that of Tell en-Naṣbeh, as a case study of an ancient economy. This site is almost certainly the settlement of Mizpah in the region of Benjamin, as detailed in biblical texts found principally in the Deuteronomistic History (Brody 2009: 116–17). My research, primarily focused on interregional interactions at Tell en-Naṣbeh and the localized mode of economy, adds to the recent model put forth by Master (2014). To quote Master (2014: 83):

> ...Any satisfactory discussion of Iron Age exchange should deal with both transactional elements and social context. This paper argues that they coexisted in economic "institutions," stable social forms that allowed people of the Iron Age to function to economic advantage. The following discussion is a first attempt to apply a "neo-institutional" economic perspective to the highland kingdoms of the southern Levant by identifying three major, overlapping contexts of exchange: the monarchy, the market, and the trade route. Though the same person or object could exist in all these spheres, each had a distinct rationale and rules of participation. Within each, the ancient inhabitants of the highland kingdoms of Israel and Judah maximized their opportunities in pursuit of a richer existence.

If we focus on Master's "three major, overlapping contexts of exchange: the monarchy, the market, and the trade route," each category is further refined when considering evidence from Tell en-Naṣbeh, a large, fortified village or town in its Iron IIB–IIC phase.[1]

As his argument is presented in a fuller fashion, Tell en-Naṣbeh has little to no place in Master's economic modeling. The excavated materials from Tell en-Naṣbeh reveal very little contact with the monarchy or state, so his first context is represented only in a meager fashion. Yet imported artifacts are found at the site that evince interregional interconnections with Naṣbeh. These imported objects must have arrived on secondary if not tertiary trade routes since the site is located far from any of the primary roads that make up another of Master's contexts of exchange. Finally, spatial analysis of the imports to Naṣbeh suggests a localized marketing system of exchange and barter, better represented in Master's final context of exchange that focuses on tiered markets. The evidence from the excavations at Naṣbeh thus nuances and adds to the model that Master develops, reframing and remodeling the House of David's economy from a bottom-up perspective allowing us to reconsider the production and exchanges of the common people who made up much of the population of this ancient patrimonial kingdom.

Site Hierarchies

Before detailing some of my archaeological analysis, it is important to establish Tell en-Naṣbeh's location in the site hierarchy of Iron IIB–IIC Judah. Archaeological settlements in the polity can be sorted into five main categories: fortresses; small villages; large, fortified villages or towns; regional administrative cities; and regal-ritual capital cities (Faust 2012: 196–205; Holladay 1995: 370–75; Keimer 2011: 65–73; see also Pierce, this volume). Naṣbeh, with its small size of three hectares, robust fortifications, agglutinated pillared houses, lack of monumental buildings, and reconstructed population of between 800 and 1000 residents, is categorized as a third-tier, large, fortified village or town (Zorn 1994: 35–42). Thus, its analysis provides insights into a non-urban,[2] non-elite set of contexts, and furthers our understanding of regionalized economy on the periphery of monarchic purview. This occurred within the small territory of northern Judah in the proximity of its royal capital city, Jerusalem, which is located just 12 km south of Naṣbeh along the trunk road that runs through the central hill country.

Contact with the Monarchy or State

Features and artifacts with probable connections to the Judean monarchy include the wall that surrounded the site in its Iron IIB–IIC phases; a relatively large number of LMLK seal impressed storage jar handles (Figure 16.1); an inscribed seal, whose owner was a "servant of the king" or royal official; and cisterns not affiliated with households. I would argue, however, that this is material evidence for punctuated influence or contact with the higher echelons of the kingdom. The massive solid wall that guarded Naṣbeh, the neighboring trunk roadway, and the northern border of the kingdom suggests a state-sponsored building project in the short-term (Figure 16.2). Whether or not some sort of royally supported garrison was maintained within the settlement is not corroborated archaeologically, and seems highly unlikely, despite biblical and extra-biblical textual attestations to interregional and international warfare with polities further north and east in the Iron IIB–IIC periods.

While the relatively high number of LMLK impressions at the site reinforces its importance as a northern boundary of the Judean kingdom in the 8th century, we are unsure of the use of the jars after their initial manufacture, use for transport of dried goods or liquids, and distribution (Keimer 2011). It should also be stressed that the 88 LMLK impressions are the equivalent of a minimum of 21–84 jars since each jar could have up to four of its handles stamped. This estimate represents a small percentage of the thousands of contemporary and later Iron IIB–IIC storage jars that are unmarked and are found throughout the site (McCown 1947: 156–60; Wampler 1947: 3–15, 129–44).

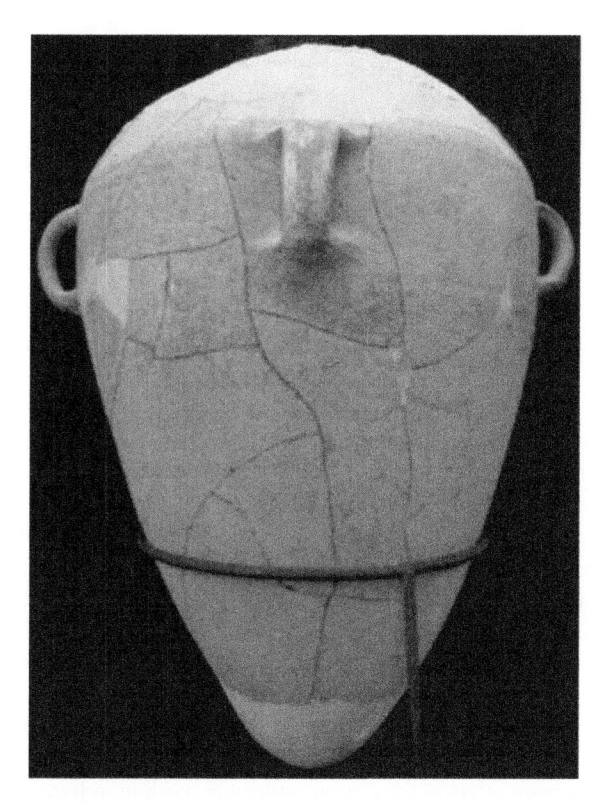

Figure 16.1 LMLK jar, with all four handles stamped; Tell en-Naṣbeh. Image courtesy of the Badè Museum, Pacific School of Religion

Figure 16.2 The settlement wall at Tell en-Naṣbeh. Image courtesy of the Badè Museum, Pacific School of Religion

An inscribed seal was discovered in a later Byzantine tomb located outside of the walls of the settlement. Clearly an Iron IIB–IIC seal based on its paleography, the seal names the owner, Ja'azaniah, as an *'eved ha-melekh*, or a servant of the king (Figure 16.3; McCown 1947: 163). This bureaucratic title suggests at least one royal official lived at, and may have been buried at, the site, out of a reconstructed population of between 800 and 1000 during the Iron IIB–IIC periods (Zorn 1994: 35–42).

Finally, there are many small, stone-lined pits in an area of the southeastern section of the site, which were constructed in a portion of the settlement newly created after the solid wall was built around the village/town (Figure 16.4). Unlike the remaining pits at Naṣbeh, these were not associated with a pillared house or household courtyard but were in an open area of the site. Zorn (2022) has recently studied these openly accessible pits in-depth and interpreted them as remains related to a state-sponsored program of taxation by the government centered in Jerusalem. This seems a probable interpretation, although such an enterprise could have been run and maintained through local control, with periodic or regular deliveries of sacks or jars of grain taking place when requested by representatives of the central authorities residing in Jerusalem.

The Judahite Economy in First Temple Times

Figure 16.3 The Ja'azaniah seal (right) and its impression (left) from Tell en-Naṣbeh. Image courtesy of the Badè Museum, Pacific School of Religion

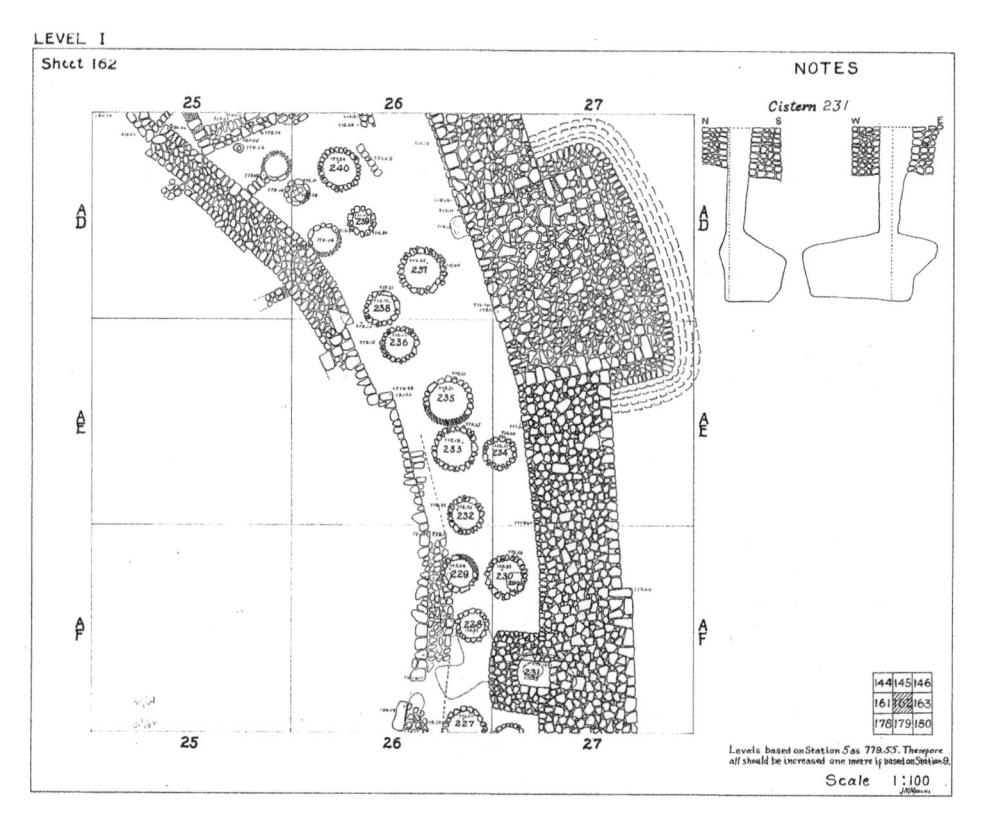

Figure 16.4 Architectural plan of southeastern squares at Tell en-Naṣbeh, featuring stone-lined pits with no associated architecture, unpublished. Image courtesy of the Badè Museum, Pacific School of Religion

Aaron Brody

Interregional Interconnections, Secondary/Tertiary Trade Routes

Despite this minimal evidence for episodic connections with the Judean monarchy, the site has artifacts that elucidate interregional interactions with neighboring polities in Phoenicia and Transjordan, suggesting foreign exchange and contacts that were not aspects of royal ventures or part of a centralized political economy. A hand full of late Iron Age Phoenician pottery vessels have been identified, two jugs and an incense burner, along with typical Phoenician glass eye-beads and other glass beads whose likely origins were along the central Levantine coast (Brody 2014a). While overall numbers are tiny, the presence of these Phoenician objects at a tertiary town/village settlement demonstrates the interconnectivity of lower-level Judean sites with the Phoenician, Mediterranean economy. Many of these Phoenician objects have ritual significance or use, such as the eye-beads' personal apotropaic qualities or the ceremonial function of the incense burner; while one of the jugs was found in the only ritual context in a five-household compound and may be interpreted as a libation vessel (Brody 2014a, 2018). These Phoenician objects may have arrived together with Cypriot artifacts uncovered at the site, which are primarily Black-on-Red juglets valued for their contents of perfumed oil and Cypriot Iron Age Bichrome wares, presumably carried by the same traders traveling upland from the Mediterranean coast.

Recent material science testing on several Judean Pillar Figurines from Naṣbeh demonstrates that they were made from the clay sources close to Jerusalem (Ben-Shlomo and McCormick 2021). These marketing connections between Jerusalem and Naṣbeh suggest that the Phoenician and Cypriot products found at the site may have been procured in the capital city, and not traded directly from the coast up to Tell en-Naṣbeh. At the same time, it is also possible that coastal traders stopped at Naṣbeh to exchange their wares prior to arrival in Jerusalem, or that goods did not move directly from the coast to the highlands but were traded in smaller segments down the lines of exchange.

Other material culture from Iron IIB–IIC Naṣbeh has clarified interregional interactions to the east, with the polities of Transjordan. Material science testing on bronze bangles (Figure 16.5) has shown them to be made from a leaded copper-tin alloy, whose copper ore was likely sourced from the mines of Wadi Feinan, with initial smelting taking place in workshops in the highland region of Edom close to the copper sources (Brody and Friedman 2007). Metrology conducted on bangles not yet sized and altered into jewelry suggests that these objects were created according to Syro-Mesopotamian and/or Phoenician, not local,

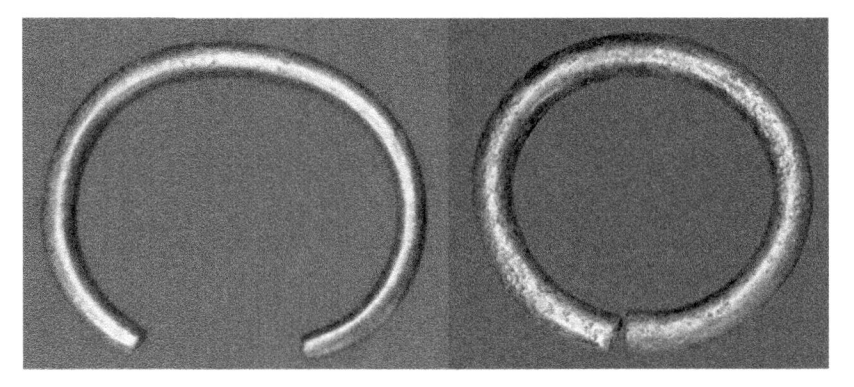

Figure 16.5 Two bronze bangles from Tell en-Naṣbeh, C-shaped (left) and O-shaped (right). Image courtesy of the Badè Museum, Pacific School of Religion, based on original images by Alon Friedman

shekel weight standards. This implies an international sophistication and intentionality of the manufacturers and consumers of these bangles, which were produced in Edom according to international measures of mass, exchanged throughout the Levant, and then sized into jewelry with economic value in terms of their metal weight and social-religious value in terms of their color, shine, and sounds made when worn as pairs.

Recently identified Ammonite painted wares and black wares from Naṣbeh further clarify the connections between Transjordan and northern Judah (Figures 16.6–16.7; Brody 2014b). The Ammonite painted wares are comprised of small and large bowls or kraters, an amphoriskos or small jars, and juglets. While the small jar and juglets may have been valued for their contents, the open vessels—the bowls and kraters—must have been prized

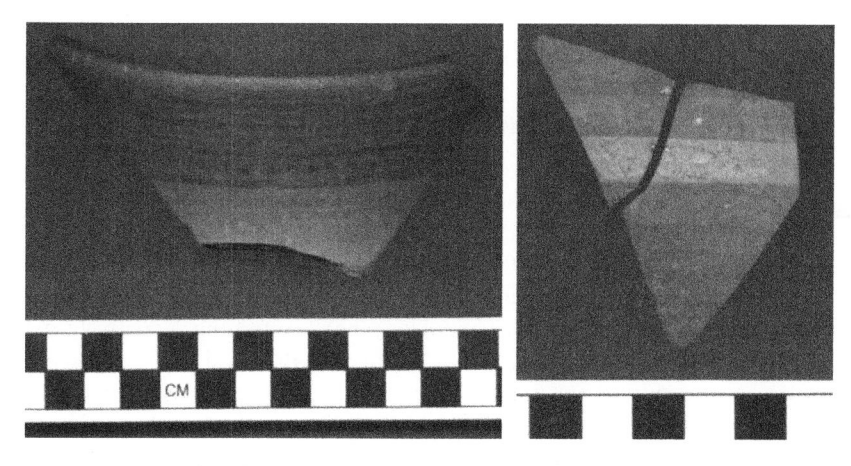

Figure 16.6 Two examples of Ammonite Painted Wares from Tell en-Naṣbeh. Image courtesy of the Badè Museum, Pacific School of Religion, based on original images by Rebecca Hisiger and Aaron Brody

Figure 16.7 Two examples of Ammonite Black Wares from Tell en-Naṣbeh. Image courtesy of the Badè Museum, Pacific School of Religion, based on original images by Rebecca Hisiger and Aaron Brody

as decorated utilitarian objects themselves since they could not have kept any contents contained in transport. Similarly, the corpus of Ammonite black wares is made up primarily of small bowls and variations on bowls, including chalices and a tripod bowl. As open vessels, these black ware ceramics were exchanged as products themselves. I have visually identified 42 vessels, or vessel fragments, from the Naṣbeh corpus as Transjordanian, and it is likely that there are other undecorated ceramic imports in the collection as well. This statistic far outnumbers the contemporary Phoenician ceramics at the site (Brody 2014a) and suggests more frequent or robust connections to the east than to the northwest. It also highlights socio-economic connections with Ammon and Edom, while texts in the Hebrew Bible and epigraphic finds highlight conflict and rivalry between Judah and the polities of Transjordan. Political enmity, however, does not preclude economic relations as commerce and social contact often continues between peoples despite antagonism among the ruling elite.

Localized Marketing System of Exchange and Barter

The contexts of the stratified examples of Transjordanian ceramics in the Iron IIB–IIC phase at Tell en-Naṣbeh may be used to elucidate the local mode of economy. The Ammonite painted wares and black wares show a relatively even distribution throughout most of the excavated portions of the site (Brody 2014b). There are no significant concentrations of these Ammonite wares, nor any signs of clustering of these imports in any particular building, compound, or specific area of the settlement. This type of patterning, a relatively even distribution of imported finds throughout a site, has been highlighted as the prime indicator of marketplace exchange in recent archaeological studies (Feinman and Garraty 2010; Stark and Garraty 2010). Similar distribution patterns of the Ammonite ceramics at Naṣbeh can be explained best by the type of open access to goods provided by marketplace exchanges.

This access to imported Ammonite ceramics is not necessarily a function of wealth. Four out of seven, or 57%, of Transjordanian wares found in architectural contexts came from three-room houses; while three out of seven, or 43%, were from larger four-room house structures (Brody 2014b). If we assume that wealthier families inhabited larger households, then the fact that Ammonite wares are less abundant in bigger domestic structures is a further indication of market exchange, as this suggests that families of different means had equal access to, and bartered for, the same types of foreign goods. This interpretation fits well with the limited textual evidence preserved in the Hebrew Bible that mentions several types of marketplaces, and varied modes of exchange, in regal/ritual centers and administrative cities (Master 2010; Nam 2012). The patterning of Ammonite imported wares at Tell en-Naṣbeh is the first material evidence presented that illustrates the utilization of market exchange in ancient Judah.

Discussion and Conclusions

Through a focus on economy and exchange in the fortified, large village or town site of Tell en-Naṣbeh, I have offered evidence that expands on Master's tripartite model of the economies of ancient kingdoms. Taking this bottom-up approach, focusing on the village and not the city, on the common and not the royal, on peripheral routes instead of main roads, I have added to the picture of the overall economies of late Iron Age Judah, an approach that can be applied to contemporary neighboring sites or polities as well. While Naṣbeh, and other third and fourth-tier settlements, exhibit very little evidence of royal contact let alone control, these village and town sites are projected to have housed over 85% of Judean agropastoralist society and generated the majority of the agricultural and pastoral products in the kingdom

(Orendi et al. 2017). Thus, Master's first context of exchange, "the monarchy," leaves the vast majority of the ancient population and the main producers out of his model. His market context of exchange is more robust, appropriately defining a tiered system of local and regional markets, which I would expand to include interregional and international markets while making room for non-royal initiative and control even between regions and nations, as is suggested by the Phoenician and Transjordanian material evidence from Iron IIB–IIC Naṣbeh (Nyman, Fogle, and Beaudry 2019). Finally, Master's third context of overlapping exchange, the trade route, needs to be further developed to include secondary and tertiary networks, like those byways that connected Tell en-Naṣbeh to the northwest to Phoenicia and to the east to Ammon. Most exchanges were likely local, within settlements themselves as households with surpluses of agricultural and pastoral goods and products gifted and bartered with their kin and neighbors. Regional exchanges of specialized craft products, such as utilitarian ceramics, between settlements were quite limited (Defonzo 2005) and may have favored these secondary and tertiary routes. Interregional and international exchanges typically favored the primary routes but are represented along secondary routes as well.

Expanding and nuancing our modeling of late Iron Age economy and exchange allows us to bring those less advantaged than the ruling elite into the picture and reveals varied tiers of differing exchange systems. These systems were held together and facilitated by a web of trade routes around which local, domestic, and imported products circulated and were distributed within, and between households, individual settlements, regions, and the polities of the late Iron Age southern Levant. Agricultural and animal products, the staples of every household's economy regardless of class, were primarily produced and consumed in a "survival subsistence economy" (Sasson 2014; see also Sapir-Hen, Gadot, and Finkelstein 2016). Regional exchanges may have circulated agropastoral products and finished goods crafted from regionally available resources such as ceramic vessels and their contents, which may have included grains, wine, or olive oil, iron agricultural tools, groundstone vessels and tools, and chipped stone tools (Brown 2014; Defonzo 2005; Ebeling and Rosenberg 2015; Gluhak and Rosenberg 2018; Gluhak, Rosenberg, and Ebeling 2016). One example of circulation between different regions within Judah can be traced through LMLK jars, which were manufactured in the Shephelah but were filled with products in the Judean settlements of Hebron, Ziph, Socoh, and *Mmšt* labeled on their handles. All four stamps are found at Tell en-Naṣbeh in the northern reaches of the kingdom at a considerable distance from the varied locations of the four sites where the jars were originally packed. Some of these local and regional exchanges would have been conducted with aid of the Judean system of weights, found at sites throughout the kingdom (Kletter 1998).

The local or regional subsistence economy coexisted with interregional marketing exchange systems for raw and finished goods not regionally available. These included imported foreign ceramics exchanged as objects, ceramic containers imported for their contents, semi-precious stone beads, bronze bangles and fibulae, shells from the Red Sea and the Mediterranean, textiles, glass beads, and glass weights, and cedar from Lebanon (Brody 2014a, 2014b; Reese 1991; Singer-Avitz 1999, 2018; Zwickel 2002). These local, regional, and interregional systems overlapped with national and imperial tributary economic systems dependent on taxation, produce from royal estates, tolls, gift exchange, tribute, and financial gains from state-sponsored warfare, all framed by a sophisticated system of silver bullion weight equivalencies and standards (Heijmans 2021; Thompson 2003). International goods and products imported into, or circulated through, Judah included ivory, carved ivories, silver bullion or *hacksilber*, silver and gold jewelry, wine, olive oil, tree resins, aromatic gums and spices, Buxus wood from Syria or Turkey, incense and spices from South Arabia and further east, semi-precious stone objects, carved tridacna shells, and dyed wool cloth (Brody 2014a, 2014b; Droß-Krüpe and Nosch 2016; Gilboa and Namdar 2015; Heijmans 2021; Holladay 1995, 2006; Singer-Avitz 1999, 2018; Steiner forthcoming; Thompson 2003; Wood, Montero-Ruiz, and Martinón-Torres 2019; Zwickel 2002).

This reframing (Feinman 2017) of our conceptualization of the ancient economy of Judah allows for a more holistic understanding of goods and products and their exchange and circulation within, and between, polities in the southern Levant. Our approach needs to be flexible enough to imagine subsistence economies, marketing economies, and tributary economies not only coexisting but intersecting and complementing, even competing with, one another; held together by a web of overland and maritime exchange routes. By the end of the late Iron Age, the routes interconnected from the southern Levant throughout the Mediterranean to the Atlantic coasts of Iberia and north Africa, and to Egypt, Kush, Assyria, Arabia, and further east to south Asia. Re-envisioning how various components of these southern Levantine segmentary, agropastoral societies functioned within differing, yet overlapping local, regional, interregional, and international exchange systems allow us to begin the important work of remodeling and reconstructing various economic foundations of the House of David.[3]

Notes

1 Presumably, the economic structures of the northern Kingdom of Israel in the Iron IIB period were similar to those of Judah, although its territory was much larger and diverse than the southern Kingdom and its interactions with the Assyrian empire differed. Hopefully, the modeling I suggest using Tell en-Naṣbeh as a case-study is applicable to the economy of the northern Kingdom, with some modifications in interregional interactions given its proximity to southern Phoenicia and southern Aram.

2 Some scholars consider Tell en-Naṣbeh to be urban or a city, see Faust 2012: 45, 72–77 and earlier references cited therein. As Faust 2012: 39–45 describes, the definition of what settlement should be interpreted as a city, or even as a town or village, is tricky. The criteria and definitions vary widely among scholars, may have varied within an ancient society over time and by region: and notions such as urban planning, state involvement in a site, and the degree of social stratification are notoriously challenging and highly interpretive. I view Naṣbeh as non-urban because it lacks any type of monumental architecture, besides the solid wall that surrounds the settlement. The buildings with the walls are all variations of pillared, three- and four-room, houses. To me, naming this type of settlement in English best maps on to our modern concepts of a town or large village; however, one that was fortified.

3 This case study glosses over probable changes in economy that occurred between the Iron IIB and IIC phases in various regions that made up the Kingdom of Judah, because of a lack of differentiation in possible phasing at Tell en-Naṣbeh. The site was excavated back in the 1920s–1930s using methods typical of the time, which were much less precise than current methodologies, and so we cannot separate out Naṣbeh's potential IIB phase from its IIC phase (Zorn 1994). A similar lack of differentiation in IIB and IIC phasing is noted for Tell Beit Mirsim, which was excavated around the same time as Naṣbeh (see comments in Finkelstein and Na'aman 2004). Changes in economy in the Shephelah in the 8th c., Iron IIB, and the 7th c., Iron IIC typically attributed to the later presence and demands of the Assyrian empire are not discernable in the remains from Naṣbeh. For an overview of those changes in the Shephelah region see Finkelstein and Na'aman 2004; for a treatment of the minimal secondary, if not tertiary, Assyrian influences in the material record at Naṣbeh, see Brody 2015.

Bibliography

Bauer, Alexander A., and Anna S. Agbe-Davies, eds. 2010. *Social Archaeologies of Trade and Exchange: Exploring Relationships Among People, Places, and Things*. Walnut Creek: Left Coast Press.

Ben-Shlomo, David, and Lauren McCormick. 2021. "Judean Pillar Figurines and 'Bed Models' from Tell En-Naṣbeh: Typology and Petrographic Analysis." *BASOR* 386: 23–46.

Boer, Roland. 2015. *The Sacred Economy of Ancient Israel*. Louisville: Westminster John Knox.

Brody, Aaron. 2009. "Mizpah, Mizpeh." Pages 116–17 in *NIDB* 4.

———. 2014a. "Interregional Interaction in the Late Iron Age: Phoenician and Other Foreign Goods from Tell En-Naṣbeh." Pages 55–69 in *Material Culture Matters: Essays on the Archaeology of the Southern Levant in Honor of Seymour Gitin*. Edited by John Spencer, Robert Mullins, and Aaron Brody. Winona Lake: Eisenbrauns.

———. 2014b. "Transjordanian Commerce with Northern Judah in the Iron II-Persian Period: Ceramic Indicators, Interregional Interaction, and Modes of Exchange at Tell En-Naṣbeh." Pages 59–93 in *"As for me, I will dwell at Mizpah…": The Tell En-Naṣbeh Excavations after 85 Years*. Edited by Jeffrey R. Zorn and Aaron Brody. Piscataway: Gorgias.

———. 2015. "Living in Households, Constructing Identities: Ethnicity, Boundaries, and Empire in Iron IIB-IIC Tell En-Naṣbeh." Pages 289–305 in *Household Studies in Complex Societies: (Micro) Archaeological and Textual Approaches*. Edited by Miriam Müller. Chicago: Oriental Institute of the University of Chicago.

———. 2018. "Materiality of Religion in Judean Households: A Contextual Analysis of Ritual Objects from Iron II Tell en-Naṣbeh." *NEA* 81: 212–21.

Brody, Aaron, and Elizabeth S. Friedman. 2007. "Bronze Bangles from Tell En-Naṣbeh: Cultural and Economic Observations on an Artifact Type from the Time of the Prophets," Pages 97–114 in *To Break Every Yoke: Essays in Honor of Marvin L. Chaney*. Edited by Robert B. Coote and Norman K. Gottwald. Sheffield: Sheffield Phoenix.

Brown, Stephanie H. 2014. "Iron in the Iron Age: The Life-Cycle of Agricultural Implements from Tell En-Naṣbeh." Pages 95–122 in *"As for me, I will dwell at Mizpah…": The Tell En-Naṣbeh Excavations after 85 Years*. Edited by Jeffrey R. Zorn and Aaron Brody. Piscataway: Gorgias. Chaney, Marvin L. 2017. *Peasants, Prophets, and Political Economy: The Hebrew Bible and Social Analysis*. Eugene: Cascade Books.

Defonzo, Ryan J. P. 2005. "Iron II Judah: An Intra-Regional Study of Production and Distribution." PhD diss., University of Toronto.

Droß-Krüpe, Kerstin, and Marie-Louise Nosch, eds. 2016. *Textiles, Trade and Theories: From the Ancient Near East to the Mediterranean*. Münster: Ugarit-Verlag.

Ebeling, Jennie, and Danny Rosenberg. 2015. "A Basalt Vessel Workshop and Its Products at Iron Age Hazor, Israel." *JFA* 40: 665–74. Faust, Avraham. 2012. *The Archaeology of Israelite Society in the Iron II*. Translated by Ruth Ludlum. Winona Lake: Eisenbrauns.

Feinman, Gary M. 2017. "Reframing Ancient Economies: New Models, New Questions." Pages 139–49 in *Eurasia at the Dawn of History: Urbanization and Social Change*. Edited by Manuel Fernández-Götz and Dirk Krausse. New York: Cambridge University Press.

Feinman, Gary M. and Christopher P. Garraty. 2010. "Preindustrial Markets and Marketing: Archaeological Perspectives." *ARA* 39: 167–91.

Finkelstein, Israel and Nadav Na'aman. 2004. "The Judahite Shephelah in the Late 8th and Early 7th Centuries BCE." *TA* 31: 60–79.

Gilboa, Ayelet, and Dvory Namdar. 2015. "On the Beginnings of South Asian Spice Trade with the Mediterranean Region: A Review." *Radiocarbon* 57: 265–83.

Gluhak, Tatjana, and Danny Rosenberg. 2018. "Back to the Source—Geochemical Data from Israel for the Provenance Analyses of Basaltic Rock Artefacts and Their Implications on Previous and Future Studies." *Archaeometry* 60: 1153–69.

Gluhak, Tatjana, Danny Rosenberg, and Jennie Ebeling. 2016. "Raw Material Variability as Archaeological Tools: Preliminary Results from a Geochemical Study of the Basalt Vessel Workshop at Iron Age Tel Hazor, Israel." *JLS* 3: 169–89.

Heijmans, Elon D. 2021. *The Origins of Money in the Iron Age Mediterranean World*. Cambridge: Cambridge University Press.

Hirth, Kenneth. 2020. *The Organization of Ancient Economies: A Global Perspective*. Cambridge: Cambridge University Press.

Holladay, John S. Jr. 1995. "The Kingdoms of Israel and Judah: Political and Economic Centralization in the Iron IIA-B (ca. 1000–750 BCE)." Pages 368–98 in *The Archaeology of Society in the Holy Land*. Edited by Thomas E. Levy. New York: Facts on File.

———. 2006. "Hezekiah's Tribute, Long-Distance Trade, and the Wealth of Nations ca. 1,000–600 BC: A New Perspective." Pages 309–31 in *Confronting the Past: Archaeological and Historical Essays on Ancient Israel in Honor of William G. Dever*. Edited by Seymour Gitin, J. Edward Wright, and J. P. Dessel. Winona Lake: Eisenbrauns.

Katz, Haya. 2008. *Land of Grain and Wine—Land of Olive Oil and Honey: The Economy of the Kingdom of Judah in the First Temple Period*. Jerusalem: Yad Izhak Ben-Zvi (Hebrew).

Keimer, Kyle H. "The Socioeconomic Impact of Hezekiah's Preparations for Rebellion." PhD diss., University of California, Los Angeles, 2011.

Kletter, Raz. 1998. *Economic Keystones: The Weight System of the Kingdom of Judah*. Sheffield: Sheffield Academic Press.

Master, Daniel M. 2010. "Institutions of Trade in I and II Kings." Pages 501–16 in *The Books of Kings*. Edited by André Lemaire and Baruch Halpern. Leiden: Brill.

———. 2014. "Economy and Exchange in the Iron Age Kingdoms of the Southern Levant." *BASOR* 372: 81–97.

McCown, Chester C., ed. 1947. *Tell en-Naṣbeh, Vol. 1: Archaeological and Historical Results*. Berkeley: Palestine Institute of Pacific School of Religion.

Miller, Marvin L., Ehud Ben Zvi, and Gary N. Knoppers, eds. 2015. *The Economy of Ancient Judah in Its Historical Context*. Winona Lake: Eisenbrauns.

Moreno Garcia, Juan Carlos, ed. 2021. *Markets and Exchanges in Pre-Modern and Traditional Societies*. Oxford: Oxbow Books.

Nam, Roger S. 2012. *Portrayals of Economic Exchange in the Book of Kings*. Leiden: Brill.

Nyman, James A., Kevin R. Fogle, and Mary C. Beaudry. 2019. *The Historical Archaeology of Shadow and Intimate Economies*. Gainesville: University Press of Florida.

Orendi, Andrea, Ladislav Smejda, Chris McKinny, Deborah Cassuto, Casey Sharp, and Itzick Shai. 2017. "The Agricultural Landscape of Tell Burna: Ecology and Economy of a Bronze Age/Iron Age Settlement in the Southern Levant." *JLE* 10: 165–88.

Reese, David S. 1991. "The Trade of Indo-Pacific Shells into the Mediterranean Basin and Europe." *OJA* 10: 159–96. Sapir-Hen, Lidar, Yuval Gadot, and Israel Finkelstein. 2016. "Animal Economy in a Temple City and Its Countryside: Iron Age Jerusalem as a Case Study." *BASOR* 375: 103–18.

Sasson, Aharon. 2014. *Animal Husbandry in Ancient Israel: A Zooarchaeological Perspective on Livestock Exploitation, Herd Management and Economic Strategies*. London: Routledge.

Singer-Avitz, Lily. 1999. "Beersheba—A Gateway Community in Southern Arabian Long-Distance Trade in the Eighth Century BCE." *TA* 26: 3–74.

———. 2018. "On Phoenicia's Trade Relations with Philistia and Judah under the Assyrian Hegemony: The Ceramic Evidence." Pages 186–215 in *The Southern Levant under Assyrian Domination*. Edited by Shawn Z. Aster and Avraham Faust. University Park: Eisenbrauns.

Skinner, G. William. 2001. *Marketing and Social Structure in Rural China*. Ann Arbor: Association for Asian Studies.

Stark, Barbara L., and Christopher P. Garraty. 2010. "Detecting Marketplace Exchange in Archaeology: A Methodological Review." Pages 33–59 in *Archaeological Approaches to Market Exchange in Ancient Societies*. Edited by Christopher P. Garraty and Barbara L. Stark. Boulder: University Press of Colorado.

Steiner, Margreet L. forthcoming. "A Closer Look: The Houses on the Southeastern Hill of Jerusalem in Economic Perspective." In *No Place Like Home: Ancient Near Eastern Houses and Households*. Edited by Laura Battini, Aaron Brody, and Sharon Steadman. Oxford: Archaeopress.

Stevens, Marty E. 2006. *Temples, Tithes, and Taxes: The Temple and the Economic Life of Ancient Israel*. Grand Rapids: Baker Academic.

Thompson, Christine M. 2003. "Sealed Silver in Iron Age Cisjordan and the 'Invention' of Coinage." *OJA* 22: 67–107.

Wampler, Joseph C. 1947. *Tell en-Naṣbeh, Vol. 2: The Pottery*. Berkeley: Palestine Institute of Pacific School of Religion.

Wood, Jonathan R., Ignacio Montero-Ruiz, and Marcos Martinón-Torres. 2019. "From Iberia to the Southern Levant: The Movement of Silver Across the Mediterranean in the Early Iron Age." *JWP* 32: 1–31.

Zorn, Jeffrey R. 1994. "Estimating the Population Size of Ancient Settlements: Methods, Problems, Solutions, and a Case Study." *BASOR* 295: 31–48.

Zorn, Jeffrey R. 2022. "Standing on Hole-y Ground: The Storage Pits at Tell en-Naṣbeh and the Role of the State." Pages 337–74 in *Material, Method, and Meaning. Papers in the Eastern Mediterranean Archaeology in Honor of Ilan Sharon*. Edited by Uri Davidovich, et al. Münster: Zaphon.

Zwickel, Wolfgang. 2002. *Edelsteine in der Bibel*. Mainz: Philipp von Zabern.

17
THE SOCIOECONOMICS OF FOOD AND FEASTING IN PRE-EXILIC ISRAEL AND JUDAH

Rebekah Welton

Food is a biological necessity for all human beings. Consequently, securing access to food was a core concern for ancient societies in which precarity and scarcity of food dominated the lives of ordinary people. As such, a large quantity of time was spent each day contributing to stable food supplies. Foodways are the culturally specific activities and meanings associated with food including diet, agriculture, pastoralism, slaughter, cooking, preserving, consumption, hospitality, feasting, and the identities and roles associated with these processes (Hastorf 2017: 14). Food thus constitutes a major component of the material culture of a given society, and as a substance that is ingested, has been termed 'embodied material culture' in that it is particularly bound up with the construction and maintenance of identity, at both individual and group levels (Dietler 2001: 72). The foodways of a particular community are inextricably linked with the social life of the group, from the status and role of individuals to the interconnected relationships between members and broader regional networks. The prominence of food in Israel and Judah is displayed in the texts of the Hebrew Bible, which are saturated with references to food and drink across all genres. The textual wealth of information relating to food must be integrated with archaeological data that have been recovered from ancient Levantine contexts and speak to the lives of ordinary people that did not participate in the formation of the ancient Hebrew texts. This chapter will provide an overview of the food and drink ancient Israelites and Judahites produced and consumed, and the significance of feasts and ritual consumption.

Diet

The following discussion recounts the main food items that ordinary Israelite and Judahites consumed while pursuing a survival subsistence strategy in their agricultural and pastoral labor (Sasson 2010: 22–23). Such a strategy entails the management of an ancient-world farmer's resource base in a way that mitigated risk and instead made optimal use of land, water, and livestock to ensure the survival of the household. This included careful management of the ratios of sheep to goats, limited use of cattle for plowing, a dependence on the lifetime products of animals (such as milk, wool, plowing power, and dung for fuel), and culling patterns that ensured these lifetime products were in secure supply. Such a strategy was likely to have included transhumance, which both widened the overall resource base of the farmer and reduced the risk of over-pasturing, disease, insect infestation, drought, and competition with other groups. This picture of agrarian-pastoral life is complicated by the fact that labor was extracted from these survival subsistence communities by the royal temple and palace to farm their own estates and to provide labor as cooks and bakers for royal consumers (Yee 2017). The diversion of this vital labor away from the rural communities increased the risk and workloads for the households affected (Yee 2017: 837). As I will demonstrate, there consequently was a wide disparity in the quality and quantity of resources between ordinary rural communities and the minority elites.

One of the most frequent finds in archaeological excavations in the southern Levant are the bones of domesticated animals, particularly goats, sheep, and cattle (Lev-Tov 2021: 77). These animals were raised primarily for the resources they provided during their lifetimes: milk, fleece, dung, and plowing power.[1] Goats and sheep provided one of the most important food resources on which ancient Israelites and Judahites depended. Milk could be processed into storable products such as cheese, butter, and yogurt, as well as being consumed as fresh or soured milk (Larkum 2016: 85).[2] Churns for processing dairy have been excavated from contexts as early as the Chalcolithic period (4500–3600 BCE) in the lower Galilee (Price et al. 2013: 185). The analyzed cooking vessel remains from Iron Age II (1000–586 BCE) cis-Jordanian sites also indicate that some soups and stews may well have been milk-based (Larkum 2016: 84).

Being a major source of protein and fat, dairy products were one of the most valuable resources the herd provided to the community, and consequently, the flocks had to be carefully managed and monitored to provide a stable supply of milk for the family (Welton 2022: 6–9). The milking of goats and sheep took place near the household structure, and therefore was likely a duty of the women of the household in addition to the processing of milk into other products, managing their storage, and organizing their distribution (Welton 2022: 9–10). Some Hebrew texts indicate the importance of dairy products, for example, Prov 27:23–27 indicates that the reward of the field will be the goats' milk that will nourish the household. It is also evident that offering dairy products to a guest was a signifier of hospitality, as we see in the stories of Abraham and his three guests (Gen 18:1) and Jael and Sisera (Judg 4:19, 5:25; cf. 1 Sam 17:17–18 and 2 Sam. 17:29). In the Hebrew Bible, dairy products are not mentioned as a part of a meal unless there is a guest being served. Because dairy products were so central to the household's daily fare, offering dairy to a guest was a gesture that socially enveloped the outsider into the household network (Welton 2020: 37–38).

Cattle were kept in low numbers as they required large amounts of fodder and water, but they were vital for preparing the ground to plant crops such as wheat and barley (Sasson 2010: 42). These grains were a major component of the diet, used in stews and porridges, brewed into beer, or ground into flour for baking bread (Ebeling 2021: 106–10). Grain could be stored easily without processing, which meant that grain-based foods were a staple of the ancient Israelite and Judahite diet year-round (Frank 2018: 163–70). In fact, grain could be stored for multiple years and thus acted as a buffer in years where harvests were less successful. Malting grain increases its caloric value, which means that the most effective use of grain was to malt it and then brew it into a thick, sweet beer. In ancient Israel and Judah beer was a primary source of calories in the form of carbohydrates and protein (Homan 2000: 84; Katz and Voigt 1984: 27). This beer, while being a primary food source, was mildly alcoholic, at about 2–4% alcohol, and could inebriate drinkers if consumed in large enough quantities. For most ancient Israelites and Judahites, beer was the most cost-effective alcohol to produce given that grain was so easily stored for long periods and thus was readily accessible at any time. Being a foodstuff produced without costly equipment in the home, beer was brewed by women and thus constituted a major aspect of Israelite and Judahite women's work (Ebeling and Homan 2008: 45–62). Beer (שכר) is frequently mentioned alongside wine in ancient Hebrew texts (Lev. 10:9; Num 28:7; Deut 14:26; Pro 31:6; Isa 28:7), but it does not receive the same amount of attention as wine—likely due to beer's association with the female domestic sphere and the greater preference of costly wine by the elite male creators of the texts (Welton 2020: 137–41). Despite this, there is one instance where beer is offered to Yahweh as part of the daily sacrifice (Num 28:7).

Like beer, bread making was a major aspect of a woman's role in the household; three hours a day would have been spent grinding grain into flour for an average household of six (Meyers 2002: 22). After the flour was produced, it was mixed with water and other ingredients like olive oil and salt, kneaded into dough, and baked into bread using a thermal installation fueled predominantly by animal dung.[3] Using grain for bread reduces the nutritional value of grain and so the energy expenditure on creating flour is instead justified because of a taste preference for bread over cooked grains in stews (Hayden, Nixon-Carcus, and Ansell 2016: 62–64). Bread starches are more quickly absorbed by the body compared to those in whole grains, meaning that bread consumption for ancient people with few other sources of sugar caused a pleasurable rush of glucose and a burst of energy (Hayden, Nixon-Carcus, and Ansell 2016: 66–67).

The preference for bread and its significance in the ancient Israelite and Judahite diet is evident in the multitude of references to bread (לחם) in Hebrew Bible texts where the term signifies food more generally (Gen 47:13; 1 Sam 30:12). Bread was also one of the most common and central components of offerings to the deities in both temple and domestic contexts (Lev 7:13; Num 6:15; Num 15:20–1; Jer 7:18). Indeed, the esteemed status of bread is also indicated by its pairing with another high-status and costly item, wine: "until I come and take you away to a land like your own land, a land of grain and wine, a land of bread and vineyards" (Isa 36:17; Deut 33:28).[4] Bread was a ubiquitous food item because being made from grain it was easily available to the majority of ancient Israelites and Judahites, but it was also valued in elite contexts because of the large quantity of labor it took to create and the pleasurable sensation bread instigated when eaten.

Lentils, peas, fava beans (broad beans), and chickpeas were the main pulse crops that supplemented grain, and their remains have been identified in the archaeological record (Mahler-Slasky and Kislev 2010: 2477–485; Mazar and Carmi 2001: 1333; Zohary, Hopf, and Weiss 2012: 80–81, 86, 89, 91). There is less archaeological evidence for items like garlic, onions, and leeks but literary evidence from Mesopotamia, and iconographic depictions from Egyptian tombs indicate that vegetable gardens were cultivated in Egypt and Mesopotamia growing melons, leeks, garlic, onion, lettuce, and possibly also beetroots and turnips (Zohary, Hopf, and Weiss 2012: 153; Potts 1997: 64–65). Garlic remains, however, have been discovered in a cave near Ein Gedi dating to the Middle Chalcolithic period (Zohary, Hopf, and Weiss 2012: 156). Awareness of some of these foods and their desirability is indicated by the literary depiction of the complaining Israelites in the wilderness who remember eating such items in Egypt: "the cucumbers, the melons, the leeks, the onions, and the garlic" (Num 11:5). Some nut varieties, such as almonds, pistachios, and walnuts, were also an accompaniment to the diet and were cultivated by ancient Israelites and Judahites (Shafer-Elliott 2021: 146–47).

Grapevines, fig trees, pomegranate trees, date palms, and olive trees were the most common fruit bearing trees. Fruit trees take years to start bearing fruit after planting, making fruit a much later delayed pay off than grain and pulse crops (Zohary, Hopf, and Weiss 2012: 114). Grapes, figs, and dates could be dried and stored for consumption later in the year.

Grapes were predominantly used to make wine; however, it was a costly endeavor (Walsh 2021: 128). Owning land for vineyards, having access to the necessary installations for the treading and straining of grapes, as well as the storage space and vessels for the wine, meant wine making was limited to the wealthier minority of society. Ordinary Israelites and Judahites would likely have had access only to small quantities of wine that likely was drunk at special occasions such as feasts, while beer would have been the more frequent alcoholic beverage. Ancient Hebrew scribes privileged wine, with vines reported as the first agricultural crop grown after the flood (Gen 9:20). Textually, wine is also a frequent element of offerings to the deity (Lev 23:13; Num 15:5) and has highly symbolic and metaphorical associations (Gen 49:11; Psalm 75:8; Isa 5:1–2).[5] The Samaria Ostraca record the distribution of high-quality "aged wine." This prestigious produce is thought to be the northern equivalent of the "wine on its dregs/lees" mentioned in ancient Judahite texts such as Ps 75:8; Isa 25:6; Jer 48:1 and Zeph 1:12. Suriano (2007: 31) speculates that the vats that have been excavated in the north, alongside the linguistic differences, highlight a possible regional variation in wine production: "One function of these extra vats, which were unique to the northern kingdom, may have been to allow a longer time-period for a portion of the newly produced wine to sit."

Olives were predominantly used for producing oil, which could be used in cooking, burnt in oil lamps to provide light, and used for anointing rituals (Exod 25:6; Lev 8:10; Num 11:8; 1 Kgs 17:12–16). There has previously been no evidence to suggest that olives were eaten whole in ancient Israel prior to the Hellenistic period, however very recent research has argued that olive pickling in seawater took place in the Middle Chalcolithic period (c. 6600 years ago) at the coastal site of Hishuley Carmel (Galili et al. 2021: 2218). It is not yet clear whether this technology was carried out at other sites, or whether it was in use in the Iron Age. Nevertheless, olive oil was an important economic resource that required specialized installations and equipment to produce, but which could be stored easily for long periods (Welch 2021: 118). As such, olive oil was likely to have been available in limited quantities to most ordinary, rural Israelites and Judahites. The "washed oil" recorded in the Samaria Ostraca appears to be, like the "aged wine," of the highest quality, which was also relatively rare compared to the "crushed oil" that was produced in larger quantities (Nam 2012: 157). These superlative gifts of wine and oil are thought to have been distributed by the Israelite king Joash, or his son Jeroboam II, to secure political power with key regional clan leaders who in return would provide safe access to valuable trade routes on the coast (Nam 2012: 160–61).

For many ordinary Israelites and Judahites, protein from fish and birds was likely a minor element of their diet. Fish was not eaten fresh. To transport fish over large distances in hot weather the fish would have to be dried, smoked, or salted to preserve it from bacterial decay and infestation from flies. Drying fish preserves it for several months, while smoking and salting allows it to remain in transit for even longer (Van Neer et al. 2004: 102). Consequently, it was possible to transport and sell preserved fish in Jerusalem and other sites at a distance from bodies of water, however, the cost of transport would probably have made fish too expensive for those who did not live in major urban centers (MacDonald 2008: 37–38). Large quantities of fish remains have been found in the City of David excavations from Iron Age II (Reich, Shukron, and Lernau 2007: 160), which may corroborate the fish markets mentioned at Jerusalem's Fish Gate in biblical texts (Zeph 1:10; Neh 3:3, 13:16; 2 Chr 33:14). Archaeological evidence does not confirm that the chukar partridge, turtledove, and pigeon were domesticated in Iron Age Israel and Judah, but instead hunted and captured from the wild (Altmann and Spiciarich 2020: 4; Fulton and Wapnish Hesse 2021: 175).

Partridges and pigeons were consumed in small quantities at Iron Age I and II sites based on the archaeological remains, but far greater quantities have been found in urban sites like Jerusalem (Altmann and Spiciarich 2020: 11). Bird meat was not a major component of diet because hunting for wild birds would have diverted significant attention and energy from the management of crops and domesticated animals. Similarly, wild animals like gazelle and deer were also hunted in small quantities, but due to the time and energy that hunting would have diverted from other necessary activities, game was not a frequent component of the diet (Fulton and Wapnish Hesse 2021: 176).

Honey appears to have been a highly valued food substance in ancient Israel and Judah but may not have been regularly accessible for ordinary Israelites and Judahites. There are two words in Hebrew which seem to refer to honeycomb: נפת which occurs five times (Ps 19:10; Prov 5:3, 24.23, 27.7; Song 4:11), and יער which occurs once in 1 Sam 14:27. דבש refers to bee honey in a number of cases: Deut 32:13 describes honey as being sucked out of a rock, a common location of bee hives; in Judg 14:8–18, Samson finds a beehive in the carcass of a lion; in 1 Sam 14:25–9 honey is found in a tree; in Ps 81:16 honey is again located in a rock, and there are several references to honey alongside honeycomb (Ps 19:10, Prov 24:13, Song 5:1). Archaeological evidence suggests that bee honey was also produced intentionally. At Iron Age IIA Tel Rehov, a total of 25 beehives have been unearthed, indicating that large-scale beekeeping was indeed practiced in Iron Age Israel (Mazar and Panitz-Cohen 2007: 202). The exact species of the honeybees at Tel Rehov were non-native Anatolian honeybees, which are much less aggressive, and produce three to eight times higher yields of honey compared to other species (Bloch et al. 2010: 11243). Maintaining the purity of the Anatolian line by preventing cross-breeding with local bees would have required sophisticated beekeeping strategies (Bloch et al. 2010: 11244), suggesting a legacy of highly skilled and experienced beekeepers. As the area around the hives had experienced destruction, and with the addition of further hives in the surrounding unexcavated areas, there could have been a total of 180 hives at Tel Rehov (Mazar and Panitz-Cohen 2007: 207). One hundred active hives could have yielded an estimated 300–500 kilograms of honey and 50–70 kilograms of beeswax per year (Mazar and Panitz-Cohen 2007: 211).

There is no mention of beekeeping in the Hebrew Bible, but honey is listed as one of the permitted first fruit offerings along with other foodstuffs that the Israelites produced, if the honey was not burnt (Lev 2:11–12). This text suggests that honey acquired from beekeeping rather than wild honey is the intended substance mentioned. The combined evidence points to a large-scale and developed strategy to produce honey and other bee products that could be sacrificed or traded.[6] The beehives uncovered at Tel Rehov are the only known examples of beekeeping in ancient Israel or Judah, and it is not currently possible to confirm how costly purchasing honey may have been. Given honey's relative rarity and the high esteem it is afforded in biblical texts (Welton 2022: 16–19), it is likely that most ordinary Israelites and Judahites did not have frequent access to large quantities of honey. The frequent expression "a land flowing with milk and honey" found in biblical texts (Exod 3:8) likely captures the idea of a plentiful and luxurious land, ranging from the vital but ubiquitous dairy products to the rarer but prestigious honey (Welton 2022).

Sheep and goats were likely slaughtered and eaten when the available land and its resources could no longer maintain the number of animals being raised. The farmer would then cull a quantity of the young males of the herd in order that females had sufficient pasturage and thus could continue to provide milk and produce future offspring. This choice also meant that young males did not deplete the supply of milk on which the human owners depended. Such a strategy has been shown to keep levels of wool, milk, and meat high and is a common approach used by pastoralists cross-culturally (Cribb 1984: 168; Sasson 2010: 39–41). Meat consumption was therefore a rare event, rather than a regular occurrence, for ordinary Israelite and Judahite pastoralists. When a herd required culling, the resulting meat could facilitate a large community gathering to enjoy the shared consumption of the rare foodstuff. Shafer-Elliott (2013: 111) has demonstrated that cooking pot types found at certain archaeological sites provide an indication of the quantities of meat eaten by rural and urban demographics, the former eating far less. Faunal remains show that rather than there being an exact age at which culling occurred, it was between the range of one and three years, as this was the age at which goats and sheep start to "cost" more to keep alive in relation to their body size (Sasson 2010: 40). While the decision to kill off members of the herd would have depended on a variety of factors—the general health of the herd, available pasturage, and milk and wool production levels—such flexibility meant at least some animals could be slaughtered at important milestones in the agricultural calendar. These agricultural milestones were marked by feasting activities.

Feasts

In ancient Israel and Judah, ritual time was inherently linked with the natural world. For ordinary farmers both growing crops and raising herds, the year was marked by their experience of the natural world, from observations of the moon and the ripening of crops to significant life cycle events such as birth and death (Davis 2020: 204).

Biblical texts such as Ps 81:3[4], 2 Kgs 4:23, and Amos 8:4–6 suggest that the New Moon (חדש) was a ritual time which was marked out by particular activities, such as blowing a horn, visiting a prophet, and/or suspending usual daily work. Some texts also indicate that food offerings were made to deities at this time of the month (Isa 1:13; Num 29:6) and that a family feasting event may also have been held (1 Sam 20:24–34). Van der Toorn (1996: 211–13) interprets the New Moon feast in 1 Sam 20 as an equivalent to the Mesopotamian *bubbulum* meal, which was a monthly family feast and a ritual time to refrain from work. It is difficult to know whether the above biblical references reflect elite or royal activities alone, or whether a wider proportion of the Israelite or Judahite population marked the transformation of the moon with ritual activities. Given that observing the moon was accessible to all communities, it does seem reasonable that the moon's cycles did mark time even for ordinary farmers, but to what extent this involved a feast is less secure. David's participation in a non-royal family meal in Bethlehem (1 Sam 20:28–29) might demonstrate that ordinary people did hold family meals at this time of the month, and some scholars have argued that the venerated ancestors of the family were believed to participate in these feasting events (Sonia 2020: 52; van der Toorn 1996: 211–18).

The wheat harvest, occurring in spring, was one of the most important agricultural events in the calendar. A successful harvest was celebrated by what is referred to as the Feast of the Harvest (קציר) in Exod 23:16. The feast displayed thanksgiving to the deity for providing a good crop of wheat—the preferred grain for making bread due to the better rise caused by wheat's higher protein content (Zohary, Hopf, and Weiss 2012: 23). A sheaf of wheat may have been offered to the deity prior to consuming any of the new produce as an act of gratitude (Lev 23:10–17; cf. Exod 23:16). Given the daily labor and constant anxiety of disease, drought, and other environmental conditions, the opportunity to rest and celebrate the relief of having a secure food supply meant that the harvest feast was an emotionally charged highlight of the year (Meyers 2012: 153–55). A larger group of people than the household unit would have congregated for a shared, commensal celebration, thus adding to the excitement of the event. This feast facilitated heightened social interactions, building intra-community networks that could assist each other by sharing food resources when needed, and facilitating the defense of local areas. The gathering of multiple communities at feasts also provided an opportunity for parents to seek out potential mates for their children (Meyers 2012: 160–61). The formation of new households, or the extension of new ones, via the partnering of younger household members, was an important activity that increased the workforce of the unit, making it more productive and resilient. Thus, feasts were important for both social cohesion and future socioeconomic stability (Greer 2021: 300).

The fruit harvest, or what Exod 23:16 calls the Feast of Ingathering (אסף), was also a significant feasting time, taking place in the autumn. This was the stage in the agricultural cycle at which fruits, such as figs, dates, and pomegranates, could be picked from their trees. Similarly, grapes and olives could also be harvested, and thus wine making and olive pressing activities could commence for those wealthy enough to own vineyards and olive orchards. Unsuccessful grape harvests in biblical texts hint at how successful harvest times might typically have been celebrated: "Joy and gladness are taken away from the fruitful field; and in the vineyards no songs are sung, no shouts are raised; no treader treads out wine in the presses; the vintage-shout is hushed" (Isa 16:10; cf. Jer 48:33; Isa 24:7–11). As the grape harvest signified the promise of wine and drunkenness, which are frequently associated with joy (Welton 2020: 202–23), it is logical that such a harvest-time celebration would emphasize joyful activities like dancing, singing, and playing instruments. Most feasts would have included the consumption of beer and wine to assist in the commensality and formation of social bonds, but it is possible that feasts associated with grapes and wine production may well have been particularly focused on alcohol consumption.

A third agricultural festival is associated with the ripening of the barley crops, which took place prior to the wheat harvest in spring. Biblical texts such as Exod 23:15 and 34:18 refer to this as the Feast of Unleavened Bread (מצות). Barley was an important grain for the beer brewing activities of the household (Hayden, Canuel, and Shanse 2013: 123), but was not as beneficial as wheat for baking risen bread. Barley was also important because it provided fodder for livestock and was hardier than wheat, meaning barley acted as a kind of "plan b" should the wheat harvest fail (Zohary, Hopf, and Weiss 2012: 52; Potts 1997: 59–60). For this reason, it is possible that the ritual act of eating unleavened barley bread prior to the wheat harvest acted as a kind of privation ritual performed to display to the deity an intense need for a successful wheat harvest (Farber 2019: 7). By conspicuously consuming the less prestigious food (flat bread rather than risen wheat bread), the aim was to make evident the dependence the ancient Israelite or Judahite agriculturalists had on the deity and thus they worked to ensure the deity did not bring disease or drought that would negatively affect the wheat in the weeks or months to come. This reasoning may provide some explanation for the command to either remove all leaven or not to eat leaven as found in Exod 12:15–20; Exod 13:3–7; Deut 16:3–4.

Later texts begin to refer to the Feast of the Ingathering as the Festival of Booths (Deut 16:13; Lev 23:34; Zech 14:16), and the Feast of the Harvest as the Day of First Fruits or Festival of Weeks (Num 28:26 cf. Lev 23:15–20) and start to associate these events with other meanings beyond simply agriculture. These later meanings served to construct Israelite identity and history in the wake of the Babylonian exile (Davis 2020; Farber 2019). The Festival of Unleavened Bread similarly comes to be associated with the history of the Israelites by combining it with the Passover, which itself appears to be a feasting event whose ritual connotations shifted over time. Biblical texts contain multiple amendments and redactions to feasts and their associated meanings. Passover is particularly affected due to the post-exilic anxieties about Israel's history and identity that found an effective expression and resolution through the construction of the story of the Exodus (Levenson 1993: 44–46; Niesiołowski-Spanò 2020: 347–48; Prosic 1999: 84–86; Van Seters 2003). It is consequently very difficult to confirm the historical existence of a pre-exilic Passover that was celebrated as an annual feast tied to the Feast of Unleavened Bread. A tentative alternative might be the existence of an ad hoc apotropaic or thanksgiving sacrifice linked to divinely granted protection and/or fertility (Niesiołowski-Spanò 2020: 346–47; Prosic 1999: 90–92).

The spring event of sheep shearing was another time of festivity given that, like the above agricultural harvests, the event marked the culmination of a year's labor and the successful procurement of a vital resource: wool. Multiple biblical texts mention sheep shearing (Gen 31:19; 38:12–13; 1 Sam 25:7; 2 Sam 13:24), but the association between sheep shearing and feasting is most apparent in the two occurrences in Samuel. There is evidence that ritualized sheep shearing feasts were practiced in comparable ancient societies, so it is reasonable to assume that ancient Israelite and Judahite pastoralists also celebrated a successful supply of wool (Geoghegan 2008: 148–51). The feasting activities involved the consumption of food, including meat from sheep or lambs, as well as drinking alcohol to bring about joyful social commensality. Some of the food intended for the sheep shearing feast in 1 Sam 25 is recounted: "Two hundred loaves, two skins of wine, five sheep ready dressed, five measures of parched grain, one hundred clusters of raisins, and two hundred cakes of figs." Feasters at both sheep shearing feasts in Samuel become merry with wine (1 Sam 25:26; 2 Sam 13:28–9). It is possible that Laban is distracted by the festivities of the sheep shearing in Gen 31:19–20, allowing Rachel to steal the household gods and flee with Jacob. Culling male animals at this time of shearing to reduce the size of the flock would have made good sense as the farmer would gain the benefit of the wool without the continued "expense" of raising additional animals that would simultaneously deplete the household's milk supply. Sacrificing animals at this particular feast thus carried an association of thanksgiving to the deity for the fertility of the flock, and their lifetime products, on which the Israelite and Judahite households depended.

Feasts were also held that were not linked to the annual cycle of agricultural and pastoral labor but were nevertheless associated with the life cycle and the socioeconomic resilience of the household unit. Events which saw the growth of the household, for example by taking a woman as a wife or by having children, celebrated the potential for future contributions of labor and thus the continuation of that household's survival and lineage. Consequently, these events were still bound up with concerns over the fertility and food of the household and fittingly were celebrated via shared consumption at feasts.

Large banquets that likely spanned several days were held to celebrate the taking of a wife as certain biblical narratives illustrate (Gen 29:27; Judg 14:12; Tob 8:19–21, 10:7). The feasts facilitated the integration of a new member who would subsequently be able to provide labor to the household, such as grinding grain, baking bread, and brewing beer. The feast was therefore a time of joy and would have included alcohol and large quantities of food, which may have been provided as part of the bride price paid by the groom's family as Mesopotamian sources suggest (Stol 2016: 112–4).

The economic considerations that pervaded the occurrence of taking a wife are perhaps illustrated by the narrative in Gen 29:15–31:21 in which the loss of Jacob's labor is a point of anxiety for Laban. Laban does not wish to lose the labor supplied by Jacob, Rachel, and Leah, and their slaves, but Jacob equally wishes to establish his own household with the labor provided by his new wives and their slaves (De-Whyte 2018: 187–88). Conception was expected to occur as quickly as possible, demonstrating the socioeconomic value of the woman who could provide offspring, and thus a larger workforce, to support the household (De-Whyte 2018: 29, 48–51).

In broader ancient Near Eastern culture, it is apparent that to secure fertility and pregnancy, sacrifices and feasts could be held in honor of the deities (De-Whyte 2018: 37–38). Similar ritual activity is perhaps preserved in several Hebrew Bible stories in which meals, feasts, or sacrifices are made to divine figures or prophets who grant pregnancy to a previously infertile couple (Gen 18:1–14; Judg 13; 2 Kgs 5:8–17). The birth of a child however does not seem to have been celebrated with much significance. By contrast, the time at which a baby is successfully weaned is deemed to be a time to celebrate with a feast or offering (Gen 21:8; 1 Sam 1:24–25). Evidence in the material culture of ancient Israel and Judah also suggests that weaning was marked by a ritual event. Heavily breasted figurines of women, sometimes referred to as Judean pillar figurines, have been recovered from Iron Age contexts and are frequently broken at their strongest part, suggesting an intentional breakage to mark the successful transition from breastfeeding to solid foods (Stavrakopoulou 2016: 357). This transition was important for the child and the household as it signified the likelihood that the baby would now survive to adulthood and thus become able to contribute to the socioeconomic labor which supplied the household with food. A weaning feast thus socially integrated the child into the productive network of the household via the shared and ritualized consumption of food, and thus signified the continued resilience and survival of the family.

The death of a member of the ancient Israelite or Judahite household would have been marked with ritual activity to mourn and commemorate the deceased (Lewis 2002: 190–94; Olyan 2004: 60; Sonia 2020: 51–64). Many texts from the ancient Near East recount offerings of food and drink for the dead, suggesting that such practices were common in the wider cultural milieu to which ancient Israel and Judah belonged (Sonia 2020: 26–50; Suriano 2021a). In the grave remains of many Judahite burial sites certain objects repeatedly turn up such as bowls, plates, ladles, food storage jars, jugs, cooking pots, and faunal remains (Bloch-Smith 1992: 72–82, 103–38; Sonia 2020: 56–63; Suriano 2021a: 322).

There are some rare occurrences of plates of lamb excavated from tombs, one in Beth-Shemesh Tomb 2 and another in a tomb at Gezer (Suriano 2021b: 129–30). Utensils and plates of food were likely left with the dead in tombs to provide them with sustenance. It is also likely that living relatives, after depositing the body, held a ritualized feast in the tomb and left the vessels and other utensils behind. This feasting and feeding of the dead was an act of commensality by the living, which likely fostered kinship bonds and positive relations with the recently dead and other ancestors (Suriano 2021a: 328). Olyan (2004: 60) has argued that invoking the name of the dead and bringing food offerings served to reconstruct the social relationship between the living and the deceased family member. Perhaps part of this resocialization involved understanding the deceased member to have become a venerated ancestor who could now participate in household life via ensuring the fertility of the land, animals, and human family (Lewis 1989: 31; Olyan 2005: 609, note 25). However, the idea that the dead had supernatural powers to engage in reciprocal acts has been contested (Schmidt 1996: 5–13; Suriano 2021a: 327).

Some biblical texts indicate such practices were normative in ancient Israel and Judah. Deuteronomy 26:14 states, "I have not eaten of it [the sacred portion of the tithe] while in mourning; I have not removed any of it while I was unclean; and I have not offered any of it to the dead." This command is the only one which relates to offering food to the dead and it is not an absolute rule outlawing all offerings to the dead. Instead, it only specifies that the tithed food should not be offered to the dead; not that it is forbidden to make offerings to the dead in general. The reason for this is likely due to the corpse impurity that would transfer to the food, it was vital that this impurity did not then become associated with the offerings made to Yahweh (Suriano 2021b: 137–38). Psalm 106:28 hints at sacrifices to the dead, albeit in a critical tone. Later texts also point to the practice of food being left on graves (Tob 4:17; Sir 30:18).

Other Ritual Consumption

Rather than an occasion for feasting like the examples I have already discussed, the *marzēaḥ* appears to be a different kind of context in which festive drinking took place. Textual references to the *marzēaḥ* originate from Ebla, Ugarit, Emar, Moab, Elephantine, Phoenicia, Nabataea, Palmyra, Rabbinic literature, and the Madaba map (McLaughlin 2001; Na'aman 2015: 215). While not necessarily referring to the same practice, references to the *marzēaḥ* span a period from the second half of the third millennium BCE to the 6th century CE—a period of 3000 years (McLaughlin 2001: 66). The term at times referred to the group members of the institution or the banquet itself and has an associated divine patron or religious association (McLaughlin 2001: 34–35, 64–65). It has also been understood to be an elite group who could own property, frequently including vineyards (McLaughlin 2001: 35, 66–68); however, more recently it has been suggested that a broader segment of society could have participated in this drinking activity (Na'aman 2015: 220–22).

The *marzēaḥ* is mentioned twice in the Hebrew Bible (Amos 6:7; Jer 16:5). This type of feast was diacritical in nature, likely being attended by elites, and had cultic functions. In Amos 6:4–7 the *marzēaḥ* participants are described as drinking wine from a large cultic vessel called a *mizrāq*, eating meat from costly animals, and lounging about enjoying music.[7] A possible *mizrāq* from Tel Dan has been identified by Greer (2010: 36 n46) and offers a possible insight into the type of vessels *marzēaḥ* feasts employed. While the occurrence of a '*marziḫu* house' in Jer 16:5–7 precedes an instruction not to perform a range of mourning customs, the *marzēaḥ* is not inherently associated with funerary or mortuary rites (McLaughlin 2001: 70–79). We must however assume that a *marzēaḥ* could feature as a locus of mourning activities as well as other occasions. Further biblical texts that do not use the term *marzēaḥ* have also been identified as likely allusions to the *marzēaḥ*, such as Judg 9:27 and 2 Kgs 9:30–37 (Na'aman 2015: 221–22), and Amos 4:1; Hos 4:16–19; Isa 28:7–8 and Ezek 39:17–20 (McLaughlin 2001: 215).

Sacrificial offerings of both meat and vegetal items such as grain, flour, bread, beer, and wine were a significant aspect of the ritual consumption of ancient Israelites and Judahites. Bread cakes and drink offerings – probably of beer – were made for a deity referred to as the Queen of Heaven (Jer 7:18; 44:17–19, 25). This ritual activity is reported as involving the whole family and that such worship of the Queen of Heaven was carried out in Judah by kings and other officials (Jer 44:17–18).[8] This household worship is particularly significant because it illustrates the ritual facilitation women could perform through their production of bread and beer (Welton 2020: 114–15).

Animal sacrifice, on the other hand, was an element of worship predominantly performed by males. For ordinary pastoral communities, the sacrifice of animals likely did not carry the same connotations as the detailed accounts of sacrifice we see in biblical texts. Instead, the ritual slaughter of an animal for more ordinary households likely signified the loss of a valued household animal on which the family had depended and was an act of thanksgiving to the deities for the household's ongoing fertility and survival (Welton 2021: 66–68). The slaughter of a domesticated animal not only facilitated the shared consumption of the meat between human household members but also included the participation of deities and venerated ancestors. The worship of specific deities acted as an identity marker of the community.

Sacrifices to deities that were deemed "foreign," or otherwise non-normative, were rendered socially deviant. Examples of so-called deviant consumption of food and alcohol may be in biblical texts such as Exod 34:14–16; Num 25:1–5; Isa 65:2–12; and 1 Sam 2:12–17, and this kind of worship may lay behind the accusation of being a זולל and a סבא (Deut 21:18–21; Prov 23:19–21, 28:7).[9]

Summary

As this discussion has demonstrated, daily life for the most part revolved around the essential need to secure food for the ancient Israelite household. The most obvious activities are those directly related to food production and preparation such as milking animals, grinding grain, and cooking meals, but other activities are also entangled with the constant and perpetual need for food security. Ritual feasting activities mark modifications to the household workforce, whether that is through gaining a woman or weaned child, or losing a person who is mourned, but fed even in death. Harvest times mark rare pauses from constant labor, providing the opportunity to enjoy the produce that household members and divine benevolence have brought to fruition. This vast amount of labor is intensified by the frequent risk of disease, drought, and famine, in addition to the extractive state which likely also added to household pressures. Food and drink marked the time of the ordinary, Israelite/Judahite household, as their production and consumption structured not just the hours of the day but also annual patterns of activity. It is this all-encompassing nature of food that affords it the rich metaphorical and symbolic power we see in ancient texts. It is additionally the reason the food and drink of Israelite/Judahite cultures should be emphasized as a significant aspect of the historical and socioeconomic context when investigating biblical texts and the lives of ordinary Israelites and Judahites.

Notes

1 The designation "lifetime products" is preferable to "secondary products" because such products were not secondary at all but rather the priority. Accordingly, so-called "primary products," such as meat and bone, are best described as "final products" (Hesse 1984: 260; Helmer and Vigne 2007).
2 For a detailed overview of the preservation of dairy products, drawing on a range of ethnographic sources, see London (2016: 120–23) and Palmer (2002).
3 Previous scholarship has referred to specific installation types such as the *tabun* or the *tannur*, however see Ebeling and Rogel (2015: 343–45).
4 All biblical quotations are taken from the NRSV.
5 For a more detailed overview of wine production and wine in biblical texts see Welton (2020: 121–36).
6 For example, Gen 43:11; 2 Sam 17:29; 1 Kgs 14:3; 2 Chr 31:5; Ezek 27:17.
7 For helpful analyses of this passage, see Greer (2007) and DeGrado (2020).
8 For further information about the Queen of Heaven, see Römer (2015: 170–72), Ackerman (2003: 461–64) and Houtman (1999: 678–80).
9 For a detailed analysis of these texts and the concept of deviant consumption, see Welton (2020: 224-82).

Bibliography

Ackerman, Susan. 2003. "At Home with the Goddess." Pages 455–68 in *Symbiosis, Symbolism, and the Power of the Past: Canaan, Ancient Israel, and Their Neighbors, from the Late Bronze Age Through Roman Palaestina*. Edited by William G. Dever and Seymour Gitin. Winona Lake: Eisenbrauns.

Altmann, Peter, and Abra Spiciarich. 2020. "Chickens, Partridges, and the /Tor/ of Ancient Israel and the Hebrew Bible." *WO* 50: 2–30.

Bloch, G., and T. M. Francoy, I. Wachtel, N. Panitz-Cohen, S. Fuchs, and A. Mazar. 2010. "Industrial Apiculture in the Jordan Valley During Biblical Times with Anatolian Honeybees." *PNAS* 107: 11240-244.

Bloch-Smith, Elizabeth. 1992. *Judahite Burial Practices and Beliefs About the Dead*. Sheffield: Sheffield Academic Press.

Cribb, Roger. 1984. "Computer Simulation of Herding Systems as an Interpretive and Heuristic Device in the Study of Kill-Off Strategies." Pages 161–70 in *Animals in Archaeology Vol. 3: Early Herders and Their Flock*. Edited by Juliet Clutton-Brock and Caroline Grigson. Oxford: British Archaeological Reports.

Davis, Andrew R. 2020. "Sacred and Ritual Times" Pages 198–206 in *The Oxford Handbook of Ritual and Worship in the Hebrew Bible*. Edited by Samuel E. Balentine. Oxford: Oxford University Press.

DeGrado, Jessie. 2020. "An Infelicitous Feast: Ritualized Consumption and Divine Rejection in Amos 6.1–7." *JSOT* 45: 178–97.

De-Whyte, Janice Pearl Ewurama. 2018. *Wom(b)an: A Cultural-Narrative Reading of the Hebrew Bible Barrenness Narratives*. Leiden: Brill

Dietler, Michael. 2001. "Theorizing the Feast: Rituals of Consumption, Commensal Politics and Power in African Contexts." Pages 65–114 in *Feasts: Archaeological and Ethnographic Perspectives on Food Politics and Power*. Edited by Michael Dietler and Brian Hayden. Tuscaloosa: University of Alabama Press.

Ebeling, Jennie R. 2021 "Grains, Bread, and Beer." Pages 99–112 in *T&T Handbook of Food in the Hebrew Bible and Ancient Israel*. Edited by Janling Fu, Cynthia Shafer-Elliott and Carol Meyers. London: T&T Clark.

Ebeling, Jennie R., and Michael M. Homan. 2008. "Baking and Brewing Beer in the Israelite Household: A Study of Women's Cooking Technology." Pages 45–62 in *The World of Women in the Ancient and Classical Near East*. Edited by Beth. A. Nakhai. Newcastle: Cambridge Scholars.

Ebeling, Jennie R., and M. Rogel. 2015. "The Tabun and Its Misidentification in the Archaeological Record." *Levant* 47: 328–49.

Farber, Zev I. 2019. "Israelite Festivals: From Cyclical Time Celebrations to Linear Time Commemorations." *Religions* 10: 323, 1–19.

Frank, Tim. 2018. *Household Food Storage in Ancient Israel and Judah*. Oxford: Archaeopress.

Fulton, Deirdre N., and Paula Wapnish Hesse. 2021. "Underrepresented Taxa: Fish, Birds, and Wild Game." Pages 171–81 in *T&T Handbook of Food in the Hebrew Bible and Ancient Israel*. Edited by Janling Fu, Cynthia Shafer-Elliott, and Carol Meyers. London: T&T Clark.

Galili, E., D. Langgut, J. F. Terral, O. Barazani, A. Dag, L. Kolska Horwitz, I. Ogloblin Ramirez, B. Rosen, M. Weinstein-Evron, S. Chaim, E. Kremer, S. Lev-Yadun, E. Boaretto, Z. Ben-Barak-Zelas, and A. Fishman. 2021. "Early Production of Table Olives at a Mid-7th Millennium BP Submerged Site Off the Carmel Coast (Israel)." *Scientific Reports* 11: 2218, 1–15.

Geoghegan, Jeffrey C. 2008. "The 'Biblical' Origins of Passover." Pages 147–62 in *Sacred History, Sacred Literature: Essays on Ancient Israel, The Bible and Religion in Honor of R. E. Friedman on His Sixtieth Birthday*. Edited by Shawna Dolansky. Winona Lake: Eisenbrauns.

Greer, Jonathan S. 2007. "A *Marzeaḥ* and a *Mizrāq*: A Prophet's Melee with Religious Diversity in Amos 6.4–7." *JSOT* 32: 243–62.

———. 2010. "An Israelite *Mizrāq* at Tel Dan?" *BASOR* 358: 27–45.

———. 2021. "Feasting and Festivals." Pages 297–318 in *T&T Handbook of Food in the Hebrew Bible and Ancient Israel*. Edited by Janling Fu, Cynthia Shafer-Elliott, and Carol Meyers. London: T&T Clark.

Hastorf, Christine. 2017. *The Social Archaeology of Food: Thinking About Eating from Prehistory to the Present*. Cambridge: Cambridge University Press.

Hayden, Brian, Neil Canuel, and Jennifer Shanse. 2013. "What Was Brewing in the Natufian? An Archaeological Assessment of Brewing Technology in the Epipaleolithic." *JAMT* 20: 102–50.

Hayden, Brian, Laurie Nixon-Darcus, and Logan Ansell. 2016. "Our 'Daily Bread'?: The Origins of Grinding Grains and Breadmaking." Pages 73–94 in *Exploring the Materiality of Food 'Stuffs': Transformations, Symbolic Consumption and Embodiments*. Edited by Louise Steel and Katharina Zinn. London: Routledge.

Helmer, D., and J. Vigne. 2007. "Was Milk a 'Secondary Product' in the Old World Neolithisation Process? Its Role in the Domestication of Cattle, Sheep and Goats." *Anthropozoologica* 42: 9–40.

Hesse, Brian. 1984. "These Are Our Goats: The Origins of Herding in West Central Iran." Pages 243–64 in *Animals in Archaeology, Volume 3: Early Herders and Their Flock*. Edited by J. Clutton-Brock and C. Grigson. Oxford: British Archaeological Reports.

Homan, Michael M. 2000. "Beer and Its Drinkers: An Ancient Near Eastern Love Story." *NEA* 67: 84–94.

Houtman, C. 1999. "Queen of Heaven." Pages 678–80 in *Dictionary of Deities and Demons in the Bible*. Edited by Karel Van der Toorn, B. Becking, and P. W. van der Horst. Cambridge: Eerdmans.

Katz, Solomon H., and Mary M. Voigt. 1986. "Bread and Beer: The Early Use of Cereals in the Human Diet." *Expedition* 28: 23–34.

Larkum, Mary K. *Clay Pot Cookery: Dairy, Diet and Class during the South Levantine Iron Age II Period*. PhD diss., University of Massachusetts Amherst, 2016.

Levenson, Jon D. 1993. *The Death and Resurrection of the Beloved Son: The Transformation of Child Sacrifice in Judaism and Christianity*. New Haven: Yale University Press.

Lev-Tov, Justin. 2021 "Animal Husbandry: Meat, Milk and More." Pages 77–98 in *T&T Handbook of Food in the Hebrew Bible and Ancient Israel*. Edited by Janling Fu, Cynthia Shafer-Elliott, and Carol Meyers. London: T&T Clark.

Lewis, Theodore J. 1989. *Cults of the Dead in Ancient Israel and Ugarit*. Atlanta: Scholars Press.

———. 2002. "How Far Can Texts Take Us? Evaluating Textual Sources for Reconstructing Ancient Israelite Beliefs About the Dead." Pages 169–217 in *Sacred Time Sacred Place: Archaeology and the Religion of Israel*. Edited by Barry Gittlen. Winona Lake: Eisenbrauns.

London, Gloria. 2016. *Ancient Cookware from the Levant: An Ethnoarchaeological Perspective*. Sheffield: Equinox.

MacDonald, Nathan. 2008. *What Did the Ancient Israelites Eat? Diet in Biblical Times*. Grand Rapids: Eerdmans.

Mahler-Slasky, Yael and Mordechai E. Kislev. 2010. "Lathyrus Consumption in Late Bronze and Iron Age Sites in Israel: An Aegean Affinity" *JAS* 37: 2477–485.

Mazar, Amihai and Israel Carmi. 2001. "Radiocarbon Dates from Iron Age Strata at Tel Beth Shean and Tel Rehov." *Radiocarbon* 43: 1333–342.

Mazar, Amihai and Nava Panitz-Cohen. 2007. "It Is the Land of Honey: Beekeeping at Tel Reḥov." *NEA* 70: 202–19.

McLaughlin, John L. 2001. *The Marzēaḥ in the Prophetic Literature: References and Allusions in Light of the Extra-Biblical Evidence*. Leiden: Brill.

Meyers, Carol. 2002. "Having Their Space and Eating There Too: Bread Production and Female Power in Ancient Israelite Households." *Nashim* 5: 14–44.

———. 2012. "The Function of Feasts: An Anthropological Perspective on Israelite Religious Festivals." Pages 141–68 in *Social Theory and the Study of Israelite Religion*. Edited by Saul Olyan. Atlanta: SBL.

Na'aman, Nadav. 2015. "Four Notes on the Ancient Near Eastern marzeaḥ." Pages 215–22 in *Open-Mindedness in the Bible and Beyond: A Volume of Studies in Honour of Bob Becking*. Edited by Marjo Korpel and Lester L. Grabbe. London: Bloomsbury.

Nam, Roger S. 2012. "Power Relations in the Samaria Ostraca." *PEQ* 144: 155–63.

Niesiołowski-Spanò, Łukasz. 2020. "The History of Passover: Changes in the Religion and Cult of the Judeans in 7th-5th Centuries BCE." *RB* 127: 338–51.

Olyan, Saul M. 2004. *Biblical Mourning: Ritual and Social Dimensions*. Oxford: Oxford University Press.

———. 2005. "Some Neglected Aspects of Israelite Interment Ideology." *JBL* 124: 601–16.

Palmer, Carol. 2002. "Milk and Cereals: Identifying Food and Food Identity Among Fallāḥīn and Bedouin in Jordan." *Levant* 34: 173–95.

Potts, Daniel T. 1997. *Mesopotamian Civilization: The Material Foundations*. Ithaca: Cornell University Press.

Price, Max D., Mike Buckley, Morag M. Kersel and Yorke M. Rowan. 2013. "Animal Management Strategies During the Chalcolithic in the Lower Galilee: New Data from Marj Rabba (Israel)." *Paléorient* 39: 183–200.

Prosic, Tamara. 1999. "Origin of Passover." *SJOT* 13: 78–94.

Reich, Ronny, Eli Shukron and Omri Lernau. 2007. "Recent Discoveries in the City of David, Jerusalem." *IEJ* 57: 153–69

Römer, Thomas. 2015. *The Invention of God*. Cambridge: Harvard University Press.

Sasson, Aharon. 2010. *Animal Husbandry in Ancient Israel: A Zooarchaeological Perspective on Livestock Exploitation, Herd Management and Economic Strategies*. London: Equinox.

Schmidt, Brian. 1996. *Israel's Beneficent Dead: Ancestor Cult and Necromancy in Ancient Israelite Religion and Tradition*. Winona Lake: Eisenbrauns.

Shafer-Elliott, Cynthia. 2013. *Food in Ancient Judah: Domestic Cooking in the Time of the Bible*. Sheffield: Equinox.

———. 2021. "Fruits, Nuts, Vegetables, and Legumes". Pages 139–55 in *T&T Handbook of Food in the Hebrew Bible and Ancient Israel*. Edited by Janling Fu, Cynthia Shafer-Elliott, and Carol Meyers. London: T&T Clark.

Sonia, Kerry M. 2020. *Caring for the Dead in Ancient Israel*. Atlanta: SBL.

Stavrakopoulou, Francesca. 2016. "Religion at Home: The Materiality of Practice." Pages 346–65 in *The Wiley Blackwell Companion to Ancient Israel*. Edited by Susan Niditch. Chichester: Wiley & Sons.

Stol, Marten. 2016. *Women in the Ancient Near East*. Translated by Helen and Mervyn Richardson. Berlin: de Gruyter.

Suriano, Matthew. 2007. "A Fresh Reading for 'Aged Wine' in the Samaria Ostraca." *PEQ* 139: 27–33.

———. 2021a. "Food, Death, and the Dead." Pages 319–34 in *T&T Handbook of Food in the Hebrew Bible and Ancient Israel*. Edited by Janling Fu, Cynthia Shafer-Elliott, and Carol Meyers. London: T&T Clark.

———. 2021b. "What Did Feeding the Dead Mean? Two Case Studies from Iron Ages Tombs at Beth-Shemesh." *AABNER* 1: 117–42.

van der Toorn, Karel. 1996. *Family Religion in Babylonia, Syria & Israel: Continuity & Change in the Forms of Religious Life*. Leiden: Brill.

Van Neer, Wim, Omri Lernau, Renée Friedman, Gregory Mumford, Jeroen Poblóme, and Marc Waelkens. 2004. "Fish Remains from Archaeological Sites as Indicators of Former Trade Connections in the Eastern Mediterranean." *Paléorient* 30: 101–48.

Van Seters, John. 2003. "From Child Sacrifice to Paschal Lamb: A Remarkable Transformation in Israelite Religion." *Old Testament Essays* 16: 453–63.

Walsh, Carey Ellen. 2021. "Grapes and Wine." Pages 125–38 in *T&T Handbook of Food in the Hebrew Bible and Ancient Israel*. Edited by Janling Fu, Cynthia Shafer-Elliott, and Carol Meyers. London: T&T Clark.

Welch, Eric Lee. 2021. "Olives and Olive Oil." Pages 113–23 in *T&T Handbook of Food in the Hebrew Bible and Ancient Israel*. Edited by Janling Fu, Cynthia Shafer-Elliott, and Carol Meyers. London: T&T Clark.

Welton, Rebekah. 2020. *"He Is a Glutton and a Drunkard": Deviant Consumption in the Hebrew Bible*. Leiden: Brill.

———. 2021. "'Know Well the Faces of your Sheep': Animal Bodies and Human Bodies." Pages 61–71 in *Life and Death: Social Perspectives on Biblical Bodies*. Edited by Francesca Stavrakopoulou. London: Bloomsbury T&T Clark.

———. 2022. "Ethnography and Biblical Studies: 'A Land Flowing with Milk and Honey' as a Case Study for Re-Contextualising a Familiar Phrase." *Biblical Interpretation* 30: 1–20.

Yee, Gale A. 2017. "'He Will Take the Best of Your Fields': Royal Feasts and Rural Extraction." *JBL* 136: 821–38.

Zohary, Daniel, Maria Hopf, and Ehud Weiss. 2012. *Domestication of Plants in the Old World: The Origin and Spread of Domesticated Plants in South-West Asia, Europe, and the Mediterranean Basin*. Oxford: Oxford University Press.

18
GENDER IN ANCIENT ISRAEL

Jennie Ebeling

While any attempt to reconstruct and understand gender roles in the past is fraught with difficulty, studying gender in the Iron Age southern Levant is particularly challenging for many reasons. Despite this, it is imperative to study gender not only because it is a basic structuring principle in individuals and societies but also because the primary textual source for this period is a source of authority for many people today that is used, as it has been for centuries, as a powerful tool of discrimination against and oppression of women and sexual and gender minorities. The biblical concepts that women and girls are inferior to men and boys and male homosexuality is a crime punishable by death, for example, limit the rights and freedoms of women and sexual and gender minorities today, even in places where the rule of law is formally separate from Judeo-Christian traditions, beliefs, and practices. In addition, the public is not particularly well informed about recent interdisciplinary research into ancient women's lives. When asked to write down their ideas about women in the biblical period at the beginning of a course on "Women in Biblical Tradition," Carol Meyers (2011: 62–63) found that college students from both religious and secular backgrounds believed that women were "'not as important as men,' 'subservient to men,' 'meant mainly for procreation,' 'inferior to men,' [and] 'marginalized.'" Scholars can respond by critically evaluating the biblical text as a source of information about real people in ancient Israel and interpreting the abundant extra-biblical sources about them for members of the public who are fascinated by the biblical world but not familiar with recent developments in the academic study of it.

Defining Sex and Gender

Definitions of sex and gender vary widely in general and in the context of the study of the ancient Near East specifically. Sex is usually believed to be biologically determined and binary – a person is either female or male and only rarely both – while gender has been understood as a cultural construction. In the past few decades, however, researchers have challenged this narrow biology-determines-sex and culture-determines-gender paradigm as well as the conceptual separation of sex from gender. Those who study sex differences in the brain, for example, argue that sex is influenced by biological, psychological, and socio-cultural factors and refute fundamental differences between female and male brains (Asher-Greve 2018: 25). In the same way, gender is no longer understood as an entirely social construct and the use of the term "gender" varies considerably across disciplines. For most who study the ancient world, however, it is the study of gender rather than sex that is the goal.

Gender roles, behaviors, and ideology vary between cultures and must be learned; as Nelson (2004: 3) succinctly puts it, "[n]o one 'has' a gender at birth." Gender studies examine how different cultures determine appropriate behaviors for biological females and males and the social construction of femininity and masculinity (Budin 2018: 524). While most individuals in antiquity, as now, identify as female or male and their gender matches the sex assigned at birth, the ancient sources – including the Hebrew Bible – indicate the existence of individuals whose gender roles cannot be understood as normative female or hegemonic male. We must, then, assume a variety of gender performances in ancient Israel as in other parts of the ancient Near East (see further Peled 2016a and essays in Svard and Garcia-Ventura 2018). At the same time, we must avoid presentism – assuming that our ways of life are the same as those in the distant past – in our understanding of ancient gender identities and roles, as well as essentialism – the idea that women and men are endowed with certain biological traits that govern behavior – in our identifications of gendered activities in ancient Israel. We must also understand the intersectional nature of gender construction and its correlation with social, economic, and political status and ethnic and religious identity (Pace 2022). A nuanced understanding of sex and gender potentially complicates investigations into ancient societies; however, it also allows for new opportunities to explore how these concepts manifested in ancient Israel and shaped the everyday experiences of its inhabitants.

History of Research

Gender studies include women's studies, masculinities' studies, and queer theory. Women's studies developed out of three "waves" known as first-wave feminism, second-wave feminism, and third-wave feminism in the mid-to-late twentieth century. First- and second-wave feminism as applied to archaeological and historical studies focused on finding women in the past, correcting androcentric biases of earlier approaches, and the historical oppression of women. These developments led to the founding of women's studies departments in universities and more sophisticated research on the roles of women in ancient societies. Third-wave feminist studies branched out into the related disciplines of women's studies, feminist studies, gender studies, and queer theory and led to the emergence of gender archaeology in the 1990s (Budin 2019: 522–24; see further Nelson 2004). Masculinities' studies also developed in the last few decades of the twentieth century in part as a response to feminist studies. Today it is an interdisciplinary research area that considers the social construction of masculinities and is not confined to biological males. Queer theory acknowledges the existence of both multiple genders and multiple sexes, including biological hermaphrodites (intersex individuals), castrated males, homosexual females and males, and individuals who adopt the gender aspects of an alternate sex (Budin 2019: 525).

While all three areas of inquiry – women's studies, masculinities' studies, and queer theory – should be part of the study of gender in ancient Israel, developments in women's studies have shaped gender studies in the ancient Near East. As Garcia-Ventura and Svard (2018: 6) note in the introduction to their edited volume *Studying Gender in the Ancient Near East*, "… women's studies formed the kernel of what nowadays is a broader and more inclusive research area, gender studies, which is devoted to not only women but to men, to the construction of gender, and to the analysis of gender relationships." However, since making women visible and writing them into history has not yet been fully accomplished in ancient Near Eastern studies, they argue for coexistence and dialogue between gender studies and women's studies rather than replacing women's studies and/or women's history with gender studies (Garcia-Ventura and Svard 2018: 6). Garcia-Ventura and Svard (2018) identify three main disciplines – archaeology, iconographic studies, and Assyriology – within gender studies in the ancient Near East and call for more interdisciplinary and inter-methodological research. The publication of several volumes in the field of ancient Near Eastern gender studies in recent years (see below) is a promising development.

The impact of these larger trends in ancient Near Eastern gender studies on the study of gender in the Iron Age southern Levant has not been great. Instead, the study of gender in ancient Israel developed out of feminist biblical studies pioneered by biblical scholars like Phyllis Trible and Phyllis Bird starting in the 1970s. Hebrew Bible scholar and archaeologist Carol Meyers was the first to combine the biblical text with archaeological discoveries to reconstruct women's lives in her 1988 monograph *Discovering Eve: Ancient Israelite Women in Context* and has published numerous studies since that have increased our understanding of women's contributions to their households and families in ancient Israel. As Nakhai (2018b: 370) notes, Meyers and other archaeologists, most of them women, have focused primarily on women's contributions to the household economy in rural contexts in their studies of Israelite women (see further below). Books on daily life and the lives of ordinary people in ancient Israel published by male scholars during the past two decades (Borowski 2003; King and Stager 2001; but see Dever 2012) provide rather limited discussions of women's daily life activities and are guilty of essentialism in their treatments of women and their experiences to varying degrees. Meanwhile, the study of gender in biblical studies has expanded beyond a focus on women and female roles in the text to include approaches in masculinities' studies, queer studies, intersex studies, and more (see further Graybill and Huber 2021).

There is potential for those who study gender in the Iron Age southern Levant to find inspiration in recent contributions to the study of gender in the ancient Near East. A review of several edited works and a special issue of the journal *Near Eastern Archaeology* published in the last five years reveals very few essays on ancient Israel. *Near Eastern Archaeology* 79/3 (2016), a special issue dedicated to gender archaeology, includes ten research articles, only one of them (Ebeling 2016) about ancient Israel; of the 20 essays in *Studying Gender in the Ancient Near East* (Svard and Garcia-Ventura 2018), only one (Nakhai 2018a) deals with gender in ancient Israel; and while there are five essays in the Ancient Israel and Biblical Studies section in the volume *Gender and Methodology in the Ancient Near East* (Budin et al. 2018) only one (Nakhai 2018b) incorporates archaeological research.

This lack of engagement of most southern Levantine archaeologists in broader studies of gender in the ancient Near East is due to several factors (Bolger 2008; Nakhai 2018a). Among the challenges Nakhai (2018a) identifies is the continuing focus on reconstructing broad historical events rather than domestic archaeology; the nature of the Hebrew Bible as an androcentric, elitist, and exceptionally complex text that is also sacred canon; and women's positions in archaeological fieldwork, academia, and professional societies. As Nakhai (2018a: 295) notes,

> Scholars committed to the study of what has been called 'gender archaeology and the archaeology of gender' tend to be scholars who are vested in the endeavor, those with a deep passion for it, because for others the rewards are insufficient. Not by chance, these scholars are most often women.

These and other factors explain why this area of inquiry has developed more slowly than one might imagine.

To be clear, studies of gender in ancient Israel – especially those that foreground archaeology – have focused primarily on heteronormative women and their roles and activities interpreted using textual, iconographic, and ethnographic sources. While approaches in masculinities' studies and queer theory have been adopted by some who study the Hebrew Bible and the ancient Near East, archaeologists working in the Iron Age southern Levant have not yet adopted these approaches. Similarly, masculinities' studies and studies of non-gender-normative individuals in biblical studies have not yet been informed by archaeological data to any great extent. Some ideas on how this might be addressed using methods employed in broader ancient Near Eastern studies will be discussed at the end of this essay.

Sources for Gender in Ancient Israel

While the Hebrew Bible has been the traditional primary source of information about gender in ancient Israel, it is a problematic and incomplete source for reconstructing real women's lives. This complex collection includes material composed and recorded over hundreds of years and it reflects the ideas and ideals of elite males living in urban settings who shared a specific and intractable theological agenda: Yahweh is the god of Israel, and the people of Israel are to worship Yahweh only. The biblical writers present the story of the people of Israel and their national god largely from the vantage point of Judah, a peripheral Levantine nation compared to the larger, wealthier, and more cosmopolitan nation of Israel to its north. The biblical writers were neither compelled to record historical events accurately nor interested in providing a manual of ancient life that would help us better understand the lives of real people who lived in ancient Israel and Judah; in fact, it is unclear if actual women's lives are documented in the text at all. Women's voices and perspectives are virtually absent, as are the perspectives of those who did not share the same narrow and privileged perspectives as those of the writers. These and other issues (see further Ackerman 2003; Ebeling 2010; Meyers 2003, 2017; Nakhai 2018a) complicate the use of the Hebrew Bible for reconstructing the lives of women in ancient Israel.

Only recently have researchers looked beyond the Hebrew Bible to extra-biblical texts and inscriptions, iconographic sources, archaeological remains, and ethnographic materials to better understand Iron Age women. Contemporary texts from neighboring lands and inscriptions from the Iron Age southern Levant like *ostraca* (inscribed pottery sherds), seals and seal impressions, and tomb inscriptions provide valuable information about the statuses of individual women and their roles in economic life. Iconographic sources range from over a thousand ceramic figurines representing females that are found in a variety of contexts in 8th–6th century BCE Judah to Assyrian wall reliefs of conquered peoples in Judah that provide unique images of women and girls. Other archaeological remains, especially those made of clay and stone, provide information about daily life in ancient Israel and have been used by some archaeologists to reveal gendered activities in household contexts (see further below). Ethnographic materials, including written and photographic descriptions of women's lives in Palestine and the surrounding area in the 19th and early 20th centuries, provide insights into ways of life in the distant past, and ethnoarchaeological studies have been useful in shedding light on crafts and technologies strongly associated with women (see further Ebeling 2010; Meyers 2013).

While these sources have strengths and weaknesses and must be evaluated carefully, Nakhai (2018a: 289–91) makes the key point that those who seek to reconstruct the lives of women in ancient Israel are quite fortunate to have a relative wealth of material at their disposal. There is thus immense potential for researchers to examine this material using approaches developed by colleagues in ancient Near Eastern studies to better understand women as well as sexual and gender minorities going forward.

Biblical Women

Before delving into a discussion of what archaeological remains can reveal about real women, let us first consider what the biblical writers offer about women, especially women who played roles that took them beyond the realm of household and family (see entries in Meyers, Craven, and Kraemer 2001 as well as Ebeling 2010; Meyers 2013; Nakhai 2018b, 2019 for more on biblical women and extensive bibliographies). We begin at the top of the social hierarchy, where we would expect to find the fewest women; indeed, while hundreds of royal women are alluded to in the text, few are named or credited with any action. According to the biblical writers, only one woman – Athaliah – ruled over Judah during the period of the monarchy (2 Kgs 11: 1–3); there were apparently no female rulers in the northern kingdom of Israel. While no Israelite/Judahite (henceforth Israelite) women are honored with the title "queen" in the biblical text, the title *gebira*, "great lady" but understood as "queen mother," was held by 18 women in Judah and one in Israel and was the highest status that an Israelite woman could attain. The most powerful of them and the sole *gebira* in Israel was Jezebel, a daughter, wife, and mother of kings who allegedly supported hundreds of prophets of Ba'al and Asherah (1 Kgs 18: 19), terrified the prophet Elijah (1 Kgs 19: 1–3), and employed an Israelite scribe and her husband Ahab's seal to frame a landowning vintner named Naboth in Jezreel (1 Kgs 21). Few kings' daughters are named and those about whom the biblical writers have much to say – for example, Saul's daughter and David's wife Michal, and David's daughter Tamar – are tragic figures. We know nothing more about these elite female biblical characters due to the complete absence of sources outside of the Hebrew Bible that confirm their existence; while extra-biblical texts and inscriptions confirm the existence of more than fifty people described in the Hebrew Bible (Mykytiuk 2017), none of them are women.

The biblical writers also describe non-royal women who held positions of leadership, including the sole female Judge, Deborah, who was a prophetess and military leader in addition to a settler of disputes (Judg 4–5). Another woman who played a significant role in Judges is Jael, who killed the Canaanite general Sisera with a tent peg in her tent (Judg 4: 21). Like Jael, the woman of Thebez described in Judges 9:50–55 uses an object nearby – in this case, a millstone – to kill Abimelech by dropping this tool of daily life on his head. Two important women who played a similar role to that of village elder and are credited with solving national crises are described in 2 Samuel: the wise woman from Tekoa (2 Sam 14:1–20) and the wise woman from Abel Beth Maacah (2 Sam 20:14–22). Three women are called prophetesses in addition to Deborah: a wife of Isaiah (Isa 8:3–4), Huldah (2 Kgs 22: 14–20), and Noadiah (Neh 6:14). Huldah is described at some length by the biblical writers and is credited with validating a scroll called "the book of the law" found in the Jerusalem temple while it was being repaired. Divinely gifted female mediums also existed; the best known – the medium of Endor – was visited by Saul in her home so he could consult with the spirit of Samuel (1 Sam 28:7–25).

A variety of other professions were available to biblical women. Women are described as perfumers, cooks, and bakers (1 Sam 8:13), midwives (Gen 35:17, 38:28; Exod 1:15–21), wet-nurses (Gen 24:59, 35:8; 2 Kgs 11:2), and prostitutes (Gen 38:13–15; Josh 6:25; Lev 19:29; Prov 29:3). They danced, sang, and played musical instruments in various contexts, including to praise Yahweh for military victories: Deborah and her military commander Barak sang a victory song after leading the Israelites to victory over the Canaanites (Judg 5:2–31), and Miriam, Moses' sister, led a group of women in a victory song after crossing the Red Sea (Ex 15:21). Women contributed to the national cult by serving at the Tent of Meeting (Ex 38:8, 1 Sam 2:22) and weaving garments for a cult statue in the Jerusalem temple (2 Kgs 23:7). Jeremiah 9:16–20 and Ezekiel 32:16 mention skilled mourning women who were summoned to lament the coming destruction of Jerusalem.

Several exemplary female characters engage in other activities that are more closely associated with men. Ruth participates in agricultural field labor, including gleaning and threshing, alongside other young women (Ruth 2: 8, 22–23); while men are believed to have engaged in most agricultural field work, the biblical text as well as ethnographic sources demonstrate that women were active participants in seasonal agricultural activities (Ebeling 2016). The Woman of Valor in Proverbs 31: 10–31 is described as an ideal wife who keeps busy caring for her household, but she also engages in the male-oriented activities of selling goods – specifically clothing items that she has produced (Prov 31:24) – and buying property and planting grapevines with her profits (Prov 31: 16).

While these and other biblical passages about women are important and resonate with many today, it is difficult to know how much they reflect ancient Israelite realities and not just the ideals of the biblical writers (Meyers 2011, 2017). However, the careful use of details in the biblical text can help us interpret the archaeological remains and bring us closer to an understanding of real women.

Ancient Israelite Women

In the past two decades, an increasing number of researchers have looked to archaeological remains as a primary source of information about the lives of women who lived in ancient Israel. Developments in household archaeology especially have been used to shed light on female activities and spaces in Iron Age houses. While predicated on the problematic assumption that women are more associated with private than public spaces, these studies take advantage of the fact that houses are relatively well-preserved and self-contained archaeological contexts where most people spent most of their time. Four-room houses located in central highland villages dating to the Iron Age I (1200–1000 BCE), ancient Israel's formative period, have been particularly attractive to researchers (e.g., Ebeling 2010; Meyers 2003, 2007, 2011, 2016). In addition to the archaeological evidence demonstrating that these small settlements were largely self-sufficient and thus relied heavily on women's domestic production, the Iron Age I is the backdrop to Judges, the biblical book with the most major female characters (other than Genesis). Stories about the important roles played by Deborah, Jael, and the woman of Thebez mentioned above, among other female characters, may indicate that women played particularly active roles in pre-monarchic society (Ackerman 2003: 175–76).

Village Households

Household food preparation and textile production loom large in studies of women's contributions to the household economy in Iron Age village settings (Meyers 2003, 2007, 2011). Most of the artifacts and installations preserved in Iron Age households are made of virtually indestructible stone and clay and can be associated with women's daily life activities. Stone grinding and pounding equipment and clay ovens evidence the preparation of cereals and baking of the staple food – bread – in the Israelite diet (Ebeling 2021). Ceramic vessels reflect the preparation, presentation, consumption, and storage of food and drink. Whorls and loom weights of clay and stone are usually all that remains of the spindles and looms used to create fabric for clothing and other uses. Although the biblical references to these activities are relatively few, women are most often the ones described engaging in grinding, baking, cooking, spinning, and weaving activities in the text (see Meyers 2016). In addition, ethnohistorical sources like descriptions of traditional village life in 19th- and 20th-century Palestine show that these were primarily female-oriented activities in domestic settings. The available evidence thus strongly suggests that these stone and clay objects and installations are associated with female contributions to the household economy during the Iron Age I.

The spaces in which artifacts and installations related to grinding, baking, cooking, spinning, and weaving are found might also be identified as female-gendered spaces. For example, the clustering of multiple grinding stone sets (Meyers 2003: 431; 2011: 85–86) and the construction of ovens near entryways, between houses, or in other shared spaces (Baadsgaard 2008) may indicate that women worked together in groups; after all, "Tedious and time-consuming tasks are typically made tolerable when done in the company of others" (Meyers 2016: 590). Women may have created these spaces by building ovens themselves or overseeing construction according to their specifications as seen in ethnographic studies of traditional clay ovens (Ebeling 2022). The proximity of whorls and weights to cooking objects and ovens in Israelite houses may further support the communal nature of women's tasks (Cassuto 2008). According to Budin (2019: 527), this "… also give[s] evidence for the extra-domestic sociability of women's work: Just as the bakers might meet up at communal ovens, so, too, 'housewives' had direct access to the area beyond the house and external social networks." Women's control of essential daily life activities may have given them power in their families and their access to female social networks would have facilitated many aspects of family and community life (Meyers 2003, 2007, 2011).

Women's everyday responsibilities in households extended to domestic religious activities (Ackerman 2016; Meyers 2005; Nakhai 2019). Although only hinted at by the biblical writers, focused as they were on the national cult, household religion comprised the primary religious experiences for most people in ancient Israel (Meyers 2017: 528). Household spaces transformed into sacred space during the performance of rituals to Yahweh, Asherah, the Queen of Heaven, and other deities. As in rituals performed in the context of the national cult, household rituals required the burning of incense as well as offerings of food and drink (Jer 7: 17–18; 44: 3–6, 15–25); these offerings were likely portions of the meals prepared by women for family members. In addition to the usual implements of daily life like ceramic vessels, ground stone tools, and ovens required to produce these offerings, a variety of specialized artifacts found in Iron Age houses – including figurines, altars, stands, amulets, and more – attest to household ritual activities. The locations of these specialized portable artifacts in household spaces associated with food preparation and textile production activities suggest that women used them. Since many women were concerned with the dangers associated with pregnancy and childbirth as well as threats to infants and children, women likely used these objects in rituals meant to protect and heal (Nakhai 2019).

Urban Settings

As Nakhai (2018b: 371) notes, much of the focus until now has been on village life and women's contributions to the rural subsistence economy and domestic religious practices rather than life in urban settings. While it is difficult to identify the archaeological remains of women's activities in larger towns and cities beyond everyday subsistence activities like food preparation and textile production, there are sources that hint at women's participation in public life in the capital cities of Jerusalem and Samaria and elsewhere. It is important to stress here that the biblical writers wrote from an urban perspective and focused on public life while physical remains of the minutiae of private life are better represented in the archaeological record. While much of what we can infer about the lives of urban women in ancient Israel derives from the biblical text (Nakhai 2018b), extra-biblical texts and inscriptions as well as figurines are among the archaeological remains that shed life on women's activities and experiences.

Epigraphic sources from archaeological contexts in the Iron Age southern Levant include *ostraca*, inscribed ceramic vessels, seals, *bullae* (lumps of clay with seal impressions), seal impressions on ceramic vessels, and tomb inscriptions. The fact that women's names were inscribed on these artifacts suggests not only that some women were literate but also that they participated in economic life. Among the 66 legible *ostraca* in the mid-8th century BCE Samaria ostraca, which record oil and wine deliveries between Samaria and communities in the tribal area of Manasseh, several include the female names Hoglah and No'ah, the names of two of Zelophehad's daughters (Num 27:1; 36:11) who were allowed to inherit their father's property. It is possible that the names of two female descendants of Manasseh are included on multiple *ostraca* because these women could inherit property as described in the biblical text and were remembered as the founders of settlements in this tribal area. In addition, several inscribed ceramic vessels found in 7th–6th century BCE Jerusalem mention women as the recipients of grain, and a complete vessel that once contained wine belonged to the "daughter of Ya'ama" according to the inscription incised on it (Meyers 2011: 92–93).

Many known Iron Age inscriptions are either small, inscribed stamp seals usually made of precious and semi-precious stones, or the impressions of these seals on *bullae* that were used to close rolled documents on papyrus or parchment. Seals could be impressed on pottery vessels to mark the ownership of the vessel and its contents as well. Most seals have a hole drilled through them so they can be worn on strings and occasionally they are preserved set into finger rings; these objects thus would have been visible symbols of status for the relatively few who owned them. While hundreds of inscribed seals and *bullae* record men's names, 12 seals include women's names. A recently published seal reading "[Belonging] to Elihana, daughter of Gael" is a rare example of a seal with a woman's name that was found in a good archaeological context in an 8th–7th century BCE administrative building in the City of David in Jerusalem ("Exceptional" 2016). A seal impressed on the handle of a jar excavated in a 7th-century BCE context in Jerusalem reads "[Belonging] to Hannah, daughter of 'Azaryah" (Meyers 2011: 94). Women who owned and used these seals must have had some of the same rights, including the ability to sign contracts and other documents and conduct business transactions, as seal-owning men.

Among the few inscribed Iron Age tombs is the so-called Tomb of the Royal Steward in the necropolis at Silwan south of the City of David in Jerusalem. The damaged inscription above its entrance reads "This is [the tomb of Sheban]iah, who is over the house. There is no silver or gold here – only [his bones] and the bones of his maidservant (who is) with him. Cursed be the man who opens this (tomb)!" (*COS* 2.54). This tomb should be identified as that of Shebna, an official during the reign of King Hezekiah who was criticized by the prophet Isaiah for commissioning a rock-cut tomb on a height (Isa. 22:15–16). The English term "maidservant" does not convey the status implied by the term *'amah*, which was an honorific referring to a woman of high status as well as a title for a woman in an official position (Meyers 2011: 96). It is thus possible that the *'amah* interred in the Tomb of the Royal Steward was a female official in the service of the royal court of Judah. If so, this inscription constitutes the only evidence outside of the Hebrew Bible for a woman who held a leadership position in ancient Israel.

Another artifact category that sheds light on women's lives is art. The vast majority of iconographic images from Iron Age Israel and Judah are clay figurines depicting females; the most common are Judean Pillar Figurines (JPFs) known from 8th–6th-century BCE Judah. JPFs are small clay figurines with either a mold-made or pinched head, large breasts, arms below the breasts, and a flaring pillar-shaped lower body. While more than 1000 examples are known from a range of archaeological contexts, most of them were found deposited as trash in domestic contexts in Jerusalem and were likely used in household rituals for healing and protection. While JPFs do not cluster in female household spaces and were not used exclusively by women (Darby 2014), as Nakhai (2018b: 376) notes, women would have needed divine protection more than men. The second most common type of Iron Age clay figurine depicts a female holding a drum. These images provide evidence for women's roles in musical traditions private and public, sacred and secular, including women's celebration of military victories as described in the biblical text (Paz 2007).

Summary and Critique: Ancient Israelite Women

The identification and appreciation of women's activities in village households and urban settings are important steps in challenging the problematic and limited information about women in the Hebrew Bible. Not only were women responsible for crucial daily life activities – including religious ones – at home, but they were also active in public life. As one would expect, women's experiences were highly variable depending on their location and situation. However, there is still a tendency toward essentialist assumptions about ancient Israelite women in scholarly and popular publications. In her discussion of the gender essentialism inherent in beliefs that women are innately maternal and that having children is a universal concern of females, Budin (2019) discredits the traditional scholarly identification of female figurines as "fertility figurines." Since depictions of pregnant females are rare in Iron Age iconography while dozens of figurines depicting females holding drums are known, she concludes that "… the women of ancient Israel were more closely associated with the celebration of successful warfare and the preservation of the state than motherhood" (Budin 2019: 530; see also Budin 2021). Not all women in ancient Israel were mothers and not all women were in stable relationships with male partners through the entirety of their adult lives. How can we learn more about those women who found themselves outside of the biblical ideal of wife and mother and how will this knowledge impact our understanding of ancient Israelite women?

Another issue is the fact that much of the research that incorporates archaeology into discussions of women in ancient Israel has appeared in journals and edited volumes read primarily by biblical scholars and researchers in adjacent disciplines and not in venues accessible to a broad audience. While it is important that those who study biblical women are aware of recent studies of household archaeology, archaeology does not appear to be more integrated into feminist biblical scholarship now than it was two decades ago (see, for example, essays in Scholz 2020b; Sherwood 2017). However, we archaeologists can do our part in parallel to advance the feminist program of interpreting the Bible "… in conversation with and in the context of the relentless and manifold issues and practices that keep the gender caste system in place even in the early part of the twenty-first century" by engaging a public that "… often mentions the Bible to establish religious, political, and socio-cultural restrictions for gendered practices" (Scholz 2020a: 22). Our time might be better spent giving public lectures for organizations like the American Society of Overseas Research (ASOR), the Archaeological Institute of America (AIA), and the Biblical Archaeology Society (BAS), as some already do, and writing for public audiences both religious and secular. Of course, those committed to the archaeology of gender are usually those privileged enough to have the time and resources to do so rather than commit full-time to more valued publication efforts that secure academic employment (Nakhai 2018a: 294–95); efforts to engage the public as well are additional commitments that many researchers – including early career and members of BIPOC communities – might not be able to afford.

Moving Beyond

A larger issue is that archaeological investigations into gender in ancient Israel have focused almost exclusively on heteronormative women. According to Pace (2022), "…any real discussion of gender going forward must take into account the wide varieties of binary (male and female) and non-binary presentations (e.g., androgyny, intersex, and transgendered) constructions possible in the human experience." There is exciting potential to utilize approaches developed in gender studies in the larger ancient Near East – where researchers have abundant and diverse textual and iconographic sources as well as archaeological remains to work with – in gender studies of ancient Israel. The following brief overview of recent studies that focus on constructions of masculinities in Neo-Assyrian art connected to Iron Age Israel and Judah illustrates such approaches.

N'Shea (2018) includes the Lachish Relief Cycle in his study of the construction of masculinity in textual and visual sources during the region of the Neo-Assyrian king Sennacherib. Among the wall reliefs found in Sennacherib's Southwest Palace in Nineveh, the Lachish reliefs include rare depictions of women and unique images of children and thus comprise important sources for understanding aspects of the urban population in 8th-century Judah. In these reliefs, the residents of Lachish are being led into exile by Neo-Assyrian conquerors in Sennacherib's presence in 701 BCE (Figure 18.1). N'Shea (2018: 331) posits that the women and children depicted in these scenes along with Judahite men, who

> are either represented in the plainest terms possible or dead and naked…reinforce the shame and humiliation of the Judahite men for having failed in their performance of masculinity, that of protecting the women and children especially. By failing to protect the women and the children, they fail in the performance of their hegemonic standard of masculinity.

A study of the children depicted in these reliefs reveals gendered differences in clothing between girls and boys. While girls are essentially smaller versions of their mothers who wear the same feminine clothing and hold the same objects, there is an emphasis on the dress of boys of different ages depicted in the reliefs, particularly in their belts: the older the boy, the more ornate and like that of an adult male his belt becomes (Garroway 2020: 48). Emphasis on details of boys of different ages may have been intended to show that the Neo-Assyrians captured not only adult males but also males of other ages and stages, and not only kingdoms and cities but families as well (Garroway 2020: 54).

Another Neo-Assyrian source depicting ancient Israelites that displays representations of hegemonic, as well as non-hegemonic, masculinity is the Black Obelisk of Shalmaneser III. Found in Nimrud and dating to the late ninth century BCE, the obelisk includes the only known image of an Israelite or Judahite king. On the second register, Jehu, king of Israel, is shown paying tribute to the king of Assyria along with 13 nearly identical male Israelite tribute-bearers. Five beardless Assyrian attendants and one bearded Assyrian official are also

Figure 18.1 Judahites being deported following the capture of Lachish. Museum no.: 124907 © The Trustees of the British Museum

part of this scene. The five beardless Assyrian attendants can probably be identified as palace eunuchs based on parallels with other images of beardless males in Mesopotamian sources (Peled 2016b: 162–63). Shalmaneser's hegemonic masculinity is thus emphasized in this scene through his subordination of other masculinities: that of his beardless male attendants and that of the subordinate vassal Jehu, who is shown prostrating himself before the king's feet (N'Shea 2018: 320).

Conclusion

Looking back through works published in the last 20 years, it is encouraging to see how our understanding of ancient Israelite women has changed; we have come a long way from studies that look to the biblical text as the only source about ancient Israelite women. This can be seen in the influential and oft-cited volume *Life in Biblical Israel* published in 2001. In Chapter 2 – The Israelite House and Household – is a four-page section called "Women" that describes women's status and roles from the perspective of the androcentric biblical writers. According to the authors,

> …The Bible was written and compiled by males who had no special interest in women's roles. They focused principally on the male aspects of life, such as warfare, governing, economy, and worship, in which women were not directly involved or to which they contributed only minimally. In addition, Israel's laws were addressed only to men. The domain of women's activities was the household, where she exercised authority in her role as mother.
>
> *(King and Stager 2001: 49)*

It is difficult to imagine the inclusion of this or a similar description in a general work about ancient Israel that incorporates archaeological evidence published today.

While researchers have made great strides to integrate household archaeology studies into considerations of women in ancient Israel, much more work needs to be done to bring the study of gender in ancient Israel to the level of studies of gender in the ancient Near East broadly. As Budin (2020: 52) argues so persuasively,

> The study of women and gender and men … in history, including ancient history, has never been so important. It is critical that we understand the origins of sexism, misogyny, and heteronormativity, as well as different ways of seeing and constructing gender identity.

This work is especially critical for understanding ancient Israelite realities, I believe, and we need to value this work even if it is not valued by the academy.

Bibliography

Ackerman, Susan. 2003. "Digging Up Deborah: Recent Hebrew Bible Scholarship on Gender and the Contribution of Archaeology." *NEA* 66: 172–84.

———. 2016. "Women in Ancient Israel and the Hebrew Bible (or Women in Ancient Israel and the Old Testament)." *Oxford Research Encyclopedias of Religion*. Online: oxfordre.com/religion/view/10.1093/acrefore/9780199340378.001.0001/acrefore-9780199340378-e-45.

Asher-Greve, Julia M. 2018. "From La Femme to Multiple Sex/Gender." Pages 15–50 in *Studying Gender in the Ancient Near East*. Edited by Saana Svard and Agnes Garcia-Ventura. University Park: Eisenbrauns.

Baadsgaard, Aubrey. 2008. "A Taste of Women's Sociality: Cooking as Cooperative Labor in Iron Age Syro-Palestine." Pages 13–44 in *The World of Women in the Ancient and Classical Near East*. Edited by Beth Alpert Nakhai. Newcastle Upon Tyne: Cambridge Scholars Press.

Bolger, Diane R. 2008. "Gendered Fields in Near Eastern Archaeology: Past, Present, Future." Pages 335–59 in *Gender Through Time in the Ancient Near East*. Edited by Diane R. Bolger. Lanham: AltaMira Press.

Borowski, Oded. 2003. *Daily Life in Biblical Times*. Atlanta: SBL.

Budin, Stephanie L. 2019. "Finding a World of Women: An Introduction to Women's Studies and Gender Theory in Biblical Archaeology." Pages 522–35 in *The Social Archaeology of the Levant: From Prehistory to the Present*. Edited by Assaf Yasur-Landau, Eric H. Cline, and Yorke M. Rowan. Cambridge: Cambridge University Press.

———. 2020. "Sex and Gender and Sex." *Mare Nostrum* 11: 1–58.

———. 2021. "Archaeology Has a Problem with Females and Figurines in Israel and the Levant." *Haaretz*, July 19, 2021. Online: www.haaretz.com/archaeology/archaeology-has-a-problem-with-females-and-figurines-1.10012823.

Budin, Stephanie Lynn, Megan Cifarelli, Agnes Garcia-Ventura, and Adelina Millet Alba, eds. 2018. *Gender and Methodology in the Ancient Near East: Approaches from Assyriology and Beyond*. Barcelona: University of Barcelona.

Cassuto, Deborah. 2008. "Bringing the Artifacts Home: A Social Interpretation of Loom Weights in Context." Pages 63–77 in *The World of Women in the Ancient and Classical Near East*. Edited by Beth Alpert Nakhai. Newcastle upon Tyne: Cambridge Scholars.

Darby, Erin. 2014. *Interpreting Judean Pillar Figurines: Gender and Empire in Judean Apotropaic Ritual*. Tuebingen: Mohr Siebeck.

Dever, William G. 2012. *The Lives of Ordinary People in Ancient Israel: Where Archaeology and the Bible Intersect*. Grand Rapids: Eerdmans.

Ebeling, Jennie. 2010. *Women's Lives in Biblical Times*. London: T&T Clark.

———. 2016. "Engendering the Israelite Harvests." *NEA* 79: 186–94.

———. 2021. "Grains, Bread, and Beer." Pages 99–112 in *T&T Clark Handbook of Food in the Hebrew Bible and Ancient Israel*. Edited by Janling Fu, Cynthia Shafer-Elliott, and Carol Meyers. London: Bloomsbury/T&T Clark.

———. "Making Space: Women and Ovens in the Iron Age Southern Levant." Pages 92-102 in *In Pursuit of Visibility: Essays in Archaeology, Ethnography, and Text in Honor of Beth Alpert Nakhai*. Edited by Jennie Ebeling and Laura B. Mazow. Oxford: Archaeopress.

Garcia-Ventura, Agnes, and Saana Svard. 2018. "Theoretical Approaches, Gender, and the Ancient Near East." Pages 1–13 in *Studying Gender in the Ancient Near East*. Edited by Saana Svard and Agnes Garcia-Ventura. University Park: Eisenbrauns.

Garroway, Kristine. 2020. "(Un)Dressing Children in the Lachish Reliefs: Questions of Gender, Status, and Ethnicity." *NEA* 83: 46–55.

Graybill, Rhiannon, and Lynn R. Huber 2021. "Introduction." Pages 1–14 in *The Bible, Gender, and Sexuality: Critical Readings*. Edited by Rhiannon Graybill and Lynn R. Huber. New York: T&T Clark.

King, Philip J., and Lawrence E. Stager. 2001. *Life in Biblical Israel*. Louisville: Westminster John Knox Press.

Meyers, Carol L. 1988. *Discovering Eve: Ancient Israelite Women in Context*. Oxford: Oxford University Press.

———. 2003. "Material Remains and Social Relations: Women's Culture in Agrarian Households of the Iron Age." Pages 424–44 in *Symbiosis, Symbolism, and the Power of the Past: Canaan, Ancient Israel, and Their Neighbors from the Late Bronze Age through Roman Palaestina*. Edited by William G. Dever and Seymour Gitin. Winona Lake: Eisenbrauns.

———. 2005. *Households and Holiness: The Religious Culture of Israelite Women*. Minneapolis: Fortress Press.

———. 2007. "From Field Crops to Food: Attributing Gender and Meaning to Bread Production in Iron Age Israel." Pages 67–84 in *The Archaeology of Difference: Gender, Ethnicity, Class and the "Other" in Antiquity—Studies in Honor of Eric M. Meyers*. Edited by Douglas R. Edwards and C. Thomas McCollough. Boston: ASOR.

———. 2011. "Archaeology—A Window to the Lives of Israelite Women." Pages 61–108 in *Torah*. Edited by Irmtraud Fischer and Mercedes Navarro Puerto, with Andrea Taschl-Erber. Atlanta: SBL.

———. 2013. *Rediscovering Eve: Ancient Israelite Women in Context*. Oxford: Oxford University Press.

———. 2016. "Women's Daily Life (Iron Age Israel)." Pages 488–500 in *Women in Antiquity: Real Women Across the Ancient World*. Edited by Stephanie Lynn Budin and Jean Macintosh Turfa. London: Routledge.

———. 2017. "Seeing Double: Textual and Archaeological Images of Israelite Women." In *The Bible and Feminism: Remapping the Field*. Edited by Yvonne Sherwood. Oxford University Press. Online: oxford.universitypressscholarship.com/view/10.1093/oso/9780198722618.001.0001/oso-9780198722618-chapter-29.

Meyers, Carol L., Toni Craven, and Ross Shepard Kraemer, eds. 2001. *Women in Scripture: A Dictionary of Named and Unnamed Women in the Hebrew Bible, the Apocryphal/Deuterocanonical Books, and the New Testament*. Grand Rapids: Eerdmans.

Mykytiuk, Lawrence. 2017. "53 People in the [Hebrew] Bible Confirmed Archaeologically." *Bible History Daily*. Online: www.biblicalarchaeology.org/daily/people-cultures-in-the-bible/people-in-the-bible/50-people-in-the-bible-confirmed-archaeologically/.

Nakhai, Beth Alpert. 2018a. "Factors Complicating the Reconstruction of Women's Lives in Iron Age Israel (1200–587 B.C.E.)." Pages 289–313 in *Studying Gender in the Ancient Near East*. Edited by Saana Svard and Agnes Garcia-Ventura. University Park: Eisenbrauns.

———. 2018b. "A World of Possibilities: Jerusalem's Women in the Iron Age (1000–586 BCE)." Pages 369–92 in *Gender and Methodology in the Ancient Near East: Approaches from Assyriology and Beyond*. Edited by Stephanie Lynn Budin, Megan Cifarelli, Agnes Garcia-Ventura, and Adelina Millet Alba. Barcelona: University of Barcelona.

———. 2019. "Women in Israelite Religion: The State of Research Is All New Research." *Religions* 10(2). Online: doi.org/10.3390/rel10020122.

Nelson, Sarah Milledge. 2004. *Gender in Archaeology: Analyzing Power and Prestige*. 2nd ed. Walnut Creek: AltaMira Press.

N'Shea, Omar. 2018. "Empire of the Surveilling Gaze: The Masculinity of King Sennacherib." Pages 315–35 in *Studying Gender in the Ancient Near East*. Edited by Saana Svard and Agnes Garcia-Ventura. University Park: Eisenbrauns.

Pace, Leann C. 2022. "Material Culture: Ancient Near East." In *Oxford Encyclopedias of the Bible*. Oxford Biblical Studies Online. Online: www.oxfordbiblicalstudies.com/article/opr/t998/e34.

Paz, Sarit. 2007. *Drums, Women, and Goddesses: Drumming and Gender in Iron Age II Israel*. Fribourg: Academic; Göttingen: Vandenhoeck & Ruprecht.

Peled, Ilan. 2016a. *Masculinities and Third Gender: The Origins and Nature of an Institutionalized Gender Otherness in the Ancient Near East*. Münster: Ugarit-Verlag.

Peled, Ilan. 2016b. "Visualizing Masculinities: The Gala, Hegemony, and Mesopotamian Iconography." *NEA* 79: 158–65.

Scholz, Susanne. 2020a. "Reading the Bible with Feminist Eyes: Introduction." Pages xxiii–lii in *The Oxford Handbook of Feminist Approaches to the Hebrew Bible*. Edited by Susanne Scholz. Oxford: Oxford University Press.

Scholz, Susanne, ed. 2020b. *The Oxford Handbook of Feminist Approaches to the Hebrew Bible*. Oxford: Oxford University Press.

Sherwood, Yvonne, ed. 2017. *The Bible and Feminism: Remapping the Field*. Oxford: Oxford University Press.

Svard, Saana, and Agnes Garcia-Ventura, eds. 2018. *Studying Gender in the Ancient Near East*. University Park: Eisenbrauns.

Times of Israel Staff. 2016. "'Exceptional' Woman's 2,500-Year-Old Seal Unearthed in Jerusalem." *Times of Israel*, 7 March 2016. Online: www.timesofisrael.com/exceptional-womans-2500-year-old-seal-unearthed-in-jerusalem/.

19
CHILDREN IN ANCIENT ISRAEL

Kristine Henriksen Garroway

Children played an important part in the ancient Israelite household. Their little beings were valued for many reasons ranging from social, economic, and legal, to emotional and religious values. A child's value stemmed from the reality that they represented the continuation of society into the next generation. Society, therefore, poured time and energy into raising the new generation. However, this job was not always easy, for children were also some of the most vulnerable members of society. The tension between value and vulnerability is evident in every area of a child's life and frames the discussion of children to follow. Drawing upon relevant texts and archaeological realia, this essay explores various stages in a child's life from pre-birth to death.

Archaeologically, much of what we know about children and their daily lives comes from the remains of the settlements where they lived (Foster and Parker 2012: 4; Meyers 2013: 103–13; Wilk and Rathje 1982; see also Zorn, this volume). There are rare instances in which a child's skeleton is found in a destruction layer, but these examples offer a frozen snapshot of the child's life. Therefore, in the same way as one envisions how the adults of the household moved and acted within the settlement, so too must one do for children. The issue becomes connecting children with the realia. Uncovering the lives of ancient Israelite children is a bit of a thought exercise in which one must compile all the possible pieces of evidence together to form a single picture. Certainly, the graves of children offer an immediate connection between a child and the items buried with them; however, mortuary contexts are not without difficulty as the living present the dead in an idealized manner (Pearson 2000).

The textual record, for its part, is fairly limited with respect to texts found in an Iron Age archaeological context. The biblical text is the principal source coming out of the region that references children with any great detail.[1] This text was created by men and has an androcentric focus and an ideological overlay focusing on the nation. While it is not easy, the goal of engaging the biblical text is to "highlight the muted children preserved therein and place them in their world" (Garroway 2018: 12). To aid in the difficult task of using the biblical text to describe children in ancient Israel, the use of ancient Near Eastern sources can also be helpful. Hays (2014: 4) states: "The Scriptures are exceedingly 'respiratory': they breathe in the culture of their times, and breathe it back out in a different form." Hays is pointing to the necessity of understanding the world of the Hebrew Bible to understand the texts therein. For example, children being mauled by she-bears (2 Kgs 2:23–24) was probably not

DOI: 10.4324/9780367815691-22

a common everyday occurrence. Yet, in looking to comparative sources from the ancient Near East (ANE) we see that the biblical story echoes both a vulnerability that children faced by virtue of their young age and the cultural imperative for children to respect their elders upon threat of bodily harm (Roth 1997: 44). Private documents and laws lay out the importance of children respecting their elders. RS 8.145, a will from Ugarit, states that if the son honors his mother, he will inherit the property, but if he curses (dishonors) her he shall be disinherited. The Sumerian Laws Exercise Tablet no. 4 states that an adoptive son who talks back to the parents saying "you are not my mother or father" will be disinherited and can be sold into slavery. The Laws of Hammurabi (LH) also state that biological and adoptive children who repudiate their parents are subject to bodily harm, the loss of a tongue, eye, or hand (LH 192, 193, 195). The "Instruction of Amenemope," dated to the Ramesside period, states: "Do not stretch out your hand to [touch] an old man or open your mouth to an elder" (COS 1.46). Ancient Near Eastern sources such as these are included here to suggest that while we cannot know the specifics of an ancient Israelite child's life, we can think about the world in which they lived and the world views that influenced their lives.

Envisioning the lives of children in ancient Israel is a complicated task. The picture we can paint is at times a gross generalization of what their lives must have been like. Surely differences in class, geographical location, socio-economic status, (dis)ability, and so forth affected the lives of individual children in much the same way as these factors do today. The best way forward, then, is to think about the "child's world," rather than individual children (Lillehammer 1989). Constructing the ancient Israelite child's world means engaging in an interdisciplinary approach that combines archaeology, biblical texts, and relevant ANE materials.[2] Each of these sources will be employed in the following discussion, which progresses through a child's life beginning with birth and ending with a child's untimely death.

The Infant (Pre-)Birth

The desire for children and the role of the divine in providing children is found throughout the biblical and ANE texts and is evidenced by the archaeological record. Children were understood as a gift from the divine. The Hebrew Bible presents both El and YHWH as the one in control of the womb, the one who opens the womb.[3] The surrounding cultures assigned different deities to the realm of fertility and womb-control; in Mesopotamia, the goddess was Inanna or Ishtar, while the Ugaritic and Canaanite texts gave this role to El and Asherah. It is not just a human desire to have children, but the desire of the gods *for* humans to have children. The command to "be fruitful and multiply" given first to Adam and Eve and then repeated to Noah in Gen 1:28 and 9:1, respectively, makes bearing children a divine imperative. So too, in the Egyptian text "The Instruction of Any", we find "It is proper to make people" (COS 1.46). Those who can bear children will receive happiness.

> Happy is the man who fills his quiver with them [children]; they shall not be put to shame when they contend with the enemy in the gate.
>
> Ps 127:5[4]

> Grandchildren are the crown of their elders, and the glory of children is their parents.
>
> Prov 17:6

> Happy is the man whose people are many, he is saluted on account of his progeny.
>
> ("Instruction of Any," COS 1.46)

Texts such as these attest to a worldview in which children are desired and valued. But what happens when a couple is infertile (Koepf-Taylor 2013; Moss and Baden 2015)? This issue is addressed time and time again in the biblical text through the barren women narratives.[5] The texts state a woman's womb was blocked and she needed God to open it.[6] A woman's barrenness was considered akin to a disability. Rachel even goes as far as to call barrenness a disgrace (Gen 30:23). Couples went to many lengths to unblock their womb. Prayer was the most common method employed. Isaac prays on behalf of Rebekah (Gen 25:21) and God responds by allowing her to conceive. Rachel also cries out to God, who "heeded her and opened her womb" (Gen 30:22). Women also turned to the magico-medical realm in hopes of curing their barrenness. The Hebrew Bible specifically references mandrakes, the love apple, as helping to get women pregnant (Gen 30:14–16; Song 7:13 [Heb. 7:14]). Mesopotamian texts address a wide range of women, from the infertile post-menopausal woman to the infertile woman of childbearing age. Techniques for opening the womb range from fumigating the vagina to inserting a pessary full of ingredients into the womb.

> You flay an edible mouse, open it up, and fill it with myrrh; you dry it in the shade, crush and grind it up, and mix it with fat; you place it in her vagina, and she will become pregnant.
>
> *(Stol 2000: 53)*

In cases where couples could not have a child, adoption and surrogates presented an alternate solution to the issue of an heir and elder care. Sarah proposes that Hagar might have a son that Sarah could count as hers (Gen 16:2), while Rachel expresses that Bilhah "might bear on my knees and that through her I too may have children" (Gen 30:3).[7] The expression "to bear on one's knees" appears again in Gen 50:23 and is alluded to in Gen 48:8–12, suggesting that this was an expression used to indicate adoption.[8] Couples might also adopt an older child or even an adult, such as Gen 15:2–4 indicates. Adoption texts spelling out the legal responsibilities of the adopting parties have not been found in ancient Israel proper but are found throughout the surrounding lands (Garroway 2014: 48–91, 254–80).

While all children were valued, texts hint that male children were especially prized. The firstborn male child would receive the special portion for the *bechor*, firstborn. As the primary heir, the son would receive a double portion of the inheritance property (Steinberg 1993).[9] It was important to have an heir so that land, as well as movable property (animals, clothing, money, and so forth), would stay within the kin group. In addition to tangible items, a man needed an heir to inherit his name. Receiving the family name meant that the child would be identified with the father's lineage and personality. The heir also had the responsibility of carrying on the father's memory after death. The Epic of Gilgamesh culminates in an expression of this important role. Bereft of his best friend, Enkidu, and with the means of living forever slipping through his hands, Gilgamesh finds hope in his newborn son as he realizes that after his death, he will live on through his son. Preference for sons also appears in Egyptian wisdom literature, "Instruction of Any": "Take a wife while you are young that she should bear a son for you" (*COS* 1.46). The Mesopotamian Instruction of Ur-Ninurta encourages piety for without it a man will not live long and "his inheritance will not be dear to him (?); a son will not be born to him" (*COS* 1.177).

While male children were desired, with a high rate of infant mortality, it seems likely that any healthy child, male or female, would be a welcomed birth. As seen above, most texts referencing the value of children highlight the male for inheritance reasons.[10] In addition to heirship, male children were able to help with farming and herding. In patrilocal, agrarian societies daughters represented a financial loss as a dowry was needed to secure their marriage (Dever 2012: 180–81; Steinberg 1993: 27). However, a daughter's marriage played a very important social role as it would create strong ties between kin groups (Steinberg 1993: 17–30). Yet, some social anthropologists conclude that when "push came to shove" female babies were much more likely to find themselves abandoned or the victim of infanticide (Nahkai 2008). Archaeologically, there is no evidence of infanticide of either males or females in the Iron Age period.

Even when a woman did become pregnant, there was always the possibility that she would miscarry. The reality of miscarriage was not lost on the writers of the Hebrew Bible. The Covenant Code concludes with the proclamation that those who uphold the covenant shall be blessed: "No woman in your land shall miscarry or be barren" (Exod 23:26). The Hebrew Bible describes miscarriages as a *nepel*, "one who has fallen out" (Exod 21:22–25; Garroway 2018: 36–39). Babylonian texts note that sorcery could cause a miscarriage and prescribe various rituals that could be done to avoid it (Stol 2000: 143). The reality of miscarriage made its way into the magico-medical canon as well. The text below is representative of procedures that could be undertaken to ensure that a pregnancy was not lost.

> If a woman is about to lose a fetus in either the first, or the second, or the third month, you dry a *hulû* mouse, crush and grind it up, (add) water three times, and mix it with oil; add *alluharu* (a mineral). You give it to her to drink, and she will not lose the fetus.
> *(Stol 2000: 28 and n13)*

There are no texts from the land of ancient Israel or the Hebrew Bible that talk about how to prevent miscarriages in quite this way. Nonetheless, one might imagine that miscarriages were common in the ancient world. While there is no data on spontaneous miscarriages, those that occur early on in a pregnancy, the remains of fetuses have been found in mortuary contexts (see below for more on childhood death.) Many fetuses found in mortuary contexts are found in jar burials, a practice whose popularity had decreased by the Iron Age. This is not to say that people did not bury fetuses or treat miscarried babies in a special way. However, without some sort of burial receptacle, their remains would be easily lost to time. These examples demonstrate that in some cases care was given to fetuses who died before reaching full term. Why some fetuses received burials and others did not remains unknown.

Birth

The birth of a child was a joyous occasion. Piecing together different sources, we find a robust set of traditions related to the birth of the newborn child. The exact gestation period varies from source to source. While Hebrew Bible does not give a specific number of gestational months or days, the ANE sources provide more details (Garroway 2018: 40–42; Stol 2000: 23–25). A Babylonian horoscope, calculating from the moment of conception, records a gestation of either 279 or 273 days (depending on the variant readings) (Sachs 1952: 51, 59). The Old Babylonian Atrahasis myth states that the birth goddess Nintu-Mami was pregnant for ten months:

> The midwives helped Nintu-Mami mount the birth stool . . . She counted ten months to determine her date. The tenth month came; Nintu-Mami went into labor.
> *(Matthews and Benjamin 2006: 36)*

The Hittite Laws also discuss gestation and birth. Hittite Law 17 says:

> If anyone causes a free woman to miscarry, [if] it is in her tenth month, he shall pay 10 shekels of silver, if it is in her fifth month, he shall pay 5 shekels of silver. He shall look to his house for it.
>
> (Roth 1997: 219)

The emphasis on the timing in the Hittite law has to do with whether the pregnancy has come to term. A woman in her tenth month was likely to give birth at any moment, and so the fine is greater. Pregnancies today are counted from the time of the woman's last menstrual cycle, and birth generally happens at the 40-week mark. The ancient texts count a little differently; any pregnancy that extended past nine months and into the tenth month would not be counted as nine months plus X number of days, but rather as ten months.

Once birthed, a newborn baby was cleaned and cared for by the midwives. Three main activities are discussed in the texts: Cutting the umbilical cord, washing the baby, and swaddling it. Ezekiel 16:4 concerns an infant who was abandoned, for whom these three things were not done: "As for your birth, on the day you were born, your cord was not cut, you were not washed with water to clean you, nor rubbed with salt, nor wrapped in wrapping (swaddled)." The Mesopotamian text "Enki and the World Order" provides a similar picture of the birthing room. In this narrative, leeks are used to stop the bleeding umbilical cord, and the child is rubbed with oil (not salt) and its mouth cleared of amniotic fluid. A hymn to Ninisinna describes midwives as conducting a sort of post-birth checkup, similar to the modern Apgar scoring (Garroway 2018: 58–61; Scurlock 1991: 148). Visual depictions of cutting the umbilical cord, cleaning the child, and swaddling it are found on multiple pieces from Mesopotamia, including a *kudurru* boundary stele from the latter part of the Kassite Period and a cylinder seal from the Neo-Babylonian period. The images on these items represent a birthing scene in a more stylized ritual setting (Garroway 2018: 63–65, Figures 2.3, 2.4, and 2.5; Van Buren 1933–34). By engaging in the acts of cleaning and swaddling the infant, a person was signaling that they were accepting responsibility for the child. Parents adopting a newborn "in its birth waters" might do these things to show the transfer of legal responsibility (Garroway 2018: 66; Wilke 1981).

Naming a Child

According to the Hebrew Bible, women and men alike named children. Sarah and Abraham name their son Isaac, "laughter" (Gen 21:2–6). Leah praises the Lord and names her fourth son Judah (Gen 29:35); Zilphah rejoices "what luck!" and names her first son Gad. Subsequently, she cries "what fortune," and names her next son Asher (Gen 30:9–13). Names from surrounding cultures also identify a child as precious to the family: "El (God) has given [a child]"; Shemaiah, "Yahweh has heard"; Nabu-apal-iddin, "Nabu has given an heir"; Išme-Dagan, "Dagan has heard [a plea for conception]"; Amenhotep, "Amun has proved to be gracious" (Byrne 2004: 138; Feucht 2001: 262; Janssen and Janssen, 1990: 14). A baby's name could also express circumstances of the birth or circumstances surrounding the birth. For example, there are names reminiscent of a difficult birth. Benjamin's name means "son of my right hand," but he was originally named Ben-Oni, "son of my affliction" (Gen 35:18). Jephthah's name means "Let the [Divine Name] open the womb;" similarly, the name Iptaṭar-lišir means "[Divine Name] has loosened the womb, let the child thrive/pass through" (Byrne 2004: 138).

Children who were born into slavery appear to have a different naming pattern. Free children were called so-and-so son/daughter of so-and-so. Slave children were only identified by their name; no patronym was given. In addition, at least as far as the biblical text indicates, free-born babies were named close to birth. On the other hand, regarding slave children, the sale documents suggest they were likely not named until they were two or three years of age. Prior to this, a slave infant was listed as a "unit" with its mother. Both would be sold together and only the mother was named. Consider the following two Neo-Babylonian period sale documents (Dandamaev 1984).

> Iddina-Nabu, son of Mušezib-Bel has voluntarily sold to Itti-Marduk-blatu son of Nabu-ahhe-iddin descendant of Egibi his slave woman, Nana-ittija and her daughter of three months, an Egyptian from his booty of the bow, for two minas of silver as the full price.
> *(Camb. 334)*

> Ibna son of Šum-ukin, of his own free will, sold Šahana and her three-year-old daughter Ša-Nana-bani to Šamaš-dannu son of Mušezib-Marduk descendant of the priest of the city of Akkad for one-half mina five shekels of silver, the price agreed upon.
> *(Nbk. 100)*

The identity of the child, therefore, remained bound up in the mother's identity until a time when it was old enough to separate from her and be viable on its own. Naming at two to three years of age seems to correspond with weaning, at which point a child could survive on its own and would be sold separately. Since there are no sale documents from ancient Israel, we cannot tell whether a similar naming process for slave children occurred there.

Caring for Infants

Most women nursed their own children, but as will be seen, there were cases when this was not possible. Nursing is an activity that can bond the child and mother, and a mother's breast is linked to comfort in Isa 66:13 and Ps 22:9 [Heb. 22:10]. There are many words used to describe the nursing infant, and as Parker (2013: 67–73) notes, these words all carry with them an aspect of vulnerability, highlighting the uncertainty that comes with not knowing if the infant would survive into childhood.

Survival was dependent upon the infant's ability to latch and properly nurse, as well as the mother's ability to produce milk. At times, these two things were at odds with each other. There were cases when the mother died, when the child was separated from the mother, or when a mother chose not to nurse so that she might increase her chances of becoming pregnant more quickly.[11] Wet-nurse contracts from the Mesopotamian world suggest that the period of nursing lasted for two to three years (Garroway 2014: 259–63). At this age, a child would also have solid food as a part of their diet. Considering that women needed to have an estimated six pregnancies to produce two children who survived to adulthood, nursing for a period of two to three years might also have served a practical purpose as an infant's immune system would benefit from the mother's milk (Meyers 2013: 98–99, 110).

Alternatives to nursing might have included an ancient form of a bottle or sippy cup. Small cups with a little spout have been found in Egyptian funerary contexts. One of the cups was made of faience and elaborately decorated with protective images (Figure 19.1). Other little cups were made of clay and looked like a tiny bowls with a pinched spout (Figure 19.2). An equivalent concept in ancient Israel might be represented by the small

Figure 19.1 Faience feeding cup for infants. Accession no.: 44.4.4, Rogers Fund, 1944, The Metropolitan Museum of Art

Figure 19.2 Clay feeding bowl for infants. Accession no.: 09.180.768c, Rogers Fund, 1909, The Metropolitan Museum of Art

juglets found in infant burials (Garroway 2014: 299–316, 2018: 101). When juglets are found in burials, they are often placed close to the infant's head as if tipping the liquid into the infant's mouth. These so-called sippy cups or bottles may have only served a ritual function. Other juglets may have had a cloth covering that would control the flow of the liquid (Avissar-Lewis 2010: 54–55, 184).

Since most infants nursed, mothers or wet-nurses could not leave the infants alone for long periods of time. Many cultures practice "on-demand" feeding rather than scheduled feedings. The latter is a creation linked to the 20th century and the invention of formula

(Bryder 2009). On-demand feeding is often linked with baby wearing and using a sling or other device to keep the infant attached to the nursing woman's body. Most visual representations of baby carriers come from the Egyptian record. The images span a wide range of dates, with examples from the 18th dynasty through the 25th dynasty. They depict both Egyptians and non-Egyptians using different kinds of baby carriers such as cloth wraps or baskets held on the head or back. In Mesopotamia, there is the possibility that long lengths of cloth were also used for swaddling. Plaques showing the birth goddess Ninhursag include a U-shaped object framing the goddess. The object might represent a long cloth wrap (like the American brand the "Moby Wrap"), wound at both ends like an ACE bandage (Garroway 2018: 92–93). Cloth does not preserve well, and no wraps have been found in the archaeological record. The Hebrew Bible, for its part, does suggest that baby carriers were used. The combination of nursing the infant while carrying it is seen in the Hebrew of Isa 66:11–13. Translations miss this connection, translating it as "you [the infant nation] shall nurse *and* you will be carried on her side, and dandled upon her knee." Inserting the word *and* takes away the imagery of an infant who is simultaneously carried [via a baby carrier] and nursing at the same time, as it seems most infants would have been.

Becoming Boys and Girls

Childhood in ancient Israel was unlike childhood in contemporary Western society.[12] Children did not receive a formal education. While it is possible some elite or royal children received scribal training, it seems that this was the exception that proved the rule (Flynn 2018: 94–100). Unlike many contemporary societies, children and adults did not spend most of their day in separate spheres (Parker 2013: 24–39). Furthermore, while there was some leisure time, as children grew, they would be increasingly incorporated into the household as participants in the household economy. Because of the gendered nature of much of ancient Israelite society, children were also expected to grow up to be women and men, in imitation of their mothers and fathers. A child's gender, therefore, affected the child's early years and the socialization process that a child underwent.

The process of passing on culture to the next generation is called enculturation. Identifying how this happened in the archaeological record is both important and difficult. Social anthropologists and archaeologists alike have commented upon the complexity of this issue: "One of the major challenges of [illuminating] the child's world […is] to throw light upon the transference of culture and tradition from one generation to another" (Lillehammer 1989: 90). Transfer of culture and tradition in ancient Israel meant adults needed to train up the next generation of Israelites. Socialization goes hand in hand with enculturation (Derevenski 1997). As children observe the actions of the adults in their lives, they learn to model their own behaviors after them. Ancient texts acknowledge this fact in their own way. The "Instruction of Amenemope" states: "If you make your life with these (words) in your heart, your children will observe them" (*COS* 1.47). Deut 6:6–9 describes enculturation in this way:

> Take to heart these instructions with which I charge you this day. Impress them upon your children. Recite them when you stay at home and when you are away, when you lie down and when you get up. Bind them as a sign on your hand and let them serve as a symbol on your forehead, inscribe them on the doorposts of your house and on your gates.
>
> *(JPS)*

The instructions in question are the commandments instructing the Israelites on how to live. Deuteronomy 6 stresses that the locus of that instruction is the home. The people for whom the instruction is meant are the children, the future generations of Israelites. A parent's job was quite literally to train up the next generation, to model for the children what it meant to be an Israelite. Deuteronomy is offering instructions on a religious and ethical level, on what makes an Israelite different than their neighbor. Children would see parents acting "Israelite" and would witness visual reminders of what it meant to be "Israelite" every time they passed through an Israelite door or gate as they saw the *mezzuzot*.

The basic unit structuring Israelite society was the *bet 'av* (Meyers 2013: 112; see Lehmann, this volume). Understanding the *bet 'av* as not only a location, the physical living space, but as a people group informs another kind of enculturation as well, one that is tied to gender (Bender 1996; Chapman 2016: 20–74). Looking to the material record for clues on the gendering process is "to consider something with a focus on gender or gender issues" (Meyers 2003: 190). Archaeologists engender a site by considering how space and objects were used by individuals (Baxter 2005; Derevenski 2000; Nelson 2006).[13] Determining the use of space and objects can be done by examining the texts, iconography, and skeletal remains of a society. Identifying gendered activities is part of the task; understanding how gender is passed on from adults to children is equally important. Gender is understood both as socially constructed and as a performance (Butler 1990; Crowley, Foley, and Shehan 2008; Nelson 2006). An adult performs gender as they conduct their day, and children both observe these actions and then enact the behaviors as they learn to become adult males and females.

Displays of gender can be seen visually in the reliefs depicting Sennacherib's siege of Lachish in 701 BCE. Lines of deported families include newborns, toddlers, young children, and older children. These reliefs show men dressed in short, belted tunics, while women wear ankle-length dresses and long hooded overcoats (Garroway 2020). It appears that a child's social age and gender dictated their style of dress, attesting to the social construction of gender. The smallest children (infants) are naked, while toddlers wear a tunic, and older children begin to dress like their older female and male counterparts.

Children and Religion

Both women and men engaged in the household religion, modeling different aspects of it for the children within the house (see Smoak this volume). Rooms with mixed ceramic assemblages of ritual and quotidian wares at Tel Jawa and Tell Halif attest to the intermingling of domestic religion with daily affairs (Daviau 2001; Hardin 2010). Religious practices for women and men might include baking offerings for various deities, pouring out libations, prayers, making sacrifices and offerings, and enacting protective rituals. According to the Hebrew Bible, there would be certain instances in which children would ask and learn from their parents about the rituals they saw conducted (Exod 12:26–27). With a culture that existed on a cyclical ritual calendar, children would witness some of these actions on a yearly basis, while seeing others conducted weekly, or even daily. Passover offers one example of a yearly ritual that was a home ritual, as well as a ritual that directly affected children.[14] The ritual requires the family to prepare an elaborate sacrificial meal, perform an apotropaic ritual to protect the children, and then quarantine within the house for an entire evening until the plague of death was no longer a threat to the firstborn child. Children are witnesses to these events and perhaps even active participants in the ritual. Children could do simple tasks like gather wood for the fire or help with the animal used for sacrifice (Jer 7:14).[15]

Household religion centered upon the family, and as seen with the Passover example, much of its focus concentrated on those members of the household who were vulnerable.[16] Pregnant women, newborn infants, and young children fell into this category, and it is no wonder with an infant mortality rate upwards of 50%.[17] Excavations have uncovered amulets of the demon Pazuzu, attacker of fetuses (Garroway 2018: 112–13). Amulets such as these could be worn by expectant mothers wishing to ward off the danger posed by malevolent demons. Other amulets were also worn as protective measures. Images of Bes, a minor Egyptian deity known for protecting pregnant women, young children, and the beds of young children, are found throughout the Levant and at major Iron Age Israelite sites (Garroway 2018: 121; Keel and Uehlinger 1998: 20–21).[18] The *wedjat* eye, another Egyptian import, was also used to protect ancient Israelite households (Garroway 2018: 127; Meyers 2013: 155).[19] Shiny objects, mirrors, and other small objects could also function as protective measures, as did lamps that would provide divine protection to ward off the demons of darkness (Job 29:4; Prov 6:20–23; Meyers 2013: 154–55).

The Deceased Child

References to childhood death and burials of infants and children represent the actualization of the fears referenced above. The child so longed for, so valuable to the family, often did not live to reach adulthood. Texts such as 1 Kgs 17 and 2 Kgs 4:17–20 demonstrate the anxiety felt when losing a son in childhood. Texts from surrounding lands also describe sick children and a desire to heal them. A letter from Mari states that "three children of Baṭaḫrum, […], all died at one time. One day they were fine, the next day they were sick, and a diviner was summoned, but to no avail" (Volk 1999: 6).[20] Another royal text calls for the king of Mari to be forewarned that upon his return home he will find his infant daughter has died (Harris 2000: 16).[21] The implication was that, like King David (2 Samuel 12), Zimri-Lim would be emotionally distraught and would need to compose himself before his subjects.

Children died from many different causes, and while the textual record can be vague on causes of death, the archaeological record provides a wealth of information. Evidence of childhood illnesses can be found in skeletal remains, especially in the dental record (Garroway 2020: 241–43). Without modern medical advances, like strong antibiotics, children succumbed to sickness and disease. Once weaned, children often died of malnutrition caused not by lack of food, but by lacking a variety of foods. A lack of vitamin D and calcium caused a major issue. Without these nutrients, children develop rickets and osteomalacia, the result of which is deformed bones. Lacking vitamin C, children's skulls could not bind and form connective tissues, so that even a small trauma in childhood could cause hemorrhaging and death. Spongy and porous bone tissues attest to iron deficiencies and a need for what today we might call a multivitamin.

While population estimates can be a bit tricky, the consensus found in the literature is that many children died, but very few of them have been identified in a mortuary context (Smith 1993). The reasons for the dearth of children abound, but it is likely that most children were buried in unmarked graves that have since been lost to the archaeological record. Within the lands of ancient Israel, when children have been found, they are discovered in multiple contexts: family tombs, caves, pits, and jars (Garroway 2014: 218–44, 2020: 255–65). While the biblical text suggests that child sacrifice was a regular practice, no evidence of cremated children or Tophet pits like those found in Carthage have been excavated in ancient Israel (Dewrell 2017).

Summary

Children represented the future of ancient Israelite society. The desire to have children can be seen in every aspect of life, from the social, to economic, to religious spheres and everything in between. The time and effort that went in to conceiving and then raising a child demonstrates the value that was placed on the child's life. Women would continue to get pregnant time after time, enduring multiple miscarriages to have a child survive until adulthood. Adults, seeking to recreate their society, actively enculturated and engendered children. Children were valuable as workers in the household and as heirs. As children grew up, the marriages contracted for them would tighten the bonds of the various kin groups. The birth of a child also represented potential stability for the parents who would need someone to take care of them in their old age. Ironically, then, the person most valued in a household could also be the person most vulnerable. Again, time and energy were poured into safeguarding these small ones. Rituals of protecting them began *in utero* and continued through birth, infancy, and a child's early years. Yet, even the best efforts might result in failure and the death of a child, at which point the desire for the valued child started the cycle all over again.

Notes

1 This study acknowledges that the biblical text was composed by many hands over a period of many years (ca. late 8th to at least the 5th century BCE).
2 For a history of scholarship on comparative research see Hays 2014: 15–38.
3 Gen 16:2, 17:15–16, 21:1–2, 29:31, 30:2; Judg 13:5; Ruth 4:12–14; 1 Sam 1:11; Job 1:21; Ps 139:13–16.
4 All translations are from the JPS unless otherwise noted.
5 Sarah, Rebekah, Rachel, Hannah, and the wife of Manoah all fall into this category.
6 Mesopotamian texts do entertain the possibility that infertility was the fault of the male (Biggs 1967: 13, 17, 18; Bullogh 1971: 191). See the discussion in Stol 2000: 148–52.
7 Given the way that women were understood to give birth in a squatting position, is possible that Bilhah might lean on Rachel for support during the birthing process (Garroway 2018: 66).
8 See the translation in the NLT, ESV, KJV, ISV, NASB.
9 The law of primogeniture was important because land was a non-renewable resource. The law of double portions meant that a person's property did not get broken up into smaller parcels too quickly.
10 The narrative of Zelophehad's daughters has been used to argue that daughters could inherit land in the case there was no son to inherit. As Aaron (2009) and Levine (2000: 357–61) have argued, the story is not about female empowerment, but about pushing the ideologies of the male government and land rights, respectively. Stol (2000: 30003) and Ben-Barak (1980: 22–33) demonstrate that female inheritance appears to be more of an ad hoc than regular practice.
11 Some women of higher social status, such as queens, did not nurse their children. For example, the Egyptians had a specific role for the official royal palace wet-nurse. King Joash's mother also employed a royal wet-nurse (2 Kgs 11:2–3).
12 Western refers to European and North American societies.
13 Spatial reconstructions of households combined with anthropological, sociological, and ethnological studies inform how spaces and objects are interpreted and assigned to men and women and in turn to children.
14 Exodus 12 describes a home ritual, moved later to the Temple. The ritual of *matzah* was a separate ritual, one that later became a yearly pilgrimage (Exod 34:18–23; Deut 16:1–17). As a home ritual, Passover is thought to stem from shepherds moving their flocks to new grazing grounds (Garroway n.d.). Schneider (2015) identified Egyptian magical overtones to the text.
15 Ethnographic reports attest to children (generally boys) in agrarian societies helping with shepherding duties and tending animals (Watson 1979: 105–12).
16 Aging members of the household, as well as those who were ill or otherwise incapacitated would also fall into the category of vulnerable individuals.

17 Ewbank and Gribble 1993; Smith and Avishai 2005: 86; Smith and Faerman 2008: 211.
18 Lachish, Gezer, Tell en-Nasbeh, Beth Shean, Megiddo, Tell Mevorakh, and Tell el-Hesi.
19 *Wedjat* eyes have been uncovered in Iron Age layers at Jericho, Gezer, Gerar, and Beersheba. Superstitions around the evil eye are reported in early 20th-century Palestine, causing villagers to keep their children dirty and unkempt as beautiful children attracted attention (Granqvist 1950: 107–11).
20 Author's translation from German.
21 While these Mari texts are a bit earlier in time, they are included to show that concern upon the death of a child is something that transcends time and space.

Bibliography

Aaron, David. 2009. "The Ruse of Zelophehad's Daughters." *HUCA* 80: 1–38.

Avissar-Lewis, Rona. "Childhood and Children in the Material Culture of the Land of Israel from the Middle Bronze Age to the Iron Age." PhD diss., Bar-Ilan University, 2010. [Hebrew]

Baxter, Judith. 2005. *The Archaeology of Childhood: Children, Gender, and Material Culture*. Walnut Creek: AltaMira Press.

Ben-Barak, Zafrira. 1980. "Inheritance by Daughter in the Ancient Near East." *Semitic Studies* 25: 22–33.

Bender, Shuna. 1996. *The Social Structure of Ancient Israel: The Institution of the Family* (beit 'ab) *from the Settlement to the End of the Monarchy*. Jerusalem: Simor.

Biggs, Robert. 1967. *ŠÀ.ZI.GA Ancient Mesopotamian Potency Incantations*. Locust Valley: Augustin.

Bryder, Linda. 2009. "From Breast to Bottle: A History of Modern Infant Feeding." *Endeavour* 33: 54–59.

Bullogh, Vern. 1971. "Deviant Sex in Mesopotamia." *Journal of Sex Research* 17: 184–203.

Butler, Judith. 1990. *Gender Trouble: Feminism and the Subversion of Identity*. London: Routledge.

Byrne, Ryan. 2004. "Lie Back and Think of Judah: The Reproductive Politics of Pillar Figurines." *NEA* 67: 137–51.

Chapman, Cynthia. 2016. *The House of the Mother: The Social Role of Maternal Kin in Biblical Hebrew Narrative and Poetry*. New Haven: Yale University Press.

Crowley, Sara, Lara Foley, and Constance Shehan, eds. 2008. *Gendering Bodies*. Lanham: Rowman & Littlefield.

Dandamaev, Muhammad. 1984. *Slavery in Babylonia: From Nabopolassar to Alexander the Great (636-331)*. Edited by M. A. Powell and D. B. Weisberg. Translated by V. A. Powell. DeKalb: Northern Illinois University Press.

Daviau, P. M. Michèle. 2001. "Family Religion: Evidence for the Paraphernalia of the Domestic Cult." Pages 199–229 in *The World of the Arameans II: Studies in History and Archaeology in Honor of Paul-Eugène Dion*. Edited by Paul-Eugène Dion. Sheffield: Sheffield Academic.

Derevenski, Joanna R. Sofaer. 1997. "Engendering Children, Engendering Archaeology." Pages 192–202 in *Invisible People and Processes: Writing Gender and Childhood into European Archaeology*. Edited by Jennie Moore and Eleanor Scott. London: Leicester University Press.

Derevenski, Joanna R. Sofaer, ed. 2000. *Children and Material Culture*. London: Routledge.

Dever, William. 2012. *Lives of Ordinary People in Ancient Israel: Where Archaeology and the Bible Intersect*. Grand Rapids: Eerdmans.

Dewrell, Heath. 2017. *Child Sacrifice in Ancient Israel*. Explorations in Ancient Near Eastern Civilizations 5. Winona Lake: Eisenbrauns.

Ewbank, Douglas, and James N. Gribble. 1993. *Effects of Health Programs on Child Mortality in Sub-Saharan Africa*. Washington, DC: National Academy Press.

Feucht, Erika. 2001. "Childhood." *OEAE* 1: 261–64.

Flynn, Shawn W. 2018. *Children in Ancient Israel: The Hebrew Bible and Mesopotamia in Comparative Perspective*. Oxford: Oxford University Press.

Foster, Catherine P., and Bradley J. Parker. 2012. "Introduction: Household Archaeology in the Near East and Beyond." Pages 1–14 in *New Perspectives on Household Archaeology*. Edited by Bradley J. Parker and Catherine P. Foster. Winona Lake: Eisenbrauns.

Garroway, Kristine. n.d. "The Origins of the Biblical Pesach." *TheTorah.com*. Online: www.thetorah.com/article/the-origins-of-the-biblical-pesach.

———. 2014. *Children in the Ancient Near Eastern Household.* Winona Lake: Eisenbrauns.
———. 2018. *Growing Up in Ancient Israel: Children in Material Culture and Biblical Text.* Atlanta: SBL.
———. 2020. "(Un)Dressing Children in the Lachish Reliefs: Questions of Gender, Status, and Ethnicity." *NEA* 83: 36–41.
Granqvist, Hilma. 1950. *Childhood Problems Among the Arabs: Studies in a Muhammadan Village in Palestine.* Helingsfors: Söderström.
Hardin, James. 2010. *Lahav II: Households and the Use of Domestic Space at Iron II Tell Halif: An Archaeology of Destruction.* Reports of the Lahav Research Project. Winona Lake: Eisenbrauns.
Harris, Rivkah. 2000. *Gender and Aging in Ancient Mesopotamia: The Gilgamesh Epic and Other Ancient Literature.* Norman: University of Oklahoma Press.
Hays, Christopher B. 2014. *Hidden Riches: A Sourcebook for the Comparative Study of the Hebrew Bible and Ancient Near East.* Louisville: Westminster John Knox.
Janssen, Jac, and Rosalind Janssen. 1990. *Growing Up in Ancient Egypt.* London: Rubicon.
Keel, Othmar, and Christopher Uehlinger. 1998. *Gods, Goddesses, and Images of God in Ancient Israel.* Edinburgh: T&T Clark.
Koepf-Taylor, Laurel. 2013. *Give Me Children or I Shall Die: Children and Communal Survival in Biblical Literature.* Minneapolis: Fortress Press.
Levine, Baruch. 2000. *Numbers 21–36: A New Translation with Introduction and Commentary.* New York: Doubleday.
Lillehammer, Grete. 1989. "A Child Is Born: The Child's World in an Archaeological Perspective." *Norwegian Archaeological Review* 22: 89–105.
Matthews, Victor, and Don Benjamin. 2006. *Old Testament Parallels: Laws and Stories from the Ancient Near East.* New York: Paulist Press.
Meyers, Carol. 2003. "Engendering Syro-Palestinian Archaeology: Reasons and Resources." *NEA* 66: 185–97.
———. 2013. *Rediscovering Eve: Ancient Israelite Women in Context.* Oxford: Oxford University Press.
Moss, Candida R., and Joel S. Baden. 2015. *Reconceiving Infertility: Biblical Perspectives on Procreation and Childlessness.* Princeton: Princeton University Press.
Nahkai, Beth Alpert. 2008. "Female Infanticide in Iron II Israel and Judah." Pages 257–72 in *Sacred History, Sacred Literature: Essays on Ancient Israel, the Bible, and Religion in Honor of Richard Elliott Freidman.* Edited by Shawna Dolansky. Winona Lake: Eisenbrauns.
Nelson, Sarah, ed. 2006. *Handbook of Gender in Archaeology.* Lanham: AltaMira Press.
Parker, Julie. 2013. *Valuable and Vulnerable: Children in the Hebrew Bible, Especially the Elisha Cycle.* Atlanta: SBL.
Pearson, Michael Parker. 2000. *The Archaeology of Death and Burial.* College Station: Texas A&M.
Roth, Martha. 1997. *Law Collections from Mesopotamia and Asia Minor.* Atlanta: SBL.
Sachs, Abraham. 1952. "Babylonian Horoscopes." *JCS* 6: 49–75.
Schneider, Thomas. 2015. "God's Infanticide in the Night of Passover: Exodus 12 in the Light of Ancient Egyptian Rituals." Pages 52–76 in *Not Sparing the Child: Human Sacrifice in the Ancient World and Beyond.* Studies in Honor of Professor Paul G. Mosca. Edited by Daphna Arbel, Paul C. Burns, J. R. C. Cousland, Richard Menkis, and Dietmar Neufeld. New York: Bloomsbury/T&T Clark.
Scurlock, JoAnn. 1991. "Baby Snatching Demons, Restless Souls and the Dangers of Childbirth: Medio-Magical Means of Dealing with Some of the Perils of Motherhood in Ancient Mesopotamia." *Incognita* 2: 137–85.
Smith, Patricia. 1993. "An Approach to the Paleodemographic Analysis of Human Skeletal Remains from Archaeological Sites." Pages 2–13 in *Biblical Archaeology Today 1990: Proceedings of the Second International Congress on Biblical Archaeology.* Edited by Avraham Biran and Joseph Aviram. Jerusalem: Israel Exploration Society, Israel Academy of Sciences and Humanities.
Smith, Patricia, and Gal Avishai. 2005. "The Use of Dental Criteria for Estimating Postnatal Survival in Skeletal Remains of Infants." *JAS* 32: 83–89.
Smith, Patricia, and Marina Faerman. 2008. "Has Society Changed Its Attitude to Infants and Children? Evidence from Archaeological Sites in the Southern Levant." Pages 211–19 in *Nasciturus, Infans, Puerulus Vobis Mater Terra: La Muerte en la Infancia.* Edited by Francesc Gusi i Jener, Susanna Muriel, and Carme Olària. Castelló: Servei D'investigacions Arquelògiques Prehistòriques.
Steinberg, Naomi. 1993. *Kinship and Marriage in Genesis: A Household Economics Perspective.* Minneapolis: Fortress Press.
Stol, Marten. 2000. *Women in the Ancient Near East.* Berlin: De Gruyter.

Van Buren, E. Douglas. 1933–1934. "Clay Relief in the Iraq Museum." *AfO* 9: 165–71.
Volk, Konrad. 1999. "Kinderkrankheiten Nach der Darstellung Babylonisch-Assrischer Keilscrifttexte." *Or* 2: 1–30.
Watson, Patty Jo. 1979. *Archaeological Ethnography in Western Iran*. Tucson: University of Arizona Press.
Wilk, Richard, and William Rathje. 1982. "Household Archaeology." *American Behavioral Scientist* 25: 617–39.
Wilke, Claus. 1981. "Noch Einmal: Šilip rēmim und die Adoption *Ina Mēšu: Neue und Alte Einschlägige Text*." *ZAW* 71: 87–94.

20
SOCIAL ISSUES IN THE ESTABLISHMENT OF BIBLICAL LAW IN THE IRON AGE

Eckart Otto

I. General Characteristics of Biblical Law in the Iron Age

For any society, law represents an indispensable instrument for strengthening its societal cohesion. Law draws its effectiveness from two basic functions of the legal sphere: settling conflicts to minimize violence on the one hand, and stabilizing the behavior of its members in socially acceptable actions by using sanctions to safeguard norms, which are vital for the endurance and survival of society on the other hand. In early societies, the norms connected with sanctions and the rules for the resolution of conflicts were handed down by way of oral traditions as the pristine form of laws. This was also the case in early Israel as a tribal society.

In state societies, these two functions of legal institutions—to solve conflicts and to preserve the observation of socially accepted norms of behavior—tend to be assumed by the state or placed under its control and supervision (Westbrook 2003). In ancient Egypt, the king's embodiment of law did not tolerate any curtailment of his competence to make legal decisions on the part of fixed laws, so that there did not exist law codes in pre-demotic Egypt. In Mesopotamia, the gods commissioned the king to implement the law and he could delegate this task to subordinate legal institutions and courts. Within this system of delegation, legal propositions were codified as a description of legal practice for educational purposes. These propositions were given a theological framing exemplifying the king's legal function and placed on public display, as in the case of the Laws of Hammurabi. In the form of scholarly texts such as the Middle Assyrian Laws, legal propositions also served to propagate legal reforms, or documented them in the manner of the Hittite Laws. However, different from biblical law, the Ancient Near Eastern laws never achieved a critical distance toward the state but were part of a royal state ideology. It is one of the most important characteristics of the legal history of Israel and Judah in the Iron Age that a process of governmental professionalization of the legal courts happened late in the preexilic period of the 8th–7th century BCE. This process of governmental takeover of lay authority is reflected by Isa 1:21–26; 3:1–9; Zeph 3:1–4 and Deut 16:18–19 and in Judean royal ideology showing the king as judge (2 Sam 15: 1–6; Ps 72). Consequently, this period of an organization of the legal sphere by the state, which ended with the Neo-Babylonian catastrophe in the 6th century BCE, remained short, so that biblical law preserved many old traits of legal lay procedures, which characterized the early biblical legal history. The legal sphere of Torah thus could become an independent counterpart to the state before it became subjected to a Torah (Deut 17: 14–20) that was theologized by priests (Otto 1994).

Many profane legal sentences of biblical law codes had their origin in orally transmitted legal narratives of particular lawsuits of settling conflicts and trials, which had happened in Israel's early legal history at local courts of nonprofessionals. These legal narratives functioned to concretize court judgments of these legal proceedings for later generations. Casuistic legal sentences—e.g., those formed by a protasis (if…) and an apodosis (then…)—were a kind of abstraction of individual items in these legal narratives that then universalized the concrete court judgments as valid for comparable cases by renouncing the specific information about the persons involved in the proceedings and the actual information of time and space of the narrated proceedings. This meant that most legal sentences of biblical law had an inner Judean and Israelite origin and were not a translation of cuneiform laws such as the Codex Hammurabi (*pace* Wright 2009).

With the formation of states in Israel and Judah in the 9th–8th centuries, started a professionalization of the legal institutions and proceedings by legal education and training of professional judges for conducting proceedings and making judgments. This training related to schools of wisdom comparable to the Babylonian house of tablets (É.DUBB.A). A text from Deir 'Alla of the 9th century BCE (Combination B l.17) shows such a connection between legal and sapiential education reading "you are responsible for *mšpṭ* (legal decision) and *mlqh/ mšl* (proverb)." In this context of the wisdom-school, indigenous legal sentences—derived from oral legal narratives of lay courts—were comparable to cuneiform legal collections, e.g. the Laws of Eshnunna (Otto 1989), collected and compiled in small legal collections of special topics (bodily injuries or material damages). It is also in this context that scribes were trained to become professional judges and that the influence of traditions of cuneiform law on biblical law by the reception of single legal sentences like those of the goring ox (Exod 22:28–32) appears. Cuneiform law also had an influence on the methods of compilation and redaction of collections of legal sentences. The small collections of law, out of which the Book of the Covenant (BC) was formed can give a good impression of these techniques influenced by those of cuneiform law (Otto 1991).

Priestly groups took over these legal collections and developed them in two directions. First, the legal collections, which the priests took over, were used to solve conflicts between families, clans, and single persons of the same social level. The priests detected the power of this law in resolving conflicts, but they used it in a context that was different from that of the original law, a society, which was economically more and more hierarchized in the states of Israel and Judah during the 9th–7th centuries BCE. The change of economy from a subsistence economy to a rent-capitalism in the states of Israel and Judah during the Iron Age caused processes of urbanization, division of labor, and a social chasm between a class of big landowners on the one side and a class of smallholders and debt slaves on the other. It was not only prophets like Amos, Micah, and Isaiah who reacted to these social developments and their fatal consequences for the coherence of the society, but also groups of scholarly educated priests, who used the power of law to resolve social conflicts between different classes in the society and to strengthen its coherence by emphasizing solidarity of the farm owners with the poor and the impoverished. These priestly authors of social law used a most effective tool for strengthening the power of their social law to resolve social conflicts and to keep a socially fractured society together. They claimed to know YHWH's will and social demands for an ethos of solidarity among the members of different social classes in Israel and Judah, and how they should deal with each other even in matters concerning the economy (Exod. 23:20–26). Second, they were used as a most effective tool to keep the society together – a theologization of originally profane law collections, which, before they were taken over by priests, served as the legal training for professional judges. The priests connected these collections with a social law, which was justified theologically by representing God's demand. The break lines of an economically hierarchized and fractured society were the gateway for a theological interpretation of the law as an expression of a divine will and opened the door for the combination of legal sentences of profane and cultic laws already in the Book of the Covenant (Otto 1988).

II. Biblical Law Codes in the Iron Age

1. The Book of the Covenant in Exodus 20–23

The title "Book of the Covenant" or "Covenant Code" for the law collection in Exod 20–23 is derived by modern biblical scholars from Exod 24:7, which describes Moses reading a book of the covenant (*sēpher ha-bĕrît*) to the people of Israel at Mount Sinai. The preexilic Book of the Covenant (BC) had a literary history of its own as a self-contained unit independent from its literary context in the Sinai pericope in Exod 19–24 and a marked literary profile of its own. It was formed out of likewise originally self-contained units of collections of casuistic laws of compensation of damages in Exod 21:33-22:14 characterized by the formulation of the apodosis by a demand of restitution or compensation ([*šāllēm*] *yĕšāllēm*) or a dispensation from restitution or compensation (*lo' yĕšāllēm*). The legal sentences of this collection define cases of compensation of loss and damages of deposits, of animals, and of the harvest in cases of negligence, alternating with laws marking off the cases of dispensation from compensation. This collection incorporated laws of deposit in Exod 22:6–14, which served as a kind of paradigm for all the other case laws in the BC reflecting the connection between early literary and legal historical developments from a law of pure compensation to an early penal law, which required punishment by multiples of compensation in cases of theft as in Exod 21:37-22:3.

A second self-contained collection of legal sentences contained laws of bodily injuries in Exod 21:18–32 (Otto 1991). In this collection laws concerning free persons in Exod 21:18,22–25,28–31 alternated with those concerning slaves in Exod 21:20–21,26–27,32 and laws demanding the death penalty in Exod 21:20,23,29, (31) alternated with those requiring compensation in Exod 21:18–19,21–22,26,30,32. Structuring the compilation and redaction of these laws this way had the function of marking off fatal from nonfatal cases that only required compensation. The *talion* formula in Exod 21:24–25 was presupposed and quoted in Exod 21:26–27, a legal sentence firmly connected to Exod 21:20–21, so that the *talion* got the function of a center by the redaction of this collection. The laws adjacent to the talion statute confirmed the death penalty in Exod 21:23 but revised it by canceling a talionic punishment of bodily injuries in favor of a compensation in nonfatal cases. The laws of bodily injuries reflected a legal historical progress and showed traits of an influence of wisdom traditions (cf. Prov 13:8–9), which indicates that they did not function as positive law in a modern sense but as part of a school curriculum of training professional judges and experts in the 9th–8th century BCE (Wells 2019). Scribes with a sapiential background also collected legal sentences of procedural law in Exod 23:1–3,6–8 (cf. Prov 17:23), which in the redaction of the BC related to rules of an ethics of solidarity with the neighbor in Exod 23:4–5. They also collected and compiled legal sentences of apodictic law in Exod 21:12–17 and 22:17–19, which were also integrated into the BC by its priestly redactors. Contrary to the casuistic law, the apodictic law in Exod 21;12–17 did not originate in court decisions, but it consisted of sentences of a family law of clans and extended families executed by the *pater familias* in the families. The cultic rules in Exod 22:17–19a were created by the priestly redactors of the BC following the form-critical paradigm of the apodictic family law in Exod 21:17–19.

Parallel to the social critique of the prophets in Israel and Judah in the 9th and 8th century BCE, which was a response to changes from an agrarian economy of independent small farmers into an economy of rent-capitalism, priestly groups took over these collections of casuistic and apodictic laws and compiled them in a new collection of the BC, giving it a comprehensive redactional structure of its own. They interpreted the originally profane laws theologically and ethically by an ethos of social solidarity and legitimized their interpretation theologically as a divine program for the coherence of society. Specifically, the priests formulated the social laws in Exod 21:2–11; 23:10–12 and then used them to frame the collections of apodictic and casuistic law within the BC. These framing laws thematized YHWH's privilege and its social consequences in a 6/7 pattern, derived from the time scheme of the Feast of Unleavened Bread. In the center of the BC its priestly redactors located legal rules of an ethics of social solidarity with the poor in Exod 22:20–26, claiming that solidarity with the poor was YHWH's demand as a compassionate and merciful God:

> You shall not exploit a stranger or oppress him, for you were strangers in the land of Egypt. You shall not mistreat any widow or orphan. If you mistreat them, they will cry to me, and I shall certainly hear their outcry to me, and my anger will burn, and I shall kill you with the sword and your wives shall become widows and your children orphans. If you lend money to my people, to the poor among you, you must not be like a moneylender to him, you must not exact interest from him. If you take your neighbor's garment in pledge, you are to return it to him before the sun is setting. It is his only clothing, the sole covering for his skin. In what else shall he sleep? Therefore, if he cries to me, I shall listen, because I am compassionate (*kî ḥannûn ʿānî*).

This theological interpretation of an originally profane law had no counterpart in cuneiform law. These sentences of a social law in Exod 22:20–26 reflected the development of a social ethics out of the legal sphere by a mixture of apodictic and casuistic formulations. The personal address also showed the strong parenetic accent of these sentences. On the other hand, they did not formulate direct legal sanctions in case such sanctions were disregarded, but instead left it to YHWH to punish those who did not care for any social ethics of solidarity. These sentences appealed to the insight of their addressees arguing for a limitation of pledge taking and appealing to a feeling of community when they were speaking of "your neighbor" and "the poor among you." But the strongest argument of the priestly authors was that YHWH himself, as an ethical idol, was a compassionate God. In Exod 22:26b the priestly redactors of the BC interpreted YHWH, the *ʾel ḥannûn*, as a solarized king god by using motives related to the preexilic Psalm 72:12–14, which was part of the liturgical literature at the temple of Jerusalem:

> For he will rescue the poor who cry out and the lowly who have no helper. He cares about the poor and the needy. He will save the lives of the poor. He will redeem them from oppression and violence, for their lives are precious for him.

This model, which speaks of a compassionate God who is full of empathy for the poor and needy, the addressees of the BC, should be emulated. Subsequently, the wealthy and strong members of the Judean society should also be compassionate with the poor and the needy.

The priestly redactors of the BC put a second cultic frame of an altar law (Exod 20:24–26) and of festival laws (Exod 23:14–19) around the frame of laws of YHWH's privilege in a 6/7 pattern and its social consequences for the male and female debt slaves in Exod 21:2–11; 23:10–12 in order to underline the theological interpretation of law in the BC.

The finale of the literary history and theological interpretation of the BC was its incorporation into the Sinai pericope in the Persian period. After most Hebrew Bible scholars worldwide have given up Wellhausen's documentary hypothesis of the sources of J, E, and P, which declared the Elohist to be responsible for the integration of the BC into a preexilic Sinai pericope, it became more and more evident that the BC was integrated into this pericope by a postexilic redaction that presupposed Deuteronomy and the P and combined Deuteronomistic and priestly motives of P. This kind of redactional activity in the Persian period was also responsible for the integration of the Decalogue into the Sinai pericope and the Deuteronomistic Deuteronomy into the Pentateuch. Under the presupposition that the formation of the Pentateuch was the product of a postexilic redaction combining Deuteronomy with the priestly source P, the formation of the Sinai pericope in its postexilic shape was derived from both these sources.

The postexilic redactors incorporated the pre-Deuteronomic BC into the post-Deuteronomistic Sinai pericope by means of their redactional technique for the postexilic Pentateuch also using the sources of their sources in Deuteronomy and P, as in Numb 13–14 and Deut 1:19–46 (Otto 2000). The pre-Deuteronomic BC was the source for Deut 12–26, and the redactors of the postexilic Sinai pericope knew this very well. Like other authors and redactors in the Pentateuch, they had an exact knowledge of its literary history. By incorporating the BC into the Sinai pericope the redactors attributed a theologically high authority to the BC as a direct revelation of YHWH at Mount Sinai, whereas Deuteronomy as its revision was "downgraded" to Moses' scriptural exegesis of the BC in the land of Moab (Otto 2012–2017: 231–38, 298–328). The reason for the attribution of such a high authority to the BC in relation to Deuteronomy was the historical knowledge of the redactors of the Pentateuch in the postexilic period that the BC was, as its source, older and more original than Deuteronomy. Out of this literary knowledge, they formed a theological argument of the degree of authority of the BC as YHWH's revelation at Mount Sinai.

2. The Preexilic Book of Deuteronomy in Deut 12–26

A sustainable foundation for the literary history of Deuteronomy is the insight that Deut 12–26 reformulated the BC; Deuteronomy was based not only on the scribal revision of single legal sentences of the BC (Levinson 1997). The redactors of the original Deuteronomy also used the redactional structure of the BC for that of Deut 12–26 and revised it according to their hermeneutics of a cult-centralization (Otto 1999: 203–382). A 7th-century date for the original version of Deuteronomy ("Urdeuteronomium")—during the reign of king Josiah—is underlined by the fact that Deut 13* and Deut 28 were subversive receptions of the Neo-Assyrian oath of loyalty to the Assyrian king Esarhaddon (Otto 2012–2017: 1959–2021; Steymans 1995), which was also sworn by the Judean king Manasseh in 672 BCE. The revision of the BC in Deut 12–26 had its main perspective in the centralization of the cultic place in Deut 12:13–19 as a hermeneutical key for all the revisions. The revision of the altar law of the BC in Exod 20:24–26 was in accord with the program of a cultic reform by king Josiah in Jerusalem and its surroundings according to 2 Kgs 23 (Otto 2012–2017: 1017–1200; Uehlinger 1995). The revision of the BC in Deut 12–26 was integrated into the subversive reception of the neo-Assyrian loyalty oath of king Esarhaddon in Deut 13 and 28. The original

Deuteronomy was based neither on collections of sources from early Israelite history nor on a Levitical sermonal practice (*pace* Von Rad 1948). The legal sentences of the BC that were affected by the centralization of the cult were revised in Deut 14–26 and all the commandments in the BC concerning the demand for solidarity with the poor and socially weak in the society of Judah were received too into the original Deuteronomy of the 7th century and revised according to the fraternal ethics of brotherhood. As in the BC, a framework comprising commandments of privilege law in the 6/7 pattern in Deut 14:22-15:23; 26:2–13* framed the order of festivals in Deut 16:1–17, which was a revision of the order of the BC in Exod 23:14–17; (34:18–26*), the rules for the organization of legal courts and procedural laws in Deut 16:18-18:5*, which was a revision of the procedural laws of the BC in Exod 23:1–3;6–8, and a block of legal revisions of BC in Deut 19:2–25:12*. The sequence of these laws was aligned with the centralization of the cult revising the legal sentences of the BC.

In Deuteronomy, the ethos of solidarity with the poor in the BC was extended to a program of fraternal social ethics of brotherhood, which granted every Judean solidarity that was normally owed only to the closest natural members of the family. With this ethics of brotherhood, Deuteronomy reacted to the dissolution of natural, genealogically legitimized ties of extended families and clans in Judah, founding a fraternal ethics in the families and clans. This dissolution was caused by the social and economic crisis in Judean society, which itself was exacerbated by Assyrian pressures in the late 8th and 7th centuries. This crisis, along with the external pressures caused the destruction of the solidarity-stabilizing cult of ancestors of extended families and clans; many Judeans lost their portions of land property because of Assyrian measures of deportation and Judean countermeasures of resettlement of parts of the Judean people living in the open land in fortified towns (Halpern 1991). In response to this development of the 7th century, every Judean, male or female, was attributed the status of a brother according to Deuteronomy. Deut 22:1–4 revised and expanded Exod 23:4–5 to a commandment concerning fraternal solidarity as a fundamental principle of Deuteronomic ethics. It required fraternal behavior even in relation to an enemy or litigant.

The commandment concerning fraternal solidarity was the foundation for a program of fraternal solidarity with the socially weak and needy. This program comprised the divine command of a regular release of debts in Deut 15:1–11* and the prohibition of taking interest from the fellow Judean in Deut 23:20–21. These commandments were part of a program of the preexilic Deuteronomy in the 7th century to overcome poverty in Judah, increased by an intensive influx of immigrants from the north. In Deut 15:4* the authors of Deuteronomy developed out of this program a utopian ideal of a society without any poverty:

> There will be no poor among you because YHWH, your God; will bless you in the land that YHWH, your God, gives you for an inheritance to possess, if only you obey the voice of YHWH and take care to do all his commandment, which I give you today. For YHWH, your God, will bless you as he promised you.

The authors of Deut 15:4–6* contradicted the developments of social crisis and turmoil by means of a social utopia of a divine promise of a society without any poverty. They described two interrelated ways of how this promise should become reality: On the one hand, YHWH would bless those who kept his command and listened to his voice, which was speaking to the addressees of Moses in Moab in the narrated time and the addressees of Deuteronomy in the time of narration in the Judean history. On the other hand, the promise, which YHWH had given by Moses' interpretation of the BC in Moab, was related to the command that creditors should release the debts to their fellow citizens as their brothers every 7th year in Deut 15:1–3:

> Every seventh year you shall practice remission of debts. This shall be the nature of the remission: Every creditor shall release what he has lent to his neighbor. He shall not harass his neighbor, his brother, because YHWH's release has been proclaimed. Of a foreigner you may exact it, but whatever of yours is with your brother, your hand shall release it.

The divine promise of a society without any poverty must not be an excuse not to release the debts with the argument that YHWH would solve all the problems of the debtors in the future. The realization of the utopian program of a society without any poverty should also depend on acts of a brotherly ethos by the Judean citizens according to God's commandments in Deuteronomy. Economic equality beyond poverty should be realized by renouncing any attempts to create wealth by taking advantage of the situation of social emergency of poor and needy fellow Judeans, as was ordered by YHWH in Deut 15:11:

> I command you: open your hand to the poor and needy brother in your land.

The command in Deut 23:20–21, not to charge any interest from a fellow Judean, complemented the commandments in Deut 15:

> You shall not lend at interest to your brother, no matter if the loan is of money or anything else that can earn interest. To a foreigner you may lend at interest, but to your brother you are not to lend at interest, so that YHWH, your God, will prosper you in everything you set out to do in the land you are entering in order to take possession of it.

This commandment was as those in Deut 15 part of the fraternal ethics in Deuteronomy, which aimed at a new way of economic behavior, different from that which was usually executed in the days of the authors of Deuteronomy. This prohibition to lend at interest was a Deuteronomic revision of the social ethics of a limitation of mortgage and the prohibition of usury in the BC in Exod 22:20–26. The Ancient Near Eastern cuneiform law knew of an institution of liable aid in distress, which the authors of Deuteronomy transformed into a general requirement of economic behavior in Judah, which paralleled Plato's economic axioms in the Nomi (742c):

> No one shall deposit money with anyone he does not trust, nor lend money at interest, since it is permissible for the borrower to refuse entirely to pay back either interest or principal.

Plato did not prohibit giving loans at interest, but he did not provide any legal security for loans and interest, and no legal protection should be granted for any contracts and claims for repayment. Such claims should not be enforceable by any legal process. The authors of Deuteronomy were stricter than Plato, prohibiting any loan at interest at all between fellow citizens in Judah. Deuteronomy spoke of damage to the Judean society caused by unlimited greed for wealth and property. Plato's focus was on the damage done to the soul of all the citizens and in the end, to all the society by greediness for wealth. Part of the Deuteronomic program to prevent economic damages by an opening schism of difference between rich and poor in Judean society was also the restriction of pledge taking in Deut 24:6,10–13,17★.

The authors of Deuteronomy believed the credit and banking system were responsible for increasing the social damages by the impoverishment of parts of the Judean society. Ancient Near Eastern societies also knew of the societal damages caused by an economy in which the rich could enlarge their wealth without any limitations while the impoverishment of the poor increased. Ancient Near Eastern states reacted by establishing the institution of irregular royal debt releases. Cuneiform law also knew of loans free of interest for neighbors in cases of emergency (Codex Ešnunna § 19); such cases had their roots in an agrarian ethics of neighborliness. The authors of Deuteronomy took up these legal institutions of Ancient Near Eastern economy and combined them with impulses they got from the revision of the social law of BC. Out of these roots, they formed a coherent program of fraternal ethics to domesticate the credit system in Judah. They replaced the genealogical justification for fraternal ethics with motives of a cultic constitution of Israel as a festival community at a central sanctuary under the inclusion of all the Judean *personae miserae*. All Judeans without any distinction of social status or gender were to participate in sacrifices at the central sanctuary (Deut 12:18). The poor, however, were due a particular degree of solidarity (Deut 14:28–29). In contrast to Mesopotamian royal edicts of restitution, which developed into pure acts of royal propaganda in the neo-Assyrian period, the Deuteronomic program of fraternal ethics remained separate from the authority of the state and had its roots in the state-critical attitude of this book.

The Deuteronomic Deuteronomy of the 7th century, as a revision of the BC, was understood as a direct expression of God's will, which was correlated to the central sanctuary; however, the loss of the temple of Jerusalem in the 6th century made it necessary during the exilic period to relocate Deuteronomy. The Deuteronomistic redactors of this period regarded Deut 12–26 as an interpretation of the Decalogue of Mount Horeb (Deut 5) in Moab. Both the BC and the original Deut of the 7th century did not mention the king and excarnated his legal function as lawgiver into YHWH's Torah (Assmann 1999). Furthermore, by formulating the Law of the King (Deut 17:14–20) Deuteronomists and post-Deuteronomistic authors of the Persian period divested the institution of kingship of all political functions and transformed the king into the first devout servant of the Torah among his people. At the same time, they domesticated a free prophecy (Deut 18:9–22) and made Moses the only arch-prophet (Deut 34:10–12). With locating the revelation of the Law at Mount Sinai and its expounding by Moses in Deuteronomy in the land of Moab even the notion of time, which the Ancient Near Eastern cultures could only conceive as royal time embodied by the king, was detached from the king following the demise of kingship, and BC and Deuteronomy were embedded in a kingless time structure of an ideal history of Israel's origins. History and law were linked together, thus creating the Torah for a postexilic Israel in the Persian period.

III. The Reception of Biblical Law of the Iron Age in the Late Babylonian and Persian Period

1. *The Decalogue in Deut 5 and Exod 20*

The designation Decalogue meaning "ten words" was derived from the late post-Deuteronomistic theory of ten commandments in Ex 20:2–17. The Decalogue in Deut 5:6–21, however, arranged the commandments in five groups of long and short commandments. It was the later version in Exod 20:2–17, which established an order of ten commandments.

This latter Decalogue was incorporated together with the BC into the post-priestly Sinai pericope in the Persian period, whereas the original Decalogue was redacted in the context of the Deuteronomistic Deut in the 6th century. After it was recognized in the 19th century that the Decalogue in Exod 20 was a literary addition to its narrative context in the Sinai pericope, biblical scholars faced the task of answering the question of the origin and dating of the Decalogue. After the answers of its dating varied in the first half of the 20th century between the Mosaic and postexilic periods, form criticism seemed to give a more stable foundation for answering these two questions. In contrast to a casuistic secular law, the prohibitions of the Decalogue as apodictic law were supposed to stem as genuine Israelite divine law from the wilderness (Alt 1959). But form criticism is not able to yield information concerning the origin of a legal sentence, but only about its functions within a legal system. A redaction-critical perspective can demonstrate that the original Decalogue in Deut 5 got its shape in a Deuteronomistic context, and that this Decalogue was subsequently revised in a perspective of the priestly source P in Exod 20 and inserted into the Sinai pericope. Instead of asking for a *setting in life* ("Sitz im Leben") of the Decalogue, one must ask for its *setting in the literature*.

Answering this question however does not yet determine the origin of the preexilic legal building blocks, out of which the Decalogue was compiled by Deuteronomistic redactors in the 6th century. We must ask for the preexilic material of the Iron Age that was used for the formation of the Decalogue. The change of speakers in the Decalogue from the first-person speech of God to a speech about God in the third person should not be traced to a secondary revision of the Decalogue because Deut 5:22 states, "YHWH spoke these words," a phrase that requires consistent divine first-person speech in the Decalogue. This change of YHWH speaking in the first person to speaking about YHWH in the third person can be better explained by the adaption of building blocks of legal traditions firmly anchored in the Iron Age Judean legal history.

Prior to Deut 5:17–19/Exod 20:13–16 being incorporated into the Decalogue the block comprised brief prohibitions without objects, which were originally an independent series of apodictic sentences of family laws:

> You shall not murder.
> You shall not commit adultery.
> You shall not steal.

These apodictic commandments were closely related to those apodictic laws of death penalty, which prohibited killing in Exod 21:12, adultery in Deut 22:22a; Lev 20:10, and kidnapping in Exod 21:16. Part of these laws was also the prohibition of violence directed against one's parents in Exod 21:15 and17, which stood behind the commandment to honor them (and also meant especially to nurture aging parents). This commandment was originally a family law that knew violence against the parents would damage the whole family and endanger its survival. The commandment of care for the aging parents in the Decalogue is grounded in the fact that the life force and soul of the family were accumulated in them so that the well-being of the family was dependent on the well-being of the parents.

The prohibition of stealing originally had the function in family law of prohibiting the kidnapping and selling of a family member. In its transmission, the theme of theft of valuables, which was rooted in casuistic law of the BC in Exod 21:37–22:3, was also incorporated into the legal range of this command. The series of prohibitions of murder, adultery, and stealing in Hos 4:2, Jer 7:9; Job 24:13–15 and the combination of these crimes in the Joseph story in Gen 37:22; 39.9; 44:8–9 reflected this expansion of the legal range of this legal sentence.

With this expansion, the block of brief prohibitions in Deut 5:17–19/Exod 20:13–16 summarized the legal traditions of apodictic family law and casuistic law of local courts. The prohibition of killing, adultery, and stealing, together with the commandment concerning the parents, form the oldest "building stone" or block for building the Decalogue. The prohibitions of bearing false witness in Deut 5:20 and Exod 20:16 associated with the other brief prohibitions were derived from the procedural law of the BC in Exod 21:1–3, 6–8, and in Deut 19:15–21. According to Babylonian and Judean procedural law, the one who was convicted of delivering a false testimony was subjected to the penalty envisioned for the falsely accused crime. In Exod 23:4–5, in connection with the procedural law in Exod 23:1–3, 6–8, an ethos of social solidarity was developed in the BC, an ethos which reacted to the social crisis in Israel and Judah, which also caused a crisis of the legal system and its procedures.

The social law in the BC assumed the function of a parenetic appeal for the protection of the poor in Exod 23:8. The Decalogue reflected this process in the linkage of the prohibition of coveting in Deut 5:21–22 and Exod 20:17 to the prohibition of bearing false witness. An older version of this prohibition, which also influenced Mic 2:2, prohibited the illegal appropriation of the neighbor's house and estate and tried during the social turmoil of the 8th and 7th century to ensure the economic foundations of agricultural life. The prohibition of coveting the wife of one's neighbor showed, as a thematic parallel to the prohibition of adultery, an anthropological shift to the inner attitude as a transition from a juridical prohibition to an ethical appeal. The conclusion of the second tablet of the Decalogue in Deut 5:22 gave all its commands the character of ethical commands.

Cultic law as the third root of biblical law in the BC and in Deut shaped also the first tablet of the Decalogue. Cultic law, including the prohibition of idol worship at a YHWH sanctuary and the prohibition of images, served the purity of the cult. The prohibition of misuse of YHWH's name in Deut 5:11 and Exod 20:7 had its origin in a cultic procedural law. The commandment of a day of rest and Sabbath in Deut 5:12–15 and Exod 20:8–11, which was rooted in privilege law of the 6/7 pattern of the Festival of Unleavened Bread expressed God's dominion over nature and the human capacity for agrarian work by singling out the seventh day as a day of rest for YHWH.

The Sabbath commandment as the center of the Decalogue in the Deuteronomistic redaction of the Decalogue of the 6th century legitimated all the decalogue theologically. By means of the Exodus formula in Deut 5:15, the day of rest commandment was linked to the introduction of the Decalogue in Deut 5:6, and was by the enumeration of those who benefited from rest in Deut 5:14 linked to the conclusion of the Decalogue in Deut 5:21. Long and short commandments alternated in the Deuteronomistic Decalogue. The prohibitions of worshipping foreign deities and of making divine images in Deut 5:7–10 constituted one long unit followed by the short unit of the prohibition of misuse of YHWH's name in Deut 5:11. The parent commandment in Deut 5:16 as a short commandment followed the long Sabbath commandment in Deut 5:12–15 and the ethical commandments formed a long unit by means of syndetic connections in Deut 5:17–21, which concluded the Decalogue. The opening of the Decalogue in Deut 5:6 with the formula of YHWH's self-presentation and the Exodus formula defined Israel, liberated by YHWH from Egypt as the realm in which the Decalogue should be valid. The salvation-historical act of deliverance—the Exodus—preceded the demand for obedience as an imperative: everybody in Israel should act according to the will of God because God had already acted in the Exodus as an act of liberation on his or her behalf. The theology of the day of rest commandment, extended from the time of harvest and plowing to the whole year, subjected all activity to God's sovereignty by singling out a Sabbath day, as did the prohibitions of idols and images.

The first commandment pointed the human addressees of the Decalogue to an active shaping of the world in accordance with God's will that was summarized in the Decalogue. The exilic perspective in the compilation of the Decalogue found expression in the fact that it put its special accent on the Sabbath commandment, which was not linked to a special sanctuary, and that the parent commandment in Deut 5:16 was placed in front of the ethical commandments in Deut 5:17–21.The family became even more important than in preexilic times in exile and diaspora, without any cultic and state institutions, and received a social key position as the entity that ordered life and was the bearer of the ethos laid out in Deut 5:17–21. In the perspective of the Deuteronomistic framework of the Decalogue in Deut 5, this applied to all Israel, independent of whether it found itself in the diaspora or in the homeland, and was placed as a summary in Deut 5 in front of the legal corpus in Deut 12–26, which should only be valid in the homeland of Israel, as Deut 12:1 clarified. In the Decalogue, the prohibitions of idols, images, and the misuse of YHWH's name, along with the Sabbath commandment, constitute a unit of duties toward YHWH.

In accordance with the Deuteronomistic structure of the Decalogue, the Deuteronomistic redactors of Deut in the 6th-century structured Deut 12:2–17:1 as a coherent block by the insertion of Deut 16:20–17:1, corresponding to the first tablet of the Decalogue (Otto 2012–2017: 1082–93). This block encompassed the major commandments dealing with cultic centralization, unity, and purity in Deut 12–13, the bill of social rights based on YHWH's privilege law in a 6/7 pattern in Deut 14–15*, and the order of festivals in Deut 16. The second tablet of the Decalogue corresponded to the order of legal sentences in Deut 17:2–26:12. The parent commandment in an opening position in the Decalogue corresponded to the order of offices in Deut 17:2–18:22. In a new Israel after the exile, religious obligations should once again be observed in the temple of Jerusalem and the institutions of legal courts, monarchy, priesthood, and prophecy should join the social institution of the family, which preserved Israel's identity during exile and diaspora. For the post-exilic redactors of the Pentateuch, who incorporated Deut into the Pentateuch, the Decalogue in Deut 5 was so important that they incorporated it into the Sinai pericope in Exod 20 and adjusted it to priestly perspectives in the priestly source P.

2. The Holiness Code in Lev 17–26

The Holiness Code (HC) in Lev 17–26 was written in the Persian period and its authors presupposed the priestly source (P) and the Deuteronomistic Deut. The HC was structured by a parenetic theological framework in Lev 18:1–5,24–30; 19:1–4; 20:7–8,22–27; 22:9,31–33;25:18–19,38,42a, 55;26:1–2, which combined themes from Deut and P under the thematic conception that Israel should sanctify itself by following the commands of the HC in order not to be "spewed" forth out of the land. But to follow the commands required sanctification by YHWH, which became tangible in the experience of the Exodus. The single laws of the HC got their theological and historical embedding by this framework. In a Torah for the laity in Lev 18–20, the sexual penal codes in Lev 18 and 20 framed a program of fraternal ethics in Lev 19. This program was an exegetical interpretation of the BC, Deut, Decalogue and Proverbs. Its framework consisted of clauses taken from the Decalogue and its climax was the commandment to love one's enemy as one was to love one's neighbor in Lev 19:18,34. A priestly Torah in Lev 21:1–22:16 followed the lay Torah; together they were framed by a sacrificial Torah in Lev 17:1–15; 22:17–30, in which Lev 17 as the introduction for the HC followed the outline of Deut and revised it under a perspective of P. A Sabbath Torah in Lev 23:3–25:55, in which Lev 24 as a post-HC supplement was inserted, consisted of an order of festivals in Lev 23 and of a program of social law of fraternal solidarity with the poor in Lev 25, consisting of laws of a redemption of debts and manumission of slaves in the Jubilee Year.

Divine promises and threats in Lev 26 in dialogue with Ezek 34 and 37 concluded the HC and YHWH's revelation in the Sinai pericope. YHWH's gift for the coming era of salvation would not be a messianic shepherd as in the Book of Ezekiel, and not a new Covenant of Peace, but would be the covenant with the patriarchs. The Sinai-generation would be held open by YHWH's fidelity despite Israel's rebellion, so that Israel could sanctify themselves through obedience to the Torah and thus dwell securely in the Promised Land. It was the intention of the HC to reconcile the laws of the Sinai pericope, BC and the Decalogue, and Deut. The priestly source P, which was limited to a cultic legislation, was supplemented by legal and ethical motives of BC and Deut, and P supplemented BC and Deut by elements of its cultic order, which were revised in the Torah for sacrifices, priesthood, and festivals. The HC thus served the scribal scholarly harmonization of the divergent law codes in the Pentateuch.

Bibliography

Alt, Albrecht. 1959. *Kleine Schriften zur Geschichte des Volkes Israel*. Munich: C. H. Beck.

Assmann, Jan. 1999. *Fünf Stufen zum Kanon. Tradition und Schriftkultur im Frühen Judentum und in Seiner Umwelt*. Münster: Lit Verlag.

Halpern, Baruch. 1991. "Jerusalem and the Lineages in the Seventh Century BCE." Pages 11–107 in *Law and Ideology in Monarchic Israel*. Edited by B. Halpern and D. W. Hobson. Sheffield: Sheffield Academic Press.

Levinson, Bernard. 1997. *Deuteronomy and the Hermeneutics of Legal Innovation*. New York: Oxford University Press.

Otto, Eckart. 1988. *Wandel der Rechtsbegründungen in der Gesellschaftsgeschichte des Antiken Israel. Eine Rechtsgeschichte des ‚Bundesbuches' Ex XX 22–XXIII 13*. Leiden: Brill.

———.1989. *Rechtsgeschichte der Redaktionen im Kodex Ešnunna und im „Bundesbuch". Eine Redaktionsgeschichtliche und Rechtsvergleichende Studie zu Altbabylonischen und Altisraelitischen Rechtsüberlieferungen*. Göttingen/Fribourg: Vandenhoeck & Ruprecht/Universitätsverlag.

———. 1991. *Körperverletzungen in den Keilschriftrechten und im Alten Tetament. Studien zum Rechtstransfer im Alten Orient*. Kevelaer/Neukirchen-Vluyn: Butzon & Bercker/Neukirchener Verlag.

———. 1994. *Theologische Ethik des Alten Testaments*. Stuttgart: Kohlhammer.

———. 1999. *Das Deuteronomium. Politische Theologie und Rechtsreform in Juda und Assyrien*. Berlin: de Gruyter.

———. 2000. *Das Deuteronomium im Pentateuch und Hexateuch. Studien zur Literaturgeschichte von Pentateuch und Hexateuch im Lichte des Deuteronomiumrahmens*. Tübingen: Mohr/Siebeck.

———. 2009. "The Holiness Code in Diachrony and Synchrony in the Legal Hermeneutics of the Pentateuch." Pages 135–56 in *The Priestly Strata of the Priestly Writings. Contemporary Debate and Future Directions*. Edited by Sarah Shectman and Joel S. Baden. Zurich: Theologischer Verlag Zürich.

———. 2012–2017. *Deuteronomium 1–34*. 4 vols. Freiburg/Breisgau: Herder.

Steymans, Hans Ulrich. 1995. *Deuteronomium 28 und die adê zur Thronfolgeregelung Asarhaddons. Segen und Fluch im Alten Orient und in Israel*. Fribourg: Universitätsverlag/Göttingen: Vandenhoeck & Ruprecht.

Uehlinger, Christoph. 1995. "Gab es eine joschijanische Kultreform? Plädoyer Für ein Begründetes Minimum." Pages 57–89 in *Jeremia und die ‚Deuteronomistische Bewegung*. Edited by Walter Groß. Weinheim: Beltz/Athenäum.

Von Rad, Gerhard. 1948. *Deuteronomium-Studien*. Göttingen: Vandenhoeck & Ruprecht.

Wells, Bruce. 2019. "Reconstructing the History of a Legal Provision." *ZABR* 25: 93–116.

Westbrook, Raymond. ed. 2003. *A History of Ancient Near Eastern Law*. Leiden: Brill.

Wright, David P. 2009. *Inventing God's Law. How the Covenant Code of the Bible Used and Revised the Laws of Hammurabi*. New York: Oxford University Press.

21
WARFARE AND INTELLIGENCE GATHERING IN ANCIENT ISRAEL

Charlie Trimm

Introduction

Warfare was a central part of life in the ancient Near East (Trimm 2017), and research on warfare has played an important role in Hebrew Bible studies (Trimm 2012). While battles are the most prominent part of warfare, battles are not won merely by what is done on the battlefield. Generals are quick to recognize that other factors, like food supplies or troop morale, play a vital role in determining victory. In this chapter, I will focus on one of those important but undervalued aspects of warfare: learning about the enemy. This field, called military intelligence, provides information about such things as the number of the enemy, their location, the kinds of enemy troops, enemy morale, and local terrain. In modern times intelligence gathering can take many forms that are based on modern technology that was unavailable in ancient times. For example, satellite imagery allows leaders to see the location of enemy troops and provides detailed maps of the area. In ancient times, intelligence gathering was largely restricted to the most basic kind of intelligence: human intelligence. This chapter will investigate various means of intelligence gathering in ancient Israel, as well as briefly looking at the practices of two of their larger neighbors: Egypt and Assyria.[1] Like other areas of warfare, this study will show not only how the gathering of military intelligence was similar in many ways to modern methods, but also how the gods played an essential role that is absent today.

For each of these three groups, I will divide human intelligence into two broad categories. First, the category of *spying* will include gathering strategic information about the enemy, generally away from the battlefield. This information may come from the foreign nationals or from a person who travels to or lives in the foreign state. The second category, *scouting*, will include gathering operational information for a campaign and tactical information near the battlefield.[2] This kind of information largely comes from scouts who were sent out before battle to learn about the enemy and the surroundings of the battlefield. The third area of military intelligence I will examine is how ancient leaders sought guidance from these *divine beings* about their enemies through such means as divination. After surveying the information, I will argue that gathering intelligence played a theological role in Israel in a way that it did not for the other countries.

Egypt

We will begin by looking at military intelligence in Egypt, though unfortunately, the details of Egyptian intelligence operations are scarce (Heagren 2010: 441–45). Evidence for spying is limited, but more information is extant for scouting. The roles of Egyptian deities in military intelligence will be excluded due to the dearth of source material concerning divination to learn about the enemy. When the gods speak to Pharaohs in the annals they promise victory, but do not communicate information about the enemy.

Spying

In general, the Egyptians seem to have valued knowing about events in the world. For example, Merenptah was praised for his ability to know what was happening everywhere in the world: "The affairs of each country are told to you while you are at rest in your palace; And you hear the speech of all nations for you have millions of ears… If one speaks—even a voice from the underworld—it reaches your ear; If one does something—and it is concealed—your eye will still observe it" (Foster 1995: 141–42). Seti I began a campaign against the Shasu when "one came to tell His Majesty" about the rebellion of the Shasu against Pharaoh (*COS* 2.4:24).

Even though Egyptians did not tend to move elsewhere to gather intelligence, some military men did so. Amenmosi was a troop captain in Retjenu during the 18th dynasty who referred to himself as the "eyes of the king of Lower Egypt and ears of the king of Upper Egypt in the foreign land of wretched Retjenu" (Cumming 1984: 190–91). The sheer number of letters from the Bronze Age imply the importance of messengers who were sent between the kings. Besides delivering messages from their masters, they most likely also gathered information on the kingdoms they were visiting (Bryce 2003: 63–75; Redford 2020). The Egyptians were also able to learn much about the world from foreigners. The Amarna Letters provide evidence of vassal kings who sought favor with Pharaoh and kept him up to date with local events in Canaan (Moran 1992). Sometimes the Egyptians were able to gather information from enemy communications. Kamose intercepted a message from the king of the Hyksos to the Nubians that sought to enlist their support against Egypt (*ANET* 555). Amenhotep II captured an enemy messenger with "a letter of clay at his throat," which provides us a picture of how messengers secured their letters (*ANET* 246).

Scouting

More evidence has been found for scouting in Egypt. The Egyptians set up military patrols at their borders as a form of defensive scouting. A group of desert nomads known as the Medjai were used as desert scouts and policemen in New Kingdom Egypt, but their close identity with the role of scout led to the word losing any ethnic association (Liszka 2012: 308–87). A Medjai patrolman described his normal routine in this way: "How great they are, the four *iteru* of travel which I make daily [42 kilometers/26 miles]; five times going up (the mountain), five times going down (the mountain); so do not let me be replaced by another!" (Darnell & Manassa 2007: 113–17). Limited evidence suggests that Egyptian scouts were mounted on horses to improve their speed (see Figure 21.1; Heagren 2010: 88–89; Rommelaere 1991: 129–32; Schulman 1957).

The Egyptians also employed scouts before battle. Quite dramatically, a late demotic papyrus records the legend of a queen calling on her younger sister to dress like a man,

Figure 21.1 Egyptian horseman. Drawing on limestone from Thebes in the Egyptian Museum. Photograph by Charlie Trimm

infiltrate the enemy camp and gather intelligence about their army (*AEL* 3:152–53). Closer to standard practice is the use of scouts by Thutmose III in his campaign culminating in the battle at Megiddo. The report at the war council concerning the entrance of enemy troops into Megiddo implies the use of scouts, and after the generals provided their input further intelligence arrived that influenced the king's decision: "Then intelligence reports [were brought] concer[ning that feeble enemy]" (*COS* 2.2A:9). Based on these reports the generals suggest a flanking attack either to the north or the south, but the Egyptian king rejected their advice and instead attacked directly against Megiddo.

The most extensive story about scouting in Egyptian records comes from Ramses II in his campaign against the Hittites at Qadesh. However, in this case, Egyptian scouting failed when they did not notice the counterespionage of the Hittites' scouts. Two Shasu spies informed Ramses II that the Hittite king remained in Hatti instead of leading his troops into battle, but this was not true as the Hittite king was at Qadesh awaiting the pharaoh and had sent these spies to mislead the Egyptian king (*COS* 2.5B:39). Later, the Egyptian intelligence service partially redeemed itself when it captured two Hittite scouts, who revealed that the Hittite king was near. In reliefs of the battle, Ramses II described the interrogation (see Figure 21.2):

> The arrival of the scout of Pharaoh, LPH, bringing 2 Hittite scouts of the despicable Fallen One of Hatti before Pharaoh, LPH. They are beaten in the (royal) presence, to make them tell where the despicable Fallen One of Hatti is.
>
> (Kitchen 1996: 19)

Such interrogation of Nubian prisoners might be recorded in several execration texts as well (Redford 2020: 326).

Figure 21.2 Relief of Ramses II at the Ramesseum showing the beating of Hittite scouts. Line drawing from James Henry Breasted, *Battle of Kadesh* (Chicago: The University of Chicago Press, 1903), pl. 1

Assyria

In contrast to Egyptian sources, the large number of Assyrian letters has allowed us a relatively clear picture of how strategic intelligence was gathered and analyzed in Assyria (Dezső 2014; Dubovský 2006, 2014; Melville 2016; Villard 2016). The Assyrians were more likely to live in foreign lands than the Egyptians, providing more opportunities to learn about those areas. Like other armies, the Assyrians employed scouts before the battle. Finally, several Assyrian kings employed divination to learn about enemy troop movements.

Spying

The ideal for the Assyrian intelligence system was that foreign nationals would provide information to Assyrians who were living in that country, who would then send that information back to the king in Assyria.[3] The royal Assyrian annals sometimes refer to the king hearing about an attack while in Assyria and then leading his army against that enemy (Leichty 2011: 15–16). According to Peter Dubovský, the ideal situation is modeled in a letter named SAA 15.186 (Dubovský 2006: 121–22).[4] Information about the movements of a "son of Zerî" was gathered by the local informant Ra'iwanu, who reported it to Shamash-abu-usur (a local provider?), who then passed it to the Assyrian governor and instructed him to "Report it to the Palace!" However, exceptions were sometimes granted, as one study showed many different people reported directly to Sargon II, perhaps as a way to keep everyone honest and to learn as much as possible about events (Dezső 2014: 234). Sometimes the informers themselves desired more direct access to the king, as illustrated by SAA 5.104.

> Three powerful men of the Kummeans have come and had an audience with me and Mar-Issar, the royal bodyguard. Here is what they said to me: "Our people may go where the king said, but your messenger should take us to the Palace. There is a matter [concerning] another country we (wish to) discuss [in] the king's [pres]ence.[…]…; we [will] not tell it to you, [n]or will we tell it to the royal bodyguard. Else if you do not take us to the Palace, sooner or later we shall say to the king: 'We spoke with the governor and the royal bodyguard, but they did not agree to bring us to the Palace.'" What are the king my lord's orders?

One of the best sources of information about military information in foreign lands would be the people who lived there. One letter informed Sargon II on conditions in Urartu from a local informant (SAA 1.32):

> […] the Itu'ean […] who […] from the city of Ištahup has now been brought to me from […]ratta. I inquired him [about the Urarṭi]ans and he told me: 'The Urarṭian [and his magnates were *defeated*] on their expedition [against] the Cimmerians, and they are very much afraid of the king, my lord. They tremble and keep silent like women, and nobody […] the forts of the king, my lord. The situation is very good.'

Foreign leaders were sometimes compelled to provide information through specific provisions in treaties (Dubovský 2006: 153–60).[5] This example comes from a fragmentary treaty (SAA 2.13).

> You shall not say: "Go and tell to that king: 'Now, the king of Assyria is marching against you, he has…ed a certain [strat]agem to use against you.'" [Nor] will you conceal from me anything that you hear, be it from the mouth of a king, or on account of a country, (anything) that bears upon or is harmful to us or Assyria, but you will write to me and bring it to my attention.

An example of a good vassal is Arije, the king of Kumme, who reported to the Assyrians the actions of Urartu and Ukku (SAA 1.29) (Dubovský 2006: 55–60). Sharru-emuranni promised to be a good vassal as well (SAA 5.243): "The king, my lord, appointed me in Qunbuna; I tell everything that I see and hear to the king, my lord, I do not conceal anything from the king."

Finally, the best way to gather information from foreign lands was to place Assyrians in those lands to gather information directly. An official called a "royal deputy" (*qēpu*) was often installed, as seen in the treaty between Esarhaddon and Baal, the king of Tyre, that said a letter from the Assyrian king could not be opened unless the *qēpu* was present.[6] Assyrian messengers could also gather information as they traveled between countries (Dubovský 2014: 266–69). The role of a messenger was not always safe; in one incident an Assyrian messenger was arrested in Babylon (SAA 18.192).

Scouting

When on campaign, the Assyrian army was accompanied by scouts (*dayyāllu*), though in some cases the word was also used for the spying category above (Dubovský 2014: 252). One letter refers to a "chief of scouts" (SAA 7.9). Sargon II instructed a subordinate about gathering intelligence (SAA 1.13):

> Don't be afraid; at the city of Urammu where you are to pitch the camp [there is] a plain which is [very] good for reconnaissance expeditions (*dayāltu*), there is [much] grass there, and it is a [good] place to rest.

Sometimes commanders complained about their scouting responsibilities, such as Illil-bani and Ashur-belu-taqqin, who thought that the land they were responsible for guarding was too large and that they needed cavalry to watch it (SAA 18.197). Other commanders noted that the extreme cold of the northern frontier made scouting difficult (SAA 19.61):

> Perhaps the king my lord will say: 'Why have you (as) Tarton not sent (a report) by the hands of a messenger?' The cold is very severe. I did send scouts (but) they turned back, saying: 'Where shall we go?' When the cold outside has *eased* (and) the cold weather has gone, they will bring a report about the enemy.
>
> (Saggs 2001: 144)

These scouts were not always Assyrian: Esarhaddon captured foreign scouts of Shubria and attached them to his army (Leichty 2011: 84). Knowing the local language was helpful for gathering intelligence, as illustrated in this letter (SAA 5.217): "The king, my lord, knows that Kubaba-ila'i masters the language. I sent him to Tikriš, and he gave us this detailed report. We are herewith sending it to the king, my lord." Deserters were also a helpful source of information (Dubovský 2006: 43–49, 2014: 258–60), as seen in this letter to Esarhaddon (SAA 10.111).

> I have written to the king, my lord, without proper knowledge of the conditions in that country. The lord of kings should consult an expert of the country and then write to his army as he deems best. Your advantage is, in any case, that there are more deserters than fighting soldiers among the enemy. When the whole army is entering, let patrols go and capture their men in the open country and then question them.
>
> (Nissinen 2003: 156–57)

The exact process of interrogating deserters is generally spoken of only in broad terms: "As to the deserters whom the governor of Der sent to me (and) about whom the king, my lord, wrote to me 'Interrogate them!'—we have interrogated them" (SAA 16.136). The Assyrians naturally faced the danger of their own troops deserting to the enemy (SAA 5.35). The fate of deserters varied. Some tried to cause more desertions among their own people (SAA 15.157) or, more frequently, assisted the Assyrians if they could keep the plunder captured in battle (SAA 15.216). However, their fate was not always positive, as SAA 15.214 records a group of deserters being sold as slaves.

Divine Beings

Divination played a significant role in military intelligence primarily during the time of Esarhaddon and Ashurbanipal. They viewed it as so important that if someone kept a divination report from the king then they would be charged with treason (SAA 16.21). Some of the divination reports involving military intelligence dealt with heavenly objects: "On the 15th day the moon and the sun were seen together: a strong enemy will raise his weapons against the land; the enemy will tear down my city gate."[7] The rituals were not merely a passive watching of the stars, but also could be an active request for information by the king. This example from Esarhaddon deals with the intentions of the Scythians.

> Will the troops of the S[cyth]ia[ns, which have been staying in the district of Mannea and which are (now) moving out from the territory] of Mannea, strive and plan? Will they move out and go through the passes [of Hubuškia] to the city Harrania (and) the city Anisus? Will they take much plunder and heavy booty from the territory of [Assyria]? Does your great divinity [know it]?[8]

Israel

Although not as much information has been preserved as for Assyria, intelligence gathering still played a key role in ancient Israel.[9] Various accounts in the Hebrew Bible refer to gathering information from other nations in a variety of ways. Likewise, other stories record how scouts operated before battle to gather information. Finally, although divination is condemned in the Hebrew Bible, in at least one case YHWH provided military intelligence to the Israelites.

Spying

The Hebrew Bible records a handful of examples of spying, although the line between this and scouting is not very clear because Israel rarely campaigned far from Canaan. In some cases, the word used to describe spying is the *piel* of the verb רגל. The word is connected to the common noun generally translated "foot," but when used as a verb it sometimes refers to spying, though it can also refer to scouting before battle.[10] The examples of Israelite spying are limited, as would befit a smaller kingdom. Unlike the larger empires of the Egyptians and the Assyrians, the smaller kingdoms had a much more localized focus and did not have as much opportunity to gather information about foreign countries. In practical terms, they also could not force other nations to provide them with information like the empires could.

Interestingly, several of the references to Israelite spies are apparently false accusations. Joseph, in his role as Egyptian overseer, accused his brothers of being spies (מרגלים) when they visited Egypt to get grain (Genesis 42). According to this accusation, they were operating as foreign nationals seeking to learn information about Egypt to bring back to Canaan. However, what the use of this information would be is unclear; indeed, the ridiculous nature of the charge might have been intended by Joseph as retribution against his brothers for their earlier mistreatment of him.[11] Likewise, the Philistines accused David of being a double agent who would turn on them, even though David had been living among the Philistines for some time and was surely not working for Saul at this point since he had sought to kill David multiple times (1 Sam 29).[12] Joab accused Abner of spying on David: "You know that Abner the son of Ner came to deceive you and to know your going out and your coming in, and to know all that you are doing" (2 Sam 3:25).[13] It is not clear if Joab's accusation is correct or not. Finally, the Ammonites accused David of sending men to Ammon not just to mourn the death of their king, but also to spy (רגל) on them (2 Sam 10:3; 1 Chr 19:3). The biblical text implies that this is a false accusation, but David would surely have welcomed information about the royal transition.

Beyond these cases, presumably, the Israelites gathered information about foreign countries in a variety of ways. Especially during the prosperous periods of the monarchy, the Israelite and Judean kings would have had extensive contacts with foreign nations. Solomon with his many foreign wives would be the most obvious example of this, but other kings would have had similar contacts. For example, Ahab married Jezebel of Sidon. The queen of Sheba not only visited Solomon but also refers to the "report" (דבר) that she had heard about him (1 Kgs 10:6). Beyond the marriages, most likely diplomatic contact continued between these kings and their neighbors, but unfortunately, more details about these contacts are lacking beyond a few hints. For example, Hiram the king of Tyre sent a letter to Solomon to tell him about his gift of a craftsman and timber in exchange for agricultural products (2 Chr 2:11–16). The king of Syria wrote a letter to the king of Israel when Naaman went to Israel to seek healing (2 Kgs 5:5). Merodach-baladan sent letters and messengers to Hezekiah, presumably to enlist him to his anti-Assyrian cause (2 Kgs 20:12). The phrase "and it was told" (ויגד) sometimes indicates learning about foreign military affairs in some unknown fashion (2 Sam 10:17; Isa 7:2). Hushai functioned as a spy in the court of Absalom for David, not only passing information back to David about Absalom's plans, but also feeding bad advice to Absalom (2 Sam 16–17). While minimal, all these texts at least show contact between Israel and other nations that might have enabled Israel to gather information about those foreign nations.

Scouting

The employment of scouts was much more common in the Hebrew Bible than spying. Stationary scouts—watchmen—are referred to occasionally in the Hebrew Bible (1 Sam 14:16; 2 Sam 13:34; 2 Kgs 9:17–18). Two different verbs are used to describe mobile scouting. First, the verb תור refers generally to investigating or searching. Job describes the wild donkey as one who "ranges (תור) the mountains as his pasture, and he searches after every green thing" (Job 39:8). The author of Ecclesiastes employs the verb as a search for wisdom (Ecc 1:13; 7:25).[14] However, as will be seen below in many cases the word תור is used for scouting before battle. Second, the word רגל, discussed above, can also refer to scouting before battle.[15]

The first reference to scouting in the Hebrew Bible is YHWH scouting for the people. After the people left Sinai, the Ark of the Covenant operated as a scout: "and the ark of the covenant of the LORD went before them three days' journey, to seek out (תור) a resting place for them" (Num 10:33). Likewise, in Deuteronomy (1:33) Moses says to the people that YHWH himself "went before you in the way to seek you out (תור) a place to pitch your tents, in fire by night and in the cloud by day, to show you by what way you should go." Ezekiel also recalls that period of Israel's history by recounting YHWH swore "I would bring them out of the land of Egypt into a land that I had searched out (תור) for them" (Ezek 20:6). This attribution of scouting to YHWH lays an important precedent for later scouting as YHWH was the one who originally performed the task for them. This does not mean that the people rejected human scouts: Moses told Hobab that he would "serve as eyes for us" in the wilderness (Num 10:31). However, while human scouts were important for retrieving information, ultimately the people were protected by YHWH.

The most important scouting story in the Hebrew Bible is the account of the 12 scouts sent into Canaan by Moses (Numbers 13–14). YHWH commanded Moses to send men to scout (תור) the land of Canaan (Num 13:1–2). There were to be 12 men, one from each tribe;

the most well-known to readers of the Bible are Joshua and Caleb (Num 13:2–16). Their instructions were given by Moses:

> Go up into the Negeb and go up into the hill country, and see what the land is, and whether the people who dwell in it are strong or weak, whether they are few or many, and whether the land that they dwell in is good or bad, and whether the cities that they dwell in are camps or strongholds, and whether the land is rich or poor, and whether there are trees in it or not. Be of good courage and bring some of the fruit of the land.
>
> *(Num 13:17–20)*

Technically, these kinds of details are probably to be viewed as the operational level rather than the tactical level since they prepare for an entire campaign rather than a specific battle.

The scouts spent 40 days walking the length of Canaan, as far north as Lebo-hamath. They also brought back grapes, pomegranates, and figs, which must have been an amazing sight for people wandering in the barren wilderness for 40 years (Num 13:21–25)! Their report, supported by the items they brought back, described the agricultural potential of Canaan very positively. However, it also included more discouraging information about the inhabitants of the land and the fortifications there: "the people who dwell in the land are strong, and the cities are fortified and very large. And besides, we saw the descendants of Anak there" (Num 13:28).

While the scouts agreed on the facts in their report, they were divided in their analysis. Caleb recommended that they attack Canaan because they would be able to conquer it, though he does not include any religious language in this initial assessment (Num 13:30). However, others of the spies recommended against conquering it (Num 13:32–33). The people of Israel listened to this negative analysis and demanded a new leader to bring them back to Egypt (Num 14:1–5). Joshua and Caleb implored the people to trust in YHWH rather than rebel against him, but the people threatened to kill them (Num 14:6–10). At that point, YHWH himself appeared and told Moses that he planned to destroy Israel and create a new nation from Moses, but Moses persuaded him not to do so on behalf of YHWH's name when he quoted YHWH's promise in Exodus 34:6–7 (Num 14:11–19). However, YHWH punished the people by condemning them to wander in the wilderness until they all died, ensuring that none of them would ever see the Promised Land (Num 14:20–35). YHWH highlighted how the analysis of the scouting report was part of the problem when he declared that the time wandering in the wilderness would be 40 years, one year per day the scouts traveled through the land of Canaan (Num 14:34). In addition, the men who brought the bad report were killed immediately, while Caleb and Joshua were the only two of that generation who would see Canaan (Num 14:36–38). The story ends on yet another tragic note as the people rebelled against YHWH's punishment and sought to enter Canaan anyway; unfortunately, the Canaanites and the Amalekites soundly defeated them (Num 14:40–45). The absence of YHWH in this attack is symbolized by the Ark of the Covenant remaining in the camp: instead of scouting ahead of them, YHWH was entirely absent from the battle. The human scouts had failed Israel and the divine scout refused to participate.

In sum, the time in the wilderness lays the foundation for the theme of scouting in the Hebrew Bible. YHWH was initially responsible for scouting ahead of the Israelites through the Ark of the Covenant. When the Israelites drew near to Canaan, he commanded that the Israelites themselves scout out the land, as a kind of test. While they were able to gather valuable information about Canaan, they failed the test. The alarming parts of the report of the scouts led the people to rebel against YHWH's entire project and threatened to undo all of YHWH's previous redemptive acts. Future scouting would always have this episode as a precedent: would learning more information about an enemy bring Israel to trust YHWH or rebel against him?[16]

The next two accounts of scouting come at the end of the wilderness wandering. Like many other parts of the narrative, this forms an inclusio around the time in the wilderness: the miraculous crossing of the Red Sea (Exod 14) corresponds to the crossing of the Jordan (Josh 3–4), the celebration of Passover is repeated (Num 9:5; Josh 5:10), and the giving of the manna begins and ends (Exod 17; Josh 5:12). Likewise, the wilderness account ends with two tales of scouting just as it began with a tale of scouting (Numbers 13–14). First, after defeating Sihon but before fighting Og, Moses sent men to spy (רגל) on Jazer, which they then conquered (Num 21:32). In neither of the major campaigns against Sihon and Og is scouting mentioned, which leaves it ambiguous why it is included in the smaller campaign against Jazer. Perhaps the smaller size of the enemy meant that more scouting was needed to gather information, in contrast to the more well-known enemy armies of Sihon and Og.

The major account of scouting after the wilderness wandering happens just after this. Before the Israelites crossed the Jordan, Joshua sent two scouts (מרגלים) to Jericho (Josh 7:2). Interestingly, they were sent "secretly" to Jericho. Since it would be redundant to say that he sent them secretly from the perspective of the people of Jericho, most likely this refers to not telling the Israelites about the scouts. Perhaps Joshua wanted to avoid a repeat of the failure of the last scouts: if the Israelites did not know that the scouts were sent, then Joshua could suppress a potentially negative report. In addition, perhaps Joshua sent two scouts this time to match the number of scouts last time who provided a good report. To further the potential discomfort from historical parallels, the spies were sent from Shittim, which was last mentioned as the place where the people of Israel had committed idolatry with the Moabites (Num 25:1) (Firth 2019: 20). The account of the scouts shows that they were rather incompetent as they were immediately discovered and must be rescued by Rahab. However, they provided a positive analysis of their report to Joshua when they return to the Israelite camp: "Truly the LORD has given all the land into our hands. And also, all the inhabitants of the land melt away because of us" (Josh 2:24). The scouts in this case provided information about the morale of the enemy: they feared Israel and their God. The disaster of the previous scouting was averted.[17]

Unfortunately, the next account involving scouting failed. After the defeat of Jericho, Joshua sent men to Ai before an attack (Josh 7:2–5). Since that chapter began with a note that the people had broken faith with YHWH (Josh 7:1), the tone is already negative. Joshua's task for the scouts was simple: "Go up and spy out (רגל) the land" (Josh 7:2). The scouts brought back a positive report: "Do not have all the people go up, but let about two or three thousand men go up and attack Ai. Do not make the whole people toil up there, for they are few" (Josh 7:3). However, when Joshua followed this recommendation, the Israelites were soundly defeated. Joshua responded in a manner like the people in the wilderness by questioning why YHWH had brought them over the Jordan (Josh 7:7), but YHWH informed them about the breaking of the command at Jericho. After the punishment of Achan, the people of Israel attacked Ai again and were victorious. No scouting is recorded with this second assault, but since Joshua employed a neighboring ravine to hide an ambush force (Josh 8:4), at least some intelligence had been gathered. The initial scouting is not condemned in this narrative and the text makes clear that the main problem is Achan's action. But the scouting, without any hint of calling on YHWH for guidance, does not seem like a positive part of this narrative. In addition, the action to attack Ai feels self-motivated and involves the Israelites trusting their own strength rather than YHWH.

The book of Judges contains two references to scouting. First, "the house of Joseph scouted out (תור) Bethel," which was formerly called Luz, and saw a man leaving the city. They convinced him to show them the secret way into the city, which led to the conquest of the city (Judg 1:23–25).[18] This account has many parallels with the Rahab story: scouts found a Canaanite in the city who helped them defeat the city. But the major difference is that instead of proclaiming the greatness of YHWH and joining Israel as Rahab does, this man took his family away and started a new city called Luz in Hittite territory to the north (Judg 1:26). In other words, the man has transported the Canaanite city to a new location. While the scouting successfully facilitated the capture of the city, it had not brought people to following YHWH (Wong 2006: 51–55).

The second story involving scouting in the book of Judges concerns the Danite scouts near the end of the book (Judges 18). Given that the book of Judges descends in a downward spiral (Wong 2006: 249–54), the location of this story near the end of the book already gives it a negative tone. This tone is intensified when the story opens with the Danites not being able to conquer their allotted territory and seeking territory somewhere else. To find this territory, they sent out five men "to spy out (רגל) the land and to explore (חקר) it" and provided them with simple orders: "Go and explore (חקר) the land" (Judg 18:2). The men happen to pass the house of Micah and were blessed by Micah's priest, but the previous chapter has already demonstrated the illegitimate nature of this particular priest (Judg 18:2–6), confirming that the men were not spiritually sensitive. The five Danites continued to the north and eventually arrived at Laish, at the northern end of the Hula Valley. Their report to their people about Laish was positive:

> Arise, and let us go up against them, for we have seen the land, and behold, it is very good. And will you do nothing? Do not be slow to go, to enter in and possess the land. As soon as you go, you will come to an unsuspecting people. The land is spacious, for God has given it into your hands, a place where there is no lack of anything that is in the earth.
>
> *(Judg 18:9–10)*

The people of Dan accepted their recommendation and sent 600 men to conquer Laish. Before that, however, they stopped at Micah's house to take the priest and the ephod for their own (Judg 18:11–26). As predicted, they were then able to take Laish because of their lack of nearby allies and renamed the city Dan, setting up Micah's carved image there (Judg 18:27–31). The scouts have accurately reported information relevant to their military concerns, but the very reason for scouting is misguided: they have not recognized the wrong ways of worshipping YHWH during their scouting mission, and they have oppressed a defenseless people.

The book of Samuel connects scouting primarily with the wilderness. When David was in the wilderness, he received a report about the Philistines fighting against Keilah, presumably the work of scouts or friendly informers (1 Sam 23:1–4). Saul likewise heard reports, such as the report about David going to Keilah (1 Sam 23:7). He instructed the people of Ziph about their scouting technique:

> Go, make yet more sure. Know and see the place where his foot is, and who has seen him there, for it is told me that he is very cunning. See therefore and take note of all the lurking places where he hides, and come back to me with sure information. Then I will go with you. And if he is in the land, I will search him out among all the thousands of Judah
>
> *(1 Sam 23:22–23)*

However, this attack on David was cut short when Saul received a report about an attack by the Philistines (1 Sam 23:27). This back and forth of scouting and reporting continues throughout the time David is in the wilderness. For example, later the people of Ziph again informed Saul about David's location (1 Sam 26:1). However, David sent scouts (מרגלים) to observe the movements of Saul; when he learned Saul's exact location he snuck into Saul's camp in the middle of the night (1 Sam 26:4–5).

The book of Kings records a few examples of scouting. Scouts informed the Aramean king Ben-Hadad that the city he was besieging had sent out troops (1 Kgs 20:17).[19] As will be discussed below, during one series of battles against Aram YHWH revealed the location of Aramean camps to Israel through Elisha several times. To combat this, the Aramean king sought to find Elisha: "And he said, 'Go and see where he is, that I may send and seize him.' It was told him, 'Behold, he is in Dothan'" (2 Kgs 6:13). The passive construction "it was told him" (ויגד לו) implies the use of scouts to learn the location of Elisha (2 Kgs 6:13). Later, the Israelites used men on horseback as scouts to investigate whether the Arameans had truly left the siege of Samaria (2 Kgs 7:13–15).

In sum, the Hebrew Bible provides many examples of tactical and operational level scouting by both Israel and their enemies. While the Hebrew Bible shows how important intelligence gathering was for armies, in typical form the Hebrew Bible also makes it a theological test. Would the people of Israel trust YHWH or the information they gathered from scouting?

Divine Beings

The role of the deity plays a minor role in intelligence gathering in the Hebrew Bible since divination was forbidden in ancient Israel (Deut 18:10; 1 Sam 15:23). Though the Urim and Thummim functioned as basic divinatory tools (Num 27:21; 1 Sam 14:41; 28:6), they are not used to provide information about the enemy. One story involving YHWH with military intelligence was when Elisha passed intelligence to the king of Israel concerning the secret gathering places of the Aramean troops; the Aramean king accused his staff of leaking secrets, but they were confident that it was through Elijah that the secret was known (2 Kgs 6:8–13). However, as noted above, YHWH scouted the way for Israel himself (Num 10:33; Deut 1:33; Ezek 20:6) and commissioned a scouting trip (Num 13:1–2).

Conclusion

As modern readers, we would like more information about military intelligence in the ancient Near East, but the texts from Egypt, Assyria, and Israel provide us with substantial glimpses. Even though they lacked sophisticated modern methods, the ancient empires and kingdoms were still able to use human intelligence quite effectively. In addition, the thoroughly religious cultures of the ancient Near East opened the door to an avenue that is not taken seriously today when it requested knowledge from the gods. Egypt exhibited knowledge of the outside world and worked to put tactical and operational intelligence into use in their campaigns. The Assyrians seem to have mastered the art of not only gathering military intelligence but also analyzing it. Israel provides a good test case of what the gathering of military intelligence looks like for a smaller kingdom: the acquisition of strategic information from foreign nations was much more limited, but many stories in the Hebrew Bible exhibit the importance attributed to tactical and operational intelligence.

However, the Hebrew Bible also theologizes military intelligence when it emphasizes that it cannot replace trust in YHWH. The people of Israel should be guided ultimately not by military intelligence, but by YHWH. Like many other areas of warfare, the goal for Israel was never merely military success. The premier example of this was the law of the king that prohibited the king from accumulating a large army or making alliances with foreign nations through marriage (Deut 17:14–17). This text serves as the basis for condemning Solomon's military expansionism (Hays 2003). Likewise, YHWH commanded Joshua to burn the captured Canaanite chariots and hamstring captured horses rather than increase the size of their army with the captured armaments (Josh 11:6) (Brueggemann 2009). I argue elsewhere the reason that YHWH never gave a divine weapon to an Israelite or Judean king, a common practice in the rest of the ancient Near East, is that such a weapon could encourage the king to trust in something besides YHWH (Trimm 2020). The texts about military intelligence fit into this pattern of placing far greater prominence on trust in YHWH than in their own strength or knowledge.

Notes

1. For intelligence gathering in other parts of the ancient Near East, see Trimm 2017: 75-96.
2. This could also be called reconnaissance; see Dubovský 2006: 243.
3. Another stream of information was through the temple system (SAA 15.161 is an example), but this was less common.
4. SAA is the abbreviation of the series State Archives of Assyria which has published many Assyrian letters.
5. For lists of all the things that the vassals were required to report to the Assyrian king and of the potential perpetrators, see Dubovský 2006: 156–58.
6. Lines iii.11–14 of SAA 2.5; COS 4.36:154. For more on the office, see Dubovský 2012.
7. SAA 8.244. Hundreds of similar examples are included in SAA 8.
8. SAA 4.23. Likewise, many other examples of this kind of questioning can be found in SAA 4.
9. Little has been written in scholarly contexts on military intelligence in Israel. One overview is in Dubovský 2006: 242–52. For an example of form criticism on spy stories, see Bauer 2000.
10. The word is also used in several other unusual ways. Absalom sent men (מרגלים) throughout Israel in preparation for his coup (2 Sam 15:10). However, unlike in other cases these men were not sent to gather information, but to disseminate information. In another two cases, the word is used in a context that requires a translation like "slander" (2 Sam 19:27; Ps 15:3). A very unusual *tifil* form is used to describe "teaching to walk" (Hos 11:3).
11. For the suggestion that the brothers could have been suspected of gathering intelligence for a great power like the Hittites or Assyrians, see Wenham 1994: 407.
12. Going the other direction, it is also possible to see Delilah as a Philistine spy, seeking to sabotage Samson the Israelite agent.
13. Unless otherwise noted, all biblical translations are from the ESV.
14. In one case, it seems to refer to traveling merchants: "now the weight of gold that came to Solomon in one year was 666 talents of gold, besides that which came from the explorers (תרים) and from the business of the merchants" (1 Kgs 10:14–15).
15. A third word sometimes used in parallel with these verbs is חפר (Deut 1:22; Josh 2:2–3).
16. The account of the scouts in Deut 1:22–46 is similar but differs most significantly in the source of the idea of sending scouts: the people instead of YHWH. However, in both versions the relevant point for the argument here remains the same as the people reject the call to enter the land, citing the terror caused by the scouts' report.
17. For the argument that an additional goal of the scouts in Jericho was to spread the news about YHWH and offer the chance of conversion, see Hess 1996: 96.
18. Interestingly, the scouts in this case are called "guards" (שמרים) rather than scouts (מרגלים).
19. Technically, the Hebrew text is missing the word "scouts," but is clearly referring to them.

Bibliography

Bauer, U. F. W. 2000. "Judges 18 as an Anti-Spy Story in the Context of an Anti-Conquest Story: The Creative Usage of Literary Genres." *JSOT* 88: 37–47.

Brueggemann, W. 2009. *Divine Presence Amid Violence: Contextualizing the Book of Joshua*. Eugene: Cascade Books.

Bryce, T. 2003. *Letters of the Great Kings of the Ancient Near East: The Royal Correspondence of the Late Bronze Age*. New York: Routledge.

Cumming, B. 1984. *Egyptian Historical Records of the Later Eighteenth Dynasty: Fascicle 2*. Warminster: Aris & Phillips.

Darnell, J. C., and C. Manassa. 2007. *Tutankhamun's Armies: Battle and Conquest during Ancient Egypt's Late Eighteenth Dynasty*. Hoboken: Wiley & Sons.

Dezső, T. 2014. "Neo-Assyrian Military Intelligence." Pages 221–36 in *Krieg und Frieden im Alten Vorderasien: 52e Rencontre Assyriologique Internationale International Congress of Assyriology and Near Eastern Archaeology Münster, 17–21. Juli 2006*. Edited by H. Neumann et al. Münster: Ugarit-Verlag.

Dubovský, P. 2006. *Hezekiah and the Assyrian Spies: Reconstruction of the Neo-Assyrian Intelligence Services and Its Significance for 2 Kings 18–19*. Rome: Pontificio Istituto biblico.

———. 2012. "King's Direct Control: Neo-Assyrian Qēpu Officials." Pages 447–458 in *Organization, Representation, and Symbols of Power in the Ancient Near East: Proceedings of the 54th Rencontre Assyriologique Internationale at Würzburg 20–25 July 2008*. Edited by G. Wilhelm. Winona Lake: Eisenbrauns.

———. 2014. "Sennacherib's Invasion of the Levant Through the Eyes of Assyrian Intelligence Services." Pages 249–92 in *Sennacherib at the Gates of Jerusalem: Story, History, and Historiography*. Edited by I. Kalimi and S. Richardson. Leiden: Brill.

Firth, D. G. 2019. *Including the Stranger: Foreigners in the Former Prophets*. Downers Grove: IVP Academic.

Foster, J. L. 1995. *Hymns, Prayers, and Songs: An Anthology of Ancient Egyptian Lyric Poetry*. Atlanta: Scholars Press.

Hays, J. D. 2003. "Has the Narrator Come to Praise Solomon or to Bury Him? Narrative Subtlety in 1 Kings 1–11." *JSOT* 28: 149–74.

Heagren, B. H. 2010. "The Art of War in Pharaonic Egypt: An Analysis of the Tactical, Logistic, and Operational Capabilities of the Egyptian Army (Dynasties XVII–XX)." PhD diss., University of Auckland.

Hess, R. S. 1996. *Joshua: An Introduction and Commentary*. Downers Grove: InterVarsity.

Kitchen, K. A. 1996. *Ramesside Inscriptions: Translated & Annotated: Ramesses II, Royal Inscriptions*. London: Blackwell.

Leichty, E. 2011. *The Royal Inscriptions of Esarhaddon, King of Assyria (680-669 BC)*. Winona Lake: Eisenbrauns.

Liszka, K. 2012. "'We Have Come to Serve Pharaoh': A Study of the Medjay and Pangrave Culture as an Ethnic Group and as Mercenaries from c. 2300 BCE until c. 1050 BCE." PhD diss., University of Pennsylvania.

Melville, S. C. 2016. "Insurgency and Terrorism in the Assyrian Empire during the Late Eighth Century BCE." Pages 62–92 in *Brill's Companion to Insurgency and Terrorism in the Ancient Mediterranean*. Edited by T. Howe and L. L. Brice. Leiden: Brill.

Moran, W. L., ed. 1992. *The Amarna Letters*. Baltimore: Johns Hopkins University Press.

Nissinen, M. 2003. *Prophets and Prophecy in the Ancient Near East*. Atlanta: SBL.

Redford, D. B. 2020. "Debriefing Enemy Combatants in Ancient Egypt." Pages 324–36 in *"An Excellent Fortress for His Armies, a Refuge for the People": Egyptological, Archaeological, and Biblical Studies in Honor of James K. Hoffmeier*. Edited by R. E. Averbeck and K. L. Younger Jr. Winona Lake: Eisenbrauns.

Rommelaere, C. 1991. *Les chevaux du Nouvel Empire Égyptien: Origines, Races, Harnachement*. Bruxelles: Connaissance de l'Égypte ancienne.

Saggs, H. W. F., ed. 2001. *The Nimrud Letters, 1952*. Trowbridge: British School of Archaeology in Iraq.

Schulman, A. R. 1957. "Egyptian Representations of Horsemen and Riding in the New Kingdom." *JNES* 16: 263–71.

Trimm, C. 2012. "Recent Research on Warfare in the Old Testament." *CBR* 10: 1–46.

———. 2017. *Fighting for the King and the Gods: A Survey of Warfare in the Ancient Near East.* Atlanta: SBL.

———. 2020. "The Sword of YHWH: The Human Use of Divine Weapons in the Ancient Near East and the Hebrew Bible." Pages 293–304 in *For Us, but Not to Us: Essays on Creation, Covenant, and Context in Honor of John H. Walton.* Edited by A. E. Miglio, C. A. Reeder, J. T. Walton, and K. C. Way. Eugene: Pickwick.

Villard, P. 2016. "Quelques aspects du renseignement militaire dans l'empire néo-assyrien." *Revue Internationale d'Histoire Militaire Ancienne* 3: 87–99.

Wenham, G. J. 1994. *Genesis 16–50.* Nashville: Thomas Nelson.

Wong, G. T. K. 2006. *Compositional Strategy of the Book of Judges: An Inductive, Rhetorical Study.* Leiden: Brill.

PART IV

Language

22
LITERACY AND SCRIBALISM IN ISRAEL DURING THE IRON AGE (CA. 1200/1150–586 BCE)

Matthieu Richelle

Ancient Israel is a unique case among the societies of the ancient Near East insofar as a whole collection of literary works from the 1st millenium BCE, the Hebrew Bible, has been transmitted by an uninterrupted tradition of handwritten copy down to modern times. By contrast, Mesopotamian literature, for instance, remained buried in the soil of Mesopotamia until modern scholarship rediscovered it. Yet when it comes to epigraphical texts from the Iron Age (ca. 1200/1150–586 BCE), the opposite is true. Compared to the innumerable Akkadian documents of that time, the corpus of Hebrew inscriptions is slim and mostly composed of brief, non-literary texts. As a result, the era of the first redactions of biblical books still contains many unknowns regarding the origins, spread, and extent of literacy. That being said, the detailed study of this corpus, set against the background of Levantine epigraphy, helps to understand the situation in its broad outlines. This chapter will successively discuss the attestations and uses of writing in the Iron Age I, often regarded as a "Dark Age," and the Iron Age II, when the Old Hebrew script flourished. Then it will address one of the most disputed questions: who read and wrote in ancient Israel and Judah?

Writing in the "Dark Age" (Iron Age I)

The Hebrew "square script" that is well known today and has been in use, with variations, for the last two millennia, did not yet exist in the Iron Age. For most of the monarchic period, more precisely from about 900 to 586 BCE, scribes used what scholars call the Old Hebrew script (or Paleo-Hebrew script). It is only during or soon after the Babylonian Exile, in the 6th century, that Judeans switched to the Aramaic script, widely used across the entire Near East, for most uses. In time, they developed it into their own local form of the alphabet, which ultimately became the "square script." The Old Hebrew script was not entirely abandoned by Judeans in the Second Temple period, but it was limited in its uses (Perrot and Richelle 2022). It was also used by the Samaritans and the Samaritan script proper stems from it.

For most of the monarchic period in Israel and Judah, therefore, it is the Old Hebrew script that proves relevant. But the question arises of its origins and of what script was used, if any, by the inhabitants of the same territories during the three centuries that separate the earliest assured attestation of Israel, about 1207 BCE (on the Merneptah stele), and the

DOI: 10.4324/9780367815691-26

emergence of the Old Hebrew script, about 900 BCE. While this period is sometimes regarded as a "Dark Age," a growing number of epigraphic findings shed some light on the use of writing at that time. It is also helpful to set this situation against the background of the changes that occurred during the transition from the Late Bronze Age (ca. 1550–1200/1150 BCE) to the Iron Age I (ca. 1200/1150–980 BCE).

A diversity of scripts were in use in the Levant in the second millennium until the end of the Late Bronze Age, including Hittite hieroglyphs and alphabetic scripts (notably the cuneiform alphabet from Ugarit), but above all cuneiform and Egyptian scripts (Sparks 2013: 76, Fig. 1). Cuneiform was used for administrative tasks, diplomatic correspondence, but also literature (Goren et al. 2009). Egyptian scripts were widely used in administrative centers like Lachish because Egypt controlled the region during the Late Bronze Age. This situation ended in the early 12th century, when the palatial system, to which a scribal apparatus was tied, collapsed during events that affected a large part of the ancient Near East. In particular, the use of the cuneiform script was virtually discontinued in the Levant, as well as the cuneiform alphabetic script. Egypt withdrew from the southern Levant a few decades later, around the middle of the 12th century.

There is one writing system, however, that was apparently not affected by the dramatic events of the 12th century, but may on the contrary have picked up steam in their wake: the Early Alphabetic script, also called the linear alphabet (as opposed to the cuneiform alphabet used in Ugarit in the 13th century BCE). It had actually been in use since the first half of the second millennium, in Egypt (where it is attested by the so-called Proto-Sinaitic inscriptions) and in the Levant (where it is attested by the so-called Proto-Canaanite inscriptions), although it spread further away, including to Mesopotamia and Yemen (Koller 2018). In time, this script was borrowed by the Greeks and the Etruscans; it is ultimately the ancestor to the Latin alphabet.

However, only brief texts have been found in the Early Alphabetic script (see Albright 1969 and Sass 1988 for classical studies). Moreover, this script was not completely standardized before the end of the second millennium. Beforehand, the texts could be written horizontally or vertically, from left to right, from right to left, or both alternatively (*boustrophedon* style); the shapes of the letters exhibited considerable variation; the stance of the letters was not fixed either, which means that they could face in various directions. Most probably, it was not standardized because it had not been adopted by a political power and "did not yet represent an official language" (Sanders 2009: 49; see also Byrne 2007: 17). Its use may have been kept low-key by scribes because the political situation forced them to mainly use Egyptian scripts or the cuneiform script (Lemaire 2008: 47), or because it was less prestigious than the systems of writing that scribes had painstakingly learned (Koller 2018: 3).

After the disruption of the early 12th century, the Early Alphabetic script now represented the main writing system in use in the Levant. A few dozen inscriptions from the 12th to the 10th centuries have been found (for inventories and dating hypotheses, see Aḥituv and Mazar 2020: 431–35; Finkelstein and Sass 2013; Lemaire 2012: 295–303; Sass and Finkelstein 2016: 25–38). During that period, it is not possible to distinguish between Phoenician, Philistine, or Hebrew inscriptions based on the script (except for the Byblian inscriptions from the 11th c.). Likewise, the meager linguistic data contained in such short texts are seldom diagnostic. Nonetheless, they give us a glimpse into the use of writing at that time.

In the northern Levant, the script was standardized in the 11th century by the Phoenicians, and they used it for royal inscriptions in Byblos in the 10th century (Rollston 2010: 19–27). In the southern Levant, most texts come from cities of the Shephelah considered to be Canaanite. The following selection of inscriptions attests a continuous scribal tradition stretching from the Late Bronze Age through the Iron I to the Iron IIA:

- Several texts come from the last stratum of the Late Bronze Age (stratum VI) at Lachish, including the Lachish jar inscription (12th c.), which seems to include a personal name, the word "scribe," and a measure of wheat indicated by signs borrowed from the Egyptian accounting system (Schniedewind 2020). At that time, Lachish was the most important city of the region, and probably an Egyptian administrative center, before its destruction ca. 1130 BCE and a subsequent gap in the settlement of roughly 200 years;
- An inscription from the 12th c. or the early 11th c. bearing a personal name (probably Jerubbaʻal) was found at Khirbet el-Raʼi, the city which took over as the main settlement center in the Shephelah after the destruction of Lachish (Rollston et al. 2021);
- A jar inscription from the 12th or 11th century (McCarter, Bunimovitz and Lederman 2011) and an ostracon from the 11th century (Lemaire 2015: 17) were found at Beth-Shemesh;
- Two inscriptions were found at Khirbet Qeiyafa: an ostracon (ca. 1000 BCE) which comprises five lines and is regarded by some as a continuous text with legal or ethical contents, but is more likely a list of personal names (Millard 2011; Richelle 2015), and the slightly later ʼIšbaʻal inscription (Garfinkel et al. 2015); it is debated whether Qeiyafa belonged to Judah or to a Philistine polity or was something else.

Other texts have been found originating from Philistia, notably an inscribed potsherd found at Qubur el-Walayda (dated ca. 1100 BCE by Lemaire [2012: 298]), from the periphery of Philistia, like the ʻIzbet Sartah abecedary (dated to the 11th century, see Lemaire 2012: 298–99), and from other parts of the southern Levant. For instance, an incision on a pottery sherd from Tel Rehov, in the Jordan Valley, is to be dated somewhere between the late 13th and the early 10th c. (Aḥituv and Mazar 2020: 415–16). An incision on a jar handle from Khirbet Raddana (15 km north of Jerusalem) is often dated to the 12th or 11th century (Lemaire 2015: 20). The Ophel pithos inscription from Jerusalem shows that the Early Alphabetic script was known there in the 10th century (after Aḥituv and Mazar 2020: 431; some prefer a date in the early 9th c.), and an inscription from Manahat, 4 km south of Jerusalem, dates from the 11th century or around 1000 BCE (Lemaire 2015: 19).

In the end, it is untenable to argue that the Early Alphabetic script was confined to the Shephelah for most of Iron I and then spread from it (as argued by Sass and Finkelstein 2013: 177). It is much more realistic to adopt a multi-center model according to which this script was more largely diffused in the Levant, perhaps radiating from Egyptian government centers, including Beth-Shean and Lachish, and from Byblos, long tied to Egypt (Naʼaman 2020).

Moreover, it is possible that the brief inscriptions on which most discussions are based only constitute the tip of the iceberg if the Early Alphabetic script was also used to write on papyrus, as a number of scholars assume or regard as possible (Amadasi Guzzo 2014; Lemaire 2008: 48; Millard 2012). Papyrus is a perishable material that rarely survives in the Levantine climate. The writing practices of the inhabitants of the Levant in the Late Bronze Age and Iron I were a legacy from their Egyptian overlords, and more precisely from the Egyptian scribes or Egyptian-trained scribes residing in the region—papyrus was a typical medium for writing among Egyptian scribes. Significantly, the lexemes used in Hebrew to designate ink, papyrus, and a number of other scribal tools and implements were borrowed from Egyptians, most probably during the New Kingdom (1549–1069 BCE; Zhakevitch 2020). It was also the time when the accounting system based on hieratic numerals, well attested in Old

Hebrew texts from the first millennium, was borrowed. The recently discovered Lachish jar inscription demonstrates that it had already happened in the 12th century; according to Schniedewind (2020: 139), "this inscription would stand at a transition point when linear alphabetic is beginning to be used administratively and when the Egyptian hieratic tradition is being adopted by alphabetic scribes."

Therefore, it seems that there was a continuous scribal use of papyrus from Iron I to Iron II. Since it is unlikely that the Egyptian scripts and language continued to be used for administrative purposes in the Levant long after Egypt's withdrawal (there are no known examples currently), it is probably the Early Alphabetic script that was used to write on papyrus, both in Byblos (Na'aman 2020: 42) and also in the southern Levant. This would provide a more plausible explanation for the rarity of the documentation in the late second millenium than the notion that the main script was still restricted to ownership marks. An indirect confirmation comes from the earliest of the Byblos royal inscriptions, namely the Ahiram sarcophagus inscription (ca. 1000 BCE), since it was written by a scribe used to writing in a cursive form of the Phoenician script (Lehmann 2008). The use of papyrus for fast writing may have been in place in Byblos for some time (Na'aman 2020: 44).

In the end, writing was present in the territories of the future kingdoms of Israel and Judah in the Iron Age I, although it must be acknowledged that we are still ignorant to a great extent about its uses and its practitioners.

Writing in the Iron Age II and the Flourishing of the Old Hebrew Script

In terms of *longue durée*, the main phenomenon that can be observed with regard to writing between the 12th and the 8th centuries BCE is the emergence of "national" (or "regional," see Lehmann 2020: 78) scripts stemming from the Early Alphabetic script, notably Phoenician in the 11th century, Old Hebrew in the early 9th century, and Aramaic in the 8th century.

There are currently two models as regards the birth of the Old Hebrew script. According to one theory, the Old Hebrew script derives from the Phoenician script from Byblos (Rollston 2010: 42–44). Because of some paleographical differences between the Byblian inscriptions and a number of alphabetic texts from the southern Levant and Syria, a variant of this hypothesis posits a second center of diffusion, perhaps Tyre (Amadasi Guzzo 2014). Either way, the strongest argument in favor of the notion that Phoenicians represented the mother script of (notably) Old Hebrew is the fact that both scripts comprise 22 graphemes, whereas the phonology of Hebrew would have required more characters to be fully expressed. The explanation would be that the Phoenicians selected the exact number of graphemes they needed, and that the Hebrew scribes just took up the Phoenician alphabet as it stood.

That said, we do not possess for the Phoenician language the same range of external documentation that is available for Hebrew to determine whether there was, or not, a perfect fit between graphemes and phonemes, so it is not entirely clear that Phoenician did not require more than 22 graphemes (Burlingame 2019: 54-55). In addition, the shorter version of the alphabet, with only 22 signs, is already attested in the late 13th century at Ugarit. Hence there is another model positing that the Old Hebrew script is not the daughter script of Phoenician but a sister, deriving in parallel from the Early Alphabetic script in which the reduction of the alphabet had already occurred (Hamilton 2014). A number of inscriptions found in the southern Levant may attest intermediary stages between the Early Alphabetic script and the Old Hebrew script. In particular, the Tel Rehov inscriptions exhibit a gradual paleographical development from Early Alphabetic to Old Hebrew, distributed over a sequence of strata dated from the 11th to the 9th century (Aḥituv and Mazar 2020; see Greene, this volume). It is at the transition between the late 10th and the early 9th centuries that the script begins to exhibit paleographical features that will be characteristic of the Old Hebrew script in later inscriptions.

Once "born," the Old Hebrew script developed and spread. It was used not only in Israel and Judah but also, for some time, in Moab, most probably because the latter country was Israel's vassal for several decades in the 9th century. As it happens, the longest text in this script is the Moabite stone (late 9th century), a basalt stone that originally bore more than 34 lines of text and commemorates the accomplishments of Mesha, king of Moab, including his victories against the Israelites (to be compared with 2 Kgs 3). To be more precise, the script of this inscription is virtually indistinguishable from Old Hebrew, although some scholars prefer to make a distinction (Puech 1988: 203 fn58).

The number of inscriptions in Old Hebrew from the 9th century BCE is very limited, but there is no doubt that most of the documents have disappeared because they were written on perishable materials such as papyrus, possibly leather, and wax tablets. Long texts may well have been written at that time, and even in the 10th century (e.g., Blum 2019; Lemaire 2015: 34; Richelle 2016; Vanderhooft 2017: 448). The oldest inscriptions in this script already bear cursive features and presuppose a practice of fast writing with ink, which is a hint that long texts were written as early as the beginning of the 9th century (Sass and Finkelstein 2016: 38), or even in the late 10th century if we take into account the most widely accepted chronology (cf. Aḥituv and Mazar 2020). Because cursivization is a gradual development that is the result of a long practice, it might point to fast writing with ink well into the 10th century. Although most of the inscriptions that have been discovered from the 10th and 9th centuries come from the territory of Israel, this is no solid reason for distinguishing between this country and Judah as regards writing, as if Judah was a sort of island deprived of substantial literacy before the 8th century (*pace* Finkelstein 2020; cf. Hogue this volume). Such an *argumentum ex silentio* proves weak in the context of the realities of Levantine writing (Richelle 2016). The Early Alphabetic script is attested in the region of Jerusalem in late Iron I, perhaps ca. 1000 BCE (Lemaire 2015: 19–20), and in Jerusalem itself in Iron IIA, probably in the 10th century, as shown by the Ophel pithos inscription. Writing technology was clearly known in Judah in the 10th and 9th centuries (Rollston 2017: 15–16). The scarcity of epigraphical findings is to be compared with the relative scarcity of archaeological findings from the Iron IIA in Judah (Aḥituv and Mazar 2020: 435), especially in Jerusalem. Moreover, although most biblical scholars hold that the bulk of biblical literature was written in Judah between the 8th century and the Persian period, and although many seals and bullae have been found, only one small fragment of papyrus has ever been discovered in this territory for these periods (Yardeni 2018: 153–54; a couple of other fragments of papyri are unprovenanced and were most likely forged). Only brief inscriptions, and no papyri, have been found in the northern kingdom of Israel, where some argue that some significant literary activity took place in the 8th century (Finkelstein 2017). In Samaria, the capital of the kingdom, most decades of that century have not yielded any single inscription, which shows that writing activity in any form is often archaeologically invisible.

From the 8th century, the documentation in Old Hebrew grows (for collections, see Aḥituv 2008; Davies 1991; Dobbs-Allsopp et al. 2005; Renz and Röllig 2016; Yardeni 2018). Monumental inscriptions are attested, although only fragments of steles from the capital cities of Samaria and Jerusalem have been discovered. The best example is the beautiful inscription from ca. 700 BCE found in the Siloam Tunnel in Jerusalem, commemorating the completion of the tunnel by the meeting of two teams working from opposite ends.

As already noted, many texts were written on papyrus, and this was the main medium used for long, literary texts. As a result, virtually no literary work in Old Hebrew script has been recovered. An ostracon (inscribed potsherd) from Horvat 'Uza (inscription No. 1) from the second half of the 7th century BCE seems to provide an exception. At Kuntillet 'Ajrud, a site located in the eastern Sinai, a few ink inscriptions on plaster from the early 8th century BCE may have included literary texts but they are so badly preserved that their interpretation remains uncertain, and the origins of the persons responsible for these texts are debated.

To get an idea of what a long, literary text looked like in the monarchic period, it is best to turn to the plaster inscriptions from the 8th century found at Deir 'Alla, in the Jordan Valley. They do not belong to the corpus of Israelite or Judean inscriptions: they are not written in Old Hebrew script but in Aramaic, and they reflect a dialect close to the Aramaic language. Yet they come from a site that was located immediately to the east of the Northern Kingdom at that time, and in a region that was alternately controlled by Israel and by Aram-Damascus. These inscriptions contain a long description of a vision given by divinities to Balaam, son of Beor, the same seer who is mentioned in Num 22–24. The layout of the text, in columns, suggests that it was copied from a scroll.

Most epigraphs found in the territories of Israel and Judah are brief texts. Seals and bullae contain personal names and sometimes titles (Avigad and Sass 1997). An exception is two silver amulets from ca. 600 BCE, found in a tomb at Ketef Hinnom (Jerusalem), bearing formulas very similar to the Priestly blessing of Num 6: 24–26. Much more common are many brief inscriptions incised on pottery or stone that indicate the ownership and/or contents of jars and other recipients. Ostraca generally contain lists of names and commodities; some of them bear messages. They were used for everyday writing. The most important collections come from Samaria, Arad, Lachish, and Horvat 'Uza. In the royal palace in Samaria, around a hundred dockets from the early 8th century record quantities of oil and wine. The Arad inscriptions (from the 9th or 8th century to the early 6th century) contain much administrative or accounting information (lists of names and commodities), and some letters as well. The same is true of the Lachish ostraca, which shed some light on the situation in an important military site in the last phase of the Judahite royal period. Such documents provide limited but precious information about the administration in Israel and Judah, some glimpses into people's day-to-day life, and linguistic data about the Hebrew spoken in the Iron Age.

In Israel and in Judah, the script naturally developed over the following centuries and epigraphers have described the paleography of ink inscriptions (Rollston 2014), seals (Herr 2014), and monumental inscriptions (Vanderhooft 2014). That said, it is important to note that lapidary inscriptions were not engraved by scribes but by masons, who copied models but did not have the same proficiency in literacy. Some of the latter may have been illiterate, but the consistency of the letterforms in monumental inscriptions renders this hypothesis questionable (Keimer 2015: 197 fn10). In addition, it is a striking fact that cursive script was used on monumental inscriptions, perhaps for aesthetic beauty (Keimer 2015: 206). It is certainly for such reasons that the Siloam Tunnel inscription reproduces broad strokes and thin strokes even though it was not made with ink. It is essential to realize that Israelites and Judeans did not have recourse to different writing systems for everyday inscriptions and for monumental writing, as did a number of other people, for instance, the Egyptians. In sum, a wide array of texts have come to light thanks to excavations and they bear witness to multiform uses of writing in ancient Israel and Judah, mostly from the 8th century on. This raises the question of who actually wrote (and read) those documents, to which we now turn.

Who Read and Wrote in Ancient Israel?

A number of scholars have argued that a relatively high proportion of the population of Israel and Judah were able to read and write (Millard 2012), at least from the 8th century onward (Demsky 2014: 90), or from the late monarchic period (Naveh 1968: 74). However, a widely held view today is that reading and writing concerned only a very limited number of people (Puech 1988; Rollston 2010: 127–35; Young 1998b). It is also plausible that various degrees of literacy coexisted (Schniedewind 2013: 104–05). The discussion rests on a number of considerations.

First, many authors have pointed out the *relative simplicity of the linear alphabet*, compared to more complex systems of writing like the cuneiform script, and claimed that it made its use accessible to a large part of the population. Yet empirical evidence reveals that acquiring proficiency in an alphabetic script requires months or even years of learning (Rollston 2006: 48–49). This does not necessarily apply to a rudimentary form of literacy, however (Schniedewind 2013: 105). It is also important to note that many inscriptions from the 8th–6th centuries BCE exhibit common orthographic and paleographic features, and some presuppose the ability to use hieratic numerals, which seems to presuppose a standardized scribal curriculum (Rollston 2006). That said, because many other inscriptions are very brief, it is not always possible to see whether their texts followed such scribal conventions. What is sure is that many inscriptions exhibit a good execution of the script.

Comparative evidence leads to mixed results. On the one hand, evidence of widespread use of an alphabetic script can be found in the tens of thousands of rock graffitis, written in Safaitic and Thamudic, found especially in the Arabic peninsula. They were not written by scribes but by shepherds during trips, as a past-time. This gives the impression of a kind of mass literacy. On the other hand, these brief texts only contain very simple information, like personal names. We now know that the more substantial texts were incised on wooden sticks (from palm-leaf stalks), with a cursive form of the script. The graffiti are merely evidence of a very basic form of literacy that subsisted alongside the fluent use of writing for commercial and administrative purposes in towns (Stein 2010). Besides, comparative data from other areas rather suggests that the use of an alphabet does not necessarily prompt widespread literacy; in fact, the estimations of the rate of literacy in Greek and Roman societies do not exceed 10–15% of the population (Harris 1989: 327–30). In Palestine, the evidence concerning writing among Jews from the Roman period also indicates a low rate of literacy (Hezser 2001: 497). A decisive factor behind the widespread use of writing is the symbolic and social capital attached to writing, which varies between cultures (Street 1984).

Second, the *wide distribution of the inscriptions* in the territories of Israel and Judah may suggest the presence of literate people in numerous sites. Moreover, inscriptions are found in all sorts of contexts, both public and domestic (Aḥituv and Mazar 2020: 435). That said, it remains possible that people had recourse to the services of scribes to write the texts they needed and incise marks of ownership on objects they owned, and then brought back these documents and items to their home or working place. That inscriptions are found in many archaeological sites could perhaps be interpreted by the hypothesis of "local clerks" present in many places to record lists and other commercial data, to be distinguished from the kind of scribes who wrote down literary texts and official documentation and correspondence.

Third, the *increase in the number of inscriptions* and their use in a *greater variety of media* in the late monarchic period suggests that more people were able to read at that time. For instance, seals were almost never inscribed before the 8th century. Many vessels bore a mark of ownership or an indication about the contents. This does not allow us to assess the spread of literacy with much precision, however.

Fourth, a number of ostraca seem to indicate that literacy spread beyond the guild of scribes to reach *a number of officials, at least in the military.* Letters exchanged between soldiers, found at Lachish, Arad, and Horvat 'Uza, favor this hypothesis. Several hands can be detected behind these texts, whereas it is unlikely that a multiplicity of scribes worked in these small fortresses; moreover, some letters mention that the soldiers wrote the texts themselves (Faigenbaum et al. 2021: 154, about Arad). An important document in this regard is Lachish ostracon No 3. Hosha'yah, a military official from (probably) the Shephelah, replies to Ya'ush, who likely was the chief soldier in Lachish. According to the most widely accepted interpretation of the ostracon, Hosha'yah quotes Ya'ush who had said: "you cannot read a letter" (or: "you did not understand it; call a scribe!"), and Hosha'yah swears that he is able to read on his own: "No one has tried to read a letter to me – ever!" (see Dobbs-Allsopp 2005: 308–14). The fact that Hosha'yah felt offended at the accusation that he was unable to read suggests that it was a relatively common skill in the higher ranks of the army. Thus it seems reasonable to posit that a number of military officials were literate in the late monarchic period.

That said, it is not that easy to find inscriptions that were demonstrably written by people that were neither scribes nor officials. In a number of cases, one may wonder if they had recourse to a scribe. Graffiti, like the inscriptions scratched on the walls of a burial cave at Khirbet Beit-Lei (8km from Lachish), perhaps in the early 6th century BCE, are examples of possible candidates, since there is no reason to assume that the persons who inscribed them happened to be scribes or military officials.

Fifth, a number of *biblical passages* are sometimes adduced to argue that a large array of people could read and write during the monarchic period (for a detailed discussion of this evidence, see Young 1998a). Besides scribes, a number of persons are said to have written or read a text: kings (see e.g. 2 Sam 11:14–15; 2 Kgs 5:7; 10:1,6; 19:14; 23:2; cf. also the prescription to read the Torah in Deut 17:19), prophets (Isa 8:1; Ezek 24:2), priests (Num 5:23; Deut 31:9–11) and Levites (Neh 8:8). However, without even raising the question of the historicity of these stories, it is worth noting that the verb "to write" (*katab*) in Biblical Hebrew often serves as a shorthand for "to have a text written by somebody else" (Nissinen 2014), and the same certainly holds true for "to read" (*qara'*). A striking example is Jeremiah, who is ordered by God to write down his oracles on a scroll (Jer 36:2) but actually has his scribe, Baruch, do it on his dictation (Jer 36:4).

A couple of specific passages seem, at first glance, to suggest that virtually anybody was supposed to be able to write. In Judges 8:14, Gideon catches "a young man (*na'ar*), one of the people of Succoth" and questions him; the young man "writes" for him the (names of the) 77 officials and elders of Succoth. Because nothing in the narrative suggests that the young man was chosen for his ability to write (the reason was rather that he was from Succoth), this verse gives the impression that any such person randomly selected in the population was able to write down personal names. Taken at face value, the scene is situated in the time of the Judges, which would be Iron I, but many exegetes would regard the narrative as a fiction from the late Iron Age or later. Still, this might provide information on the realities of the time when it was written. However, here again, the verb "to write" is equivocal. Furthermore, some have noted that *na'ar* can designate a large range of roles, including servant, attendant, or official (Young 1998a: 250). In any case, the kind of literacy that is evoked is "name literacy," it does not point to a high level of literacy.

According to Deuteronomy, the Israelites are required to write the laws of Moses "on the doorposts of your house and on your gates" (Deut 6:9; 11:20). But this does not mean that all the inhabitants of Judah were able to read texts in, say, the 7th century (the usual dating of the earliest core of Deuteronomy). In addition to the "ideal" or "utopic" perspective of this text, such a reference to inscriptions is more realistically explained by the iconic dimension of writing (Carr 2005: 121–22); even today, the presence of inscriptions in Hebrew and Latin in synagogues and churches does not mean that any participant in the religious services are able to read the texts. In the end, the biblical data do not enable us to determine who was able to read and write in the monarchic period beyond scribes and possibly some officials.

To conclude so far, there is no unequivocal evidence for widespread literacy beyond scribes and officials in ancient Israel and Judah during the Iron Age, at least as long as we are speaking of a substantial level of literacy, enabling a person to write messages, for instance. Yet there is a widespread presence of writing in these countries. It remains possible that lower forms of literacies existed and that a number of people had the ability to write their own name, a few words, perhaps lists, but it so happens that the unequivocal data mostly points to the work of trained scribes and officials. It is also possible that a greater number of people were able to read but not to write. By nature, however, this cannot be observed on inscriptions. The increase in the variety of inscriptions and media may, however, suggest a growing number of people able to read at least brief inscriptions. In the end, it is the work of the scribes that is best illuminated by the documentation.

What do we know about scribes in monarchic Israel and Judah? Only a few are named in the Hebrew Bible, notably David's scribe (named Seraiah in 2 Sam 8:17, Sheva in 2 Sam 20:25, and Shavsha in 1 Chr 18:16) and Solomon's scribes (Elihoreph and Ahijah, sons of Shisha, in 1 Kgs 4:3). If Shisha is the same person as David's scribe, then this suggests that the scribal office was, at least in some cases, a hereditary profession. Another interesting case is the role played by Jeremiah's scribe, Baruch son of Neriyah (Jer 36) since it suggests that even such a skillful person as this prophet had recourse to a professional scribe to draft his oracles on a scroll.[1] While there were female scribes in Mesopotamia (Stol 2016: 367–71), it is not clear whether this was also the case in Israel and Judah. A possible hint is the mention of "the sons of *hassopheret*" in Ezra 2:55; the latter Hebrew word could mean "female scribe," although such a reference, without any personal name, seems unusual.

Much ink has been spilled by modern scholars to try and understand how their early predecessors spilled their own ink. The Hebrew Bible provides precious information on the tools used by scribes and the medium on which they wrote (Zhakevitch 2020). The epigraphical data indicate that scribes used rush brushes to write, as opposed to the reed pen that was adopted later, in the Hellenistic period (Longacre 2021). The use of a chisel-shaped broad-nib pen enabled fast writing and had calligraphic consequences (Lehmann 2020: 84–87; van der Kooij 1986); notably, it facilitated shading in the calligraphy, that is, variations in the thickness of the strokes, as can be observed in ink inscriptions.

How did scribes learn to write? It has been suggested that some buildings or rooms served as schools, especially in locations where abecedaries have been found (Lemaire 1981). However, because it seems difficult to establish that any specific place in Israel or Judah fulfilled this function, this hypothesis is rarely adopted today. Perhaps, like in Ugarit, "schools formed around individual scribes in a domestic setting, where these very scribes (…) not only taught but carried out their duties" (Hawley, Pardee, and Roche-Hawley 2015: 246). In other words, we do not need to hypothesize that specific public buildings were devoted to the training of scribes; what really mattered was the presence of an experienced scribe and a few tools.

As a result, recent research has focused on the *curriculum* followed by apprentices, regardless of the precise setting where it took place. Two kinds of evidence shed light on the way they were trained. First, abecedaries and scribal exercises. The former constitutes the most evident testimonies of the presence of apprentices. Abecedaries have been found in various places. Some of them were models written by a teacher, others were attempts at imitation made by apprentices. On Pithos B from Kuntillet 'Ajrud, dated to the early 8th century BCE, we see no less than four abecedaries, numbered 3.11–14 in the *editio princeps* (Aḥituv, Eshel, and Meshel 2012). Schniedewind writes that "Inscriptions 3.12 and 3.14 are written in red ink in a flowing, elegant hand, whereas Inscriptions 3.11 and 3.13 are written in black ink reflecting a more basic hand." The former are likely the work of a teacher, and the latter of beginners. Interestingly, in Egypt, master scribes sometimes used red ink to make corrections on the work of apprentices (Schniedewind 2019: 28–29). On the same pithos, a student also practiced the writing of several signs, notably the letter *yod* and hieratic numerals, in particular, the sign for "70". Intensive training in hieratic numerals, alongside signs for measures and commodities, is attested on four ostraca from Kadesh Barnea (Tell el-Qudeirât) dated to the 6th century BCE. One of them lists key numerals from 1 to 10,000 (Aḥituv 2008: 210–12). Yet another case where we can see both the hand of a teacher and that of an apprentice is a stone inscription found in the City of David and dated to the 7th century BCE. It contains a name written twice, first by an experienced and then by a beginner's hand (Rollston 2012). The presence, on the same document, of a model text written by a trained scribe and of an exercise by an apprentice, echoes practices that are well attested in Mesopotamia and in Egypt.

Other epigraphs were likely written by persons with limited practice. Such is the case, for instance, of the so-called "*mpqd* ostracon" from Tel 'Ira, dated to the 7th century BCE: "the bold script written in uneven lines seems to be the work of a non-professional, unskilled scribe, who, although being familiar with the formal cursive Hebrew script, apparently did not have much practice in writing" (Yardeni 2018: 160). Similarly, the so-called "Ahiqam ostracon" from Horvat 'Uza exhibits crude handwriting (Mendel-Geberovitch 2011: 57). Such situations raise the question of whether we are dealing with texts inscribed by "early career scribes" or by other kinds of professionals who had acquired training to write down some records, but whose job proper was not to be a scribe. It is not always possible to tell. But the context sometimes favors the latter possibility, as in the two inscriptions just mentioned, since they come from fortresses. In the case of the Ahiqam ostracon, Mendel argues that it was written by a lower-rank soldier (Mendel-Geberovitch 2011: 57–64).

It is likely that the training of scribes in Israel and Judah could include several stages enabling them to acquire skills of increasing complexity, as in other societies from the Near East, from the ability to write down ownership marks as well as lists of names and commodities, to the use of hieratic numerals for bookkeeping, to the ability to write messages and finally the ability to write literary works. The evidence concerning the most advanced part of the curriculum is slim but likely included memorization and recitation of texts (Carr 2005; Schniedewind 2019). It is likely that some scribes only learned the first stages of the curriculum while others also went on to acquire higher levels of literacy.

Although much eludes our knowledge due to the lack of preservation of documents, the evidence provided by the epigraphical findings and by the Hebrew Bible sheds precious light on the multifaceted writing tradition in the territories of Israel and Judah. While it seems that only a limited part of the population was literate in a meaningful way, writing was important in these cultures, and the manifold uses of writing by its practitioners were enough to leave a limited but rich and varied documentation that is ever-growing with new discoveries.

Note

1 Several unprovenanced seals and bullae in Old Hebrew script also mention scribes (Avigad and Sass 1993: 57–58, 175), including two bullae of "Baruch, son of Neriyahu, the scribe," but their authenticity is questionable (for the Baruch bullae, see Goren and Arie 2014).

Bibliography

Aḥituv, Shmuel. 2008. *Echoes from the Past: Hebrew and Cognate Inscriptions from the Biblical World*. Jerusalem: Carta.

Aḥituv, Shmuel, Esther Eshel, and Ze'ev Meshel. 2012. "Chapter 5: The Inscriptions." Pages 73–142 in *Kuntillet 'Ajrud (Ḥorvat Teman): An Iron Age II Religious Site on the Judah-Sinai Border*. Edited by Ze'ev Meshel. Jerusalem: Israel Exploration Society.

Aḥituv, Shmuel, and Amihai Mazar. 2020. "Inscriptions on Pottery." Pages 415–39 in *Tel Rehov: A Bronze and Iron Age City in the Beth-Shean Valley*, vol. 4: *Pottery Studies, Inscriptions and Figurative Art*. Edited by Amihai Mazar and Nava Panitz-Cohen. Jerusalem: Institute of Archaeology, Hebrew University of Jerusalem.

Albright, William Foxwell. 1969. *The Proto-Sinaitic Inscriptions and Their Decipherment*. Cambridge: Harvard University Press; London: Oxford University Press.

Amadasi Guzzo, Maria D. 2014. "'Alphabet insaisissable:' Quelques notes concernant la diffusion de l'écriture consonantique." *Transeuphratène* 44: 67–86.

Avigad, Nahman, and Benjamin Sass. 1997. *Corpus of West Semitic Stamp Seals*. Jerusalem: Israel Exploration Society. Jerusalem: Israel Academy of Sciences and Humanities/Israel Exploration Society/Institute of Archaeology, Hebrew University of Jerusalem

Blum, Erhard. 2019. "Institutionelle und kulturelle Voraussetzungen der Israelitischen Traditionsliteratur." Pages 3–44 in *Tradition(en) im Alten Israel: Konstruktion, Transmission und Transformation*. Edited by Ruth Ebach und Martin Leuenberger. Tübingen: Mohr Siebeck.

Burlingame, Andrew. 2019. "Writing and Literacy in the World of Ancient Israel: Recent Developments and Future Directions," *BiOr* 76: 45-74.

Byrne, Brian. 2007. "The Refuge of Scribalism in Iron I Palestine." *BASOR* 345: 1–31.

Carr, David M. 2005. *Writing on the Tablet of the Heart: Origins of Scripture and Literature*. New York: Oxford University Press.

Davies, Graham I. 1991. *Ancient Hebrew Inscriptions*, Vol. 1: *Corpus*. Cambridge: Cambridge University Press.

Demsky, Aaron. 2014. "Researching Literacy in Ancient Israel—New Approaches and Recent Developments." Pages 89–104 in *"See, I Will Bring a Scroll Recounting What Befell Me" (Ps 40:8): Epigraphy and Daily Life from the Bible to the Talmud*. Edited by Esther Eshel and Yigal Levin. Göttingen: Vandenhoeck & Ruprecht.

Dobbs-Allsopp, F. W., J. J. M. Roberts, C. L. Seow, and R. E. Whitaker. 2005. *Hebrew Inscriptions: Texts from the Biblical Period of the Monarchy with Concordance*. New Haven: Yale University Press.

Faigenbaum-Golovin, Shira, et al. 2016. "Algorithmic Handwriting Analysis of Judah's Military Correspondence Sheds Light on Composition of Biblical Texts." *PNAS* 113: 4664–69. DOI: 10.1073/pnas.1522200113.

Finkelstein, Israel. 2017. "A Corpus of North Israelite Texts in the Days of Jeroboam II." *HeBAI* 6: 262–89.

———. 2020. "The Emergence and Dissemination of Writing in Judah." *Semitica et Classica* 13: 269–82.

Finkelstein, Israel, and Benjamin Sass. 2013. "The West Semitic Alphabetic Inscriptions, Late Bronze IIA to Iron IIA: Archaeological Context, Distribution and Chronology." *HBAI* 2: 149–220.

Garfinkel, Yosef, M. R. Golub, H. Misgav, and S. Ganor. 2015. "The 'Išba'al Inscription from Khirbet Qeiyafa." *BASOR* 373: 217–33.

Goren, Yuval, and Eran Arie. 2014. "The Authenticity of the Bullae of Berekhyahu Son of Neriyahu the Scribe." *BASOR* 372: 151–53.

Goren, Yuval, et al. 2009. "A Provenance Study of the Gilgamesh Fragment from Megiddo." *Archaeometry* 51 (2009): 763–73.

Hamilton, Gordon A. 2014. "Reconceptualizing the Periods of the Early Alphabetic Scripts." Pages 30–55 in *"An Eye for Form": Epigraphic Essays in Honor of Frank Moore Cross*. Edited by Jo A. Hackett and Walter E. Aufrecht. Winona Lake: Eisenbrauns.

Harris, William V. 1989. *Ancient Literacy*. Cambridge: Harvard University Press.
Hawley, Robert, Denins Pardee, and Carole Roche-Hawley. 2015. "The Scribal Culture of Ugarit." *JANEH* 2: 229–67.
Herr, Larry G. 2014. "Hebrew, Moabite, and Edomite Seal Scripts." Pages 187–201 in *"An Eye for Form": Epigraphic Essays in Honor of Frank Moore Cross*. Edited by Jo A. Hackett and Walter E. Aufrecht. Winona Lake: Eisenbrauns.
Hezser, Catherine. 2001. *Jewish Literacy in Roman Palestine*. Tübingen: Mohr Siebeck.
Keimer, Kyle H. 2015. "The Impact of Ductus on Script Form and Development in Monumental Northwest Semitic Inscriptions." *UF* 46: 189–212.
Koller, Aaron. 2018. "The Diffusion of the Alphabet in the Second Millennium BCE: On the Movements of Scribal Ideas from Egypt to the Levant, Mesopotamia, and Yemen." *JAEI* 20: 1–14.
Lehmann, Reinhard G. 2008. "Calligraphy and Craftsmanship in the Ahirom Inscription: Considerations on Skilled Linear Flat Writing in Early First Millennium Byblos." *MAARAV* 15: 119–64.
———. 2020. "Much Ado About an Implement! The Phoenicianising of Early Alphabetic." Pages 69–90 in *Understanding the Relations between Scripts II: Early Alphabets*. Edited by Philip. J. Boyle and Philippa M. Steele. Oxford: Oxbow Books.
Lemaire, André. 1981. *Les écoles et la formation de la Bible dans l'ancien Israël*. Göttingen: Vanderhoeck und Ruprecht.
———. 2008. "The Spread of Alphabetic Scripts (c. 1700–500 BCE)." *Diogenes* 218: 44–57.
———. 2012. "West Semitic Epigraphy and the History of Levant during the 12th–10th Centuries BCE." Pages 291–307 in *The Ancient Near East in the 12th–10th Centuries BCE: Culture and History*. Edited by Gershon Galil et al. Münster: Ugarit-Verlag.
———. 2015. "Levantine Literacy (ca. 1000–750 BCE)." Pages 11–45 in *Contextualizing Israel's Sacred Writings: Ancient Literacy, Orality, and Literary Production*. Edited by Brian B. Schmidt. Atlanta: SBL.
Longacre, Drew. 2021. "Comparative Hellenistic and Roman Manuscript Studies (CHRoMS): Script Interactions and Hebrew/Aramaic Writing Culture." *COMSt Bulletin* 7: 7–50.
McCarter, P. Kyle., Shlomo Bunimovitz, and Zvi Lederman. 2011. "An Archaic Ba'l Inscription from Tel Beth-Shemesh." *TA* 38: 179–93.
Mendel-Geberovitch, Anat. 2011. "Who Wrote the Ahiqam Ostracon from Ḥorvat ʿUza?" *IEJ* 61: 54–67.
Millard, Alan. 2011. "The Ostracon from the Days of David Found at Khirbet Qeiyafa." *TynBul* 62: 1–13.
———. 2012. "Scripts and Their Uses in the 12th–10th Centuries BCE." Pages 405–12 in *The Ancient Near East in the 12th–10th Centuries BCE: Culture and History*. Edited by G. Galil et al. Münster: Ugarit-Verlag.
Na'aman, Nadav. 2020 "Egyptian Centres and the Distribution of the Alphabet in the Levant." *TA* 47: 29–54.
Naveh, Joseph. 1968. "A Palaeographic Note on the Distribution of the Hebrew Script." *HTR* 1968: 68–74.
Nissinen, Martti. 2014. "Since When Do Prophets Write?" Pages 585–606 in *In the Footsteps of Sherlock Holmes: Studies in the Biblical Text in Honour of Anneli Aejmelaeus*. Edited by Kristin de Troyer, T. Michael Law, and Marketta Liljeström. Leuven: Peeters.
Perrot, Antony, and Matthieu Richelle. 2022. "The Dead Sea Scrolls' Paleo-Hebrew Script: Its Roots in Hebrew Scribal Tradition." Pages 1–74 in *The Hebrew Manuscripts: A Millennium*. Edited by Elodie Attia and Antony Perrot. Leiden: Brill.
Puech, Emile. 1988. "Les écoles dans l'Israël pré-exilique: Les données épigraphiques." Pages 189–203 in *Congress Volume Jerusalem 1986*. Edited by John A. Emerton. Leiden: Brill.
Renz, Johannes, and Wolfgang Röllig. 2016. *Handbuch der Althebräischen Epigraphik: Die Althebräischen Inschriften*, 2 vols. Darmstadt: Wissenschaftliche Buchgesellschaft.
Richelle, Matthieu. 2015. "Quelques nouvelles lectures sur l'ostracon de Khirbet Qeiyafa." *Semitica* 57: 147–62.
———. 2016. "Elusive Scrolls: Could Any Hebrew Literature Be Written Prior to the Eighth Century B.C.E.?" *VT* 66: 556–94.
Rollston, Christopher A. 2006. "Scribal Education in Ancient Israel: The Old Hebrew Epigraphic Evidence." *BASOR* 344: 47–74.
———. 2010. *Writing and Literacy in the World of Ancient Israel. Epigraphic Evidence from the Iron Age*. Atlanta: SBL.

———. 2012. "An Old Hebrew Stone Inscription from the City of David: A Trained Hand and a Remedial Hand on the Same Inscription." Pages 189–96 in *Puzzling Out the Past: Studies in Northwest Semitic Languages and Literatures in Honor of Bruce Zuckerman*. Edited by Marilyn J. Lundberg, Steven Fine, and Wayne T. Pitard. Leiden: Brill.

———. 2017. "Epigraphic Evidence from Jerusalem and Its Environs at the Dawn of Biblical History: Methodologies and a Long Durée Perspective." Pages 7–20 in *New Studies in the Archaeology of Jerusalem and Its Region: Collected Papers*, vol. 11. Edited by Yuval Gadot et al. Jerusalem: Israel Antiquities Authority, Hebrew University of Jerusalem.

Rollston, Christopher. A., Y. Garfinkel, K. H. Keimer, G. Davis, and S. Ganor. 2021. "The Jerubba'al Inscription from Khirbet al-Ra'i: A Proto-Canaanite (Early Alphabetic) Inscription." *JJAR* 2: 1–15.

Sanders, Seth. 2009. *The Invention of Hebrew*. Urbana: University of Illinois Press.

Sass, Benjamin. 1988. *The Genesis of the Alphabet and Its Development in the Second Millennium B.C.* Wiesbaden: Harrassowitz.

Sass, Benjamin and Israel Finkelstein. 2013. "The West Semitic Alphabetic Inscriptions, Late Bronze II to Iron IIA: Archeological Context, Distribution and Chronology." *HBAI* 2: 149–220.

———.2016. "The Swan-Song of Proto-Canaanite in the Ninth Century BCE in Light of an Alphabetic Inscription from Megiddo." *Semitica et Classica* 9: 19–42.

Schniedewind, William M. 2013. *A Social History of Hebrew: Its Origins Through the Rabbinic Period*. New Haven: Yale University Press.

———. 2019. *The Finger of the Scribe: How Scribes Learned to Write the Bible*. New York: Oxford University Press.

———. 2020. "The Alphabetic 'Scribe' of the Lachish Jar Inscription and the Hieratic Tradition in the Early Iron Age." *BASOR* 383: 137–40.

Sparks, Rachel T. 2013. "Re-Writing the Script: Decoding the Textual Experience in the Bronze Age Levant (c.2000-1150 BC)." Pages 75–104 in *Writing as Material Practice: Substance, Surface and Medium*. Edited by Kathryn E. Piquette and Ruth D. Whitehouse. London: Uniquity Press.

Stein, Peter. 2010. "Literacy in Pre-Islamic Arabia: An Analysis of the Epigraphic Evidence." Pages 255–80 in *The Qur'ān in Context: Historical and Literary Investigations into the Qur'ānic Milieu*. Edited by Angelika Neuwirth, Nicolai Sinai, and Michael Marx. Leiden: Brill.

Stol, Marten. 2016. *Women in the Ancient Near East*. Boston: de Gruyter.

Street, Brian V. 1984. *Literacy in Theory and Practice*. New York: Cambridge University Press.

van der Kooij, Gerrit. 1986. *Early North-West Semitic Script Traditions: An Archaeological Study of the Linear Alphabetic Scripts Up to c. 500 B.C.; Ink and Argillary*. PhD diss., Leiden University.

Vanderhooft, David S. 2014. "Iron Age Moabite, Hebrew, and Edomite Monumental Scripts." Pages 107–26 in *"An Eye for Form": Epigraphic Essays in Honor of Frank Moore Cross*. Edited by Jo A. Hackett and Walter E. Aufrecht. Winona Lake: Eisenbrauns.

Yardeni, Ada. 2018. *The National Hebrew Script Up to the Babylonian Exile*. Jerusalem: Carta.

Young, Ian M. 1998a. "Israelite Literacy: Interpreting the Evidence: Part I." *VT* 48: 239–53.

———. 1998b. "Israelite Literacy: Interpreting the Evidence: Part II." *VT* 48: 408–22.

Zhakevitch, Philip. 2020. *Scribal Tools in Ancient Israel: A Study of Biblical Hebrew Terms for Writing Materials and Implements*. University Park: Eisenbrauns.

23
MORE THAN THE SUM OF THEIR PARTS

Multimodality and the Study of Iron Age Inscriptions

Alice Mandell

Introduction

Inscriptions enable scholars to reconstruct different phases and varieties of Northwest Semitic scripts and languages, and they can be informative about the geopolitical, royal, and scribal histories of this region (Sanders 2009; Rollston 2010; Schniedewind 2013; 2019; Mandell 2022a). Recent scholarship into text-audience interactions and literacy also highlights the importance of engaging with questions about the material, visual, spatial, and social dimensions of writing (Piquette and Whitehouse 2013; Mandell and Smoak 2017, 2018; Richey 2021). Such scholarship reminds us that these important aspects of ancient inscriptions should not be relegated to the periphery of scholarly attention. When we focus solely on the linguistic meaning of a text, we implicitly limit the scope of its meaning to ways in which ancient audiences engaged with a text's words; that is, literacy and textual engagement and access are restricted to a person's ability to write or read. When we analyze inscriptions more holistically, we see the limitations of the assumption of the primacy of written language over other aspects of textual production, design, and communication. Ancient texts were not always made to be read, and their words were not always how they made meaning.

Multimodality is an approach that gives scholars a richer window into diverse ways in which ancient people made, used, engaged with, and valued texts. This approach highlights the range of ways that texts function as communication media through multiple "modes" of texts, that is, through their different semiotic resources that make meaning and communicate this meaning to audiences (Kress and van Leeuwen 2021). Modes are the linguistic, visual, material, and contextual properties of texts that make meaning, from which "people draw on and configure in specific moments and places to represent events and relations" (Jewitt 2017: 2). Thus, a text's form, materials, design, layout, and composition as well as its script, language variety, and orthographic characteristics impart meaning to the text and communicate this meaning to its audiences.

This approach also emphasizes the importance of considering how the different properties of texts are interconnected (for example, the use of color or a font style to highlight a particular word, thereby layering a linguistically marked word with a visual cue that signals its importance). Bezemer and Kress describe how modes are interconnected in texts in the following way:

Meanings are made in a variety of modes and always with more than one mode. Modes have differing modal resources. Writing, for instance, has syntactic, grammatical, and lexical resources, graphic resources such as font type, size, and resources for "framing," such as punctuation. Writing might make use of other resources, for instance, the resource of color. Speech and writing share aspects of grammar, syntax, and lexis.

(2008: 171)

A text's modes are determined by their individual and cumulative affordances; their properties and different capabilities, limitations, and ranges of possible meaning impact the ways that audiences engage with and encounter texts (Bezemer and Kress 2008: 168–69; 171–72). This approach also draws attention to the social location in which audiences engage with texts as an important factor in their meaning, and in their range of possible functions in different social spaces (Jones 2017). This approach therefore accounts for the important ways that the lived context of an ancient text and its audience's engagement with it also determined its range of meaning and use.

In order to outline the benefits of a multimodal approach to the study of ancient Hebrew inscriptions, this chapter will offer: (1) a summary of developments in literacy studies and in the study of texts as visual media that have paved the way for this approach; (2) a discussion of how the multimodality perspective enriches our analysis of less linguistically informative texts; and (3) two case studies that demonstrate how this approach can be meaningfully applied to the study of two different sets of dedicatory inscriptions that represented people before the Israelite god. Analysis of an inscribed stone basin from the Iron II site of Kuntillet 'Ajrud, and the inscriptions set into the High Priest's clothing in Exodus 28 and 39. These two case studies demonstrate that we cannot fully understand the communicative scope of these inscriptions or their ritual logic without recourse to an exploration of their multimodality.

Theoretical Approach: New Literacy Studies and The Multimodality Perspective

Since the mid-1990s, research in sociolinguistics, literacy and education, writing systems research, and visual design has taken a new direction, largely because of the increasingly complex and dynamic literacy practices in the modern era. Scholars have sought to better understand the socially situated nature of literacy and to explore the diverse ways in which people engage with written language and with communication media (Trimbur and Press 2015). Scholarship in the branch of literacy studies known as New Literacy Studies paved the way for the extension of the study of literacy to the diverse ways that a group's literacy practices are interconnected to particular social and cultural settings (Scribner and Cole 1981; Street 1984; Street 1993; Barton, Hamilton, and Ivanič 2000; Gee 2015). Literacy practices—"what people do with literacy"—not only encompass the ability to make or read texts but also include all practices where people engage with, encounter, and even talk about texts (Barton and Hamilton 2000: 7). By adopting this more nuanced and inclusive understanding of the range of literacies (pl.) that can coexist in ancient communities, we are better positioned to study ancient inscriptions as indices of a broader range of literacy practices, which of course not only included the writing and reading of texts but also other forms of engagement with texts and inscribed things.

The multimodality perspective into texts highlights that language is not always the primary mode through which people engage with texts, and it considers the other semiotic modes that have the potential to engage audiences. One important assumption is that written media are extensions of conventions of visual and representational communication, and as such, they are tied to the other semiotic ideologies and modes of communication in a community (Kress and van Leeuwen 2021). By way of example, in speech, this approach to conversation analysis highlights how we communicate through our words and through a range of sound and movement-based strategies that can add meaning to our words. The multimodality of spoken communication includes the kinetic, gestural, and performative dimensions of our speech practices. When speaking, we might use our body to gesture or to create meaning by our proximity or distance to an audience, or we might use the tone or volume of our voices to add emphasis, for example.

Texts are also multimodal, yet their semiotic properties are bound to the media and materiality of the text object. They not only communicate meaning through their words but also through their materials, spatial organization, and design (e.g., through a choice in font style, underlining or other marks, or a choice in color), and through any images, markings, and other inscribed signs that are a part of a text's composition (Kress and van Leeuwen 2021). The process of transduction describes how the semiotic meaning connected to one mode can be transferred into another mode in a different medium; in this new form, the mode might take a completely different form, and yet communicate a similar meaning (Bezemer and Kress 2008: 169). Transduction explains the choices that writers make when they adopt strategies from speech or oral performance and adapt them to express similar meaning in a text.[1]

In the same way that gesture, gaze, the proximity of people in conversation and their movements, and their facial expressions have semiotic power in conversation, in *writing* we can think of the text's medium, size, scale, color, and other design elements, and its placement as contributing to its meaning and to the ways in which audiences engage with its multimodality. For example, critical passages in a text can be marked visually through their layout and design in a way that highlights their linguistic meaning and rhetorical significance.

This approach offers a way to analyze ancient texts beyond their words, to extend to the ways in which they communicate through their form, materiality, design, and spatial contexts, and what audiences bring to their engagement with a text. Equally critical to the communicative power and meaning of a text as its words or design is its context, which should not be relegated to the periphery of scholarly attention. Indeed, the "site of display" of a text can be the primary mode by which audiences engage a text and access its other modes of meaning (Bezemer and Kress 2008: 173–174; but also 182–190). A text's site of display also impacts the ways that people engage with each other in enacting literacy practices (Jones 2017). This understanding also highlights the primacy of a text's context, as changes to the site of display of a text can change its meaning and the way that audiences engage with it, even when its words remain unchanged.

The application of the "multimodal" turn in the study of writing and literacies to the study of ancient inscriptions calls for analysis of their production, design, script, and the interplay of their linguistic content and its communicative aims, and the orthographic practices in play in the text. In this way, this approach decenters language as the primary mode of how texts communicate and considers the way that written language is interconnected to the broader visual "grammar" inherent in texts (Kress and van Leeuwen 2021). One benefit to this application is that it avoids the pitfalls of thinking about ancient cultures as bifurcated between literate and non-literate people. A critical takeaway is that the designs and contexts of inscriptions can be studied as evidence for the diverse uses of texts in ancient communities. Rather than limit the analysis of inscriptions to the traditional pillars of linguistic and script analysis, this approach therefore calls for a holistic analysis of ancient inscriptions as complex communication media that derived meaning from their social and physical contexts of use.

Another advantage is that this approach shifts our gaze and our assumptions when we inspect ancient texts. When we study ancient Levantine inscriptions as multimodal things, we inherently ask a different set of questions than when we approach these same texts only as vehicles for linguistic expression: How do inscriptions reflect the interface of writing as language and writing as visual culture? In what ways were the designs of texts related to their linguistic content? How did these different facets of texts impact a text's meaning? How can we study texts and their affordances more holistically to anticipate how ancient audiences of diverse literacies might have engaged with ancient inscriptions? And, what can we learn about the design, content, and different contexts of inscriptions to better understand their situated use in ancient communities?

This approach therefore has several important implications for how we can analyze the different properties of ancient texts:

1. The multimodality perspective asks us to pay close attention to how texts are designed and made, and how their form, composition, and layout communicate meaning and function to audiences. The design and materiality of a text and its setting impact a text's meaning and the expectations of its audience about what it "says" as well as what it does or what it is supposed to do.

2. This approach highlights the interconnections and interdependence of the diverse semiotic resources in a text (e.g., how a color may be used to highlight a key word or phrase or may have meaning in and of itself that informs the linguistic content [Puhalla 2014: 195–214, esp. 211–212; cf. Houston et al. 2009]). Moreover, texts are more than the sum of their parts, and the relationships between modes are in and of themselves vehicles for communication. For example, a text's visual and verbal communicative modes are interconnected systems, as a text's script and the writer's orthographic choices draw from ideas about the written materialization of language that intersect with a group's conventions of visual and material culture.

3. Another important takeaway is that the properties and meanings associated with particular modes in texts are in flux. The meaning of a text is interconnected to its material and visual properties, but texts are also informed by changes in the social and spatial settings in which they are used, displayed, or encountered, as well as by the varying literacies of their audiences. Such an understanding opens the study of inscriptions to a more fluid set of meanings, as ancient writings changed in their meaning and in their reception by ancient audiences.

4. Rather than privilege the ways in which literate (so-called) elites read inscriptions, this approach is inclusive of how ancient texts communicated to a broader range of ancient audiences in ways beyond linguistic communication. One person viewing a text might associate a certain linguistic, visual, or material property of a text with a particular social status, state, or social function; another person may not have been able to access any of these modes of meaning, much less all of them simultaneously. Indeed, the inscriptional record indicates that ancient writings were crafted by people with varying literacies. Not all writers were scribes or masters of the local script and written language; some writers created texts in the limited scope of their professions or used texts in limited ways. Comparably, the audiences of texts included readers (in the common sense of how we use this word today) and people who had more limited access to written language, yet who engaged with written media.

Alice Mandell

Analyzing Dedicatory Inscriptions Through the Framework of Multimodality

The multimodality perspective enriches our study of ancient literacy practices, particularly those involving inscriptions that are short, or formulaic, or that are less linguistically informative texts that offer a more limited range of grammatical data for analysis. In the study of the epigraphic evidence from the Iron Age southern Levant, much of the scholarly focus has been upon inscriptions from a royal provenance, which speak to the power of ancient rulers or elites to commission scribes and masons, and to the power of writing to communicate the reach and might of elites. For example, stone inscriptions such as the Mesha and Tel Dan stelae are particularly valued in the study of southern Levantine inscriptions because these are planned monumental texts that reference kings and perhaps even events alluded to in the biblical text. And yet, it is important to remember that most of the writings from the Iron Age southern Levant are not royal, or what might be called "monumental" in terms of their form, design, scale, size, or content (Smoak and Mandell 2019). Indeed, much of the inscriptional evidence that we have reflects literacy practices connected to the use of writing in diverse contexts, and to the production of short inscriptions: for example, the use of inscribed seals, writing on vessels as a means of labeling content or to mark aspects of exchange or administration, as well as the use of writing in ritual contexts to represent individuals or to mark ritual vessels.

Inscriptions that are written in the local linear, alphabetic scripts which are short and/or linguistically sparse texts, or which were created with less concern for their legibility, offer a productive and incredibly diverse data set for understanding ancient literacies. This grouping of communication media includes inscribed objects that moved through economic and social networks, such as short texts used in administration (such as seals, seal impressions, or labels), and those which were more static such as inscriptions incorporated into the walls or architectural features of built spaces in tombs. This diverse inscriptional material gives insight into literacy practices that were a part of the fabric of everyday life in local economies, administration, and rituals (Mandell and Smoak 2017, 2018; Mandell 2018).

The study of dedicatory inscriptions benefits from the approach outlined in this chapter. Such inscriptions often present, at face value, as a linguistically improvised text type, in the sense that they typically comprise formulaic language and often do not have the grammatically rich clauses found in other text types (e.g., letters or royal inscriptions that describe the exploits of kings). Despite their limited content, such inscriptions offer a window into the important role that writing played in religious life in ancient Israel and Judah. They convey important information about the literacy practices of people who were not necessarily scribes, priests, or royal elites, yet who valued the power of writing enough to dedicate their time and resources to develop inscriptions that would represent them before deities (Mandell 2018).

In order to demonstrate how the framework of multimodality can be applied to diverse inscribed dedications, I offer here an analysis of two "short" Hebrew inscriptions: an inscribed stone bowl from Kuntillet ʿAjrud; and, the two sets of inscribed precious stone inscriptions on Aaron's uniform that are described in Exodus 28 and 39. These inscriptions are dedicatory writings that served two main ritual functions: (1) they communicated that the inscribed object was dedicated by specific people to YHWH's cult, and (2) they signified that the inscribed objects represented the named individuals in YHWH's presence. Inscribed dedications in the southern Levant typically comprised of a personal name, identifying the person who commissioned the dedication, or the person who was meant to be represented in

Multimodality and the Study of Iron Age Inscriptions

the god's presence by the inscribed object or text. Dedicatory inscriptions frequently use the stock formula: *l*-PN, "for PN," which can be expanded by the inclusion of the patronymic formula *bn* PN (son or descendant + personal name). This base dedicatory formula can also be expanded with a reference to the deity being appealed to, and/or a reference to the very object itself that is inscribed and that was used as a ritual object to represent a worshiper. This formula can also include directives about what the inscription is supposed to do, for example, to enact a blessing on the person named in the inscription. The power of such inscribed objects seems to have been activated when the dedication was placed in a space connected to the cultic practice of a particular god (or gods) and then was most likely complemented by an oral invocation.

The Multimodality of an Inscribed Stone Bowl Dedication from Kuntillet 'Ajrud

The site of Kuntillet 'Ajrud operated as a fort from at least the late-9th–mid-8th centuries BCE, though, it may have been founded as early as the late 10th (Meshel 2012b: 3–10; Carmi and Segal 2012: 61–64; Schniedewind 2017: 134–145). Its geopolitical context, ceramics, inscriptional remains, and the royally themed wall murals connect its founding to the growing power and trade ambitions of the kingdoms of Israel and Judah in the Negev region (Ornan 2016). To this, we can add that the evolution of the entrance of Building A from a broad room into a bench room used for ritual practice speaks to the importance of this multivalent site that expressed the protective power of the gods and more distant kings (Mandell 2012, 2021).

Building A is of particular interest as diverse inscriptions were found on the walls and on vessels in several of the building's rooms. The inscriptions' language, orthography, and script, coupled with the ceramics, suggest that the northern Kingdom of Israel controlled the site. At the same time, storage jars from the area of Jerusalem were discovered at this site, suggesting that Kuntillet 'Ajrud was provisioned by the ruling family in Jerusalem; this might suggest that this southern site was jointly operated by the kings of Israel and Judah.

With this backdrop in mind, we can now turn to the multimodality of an inscribed stone basin discovered in Building A (Kuntillet 'Ajrud [KA] 1.2; Figure 23.1). This inscribed vessel was discovered in the easternmost entrance of the southern storeroom (Aḥituv, Eshel,

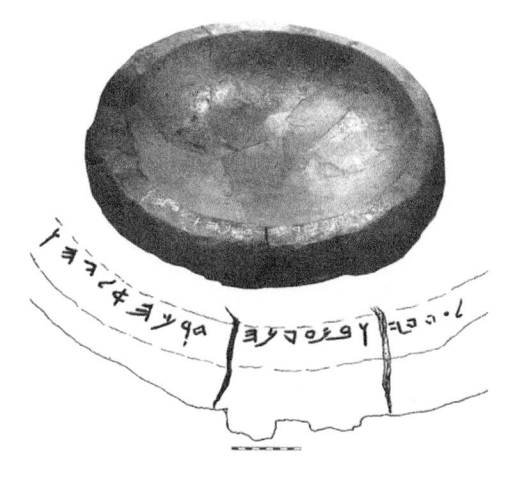

Figure 23.1 Photo of the stone basin from Kuntillet 'Ajrud, with a line drawing of its incised rim (courtesy of the Israel Exploration Society)

and Meshel 2012: 76–77). The excavators note that it was found in a pile of debris, which suggests that it was "thrown there from another part of the building" (Aḥituv, Eshel, and Meshel 2012: 76); they propose that this basin was originally on the second floor (Meshel and Goren 2012: 52).

The inscription was incised into the stone basin, which makes it difficult to establish if it was inscribed at the time that the basin was created.[2] Nevertheless, in the case of KA 1.2, its large size (nearly 1 meter in diameter) and heavy weight (150 kg) suggest that once this vessel was inscribed, it was stationary and prominent as a large, inscribed object.

The inscription on the rim of the basin reads:

לעבדיו בן עדנה ברכ הא ליהו

"(Stone Basin) Belonging to *Ōbadyāw*, son of *ʿAdnā*. May he be blessed by YHW."

This dedicatory formula includes the identification of the person that the basin represents, followed by their patronymic identification. It also includes a verb of blessing *brk* and a reference to the deity using a northern orthography: YHW. This deity is identified as the agent of blessing. Based on this formula and its context, this inscription can be understood as a ritual text that enacts a blessing on *Ōbadyāw*, son of *ʿAdnā* by invoking YHW. While the basin itself is not referred to directly in the inscription, the dedicatory formula implies that it is what is being dedicated by *Ōbadyāw* to his god. The inscription therefore connects this individual to the object, and the vessel becomes a representation of the owner before the deity.

While this inscription is "short"—comprised of merely the dedicatory formula—the object itself speaks through its form, material, weight, and its script and orthography in a way that complements the words of this inscription. The inscription's placement on the rim of the vessel communicates, through its very location and prominence, that this vessel served a special function: That of a dedicated vessel. Its location on the presumed most visible part of the vessel also suggests that the inscription's layout was designed to solicit blessings on *Ōbadyāw*'s behalf. We might add that the writing of the divine name was iconic of the cult of Israel's god and operated as a sign signifying that this was a ritual object. In this way, we might imagine that this word stood out and communicated that this object was a dedicated thing, even to those unable to read the other words of this inscription, but who could recognize the divine name YHW. The dedicatory formula in this inscription coupled with the use of the 3ms independent pronoun indicates that the verb of blessing *brk* is a G-stem passive participle: "blessed be he [*Ōbadyāw*] to YHW" (Aḥituv, Eshel, and Meshel 2012: 127). Yet, when we think about the way that writing represents not merely language but ideas, we might also consider the possibility that this verb was a visual sign serving a polyvalent purpose that may also have led any person engaging with this object to bless the person that it represented. In other words, the verb not only enacted YHW's blessing on this individual but also communicated to people who saw the inscription that they too should bless him.

The multimodality perspective also calls for consideration of the visual and iconic properties of the ways that language is materialized into a text. In this vessel's inscription, the orthography and style of the script were not neutral but were signifiers of northern identity. The divine name is written as YHW and not YHWH, which is the standard orthography in Judah; also, the theophoric element in the personal name, *Ōbadyāw*, is written as -*yw* rather than -*yhw* (Aḥituv, Eshel, and Meshel 2012: 76–77). This difference in orthographic practice is a diagnostic feature that differentiates writing practices in Israel and Judah; it operates both visually and linguistically to signal the writer or vessel owner's connection to the northern kingdom.

When we turn to the features of the script, certain letter forms on this stone vessel align with inscriptions dating to the late 10th–early 9th century BCE, whereas other forms are also attested in the late 9th–early 8th century BCE. Specifically, the *'aleph*, *heh*, and *kaph* find parallels in Phoenician inscriptions, and those dated to the 10th century (e.g., the Gezer Calendar; Aḥituv, Eshel, and Meshel 2012: 77). Another inscription (KA 1.1) found in the northeastern corner bench room is similarly inscribed with a personal name on the vessel's rim; this vessel also features graphemes that are paralleled in Phoenician inscriptions, and in the Gezer Calendar (Aḥituv, Eshel, and Meshel 2012: 75). The script style of the inscription has largely been studied as a reflection of its date, its stone medium, or the inexperience of the writer. For example, Schniedewind has argued that this inscription should be dated to the late 10th century and is evidence for an earlier phase of this site (2017: 136–137). Another, not mutually exclusive, possibility is that these graphemes were written in a less cursive style because of both the technical aspects of writing this inscription and its location on the rim of a stone vessel. The tools and stone medium, and perhaps, the writer's lack of skill, may have occasioned the less cursive letter forms (Aḥituv, Eshel, and Meshel 2012: 75).

Another possibility is that the ritual function of the inscription and its stone medium conditioned the form of the script and led to the script's less cursive letter forms. That is, the shape of the script was a feature of the inscription's design as a text that communicated the ritual function of the basin. According to this interpretation, the inscriber employed an older, and less cursive script style, perhaps even in emulation of the script used by Israel's Phoenician neighbors, because this was a high register script that imparted an accordingly high status to the object and to the person that it represented.[3] In this way, approaching inscriptions from the perspective of multimodality enriches the analysis of a simple inscription on a vessel, and offers insight into the ways that the design of the text was entangled with the ritual logic underlying the vessel's function.

The Multimodality of the Inscriptions on Aaron's Inscribed Uniform in Exodus 28 and 39

The multimodality perspective can also be implemented in the analysis of ekphrastic descriptions of texts and literacy practices. Indeed, some of the most important texts in the study of ancient Israelite religion are only accessible through engagement with the literary descriptions of these texts, their crafting, and their use. For example, the form, content, and also the broader literary context of the Decalogue in Exodus 20 channel the monumentality of royal inscriptions in the ancient Near East (Hogue 2019). In its unique literary frame, the Decalogue "co-opts" the associations of power around monumental royal stelae, and attributes this power to YHWH, who takes the assumed role of Israel's leader and king (Hogue 2019: 85).

This approach also offers insight into the descriptions of the crafting and design of dedicatory inscriptions that are set into the High Priest's uniform in the priestly source's account of the building of the Tabernacle in Exodus 28 and 39. These inscribed garments are detailed in YHWH's orders regarding their make and meaning in Exod 28; they are then crafted in Exod 39. While this inscribed uniform is only available through textual analysis, we can still use the details that the biblical writers provide us to analyze their properties as inscriptions, and also as texts that do ritual work in YHWH's presence.

The inscribed uniform communicates Aaron's status and the important role of the priesthood, both within the Tabernacle and implicitly in YHWH's temple. While wearing these inscribed garments, the High Priest is not merely a representative of the priesthood, Israel, or YHWH, but his inscribed body becomes a material part of the cultic activity in the Tabernacle (Mandell 2022a, 2022b). The material, design, and colors of Aaron's uniform (e.g., the types of woven fabric, and use of gold, blue, purple, and crimson threads) materially connect his body and his ritual work to the holiest areas of the Tabernacle (Haran 1978: 149–204; esp. 158–165, 212).

Exodus 28 and 39 also provide a wealth of detail regarding the design, crafting, and ritual significance of the three sets of inscriptions that are placed in Aaron's garments. The two inscribed stones on the shoulder piece and the 12 inscribed stones on the breast piece form two inscriptional displays that represent Israel on Aaron's uniform, on the upper half of his body. A third inscriptional display with the words קֹדֶשׁ לַיהוָה "dedicated to YHWH" adorns his headdress and marks Aaron himself as a ritually consecrated thing.

Together, these inscriptions communicate that Aaron is set apart from other priests for YHWH's cultic service in the Tabernacle. The multimodality perspective also draws attention to the way in which the visual display of Aaron's clothing is complemented by the sound of the bells on his robe (Exod 28: 33–35; 39:25–26). The understanding in this narrative is that the bells make music as he moves in the Tabernacle space (Houtman 1990). He therefore stands out from the other ritual vessels and implements as he enacts his ritual work in the Tabernacle (Mandell 2022a, 2022b).

Multimodality highlights the importance of the designs of the unique individual properties of each inscription and their meaning as a unified inscriptional display on Aaron's clothing. The script design (that of a seal inscription) and the layout of these texts on particular locations on Aaron's body when he wears his uniform (his head, shoulders, and chest) also emerge as significant modes of these inscriptions. The visual and spatial aspects of the inscriptions contribute to the argument that is crafted in this story that Aaron (and any high priests after him) are authorized to do two forms of representational work in YHWH's shrine: to represent Israel and to fulfill the role of ritual vessels dedicated to YHWH's service.

Significance can be ascribed to the differences between the stone and golden ornament inscriptions, and it can be suggested that they were salient and meaningful to the writers and the ancient audiences of this narrative. Despite the similar function of the inscribed stones, there are key differences in the design of the shoulder and chest piece stone dedications that are not explained in the narrative. The first set of inscriptions comprises two inscribed precious stones of the same type, which are each inscribed with six of the names of Israel's sons according to their birth order; the two stones are then set into the ephod, specifically on Aaron's two shoulders (Exod 28:6–12; 39:6–7). The second set of inscribed dedications also represents Israel before YHWH yet is comprised of 12 different precious stones that are each individually inscribed with a tribal name. The 12 stones are arranged in four rows (three stones in each row) and are incorporated into Aaron's chest piece (Exod 28: 15–30; 39:10–14).

Much attention is paid in this narrative to the stone types, their location on Aaron's uniform, and to their script, whereas we do not know much about the placement of the names on the stones, or the reasons for the pairing of particular names and stone types.[4] Yet, we can imagine that these associations were known and infused the inscriptions with meaning that went beyond their mere words. For example, a close reading of the text highlights the potential for difference in the names inscribed into the two sets of stone dedicatory inscriptions in Aaron's uniform: the two shoulder piece stones are to be inscribed with the names of Israel's sons (that is, Jacob's sons) according to their birth order in Exod 28:9–10 and 39: 6–7; however, in the instructions in Exod 28: 21 and 39:14, the second set of precious stones are to be inscribed with the names of Israel's 12 tribes, which might indicate a different set of names (MacDonald forthcoming).[5] This set of inscriptions also differs from the shoulder stones due to its placement on the chest piece, which interconnects the stones to the power and meaning of the Urim and the Thummim (Guillaume 2013; van Dam 1997: 215–55). This might then suggest a difference in the representational power of the two sets of stones, which is articulated in these details of their crafting and design, but not in YHWH's instructions to Moses.

We can now turn to the details in this narrative regarding Aaron's headdress inscription, which is described as an inscribed golden flower (Exod 28:36–38; 39:30). Again, the details of this text mark it apart from the other two sets of inscriptions: it is metal, it is shaped like a flower (most likely a rosette), and it is located on Aaron's headdress. Moreover, this golden ornament is inscribed with a different type of dedicatory text that marks an object as something dedicated to the cult of a particular god that is to be used for service. The words of this inscription reference YHWH and indicate that Aaron and any future wearer of the inscription are "dedicated" to this god's service.

When these inscriptions are analyzed as multimodal objects, it becomes clear that they communicate their ritual power not merely through their words, but also through their costly and colorful materials, their design, the details regarding their script (in the manner of seal inscriptions), and their placement on the High Priest's uniform; to this, we can add that these inscriptions also derive meaning as texts made to move with Aaron when he wears this uniform in his ongoing cultic work in the Tabernacle. The focus on these particular facets of their design imparts significance to these inscriptions in this story that extends their authority beyond the meaning that YHWH ascribes them.

This analysis also highlights how the design of the three sets of inscriptions works together with their words to enable Israel to be appropriately represented in the Tabernacle. The richness of the visual experience of Aaron's dress, which is expressed through the reference to diverse stone types from different reaches of the ancient world, articulates the High Priest's power and vast resources (Zwickel 2002). The juxtaposition of the precious materials used to create Aaron's uniform interconnects his office and authority with access to trade and to the procurement of these fabulous materials and the dress designs of ancient Near Eastern elites (Nihan and Rhyder 2018; Imes 2019).

The repeated reference to the "seal" like script of the three sets of inscriptions in Exod 28 and 39 unifies the inscriptions as having a shared visual design, despite the differences in their media. The attention to their script style also connects the three sets of inscriptions to a host of inscriptional and ritual practices involving seals. The high degree of skill needed to produce seals is referenced through the elite status and cross-specialization of the craft specialists making these three sets of inscriptions. In Exod 28:22–23, Bezalel and Oholiab are entrusted with making the vestments and the inscriptions (see also Exod 39:6, 14, and 30).

Comparative analyses of Israel's dedications have highlighted how the inscribed stones are best paralleled by precious stone seals, which could also be used as votives (Propp 2006; Tigay 2007; Frevel 2008; Nihan and Rhyder 2018). The golden blossom of the headdress ornament is most likely a stylized rosette, a well-known emblem of elite dress in the ancient Near East (Oppenheim 1949; Cahill 1997; Imes 2019). And yet, the very form of this inscription and its script also interconnect this inscription to sealing practices and to royal authority. In late monarchal Judah, the rosette was also used in royal seals (Cahill 1995; Koch and Lipschits 2013). Together, the seal-script and rosette design of this inscription work together as a visual means of connecting Aaron to the ritual and administrative power of seals.

It is also implied in this narrative, in the crafting of the stones in a hard medium, that these objects were made to be permanent representatives of the tribes; furthermore, their placement on Aaron's clothing in a restricted-access space (under YHWH's watchful gaze) communicates that these seals are forever protected from change or re-carving. Were these seal-script inscriptions executed on lesser materials, such as less costly stones, bone, or clay by lesser craftspeople, their message of power would have been quite different. The description of the creation of the stone dedications communicates their role as eternal ambassadors for Israel in YHWH's presence.

The materials used to make these inscriptions—precious stones and gold—also speak to the importance of these inscriptions as an eternal part of the apparatus of the Tabernacle and of the High Priest's ritual regalia. Nihan and Rhyder (2018: 56, 62) have also proposed that the inclusion of these precious stones in Aaron's uniform connects his dress to that of the clothing of deity statues, which speaks to the ascending role of the High Priest, not as a god, but as "a superhuman agent" that is interconnected to the divine in a way unlike other Israelites.

Here we can turn to the broader literary context of these inscriptions in the Priestly Source's description of the Tabernacle to evaluate their unique purpose and design.[6] The multimodality perspective highlights the importance of the shifting site of display of these inscriptions. We therefore have a text—the narrative framework of the Tabernacle building story in Exodus—that creates three texts—two inscribed stone displays and an inscribed golden inscription—drawing on inscriptional practices outside of this story. This text then sets them into the moving body of Israel's High Priest where they represent Israel in perpetuity.

In this narrative, it is significant that Israel's dedications are not just placed in the Tabernacle, but are texts designed to move with Aaron. As Gudme writes, the Tabernacle narrative describes "a traveling deity that can be worshiped in every place, because his dwelling place and cult are preserved in the text" (2014: 14). The inscriptions, as described in Exod 28 and 39 are inherently mobile, as they are a part of Aaron's uniform, and move with him; and yet, they are a permanent part of his uniform and are bound to the Tabernacle as they are an eternal part of its cultic apparatus.

The layout of these three sets of inscriptions on Aaron's uniform also emerges as a significant part of their design. They are placed on Aaron's body when he wears his uniform, rather than into stationary objects or into actual signet rings or seals worn as inscribed jewelry. Their incorporation into the High Priest's uniform differentiates these inscriptions from any other ritual texts, as they are only able to be worn by the person who holds this sacred office in YHWH's shrine. Moreover, the layout of the texts is also important to the ritual logic of these dedications: it mimics the placement of inscriptions on the rims and upper extremities of ritual vessels in the southern Levant, which suggests that through these inscriptions, Aaron becomes, in a sense, a dedicated vessel in YHWH's shrine (Mandell 2022a, 2022b).

By tethering these dedicatory texts onto the High Priest's body, they become subject to his daily agenda. They move with Aaron and thereby participate in his ritual activities in the Tabernacle. In this way, these inscriptions and the inscriptional practices that they represent become bound to priestly time and to the sacred calendar of Israel's High Priest. This transformation in ritual practice is also reflected in YHWH's instructions that these garments are meant to be timeless like the Tabernacle itself; they are to be passed down to Aaron's descendants. Instead of individual dedications that represent specific individuals, the inscribed names on the stone inscriptions are designed to represent Israel's past, contemporary, and future generations.

These inscriptions serve to further the power of the High Priest that is expressed in the broader narrative arc of the Priestly Source, authorizing him and his descendants as the solely authorized mediators between Israel and their god, in part through the power of ritual texts.

This narrative seems to speak to a post-monarchal context, where the high priesthood stakes a claim on a new domain of power. As Nihan and Rhyder write, Aaron's inscribed clothing:

> blends elements of royalty with a new type of hegemonic power, which is defined entirely in and through the sanctuary. In other words, the high priest does not merely substitute the king but, rather, embodies a distinct post-monarchic *temple* paradigm, in which a king is no longer needed.
>
> *(2018: 62)*

When we turn to the world that lies behind this story and study this inscribed uniform as a signifier for the authority of Israel's High Priest, we can see that Aaron's clothing is a multimodal and multivalent statement about the High Priest's prominence and power. The intricate and costly uniform speaks to the economic and political power of the high priesthood, through the costly materials and other royal aspects of the uniform's design. All of these facets of Aaron's uniform in this narrative communicate the unique role of the high priesthood, perhaps speaking to a time when Israel's kings or other forms of leadership were less relevant in the Second Temple Period (Frevel 2012; Nihan and Rhyder 2018).

The design of these inscriptions communicates Aaron's preeminent role in YHWH's cult as a figure who is the only person that can serve YHWH and represent Israel before their god in his cultic center. The site of display of Israel's dedications, Aaron's moving body, is not only critical to the ritual logic of the priestly vision of the Tabernacle but also to the role of the High Priest that is articulated in this narrative.[7] The stones are the unique inscriptions made to be a permanent part of the Tabernacle apparatus, and they are bound to the High Priest's clothing. They therefore occupy prime real estate as the only dedications that enable people outside of the Tabernacle to access YHWH's presence inside of a highly restricted space, which was accessed only by Israel's priests. Israel is dependent upon the inscriptions that Aaron wears for their representation before YHWH; they are then also dependent upon Aaron and Israel's future high priests, who are the only people authorized to wear these texts in the Tabernacle.

We can summarize what these inscriptions "do" in this narrative as multimodal texts that become tied to Aaron's regalia and to his power. Exodus 28 and 39, which describe Aaron's inscribed uniform, recontextualize established inscriptional practices into a priestly framework to connect their efficacy to the authority of the High Priest. These inscriptions legitimize Aaron as a textual intermediary between Israel and YHWH; his body thus takes over the role of inscribed dedications and vessels in ritual spaces. In this way, the Tabernacle story connects the High Priest to the authority of diverse ritual texts and the pivotal role that they played in ritual spaces outside the literary frame of this story. In this new framework (the literary space of the Tabernacle), the movement of the High Priest's body ritualizes these inscriptions as priestly writings when he moves and does his cultic work. In this way, this narrative construes an ideal of sacred text that is mobile yet bound to the corporate body of the priesthood. The high priesthood, under Aaron's line, is framed as the bearer and guardian of ritual and textual authority, perhaps speaking to the evolving power of the priesthood in the Second Temple Period.

Conclusion: Multimodality and the Study of Ancient Northwest Semitic Inscriptions

The multimodality perspective, as applied to the study of ancient inscriptions, is an approach that highlights the importance of analyzing inscriptions more holistically: this includes a text's language variety and orthography, but also its non-linguistic modes, such as the text's visual and spatial properties (e.g., the script, layout and scale, spatial orientation, and other design features), and importantly, its socially situated context when it engages an audience.

The deeper consideration of the multimodality of texts grounds the study of inscriptions in the broader literacy practices of these ancient communities. Most importantly, it places value on the ways that these texts would have been "read" by diverse audiences, with different levels of access to their linguistic content. This approach allows us to appreciate the inherent fluidity of meaning that was created by the interactions of ancient texts and diverse ancient people through their content, their design, and their contexts. An additional advantage is that this approach is applicable to ancient texts that are described in other texts, and which otherwise offer us a more limited range of analysis.

Notes

1 For example, cursing in speech is represented in different ways in written media, including using symbols (known as grawlixes or obscenions). In audiovisual media, spoken curses in a film or TV show, for example, can be transcribed directly, or represented by alternative spellings or even words that are considered more mild (*f-ing* or *effing*); or they can be subtitled using grawlixes or emoticons (a string of "typographical marks" that stand as a representation of a range of curse words, such as @#*?$*!); or they can been expressed by "bleeping," a standardized noise that stands in for a curse or language that is censored. See Cintas 2012.
2 This is unlike inscriptions on ceramic vessels, which offer a clearer timeline for the moment of writing (before/after the vessel was fired), and subsequently can suggest a close relationship between the vessel maker and the writer, or even that they were the same person.
3 This perspective might also explain the use of this "northern" style in certain letter forms on this vessel, but also the use of the Phoenician, or rather, northern style script in the ink display inscriptions on the walls of the site (e.g., in KA 4.1, 4.2, and 4.3), which were inscribed in black ink in a Levantine-style script that is associated with Phoenician writing, but are Hebrew and written according to Judean orthographic practices (Aḥituv, Eshel, and Meshel 2012: 105–22; 126–27). It is likely that this northern script operated iconically as a part of the design of the wall decorations, to visually connect this wilderness site to the northern ruler that it represented. We might also consider the use of this high register script, used by diverse elites in the Levant and in Anatolia, to communicate the ruler's power and membership among an international network of elites (Mandell 2021: 274).
4 For a summary of later traditions about the meaning and placement of the stones, see Houtman 2000: 487, 497–98, 502–03.
5 For example, the chest piece stones which are written with tribal names would include not Joseph, but Joseph's sons, who are the fathers of the tribes of Ephraim and Manasseh.
6 We might also ask, why are there no inscribed ritual vessels in the description of the construction of YHWH's temple in Jerusalem in 1 Kings 6-8. We would expect any inscriptions to be in later cultic buildings (following the chronology presented in the world of the text, where the Tabernacle is essentially a proto-temple). And yet, there are *no* ritual writings in the Temple building narrative in 1 Kings 6-8 and *three* inscriptions created in the Tabernacle story (!).
7 For an assessment of the different traditions about the High Priest's clothing, see MacDonald 2019.

Bibliography

Aḥituv, Shmuel, Esther Eshel, and Ze'ev Meshel. 2012. "The Inscriptions." Pages 73–142 in Meshel 2012a.

Barton, David, and Mary Hamilton. 2000. "Literacy Practices." Pages 7–14 in *Situated Literacies: Reading and Writing in Context*. Edited by David Barton, Mary Hamilton, and Roz Ivanič. London: Routledge.

Barton, David, Mary Hamilton, and Roz Ivanič, eds. 2000. *Situated Literacies: Reading and Writing in Context*. London: Routledge.

Bezemer, Jeff, and Gunther Kress. 2008. "Writing in Multimodal Texts: A Social Semiotic Account of Designs for Learning." *Written Communication* 25: 166–95.

Cahill, Jane M. 1995. "Rosette Stamp Seal Impressions from Ancient Judah." *IEJ* 45: 230–52.

———. 1997. "Royal Rosettes Fit for a King," *BAR* 23: 48–57, 68–69.

Carmi, Israel, and Dror Segal. 2012. "¹⁴C Dates from Kuntillet 'Ajrud." Pages 61–64 in Meshel 2012a.

Cintas, Jorge Díaz. 2012. "Clearing the Smoke to See the Screen: Ideological Manipulation in Audiovisual Translation," *Meta* 57: 279–293.

Frevel, Christian. 2008. "Gifts to the Gods? Votives as Communication Markers in Sanctuaries and other Places in the Bronze and Iron Ages in Palestine/Israel." Pages 25–48 in *"From Ebla to Stellenbosch" Syro-Palestinian Religions and the Hebrew Bible*. Edited by Izak Cornelius and Louise Jonker. Wiesbaden: Harrassowitz.

———. 2012. "On Instant Scripture and Proximal Texts: Some Insights into the Sensual Materiality of Texts and their Ritual Roles in the Hebrew Bible and Beyond." *Postscripts* 8: 57–79.

Gee, James Paul. 2015. *Social Linguistics and Literacies: Ideology in Discourses*. 5th ed. London: Routledge.

Gudme, Anne K. de Hemmer. 2014. "Dyed Yarns and Dolphin Skins: Temple Texts as Cultural Memory in the Hebrew Bible." *Jewish Studies* 50: 1–14.

Guillaume, Phillipe. 2013. "Aaron and the Amazing Mantic Coat." Pages 101–17 in *Studies on Magic and Divination in the Biblical World*. Edited by Helen R. Jacobus, Anne K. de Hemmer Gudme and Phillipe Guillaume. Piscataway: Gorgias.

Haran, Menahem. 1978. *Temples and Temple-Service in Ancient Israel*. Oxford: Clarendon Press.

Hogue, Timothy. 2019. "The Monumentality of the Sinaitic Decalogue: Reading Exodus 20 in Light of Northwest Semitic Monument-Making Practices." *JBL* 138: 79–99.

Houston, Stephen C., Brittenham, Claudia, Mesick, Cassandra, Tokovinine, Alexandre, and Warinner, Christina 2009. *Veiled Brightness: A History of Ancient Maya Color*. Austin: University of Texas Press.

Houtman, Cornelis. 1990. "On the Pomegranates and the Golden Bells of the High Priest's Mantle." *VT* 40: 223–29.

———. 2000. *Exodus*. Kampen: Kok Pharos.

Imes, Carmen Joy. 2019. "Between Two Worlds: The Functional and Symbolic Significance of the High Priestly Regalia." Pages 29–62 in *Dress and Clothing in the Hebrew Bible: "For All Her Household are Clothed in Crimson."* Edited by Antonios Finitsis. T&T Clark: New York.

Jewitt, Carey. 2017. "Introduction. Handbook Rationale, Scope and Structure." Pages 1–8 in *The Routledge Handbook of Multimodal Analysis*. 2nd ed. Edited by Carey Jewitt. London: Routledge.

Jones, Rodney H. 2017. "Technology and Sites of Display." Pages 139–51 in *The Routledge Handbook of Multimodal Analysis*. Edited by C. Jewitt. 2nd edition. London: Routledge.

Koch, Ido, and Oded Lipschits. 2013. "The Rosette Stamped Jar Handle System and the Kingdom of Judah at the End of the First Temple Period." *ZDPV* 129: 55–78.

Kress, Gunther, and Theo van Leeuwen. 2021. *Reading Images: The Grammar of Visual Design*. 3rd ed. London: Routledge.

MacDonald, Nathan. 2019. "The Priestly Vestments." Pages 435–48. In *Clothing and Nudity in the Hebrew Bible*. Edited by Christoph Berner, et al. London: Bloomsbury.

———. forthcoming. *The Making of the Tabernacle and the Construction of Priestly Hegemony*. Oxford University Press.

Mandell, Alice. 2012. "'I Bless You to YHWH and His Asherah'— Writing and Performativity at Kuntillet 'Ajrud." *MAARAV* 19: 131–62.

———. 2018. "Reading and Writing Remembrance in Canaan: Early Alphabetic Inscriptions as Multimodal Objects." *HBAI* 17: 95–126.

———. 2021. "'Top-Down' and 'Bottom-up' Monumentality at Kuntillet 'Ajrud: The Evolution of the Benchroom at Kuntillet 'Ajrud as a Ritual Space." *HBAI* 10: 257–82.

———. 2022a. "Aaron's Body as a Ritual Vessel in the Exodus Tabernacle Building Narrative." Pages 159–81 in *New Perspectives on Ritual in the Biblical World*. Edited by Laura Quick and Melissa Ramos. London: Bloomsbury T&T Clark.

———. 2022b. "Writing as a Source of Ritual Authority: The High Priest's Body as a Priestly Text in the Tabernacle Building Story." *JBL* 141: 43–64.

Mandell, Alice, and Jeremy D. Smoak. 2017. "Reading and Writing in the Dark at Khirbet el-Qom: The Literacies of Ancient Subterranean Judah." *NEA* 80: 188–95.

———. 2018. "Reading Beyond Literacy, Writing Beyond Epigraphy: Multimodality and the Monumental Inscriptions at Ekron and Tel Dan." *MAARAV* 22: 79–112.

Meshel, Ze'ev. 2012a. *Kuntillet 'Ajrud (Horvat Teman). An Iron Age II Religious Site on the Judah-Sinai Border.* Jerusalem: Israel Exploration Society.

———. 2012b. "The Site: Location, Environment, and Exploration." Pages 3–10 in Meshel 2012a.

Meshel, Ze'ev, and Avner Goren. 2012. "Architecture, Plan and Phases." Pages 11–60 in Meshel 2012a.

Nihan, Christophe, and Julia Ryder. 2018. "Aaron's Vestments in Exodus 28 and Priestly Leadership." Pages 45–67 in *Debating Authority: Concepts of Leadership in the Pentateuch and the Former Prophets.* Edited by Katharina Pyschny and Sarah Schulz. Berlin: De Gruyter.

Oppenheim, A. Leo. 1949. "Golden Garments of the Gods." *JNES* 8: 172–93.

Ornan, Tally. 2016. "Sketches and Final Works of Art: The Drawings and Wall Paintings of Kuntillet 'Ajrud Revisited." *TA* 43: 3–26.

Piquette, Kathryn E., and Ruth D. Whitehouse, eds. 2013. *Writing as Material Practice: Substance, Surface and Medium.* London: Ubiquity.

Propp, William H. 2006. *Exodus 19–40: A New Translation with Introduction and Commentary.* New York: Doubleday.

Puhalla, D. 2014. "Colour Language Hierarchy." Pages 195–214 in *Visual Communication.* Edited by David Machin. Berlin/Boston: de Gruyter.

Richey, Madadh. 2021. "The Media and Materiality of Southern Levantine Inscriptions: Production and Reception Contexts." Pages 29–39 in *Scribes and Scribalism.* Edited by Mark Leuchter. London: T&T Clark.

Rollston, Christopher A. 2010. *Writing and Literacy in the World of Ancient Israel: Epigraphic Evidence from the Iron Age.* Atlanta: SBL.

Sanders, Seth L. 2009. *The Invention of Hebrew.* Chicago: University of Illinois.

Schniedewind, William M. 2013. *A Social History of Hebrew: Its Origins Through the Rabbinic Period.* New Haven: Yale University.

———. 2017. "An Early Iron Age Phase to Kuntillet 'Ajrud?" Pages 137–46 in *Le-ma'an Ziony: Essays in Honor of Ziony Zevit.* Edited by Frederick E. Greenspahn and Gary A. Rendsburg. Eugene: Cascade Books.

———. 2019. *The Finger of the Scribe: How Scribes Learned to Write the Bible.* Oxford: Oxford University.

Scribner, Sylvia, and Michael Cole. 1981. *The Psychology of Literacy.* Cambridge: Harvard University Press.

Smoak, Jeremy D., and Alice Mandell. 2019. "Texts in the City: Monumental Inscriptions in Jerusalem's Urban Landscape." Pages 309–42 in *Size Matters: Understanding Monumentality Across Ancient Civilizations.* Edited by Federico Buccellati, et al. Berlin: Transcript.

Street, Brian V. 1984. *Literacy in Theory and Practice.* Cambridge: Cambridge University Press.

———. 1993. *Cross-Cultural Approaches to Literacy.* Cambridge: Cambridge University Press.

Tigay, Jeffrey. 2007. "The Priestly Reminder Stones and Ancient Near Eastern Votive Practices." Pages 339–55 in *Shai le-Sara Japhet: Studies in the Bible, Its Exegesis and Its Language.* Edited by Moshe Bar-Asher, et al. Jerusalem: Bialik.

Trimbur, John, and Karen Press. 2015. "When was Multimodality? Modality and the Rhetoric of Transparency." Pages 17–42 in *Multimodality in Writing.* Edited by Arlene Archer and Esther Breuer. Leiden: Brill.

van Dam, Cornelis. 1997. *The Urim and Thummim: A Means of Revelation in Ancient Israel.* Winona Lake: Eisenbrauns.

Zwickel, Wolfgang. 2002. "Die Edelsteine im Brustschild des Hohenpriesters und Beim Himmlischen Jerusalem." Pages 50–70 in *Edelsteine in der Bibel.* Edited by Wolfgang Zwickel. Mainz am Rhein: Verlag Philipp von Zabern.

24
SOCIO-POLITICAL GLEANINGS FROM NORTHWEST SEMITIC PALEOGRAPHY

The Inscriptions from Tel Reḥov, as a Test Case

Nathaniel E. Greene

Introduction

The emergence of writing in the southern Levant has occasioned considerable discussion.[1] Indeed, the dawn of the Iron Age in the wake of the Late Bronze Age collapse created social and political voids that needed to be filled with new offices and newly reimagined[2] or emergent modes of social structuration to manage and control people, resources, and technologies alike. As the Levantine economy adjusted to what appears to our eyes as the outright dissolution of major Bronze Age powers (Cline 2014; Kuhrt 1995: 385; Sergi 2019), new forms of communication and control emerged that would eventually contribute to the birth of the kingdoms of Israel and Judah alongside the textual traditions that emplotted their respective identities. Inseparable from this process was the development of a literate class of scribes—without a doubt, social elites—who received and developed the primary technology[3] of alphabetic writing.

It is no secret, however, that the epigraphic evidence from the Iron Age that would attest to these processes is scant, consisting primarily of short and often enigmatic texts that range in "genre" from economic inscriptions like receipts or inventories to name tags and prestige items. As Malena (2021: 13, 19) has recently suggested,

> Our limited corpus makes clear that the creation of inscriptions during this period was in fact a rarity. At the same time, there is sufficient evidence of the demand for a scribe's service, at least in certain circles. According to the current body of evidence, a significant aspect of the scribe's work was documenting personal names.

Malena (2021: 19) goes on to suggest that "the use of scribes in the late eleventh and tenth centuries coincided with uncommon wealth and status and that writing was used to demonstrate ownership or patronage of some kind." Limitations of the extant data have often been overstated, however.[4] Malena is correct in observing that there was a demand for writing; however, her pointed focus on the textual content of the corpus in view comes at the expense of broader, contextual considerations and specific paleographic data in particular. To that end, her work is illustrative of many studies (several are cited above) that point to these

DOI: 10.4324/9780367815691-28

apparent limitations as being illustrative of the full extent of the scribal office. While it is certainly important to hold the extant data in view, such approaches have had the concomitant effect of inhibiting scholars from being able to capture the full value that data has to offer us.

By asking questions about the state of writing in a more comprehensive manner—inquiring specifically about the development of script traditions during the late 10th and early 9th centuries BCE, how those traditions are evidenced in accessible media, and what media-related data can tell us about scribal activity—we can cast off such fetters that have precluded more robust proposals about scribal potential and productivity earlier in Israel's existence than those with which many have previously been comfortable. Furthermore, movement in ancillary fields over the past 20 years—especially anthropological work in archaic state formation—should compel us to approach the epigraphic data with fresh eyes to reconsider both (a) the social roles and spaces occupied by literate individuals and (b) what their work can tell us about ancient societies that were no doubt more complex and layered than we often give them credit. In this light, it is vital to give consideration to the fact that the extant corpus of Old Hebrew inscriptions is not only the product of individual application of artisanal skill but also of larger and more complex socio-political processes that necessitated their execution.

Thus, the present article will attempt to broach questions of method and implication by way of a targeted study on a smaller cross-section of inscriptions that have been found over the course of the past 25 years at Tel Reḥov. Even though these inscriptions are brief and enigmatic, they are illustrative of how we can theorize West Semitic script development adjacent to larger, regional and socio-civic organization. Careful consideration of not only specific, observable paleographic features but also of media and scribal method should allow us to draw more confident conclusions about how and where early Hebrew scribes employed their craft. Additional consideration of difficulties presented by the particularities of writing media should also enhance our understanding of scribal praxis in the 10th and 9th centuries BCE.

After considering archaeological and paleographic contexts, I will propose that the discernible cursive features in the inscriptions from Tel Reḥov have heretofore been underappreciated and are directly indicative of an Israelite scribal apparatus capable of much more than name tags or object markers. Instead, these scribes, who participated in complex social networks that included a range of people and who worked with a greater breadth of media than merely pottery, employed their craft frequently and in a sophisticated enough manner so as to contribute substantially to the development of what would eventually come to be the Old Hebrew "national script."[5] That is, the cursive features in the Reḥov inscriptions show us, in no uncertain terms, that these inscriptions were the product of a larger culture of writing with enough social and political support to occasion the refinement of the alphabetic technology in use at the time. The argument below will progress first by providing a brief overview of basic parameters for understanding early alphabetic writing and paleographic method. Next, I will place the inscriptions within their archaeological context. Then, I will turn to a brief assessment of each inscription from the site, noting salient paleographic features while drawing particular attention to various interpretive cruxes. Finally, I will synthesize the foregoing data into a proposal about scribal capability, social location, and education during the Iron II—especially the Iron IIA.[6]

Preliminary Considerations

By way of a brief overview, the following statements may be made concerning scribes and scribal praxis in Iron Age Israel. These statements are not novel and have been noted in numerous places (Cross 2003a, 2003b, 2003c; Naveh 1987; Parker 2018; Rollston 2006, 2010 to name just a few), but bear repeating here to contextualize properly both southern Levantine scribes and the discussion to follow.

- Literacy rates throughout the Iron Age were generally rather low. (See especially, Rollston 2010: 134). Less convincing are arguments to the contrary such as those of Hess (2006: 342–46) due simply to the complex and lengthy nature of scribal education during the Iron Age[7].
- Literate individuals would have almost exclusively been social elites or tied to officialdom in some capacity (Byrne 2007: 23; Rollston 2010: 134; Malena 2021: 19).
- Until such a time as scribal training became both more formalized and widespread (thus leading to a greater amount of standardization), writing was employed in *sinistrograde*, *dextrograde*, *boustrophedon*, or in *columnar* fashions. Within West Semitic contexts specifically, *sinistrograde* writing eventually became the dominant direction of writing. It is generally accepted that it was not until Phoenician standardization that writing direction and grapheme stance became settled and more universally consistent (Cross 2003b 322–23; Rollston 2010: 19; Parker 2018: 3–4). Grapheme stance would, however, continue to evolve in some cases (e.g., the clockwise rotation of *bet* in the Old Hebrew script).
- Writing could be executed through several different writing tools—styli, perhaps of reed or even metal, brushes, chisels, etc. (Richey 2021).
- Writing could be applied to a variety of surfaces (stone, pottery, papyrus, plaster, vellum, walls as within tombs or caves) and either incised or brushed on with ink. In some cases, such as Palmyra in later antiquity, incised letters could be filled in or highlighted with paint (especially red; Richey 2021: 37).
- The context in which writing appeared (i.e., within tombs, on prestige objects, on pottery or papyrus, etc.) necessarily conditions how we should understand and interpret the inscriptions that are available to us. On this point, Mandell and Smoak (2019: 11) have helpfully noted that "by paying more attention to the social and physical spaces of these things and practices, we can better understand the multiple ways in which 'historically distinctive disciplines and forces' informed them."
- In northwest Semitic contexts, typological features of the more rapidly written cursive forms of scripts influenced the more conservative lapidary forms; however, this process was slow (Rollston 2008: 76–77; *contra* Sass 2005: 49).

More recently, studies in northwest Semitic epigraphy have begun focusing less on the linguistic aspects of inscriptions and more on the materiality of epigraphic realia. As Richey (2021: 39) has recently noted, "the privileging of epigraphic linguistic content tends to produce conclusions that might have been made from any textual source." This is not to say that the linguistic elements of a given epigraph are of lesser importance at this juncture in scholarly conversations—something Richey is keenly aware of; but, rather, that linguistic data and grapheme morphology have been too heavily foregrounded and that a more comprehensive approach to southern Levantine epigraphy requires due consideration of the material context in which we find ancient, un-curated textual artifacts. While there are certainly linguistic elements worth consideration within the Reḥov corpus, they also present a fertile ground for applying the work of Mandell and Smoak (2019) as well as Richey (2021).

Reḥov in Context

The site appears to have been built originally during the LB I (ca. 15th century BCE: Mazar 2020: 75). Significantly, its founding may have occurred amid a larger, regional decline in city building. While this is at a substantial chronological distance from the period under consideration here (i.e., the early Iron II), the likely Egyptian influence on the site during the LB bears consideration. Egyptian regional control in this period is discernible at sites neighboring Reḥov such as Pella and Tell Abu-al Kharaz (to say nothing of the Egyptian garrison at Beth-Shean). According to the excavators, Reḥov was "most probably the center of a Canaanite city-state, administered by a local ruler who perhaps controlled a large part of the Beth-Shean Valley and some adjacent territory… while being under the supreme control of the Egyptian governor at Beth-Shean" (Mazar 2020: 75). At present, no destruction layers have been uncovered that interrupt the occupation of the site between the LB and Iron II (Mazar 2020: 79, 85–86). Over the course of the life of Tel Reḥov, the site was connected to various trade routes. Most prominently, these routes were oriented east-west and connected Reḥov to coastland sites like Akko and Dor on the eastern Mediterranean coast. North-south trade routes were also in play, supported by the discovery of Anatolian bee species in the apiary (Mazar 2020: 101–03).

Importantly, Egyptian administration and influence over the southern Levant left their mark in the material culture record even after its withdrawal from the region. Egyptian remains include, but are not limited to, scarabs, amulets, fish remains, and at least four seals that date to the Iron IB and more to the Iron II (Mazar 2020: 82, 105). These finds point to a sustained economic relationship which must have included "thriving trade" (Mazar 2020: 105). Such a relationship no doubt brought with it the use of papyrus, although this must remain circumstantial at this juncture.

Though various aspects of socio-political structuration in the region collapsed at the end of the LB, material culture production persisted, as evidenced by such things as the genetic relationships between LB and early Iron Age pottery forms as well as (and importantly for this essay) Proto-Canaanite, Canaanite, and Phoenician script morphologies. Suffice it to say for now that due to its location, size, and the circumstances surrounding its founding and occupation history, the stage was set for scribal activity during the Iron II beyond what we might hope the current finds and assemblages might show us more directly.

The Inscriptions from Tel Reḥov[8]

Eleven inscriptions were recovered in Iron Age levels at Tel Reḥov (Ahituv and Mazar 2014: 40; Lemaire 2007: 280).[9] These inscriptions appeared in Str. VI–IV and date to the 10th–9th c. BCE.[10] They consist primarily of nametags with a handful of sherds bearing only single graphemes. Despite the small and fragmentary nature of the Reḥov corpus, some rather substantial paleographic comments may be made about how the scribes responsible for these inscriptions operated. Such paleographic commentary, furthermore, may be extrapolated to allow for larger claims about more granular scribal activity—i.e., its frequency, modality, media, and to a limited extent, accessibility.

Reḥov 1

While a reading of 'ayin for the o-shaped grapheme makes good sense, the second grapheme is less legible (Figure 24.1). It may initially appear that *yod* is a possibility (Parker 2018: 132); however, as Rollston has indicated to me (personal communication), microscopic observation of the inscription suggests that it is not possible to definitively conclude that this

The Inscriptions from Tel Reḥov, as a Test Case

Figure 24.1 Reading: *'ayin-[yod?]* (Ink on pottery. Stratum VI. Courtesy of Amihai Mazar)

grapheme represents the "z-shape" expected for *yod* at this time. Regardless, it is worth noting here that at least the *'ayin* exhibits a softer amount of curvature (relative to some of the inscriptions incised into fired pottery discussed below). That is, what is present here in the ink is not rigid or sharp and perhaps speaks to a certain level of ability on the part of the person responsible for writing on the sherd. Indeed, this is what we would reasonably expect to see in an ink-on-pottery inscription.

Reḥov 2

This jar is incised twice with what we can safely reconstruct as the same name on opposite sides. Figure 24.2 below illustrates the instance with the full name while Figure 24.3 shows

Figure 24.2 Reading: *mt'|* (Incised after firing. Stratum VI. Coutresy of Amihai Mazar)

Figure 24.3 Reḥov 2. Incised after firing. Stratum VI. Courtesy of Amihai Mazar

the opposite side of the jar where only traces of the upper left arm of *taw*, the majority of *'alef*, and the entirety of the vertical stroke to the left of *'alef* (possibly a numeral—see Ahituv and Mazar 2013: 207) remain. *Mem* appears in its Proto-Canaanite form, lacking a tail and comprised of four zig-zag segments. It is not preserved on the opposite side of the jar. There is no curvature or tail-elongation discernible for any grapheme represented here. The letters appear to have been incised more slowly given the less precise lower oblique of *'alef*.

Reḥov 3

Ahituv and Mazar (2020: 419) note that Reḥov 3 (Figure 24.4) was inscribed after the pot was broken as it appears on what would have been the interior of the jar. The *lamed* itself is angular and appears nicely formed, but it is impossible to determine the skill level of the scribe based on a single grapheme.

Reḥov 4

Reḥov 4 (Figure 24.5) is roughly hewn; there is a marked angularity to every letter. At the same time, *lamed* and *nun*, which are clear, appear to have been precisely incised. There are additional surface abrasions that render convincing decipherment of the final grapheme difficult. Yardeni and others have suggested that one letter appears on top of another (Ahituv and Mazar 2014: 42). Yardeni has specifically read *yod* atop *mem*. Other possibilities include *ḥet* on top of *mem*, but probably not *nun*. The angularity of the graphemes is no doubt a function of the fact that it was incised after firing.

Reḥov 5

Reḥov 5 (Figure 24.6) is read clearly. Because it was incised before firing, we can make a few substantive comments about ductus. We should take note of the nicely curved *lamed*, which is

Figure 24.4 Reading: *l* (Incised after firing. Stratum VI. Courtesy of Amihai Mazar)

Figure 24.5 Reading: *ln[ḥ?]/[m?]* (Incised after firing. Stratum VI. Courtesy of Amihai Mazar)

a notable difference from most of the other inscriptions except Reḥov 7—as well as the parallel inscription from Tel ʿAmal (Ahituv and Mazar 2014: 43). Furthermore, this particular inscription exhibits a handful of more developed features—namely, the lengthy, oblique tails, the clockwise rotation of the stances, and the kerning between *nun* and *mem*, allowing their tails to extend in near-parallel to the left (Parker 2018: 131). The extensive upper arm of the *lamed* extends above the ceiling line from which we would otherwise expect the letters to "hang"

Figure 24.6 Reading: *lnmš* (Incised before firing. Stratum V. Courtesy of Amihai Mazar)

Figure 24.7 Reading: *lšq[y?]nmš* (Incised after firing. Stratum IV. Courtesy of Amihai Mazar)

(Parker 2018: 130n561). The *nun* of this inscription exhibits a stance that has rotated clockwise from the more upright exemplar in Reḥov 4; taken in concert with the paleographic data from Reḥov 4, there is clear development and concomitant refinement of writing style. It is difficult to tell, however, what proportion of these differences were driven by media considerations (i.e., whether incised before or after firing). There is a comparable inscription from Tel ʿAmal that exhibits notably similar letter morphology; however, it is important to note that we should expect synchronic variation even from the hand of the very same scribe as no person is truly capable of writing *exactly* the same letter form multiple times—especially in a context as seemingly expedient as name-tagging pre-fired pottery. (Thus, we might appeal instead to a certain graphemic *Gestalt*—or, to put it another way, the range of acceptable synchronic variations of a given letter.) As far as the relationship between this particular inscription and the one from Tel ʿAmal is concerned, it is certainly possible that they came from the same scribe; however, it is equally possible that they came from a scribe with equivalent training and style. Alternatively, pottery could easily have been incised at one location and later transported to other sites.

Reḥov 6

Reḥov 6 (Figure 24.7), one of the longer inscriptions from the tel, has been restored from a combination of four sherds of a larger "Hippo type" jar (Aḥituv and Mazar 2014: 44). It contains seven graphemes, most of which appear in forms that we would otherwise expect during the 9th century BCE and is easily read as the graphemes are almost all entirely clear and legible. The inscription should be (tentatively) read lšq[y?]nmš. Aḥituv and Mazar (2014: 44) suggest that "the first three letters were incised in a somewhat different manner from the other four, being more carefully executed and running in a slightly different direction." This description, however, does not offer much in the way of explanation for why this might be the case. I am not convinced that there are substantial skill-related discrepancies between the first and second halves of the inscription. Regarding writing direction, while there is another inscription from Reḥov that preserves "ruling" lines (of a sort, see Reḥov 11), there do not appear to be any anchors to which the scribe was moored in Reḥov 6, and thus minor amounts of deviation or curvature should be expected. Second, the "less carefully executed" portion of the inscription appears as such only in places where the scribe was forced to draw semi-circular portions of letters (rather than gradual curves). Having been incised after firing, one could surmise that both *lamed* and *qop* suffered from the scribe's difficulty with the material at hand. Pointing us to this conclusion might be the discrepancies in graphemic morphology between inscriptions incised before as opposed to after firing. The extant inscriptions from Reḥov that were incised prior to firing, hailing both from Strata V and IV, do exhibit much finer dexterity, especially with curved letter segments (cf. Reḥov 5, 7, 9, and 10).

Reḥov 6 has occasioned additional discussion due to the exceptional fourth grapheme which has been interpreted in several ways. Wimmer (2008) understood it to be the Hieratic numeral 70; Mazar and Aḥituv (2020: 422), however, rightly point out that this would make for a syntactically impossible construction. Following Yardeni, it could be a stylized form of *yod* (Aḥituv and Mazar 2020: 422; Mazar and Aḥituv 2014: 44; see also Parker 2018: 190). *Yod* does appear to be the most likely reading of the proposals thus far. Such a reading accords with at least one Aramaic lexeme—šqy', "cup bearer" (*DNWSI*: 1186)—attested in Official and Palmyrene Aramaic.

If this is actually a *yod*, the studies that have adopted this reading have not put forth any proposals explaining why the grapheme appears in such an odd or unique form as it does here. As noted above, Rollston has convincingly shown that scribes of the southern Levant underwent substantial and lengthy training to hone their craft, giving rise to a noteworthy consistency in letter forms (see also Rollston 2012: 193–96). However, as far as I am aware, no study has considered whether scribes were free to deviate from their training for the sake of expediency, limitations of media, or other similarly conditioning factors.[11] That is to say, while there certainly appears to have been "standards and practices" within the larger epigraphic corpus, inscriptions such as this one maintain an almost unique style—thus, synchronic variation. While we cannot definitively determine the ductus—the order, number, and direction of strokes—in this inscription, there does seem to be a particular scribal "style" employed here where the scribe utilized "check marks" (Parker 2018: 192–93) in forming certain parts of or even entire letters: the head of *mem* and *nun* each consist of either 2 or 1 check mark(s) respectively, *šin* consists of two contiguous check marks, etc. This more "angular" style of writing would have no doubt been more easily incised into fired clay, an effect that is evident also in Reḥov 4. Finkelstein and Sass (forthcoming) have observed a mixture of letter types that they suggest speaks to a "supraregional cursive" stage of development; however, as they note, this understanding awaits further consideration and, ideally, data to support it as well.

Reḥov 7

Reḥov 7 (Figure 24.8) was incised into wet clay before firing. Overall, it was very nicely executed with each grapheme exhibiting the refined nature of the scribal hand. Most of the inscription is clearly read despite the numerous breaks in the pottery. The only exception to this is the fifth letter—reasonably reconstructed as a *qop* based on the traces of the tail and right side of the head that remain. Indeed, *qop* also makes for a reasonable reading from linguistic and onomastic perspectives, yielding a reading of a PN ʾilṣadaq.

While it was found in the same stratum as Reḥov 6, there is a remarkable difference in style, highlighting a range of acceptable letter forms. Compare, for example, the contiguous check marks of the *šin* of inscription 6—the second of which joins the first just over midway up the left oblique stroke of the first check—whereas the two halves meet at the apex of the *šin* of inscription 7. Similarly, we might note the varied angles of the oblique strokes on *ṣade*, all of which depart at different angles that are smoothly connected—derivative, no doubt, of the fact that the scribe was operating in pre-fired clay and was able to reproduce more effectively the forms that would have appeared in ink-based writing of the same period (cf. Reḥov 5, just above).

Reḥov 8

Reḥov 8 (Figure 24.9) preserves three complete letters and traces of at least three others. The *mem*s are complete and legible; two ʿ*ayin*s, while one is not perfectly complete, are read confidently as well. Traces of the tails of intervening letters in the middle of the inscription are all that remain of the others. This is the first inscription in the Reḥov corpus that exhibits a clear bend in the tail of *mem*—a feature Parker (2018: 192) has observed as parallel to instances in the Mesha inscription (*KAI* §181). It is possible that such a bend is detectable in Reḥov 6 at the terminus of the tails of *mem* and *nun*, but not to any comparable degree as observable here. Both instances of ʿ*ayin* have a small tail on the bottom right-hand side—a function of the imperfect circular form to be expected in this period (compare the ʿ*ayin* in the following inscription; contrast the exemplar in Reḥov 1)—but the tick itself is not typological (Parker 2018: 194n884), although this form anticipates the open-headed form of _ ʿayin_s from later periods. The letter forms here are comparable to those in Reḥov 6, most notably the head of the *mem*.

Figure 24.8 Reading: ʾlṣd[q]šhly (Incised before firing. Stratum IV. Courtesy of Amihai Mazar)

The Inscriptions from Tel Reḥov, as a Test Case

Figure 24.9 Reading: *m*[ʿ...]ʿ (Incised after firing. Stratum IV. Courtesy of Amihai Mazar)

Figure 24.10 Reading: [*lʾl*]*yš*ʿ (Ink on pottery. Stratum IV. Courtesy of Amihai Mazar)

Reḥov 9

Unique among the Reḥov inscriptions, the ninth epigraph consists of four more or less complete graphemes and traces of two additional tokens (Figure 24.10). The excavator and site epigrapher have read this as the personal name *'lyš'* ("Elisha"), going so far as to connect this inscription to the prophet of biblical fame, Elisha, stating:

> We conjecture, with due caution and fully aware of the problems inherent in such an identification, that the Elisha mentioned in our inscription is the prophet Elisha son of Shaphat, 'a holy man of God' (2 Kings 4:9), who appears to have been a 'miracle worker' and a holy man in the eyes of his contemporaries. Ahituv and Mazar 2020: 428 and in other publications of the ostracon.

The reading of the name on its own is tentatively sound on paleographic grounds, and Mazar and Ahituv do well to make the suggestion with the appropriate caveats. I am much less confident that any substantial connection can be drawn between this ostracon and the biblical prophet; however, if this ostracon were able to be substantially connected to the biblical prophet, this would truly be exceptional.

Palaeographically, the following characteristics are noteworthy: A tail appears on both *'ayin*s, as noted above, and slight curvature appears in the formation of *šin*. We can get a slight sense of the type of tool used to write this inscription in that there is an almost calligraphic quality to the formation of some of the letter strokes. Those strokes that appear oriented more horizontally tend to be thinner while vertical strokes are clearly thicker. This suggests that the writing implement had a somewhat flat and squared tip, functioning not unlike the nibs on modern calligraphy pens. *'Ayin* in particular was formed with two strokes of the brush—two oppositely facing half circles. The left half circle has clearly become dominant in this scribal hand—with the right side appearing as a nearly vertical stroke the right side more or less vertical stroke and thus creating a distinctive tail that appears also to be present in Reḥov 8.

Figure 24.11 Reading: *b* (Incised before firing. Stratum IV. Courtesy of Amihai Mazar)

Reḥov 10

Reḥov 10 (Figure 24.11) is a nearly intact *bet*. The spine curves nicely down into the foot as it extends to the left. The damming of the clay (Rollston 2010: 146) makes it apparent that this letter was formed by beginning where the horizontal stroke of the head connects to the spine, moving the stylus to the left before turning upward and to the right and forming the head before swooping down and to the left to form the spine and foot in one motion. The excavators note that the sherd could have been a part of several different objects and, as a result, the stance of the letter is more difficult to discern. *Bet* in Hebrew does eventually begin to recline (i.e., rotate clockwise); however, that feature does not appear to become salient until the 8th c. BCE (Parker 2018: 96, 215). It is further unclear what the *bet* was intended to indicate. It is possible that it is an abbreviation for something like the measurement *bath* (cf. Arad 1 l. 3, which reads *yyn. b* \ "one bath… of wine"). While it is not possible to substantiate such a reading beyond speculation, the use of abbreviations would necessitate substantial enough familiarity with both a language and writing system to support its use.

Reḥov 11

Despite its fragmentary nature, Reḥov 11 (Figure 24.12) provides important insight into the material production of inscriptions on pottery as well as the professional interactions enjoyed

Figure 24.12 Reading: [š] (Incised before firing. Stratum IV. Courtesy of Amihai Mazar)

by scribes at Reḥov. The fragmentary incisions may tentatively be understood as *šin*—perhaps even the final letter in the name NMŠ. Importantly for this inscription, however, is the fact that the remaining traces are situated between a set of what Ahituv and Mazar (2014) understand to be "potter's marks." Because the letter was incised before firing, we can state definitively that it was placed on the vessel after the potter's marks—note especially where the upper left segment bisects the upper potter's mark. This allows us to reconstruct the following process for the creation of this fragmentary vessel. After forming the jar, the potter would have added the horizontal marks and, presumably, any additional decorative features that would have figured in the final form of the jar. A scribe could then step in to incise it with whatever content had been solicited by the patron responsible. Of course, there is no telling if this scribe would have been local to Reḥov or if the clay object would have been brought in from outside. It is also possible that the potter was responsible for adding the letters, perhaps after being given a copy on another piece of media from which to copy the letters. Finally, while it was common to use ceiling lines in the production of Iron Age West Semitic inscriptions (Rollston 2010: 145), the fragmentary *šin* here was intended to fit neatly between the jar lines rather than hanging from or resting upon a specific ruling line.

Synthesis: The Importance of the Presence of Cursive Features in the Reḥov Inscriptions

Having considered the inscriptions from Reḥov and the paleographic data they contain, we can now turn to a discussion of what value these data have for our understanding of scribes, how and with whom they worked, and what impact paleographic data should have on our understanding of a broader southern Levantine writing culture. It will become clear over the course of this discussion that the scribal art and profession during the Iron II was engaged in activities that contributed directly to the social, political, and economic development of early Israel. Unfortunately, a paucity of linguistic features limits discussion of the *language* of the Reḥov inscriptions as anything other than "West Semitic" (Ahituv and Mazar 2014: 60–61). The following discussion will therefore focus on synthesizing data concerning letter morphology and environment, scribal method and capability, and social location.

Overall, the development of paleographic thought as it pertains to the Reḥov inscriptions has been even-handed and cautious. Still, some more specific observations are merited. Ahituv and Mazar (2014: 45) note the paleographic differences between Reḥov 5 and 6 in how they each represent the personal name NMŠ. They suggest that "it is possible that the reason for this discrepancy is chronological… Alternatively, the difference might be due to the style of writing." Indeed, the inscriptions were found in different strata—V and IV respectively; but they were also incised in different manners—i.e., before and after firing. One could speculate that the clockwise rotation of letter stance and resultant kerning apparent in Reḥov 5 (paralleled in the inscription from Tel ʿefor) was unique to a specific scribe under the employ of NMŠ—whether that be an individual or family name.

Overall, however, what we see in the inscriptions from Reḥov are observable developments in southern Levantine writing traditions over the course of years and anticipatory of later forms found at places like Samaria, Lachish, and Arad. The data from Reḥov reflect the influence of cursive writing. We should therefore consider the role of cursive developments in our understanding of the inscriptions under present consideration. These developments were in part a function of the media being used to create them which, in turn, determined the type of tools employed by the scribe.

Three different methods were used to inscribe pottery at Tel Reḥov: Incision before firing, incision after firing, and ink on fired pottery. Based on the available inscriptions, there was no preferred method; instead, the method appears to have been decided based on expediency and context. Pots were not always fashioned with an epigraph in view—hence incising after firing—or perhaps this was the result of a scribe's availability. Scribes utilized styluses for incising pottery and brushes or pens of some sort to write in multiple colors of ink, namely, black (Reḥov 1) and red (Reḥov 9). The use of black ink was no doubt much more common in the southern Levant (e.g., Samaria, Lachish, and Arad ostraca) while red ink is attested elsewhere, such as in the Deir 'Allā plaster texts and, in later antiquity, red pigment came to be used to fill in incised graphemes at places such as Palmyra. When writing in ink, at least on the ostraca from Reḥov, scribes appear to have used specialized pens that allowed for the more artful rendering of letters, the forms of which offer further insights on cursive developments within the region.

Cursive features are those features that develop naturally from initially fleeting features of an individual's handwriting—first in ink and arising from extraneous or additional dragging of the writing implement beyond the "ideal form" of a given grapheme (Rollston 2010: 146). Such features are a result of finding more convenient ways to write and streamline the overall writing process. It is only over time that such features evolve from ephemeral idiosyncrasies to permanent, salient features of a given grapheme as they are passed from teacher (most likely a father) to student (most likely a son; see Carr 2005: 130). (Importantly for paleographic method: not every idiosyncratic feature evolves to become a salient, typological feature for a given script series.) Exemplary cursive features that develop within the Old Hebrew script include, but are not limited to, (1) elongated tails that swoop to the left (rather than remaining straight, as in Phoenician; cf. the tails of letters like *mem* in the Mesha and Kerak Inscriptions), (2) the "tick" that forms on the far right extremity of the lower oblique stroke of Old Hebrew *'alef* (see the *'alef* of the Royal Steward Inscription); (3) the loss of the "bent knee" shape of the down stroke of *bet*; and (4) and the ticks that develop on the right extreme of the horizontal strokes in the head of Old Hebrew *samek* (see both Lachish and Arad ostraca for examples).[12] Such features are known to have enjoyed their origins in ink-based writing, developing slowly and then appearing in contexts less suitable for cursive forms such as being etched into hard surfaces where rapid writing was not feasible (note the arguments for a slow pace of script development in Rollston 2008) (Figure 24.13). Later,

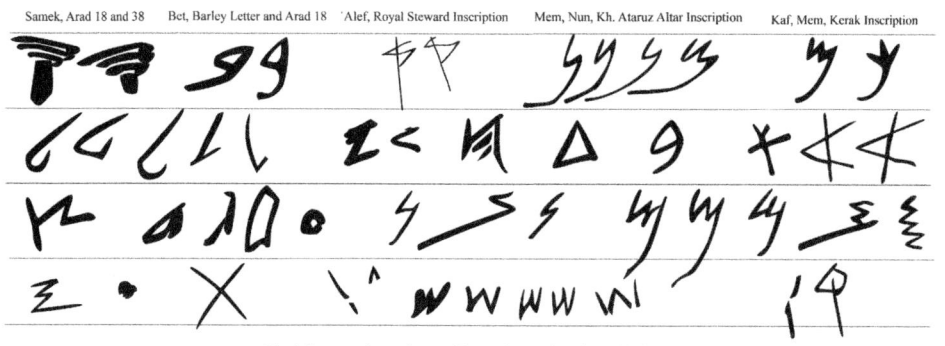

Line 1: Representative graphemes with exemplary cursive paleographic features.
Lines 2–4: Graphemes from Reḥov Corpus in alphabetic order.

All drawings here by the author. Graphemes represented above are not to scale and register lines are not indicative of putative ceiling or floor lines of actual inscriptions.

Figure 24.13 Cursive Developments within the Old Hebrew Script

more developed letter forms were doubtless anticipated by earlier inscriptions such as the ʿore d Ṣarṭah abecedary, the Qubur al-Walaydah Bowl, and the Qeiyafa ostracon (to name only a few)—inscriptions that exhibit far fewer cursive features (if any at all).

The paleographic data recoverable from the Reḥov corpus in particular makes it clear that cursive features were present during the Iron IIA. This includes the lengthened, and occasionally curved, tails of letters like *mem* and *nun* (Reḥov 5, 6, and 8), the curvature present in the spine and foot of *bet* (Reḥov 10), and letter environment conditioned kerning (see especially in Reḥov 5). These features contribute to why Rollston has described the Reḥov inscriptions as, at least in part, representing an instantiation of "the fledgling, but distinctive, Old Hebrew script" (2016: 33; also compare the Moabite altar from Kh. ʿAtaruz [Bean et al. 2019: 230]).[13] Scholars such as Millard (1998), Richelle (2016), and Rollston (2016) have all appropriately (albeit tentatively) suggested that there was likely a greater amount of writing than formally attested in the epigraphic record. Significantly, the state of writing in the Iron II at a site as complex and integrated as Reḥov provides supporting evidence and allows the following conclusion: for cursive features to appear in this cross-section of the epigraphic record, sufficient writing must have been taking place beyond that which is directly evidenced in the epigraphic record. Second, that writing must have been done primarily in ink on either potsherds or (perhaps more likely) papyrus or vellum—the latter of which would have been lost to history due to their perishability (see Richey 2021: 35 where she refers to papyrus as "the pride and joy of southern Levantine scribalism;" similarly, see Richelle 2016: 564).[14] Third, the paleographic features discussed above are not present in epigraphic remains that can be securely dated to earlier periods within the same region. Thus, these features cannot at this time be considered inherited; instead, they are innovations in writing that could have resulted only from the extensive application of writing technology beyond our observable dataset. We can therefore be confident that the name tags and other short epigraphs that comprise the majority of the *extant* early Iron Age epigraphic corpus in reality represent only a portion of the actual writing that was being done. As a result, any model of Iron Age scribalism that utilizes only the extant inscriptions—as well intentioned and judicious as such models indeed are—cannot adequately account for the full spectrum of factors influencing the development of writing during this period. Ultimately, this writing culture must have been productive enough, in media more predisposed to cursive writing styles, in order that such features would have made their way into scripts used either formally at Reḥov or at nearby sites with which Reḥov would have been engaged in some social, political, religious, or economic form. I am therefore in full agreement with Ahituv and Mazar (2020: 435) and their suggestion that "it is thus untenable to claim that writing was limited only to the state's elite, although we cannot claim that literacy was widespread."

Further, taking seriously Richey's (2021: 36–37) observations about media focused epigraphy as it pertains to textual production, we should also begin asking questions about our own expectations for the epigraphic record. While scholars such as Sanders (2009), Dobbs-Allsopp and Pioske (2019), and Malena (2021)[15] have made substantive and productive arguments about theoretical processes such as vernacularization, "textual modeling" (i.e., scribes modeling their work off of foreign influence), and scribal social location, we must ask questions about the kinds of media we should expect to be associated with things like narrative or poetic composition. Looking beyond the text *qua* text, what, precisely, are the types of media that would have been used to create texts that more closely resemble the kinds of literature we find within, say, biblically oriented corpora?

Similarly, Ahituv and Mazar (2014: 63) have done well to speak to a variety of different spaces where the Reḥov inscriptions were found: "a cultic area (No. 8), a dwelling that might have been a patrician house (No. 6), an average house (No. 7), a building with a unique plan

(No. 9) and in the apiary (No. 5)." It is certainly possible that some or even many of these inscriptions were brought to the site from other locales; the key point here, however, is that several of the inscriptions were discovered in "various everyday settings" (Ahituv and Mazar 2014: 63) rather than contexts that would point to more administrative or official capacities. While this does not definitively prove that they were made on site, it would seem more likely to me that incoming shipments fulfilling administrative or bureaucratic purposes would be stored in equivalent "public works"[16] locations on the site. Thus, the inscriptions, taken in concert with their archaeological contexts, grant valuable insight into the social spheres impacted by and engaged with scribal activity. Such a variety of find locations indicates that writing played a role in an equally variegated life at Tel Reḥov and that access to scribes was not as unattainable or out of reach as many have previously suggested.

In that light, nearly every study on scribal practice in the southern Levant has made some form of the claim that scribes would have been rather expensive to hire and, as a result, their patronage would have been restricted almost exclusively to elite retainers (e.g., Byrne 2007: 22–23; Malena 2021: 14). In such models, to become a scribe was to undergo a lengthy and rather rigorous education (Carr 2005; Rollston 2006, 2010, 2015). This education would have most likely taken place within the home and not within a centralized "school" (compare, however, outdated models such as Jamieson-Drake 1991; see more recently and relevantly, Rollston 2012 and 2015 and bibliography there). Because training was so lengthy and rigorous, few people would have been able to pursue it. Additionally, the materials required to create "texts" (a term used loosely here) would have been costly.[17] Therefore, to hire a scribe would have been beyond the capabilities of the average Israelite. This claim, while certainly reasonable on its surface, should occasion more consideration. After all, a significant amount of data about the Iron Age Levantine economy is simply inaccessible. What would the "going rate" have been for the composition of a brief letter on a potsherd or scrap of papyrus? How long would it really have taken, for example, for a scribe to compose something comparable to Lachish 3—as just one example?[18] How much was a scribe paid for the composition of this letter? Did scribes only accept hard currency or were they amenable to receive goods or services in exchange for hiring out their talents? Papyrus or vellum may have been expensive to acquire for writing purposes, but potsherds would have been relatively ubiquitous and provided a cheaper avenue for the less well-off to secure. Additionally, throughout all these considerations there is a consistent risk that scholars are retrojecting notions of modern exchange onto ancient societies. We have no evidence that scribes were retained exclusively and without the ability to hire themselves out for smaller projects. Thus, it is equally possible that an average Israelite of the Iron II period could have traded with scribes in various para- or non-elite contexts to suit whatever "smaller" needs that may have arisen.

We should also consider anew the oft-repeated "fact" (but, perhaps better: "factoid"—see Yoffee 2005: 6) that a perceived dearth of genre variety in early Iron Age northwest Semitic inscriptions means that scribes were primarily or exclusively engaged in the practice of name-tagging or creating prestige objects such as the Aḥiram sarcophagus (Sanders 2009: 79–83; Malena 2021: 19; on the inception of alphabetic royal inscriptions, see Dobbs-Allsopp and Pioske 2019: 8, 16–17). The argument leveraged to arrive at such a conclusion, however, appears to be circular in nature: only certain types of inscriptions have been discovered and therefore these were the only types of writing scribes at this time were capable or even in need of producing (see also van der Toorn 2007: 82).

We would not expect, however, to come across an epistle etched into the side of an arrowhead in the same way that we would be unlikely to dig up a treaty or quitclaim incised into a collared rim storage jar.[19] That is to say, the material culture remains that are most likely to have survived the past 3000 years are exactly the kinds of objects prone to being marked with names or considered prestige objects. This does not mean that scribes were incapable of greater or more complex work or that such work was not in the scribal purview of the Iron II.

Finally, further considerations of Israel's development as a secondary state reinforce the idea that writing would have been available at a period earlier in its formation than other primary states that would have influenced it. Indeed, Israel—and, more importantly for the present discussion, the writing system it came to adopt—did have a "navel," to borrow Ernest Gellner's (1996) analogy, at least in the sense that as a secondary state, Israel inherited and borrowed concepts, technology, politics, and cultural expressions (to name only a few things) from larger and older "states"[20] in its immediate vicinity. Antecedent cultural expressions from outside of Israel contributed to Israel's own emergence. In fact, very few socio-political systems in human history can actually be said *not* to have a navel in this respect—thus the alphabet is no different as its outgrowth and evolution from the dawn of the Iron Age was a natural and genetic process.[21] To Gellner's (1996) point, it is not the presence or absence of the navel that matters. Rather, it is the presence of ongoing biological processes like digestion and blood circulation (to utilize his metaphor) that matter. In the case of Reḥov, the "biological" process of script development is clearly discernable. It speaks to a writing culture inseparable from but vital to a larger socio-political body (or, perhaps better, "bodies") that grew and changed alongside those who employed it.

Notes

1 See, variously, Byrne 2007; Carr 2005; Finkelstein and Sass 2013; Hess 2006; Jamieson-Drake 1991; Richey 2021; Rollston 2006, 2015, 2016; Sanders 2009; van der Toorn 2007; Whisenant 2013; see especially Parker 2018 for a comprehensive treatment of Old Hebrew and Aramaic paleography.
2 Rather than simply "new" as Younger (2016: 63) notes, "structures of the socially constructed groups of the second millennium continued into the first." While his focus here is on Aramean social systems, his perspective can no doubt be extrapolated to the larger eastern Mediterranean, as evidenced by the continuation of other social expressions such as pottery forms and, especially for the purposes of this essay, alphabetic writing. On the matter of contextualizing such scribal enterprise within larger state formation processes in the southern Levant, see Greene forthcoming.
3 By "primary technology," I mean tools or crafts that were developed first in other social and political locations by primary "state" entities that were then available to be adopted by and adapted for secondary—always in some manner derivative—spheres. See Greene forthcoming where this terminology is explained in greater detail.
4 Interestingly, Malena (2021: 14n3) restricts her study to inscriptions only while admitting that "This essay focuses on inscriptions, but for a fuller picture one must also consider seals and clay bullae, which testify to the existence of scrolls and the demand for scribes." She is correct in highlighting the need for epigraphers to consider data well beyond merely the text of inscriptions by itself—a fact that is emphasized excellently in Richey's (2021: passim) article in the very same volume. Further, Malena's model ties scribes closely to state enterprise—a rather broadly adopted assumption that I have problematized in Greene forthcoming.
5 I am here employing the term "national script" for the sake of the present argument, though see n12 below for a critique of such terminology.
6 This essay follows the Mazar's (2011: 105–11) "Modified Conventional Chronology"; see also Lee et al. 2013: 731–40.
7 Literacy, in this essay, follows Rollston's definition and requires more substantial ability to employ a writing system than simply writing one's own name—especially at sites like Reḥov, where the apparent scribal hands are rather clearly refined and particularly dexterous (see, especially, Reḥov 5, 7, 8, and 9 below).
8 All images used here come from Mazar 2020 and are used with permission.
9 Ahituv and Mazar (2020: 106) note that the total number of inscriptions may in fact be 12—two of the finds ("inscriptions" 11 and 12 in Ahituv and Mazar 2020: 415, 429–30) are debatable.

I have included the eleventh inscription in the discussion below because the traces that appear there seem likely to be remnants of a *šin* and these traces likely connect it to the personal name NMŠ; however, I have not included the 12th as there are no clear paleographic features that allow it to be classified alongside the others. Additionally, a Proto-Canaanite inscription was discovered in a surface survey of the site in 1939. This inscription, while certainly important for conversations pertaining to writing culture in the southern Levant, will not be considered here.

10 Parker (2018: 191) concludes that the script of the inscriptions from stratum IV is favorably compared to the Old Hebrew script (as evidenced elsewhere such as the Mesha Stele, *KAI* §181) and that this collection of epigraphs represents "the largest corpus of ninth-century Hebrew inscriptions recovered to date."

11 On possible tool-based explanations of paleographic phenomena in monumental inscriptions, see Keimer 2015. Keimer's approach helpfully considers the tools available to stone masons to produce monumental inscriptions and how those tools could have impacted the development of Northwest Semitic script traditions. I maintain a perspective closer to Naveh (1987) and Rollston (2010) on this matter and understand script development to have been primarily derivative of cursive developments in non-monumental contexts.

12 Some of these features do not develop until after the Reḥov inscriptions. The main point here is the way cursive features make their way into a given writing system.

13 The concept of "national scripts" has, since at least the work of Naveh (1987: 9, 53) persisted as the consensus model for understanding the various divergent writing traditions in Northwest Semitic contexts. That is, it is generally accepted that the Phoenician script was the *Mutterschrift* for its Hebrew and Aramaic *Tochterschriften* (Rollston 2010: 20–46). Jeremy M. Hutton and I are in the process of problematizing the notion of "national scripts" in the context of scribal activity vis-à-vis "state" (but, better, "socio-political") enterprise in the Levant (Greene and Hutton in preparation).

14 Other education related media such as wax boards were also available. Additionally, I should note that I am comfortable pushing the ceiling for papyrus use in the Levant higher than Richey has noted in her work. Economic connections to other sites—both coastal and inland—and concomitant presence of Egyptian material culture objects at Reḥov make it likely to me that papyrus was in use despite a lack of other evidence we would otherwise hope to find. Texts like the Report of Wenamun detail Egyptian activity in the Iron Age Levant alongside writing in Semitic contexts—specifically Phoenician (see K. V. L. Pierce, this volume). Further, anepigraphic evidence from other sites in the larger region—such as the clay bullae discovered at Kh. Summeily (see Hardin, Rollston, and Blakely 2014) and ongoing copper mining at Timna and Kh. en-Naḥash (see Holladay and Klassen 2014: 41)—provide additional, albeit indirect, support for such conclusions.

15 Malena (2021: 14, note 5) maintains, for example,

> that scribal activity would have been a tool of the elite in the process of social change and not easily acquired or readily available to a broader population ... With this model, we should expect small numbers of inscriptions and other 'luxury items' for some time, which produces a better correlation between the data and interpretation.

16 On the interpretation of public works as it pertains to scribal social location, see my discussion of dual processual state formation theory in Greene forthcoming.

17 Note that the model also almost exclusively focuses on the *student* and pays little attention to the *teacher*.

18 For a study on the work rate and produce of individual cuneiform scribes, see Tanret 2004. The case of Lachish 3 is particularly interesting in this context as it raises several additional questions about affordability, access, and scribal purview. While Hoshaiah insists that he does not need anyone to *read* letters for him ($\sqrt{q\text{-}r\text{-}'}$), the act of writing *qua* writing is not immediately a concern within the plain sense of the letter. It is no doubt possible that Hoshaiah could have been able to write; it is equally possible, however, that he hired someone to write on his behalf. N.B.: Reading literacy does not immediately assume writing literacy (Fitzgerald and Shanahan 2010).

19 An exception to this might be the Tel Siran Bottle. This inscription, however, is dedicatory and was presumably for display, in a manner similar to the Royal Byblian inscriptions.

20 The definition of this term is widely contested. See Greene forthcoming.

21 Gellner (1996: 101) artfully suggested, "Some nations have navels, some achieve navels, some have navels thrust upon them. Those possessed of genuine navels are probably in a minority, but it matters little. It is the need for navels engendered by modernity that matters."

Bibliography

Ahituv, Shmuel, and Amihai Mazar. 2013. "The Inscriptions from Tel Reḥov and Their Contribution to the Study of Script and Writing during Iron Age IIA." *Maarav* 20: 205–46.

———. 2014. "The Inscriptions from Tel Reḥov and Their Contribution to the Study of Script and Writing During Iron Age IIA." Pages 39–68 in *"See I Will Bring a Scroll Recounting What Befell Me" (Ps 40:8): Epigraphy and Daily Life from the Bible to the Talmud. Dedicated to the Memory of Prof. Hanan Eshel*. Edited by Esther Eshel and Yigal Levin. Göttingen: Vandenhoeck & Ruprecht.

———. 2020. *Tel Reḥov: A Bronze and Iron Age City in the Beth Shean Valley. Volume IV, Pottery Studies, Inscriptions, and Figurative Art*. Jerusalem: Hebrew University of Jerusalem.

Bean, Adam, Christopher A. Rollston, P. Kyle McCarter, and Stefan J. Wimmer. 2019. "An Inscribed Altar from the Khirbat Ataruz Moabite Sanctuary." *Levant* 50: 211–36.

Byrne, Ryan. 2007. "The Refuge of Scribalism in Iron I Palestine." *BASOR* 345: 1–31.

Carr, David M. 2005. *Writing on the Tablet of the Heart: Origins of Scripture and Literature*. Oxford: Oxford University Press.

Cline, Eric H. 2014. *1177 B.C.: The Year Civilization Collapsed*. Princeton: Princeton University Press.

Cross, Frank M. 2003a. "The Evolution of the Proto-Canaanite Alphabet." Pages 309–12 in *Leaves from an Epigrapher's Notebook: Collected Papers in Hebrew and West Semitic Palaeography and Epigraphy*. Winona Lake: Eisenbrauns.

———. 2003b. "The Origin and Early Evolution of the Alphabet." Pages 317–29 in *Leaves from an Epigrapher's Notebook: Collected Papers in Hebrew and West Semitic Palaeography and Epigraphy*. Winona Lake: Eisenbrauns.

———. 2003c. "Alphabets and Pots: Reflections on Typological Method in the Dating of Human Artifacts." Pages 344–50 in *Leaves from an Epigrapher's Notebook: Collected Papers in Hebrew and West Semitic Palaeography and Epigraphy*. Winona Lake: Eisenbrauns.

Dobbs-Allsopp, F. W., and Daniel Pioske. 2019. "On the Appearance of Royal Inscriptions in Alphabetic Scripts in the Levant. *Maarav* 23: 389–442.

Finkelstein, Israel, and Benjamin Sass. 2013. "The West Semitic Alphabetic Inscriptions: Late Bronze II to Iron IIA: Archaeological Context, Distribution and Chronology." *HBAI* 2: 149–220.

———. Forthcoming. "The Exceptional Concentration of Inscriptions at Iron IIA Gath and Rehob and the Nature of the Alphabet in the Ninth Century." In *Oral et écrit Dans le Proche-Orient Ancien: Les Processus de Rédaction et D'édition. Actes du Colloque Organisé par le Collège de France, Paris, les 26 et 27 mai 2015*. Edited by Thomas Römer, et al. Leuven: Orbis Biblicus et Orientalis.

Fitzgerald, Jill, and Timothy Shanahan. 2010. "Reading and Writing Relations and Their Development." *Educational Psychologist* 35: 39–50.

Gellner, Ernest. 1996. "Ernest Gellner's Reply: 'Do Nations Have Navels?'" *Nations and Nationalism* 2: 366–70.

Greene, Nathaniel E. Forthcoming. *Warlord and Scribe: The Nascent Israelite State beneath Its Textual Veneers*. University Park: Eisenbrauns.

Greene, Nathaniel E., and Jeremy M. Hutton. In Preparation. "The Rise of National Scripts in the Iron II: A Proposal."

Hardin, James W., Christopher A. Rollston, and Jeffrey A. Blakely. 2014. "Iron Age Bullae from Officialdom's Periphery: Khirbet Summeily in Broader Context." *NEA* 77: 300–03.

Hess, Richard S. 2006. "Writing About Writing: Abecedaries as Evidence for Literacy in Ancient Israel." *VT* 56: 342–46.

Holladay Jr., John S., and Stanley Klassen. 2014. "From Bandit to King: David's Time in the Negev and the Transformation of a Tribal Entity into a Nation State." Pages 31–46 in *Unearthing the Wilderness: Studies on the History and Archaeology of the Negev and Edom in the Iron Age*. Edited by Juan Manuel Tebes. Leuven: Peeters.

Jamieson-Drake, David. 1991. *Scribes and Schools in Monarchic Judah: A Socio-Archaeological Approach*. Sheffield: Sheffield Academic Press.

Keimer, Kyle H. 2015. "The Impact of Ductus on Script Form and Development in Monumental Northwest Semitic Inscriptions." *UF* 46: 189–212.

Kuhrt, Amélie. 1995. *The Ancient Near East c. 3000–350 B.C.* 2 vols. New York: Routledge.

Lee, Sharen, Christopher Bronk Ramsey, and Amihai Mazar. 2012. "Iron Age Chronology in Israel: Results from Modeling with a Trapezoidal Bayesian Framework." *Radiocarbon* 55: 731–40.

Lemaire, André. 2007. "West Semitic Inscriptions and Ninth-Century BCE Ancient Israel." Pages 279–303 in *Understanding the History of Ancient Israel*. Edited by H. G. M. Williamson. London: The British Academy.

Malena, Sarah. 2021. "Influential Inscriptions: Resituating Scribal Activity during the Iron I-IIA Transition." Pages 13–27 in *Scribes and Scribalism*. Edited by Mark Leuchter. London: T&T Clark.

Mandell, Alice, and Jeremy D. Smoak. 2019. "The Material Turn in the Study of Israelite Religions: Spaces, Things, and the Body." *JHS* 19. Online: doi.org/10.5508/jhs29397.

Mazar, Amihai. 2011. "The Iron Age Chronology Debate: Is the Gap Narrowing? Another Viewpoint." *NEA* 74: 105–11.

———. 2020. *Tel Reḥov: A Bronze and Iron Age City in the Beth Shean Valley. Volume I, Introductions, Synthesis and Excavations on the Upper Mound*. Jerusalem: Hebrew University of Jerusalem.

Millard, Alan. 1998. "Books in the Late Bronze Age." Pages 171–79 in *Past Links: Studies in the Languages and Cultures of the Ancient Near East Dedicated to Professor Anson F. Rainey*. Edited by Shlomo Izre'el, et al. Winona Lake: Eisenbrauns.

Naveh, Joseph. 1987. *The Early History of the Alphabet*. Jerusalem: Magnes Press.

Parker, Heather Dana Davis. 2018. "The Levant Comes of Age: The Ninth Century BCE Through Script Traditions." Online: www.academia.edu/36755960/PARKER_LEVANT_COMES_OF_AGE_PARTI_05312018_docx.

Richelle, Mathieu. 2016. "Elusive Scrolls: Could Any Hebrew Literature Have Been Written Prior to the Eighth Century BCE?" *VT* 66: 566–94.

Richey, Madadh. 2021. "The Media and Materiality of Southern Levantine Inscriptions: Production and Reception Contexts." Pages 29–39 in *Scribes and Scribalism*. Edited by Mark Leuchter. London: T&T Clark.

Rollston, Christopher A. 2006. "Scribal Education in Ancient Israel: The Old Hebrew Epigraphic Evidence." *BASOR* 344: 47–74.

———. 2008. "The Dating of the Early Royal Byblian Phoenician Inscriptions: A Response to Benjamin Sass." *Maarav* 15: 57–93.

———. 2012. "An Old Hebrew Stone Inscription from the City of David: A Trained Hand and A Remedial Hand of the Same Inscription." Pages 189–96 in *Puzzling Out the Past: Studies in Northwest Semitic Languages and Literatures in Honor of Bruce Zuckerman*. Edited by Marilyn J. Lundberg, et al. Leiden: Brill.

———. 2015. "Scribal Curriculum in the First Temple Period: Epigraphic Hebrew and Biblical Evidence." Pages 71–101 in *Contextualizing Israel's Sacred Writings: Ancient Literacy, Orality, and Literary Production*. Edited by Brian B. Schmidt. Atlanta: SBL.

———. 2016. "Inscriptional Evidence for the Writing of the Earliest Texts of the Bible—Intellectual Infrastructure in Tenth- and Ninth-Century Israel, Judah, and the Southern Levant." Pages 15–46 in *The Formation of the Pentateuch: Bridging the Academic Cultures of Europe, Israel, and North America*. Edited by Jan C. Gertz, et al. Tübingen: Mohr Siebeck.

Sanders, Seth L. 2009. *The Invention of Hebrew*. Urbana: University of Illinois Press.

Sass, Benjamin. 2005. *The Alphabet at the Turn of the Millennium: The West Semitic Alphabet ca. 1150–850 B.C.E.* Tel Aviv: Yass Publications in Archaeology.

Sergi, Omer. 2019. "The Formation of Israelite Identity in the Central Canaanite Highlands in the Iron Age I-IIA." *NEA* 82: 42–51.

Tanret, Michel. 2004. "The Works and the Days . . . On Scribal Activity in Old Babylonian Sippar-Amnānum." *RA* 98: 33–62.

Van der Toorn, Karel. 2007. *Scribal Culture and the Making of the Hebrew Bible*. Cambridge: Harvard University Press.

Whisenant, Jessica. 2013. "Let the Stones Speak! Document Production by Iron Age West Semitic Scribal Institutions and the Question of Biblical Sources." Pages 133–60 in *Contextualizing Israel's Sacred Writings: Ancient Literacy, Orality, and Literary Production*. Edited by Brian B. Schmidt. Atlanta: SBL.

Wimmer, S. J. 2008. "A New Hieratic Ostracon from Ashkelon." *TA* 35: 65–72.

Yoffee, Norman. 2005. *Myths of the Archaic State: Evolution of the Earliest Cities, States, and Civilizations*. Cambridge: Cambridge University Press.

Younger, K. Lawson. 2016. *A Political History of the Arameans: From their Origins to the End of Their Polities*. Atlanta: SBL.

25
LANGUAGE IN ISRAEL AND JUDAH
A Sociolinguistic Reappraisal

Timothy Hogue

A tongue-in-cheek axiom in linguistics posits that the key difference between a language and a dialect is that a language has an army and a navy. For ancient Israel, I would offer instead that a language is a dialect with a king and a god. These are also primary factors in distinguishing languages such as Ammonite, Moabite, Edomite, and Samʿalian. All quips aside, the principle holds that even traditional linguists tend to differentiate languages on social grounds rather than purely linguistic ones. Otherwise, why should Israelite and Judahite both be treated as dialects of "Hebrew" while the supposedly mutually intelligible Moabite is excluded? These metalinguistic labels tell us more about the social relationships between polities (at least in the minds of modern scholars) than about concrete linguistic features. Sociolinguistics can reframe this discourse by bringing historical linguistics, philology, and epigraphy into conversation with anthropology, sociology, archaeology, and a growing set of other methods. Reframing the data from ancient Israel in this way will allow us to see that the languages we find were complex material practices that were inextricable from the people and institutions that used them. While the earliest language practices attested in ancient Israel are diverse and suggest a lack of standardization, a standard Israelite language was eventually created under the auspices of the kingdom of Israel. When Israelite scribes brought this practice to Jerusalem after the fall of Samaria, they revolutionized Judahite writing as well.

Introduction: The Sociolinguistics of Writing

The primary difficulty in approaching language in ancient Israel is that the only data available comes from texts—not speakers, readers, or writers. A text may be understood as a simulation of speech, but an accurate simulation requires culturally situated knowledge of linguistic features and their manner of representation (Bottineau 2010: 273). Because writing transcends the spatial and temporal constraints of speech, we now lack most of the culturally situated knowledge needed to voice ancient texts (Coulmas 1989: 7–8; Ong 1992). Furthermore, written language is much more than a simulation of speech or a representation of vocabulary and grammar. It is a technical practice embedded within particular social networks. Therefore, analyzing the languages of Israel requires an approach that combines archaeology and philology.

Sociolinguistics provides a bridge between archaeological and philological data because it recognizes that language is primarily a social, material practice. Language falls within the broader category of material culture. This is especially obvious in the case of written language, but it is true of all language. Speech is ultimately a physical activity, and even speaking 'in our heads' can only proceed when we simulate that physical process (Gahrn-Andersen 2019: 175; Heidegger 1982: 114; Hutchins 2005: 1573–76). In the case of writing, language is materialized by the manipulation of tools and surfaces via manual gestures to produce an artifact (Bottineau 2010: 273–75). The notion of a language as a discreet, identifiable collection of linguistic features tied to a particular place and time has thus been increasingly problematized. Sociolinguistics posits instead that language is a socially motivated practice driven by various relationships and interactions (Cf. Fishman 1970, 1972; Labov 1994, 2001, 2010).

"Language" has accordingly been reinterpreted as a verb by many researchers. We are now less concerned with a community's language than with their practices of *languaging*. As Jan Blommaert (2016: 244) summarizes:

> These developments have refocused sociolinguistic analysis, from reified notions of language (and dialect, sociolect, etc.) to a new kind of unit: an ideologically configured and indexically ordered set of specific linguistic-semiotic resources...dynamically developing as "repertoires" in the course of people's social lives, and deployed in highly context-sensitive metalinguistically regimented social practices.

These "linguistic-semiotic resources" include the features to which language is typically reduced: lexicon, morphology, phonology, syntax, etc. But these also include the people who practice language, their tools and materials, and the social networks that afford and constrain these resources and practices (Lillis 2013: 100–23). As such, languaging is always ideologically motivated by interactions and relationships within these networks. All language practices—whether speaking face to face or writing a chapter on language in an edited volume—involve decisions about what matters and what does not (Bottineau 2010: 269–70; Irvine and Gal 2000). More than this, languaging is a means of proposing new ideologies. It performatively brings about new interactions and relationships, and is thus simultaneously motivated by and constitutive of ideology (Bottineau 2010; Gahrn-Andersen 2019: 175–82; Hodder and Mol 2016: 1067; Sanders 2009: 118).

It is important to keep in mind that the resources utilized in writing in ancient Israel were scarce and therefore easy to constrain within certain hubs in social networks. Lillis (2013: 111–12) calls these hubs *brokers* and *pivots*. Brokers afford and constrain access to resources necessary for writing. In the ancient world, we encounter brokers in the form of elites who possess and control the movement of materials, means of hiring scribes, and the human labor force necessary to create the tools, surfaces, and spaces for writing. These elites could be royals, but ancient Israel also attests writing brokered by administrative officials, military leaders, priests, prophets, and merchants. We encounter pivots in the form of scribes and other craftsmen. These specialists controlled the technical knowledge necessary to execute writing.

Elites organized themselves around centering institutions—such as polities, temples, and schools—that prescribed and proscribed writing practices (Lillis 2013: 113–15). Ancient centering institutions tended to act as gravitational points, pulling scarce writing resources toward them (Osborne 2013: 783–5). Resources followed various trajectories relative to the pull of centering institutions. These trajectories could be pulling toward or accommodating a center or else pulling away from or resisting a center (Lillis 2013: 133–34).

These trajectories must be considered to accurately reconstruct the social import of specific instances of writing. With this network approach to languaging in mind, I turn to the languaging of ancient Israel.

Languaging in Ancient Israel Before the 8th Century BCE

Israel and Judah are sometimes treated together as a relatively uniform speech area dominated by a language called "Hebrew." Archaeological evidence, however, suggests quite the opposite. Israel and Judah were populated by diverse speech communities who occasionally donated their verbal resources to the development of written languaging. The spread of one written language rather than another attests not to the extension of a speech community but to the success of particular centering institutions. Therefore, throughout this chapter, I will avoid as much as possible the label "Hebrew." Admittedly, this is the conventional label for Israelite and Judahite epigraphic materials, and these do display remarkable consistency with the texts in the Hebrew Bible. However, the term is unattested from this period; its earliest occurrence was only after the Bar Kochba Revolt in 135 CE (Schniedewind 2013: 5). Especially if metalinguistic labels are reifications of language ideology, we should be careful of projecting later ideologies into the past in our descriptions. Furthermore, the use of the term "Hebrew" fails to acknowledge the geographic and diachronic variation in the materials it aims to describe. I will therefore use the term Judahite to refer to the epigraphic traditions associated with the kingdom of Judah, based on the usage of this term in 2 Kgs 18:26. By analogy, I use the term Israelite to refer to the epigraphic traditions associated with the kingdom of Israel based in Samaria.

The preoccupation with "Hebrew" also obscures the diversity of written varieties attested in ancient Israel. An identifiably Israelite writing system using a unique script and the linguistic features typically associated with Hebrew does not appear until the 8th century. Prior to this period, writing in Israel was much more varied, consisting of inscriptions in several Northwest Semitic dialects. While these undoubtedly reflect some of the spoken diversity of the region, writing permits the transmission of linguistic features beyond their original place and time. It also tends to utilize verbal resources to accomplish social functions and goals distinct from those of speech communities (Coulmas 1989: 12–14; Lillis 2013: 105–57). This will be readily apparent if we begin by considering some of the writing practices attested in Israel before the emergence of Israelite writing proper.

Canaanite Writing in the 11th–10th Centuries BCE

Writing in early Iron Age Israel must be understood against the backdrop of the power vacuum created by the exit of the Great Powers of the Late Bronze Age from the region. One consequence of this was the dislocation of scribes from the imperial networks that formerly employed them. In the ensuing centuries, scribal practice was much more limited, but it did survive and adapt to this new context. Most notably, cuneiform and Egyptian hieroglyphic writing were essentially replaced by the linear alphabet, though aspects of the earlier scribal practices were maintained in this new idiom (Burke 2020: 59–62). The inscriptions from this period are difficult to classify with any precision. Territorial polities were nearly non-existent in the southern Levant at this time, so scribes instead attached themselves to local elites and engaged in highly localized practices (Byrne 2007).

A key example of these localized scribal practices is the Khirbet Qeiyafa Ostracon. This artifact dates to the late 11th or early 10th century and was discovered at Khirbet Qeiyafa approximately 30 km from Jerusalem (Garfinkel et al. 2015). In a recent study, Donnelly-Lewis (2021) identified it as the earliest "Hebrew" inscription. However, he admits that the inscription is "archaic" and "dialectal." He reads the inscription as a judicial document, in which the text's broker reports having been summoned in regards to a local dispute (Donnelly-Lewis 2021). In addition to the idiosyncratic dialect, the script matches no other inscriptions, and the ductus is a piece of locally produced pottery. This all suggests that the only center prescribing the practices in the Khirbet Qeiyafa Ostracon was located at Khirbet Qeiyafa itself.

Only one piece of evidence may warrant viewing the Khirbet Qeiyafa Ostracon as indicative of a non-local broker for its writing. Donnelly-Lewis reads line 4 of the inscription as follows:

'qm wyqmy bd mlk
I will appear, since he summoned me by (the authority of) the king.

This interpretation of *bd mlk* would indicate the connection of a royal center to Khirbet Qeiyafa. Given the date of the inscription, the king referenced here would be one of the earliest in ancient Israel. However, Donnelly-Lewis admits that this interpretation is conjectural. Equally plausible is the option to read BDMLK as a personal name—that of a local elite summoning the author of this document (Donnelly-Lewis 2021; Millard 2011: 11). In general, any attempt to identify the elite brokers of inscriptions from this period must remain tenuous. What is clear is that resources tended to be clustered locally rather than oriented toward centering institutions elsewhere. If royal brokers were involved, they likely appropriated local practices rather than imposing trans-local standards.

A similar case of localized scribalism comes from Tel Gezer, also 30 km from Jerusalem. The Gezer Calendar (Figure 25.1) is an inscribed limestone tablet that has been dated paleographically to the 10th century BCE. Once thought to be the earliest "Hebrew" text, it has more recently been argued that both the script and language of the inscription are Phoenician (Naveh 1987: 65; Pardee 2013; Rollston 2010: 29–31). While the script does appear to share commonalities with other examples from this period, it is hard to speak about the language with certainty (Schniedewind 2005: 406). On the one hand, "Phoenician" like Hebrew is an anachronism covering both regional and diachronic diversity in the inscriptions it labels (Schniedewind 2013: 54–56). On the other hand, many features of the inscription are highly idiosyncratic. For example, the inscription contains the unusual form *yrḥw* "two months," apparently an otherwise unattested dual formation. On these grounds, Pardee (2013) allows that the inscription might simply be considered "Canaanite."

The content of the Gezer Calendar has most recently been analyzed as a lexical list—a pedagogical tool used to train scribes in vocabulary. The specifics of the list actually appear to derive from Mesopotamian educational practice, providing one example of the continuation of cuneiform scribal practice in the Levant (Burke 2020: 62). The use of local limestone buttressed this educational function because it allowed the tablet to function as a palimpsest that could be erased and reused to repeat the exercise (Schniedewind 2019: 80–85). The educational function of this tablet speaks to the presence of a centering institution in the form of a local scribal school. It is more difficult to speak of any elite brokers for this inscription with certainty, but there is one intriguing possibility.

The most recent excavators argue that the fortification of Gezer during this period and the construction of its administrative buildings is consistent with other evidence for the westward expansion of the nascent polity at Jerusalem (Ortiz and Wolff 2012, 2021).

Figure 25.1 The Gezer Calendar

Gezer is famously associated with King Solomon, who was gifted the city by the Pharaoh Shoshenq in 1 Kgs 9:15–17 (Dever 2021; see also K. V. L. Pierce, this volume). If this interpretation is correct, it indicates a particular relationship between monarchic power and writing in this period. Both the Gezer Calendar and the Khirbet Qeiyafa Ostracon (Figure 25.2) reveal highly localized writing practices that are inconsistent with each other, not to mention other sites. If the kings in Jerusalem were brokering this writing, they were apparently neither prescribing nor proscribing languaging. This attitude toward writing is consistent with Mazar's proposal that the early Davidic polity be understood as a "tribal alliance, lacking a centralized administration and hierarchal society yet having an impact on extensive territories" (Mazar 2021: 260; cf. Keimer 2021). In contrast, the 9th century witnessed the emergence of new elite attitudes toward writing, culminating in the development of standardized languaging practices.

Moabite and Aramaic in the 9th Century BCE

The Mesha Stele is a basalt stele dating to the mid to late 9th century BCE. It was found out of context at Dibon (modern Dhiban), but the stele's inscription strongly implies that it was originally erected at that site. This is an important example of monumental writing, and this must inform our understanding of its function. Levantine monuments of this type were

Figure 25.2 Drawing of Khirbet Qeiyafa Inscription. Courtesy of Brian Donnely-Lewis

specifically deployed in order to drive ideology and identity formation (Hogue 2021a). The stele appeared during an innovative time in the history of monument-making in the Levant. While monumental inscriptions had been utilized to project sovereignty over cities prior to the 9th century and still afterwards, it was during the late 9th century and first half of the 8th that these inscriptions were used to configure territories (Gilbert 2011: 130–31; Hogue 2019a: 76–86; Shafer 2007: 135). The Mesha Stele's inscription narrates the deeds of King Mesha of Moab, who by his own account was instrumental in the creation of a territorial polity of Moab in the Iron Age (see Porter, this volume). Significantly, Mesha's primary enemy in the inscription is Israel, but he also records fighting the Gadites and possibly Judah as well, if the reading in line 31 of *bt dwd* "House of David" is correct (Lemaire 1994). The Mesha Stele thus provides evidence for languaging in territory formerly associated with Israel and specifically for a language practice defined in part in opposition to Israel.

The linguistic features of Moabite are remarkably similar to those known from Israelite and Judahite in the following century (Garr 2004: 228–29). So close is Moabite to these varieties, that some scholars even propose that they were mutually intelligible (Garr 2004: 228–32; Schwartz 2005: 58; Young 1993: 39). The script of the inscription is so similar to that of Samaria in the 8th century that Joseph Naveh remarked, "Strange as it may seem, the first distinctive features of Hebrew writing can be discerned in the scripts of the ninth-century Moabite inscriptions" (Naveh 1987: 68). Subsequent scholarship has thus assumed that the writing practices of Moab were appropriated from Israel (Sanders 2009: 124; Sass 2005: 88). However, this conclusion involves comparing a carved stone inscription to cursive inscriptions written in ink on pottery, a practice involving very different tools and techniques (Keimer 2015: 197; Schniedewind 2005: 406). Even if there is a connection between the two styles, given the apparent absence of standardized writing in 9th century Israel, we must consider also that the transfer happened in the opposite direction.

What is most important, however, is Mesha's conscious use of writing to propose a new political identity to his subjects in Moab (Sanders 2009: 114). Mesha identifies himself in lines 1–2 as *hdbny* "the Dibonite" and claims Dibon as the very center of his kingdom. In the narrative, the rest of Moab seems to be ranked in terms of its need to be tamed based on its relative distance from Dibon (Routledge 2000, 2004: 133–53). We might accordingly conclude that Moabite was actually a prestige language based on the local variety of Dibon. Prestige languages are varieties selected by centering institutions for use in contexts such as commerce, administration, and education (Fishman 1972: 286–93; Polak 2006: 592). By contrast, Mesha is actively resisting the political program of Israel. Viewed in this light, the use of some apparently local features in the writing – for example, the Gt stem *w'lthm* "and I made war" (line 11) or masculine plural -*n*– suggests a resistance to other prestige varieties. If aspects of this languaging were indeed appropriated from Israelite, the incorporation of some unique features might imply that Moabite is actually an anti-language—a practice designed specifically for the purpose of resisting Israelite (Schniedewind 1999: 239). Mesha's ideology of Moabite independence from Israel is performed by the Moabite language itself.

A similar political function can be seen in the use of Aramaic in the Tel Dan Stele (Figure 25.3). This was a royal monument erected at Tel Dan by the Aramaean king Hazael in the late 9th century BCE. Its inscription is an apology of Hazael legitimating his rule in Dan (Knapp 2015: 277–300; Suriano 2007). Tel Dan was one of the northernmost cities historically associated with the kingdom of Israel. Hazael conquered it and used his inscription to explicitly narrate having killed the king of Israel as well as the king of Judah (here called *bytdwd* "the House of David" in line 9). It was later recaptured by the Israelites, who summarily destroyed Hazael's inscription, demonstrating its continued relevance to processes of political formation (Hogue 2021b). This inscription can tell us essentially nothing about

Figure 25.3 Tel Dan Stele. Photo by Gary Todd

the speech community at Tel Dan, but it serves as a key example of languaging to propose a particular ideology.

Like the Mesha Stele, this is another example of monumental writing. In particular, inscriptions like those found at Tel Dan were erected in newly acquired cities to propose social structures relative to political centers elsewhere (Green 2010: 164–66; Hogue 2019b: 96–97). The Tel Dan stele was strategically erected at a newly conquered city in Israel to project a Damascene perspective into that space, thus reconfiguring it as Aramaean territory. The use of Aramaic on the stele, then, does not represent an attempt to accommodate a local speech community, but the proposition of Aramaean ideology in formerly non-Aramaean territory.

The use of Aramaic on the Tel Dan Stele serves as a concrete example of a prestige language developing in connection to a polity-centered ideology. It is reasonable to suspect that the so-called "national languages" of Israel, Judah, Aram, Moab, Ammon, and Edom did originally derive from local varieties, probably those favored by speech communities in the primary urban centers of these polities (Parker 2002: 44). But these varieties were co-opted as "a medium for top-down genres of sovereignty" (Sanders 2009: 105). They were not deployed to maximize understanding among a particular speech community, but rather these "first deliberate vernaculars are royal tools" (Sanders 2009: 106). These were used in order to propose a territorial language—probably one that did not exist prior to this instantiation—in tandem with a particular political identity (Sanders 2009: 118).

The Rise and Fall of Standard Israelite

The resources utilized in Israelite writing first appeared in the 9th century, but the trajectories of these resources were quite different from the examples considered above. Most notably, none of the 9th-century inscriptions from Israel suggest the political use of language to enact territorial ideologies—that is, standardization. A fragment of an inscribed stele discovered at Samaria demonstrates the use of monumental writing in ancient Israel, but non-royal elites were also known to erect monumental steles in royal cities so this cannot be taken as definitive evidence for standardization (Figure 25.4; Gilibert 2011: 96). The 9th century monumental stone bowls from Kuntillet Ajrud show consistent Israelite spelling (as seen in the consistent use of the theophoric -*yw* in names such as ʿ*bdyw*, *šmʿyw*, and *ḥlyw*) and letter forms approaching those of the later Israelite script, but they only explicitly identify non-royal brokers (Ahituv, Eshel, and Meshel 2015: 75–78; Meshel, Carmi, and Segal 1995; Schniedewind 2017).

Some small finds from the 9th century may provide circumstantial evidence for royally brokered writing. A potential "administrative center" uncovered in Jerusalem attests 170 clay bullae with seal impressions as well as other artifacts suggestive of administrative practices, such as a calendrical device used to count days. Though uncovered in Jerusalem, the excavators proposed that this center might have been established after the Omride princess Athaliah married into the Judahite royal family. This office may have been used to send and receive letters from Samaria as well as urban centers in Phoenicia, but no writing was found on any of the associated artifacts (Reich, Shukron, and Lernau 2007: 156–63). Further north, a storage jar found at Tell el-Hammah is inscribed with the name ʾ*ḥʾb* "Ahab," but the lack of title or patronymic makes it impossible to determine whether this refers to the Omride king (Aḥituv and Mazar 2016: 235). A stamp seal is known that may be inscribed with the name of Ahab's queen Jezebel (Avigad and Sass 1997: 275). The date of this seal is contested, however, because it is unprovenanced and the relationship between its iconography and inscription is unusual and permits multiple interpretations (Korpel 2008; Rollston 2009).

Figure 25.4 Fragmentary stele from Samaria. Photo by Gary Todd

Lemaire is probably correct to note that the narratives of political catastrophes in 9th century Israel and Judah presented in the Aramaean, Moabite, and biblical texts reflect a real period of instability that prevented standardized languaging akin to that of Aram and Moab (Lemaire 2007: 298). This did not prevent local elites from brokering languaging practices, however.

Perhaps the best example of localized languaging in 9th century Israel is the corpus from Tel Reḥov: a site in the Beth-Shean Valley. These inscriptions are short and essentially provide no analyzable verbal resources. The only possible exception to this is an inscription on a storage jar that may read *lšqy nmš* "(belonging) to the cupbearers of Nimshi." If this reading is correct, it preserves the Aramaic word for cupbearer as opposed to the expected Israelite form *mšqh* (Aḥituv and Mazar 2016: 216; Bloch 2017: 88–90). The other peculiarity in this inscription is that the fourth letter is a hitherto unknown form of the letter *yod*. Unique letter forms have been identified in at least two other inscriptions from this site, testifying to a localized scribal practice (Schniedewind 2005: 408–89). The broker of this inscription, Nimshi, is also mentioned in an inscription found in an apiary at Tel Rehov and on a storage jar from Tel Amal, but these inscriptions exhibit more archaic script features than the cupbearer inscription (Aḥituv and Mazar 2016, 45; Mazar 2018, 46). A diachronic analysis of written languaging at Tel Reḥov reveals localized developments in script, consistent brokering by non-royal elites in different periods, and perhaps the co-option of the prestige verbal resources of Aram.

Mazar suggests that Nimshi was a merchant or merchant-clan that traded honey, and that this figure is perhaps to be identified with the eponymous ancestor of Israel's Nimshide dynasty. This identification is attractive given the co-occurrence at the site of a display inscription in a cultic building brokered by a religious leader named Elisha. Incidentally, Tel Reḥov is immediately north of Abel Meholah: the birth place of the biblical prophet Elisha, who was active during this period and was instrumental in orchestrating the Nimshide coup (2 Kgs 9:1–3) (Aḥituv and Mazar 2016: 48–50). If the Nimshide kings were in fact related to the broker(s) at Tel Reḥov, perhaps they brought earlier elite attitudes toward writing with them to Samaria, where they developed Israel's first standardized languaging practice (Sass 2005: 59).

Israelite: The Hegemony of Samaria

One of the earliest and largest samples of standardized Israelite writing are the Samaria Ostraca. These 102 ostraca record the movement of prestige items under the auspices of an 8th-century Israelite king, now usually identified as Jeroboam II. The Samaria Ostraca attest to a community of scribes in the employ of the Israelite monarchy at its central city, but this community may have been surprisingly small. A recent study applied algorithmic handwriting analysis to these artifacts. This forensic method combines image processing with machine learning to distinguish between different samples of handwriting and thus determine how many writers were responsible. Algorithmic handwriting analysis of 31 of the legible ostraca strongly suggests that they were produced by only two scribes (Faigenbaum-Golovin et al. 2020). The restricted number of scribes active in this administrative operation suggests that the Samarian scribes were an elite and contained group. As pivots for Israelite writing, this elite group played a significant role in restricting access to the technical skills necessary to produce Israelite writing.

Nam (2013) analyzes the Samaria Ostraca as recording gifts of aged wine and fine oil from the Israelite royal family to clan leaders within 5–12 km of the city. These gifts demonstrated the power of the Israelite king not only through his possession of such goods but also through his successful control of the labor necessary to procure them. Furthermore, these gifts increased the king's prestige and hegemony over the recipient clans. Nam argues that the Samaria Ostraca's lack of values for these goods implies a gift exchange that did not entail reciprocity in kind. Rather, the king gained social capital by offering gifts to clan leaders that they could not procure for themselves. These gifts thus created asymmetrical political and economic ties between the king and these elites. These elites could in turn promote submission to the Israelite king in the regions adjacent to their clans.[1] This function of buttressing regional hegemony should factor into our understanding of the trajectories of linguistic features in these texts.

The ostraca demonstrate and indeed project the Israelite king's ability to harness scarce material resources, labor, and social capital. Therefore, it is highly likely that the verbal resources of these ostraca reflect the prestige language of the Israelite court. The purpose of writing these ostraca was to project the Israelite king's hegemony over nearby clans and to extend his power to even further regions. This languaging performs an ideology of Israelite identity by tying these groups and regions together under a single ruler in Samaria. This same purpose holds for other major examples of Israelite writing, but I will focus on one of the most informative—the inscriptions from Kuntillet Ajrud.

The inscriptions at Kuntillet Ajrud must be considered in light of the site's political and economic function. The site is in northeastern Sinai 15 km west of the Darb el-Ghazza—the western branch of the Arabian trade route leading to the Mediterranean Sea. The script and linguistic features of the ink inscriptions on pottery are remarkably consistent with those of Samaria, despite the location of Kuntillet Ajrud far to the south. The inscriptions even explicitly mention Samaria in blessing formulae (Schniedewind 2019: 33). The site fits into a growing picture of Israel's expansion under Jeroboam II. The Nimshides were transforming

Israel into an empire at this time. In addition to Kuntillet Ajrud, archaeological evidence points to Israel's presence at Tell el-Kheleifeh and Kadesh Barnea to control more nodes on the western branch of the Darb el-Ghazza. Furthermore, Jeroboam II captured nodes on the eastern branch of the route along the King's Highway in Transjordan, and he may have even imposed vassalage on Ammon, Moab, and Edom. Judah also seems to have become an Israelite vassal during this time, with the kings Amaziah and Uzziah acting as Jeroboam's proxies (Finkelstein 2020). Kuntillet Ajrud was one piece of this burgeoning imperial program.

Though originally interpreted as cultic in nature, Schniedewind has offered a more compelling interpretation of the ink inscriptions on pottery at Kuntillet Ajrud as examples of scribal curriculum. These inscriptions consist of partial abecedaries, numerical exercises, lexical lists, practice letters for learning epistolary conventions, and even exercises in literary composition. These inscriptions are written in both red and black ink, each corresponding to different hands. The black ink inscriptions are more rudimentary, reflecting the writing of students. The red ink inscriptions are more sophisticated, and these appear to represent the corrections or models set down by a master scribe (Schniedewind 2019: 23–48).

The use of Israel's prestige language, the location of the site near the Darb el-Ghazza, and its place within Jeroboam's larger imperial strategy all point to the teaching of writing here as a means of extending a pro-Samaria ideology to the south. This writing—and especially the apparent training of new scribes—indicate the enactment of Israelite territoriality in this region. As in the case of Tel Dan, this does not reflect the practices of a local speech community in the south but the performance of Israelite hegemony by means of standardized languaging.

Judahite: New Trajectories for Israelite Writing in Jerusalem

In Judah before the late 8th century, there are no identifiably "Hebrew" inscriptions—that is, texts utilizing the Samarian script and linguistic features otherwise known from Israelite texts or the biblical corpus (Finkelstein and Silberman 2006: 263; Fleming 2012: 302–23). The most important early inscriptions that might be examples of Judahite writing are the ostraca from Tel Arad in the Beer Sheba Valley (Figure 25.5). The dating of the inscriptions at Tel Arad is entangled in the high-low chronology debate, but both groups agree that the ostraca from Stratums XI and X date before Hezekiah. Unfortunately, these early ostraca preserve no verbal resources, and their paleography is problematic for typologies assuming the unified development of Hebrew. Arad 67, for example, was originally dated to the 9th century based on stratigraphy at the site, and aspects of its script—especially the letters *aleph* and *kaph*—may corroborate this date. However, the excavators dated the inscription paleographically to the late 8th century based on other peculiarities (Schniedewind 2005: 409–10). It is worth noting that Arad 67 is the only potentially early ostracon from the site that includes a *-yhw* theophoric, which would be the only definitively Judahite aspect of its writing. If the inscription is from the 9th century, then it may be taken as evidence of the early development of some Judahite writing practices independent of Israelite.

Regardless of how we interpret Arad 67, features of the Arad ostraca that resemble Israelite writing may simply be evidence of Israelite hegemony in the south. Judah was an Israelite vassal in the 9th and early 8th centuries, and some of the pottery at the Israelite fort at Kuntillet Ajrud has been shown to originate in the Beer Sheba Valley (Gunneweg, Perlman, and Meshel 1985; Na'aman 2017: 88–89). It is logical to assume that the Israelites would attempt to control the Beer Sheba Valley as part of their larger economic strategy under the Nimshide dynasty, but the nature of this control is currently unknown (Daniels 2020;

Figure 25.5 Arad letter, 6th century BCE. Photo by Gary Todd

Tebes 2018: 178–81). Perhaps they merely utilized pre-existing garrisons in the region to protect their own interests. Other early examples of writing from Judah bear out this understanding of Israelite hegemony driving their languaging practices.

Two unprovenanced seals mention the Judahite king Uzziah (ca. 783–742 BCE) and may evidence scribal activity in Jerusalem prior to the fall of Israel. The seals read as follows:

lšbnyw ʿ
bd ʿzyw
"Belonging to Shebanyaw, servant of Uzziyaw"
l'byw ʿbd
ʿzyw
"Belonging to Abiyaw, servant of Uzziyaw"

(Avigad and Sass 1997: 50–51)

Notably, every name in these seals—including that of the Judahite king—is spelled using the Israelite theophoric *yw* rather than the expected Judahite *yhw*. Because Uzziah is a known Judahite figure, this is likely not reflective of a dialectal difference or ethnic affiliation in this case. Rather, this reflects the position of Uzziah and Judah as a vassal to Jeroboam II. The languaging of Judahite elites at this time was apparently that of Israel—their suzerain. The imposition of a written language on a vassal is not an unknown practice in the Levant. Only a few decades later, King Bar-Rakib of Samʿal adopted Aramaic in deference to his Assyrian suzerain, even though Samʿalian was still a viable option (Hogue 2022). While the spoken varieties of Jerusalem and Samaria likely shared some similarities, this example is not evidence of shared linguistic features. The writing of names was especially wrapped up in processes of identity formation, and yet here these Judahite elites forgo their native theophoric to accept a prescription from Samaria (Schniedewind 2019: 33). The broker of this writing was the Israelite king and so the prescriptions evidenced here accommodate those of Samaria and astoundingly resist the expected practice of Jerusalem. This Samarian influence would continue to operate even after Israel's fall.

Israel was conquered and incorporated piecemeal into the Assyrian empire between 732 and 722 BCE. Around the same time, Judah experienced a great leap forward. The population of the polity doubled, the population of Jerusalem alone increased by a factor of 10, and economic, technological, and political advancements transformed Judah (Finkelstein 1999). These changes have often been explained by the possible immigration of Israelite refugees to the south (Burke 2012: 279–80; Finkelstein and Silberman 2006: 261–65). This is corroborated by seals from Jerusalem and its environs attesting Israelite names written in the Israelite script. For example, multiple seal impressions bearing the name *mnḥm bn ywbnh* "Menaḥem son of Yobana" have been found at Jerusalem, Tell el-Judeideh, Beth Shemesh, Ramat Raḥel, Lachish, and Gibeon (Avigad and Sass 1997: 248–49). Not only was this individual's name shared with an Israelite king, but his father's name also clearly uses the Israelite theophoric *yw* rather than the Judahite *yhw*. These seals and others like them suggest that some Israelite refugees or their children rose to high office in Judah after the fall of Samaria. These individuals undoubtedly facilitated the transfer of Israelite technologies, such as the stone olive press already known from 9th and 8th century Israel but which first appeared in Judah during this period (Finkelstein and Silberman 2006: 265–69). The appearance of Israelite writing in Judah during this time is just this sort of technology transfer. It demonstrates the movement of Israelite scribes and their conventions to Judah.

One final seal is worth considering regarding the transfer of Israelite scribal practice to Judah. A seal found in Beth Shemesh reads *lʾlyqm nʿr ywkn* "belonging to Elyaqim, Apprentice of Yawkin" (Avigad and Sass 1997: 243). While this individual's name is not identifiably Israelite or Judahite, his master's name includes the Israelite theophoric *yw*. This reveals that an Israelite administrator trained this figure—possibly a scribe—and also that this relationship was considered important enough to appear on a seal in place of the expected patronymic. Israelite refugees had brought Israel's administrative and scribal practices to Judah, and social connections to these individuals apparently came with significant prestige. The refugees were the initial pivots of Judahite writing. In essence, the Israelites taught the Judahites to write in "Hebrew" or more accurately Israelite. Whatever writing practices may have existed in Judah prior to this point, they were completely transformed by this interaction. The result was the accommodation of Israelite writing to the linguistic features of the speech community in Jerusalem. This led to the development of a new written language—Judahite.

The end of the 8th century and the beginning of the 7th century was apparently a period of languaging diversity in Judah. This can be seen most clearly in the Siloam Tunnel Inscription (Figure 25.6). This inscription describes the cutting of a tunnel used to bring water

Language in Israel and Judah: A Sociolinguistic Reappraisal

Figure 25.6 Siloam Tunnel Inscription (replica in the Israel Museum). Photo by Gary Todd

into Jerusalem in the late 8th century. Rendsburg and Schniedewind (2010) have argued that the inscription contains at least three dialectal features of Israelite (Israelian Hebrew in their terminology) that are distinct from Judahite. These are the forms *rʿw* "his fellow" and *hyt* "it (fem. sing.) was" and the lexeme *mwṣʾ* "water source." They conclude that the scribe was an Israelite who utilized features of his native spoken variety in the inscription.

The fact that the Siloam Tunnel Inscription preserves dialectal features of Israelite is less surprising than the fact that the Judahite brokers of the inscription allowed this. The creation of this tunnel was a major undertaking that must have been commissioned by a powerful elite with a lot of capital. Even though this elite is never named in the inscription, it is highly likely that the scribe was hired by the same individual who commissioned the tunnel. There is little reason to doubt the Hebrew Bible's identification of this broker as Hezekiah (2 Kgs 20:20; 2 Chr 32:30). We thus see an Israelite pivot working for a Judahite broker, but one who was in this case unconcerned with prescribing the use of particular verbal resources. This may serve as an example that the choice of verbal resources can be motivated by other semiotic resources, in this case space and light. The Siloam Tunnel Inscription was carved six meters from the tunnel's outlet within the tunnel itself. It would therefore have been unreadable in antiquity unless the reader knew the location of the inscription and brought a sufficient light source. In cases like this, writing was executed to communicate visually but not necessarily verbally, and so Israelite verbal resources were not proscribed in its execution (Smoak and Mandell 2017).

Even though the writing was produced as part of a civil project in Jerusalem, in the dark Samaria could continue to wield influence from beyond the grave, as it were. This recalls Bar-Rakib's use of the old prestige language Samʾalian in an inscription (Figure 25.7) erected outside of his city, even though he had switched to Aramaic in his public display

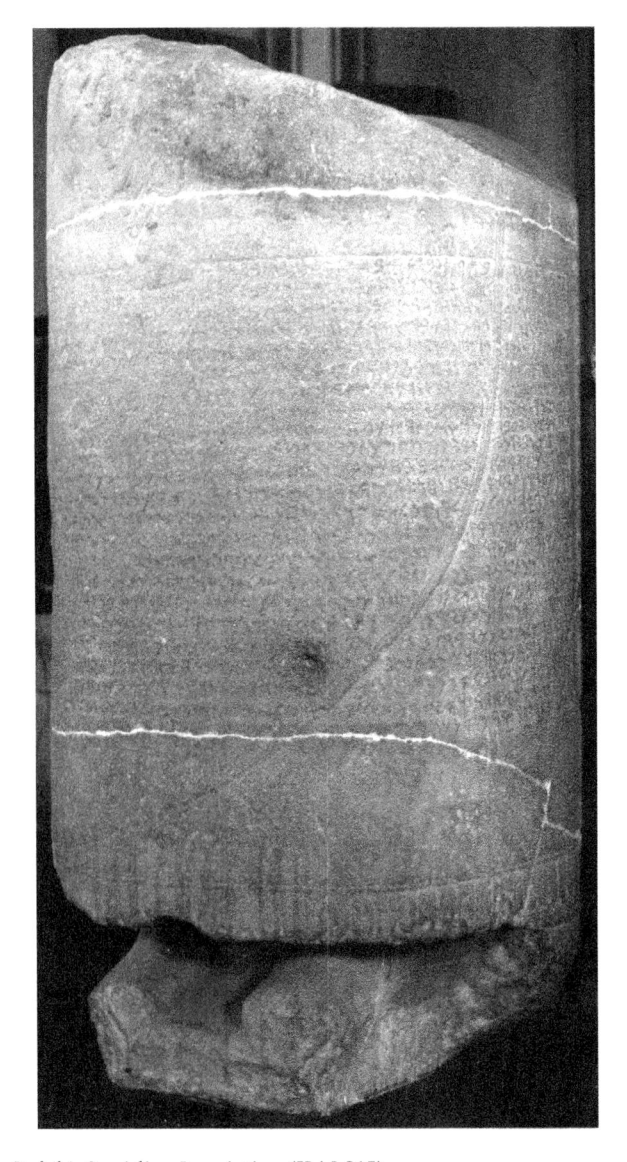

Figure 25.7 Bar-Rakib's Sam'alian Inscription (KAI 215)

inscriptions (Hogue 2022). Similar codeswitching is apparent in Jerusalem during the same period.

The appropriation of Israelite resources to develop a new Judahite languaging practice is apparent in the Royal Steward Inscription (Figure 25.8). If the reconstruction of the name in this inscription as *šbnyhw* "Shebnayahu" and the identification of this figure with Isaiah 22:15–19's Shebna is correct, then this was the royal steward of Hezekiah, and the inscription must date to the same period as the Siloam Tunnel Inscription.[2]

This is an exquisitely executed monumental display inscription, attesting to the concerted work of an expert scribe and stonemason. Most notably, the script is a lapidary style that is unattested up to this point in Judah but known from Samaria (Rollston 2010: 55). Even the

Figure 25.8 The Shebna (or Royal Steward) Inscription, 7th century BC. Museum no.: 125205 © The Trustees of the British Museum

Siloam Tunnel Inscription made use of a more cursive-style script (Smoak and Mandell 2019: 320–27). This lapidary style required not only specific technical knowledge but also a very specific set of iron chisels to execute correctly (Keimer 2015). The script and the tools and skills necessary for executing it must have been transmitted to Judah by Israelite scribes and artisans, but the inscription attests no Israelite linguistic features. As in the Siloam Tunnel Inscription, the sociotechnical resources derive from elsewhere, but the verbal resources now reflect those of the inscription's Judahite broker.

The ensuing century witnessed the flowering of Judahite as a true standard like those of Israel, Moab, and Aram. The script shows signs of transition at the end of the 8th century, before taking on a form more distinct from its Israelite precursor in the 7th (Rollston 2010: 98–103). We also find a wealth of inscriptions from a large number of sites, suggesting a high level of literacy (Shaus et al. 2020: 10). The uniformity of the inscriptions undoubtedly reflects the high degree of centralization in Judah during this period (Fleming 2012: 18). The Arad letters from the turn of the 6th century provide one example of this. This fortress attests writing produced by at least 12 different scribes based on algorithmic handwriting analysis of only 18 inscriptions (Shaus et al. 2020). This is an amazing development from the two scribes of the Samaria Ostraca two centuries earlier. This substantial number of scribes at a single site along with the considerable number of inscriptions from this period demonstrates the remarkable success of scribal education under the aegis of the Judahite court. We must recall that such uniformity of writing suggests a strong accommodation of centering institutions, not a widespread speech area. The texts at Arad, for instance, attest to a complex hierarchy headed by the Judahite king (Shaus et al. 2020: 9–10). The use of an apparently standardized Judahite writing in these inscriptions was one means of reifying this hierarchy.

Conclusions: The Social Prehistory of Hebrew

Every example of written language from ancient Israel and Judah required manifold resources. Linguistic features were caught up with technical skill and training, materials, tools, labor, and the economic and political structures that afforded and constrained all of these. Writing is thus always performed with particular functions and goals in mind. It always involves choices about what matters and what does not, about what is appropriate and what is not. It is never the expression of an abstract, pre-existing grammar separate from any particular social context. Approaches to writing in ancient Israel must always keep such social factors at the forefront of their analyses to avoid reductionistic and anachronistic assumptions about their character. Sociolinguistics allows us to refocus our inquiry from the *languages* of

Israel and Judah to their *languaging*. This makes it possible to treat ancient Israelite and Judahite languaging as dynamic and constantly evolving social practices without reducing them to their linguistic features alone.

While ancient Israel and Judah attest a diverse set of languaging practices, none were more successful than Israelite and Judahite. The widespread use of Israelite attests to the success of its scribal education and political organization. Israelite was so influential a practice that it even survived the demise of the kingdom of Israel when it was transmitted to Judah by refugees and there appropriated by local elites. In this new center, Israelite scribal practice was transformed into a new written language—Judahite. While Judah would never be as politically successful as Israel, the highly centralized polity facilitated the creation of a remarkably successful educational apparatus. This made Judahite into an even more widely attested practice than Israelite. All this came to a crashing halt at the beginning of the 6th century, however. As the Babylonians decimated Judah and deported much of its population, Judahite writing essentially died (Schniedewind 2004: 139–47, 2013: 126–33). Despite this, many of the linguistic and literary resources of Israel and Judah were appropriated later, but along quite different trajectories in new social networks. It was from within this continuing cycle of reappropriations that Hebrew and the modern study of its antecedents emerged.

Notes

1 A similar function is actually attested for the distribution of wine to Israelite emissaries by the Assyrians during this same period (Aster 2016).
2 This identification is based on the similarity of the two names and the prophet's rebuke of Shebna for constructing a lavish tomb (Suriano 2018: 108–11 with references).

Bibliography

Ahituv, Shmuel, Esther Eshel, and Zeev Meshel. 2015. "The Inscriptions." Pages 71–121 in *Kuntillet 'Ajrud: An Iron Age II Religious Site on the Judah-Sinai Border*. Edited by Ze'ev Meshel. Jerusalem: Israel Exploration Society.

Ahituv, Shmuel, and Amihai Mazar. 2016. "The Inscriptions from Tel Reḥov and Their Contribution to the Study of Script and Writing During Iron Age IIA." *Maarav* 20: 205–46.

Aster, Shawn Zelig. 2016. "Israelite Embassies to Assyria in the First Half of the Eight Century." *Biblica* 97: 175–98.

Avigad, Nahman, and Benjamin Sass. 1997. *Corpus of West Semitic Stamp Seals*. Jerusalem: Israel Academy of Sciences and Humanities.

Bloch, Yigal. 2017. "Aramaic Influence and Inner Diachronic Development in Hebrew Inscriptions of the Iron Age." Pages 833–112 in *Advances in Biblical Hebrew Linguistics: Data, Methods, Analyses*. Edited by Adina Moshavi and Tania Notarius. Winona Lake: Eisenbrauns.

Blommaert, Jan. 2016. "From Mobility to Complexity in Sociolinguistic Theory and Method." Pages 242–59 in *Sociolinguistics: Theoretical Debates*. Edited by Nikolas Coupland. Cambridge: Cambridge University Press.

Bottineau, Didlier. 2010. "Language and Enaction." Pages 267–306 in *Enaction: Toward a New Paradigm for Cognitive Science*. Edited by John Stewart, Olivier Gaprenne, and Ezequiel Di Paolo. Cambridge: MIT Press.

Burke, Aaron A. 2012. "Coping with the Effects of War: Refugees in the Levant During the Bronze and Iron Ages." Page 263–88 in *Disaster and Relief Management: Katastrophen Und Ihre Bewältigung*. Edited by Angelika Berlejung. Tübingen: Mohr Siebeck.

———. 2020. "Left Behind: New Kingdom Specialists at the End of Egyptian Empire and the Emergence of Israelite Scribalism." Pages 50–56 in *"An Excellent Fortress for His Armies, a Refuge for the People": Egyptological, Archaeological, and Biblical Studies in Honor of James K. Hoffmeier*. Edited by R. E. Averbeck and K. Lawson Younger Jr. University Park: Eisenbrauns.

Byrne, Ryan. 2007. "The Refuge of Scribalism in Iron I Palestine." *BASOR* 345: 1–31.

Coulmas, Florian. 1989. *The Writing Systems of the World*. Oxford: Blackwell.
Daniels, Quinn. 2020. "The Activity of the Kingdom of Israel South of Judah." Paper presented at the annual meeting of ASOR. November 21, 2020.
Dever, William G. 2021. "Solomon, Scripture, and Science: The Rise of the Judahite State in the 10th Century BCE." *JJAR* 1: 102–25.
Donnelly-Lewis, Brian. 2021. "The Khirbet Qeiyafa Ostracon: A New Collation and Translation on the Basis of the Multispectral Images." Paper presented at the annual meeting of SBL. San Antonio, November 2021.
Faigenbaum-Golovin, Shira, Arie Shaus, Barak Sober, Eli Turkel, Eli Piasetzky, and Israel Finkelstein. 2020. "Algorithmic Handwriting Analysis of the Samaria Inscriptions Illuminates Bureaucratic Apparatus in Biblical Israel." *PLoS ONE* 15: e0227452. Online: doi.org/10.1371/journal.pone.0227452.
Finkelstein, Israel. 1999. "State Formation in Israel and Judah: A Contrast in Context, a Contrast in Trajectory." *NEA* 62: 35–52.
———. 2020. "Jeroboam II in Transjordan." *SJOT* 34: 19–29.
Finkelstein, Israel, and Neil Asher Silberman. 2006. "Temple and Dynasty: Hezekiah, the Remaking of Judah and the Rise of the Pan-Israelite Ideology." *JSOT* 30: 259–85.
Fishman, Joshua A. 1970. *Sociolinguistics: A Brief Introduction*. Rowley: Newbury House.
———. 1972. *The Sociology of Language: An Interdisciplinary Social Science Approach to Language in Society*. Rowley: Newbury House.
Fleming, Daniel E. 2012. *The Legacy of Israel in Judah's Bible: History, Politics, and the Reinscribing of Tradition*. Cambridge: Cambridge University Press.
Gahrn-Andersen, Rasmus. 2019. "But Language Too Is Material!" *Phenomenology and the Cognitive Sciences* 18: 169–83.
Garfinkel, Yosef, Katharina Streit, Saar Ganor, and Paula J. Reimer. 2015. "King David's City at Khirbet Qeiyafa: Results of the Second Radiocarbon Dating Project." *Radiocarbon* 57: 881–90.
Garr, W. Randall. 2004. *Dialect Geography of Syria-Palestine 1000–586 BCE*. Winona Lake: Eisenbrauns.
Gilibert, Alessandra. 2011. *Syro-Hittite Monumental Art and the Archaeology of Performance: The Stone Reliefs at Carchemish and Zincirli in the Earlier First Millennium BCE*. Berlin: de Gruyter.
Green, Douglas J. 2010. *"I Undertook Great Works": The Ideology of Domestic Achievements in West Semitic Royal Inscriptions*. Tübingen: Mohr Siebeck.
Gunneweg, Jan, Isadore Perlman, and Zeev Meshel. 1985. "The Origin of the Pottery of Kuntillet 'Ajrud." *IEJ* 35: 270–83.
Heidegger, Martin. 1982. *On the Way to Language*. New York: Harper & Row.
Hodder, Ian, and Angus Mol. 2016. "Network Analysis and Entanglement." *JAMT* 23: 1066–94.
Hogue, Timothy. 2019a. "The Eternal Monument of the Divine King: Monumentality, Reembodiment, and Social Formation in the Decalogue." PhD diss., University of California, Los Angeles.
———. 2019b. "The Monumentality of the Sinaitic Decalogue: Reading Exodus 20 in Light of Northwest Semitic Monument-Making Practices." *JBL* 138: 79–99.
———. 2021a. "Thinking Through Monuments: Levantine Monuments as Technologies of Community-Scale Motivated Social Cognition." *CAJ* 31: 1–17.
———. 2022. "In the Midst of Great Kings and Small Finds: The Transmission of Monumental Discourse at Iron Age Sam'al." *MTC* 1: 14–54.
———. 2021b. "With Apologies to Hazael: Theater, Spectacle, and Counter-Monumentality at Tel Dan." In *Ritual Space and Ritual Text: New Perspectives on Monumentality and Monumental Texts in the Southern Levant*. Edited by Jeremy D. Smoak, Alice Mandell, and Lisa Joann Cleath. Tübingen: Mohr Siebeck. pp. 243–256
Hutchins, Edwin. 2005. "Material Anchors for Conceptual Blends." *Journal of Pragmatics* 37: 1555–77.
Irvine, Judith T., and Susan Gal. 2000. "Language Ideology and Linguistic Differentiation." Pages 35–83 in *Regimes of Language: Ideologies, Polities, and Identities*. Edited by P. Kroskrity. Santa Fe: School of American Research Press.
Keimer, Kyle H. 2015. "The Impact of Ductus on Script Form and Development in Monumental Northwest Semitic Inscriptions." *UF* 46: 189–212.
———. 2021. "Evaluating the 'United Monarchy' of Israel: Unity and Identity in Text and Archaeology." *JJAR* 1: 68–101.
Knapp, Andrew. 2015. *Royal Apologetic in the Ancient Near East*. Atlanta: SBL.
Korpel, Marjo C. A. 2008. "Queen Jezebel's Seal." *UF* 38: 379–98.

Labov, William. 1994. *Principles of Linguistic Change, Volume 1: Internal Factors*. Language in Society. Malden: Wiley-Blackwell.

———. 2001. *Principles of Linguistic Change, Volume 2: Social Factors*. Language in Society. Malden: Wiley-Blackwell.

———. 2010. *Principles of Linguistic Change, Volume 3: Cognitive and Cultural Factors*. Language in Society. Malden: Wiley-Blackwell.

Lemaire, André. 1994. "'House of David' Restored in Moabite Inscription." *BAR* 20: 30–37.

———. 2007. "West Semitic Inscriptions and Ninth-Century BCE Ancient Israel." Pages 279–303 in *Understanding the History of Ancient Israel*. Edited by H. G. M. Williamson. Oxford: Oxford University Press.

Lillis, Theresa. 2013. *The Sociolinguistics of Writing*. Edinburgh: Edinburgh University Press.

Mazar, Amihai. 2018. "The Iron Age Apiary at Tel Reḥov, Israel." Pages 4–49 in *Beekeeping in the Mediterranean—From Antiquity to the Present*. Edited by Fani Hatjina, Georgios Mavrofridis, and Richard Jones. Greece: Nea Moudania.

———. 2021. "The Beth Shean Valley and Its Vicinity in the 10th Century BCE." *JJAR* 1: 241–71.

Meshel, Zeev, Israel Carmi, and Dror Segal. 1995. "^{14}C Dating of an Israelite Biblical Site at Kuntillet Ajrud (Horvat Teman)." *Radiocarbon* 37: 205–12.

Millard, Alan. 2011. "The Ostracon from the Days of David Found at Khirbet Qeiyafa." *TynBul* 62: 1–13.

Na'aman, Nadav. 2017. "In Search of the Temples of YHWH of Samaria and YHWH of Teman." *JANER* 17: 76–95.

Nam, Roger. 2013. "Economics and the Bible." Pages 259–67 in *The Oxford Encyclopedia of Biblical Interpretation*. Edited by S. McKenzie and David Garber, Jr. Oxford: Oxford University Press.

Naveh, Joseph. 1987. *Early History of the Alphabet: An Introduction to West Semitic Epigraphy and Paleography*. Jerusalem: Magnes Press.

Ong, Walter J. 1992. "Writing Is a Technology That Restructures Thought." Pages 293–320 in *The Linguistics of Literacy*. Edited by Pamela A. Downing, Susan D. Lima, and Michael Noonan. Amsterdam: John Benjamins.

Ortiz, Steven M., and Samuel R. Wolff. 2012. "Guarding the Border to Jerusalem: The Iron Age City of Gezer." *NEA* 75: 4–19.

———. 2021. "New Evidence for the 10th Century BCE at Tel Gezer." *JJAR* 1: 221–40.

Osborne, James F. 2013. "Sovereignty and Territoriality in the City-State: A Case Study from the Amuq Valley, Turkey." *JAA* 32: 774–90.

Pardee, Dennis. 2013. "A Brief Case for Phoenician as the Language of the 'Gezer Calendar.'" Pages 226–46 in *Linguistic Studies in Phoenician*. Edited by Robert D. Homstedt and Aaron Schade. Winona Lake: Eisenbrauns.

Parker, Simon B. 2002. "Ammonite, Edomite, and Moabite." Pages 43–60 in *Beyond Babel: A Handbook for Biblical Hebrew and Related Languages*. Edited by John Kaltner and Steven L. McKenzie. Atlanta: SBL.

Polak, Frank H. 2006. "Sociolinguistics and the Judean Speech Community in the Achaemenid Empire." Pages 589–628 in *Judah and the Judeans in the Persian Period*. Edited by Oded Lipschitz and Manfred Oeming. Winona Lake: Eisenbrauns.

Reich, Ronny, Eli Shukron, and Omri Lernau. 2007. "Recent Discoveries in the City of David, Jerusalem." *IEJ* 57: 153–69.

Rendsburg, Gary A., and William M. Schniedewind. 2010. "The Siloam Tunnel Inscription: Historical and Linguistic Perspectives." *IEJ* 60: 188–203.

Rollston, Christopher A. 2009. "Prosopography and the YZBL Seal." *IEJ* 59: 86–91.

Rollston, Christopher A. 2010. *Writing and Literacy in the World of Ancient Israel: Epigraphic Evidence from the Iron Age*. Atlanta: SBL.

Routledge, Bruce. 2000. "The Politics of Mesha: Segmented Identities and State Formation in Iron Age Moab." *JESHO* 43: 221–56.

———. 2004. *Moab in the Iron Age: Hegemony, Polity, Archaeology*. Archaeology, Culture, and Society. Philadelphia: University of Pennsylvania Press.

Sanders, Seth. 2009. *The Invention of Hebrew*. Urbana: University of Illinois Press.

Sass, Benjamin. 2005. *The Alphabet at the Turn of the Millennium: The West Semitic Alphabet CA. 1150–850 BCE—The Antiquity of the Arabian, Greek and Phrygian Alphabets*. Tel Aviv: Emery and Claire Yass Publications in Archaeology.

Schniedewind, William M. 1999. "Qumran Hebrew as an Antilanguage." *JBL* 118: 235–52.

———. 2004. *How the Bible Became a Book: The Textualization of Ancient Israel.* Cambridge: Cambridge University Press.

———. 2005. "Problems in the Paleographic Dating of Inscriptions." Pages 405–12 in *The Bible and Radiocarbon Dating: Archaeology, Text and Science.* Edited by Thomas E. Levy and Thomas Higham. London: Equinox.

———. 2013. *A Social History of Hebrew: Its Origins Through the Rabbinic Period.* New Haven: Anchor Yale Bible Reference Library.

———. 2017. "An Early Iron Age Phase to Kuntillet ʿAjrud?" Pages 134–46 in *Le-Maʿan Ziony: Essays in Honor of Ziony Zevit.* Edited by Frederick E. Greenspahn and Gary A. Rendsburg. Eugene: Cascade Books.

———. 2019. *The Finger of the Scribe: How Scribes Learned to Write the Bible.* Oxford: Oxford University Press.

Schwartz, Seth. 2005. "Hebrew and Imperialism in Jewish Palestine." Pages 53–84 in *Ancient Judaism in Its Hellenistic Context.* Edited by Carol Bakhos. Leiden: Brill.

Shafer, Ann. 2007. "Assyrian Royal Monuments on the Periphery: Ritual and the Making of Imperial Space." Pages 133–60 in *Ancient Near Eastern Art in Context.* Edited by Jack Cheng and Marian H. Feldman. Leiden: Brill.

Shaus, Arie, Yana Gerber, Shira Faigenbaum-Golovin, Barak Sober, Eli Piasetzky, and Israel Finkelstein. 2020. "Forensic Document Examination and Algorithmic Handwriting Analysis of Judahite Biblical Period Inscriptions Reveal Significant Literacy Level." *PLoS ONE* 15: e0237962. Online: doi.org/10.1371/journal.pone.0237962.

Smoak, Jeremy D., and Alice Mandell. 2017. "Reading and Writing in the Dark at Khirbet El-Qom: The Literacies of Ancient Subterranean Judah." *NEA* 80: 188–92.

———. 2019. "Texts in the City: Monumental Inscriptions in Jerusalem's Urban Landscape." Pages 309–44 in *Size Matters: Understanding Monumentality Across Ancient Civilizations.* Edited by Federico Buccellati, Sebastian Hageneuer, Sylva van der Heyden, and Felix Levenson. Bielefeld: Verlag.

Suriano, Matthew. 2007. "The Apology of Hazael: A Literary and Historical Analysis of the Tel Dan Inscription." *JNES* 66: 163–76.

———. 2018. *A History of Death in the Hebrew Bible.* Oxford: Oxford University Press.

Tebes, Juan Manuel. 2018. "The Southern Home of YHWH and Pre-Priestly Patriarchal/Exodus Traditions from a Southern Perspective." *Biblica* 99: 166–88.

Young, Ian. 1993. *Diversity in Pre-Exilic Hebrew.* Tübingen: Mohr Siebeck.

26
THE COMPOSITION OF THE HEBREW BIBLE

Process in the Production of Israelite Literature[1]

Joel S. Baden

Introduction

The Hebrew Bible, as an identifiable entity, comprises the Pentateuch, the historiographical work from Joshua-Kings known as the Deuteronomistic History, the major prophets Isaiah, Jeremiah, and Ezekiel, the minor prophets collected in what is called the Book of the Twelve, and the diverse collection of the Writings, which includes the poetic collections of Psalms, Lamentations, and Song of Songs, the wisdom books of Proverbs, Ecclesiastes, and Job, the narratives of Ruth, Esther, and Daniel, and the historiographical books of Ezra, Nehemiah, and Chronicles. In the preexilic period, virtually none of these existed in the form in which we now have it; certainly, none of the larger blocks was connected with any other. We thus cannot speak in any meaningful way of a preexilic Hebrew Bible; indeed, even over half a millennium later, there was still no fixed canon (see Mroczek 2016). Rather, we are dealing in this period with the building blocks, of various sizes and shapes, of what would eventually become the Hebrew Bible.

For the purposes of this overview, we will deal only with the production of written text. This is not at all to deny the existence of oral tradition in ancient Israel; on the contrary, as we will see, oral tradition formed the backbone of much of what would become proto-biblical literature. Our ability to describe and discuss orally generated and transmitted materials, however, is constrained by the obvious lack of data, not just about the content of oral tradition but also about its means of production and dissemination. Thus, as useful as the methods of tradition criticism and cultural memory are for explaining some of the phenomena we see in the Bible, they are so largely heuristically. Oral tradition is like the dark matter of Israelite literary production: its existence is required by the visible evidence—that is, the written text—but it is itself almost entirely inaccessible.

In a sense, the same can be said about the actual material production of texts in ancient Israel. Despite a spate of recent studies, we have no direct evidence for any aspect of Israelite scribal production in the preexilic period.[2] Instead, data from neighboring cultures are imported as a potential analogy to Israelite scribalism. While this data may be useful for determining likely parameters for scribal practice, it cannot be taken as a direct window on Israelite scribalism (Sanders 2017).[3] Of course, we must recognize that there was scribalism of some sort in Israel: individuals in the Bible are identified as professional scribes, scrolls are commanded to be written and copied, and reference is made to various written materials. All literary production in ancient Israel belonged to the elite literate classes and the scribal professionals attached to them.

A final caveat: in discussing the composition of the texts that would eventually make up the Hebrew Bible, we cannot—or at least should not—attribute texts to individual authors. This is true both for the authors putatively named in the texts themselves, such as Amos or Hosea, and for the presumptive unidentified authors and editors responsible for texts such as Deuteronomy or early collections of psalms, for example. Of course, we cannot deny that at some point an individual or group of individuals physically committed words to papyrus. Such figures are, however, lost to us, and attempts to identify them are primarily exercises in wishful thinking. Our interest in the question of authorship is not native to ancient Israel, and the desire to attach individual identities, whether named or not, to various literary compositions is mostly an expression of a modern need to align text with biography, with intent, and with the notion of the genius.

Thus, rather than speak of authors or editors, it is more appropriate and productive to refer to literary processes and functions. In important ways, this approach should mitigate some of the ongoing disputes that plague certain corners of biblical studies, particularly regarding the composition of the Pentateuch. While disagreements about the details of particular literary histories are endemic in the field, there remains broad agreement regarding the existence of base texts and the application of these various processes to them (Schmid 2011: 17–30). The pages that follow will outline and define four major processes of literary production in preexilic Israel—text creation, assemblage construction, revision, and redaction—as variously exemplified in the major corpora of biblical literature. These processes are not to be understood as representing a linear progression of literary production. Some texts participate in only one or two processes; some texts participate repeatedly in one process or another. Furthermore, as we will see, the lines between these processes can be decidedly blurry. Nevertheless, most textual production in preexilic Israel falls into these categories, and it is hoped that the basic taxonomy presented below will help clarify the nature of the literary activity that led to the textual building blocks for what would eventually become the Hebrew Bible.

Defining Literary Processes

In this section, I provide a rough overview of the four main literary processes evident in the biblical text, with some methodological considerations regarding their identification and potential scope. These discussions will form the background for the subsequent treatment of the texts themselves.

Text Creation

By text creation, I mean the process by which an independent textual unit is composed. It is important to distinguish between a textual unit and what is often called a literary unit. Literary units are, or can be, divisions within a single text, identified on the basis of form, genre, structure, or content: an episode in a larger narrative, a topical discussion in a legal collection, a prophetic oracle, or an individual psalm. While it is of course possible for a literary unit to have once also been an independent textual unit, the identification of the former does not necessarily lead to the necessity of the latter. That is, the ability to recognize formal literary markers within a text does not provide any basis for a claim about its compositional history.[4] Shakespeare's plays are full of distinctive literary units: speeches, soliloquies, poems, etc.; yet we would hardly suggest dividing his texts into separate pieces on such a basis.

Just as literary units are not to be blithely identified with textual units, so too the possibility of a text form existing as an independent material text in ancient Israel is not to be identified with any given example of that text form found in the biblical corpus. Individual scrolls of ritual instruction, for example, may have existed in ancient Israel; we do not have those scrolls preserved in the biblical text, even when the biblical text might draw on or even explicitly allude to the genre (e.g., in Lev 6–7). Another example of this is the genealogy: it is certainly imaginable that standalone genealogical texts existed in ancient Israel, yet none of the preexilic genealogies can be lifted from their narrative contexts and reckoned as actual examples of such independent textual units.

A distinction must be made between, on one hand, the possibility, even probability, of a wide range of texts and processes of text creation in ancient Israel, and on the other the evidence, or lack thereof, that any given part of the Hebrew Bible itself was a previously independent textual unit. Thus, for example, we may recognize in the non-priestly Jacob cycle a series of literarily isolatable units; this does not mean that those literary units were once independent texts (*contra* Blum 1984). Even as we recognize the literary coherence of a Jacob cycle, and the potential for such a text type to have existed as an independent textual unit, we are not compelled to therefore assume that there was once a textually independent Jacob cycle.

Materiality is not irrelevant. Unlike Mesopotamia or Ugarit, which used clay as the primary textual medium, in preexilic Israel literary texts were written on papyrus (Haran 1982, 1983, 1984). While we have short texts preserved independently—the brief Ugaritic text RS 24.258, for example, or the Gezer Calendar from Israel—they are, notably, inscribed texts, and do not survive the conceptual shift to papyrus. We are forced to imagine a single sheet—perhaps a half-sheet or less; practically no more than a scrap—dedicated to one such independent text (Baden 2012: 59–60). The very short literary unit does not lend itself particularly well to the assumption of textual independence.

One of the common fallacies in biblical scholarship, emerging from work done in the early 20th century, is the notion that the earliest stages of biblical composition were necessarily the simplest, both in content and in genre. Mixed-genre texts—whether psalms that do not conform to the standard form-critical designations or longer texts that incorporate both poetry and prose, narrative and ritual—are often understood as later literary products almost by definition.[5] Yet though we may assume that a given genre, in theory, must develop independently before being combined with any others, this does not mean that a newly written text cannot combine multiple genres. We moreover have ample attestations of mixed-genre texts that predate the Bible, from the aforementioned RS 24.258, which combines a brief narrative poem with a medicinal prescription, to the Sumerian (and later Neo-Assyrian) versions of Adapa, which include both myth and incantation (Sanders 2017: 41, 66).

The process of text creation in the preexilic period is thus not limited only to the production of small, generically consistent, form-critically isolated literary units. It extends from the individual poem or prophetic oracle through much larger, multi-genre literary complexes. Although the former may be easier to identify, and certainly less controverted in scholarship, the latter is just as plausible on both literary and literary-historical terms. Most importantly for our purposes, the two in fact participate in the same compositional process: that is, the creation of an entirely new textual unit.

Assemblage Construction

Assemblage construction is defined here as the gathering together of multiple previously independent textual units into a new single text with minimal editorial reworking.

The clearest instances of this come from generically coherent corpora: collections of psalms, or perhaps of prophetic oracles, which may be understood as essentially anthologies. The biblical text attests to such collections outside itself: repeated references are made to the "Annals of the Kings of Israel/Judah" (1 Kgs 14:19, 29) suggesting that such annals—fair examples of textual assemblages—were a known phenomenon in ancient Israel. The "Book of Jashar" (Josh 10:13; 2 Sam 1:18) would similarly seem to have been a collection of poems.

Yet a strict logic of viewing all such generic collections as the product of the assemblage of preexisting textual units quickly breaks down. What may seem reasonable in the case of the psalms is considerably less so when one turns to, for example, legal corpora. The Covenant Code in Exod 21–23 is, of course, a collection; yet the individual laws, or legal discussions, that are collected therein—the foundational literary units—can hardly be imagined to have had a prior independent textual existence. We are almost required to assume that the first textualization of most laws occurred in the process of creating a collection thereof.

The appearance of assemblage construction is therefore not always aligned with its actual instantiation as a literary process. The ostensibly textual assemblage may in fact be a written distillation of a prior process of oral anthologizing, whether it be of a particular prophet's speeches, for example, or of traditions relating to Israel's early history. Both the creation of new material and the collecting of that material can take place on both the oral and written levels. It is thus the case that the distinction between text creation and assemblage construction is not always secure. That is, an individual poem may be the base unit of textual production, but so too might a collection of poems that previously existed only in oral form. Genre-centered corpora, equally alongside individual literary units, thus may belong also to the process of text creation. As noted above, this may be clearest in the Bible in the case of a collection of laws, but more modern examples, such as the work of the Grimm brothers, illustrate the mechanisms by which individual oral exemplars of a genre can be textualized first in anthology.

Unlike text creation, assemblage construction can occur more than once in any given corpus. Thus, we may well imagine—indeed, we have reasonably clear evidence for—collections of collections. In one sense, the entire biblical corpus—though a distinctly postexilic product—is just such a multi-tiered assemblage.

Textual Revision

The process of textual revision, like that of assemblage construction, presupposes an already extant text, be it an isolated unit like an individual psalm or an assemblage thereof, or a larger individual unit (such as a legal corpus). This broad category includes supplementing, reframing, updating, glossing, and so on. The potential rationales for textual revision are almost limitless, and—despite the fervent attempts of some scholars—largely inaccessible to us. Multiple motivations might be assigned to any given revision; and multiple types of revision might be sensible for any presumed motivation. It is thus safest to observe textual revision with a wide lens, as it were. Regardless of motivation, or method of revision, all such examples share in the process of making changes to a preexisting text while still preserving the fundamental shape and identity of that original text. In textual revision—as opposed to redaction—new materials added to existing texts are understood to have been composed for the purpose of revision, rather than to have stood independently.

Textual revision can occur on a very large scale or a very small one. The addition of a superscription to a psalm, for example, entails the insertion of as few as two words (e.g., Ps 11:1). The expansion of the original priestly document of the Pentateuch (P) with what we call the

Holiness material (H), by contrast, was a near-comprehensive rewriting, expanding the base text by perhaps a third. Though these examples may seem widely disparate in their effect on the text, they are essentially identical in both process and function: both expand an existing text such that the reader's experience is necessarily different, framed by the new material.

Key is the recognition that these changes to the reader's experience are, from the perspective of the reader, imperceptible as changes. That is, while textual revision may leave some telltale literary evidence that we as modern scholars can analyze and appreciate, only a reader familiar with both the original text and the revised text would identify what they were reading as "changed." The revisions in a text are not marked as such—not highlighted, underlined, or in a different font. They are, for all practical purposes, invisible. In addition, it is thus equally important to acknowledge that many—potentially even most—textual revisions remain unrecognized, and unrecognizable. We should assume that innumerable changes have been made to our texts that we will never be able to identify as such.

As a literary process, textual revision offers a certain ambivalence toward the authority of the original text. On the one hand, it is deemed valuable enough to be maintained, rather than simply replaced or discarded in favor of something new. On the other hand, it cannot have achieved the kind of textual authority that is traditionally associated with the Bible; that is, the text is manifestly not fixed or unalterable. It is likely, given the evidence for widespread textual revision in virtually every preexilic text and corpus, that no such extreme sense of textual authority is attached to any preexilic literary materials (Mastnjak 2016).

The reworking of a preexisting text is not, of course, a one-time process. Until a moment of canonical fixity—a moment which did not come for many centuries after the exile—texts could be, and were, revised in an ongoing manner. The corpora in which such continuous revision is readily apparent provide a basis for the assumption that the same is true for those in which multiple stages of revision are not visible to the naked eye, as it were. Whatever little we might be able to say about scribal practice in ancient Israel, it seems highly probable that those texts produced by and for the literate elite—that is, the sorts of texts we find in the Bible, rather than ones we might label as ephemera, such as letters or economic documents—were copied and recopied, revised and re-revised, within the scribal and intellectual circles that produced and valued them. In this sense, our ability to assign a date to the composition of any biblical text is compromised by the strong likelihood that, whether literarily obvious or not, the text has gone through many stages of growth and change and belongs more to a continuous school than to any individual author or moment in time.

Redaction

As distinguishable from textual revision, the main identifying feature of redaction is the bringing together of preexisting independent texts to create a new, ostensibly unified, literary product. It is the appearance of unity that distinguishes redaction from assemblage construction: while anthologizing a collection of psalms is indeed the bringing together of preexisting independent texts, those texts remain identifiably distinct. Redaction, by contrast, as defined here, obscures the original independence of its constituent textual units. Again, we as modern scholars may be capable of detecting the seams in a redacted text, but a casual reader, or one not concerned with diachronic analysis, will read with, rather than against, the form of the text. The pre-critical history of reading is a relatively easy guide to this distinction: while everyone has always been capable of recognizing the individual psalms as independent compositions, the various sources employed in the composition of the Pentateuch went unidentified for 2000 years.

Redaction and textual revision are also close neighbors. The composition of the book of Isaiah is a good example of how the two processes may be interchangeable depending on the position of a given scholar. Was Second Isaiah an independent prophetic work only subsequently attached to the text of First Isaiah? Then perhaps redaction is the more accurate description. Or was it perhaps written to expand on and update the prophecies of First Isaiah? If so, then textual revision is more apt. Similarly, in the history of scholarship on the priestly pentateuchal materials, the status of H has shifted from redaction to textual revision, as scholarly opinion on its potential independence from P has moved decidedly toward the negative.

Like textual revision, redaction exhibits a mixed attitude regarding the authority of the texts being brought together. Redaction both preserves and obscures its constituent parts and can do so in various degrees. Preservation can be partial or nearly complete; the source materials are sometimes manifest to the critical reader, sometimes almost entirely obscured.

Thus, redaction may also share features with text creation. A new whole is being formed: a work (as distinguished from a text[6]) that did not exist previously. Similarly, the creation of a new text may incorporate some preexisting material in a manner that looks much like redaction. We may assume that the blessing of Jacob in Gen 49, for instance, existed as an independent textual unit; when the J Pentateuchal document was being written, this independent poetic text was included therein. Although not technically the combination of two previously independent units, we do have to reckon here with the literary recontextualization of one text into another. This is text creation with a semi-redactional element, perhaps. The lines, as noted above, can be blurry.

The processes described above are meant to be broad rubrics, useful categories for understanding the composition of literary texts in preexilic Israel. They are roughly descriptive—that is, based on the kinds of evidence we find in the literary record—rather than prescriptive, determined by any external sense of what ancient literary practices are imaginable or "permitted," or limited by any sort of "empirical" comparison with other ancient Near Eastern literary materials. The overall picture is one of a wide variety of potential processes of textual production, not always cleanly distinguishable from each other. Further, as we will see in the following section, this set of categories is untethered to either absolute or relative chronological dating. While text creation is the necessary starting point, what text creation looks like can be quite varied—and what happens to a text after it has been created is in no way a linear progression. Each text, and each corpus, has its own trajectory.

The Preexilic "Biblical" Texts of Ancient Israel

In this section, we will examine the various texts and corpora of preexilic Israel preserved in the Hebrew Bible, with an eye toward understanding their composition, not through a purely historical lens, but as manifestations of the literary processes described in the preceding pages. At the heart of this approach is the recognition that with very few (if any) exceptions, our ability to precisely date biblical texts is virtually non-existent (Sommer 2011), an inability significantly compounded by the likelihood, verging on certainty, that the texts we have, in whatever stage we want to observe them, are the product of schools rather than individuals, of ongoing processes of revision rather than fixed in time or space. A further limitation is placed on us by the constraint of focusing on the preexilic period of textual production, as the sharpest conceptual or ideological distinctions across the biblical materials are those between the major blocks of preexilic, exilic, and postexilic texts; it is considerably more difficult to clearly distinguish any sort of diachronic ideological shifts among preexilic writings alone. What is identifiable, by contrast, are some—not all—of the literary processes by which these texts achieved their various forms, processes that left their marks in the literary record itself.

Psalms

Perhaps the simplest of the corpora with which to start is the psalms. Though the canonical book of Psalms is clearly a postexilic text (and even then an open one, as the supplementary psalms in both the Septuagint and the Dead Sea Scrolls make clear), it is quite likely that the majority of the first two books of psalms, Pss 1–72, are of preexilic origins.

From a standpoint of process, we may assume, at least as a starting point, that individual psalms constituted one basic unit of text creation. Whether we attribute these, as was common in the 20th century, to the liturgy of the temple cult or to some other less-defined locus of production, the overlap between internally consistent content, formal and structural cohesion, and form-critical literary isolation suggests that here we have a case of a literary unit that was—or could certainly be imagined having been—also an independent textual unit.

While it is reasonable to presume that psalms as a genre, and maybe even some of the psalms in the Bible, originated essentially as improvised oral performances, perhaps in a cultic setting, the psalms that we have in our text are not to be identified directly with the words of a worshipper at a sanctuary. They are, instead, distinctively literary—though such a label does not necessarily exclude the possibility of oral composition.

There is little to no evidence that any of the individual psalms went through any substantial textual revision (though see below). This is not to exclude the possibility, of course; it is rather to recognize that any such reworking, if any took place, has left little to no trace in our text. Form-critical considerations have at times led scholars to find evidence for the expansion of psalms, particularly where one psalm seems to employ multiple genres—the combination of lament and hymn in Ps 22, for example (Lyons 2015). Such analyses, however, tend to rely on a restrictive view of literary composition, and fundamentally mistake form criticism for literary criticism.

Assuming that the unit of text creation was the individual psalm, we can thus readily recognize that the second major literary process at work here is assemblage construction, for which we have abundant internal evidence. The canonical text is subdivided into five smaller books, marked (in the case of the first four) by the addition of brief doxologies concluding with the word "Amen" (Pss 41:13; 72:19; 89:53; 106:48). These may in fact represent a later division of the book, but there are other internal markers that illustrate, if not the actual earlier assemblages out of which the canonical book was formed, at least the sorts of textual assemblages that are likely to have existed at an earlier stage of the book's formation: the statement that "The prayers of David, son of Jesse, are concluded" in Ps 72:20, which appears to be the formal ending to the group of Pss 51–72, all of which have a superscription ascribing them to David, or the psalms said to be "of Asaph," in Pss 73–83.

Insofar as the superscriptions seem to be linked to assemblages, we may surmise that between text creation and assemblage construction there was, in some cases at least, a minor form of textual revision at work in the adding of those superscriptions. The relative order of processes is not at all fixed here (or, as we shall see, almost anywhere). Just as there seems good reason to think that some superscriptions preceded some assemblages, so too it is clear that some superscriptions were added after the psalms were anthologized: the Septuagint adds an "of David" superscription to 12 psalms where the Masoretic text lacks one, suggesting an ongoing literary revision. The aforementioned doxologies are another indication of textual revision, not on the level of the individual psalm, but aligned rather with assemblages of psalms.

We should also allow for the possibility that some, if not all, psalms existed only in oral form before being written down as part of a larger anthology. The materiality of potentially independent psalms is also relevant to this discussion, especially when we consider the shorter psalms, such as the five-verse Ps 15, for example (see the discussion above). We might posit, then, that some psalms may have been composed and transmitted orally before being transcribed as part of a larger collection. One potential locus for such considerations would be the parallel texts of Ps 18 and 2 Sam 22, where we have what is manifestly the same poem in two distinct variant forms. This phenomenon might be accounted for on text-critical grounds, whether we describe it as textual corruption or in less pejorative terms; it may, however, also be a case of a poem that previously circulated only orally and was given its written form in two independent textual recensions. As noted in the introduction above, we must reckon both with the uncertainty that comes with recourse to orality and with the certainty that there was indeed a predominant orality in ancient Israelite culture.

In this second scenario, the processes of text creation, textual revision, and assemblage construction would be almost coterminous. A set of originally independent oral compositions would be transcribed, grouped together by means of superscription (which may have already been attached even at the oral stage), and thus brought into the textual world as an already formed collection of psalms. Neither this nor the more linear possibility presented above—creation and/or transcription of an individual psalm, the subsequent adding of a superscription, and finally the anthologizing of similarly titled psalms—is necessarily more probable. Indeed, both may well have taken place, subsequently or simultaneously.

Finally, we may note that some assemblages are themselves constructed out of previous assemblages. The "Psalms of David" in Pss 53–72, assuming that they had independent existences as a small anthology, have themselves been subsumed into a larger anthology of psalms (whether aligned with the internal book divisions of the canonical text or not).

Prophets

The composition of the prophetic texts was decidedly complex, and its specific trajectory unclear for any given book and surely not identical across the entire prophetic corpus. The basic unit of prophecy is the prophetic speech; at least, that is the conceit of the prophetic books, as well as the narratives about prophets found elsewhere in the Bible. These are, following the same conceit, oral compositions, whether improvisational or constructed in advance, and what we have in our texts is essentially a transcription of a prophet's words. An open question is the extent to which our texts are in fact to be understood as being, or having been at some point, such transcriptions, or whether they are in fact entirely literary compositions, merely taking on the voicing and characterization of a prophet, participating in the literary genre of the prophetic text rather than being based in any realia.

To a degree, the literary processes involved may be the same in either case. The isolation of the individual prophetic speech as a literary unit is for the most part relatively straightforward. We can at least heuristically presume that some prophetic oracles were written down and disseminated as independent textual units. The postexilic oracle against Edom that constitutes the single chapter of the book of Obadiah stands as a potential exemplar. So too, though somewhat less clearly, does Jer 51, in which a scroll is said to be produced that contains only an oracle against Babylon—presumably the same oracle found in that chapter.

Though Jeremiah's scroll is said to have been immediately destroyed, the process described there assumes the feasibility of a single, contained prophetic speech transcribed into text.

If the existence of independent prophetic speech-texts is granted, we might well presume that prophetic oracles were similarly collected into assemblages, oriented around the attributed (whether or not actual) speaker of the material. Thus, in theory, those oracles attributed to Isaiah—against Babylon, Moab, Damascus, Egypt, Tyre, and others in Isa 15–23—could well have been, like Obadiah or the oracle against Babylon in Jer 51, independent scrolls, collected into a compilation of Isaianic oracles against the nations, a compilation that itself would then be taken up into the larger corpus of Isaianic literature.

Yet it is equally likely that—as was suggested for the psalms above—the various oracles and other speeches attributed to a prophet were disseminated only in oral form before being written down for the purpose of their inclusion in a larger collection of that prophet's sayings. Here we again have some evidence from Jeremiah. In Jer 36, we find the narrative of Jeremiah's scribe, Baruch, writing down in a scroll (twice!) all of Jeremiah's prophecies to that point in his prophetic career. While we should certainly recognize that this text is hardly to be taken as "historical"—it is, of course, itself a literary presentation of a literary phenomenon—it does point to the likely reality of the process of textualization of a collection of prophetic material previously delivered, and presumably preserved and transmitted only orally. In light of both Jer 51 and 36, it seems that we are dealing not with an either/or but with a both/and situation: both prophetic speeches written and disseminated individually and prophetic speeches transmitted only orally until being transcribed *en masse*.

There is abundant evidence of textual revision throughout the prophetic corpus. Several prophetic texts have been expanded considering historical events. Because prophetic texts were so often explicitly reflections of and responses to specific historical circumstances, their continued relevance was maintained by updating them, either within the text or in supplemental material at the end of the work. The oracles against Babylon in Isa 13–14, in referring to Babylon, are manifestly later than the original 8th-century prophet. Prophecies directed against the northern kingdom of Israel have, in the wake of the destruction of the north at the end of the 8th century, been supplemented with references to the southern kingdom of Judah (Hos 8:14), or, in the wake of the destruction of Judah at the beginning of the 6th century, with references to the restoration of the Davidic monarchy (Amos 9:11–15). Whether such expansions occurred before or after the prophetic collection was formed is unclear.

One must obviously reckon too with the interweaving of oracles ostensibly from the prophet and narratives about the prophet. Such narratives seem, at times, to have had a textual existence of their own outside the context of the canonical book. An illustrative example is the repetition of Jeremiah's speech at the temple, found in both Jer 7 and 26 in two close, though not identical, narrative forms. The combination of prophetic speech and narrative could be the result of assemblage construction, the gathering together of material related to the prophetic figure; it could just as well be the product of textual revision, earlier texts being expanded with later additions—though it is important to recognize that we need not attribute poetic or first-person material to an earlier layer and narrative or third-person material to a later one. Most likely, what we have is a combination of both literary processes, happening in an ongoing and mutual way. Jeremiah, at least, further presents us with a fairly clear-cut case of extensive textual revision, as evident in the deuteronomistic material that pervades the book.

The superscriptions to some of the prophetic books, like those of the psalms, are also the product of textual revision. In some cases, we may also recognize in that act of textual revision an accompanying process of assemblage construction: the introductory verses of Amos,

Hosea, Micah, and Isaiah are similar enough that it is reasonable to presume that they were created to tie the four 8th-century prophets together. Though potentially simultaneous as a literary event, these should still be recognized as distinct literary processes.

Deuteronomistic History

Though the latest major developmental stage of the Deuteronomistic History (Dtr) took place in the exile (as that is where its final narratives are set), it has long been argued that there were earlier editions, whether Hezekian or Josianic or both. In any case, significant parts of Dtr's compositional process belong to the preexilic period.

Here it is perhaps best to work backward from the (nearly) final text. Dtr as a corpus is the product of redaction. A wide array of previously independent source texts have been worked together into a broad history of Israel from Joshua through the exile, and overlaid with a consistent theological framework, most evident in the recurring speeches and narratorial explanations that litter the text and justify the course of Israel's past as the working out of the reward-and-punishment scheme detailed in Deuteronomy (e.g., Josh 1:6–8; Judg 2:11–19; 1 Kgs 2:3–4; 2 Kgs 17:7–24, et al.). Here, then, we have simultaneous redaction and textual revision: both combination and framing expansion.

Scholars have proposed a number of sources underlying Dtr. These include such texts as the Ark Narrative, the Succession Narrative, a cycle of stories about Israel's judges, continuations of the Pentateuchal sources J, E, and P (see next section), and a variety of potential annals and other historical records. Each of these, in turn, has its own compositional history. A full description of each would require a book-length analysis; here we may concentrate on one or two as representative.

Embedded in the book of Judges is a cycle of narratives about localized military leaders (Judg 3:5–16:31). It has long been recognized that the text in its current form, with each successive judge introduced by a scheme of Israelite apostasy and repentance, represents a later theological framework, probably attributable to Dtr, overlaying originally independent historiographical material. When the Dtr material is removed, what remains is, ostensibly, a collection of accounts of Israel's judges: potentially an assemblage.

Within this assemblage are literary units ranging from full multi-episode narratives (Gideon, Judg 6–8; Abimelech, Judg 9; Jephthah, Judg 11:1–12:7; Samson, Judg 13–16) to extended single episodes (Ehud, Judg 3:15–30; Deborah, Judg 4–5) to mere notices (e.g., Ibzan, Elon, and Abdon, Judg 12:8–15). Certainly, some of the lengthier accounts may well have existed in written form as independent texts, though we should not be too quick to equate length with textuality. The shorter notices, however, are harder to imagine as their own textual units: what kind of existence could be proposed for the two verses about Tola in Judg 10:1–2, for instance? We may thus be faced with a combination of both previously written and previously only oral material—a combination, in other words, of assemblage construction and text creation.

Narrowing our gaze even further, the account of Deborah comprises two distinct sections: the prose narrative in Judg 4 and the poem of Judg 5. The original independence and antiquity of Judg 5 have long been recognized, on grounds of both language and content. It seems most likely that the prose account is based on the older poem; yet the literary processes by which we ended up with both in our present text are not as evident. The prose may have been written as an introduction to the earlier poem, in which case this would be textual revision of a sort. The prose may have been written separately, as part of the broader anthology of the judges, and the poem on which it was based was inserted to accompany it, thus some combination of redaction and textual revision.

It is also, however, conceivable that the poem had never been written down before it was set in its place in the Judges cycle. Oral transmission of older materials did not cease upon the advent of writing; there is no prima facie reason why an ostensibly ancient tribal poem such as Judg 5 would require textualization to be preserved until its later reuse. A modern analogy would be a novel in which a parent sings a nursery rhyme to their child: such songs are still primarily passed down orally and could thus be incorporated into a novel without recourse to a prior written version—even if such a written version may have also existed. Oral transmission also in no way precludes the preservation of older, even archaic, language; again, to use the nursery rhyme analogy, when children to this day recite "Jack and Jill," they use the word "crown" for "head," though such usage is decidedly not contemporary.

A different combination of literary processes seems to have been at work in at least some of the David material in 1 Sam 16-1 Kgs 2. There are clear Dtr overlays (e.g., 1 Kgs 2:3–4); there seems to be a pro-Solomon layer as well (e.g., 2 Sam 7). Both of these fall under the category of textual revision. At the core of the text is an apology for David. This apology, however, contains some doublets (e.g., 1 Sam 24 and 26) and contradictions (e.g., 1 Sam 16 and 17) that suggest that it may be the product of the redaction of two previous such texts, or perhaps two editions of the apology for David. The David story includes independent poetic pieces (2 Sam 1:19–27; 22; 23:1–7) as well as what looks like a potentially independent collection of stories about David's warriors (2 Sam 23:8–39), which may have been previously oral or written, and which may have entered the text at any number of points. And there are examples of textual revision apart from the Dtr framing that similarly are not necessarily attributable to any specific moment in the process (e.g., 1 Sam 25:1a).

Pentateuch

In the preexilic period, there was no Pentateuch. The Pentateuch as we now have it did not come into existence until the 5th century BCE at the earliest. What existed in the preexilic period, however, were the sources that would eventually be combined to form the Pentateuch: the independent texts that scholarship has labeled J, E, P, and D. Each has its own literary history, with unique combinations of materials and processes.

D, the source found entirely within the canonical book of Deuteronomy, consists of two core pieces: the laws of Deut 12–26 and 28, and the poem of Deut 32:1–43, each a product of text creation. Either or both of these may have once been independent texts (on the laws, see below), and both may have gone through their own internal processes of textual revision. Both were subsequently taken up into a broader composition that included substantial framing material, thus exhibiting both redaction and textual revision—or, if the legal and poetic material did not have a prior independent existence, text creation. This occurred, however, in two distinct editions, as is evident, for example, from the two introductory frames (Deut 1:1–4:40, 44 and Deut 4:45-11:32). The two editions of D were then combined, through redaction, into a single D document.[7] Throughout D we also find a number of further textual revisions, supplements, and expansions of varied natures, from historical notices (e.g., Deut 2:10–12, 20–23) to canonically minded "corrections" (e.g., Deut 2:14–16) to glosses (e.g., Deut 3:9) to theological discourses (e.g., Deut 4:15–31) to narrative insertions (e.g., Deut 27). As is often the case, it is not always clear at what stage in D's literary history these revisions occurred.

P is, in terms of genre, a highly variable text, comprising, inter alia, narrative, genealogy, ritual law, building instructions, and census lists. Here it is important to recognize that generic distinctions, and the literary units that are identified to match them, are not necessarily indications of previously independent texts. Most often disputed in this regard are the ritual laws of Leviticus 1–7, 11–15. We might certainly assume that the priestly ritual instructions existed as an independent textual unit before being taken up into the broader priestly document. There does appear to be some evidence that smaller sub-units of the ritual instructions may have had their own independent existence. Scholars have noted particularly the designations in Lev 6–7, "This is the torah of X offering," and suggested that in fact these were once standalone scrolls of ritual instruction, to be consulted by the priests (Haran 1983: 115; Knohl 2007: 68). The discovery of similar ritual texts in Ugarit is especially relevant in this regard and might suggest a process of assemblage construction.

Yet caution is required here. The language used in Lev 6–7, and the comparative evidence, may point us toward the presumptive existence of such scrolls in ancient Israel. That is not to say that the literary units of Lev 6–7 are, in fact, precisely those scrolls. It is clear, rather, that the various individual sacrificial instructions in Lev 6–7 cannot be simply lifted from their current literary context and read independently, as they build on and refer to one another ("The guilt offering is like the purification offering," Lev 7:7, e.g.). This is true of the entire block of priestly ritual instruction: whatever potential ritual text types or genres they may be drawing from, their literary interdependence in their present form militates against the possibility that we actually have earlier independent textual units preserved, as if in amber, within the larger complex. Rather, here the independent unit of text creation is, at a minimum, Lev 1–7, 11–15.

Here again, however, even if we grant the theoretical possibility of some independent ritual material, the ritual texts found in Leviticus cannot have stood alone. They are dependent on the Tabernacle construction that precedes them and are integrated into the overarching P narrative (Feldman 2020). Indeed, P, as a whole, is so thoroughly consistent, coherent, and continuous that no literary unit within it is easily identifiable as having existed as a prior independent text.

What is clear about P, however, is that its original core was supplemented through repeated processes of textual revision. The most significant of these is the expansion known to scholarship as H, centered on the legal material of Lev 18–26 but extending throughout the priestly text (Exod 12:14–20, 24–27; Lev 16:29–34a, e.g.). Further textual revisions may be identified in, for example, the sacrificial prescriptions of Num 28–29, or the genealogy of Moses and Aaron in Exod 6:13–30.

The J document is also generically diverse: it is predominantly narrative but includes significant poetic texts (Gen 49; Exod 15; Deut 33) as well as some genealogical material (Gen 4:17–26, e.g.). Regarding the poems, the same probabilities and caveats that we saw in the case of Judg 5 apply here as well. It is often argued that J should be understood primarily as an example of redaction and textual revision: that what we have here is in fact an overarching framework given to independent narrative units, identified through a combination of form and tradition criticism. We have, of course, examples of independent narrative texts, whether in prose or poetry, from the ancient Near East, such as Gilgamesh or the Baal cycle. It is thus certainly theoretically possible that in ancient Israel there were also independent narrative texts, though as noted above the issue of materiality places some potential limits on the imagined length of such. Thus an independent narrative of Jacob's theophany at Bethel claimed by some to reside at the core of Gen 28, for example (see Blum 1984), would be difficult to imagine. Within the Bible itself, perhaps the shortest recognizable independent narrative textual unit is at least a couple of chapters long: Jonah (without the embedded prayer of Jonah 2), for example, or, from a postexilic example, the four chapters of Ruth.

Given its somewhat episodic nature, J can be read as something like an assemblage: a chronologically arranged collection of stories about Israel's ancestors. While this may have some truth to it, it is so only on the level of oral tradition. Whatever stories J had at hand, they show no indication of having been textualized prior to their inclusion in the J story. This is true of both P and E as well. The basic unit of text creation for J is, in fact, fundamentally the entirety of the J document. Like every other text, of course, J is also likely to have undergone some textual revision, though it is less apparent in J than elsewhere. A commonly proposed example is Gen 2:10–14, which hardly sticks out from its context in the same way that H does from the original core of P.

Finally, the E document similarly comprises extensive narrative, along with, most notably, a major legal corpus in the Covenant Code of Exod 21–23. Again, we can presume that E has undergone significant textual revision, but it is even less discernible here than in J. The Covenant Code, however, is regularly held up as an example of an independent textual unit that has been incorporated into a narrative frame, and so is worth a moment of attention.

Considering the abundant comparative ancient Near Eastern evidence, one hardly needs to make the case for the legal collection as a potential standalone textual unit. Even for those who argue for an exceedingly close literary connection between the laws and their narrative frame, it is essentially unproblematic to imagine that the laws existed, in independent written form, at some point prior to their inclusion in a broader literary context. Indeed, such a claim can lend support to the notion that the promulgation of the preexisting laws was in fact the aim of the framing material. (The commonly held alternative, that the narratives preceded the laws, is based on a fundamentally anti-Semitic evolutionary framework popular in 19th-century German Protestant thought, one that has unfortunately lingered in scholarship down to the present.) We need not, however, imagine any significant temporal gap between the laws and their frameworks. This is, in part, why a focus on process, rather than on "hands" or "authors/editors," is helpful. Text creation, framing, revision—all could in theory be done by the same "hands" for any given literary material, but the processes are distinct, and can be separated to an extent from chronological claims.

The Pentateuchal sources provide the best evidence for multi-genre text creation. Even if we set aside the ritual instructions and the law codes of the Pentateuch as having been originally independent textual units, the Pentateuchal sources still comprise narrative prose, genealogy, poetry, etiology, and more. Again, any or all of these may have been generated and transmitted orally at first. Indeed, the purely narrative material of the Pentateuchal sources, even without any of the other genres, is clearly the textual manifestation of previously independent oral traditions. But while we may recognize that, for example, the narrative of Eden, the narrative of Cain and Abel, the genealogy-cum-etiologies of Cain's descendants, the song of Lemech, the narrative about the union of the divine beings and the daughters of men, the flood narrative, the story of Noah's drunkenness, and the narrative of the Tower of Babel—that is, the various narrative units of the J primeval history—almost certainly all derive from previously independent oral traditions, none can be ascribed to a previously independent text. So too, *mutatis mutandis*, for the E and P sources. Indeed, given the broad similarities among the various Pentateuchal sources more generally, it is most likely that those independent oral traditions had already been assimilated, still at an oral stage, into a lengthier narrative arc of Israel's early history. The units of textual composition for all this material, generically blended though they may be, are the Pentateuchal documents as wholes.

Conclusion

Though this essay has concentrated on the preexilic stages of the Bible's composition, it should be readily apparent that all the processes described above continued on into the postexilic period, and beyond. There was abundant new text creation, from Ruth to Daniel to Esther to Ecclesiastes and Job. Assemblage construction can be seen in the creation of the prophetic corpus as a whole, as well as in the ongoing expansion of the psalms collection, and potentially in the development of Proverbs (see the headings to ostensibly independent sub-collections in Prov 1:1; 10:1; 25:1; 30:1; 31:1). Textual revision is almost universally recognizable in every corpus and almost every individual text, often with an eye toward a growing (if only preliminary) sense of canon (e.g., Mal 3:22; Deut 34:11–12). Redaction is, of course, most obvious in the Pentateuch, which, even post-redaction, continued to undergo textual revision (e.g., Exod 34:10–27).

The foregoing has not attempted to be comprehensive in its treatment of the entire biblical corpus. The intent here was to provide a broad taxonomy of the types of literary processes that were at work in the creation of ancient Israelite literature, with the understanding that those texts not described in detail here could be understood in a similar manner. Above all, the purpose of thinking about biblical composition in this somewhat abstracted way is to step back from the pervasive focus in biblical scholarship on issues of who wrote these texts and when they did so and concentrate more on the question of how. Who and when are questions that can be answered with any specificity or accuracy only very rarely, or in very broad terms, and the disagreements among scholars are ubiquitous, dependent on all sorts of assumptions and intellectual positions. Of course, such assumptions and positions are unavoidable, and this essay is of course dependent in large part on my own. However, the processes described here are common to virtually every reconstruction of the Bible's history and can be adjusted in line with almost any specific scholarly argument.

Thus, we may, in what I hope are fruitful ways, have a conversation separate from, if parallel to, the constant disagreements about when a particular text was created, collected, expanded, or redacted, and more about the basic fact of that text's creation, assemblage construction, textual revision, and redaction. Perhaps it may allow for a more specific discourse about what exactly is happening in the text, rather than when or by whom it was brought about. When we see a literary process, we can understand it in light of similar processes elsewhere, either by comparison or contrast. And even when we postulate processes occurring in combination, we can identify the component steps, and recognize them as participating in modes of literary production that span Israelite history and literature.

Notes

1. My thanks to Seth Sanders for his thoughtful suggestions on this essay.
2. For comparative studies of Israelite scribalism, see, *inter alia*, Carr 2005; Schniedewind 2019; van der Toorn 2007.
3. If we knew nothing of Israelite cultic ritual, we would be quite mistaken to take, for example, Mesopotamian rituals as a model.
4. Contra Rendtroff (1990) and the broader school of scholarship that followed him. See especially the crucial sentence: "The Pentateuch as a whole as it lies before us is no longer the point of departure, but rather the concrete individual text, the 'smallest literary unit'" (Rendtroff 1990: 23). Note the equation of "literary unit" with "individual text."
5. This understanding derives largely from the work of Gunkel (1901).
6. On the distinction of work and text (and manuscript), see Lied (2015).
7. Proposed originally Wellhausen (1963: 193), this position is argued in more detail by Haran (1996-2008, 2:54–58; Hebrew).

Bibliography

Baden, Joel S. 2012. *The Composition of the Pentateuch: Renewing the Documentary Hypothesis.* New Haven: Yale University Press.

Baden, Joel S., and Jeffrey Stackert. forthcoming. *Deuteronomy.* Stuttgart: Kohlhammer.

Blum, Erhard. 1984. *Die Komposition der Vätergeschichte.* Neukirchen-Vluyn; Neukirchener Verlag.

Carr, David. 2005. *Writing on the Tablet of the Heart: Origins of Scripture and Literature.* Oxford: Oxford University Press.

Feldman, Liane. 2020. *The Story of Sacrifice: Ritual and Narrative in the Priestly Source.* Tübingen: Mohr Siebeck.

Gunkel, Hermann. 1901. *Legends of Genesis.* Chicago: Open Court.

Haran, Menahem. 1982. "Book-Scrolls in Israel in Pre-Exilic Times," *JJS* 33: 161–73.

———. 1983. "Book-Scrolls at the Beginning of the Second Temple Period: The Transition from Papyrus to Skins." *HUCA* 54: 111–22.

———. 1984. "More Concerning Book-Scrolls in Pre-Exilic Times," *JJS* 35: 84–85.

———. 1996–2008. *The Biblical Collection.* 3 vols. Jerusalem: Magnes Press. (Hebrew)

Knohl, Israel. 2007. *The Sanctuary of Silence: The Priestly Torah and the Holiness School.* Winona Lake: Eisenbrauns.

Lied, Liv. 2015. "Text–Work–Manuscript: What is an 'Old Testament Pseudepigraphon'?" *JSP* 25: 150–65.

Lyons, Michael. 2015. "Psalm 22 and the 'Servants' of Isaiah 54; 56–66." *CBQ* 77: 640–56.

Mastnjak, Nathan. 2016. *Deuteronomy and the Emergence of Textual Authority in Jeremiah.* Tübingen: Mohr Siebeck.

Mroczek, Eva. 2016. *The Literary Imagination in Jewish Antiquity.* New York: Oxford University Press.

Rendtroff, Rolf. 1990. *The Problem of the Process of Transmission in the Pentateuch.* Sheffield: JSOT.

Sanders, Seth. 2017. *From Adapa to Enoch: Scribal Culture and Religious Vision in Judea and Babylon.* Tübingen: Mohr Siebeck.

Schmid, Konrad. 2011. "Has European Scholarship Abandoned the Documentary Hypothesis? Some Reminders on Its History and Remarks on Its Current Status." Pages 17–30 in *The Pentateuch: International Perspectives on Current Research.* Edited by Thomas B. Dozeman, Konrad Schmid, and Baruch J. Schwartz. Tübingen: Mohr Siebeck.

Schniedewind, William. 2019. *The Finger of the Scribe: How Scribes Learned to Write the Bible.* Oxford: Oxford University Press.

Sommer, Benjamin D. 2011. "Dating Pentateuchal Texts and the Perils of Pseudo-Historicism." Pages 85–108 in *The Pentateuch: International Perspectives on Current Research.* Edited by Thomas B. Dozeman, Konrad Schmid, and Baruch J. Schwartz. Tübingen: Mohr Siebeck.

van der Toorn, Karl. 2007. *Scribal Culture and the Making of the Hebrew Bible.* Cambridge: Harvard University Press.

Wellhausen, Julius. 1963. *Die Composition des Hexateuchs und der historischen Bücher des Alten Testaments.* Berlin: G. Reimer, 1885. Repr., Berlin: de Gruyter.

PART V

Religion

27

RELIGION IN THE HOUSE IN ANCIENT ISRAEL

Jeremy D. Smoak

Introduction

The description of Isaac's blessing of Jacob in Gen 28 offers a rich picture of religion's embeddedness within the Israelite household.[1] Instead of fixing religion within a discrete space in the dwelling, the text alludes to its fluidity, portability, and infusion with the family's lifecycle. The text threads together a cultural memory of religion by focusing on the way that the ritual of blessing integrates the family's lifecycle within the house's dependence on the family field. That the narrative locates the story in a household context is explicit in the statement that Rebekah took Esau's best clothes which were with her "in the house" (בבית) (27:15). Following this statement, the story focuses upon sensory experience and the ways in which the house opens up to other spaces around the family dwelling. When Isaac catches the smell of his son Jacob's clothes, he blesses him and says, "…the smell of my son is like the smell of a field that Yahweh has blessed" (v. 27). This verse locates religion within olfactory experience as the smell of Jacob's body triggers and mediates Isaac's experience of divine blessing (Avrahami 2012: 103). The following verses further connect this experience of blessing to feasting, as Isaac consumes the game from his son's hunt and drinks the family wine. What results is a textual tapestry of the way that the act of blessing threaded religion within the fabric of the family's daily life and transgenerational relationships.

This text reminds us that while we may be tempted to look for a "space" for religion in the Israelite house, the most characteristic feature of religion in this space was its deep integration within the materials of the dwelling and the routines and lifecycles of the family. To put it differently, the house was the place *par excellence* where religion infused the family's daily sustenance and the family's transgenerational relationships (Ackerman 2014; Meyers 2014; Zevit 2014; Stavrakopoulou 2016). The story of Isaac's blessing integrates the smell of clothing and the family field, the taste of food, and the touch of family, and it anticipates the patriarch's death and burial in the family tomb. The text also points to religion's entangled relationship with the various installations related to food processing, consumption, and other household activities.

The description of Isaac's blessing of Jacob in this text also emphasizes the role that sensory experience plays in religious experience. Smell, taste, and feel mediate Yahweh's blessings as the text describes the family's house as a *sensescape*. To refer to the house as a sensescape is to imagine it as a sensory envelope for the bodies that inhabited it and to consider how both the natural and built environment of the dwelling participated in the formation of religious experience (Howes and Classen 2013; Thomason 2016). Religion according to this text is something that integrates time and space for the family and something that permeates the skin to lodge blessing in the body. In this way, the text also challenges a view of household religion that would categorize religious experience too narrowly within the walls of a dwelling. The story draws attention to the way in which the house opens up to other spaces, its setting within the natural landscape, and the portability of the house's materials. It also reminds us that it was not only the durable objects that made the house the center of religion but mostly those portable, fragile materials and those fleeting gestural acts that produced religion (Carroll 2016).

The story of Isaac's blessing is likely not the first biblical text that scholars consider when looking for religion in the Israelite house. Studies more commonly focus upon those texts that allude to objects or fixtures within the domestic dwelling (see Zevit 2001: 201–41; Albertz and Schmitt 2012: 57–219). While these are crucial avenues of inquiry, they also reflect certain legacies in the study of religion that continue to haunt the house. Behind some of the search for terminology to define religion in this space stand the legacies of earlier conceptualizations of religion, which tended to bifurcate religious practice in categories such as "official" vs. "popular" or "sacred" vs. "profane" (see Zevit 2003; Gudme 2010; Stavrakopoulou and Barton 2010). Part of this legacy manifests itself in the search for a bounded space for religion in the house rather than an emphasis upon its fluidity and embeddedness into diverse aspects of the family's daily tasks and relationships.

While recent studies have challenged these older paradigms, we might take such advances further by asking how religion in the house was characterized by its integration, embeddedness, and ephemerality (Nakhai 2011). Indeed, we might struggle to locate religion because we do not ask how the taste or smell of a meal mediated divine experience. While a focus upon temple religion may support Rudolf Otto's idea of the holy as something "Other," a focus upon the family meal offers a window into religion that becomes internalized in the body and renders the divine "hyperpalatable" (Blumberg-Kraus 2010). By drawing attention to these aspects of religion we can complement recent studies on gender and household economies with three additional foci: religion's integration in the house; the house's function as a sensescape of religion; and the house's relationship to the family tomb.

Religion's Integration

As noted above, the story of Isaac's blessing of Jacob focuses upon religion's integration within the daily lives of its members and within the transgenerational relationships of the family. Whereas other biblical texts offer glimpses of religious installations in the house, this story emphasizes religion's attachment to clothing, food, drink, and rights of inheritance. The text functions as a window into family religion *par excellence* because it situates religion around a meal and the rituals of inheritance rather than around a temple or local altar (Ebeling 2010; Meyers 2012; Shafer-Elliott 2012). The performance of the blessing gathers the mundane and ephemeral in the house into a celebration in which everything in the space coheres within the divine blessing of the family field. Repeated references to Yahweh's blessing of the family and Isaac's act of blessing are interwoven in the narrative with the description of the preparation and consumption of a meal. Whereas the archaeological evidence would give us a picture of the various dishes and vessels used in the meal, the text focuses upon the way that blessing integrates religion with the activities of the different members of the family and the meal's sensory stimuli.

When we turn back to the archaeological evidence for domestic life, we can see how the archaeological materials complement this textual picture of family religion as diffused throughout the house (see Albertz and Schmitt 2012: 57–219). In most houses, there is no clear evidence of a differentiation between "sacred" and "profane" space. Instead, religion was expressed through the things used in the different spaces of the house, as well as their range of meanings. The Israelite house and the assemblages found in such spaces reflect their inherent flexibility to adapt to the needs of a highly multipurpose and multigenerational space (Stavrakopoulou 2016: 349–50). Such fluidity and ambiguity is what makes identifying cult corners and other areas thought to be set aside for cult so difficult to locate, as the things of the Israelite house were used for diverse purposes.

The story of Isaac's blessing also highlights the ways in which the body's movement between the house and other spaces outside of the house created household religion. This means that our consideration of religion in the Israelite house might not focus primarily upon its difference or isolation from community and state religion, but instead upon the ways in which it mapped religious performances at larger settings (i.e., communal altars, temples, etc.). Indeed, it is important to remember that the house served as the primary map through which ritual action was conveyed and understood in larger religious settings. As Meyers observes, "household offerings provided the model for the sacrificial regime at communal shrines…the food and drink of temple sacrifice were household staples writ large, with household dietary regimens being the precursors of sacramental ones" (2017: 12). In the story of Isaac's blessing, we can see glimpses of how this mapping played out in the household. The description of Isaac, Rebekah, and Jacob preparing and partaking of a meal as part of the performance of blessing models certain aspects of sacrificial rituals at larger communal sanctuaries.

More recent studies examine how practices of sustenance and protection infused religion within the house and its members, with a particular focus upon the ritual knowledge and expertise of women (Meyers 2005, 2007, 2012, 2013, 2017; Ackerman 2008, 2012, 2014, 2016; Nakhai 2008, 2011, 2014a, 2014b; Ebeling 2010). Such studies emphasize the significance of studying the house as a gendered space, both in the sense that it was experienced differently by women and men, but also in the sense its spaces were gendered based upon the distribution of labor, expertise, and practice (Meyers 2007; Ebeling and Homan 2008; Gudme 2014; Chapman 2016). This is an important step in approaching the topic of domestic religion because it highlights how religious experience related to the distribution of labor and the use of spaces by specific members of the household.

We can turn to the excavations of domestic dwellings at the Iron Age site of Tell el-Farah (N) to illustrate these aspects of religion in the house. The excavations at the site offered a picture of residential patterns and the layout of early Iron Age dwellings (de Vaux 1961; Finkelstein 2012). Located in the highlands of Samaria, the site sits about 11 kilometers to the northeast of Shechem and is most likely the biblical city Tirzah, one of the early capitals of the northern kingdom. Stratum 7b, which the excavators dated to the 10th century BCE, contained an array of artifacts located in domestic enclosures. Such artifacts include what is now known to be a typical assemblage associated with the space of 10th century houses in ancient Israel, including model shrines, jewelry, incense stands, harnessed horse figurines, arrowheads, zoomorphic vessels, beads, woman with tambourine figurines, bovine heads, cow nursing calves, and various forms of amulets (Albertz and Schmitt 2012: 95–97).

In House 440, excavators discovered an abundant assortment of objects that are easily associated with religious behavior, among other objects whose association is not as readily identifiable (Willett 1999: 118–33). The structure had been built in the typical "four-room" style, with a main courtyard that provided access to several smaller rooms on both sides of the enclosure (see Zorn, this volume). Just inside the doorway that provided access between the street and the courtyard of the house, excavators discovered a zoomorphic vessel, an alabaster pendant, a nursing female figurine, a harnessed horse head, and six beads next to an oven to the west of the entrance (Willett 1999: 125). A model shrine was discovered in a room to the east of the house's entrance, and toward the rear of the courtyard along the western side of the courtyard, excavators found a female-with-tambourine figurine on the floor near a stone bench built against the wall.

Evidence for domestic cult activity is also especially prominent in the artifacts discovered in Stratum III at Lachish, dating to the 8th century BCE (Tufnell 1953; Willett 1999: 335). These artifacts come from domestic structures built near the city gate and palace. The relevant domestic structures include House 1002, 1003, 1008, and House 1032. The artifacts uncovered in House 1002 included an eye amulet, a bone sacred eye scaraboid, cooking pots, lamps, a bone spatula, and weaving tools. House 1003 contained a blue faience bead, cooking pots, a chalice, a lamp, and several ceramic items used for food preparation. House 1032 also preserved an assortment of smaller artifacts that likely served apotropaic functions. These included several amulets, including two eye amulets, a faience amulet, a bone pendant with ring-and-dot designs, six beads, a shell fragment, and a cowrie amulet (Willet 1999: 335). In addition, the remains of a hand-modeled goddess head originally attached to a ceramic vessel were discovered in the room. The majority of small artifacts discovered in these houses at Lachish evidence the importance of using beads, bones, shells, and various types of amulets for personal protection against various forms of danger that threatened the house and household (Willett 1999: 292–388; Limmer 2007; Garroway 2018).

The objects discovered in these contexts also show that a major concern of domestic religion was the protection of the household. Comparative evidence demonstrates that the concern of many of such objects would have been directed toward the health of children and women, especially concerns over reproduction. On average women lived about ten years less than men and about 30% of children did not survive to the age of three (Nakhai 2018: 109). This meant that a major focus of the strategies of protection in this space would have been concerned with the rites of reproduction and the health of newborn and young children. Bes amulets are especially prominent in the repertoire of amulets from the Iron Age southern Levant. Such amulets are also widely known from Egypt and there is some evidence that they had a specific application to the protection of women and children during childbirth (Pinch 1983: 405–14; Andrews 1994: 40; Ebeling 2010: 106).

The House as a Sensescape

In the story of Isaac's blessing, we see the way that the act of blessing is infused with the preparation and enjoyment of a meal (Gen 27:1–40). The story alludes to this dynamic of household religion by focusing upon the sensory experiences of the family meal. The movement of the text proceeds from an emphasis upon Isaac's consumption of "the savory food" (המטעמים) to references to the "smell" (ריח) of a field to "the dew of heaven" (טל שמים), "the fatness of the earth" (שמני הארץ), and "plenty of grain and wine" (רב דגן ותירש). These allusions to the family's sustenance are interlaced with references to Jacob's voice, the feel of Esau's skin, and the interactions that he has with family. As we see in this example, instead of focusing upon the vessels and dishes involved in the meal, the text draws attention to the way that its smell and taste blended sensory experiences into the performance of blessing.

We might broaden our focus therefore to ask how the house functioned as a *sensescape*, that is, a place where the senses were especially attuned to the space's sensory affordances.[2] As noted in the introduction, this means to take seriously the agency of the house as a space that acted upon the household in order to create religion. As Betts (2017: 6) summarizes, "like people and objects, places are embodied and have agency. The visual cues, textures, and other haptic affordances, sounds, smells, and tastes (whether permanent or transient) present in spaces help to characterize them as places, and consequently give them affective properties…." To refer to the house as a sensescape also means to think of it as the location where the senses were most effectively integrated to activate religious experience. The term sensescape forms a heuristic model for considering the variety of sensory affordances that a place possesses and the ways in which they press upon a person in order to communicate meaning. As Meyer et al. (2010: 209) emphasize, "the body enters integrally into every feeling, thought, emotion, and perception that human beings have…And bodies are the medium of social experience, the gateway to the social bodies to which individuals belong, with which they identify, through which they feel and perceive themselves, others, and the divine." A serious consideration of the way in which religion was infused within the house and its activities pushes us therefore to reconstruct how the house was *sensed* as a place of religion.

When we look back at the descriptions of the meal in the story of Isaac's blessing we cannot be certain of the nature of the "house" imagined in this narrative. However, the text has constructed the place of eating as a place of ritual and of the performance of kinship. Ebeling emphasizes that "early Israelite household cult activities probably centered on 'table manners' or the ritual actions that take place around meals, including offering a portion of food and drink to the gods…" (2010: 75; also van der Toorn 1996: 30). The infused or integrated character of religion in the house meant that religion was most fully activated by the meal and anchored in the practices of meal preparation and consumption wherever they took place.

While past studies have focused upon the expertise, labor, and production of food in the house, a material religion approach to domestic religion would ask how the sensory experience of all these actions as well as the act of tasting and smelling the food forged religious experience. Recent studies have highlighted the ways in which olfactory experience, for example, creates notions and triggers memories of space (Porteous 1985; McHugh 2011). Such studies emphasize the power that smell plays in generating strong attachments to places. A focus upon the senses also challenges the tendency to define religion in the house *within* the walls of the dwelling as such sensory stimuli can permeate the walls of the structure and bring the smell of the harvest and the light of daybreak into the house.

Scholars often lament that one of the great challenges of identifying religion in the house has to do with the very nature of the evidence. Most of the material expressions of religious practice in such spaces were organic and do not survive time. As Houston and Taube emphasize, "…sight, sound, touch, hearing, and smell are not ordinarily the concern of archaeologists, since the senses do not leave vestiges that can readily be accessed" (2000: 261). As a result, we should acknowledge at the outset the very limited picture that the *archaeological record* provides us of religion in the house. We should assume *a priori* that religion's material expressions in this space were much fuller than the recovery of the past allows us to visualize and study.

At the same time, advances in chemical analysis are providing a fuller picture of the role that organic materials played in religious experience in the house. Studies have long noted the role that aromatics such as incense played in Israelite religion (Haran 1960; Nielsen 1986). More recent studies are pointing to the role that hallucinogens played in religion in ancient Israel and surrounding regions. Recent organic residue analysis of material from an altar at the shrine at Tel Arad detected traces of cannabinoids and terpenoids along with residues of animal dung (Arie, Rosen, and Namdar 2020). The presence of cannabinoids on the altar strongly indicates that the burning of cannabis formed part of the rituals of the temple at the site. Heating and burning the cannabinoids on the altar would have released active compounds that would have been inhaled by those at the temple in order to produce a psychoactive effect. The discovery of residue of frankincense on the larger altar at the site demonstrates that both functioned as incense altars and connects their use to the incense altars from domestic contexts.

Similar analysis of organic residues discovered in several chalices from houses at Tell es-Ṣafi not only provide new insight into the function of such objects but also the way that religion in that space was mediating by inhaling and perhaps digesting hallucinogens (Gadot et al 2014: 55–56). The analysis of the chemicals found in the chalices evidenced traces of the parent-compound trimyristin. The compound trimyristin is abundant in plants that cause hallucinogenic effects when inhaled or digested. At several other sites, we find incense altars near different types of objects related to domestic activities, such as figurines, lamps, and standing stones. At Tel Halif, incense altars have been discovered near vessels and installations used for food preparation and consumption (Bang et al. 2017). This evidence reminds us again of the deep integration of religion in the house as the smell of incense together with the experience of the flavor of food rendered the meal one of the most powerful and memorable experiences of religion.

That so many biblical texts preserve memories of festival meals reflects the power that the meals served as a mediator of religious identity in the house. It was the meal—as MacDonald (2008: 79–81) notes—that helped the Israelites "remember" and forge an identity around the celebration of the annual harvests as Yahweh's blessing. Specific foods come to be associated with religious festivals, ceremonies, and other religious rites. MacDonald (2008: 71–77) has detailed the specific ways in which the biblical texts connect the memory of Yahweh's benevolent deeds to Israel with rituals of eating during specific festivals both at the sanctuary and at the home. The eating of certain foods at such celebrations became a powerful way in which the family and community "inscribed" and "incorporated" the memory of Yahweh's blessings upon Israel. Certain foods were viewed as the manifestation of divine blessings, while others—or the lack of food—mediated divine cursing.

When we put all of this together, we can imagine the way in which the house during a meal served as a sensory envelope for the body. Religion in this space was most fully anchored around the table and most fully activated by the meal. In this familiar space, smelling and seeing the food just before tasting and consuming it while gathered with family and the family gods merged the senses so that the meal could render the divine "hyperpalatable." Although the biblical texts cannot reconstruct the sensory stimuli associated with this experience, they provide small glimpses of how the meal mediated religion. We can turn to Deut 4:28 in order to imagine how the meal and its setting in the house produced an inter-sensorial experience. The verse alludes to gods made of wood and stone—perhaps the biblical *teraphim*—who do not *see, hear, eat,* or *smell*. While here in Deuteronomy the verse has a polemical tone, it preserves an important glimpse of the role that the meal as an intersensorial experience played in mediating religion. The verse likely alludes to the presence of the household gods (i.e., "gods made of wood and stone") gathered around the family meal with the family as the members of the household feed themselves *and them*. We can use the allusion to the family gods here in the verse to imagine the setting of the family and their gods in the domestic enclosure saturated with the smell of the meal mingling with incense, seeing each in the space of the room, hearing each other talk, and tasting the sweetness of the blessings of the gods.

Blessings in the House and in the Tomb

The larger coherence of the story of Isaac blessing Jacob revolves around the role that blessings played as part of inheritance rituals in anticipation of death. This is not surprising given that blessings are most often associated with departures in the biblical texts (Gen 24:60, 47:10; 1 Kgs 8:66). In the story of Isaac's blessing, the patriarch's blessing anticipates his own final departure in death and his eventual movement from the house to the family tomb. At the outset of the story, Isaac states: "I am now an old man and do not know *the day of my death*" (Gen 27:2). Two verses later he connects his desire to bless Esau with the following request, "prepare for me the kind of tasty food I like and bring it to me to eat, so that I may give you my blessing *before I die*" (Gen 27:4). In this verse, the connection between blessing and death is framed by the preparation and consumption of a meal. Rebekah reiterates the connection between blessing and death in her request for Jacob to bring her two young goats so that she may prepare a meal (Gen 27:9–10). The sensory experience of this food and the other sensory aspects of the ritual of blessing infused religion with a type of portability and ephemerality that fused the house and the tomb.

We can also think of Isaac's blessing of Jacob as not only a transfer of inheritance understood in economic terms discretely conceived, but also in a more holistic sense. The giving of blessing according to this text involves the transfer of the house's powers understood as the bundling of everything that has produced the family's wealth and ensured the family's protection and survival. This explains much of the architecture of our narrative and the way that it focuses upon how the description of the act of giving a blessing gathers into its frame much of the household's economy, sustenance, and progeny. The references to the field and the house, the food and the drink, and the different members of the family form the building blocks of this narrative centered upon blessing. This is where an understanding of religion's fluidity and embeddedness becomes especially important as it brings into sharp focus the way that the act of blessing conjured and transferred the power of the house for a new generation.

When we turn back to the archaeological record, we can look to the site of Ketef Hinnom for further illustration of the role that blessings played in association with death and burial (Barkay 1992; Suriano 2018). The site is an elite mortuary complex dating to the late Iron Age located just outside of the Old City walls of Jerusalem (Barkay 1994). The tomb repositories discovered at the site provide some of the richest glimpses of the types of personal possessions that were buried with the dead in this period (Suriano 2018: 88–90). As such, the objects discovered in this space offer a picture of the many things of the house that functioned as part of domestic religion that were buried with the dead in the family tomb. In many cases, the assemblages discovered in such repositories parallel the assemblages characteristic of domestic enclosures, though there are generally fewer cooking pots and storage jars represented (Bloch-Smith 2009: 125–29). Assemblages from mortuary contexts include layers of pottery vessels, all types of figurines, model furniture, amulets, seals, weapons, and a variety of other objects also found in domestic contexts. Compared to domestic contexts, the assemblages in tombs contain more vessels related to the consumption rather than preparation of food and drink, lamps, and items of personal adornment.

The tomb assemblages described above provide the context for understanding the meaning of two inscriptions that were discovered in one of the repositories in the mortuary complex at Ketef Hinnom. While offering a different use of blessings than that found in the text about Isaac's blessing, these two inscriptions provide a window into how blessings were recontextualized to serve a function in death (Lewis 2012). The inscriptions are miniature metal scrolls that were designed to be suspended from the neck as amuletic jewelry. Amulet 1 measures about 27.5 mm. in length while Amulet 2 is considerably smaller, measuring about 11.5 mm. in length. When the amulets were unrolled it was discovered that both objects contained inscriptions with several lines of text in Paleo-Hebrew script including blessings with striking parallels to the biblical priestly blessing of Numbers 6:24–26. The revised edition of the amulets also clarified that both amulets contained statements about Yahweh's ability to ward off Evil (Barkay et al. 2003). Paleographic and linguistic analysis of the inscriptions suggests that the amulets date to the period of the late Judean monarchy in the late 7th or early 6th century BCE (Barkay et al. 2004; Aḥituv 2012).

The relevance of the amulets to domestic religious concerns is readily apparent in the language of the inscriptions. While the inscriptions were rolled up and hidden and not meant to be read, they direct their language to concerns over individual blessing and protection (Smoak 2019). Both amulets contained the names of their owners at the top of the inscriptions. That they were inscribed on a tiny scroll of metal and placed around the neck rather than displayed for people to see points to their function in domestic religion (Lewis 2020: 43). The amulets were likely placed with the deceased in the tomb because they had functioned as personal possessions of their owners in life. A brief description of their inscriptions draws further attention to their function in domestic religion.

Amulet 1 reads:

> [For PN]-iah . . .[3] the grea[t . . . who keeps][4] the covenant and[5][g]raciousness toward those who love [him] and[6] those who keep [his commandments . . .[7] . . . the eternal [. . .][9] [the] blessing more than any[10] [sna]re and more than evil.[11] For redemption is in him.[12] For Yahweh[13] is our restorer [and][14] rock. May Yahweh bless[s][15] you and[16] [may he] guard you.[17] [May] Yahweh make[18] [his face] shine...

Amulet 2 reads:

> [For PN, (the son/daughter of) xxxx][1]h/hu. May h[e]/[2]sh[e] be blessed by Yahweh,[3]the warrior [or: helper] and[4] the rebuker of[5][E]vil: May Yahweh bless you,[6]keep you.[7]May Yahweh make[8]his face shine[9]upon you and[10]grant you p[ea]ce.

The first two lines of the inscription on Amulet 1 direct a blessing toward an individual: "May h[e]/sh[e] be blessed by Yahweh." The very top of the inscription on Amulet 1 may also preserve traces of the theophoric element of a personal name (Barkay 1994: 159). The covenantal statements about Yahweh's faithfulness to those who love him in Amulet 1 also direct their focus toward individual concerns. As Barkay et al. (2004: 68) concluded, "the use of confessional statement in Ketef Hinnom I...introduces a context associated with personal piety and family life—that of family tomb and burial or an individual." In the context of the amulets, the second person pronominal suffixes in the blessings ("bless *you*," "keep *you*," "shine upon *you*," "grant *you* peace") direct Yahweh's protection toward the amulets' owners. The concern is not corporate—as in the use of the blessing in the biblical texts—but instead individual: *you* here in this context directs Yahweh's shining face toward the health and protection of the individual body. In this way, the second person suffixes in the blessing give verbal expression to what the feel of the amulets upon the body conveyed for their wearers, and the shine of the silver conveyed that Yahweh's blessings and protection manifested themselves upon the individual.

A material religion approach reminds us that the materiality and design of these tiny scrolls would have been the primary means by which they communicated meaning for their owners.[3] More than a backdrop to their words, the chemical purity of the precious metal and the visual quality of its shine conveyed notions of divine blessing and protection (Smoak 2021). While the silver would have indexed the wealth and perhaps prestige of their wearers, refined silver also held a ritual application in the use of amulets. Several biblical texts associate refined silver with covenant devotion to Yahweh (Jer 6:27–30; Mal 3:3; Zech 13:9; Holladay 1986: 228–33). Such texts connect refined silver to the status of an individual who has been tested by God and found ritually pure (see also Prov 17:3; Fox 2009: 625). Silver was valued for its associations with cultic purity, divine presence, and ritual efficacy (Benzel 2015).

The tiny size of the amulets and their design as scrolls with divine words mediated the divine presence of Yahweh for their wearers. Their surfaces created an experience of divine words at the fingertips that felt smooth, pure, straight, and perhaps most importantly, within arm's reach. Feeling the chemical purity of the silver at the touch of the fingers while catching the glimmer of their shine presenced Yahweh's blessing and protection for their owners. They transposed language associated with temple ritual to the stage of the individual body (Smoak 2021). By placing the silver scrolls onto the upper part of the chest their wearers set Yahweh's words of blessing upon their hearts. As expressions of personal religious devotion, the amulets also played an important role in producing notions of religion in the house. They expressed not only personal piety, but as personal adornment, they played active roles in constructing the relationship between personal identity and familial identity (Albertz and Schmitt 2012: 412; Quick 2021: 145–46).

The act of placing the amulets in the tomb with the dead then served to further the association of the tomb, or the "house of eternity," with the family dwelling. Barkay noted that over a thousand objects were discovered in the space where the amulets were discovered (1994). The objects included 263 complete pottery vessels, fragments from jewelry made of iron, bronze, silver, gold, shells, arrowheads, bone and ivory objects, lamps, beads, a coin, a seal, and several glass and alabaster objects. Barkay emphasized the pottery vessels from the repository were mostly of the type used in mortuary contexts—vessels for lighting, wine, or perfume (1994). The discovery of the two amulets among the different objects listed here provides the context for understanding their meaning in the tomb. They adorned the dead as they had adorned the living, but in this new context, the durability of the silver was amplified against the body's transition to the afterlife. We might also reflect back upon the story of Isaac one last time here and imagine how these many objects in the tomb reflect the types of vessels that would have been used in the preparation and consumption of a meal. While the blessings on the two amulets had an explicitly personal function related to the bodies of the deceased they adorned, we can also imagine how their placement on the dead by living kin transferred divine blessings to the house of eternity.

Conclusion

Ending with an emphasis upon the relationship between tomb and house also returns us to the house and a focus upon the immateriality of religion. While we often focus upon the house as a place of sustenance and protection, the house for some and at varying times conjured feelings of ambivalence and loss. It reminds us that the house is the space where people were most aware of the role that the *presence of absence* played in religion (Meyer 2012: 104). The pain of the loss of family and the resulting silence or the loss of one's house produced pervasive cognitive dissonance as well as shared social experience. While absence is more difficult to identify and visualize through the material remains in the archaeological record, the textual evidence provides a variety of glimpses of the house as a conflicted, ambivalent, and haunted space as the loss of family left a palpable presence for those who continued to live in the family dwelling. The various rites of mourning that the biblical texts connect with the house and the household point not only to the importance of such rituals but also to the deep imprint that they left upon cultural memory (Gen. 37:34; 2 Sam. 1:11–12; Jer. 6:26, 16:17).

The fact that so many biblical curses direct their threats toward the destruction or loss of houses point to the way that religion infused both the fears and realities associated with the absence of family and the experience of exile and in this way the great ability of the house to become home. Indeed, one of the most persistent curses preserved in the biblical texts is the threat of the loss of one's house (Deut. 28:30; Amos 5:11; Zeph. 1:13; Smoak 2008). It is, after all, this conflicted and ambivalent character and memory of the house that allowed Isaiah 65 to idealize return from exile in the following words:

> No more shall there be in it an infant that lives but a few days,
> or an old person who does not live out a lifetime;
> for one who dies at a hundred years will be considered a youth,
> and one who falls short of a hundred will be considered accursed.
> They shall build houses and inhabit them; they shall plant vineyards and eat their fruit.
> They shall not build and another inhabit; they shall not plant and another eat;
> for like the days of a tree shall the days of my people be,
> and my chosen shall long enjoy the work of their hands.

This text also illustrates well the larger point made in the present study about religion in the house as it describes Yahweh's blessing as something that permeates and fuses the labor and activities of the family with the materials of the house and the human lifecycle.

Notes

1. It is beyond the scope of the present paper to discuss the composition and date of the present passage. For summary and discussion, see Coats 1983: 199–200; Blum 1984: 84–85; Carr 1996: 85–86.
2. For discussion of recent studies on the senses in religion and archaeology, see Skeates and Day (2020); Day (2013); Hamilakis (2011).
3. For a helpful introduction to a focus upon materiality in the study of religion, see Raja and Rüpke (2015: 3–4); Hazard (2013: 58–78). For more specific application in the study of Israelite religion, see Mandell and Smoak (2019: 1–42).

Bibliography

Ackerman, Susan. 2008. "Household Religion, Family Religion, and Women's Religion in ANCIENT ISRAEL." Pages 127–58 in *Household and Family Religion in Antiquity*. Edited by J. Bodel and S. M. Olyan. Malden: Blackwell.

———. 2012. "Cult Centralization, the Erosion of Kin-Based Communities, and the Implications for Women's Religious Practices." Pages 19–40 in *Social Theory and the Study of Israelite Religion: Essays in Retrospect and Prospect*. Edited by S. M. Olyan. Atlanta: Society of Biblical Literature.

———. 2014. "Women's Rites of Passage in Ancient Israel: Three Case Studies (Birth, Coming of Age, and Death)." in Pages 1–32 in *Family and Household Religion: Toward a Synthesis of Old Testament Studies, Archaeology, Epigraphy, and Cultural Studies*, Edited by R. Albertz, B. A. Nakhai, S. M. Olyan, and R. Schmitt. Winona Lake.: Eisenbrauns.

———. 2016. "Women and the Worship of Yahweh in Ancient Israel." Pages 189–97 in *Confronting the Past: Archaeological and Historical Essays on Ancient Israel in Honor of William G. Dever*. Edited by S. Gitin, J. E. Wright, and J. P. Dessel. Winona Lake: Eisenbrauns.

Aḥituv, Shmuel. 2012. "A Rejoinder to Nadav Na'aman's 'A New Appraisal of the Silver Amulets from Ketef Hinnom," *IEJ* 62: 223–32.

Albertz, Rainer, and Rüdiger Schmitt. 2012. *Family and Household Religion in Ancient Israel and the Levant*. Winona Lake: Eisenbrauns.

Andrews, Carol. 1994. *Amulets of Ancient Egypt*. London: British Museum Press.

Arie, Eran, Baruch Rosen, and Dvori Namdar. 2020. "Cannabis and Frankincense at the Judahite Shrine of Arad." *TA* 47: 5–28.

Avrahami, Yael. 2012. *The Senses of Scripture: Sensory Perception in the Hebrew Bible*. New York: T & T Clark.

Bang, Seung Ho, Oded Borowski, Kook Young Yoon, and Yuval Goren. 2017. "Local Production and Domestic Ritual Use of Small Rectangular Incense Altars: A Petrographic provenience Analysis and Examination of Craftsmanship of the Tell Halif Incense Altars." Pages 171–92 in *Gods, Objects, and Ritual Practice*. Edited by S. Blakely. Atlanta: Lockwood Press.

Barkay, Gabriel. 1992. "The Priestly Benediction on Silver Plaques from Ketef Hinnom in Jerusalem," *TA* 19: 139–91.

———. 1994. "Excavations at Ketef Hinnom in Jerusalem." Pages 85–106 in *Ancient Jerusalem Revealed*. Edited by Hillel Geva. Jerusalem: Israel Exploration Society.

Barkay, Gabriel, Marylin J. Lundberg, Andrew G. Vaughn, Bruce Zuckerman, and K. Zuckerman. 2003. "The Challenges of Ketef Hinnom: Using Advanced Technologies to Reclaim the Earliest Texts and their Contexts," *NEA* 66: 162–71.

Barkay, Gabriel, Andrew G. Vaughn, Marylin J. Lundberg, and Bruce Zuckerman. 2004. "The Amulets from Ketef Hinnom: A New Edition and Evaluation," *BASOR* 334: 41–71.

Betts, Eleanor. 2017. *Senses of Empire: Multisensory Approaches to Roman Culture*. New York: Routledge.

Bloch-Smith, Elizabeth. 2009. "From Womb to Tomb: The Israelite Family in Death as in Life," Pages 122–31 in *The Family in Life and in Death: The Family in Ancient Israel, Sociological and Archaeological Perspectives*. Edited by P. Dutcher-Walls. New York: T & T Clark.

Blum, Erhard. 1984. *Die Komposition der Vätergeschichte*. Neukirchen-Vluyn: Neukirchener Verlag.

Blumberg-Kraus, Jonathan. 2010. "'Truly the Ear Tests Words and the Palette Tests Foods,' (Job 12:11)." Pages 42–51 in *Food and Language: Proceedings of the Oxford Symposium on Food and Cookery 2009*. Edited by Richard Hosking. Devon: Prospect Books.

Carr, David. 1996. *Reading the Fractures of Genesis: Historical and Literary Approaches*. Louisville: Westminster John Knox.

Carroll, Timothy. 2016. "Im/material Objects: Relics, Gestured Signs, and the Substance of the Immaterial." Pages 119–32 in *Materiality and the Study of Religion: The Stuff of the Sacred*. Edited by T. Hutchings and J. McKenzie. London: Routledge.

Chapman, Cynthia. 2016. *The House of the Mother: The Social Roles of Maternal Kin in Biblical Hebrew Narrative and Poetry*. New Haven: Yale University Press.

Coats, George. W. 1983. *Genesis, with an Introduction to Narrative Literature*. Grand Rapids: Eerdmans.

Day, Jo., ed. 2013. *Making Senses of the Past: Toward a Sensory Archaeology*. Carbondale: Southern Illinois University Press.

Ebeling, Jennie R. 2010. *Women's Lives in Biblical Times*. London: T & T Clark International.

Ebeling, Jennie R., and Michael M. Homan. 2008. "Baking and Brewing Beer in the Israelite Household: A Study of Women's Cooking Technology." Pages 45–62 in *The World of Women in the Ancient and Classical Near East*. Edited by B. A. Nakhai. Newcastle upon Tyne: Cambridge Scholars.

Finkelstein, Israel. 2012. "Tell el-Farah (Tirzah) and the Early Days of the Northern Kingdom." *RB* 119: 331–46.

Fox, Michael. 2009. *Proverbs 10–31: A New Translation and Introduction and Commentary*. New Haven: Yale University Press.

Gadot, Yuval, Israel Finkelstein, Mark. Iserlis, Aren M. Maeir, Pirhiya Nahshoni, and Dvori Namdar. 2014. "Tracking Down Cult: Production, Function and Content of Chalices in Iron Age Philistia," *TA* 41: 55–76.

Garroway, Kristine Henrickson. 2018. *Growing Up in Ancient Israel: Children in Material Culture and Biblical Texts*. Atlanta: SBL.

Gudme, Anne Katrine. 2010. "Modes of Religion: An Alternative to 'popular/official' Religion." Pages 77–104 in *Anthropology and the Bible: Critical perspectives*. Edited by E. Pfoh. Piscataway: Gorgias.

———. 2014. "Inside-Outside: Domestic Living Space in Biblical Memory." Pages 61–78 in *Memory and the City in Ancient Israel*. Edited by D. Edelman and E. Ben Zvi. Winona Lake: Eisenbrauns.

Hamilakis, Yannis. 2011. "Archaeologies of the Senses." Pages 208–25 in *The Oxford Handbook of the Archaeology of Ritual and Religion*. Edited by T. Insoll. Oxford: Oxford University Press.

Haran, Menahem. 1960. "The Uses of Incense in Ancient Israelite Ritual." *VT* 10: 113–29.

Hazard, Sonia. 2013. "The Material Turn in the Study of Religion," *Religion and Society: Advances in Research* 4: 58–78.

Holladay, William L. 1986. *Jeremiah: A Commentary on the Book of the Prophet Jeremiah (Chapters 1–25)*. Philadelphia: Fortress.

Houston, Stephen D. and Karl A. Taube. 2000. "An Archaeology of the Senses: Perception and Cultural Expression in Ancient Mesoamerica." *CAJ* 10: 261–94.

Howes, David, and Constance Classen. 2013. *Ways of Sensing: Understanding the Senses in Society*. London: Routledge.

Lewis, Theodore. 2012. "Job 19 in the Light of the Ketef Hinnom Inscriptions and Amulets." Pages 99–113 in *Puzzling Out the Past: Studies in the Northwest Semitic Languages and Literatures in Honor of Bruce Zuckerman*. Edited by S. Fine, M. J. Lundberg, and W. T. Pitard. Leiden: Brill.

———. 2020. *The Origin and Character of God: Ancient Israelite Religion through the Lens of Divinity*. Oxford: Oxford University Press.

Limmer, Abigail. "The Social Function and Ritual Significance of Jewelry in the Iron Age II Southern Levant." Unpublished PhD diss., University of Arizona, 2007.

MacDonald, Nathan. 2008. *Not Bread Alone: The Uses of Food in the Old Testament*. Oxford: Oxford University Press.

Mandell, Alice, and Jeremy Smoak. 2019. "The Material Turn in the Study of Israelite Religions: Spaces, Things, and the Body." *JHS* 19: 1–42.

McHugh, John. 2011. "Seeing Scents: Methodological Reflections on the Intersensory Perception of Aromatics in South Asian Religions." *History of Religions* 51(2): 156–77.

Meyer, Brigit, David Morgan, Chris Paine, and Brent Plate. "The Origin and Mission of Material Religion." *Material Religion* 40(3): 207–11.

Meyer, Morgan. 2012. "Placing and Tracing Absence: A Material Culture of the Immaterial." *JMC* 17: 103–10.

Meyers, Carol. 2005. *Household and Holiness: The Religious Culture of Israelite Women*. Minneapolis: Fortress.

———. 2007. "From Field Crops to Food: Attributing Gender and Meaning to Bread Production in Iron Age Israel." Pages 67–84 in *The Archaeology of Difference: Gender, Ethnicity, Class, and the "Other" in Antiquity: Studies in Honor of Eric M. Meyers*. Edited by D. R. Edwards and C. T. McCullough. Boston: American Schools of Oriental Research.

———. 2012. *Rediscovering Eve: Ancient Israelite Women in Context*. New York: Oxford.

———. 2014. "Feast Days and Food Ways: Religious Dimensions of Household Life." Pages 225–250 in *Family and Household Religion: Toward a synthesis of Old Testament Studies, Archaeology, Epigraphy, and Cultural Studies*. Edited by R. Albertz, B. A. Nakhai, S. M. Olyan, and R. Schmitt. Winona Lake: Eisenbrauns.

———. 2017. "Contributing to Continuity: Women and Sacrifice in Ancient Israel." Pages 1–19 in *Women, Religion, and the Gift: An Abundance of Riches*. Edited by Morny Joy. Basel: Springer.

Nakhai, Beth Alpert. 2008. *The World of Women in the Ancient and Classical Near East*. Newcastle upon Tyne: Cambridge Scholars.

———. 2011. "Varieties of Religion Expression in the Domestic Setting." Pages 347–60 in *Household Archaeology in Ancient Israel and Beyond*. Edited by A. Yasur-Landau, J. R. Ebeling, and L. B. Mazow. Leiden: Brill.

———. 2014a. "The Household as Sacred Space." Pages 53–72 in *Family and Household Religion: Toward a Synthesis of Old Testament Studies, Archaeology, Epigraphy, and Cultural Studies*. Edited by R. Albertz, B. A. Nakhai, S. M. Olyan, and R. Schmitt. Winona Lake: Eisenbrauns.

———. 2014b. "Mother-and-Child Figurines in the Late Bronze-Persian Period Levant." Pages 165–98 in *Material Culture Matters: Essays in the Archaeology of the Southern Levant in Honor of Seymour Gitin*. Edited by J. Spencer, R. Mullins, and A. Brody. Winona Lake: Eisenbrauns.

———. 2018. "When Considering Infants and Jar Burials in the Middle Bronze Age Southern Levant." Pages 100–28 in *Tell it in Gath: Studies in the History and Archaeology of Israel: Essays in Honor of Aren M. Maeir on the Occasion of his Sixtieth Birthday*. Edited by I. Shai, J. R. Chadwick, L. Hitchcock, A. Dagan, C. McKinny, and J. Uziel. Münster: Zaphon.

Nielsen, Kjeld. 1986. *Incense in Ancient Israel*. Leiden: Brill.

Pinch, Geraldine. 1983. "Childbirth and Female Figurines at Deir el-Medina and el-'Amarna." *Or* 52: 405–14.

Porteous, J. D. 1985. "Smellscape." *Progress in Physical Geography: Earth and Environment* 9(3): 356–78.

Quick, Laura. 2021. *Dress, Adornment, and the Body in the Hebrew Bible*. Oxford: Oxford University Press.

Raja, R., and J. Rüpke. 2015. "Archaeology of Religion, Material Religion, and the Ancient World." Pages 1–26 in *A Companion to the Archaeology of Religion in the Ancient World*. Edited by R. Raja and J. Rüpke. Malden: John Wiley & Sons.

Shafer-Elliott, Cynthia. 2012. *Food in Ancient Judah: Domestic Cooking in the Time of the Hebrew Bible*. Sheffield: Equinox.

Skeates, Robin and Jo Day, eds. 2020. *The Routledge Handbook of Sensory Archaeology*. London and New York: Routledge.

Smoak, Jeremy D. 2008. "Building Houses and Planting Vineyards: The Inner-biblical Discourse on an Ancient Israelite Wartime Curse." *JBL* 127: 19–35.

———. 2019. "Wearing Divine Words: In Life and Death." *Material Religion* 15(4): 433–55.

———. 2021. "You Have Refined Us Like Silver is Refined (Ps. 66:10): Yahweh's Metallurgical Powers in Ancient Judah." *AABNER* 1(3): 81–116.

Stavrakopoulou, Francesca. 2016. "Religion at Home: The Materiality of Practice." Pages 347–65 in *The Wiley Blackwell Companion to Ancient Israel*. Edited by S. Niditch. Malden: John Wiley.

Stavrakopoulou, Francesca, and J. Barton, eds. 2010. *Religious Diversity in Ancient Israel and Judah* London: T&T Clark.

Suriano, Matthew J. 2018. *A History of Death in the Hebrew Bible*. New York: Oxford University Press.

Thomason, Alison K. 2016. "The Sense-scapes of Neo-Assyrian Capital Cities: Royal Authority and Bodily Experience." *CAJ* 26: 243–64.Toorn, Karel van der. 1996. *Family Religion in Babylonia, Syria and Israel: Continuity and Change in the Forms of Religious Life*. Leiden: Brill.

Tufnell, Olga. 1953. *Lachish III: The Iron Age*. London: Oxford University Press.

Vaux, Roland de. 1961. "Les fouilles de Tell el-Far'ah: Rapport préliminaire sur les 7e, 8e, 9e campagnes, 1958–1960." *RB* 68: 557–92.

Willett, Elizabeth. A. R. "Women and Household Shrines in Ancient Israel." Unpublished PhD diss., University of Arizona, 1999.

Zevit, Ziony. 2001. *The Religions of Ancient Israel: A Synthesis of Parallactic Approaches*. London: Continuum.

———. 2003. "False Dichotomies in Descriptions of Israelite Religion: A Problem, Its Origin, and a Proposed Solution." Pages 223–35 in *Symbiosis, Symbolism, and the Power of the Past: Canaan, Ancient Israel, and their Neighbors from the Late Bronze Age through Roman Palaestinae*. Edited by W. G. Dever and S. Gitin. Winona Lake: Eisenbrauns.

———. 2014. "The Textual and Sociological Embeddedness of Israelite Family Religion. Who are the Players? Where Were the Stages?" Pages 287–314 in *Family and Household Religion*, ed. R. Albertz, B. Nakhai, S. M. Olyan, and R. Schmitt. Winona Lake: Eisenbrauns.

28
VISUAL CULTURE AND RELIGION IN ANCIENT ISRAEL AND JUDAH

Christoph Uehlinger

The very idea that the religion(s) of ancient Israel and Judah should be associated with visual culture, images, and iconography may seem counter-intuitive to readers used to thinking about Israelite religion in terms of worship of (and belief in) a single deity, Yahweh, whose explicit demand in the so-called "Decalogue" was that he not be associated in ritual with other deities, nor represented as a cult statue, or visualized by "any manner of likeness, of anything that is in heaven above, or that is in/on the earth beneath, or that is in the water under the earth" (Exod 20:4; par Deut 5:8). In contrast, modern scholarship posits that the Decalogue's prohibition expresses the programmatic ideal of a "post-exilic" priestly-scribal elite rather than actual ritual practice among Israelites and Judahites during the first half of the first millennium BCE. That "preexilic" Israelite and Judahite religion and culture at large were far from aniconic (literally, "imageless") has been demonstrated based on several threads of data and arguments. First, the Hebrew Bible itself is full of texts that refer to visual imagery in one way or another (Schroer 1987). Second, archaeological data from the southern Levant, and more specifically from territories controlled by the Israelite and/or Judahite polities (whether pre-state or monarchic) during the Iron Age, attest to a wide repertoire of figurative visual art and culture, some of which relate rather obviously to religion—both practice and imagination (Keel and Uehlinger 1998; Schmitt 2020). Third, ancient Hebrew inscriptional data (and biblical texts) point to patterns of religious practice so well-fitting what we know from other ancient Levantine societies that the very notion of a fundamentally different and distinct Israelite or Judahite mindset has become increasingly difficult to support. The effect is that, fourth, many scholars tend to construe ancient Israelite and Judahite religion as sub-set(s) of ancient Levantine religion (Uehlinger 2015). Much historical-critical de- and reconstruction has led some scholars to convert biblical normativity into its assumed historical opposite, something highlighted by recent attempts to identify images as actual visual representations of Yahweh (see below). While such an identification remains highly hypothetical for the time being, to consider the relationship of visual culture and religion in ancient Israel and Judah is all but a subject for revisionists, having developed over the last decades into an almost obvious, necessary, and challenging task for critical contemporary scholarship on "ancient Israel" in its southern Levantine context (Uehlinger 2019).

Preliminaries

Before approaching the subject frontally, we should pause and reflect how this task can be best approached in line with state-of-the-art theory on the one hand, and historical data on the other. To begin, I clarify some key concepts used in this chapter, especially "visual culture," "iconography," and "religion," but also "ancient Israel and Judah." This will be followed by explanations of how this chapter selects and organizes the data on which its main arguments rest.

Iconography vs. Visual Culture

Iconography typically refers to the study of mainly figurative art, the recognition of individual features, motifs, and subject matter within pictorial compositions as well as their correlation and identification with themes and plots known from literature, mythology, etc. In its most elementary sense, the task of iconography consists of collecting and establishing the repertoire of visual motifs attested at a given place (or region) and period. For the present purpose, we might ask what were the most representative motifs and entities (deities, humans, animals and *Mischwesen*, natural and human-made objects, etc.) pictured in and on images that circulated in ancient Israelite and Judahite society during the Iron Age? To be distinguished from iconography, *iconology* questions images about their meanings and the ideologies they convey in and for a particular society: why and to what end would that society (or a particular milieu, e.g., a king and his court, a traders' network, or a community of craftsmen) favor this or that selection of iconographical motifs and scenes available at any given time?

The concept of *visual culture* (with its corollary "Visual Culture studies") points to a significant move within disciplines traditionally concerned with images and pictures, such as art history or visual media studies, from a privileged concern with products of elite culture and its consumption among the fortuned and connoisseurs, toward a more social-scientifically minded search for the uses and functions of images in society at large, including so-called popular culture. In a visual culture approach, images, imagery, and visual arrangements in the widest sense are studied as media meant to attract people and to engage them in specific practices, whether of looking and recognizing, interacting or believing, to rule or to obey. Images are not simply taken as givens to look at, but are approached as conveyed by artifacts, which themselves result from transformative labor as products of craftsmen and artists driven by skill as much as interest and patronage. On a more hermeneutical level, images are today regarded not simply as figurative "representations" of something or someone, but as devices employed to render present ("presentify") something or someone, to give a form to what (or who) would otherwise be absent—a material presence or a body with which people might communicate and interact, both physically and through their imagination.

In the context of this chapter, to look for visual culture (more specifically: *material* visual culture) rather than images or iconography alone entails that while we may consider images of gods or goddesses a significant part of our study, we should be concerned with a far wider array of meaningful data. An intentionally erected standing stone, a stela, even if "aniconic" (that is, devoid of any figurative, sculptured, or painted image), the façade of a monumental building or a conspicuously arranged city gate can all be regarded as part of visual culture broadly understood. Equally important, we should always consider images as material artifacts, or parts thereof; that is, not only in terms of the cognitive concepts they may convey, but intimately related to the actual physical objects (their material and affordances, dimensions, functions, and use) on which they appear.

Christoph Uehlinger

What Data of Ancient Visual Culture Should We Count as "Religious"?

However commonplace it may be for scholars and laypeople to speak about "ancient Israelite or Judahite religion," such a thing did not exist in antiquity. "Religion," as used to designate a discrete field of social organization concerned with collective, communal, or individual beliefs and practices (involving non-empirical entities such as deities, demons, angels, etc.) and distinguished from, e.g., politics or economy, is a modern concept shaped by the peculiar pathways taken by (Western) societies from late antiquity to the present. That ancient Semitic languages including ancient (and biblical) Hebrew have no semantic equivalent for "religion" should therefore not surprise us, regardless of how our conceptual apparatus may otherwise depend on biblical or non-biblical languages and literature (even the phrase "to fear God" cannot serve as a simple placeholder). To insist on the huge gap separating the modern concept of "religion" from any hypothetically conceivable ancient Israelite or Judahite historical reality is to remind us that when searching for "religion" among the data that will potentially inform us, we apply our own categorial framework and select the data according to modern scholars' choice. The choice is not all haphazard or futile. It is perfectly legitimate to pragmatically inquire (Aldenderfer 2012) how ancient Israelites and Judahites (some of whom may not have considered themselves as such in the first place) situated themselves in their natural and social environment, a world they experienced in terms of threats, duties, and rewards partly influenced by non-empirical entities; how they imagined and visualized deities and demons on which they relied or which they feared; and under what circumstances, in what settings, and by what ritual practices they would have engaged with them.

How should we select among the myriads of archaeologically recovered data those potentially relevant for our inquiry? This chapter suggests that we distinguish between three distinct kinds of data:

- those we classify as religion-related because of the special context from which they were recovered, e.g., shrines; and/or which indicate religiously ceremonial function because of particular types or assemblages of objects pointing to a special emphasis on ritualization;
- special object genres we tend to attribute to ritual practices and ritualization (such as altars, offering stands, or shrine models);
- other items whose use and purpose were not necessarily religion-related, but whose iconographical decorum features non-empirical entities, scenes of ritual intercourse, or symbols for blessing, good health, protection, etc.

Israelite and Judahite Religion and Visual Culture?

A last word of caution is needed to problematize the two ethno-political adjectives qualifying the term "religion" in the title of this chapter. The epistemological precedent for the distinction of "Israelite" vs. "Judahite" is of course set by the Hebrew Bible and its literary *mise en scène* of an ethno-history focusing on a single *ethnos* ("the children of Israel") split, for much of its pre-exilic history, into two distinct polities and territories. Far from being inventions of the biblical historiographers' minds, the two polities and some of their kings are mentioned extensively in extra-biblical inscriptions. The sensitive issue at stake here is that biblical historiography correlates their historical destiny to notions of right vs. wrong behavior *vis-à-vis* Yahweh, the god of (all) Israel, and his putatively preferred residence-temple in Jerusalem. In other words, exclusive worship of one deity and at one single sanctuary are construed as the two paramount criteria to distinguish right from wrong religious obedience, in a framework that is both ethnically and politically defined. Moreover, the two polities are construed as surrounded by other "nations" which follow deities of their own such as Baʿal, Chemosh, or Dagon. Following the basic opposition of "one god – one people or polity" vs. "other deities and nations," scholars have long conceived southern Levantine religion of the first millennium BCE almost exclusively in terms of "national religions," and they continue to do so even when they deal with aspects of religion that do not necessarily relate to state politics (see Schmitt 2020 for the latest installment of such a framework).

The main problem of this approach, apart from its exaggerated reliance on biblical historiography, is that religion at the time would have found a multitude of different expressions at various levels of society, from state to region, or village, through trade and guilds to family and even individuals (Barton and Stavrakopoulou 2010; see Pierce and Keimer this volume). One of the most sophisticated recent treatments of this complexity (Albertz and Schmitt 2012: ch. 4) distinguishes no less than eight different levels (with 13 sub-types) of religious organization, concern, and practice. Not always can archaeological data be precisely correlated with one of these levels, but the model may serve as a reminder that much of ancient religion related to everyday concerns and the uncertainties of people's lives (from birth to death, from the blessing of crops to the welfare of herds), with little to qualify specifically as "Israelite" or "Judahite."

Another, methodological problem related to the notion of "national religion(s)" and to the still fragmentary nature of evidence is whether we restrict our study of visual culture exclusively to the territories controlled at any given time by the polities of Israel and Judah; or whether we allow ourselves to consider data recovered outside these territories and ask, be it only for heuristic purposes, whether a certain feature, item or object genre (a certain type of statuary, a figurative stela, a shrine model, a cult symbol, etc.) attested in neighboring areas should be expected to have also been known and used in Israel and Judah. Think for instance of the rich iconographic repertoire (human figures, animals, trees, etc.) figured on the ritual objects recovered from a favissa dated to the Iron Age IIA at Yavneh: should we consider these an expression of exclusively and specifically "Philistine" religion, and hence irrelevant for the study of the religion and visual culture of "Ancient Israel?" Or should we infer from such data that the concern for the blessing of families, herds, and crops was shared by all inhabitants of the southern Levant who engaged in agriculture and animal husbandry, and that Israelite and Judahite farmers would have known similar, if not identical means to represent materially and visually what for them counted most in their everyday lives? Depending on how we deal with and answer this methodological question, our reconstruction will be either broad or restricted, inclusive or exclusive. The path here taken is to privilege data from locations that we can historically relate to the Iron Age polities of Israel and Judah, but to keep in mind all neighboring regions as a heuristic and comparative horizon; and to span the full spectrum, if selectively, from "official" state religion to less conspicuous, almost "everyday" religious practices and related imagery.

A special concern for scholars has long been whether figurative or symbolic representations of the main Israelite/Judahite deity Yahweh (and a possible female companion) can be positively identified in the material and visual record (see below for a brief discussion of this question).

Visual Culture in Contexts Related to "Religious" Ritual

The first approach to religion-related visual culture is to look for it in places where we would "expect" it because we think of those places specifically as locations of religious ritual: temples and shrines, outdoor cult places and wayside sanctuaries, or gate areas for public expressions of ritual; production areas, living quarters and tombs for more restricted practices; and, perhaps somewhere in between, places where full- or part-time specialists (men or women) would have operated, such as diviners soliciting ancestors or other spirits, healers, and exorcists (see Halbertsma and Routledge 2021 for important methodological reflections on how to identify "religious architecture").

State-run, Monumental Contexts

Positive archaeological evidence for temples in ancient Israel and Judah is so far not overwhelming (see Pierce and Keimer this volume), yet they existed beyond reasonable doubt (Koch 2020). Remains of a monumental temple structure were recovered at Tel Dan in Str. IV–II (Iron Age IIB). Although found south of the city gate, which is physically unrelated to the temple, two bronze "plaques" that may originally have belonged to standards are particularly interesting from the point of view of visual culture and religion. Dated to the late 9th or early 8th century, both show ritual scenes in which a male worshipper faces a major deity, one (Figure 28.1a) sitting on a throne, the other (Figure 28.1b) standing on a bull. While both items reflect various degrees of typically northern "influence" or tradition, plaque A has good comparanda from North Syria, whereas plaque B, which seems to be the work of a lesser skilled, possibly local craftsman, is more idiosyncratic and intriguing. The disc held by the deity on plaque B probably represents a ring, an expression of the deity's authority; the rays emerging from the deity's shoulders seem to indicate wings; while the spikes on the garment are more difficult to interpret even if they suggest a somehow aggressive attire. The overall impression is that of a winged male storm god (rather than a female goddess such as Anatolian Kubaba, *pace* Ornan 2006) standing on a bull, his attribute animal – an image a reader of the Hebrew Bible is tempted to connect with cultic imagery mentioned in 1 Kgs 12:28–29, notably in relation to Yahweh as Israel's state deity. Depictions of an anthropomorphic figure standing on a bull occur on Iron IIB stamp seals from Samaria and other sites (see below, Figures 28.11.1–4). An earlier witness for the importance of (proto-)"Israelite" bull iconography is the bronze figurine discovered at an open-air sanctuary in the Dothan region dated to the Iron Age I (Figure 28.2).

A different tradition of divine bull iconography is attested on stelae recovered from a monumental gate complex of 8th-century et-Tell ("Bethsaida"). The more elaborate of these (literally the image of an image) displays what must have been a major cult emblem composed of a pole surmounted by a bull's head, whose horns are stylized like a lunar crescent, with an additional sword and textile bands attached to the pole (Figure 28.3). The emblem combines features of a storm god with lunar and warrior symbolism – a typically Aramean or Inner Syrian composite distinct from the coastal (Canaanite and Phoenician) Baʻal tradition. Comparanda are known from the Golan (two "stick figures" carved in a wall boulder close to the entrance of an early Iron Age fortress near Hispin), the wider Hauran region, and from further north; given their distribution, the emblem most probably represented a major regional deity, perhaps Hadad of Damascus, rather than a specifically Geshurite deity as hypothesized by the excavators of et-Tell.

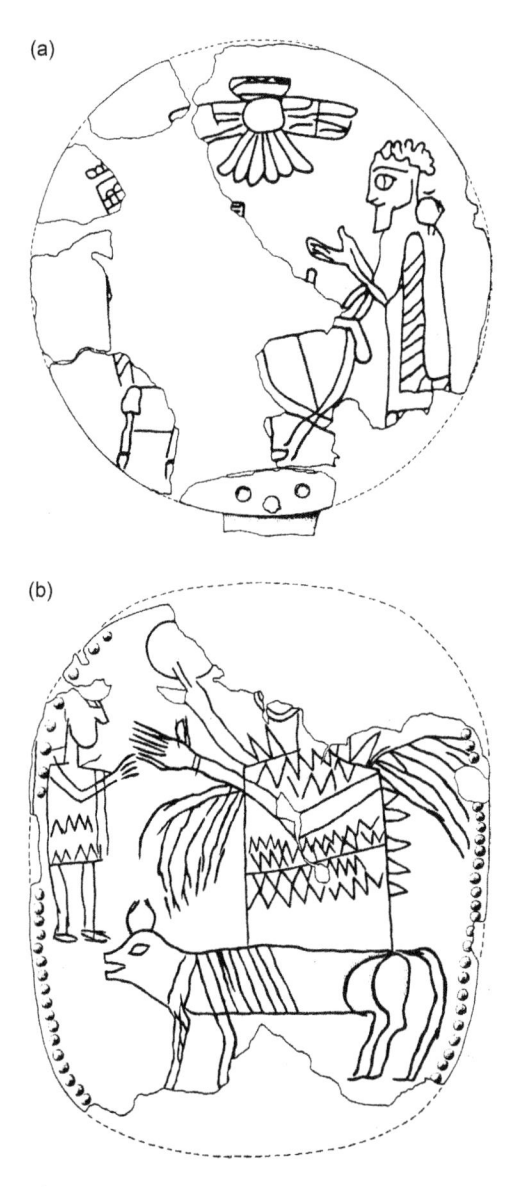

Figure 28.1 Two bronze plaques (mirrors?) from Tel Dan, Structure B south of main city gate, Iron Age IIB, late 9th or 8th cent.: (a) Plaque A, diameter 8.7 cm (Biran 1999: 53, Figure 12); (b) Plaque B, 9 x 7.6 cm (ibid.: 54, Figure 14; courtesy Nelson Glueck School of Biblical Archaeology, Jerusalem)

Regarding Judah, the recently excavated temple at Tel Motza, located only 7 km northwest of Jerusalem, operated in several phases between the late 10th and the 6th century (Kisilevitz and Lipschits 2020). The monumental building must have made a striking visual impression when seen from the valley and may by itself be considered an important aspect of local visual culture. Ritual-related objects at the site include (for the time being) the fragmentary remains of a limestone relief showing two legs of an anthropomorphic figure, an elaborate cult stand decorated with lions at the base and flower petals at the top, terracotta

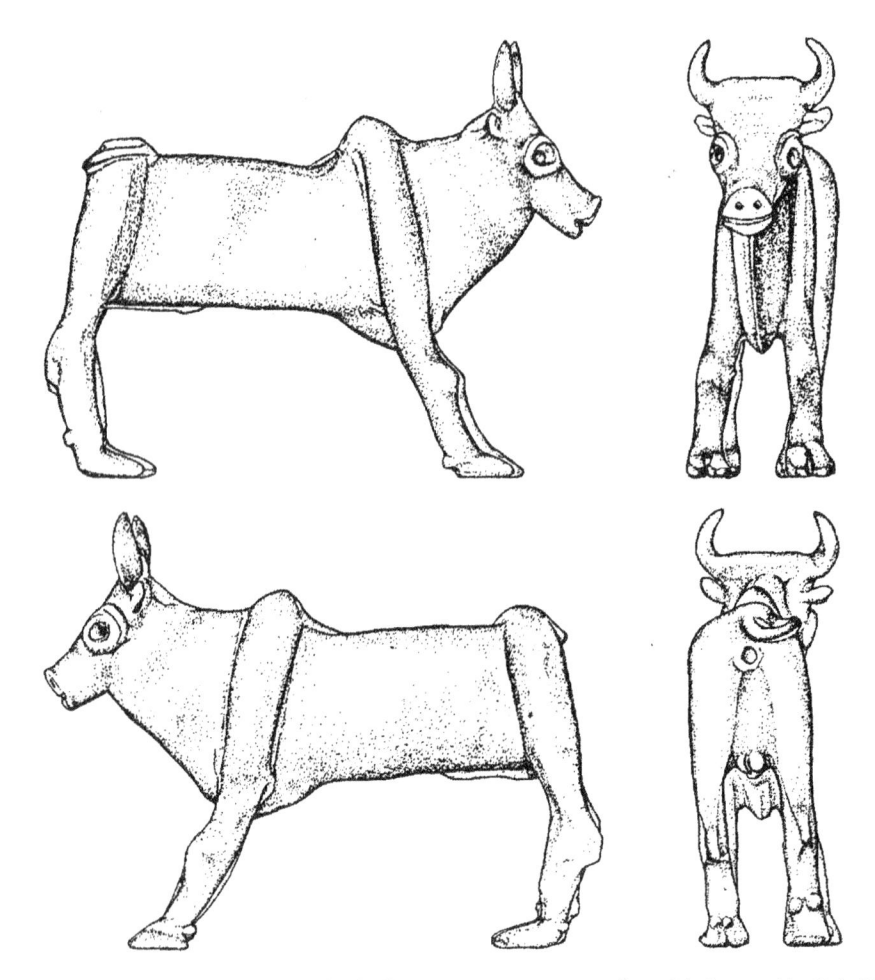

Figure 28.2 Bronze statuette of a Zebu bull, H 12.4 x L 17.5 cm; from Dhahrat et-Tawileh "Bull site," an open-air sanctuary in the Dothan region; Iron Age I, 12th cent. (Mazar 1982: 30, Figure 2A–B; courtesy Amihai Mazar, Jerusalem)

figurines of both horse riders and horses, bearded male terracotta heads which may originally have been part of small statuettes or of a stand, and a conoid stamp seal showing a bowman and a running horse. The bold suggestion to identify the small male heads with Yahweh is premature and has been rightly criticized by the excavators. Far more importantly, the overall data currently known point to the existence, next to Jerusalem, of another temple besides the one at Jerusalem (which we know only from the Hebrew Bible), something that contributes significantly to our knowledge of Iron Age II Judahite religion.

Another long-known example is the temple that was part of the Judahite fortress of Arad during the Iron Age IIB. Its center of ritual attention (or "holy of holies") contained a carefully worked standing stone that showed traces of red color, which may denote blood for "life" and thus was meant to materialize the life-holding and life-giving presence of the major deity associated to this shrine: Yahweh. We should not assume that a standing stone was considered the only acceptable way for Judahites to materialize Yahweh's presence. The Arad arrangement suggests that such a relatively modest investment was deemed sufficient for a regional sanctuary located on the southeastern periphery of the Judahite state. Note that the temple's courtyard

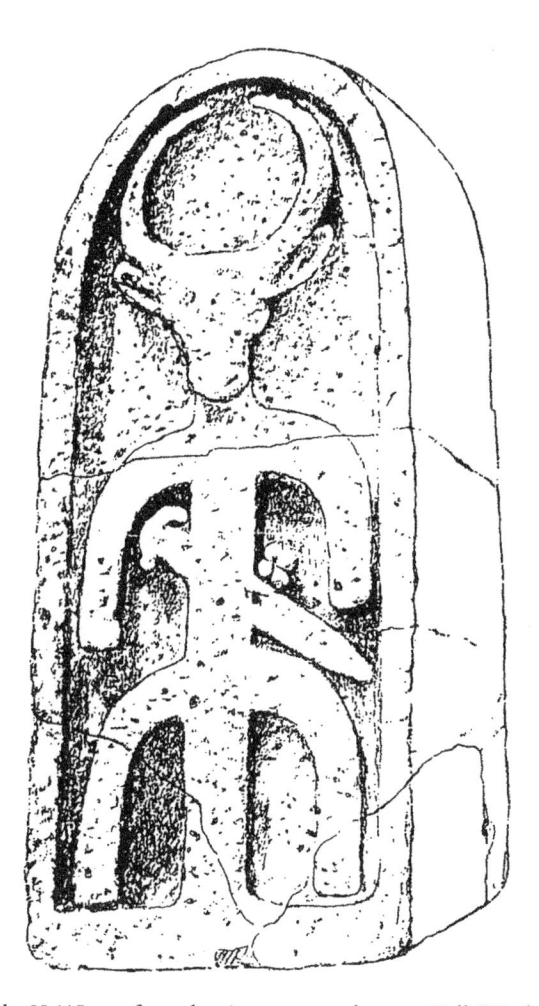

Figure 28.3 Basalt stela, H 115 cm, from the city gate complex at et-Tell ("Bethsaida"); Iron Age IIB, 8th cent. (Bernett and Keel 1998: 96, Figure 1d; drawing Bethsaida Excavations Project, courtesy Orbis Biblicus et Orientalis)

also yielded remains of typical Judahite pillar figurines, which are often disregarded in scholarly discussions about this structure. They clearly indicate an overlap of practices related to both state administration (and thus, "official" religion) and household-and-family concerns.

Intra- and Extra-mural Shrines

In addition to (a few) monumental structures, excavations have pointed to smaller buildings, generally located within towns and near gates and/or living quarters that seem to have been used primarily for ritual purposes. Examples include buildings at Megiddo, Taanach, Tell el-Farʿah (N), Tel Reḥov, Khirbet Qeiyafa, Lachish, and others. Distinctive assemblages of offering stands, vessels, rattles, etc., at times associated with offering tables, altars, standing stones, or portable shrine models, point to the role such structures played for rituals probably performed by semi-professional, part-time experts (whether male or female). Shrine models and offering stands represent the iconographically most sophisticated objects to date from such contexts; they will be discussed in the following section.

Rich assemblages of objects, many of which are explicitly iconic, have also been recovered in extra-mural shrines such as Ḥorvat Qiṭmit in the northern Negev, a region whose control was disputed between Judah and Edom, En Ḥaṣeva in the central Arabah, and in Wadi ath-Thamad in northern Moab. The three-horned head of a goddess from Qiṭmit may illustrate that anthropomorphic cultic statuary produced from clay could appropriately represent a deity despite being a cheaper material. Among the most conspicuous objects found at Qiṭmit, En Ḥaṣeva, and elsewhere (most notably Transjordan) are standing vessels elaborated by sculptor-potters into anthropomorphic figures; most of them may have represented worshippers, but since they support an offering bowl on their head, and some carry weapons (which would seem inappropriate for worshippers), at least some of these figures could well have been recipients of offerings themselves. Such vessel figures remain unattested in clearly identified "Israelite" or "Judahite" contexts. The methodological conundrum is whether this type of anthropomorphic vessel was produced among Israel's and Judah's neighbors only, or whether similar finds may also be expected to surface at sites within the borders (including, but not necessarily, so-called "fringe areas") of Israel and Judah. The most responsible scholarly attitude is to refrain from both simplistic and purely speculative answers and not to exclude options *a priori*.

Production Areas and Living Quarters

It is often (religion-related) ritualization, i.e., practice rather than an *a priori* assigned function, that renders a given setting "religious" (Halbertsma and Routledge 2021). As ancient craftsmen could engage in ritual practices to enhance the outcome of their professional activities and/or travels, it comes as no surprise that specifically dedicated workspaces and production areas may at times display ritual-related remains. Such locations have been identified at several places (e.g., Tell eṣ-Ṣâfi/Gath, Tel Reḥov, Taanach, and in Wadi ath-Thamad) in relation to very different industrial activities ranging from beekeeping or weaving to metallurgy. Whether the scholarly concept of "industrial cult" captures the entanglements of work and religion in adequate terms is a matter of a debate which will require more nuanced theoretical reflection in the future. In the words of Halbertsma and Routledge (2021: mp.17), "making things and making offerings were linked activities that shared the same architectural spaces in the Iron Age of the Southern Levant. This is only problematic if we start from the position that religious and secular spaces are categorically distinct." The latter-mentioned position may work for modern (Western) societies, but we should not impose it on ancient data.

Much attention has been devoted over the last decades to a better understanding of household and family religion (see Smoak this volume). To identify household religion in material evidence, a checklist approach identifying special artifacts as related to religious practice seems somehow inevitable, although what counts as "religious" will ever be disputed: figurines, furniture models, rattles, etc. are generally counted among the more explicit markers of religious (or "magic") ritual practices performed within households. Seals and amulets may convey religiously relevant iconography, but their presence in an assemblage does not render that context religious *per se*. The same holds for precious ivory carvings that once decorated luxury furniture, jewelry boxes, or cosmetic utensils: how far should we go when classifying them, even when the subject matter of such carvings looks most straightforwardly religious, e.g. when it figures "Egyptianizing" deities or winged composite beings flanking a stylized tree? Is it appropriate or not to describe a cosmetic spoon elaborately carved from

Visual Culture and Religion in Ancient Israel and Judah

bone from Hazor (Figure 28.4a), whose primary function was no doubt to serve an elite lady's concern for beauty, in terms that acknowledge the sliding overlaps of a profane value and religion (in this case goddess) related symbolism? Note the astute combination of the stylized tree with a female face and birds, and the dialectics of hide-and-show when you

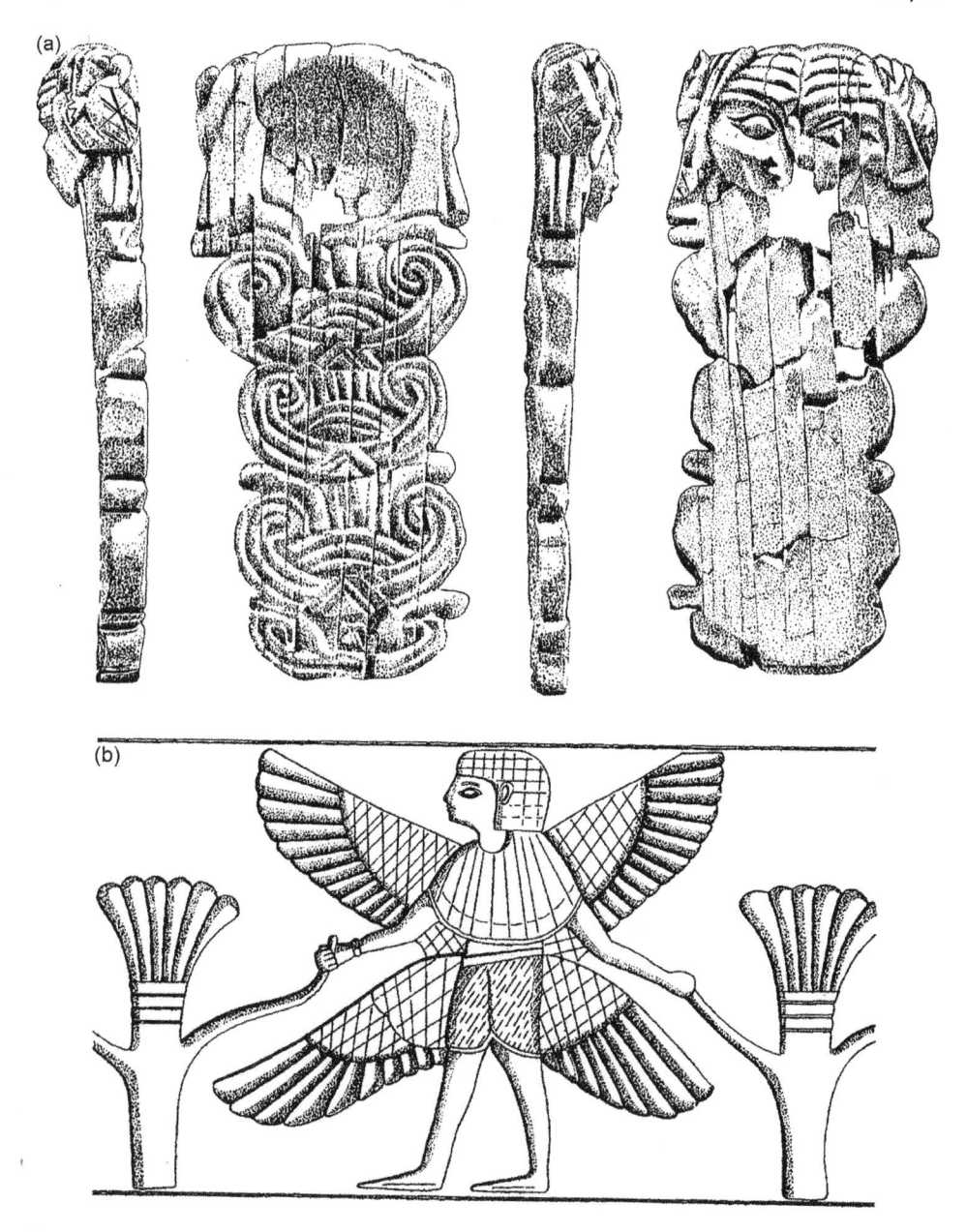

Figure 28.4 (a) Cosmetic spoon made of ivory, H 14 cm, from Hazor, Area A, Building 241/1, Str. VI, 8th cent. (Keel and Uehlinger 1998: 200, Figure 214). (b) Fan handle made of bone, H 18 cm, from Hazor, Area A, Building 48, Str. VI, 8th cent. (Keel and Uehlinger 1998: 196, Figure 210). (c) Ivory pyxis, H 7.2 cm, from Hazor, Area B close to citadel, Str. VA, late 8th cent. (Keel and Uehlinger 1998: 238, Figure 234a)

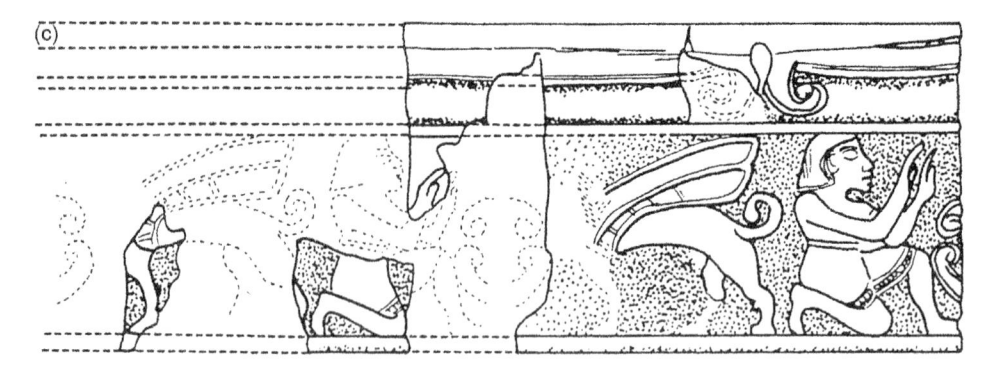

Figure 28.4 (Continued)

turn the object in your hand. Should we consider the contemporary image of a four-winged youth sculptured on a bone handle from the same site (Figure 28.4b) in our inquiry? Another scene representing a kneeling man worshipping or blessing a stylized tree in the company of a winged sphinx, carved on a slightly later ivory pyxis from the same site, can hardly be considered "non-religious" (Figure 28.4c). Whether or not such data are relevant for the (re)construction of ancient Israelite "religion" will probably always be disputed, and rightly so. The task, in my view, is to remain attentive to degrees of overlap and potential allusion, the interpenetration of religious imagination and everyday concerns, rather than to hinder scholarly imagination by clear-cut modern dichotomies and the anachronism of religious versus secular.

Tombs

Funerary practices have always been considered a major domain of religion, ancient and modern, since they structure that most fundamental boundary separating the living from their dead. Tombs are thus considered spaces of religious engagement almost by definition. Studied from the point of view of visual culture, they present a special case since graves are only open, and their contents visible, on the very occasion a person is buried; and rock-cut tombs are generally dark spaces, where lamps are needed to experience space and to recognize a burial cave's interior and paraphernalia for the funerary ritual. It can be interesting for our inquiry to observe whether the spatial organization and potential decoration of a tomb stress the latter's character as an "otherspace" or suggest continuity with a family's home. Both options are represented in the archaeological record and are especially well-documented in Judah during the Iron Ages II and III (10th–6th centuries BCE). In a 9th-century tomb near Tel Eton, two crudely hewn guardian lions flanking the entrance look toward the chamber rather than toward the exit of the tomb; they seem to protect the living from potential harm provoked by wandering spirits rather than keep away robbers from the grave: a fine example for a tomb considered as "otherspace." More frequently, however, bench tombs allowing the deposition of vessels for drinking and meals, lamps and figurines stress the continuity of the "house of a father" and a sense of a community embracing both the living and the dead.

Religion-related Artifacts and Their Iconography

Shrine Models (Portable Shrines) and Cult Stands

That portable shrine models and cult stands, generally made of terracotta or (less frequently) stone, relate to religion and religious ritual seems obvious and beyond dispute. Shrine models are equally attested in Israel (Tel Rekhesh, Tell el-Far'ah [N], Gezer), Judah (Khirbet Qeiyafa), and neighboring regions. They reflect a common Near Eastern tradition that can be traced far back into the Bronze Age, giving a strong sense of continuity between Bronze Age ("Canaanite") and Iron Age practices and beliefs (Muller 2002; Katz 2016). It has been hypothesized that shrine models partly compensated for the decline of urban temples in the transition from the second to the first millennium BCE; however, since the tradition coexisted with urban temples during the Bronze Age and evidence for Iron Age temples is increasing, the process cannot be viewed in terms of replacement. Still, whether to perform a ritual within a specifically dedicated building or to perform it by engaging a miniature model of such a building implies a difference of scale in several respects: the building itself, the number of participants involved, and the nature and quantity of offerings. Rituals engaging shrine models seem to require a slightly different cognitive stance regarding the presence and proximity of an addressee (the deity) and communication with him or her through the ritualist's manipulative actions.

Shrine models usually represent an interior space (*naos*), and there is often a device indicating that they could be opened or closed. Unfortunately, not a single Iron Age shrine model from the southern Levant has been found together with its original content (a statuette, a figurine, a piece of wood…). That said, it seems unlikely that we should construe these containers as deliberately empty, not least since some earlier items from the second millennium did indeed contain a statue. Shrine models can be classified according to their shape and degree of iconographic sophistication, and the motifs used for their decoration inform about specific concerns and potential meaning. As it happens, some more spectacular items have surfaced through the antiquities market, and thus from illegal digging that severed the objects from their context; to what extent they should be included or not in the discussion is disputed. If we concentrate on properly excavated examples, we can still make several interesting observations: A pair of pillars or pilasters topped by palmettes are often represented flanking the *naos*; they are sometimes supported by lions or enhanced by human (generally female) figures. The corniche of a conspicuous item from Tell el-Far'ah (N) (Figure 28.5), found in a pit (a *favissa?*) inside a non-domestic building next to the city gate and piazza, displays a crescent or veil above which dotted bands may signify rain, pointing to the possible use of the model in communal fertility rites (a notoriously vague concept employed here *faute de mieux*; cf. Ziffer 2019). Another more recently found item from Khirbet Qeiyafa has been used to clarify architectural terminology from the description of Solomon's temple (1 Kgs 6; Garfinkel and Mumcuoglu 2016). The most interesting aspect of that exercise is to remind us that despite their difference in size, temples and shrine models share basic assumptions about divine presence, namely that it can be materialized and housed within a ritually confined space, and that ritual intercourse does not necessarily require a monumental infrastructure.

Cult stands are known from many sites in Israel (e.g., Beth-Shean, Tel Reḥov, Taanach) and Judah (most notably, a fragment from the City of David, Jerusalem). In terms of artifact genre, they are close relatives of shrine models, and they too contribute significantly to our understanding of ancient Israelite religious imagery and cultural values. Two stands from Taanach have attracted the most attention and discussion because of the complexity of their

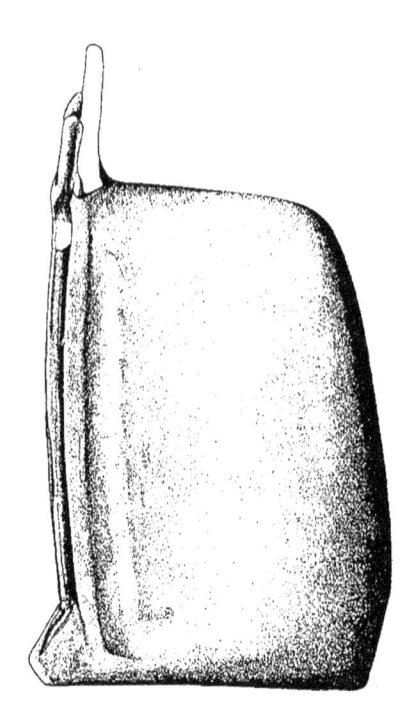

Figure 28.5 Terracotta shrine model, H 20.8 cm, from a pit in Building 149B at Tell el-Farʿah (North), Str. VIIB, Iron Age IIB, mid-9th to 8th cent. (Muller 2002: II 147, Figure 143 e, f)

decorum. For reasons of space, we can only briefly discuss one of them here (Figure 28.6). It is built as a square tower in four storeys or registers topped by a bowl on which offerings could be placed. The bottom register shows a nude woman holding two lions by their ears (mistress of lions). The second register has two human-faced, winged sphinxes; whether the empty space between them can be interpreted as indicating an entrance is unclear. The third register features a stylized tree nourishing two upright goats, flanked by a pair of lions that closely resemble those of the bottom register. The top register shows the most complex arrangement. In the center, a winged disc hovers above a striding quadruped (variously interpreted as a bull calf or a horse). These are flanked by pillars ending in outward-turned volutes, next to which a smaller feature may indicate a stand. Either side features again a winged sphinx, whose heads were less carefully shaped than those of the second register since they would hardly have been seen from the front. Not surprisingly, this remarkable artifact has given rise to several interpretations. Viewed as signifying sacred space, some authors construe the arrangement of registers in terms of succession from outer to inner space and a gradual increase of sanctity. One could be tempted to interpret register three as a representation of the supreme deity's *asherah* (cultic tree). Others have favored a cosmological interpretation, associating the bottom register with the netherworld and the top with heaven (or the holy of holies in a temple) as the ultimate realm of divinity. Both readings concur in assuming gradually increasing sanctity, and both understand the top register as the decisive one for identifying the deity for whose provision this cult stand would have served. Whether viewed as a bull calf or a horse, the quadruped by its association with the winged disc must have represented a major deity. More "biblicist" and, in my view farfetched, readings of the cult stand tend to put more emphasis on voids (e.g., between the two sphinxes of register

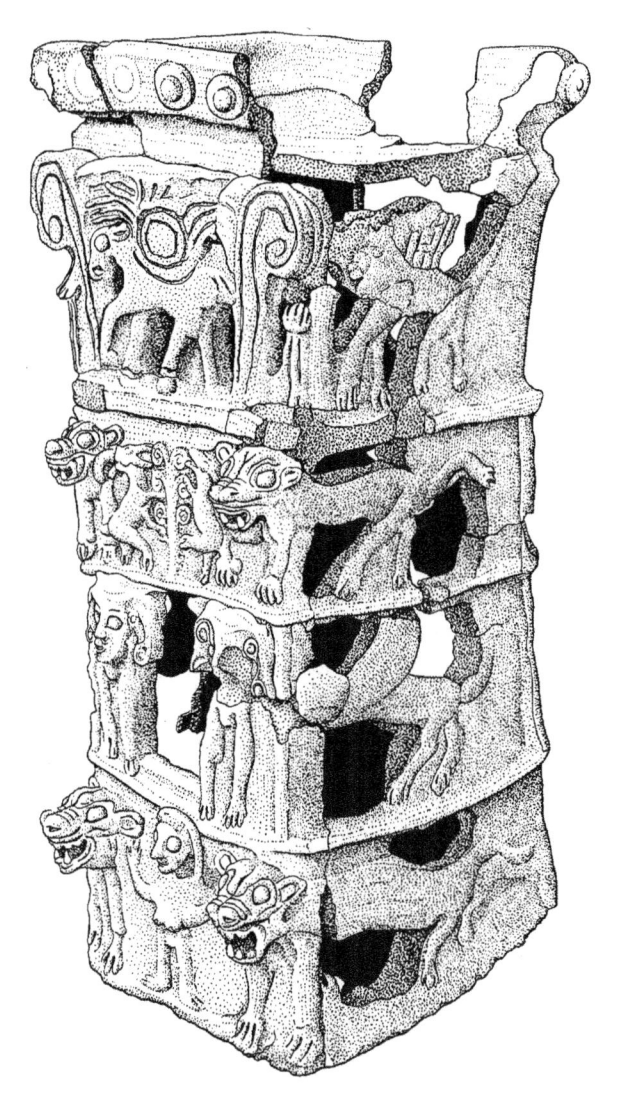

Figure 28.6 Terracotta offering stand, H 53.7 cm, from Taanach, Area SW 2–8, Iron Age IIA, late 10th/early 9th cent. (Keel and Uehlinger 1998: 159, Figure 184; drawing Gisela Tambour)

two) and what is thought *not* to be represented (namely, an anthropomorphic deity) than on what there *is* emphatically represented.

The issue at stake behind such differing scholarly attitudes is how we consider the basic relationship of "Canaanite" and "Israelite" religion in the first place. That this iconographically sophisticated and technically elaborate object reflects and perpetuates local "Canaanite" tradition is beyond dispute, but only a biblically biased perspective will take this to imply that we should therefore consider it less or not entirely "Israelite," or if "Israelite," we should narrow down its implications. If we look primarily at what *is* there to view, artifacts of this kind allow us to recognize the fundamental continuity between "Canaanite" and "Israelite" religion and to acknowledge how deeply the latter was rooted in its Levantine cultural matrix.

Statuary and Figurines

Cult statues are often considered a paramount feature of ancient Near Eastern ("polytheist" and "idolatrous") ritual and religion, against which normative biblical religion is then construed as "aniconic." From a religio-historical and visual culture-oriented perspective, such a straightforward dichotomy does not do justice to either side of the opposition. On the one hand, scholars have offered nuanced accounts of how deity and material image were conceptually distinguished in ancient Near Eastern religion, the latter being meant, once ritually induced, to function as a medium for proper communication and interaction with ritual specialists, and only rarely for laypeople to see and meet on special occasions. On the other hand, contemporary scholarship has been increasingly attracted to the idea that ancient Israelites and Judahites represented Yahweh as materialized in a cult statue (see below). This is what the biblical "golden calf" tradition and other texts referring to Israelite "idolatry" suggest in the first place.

No example of an elaborate composite cult statue has survived from the Iron Age southern Levant, a fact that should not surprise us too much. Material remains of ancient cultic statuary are extremely rare all over the ancient Near East, not least because they were subject to plunder and destruction. It has been suggested, however, that sculptures from the palaces of Assyrian kings Tiglath-pileser III, Sargon II, and Sennacherib depict the capture of anthropomorphic cult statuary from Gaza, Ashkelon (Figure 28.7a–b), and possibly Samaria (Uehlinger 1998). While some of these identifications have been contested (not always on convincing grounds), the Assyrian sculptures provide a welcome illustration of how anthropomorphic cult images could vary in size, from almost human-sized (and thus necessarily composite) to smaller and probably mono-material; that some of them may have been clothed; and that some would be placed in boxes or shrine models as described above. The same would apply to theriomorphic cult images.

Bronze statues of anthropomorphic deities (usually recognizable as such by horns emerging from the head or by a horned headdress) and of animals (understood as theriomorphic representations of a deity or simply his or her attribute animal, see above Figure 28.2) have

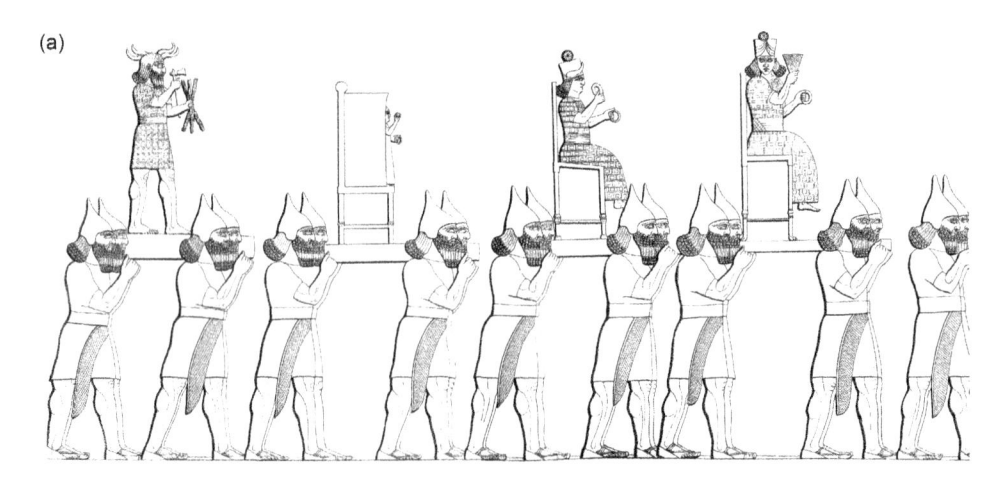

Figure 28.7 (a) Statues of Levantine deities, arguably the gods of king Hanun of Gaza, carried away as booty by Assyrian soldiers; Nimrud/Kalhu, Central Palace of Tiglathpileser III, ca. 830 BCE (Uehlinger 2002: 124, Figure 5). (b) Statues of Levantine deities carried away by Assyrian soldiers, arguably from Ashkelon; Nineveh, Southwest Palace of Sennacherib, ca. 700 BCE (Uehlinger 1997: 126, Figure 46)

Figure 28.7 (Continued)

been found in much greater numbers in Bronze Age than in Iron Age contexts, where most may represent heirlooms of an earlier period. Such statues often perpetuate the tradition of the "smiting god" (confirmed by the Assyrian sculptures just mentioned), an attitude we may consider to have represented one of two main options for figuring major state deities, the other showing the deity enthroned with or without flanking animals. Depending on availability and artisanship, other materials such as ivory (see Figure 28.8, a fragmentary ivory statuette from Tel Reḥov, which originally represented a sitting king or deity), wood, clay, or stone would have offered various alternatives. As mentioned above, a deity could also be represented by a cult standard or emblem (see Figure 28.3), or, as in Arad, simply by a standing stone.

Clay figurines are much better represented in the archaeological record than figurines made of more precious materials. Depending on the context and circumstantial evidence, they have been interpreted as votives, symbols of welfare and blessing, or even toys (see Darby and de Hulster 2021 for a recent supra-regional assessment). Most conspicuous among them, horse-and-rider figurines reflect a typically male symbol of status, strength, power, and possibly mobility, based on the impact armed equestrians would have made on a society used to donkeys both to carry loads and for transportation. Female figurines are usually understood as concerned with fertility and sexual attractivity, not least because of the female's nakedness and/or gestures, e.g., supporting her breasts. Interestingly, however, figurines from the Northern hill country and Judah show a preference for clothed rather than naked women. Whenever paint is preserved on Judahite pillar figurines (Figure 28.9a–b), it was used to highlight jewelry and thus emphasize the wealth, beauty, and strength of what must

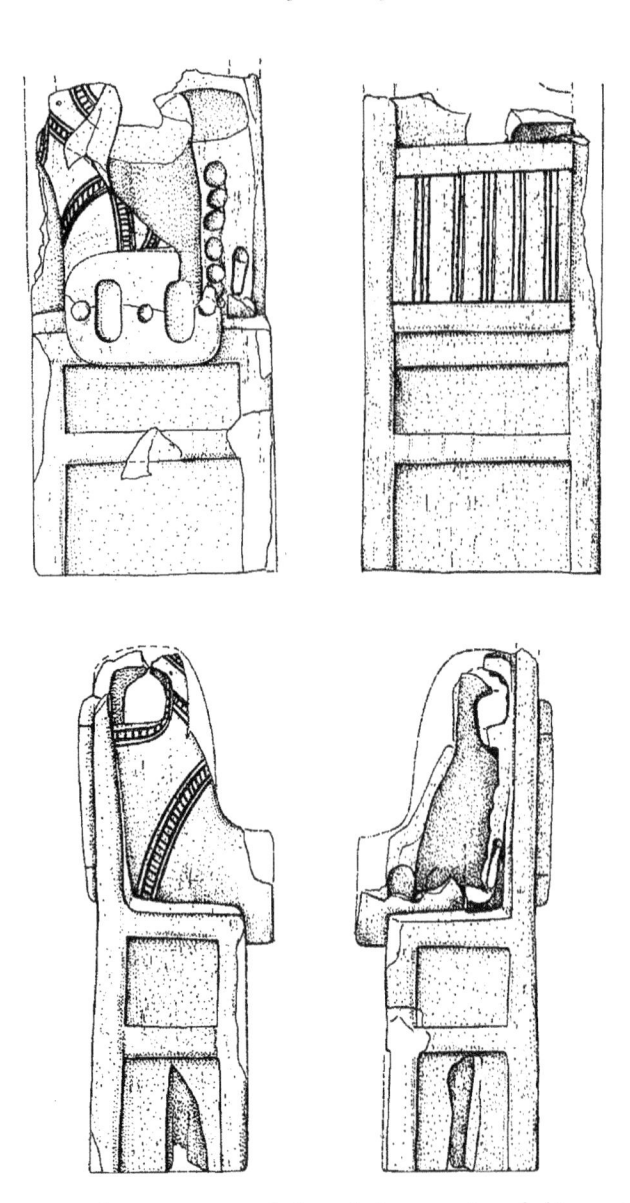

Figure 28.8 Fragmentary ivory statuette made from the lower canine of a hippopotamus, H 8.5 cm, showing a seated, probably royal figure; Tel Reḥov, Area C, Str. C-1a (= IV), Iron Age IIA, late 9th cent. (Mazar 2022: 511, Figure 32.1; courtesy Amihai Mazar, Jerusalem)

have been regarded as a strong woman *par excellence*. Whether or not these represent a deity (Asherah rather than Astarte) remains disputed. An intriguing scene figured on an 8th- or early 7th-century stamp seal from Lachish (Figure 28.9c) shows an elegantly clothed male ritualist gesturing toward a breast-offering lady reminiscent of the attitude of the pillar figurines, surmounted by a winged sun and accompanied by a monkey and a twig. In the absence of supporting evidence, the seal alone cannot carry the burden of proof to consider all Judahite pillar figurines' images of Asherah, but it invites us to remain circumspect and not dismiss the Asherah hypothesis all too quickly.

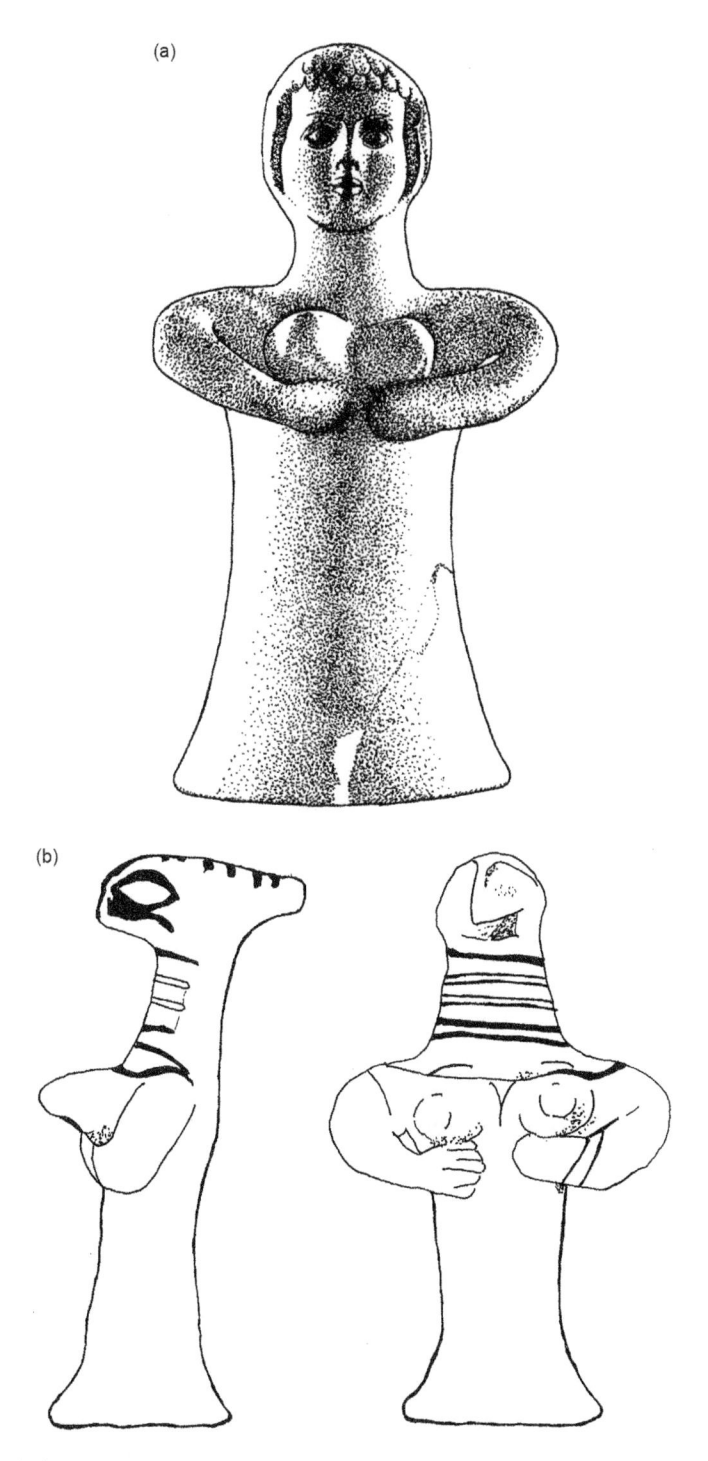

Figures 28.9 (a–b) Two Judahite pillar figurines, one with molded (Lachish), the other with pinched-nose head (Beersheba), the latter with remains of paint; Iron Age IIB, late 8th century. (Schroer 2018: Figures 1544 and 1545). (c) Stamp seal ("scaraboid") from Lachish, unstratified, probably 7th century (Keel and Uehlinger 1998: 330, Figure 323)

(c)

Figures 28.9 (Continued)

Religion-related Motifs on Non-ritual Artifacts

As argued in the introduction to this chapter, "religion" broadly understood can be studied in terms of practices, which are archaeologically best documented through contexts and assemblages that relate to ritual activity; or in terms of "beliefs" about non-empirical entities impacting individuals or groups and their environment in positive or negative ways. Scenes of ritual intercourse with such entities, as well as symbols for blessing, good health, protection, etc. are attested outside of strictly ritual settings and in various kinds of image genres, to which we shall turn in this section.

Wall Paintings, Drawings, and Graffiti

How little we know of the visual decoration of ancient Levantine elite architecture (from palaces and banqueting halls to cultic venues) has been highlighted by the paradoxically spectacular finds from Kuntillet ʿAjrud, a caravanserai dated around 800 BCE run by the Israelite state administration and possible partners in the northwestern Sinai as a station on the trade route connecting the southern coastal plain to the Red Sea (Meshel et al. 2012). Fragments of wall paintings include the image of an enthroned royal figure (Figure 28.10a) most strikingly placed in the structure's gate area where any visitor would pass by and the depiction of a city or fortress guarded by two men in an adjacent meeting hall. Ink drawings applied on two pithoi (Figure 28.10b–c) are best understood as sketches for other wall paintings that have not survived (Ornan 2016). They show typical motifs referring to state apparatus (a horse-driven chariot) and entertainment (a sitting lyre player), icons of welfare and blessing (e.g., pairs of goats nibbling on a stylized tree, cows with their suckling calf), animals in the wild (lions, a bear, a boar), a procession of men with hands raised for greeting

Figure 28.10 (a) Wall painting from Kuntillet ʿAjrud, entrance area, showing a seated royal figure holding a lotus flower (H 32 cm); Iron Age II B, ca. 800 (Meshel et al. 2012: 191, Figure 6.39). (b–c) Various ink drawings and inscriptions sketched on two pithoi from Kuntillet ʿAjrud: Pithos A from the so-called bench room in the inner gate area, Pithos B from close by in the inner courtyard; Iron Age II B, ca. 800 (Meshel et al. 2012: 87, Figure 5.24 and 92, Figure 5.35; drawings reproduced courtesy Zeʾev Meshel, Tel Aviv)

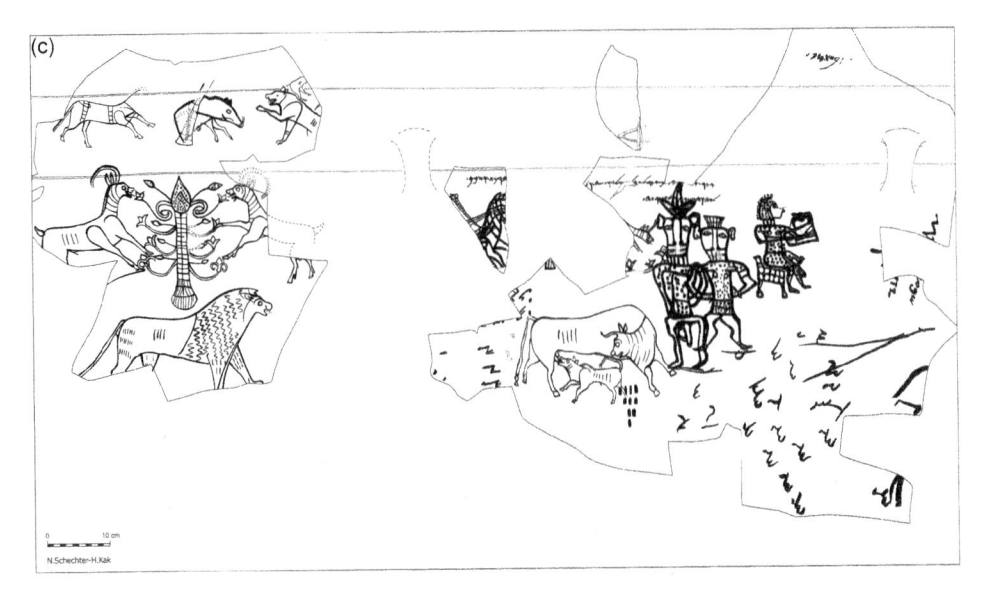

Figure 28.10 (Continued)

or blessing, and two anthropomorphic divine figures that are sometimes taken to represent "Yahweh and his Asherah" (mentioned in several blessing formulae at the site) but probably best understood as variant drawings of Bes, an Egypto-Canaanite protective demon, and possibly a female variant thereof. A direct relationship between these drawings and the inscriptions seems intrinsically improbable, apart from the fact that both media show a concern for the well-being of people who apparently identified as worshippers of Yahweh, both at Samaria and in the southern lands of Teman. What these drawings demonstrate most vividly (and in the middle of nowhere) is how much Israelite elites down to the ranks of traders and outpost military personnel participated in the consumption of the diverse and sophisticated visual *koine* they shared with other elites throughout the southern Levant. To postulate the existence of similar works of interior design in more centrally located environments is a most reasonable hypothesis rather than an educated guess, let alone speculation. It is most vividly supported by the famous ivory carvings from Samaria, the capital of the kingdom of Israel.

Ivory Carvings and Other Luxury Items

However fragmented and unfortunately recovered from a non-indicative, secondary archaeological context, the ivories from Samaria represent the second largest hoard of objects of this kind ever discovered in the Middle East (the most important being ivory carvings from various locations assembled and found in Assyrian storerooms at Kalhu/Nimrud). They once decorated luxury furniture, from couches, stools, and tables to boxes and caskets, which must have made a major effect on those who used them, for instance when elite persons gathered for banquets and receptions. The figurative repertoire of these ivories includes Egyptianizing divine, so-called "semi-divine" and hybrid beings of the same kind as those represented in contemporary glyptics (see below) and metalwork, royal figures, animals in combat, peacefully suckling, or nibbling, etc. The meaning and function of these luxury items, primarily aesthetic and lavishly demonstrative, should neither be considered "religious" in a qualified sense nor be related to explicitly ritual concerns (Suter 2011). Nevertheless, they contribute indirectly, via their appeal to aesthetics and a richly variegated imagination, to our understanding of the ancient Israelite worldview and sense of good life. In the present context of a chapter focusing on visual culture, we should emphasize that whereas earlier studies tended to regard these ivories (and related work in bone and wood) as Phoenician imports, current scholarship posits that Israelite craftsmen probably participated in their production (Naeh 2015). Ivory work of slightly later date, some of which is more indebted to North Syrian or even Assyrian models, has recently surfaced in Jerusalem (Avisar et al. 2022). We may thus safely assume that the Jerusalem elites, too, had their share in Levantine luxury arts, if on a slightly more modest scale than their predecessors in Samaria.

Seals

Seals and seal impressions dated to the Iron Age number in the thousands (Keel 1995–2017); most of them are stamp seals, against only a handful of cylinder seals. Given the strict confines of a stamp's sealing surface, the base engravings of anepigraphic stamp seals represent single-scene images or a combination of meaningful symbols of luck or protection. In spite or partly because of the necessarily condensed character of seal images, which implied the necessity of motif selection, seals offer valuable means to study the tides of political, economic, and cultural contacts and their impact on the local symbol system. Specificities of material, shape, chronological range, and geographic distribution allow scholars to define groups, often of restricted diffusion, and thus to study the motifs and symbols that mattered most to people inhabiting a certain region at a certain time. If the diachronic account of major developments in the repertoire of Levantine stamp seal iconography offered by Keel and Uehlinger (1998) remains largely valid today, more recent findings have obviously added nuance and additional evidence (see Keel 2012 for an essentially glyptics-based attempt to contextualize various cult practices and other aspects of religion in Iron Age II Jerusalem).

Within the limits of this chapter, we can only highlight some of the most conspicuous features and tendencies. To begin with, a group of coarsely cut scarabs and plaques dubbed "Post-Ramesside Mass Production," best represented in the southern coastal plain and bridging the period from the late second to the early first millennium, features motifs centered on the name of Amun (whose temple at Gaza may have been involved in the group's production and/or diffusion), but also the Canaanite gods Baʿal(-Seth), Resheph and possibly a female goddess (Koch 2021: 120–23) alongside scenes of royal hunt and striding lions. In contrast, local limestone conoids from the hill country show a clear preference for the depiction of caprids, occasionally suckling their kid, and plants – all motifs pointing to an animal-based herding economy and unrelated to any memory of Egyptian colonialism. The close relation of herders to their flock is also reflected in images depicting a human figure facing a caprid. Two such figures raising their hands on either side of a tree may relate to tree worship at extra-mural "high-places."

During the Iron Age IIB, scaraboids from Samaria and other sites display an anthropomorphic deity on a bovine, joining evidence discussed above to confirm the significance of storm god imagery in northern Israel (Figure 28.11a–e). A more southern group of seals typically made of bone and carved in a most characteristic style seems to perpetuate post-Ramesside

Christoph Uehlinger

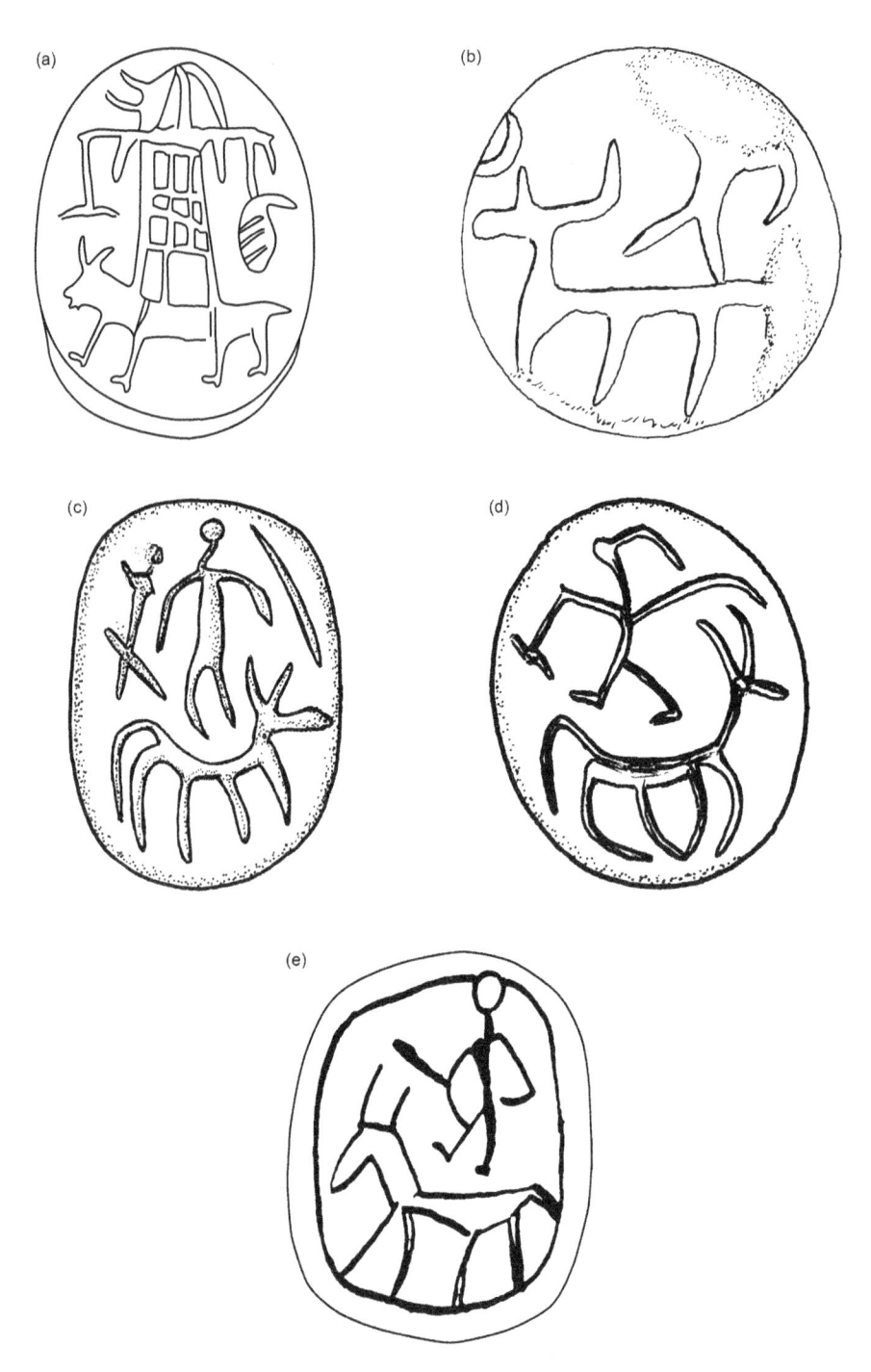

Figures 28.11 (a–e) Anthropomorphic, male divine figure(s) on a bull as represented on various locally produced stamp seals (a scarab, a conoid, and scaraboids) from (a) Jericho (CSSL no. 60), (b) Gibeon (CSSL no. 20), (c-d) Samaria (CSSL nos. 8, 49) and (e) Lachish (CSSL no. 127); Iron Age I-IIB, 10th to 9th cent. (courtesy Stamp Seals from the Southern Levant Project)

Figures 28.12 (a–d) Solar symbolism on Israelite and Judahite scarabs, scaraboids and bullae dated to the mid- to late 8th century: (a) Samaria (CSSL no. 6); (b) Shechem (CSSL no. 7); (c) Lachish (L=ḤMLK SMK, CSSL no. 209); (d) Jerusalem (L=ḤZQYHW•ʾḤZ•M LK•YHD[H]; CSSL no. 495a) (courtesy Stamp Seals from the Southern Levant Project). (e–f) Solar symbolism on seal impressions made with *LMLK* (royal) stamps on the handles of jars used by Judahite officials to collect taxes for the Assyrian administration, late 8th cent.: (e) flying scarab, (f) winged sun disc (courtesy Ido Koch, Tel Aviv)

motifs yet indicates a new stance toward Egypt: base designs figure men greeting an oval cartouche or two containing unreadable signs that mimic Egyptian royal names, men joining in pairs or groups of three, or emblematic animals such as a lion, a falcon or vulture, and a rather un-Egyptian billy goat. Currently best represented in the Shephelah and the southern coastal plain, this group's somehow idiosyncratic fusion of Canaanite and Egyptian elements reflects a local network rather than one directly dependent on Egypt (Münger 2022).

Slightly later seals again from the Northern kingdom display strong affinities with both Phoenician and Aramean glyptics. The former is characterized by "Canaanite" motifs and a creative adoption of Egyptianizing symbolism (e.g., in the depiction of a four-winged youth, falcon-headed sphinxes, two-winged uraei, or the Horus child in a flower) also known from local bone and ivory work. The latter operates in images of a roaring lion ready to attack, as on a famous seal once owned by Shemaʿ, minister of king Jeroboam II, from Megiddo. Despite occasional leonine metaphors used for Yahweh in the Hebrew Bible (e.g., Am 1:2: "the Lord roars from Zion"), an identification of such images of roaring lions with Yahweh seems unwarranted.

It is well known that Jerusalem and Judah experienced Israelite preeminence during the 9th and early 8th centuries but then took advantage of the progressive Assyrian dismantling of the northern kingdom and turned into one of the region's major polities during the last decades of the 8th century. Judahite seals, bullae from the royal palace, and the famous *LMLK* seal impressions reflect this process and demonstrate how closely Jerusalem's ruling elite at that time defined itself through "Egyptianizing" symbols previously enculturated in the Northern kingdom, such as the flying beetle or the winged sun disc (Figure 28.12a–f). While these seals tell little about religion *per se*, they point to a general significance of solar symbolism as a central cultural (and certainly royal) concern, a preference that seems to have changed somehow in the wake of the Assyrian conquests. One of the more prominent icons on 7th-century seals is the cult symbol of the moon god of Harran in North Syria, whom the Sargonid kings, especially Esarhaddon, considered the divine patron and protector of the empire's expansion to the West and into Egypt. Cultic service to this god, represented by a lunar crescent with two characteristic tassels, is attested in a variety of visual media: a temple at Ammonite Rujm el-Kursî, a crescent-shaped standard at Tel Sera, and numerous seals and seal impressions from many quarters of the southern Levant, including Jerusalem (Keel and Uehlinger 1998: §§ 173–77; Moriconi 2018; see Koch this volume). An anthropomorphic version of the moon god, so far only attested in the southern Levant, shows him enthroned and traveling in a heavenly boat. A conspicuous seal with that motif, bought in Jerusalem in the early 20th century, once belonged to a certain Elishamaʿ ben Gedalyahu, who may have been a member of king Manasseh's ruling elite (Figure 28.13). A side effect of Assyrian control over the Levant, accompanied by significant population exchanges, is that Mesopotamian deities make their appearance in the glyptic record—Ishtar is represented anthropomorphically, while others like Marduk or Nabû are represented via their cult emblems in scenes of worship. In the absence of clear markers of local production, it is difficult to evaluate to what extent such scenes mirror actual ritual practices performed in the Levant proper; most owners of the relevant seals will have received them through their office in an imperial administration network.

Inscriptions, usually the seal owner's name and patronym, and occasionally rank or occupation, appear alongside images and symbols from the mid-8th century; by the end of the century, they tend to become the more prominent feature of a seal's base engraving,

Figure 28.13 Anepigraphic side of bifacial Judahite seal L= 'LŠMʿ BN GDLYHW (7th century BCE), bought in Jerusalem at the turn of the 20th cent. CE (Keel and Uehlinger 1998: 308, Figure 306a)

especially in Judahite glyptics, to the point of displacing figural motifs altogether in the late 7th and early 6th centuries. Whether this development participated in the rise of less image- and more name-related notions of the deity and the mediation of divine presence (cf. deuteronomistic so-called "Name theology", see Lewis 2020: 379–92) is a matter of debate.

Amulets

The last class of artifacts to be mentioned in this chapter are amulets (Herrmann 1994–2016), the bulk of which can be divided into amulets made of faïence or similar composite material versus amulets made of locally available material such as bone or wood. The former, produced from clay molds, are generally of Egyptian origin. They may represent Egyptian deities, among whom lion-headed Sekhmet, Isis suckling her child and Nefertem seem to have been most popular during the Iron Age, apotropaic and protective demons such as Bes and so-called *pataikoi* dwarfs, various animals, signs of luck and well-being (in the shape of a Horus eye), appropriate hieroglyphs, or vegetals. Different amulets could be assembled in bracelets and necklaces or carried in a pouch and combined with stamp seals and beads. To what extent the use of an amulet featuring an Egyptian deity would have implied an individual's conscious choice and implied a sense of personal relationship with that deity is unknown. With the region's increasing exposure to Assyria in the late 8th and 7th centuries, metal amulets with the head of Pazuzu, another protective demon, became available but remained rare. As for locally produced amulets, a figurative type representing a nude woman in a posture also known from clay plaques seems to have been favored in the southern coastal plain rather than in Judah or Israel proper, where non-figurative pendants seem to have been preferred.

Images of Yahweh (and his Asherah)?

Whether the biblical so-called "ban on images" is directed against the worship of images of other gods alongside Yahweh, or whether it also (if not primarily) prohibits the manufacture of an image for the cult of Yahweh himself has been debated by generations of biblical exegetes. In fact, numerous biblical texts condemn the (for their authors, improper) use of imagery for the cult of Yahweh, which seems to imply that such imagery existed; this in turn raises the question of whether images of this god can be positively identified in the material visual record of Iron Age Israel and Judah (see Lewis 2020: 287–426, titled "The Iconography of Divinity: Yahweh," for a broad and nuanced assessment). The finds from Kuntillet ʿAjrud, where blessing formulae mentioning Yahweh of Samaria and Yahweh of (the) Teman alongside "his Asherah" occur in a context that also brought to light a rich array of figurative iconography (see above), have fueled various suggestions to that effect. Some of these rise and disappear only to rise again a decade or generation later; while others are made once and stay on the records as possible options, without however achieving favorable consensus. One of the first hypotheses, published in 1902 by the German scholar Gustav Dalman, concluded from the Yahwist patronym on the seal of Elishamaʿ ben Gedalyahu (Figure 28.13) that the enthroned, bearded figure engraved on the seal's base represented the god Yahweh; methodologically speaking, the argument carries little weight (although the identification cannot be positively ruled out). The finds from Kuntillet ʿAjrud immediately led some scholars to suggest that the two anthropomorphic hybrid figures drawn on Pithos A (above, Figure 28.10b) might represent Yahweh and his female companion Asherah, the figure on the right displaying clearly (if perhaps secondary) female attributes (most notably, breasts). The debate on these figures has produced anything from totally unreceivable to theoretically sophisticated arguments. Among the former is that the left figure's headdress should represent bovine horns or the tail between the same or both figure's legs a phallus. That the figures reflect Bes iconography cannot be doubted, so the decisive question is whether one considers it a plausible option that Yahweh (and his Asherah) should be represented in the gear of Bes (as once more argued by Thomas 2016) and, if so, why. Similar reservations are raised by the bold suggestion to recognize Yahweh and his Asherah in a graffito scratched in a rather crude manner into a late Iron Age potsherd from Jerusalem (Gilmour 2009) – perhaps no more than a love charm was intended (Lewis 2020: 309–13). Yet another suggestion, by the present writer, compared the syntax of the "Yahweh and his Ashera" formula to the visual syntax of an equally unique Judahite terracotta group representing a standing female (or young male?) figure accompanied by lions next to a sitting, bearded deity – alas, the object is unprovenanced and can only be very generally designated as Judahite (Figure 28.14).[1]

The problem is complicated by the fact that, in the process of being promoted from a local and regional deity (perhaps represented and/or imagined differently in different regions, temples, and shrines) to a supreme and eventually all-encompassing god (Lewis 2020), Yahweh attracted a great number of different roles and attributes, which cannot *ex post* be reduced to a single iconographical prototype. While some texts of the Hebrew Bible imagine Yahweh as a smiting warrior god, others present him enthroned and accompanied by a divine council, an entourage most vigorously denied or rejected by still other texts. As shown

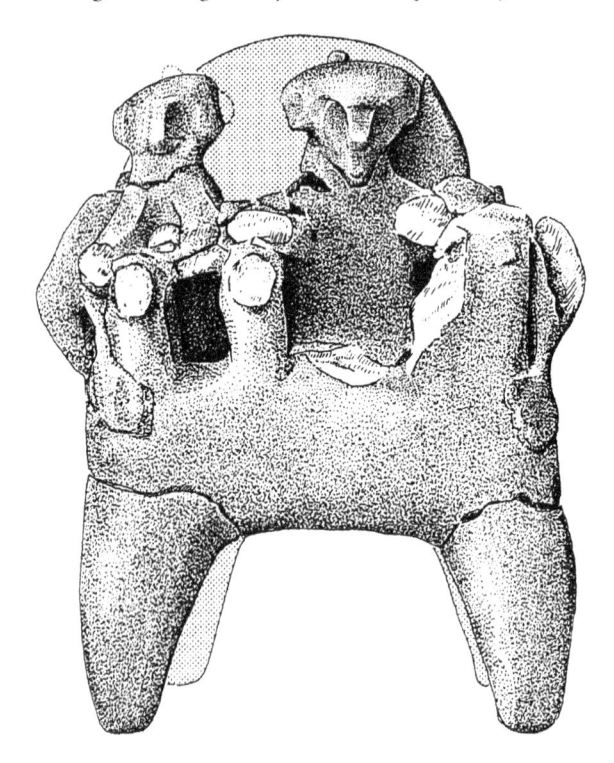

Figure 28.14 Terracotta group showing a standing, beardless figure flanked by quadrupeds (lions?) next to a seated, bearded figure; the undefined feature to the right could represent a standing stone. The special (sacred) character of the composition is suggested by the conspicuous elevation on four legs (Uehlinger 1997: 150, Figure 61; courtesy Orbis Biblicus et Orientalis)

by Keel in groundbreaking studies, some biblical texts invite close comparison with roughly contemporary iconography: e.g., the lampstand described in the vision of Zech 4 correlates rather well with the cult standard of the moon god mentioned above (Keel 1977); and Yahweh's engagement with ostriches in Job 39:13ff can be brought into a productive conversation with the "master of ostriches" attested on numerous Iron Age stamp and cylinder seals (Keel 1978). The latter correlation, however, does not allow us in turn to identify any image of a "master of ostriches" (nor perhaps *the* "master of ostriches" if there ever was only one) with Yahweh "from Teman" nor, for that matter, with his Edomite fellow Qaus. The variety of biblical images, role types, and metaphors produce a mosaic screen which tends to obscure earlier, primary image(s) of Yahweh that must have existed in Israel and Judah during the Iron Age – to the effect that *we* cannot identify them with certainty (Berlejung 2017).

To conclude, a massive and continuously growing amount of data support the recognition that Israelite and Judahite society, culture, and religion during the Iron Age enjoyed a full share in the southern Levant's rich and variegated visual culture (Schroer 2018). The assumption that the cult of Yahweh should have been programmatically aniconic has during recent decades lost its plausibility, not least because of increasing scholarly exposure to and engagement with relevant visual culture. There were regional differences between the religious iconographies of Israel and Judah, the southern lands of Teman, and other neighboring regions. Some special icons may have worked as identity markers of sorts to regional communities, contributing to the distinction of one region's, temple's, or shrine's material visual image of Yahweh from others. It stands to reason that, although we are not yet able to identify him with ultimate certainty in the visual record, Yahweh, the main deity served in Iron Age Israel and Judah, *is* figuratively represented among the dozens and hundreds of first-millennium images available, discussed here only in the most approximate and summary way.

Note

1 The claim for a Judahite provenance is based on petrographic analysis, stylistic comparison with pitched-nose coroplastics, and the artifact's documented acquisition within an assemblage of Judahite figurines and vessels typical of the late 8th and early 7th centuries.

Bibliography

Albertz, Rainer, and Rüdiger Schmitt. 2012. *Family and Household Religion in Ancient Israel and the Levant*. Winona Lake: Eisenbrauns.

Aldenderfer, Mark. 2012. "Envisioning a Pragmatic Approach to the Archaeology of Religion." *APAAA* 21: 23–36.

Avisar, Reli, et al. 2022. "'Jerusalem Ivories': Iron Age Decorated Ivory Panels from Building 100, Giv'ati Parking Lot Excavations, and Their Cultural Setting." *'Atiqot* 106: 57–74.

Barton, John, and Francesca Stavrakopoulou, eds. 2010. *Religious Diversity in Ancient Israel and Judah*. London: T&T Clark.

Berlejung, Angelika. 2017. "The Origins and Beginnings of the Worship of YHWH: The Iconographic Evidence." Pages 67–92 in *The Origins of Yahwism*. Edited by Jürgen von Oorschot and Markus Witte. Berlin: De Gruyter.

Bernett, Monika and Othmar Keel. 1998. *Mond, Stier und Kult am Stadttor: Die Stele von Betsaida (et-Tell)*. Fribourg and Göttingen: University Press/Vandenhoeck & Ruprecht.

Biran, Avraham. 1999. "Two Bronze Plaques and the *ḥuṣṣot* of Dan." *IEJ* 49: 43–54.

Darby, Erin D., and Izaak J. de Hulster eds. 2021. *Iron Age Terracotta Figurines from the Southern Levant in Context*. Leiden: Brill.

Garfinkel, Yosef, and Madeleine Mumcuoglu. 2016. *Solomon's Temple and Palace: New Archaeological Discoveries*. Washington, DC: Biblical Archaeology Society.

Gilmour, Garth. 2009. "An Iron age II Pictorial Inscription from Jerusalem Illustrating Yahweh and Asherah." *PEQ* 141: 87–103.

Halbertsma, Diederik J. H. and Bruce Routledge. 2021. "Between Rocks and 'High Places': On Religious Architecture in the Iron Age Southern Levant." *Religions* 12(9): 740. Online: doi:10.3390/rel12090740.

Herrmann, Christian. 1994–2016. *Ägyptische Amulette aus Palästina/Israel*. Vols. I–IV. Fribourg and Göttingen: University Press/Vandenhoeck & Ruprecht.

Katz, Hava. 2016. *Portable Shrine Models: Ancient Architectural Clay Models from the Levant*. Oxford: British Archaeological Reports.

Keel, Othmar. 1977. *Jahwe-Visionen und Siegelkunst: Eine neue Deutung der Majestätsschilderungen in Jes 6, Ez 1 und 10 und Sach 4*. Stuttgart: Katholisches Bibelwerk.

———. 1978. *Jahwes Entgegnung an Ijob. Eine Deutung von Ijob 38–41 vor dem Hintergrund der zeitgenössischen Bildkunst*. Göttingen: Vandenhoeck & Ruprecht.

———. 2012. "Paraphernalia of Jerusalem Sanctuaries and Their Relation to Deities Worshiped Therein during the Iron Age IIA-C." Pages 317–42 in *Temple Building and Temple Cult: Architecture and Cultic Paraphernalia of Temples in the Levant (2.-1. Mill. B.C.E.)*. Edited by Jens Kamlah. Wiesbaden: Harrassowitz.

———. 1995–2017. *Corpus der Stempelsiegel-Amulette aus Palästina/Israel: Vom Neolithikum bis zur Perserzeit. Einleitung* and Vols. 1–5. Fribourg and Göttingen: University Press/Vandenhoeck & Ruprecht.

Keel, Othmar, and Christoph Uehlinger. 1998. *Gods, Goddesses, and Images of God in Ancient Israel*. Philadelphia: Fortress.

Kisilevitz, Shua, and Oded Lipschits. 2020. "Tel Moẓa: An Economic and Cultic Center from the Iron Age II (First Temple Period)." Pages 295–312 in *The Mega Project at Motza (Moẓa): The Neolithic and Later Occupations up to the 20th Century*. Edited by Hamoudi Khalaily et al. Jerusalem: Israel Antiquities Authority.

Koch, Ido. 2020. "Southern Levantine Temples during the Iron Age II: Towards a Multivocal Narrative." *Judaïsme ancien/Ancient Judaism* 8: 325–44.

———. 2021. *Colonial Encounters in Southwest Canaan during the Late Bronze Age and the Early Iron Age*. Leiden: Brill.

Lewis, Theodore J. 2020. *The Origin and Character of God: Ancient Israelite Religion through the Lens of Divinity*. Oxford: Oxford University Press.

Mazar, Amihai. 1982. "The 'Bull Site' – An Iron Age I Open Cult Place." *BASOR* 247: 27–42.

———. 2020. "An Ivory Statuette Depicting an Enthroned Figure." Pages 509–17 in *Tell Reḥov: A Bronze and Iron Age City in the Beth-Shean Valley. Vol. IV: Pottery Studies, Inscriptions, and Figurative Art*. Edited by Amihai Mazar and Nava Panitz-Cohen. Jerusalem: Israel Exploration Society.

Meshel, Zeev et al. 2012. *Kuntillet ʿAjrud (Ḥorvat Teman): An Iron Age II Religious Site on the Judah-Sinai Border*. Jerusalem: Israel Exploration Society.

Moriconi, Alessandro. 2018. "Rising Moon at Tell eš-Šerīʿa/Tel Seraʿ: A Neo-Assyrian Bronze Crescent Standard and the Iconography of the Moon God Sîn of Ḥarrān in Southern Levant. Ritual Paraphernalia and Military Insignia?" *AeL* 28: 409–18.

Muller, Béatrice. 2002. *Les « maquettes architecturales » du Proche-Orient ancien*. Beyrouth: Institut Français d'Archéologie du Proche-Orient.

Münger, Stefan. 2022. "Judäo-israelitische Knochensiegel der Eisenzeit II. Ägyptische Ikonographie und kanaanäisches Erbe." Pages 45–58 in *Ägypten und Altes Testament. Fachtagung, 40 Jahre ÄAT", München, 6.–7. Dez. 2019*. Münster: Zaphon.

Naeh, Liat. 2015. "In Search of Identity: The Contribution of Recent Finds to Our Understanding of Iron Age Ivory Objects in the Material Culture of the Southern Levant." *AoF* 42(1): 80–96.

Ornan, Tallay. 2006. "The Lady and the Bull: Remarks on the Bronze Plaque from Tel Dan." Pages 297–312 in *Essays on Ancient Israel in Its Near Eastern Context: A Tribute to Nadav Naʾaman*. Edited by Yairah Amit et al. Winona Lake: Eisenbrauns.

———. 2016. "Sketches and Final Works of Art: The Drawings and Wall Paintings of Kuntillet ʿAjrud Revisited." *Tel Aviv* 43(1): 3–26.

Schmitt, Rüdiger. 2020. *Die Religionen Israels/Palästinas in der Eisenzeit. 12.–6. Jahrhundert v. Chr*. Münster: Zaphon.

Schroer, Silvia. 1987. *In Israel gab es Bilder. Nachrichten von darstellender Kunst im Alten Testament*. Göttingen: Vandenhoeck & Ruprecht.

———. 2018. *Die Ikonographie Palästina/Israels und der Alte Orient: Eine Religionsgeschichte in Bildern. Vol. IV: Die Eisenzeit bis zum Beginn der achämenidischen Herrschaft*. Basel: Schwabe.

Suter, Claudia. 2011. "Images, Tradition, and Meaning: The Samaria and Other Levantine Ivories of the Iron Age." Pages 219–41 in *A Common Cultural Heritage: Studies on Mesopotamia and the Biblical World in Honor of Barry L. Eichler*. Edited by Grant Frame et al. Bethesda, MD: CDL Press.

Thomas, Ryan. 2016. "The Identity of the Standing Figures on Pithos A from Kuntillet ʿAjrud: A Reassessment." *JANER* 16: 121–91.

Uehlinger, Christoph. 1997. "Anthropomorphic Cult Statuary in Iron Age Palestine and the Search for Yahweh's Cult Images." Pages 97–156 in *The Image and the Book: Iconic Cults, Aniconism, and the Veneration of the Holy Book in Israel and the Ancient Near East*. Edited by Karel van der Toorn. Leuven: Peeters.

———. 1998. "'…und wo sind die Götter von Samarien?' Die Wegführung syrisch-palästinischer Kultstatuen auf einem Relief Sargons II. in Khorsabad/Dur-Sharrukin." Pages 739–76 in *„Und Mose schrieb dieses Lied auf…". Studien zum Alten Testament und zum Alten Orient*. Edited by Manfried Dietrich and Ingo Kottsieper. Kevelaer: Butzon & Bercker and Neukirchen-Vluyn: Neukirchener.

———. 2002. "Hanun von Gaza und seine Gottheiten auf Orthostatenreliefs Tiglatpilesers III." Pages 94–127 in *Kein Land für sich allein. Studien zum Kulturkontakt in Kanaan, Israel/Palästina und Ebirnâri für Manfred Weippert zum 65. Geburtstag*. Edited by Ulrich Hübner and Ernst Axel Knauf. Fribourg and Göttingen: University Press/Vandenhoeck & Ruprecht.

———. 2015. "Distinctive or Diverse? Conceptualizing Ancient Israelite Religion in Its Southern Levantine Setting." *HBAI* 4: 1–24.

———. 2019. "Beyond 'Image Ban' and 'Aniconism': Reconfiguring Ancient Israelite and Early Jewish Religion\s in a Visual and Material Religion Perspective." Pages 99–123, 286–7, 304–7 in *Figuration and Sensation of the Unseen in Judaism, Christianity and Islam: Contested Desires*. Edited by Birgit Meyer and Terje Stordalen. London: Bloomsbury Academic.

Ziffer, Irit. 2019. "Moon, Rain, Womb, Mercy: The Imagery of the Shrine Model from Tell el-Farʿah North—Biblical Tirzah." *Religions* 10: 136. Online: doi:10.3390/rel10020136.

29

THE ARCHAEOLOGY OF ISRAELITE CULT

Yahwisms across Space and Time

George A. Pierce and Kyle H. Keimer

Introduction

Israelite religion has been accepted as an element that unified and promoted interaction between disparate clan and tribal groups in the subregions of the southern Levant from the Huleh basin in the north to the Negev in the south and parts of Transjordan – at least according to the biblical narrative. With some exceptions, the Israelite cult was to be centered on a specific sanctuary, at first portable (the tabernacle) then later more permanent (the Jerusalem temple). Exceptions to this centrality, especially during the period of the divided monarchy, are noted as aberrant and drew condemnation from the biblical authors writing from a male, Yahwistic, Jerusalem-centric position. The dominating framework for interpreting archaeological data related to cult for most of the 19th and 20th centuries was based on the biblical text because the "code," to borrow a term from Levi-Strauss, for interpretation is recorded therein.

It is now sufficiently clear, however, that even with a code there are lacunae both in that code itself and in the archaeology being decoded. As such, and despite precedence, we have chosen to work within an anthropological framework that allows us to address some of these lacunae, even if on a more theoretical basis.

Rappaport (1971a) divided religion into three interrelated categories, namely: ultimate sacred propositions, ritual, and religious experience.[1] These three aspects of religion form a system that informs and affects socio-economic and ecological processes. Israelite society, like all other societies, had "ultimate sacred propositions" – completely unverifiable beliefs that are held as unquestionable truths by the faithful (Rappaport 1971a: 69, 1971b: 28). For ancient Israel, the primeval histories, such as those recorded in Genesis 1–11, may be interpreted as foundational propositions, with other portions of the Hebrew Bible (e.g., legal codes, wisdom literature, or prophetic oracles) detailing other sacred propositions.

Rituals are defined as religious acts that are performed in a particular way to evoke a religious experience. Certain constructs may be tied to rituals such as the necessity of sacrifice and the veneration of the deity for whatever purpose (e.g., fertility, divine blessing, and/or spiritual atonement/redemption). Rituals can be categorized as either *ad hoc* rituals like divination or consultation of the deity or sacrifices that are done at significant times but not on a schedule, or *calendric* rituals occurring at specific times, often yearly, as part of an established, or official, cult.[2] Both categories of ritual can be understood for biblical Israel by using: (a) the biblical text for calendric and prescribed ad hoc rituals; and (b) archaeology for ad hoc rituals either not described or not endorsed by the biblical authors.

Embedded as part of the regular cycle of life within a social group, the function of ritual is to produce a numinous religious experience focused on contact with the supernatural and centered on feelings rather than rational thought to verify the ultimate sacred propositions held by the community. Such rituals may require paraphernalia and a locus of activity and be performed enough times to leave an archaeological signature no matter how faint (e.g., cannabis and frankincense on the small altars at Arad; Arie, Rosen, and Namdar 2020). Still, after nearly two centuries of research on ancient Israel, there are archaeological imprints for which we do not understand the ritual/ritual behavior, and there are rituals described in the text for which we have no archaeological signature (e.g., Passover). Moreover, many artifacts considered to be "cultic" – i.e., they played a role in ritual or ritualization – were recovered from problematic contexts. Alternatively, specific features at a site convey little due to their dissimilarity to features or rituals described in the Hebrew Bible. Yet, despite these issues, rituals convey information about group solidarity, regulate and adjust animal populations, and disseminate other information about the human population engaged in the ritual (Bergen 2007).

Ritual, then, serves as a focal point between religion and society by "upholding and reaffirming at regular intervals the collective sentiments and the collective ideas which make [the social group's] unity and its personality" (Durkheim 1915: 474–75). The question for archeologists, then, is to ask what information was being transmitted by a particular artifact or feature that may have been ritually utilized (Flannery 1976: 333). The answer may be provided by the archaeological context, or in the case of ancient Israel, also intimated by the biblical text.

The archaeological context may suggest certain levels of information both for the ancient participants and for modern archaeologists, although that information may be different for these two groups based on perspective and interpretation. For example, artifacts and features that were likely in public buildings or areas could convey knowledge about the community, items found in elite contexts may reveal the piety and the status of the owner, and cultic objects found in domestic contexts may either indicate sodality and rituals within the surrounding community or the personal piety of an individual or group in that household. Further, operational models of ancient religion are derived from the analyst's viewpoint to discover the cognized models that would provide the motivations and understandings of actions within societies from the perspective of those being analyzed (Drennan 1976: 345).

Ritual activity is characterized by its fluid and dynamic behaviors (Insoll 2011: 3). To this end, it is more pertinent as we consider Israelite cult over the course of the Iron Age, from ca. 1200–586 BCE, to think in terms of ritualization. "From an archaeological perspective, this allows us to reorient our questions from 'is this ritual?' to 'what is being ritualized, to what degree, by what means and with what effect?'" (Halbertsma and Routledge 2021: 8). Adopting such a framework allows us to utilize the archaeological remains to better ask questions such as: what were ancient Israel's ultimate sacred propositions and how might those propositions be reflected in surviving material culture and architecture; in what ways might archaeology reflect changes in those beliefs and associated rituals over the course of Israel's existence as an entity from its mention in the Merenptah Stele to the Babylonian conquest of Jerusalem; and in what ways did rituals evoke experiences that influenced or justified social, economic, or ecological changes throughout the history of ancient Israel (and Judah)?

The biblical texts, of course, provide many details for answering these questions, but these texts also obfuscate certain aspects due to later redactions, ideology, and other historical happenstance. Having an external (archaeological) record by which to evaluate the biblical narrative is extremely significant and helpful for tracking Israelite cult (as ritualized action that expresses belief). At the same time, however, the archaeological remains are not necessarily a panacea for textual ambiguities or expressions. The archaeological remains must be interpreted within their broader original ancient Near Eastern context, within a pan-Israelite context, and within appropriate modern theoretical frameworks that allow for meaningful understanding. Even then, collocating the archaeological remains with textual expressions is not easy or even possible in some instances.

Therefore, this article focuses on ritual and cult in an archaeological context and interpretation, drawing on the biblical text for possible "codes" of interpretation.[3] Following a discussion of methodology, we examine ritualized space in ancient Israel and present a case study of cultic areas and buildings with regards to their physical locations within their respective sites and the buildings' orientations.[4] Following Zevit (2001: 14–15), we are better suited to speak of Israelite religions, or the Yahwisms of ancient Israel. Israelites and Judahites both understood their origins, arguably, with an ancestor named Jacob/Israel even as their responses to YHWH were not uniform despite clear evidence of their affirmation of YHWH and his value within their worldview.

Methodological Concerns

The challenge of articulating the archaeologies of Israelite cult is two-fold: first, we must determine which archaeological objects/architecture played a role in cultic ritual; and second, we have to determine which specific cultic architecture, space, and/or objects should be associated with ancient Israel as opposed to their neighbors (Canaanites, Philistines, Arameans, etc.).[5] This is a difficult endeavor as is becoming ever clearer; ancient Israel interacted with its neighbors, sharing ideas and practices common throughout the ancient Near East. Sometimes Israel adopted these practices, other times they purposefully rejected them and established their own specific expression.[6] Like other aspects of Israelite culture and society, the significance in this study, and others in this volume, lies in determining what was common to all ancient Near Eastern people groups, or even to the human religious experience, and what was particular to Israel and Judah. As Israelite cultic space can be delineated, we can begin to address questions such as: did Israelite ritual action differ from that of its neighbors? How did cultic (ritual) activities serve to unite or divide the social groups that made up ancient Israel? How did cultic activities influence the local economy and intra-regional exchange networks?

Traditional approaches to the archaeology of Israelite cult have often sought to categorize and delineate what constituted cultic architecture and materiél (Albertz and Schmitt 2012; Coogan 1987; Faust 2010; Gilmour 1995; Holladay 1987; LaRocca-Pitts 2001; Nakhai 2001). While such studies have provided many useful insights, some tend to flatten the material (and sometimes the textual representation of Israelite cult) into convenient (albeit, sometimes very complex) categories that are understood to be discreet *and diachronically stable*. Moreover, the use of non-standard terms for the same buildings or types of buildings has led to an oversimplification of past human activity (Halbertsma and Routledge 2021: 6).

The problem with such taxonomic approaches is that there are an ever-growing number of outliers, whether this be the form of structures identified as cultic, or the presence of what have been identified as cultic vessels in non-cultic, domestic contexts. Several recent studies have shown that religious and secular activities can occur in the same places and can utilize many of the same objects (cf. already Amiran 1970: 302; Halbertsma and Routledge 2021: 4; see Smoak, this volume). Thus, either what has been identified as cultic has been done so incorrectly by modern scholars, or Israelite cultic expression was far more variegated than has traditionally been allowed for, or possibly both concomitantly. Therefore, approaches that also integrate behavior allow for greater nuance and flexibility when delineating and discussing ancient Israelite cult (e.g., Hawkins 2012; Zevit 2001; cf. Renfrew 1985). Such studies also align with the fact that belief systems are not always expressed in the material culture and/or religious actions "are not always clearly separated from the other actions of everyday life" (Renfrew and Bahn 2004: 416). Zevit states that "archaeology enables us to study the material remains of cult practice and then to infer from them the various activities of people engaged with the objects. Sometimes, it may even be possible to infer or guess at some aspects of the belief expressed through these practices" (2001: 81). We build upon such studies, integrating the archaeological remains with behavioral patterns.

It is essential to recognize that the issue of identifying cultic locations and architecture is complicated by the fact that ritual behaviors that create cultic space can manifest differently on the grand/public scale, the clan or household level, and even the individual level. Implied within this is the fact that rituals may change over time and/or they may look different in various regions.[7] Cultic locations change over the course of time from the pre-monarchic to monarchic periods, and within the monarchic period as well, as sites experience sacralization and desacralization according to various ritual needs or religious reforms (see Figure 29.1). With this in mind, cultic space must be articulated on a scalar level: cultic landscape(s); cultic buildings; cultic spaces within buildings; and cultic objects. Establishing the cultic nature of a space is tied to the ritualized actions that would have taken place there. Ritualization can be ascertained through several avenues, including the formality, fixity, and repetition of actions taking place in the space (Bell 1992: 90–91), and/or, as Halbertsma and Routledge (2021: 8) point out: "elaboration, iconicity (or aniconicity), sensorial enhancement, isolation/singularity, cost, scale (e.g., monumentality or miniaturization) and quantity." Archaeological materials can shed light on ritualized spaces, and, when read in conjunction with biblical and/or ancient Near Eastern texts, ritualized actions that would have imbued those spaces with cultic quality. The challenge with the biblical texts, as has already been expressed above, is allowing for multifarious expressions of cult and ritualization over the course of Israel's history while at the same time holding such expressions in tension with the idealized expression of some biblical authors. Additionally, we would do well to remember that texts about rituals (e.g., Lev 1–7) are different from rituals themselves, and we must assess the purpose of the text prescribing or proscribing the ritual (Bergen 2007: 580).

Ritualized Space in Ancient Israel

While space does not allow a full treatment of ritualized spaces in ancient Israel (they will be addressed in our forthcoming monograph on Israelite cult), we will list several spaces/objects that we believe were cultic, each garnering that label due to a confluence of various archaeological data: the ceramic repertoire, the architecture, use of space, and presence of small finds.[8] For the present, after a brief discussion of each type of ritual space, we will then present one case study on the cultic landscape in ancient Israel over the course of the Iron Age to illuminate how a combination of the archaeological remains and behavioral considerations provide a fruitful way by which to discuss ancient Israelite cult.

Cultic Landscape(s)

While this first category does include some structures, its focus is on the cognitive landscape(s) as perceived by ancient Israelites, tantamount to open-air cult spaces and/or regional

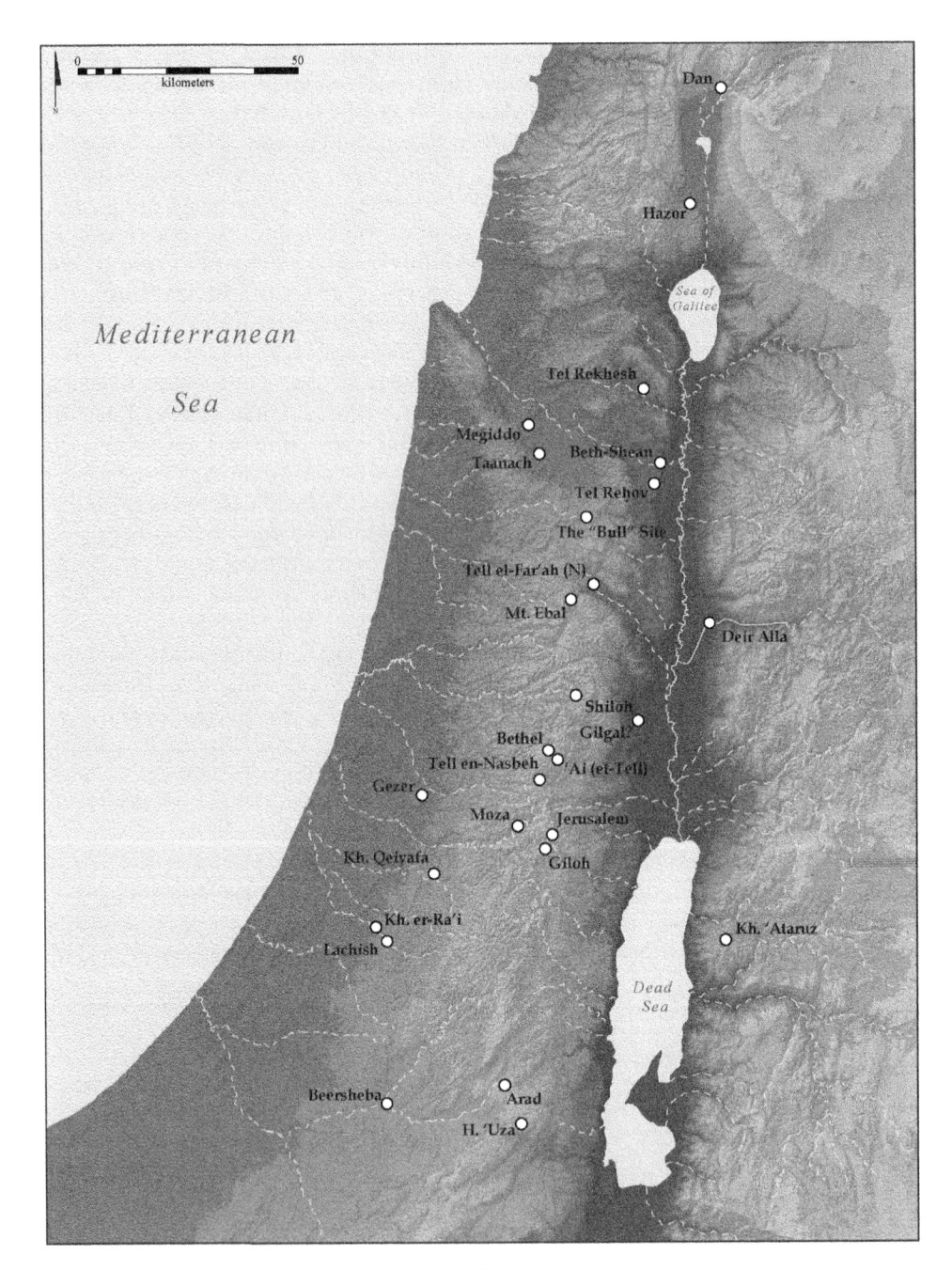

Figure 29.1 Map of cultic sites mentioned in the chapter

cult space where multiple clans/tribes could participate in various rituals. In some instances, "high places" and/or cultic sites were located on hill tops. These would likely have been visually commanding, although some "high places" identified by archaeologists are not at the highest places in a landscape or at a site. Topographic elevation in ancient Israel, and the ancient Near East in general, meant closeness to the deity (or deities) and could ritually transform the natural element (a mountain or high hill) into the cosmic mountain, representative of the "foundation of the earth" (Wiercinski 1977: 72).

This category of cultic space is marked by broad access for various groups. Such spaces were demarcated by temenos walls, indicating their cultic nature and that there is a graded access to the space within the temenos wall, but such spaces could still accommodate larger groups of people than could cultic spaces within settlements. Specific high places would have served broad geographical regions and the tribes/clans that occupied those regions. There was a sacred landscape that would have been known; Israelites in the Iron Age I would have known where to go for specific ritual activity (e.g., Mt. Ebal, the "Bull Site," altars near Shiloh or Zorah) (Table 29.1).

Another aspect of cultic landscapes, and one to which we will return for our case study, is the location of cultic space within a given site. In the Iron Age I and II, there appears to be a preference for cultic space being located at the northern end of a site. There are some outliers, but the pattern applies to many cultic spaces that appear within sites.

Table 29.1 Open-air cultic places/landscapes

Site	Structure	Notes
Mt. Ebal structure (Stratum I B)	Altar complex	Str. I B; Str. II has been interpreted to include a *favissa* along with a 4-room house where cultic personnel may have lived (Hawkins 2012: 32–38).
Dhahrat et-Tawileh (the "Bull Site")	Altar complex?	Elliptical enclosure encircled by a fieldstone wall; opposite three massive stones forming a wall in the south-eastern portion of the enclosure a large stone set on its long edge may have functioned as a *massebah* or a simple altar. To the north of this stone lay a stone-paved area, from which some sherds, an unidentified bronze object (handle of a mirror?), and part of a square ceramic cult vessel (incense burner or model shrine) were recovered (Mazar 1982: 34–35).
Giloh (Building 105, Area G)	Altar complex?	Mazar (1990: 84) interprets the building as the platform of a tower with parallels to the Mt. Ebal structure; Hawkins (2012:113–16) proposes that the platform may have been an altar complex like the Mt. Ebal structure.
Altar near Tel Shiloh	Open-air shrine?	Rock-hewn altar 1.5 km west of Shiloh with corners oriented to cardinal compass points; no other architecture or finds in the immediate context, but similar in construction to altars at Arad (Str. XII) and "Manoah's altar" at Zorah (Elitzur and Nir-Zevi 2003: 32–33).
Gilgal	Open-air shrine?	Textual evidence indicates that *gilgalim* appear to be places of cultic activity (see Hawkins 2012: 118–22; proposed *gilgalim* include: el-'Unuq and Bedhat esh-Sha'ab).
Bethel	Open-air shrine	Elevation Point (E.P.) 914, located 900m northeast of Beitin is a 70 x 70m flattened area with surrounding walls. Pottery from the 9th–8th century, three figurines, and animal bones were excavated. Based on biblical descriptions, geographic location, and the archaeology, it is proposed as the most likely location for Bethel's cultic area (see Tavger 2021).
Tel Reḥov	Open-air sanctuary	Area E (Str V-IV); Building EB, into which a platform with standing stones is incorporated, does have a plastered room with Phoenician seal impressions impressed into the plaster. It is unclear whether we should consider Building EB itself cultic space, or just the platform, which appears to be connected to the open space to the NE where an offering (?) stone and pottery altar were found. Mazar (2020: 108) identifies Building EB as a *lishkah* where communal and/or ritual meals were held.

One element of this category that needs further research, but which can only be touched upon briefly in this context, is the evolution of cultic landscapes from the Bronze Age through the end of the Iron Age. This involves tracing the creation and de-creation of cultic space in the southern Levant. For instance, the Mt. Ebal structure operated during the early Iron Age I but fell out of use after this. Was it replaced by another structure in a different location? Alternatively, what prompted the construction of a bamah and altar at Arad (Str. XII) and the later sanctuary in the fortress? Concerning the Motza structure, why was this built so near to Jerusalem and in such a low spot in the topography in contrast to other altar complexes or shrines? To address such questions requires articulating numerous variables, including the role of the palace or the Jerusalem (or Israelian) priesthood in centralizing, directing, and impacting the cult.

Cultic Buildings

These are structures established for cultic purposes alone and which are entirely given to cultic space – the term "temple" is appropriate (Table 29.2). In this regard they are separate from the next category, which distinguished spaces within buildings, recognizing that the buildings in which cultic space is found could (and likely did) serve multiple purposes. It is not always possible to ascertain whether an entire building served a (strictly) cultic function, or if only a portion of a building was considered cultic space. This issue needs further research, but for the purpose of our current discussion, we have chosen to be minimalistic in identifying entire buildings as cultic unless cultic remains were recovered from more than one space within the building.

Table 29.2 Selected examples of cultic structures

Site	Structure	Notes
Jerusalem	Temple complex	No archaeological remains; the temple and its surrounding complex north of the City of David and near the palace is described in 1 Kgs 6–7.
Motza	Temple complex	Fragmentary remains of a cultic building, identified as a temple, with an altar in a courtyard to the east of the building's entrance (Kisilevitz and Lipschits 2020).
Arad	Temple	Temple with courtyard and altar, holy place, and holy of holies. The holy of holies contained a standing stone and two stone incense altars (Herzog 2002).
Dan	Temple complex	We assume one could enter the building identified as a temple even though no remains from the earliest phases are preserved. The altar is situated directly to the south, and there are surrounding rooms in which cultic paraphernalia were found. The confluence of data suggests that the square platform is the foundation for a shrine/building/temple.
'Ataruz	Temple complex	A temple complex was established in the late 10th/early 9th c. and continued to operate until the mid-9th c. at which point it was destroyed and replaced by a Moabite shrine (Ji 2012, 2018; Ji and Schade forthcoming)
Tel Reḥov	Building CP (Str. IV)	This building has a unique plan, but several cultic items were found in multiple rooms. Mazar (2020: 108–09, 125) suggests a cultic function for this building, which was where the "Elisha" inscription was recovered.

Differentiating cultic buildings from non-cultic buildings is possible through a consideration of the architectural plan viewed in conjunction with the small finds, inscriptions, and/or other iconographic remains. As such, certain architectural plans (e.g., the temple *in antis*) have been securely identified as demarcating ritual space. Such buildings are noticeably different from domestic structures in plan and, often, in associated small finds.

Cultic Spaces within Buildings

The separation of this category from the preceding is of course imposed in some instances where the complete plan of a building is unknown. Also, it is not always possible to distinguish whether a single cultic room (as these spaces are typically labeled) should be considered a stand-alone cultic structure, or if it is part of a larger structure. Equally important to consider, is whether an entire structure that does attest to cultic space should be considered a temple or if the structure was multipurpose. In the current classification, entire structures that have some cultic space, but for which it is unclear if they are actually temples, are included in this category (e.g., Megiddo Building 2081; Khirbet Qeiyafa Building C10). Also falling into this category are the so-called "gate shrines" that have been identified at a number of sites but which may have been more extensive than attested archaeologically (Table 29.3).

Table 29.3 Selected examples of cultic spaces within buildings

Site	Room/structure	Notes
Ai	Iron I shrine (Locus 65)	
Kh. Qeiyafa	1 Cultic Building?/space within Building (Building C10) 2 Gate Shrine 3 Space in Building C3	in gate; near gate; private building
Kuntillet 'Ajrud	NW Corner room?	Possible *massebot* were found in the NW corner room of the structure.
Jerusalem	Cave 1 (7th c.)	
Lachish	1 Room 49[1] (Str. V) 2 Gate Shrine (Str. III)	
Megiddo	Room 2081 (Str. VA/IVB)	
Beersheba	Gate shrine(?)	
H. 'Uza	Cultic room south of gate	
Tel Reḥov	1 Within the Apiary (Str. V) 2 Building CF (Str. IV)	

1 Aharoni (1975) originally excavated and proposed the form of this room, dated by him to Str. V. Four cultic stands, two stand-bowls, a stone altar (with collar; unlike Megiddo and Hazor), 8 chalices, 3 lamps, 2 dipper juglets, 8 jugs, 3 cooking pots, 14 bowls, and 1-2 store jars were recovered from this room. Ussishkin (2004: 105-109) reevaluated this interpretation and argues that no such cult room existed. Instead, the cultic objects were located in a pit from Str. IV that was unidentified by Aharoni. While Ussishkin is certainly correct that Aharoni's original reconstruction of Room 49 is incorrect, the idea that there is simply a cultic pit or favissa, is problematic in itself. Both stands and the stone altar were clearly laying on the plaster floor of the room, and there is no clear evidence for a pit in the published photos from Ussishkin 2004 or Aharoni 1975. Walls 8 and 9 certainly do not belong to the same phase as floor 10, which is associated with Walls 1-4. Aharoni's proposed opening in the northeastern wall of the room can be refuted by the fact that it is one continuous wall with what appears to be a segment of mudbrick left unexcavated.

Cultic Objects

Identifying cultic objects is as challenging as identifying cultic architecture. There are some factors that help identify objects as cultic: (1) location in a cultic building; (2) form or plastic decoration that shares elements with known religious iconography; (3) containing residue of compounds meant to heighten senses of perception or alter the participant's mind; and (4) unique shape for which a specific function may not be clear (Table 29.4).[9]

Table 29.4 Selected categories of objects with cultic functions

Cultic items/features	Site(s)	Notes
Model shrine	The "Bull Site"(?), Kh. Qeiyafa, Tel Reḥov, Kh. er-Ra'i, Tel Rekhesh, Dan, Tell el-Far'ah (N), Tell en-Nasbeh	
Portable altar	Kh. Qeiyafa; Beersheba (?), Tel Reḥov, Megiddo, Lachish	
Ceramic (incense) stand	Kh. Qeiyafa, Taanach, Jerusalem, Lachish(?),Tell en-Nasbeh	For Lachish, Ussishkin (2004: 86) questions whether the stands carried away by Assyrian soldiers should be understood as cultic when they are considered in the context of the other items being carried away.
Figurines	Kh. Qeiyafa, Jerusalem, Motza	
1. Male	1 male—Qeiyafa, Motza	
2. Female	2 female –Dothan (gold plaque)	
3. Zoo morphic	3 zoomorphic – the "Bull Site," Tel Reḥov, Tell en-Nasbeh	
Standing stones (*masseboth*)	Kh. Qeiyafa, Kh er-Ra'i (?), Dan, Lachish (?), Arad, Kuntillet 'Ajrud (?), Kh. al-Mudayna; Tell el-Farah (N)	(?)=The identification of some stones as *masseboth* is uncertain
"*Asherim*"	Locus 81 (Str. V)	The charred remains of what appeared to be an olive wood pole were found next to a possible standing stone.
Cultic vessels	1 Cup-and-saucer vessels – Tel Reḥov, Kh. Qeiyafa, Arad, Jerusalem 2 Zoomorphic vessels – Dothan, Beth Shean, Kh. Qeiyafa, Tel Reḥov 3 Libation vessels – Kh. Qeiyafa	
Cultic inscriptions/ graffiti	Kuntillet 'Ajrud; Deir 'Alla; Kh. Beit Loya; Kh. el-Qom	
Favissa(e)	Mt. Ebal(?)	Two large favissae have been excavated at En Hazeva and Yavneh, though neither site is Israelite.
Multi-spouted lamps	Dan, Dothan, Megiddo, Taanach, Tell es-Safi, Gezer, Lachish	

The Archaeology of Israelite Cult: Yahwisms across Space and Time

Ritualized Space and Orientation: A Case Study

The landscape of ritual space is not something that has been fully addressed in studies on ancient Israel's cult. As such, there is fruitful ground to plumb for insight into ancient Israel's ritual conception of their space. Zevit (2001: 250) raised the question of whether Israelite temples were always located on the northern side of sites. It was an interesting musing that has not been taken up since, so we examined the location of cultic spaces with respect to their location within Israelite sites across the Iron Age.

Based on additional sites excavated since the publication of Zevit's volume, it appears that there is now substance for claiming that ancient Israel, from at least the late Iron Age IIA, preferred a northern location for their cultic space(s) within any given site where practical. Israelite cultic buildings, complexes, and/or enclosures discovered over the past 20 years are all located on the northern (northwest, and/or northeast) side of their respective sites (see Table 29.5). Our analysis revealed that cultic structures and buildings/complexes dated to the Iron Age I to IIA were located in various areas at each site with Khirbet Qeiyafa having

Table 29.5 Locations and orientations of select cultic structures

Site	Location of cultic structure at site	Orientation of cultic structure (entrance)	Notes
Iron I–early Iron IIA			
Mt. Ebal	NE	SW	Corners oriented to cardinal points
'Ai	Center (L.65)	E	
Hazor	W (Area B); E (Area A, L.8400 and L.80019)	N; E	L.8400 is a standing stone with offering slabs to the east. L.80019 is a rounded installation of miniature *masseboth*, located on the northern side of L.8400.
Kh. Qeiyafa	SE (Building C3); S gate; S (Building C10); W (Building D100)	NW?; E; N?; E?	Buildings C3, C10, and D100 were likely entered from the center of the site
Iron II – Northern (Israelite) Sites			
Dan	N	S	
Megiddo	NW (Building 2081); E (Building 338)	SE; W	
Tel Reḥov	NW (Building CP); NE (Building EB+courtyard)	E; ?	
'Ataruz	–	SE	The early phase of the site appears to be comprised of the cultic structure alone. After it is rebuilt as a Moabite shrine, the cultic area is in the center of the site
Iron II – Southern (Judahite) Sites			
Arad	NW	E	
Jerusalem	N	E	Based on 1 Kgs 6–7
Tel Motza	NW(?)	E	

numerous cultic rooms in the buildings along the southern end of the site. During the Iron Age II, Israelite sites such as Tel Dan, Megiddo (Building 2081), and Tel Reḥov (Building CP, Str. IV) had cultic spaces built in their northern portions.[10] Sites in Iron II Judah, namely, Arad, Motza, and Jerusalem, have cultic structures or complexes in the northern parts of the sites. The locations of cultic structures and buildings/complexes dated to the Iron Age I to early IIA were not as standardized. Some appear in the north of a site (e.g., Mt. Ebal), but others, such as the cultic rooms at Khirbet Qeiyafa, appear along the southern or eastern ends of the site.

This northern preference for cultic space is one feature that ties together Israel's cultic landscape, in the pre-monarchic, united monarchic, and divided monarchic periods. At the same time, when we consider the orientation of the specific cultic buildings/rooms, we see a divergence between northern Israelite and southern Judahite sites: cultic sites in the northern kingdom of Israel are generally oriented to the south(east) – that is, the entrance to the cultic space is on the south(east) – while cultic sites in the southern kingdom of Judah are oriented to the east. This pattern is particularly apt for cultic buildings. Cultic spaces within buildings are a bit more fluid in their orientation, but further research is needed to bear out how accurate this may be. For instance, Building CP at Tel Reḥov (Str. IV) appears to be entered from the east. However, once inside, the northwest corner room, which appears to be a space of focus, can be entered from the east or the south.

With the pattern of placement and access provided by archaeology (as well as text and tradition in the case of Jerusalem), the interpretive code as to why cultic complexes or structures are located in the northern part of sites may be adduced from the biblical text and ecology. A cursory examination of the term "north" (צָפוֹן) in the Hebrew Bible shows its use as a cardinal direction and recognition of the north as a direction from which precipitation and seasonal, cooler winds blow (Prov 25:23; Qoh 1:6; Song 4:16).[11] Thus, the location of cultic complexes or buildings on the north may have a physical element related to the winds underlying their placement. Moreover, although some biblical texts indicate a perception of YHWH originating from Mt. Seir or the area of Edom (Deut 33:2; Judg 5:4–5; Hab 3:3), other texts also show the deity's association with the north within an Israelite mindset. In a speech in Job 37:22, Elihu states:

מִצָּפוֹן, זָהָב יֶאֱתֶה; עַל-אֱלוֹהַּ, נוֹרָא הוֹד

Out of the north comes golden splendor; around God is awesome majesty.

The "north" as the co-location of YHWH and the temple on Mt. Zion is also extolled by the psalmist in Ps 48:2–3 (English vv. 1–2):

גָּדוֹל יְהוָה וּמְהֻלָּל מְאֹד-- בְּעִיר אֱלֹהֵינוּ, הַר-קָדְשׁוֹ.
יְפֵה נוֹף, מְשׂוֹשׂ כָּל-הָאָרֶץ: הַר-צִיּוֹן, יַרְכְּתֵי צָפוֹן; קִרְיַת, מֶלֶךְ רָב.

"Great is the Lord and greatly to be praised in the city of our God, His holy mountain. Beautiful in elevation, is the joy of all the earth, Mount Zion, in the far north, the city of the great King."

Additionally, Ezekiel's vision of the glory of YHWH with its accompanying storm, cloud, and fire imagery came from the north (Ezek 1:4). Thus, while some texts indicate an origin for YHWH in Edom or Sinai, some biblical authors associated the deity with the north in some way that may be associated with the sacrificial instructions in Lev 1:11. Whether this particular correlation equals causation in the case of locating cultic structures in the northern parts of sites, or these examples are reflecting, or were influenced by, the extant cultic landscape cannot be presently determined.

Of significance is the fact that the location of religious precincts in the capital cities was close to the palace (Jerusalem and likely the temple of Baʻal at Samaria mentioned in 1 Kgs

16:32–33 and 2 Kgs 10:21), which seems to indicate that the monarch functioned as the head of the cult (Solomon, Jeroboam, Ahab and Jezebel, Jehu, Athaliah, Hezekiah, Manasseh, Josiah) albeit titular in most cases, being approved by religious officials (such as priests and prophets) but also initiating and fostering the state support of cultic rituals performed by priests. In contrast, the sanctuaries at Dan and Bethel built by Jeroboam (1 Kgs 12:26–33), while not located near the royal residence at Shechem, probably marked Israel's borders, delineating Jeroboam's kingdom, and in the case of Bethel, also likely drew on shared cultural memory of Jacob, the eponymous ancestor of Israel, and his experiences at Bethel (Gen 28, 35; Tavger 2021).

It is also noteworthy that the orientation of Israelite and Judahite cultic spaces are different from those of the Philistines, which tend to favor a northward orientation (e.g., Tel Qasile Temples 300, 131, 319(?); Ekron Temple 350).[12] Phoenician cultic space is poorly represented, but if we understand Tel Michal to be representative of Phoenician cultic influence, then the fact that the cultic building there, located to the SE of the high tell, is oriented to the SE may indicate that there was a shared sense of cultic space between the Phoenicians and northern Israelites. If such a parallel is in fact correct, it coheres nicely with the fact that the northern kingdom of Israel had close ties to the Phoenician kingdom of Tyre, if not other Phoenician cities in the Iron Age, according to the biblical text.

Toward a Synthesis of Israelite Cult

This is the first step in a larger study of cults in Bronze Age Canaan and Iron Age Israel that will also include a consideration of desanctification and its effects on society. There are many aspects related to Israelite cult and belief that we have not touched upon but which warrant much further discussion or development, e.g., the similarity and distinctions between other West Semitic sacrificial rituals and those of Israel (Smith 2002: 22–23); iconography and its distribution (see Uehlinger, this volume); shifts or changes that occurred between the emergence of Israel and development of kingship; rituals that reified the Davidic monarchy or established new dynasties in the northern kingdom of Israel; mortuary cults (but see Ilan 2017 for a recent summary of evidence and bibliography); and the desanctification of objects or places. For example, we do see a decommissioning of cultic locations outside of Jerusalem in the late 8th century BC such as Arad, Beersheba, and Motza, and the desanctification of shrines and religious objects in Jerusalem (e.g., Nehushtan; 2 Kgs 18:4). This does not necessarily have to be solely a religious reform, even though the biblical texts make this claim. The closure of these sites could have been a political reform meant to create a more centralized power structure in the face of Assyrian pressure and the immigration of northern Israelites into Judah. Additionally, the reliefs from Sennacherib's conquest of Lachish show Assyrian soldiers carrying away cultic paraphernalia. This has been seen as evidence negating/disputing the biblical claims that Hezekiah conducted all-encompassing religious reforms. However, as in the case of how monotheism may be represented in the archaeological record, it may be that the universalizing language of the text does not assume every single place was closed, particularly at the ever-important site of Lachish.[13]

Our brief case study here and proposed longer study should demonstrate that the ultimate sacred propositions held in common by ancient Israel (and Judah) throughout the Iron Age are attested textually and archaeologically. The rituals that would have produced a religious experience may have been performed in different ways reflected in the archaeological record by various ritual paraphernalia such as iconic cult stands, aniconic cult stands, zoomorphic or anthropomorphic figurines, model temple shrines, or other artifacts deemed "cultic," evincing flexibility in approaches to experiencing the divine. The plurality of cultic expression in ancient Israel diachronically and regionally is clear, and when we consider the biblical text there are interesting elements that we must address. Could it be that the different Levitical clans, established in specific tribal areas, each developed their own cultic expression?

Despite there being unifying sacred propositions, including the preeminence of YHWH, the religious experience is variable. Such variability could serve several purposes, such as fostering or eliminating group cohesion. Giles de Rapper (2010: 259) notes that shrines are "places where the social production of the border takes place."[14] As noted in the case study, the cultic landscape in the northern kingdom of Israel differed from cultic space in Judah on a political level when comparing the shrines at Dan and Bethel to the contemporary temple complex at Jerusalem. However, at the local and individual level, except for the orientation of cultic space, there are no clear archaeological markers that distinguish northern Israelite cult from southern Judahite cult. The fact that Jeroboam created two cultic contexts where Yahweh was worshiped, is evident from the archaeological remains (Greer 2013) and from the biblical text (1 Kgs 12:25–32). Religion both unified Israel and yet divided it because the Judahite authors viewed the north as heterodox or apostate. The differences in cult expression and praxis should not necessarily be understood as differences in overarching beliefs; in particular, that related to the idea of monotheism. In this regard, Miller's idea of heterodox Yahwism, which is "an amalgam of [pure Yahwism blended with foreign elements], together with particular practices that came into conflict with some of the facets of more orthodox Yahwism or were not customarily a part of it" (2000: 51), should be reevaluated.

Similarities in cultic assemblage and behavior, as best as can be reconstructed via archaeology, suggest greater alignment of ritual action across the north and south. In this regard, the popular view held in previous generations that there was an "official cult" and a "popular cult" has credence, though the politicization of cult which is ascribed to the official cult is not necessarily antithetical to the popular cult because each prescribes and proscribes different ritual behavior and is meant to address different beliefs. What we see is not Yahwism, but *Yahwisms* – different practices for different people and times and locations. The Yahwisms of ancient Israel and their accompanying rituals and sacred experiences, which could be employed to divide Israel and sever bonds to serve a socio-political purpose, greatly served to establish networks within society, strengthening and uniting the various clans and tribes of Israel despite geographic and political differences.

Notes

1 Rappaport's definition is complimented by that of Zevit, which sees religion (particularly Israelite religions) as the "varied, symbolic expressions of, and appropriate responses to, the deities and powers that groups or communities deliberately affirmed as being of unrestricted value to them within their worldview" (2001: 15). Religion for both includes, and is the cumulative expression of belief, action, and meaning.
2 The term "cult" refers to the praxis of ancient Israelite religion and is essentially ritual in action. "Israelite" throughout this chapter refers to both Israel and Judah; when the northern kingdom of Israel and its practices are the subject, it will be referred to as "the northern kingdom of Israel" or simply, "the northern kingdom."
3 For a treatment of ritual in relation to the biblical text, see Belnap, this volume.
4 Our examination here is the first step in a much larger study of cult in Iron Age Israel that will also include a consideration of material culture reflecting ritual, regional iconography, ritual practices established local and interregional social and economic networks, and desanctification and its effects on society.
5 Such questions have been treated most extensively by Zevit (2001: 81–121).

6. See Walton (2018: 333–35) for a discussion of the various ways Israelite religion operated in its ANE context. For this paper, sites accepted as Israelite/Judahite are accepted as such and sites identified as Philistine, Edomite, etc. are accepted as such. Our future monograph on Israelite cult will include a full discussion and assessment of the accuracy and applicability of such labels.
7. We are not suggesting an evolution in Israelite ritual behavior from simplistic open-air shrines or altars to highly ordered, temple-centric ritual systems overseen by priests governed by sacred propositions embedded in codes. Rather, we are examining the various components of the ritual and cult to take "snapshots" of specific instances to see what, if any, development happens in cultic architecture and material culture, viewed together with the relevant texts as assemblages (see Pioske, this volume).
8. The examples given in each of the tables are indicative of a category, but the tables are not necessarily comprehensive.
9. The last factor, a shape with an unknown function, is ambiguous at best and falls within the well-known humorous observation that if an archaeologist is unsure of an object's function, it was probably cultic.
10. The cultic complex at Khirbet 'Ataruz is dated to the 10th–9th century BCE and is destroyed in the mid/late 9th century. It is rebuilt and the site appears to expand to the north and east. Presently, it appears that the site was a stand-alone cultic complex until this expansion, but there is much late disturbance at the site that hinders understanding of the earlier periods.
11. Other references to north as a direction/place include the placement of the Table of Shewbread (Exod 26:35), while the Holiness Code indicates that sacrificial animals should be slaughtered on the north side of the altar (Lev 1:11). Further, the oracles of Joel, Isaiah, Jeremiah, and Ezekiel use "north" to refer to the direction from which the Assyrians and Babylonians would conquer Israel and Judah. The same generalized term is used for the location from which scattered Israelites would be gathered in the prophetic utterances of Isaiah, Jeremiah, and Zechariah as well as Ps 107:3.
12. The Iron I temple at Tell es-Safi, Area A, is fragmentary making it difficult to discern from which side it was entered. Still, the fact that its corners are orientated to the cardinal points precludes that it was entered from the east.
13. Universalizing language is common in relation to many topics in the Bible and the broader Near Eastern literature (e.g., military conquest).
14. Berlin (2021: 147) calls them "signposts, material adjuncts to topography."

Bibliography

Aharoni, Yohanan. 1975. *Lachish: The Sanctuary and Residency (Lachish V)*. Tel Aviv: Tel Aviv University Institute of Archaeology.

Albertz, R. and Schmitt, R. 2012. *Family and Household Religion in Ancient Israel and the Levant*. Winona Lake: Eisenbrauns.

Amiran, Ruth. 1970. *Ancient Pottery of the Holy Land: From Its Beginnings in the Neolithic Period to the End of the Iron Age*. New Brunswick: Rutgers.

Arie, Eran, B. Rosen, and D. Namdar. 2020. "Cannabis and Frankincense at the Judahite Shrine of Arad." *TA* 47: 5–28.

Bell, Catherine. 1992. *Ritual Theory, Ritual Practice*. Oxford: Oxford University Press.

Bergen, W. 2007. "Studying Ancient Israelite Ritual: Methodological Considerations. *Religion Compass* 1: 579–86.

Berlin, Andrea M. 2021. "The Upper Galilee and the Northern Coast." Pages 145–75 in *The Middle Maccabees: Archaeology, History, and the Rise of the Hasmonean Kingdom*. Edited by Andrea M. Berlin and Paul J. Kosmin. Atlanta: SBL.

Coogan, Michael D. 1987. "Of Cults and Cultures: Reflections on the Interpretation of Archaeological Evidence." *PEQ* 119:1–8.

de Rapper, Gilles. 2010. "Religion on the Border: Sanctuaries and Festivals in Post-Communist Albania." Pages 247–65 in *Religion and Boundaries. Studies from the Balkans, Eastern Europe and Turkey*. Edited by Galia Valtchinova. Istanbul: Isis Press.

Drennan, Robert D. 1976. "Religion and Social Evolution in Formative Mesoamerica." Pages 345–68 in *The Early Mesoamerican Village*. Edited by Kent V. Flannery. San Diego: Academic Press.

Durkheim, Émile. 1915. *The Elementary Forms of Religious Life*. New York: Free Press.

Elitzur, Yael, and Doron Nir-Zevi. 2003. "A Rock-Hewn Altar near Shiloh." *PEQ* 135: 30–36.

Faust, Avraham. 2010. "The Archaeology of Israelite Cult: Questioning the Consensus. *BASOR* 360: 23–35.

Flannery, Kent V. 1976. "Contextual Analysis of Ritual Paraphernalia from Formative Oaxaca." Pages. 333–45 in *The Early Mesoamerican Village*. Edited by Kent V. Flannery. San Diego: Academic Press.

Gilmour, Garth H. 1995. "The Archaeology of Cult in the Southern Levant in the Early Iron Age." Ph.D. diss., University of Oxford.

Greer, Jonathan S. 2013. *Dinner at Dan: Biblical and Archaeological Evidence for Sacred Feasts at Iron Age II Tel Dan and Their Significance*. Leiden: Brill.

Halbertsma, Diederik J. H., and Bruce Routledge. 2021. "Between Rocks and 'High Places': On Religious Architecture in the Iron Age Southern Levant." *Religions* 12: Article 740. Online: doi.org/10.3390/rel12090740.

Hawkins, Ralph K. 2012. *The Iron Age I Structure on Mt. Ebal: Excavation and Interpretation*. Winona Lake: Eisenbrauns.

Herzog, Ze'ev. 2002. "The Fortress Mound at Tel Arad an Interim Report." *TA* 29: 3–109.

Holladay, John S. 1987. "Religion in Israel and Judah Under the Monarchy: An Explicitly Archaeological Approach." Pages 249–99 in *Ancient Israelite Religion: Essays in Honor of Frank Moore Cross*. Edited by Patrick D. Miller, Paul D. Hanson, and S. Dean McBridei. Philadelphia: Fortress.

Ilan, David. 2017. "Iron Age Mortuary Practices and Beliefs in the Southern Levant." Pages 51–66 in *Engaging with the Dead: Exploring Changing Human Beliefs about Death, Mortality and the Human Body*. Edited by J. Bradbury, and C. Scarre. Oxford and Philadelphia: Oxbow Books.

Insoll, Timothy. 2011. "Introduction: Ritual and Religion in Archaeological Perspective." Pages 1–7 in *Oxford Handbook of the Archaeology of Ritual and Religion*. Edited by Timothy Insoll. Oxford: Oxford University Press.

Ji, Chang-Ho. 2012. "The Early Age II Temple at Hirbet 'Atarus and Its Archecture and Selected Cultic Objects." Pages 203–22 in *Temple Building and Temple Cult: Architecture and Cultic Paraphernalia of Temples in the Levant*. Edited by Jens Kamlah. Wiesbaden: Harassowitz.

———. 2018. "A Moabite Sanctuary at Khirbat Ataruz, Jordan: Stratigraphy, Findings, and Archaeological Implications." *Levant* 50: 173–210.

Ji, Chang-Ho, and Aaron Schade. "The Iron IIB Period at Khirbat 'Ataruz." *Studies in History and Archaeology of Jordan* 14, forthcoming.

Kisilevitz, Shua and Oded Lipschits. 2020. "Tel Moẓa." *HA-ESI* 132. Online: http://www.hadashot-esi.org.il/report_detail_eng.aspx?id=25702&mag_id=128.

LaRocca-Pitts, E. C. 2001. *"Of Wood and Stone": The Significance of Israelite Cultic Items in the Bible and Its Early Interpreters*. Winona Lake: Eisenbrauns.

Mazar, Amihai. 1982. "The 'Bull Site': An Iron Age I Open Cult Place." *BASOR* 247: 27–42.

———. 1990. "Iron Age I and II Towers at Giloh and the Israelite Settlement." *IEJ* 40 (2/3): 77–101.

———. 2020. "The Tel Reḥov Excavations: Overview and Synthesis." Pages 69–140 in *Tel Reḥov: A Bronze and Iron Age City in the Beth-Shean Valley. Volume I, Introductions, Synthesis and Excavations on the Upper Mound*. Edited by Amihai Mazar and Nava Panitz-Cohen. Jerusalem: The Institute of Archaeology of the Hebrew University of Jerusalem.

Miller, Patrick D. 2000. *The Religion of Ancient Israel*. Louisville: Westminster John Knox.

Nakhai, Beth Alpert. 2001. *Archaeology and the Religions of Canaan and Israel*. Boston: ASOR.

Rappaport, Roy A. 1971a. "Ritual, Sanctity, and Cybernetics." *American Anthropologist* 73: 59–76.

———. 1971b. "The Sacred in Human Evolution." *Annual Review of Ecology and Systematics* 2: 23–44.

Renfrew, Colin. 1985. *The Archaeology of Cult: The Sanctuary at Phylakopi*. London: Thames and Hudson.

Renfrew, Colin, and Paul Bahn. 2004. *Archaeology Essentials: Theories, Methods, and Practice*. London: Thames and Hudson.

Smith, Mark S. 2002. *The Early History of God: Yahweh and the Other Deities in Ancient Israel*. Grand Rapids: Eerdmans.

Tavger, Aharon. 2021. "And He Called the Name of that Place 'Bethel' (Gen 28: 19): Historical-Geography and Archaeology of the Sanctuary of Bethel." Pages 221–43 in *The History of Jacob Cycle (Genesis 25–35): Recent Research on the Compilation, the Redaction and the Reception of the Biblical Narrative and Its Historical and Cultural Contexts*. Edited by B. Hensel. Tübingen: Mohr Siebeck.

Ussishkin, David. 2004. "A Synopsis of the Stratigraphical, Chronological, and Historical Issues." Pages 50–119 in *The Renewed Archaeological Excavations at Lachish (1973–1994)*. Edited by David Ussishkin. Tel Aviv: Institute of Archaeology, Tel Aviv University.

Walton, John H. 2018. "Interactions in the Ancient Cognitive Environment." Pp. 333–39 in *Behind the Scenes of the Old Testament: Cultural, Social, and Historical Contexts*. Edited by Jonathan S. Greer, J. W. Hilber, and John H. Walton. Grand Rapids: Baker Academic.

Wiercinski, Andrzej. 1977. "Pyramids and Ziggurats as the Architectonic Representations of the Archetype of the Cosmic Mountain." *Katunob* 10: 72.

Zevit, Ziony. 2001. *The Religions of Ancient Israel: A Synthesis of Parallactic Approaches*. London: Continuum.

30
THE ROLE OF RITUAL IN BIBLICAL NARRATIVE

Dan Belnap

A fundamental aspect of ancient Israel was the ritualization of their environment(s), providing structure for their relationships with one another and more particularly, the divine. The biblical text is replete with descriptions of and allusions to ritualized activities, both within the cult and without.[2] Of course, the exact nature or utility of the ritual behavior cannot be confirmed via the biblical text alone, the text being separated from actual praxis. Moreover, the text is not objective, but polemical, reflecting pro-Yahwistic, cultically positive voice(s). Thus, what is legitimate ritualization versus illegitimate praxis is necessarily influenced by the biblical voice(s). Moreover, as noted above, ritual behavior present within the text necessarily remains a literary construction. Even if these practices were performed at one time, the version we have is a later, literarily produced one. Thus, rather than determining whether the ritual behavior described within the text was an actual ritual performance, a more productive approach may be determining the function of the description with the literary context.[3]

In light of this, ritual narratives can be identified as one of three general categories: (1) prescriptive texts, or those texts/narratives in which the ritual performance is found within instruction concerning the performance and as such represents an idealized version of the ritual behavior; (2) descriptive texts, or those texts/narratives that are presumed to describe actual ritual performance, and which often indicate efficacious vs. inefficacious ritual; and (3) "divine" texts, or those texts/narratives in which divine ritual activity, either situated in the divine realm or mortal realm, are described. This chapter explores the value of approaching biblical ritual from the perspective of the categories provided above, by a review of two such narratives, the anointing of Aaron and his sons and the Saulide narrative, and how the categories mentioned above interweave throughout the narratives, suggesting that in doing so, we gain a greater understanding as to what ritual meant for ancient Israel.

Example 1: The Anointing of Aaron and his Sons

The first such narrative is the anointing of the tabernacle and Aaron and his sons, described in both Exodus 40 and in Leviticus 8. The narrative begins with the instructions concerning the preparation and sequence for the performance. The instructions were received by Moses and given by God directly to Moses. Thus, even before one reviews the instruction, one is already presented with a "divine" text, with God as a ritual participant providing the instruction. Though often acknowledged, God as provider of ritual instruction, and thus as an agent of ritual activity, is often overlooked. In fact, the Hebrew Bible is replete with ritual instructions given by deity. This instruction may be divided into two types: (1) ritual instructions that provide a reason or expected result for the ritual activity (e.g., the *ḥaṭṭāʾt* sacrifices in Leviticus 3); and (2) ritual instructions that do not provide the reason or result (e.g., Genesis 15, where God simply tells Abraham to give him a series of animals).

The divine origin and presentation of ritual instructions from deity to chosen mortal recipient(s) speaks to the crucial role that the ritual plays in the relationship between humankind and the divine community, particularly in the facilitation of that relationship. Yet this highlights an intriguing question, namely, where does ritual instruction and the subsequent ritual behavior fit within God's choices of interaction? If God can interact in other ways than ritual, such as dreams and visions, then what mortal-divine interaction is made more efficacious through ritual than through other means? Unfortunately, the answer to this question is not altogether clear and can only be adduced by context. Still, some generalizations can be assumed. Though disparate from one another, the purpose behind the ritual instruction, say, in Genesis 15 and in Genesis 35—where God gave Jacob ritual instructions to go to Bethel and build an altar—and the ritual instructions of Exodus 40, all presume that God wished to meet and interact with his people in a way that dreams or visions cannot. Moreover, since the rituals performed are done by the mortals, it suggests that the purpose of the ritual is to sanctify the individual to enter the presence of God. Thus, the ritual instructions provided by God are not necessarily meant to appease God's appetite or soothe his emotions, but instead are so humans could become sanctified enough to withstand God's presence.

The instruction in Exod 40:1–16, which is both a "divine" text and a prescriptive text, represents a dedicatory sequence in which anointing was the primary act. It is then followed by a descriptive section, vv. 17–33, in which the tabernacle was set up, including the lighting of the lamp and the placing of incense on the altar within the tabernacle, and the offering of initial sacrifices (burnt offering and grain offering). Presumably, though not mentioned explicitly here, the tabernacle was then anointed, followed by Aaron and his sons being washed, invested, and anointed. This descriptive text is then followed by the results of the dedication, vv. 34–38, specifically that the divine presence was now present in the tabernacle. The emphasis on the anointing of the tabernacle and those items associated with it, including Aaron and his sons, indicates its importance in the overall narrative. Significantly, unlike many other actions associated with the tabernacle, the anointing process begins with those items that will be in the holiest space and moves outward consecutively into less sacred space—the tabernacle and its items were anointed first, followed by the altar of burnt offering, and then the laver.

Exodus 30 may further illuminate the anointing sequence. Following the instruction and recipe for the anointing oil, Moses was told that the oil would be used to anoint the tabernacle and the ark (v. 26), then, following a clockwise order, the table of the bread of presence, the lamp, and the altar of incense (v. 27), ending with the altar of burnt offering, and the laver (v. 28; Klingbeil 1995). Thus, the list begins with the furniture in the holiest space, moves to those items in the successively less holy space, and ends with those items in the courtyard, the least holy space of the tabernacle. Finally, like the instruction in Exodus 40, the priests were anointed as well. While the text does not explicitly say that this was to be the order of the anointing process, the order of the list suggests that in fact this was the order of the anointing.[4]

Leviticus 8 is the descriptive text of the tabernacle's dedication. The order of the dedication procedure begins differently than the instruction, with Aaron's washing and investiture in the priestly garb taking place first (vv. 6–9). This is then followed by the order outlined in Exodus 40, with the tabernacle and items associated within being anointed (v. 10) followed by the anointing of the altar of burnt offering and the laver (v. 11), and then the anointing of Aaron (v. 12). The initial anointing sequence is then followed by a second anointing sequence, not reflected in the earlier prescriptive passages in Exodus 30 and 40. Beginning in verse 22, the manipulation of the consecration ram is described, the penultimate element being the mixing of the blood with the anointing oil, which is then spritzed on Aaron, his sons, and their clothing. While not exactly an anointing in that the mixture is spritzed rather than poured out, the function of the secondary placement of the anointing oil reinforces the purpose of the first anointing, namely to sacralize the priest and his accoutrements.

Although the prescriptive and descriptive texts differ in aspects, the overall emphasis on the act of anointing and the way the anointings took place may indicate that the anointing of the priest and the tabernacle was understood as ritual activity performed by God himself. While it is clear from the text that it is Moses who anoints the tabernacle and Aaron and his sons, several elements within the ritual narrative suggest that Moses may be viewed as a divine "stand-in." This substitution is explicit in Exod 4:16, where Moses is told that he would be "god" to Aaron while Aaron would be as a prophet, or the one who speaks the words of God. Similarly, in Exod 7:1, God announces that Moses would be "god" in relation to Pharaoh and Aaron would be his prophet. Considering the above, it is possible that Moses-as-god is also in play for the dedication of the tabernacle, with Moses' acts recognized as if God himself were doing them (Meeks 1970). God-as-anointer is in fact found elsewhere in the Hebrew Bible. Psalm 45 includes a scene in which the subject is anointed by "God, even your God, with the oil of joy" (v. 7).[5] In Ps 89:20, the reader is told David was anointed by God with God's anointing oil. The actual anointing of David is described in 1 Samuel 16, where he is anointed by Samuel; however, the relationship of these two passages suggests that, like Moses, Samuel is to be understood as God's representative, thus his actions are to be seen as God's actions.

Elements of the rite itself also intimate its divine performance. As noted earlier, the anointing sequence described in Exodus 30, 40 and performed in Leviticus 8 began from the innermost holy space, in which God's own presence was to be found, and moved from that space to increasingly less holy space until ending at the laver in the tabernacle courtyard. This inward to outward progression was the inverse of normal priestly cultic movement which may be characterized as an outward progression toward a more holy space. In terms of the dedication, both movements are performed, with the anointing moving outward from the holy of holies and Aaron and his sons moving inward from the courtyard laver which may suggest that the sanctifying of the tabernacle was not meant to separate the tabernacle from its mundane construction, but to facilitate the joining of the mortal/divine realms with God's anointing "impressing" his presence throughout the tabernacle while providing the means for humankind to move through increasing holy space by virtue of the other rites.

The non-iterative performance of anointing was also significant. Unlike the other acts performed in the *sancta*, anointing only took place once. Outside of the description in Leviticus 8, no mention is made of the tabernacle being anointed again. Similarly, once the priest was anointed, there is nothing that suggests of a necessity to be anointed again. Instead, the initial act of anointing had lasting efficacy. This contrasts with most, if not all, of the other cultic acts performed, which were iterative in nature (e.g., continual washing by the priests, the *tāmîd* rites). The continuing efficacy of the anointing rite as opposed to the need to perform the other rites on a continual basis seems to highlight the difference in purpose between the two types of rites. The iterative nature of the rites is precisely because God does not perform them, and they thus lose their efficacy with passing time and circumstances which necessitate their repeated performance. God, on the other hand, cannot become unsanctified. His sanctified state never changes and thus what he changes is permanently changed (Fleming 1998: 407).

This non-iterative aspect, reflected in lasting efficacy, of the anointing rite is noted in later passages which note the permanently changed status of the priest. In Lev 10:7, following the death of his two sons, Nadab and Abihu, Aaron is told that he cannot mourn in the normal fashion for his sons: כי שמן משחת יהוה עליכם ("because the oil of YHWH's anointing is upon you"). Similarly, Lev 21:10, 12, which repeats the same mourning injunctions for priests, states that these injunctions apply because the priest had been anointed, with v. 12 noting that this is so: כי נזר שמן משחת אלהיו עליו ("because the crown of the oil of your God's anointing is on you"). In both instances, the anointing is the express reason given as to why the priest is not allowed to mourn. Moreover, the injunction is in force the moment the priest is anointed and remains in effect until his death, thus indicating the lasting efficaciousness of the anointing's performance. It is also worth noting that both references either indicate the anointing is God's or that the oil itself is God's possession; either way, the anointing is a divinely enacted performance.

While the anointing narratives present several specific insights into Israelite beliefs concerning ritual and ritual actors, specifically recognizing God as a primary actor, they may also provide a greater narratological function, especially when compared with the subsequent narratives, such as the descriptive narrative that immediately follows—the deaths of Nadab and Abihu (Lev 10), which establish the importance of the *tāmîd* rites. According to Leviticus, following the successful dedication of the tabernacle and the first set of offerings made by Aaron as recorded in Chapters 8–9, at some undisclosed time Aaron's sons, Nadab and Abihu, offer "strange fire" on the altar of incense. The exact nature of "strange fire" is not defined, but the result of Nadab's and Abihu's actions is unambiguous: "and fire came out from the presence of YHWH and devoured them [the sons] and they died before YHWH" (v. 2). While it is unclear whether the failed performance happened on the day of the dedication or later, the placement of the text immediately following the divine approval of such suggests that it should be understood as such and therefore presents an intriguing juxtaposition of efficacious ritual performance (the dedication of which God's anointing plays a central role) followed by an inefficacious performance (the offering of "strange fire" and subsequent death). At the heart of both narratives are the role of two ritual acts. For the dedication it is the role of the divinely performed, non-iterative rite of anointing, for the "strange fire" narrative it is the mortally performed, iterative (*tāmîd*) rite of incense burning.

Exodus 30:1–10 records the construction, placement, and primary rite associated with the altar of incense. According to 30:6, we are told specifically that the altar was to be placed before the veil separating the holy of holies from the holy place. As for the rite itself, it is described in vv. 7–8:

> Aaron shall burn the sweet incense: every morning when he tends to the lamps he shall burn it. And when Aaron lights the lamps in the evening, he shall burn the incense always before the Lord through the generations (lit., your generations).

Though the instructions are short, we learn four important elements about the rite: the time and the location of this performance, its placement within a larger ritual series, and the repetitive, iterative nature of its performance. The first two, the time and location, also highlight its liminal nature as the liminality of the incense offering is recognized in both the temporality of the practice—the incense is offered during the "betwixt and between" time of dawn and dusk, when it is not quite day and it is not quite night—and in the location of rite—the location being between the holy of holies and the rest of the holy place, or at the "threshold" of the holy of holies.[6] This liminal rite was part of a larger ritual series, which included the dressing of the lamps and the offering of the daily *ʻolâh*, also noted by their performance during the liminal periods of dawn and dusk. The final element, the repetitive, daily iteration of this rite, appears to highlight the 'mortal' significance of the rite and may be contrasted with the anointing. Whereas the anointing is done by God once, reflecting the lasting efficaciousness of God's actions, the offering of incense had to be done repeatedly, daily even, suggesting that the liminal, iterative rites were necessary mortal rites to keep the divine-mortal communication lines open.[7] This may be confirmed in Ps 141:2, where the daily burnt offering and the incense offering are associated with prayer: "Let my prayer be set forth before you like incense and the lifting up of my hands as the evening sacrifice."

As the descriptive text in Leviticus 10 points out, the *tāmîd* rite of the incense burning was performed incorrectly by Nadab and Abihu as they offered "strange fire." What exactly strange fire is not clear. The two most common explanations are that either the two offered inappropriate incense (incense that was not prepared according to the formula recorded in Exodus 30), or they did not take the coals or the burning from the altar of burnt offering to start the rite.[8] What is clear is that some type of ritual impropriety associated with strangeness was done. Significantly, God himself explains why the ritual failed in 10:3:

ויאמר משה אל אהרן הוא אשר דבר יהוה לאמר בקרבי אקדש על פני כל העם אכבד

The exact meaning of this observation is not clear as the *niphals* could be read as either passive or reflexive constructions. If passive, then the passage could be translated as: "Moses said unto Aaron, This is what the Lord declares, saying: by those who approach me I will be sanctified, and before the face of all the people I will be glorified"; if reflexive, then a reading of: "Moses said to Aaron, this is what the Lord declares, saying: To those who are near me I sanctify myself, and glorify myself before all the people." Of course, it is also possible that one is reflexive and the other passive and vice versa, providing a possibility of four different readings.

Though either rendering works, reading the verbs as reflexives seems to reflect the nature of God better in that God does not need glory to be given him from Israel nor does he need to be sanctified by the priests. Instead, the purpose of the instruction appears to highlight that both Israel and the priest need to be aware that God is continually sanctifying and glorifying. The latter action had already taken place in Chapter 9 as all of Israel had seen God 'glorying' at the dedication of the temple. Thus, the instruction in 10:3 may be understood as a warning that God is always sanctifying or being holy and that the tabernacle must always be understood as a location in which his sanctifying presence should always be expected and sanctification is therefore continually happening, even during the normal, prosaic *tāmîd* sequence; the tabernacle having been prepared for this continual presence via the dedicatory ritual sequence of anointing. Thus, even though the failure is tragic, it highlighted the efficacy of the anointing rite, and thereby reinforced the efficacy of the entire ritual system. If it had not been for the aberrant praxis, the ritual would have had the effect that it was meant to have.

The significance of both narratives, the interaction of the two narratives with each other, and the prescriptive, descriptive, and "divine" texts that make up these narratives, come back into play with the instruction concerning the day of atonement in Leviticus 16. The instruction begins with a direct allusion back to the "strange fire" narrative:

וידבר יהוה אל משה אחרי מות שני בני אהרן בקרבתם לפני יהוה וימותן

And YHWH spoke to Moses after the death of the two sons of Aaron, when they approached ("offered before"?) the presence of YHWH and died.

The setting is then followed by a warning to Aaron that he is not to enter the holy of holies any time he wants: כי בענן אראה על הכפרת ("because in the cloud I will appear on the *kapporet*"). What is meant by the "cloud" is not provided, but the preceding allusion to the "strange fire" incident suggests that it is the cloud of incense created when incense was placed on the altar of incense. If this is the case, then the purpose of the incense *tāmîd* rite was to provide the environment (the "cloud") by which God's presence will be continually present (the 1st person, singular imperfect of ראה indicating a durative aspect).

What then follows the warning is the prescriptive instruction as to how Aaron, and thus any high priest, could successfully enter the presence of God. Though this is associated with the day of atonement, it is worth noting that the instructions' explicit connection to the day of atonement appears late in the chapter (v. 29). Even then, that instruction is within the framework of the anointing narrative as the atonement made was to be done by: הכהן אשר ימשח ("the priest who was anointed," v. 32). Thus, the day of atonement rites are efficacious because of both the efficacious *tāmîd* rites performed by the mortal priest and the efficacious anointing rite performed by God earlier. The interaction of the two narratives, the anointing narrative, and the "strange fire" narrative, synthesize in Leviticus 16, thus demonstrating the role of both the divine and the mortal in performing the rites in such a manner by which atonement can take place and God may appear before his chosen priest. By exploring the interplay between the prescriptive and descriptive elements of the different narratives and thereby the interplay between the narratives themselves, which may now include the prescriptive text of Leviticus 16, we may gain a greater understanding both of what the function of the cult was and the expected result of cultic behavior for those who compiled the Hebrew Bible.

Example 2: The Rise and Fall of Saul

Unlike the first example, which focuses on ritual narratives associated with the cult, the second example demonstrates the role of ritual within political narratives of the Hebrew Bible, specifically the narrative of Saul's ascendancy and demise. Again, the interplay between prescriptive and descriptive ritual texts, and efficacious vs. inefficacious ritual behavior, highlight the way ritual was used narratively, in this case, to present a historiography. Saul's rise and fall is a literary construction writ out in 1 Samuel, but it is marked by his encounters and participation in ritual events; some highly 'successful' and others abject failures. In particular, the three scenes of ritual interaction at Gilgal plot out his trajectory through one success and two failures. In so doing, it is possible to get a glimpse, even if it is fictional, of the actual ritual life of Israel as well as the fragility by which ritual success could be achieved.

The narrative begins with Saul's initial encounter with Samuel (1 Sam 9). After a futile search for the family's lost equids, Saul's servant suggested that they ask a "man of God" who is in the nearest town. Encountering the city's young women upon arrival Saul and his servant are informed that Samuel was indeed there for a communal sacrifice which was to take place at the *bāmāh* and that Saul should be able to find Samuel before he goes up to the high place and the eating commences, for, the young women explain, the community will not eat until the prophet arrives because he would give a blessing first. With that, Saul entered the city and met Samuel, who invited the young man to share the meal with him following the sacrifice whereupon he would give prophetic instruction. Samuel then sent Saul on before him to the high place. The meal, like the sacrifice, appears to have been a communal activity though one dependent upon the invitation. Saul, as the special guest, was given a preferred portion. Thus, the Saulide narrative is introduced by a ritual system consisting of four elements: assembly, sacrifice, divine pronouncement/blessing, and feasting. Besides these elements, the overall system also includes private and public components; the sacrifices and blessing being public, while the feasting appears to have been a more private affair.

Though the text does not state so explicitly, the ritual event was understood as efficacious, with the expectation that it would provide a positive benefit to the community in general, in the form of the blessing, and the invited guests specifically, to whom individual prophetic instruction will be given. This expectation is noted through the proper conduct of the participants who waited for Samuel to arrive, offer the sacrifice, and give his blessing before feasting. Though Saul is an outsider, he too followed the ritual protocol and was subsequently promised greater instruction the following day.

The next day continued the ritual event as Saul and Samuel went to the edge of the city at dawn where Samuel anointed Saul and prophesied concerning the initial crisis, letting Saul know that it was already resolved, as well as Saul's forthcoming change in status and ability. This transformation would be recognized when Saul, upon encountering a group of ecstatic prophets, would have the spirit of God fall upon him (see Aster, this volume). In doing so, he "turned into another man" (1 Sam. 10:6). This new identity, noted by Saul's ability to engage in ecstatic prophetic practice, included a new divinely appointed authority. Finally, Saul was given a set of instructions which paralleled his initial ritual experience, namely that he was to go before Samuel to a designated ritual locale, in this case, Gilgal, wait for Samuel who would come and offer sacrifice, then provide the expected divine instruction (i.e., blessing). As to when this was to happen is undetermined. While one may assume an immediate, one-time fulfillment, later events, as well as the presence of the pattern in the initial scene, suggest that this was a general set of instructions repeated on a regular basis.

The rituals of this second day in the narrative were as efficacious as the rituals performed the day before. Anointed at a ritually significant locale and time—the liminal space-time of the city boundary and at dawn—Saul was promised a transformation via his anointing that in fact does take place. Saul's prophetic experience among the itinerant prophets aptly displays the new identity, an identity in which he now may interact directly with God himself. So significant and striking is this transformation and the requisite abilities, enacted through the ritual process of anointing and prophecy, that a proverb arises "Is Saul also among the prophets?" Though this proverb will be used negatively later, here it signifies the efficacious nature of Samuel's and Saul's ritual behavior. It also demonstrates that Saul, through his proper behavior, became as one of the prophets, and was thus able to engage in some limited ritual displays without requiring permission from Samuel. The success of the two-day ritual events, coupled with how the text explicitly links the proper ritual behavior of the participants to an efficacious result, provides a precedent by which the similarly described, but yet to be performed, ritual events at Gilgal could be made efficacious. Like dominoes lined up, ritual behavior determined not only the outcome of that specific ritual event but affected later ritual outcomes. This "cascading" aspect operated both with positive, efficacious rituals, like the ones described above, as well as negative, inefficacious rituals, as will be described below.

The positive consequences of the ritual events play out over ensuing crises that demonstrate Saul's anointed status. The first of these is the potential destruction of the Jabesh-Gilead community. When he heard of their plight, "the spirit of God" fell, or rushed, over him. Saul's immediate action was to slaughter two oxen and send pieces of the carcasses to the different Israelite communities (1 Sam 11:6–7). Such ritual procedure is found elsewhere in the Hebrew Bible, notably in Judges 19 which records the cutting up of a Levite's female companion following her death at the hands of the inhospitable Gibeah community. Not surprisingly, the quartering and sending out of the woman's body parts horrified Israel, yet it appears to have been effective as Israel gathered to hear the Levite's complaint. As to the specific meaning of the Levite's act, the text does not provide an explanation, but Saul's bovine quartering and sending forth does: "whosoever does not come to Saul and to Samuel, so shall be done to his oxen" (v. 7). The act appears to be a reciprocal one in which similar repercussions to the slaughtered animal are promised if participation does not occur (Vikberg 1992: 65–67).

This particular rite does not seem to be specific to ancient Israel but can be found elsewhere in the ancient Near East. Sefire Stele 1, line 40, records: "Just as this calf is cut in two, so may Matiel be cut in two, and his nobles be cut in two." Considering 1 Samuel 11 and the Sefire text, the assumption is that a similar meaning can be applied to the Gibeah situation, in that the one who does not respond will be cut up just as the woman has been cut up. In any case, the Gibeah situation was resolved as Israel gathered at Mizpeh and vowed that any Israelite who does not participate in the purge of the tribe of Benjamin would be destroyed. Jabesh-Gilead, which did not do so, was slaughtered with its young women being taken to serve as wives to the survivors of Benjamin thereby preserving the tribal unit. While much of Judges could be explored via ritual failure noted by the accelerated degradation of rites of hospitality, culminating in the Gibeah incident, the conclusion of Israel's behavior was the social disorder in which "every one does that which they believed to be right in their own eyes" (Judg 21:25). What is also significant is that ritual reciprocity is at the center of the performance, as the original quartering event which led to the destruction of Jabesh-Gilead, was now resolved via the same, but proper, ritual performance, resulting in the deliverance of Jabesh-Gilead. In a similar manner, the response of Israel to Saul's ritualized quartering and sending out of the bovine led to the deliverance of Jabesh-Gilead and a subsequent gathering at Gilgal where a renewal of the kingdom takes place.[9]

The renewal follows a familiar pattern, in which Saul goes before Samuel, sacrifices are made, a feast is experienced via the peace offerings, and Samuel gives a divine pronouncement. Already recognized as one anointed for Israel, Samuel now declares that God had set Saul as king. Continued allegiance to both God and king would allow God's further beneficence, but disobedience and rebellion to either would result in the hand of the Lord being brought against them. Up to this point, proper ritual behavior had netted positive results for Saul. Following Samuel's ritual instruction Saul was chosen by God as one anointed, which includes both civic and quasi-priestly/prophetic responsibilities, as well as the ability to receive the spirit of God. This authority was demonstrated by his successful performance of the quartering ritual and its expected results, the unity of purpose for Israel, which in turn allowed Saul to overcome earlier ritual errors. Finally, by following the original instructions the first Gilgal event culminated in Saul's divine election by which he was selected as king. While all these ritual actions impacted Saul directly, these rituals were also public, communal events which meant they had also positively impacted the greater community of Israel.

Such rituals also reveal an unspoken understanding of the efficacy of Israel's ritual behavior by the author(s)/redactor(s). The primary ritual system of assembly, sacrifice, divine pronouncement/blessing, and feasting, performed in the prophet's city and at Gilgal, suggests a common communal experience, one in which the primary purpose was to gain the divine blessing. Proper ritual protocol determined the success of this ritual form and therefore can be expected to have been performed in this manner in the local communities. The apparent relationship between the quartering rite in Judges and the Saulide variant suggests that later Israelite schools of thought recognized the significance of ritual reciprocity, in which earlier ritual failures could be righted by performing a subsequent, similar rite. Thus, the ritual descriptions within the narrative speak to a larger, general ritual understanding.

This is significant as the narrative turns from positive ritual performances and their outcomes to rituals that go awry, leading to successive ritual failures. The first couple years of Saul's reign appear to have been quiet and stable, noted by his institution of a state military with Saul leading one cohort and Jonathan his son leading the other. At some point during this time, Jonathan successfully captured a Philistine stronghold, an episode that concluded with Saul gathering Israel at Gilgal. It may seem as if this second Gilgal event is simply the conclusion of a successful military excursion similar in function to the first Gilgal event, which also occurred at the end of a successful military clash and which concluded hostilities. However, it is also possible that a Gilgal convocation was a regular occurrence since not only did the first event occur following battle but also coincided with the beginning of the wheat harvest. Thus, meeting at Gilgal corresponded with the agricultural calendar and therefore may have had another purpose outside of the apparent military function. In any case, Saul convened the people a second time at Gilgal, expecting the arrival of Samuel. During the weeklong event, a crisis emerged as word was received that the Philistines maneuvered into the Michmash/Bethel region, scattering the local Israelite communities. Perhaps fearing further fractures in Israel's unity or that waiting longer would jeopardize his ability to respond effectively, on the seventh and final day, Saul proceeded to offer sacrifices without the presence of Samuel, presumably with the assumption of receiving the divine pronouncement that followed the sacrificial procedures. Just as he did so, Samuel appeared over the hill (1 Sam 13:1–10).

While this appearance has a certain narratological flair, indeed the entire scene is one in which the tension is intensified, it also indicates that the ritual performance this second time at Gilgal may be understood to be a failure. Grime's typology of ritual failure is particularly useful for recognizing the complete breakdown of this event (1990: 205–07). The first and most prominent problem is what Grime terms a "misapplication," or a ritual act that is not performed by the appropriate authority. Although Saul may be the Lord's anointed, this designation was contingent on the ritual instructions given by Samuel which denoted a clear hierarchy of authority for the performance of this particular ritual system. It does not matter whether Saul's threefold reasoning as to why he offered the sacrifice was sound, they did not negate the assumption of authority that he simply did not have. The second problem with this ritual event stems directly from the misapplication mentioned above, as Saul's unauthorized performance leads to a "violation" in which the ritual is effective but demeaning. In this case, the result is a negative pronouncement rather than a positive one in which Saul is told that there would be no dynastic continuity following his own reign. There is also the presence of a "hitch" in that the ritual process is not completed. In prior descriptions, burnt offerings were offered up with peace offerings, thus implying a feast among the participants. While the narrative states that Saul offered the burnt offerings, the peace offerings are not mentioned suggesting that they were either not offered, or their positive function was no longer possible.

Finally, although not a part of the ritual proper, this event marks the beginning of several future ritual failures. Grimes notes a type of specific ritual failure by which the failed ritual affects more than its own prescribed function and performance, but the effect noted above differs in that failure follows even after the original event is concluded, reflecting how specific ritual events fit within larger ritual systems as well as the ritual reciprocity noted earlier. The concern revealed is that a specific ritual failure creates conditions in which later, unrelated ritual events also fail jeopardizing the overall system's integrity. In other words, this cascading effect suggests that there was no failsafe or redundancy by which the system could isolate the specific event thereby limiting the damage. As we shall see, the only way to resolve this cascade is to simply start over the entire ritual process (Belnap 2008: 191–97).

The consequences of the ritual's failure are experienced almost immediately as the next narrative scene highlights Saul's inability to enact efficacious ritual behavior. His attempts to strengthen his own authority and engender greater social unity via ritual accelerate the erosion of both. Again, this happens within another context of military engagement against the Philistines—Jonathan decided to engage with the Philistines with only his armor-bearer and without informing anyone what he had done. Unaware of his son's actions, Saul sought divine aid by engaging with the priest and the Ark of Covenant, yet before any answer was given, Jonathan's engagement turned the battle. While the outcome was successful, the inaction of the priest and the non-reception of the divine pronouncement via the ark remained unresolved. Moreover, the reader is told that prior to the battle Saul had pronounced a curse upon any who ate prior to evening. Fasting is found throughout the Hebrew Bible and was in fact associated with both unification of the community and the seeking of divine aid, thus one can see its utility in the context of the conflict. Saul had turned its potentially positive value into a negative by assigning a curse to its performance. Moreover, it was ill-advised, taxing the actual physical strength of those who performed it. Thus, any positive unification was erased by the strictures Saul placed upon its performance and non-performance.

The negative results were striking. Jonathan, who was not present for Saul's instructions, unknowingly ate some honey following the battle, while those who did fast, hungry from the day of fasting and battle, fall on the Philistine livestock, slaughtering and eating the animals in such a manner that they consumed some of the animal's blood. The narrator does not need to explain to the reader how this is a ritual transgression; it is simply described and left as a stark example of how much control Saul has lost.[10] Saul attempted to redress the issue by gathering a stone and slaughtering the rest of the animals properly, but for those who had already consumed, this was an empty act and thus indicates a "gloss" within Grimes' typology which is itself a "flop" in that it fails to produce the appropriate mood and may be deemed "ineffectual" by simply not resolving the issue at hand. Moreover, the narrator states that this was the first time Saul had built an altar. While no moral exposition follows, this observation placed where it is in the narrative is not meant to be understood as a positive development, but instead acts as an indictment against Saul as the hastily constructed altar is an attempt at a stopgap. More damning is the consequence of ritual contagion. One cannot imagine a worse ritual scenario for Saul and Israel. Saul's inability to gain divine instruction alongside his ill-considered curse which fractures rather than unifies his people, has led to serious infractions by his people against the greater cultic ritual system and its primary injunction to not ingest blood.

The situation worsened as Saul then suggested a nighttime attack against the Philistines, as an attempt to rally his people once more. This too fails as the people respond that Saul should do whatever he wants to. The severity of this answer may be noted by its usage at the end of Judges reflecting the state of Israel after successive ritual failures in which Israel is collectively described negatively, the narrator noting that "every one did that which was right in their own eyes" (Judg 21:25). Intriguingly, Israel's state is described as such because "there was no king in the land." As noted earlier, the relationship between Judges and the Saulide narrative has long been noted. It is possible that a similar indictment is subtly being made here, i.e., that Saul is no longer recognized with authority, thus everyone, including Saul, may do what they want. Perhaps gauging the people's mood, the priest suggested finding out the divine will regarding this plan, but when sought via the Ark, the answer was contrary to

Saul's will emphasizing the divide between himself and God. At this point, Saul appeared to recognize something was wrong and proceeded to find the fault through lot casting. When the lot falls upon Jonathan, and Jonathan confesses that he had not fasted, Saul was now faced with the necessity of killing his son to fulfill the vow. The people then acted against Saul, refusing to let him kill the hero of the day. By the end of this day, Saul had experienced over half of Grime's typology of ritual failure including insincerity and breach as he did not go through with his intent, along with the characteristics of gloss, flop, ineffectuality, and contagion noted earlier.

A chance to reverse the ritual misfortunes is the setup for the next scene in the Saulide narrative as Samuel, who has been absent since the second Gilgal event, gave Saul explicit instructions concerning Saul's expedition against the Amalekites, in that all living things were to be killed. Samuel also gave Saul a clear reminder that his anointing was contingent on his obedience to Samuel's and the Lord's authority, the implication being that Saul could restore his own authority by following the instructions. Again, Saul was militarily victorious, but instead of engaging in the *ḥerem*, he preserved the life of the Amalekite king. Saul and the people also kept the best of the livestock before traveling to Gilgal without Samuel's approval in an apparent attempt to repeat the efficaciousness of earlier Gilgal events.

In this case though, the performance was a failure before it even began. First, Saul had disregarded the specific instruction by retaining the livestock thereby invalidating the performance of any sacrifice with the captured livestock. Moreover, Saul has not just indicted himself, but also his entire people; his ritual behavior was leading all to disobey the Lord. While the ritual system associated with Gilgal required Saul to go before Samuel as per the original instructions, it also required Saul to do so at the request of Samuel, which, in this case, had not happened. In fact, the text suggests that Samuel was set to meet Saul at Carmel, only to find that Saul had gone on, thus forcing Samuel to follow. This suggests a new typological element in which what could be called the ritual flow, or smoothness or harmony, of the ritual sequence, is interrupted and rather than being harmonious, becomes jarring and forced.

What follows is another negative divine pronouncement by Samuel beginning with the declaration, "to obey is better than sacrifice" (1 Sam 15:22). It bears noting that while this is often understood as a later critique against ritual praxis, within the narrative arc, obedience to the divine will is included in the ritual instruction given at the time Saul was chosen and anointed; Saul's ritual efficacy was contingent upon his adherence to God's word. Thus, rather than being a higher religious ethos, obedience was completely necessary for proper ritual performance. This declaration is then followed by the pronouncement that Saul was in rebellion against God and that as such he had lost his kingship. The scene ends with Saul begging Samuel's participation to not lose face before the gathered Israel.

While Samuel agreed to do so, he also ritually humbled Saul by killing Agag, the Amalekite king, and cutting him into pieces, an apparent variation of the earlier quartering/unification rites Saul had performed earlier, with an attendant reciprocal curse formula; "as your sword made women childless, so shall your mother be childless." As the function of this rite earlier appears to have been to engender unity among the gathered, one may assume that the same function is at play here. Yet, since the people are already gathered it does not appear to be unity among the people that is sought. Instead, the observation that Samuel did this "before the Lord" suggests that the unity sought for was a reunification between God and Israel and an indictment against Saul who had breached that unity through his ritual failures. By the end of this third Gilgal event, Saul has been effectively stripped of his kingship, at least in the eyes of God.

Having effectively quarantined Israel from further failures, Samuel restored the overall system by anointing another individual. In this sense, the system is rebooted through another sacrificial feast event, this time at Bethlehem, followed by David's selection and subsequent possession of the "spirit of God." Yet, while greater Israel was no longer affected by Saul's behavior, Saul himself continued to experience the cascading effect as he sought divine instruction, even after the pronouncement. According to the narrator, "when Saul inquired of the Lord, the Lord answered him not, neither by dreams, nor by Urim, nor by prophets" (1 Sam 28:6). Having no recourse through any of the legitimate ritual means, Saul did not take this as a warning, but instead turned to an unorthodox, illegitimate praxis that he in fact had condemned earlier. While much has been written on the necromancy that follows, the similarities between this event and the original event are significant, particularly in the giving of a prophetic pronouncement via the spirit of Samuel and the subsequent feast of the calf and unleavened bread, which resembles sacrificial items. However, whereas the earlier one is efficacious and leads to a positive outcome, this event results in a negative outcome in which Saul was told that he is God's enemy and would therefore die soon. As such, it is a "violation" according to Grimes' typology and bookends Saul's experience with the primary ritual system experienced in the prophet's city and subsequent Gilgal events.

Unfortunately, it is not the last ritual failure of the narrative. As promised, in the next Philistine/Israelite engagement, Saul was killed. When his corpse was found, the Philistines "cut of his head, and took off his armor" sending it around to all their communities. Just as the encounter with the witch of Endor represents a version of the primary ritual system (assembly/meeting, sacrifice, divine pronouncement/blessing, feasting), the defilement of his corpse reflects the secondary ritual forms for the purpose of unity found throughout the narrative, specifically the quartering and sending forth, but whereas now instead of unifying Israel, Saul unifies the Philistines, a complete "misframing" of the ritual procedure that completes Saul's narrative arc.

While Saul's narrative is of value to ritual studies for several reasons, including a window in the ritual life, or at least the imagined ritual life of local Israelite communities, it is the depiction of Saul's ritual failures that provide an understanding as to the significance of ritual and the perceived effects it had on individuals and communities alike. The role of reciprocity, the threat of contagion and cascading, and the inherent desire for ritual "smoothness" all indicate that ritual was both understood within a larger worldview in which order was sought for and obtained via ritual processes and recognized as a potential threat to that overall order. In this manner, the narrative of Saul may be understood not so much as history, but more as a series of lessons by which the reader recognized the inherent power, and danger, of their own ritual experience.

Conclusion

As the two examples above demonstrate, ritual and ritual performance play fundamental roles in the framing and construction of entire narratives. Moreover, the presence of both prescriptive and descriptive texts within those narratives suggests that one of the primary roles of these narratives is to highlight the tension between divine will and mortal performance. This is particularly true with those narratives that present ritual failures in which the ideal prescriptive instruction is contrasted with the descriptive failure to perform the ritual sequence correctly. This in turn often may lead to a "divine" text, in which God takes a corrective role. In the anointing narratives this results in instruction as to how to engage with God directly successfully as noted in the Day of Atonement instructions (Lev 16).

In the Saulide narrative, although God is not physically present in the same way promised in Leviticus, his corrections were presented through the prophet Samuel and eventually reflected in God's election of David because of Saul's failures. Although only two examples are examined here, the narratological usage of ritual suggests that other narratives may be approached through the categories of prescriptive, descriptive, and "divine" ritual texts. The Davidic narrative arc, for instance, suggests that it too was structured using ritual behavior to trace the ascendancy and downfall of David. Similarly, the Hezekiah/Assyria narrative may also be viewed via the performance of ritual by Hezekiah and the formal acts and speech of the Rabshakeh. Like the examples above, these too contain prescriptive and descriptive texts as well as "divine" text scenes by which human failure was rectified. This narratological pattern suggests that to the biblical author(s)/redactor(s), ritual was a primary means by which one could understand and interact with God. Thus, the use of ritual in the framing of these narratives, and the archaeological correlates (see Keimer and Pierce, this volume) may be one of the more useful tools for the biblical scholar and archaeologists looking to understand the biblical text.

Notes

1. In the Hebrew bible, this category may be understood to primarily indicate mortal/divine interaction as narratives or scenes situated in the divine realm or with only divine beings are extremely rare (e.g., Genesis 1, Psalm 82, Job 1). Elsewhere in the ancient Near East, such interaction is much more common (the Ugaritic Baal Cycle, *Enuma Elish*) and therefore this category more accurately describes the ritual behavior that takes place among deities and by deities.
2. For an archaeological perspective on ritual and its traces in material culture and architecture, see Keimer and Pierce, this volume.
3. Two recent studies have emphasized similar sentiments; see Feldman 2020 and Watts 2021.
4. If the ritual movement within the anointing of Exodus 30 is correct, then it is possible that the east to west movement reflected an attempt to harmonize the anointing with the movement of the cosmos at large. Certainly, harmonization with the cosmos existed architecturally in ancient Near Eastern temples between the conceptual locations of heaven and earth and some have suggested similar harmonization existed in Israelite domestic structures (Faust 2001).
5. All English translations of the Hebrew Bible are the author's.
6. It is possible that the liminality of this rite is also expressed in the spatiality of the altar of incense. Physically, the altar of incense, while part of the holy place, is situated before the veil and is the closest item to the holy of holies except for the veil (which is itself the ultimate symbol of liminality). Many have noted that gradation of space within the temple from profane states to holy states (Jenson 1992). This gradation would suggest that space closer to the holy of holies is more holy than space that is farther away. The altar's position of "holier than," but "not as holy" suggests that liminality would exist spatially as well in the rituals of the incense offering (Klingbeil 2007).
7. Houtman (1992) also notes this function of the incense, though he focuses on the incense as a marker of divine presence.
8. Jenson states: "in the illegitimate offering of Nadab and Abihu (Lev. 10.1–3), it is probably not the incense but the fire that is alien. Fire not taken from the altar of burnt offering lacks the necessary holiness for the holy incense offering" (1992: 111).
9. The relationship between Judges 19–21 and the Saulide scene has long been recognized, with many understanding Judges 19–21 to be an anti-Saulide (and therefore, pro-Davidic) narrative. For a summary of scholarship concerning this approach, see Peterson 2015–16 and Milstein 2016. While the anti-Saulide element may be there, as we shall see the quartering scene finds it apotheosis in Saul's own quartering done by the Philistines at the end of the Saulide narrative arc.
10. Similarly, in Judges 19–21 the text does not state explicitly what the wrongdoing was, instead it just presents the events letting the reader recognize for themselves the horrific wrongdoing. In these cases where the narrative does not provide explicit condemnation, recognizing the entire narrative, particularly the inefficaciousness of the actions, is necessary.

Bibliography

Belnap, Dan. 2008. *Fillets of Fatling and Goblets of Gold: The Use of Meal Events in the Ritual Imagery in the Ugaritic Mythological and Epic Texts*. Piscataway: Gorgias Press.

Faust, Avraham. 2001. "Doorway Orientation, Settlement Planning, and Cosmology in Ancient Israel During Iron Age II." *OJA* 20: 129–55.

Feldman, Liane M. 2020. *The Story of Sacrifice: Ritual and Narrative in the Priestly Source*. Tübingen: Mohr Siebeck.

Fleming, Daniel. 1998. "The Biblical Tradition of Anointing Priests." *JBL* 117: 401–14.

Grimes, Ronald. 1990. *Ritual Criticism: Case Studies in its Practice, Essays on its Theory*. Columbia: University of South Carolina Press.

Houtman, C. 1992. "On the Function of the Holy Incense (Exodus XXX 34–8) and the Sacred Anointing Oil (Exodus XXX 22–33)." *VT* 42: 458–65.

Jenson, Philip Peter. 1992. *Graded Holiness: A Key to the Priestly Conception of the World*. Sheffield: JSOT Press.

Klingbeil, Gerald A. 1995. "Ritual Space in the Ordination Ritual of Leviticus 8." *JNSL* 21: 59–82.

———. 2007. *Bridging the Gap: Ritual and Ritual Texts in the Bible*. Winona Lake: Eisenbrauns.

Meeks, Wayne A. 1970. "Moses as God and King." Pages 354–69 in *Religions in Antiquity: Essays in Memory of Erwin Ramsdell Goodenough*. Edited by Jacob Neusner. Leiden: Brill.

Milstein, Sarah J. 2016. "Saul the Levite and his Concubine: The 'Allusive' Quality of Judges 10." *VT* 66: 95–116.

Peterson, Brian Neil. 2015–2016. "Judges: An Apologia for Davidic Kingship? An Inductive Approach." *McMaster Journal of Theology and Ministry* 17: 3–46.

Viberg, Åke. 1992. *Symbols of Law: A Contextual Analysis of Legal Symbolic Acts in the Old Testament*. Stockholm: Almqvist & Wiksell.

Watts, James W. 2021. "Texts are Not Rituals, and Rituals are not Texts, with an Example from Leviticus 12." Pages 172–87 in *Text and Ritual in the Pentateuch: A Systematic and Comparative Approach*. Edited by Christophe Nihan and Julia Rhyder. University Park: Eisenbrauns.

31
ISRAELITE PROPHECY FROM ITS ORIGINS TO THE EXILE

Shawn Zelig Aster

Much of the Hebrew Bible is the product of prophetic schools. This essay will survey the societal role filled by the prophet and the ways in which prophetic literature interacted with political and social realities. While in popular parlance prophecy is often equated with an ability to see the future, Biblical prophecy more often focuses not on knowing the future, but on understanding the present. We will first examine the sources of the prophet's authority, then move to discuss the societal role filled by the prophet and the interaction of prophets and political forces.

The Hebrew Bible contains at least 15 books named after prophetic figures (excluding Daniel, a book whose final form is much later than that of the other books named after prophets). As can be expected, different prophetic corpora emphasize different ideas. Nevertheless, there are many points of agreement among the prophets whose words are preserved in the Hebrew Bible. Many prophets, especially those active in the eighth to 6th centuries BCE, preserved the traditions of earlier Israelite society.

What were these traditions, of which the prophets deemed themselves tradents? We will discuss these in detail later in this essay, but we should note at the outset that these traditions idealized Israelite life as it existed before the establishment of an Israelite monarchy with an administrative apparatus.

Biblical Israel's pre-monarchic period saw important political changes as well as the genesis of its most important religious ideas. We begin by describing the political changes. In this pre-monarchic age (referred to by archaeologists and historians as the Iron Age I, the period of the 12th to the 10th centuries BCE), Israelite society dissociated itself from the vassalage system of the Egyptian empire. This vassalage system had controlled Canaan, by means of local Canaanite rulers, from at least the 15th century BCE until sometime in the late 12th century BCE. Among the earliest texts to hint at this system of Egyptian control by means of local Canaanite rulers are the Execration Texts of the 20th century BCE. In these texts, Egyptian rulers curse Canaanite rulers by inscribing their names on pottery and smashing it; the Canaanite rulers so cursed were presumably those disloyal to the Egyptians.[1] Evidence for vassalage in the form of narratives of Egyptian conquest and Canaanite rebellion comes to us from the writings of Pharaoh Thutmose III and his successors in the 15th c. BCE.[2] The clearest archival evidence for this vassalage comes to us from the Tel El-Amarna letters of the 14th century BCE. The system of Egyptian control continued, in some parts of Canaan, until late in the 12th century BCE, and ended gradually.[3] While it lasted, this vassalage system meant that Canaan's resources were exploited by the Egyptian empire. In eschewing this vassalage system, early Israelites enjoyed the advantage of using Canaan's resources directly for their own benefit, but accepted the disadvantage of being less integrated into international systems of trade and mutual defense.[4]

The rejection of Egyptian vassalage had ideological consequences, not only practical ones. Rejecting the vassalage of the Egyptian imperial system (or that of the Egyptian king's rivals in the Hittite empire) meant rejecting the ownership of the land of Canaan by these kings; Egyptian vassalage meant accepting that the Egyptian king owned the land, as is clearly expressed in many of the El-Amarna letters.[5]

One of the earliest recorded expressions of Israelite thought, the Song of the Sea in Exodus 15, contrasts the sovereignty of YHWH with the sovereignty of the Egyptian king. It follows from this important text that at least some early Israelites recognized YHWH as the sovereign of Canaan. A clear expression of this idea appears in Exod 15:13–18, which describes how YHWH became Sovereign of Canaan. In place of a human sovereign, YHWH was seen as having allocated the land and its resources to the Israelites on the basis of tribal and sub-tribal divisions. Therefore, no human king is the owner of the land's resources. Since division of the land does not depend on a king or an imperial sovereign, a more egalitarian division of the land among the different *pater familias* of tribal and sub-tribal units emerged.

In understanding these ideals, we should recognize that theological and political ideologies are completely intertwined. Acknowledgment of YHWH's sovereignty paralleled acknowledging an emperor's sovereignty, which was exclusive within the territory he controlled. Therefore, acknowledging YHWH's sovereignty was seen as incompatible with acknowledging the sovereignty of other gods. Prophetic texts often portray the worship of other gods as gross disloyalty to YHWH, who granted the land to the Israelites (e.g., Jer 2:4–13).

But these early Israelite ideals of Divine Sovereignty over Canaan were tested, from their inception, by political realities. As Israelite society developed, it encountered new imperial actors. In the Iron Age II (10th–early 6th centuries BCE), the Israelite kingdoms that developed encountered such imperial actors as the Arameans, the Assyrians, and the Babylonians. Like the Egyptians, these were polities that came from outside Canaan and asserted control over its resources. Necessarily, the kings of Israel and Judah in the Iron II abandoned or compromised on many of the early Israelite ideals, especially the idea that the king did not own the land's resources. As we will see below, the kings needed to assert control over the land's resources both to maintain their kingdoms and to fulfill the demands for resources expressed by the imperial actors.

Nevertheless, many prophetic texts, dating from the 8th–early 6th centuries BCE, assert the importance of the earlier ideals of Divine Sovereignty, limiting the king's ownership of the land. The emphasis on these early ideals unites many of the different prophetic literary corpora in the Hebrew Bible into what we can call the Israelite prophetic tradition.

This prophetic tradition stood therefore as an alternative to the political chain of the Israelite monarchies. It provided a different way of integrating political realities with religious ideals. As noted, by the 8th century BCE, Israelite and Judahite kings came under pressure from empires that claimed sovereignty over the land. Prophets, on the other hand, because they had no temporal authority, rarely interacted directly with these empires. Kings and prophets, therefore, represent two different ways of dealing with the changes Biblical Israel experienced in the 8th to 6th centuries. In the following section, we will explore how prophetic authority emerged and how prophets and kings interacted.

Sources of Prophetic Authority

The prophet's authority has two sources. One is his/her position as part of the prophetic tradition whose general ideological outline was described above. As is widely recognized, prophetic texts frequently reference earlier prophetic texts, as well as the literature of the Pentateuch.[6] They do this in order to situate themselves more clearly within the prophetic tradition and to show that their texts amplify earlier ones. The references to the Torah connect later prophets with Moses, the ultimate prophet (Num 12:7–8; Deut 34:10), viewed as the founder of the Israelite prophetic tradition (Deut 18:15).

Like other prophets, Moses is portrayed as explaining to both Israelites and others the reality through which they are living, the reasons for political, social, and military events, and the ways God expects people to react at any given moment. But he has a unique role, which he does not share with other prophets: he conveys legislation, much of which (especially in Deuteronomy) encapsulates the social ideals described above. Although he conveys legislation, he does not legislate; Moses can publicize legal material which he receives from God but is nowhere portrayed as legislating on his own. The distinction is important and demonstrates the second (and more important) source of prophetic authority: prophetic authority derives from the perception that the prophet receives Divine communication.

The prophet's authority rests on the perception that s/he has a unique connection with God, allowing him/her on the one hand to receive communication from God in some fashion, and on the other the unique ability to intercede with God on behalf of people (as in Gen 20:7). Since the prophet's authority rests on this unique connection, and since God's choice of prophets are nowhere portrayed as tethered to any dynastic or political structure, the prophet's authority is independent of these structures.

There is no clear description of how and why God chooses a particular individual as a prophet. We are told very little about the nature of this communication: one of the few descriptions of it appears in Num 12:6, where we are told that prophets other than Moses receive communication in visions or dreams. The passage argues that communication from God is so overwhelming an experience that humans (other than Moses) cannot undergo this experience without the distance from consciousness created by a vision or dream. This fits with Jeremiah's description of the experience in Jer 23:9: receiving prophetic communication requires him to enter an altered state of consciousness.

Narratives of "Prophesying"

Several narratives in Samuel and Kings, books assigned to the Deuteronomistic history, portray the prophetic experiences of incipient prophets. They receive communication from God in a trance-like state, sometimes accompanied by music.

One such narrative appears in 1 Sam 10:5. On the way to becoming the first king of Israel, Saul is said to encounter a group of prophets-in-training (lit., "sons of the prophets") who descended from the high-place at Gibeath-Elohim accompanied by musicians, while "prophesying." The act of "prophesying" meant entering into a state of altered consciousness. Saul is said to become "a different man" in 1 Sam 10:6.

The same verb, "prophesying" is used in 1 Sam 19:20–24 to describe the actions of the messengers sent by Saul to trap David, Saul's rival. A spirit descended upon them, and they became unable to fulfill their mission. Saul himself was affected by the same spirit (1 Sam 19:24) and began to act ecstatically rather than rationally. As before, "prophesying" is conncected with a state of altered consciousness, which the people considered evidence of receiving Divine communication.

Both narratives portray the experience of prophesy as an experience disconnected from regular existence, and tie into Jeremiah's description of his prophetic experience. But equally importantly, both narratives portray the first king of Israel as being "among the prophets," (1 Sam 10:11 and 19:24). No later kings of Israel or Judah are so described, even those given highly favorable descriptions in the Deuteronomistic history.

Besides being the only king "among the prophets," Saul is notable for being the only king with no administrative apparatus. This is clear from the narratives about him. When he seeks to draft Israelites to fight the Ammonites (1 Sam. 11:7–10), he has no salaried army leaders to draft and lead the fighters. Later in his reign, Saul is described as distributing patronage among a small group of loyal servants (1 Sam. 22:7). Nowhere is he described as enforcing a *corvée* or collecting taxation, as Solomon did.[7]

In other words, Saul is not described in the biblical narrative as acting as though he owned the land or had exclusive rights to its resources. Because this early king does not act as though he owns the land, he can be described as a prophet. As a non-resource-extracting king, Saul is worthy of a place among the prophets. Later kings, who asserted their ownership of the land through an administrative apparatus, extracting resources and enforcing a *corvée* on the population, had clearly diverged from the prophetic tradition and are never described as "prophesying."

False and True Prophets in the Deuteronomistic History

The tension between the prophetic tradition, which argues for limited monarchic authority, and the understandable tendency of kings to expand their authority emerges from other narratives in the book of Kings and in prophetic narratives.

We find several narratives which contrast "prophets of the Lord" with "false prophets." These narratives tend to correlate the "false prophets" with those supported by the monarchy who also advocate (understandably) expanded authority for the king. In contrast, they correlate the "true prophets" with those who limit royal authority.

We should note at the outset that the unstructured and somewhat-amorphous nature of prophetic authority meant that there were few clear litmus tests available to a believer to discern true prophets from false ones. Above, we described two sources of prophetic authority: (a) a perceived channel of communication with God, and (b) operating as part of a prophetic tradition. Are either of these channels useful to the believer in distinguishing "false" from "true prophets"? Deuteronomy's legal code argues that only the second of these can be used. Deuteronomy 13:2–6 describes a prophet who can indeed provide signs attesting to his communication with God, but who advocates worshipping deities other than YHWH, thus setting him apart from the prophetic tradition Deuteronomy seeks to portray as legitimate. Deuteronomy thus uses a prophet's loyalty to the prophetic tradition as a litmus test for distinguishing false prophets from true ones.

In those verses, Deuteronomy portrays later prophets as "like" Moses, enjoining Israelites to obey only those who continue in the legal tradition of Deuteronomy.

Prophetic narratives in the Deuteronomistic history also use the prophet's loyalty to this chain of prophetic tradition as a litmus test, meant to distinguish between "false" and "true" prophets. Thus, subsequent "true" prophets, such as Ahijah of Shiloh (1 Kgs 14: 1–18) and Elijah (1 Kgs 19–2 Kgs 2) are portrayed as supporting Deuteronomy's program of monotheism and extirpating any cultic worship outside of Jerusalem. "False" prophets, as we see below, invariably support royal prerogative.

The contrast between "false" and "true" prophets is most clearly shown in several narratives in the Elijah cycle, concerning Ahab, who ruled the northern kingdom of Israel in the first half of the 9th century BCE. He made his kingdom into an active participant in the shifting regional system of alliances. On the one hand, he formed an alliance with the Phoenician rulers, marrying Jezebel, the Phoenician king's daughter, according to 1 Kgs 16:31. On the other, he joined an alliance that opposed Assyrian expansion into the Levant, according to the Kurkh monolith of Assyrian king Shalmaneser III.

The first of these Elijah narratives to contrast prophets is the "face-off" at Mount Carmel described in 1 Kings 18. Verse 19 contrasts a group of "450 prophets of Baal and 400 prophets of Asherah, who eat at Jezebel's table" with Elijah. The narrative contrasts Jezebel's support of the prophets of Baal and Asherah with her persecution of the prophets of YHWH, of whom Elijah alone remains active. Elijah argues against any attempt to syncretize worship of YHWH with that of other deities, declaring "until when are you shifting from one joint to the other: if YHWH is God, follow Him, and if Baal, follow him" (1 Kgs 18:21). The narrative thus illustrates the lack of state support, in Ahab's period, for prophets who support Deuteronomy's program of recognizing YHWH as the sole God.

A second narrative, that of Naboth, in 1 Kings 21, highlights how Elijah represents traditional limits on royal prerogatives. In that narrative, Ahab demands of a commoner, Naboth, the surrender of his vineyard to the king. Naboth refuses, and Ahab feels that he does not have the prerogative to seize the vineyard. Jezebel rejects Ahab's view and represents the view, standard in the Near East, that the king is the master of the land. She therefore demands of Ahab that he "do kingship in Israel" (1 Kgs 21:7). She then has Naboth killed, and Ahab seizes his vineyard. Elijah appears and accuses Ahab of both murdering Naboth and profiting from ill-gotten gain: "Have you murdered and inherited?" (1 Kgs 21:19). Elijah clearly represents the view that kings do not have ownership of all land in their kingdom.

The third narrative does not involve Elijah per se, but narrates the clash between "false" prophets supported by Ahab's kingdom and a "true" prophet. In preparing for war with Aram, Ahab makes inquiries regarding the likelihood of his success in war of 400 state-supported prophets (1 Kgs 22:6, 12), who unanimously declare their support for the war. On some level, however, Ahab does not trust these state-supported prophets, and at the urging of King Jehoshaphat of Judah, he inquires further of Micaiah son of Imlah, despite the fact that "he never prophesies good to me, only bad" (1 Kgs 22:8). As expected, Micaiah tells the king that "YHWH has planned evil for you" (1 Kgs 22:23). Although Micaiah's words are contradicted by Zedekiah (apparently a leader of the 400 state-supported prophets), Ahab considers Micaiah's words worthy of attention. Ahab attempts to evade his evil fate by disguising himself in war, but Micaiah's report of God's plans is portrayed as accurate, and Ahab is killed in this war. This narrative illustrates the unquestioning support that state-supported prophets provide for royal initiatives, but also calls into question whether the same royals who provided this support trusted the prophets they financed.

Royal Prerogative Clashes with Prophetic Tradition

Clashes between prophets representing the prophetic tradition and proponents of royal prerogatives appear in several other biblical corpora. Below we will examine such clashes in Amos.

The famous clash between Amos the prophet and Amaziah, the priest at Bethel, is narrated in Amos 7:10–17. The narrative is set in the first half of the 8th century BCE, at the time of the reign of Jeroboam II over Israel. Despite the power of Jeroboam's kingdom, Amos prophesied its demise: "The high places of Isaac shall become desolate, and the temples of Israel will be destroyed, and I shall rise against the house of Jeroboam with the sword" (Amos 7:9). Amaziah viewed Amos' prophetic activity as an attack on the king. Furthermore, he demanded that Amos cease prophesying at the Bethel shrine, claiming that the shrine belonged to the king (Amos 7:12). At the Bethel shrine, Amaziah argued, only royally-sanctioned cultic personnel were permitted to perform.

Amaziah clearly considered Amos a prophet-for-hire. He demanded that Amos leave Bethel and go to Judah, where he would earn his bread prophesying (Amos 7:11). Amos responds by denying that he is a prophet. He does not mean that he does not receive communication from God, but rather denies that he is a prophet-for-hire, affirming that he has other sources of income: "I am neither a prophet nor the son of a prophet, but rather a herder and tender of sycamore trees" (Amos 7:14–15).

The clash between Amos and Amaziah is really over whether prophets can exist without royal financial support. Amaziah appears to deny the existence of any independent prophets, and seems to deny the existence of the whole chain of prophetic tradition discussed above. Taken in the context of the ancient Near East, this is an entirely reasonable position: nearly all of our evidence for prophecy in the ancient Near East outside of ancient Israel relates to state-supported prophets. The greatest collection of prophetic texts comes from ancient Assyria, where prophets were paid by the king and expected to deliver prophecies encouraging his exploits (Parpola 1997).

But Israel's prophetic tradition included prophets who stood in counterpoint to the royal establishment, and who were not supported by the king. In this respect, as in many others, Israel's religious tradition differs from that of much of the ancient Near East. Among these independent prophets were Amaziah's opponent Amos, Ahab's opponent Elijah, and Ahijah the opponent of Jeroboam I. Each of these prophets left a substantial mark on the biblical literary record. We know little of how precisely they supported themselves, but the biblical narratives about them suggest that they were respected and regarded as authentic purveyors of God's word both by the king and by the general public of their time.

The portrayal of Israel's prophets above is entirely based on literary evidence in the Bible. But many scholars have argued that texts such as Amos and the Deuteronomistic history were composed almost entirely after the middle of the 7th century BCE. Therefore, these scholars hold that these texts can provide little information about Amos in the 8th century, Elijah in the 9th century, or about earlier periods. In my view, there is sufficient evidence to date the composition of Amos to the 8th century, and the composition of much of the Deuteronomistic history to the 9th and 8th centuries BCE.[8]

Nevertheless, it is important to show extra-biblical evidence demonstrating that a tradition of prophets who were not part of the royal court existed in Israel not later than the 8th century. Archaeological evidence for the existence of such prophets will be discussed below. However, first, it is necessary to discuss the extensive literary product left to us by two prophets who lived later than Amos: Isaiah in the 8th century BCE and Jeremiah in the late 7th and early 6th centuries.

Isaiah and Jeremiah as Independent Prophets Advising the King

Both Isaiah and Jeremiah dealt with the encounters between the kingdom of Judah and the far more powerful Mesopotamian empires. In Isaiah's period, Assyria was the reigning empire, while Babylonia was the most powerful empire for much of Jeremiah's period. Each advised the kings of their time as to the appropriate steps to take in negotiating Judah's relationship with these empires. Although their advice was clearly sought out by the kings of their time, and they were clearly respected by these kings, neither prophet felt obligated to support all of the king's policies. Each severely critiqued several of the steps taken by the kings of their period in dealing with the Mesopotamian empires and maintained a clear position independent of royal influence.

The positions of both Isaiah and Jeremiah combine a commitment to a traditional desire to eschew entanglement with empire with a clear sense of pragmatism and an awareness of the limits which Judah's weakness imposed on it.

One of the earliest narratives of Judah's interactions with Assyria appears in Isaiah chapters 7 and 8, which narrate events surrounding the "Syro-Ephraimite Crisis" of c. 734 BCE. In this period, Assyria advanced into the southern Levant, and most of the kingdoms of the region became Assyrian vassals. In contrast, Aram-Damascus under Rezin and the kingdom of Israel under Pekah son of Remaliah refused to become vassals. They formed an "Anti-Assyrian Alliance" designed to block the Assyrian advance and sought to force Judah to join their alliance.[9] Ahaz, king of Judah, was pressured to join this Anti-Assyrian Alliance but felt that he might receive greater backing were he to become vassal to Assyria.

In this context, Isaiah cautioned: "Refrain from activity, and keep calm, do not fear, and let your heart not become soft as a result of these two smoking firebrands, in the anger of Rezin and Aram and the son of Remaliah" (Isa 7:4). Isaiah clearly advised against joining the Anti-Assyrian Alliance but also advised against becoming a tributary vassal to Assyria. A few verses later, Isaiah is recorded as saying "YHWH will bring upon you, your nation, and your father's house a period which has not occurred since Ephraim left Judah: the king of Assyria" (Isa 7:17). Isaiah clearly saw the danger of Assyrian invasion, which resulted directly from Judah's becoming vassal to Assyria and then failing to pay the very substantial tribute payments demanded by Assyria. Opposed both to the Anti-Assyrian Alliance and to becoming vassal to Assyria, Isaiah was left in the uncomfortable position of advising Ahaz to maintain Judah's political neutrality.[10]

What is important for our purposes here is that Isaiah was consulted by Ahaz, king of Judah, but he was clearly able to articulate political advice that flew in the face of Ahaz' policies. Isaiah was a prophet who gave counsel against the views of the king and who was not required to follow royal policies. Ahaz ignored Isaiah's advice, and became vassal to Assyria, with serious consequences for Judah's future. Yet Isaiah's independent status was maintained, and Isaiah continued to advise Ahaz' son Hezekiah, who dealt with these consequences.

Likewise, the independence of the prophet is clearly evident in the prophecies of Jeremiah, who advised the last kings of Judah, in the period in which Judah was threatened by the Babylonian conquest. The stories of Jeremiah's dialogues with Zedekiah, the last king of Judah, during the final siege of Jerusalem in 587 BCE, clearly illustrate that the prophet was on the one hand consulted and respected by the king, and on the other, able to give advice that differed markedly from the king's political program. One of the most poignant dialogues appears in Jer 38:14–28. Zedekiah is said to ask Jeremiah how to respond to the Babylonian siege, whereupon Jeremiah opposed Zedekiah's futile attempts to resist Babylon:

> *If you will go out to the officers of the king of Babylon, you will live and the city will not be burned, and you will survive along with your house. But if you will not go out to the officers of the king of Babylon, the city will be given into the hands of the Chaldeans, and they will burn it, and you will not escape from their hands.*
>
> (Jer 38:17–18)

Zedekiah strongly opposed surrender to Babylon, going so far as to express fear of being tortured by Judahites who had surrendered against his advice (Jer 38:19). Jeremiah nevertheless advocated an entirely different policy.

Isaiah and Jeremiah in Archaeological Evidence?

Archaeological evidence cannot in any way affirm or call into question specific prophecies of Isaiah or of Jeremiah. But interesting pieces of historical evidence indicate quite clearly that each of these prophets was a historical figure. We cannot extrapolate from the existence of these two historical figures to demonstrate unquestionably the existence of earlier prophets. But the evidence for Isaiah and Jeremiah as historical figures should at least give us pause before we call into question the existence of the earlier prophets discussed above.

In discussing the historical Isaiah, the most dramatic piece of evidence is a bulla discovered in the Ophel area of the ancient city of Jerusalem, during archaeological excavations directed by the late Dr. Eilat Mazar, and published in Mazar 2018. The text of the bulla reads "belonging to Isaiah the prophet."[11] Because of the disturbed archaeological context, a precise date for the bulla is not possible, but the shape of the letters suggests an 8th-century BCE date. The bulla clearly indicates that a prophet named Isaiah lived in 8th-century Jerusalem, and was a sufficiently highly ranked member of the social elite to have his own signet ring.

While that specific bulla is indeed the most dramatic evidence for the historical Isaiah, we have much more detailed evidence for this important historical figure. Much can be learned from comparing the language of many of the passages in Isaiah 1–39 with the language of the Assyrian royal inscriptions of the 8th century BCE. The language of many of these passages shows knowledge of the Assyrian inscriptions (see Aster 2017; Machinist 1983). Since the Assyrian inscriptions were only known in the late 8th and early 7th centuries BCE, and were then unknown until the 19th century CE, it follows that the passages in Isaiah 1–39 which show awareness of these inscriptions were themselves written in the late eighth and early 7th centuries BCE.

The author of these passages, who is often called "Isaiah of Jerusalem," learned the contents of Assyrian royal inscriptions from emissaries sent by the kings of Judah from Jerusalem to Assyria in the late 8th century. These emissaries returned to Jerusalem and reported to the royal court on the contents of Assyrian texts.[12] Isaiah's knowledge of the Assyrian texts' contents strongly suggests that he was part of Jerusalem's political elite in the late 8th century, since it was to this elite that the emissaries returned with their reports. His status as a member of this elite was already suggested by Machinist (1983), and the discovery of the Isaiah bulla strongly suggests the existence of such a historical figure. As a member of Jerusalem's political elite, he would certainly have had his own signet ring. Thus, the archaeological and textual evidence converge in supporting the existence of a person named Isaiah in Jerusalem in the late 8th century BCE, who was known as a prophet. The textual evidence strongly suggests that his positions on dealing with Assyria were often at odds with those of the king.

The archaeological evidence for Jeremiah as a historical figure is less specific, but no less interesting. It comes from the Lachish letters, unearthed at the biblical city of Lachish in 1935.[13] The letters date from the stratum immediately preceding the final destruction of the city c. 587 BCE. Most of them are letters sent to the commander at Lachish, an important fortress-city, by a subordinate located at a different city in the region, probably Mareshah.

Letter 2 details the challenges facing the subordinate in fulfilling the commander's orders. He insists that he has read the commander's instructions, and then tells of his woes: the head of the army, Conaiah son of Elnathan, has gone down to Egypt (presumably to try to obtain military aid, but perhaps in an attempt to escape Judah's defeat). Conaiah took a group of soldiers away from the subordinate's position, leaving the subordinate with less manpower to fulfill his military obligations. The military picture emerging from this letter is certainly bleak. In the last three lines, the subordinate discusses a further problem facing him:

> *I have sent to you, my master, the message of Tobiah, the king's servant, which reached Shallum son of Jaddua from the prophet, saying "Refrain from action."*

We cannot know the name of the prophet who sent this message, but the prophet's message is recorded in these lines: "Refrain from action." The message "refrain from action," shared with a military commander close to the time of the final Babylonian attack on Jerusalem in 587 BCE, seems to indicate that officials should refrain from opposing Babylonian attacks. Such a strategy would fit closely with Jeremiah's instructions to Zedekiah recorded in Jeremiah 38 and discussed above. Jeremiah advised surrendering Jerusalem and ceasing resistance to Babylon. The unnamed prophet referenced in the last lines of Lachish letter 2 also advises his interlocutor to refrain from action. We cannot definitively identify this prophet with Jeremiah, but it would appear that he advocated a similar strategy.

Regardless of who this prophet was, it is certain that this document describes a prophet operating with a certain degree of independence. The prophet did not communicate his message directly to the king but rather approached Shallum son of Jaddua with his message, which was later communicated to the king's servant Tobiah. He was therefore not "under the thumb" of the king, serving as a personal prophet to him. We do not know anything about the relationships among Tobiah, Shallum, and the prophet, but it does appear that the unnamed prophet, who certainly was active at the same time as the biblical figure Jeremiah, enjoyed independence in communicating his messages during wartime.

The archaeological evidence for Isaiah of Jerusalem and for the unnamed prophet of Jeremiah's time shows that prophets with some degree of independence from the royal court existed in Judah in the 8th to 6th centuries BCE.

A Chain of Prophetic Tradition in Historical Reality

What can we know, then, about a chain of prophetic tradition in Biblical Israel and Judah? The cumulative weight of evidence presented here strongly suggests that prophets operated in Israel and Judah without necessarily requiring royal authorization for their prophecies, and without necessarily being financially supported by the royal court.

One can question how early this tradition of independent prophets emerged, and whether later writers retrojected these prophets into the 10th and 9th centuries BCE. However, such independent prophets seem to have existed not later than the 8th century BCE. It would be strange for independent prophets to have emerged just at the moment when Israel and Judah came under the sway of the powerful Assyrian and Babylonian empires. The prophets of the 8th century whom we have discussed (Amos and Isaiah) and of the late 7th and 6th centuries (Jeremiah) clearly represented an anti-imperial point of view. This is evident in several ways. First, they saw imperial rule over Israel and Judah as negative. Second, they argued against concentrating power in the hands of the king and the economic elite, who stood to benefit from submission to the empires. Their speeches against the concentration of power in the hands of the local economic elite can be found, for example, in Amos 4:1–3, Isa 1:10–17, and Jer 34:8–22. Third, the narratives discussed above show that each of these prophets advocated limited authority for the local king and opposed unlimited royal prerogatives; limited royal prerogative is incompatible with the structure of the imperial system and vassalage.

It seems unlikely that a social force of independent prophets, dedicated to limiting the power of the elite, opposed to imperial power structures, and claiming legitimacy based on their allegiance to an earlier tradition, would emerge *ex nihilo* in the 8th century BCE, at the precise moment when Israel and Judah encountered empires intent on imposing such power structures on them. It is far more reasonable to posit, following the Biblical narratives, that such a tradition of prophets in the 8th century BCE drew on earlier traditions and social ideals.

I freely admit that we lack hard extra-biblical evidence for prophecy in Israel and Judah in the 10th and 9th centuries BCE. But the existence of independent prophets in these centuries, who formed part of the chain of prophetic tradition described here, fits well into the existing evidence. These prophets, among whom the Deuteronomistic history names Ahijah and Elijah, link what we know of the social ideals of early, pre-monarchic Israel in the Iron Age I, to what we know of the prophetic tradition in the 8th, 7th, and 6th centuries BCE.[14]

As discussed at the outset, there is clear extra-biblical evidence for the underlying egalitarian ethos of pre-monarchic Israel. It is quite clear that the settlements that emerged in the highlands of central Palestine in the Iron Age I had limited social stratification and were not under the control of an empire. Out of these settlements, Early Israel emerged. Many aspects of "Early Israel" are debated in scholarship, from the nature of that monarchy to the question of Israel's origins. But the eschewing of empire and the limited social stratification are entirely clear (see references above to Dever 2003; Faust 2006).

The chain of prophetic tradition described in Deuteronomy and the Deuteronomic history books fits well into the period between pre-monarchic Israel and the 8th century and fills the gap in evidence in the 10th and 9th centuries BCE. As discussed, Deuteronomy 18:15 portrays later prophets as "like" Moses and enjoins the Israelites to obey them. The books of Samuel and Kings then portray the "true" prophets as those who follow the Deuteronomic tradition attributed to Moses. In these books, these "true" prophets are portrayed as opposing the expansion of royal privilege, whether the royal privilege is expressed by expropriating private land, or through forming alliances with empires which benefit the local king, or by defeating enemies and seizing territory. The political position taken by the true prophets in these stories fits with the Deuteronomic ethos of a society with few social hierarchies and with a relatively egalitarian social structure.[15] The prophetic tradition in Israel, therefore, forms a counterpoint to royal privilege, and a way of carrying into future generations some of the social ideals of pre-monarchic Israel.

Notes

1 For more on the Execration Texts, see Rainey and Notley 2006: 50–58.
2 For more on Thutmose III and his successors, known as the eighteenth dynasty, see Notley and Rainey 2006: 65–75.
3 Weakened by internal disputes in Egypt and by the rise of the Sea-Peoples in Canaan, Egypt largely withdrew from Canaan late in the 12th century BCE (or possibly early in the 11th c.), and Canaanite city-state rulers who had supported Egypt, such as the king of Megiddo, ceased to exercise control by the middle of the 11th century BCE. For more on the end of Egyptian and Canaanite Megiddo, from an archaeological point of view, see Finkelstein et al. 2017: 280.
4 For more on early Israel's social system, see Faust 2006: 54–111, 161–91, and for background, Dever 2003.
5 For more on these letters, see Moran 1992.
6 For a clear summary of this tendency, see Sommer 1998.
7 Even David has a small group of administrators (2 Sam 8:16–18) and salaried army personnel (2 Sam 23:8–39). But Saul has neither of these. For more on the early monarchy and contrasts with later monarchs in Israel, see Provan, Long, and Longman 2003: 193–258.

8 On the incorporation of documents from the ninth and 8th century BCE into the book of Kings, see Cogan 2000: 97–99. It is hardly possible to read of Ahab's descendants' interactions with Mesha (2 Kgs 1:1 and 3:4) without recognizing that the author of Kings knew historical information from the 9th century BCE. On the date of Amos, see Andersen and Freedman 1989: 18–23, 98–138.
9 For more on the history of this period, see Aster 2017: 82–87.
10 For more on Isaiah's advice in this period, see Aster 2017: 87–113.
11 This is the most likely reading of the letters preserved. The word "Isaiah" is fully preserved, but the word "prophet" lacks the last letter. As Misgav 2018 argues, the circumstantial evidence in favour of reading this word as "prophet," and reconstructing the last letter accordingly, is powerful.
12 For more on these emissaries, see Aster 2017: 41–80.
13 Full text of these is available in Ahituv 2008.
14 No concrete evidence can be cited to prove the historicity of any of these prophets. It is interesting that the name Elisha appears on an inscription at Tel Rehov dated to the 10th or 9th centuries BCE, found in a room with incense altars (Mazar and Panitz-Cohen 2020). Tel Rehov is close to the location of Abel-Meholah, the hometown of Eilsha the prophet, who was Elijah's successor. But the very popularity of the name Elisha prevents us from being sure that the Elisha of this inscription was the prophet. The name Elisha appears in many other inscriptions, including later ones found at Lachish and Samaria.
15 For more on Deuteronomy's ethos, see Berman 2008.

Bibliography

Ahituv, Shmuel. 2008. *Echoes from the Past: Hebrew and Cognate Inscriptions from the Biblical Period*. Jerusalem: Carta.

Andersen, Francis I., and David N. Freedman. 1989. *Amos*. New York: Doubleday.

Aster, Shawn Zelig. 2017. *Reflections of Empire in Isaiah 1–39: Responses to Assyrian Ideology*. Atlanta: SBL.

Berman, Joshua. 2008. *Created Equal: How the Bible Broke with Ancient Political Thought*. Oxford: Oxford.

Cogan, Mordechai. 2000. *I Kings*. New York: Doubleday.

Dever, William G. 2003. *Who Were the Early Israelites and Where Did They Come From?* Grand Rapids, MI: Zondervan.

Faust, Avraham. 2006. *Israel's Ethnogenesis: Settlement, Interaction, Expansion, and Resistance*. London: Equinox.

Finkelstein, Israel, Eran Arie, Mario A. S. Martin, and Eli Piasetzky. 2017. "New Evidence on the Late Bronze/Iron I Transition at Megiddo: Implications for the End of Egyptian Rule and the Appearance of Philistine Pottery." *AeL* 27: 261–80.

Machinist, Peter. 1983. "Assyria and Its Image in the First Isaiah," *JAOS* 103: 719–37.

Mazar, Eilat. 2018. *The Ophel Excavations to the South of the Temple Mount 2009–2013*. Jerusalem: Shoham.

Mazar, Amihai, and Nava Panitz-Cohen. 2020. *Tel Rehov: A Bronze and Iron Age City in the Beth-Shean Valley*. Jerusalem: Institute of Archaeology of the Hebrew University of Jerusalem.

Misgav, Haggai. 2018. "The Yesha'yah[u] /Nvy[?] Bulla and Its Significance: Principles for an Analyzing Archaeological Epigraphic Find." *City of David: Studies of Ancient Jerusalem, 2018*. Online: https://www.academia.edu/37425997.

Moran, William, ed. 1992. *The Amarna Letters*. Baltimore: Johns Hopkins.

Parpola, Simo. 1997. *Assyrian Prophecies*. Helsinki: University of Helsinki.

Provan, Iain, V. Philips Long, and T. Longman III. 2003. *A Biblical History of Israel*. Louisville, KY: Westminster John Knox Press.

Rainey, Anson F., and Steven Notley. 2006. *The Sacred Bridge: Carta's Atlas of the Biblical World*. Jerusalem: Carta.

Sommer, Benjamin D. 1998. *A Prophet Reads Scripture: Allusion in Isaiah 40–66*. Stanford: Stanford University Press.

32

DEATH AND AFTERLIFE

Christopher B. Hays

Introduction

Cultural practices surrounding death give us some of the richest testimonies to life in the ancient world. Psychological factors play a role: death poses the ultimate existential challenge and elicits investment in expressing what a culture believes and values. The belief in the importance of an enduring testimony to those who have died was widely held in the ancient world, and so material remains related to burials are typically a major feature of archaeological data.

Ancient Israel and Judah, however, pose some problems that have led to competing interpretations of what Israelites and Judahites believed. The relative scarcity of the data (see below) is one factor—there are few excavated burials compared to, say, Egypt, with its myriad elite tombs built out of rock, and its parching climate that preserved papyri and art. The pressure of ideologies, both ancient and modern, also leaves a confusing imprint on the data. The primary textual source, the Hebrew Bible, is a "curated" artifact that was edited and overwritten for centuries; and today, multiple living religions trace their lineage to this document and the people who wrote it. This means that identities are felt to be at stake in historical reconstructions.

The most basic questions involve (1) the *distinctiveness* of Israelite and Judahite beliefs since various biblical texts assert that Israel's religion was different from its neighbors; and (2) the degree of *unity or diversity* within the religious beliefs and practices among the people. Given the nature and extent of the data, it is inevitable that interpretations vary significantly, at least in their major emphases. The present essay surveys the data briefly and then closes with a discussion of recent debates (esp. since Hays 2011).

Diversity in Ancient Near Eastern Context

Judahite burial practices and beliefs about death were complex. They had distinctive emphases—every culture is "distinctive" in its basic historical particularity—but they were as diverse as the nation itself. A look at the mortuary cultures of other ancient Near Eastern nations helps to bring that diversity into focus; the perspective they offer is particularly important because of the relative dearth of Iron Age Levantine inscriptions.

Particularly important are the texts from Late Bronze Age Ugarit, on the coast of present-day Syria; these attest funerary and mortuary rituals for the care of the dead and the invocation of divinized royal ancestors to request their blessings. Ugaritic tombs also appear designed to allow cults of the dead to be carried out—with unsealed doors and windows, lamp niches, and offering jars. In the same period, Hatti royalty practiced one of the most elaborate royal burial rituals known in the ancient Near East outside Egypt, lasting 14 days and including food and drink offerings, a statue of the deceased, and cremation of the body. Other aspects of Hittite imperial mortuary religion were shared with Mesopotamia and Egypt: the role of the sun god as royal psychopomp; the belief in an afterlife where food and drink are scarce; the fear of the neglected dead; and the practice of necromancy.

The past decade has seen significant advances in understanding the burial practices of nations such as the Phoenicians and Philistines that were even nearer to Israel and Judah. It is necessary to speak broadly since the present context will not permit a detailed discussion: Earlier theories about the relatively well-defined burial types of these coastal neighbors have been rendered impossible to maintain considering ongoing discoveries of diverse burials.

In her extensive survey of variability in Phoenician mortuary practices, Dixon (2013: 568) concludes that "we can no longer speak meaningfully about a 'duality' of mortuary practices. Most inhabitants of the central coastal Levant had much more choice than simply to cremate or to inhume their dead."

The Philistine case is similar: In the recent discovery of a large Philistine cemetery in Ashkelon (Master and Aja 2017), the most common burial form was the simple pit interments, but cremation burials in jars and stone tombs were also found. A broader look at the data from various sites led Uziel and Maeir (2018: 20) to conclude that

> as has been shown in almost every study of the Philistines in the past forty years, Philistine culture was in a constant state of development and change, from the Iron Age I and through to the end of the end of the seventh century B.C.E.,

and that "the diversity of the Philistine culture ... is reflected in the diversity in burial types, mortuary offerings, and who was placed where. These are indications of various groups within the Philistines, bringing different customs with them" (Uziel and Maeir 2018: 20). Fairly recently, analyses of burials spoke of strong correlations between burial types and nationality,[1] so this emphasis on *intra*national cultural diversity is important. One must expect a similar scenario in Judah. It may have been marginally less diverse than coastal nations with far-flung trade contacts, but its ethnic diversity is reflected pervasively in the historical accounts that Judah rendered to itself—from the "mixed multitude" that came out of Egypt (Exod 12:38) to the international character of David's administration and military, and from the foreign wives for whom Solomon built temples (2 Kgs 11) to the Phoenician workmanship of his own temple (1 Kgs 5).

The diversity of ancient burial styles surely reflected somewhat diverse beliefs about the afterlife. One of the major hopes for royalty and elites in the Levant was that they could rise from the dead and feast in the afterlife. (This is, of course, consistent with Egyptian and Mesopotamian beliefs of great antiquity.) One early example of this from the Phoenician sphere is the sarcophagus of Ahiram of Byblos, from the early 10th century BCE. On it, women are depicted in mourning at the ends of the coffin, and the deceased king is portrayed sitting on a throne receiving funerary offerings. The inscription warns against disturbing the burial, a common concern known also from 8th- and 7th-century Aramaic inscriptions.[2] As in Egypt, it was important for the burial to be intact for the dead to enjoy the afterlife.

Other Levantine coffin inscriptions also attest to the expectation of a supernatural afterlife. That of Panamuwa, king of the Aramean state of Sam'al in the 8th century, instructs whichever of his sons inherits the throne to make sacrifices and say to Hadad: "May the soul of Panamuwa eat with you, and may the soul of Panamuwa drink with you" (COS 2.36: 157). A text on the sarcophagus of Tabnit of Sidon from the 5th century also attests to the hope of a place among the divinized dead: "If you ... open my cover and disturb me, may you have no ... resting-place with the Rephaim" (COS 2.56: 182).

Neo-Hittite mortuary stelae from the same timespan also attest to the expectation of care and enjoyment in the afterlife. In one, the Katumuwa Stele from Zinçirli, the decedent calls for mortuary banquets "for my soul that is in this stele" (Pardee 2009: 53–54). The soul was not only believed to survive apart from the body but also to somehow be resident in the monument. The archaeological context of the Katumuwa Stele has been interpreted as a mortuary chapel, one of perhaps a number in the Syro-Hittite sphere. Similar cultic sites have been tentatively identified in Moabite regions and hypothesized to have hosted feasting in cults of the dead. These mortuary chapels were not burial sites. No remains have been found with the Neo-Hittite stelae; instead, large-scale cremation cemeteries have been found in cities such as Carchemish and Hamath.

Another informative aspect of the Neo-Hittite stelae is that they reflect beliefs among a broader group of elites that had previously been attested mostly for kings in the Levant. It is unlikely that the number of people who expected to enjoy a happy afterlife increased. Compare ancient Egypt: afterlife texts were restricted to royalty in the Old Kingdom, and a "democratization of the afterlife" was theorized—but that theory has now been discredited (Smith 2009), and it should not be adopted for the Levant either. Instead, access to writing increased in the first millennium BCE, giving more people the means to record their hopes. In earlier nonroyal burials, comparatively simple burial practices such as the inclusion of clothing, jewelry, and food and drink, reflected a similar desire to ensure the flourishing of the dead in the next life.

Archaeology of Burial in Judah

A discussion of mortuary practices and beliefs focuses by necessity on Judah rather than the northern kingdom of Israel. This is both because of the sparseness and diversity of archaeological data on burials in the north (Kletter 2002 Faust 2013; Yezerski 2013; Lehmann and Varoner 2018), and because the biblical text, our primary source for the religion, is overwhelmingly a Judahite product despite its sporadic incorporation of northern traditions. It is possible that rock-cut royal tombs have been identified under the palace in Samaria (Franklin 2013), but since they were found empty and uninscribed, this remains less than certain.

One reads often (including in some of my earlier work) that the bench tomb was the characteristic Judahite form of elite burial, or even that "[b]urying the dead in a certain way became part of being Judahite" (Suriano 2018: 129). A bench tomb was a man-made room cut into rock, commonly rectangular and on the order of five meters per side, with low benches protruding from the perimeter walls. In more complex examples, additional rooms could be added. Normally a body was laid out on one of the stone benches, and when it decomposed, the bones were brushed into a charnel pit to make room for the next burial. Bench tombs were essentially deluxe, costly interpretations of the cave tombs that were previously popular but seem to have been phased out during the Iron II period.

It is difficult, however, to argue that the bench tomb was a defining aspect of Judahite identity when so few were apparently buried in this way. It is generally recognized that the bench tomb was limited to a small and elite subset of the population—perhaps 5% (Bloch-Smith 2018: 265–66). Fewer than 250 graves in the southern highlands of Judah have ever been identified, and even though the bench tomb is indeed the characteristic form of burial within this tiny sample, this leaves most of the Iron Age Judahite burials out of the accounting.

Common people tended to bury their dead in simple pit graves, perhaps in a field owned by the family (2 Kgs 23:6; Jer 26:23; 31:39–40). Pit graves become nearly "invisible" to archaeology, although some have been excavated. As Bloch-Smith (2018: 366) has pointed out, "[T]he recovered remains may not represent the range of Israelite burial practices," and suggests that "massive, communal burial grounds may yet be located." By contrast, given the detailed way in which the modern state of Israel has been surveyed, it is unlikely that there are hundreds of unrecognized bench tombs still waiting to be found.

Nevertheless, the bench tomb was a significant symbol; Suriano (2018: 97) argues that its structure and practices pointed to a "constructed sense of collective ancestry." A tomb was a symbol of a family's endurance and hoped-for permanence, and graves may even have marked the boundaries of its land (Stavrakopoulou 2010).

Bench tombs varied in wealth and fineness, but most were undecorated. There were exceptions, however. For example, some tombs in Silwan and on the grounds of the Saint-Étienne priory in Jerusalem included bathtub coffins akin to Egyptian sarcophagi, and no charnel pits; these were clearly intended to ensure an undisturbed personal afterlife, just as many Egyptian and Phoenician tombs did. Other Judahite bench tombs included iconographic details that also suggest unusual beliefs about the afterlife. A couple of the Saint-Étienne's benches have what seem to be womb-like Hathor-wig headrests, perhaps reflecting a belief in the afterlife as rebirth (Hays 2012). At Tel 'Eton there was a face with a gaping mouth carved in relief on the wall, possibly revealing the common belief in death as a great swallower (Hays 2018), which is attested in the biblical text (e.g., Isa 5:14; Num 16:30–34). When Isaiah condemned the Judahite high official Shebna in Isa 22:16 for building a *miškan* for himself in the rock in a location where he has no family buried (Hays 2010), this reflected a live debate within the culture: the prophet viewed the official's ambitious hopes for the afterlife as hubristic. The condemnations of such variant beliefs would often have had no effect, however, like prophets' condemnations of Asherah worship.

Judahite tomb inscriptions sometimes identify the tomb's owner and/or seek to ward off robbers, similar to those of the Phoenicians. For example, the tomb of the Royal Steward inscription at the Silwan cemetery tells potential robbers that there is "no silver and no gold, only his bones and the bones of his slave-wife with him," adding, "Cursed be the man who opens (this)!" (COS 2.54). There are also multiple preexilic inscriptions in tomb contexts that sound like excerpts from psalms. For example, Khirbet el-Qôm 3 reads, "Blessed be Uriyahu by YHWH/ and from his enemies, by his Asherah, save him" (COS 2.52). Khirbet Beit Lei 6 prays, "Attend, Yah, O gracious God! Acquit, Yah, O YHWH!." And Khirbet Beit Lei 7 implores, "Save, O YHWH!" (*COS* 2.53). These are all prayers that one might well expect someone living to pray if there were no afterlife, but they are inscribed on tomb walls, and they seem to refer to afterlife hopes.

Grave provisioning was practiced consistently by Judahites, mostly commonly pottery jars and bowls intended to provide food and drink for the dead. Other goods included travel gear, food, jewelry and amulets, and assorted household items. Various clasps found among the remains indicate that the dead were clothed and wrapped in cloaks. Female figurines made of clay were also commonly placed in burials; these "Judean Pillar Figurines" remain among the most contested in ancient Israelite religion. These female statuettes, made of clay and often with exaggerated breasts, appear widely throughout Judah during the Iron Age. The significance of these remains in dispute, but one prominent theory is that they were related to protection or healing (Darby 2014: 402–405), as were similar Egyptian items (Waraksa 2008). If so, their frequent presence in tomb contexts provocatively suggests that that protection might have been thought relevant in the afterlife.

Related hopes were expressed in amulets such as the silver ones from Ketef Hinnom, found in an Iron Age tomb outside Jerusalem and dated to the end of the 7th century BCE (Barkay 1990; Smoak 2015). The texts engraved in them seek God's blessing, with language echoing the Aaronic blessing of Num 6:24–27. Each of the amulets also bears a prayer preceding the blessing. They express concerns about "enemies," and ask YHWH to "acquit" the bearers and to "save" them. One asserts that Yahweh will protect the wearer from "*every* snare and from (the) evil" (מכל פח ומהרע). These were presumably worn both in life and in death; their desire for comprehensive protection reflects that the dead were thought to need YHWH's blessing and help as much as the living.

Death and Afterlife in the Hebrew Bible

Because of the challenges inherent in the data, there has been a long debate over the beliefs about death and afterlife in Israel and Judah.[3]

The biblical texts require critical assessment. They include statements (e.g., about the finality of death and the powerlessness of the dead) that probably ran *counter* to commonly held beliefs. Despite the unifying work of scribes and redactors, particularly of the Deuteronomistic and Priestly schools, ample indication of religious diversity remains in the Bible. It is quite possible to discern a society that, as a matter of course, cared for its dead, practiced necromancy, worshiped chthonic gods, knew very well about the religions and mythologies of its neighbors (at least at upper levels of society), and was not overly influenced by the orthodoxies of priests and prophets.

Burial in the Texts

Biblical law codes say almost nothing about burial; the only instruction in the Torah related to it is that the one who is executed and hung on a tree must be buried the same day (Deut 21:23). Nevertheless, burials are prominent features of the biblical narratives. In Genesis, variations on the formula, "he died and was gathered to his people," reflect the secondary gathering of bones that characterized family cave and bench tombs. Abraham (25:8), Ishmael (25:17), Isaac (35:29), and Jacob (49:33) are all buried in this way, as are Aaron and Moses later (Num 20:24–26; Deut 32:50).

Biblical authors often showed sensitivity to diachronic changes and cultural differences in burial customs. Abraham's acquisition of a burial cave at Machpelah in Genesis 23 is consistent with premonarchic practice, and the embalming and mourning of Jacob and Joseph (Gen 50:2–3, 26) reflect an awareness of Egyptian practices. The erection of a memorial for Rachel (Gen 35:20) resonates with the theory that standing stones on high places were part of ancestor worship (Albright 1957). The burial places of many prominent figures are recorded, including Miriam, Aaron, Joshua, Gideon, and all the judges after him. It is remarkable, then, that Deut 34:5–6 insists that "no one knows where [Moses's] grave is, to this day." This may have been intended to discourage religious activities at his tomb.

The burials of Israelite and Judahite kings are routinely recorded in the historical books. In 1–2 Kings, the recurrent formula "he slept with his ancestors" reflects a peaceful death and normal burial. Most kings are said to be buried in their capital cities, e.g., David and Solomon in the City of David (1 Kgs 2:10; 11:43) and Omri in Samaria (1 Kgs 16:28). Even kings slain in battle were returned by chariot to Jerusalem and buried there if at all possible (e.g., Ahaziah in 2 Kgs 9:28; Josiah in 2 Kgs 23:30). The importance of proper burial for royalty is emphasized by the restoration of divine favor to Israel after Saul and Jonathan are buried (2 Sam 21:14).

The royal tombs in Jerusalem have never been conclusively identified, and they may have been quarried away and lost. It has been suggested that Davidic rulers re-used the rock-cut Canaanite tombs down the slope from the Temple Mount, but Ezekiel 43 suggests that some Judahite kings were instead buried in or adjacent to the Jerusalem temple. Most of the Judahite kings up to Ahaz are said to have been "buried in the city of David," but this formula abruptly disappears after that point. It may be that by this late period the original royal necropolis was full since royal remains probably were left intact and not gathered to the pit. This is consistent with Josiah's burial "in his (own?) tomb" (2 Kgs 23:30).

Na'aman (2004) has argued that the place of the Judahite kings' burials was moved for religious reasons. It is written in 2 Kgs 21:18, 26 that Manasseh and his son Amon were buried in "the garden of Uzza." Na'aman asserts that this is the same as the "garden of the king" in 2 Kgs 25:4; Jer 39:4; 52:7 and Neh 3:15, and that it was established by Hezekiah as a royal burial ground outside the City of David in contrast to the earlier royal tombs near the palace. He views this as part of Hezekiah's reform program (2 Kgs 18:4, 22) and as a response to the priestly revulsion at the proximity of royal burials to the temple.

Chronicles is more selective and detailed about burial information and differs from Kings in its reports about several rulers, denying them placement in the royal tombs on the basis of impurity due to sickness (e.g., Jehoram in 2 Chr 21:20; Uzziah in 26:23) or wrongdoing (Ahaz in 28:27). The account of Asa's burial (2 Chr 16:14) says that "They laid him on a bier that had been filled with various kinds of spices prepared by the perfumer's art; and they made an exceedingly great fire." This may indicate that Asa was cremated, perhaps because disease had rendered him impure for burial (2 Chr 16:12).

Some aspects of Judahite royal burial remain mysterious. For several kings who were murdered, no burial information is noted. (The murdered may have been counted among the unhappy dead, and thus not buried with the other kings.) And unlike the women of the Genesis narratives, there is no mention of other family members being buried with kings of Israel or Judah, although a few nonroyal burials in other places are recorded (2 Sam 3:32; 4:12; 17:23; 19:38; 1 Kgs 2:34) (Bloch-Smith 1992: 116).

Despite the lack of instruction about how to bury the dead, it is quite clear throughout that the *lack* of proper sepulture and mourning was viewed as a horrible fate, as in the curse of Deut 28:26: "Your corpses shall be food for every bird of the air and the beasts of the earth, and there shall be no one to frighten them away" (cf. also 1 Kgs 13:22; 14:11–13; 2 Kgs 9:10; Ps 79:3; Eccl 6:3; Isa 14:19–20; Ezek 29:5). The threat of exposure is a particularly persistent theme in Jeremiah (Jer 9:22; cf. 7:33; 8:1–2; 14:16; 16:4; 19:7; 22:18; 26:23; 36:30).

Beyond mere non-burial, there was "anti-burial," or the abuse of the corpse. Exceptionally, there are references to burning kings, or their remains, in vengeance (Amos 2:1; Isa 30:33). Other examples include hanging Saul and Jonathan's corpses on a wall (1 Sam 31:10), and the devouring of Jezebel's corpse by dogs (2 Kings 9).

I have proposed the following hierarchy of burial types, from most to least desirable, as a modification of S. Olyan (2005):

1   Individual burial in a personal tomb
2   Honorable burial in the family tomb
3   Honorable interment in a substitute for the family tomb
4   Dishonorable forms of interment
5   Non-burial
6   Anti-burial

Mourning and Funerary Feasting

The biblical text portrays Israelite and Judean customs of mourning and lamentation as very similar to those of their neighbors (Nutkowicz 2006: 27–61). A variety of terms are used to refer to mourning in the Hebrew Bible (אבל, ספד, נהה, שחח, קדר, הילל, and אניה—not all of which are limited to mourning the dead), but a coherent picture nevertheless emerges (Anderson 1991; Olyan 2004).

Large numbers of mourners were a marker of a successful life since lack of mourning was seen as a curse (Job 27:13; Ps 78:64; Jer 16:4; 25:33). At the death of a prominent person, a whole family (Zech 12:12) or tribe (Num 20:29) would ideally gather. Indeed, allowing for hyperbole and the legendary character of certain texts, a whole nation might be said to gather (Gen 50:10; Deut 34:8; 1 Sam 25:1; 1 Kgs 14:18)—though in reality, a maximum turnout would have included *representatives* from the whole nation, as the Neo-Babylonian king Nabonidus described in the case of his mother's burial.

Vocal weeping and wailing (e.g., Jer 4:8) were central to mourning. Professional mourners seem to have been employed in some cases: "Call for the mourning women to come; send for the skilled women to come; let them quickly raise a dirge over us, so that our eyes may run down with tears" (Jer 9:16–17; cf. Amos 5:16). The meter and poetic form were also somewhat formalized, as in Ezek 19:14: "this is a lamentation (*qînâ*), and it shall be (used as) a lamentation (*qînâ*)" (see also 27:2, 32; 28:12; 32:2, 16; Amos 5:1; 2 Chr 35:25, etc.; Budde 1882; Garr 1983). The cry *hôy* (Jer 22:18; 34:5; Amos 5:16) also seems to have been typical of laments, although this sense was lost in later periods (Janzen 1972). A para-canonical written text of laments is referred to in 2 Chr 35:24, but no such text survived.

Mourning was accompanied by physical manifestations, including a bowed posture (Ps 35:13); shaving of the head or disheveling of the hair (Ezek 27:31; Amos 8:9); the tearing of garments (Gen 37:34; 2 Sam 1:11; Joel 2:12); the donning of sackcloth or other specific "mourning garments" (2 Sam 14:2; Jer 4:8; 6:26; Joel 1:8); and the smearing of ashes on the body (Jer 6:26; Job 2:8). Through self-abasement, one acted out one's link to the dead. Some extreme expressions of mourning were condemned, however: for example, gashing flesh is portrayed as a foreign practice in Jer 49:3 and is specifically prohibited (Lev 19:28; Deut 14:1). Mourning might also be accompanied by fasting (2 Sam 12:23; Ps 35:13).

No single answer emerges about the traditional length of the period of mourning. Often the length of time is not specified; when it is, it ranges from one or two days (Sir 38:17), to seven days (Gen 50:10; Sir 22:12), and up to 30 days (Num 20:29; Deut 34:8).

Specific public mourning festivals are reported to have arisen in specific periods to honor certain people such as Josiah (2 Chr 35:24–25) and Jephthah's daughter (Judg 11:39–40). Zechariah 7:3–5 refers to a custom of mourning in the fifth and seventh months, almost certainly related to the destruction of Jerusalem in the fifth month.

Scattered references suggest that there were dedicated spaces for mourning and the cultic functions associated with burials. Ecclesiastes 7:2, 4 mentions a "house of mourning" (*bêt 'ēbel*), and Judah seems to have a known venue called the *bêt marzēaḥ* in which funerary feasting could take place (McLaughlin 2001). A similar institution was known at Ugarit and seems to have been traditional in Levantine cultures. Jeremiah 16:4–7 clearly locates this place in a funerary context. It prophesies widespread deaths and forbids mourning for them: "Do not enter the house of mourning (בית מרזח), or go to lament, or bemoan them." It goes on to proscribe "breaking bread for the mourner, to offer comfort for the dead," as well as "giving them the cup of consolation to drink for their fathers or their mothers." Since the *marzēaḥ* is implicitly condemned in both its biblical attestations (cf. Amos 6:7), it may well have been viewed by Yahwistic prophets as inappropriate and as a threat to YHWH's worship because it could involve necromantic invocation of the ancestors.

The Corpse

Dead bodies could be perceived as ritually impure in ancient Judah; but on the other hand there are intimations that they were thought to have supernatural powers. The Priestly legislation is particularly concerned about defilement of the living by the dead—any person is made ritually unclean for seven days by contact with a human corpse (Num 19:11–16; 31:19), making it arguably the most powerful form of impurity. Even the one who touches a person defiled by a corpse is unclean for a day (Num 31:22)! Impurity extends beyond human corpses to animal corpses (Lev 11:31). In keeping with the phenomenon of gradations of holiness, priests are allowed to handle the corpse only of close relatives (Lev 21:1–2), and the high priest is not allowed any contact at all with the dead (Lev 21:10–11).

Authors influenced by Priestly theologies, such as Ezekiel (6:5; 44:25) and Haggai (2:13–14), also allude to defilement by dead bodies, but the theme is absent from the Covenant Code and the Deuteronomic Code. Thus the extent of this ideology may have been more limited than some discussions would suggest.

The potential power of bones is seen most vividly in the resurrection miracle of Elisha's bones (2 Kgs 13:21: "as soon as the man [being buried] touched the bones of Elisha, he came to life and stood on his feet"). It is also suggested by the desire of the prophet from Bethel to be buried with the bones of the unnamed man of God (1 Kgs 13:31). Furthermore, the Bible's interest in the remains of Joseph (Gen 50:25; Exod 13:19) and Saul (2 Sam 21:12–14), in addition to reflecting the preference for burial with one's family, may also be evidence of similar beliefs about the power of bones that have been obscured in the present form of the text.

Sheol and the Underworld

In the Hebrew Bible, the underworld is known primarily by the name Sheol, which is essentially unique to Hebrew and is of uncertain etymology. Sheol is characterized as deep (Deut 32:22; Job 11:7), or even as a pit deep underwater (Ezek 28:8). It is dark (Job 17:13; 38:17; Ps 23:4; 88:6; 143:3; Lam 3:6) and dusty (Ps 22:16, 30; 30:10; Job 17:16; Dan 12:2). These naturalistic descriptions are consistent with negative portrayals of the world of the uncared-for dead especially in Mesopotamian culture.

Other terms also are used for the underworld in the Hebrew Bible. "Abaddon" ("destruction") occurs primarily in poetic contexts (Job 26:6; 28:22; 31:12; Ps 88:12; Prov 15:11; 27:20). More naturalistically, the underworld was known in Hebrew as "the pit" (Ps 28:1, etc.) and "the earth" (Jonah 2:7; Ps 22:30; 71:5; Jer 17:13; etc.). This is only a small sample of the numerous poetic images that could be used for the underworld.

In a few cases, the underworld was perceived to have levels, as in the societies of the living, as is reflected in Mesopotamian texts like the Standard Babylonian Gilgamesh Epic (Tablet XII), Nergal and Ereshkigal, and the Underworld Vision of an Assyrian Prince. Distinctions among the dead are perceptible in Isa 14's description of glorified deceased kings, and in Ezek 32's gradated list of destroyed nations (Wells and Hays 2020). In such cases, "the Pit," or even "the extremities of the Pit," may be used for those most severely judged.

Suriano (2018: 243–47) has proposed understanding Sheol from the perspective of liminality, primarily on the basis of Pss 16, 49, 88, and 116. He argues that dying was seen as a process, and that Sheol was not a permanent destination for most of the dead, but a temporary state through which they must pass. In this view, Sheol corresponds with the corpse's time decomposing alone on the bench, after which the deceased was reunited with the dead kin by being gathered to the charnel pit. While this may work in certain cases, texts like Ps 16:10; 30:4; Isa 14:15; 38:18; and Ezek 31:16 equate Sheol with the Pit—a final destination. It is not to be expected that the portrayal of Sheol in the Bible should be consistent everywhere.

Gods and the Underworld

Death is personified quite clearly at times in the Bible. One of the most famous references to the swallowing god of Death is found in Isa 5:14 (see also Hab 2:5; Job 28:22; Ps 49:14; Hos 13:14; Jer 9:20). It does not appear, however, that Mot had a cult in Judah, Israel, or Ugarit. Thus in West Semitic religions he functioned less as a God than as a kind of demon. Job 18:13–14 refers to a demonic attack by "the firstborn of Death (בכור מות)" and "the king of terrors (בלהות למלך)." Other demonic powers related to death included Rešeph ("Plague"), a deadly henchman of YHWH in Hab 3:5 (cf. Ps 78:48–49). And insofar as wastelands were viewed as a place the unburied dead haunted as in other ancient Near Eastern cultures, the images of Lilith (Isa 34:14) and various demonic wild animals (e.g., Ps 22:13–19) might be considered as reflections of afterlife beliefs. Otherwise, there is little explicit link in the Bible between demons and the dead.

The chthonic deity Malik/Molek was certainly known to the Israelites (Lev 18:21; 20:2–5; 2 Kgs 23:10; Jer 32:35; Isa 57:9 [emended]). Molek is repeatedly portrayed as a god who received child sacrifices (Ezek 16:21; 23:37–39; see Heider 1985; Day 1989). Child sacrifice is well attested in the ancient world, especially in times of crisis. King Mesha of Moab sacrifices his firstborn son (2 Kgs 3:27) and a battle turns in his favor; similar child sacrifices are attested through remains of child sacrifices with votive inscriptions in Phoenician cities such as Carthage (Garnand forthcoming). The intrabiblical debate about child sacrifice is large and complex (see Levenson 1993; Dewrell 2017).

The idea that YHWH had no commerce with death and the underworld in the mainstream preexilic religion is another oft-repeated oversimplification. God's authority over the underworld is expressed in different ways in Amos 9:1–2; 1 Sam 2:6; Deut 32:39; Prov 15:11; Ps 139:6–7 and Job 26:6; 38:17. Given the development of monotheism in Israel and Judah, it was inevitable: YHWH had to be the god of the underworld because there was "no other" (Isa 45:5–6, etc.).

Afterlife

The Hebrew Bible is distinguished from other ancient Near Eastern (ANE) literature by its polemic against the power of the dead. The dead, it is said, do not praise (Ps 30:10; 88:10; etc.); instead they "go down into silence" (Ps 115:17), and are forgotten (Pss 31:13; 88:5; Job 24:19–20). They know nothing (Eccl 9:5, 10) and sit in darkness (Lam 3:6). These ideas can also be inferred from pessimistic texts in Mesopotamia and even Egypt, but Judahite authors made it one of the primary ideologies in the biblical text.

Past scholarship often treated these biblical statements as theologically normative (Schmidt 1994, 267–73; Johnston 2002: 141–42, 193–95). However, it is important to note their rhetorical contexts: In the Psalms, they represent laments and cries intended to motivate God to save, especially by means of desire for praise (cf. Num 14:11–20). The Ecclesiastes and Job references are from pessimistic wisdom literature and do not reflect universally held beliefs (cf. Eccl 3:21).

Nevertheless, Sheol was a symbol of sorrow (Gen 42:38; 44:29–31) and is often described as the end of all people (Ps 89:48; cf. Eccl 8:8). Although other hopes existed for the afterlife, certainly one view was that the grave was the end.

There is also no question that revivification from death is attested in the Hebrew Bible—Psalmists do not only seek God's salvation *prior* to death (e.g., Ps 13:3: "Give light to my eyes, *lest* I sleep the sleep of death"; also 28:1; 143:7), they also sometimes state quite clearly that God redeems from death (e.g., Ps 56:14: "You have delivered my soul from death"; also Pss 9:14; 49:15; 68:21; 103:4; Hos 13:14; Lam 3:55–58) and brings people up from Sheol (Pss 30:3; 86:13; Jonah 2:2). YHWH's authority over death is narrativized in the story of Elisha and the Shunammite woman (2 Kgs 4:32–37; cf. 8:5). The man of God channels YHWH's power to raise the dead boy. Jehoram's question, "Am I God, to give death or life?" (2 Kgs 5:7) reflects the same assumption about YHWH's power.

Another set of texts spanning a fairly wide historical period uses the image of revivification to express national deliverance (Levenson 2006). This was in line with a lengthy tradition of subordinates expressing gratitude to their sovereigns in extravagant terms: Vassals to Egypt, Hatti, Assyria, and Persia all thanked emperors for bringing them back from the dead (Hays 2019: 68–94). This was also consistent with longstanding traditions about the gods' power to revive the dead. The earliest of these is Hos 6:1–2, in which the speaker asserts that although God struck Israel down, "After two days he will revive us (יחינו);/ on the third day he will raise us up (יקמנו), / that we may live before him." This reflects a hope for the restoration of the northern kingdom after its fall in the 8th century. The same hope is expressed in a different way by 7th-century authors in Isaiah, in their efforts to reincorporate the northern territory into Josiah's kingdom after the collapse of Assyrian power in the region. It exhorts the north to confess its failings (26:18), and then goes on to promise: "Your dead shall live, your corpses shall rise" (26:19). Ezekiel 37 picks up and elaborates this same motif, this time in a message to the Judean exiles: its cinematic imagery of the dry, disarticulated bones in the valley coming back together and taking on flesh is a detailed reversal of the process of decomposition and removal in a bench tomb. The revivification of the bones symbolizes the hope of "the whole house of Israel" that they are not "cut off completely," but can be brought back from the dead (37:11–12).

By the time of Dan 12 in the 2nd century BCE, these accounts of national restoration as revivification were colored by sectarian divisions and an apocalyptic worldview. Rather than holding out resurrection to all, corporately, Dan 12:2–3 is dualistic, distinguishing between "the wise" who will "awake ... to everlasting life," and the others who will then face "shame and everlasting contempt." This image of awakening to judgment and possibly a blessed afterlife is farther along the continuum toward the NT doctrine of the general resurrection (e.g., Rom 14:10–11), but it also resonates profoundly with Egyptian afterlife beliefs that were well developed long before Israel existed.

Past scholarship has sought to fit the data into an evolutionary model, in which the later Jewish and Christian doctrine of resurrection was a pinnacle and an innovation emerging in the Hellenistic period. This theory is simply not sustainable in light of the broad historical extent of these ANE and biblical traditions regarding revivification. Although the "doctrine of resurrection" became a matter of religious self-definition only in the later period, it appears that various Israelites and Judahites believed in resurrection and afterlife even in the preexilic period. Given that some of the dominant voices in the Hebrew Bible—the Priestly and Deuteronomistic authors—were in different ways skeptical of mortuary religion and mythology about the dead, it is not surprising that these features are "minority reports" in the Bible as we have it.

Nevertheless, certain venerable material like the early Psalms preserves fragments of those ideas. The king is promised eternal life in the company of the chief god, just like those of surrounding Levantine nations: "He asked you for life; you gave it to him—length of days forever and ever" (ארך ימים לעולם ועד; Ps 21:4, cf. 16:9–11). Early Psalmists expressed the king's desire to dwell securely in his burial by the Temple (15:1, 5; 16:9), and to behold God and feast in his presence (17:15; 21:7 (MT); 23:5–6). The judgment of the dead—usually associated with the widely-known Egyptian image of weighing of the heart—is also referred to by various biblical authors (Prov 21:2; Job 31:6; Ps 17:3). Some of the statements of innocence in the aforementioned early psalms (e.g., 17:4–5; 15:2–5) may be compared with the "negative confessions" of Egypt's afterlife books such as Book of the Dead 125. These should probably not be considered foreign influences, so much as simply part of Israel and Judah's ancient cultural heritage.

The Rephaim

Numerous biblical references to the Rephaim (רפאים) attest that Israel clearly knew of the common Syro-Palestinian belief in a group of supernatural dead. The term is cognate with the Ugaritic *rāpi'ūma*, divine healers/protectors who were summoned in royal ceremonies to bless the ruling dynasty (e.g., KTU³ 1.161).[4]

The Hebrew Rephaim fall into two categories: They are sometimes reckoned as a mythic ancient tribe (Gen 14:5; 15:20; Deut 2:11) of giants (Deut 3:11), and at other times the term refers to the assembled dead. This group of the dead is sometimes royal in nature (Isa 14:9), but in most cases, their rank is not specified, so that they may include any and all of the dead: "[the strange woman's] house leads down to death and her paths to the רפאים" (Prov 2:18; cf. Job 26:5; Ps 88:10; etc.). It is possible either that the ancient term for the mighty dead seemed natural to apply to a defunct tribe of giants, or that the term originally referred to human rulers who were thought to be divinized at death, and that use of the term eventually expanded to include all the dead.

The etymology of רפאים from רפא indicates that the Hebrew term had its roots in a belief in the powerful dead; but these powers are not often reflected in the biblical text. In particular, the fear of the wrath of the dead that was prevalent in Mesopotamia seems to have been as muted in Israel and Judah as it was in Ugarit.

Necromancy

Necromancy provides a major contrast to the Bible's assertions of the powerlessness of the dead. It is clear that the dead were viewed as a potential source of divinatory knowledge. Necromantic practices are banned or condemned in various strata of biblical literature, including the Holiness Code (Lev 19:31; 20:6, 27), the Deuteronomic Code (Deut 18:11) and Deuteronomistic History (2 Kgs 21:6), and Chronicles (1 Chr 10:13–14). It is also among the practices said to have been abolished by Josiah in his reforms (2 Kgs 23:24).

The story of Saul and the necromancer in 1 Sam 28 is a unique narrative description of a necromantic consultation. Despite its negative portrayal of Saul and of necromancy, the story makes no effort to deny that it "worked": Samuel is summoned, and he correctly foretells Saul's future. This is consistent with the henotheistic ideology of much of the Hebrew Bible: for the most part, biblical authors acknowledged other supernatural powers, but they forbade the people from worshiping them (e.g., Deut 6:4–5, 14).

The female diviner in 1 Sam 28 is called a "mistress of an ʾôb"—and although this term is also used in various legal prohibitions, in Josiah's reform, and in Isaiah (8:19; 19:3; 29:4), it is poorly understood. It seems to be used in various ways, most likely it denoted *both* a spirit of the dead and a cultic object used in necromancy.[5]

Israelites and Judahites used figurines representing ancestors in divination: in other contexts, these are called *teraphim* (Ezek 21:26; Zech 10:2). The *teraphim* were clearly physical objects of some sort (Gen 31:19–35; Judg 17:5, 18:14–20; 2 Kgs 19:11–17) and were probably once an accepted part of Israelite family religion. They are not explicitly condemned in the legal codes, but only in 1 Sam 15:23 (a difficult text) and the report of their removal by Josiah in 2 Kgs 23:24.

Why were ancestor cults eventually condemned by various biblical authors? Most basically, necromancy had the potential to come into conflict with central forms of Yahwistic divination, especially prophecy. Based particularly on the Isaianic references, it appears that the 8th-century prophets were among the first to focus on the practice (Smith and Bloch-Smith 1988). Changing socio-political conditions in Judah under Assyrian domination, which altered family patterns and strained the authority of elders, may have given the condemnations additional force (Blenkinsopp 1995; Douglas 2004).

Care for the Dead

Historians of religion had long theorized that Israelite religion included veneration of the dead. In particular, the turn of the 12th century saw great interest in cults of the dead and their relevance to ancient Israel. The description of the dead as weak in the Old Testament was chalked up to a Yahwistic critique of folk religion. This view was challenged in the mid-20th century by various theologians arguing that Israelite religion was, even from its origins, quite distinctive from its environment. However, an important article by Brichto (1973) argued that kin, cult, land, and afterlife formed a foundational biblical thought complex—that Israelite families believed that the dead depended on them, and that they in turn depended on the blessing of the dead to remain and flourish on their ancestral land—much like ANE royal dynasties. David's "yearly sacrifice for all the family" (1 Sam 20:6) and even the commandment to "honor father and mother" (Exod 20:12 || Deut 5:16) suggested to him mortuary ritual (cf. also Prov 20:20; 24:20; 30:11).

In the ANE, care for the dead most commonly took the form of providing food and drink. Analysis of food remains in burials cannot determine the extent of ancestor cults, since those cults were commonly practiced apart from tombs, as the aforementioned Katamuwa Stele reflects.

Offerings to the dead are mentioned negatively in Deut 26:14 and Hos 9:4, and some scholars have concluded that they were not a significant part of religious life in Israel (e.g., Johnston 2002). It is also possible to argue that these passages are not condemning mortuary care as such, but rather its combination with the cult of YHWH. Sonia (2020: 128) goes so far as to argue that "there is no systematic condemnation of commemoration and care for the dead in the Hebrew Bible." This view, however, requires making strong distinctions between necromancy, the *teraphim*, and ancestor cult. The former two clearly came to be condemned by the 8th (Isa 8:19–21) and the 7th (2 Kgs 23:24) centuries, respectively. Nihan (2012) has shown that the compatibility of ancestor cult and Yahwism was assumed in the earliest biblical law collections, but increasingly excluded in later ones, beginning with Deuteronomy. Thus, although the data is admittedly complex, the best conclusion is the more traditional critical one that necromancy, the *teraphim*, and ancestor cult were interrelated (van der Toorn and Lewis 2015) and eventually viewed negatively. Granted that the main concern of Deut 26:14 and Hos 9:4 is not to ban mortuary religion, it is still hard to deny that the Deuteronomistic centralization of worship and socioreligious authority is consistent with suspicion of religious practices that were beyond central control.

Others have minimized the significance of cults of the dead in Israel and Judah by arguing that offerings to the dead indicate their neediness and weakness (Schmidt 1994; Suriano 2018: 161–82). However, Scurlock (1997) has cogently demonstrated that the neediness and power of the dead are far from mutually exclusive; it was the perceived neediness of the dead that made them potentially angry and dangerous, so as to require cultic care much as a deity would.

Conclusion: Diversity and Distinctiveness

Death and afterlife in ancient Judah is a more complex and interesting topic than many have been accustomed to thinking. The gloom of Sheol and the familial symbolism of the bench tomb dominate the scholarly literature in much the same way that the Priestly and Deuteronomistic authors sought to dominate the biblical literature. Neither archaeological nor biblical nor comparative data allows us to suppose, however, that the reality on the ground was anything other than complex. Right alongside the dominant literary-theological traditions, there existed familial ancestor cults wherever there were the means to maintain them, reflecting diverse hopes and mythologies about the afterlife.

Notes

1 Various cultural and even geological considerations determined decisions about burial types, in addition to religious ones. In her foundational study, E. Bloch-Smith (1992: 63) associated Egyptians with pit burials, cist graves, and anthropoid coffins; the Assyrians with bathtub coffins; Phoenicians with cremation or inhumation; and the people of the highlands with cave tombs. Bloch-Smith (1992: 55) did also observe that diversity was visible in larger, cosmopolitan cities, so this point should perhaps be elaborated further.
2 For the coffin reliefs, see *ANEP* plates 631, 633. For the inscription, KAI 1. For similar themes, see *KAI* 215 (Panammuwa), 225 (Sinzeribni), and 226 (Si'gabbar).
3 For a detailed review, see Hays 2011: 133–92.
4 Nearly all of the biblical occurrences reflect the consonantal root רפא, "to heal," but the vowel pointing is not the Qal active participle that one would expect (רֹפְאִים). The Masoretic pointing reflects a perpetual *qere* as if רפאים were from the root רפה, "to sink down, be weak," deliberately obfuscating the meaning.
5 It may ultimately derive from a Middle Egyptian term for (often deceased) kin, *3bwt* (Hays and LeMon 2009), though the closer cognate in Heb. אבות, "fathers" is also suggestive.

Bibliography

Albright, W. F. 1957. "The High Place in Ancient Palestine." Pages 242–58 in *Volume du Congrès: Strasbourg 1956*. Edited by G. W. Anderson. Leiden: Brill.
Anderson, Gary A. 1991. *A Time to Mourn, a Time to Dance: The Expression of Grief and Joy in Israelite Religion*. University Park: Pennsylvania State University Press.
Barkay, Gabriel. 1990. "The Cemeteries of Jerusalem in the Days of the First Temple Period." Pages 102–23 in *Jerusalem in the Days of the First Temple*. Edited by D. Amit and R. Goren. Jerusalem: Yad Izhak Ben-Zvi. (Hebrew).
Blenkinsopp, Joseph. 1995. "Deuteronomy and the Politics of Post-Mortem Existence." *VT* 45: 1–16.
Bloch-Smith, Elizabeth M. 1992. *Judahite Burial Practices and Beliefs about the Dead*. Sheffield: JSOT Press.
———. 2018. "Death and Burial in Eighth-Century Judah." Pages 365–66 in *Archaeology and History of Eighth-Century Judah*. Edited by Zev I. Farber and Jacob L. Wright. Atlanta: SBL Press.

Brichto, Herbert Chanan. 1973. "Kin, Cult, Land and Afterlife—A Biblical Complex." *HUCA* 44: 1–54.

Budde, Karl. 1882. "Das hebräische Klagelied." *ZAW* 2: 1–52.

Darby, Erin. 2014. *Interpreting Judean Pillar Figurines: Gender and Empire in Judean Apotropaic Ritual.* Tübingen: Mohr Siebeck.

Day, John. 1989. *Molech: A God of Human Sacrifice in the Old Testament.* Cambridge: Cambridge University Press.

Dewrell, Heath D. 2017. *Child Sacrifice in Ancient Israel.* Winona Lake: Eisenbrauns.

Dixon, Helen M. "Phoenician Mortuary Practice in the Iron Age I-III (ca. 1200–ca. 300 BCE) Central Coastal Levant." PhD diss, University of Michigan, 2013.

Douglas, Mary. 2004. "One God, No Ancestors, in a World Renewed." Pages 176–95 in *Jacob's Tears: The Priestly Work of Reconciliation.* Oxford: Oxford University Press.

Faust, Avraham, and Shlomo Bunimovitz. 2008. "The Judahite Rock-Cut Tomb: Family Response at a Time of Change." *IEJ* 58: 150–70.

Faust, Avraham. 2013. "Early Israel: An Egalitarian Society." *BAR* 39: 45–49, 62–63.

Franklin, Norma. 2013. "The Tombs of the Kings of Israel: Two Recently Identified 9th-Century Tombs from Omride Samaria." *ZDPV* 119: 1–11.

Garnand, Brien. forthcoming. "Phoenician Synthesis: Patterns of Human Sacrifice and Problems with Ritual Killing." In *Ritual Killing and Human Sacrifice in Antiquity.* Edited by Karel C. Innemée. Leiden: Sidestone Press.

Garr, W. Randall. 1983. "The *qinah*: A Study of Poetic Meter, Syntax and Style," *ZAW* 95: 54–75.

Hays, Christopher B. 2010. "Re-Excavating Shebna's Tomb: A New Reading of Isa 22:15–19 in Its Ancient Near Eastern Context." *ZAW* 122: 558–75.

———. 2011. *Death in the Iron Age II and in First Isaiah.* Forschungen zum Alten Testament 79. Tübingen: Mohr Siebeck.

———. 2012. "'My Beloved Son, Come and Rest in Me': Job's Return to His Mother's Womb (Job 1:21a) in Light of Egyptian Mythology." *VT* 62: 607–21.

———. 2018. "Swallowing Death at Tel 'Eton," *JNSL* 44: 103–16.

———. 2019. *The Origins of Isaiah 24–27: Josiah's Festival Scroll for the Fall of Assyria.* Cambridge: Cambridge University Press.

Hays, Christopher B., and Joel M. LeMon. 2009. "The Dead and Their Images: An Egyptian Etymology for Hebrew 'ôb." *JAEI* 1: 1–4.

Heider, George C. 1985. *The Cult of Molek: A Reassessment.* Sheffield: JSOT Press.

Janzen, Waldemar. 1972. *Mourning Cry and Woe-Oracle.* Berlin: De Gruyter.

Johnston, Philip S. 2002. *Shades of Sheol: Death and Afterlife in the Old Testament.* Downers Grove: InterVarsity.

Kletter, Raz. 2002. "People without Burials? The Lack of Iron I Burials in the Central Highlands of Palestine." *IEJ* 52: 28–48.

Kloner, Amos. 2004. "Iron Age Burial Caves in Jerusalem and Its Vicinity." *BAIAS* 19–20: 95–118.

Lehmann, Gunnar, and Oz Varoner. 2018. "Early Iron Age Tombs in Northern Israel Revisited." *TA* 45: 235–72

Levenson, Jon D. 1993. *The Death and Resurrection of the Beloved Son: The Transformation of Child Sacrifice in Judaism and Christianity.* New Haven: Yale University Press.

———. 2006. *Resurrection and the Restoration of Israel.* New Haven: Yale University Press.

Master, Daniel M., and Adam J. Aja. 2017. "The Philistine Cemetery of Ashkelon." *BASOR* 377: 135–59.

McLaughlin, John L. 2001. *The Marzēaḥ in the Prophetic Literature: References and Allusions in Light of the Extra-Biblical Evidence.* Leiden: Brill.

Na'aman, Nadav. 2004. "Death Formulae and the Burial Place of the Kings of the House of David." *Biblica* 85: 245–54.

Nihan, Christophe. 2012. "La polémique contre le culte des ancêtres dans la Bible Hébraïque: Origins et Fonctions." Pages 139–73 in *Les vivants et leurs morts: Actes du colloque organizé par le Collège de France, Paris, les 14–15 Avril 2010.* Edited by Jean-Marie Durand, Thomas Römer, and Jürg Hutzli. Fribourg/Göttingen: Academic/Vandenhoeck & Ruprecht.

Nutkowicz, Hélène. 2006. *L'Homme face à la mort au royaume de Juda: Rites, pratiques, et représentations.* Paris: Cerf.

Olyan, Saul M. 2004. *Biblical Mourning: Ritual and Social Dimensions.* Oxford: Oxford University Press.

———. 2005. "Some Neglected Aspects of Israelite Interment Ideology." *JBL* 124: 601–16.
Pardee, Dennis. 2009. "A New Aramaic Inscription from Zincirli." *BASOR* 356: 51–71.
Ribar, J. W. "Death Cult Practices in Ancient Palestine." PhD diss., University of Michigan, 1973.
Schmidt, Brian B. 1994. *Israel's Beneficent Dead: Ancestor Cult and Necromancy in Ancient Israelite Religion and Tradition.* Tübingen: Mohr Siebeck.
Scurlock, Jo Ann. 1997. "Ghosts in the Ancient Near East: Weak or Powerful?" *HUCA* 68: 77–96.
Smith, Mark. 2009. Democratization of the Afterlife. *UCLA Encyclopedia of Egyptology.* Online: https://escholarship.org/uc/item/70g428wj.
Smith, Mark S., and Elizabeth Bloch-Smith. 1988. "Death and Afterlife in Ugarit and Israel." *JAOS* 108: 277–84.
Smoak, Jeremy D. 2015. *The Priestly Blessing in Inscription and Scripture: The Early History of Numbers 6:24–26.* New York: Oxford University Press.
Sonia, Kerry M. 2020. *Caring for the Dead in Ancient Israel.* Archaeology and Biblical Studies 27. Atlanta: SBL.
Stavrakopoulou, Francesca. 2006. "Exploring the Garden of Uzza: Death, Burial and Ideologies of Kingship." *Biblica* 87: 1–21.
———. 2010. *Land of Our Fathers: The Roles of Ancestor Veneration in Biblical Land Claims.* London: T&T Clark.
Suriano, Matthew. 2018. *A History of Death in the Hebrew Bible.* New York: Oxford University Press.
Uziel, Joe, and Aren M. Maeir. 2018. "Philistine Burial Customs in Light of the Finds at Tell Es-Sâfi/Gath," *NEA* 81: 19–21.
van der Toorn, Karel, and Theodore Lewis. 2015. "תרפים." *TDOT* 15: 777–89.
Waraksa, Elizabeth. 2008. "Female Figurines (Pharaonic Period)." *UCLA Encyclopedia of Egyptology.* Online: https://escholarship.org/uc/item/4dg0d57b.
Wells, Sara, and Christopher B. Hays. 2020. "Gradations of Degradation: Ezekiel's Underworld as a Temple of Doom," *Old Testament Essays* 33: 490–514.
Yezerski, Irit. 2013. "Iron Age Burial Customs in the Samaria Highlands." *TA* 40: 72–98.

PART VI

Israel Among the Nations

33

AMORITES AND CANAANITES

Memory, Tradition, and Legacy in Ancient Israel and Judah

Aaron A. Burke

Introduction

One important aspect of the Hebrew Bible is its preservation of Israelite but more so Judean, cultural memories and worldviews.[1] Various groups mentioned in the Bible, like the Amorites and Canaanites, fall into a traditional category as Israel's most ancient enemies and purveyors of archaic indigenous traditions, foremost of which were their unorthodox cult practices. The challenge in addressing their historical and cultural significance for Israel, Judah, and their neighbors is, however, the need to disambiguate predominantly pejorative biblical characterizations of Amorites dated to the late Iron Age from their referents, while seeking to understand how such perceptions may have evolved. If one does not simply conclude, for example, that a later collective identity relates to an earlier one in name only, which is almost never the case, then a framework must be articulated that explains the historical relationship between them. This chapter, therefore, seeks to apply such a framework for the consideration of the importance of Amorite and Canaanite traditions to both the biblical narrative and the archaeological record of the southern Levant.

Several considerations frame this enterprise. First, in order to avoid catchall approaches to collective identities that often freight later references with earlier meanings, biblical references, first and foremost, must be contextualized in their Iron Age historical setting. Contemporaneous use of these names in ancient Near Eastern sources during the Iron Age must take precedence over earlier uses, of which biblical writers were most often likely to be unaware. Underlying this, to the extent that we can determine, we must ask: what did the group label mean at the time of writing a specific book? Related to this, how was this label applied in this period outside of the southern Levant? Second, it is necessary to consider the actual associations biblical writers are likely to have assumed between groups and particular cultural traditions, and how that informed their references to these groups. Finally, it is then possible to consider the ways in which earlier cultural traditions like those of Amorites and Canaanites influenced those of Israel, Judah, and their neighbors apart from the issue of biblical characterizations of these groups. In so doing it is necessary to remain aware that later groups were themselves not necessarily cognizant—and many were likely entirely unaware—of the actual influence of specific groups upon many of their own traditions. Although on the surface this seems a straightforward even traditional approach, the perspective offered in this essay departs significantly from previous discussions of Amorites and Canaanites by reconciling a synchronic Near Eastern view of Amorites during the Iron Age with an understanding of the cultural, often material, legacy of Bronze Age traditions that can be traced back to Middle and Late Bronze Age Amorite traditions. This approach makes it more likely that we can understand diachronic changes in the application of the terms Amorite and Canaanite across the world of ancient Israel. Consequently, it is possible to identify *both* a coherent understanding of Iron Age biblical traditions concerning Amorites and Canaanites *and* a material legacy that can be attributed to them in the archaeological record of the southern Levant during the Iron Age.

In what follows, I argue that the term "Canaanite" in the Bible serves, first and foremost, as simply a demonym for the population of the southern Levant while eliding many of the cultural traits of various pre-Israelite populations. By comparison, "Amorite" was deployed in reference to a specific, culturally-bounded group, which is largely consistent with earlier Bronze Age traditions and resulted from the maintenance of distinct cultural memories of the Amorites across the ancient Near East. This approach, therefore, brings together the contributions of Amorite culture and its institutions during the second millennium, a broader understanding of the reception of Amorite traditions during the first millennium, and the manner in which Judah viewed itself within this cultural and historical legacy during the late Iron Age.

Canaanites and the Bible

In this section, the basis for recognizing Canaanites as a demonym (a term referencing a population of a space, principally a region) rather than an ethnonym (an ethnic construct) is outlined to illustrate the functional contrast that existed between it and the usually more meaningful deployment of identities like Amorites. The reason for this distinction is that, despite biblical references qualifying Canaan as the "land of the Canaanites," there is much less evidence to suggest that "Canaanite" was employed as an ethnonym within the Levant, specifically outside of the biblical imagination. As a label for a population rather than a region, it is remarkably rare among second-millennium sources. In almost every one of the attested uses of Canaan, it points principally to a geographic area (i.e., "land of Canaan"; see Rainey 1996), which can be no more precisely defined than it is in the Bible. To press the geographic label further is to ask limited references among sources from Mari, Alalakh, Ugarit, Mitanni, and Egypt (including the Amarna letters) to do what they cannot, and risks constructing a definition far narrower than the evidence warrants.[2] As attested in Akkadian and Egyptian sources for the Bronze Age, town names comprised the most common basis for individual identification and, consequently, the generation of ethnonyms, a tradition that is well in evidence in the Bible. As a result of this, it seems reasonably clear that from the Middle Bronze Age on Canaan was at best a local term for the geographic region that more or less encompassed an area identified today as the southern Levant.

That Canaan represents an ill-defined toponym that was elevated to a status as a demonym-cum-ethnonym in the writing of the Hebrew Bible is nowhere clearer than in the so-called Table of Nations in Gen 10. Alongside references to Canaanites and Amorites among Israel's traditional enemies, which usually appear among Deuteronomic texts (e.g., Deut 7:1), Canaan's inclusion here serves to articulate the conceptual relationship between Canaanites and Amorites from a late Judean perspective, which may date as late as the 5th century BCE.

[15] Canaan sired Sidon, his firstborn, as well as Heth (i.e., the Hittites),[16] the Jebusites, the Amorites (Heb. *'emorī*), the Girgashites,[17] the Hivites, the Arkites, the Sinites,[18] the

Arvadites, the Zemarites, and the Hamathites. (Thereafter the Canaanite clans were dispersed.[19] The territory of the Canaanites extended from Sidon toward Gerar until Gaza, and toward Sodom, Gomorrah, Admah, and Zeboiim, as far as Lasha.)

Gen 10:15–19 (author's translation)

Canaan's stature within this genealogy is in parallel to those of Cush (10:8) and Egypt (10:13),[3] each of which seems to function principally to identify geographic regions, which were inhabited by various groups that are identified as their progeny. In this arrangement, Amorites were also residents in Canaan (10:15), along with many of Israel's other traditional enemies, the Hittites, Jebusites, Girgashites, and Hivites (10:16–17). Yet, Sidon and Arvad, famous cities of the Iron Age Phoenician heartland, were also reckoned a part of Canaan.[4] Whatever the final verdict may be on the dating of this tradition,[5] there is considerable accordance throughout the Bible regarding Canaan's territorial breadth. Furthermore, by contrast with Amorites and Hittites, no named individual is ever identified as "the Canaanite" in the Hebrew Bible,[6] and more general uses of it do not commend them as an ethnonym, despite scholars' persistence in employing it as a "catchall" term for Canaan's Late Bronze Age population. As a label, Canaanite had no notable emic value and for this reason it is of little use to scholarly discussions.

In sum, as indicated by isolated inscriptions on Hellenistic coins from Beirut, which point to the emergence of an imagined "Canaanite" identity in the face of intensifying contacts with the Greek world, there is no evidence for an earlier self-ascription as "Canaanite." Thus, there are no early sources upon which we may expect biblical authors to have drawn for an articulation of Canaanites as an ethnic or cultural group, and the respective terms therefore assume a role in establishing the "other" during the Iron Age. During the Iron Age, with respect to its geographic identification, the situation is analogous to that for Amorites, namely that Amurru like Canaan was understood principally as a toponym from which the demonym was revived. However, as will be clarified later, a significant difference between these terms is that while Canaan is not attested among Neo-Assyrian toponyms—and may thus not have been remembered outside the Levant—the toponym Amurru continued in use outside the Levant during the Iron Age.

Amorites and Iron Age Traditions

While in the Bible Canaan functioned principally as a geographic label from which the cultural label Canaanite was derived and then ascribed to its diverse populations and their traditions, the term Amorite was employed in more specific ways that are seemingly reflective of the broader use and prevalence of the term during the Iron Age, as especially witnessed among Neo-Assyrian sources. Among Neo-Assyrian sources, Amurru can be identified as a relatively specific geographic region in the northern Levant (Bryce 2009), and the "land of Amurru" (KUR MAR.TU.KI) was a somewhat amorphous region that seems to have been roughly equivalent to the northern Levant and was bounded by the upper or western sea (i.e., the Mediterranean).[7] This continued the use inaugurated already in the inscriptions of Middle Assyrian kings from as early as the reign of Tiglath-pileser I (1114–1076 BC), when Amurru evidently included the Phoenician coast.[8] This meaning seems to have expanded upon the location of the earlier kingdom of Amurru, which is mentioned during the Late Bronze Age in the Amarna letters and still earlier in the Mari letters of the Middle Bronze Age. No extrabiblical sources refer to Amurru further south during the Iron Age. As such, this toponym may have been somewhat familiar to Israelites and Judeans, certainly to the courts of both nations, not the least because of their participation in military alliances against Shalmaneser III in the mid-9th century, as recorded on the Kurkh Monolith,[9] and Assyrian expansion that persisted for more than a century until the eventual conquest of Samaria.

Of interest to the question of what Amorite identity may have signified during the Iron Age are several other references to Amorites among Neo-Assyrian sources. These include copies of Assyrian King Lists from Nineveh and Dur-Sharrukin (Khorsabad) where Amorites of the early second millennium BCE were reckoned ancestors in the line of Assyrian kings (COS 1.135). Among them are tallied 17 kings who together are described as "kings who lived in tents." In addition to this, there are copies of Assyrian proverbs from the library of Ashurbanipal (ca. 630 BCE) of uncertain meaning but which, nevertheless, appear to continue to propagate literary stereotypes of Amorites, notably the suggestion of role-swapping between husband and wife, which it may be argued was intended to impugn Amorite social mores (Lambert 1960, 225). Although it is unclear if this was part of a wider circulation of traditions associated with Amorites, it seems significant that this particular proverb even appears to have been preserved more than 2000 years later in a series of pronouncements against the "ways of the Amorite" that are found in the Talmud (Shabbat 67b:2).[10] Together these references may point to a cultural-historical familiarity associated with reference to Amorites as an ethnos of hoary past since no contemporary individual or group is identified as an Amorite among Neo-Assyrian or other sources.

Analogous to the pattern suggested for Neo-Assyrian references to the location of a place known as Amurru, a geographically-centered understanding of Amorite identity also appears to have served as the principal basis for the reanimation of "Amorite" as an ethnonym by biblical authors during the Iron Age. The expression "land of the Amorites" occurs four times, though exclusively in reference to the territory of Sihon east of the Jordan (e.g., Num 21:31; Josh 24:8). Joshua 10:5 refers more generally to "Amorite kings" of "the hill country" in Cisjordan (i.e., at Jerusalem, Hebron, Jarmuth, Lachish, and Eglon), but also evidently included the inhabitants of Gibeon who, during the reign of David, were also identified as Amorites (2 Sam 21:2). Sihon king of Heshbon (Num 21:21) and Mamre of Hebron (Gen 14:13) are the only two named individuals remembered as "Amorite" in biblical tradition (though also perhaps Og of Bashan by association with Sihon, Deut 3:8–11). Almost all other references to Amorites were applied in an inclusive and vague manner alongside Israel's traditional enemies; of 27 occurrences of such lists, Canaanites appear in all but two and Amorites appear in all but four (Ishida 1979). Indeed, here it is notable that although emphasis is often placed in biblical tradition on the Israelite conquest of the "land of the Canaanites" (Exod 13:11), in such instances this seems to be only a shortened form of fuller variants that qualify the populations of Canaan as "the Hittites, the Amorites, the Perizzites, the Hivites, and the Jebusites," who were the inhabitants of "a land flowing with milk and honey," as in Exod 3:17 (also 3:8).[11] Otherwise, the far more common expression "the land of Canaan" seems to have been intended most often as a geographic term (e.g., Gen 11:31 passim) and should not be read a priori as equivalent to references to "Canaanites" as a population.

This geographical understanding, which is also in evidence as early as the 8th century among the prophets, was later represented in the Judean political geography, which was articulated in Genesis 10, as discussed earlier. There the Amorites are recounted as descendants of Canaan, the personified son of Ham, who was one of Noah's sons (Gen 10:6). The 8th century prophets make mostly passing references to the Amorites (Isa 17:9), though they were evidently legendary enemies of Israel of exceeding physical size who possessed the land (Amos 2:9).[12] Ezekiel's declaration in the 6th century concerning Jerusalem's cultural pedigree can be read as a stinging indictment of the perception of Judah's embrace of archaic practices associated with Canaan's indigenous communities.

> Thus says the lord Yahweh to Jerusalem:
> "Your origin and your birth are in the land of the Canaanites;
> your father was the Amorite and your mother a Hittite."
>
> *Ezek 16:3 (author's translation)*

Alongside the repudiation of Canaanite cult practices, Amorite cultic practices (e.g., Gen 15:16; 1 Kgs 21:26; 2 Kgs 21:11) and their gods (e.g., Josh 24:15) were also singled out to be rejected by Yahwists. Despite biblical assertions of Amorites as early inhabitants of Canaan (e.g., 1 Sam 7:14; 2 Sam 21:2), the primary deployment of these group names center on the geographic realities of Judah in the late Iron Age.

In light of the context for the biblical use of the labels Canaan/Canaanite(s) and Amorite(s) during the Iron Age, it is worthwhile to reconsider the implications of a more nuanced understanding of these two terms that are afforded by extrabiblical traditions. The limited utility of the term Canaanite in archaeological analyses have been noted, owing largely to its general application as a moniker for all of Canaan's inhabitants during the Late Bronze Age (e.g., Killebrew 2005: 94). Thus, it emerges that rather than an ethnonym or even a social identity, the label "Canaanite" in such contexts is better identified as a demonym, in this case as a term that references the entire population of Canaan.

Various occurrences of the term "Amorite" among biblical texts, as discussed earlier, suggest that in some instances it too functioned as a demonym. However, references to specific individuals and other groups as Amorite, in a manner that qualifies subsets of Canaan's population suggests it was used in a more restricted sense (e.g., of the highlands in biblical tradition or Gibeon's population) and thus employed as a term with a more specific meaning.[13] For such an understanding, we find evidence not only among Neo-Assyrian references to a region called Amurru but also among Iron Age references both within and outside of biblical tradition that reveal extant cultural memories of Amorites, which correlate with historical contexts that predated Israel's existence. Indeed, as discussed below, a legacy of Amorite traditions dating back to the Middle Bronze Age contributed to Canaan's cultural mosaic beyond the end of the Late Bronze Age and, thereby, played a formative role in the construction of Israel's identity.

Reconsidering the Place of Amorites in Biblical Studies

Since the mid-20th century, Amorites and Canaanites have often been discussed in similar contexts and often treated as veritable synonyms in biblical literature. In *Amorites and Canaanites*, Kathleen Kenyon (1966) made explicit the basis for her retrojection of the label "Canaanite" from biblical references to the population of pre-Israelite Canaan of the Late Bronze Age (ca. 1550–1100 BCE) and back into the Middle Bronze Age (ca. 2000–1550 BCE). She did so on the grounds of the cultural continuity identified in the archaeological records of the Middle and Late Bronze ages (Kenyon 1966: 1–5). This view reflected the consensus of scholars like William F. Albright in which "Canaanite" was generally recognized as a geographically derived term that could be applied inclusively, therefore, to refer to the population of Canaan (i.e., as a demonym). This was done, however, under the assumption that so-called Canaanite traditions of the Late Bronze Age persisted from the Middle Bronze Age, a period associated with Amorite cultural traditions. While this understanding can be said to be generally well reasoned, it required more explanation than could be offered at the time, and it is not clear that most scholars since then have fully considered the interpretive implications associated with identifying Canaan's Late Bronze Age population as ethnically Canaanite (see critique in Lemche 1991).

As a result of inheriting this reasoning, biblical scholarship has addressed the Amorites in a rather schizophrenic fashion. On the one hand, biblical scholars in the 20th century regularly sought to establish direct connections between biblical references to Amorites (and other appellations associated with Amorite groups in the Bible) and the early history of Israel, especially within the patriarchal narratives in Genesis. Much has been written, for example, seeking to identify Abram's departure from Mesopotamia as a broad reflection of Amorite origins with attendant reconstructions of the cultural and historical contexts as well as the chronology of the patriarchal narratives. Unsurprisingly, these were among the earliest efforts of biblical archaeology to be widely challenged, largely for sidestepping the relevant contributions made by textual criticism during the prior century (Thompson 1974; Van Seters 1975). Overlooked were not only anachronisms throughout these narratives but also the overriding, often forced, etiological character of these texts, which in more recent scholarship has been appropriately framed as cultural memories or myths, which are recognized to serve an important role in articulating both Israel's and Judah's prehistory (Hendel 2005: 2010). Still, owing to the frequency of references to Amorites and their location as one of Canaan's inhabitants before Israel, they continue to be included in broad treatments of the peoples of the Bible (Liverani 1973; Fleming 2016).

On the other hand, biblical scholars with firm groundings in ancient Near Eastern studies also recognize that Amorites, who in their own right played an outsized role in the ancient Near East in the second millennium (Burke 2021a), likely played some role in shaping the cultural landscape of Israel and Judah during the first millennium. The emphasis, until recently at least, has been principally on how tribalism and pastoralism among Amorite groups of the early second millennium at Mari contribute to our understanding of these phenomena in ancient Israel (see Fleming 2012: 202–19 and bibliography therein). This effort is an outgrowth of previous work to understand the biblical patriarchs as pastoralists and the patriarchal age as tribal—more so than during the monarchic period, for example—based on readings of the patriarchal narratives, despite that they too were products of the late Iron Age. Although the extensive exploration of these subjects has borne much fruit (see Fleming 2016 and bibliography therein), it has resulted in the all-too-frequent elision of pastoralism, tribalism, and Amorite identity that has pervaded Near Eastern studies (e.g., Porter 2012). This is understandable considering the sheer size and scope of the Mari corpus that has become, effectively, the backbone of Amorite studies. However, such efforts have too often propagated comparisons of Israel's agropastoral economy and that of the highly specialized, large-scale pastoralist economies of the Mesopotamian steppe as they are known from the Mari archive. In this context, these comparisons result from the assumption that the patriarchal narratives accurately represent Israel's Iron Age economy, rather than an *idealization* of Israel's origins. This also fails to account for the fact that the etiological purpose of Genesis engenders no confidence in it as a *historical* source and as a result, it becomes an unreliable source by which to reconstruct a historical picture of the region's society and economy *before* the late Iron Age. Such efforts, for example, have mistakenly retrojected the environmental conditions of the highlands during the late Ottoman period—when the region was deforested and covered to a large extent by grassy terraces on which only small herds from nearby villages and farmsteads could be sustained (though to the peril of reforestation)[14]—as representative of the highlands during the Iron Age. However, the highlands until the early Iron

Age probably consisted of a traditional Mediterranean forested landscape that also typified the Middle Bronze Age, which was increasingly employed for horticulture and viticulture.[15] In short, what we know of the Iron Age highlands, and certainly that of any earlier period, is not commensurate with a highland open to extensive grazing as would be required for sustaining a Mari-like, pastoralist economy.

Concerning comparisons between the Israelite economy and that of Amorite communities, reliance on Mari has reified the association between pastoralists and Amorites that typified Mesopotamian studies during the 20th century (Burke 2021a: 90–91). As such, stereotypes, often derived from tropes occurring among select texts, have been adopted as representations of pastoralists (see discussion in Porter 2012). Further, Mari's pastoralist economy was likely rather unique even within the Near East (Arbuckle and Hammer 2018: 420–24). Yet, were we to consider the Amorite communities closer in time to that of Israel, like Late Bronze Age Ugarit (Buck 2020), we find arguably broader and more diverse economies that serve as a better point of comparison. These were village-based economies reliant on rainfed agriculture and supplemented by small-scale, mostly local pastoralism, now commonly referred to as agropastoral. As a result, many scholarly efforts to relate Amorites to the biblical tradition have reified the characterization of Israelite and Amorite economies as principally pastoralist, which they have assumed is further supported by a related vocabulary for social structures and customs. However, both economies are fundamentally agropastoralist, varying only in the extent to which they engaged in these two broad sectors of their economies.

With respect to the question of tribal social structure, what we know of Amorite social organization is only a useful frame of reference insofar as the Mari texts provide an unparalleled and extensively documented example of traditional, rural tribal society in the West Semitic tradition. It is worth keeping in mind that outside of the Hebrew Bible we possess no Iron Age sources from the Levant (i.e., not from any of Israel's or Judah's neighbors) with which to compare our reconstruction of Israelite society as portrayed in the Bible. Was it also radically different than the third-millennium societies that preceded it in the Levant or those of the Late Bronze Age, like Ugarit? Not likely. While there remain useful and important points of comparison (for a detailed discussion, see Fleming 2004: 24–103), these are more general in character and owe more to the wider cultural milieu out of which Israel emerged at the end of the second millennium BCE. Rather, these comparisons do suggest that Israel, Judah, and neighboring groups can be seen to owe something to second-millennium traditions that preceded their own, which can be identified with Amorites (Fleming 2012). In this context, explorations of groups like the Arameans, for example, might also be revisited for the observations they may afford concerning an analogous, first-millennium group that would also have shared in this Amorite "cultural stream."[16] Nevertheless, up to the present these approaches, while touching upon relevant strands for fleshing out any relationship between Israel of the Iron Age and the Amorites of antiquity, largely fail to account for the precise manners by which references to Amorites entered biblical tradition. This is in part due to a lack of consensus on so many aspects of the textualization of Israelite tradition in biblical scholarship, but also because of a lack of familiarity with the archaeological and broader cultural history of the ancient Near East that makes possible a more nuanced approach for understanding how Amorites factored into both ancient Israel's cultural memory and may have impacted Israelite traditions.

If one thing is clear from this brief survey, it is that by the Iron Age the term Amurru no longer possessed any particular association with either pastoralism or tribalism, as had been the emphasis of earlier biblical scholarship. In sum, biblical references to Amorites as among the remaining inhabitants of parts of Canaan by the Late Bronze Age seem most often to have rendered a known geographic label as a demonym. Less frequently, the Bible referenced specific groups identified as Amorites, who were listed as one of several groups inhabiting Canaan before the Israelites. It is perhaps this observation that warrants consideration of the broader cultural context that is the tangible, material contribution of Amorites to the world of ancient Israel, quite apart from, and in spite of, the portrayal of Amorites in biblical literature.

An Amorite Legacy and Its Reception

While an Iron Age context for the reading of references to Amorites in the Hebrew Bible clarifies many issues, consideration of the cultural trajectory of Israel, Judah, and their neighbors during the Iron Age reveals that they were also heirs to a significant cultural legacy that is to be attributed to the Levant's Bronze Age inhabitants. Much of this legacy reveals a discernible antiquity that traces back to the early second millennium BCE (e.g., Burke 2021b), exposing a variety of Israelite traditions as part of a cultural koine or "cultural stream" that took shape during a period of Amorite patronage in the Middle Bronze Age (Burke 2014). Of great importance to this situation is that these were the prevailing circumstances whether or not the Iron Age inhabitants of the Levant were aware of this prehistory and its implications. As the earlier quote from Amos suggests, there may have been a vague sense of such a heritage that was attributed to Amorites and other cultural groups. However, as illustrated with respect to religious traditions, Amorites were almost exclusively painted in a negative light by biblical authors. Even so, various other unacknowledged traditions within Israelite and Judean societies were also arguably influenced by Amorite cultural institutions, which were most conspicuous at the peak of Amorite social power during the late Middle Bronze Age, as exemplified among a range of monuments large and small (Burke 2021a: 257–344). Consequently, this Amorite koine, like a painting's canvas, contributed indelibly to the cultural palimpsest of first-millennium Levantine communities. To the extent that the Levant's inhabitants were aware of the origins of these traditions, their engagement with them varied significantly. They could appropriate and modify these traditions, reject them, or be entirely indifferent to them if often only because they were entirely unaware of the influences of these early traditions upon what they would likely have myopically identified as core elements of their own traditions.[17]

In the absence of a longue durée perspective concerning the customs and traditions of these Iron Age populations, the contributions of Amorites to the shaping of Levantine traditions too often have been overlooked, misattributed, or minimized. Yet, whether considering the realm of kingship, jurisprudence, cult, or burial customs, for instance, Amorite customs extensively shaped Levantine cultural traditions by the end of the Bronze Age. This is not to say, of course, that other distinct influences are not also evident from neighboring regions such as Egypt, Anatolia, or Mesopotamia, nor that other local traditions did not persist. Rather, such influences on ancient Israel and its neighbors largely occurred sporadically and mostly in the wake of a significant Amorite cultural stream, which arguably shaped many of the most identifiable substrates of Levantine cultural traditions during the first millennium BCE. In what follows, attention is given to a variety of Amorite-style monuments that persisted during the Iron Age in the southern Levant: royal inscriptions, direct-axis temples, stelae, and royal burial traditions.

Iron Age royal inscriptions are likely among the most conspicuous monuments of royal patronage within an Amorite tradition. The accomplishments they record find their echo in documents like one proclaiming the deeds of Yahdun-Lim, written on a foundation tablet at Mari (*COS* 2.111).[18] Among the accomplishments attributed to him, and mirrored among other Old Babylonian inscriptions associated with Amorite rulers, were canal excavation, fortification construction, the erection of stelae, the conduct of expeditions, the subjugation of enemy lands, and temple construction. While all of these do not possess easily discernible archaeological correlates, they are prominent in the Hebrew Bible especially in association with, for example, the founders of the Judean and Omride dynasties. Among the imagery with strong associations with earlier Amorite rule is, for example, the identification of the king as a shepherd to his people (Burke 2021a: 194; e.g., 2 Sam 5:2). While no monumental stelae recording the deeds of Israelite or Judean kings have been identified yet, that the genre of royal inscriptions extolling kingly deeds was likely an inherited archetype is illustrated both by biblical literature and in the most famous example of a stele so far identified, namely the stele of Mesha from the 9th century BCE. Despite the absence of examples of such inscriptions for Judean kings, efforts were made to remember similar accomplishments, as evidenced in the book of Kings (1 Kgs 9:15–22). Much like the inscription of Yahdun-Lim, this dedicatory inscription memorializes Mesha's kingship, his lineage, his patron god, the military defeats of his enemies, his construction of cities, restoration of water systems, and various other monumental building programs (*COS* 2.23). There is ample evidence for a genre of royal Iron Age Levantine inscriptions, whether or not inscribed on stelae identical to that of Mesha, like the 9th century Aramaic inscription of Hazael from Tel Dan (*COS* 2.39), as well as fragments of other Moabite inscriptions (*COS* 4.19 and 4.20).

Aside from commemorative stele and plaques, the concept of legal traditions inscribed on stelae that could be publicly consulted also originated in the early second millennium when collections of laws were frequently erected in public spaces by rulers (Burke 2021a: 319–22). The idea of laws inscribed on stelae seems to underlie the portrayal of the reception of Israelite law in the Sinai narrative within which Israelite laws were inscribed on stone "tablets" (Exod 24:12; 31:18; 34:1). Although there is little consensus on the exact antiquity of Israelite law as presented in the Bible, law collections associated with various Amorite rulers—Hammurabi foremost among them—were copied and recopied for a millennium thereafter, with copies appearing in the library of Ashurbanipal (Roth 1995). Although Middle Assyrian laws likely played a role in Neo-Assyrian legal practices, it is curious that no Neo-Assyrian law collections or copies of them have ever been identified (Radner 2003). Consequently, one is inclined to see the influence of Old Babylonian legal traditions, which were known widely within Neo-Assyrian scribal circles, as significant to biblical legal tradition as well, whether they were transmitted through Levantine circles or, perhaps more likely, canonized during the Iron Age with a certain awareness of Old Babylonian traditions.

The most conspicuous monuments of an Amorite legacy were direct-axis temples, which demonstrate a direct evolution from the Middle Bronze Age through the Iron Age (Figure 33.1). The most famous Iron Age example is, of course, the temple for Yahweh in Jerusalem that was constructed by Solomon that is described in 1 Kgs 6. While the temple of Yahweh certainly possessed analogs among Iron II temples like those at Arad and Moza, its forebears are actually to be found among Middle and Late Bronze Age temples in the Levant, which are variously referred to as belonging to the "migdol" (i.e., tower) or Syrian type (Mazar 1992, see esp. figure 3). By the Middle Bronze Age, the type was widespread in the Levant and Mesopotamia (Burke 2021a: 302–17), having originated during the third millennium, as most clearly demonstrated at Ebla (d'Andrea 2019: 20–24). Iron Age examples of this temple type in the Levant (see Mazzoni 2002) include those at Tell Ta'yinat (Haines 1971: 53–55), 'Ain Dara (Abou Assaf 1990), the Aleppo citadel (Kohlmeyer 2000),

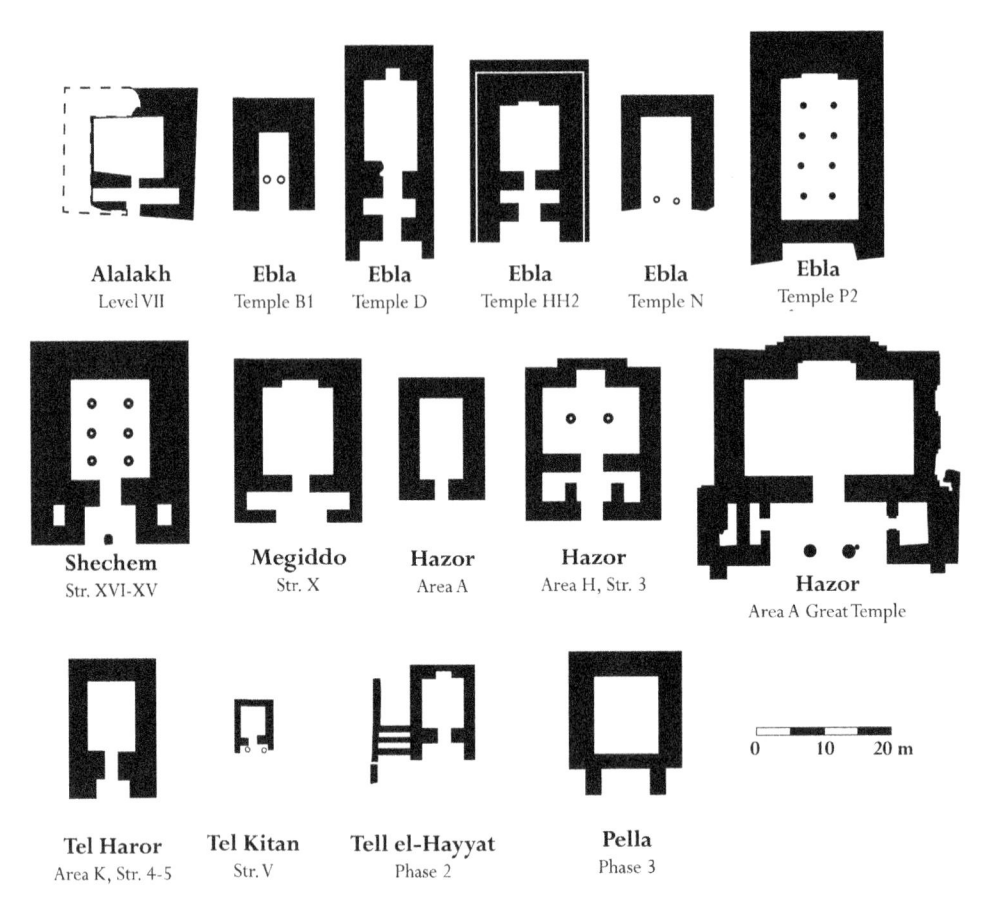

Figure 33.1 Middle Bronze Age temples in the Levant (after Burke 2021: figure 5:10)

Tell Mastuma (Nishiyama 2012), Karkemish (Woolley and Barnett 1952: 167–75, 210–14), Arad (Aharoni 1993: 83–84), and Tel Moza' (Kisilevitz 2015). In keeping with Levantine prototypes, the Solomonic temple is described as possessing an open precinct in front and like the Late Bronze Age temple at Hazor also featured a large altar for sacrifices (Lev-Tov and McGeough 2007).

From the Middle Bronze Age onward, standing stones (Akk. *sikkanu*) were popular monuments in many Amorite cultic contexts (Durand 2005). This also was the case in the Levant during the same period, likely due to the ready availability of such natural elements. Although these were anepigraphic, they often appear in temple contexts, sometimes even propped against their facades (Burke 2021a: 137). Although the employment of these stelae during the period of the Judean monarchy (Heb. *maṣṣebôt*) was derided by Yahwists (2 Kgs 18:4; 23:14) because of their specific associations with deities like Baal (2 Kgs 3:2), they were remarkably persistent elements in cultic contexts throughout Israel and Judah during the Iron Age. Such stelae even appear in the "holy of holies" of the Judean temple at Arad (Aharoni 1993: 83–84) and have been identified at Tel Moza, and many more examples are known from a wide variety of cult installations throughout the southern Levant during the Iron Age (Bloch-Smith 2015 and bibliography therein). It is unclear, though, if the pillars (Heb. *amudîm*) located in the portico of Solomon's temple, which were named Boaz and

Jachin (1 Kgs 7:21), are also to be identified as *maṣṣebôt* since a different Hebrew term is used to describe them, or if they were structural as attested in the Bronze Age temple at Hazor (Figure 33.1). Nevertheless, standing stones, mostly aniconic, were an enduring element in ritual activities for various deities, as had been the case with the Amorite *pagrû* rite associated with the god Dagon, which persisted at Ugarit until the end of the Late Bronze Age (e.g., Pardee 2002: 123–25).

Other practices such as the intramural burial of royalty, like the kings of Judah (e.g., 1 Kgs 2:10) who were presumably buried under the palace in the City of David, may likewise be suggested to originate in a second-millennium milieu (Zorn 2006). Although continuity is often said to dominate burial practices in Canaan, intramural residential funerary chambers first appeared only in the early Middle Bronze Age (Gonen 1992) in the Levant, likley owing their influence to Amorite social groups (Burke 2021a: 289–93, 322–27). Even though they exhibit some variation, from sub-floor inhumations to corbel-vaulted hypogea, this period across much of the Near East witnessed a new and distinct emphasis on residential burials especially among elites (Laneri 2014; Valentini 2016), even as extramural, communal burial chambers were also employed, as in the Levant. Nevertheless, many of the extramural burials of the late Iron Age outside Jerusalem, for example, actually exhibit greater affinity to Middle and Late Bronze Age burial practices than they do to earlier Iron Age burial traditions, especially with respect to their plan, approach, kinship, and function.[19]

Despite the relative ease with which earlier traditions like those mentioned above can be identified, other influences of Amorite tradition are only preserved in biblical narratives. Indeed, while the seeming ubiquity of some of these traditions has sometimes led to their qualification as generally ancient Near Eastern in character, this is a rather useless classification that stops short of actually seeking the cultural and historical origins of these traditions, which are of importance to the work of text critics, biblical historians, and archaeologists alike. Recognizing the late Iron Age to Persian Period contexts for the writing of the Hebrew Bible, various allusions to practices often discussed in connection with Amorites in earlier periods are notable. Among these are the occurrence of Middle Bronze Age personal names with Yahwistic elements (Finet 1993b: 20), the esteem given to the donkey in Levantine society and economy from the late third millennium on (Lafont 2000; Way 2010), the place of donkey sacrifice in ritual among Amorite and biblical traditions (Finet 1993a), and arguably even lion imagery as associated with Yahweh (Burke 2021a: 195; cf. Strawn 2009). The above examples suffice to illustrate some of the more conspicuous and tangible elements of the influence of an Amorite legacy and to underscore that much more research into these individual traditions is warranted, with the hope that they will improve our understandings of certain elements among biblical traditions.

Conclusions

Despite early and overly optimistic scholarly efforts to identify the biblical patriarchs as historical figures among Amorite communities of the Middle Bronze Age, there remains a legitimate basis for seeking to identify early cultural influences that shaped first-millennium Levantine societies. While there is a long-accepted tradition of identifying aspects of cultural continuity across the archaeological records of the Bronze and Iron Ages in the southern Levant and the ancient Near Eastern character of many biblical traditions, it is necessary to further consider the specific manner in which each of these traditions came to be preserved in the Bible. In some cases, there are reasons to suggest that cultural memories associated with Amorites circulated widely during the Iron Age and that these were assimilated by biblical writers. In other cases, cultural practices persisted that suggest a cultural legacy owed by first-millennium Levantine societies to an Amorite oikoumene that prevailed during the first half of the second millennium. Outside of a limited number of biblical references, however, the challenge remains to discern to what extent the Levant's Iron Age inhabitants could attribute particular practices to specific groups like the Amorites.

Notes

1. I would like to thank Adam Miglio, Jeremy Smoak, and Kyle Keimer for helpful remarks on an early draft of this work. Any errors herein remain my own.
2. For Mari, see A.3552 (*COS* 4.50).
3. Put's descendants are omitted.
4. The absence of a reference to Tyre here or elsewhere in Genesis, points to its relative unimportance from the Achaemenid period onward when Sidon ascended politically and received control of Dor and Jaffa to its south in the 5th century BCE (*COS* 2.57), when it also seems to have exerted influence over this coast, as perhaps reflected in Gen 10:19.
5. The reflection of the relationship of Ham vis-à-vis Canaan, his progeny, is almost certainly a memory of Egypt's short-lived control of Canaan during the late 7th century BCE under the Saite Dynasty, which was quickly replaced by the Babylonian empire (Redford 1992: 430–69).
6. By contrast, there are references to named Hittites (e.g., Ephron the Hittite in Gen 23:10) and Amorites.
7. For Neo-Assyrian period references to "Amurru" from reign of Shalmanesser III on, see *RIMA* 3 and *RINAP* volumes. At least one reference to the "army of Amurru" in the reign of Adad-nirari (*RIMA* 0.104.2011) likely references a coalition of kingdoms in this region.
8. *RIMA* 0.87.3; 0.87.10.
9. *RIMA* 0.102.2.
10. Concerning the "ways of the Amorite" criticized in the Talmud, see Tosefta Shabbat 67a and 67b.
11. Of these various "land of ethnonym" constructs, the "land of the Hittites" occurs four times and is located north and associated with Hatti of the Neo-Assyrian period and not in Anatolia (e.g., Josh 1:4), while the "land of the Perizzites" occurs only once (Josh 17:15).
12. The identification of former, largely dispossessed populations of Canaan, including the Amorites, as giants is an important theme in biblical tradition (Hendel 2021).
13. This would also be the case for Hittites, Hivites, Girgashites, and Jebusites within the biblical text, quite irrespective of the accuracy of these labels or historical reality of these identities. Whether imagined or not, various of these groups were identified with more specific geographic areas *within* Canaan.
14. See Kark and Levin (2013).
15. See Finkelstein and Langgut (2014, 2018) and Langgut et al. (2014), among other studies.
16. See Fleming (2016: 27–28), now also Younger (2017: 35–107). Concerning the use of the term "cultural stream," see Fleming (2012: 202–19).
17. As invoked here, the "logic of demand, rejection, or indifference" is articulated by Michael Dietler (2010: 66–74).
18. See also *RIME* 4.6.8.2.
19. It is certainly likely that extramural burial chambers of the Middle Bronze Age, which were analogous to their intramural counterparts and cannot be distinguished by their contents, were in many cases simply the result of the limits of space experienced by tell-based communities seeking to bury their dead.

Bibliography

Abou Assaf, Ali. 1990. *Der Temple von 'Ain Dara*. Mainz am Rhein: Philipp von Zabern.

Aharoni, Miriam. 1993. "Arad: Israelite Citadels." Pages 82–87 in vol. 1 of *NEAEHL*. Edited by E. Stern. New York: Simon and Schuster.

Arbuckle, Benjamin S., and Emily L. Hammer. 2018. "The Rise of Pastoralism in the Ancient Near East." *JAR* 27: 391–449.

Bloch-Smith, Elizabeth. 2015. "Massebot Standing for Yhwh: The Fall of a Yhwistic Cult Symbol." Pages 99–115 in *Worship, Women and War: Essays in Honor of Susan Niditch*. Edited by John J. Collins, T. M. Lemos and Saul M. Olyan. Providence: Brown University.

Bryce, Trevor R. 2009. "Amurru." Pages 41–42 in *The Routledge Handbook of the Peoples and Places of Ancient Western Asia: From the Early Bronze Age to the Fall of the Persian Empire*. Edited by Trevor R. Bryce. London: Routledge.

Buck, Mary Ellen. 2020. *The Amorite Dynasty of Ugarit: Historical Implications of Linguistic and Archaeological Parallels*. Leiden: Brill.

Burke, Aaron A. 2014. "Entanglement, the Amorite koiné, and Amorite Cultures in the Levant." *ARAM* 26: 357–73.

———. 2021a. *The Amorites and the Bronze Age Near East: The Making of a Regional Identity*. Cambridge: Cambridge University Press

———. 2021b. "Toward the Reconstruction of a Sacred Landscape of the Judean Highlands." *JANER* 21:1–41. doi: 10.1163/15692124-12341317.

d'Andrea, Marta. 2019. "Before the Cultural *Koinè*: Contextualising Interculturality in the 'Greater Levant' during the Late Early Bronze Age and the Early Middle Bronze Age." Pages 13–45 in *The Enigma of the Hyksos I: ASOR Conference Boston 2017–ICAANE Conference Munich 2018—Collected Papers*. Edited by Manfred Bietak and Silvia Prell. Wiesbaden: Harrassowitz.

Dietler, Michael. 2010. *Archaeologies of Colonialism: Consumption, Entanglement, and Violence in Ancient Mediterranean France*. Berkeley: University of California Press.

Durand, Jean-Marie. 2005. *Le culte des pierres et les monuments commémoratifs en Syrie amorrite*. Paris: SEPOA.

Finet, André. 1993a. "Le sacrifice de l'âne en Mésopotamie." Pages 135–42 in *Ritual and Sacrifice in the Ancient Near East*. Edited by J. Quaegebeur. Leuven: Peeters.

———. 1993b. "Yahve au royaume Mari." Pages 15–22 in *Circulations des monnaies, des merchandises et des biens*. Edited by Y. Mansef. Bures-sur-Yvette: Groupe pour l'étude de la civilisation du Moyen-orient.

Finkelstein, Israel, and Dafna Langgut. 2014. "Dry Climate in the Middle Bronze I and Its Impact on Settlement Patterns in the Levant and Beyond: New Pollen Evidence." *JNES* 73:219–34.

———. 2018. "Climate, Settlement History, and Olive Cultivation in the Iron Age Southern Levant." *BASOR* 379:153–69.

Fleming, Daniel E. 2004. *Democracy's Ancient Ancestors: Mari and Early Collective Governance*. New York: Cambridge University Press.

———. 2012. *The Legacy of Israel in Judah's Bible: History, Politics, and the Reinscribing of Tradition*. Cambridge: Cambridge University Press.

———. 2016. "The Amorites." Pages.1–30 in *The World around the Old Testament: The People and Places of the Ancient Near East*. Edited by Bill T. Arnold and Brent A. Strawn. Grand Rapids: Baker Academic.

Gonen, Rivka. 1992. "Structural Tombs in the Second Millennium B.C." Pages 151–60 in *The Architecture of Ancient Israel: From the Prehistoric to the Persian Periods*. Edited by Aharon Kempinski and Ronny Reich. Jerusalem: Israel Exploration Society.

Haines, Richard C. 1971. *Excavations in the Plain of Antioch II*. Chicago: University of Chicago Press.

Hendel, Ronald S. 2005. *Remembering Abraham: Culture, Memory, and History in the Hebrew Bible*. Oxford: Oxford University Press.

———. 2010. "Cultural Memory." Pages 28–46 in *Reading Genesis: Ten Methods*. Edited by Ronald S. Hendel. Cambridge: Cambridge University Press.

———. 2021. "The Landscape of Memory: Giants and the Conquest of Canaan." Pages 263–88 in *Collective Identity and Collective Memory: Deuteronomy and the Deuteronomistic History in Their Context*. Edited by Johannes U. Ro and Diana Edelman. Berlin: De Gruyter.

Ishida, Tomoo. 1979. "The Structure and Historical Implications of the Lists of Pre-Israelite Nations." *Biblica* 60:461–90.

Kark, Ruth, and Noam Levin. 2013. "The Environment in Palestine in the Late Ottoman Period, 1798–1918." Pages 1–28 in *Between Ruin and Restoration: An Environmental History of Israel*. Edited by Daniel E. Orenstein, Alon Tal and Char Miller. Pittsburg: University of Pittsburgh Press.

Kenyon, Kathleen M. 1966. *Amorites and Canaanites, The Schweich Lectures of the British Academy, 1963*. Oxford: Oxford University Press.

Killebrew, Ann E. 2005. *Biblical Peoples and Ethnicity: An Archaeological Study of Egyptians, Canaanites, Philistines, and Early Israel 1300–1100 B.C.E*. Atlanta: SBL.

Kisilevitz, Shua. 2015. "The Iron IIA Judahite Temple at Tel Moza." *TA* 42:147–64.
Kohlmeyer, Kay. 2000. *Der Tempel des Wettergottes von Aleppo*. Münster: Rhema.
Lafont, Bertrand. 2000. "Cheval, âne, onagre et mule dans la haute historire mésopotamienne: quelques données nouvelles." *TopoiSupp* 2:207–21.
Lambert, Wilfred G. 1996. *Babylonian Wisdom Literature*. Oxford: Oxford Clarendon, 1960. Repr., Winona Lake: Eisenbrauns.
Laneri, Nicola. 2014. "Locating the Social Memory of the Ancestors: Residential Funerary Chambers as Locales of Social Remembrance in Mesopotamia during the Late Third and Early Second Millennia BC." Pages 3–10 in *Contextualising Grave Inventories in the Ancient Near East*. Edited by Peter Pfälzner, Herbert Niehr, Ernst Pernicka, Sarah Lange and Tina Köster. Wiesbaden: Harrassowitz.
Langgut, Dafna, Frank Harald Neumann, Mordechai Stein, Allon Wagner, Elisa Joy Kagan, Elisabetta Boaretto, and Israel Finkelstein. 2014. "Dead Sea Pollen Record and History of Human Activity in the Judean Highlands (Israel) from the Intermediate Bronze into the Iron Ages (~2500–500 BCE)." *Palynology* 38:280–302.
Lemche, Niels Peter. 1991. *The Canaanites and Their Land: The Tradition of the Canaanites*. Edited by David J. A. Clines and Philip R. Davies. Sheffield: JSOT.
Lev-Tov, Justin, and Kevin McGeough. 2007. "Examining Feasting in Late Bronze Age Syro-Palestine through Ancient Texts and Bones." Pages 85–111 in *The Archaeology of Food and Identity*. Edited by Katheryn C. Twiss. Carbondale: Southern Illinois University Carbondale.
Liverani, Mario. 1973. "The Amorites." Pages 100–33 in *Peoples of Old Testament Times*. Edited by Donald J. Wiseman. Oxford: Clarendon.
Mazar, Amihai. 1992. "Temples of the Middle and Late Bronze Ages and the Iron Age." Pages 161–87 in *The Architecture of Ancient Israel: From the Prehistoric to the Persian Periods*. Edited by Aharon Kempinski and Ronny Reich. Jerusalem: Israel Exploration Society.
Mazzoni, Stefania. 2002. "Temples in the City and Countryside: New Trends in Iron Age Syria." *DamM* 13:89–99.
Nishiyama, Shin'ichi. 2012. "A Local Temple in the Iron Age Village? Reassessing a Building Complex at Tell Mastuma in the Northern Levant." *Orient* 47: 91–123.
Pardee, Dennis. 2002. *Ritual and Cult at Ugarit*. Edited by Simon B. Parker. Atlanta: Scholars Press.
Porter, Anne. 2012. *Mobile Pastoralism and the Formation of Near Eastern Civilizations: Weaving Together Society*. Cambridge: Cambridge University Press.
Radner, Karen. 2003. "Neo-Assyrian Period." Pages 883–910 in *A History of Ancient Near Eastern Law*. Edited by Raymond Westbrook and Gary M. Beckman. Leiden: Brill.
Rainey, Anson F. 1996. "Who Is a Canaanite? A Review of the Textual Evidence." *BASOR* 304:1–15.
Redford, Donald B. 1992. *Egypt, Canaan, and Israel in Ancient Times*. Princeton: Princeton University Press.
Roth, Martha T. 1995. "Mesopotamian Legal Traditions and the Laws of Hammurabi." *Chicago-Kent Law Review* 71: 13–39.
Strawn, Brent A. 2009. "Whence Leonine Yahweh? Iconography and the History of Israelite Religion." Pages 51–85 in *Images and Prophecy in the Ancient Eastern Mediterranean*. Edited by Martti Nissinen and Charles E. Carter. Göttingen: Vandenhoeck & Ruprecht.
Thompson, Thomas L. 1974. *The Historicity of the Patriarchal Narratives: The Quest for the Historical Abraham*. Berlin: De Gruyter.
Valentini, Stefano. 2016. "Vaulted *Hypogea* during the Middle Bronze Age: A Perfect Example of the Intra-Muros Multiple Tomb in Mesopotamia." Pages 217–40 in *How to Cope with Death: Mourning and Funerary Practices in the Ancient Near East. Proceedings of the International Workshop, Firenze, 5th-6th December 2013*. Edited by Candida Felli. Florence: ETS.
Van Seters, John. 1975. *Abraham in History and Tradition*. New Haven: Yale University.
Way, Kenneth C. 2010. "Assessing Sacred Asses: Bronze Age Donkey Burials in the Near East." *Levant* 42: 210–25.
Woolley, Charles Leonard, and Richard D. Barnett. 1952. *Carchemish: Report on the Excavations at Djerabis, Part III, The Excavations in the Inner Town; The Hittite Inscriptions*. London: Trustees of the British Museum.
Zorn, Jeffrey R. 2006. "The Burials of the Judean Kings: Sociohistorical Considerations and Suggestions." Pages 801–20 in *"I Will Speak the Riddles of Ancient Times": Archaeological and Historical Studies in Honor of Amihai Mazar on the Occasion of His Sixtieth Birthday*. Edited by Aren M. Maeir and Pierre de Miroschedji. Winona Lake: Eisenbrauns.

34

NEW KINGDOM EGYPT AND EARLY ISRAEL

Entangled Identities

Aaron A. Burke

Introduction

The question of the historicity of the Exodus narrative and its implications for understanding Egypt's role in shaping the identities of ancient Israel and Judah has attracted serious interest by biblical scholars, especially exploration of the exodus of Israel from Egypt as a historical event (Friedman 2017; Hoffmeier 1997, 2005; Levy, Schneider, and Propp 2015). In such discussions, evidence for Egyptian or Egyptian-inspired customs in ancient Israel or Judah, whether surfacing in the Hebrew Bible or within contemporaneous archaeological contexts, is often assumed to provide authentication for the Israelite exodus and is thus seen to further confirm this event as the primary vector that accounts for Egyptian influence upon Israel's cultural traditions. Unfortunately, this has also likely contributed to a neglect of what is undoubtedly the most substantive and enduring episode of Egyptianizing influence on Canaan, early Israel, and its traditions, namely more than four centuries of Egyptian New Kingdom imperial intervention in Canaan during the Late Bronze Age (LBA), ca. 1550–1100 BC.[1] This essay seeks to address the influence of the Egyptian New Kingdom from early Israelite tribal identities to later Judean traditions during the Iron Age by considering specific outcomes resulting from Egyptian intervention, the social entanglements that accompanied it, and the ensuing effects of the disappearance of this order after the end of the 12th century.

Despite earlier episodes of Egyptian influence in the Levant, New Kingdom rule contributed to a range of intensive social interactions over a protracted span of time that left an indelible imprint upon the social experience of Canaan's inhabitants and, consequently, upon early Israelite identity and its traditions thereafter. In many cases, emergent traditions were the result of the presence of different communities of practice during the LBA, notably specialists such as administrators and warriors affiliated with Egyptian imperial intervention during the New Kingdom. In other cases, recurring conflict and the flight of populations from urban centers during conflicts surrounding Egyptian rule contributed to ideal conditions for the formation of new social and political identities, both resulting from Egyptian intervention.

Throughout this essay, cultural influences identified as Egyptian are referred to as *Egyptianizing*, a classification that includes the widest range of possible traditions associated with Egyptian influence, irrespective of whether or not the specific agents behind these influences can be identified with certainty, since it is possible that they may be agents of the Egyptian empire irrespective of whether they are identified as culturally Egyptian themselves (e.g., Nubians, Sherden). This encompassing term therefore seeks to avoid assumptions about agency while identifying the fullest range of possible evidence for cultural influences that may be attributed to the presence of individuals accompanying Egyptian intervention, since this could vary from inhabitants of the Delta and Nile Valley to mercenaries like Nubians and Mediterranean groups often referred to as Sea Peoples. Nevertheless, where evidence permits, some speculation as to the agents behind these exchanges is relevant to understanding the outcomes of interactions since they have the potential to reveal how extensive and enduring certain traditions were among later Iron Age states like Israel and Judah. Out of the imperative to contain the scope of this essay, literary traditions that are suggested to have been influenced by Egyptian traditions are left aside (e.g., see Schniedewind 2019: 118–37).

New Kingdom Rule and the Transformation of Canaan

After a period of nearly 350 years without substantive evidence for the direct presence of any significant number of Egyptians in Canaan, military intervention by Egypt followed the expulsion of the Asiatic (i.e., Amorite) rulers of Dynasty 15, who had inhabited Avaris in the eastern Nile Delta and who are commonly known as the Hyksos. The reunification of Egypt during the early Eighteenth Dynasty ushered in a period of territorial expansion that gradually led to formalized territorial control, as the New Kingdom Egyptian empire, of large parts of both Nubia and the Levant (Morris 2018: 117–221). Although the motivations for empire in Canaan during the LBA remain debated (Ahituv 1978; Na'aman 1981), they likely evolved over this period. Early Egyptian campaigns in the Levant consisted largely of ad hoc raids with no clear concern for empire building (Burke 2010; Höflmayer 2015).

Only in the wake of Thutmose III's defeat of a large Levantine coalition led by the king of Kadesh at Megiddo, ca. 1460 BCE (Spalinger 2005: 83–101), does substantive evidence emerge of a deliberate effort to orchestrate a permanent Egyptian occupation of Canaan (Morris 2005). This began with the construction of fortresses and the installation of accompanying garrisons at key sites, and with them the first appearance of a number of Egyptian monuments. Settlements like Jaffa and Beth-Shean emerge as central nodes in a growing network of Egyptian settlements that would eventually peak during the Ramesside period in the 13th century BCE. By that point, numerous Egyptian residences reveal the presence of a large cadre of Egyptian officials and a network of smaller farmsteads and settlements throughout Canaan (Oren 1984), such as Aphek in Jaffa's hinterland (Gadot 2010). These were intended to support almost annual Egyptian military campaigns that were required to maintain control of Canaan through episodes of resistance, the results of which are conspicuously portrayed on New Kingdom temples as at Karnak (Burke 2009). The overall impact of Egyptian intervention ranged from major disruptions to the settlement pattern, recognized mostly in a decline in the total settled area (i.e., population) owing to the repeated destruction of so many sites (Gonen 1984), to the enslavement and likely deportation of a significant portion of Canaan's population to Egypt, and shifts in settlement within the Levant (Burke 2018). The end of Egyptian rule came in the final quarter of the 12th century (after 1125 BCE), a date that is now supported by a robust set of radiocarbon dates for the final destruction of the fortress in Jaffa, Egypt's principal harbor and fortress along Canaan's central coast (Burke et al. 2017: 118–20).

Egyptian intervention in Canaan during the New Kingdom, lasted more than 400 years. Very importantly, this represented a period of the most intensive Egyptian presence in

Canaan during all of the Bronze Age, affecting a wide range of local traditions owing to extensive entanglements with so many agents of the Egyptian empire. The reasons for this are twofold. On the one hand, through conquest and violence, Egypt is clearly implicated in the erosion of local institutions and their traditions, through both the demographic decline in Canaan's population during the LBA and the deliberate destruction of institutions that accompanied the persistent destruction of towns and villages. Although often overlooked in discussions of LBA "collapse," the Egyptian empire was the catalyst that brought about a cultural sea change in Canaan that would lay the foundation for Israel's emergence. On the other hand, the extensive footprint of the Egyptian imperial presence, which was embodied in its varied personnel, exposed Canaan's inhabitants to a range of foreign traditions that permanently shaped many, if not most, local traditions.

The Disruption of Canaanite Traditions

Under Egyptian rule, persistent warfare and accompanying declines in Canaan's population due to death and deportations, alongside the annexation of land, and the imposition of economic obligations all challenged existing political orders and stretched Canaan's social and economic fabric, as well as its existing political order (Panitz-Cohen 2014). While other factors, including natural phenomena such as drought (e.g., Kaniewski et al. 2019), are often implicated in the decline of Canaan's palatial order, no factor during the LBA was more persistently significant to Canaan's cultural trajectory than Egyptian intervention. A major result of New Kingdom intervention was the fundamental erosion of Canaan's social, economic, and political institutions, which at the start of Egyptian rule had experienced nearly 500 years of steady patronage, often at the hands of Amorite rulers (Burke 2021: 257–344). The resultant Amorite *koine* comprised distinct approaches to, for example, war, cult, burial, legitimation, law, scribalism, and kinship (see Burke this volume). Although these traditions were not eradicated by Egyptian occupation, by the end of the Bronze Age their collective significance was seriously undermined because of Canaan's altered social landscape. A significant demographic decline in the region's population, a disruption in cultural ties with the northern Levant and Mesopotamia, and the introduction of new traditions all contributed to these circumstances.

The disruption of enduring cultural institutions is often only given superficial consideration in discussions of the decline of the LBA, primarily due to materialist concerns with economic and political narratives associated with elites in which material correlates are viewed as direct evidence for the decline of robust trade networks and palatial economies (e.g., Cline 2014). However, as material markers of the economic connections that Egyptian-occupied Canaan maintained, these imports are to some extent misleading as markers since they represent only one facet of Canaan's diverse economy. Long-distance trade, which originated during the Middle Bronze Age (MBA), was almost exclusively rooted in the palace and was not therefore a byproduct of the LBA. Furthermore, the LBA witnessed shifts in loyalties by Canaan's rulers both toward, but also occasionally away from, Egypt. A more accurate reflection of this trade's relationship to Egyptian control would recognize that the falloff in this trade with Canaan resulted from the decimation of Canaan's palaces as Egypt struggled to maintain control of Canaan. Nevertheless, while conspicuous markers of trade (e.g., imported ceramic vessels) fall off drastically, suggesting that royally-sponsored, long-distance trade declined, the persistence of trade during the early Iron Age may be marked by the remains of perishable items as evidenced by residue analyses (personal communication, Kyle Keimer 2021). Similarly, much of the social dynamism that is often implicated in this cultural shift in Canaan centered on foreign agents, be they Aegean, Cypriot, or Philistine (see Panitz-Cohen 2006), who are more conspicuous as mercenaries and foreign fighters than as merchants. These individuals did not disappear and in some cases became only more conspicuous with Egypt's retreat. In other words, whether we are speaking of Egyptianizing influences resulting from the presence of Egyptians or the presence of Philistines and other foreign groups, the archaeological evidence suggests that conflict was the principal context responsible, directly and indirectly, for the creation of the most substantive and enduring social influences (e.g., destructions of communities, garrisons, foreign warriors) on Canaanite society during the LBA and into the early Iron Age (EIA).

The destruction of many sites at the hands of the Egyptians and, more generally, as a result of Egypt's struggle for Canaan by the end of the LBA further reduced both the physical remains of many local institutions and the number of their officiants and participants. Palaces as at Hazor and Megiddo (VIIB), for example, which had flourished throughout the LBA and thus embodied continuity with the MBA, were destroyed. Correlating with this, the scribal use of Akkadian vanished with the demise of these centers, and cuneiform as a writing system was abandoned in the Levant until its limited reintroduction in the Neo-Assyrian period (Horowitz, Oshima, and Sanders 2018: 18). The destruction of long-lived, ancient temple sanctuaries accompanied that of palaces at these sites. Few of the many LBA temple complexes, many of which had persisted from the MBA, survived Egyptian rule. The unimpressive attempts to reconstruct palaces and temples, reveal the erosion of local social power that followed in the wake of these destructions (Zuckerman 2007). The gradual decline of palaces and temples was also accompanied by a decline in defensive efforts by most Canaanite communities (Kempinski 1992: 136–40). Having maintained a scaffold of fortifications centered on the continuity of gate architecture from the end of the MBA, repeated stress on settlement defenses during the LBA and the erosion of Canaanite palatial power meant that efforts to maintain and rebuild fortifications were inadequate, and no real innovation is attested (Burke 2008: 80–84).

Accompanying disruptions to royal and cultic traditions, sedentary communities and Canaan's urban centers experienced significant ruptures of longstanding cultural traditions. By the end of Egyptian rule, family burial caves, in many cases a continuous locus of kin identity from the MBA, were almost entirely abandoned (Gonen 1992a: 41–69). Alongside the abandonment and destruction of settlements, these stand as some of the clearest data for the displacement of populations resulting from warfare. In other cases, some cemeteries that appear to lack clear connections to nearby contemporaneous settlements may have continued to be used by dislocated groups even after the abandonment of nearby towns.[2] Not surprisingly, Egyptian imperial control of southern Canaan also contributed to a broad decline in Canaan's ties with the northern Levant, which itself had fallen under Hittite imperial control. This effected a fragmentation across a range of curated cultural exchanges that had predated these empires. As such, the changes brought about by Egyptian intervention disrupted ancient political, social, and economic ties, eroding vestiges of patronage of political and social institutions by local groups.

To a large extent, this disruption represented the unwinding of Amorite social power (Burke 2021: 367–69). Its subsequent replacement during the LBA was mostly ad hoc and sometimes occurred at the hands of upstart rulers. As represented by Canaanite correspondence with the Egyptian court already during the Amarna period (14th century BCE), emergent regional leaders, often 'apiru-and thus lacking ties to the *régimes anciennes*—grappled to legitimate their ascendance under Egyptian rule. Protracted circumstances such as these also created a context for greater visibility of previously less conspicuous traditions. Alphabetic writing, for example, which was in use prior to the LBA experienced a rapid and widespread adoption during the EIA (Rollston 2019: 373–76), a development that correlates with the contemporaneous disappearance of Egyptian rule and the decline of Canaanite patronage of Akkadian scribal traditions.

Social Entanglement and the Introduction of Egyptian Traditions

In the wake of Thutmose's decisive victory over the king of Kadesh and his coalition, the presence of a range of personnel associated with Egypt's military occupation can be identified through a combination of epigraphic and archaeological sources. Among these occupations were, of course, soldiers and administrators, but also cooks, potters, architects, and cult officials. Each of these capacities provided opportunities for the introduction of unique sets of customs in the context of imperial occupation and administration. As a result, part and parcel of the disruption of some ancient traditions, social and economic changes wrought by the footprint of New Kingdom intervention included the introduction of a range of craft traditions some of which have left identifiable traces on local traditions, including ceramic manufacture, textile production, metallurgy, scribalism, and iconography.

In the realm of ceramics production, Egyptian influences included the introduction of certain forms as well as techniques of manufacture. Forms like cup-and-saucer bowls, which first appear in the LBA and are widely considered to be of Egyptian origin (Martin 2011: 88–89), persisting throughout the Iron Age (Uziel and Gadot 2010). Ceramic spinning bowls, which were introduced with the Egyptian New Kingdom assemblage (Martin 2011: 45–46) and are associated with flax spinning for local linen textile production, also continued in local use until the late Iron Age (Mazar 2015: 10, pl. 1.1.4). Egyptian ceramic technology has also been identified as an important influence on local Canaanite ceramic production during the LBA, which up to that point still reflected the overwhelming persistence of MBA traditions (Mullins and Yannai 2019: 151–52). Changes included an increasing coarseness in fabric and a thickening of vessel walls, as in the case of simple bowls, which were produced on slower wheels resulting in an increase in their clunkiness, which may actually have made the wares more durable. Influences on local production likely also included the reintroduction of straw-temper in ceramic production (Martin 2011: 98–99), as well as red-slipped and red-banded decoration by the end of the LBA (Panitz-Cohen 2009: 201–02).

The tools of writing in the southern Levant may be the clearest case of lasting Egyptian influence upon Canaan from the LBA. As evidenced from Iron Age bullae preserving the impressions of papyrus scrolls, papyrus is exposed as an example of a writing medium borrowed from Egypt, where it was in use, of course, well before the Iron Age. Furthering the argument for the borrowing of this technology and the influence of Egyptian scribalism in the wake of the New Kingdom is the lexicon of scribal terms in Hebrew for the scribe's toolkit, namely the terms for papyrus, pen, ink, and writing palette (Schniedewind 2013: 56–60). The adoption of red and black ink color distinctions in scribal training, Hieratic numerals, and technical terms for items such as the "seal," "signet ring," and different measurements all point to the pervasive influence of Egyptian scribal administrators (Schniedewind 2019: 40–41, 46–47, 130–33). The New Kingdom text *The Craft of the Scribe*, for example, provides insights into the expectations and experiences of the military scribe in Egyptian service in the Levant (COS 3.2). This individual, who was also identified with the Semitic term *mahir* (warrior), was tasked with a wide range of logistical responsibilities and was evidently required to command a vast linguistic, geographic, political, and cultural knowledge of the Levant in order to carry out his duties. It is likely that several such individuals remained in

Canaan after Egypt's departure (Burke 2020: 59–62). Several other Egyptian loanwords (Lambdin 1953) may also owe their preservation in Hebrew to the post-imperial moment, when Hebrew and other national languages emerged from various Canaanite dialects. In this context, it is also noteworthy that cylinder seal technology, like Akkadian—with its Mesopotamian associations—was abandoned.

It is little wonder that in the wake of the centuries-long intervention of the Egyptian empire Canaan's iconographic repertoire adopted a range of traditional Egyptian symbols and iconography. The most conspicuous evidence of this is the appropriation of various elements and motifs within locally-produced Levantine ivories from the LBA onward (Feldman 2009: 179–80). Ivory inlays for furniture found in 8th-century contexts at Samaria expose the repertoire of Egyptian iconography with which elite households were familiar, if also to a lesser degree the wider public of southern Levantine societies (Crowfoot and Crowfoot 1938). These symbols, among others, include adaptations of the lotus, sphinx, and palmette motifs. In addition to their pervasive influence on ivory production, seals, architecture, and statuary drew upon these motifs as well (Wright 2018: 160), and allusions to this iconography, of course, also appear within biblical literature of the late Iron Age (Wright 2018: 163). Some of these motifs also appear among EIA stamp seals (Shuval 1990). Among carved seals and sealings, such as the *lmlk* seals of the late 8th century BCE but also from Ammon and elsewhere appear the winged sun-disk and winged beetle, as well as the uraeus. Similarly, Egyptian crowns persisted to influence depictions from Baal statuary of the LBA at Ugarit through to the headdresses of Ammonite statuary during the Iron Age.

The introduction of the range of traditions suggests the degree to which social entanglements existed between agents of Egypt's imperial presence and Canaan's inhabitants during the LBA. Indeed, a wide variety of personnel composed New Kingdom Egypt's footprint in Canaan and provided many individual vectors for Egyptianizing traditions to influence different local crafts. As becomes clear from the record of Egyptian strongholds in Canaan with those from Egypt itself over several hundred years during the LBA, a constant influx of new personnel accompanied New Kingdom administration and this resulted in a seemingly regular synchronization of local imperial styles with contemporary Egyptian traditions and fashions, most evident in the correlations between the Egyptian ceramic repertoire of both Egypt and Canaan. Interestingly, there is no evidence to support interpreting this Egyptianizing presence as simply the emulation of Egyptian practices by Canaanite elites (contra Higginbotham 2000). Instead, there is ample evidence to clarify the character of an Egyptian New Kingdom presence composed of a range of personnel (see Morris 2018: 203–04). It is important to consider that the many such individuals who likely remained in Canaan after Egypt's official departure, contributed to an eclectic community of specialists of various cultural backgrounds (Burke 2020). Thus, added to the occupational diversity represented among Egyptian personnel was the ethnic and social diversity inherent to the composition of the New Kingdom military (Spalinger 2005: 264–77). While many were recruited doubtlessly from Egypt proper, Nubians (*medjay*), Aegean groups (e.g., Sherden), Hittites, and Hurrians (i.e., *maryannu*) were also present among Egypt's archers, foot-soldiers, and charioteers. It is important to acknowledge then that EIA Canaan exhibited a mixed cultural heritage that was in considerable measure the direct result of Egyptian intervention as well as foreign efforts to assist in resistance to it, a characterization in line with biblical memories of a "mixed crowd" that were part of the Israelite exodus (*NRSV*, Exod 12:38).

As in the case of military personnel, questions must be entertained about the degree of Egyptian cultic influence on Canaan's inhabitants. One such question emerges in relation to the identity of the Levites in Israelite society. R. E. Friedman, for example, asserts that the Levites were the Israelites who most likely participated in an actual exodus from Egypt (Friedman 2017). This, he suggests, is based on the observations that of all the Israelite tribes the Levites possessed more etymologically Egyptian names, that the Levites were central to the Song of the Sea, and yet that they were also absent in the Song of Deborah. Friedman justifies this characterization on the basis of the identification of particular attributes of Israelite cult with Egyptian traditions, namely the tabernacle (after Homan 2002) and the Ark of the Covenant (e.g., Noegel 2015), as well as the adoption of the practice of circumcision (which Egyptians also did), and biblical traditions that reflect understandings of Egyptian traditions, such as magic, as many scholars have discussed for a century. Of course, it must be acknowledged that the various sources traditionally associated with the Levites, such as the so-called E and P strands of authorship, are also considered late by many scholars (i.e., after the fall of Judah in 586 BCE), making it more difficult to be certain when and under what conditions these traditions might have entered biblical narratives.

Quite apart from the biblical evidence for the possible identification of the influence of Egyptian imperialism on Iron Age southern Levantine cult traditions, the line of inquiry is certainly warranted. This is particularly so considering the range of other evidence for Egyptian cult that persists in the EIA that suggests the presence of such individuals. These include remains of some unique Egyptian finds from Iron I contexts at Ekron (Brandl 2016a, b), which can perhaps be associated with the presence of an Egyptian-trained scribe after the departure of Egypt (Burke 2020: 57). Questions might also be asked about the extent of the association of Egyptian amulets (i.e., *wadjet* and divine Egyptian images) with individuals whose lineages might have been affiliated with earlier Egyptian rule. Notions of trinkets wherein such amulets were simply souvenirs or bobbles are likely anachronistic. Indeed, the aniconism that largely typifies material culture of the EIA, when compared with the LBA, might be read at least in part as a reaction to the iconography of the Egyptian empire, with a biblical ascription of this cultural trend narrowing to Israelite, if mostly Judean, rejection of Canaanite symbolism.

Israel and Social Trajectories after Egyptian Rule in Canaan

Evidence of Israel's direct relationship to and interaction with New Kingdom Egypt is unequivocally established by a single source, the Merneptah Stele, which reports on the earliest historical encounter with a group that is referred to as "Israel" (*COS* 2.6). At a minimum this reference, dated ca. 1207 BC, provides clear evidence of the existence of a group known as Israel, which resisted Egyptian imperial rule in southern Canaan. For this reason, Israel, in its earliest incarnation and whatever it may later represent, perhaps best and most simply represents a military alliance. Consequently, quite beyond the question of the historical existence of an entity known as Israel out of which one would seek to identify the Israel of later biblical narratives, this reference serves as the basis for a series of important, if basic, conclusions concerning Israel's relationship to Egyptian rule and its early identification as a political coalition in resistance to Egypt.

First, Israel as an entity emerged not later than the second half of the 13th century BCE and directly from the context of Egyptian rule. Thus, Israel's early identity should be sought in the conditions that shaped the cultural trajectories of membership in this early Israel at the end of New Kingdom rule, during the 13th century BCE. Slavery and forced migration, key elements in the Exodus tradition, were central elements of the Canaanite experience under Egyptian rule (Killebrew 2017). As such, the experience of slavery and Egyptian control played, unsurprisingly, an important role in the shared experience of Canaanites

(Hendel 2001, 2015). This also included a shared experience in flight from these circumstances, namely as refugees, a largely understudied phenomenon. The flight of many of Canaan's inhabitants to less populous parts of the Canaanite countryside during the 12th century followed the decline in Egyptian military power as the New Kingdom ended, making the refugee experience in Canaan resonant with an emerging Israelite identity. As I have outlined elsewhere, the highlands of the southern Levant are readily identified as a refuge for lowland inhabitants in the transition between the end of the LBA and the EIA (Burke 2018). The settlements are characteristically short-lived and consist largely of utilitarian ceramic assemblages, reflecting rather small, isolated, short-term agropastoralist settlements, sometimes in the most marginal and certainly less visible fringes of the highlands. The wider context for such resettlement of displaced persons is further established by the widespread and contemporaneous phenomena of the appearance of squatter occupation within urban centers and subterranean storage pits and silos at most sites, which together point to broader concerns like physical protection and food insecurity.

Second, Israel's earliest identity is principally one of military resistance to Egyptian rule that emerges in the context of the formation of a military alliance (Mullins 2015: 522–23), and thus it is to be expected that cultural memories of Israel's origins would feature a central place for Egypt. There was no corner of Canaan that was unaffected by Egyptian rule, though some areas, principally those away from its transit corridors, certainly did offer greater refuge. Inseparable from this is the role that violence played in the relationship between Egypt and Canaan's inhabitants, notably in the context of resistance and its role in the consolidation of identity, but also the effective reorganization of group solidarity. Regular destructions of sites throughout Canaan during the LBA, repeated Egyptian campaigns to quell resistance and rebellions, and the destruction of Egyptian sites, all with increasing frequency by the 12th century illustrate that violence and resistance shaped the lives of Canaan's inhabitants under Egyptian rule (see Burke et al. 2017). At a minimum, earliest affiliation with Israel required participation in and support of active resistance to Egyptian rule as organized by this new coalition, a situation analogous to that which permeates the narratives of Israel's early military leaders in the book of Judges. Thus, there is ample ground for understanding why violence, resistance, and military action also play such a prominent role in the early biblical narratives associated with Israel's rise at the end of and immediately after Egyptian rule, as in the book of Joshua but especially in that of Judges.

Finally, acknowledging Israel's identity in relation to its resistance to Egypt complicates traditional identifications of Israel as an ethnic group based principally on the characteristics of a single group of highland settlements (e.g., Finkelstein 1988; Stager 1998; Faust 2006). If as even the book of Judges recounts, the tribal constituencies of the political entity known as Israel were dispersed across Canaan's varied geography, the highlands offered but one side of this emerging identity and the suggestion of "type fossils" based on the material culture of these settlements can, at best, only provide insights regarding some of Israel's constituency, namely the groups or tribes inhabiting this region.

As evidenced by the Merneptah Stele, at the end of the LBA the label "Israel" cannot be unequivocally limited to the identification of a specific region or the whole of what would later constitute monarchic Israel, as the term was identified by later biblical authors in the 7th century BCE. Although a case may be made for suggesting Israel's association with the region of Samaria (Mullins 2015: 523), the stele's narrative does not itself provide this level of geographic resolution. It is fair to say that as something approximating a political or military alliance, Israel represented an ideology. In the context of widespread resistance to Egyptian rule in the late stages of New Kingdom control of Canaan, various subsequent groups could lay claim to the cultural legacy of this resistance (Hendel 2001). This complicates unilinear reconstructions that explain that Judah claimed a predominantly Israelite (i.e., northern) tradition regarding its relationship to Egypt to explain why Judah's bible propagated the exodus tradition (contra Finkelstein 2013). Judah may have been smaller, but could likewise claim its role and stake in a wider resistance to Egyptian rule. Considering the various trajectories that different regions in Canaan experienced in the wake of the demise of Egyptian control we have reason to conclude that different groups reckoned their relationship to Egypt in analogous ways, and that triumphalist narratives as in the book of Exodus would emerge to embody the plights of those who resisted and fled from Egyptian rule.

Conclusion

While it is certainly true that Egyptian influences are less conspicuous than the influences of the customs of Canaan's other and probably more numerous LBA inhabitants, the chronological synchrony between Israel's earliest appearance and the end of New Kingdom rule requires that greater consideration should be given to Egypt's role in the creation of the context for Israel's emergence. And, although some Egyptian influences are more conspicuous than others, they can nonetheless be identified across a range of crafts and traditions in Canaan in the immediate aftermath of the departure of Egyptian imperial rule. Nevertheless, ample space remains for a more thorough consideration of the impact of Egyptian rule on the shaping of different local traditions.

Notes

1 The periodization of Canaan in the Late Bronze Age employed here identifies the 12th century as Late Bronze Age (i.e., LB III) rather than as the Iron Age IA (see Panitz-Cohen 2014).
2 Early explanations suggested their associations with nomadic groups (Gonen 1992b, 148-149), which overemphasized the role of pastoral nomadism and now appear incorrect (see Arbuckle and Hammer 2018).

Bibliography

Ahituv, Shmuel. 1978. "Economic Factors in the Egyptian Conquest of Canaan." *IEJ* 28: 93–105.
Arbuckle, Benjamin S., and Emily L. Hammer. 2018. "The Rise of Pastoralism in the Ancient Near East." *JAR* 27: 391–449.
Brandl, Baruch. 2016a. "The Thoth Baboon Statuette: The Inscription and Its Dating." Pages 462–66 in *Tel Miqne-Ekron Excavations 1985–1988, 1990, 1992–1995: Field IV Lower—The Elite Zone, The Iron Age I and IIC, The Early and Late Philistine Cities*. Edited by Trude Dothan, Yosef Garfinkel and Seymour Gitin. Winona Lake: Eisenbrauns.
———. 2016b. "Two Scarabs and Two Finger-Rings from Iron Age I Contexts." Pages 503–509, 595 in *Tel Miqne-Ekron Excavations 1985–1988, 1990, 1992–1995: Field IV Lower—The Elite Zone, The Iron Age I and IIC, The Early and Late Philistine Cities*. Edited by Trude Dothan, Yosef Garfinkel and Seymour Gitin,. Winona Lake: Eisenbrauns.
Burke, Aaron A. 2008. *"Walled Up to Heaven": The Evolution of Middle Bronze Age Fortification Strategies in the Levant*. Winona Lake: Eisenbrauns.
———. 2009. "More Light on Old Reliefs: New Kingdom Egyptian Siege Tactics and Asiatic Resistance." Pages 57–68 in *Exploring the Longue Durée: Essays in Honor of Lawrence E. Stager*. Edited by J. David Schloen. Winona Lake: Eisenbrauns.
———. 2010. "Canaan under Siege: The History and Archaeology of Egypt's War in Canaan during the Early Eighteenth Dynasty." Pages 43–66 in *Studies on War in the Ancient Near East: Collected Essays on Military History*. Edited by Jordi Vidal. Münster: Ugarit-Verlag.

———. 2018. "The Decline of Egyptian Empire, Forced Migration, and Social Change in the Southern Levant, ca. 1200–1050 B.C." Pages 229–49 in *The Archaeology of Forced Migration: Conflict-Induced Movement and Refugees in the Mediterranean at the End of the 13th c. BC*. Edited by Jan Driessen. Louvain-la-Neuve: Presses Universitaires de Louvain.

———. 2020. "Left Behind: New Kingdom Specialists at the End of Egyptian Empire and the Emergence of Israelite Scribalism." Pages 50–66 in *"An Excellent Fortress for his Armies, a Refuge for the People": Egyptological, Archaeological, and Biblical Studies in Honor of James K. Hoffmeier*. Edited by Richard E. Averbeck and K. Lawson Younger. University Park: Eisenbrauns.

———. 2021. *The Amorites and the Bronze Age Near East: The Making of a Regional Identity*. Cambridge: Cambridge University Press.

Burke, Aaron A., Martin Peilstöcker, Amy Karoll, George A. Pierce, Krister Kowalski, Nadia Ben-Marzouk, Jacob Damm, Andrew Danielson, Heidi Dodgen Fessler, Brett Kaufman, Krystal V. L. Pierce, Felix Höflmayer, Brian N. Damiata, and Michael W. Dee. 2017. "Excavations of the New Kingdom Egyptian Fortress in Jaffa, 2011–2014: Traces of Resistance to Egyptian Rule in Canaan." *AJA* 121: 85–133.

Cline, Eric H. 2014. *1177 B.C.: The Year Civilization Collapsed*. Princeton: Princeton University.

Crowfoot, John Winter, and Grace Mary Hood Crowfoot. 1938. *Early Ivories from Samaria, Reports of the Work of the Joint Expedition in 1931–1933 and of the British Expedition in 1935, 2*. London: Palestine Exploration Fund.

Faust, Avraham. 2006. *Israel's Ethnogenesis: Settlement, Interaction, Expansion and Resistance, Approaches to Anthropological Archaeology*. London: Equinox.

Feldman, Marian H. 2009. "Hoarded Treasures: The Megiddo Ivories and the End of the Bronze Age." *Levant* 41: 175–94.

Finkelstein, Israel. 1988. *The Archaeology of the Israelite Settlement*. Jerusalem: Israel Exploration Society.

———. 2013. *The Forgotten Kingdom: The Archaeology and History of Northern Israel*. Atlanta: SBL.

Friedman, Richard Elliott. 2017. *The Exodus: How It Happened and Why It Matters*. New York: HarperOne.

Gadot, Yuval. 2010. "The Late Bronze Egyptian Estate at Aphek." *TA* 37: 48–66.

Gonen, Rivka. 1984. "Urban Canaan in the Late Bronze Period." *BASOR* 253: 61–73.

———. 1992a. *Burial Patterns and Cultural Diversity in Late Bronze Age Canaan*. Winona Lake: Eisenbrauns.

———. 1992b. "The Late Bronze Age." Pages 211–57 in *The Archaeology of Ancient Israel*. Edited by Amnon Ben-Tor. New Haven: Yale University.

Hendel, Ronald S. 2001. "The Exodus in Biblical Memory." *JBL* 120: 601–22.

———. 2015. "The Exodus as Cultural Memory: Egyptian Bondage and the Song of the Sea." Pages 65–77 in *Israel's Exodus in Transdisciplinary Perspective: Text, Archaeology, Culture, and Geoscience*. Edited by Thomas E. Levy, Tammi J. Schneider and William H. C. Propp. New York: Springer.

Higginbotham, Carolyn R. 2000. *Egyptianization and Elite Emulation in Ramesside Palestine: Governance and Accommodation on the Imperial Periphery*. Leiden: Brill.

Hoffmeier, James K. 1997. *Israel in Egypt: The Evidence for the Authenticity of the Exodus Tradition*. New York: Oxford University Press.

———. 2005. *Ancient Israel in Sinai: The Evidence for the Authenticity of the Wilderness Tradition*. Oxford: Oxford University Press.

Höflmayer, Felix. 2015. "Egypt's 'Empire' in the Southern Levant during the Early 18th Dynasty." Pages 191–206 in *Policies of Exchange: Political Systems and Modes of Interaction in the Aegean and the Near East in the 2nd Millennium B.C.E.*. Edited by Birgitta Eder and Reginen Pruzsinszky. Vienna: Österreichischen Akademie der Wissenschaften.

Homan, Michael M. 2002. *To Your Tents, O Israel!: The Terminology, Function, Form, and Symbolism of Tents in the Hebrew Bible and the Ancient Near East*. Leiden: Brill.

Horowitz, Wayne, Takayoshi Oshima, and Seth Sanders. 2018. *Cuneiform in Canaan: The Next Generation*. 2nd ed. University Park: Eisenbrauns.

Kaniewski, David, Nick Marriner, Joachim Bretschneider, Greta Jans, Christophe Morhange, Rachid Cheddadi, Thierry Otto, Frédéric Luce, and Elise Van Campo. 2019. "300-year Drought Frames Late Bronze Age to Early Iron Age transition in the Near East: New Palaeoecological Data from Cyprus and Syria." *Regional Environmental Change*. Online: doi: 10.1007/s10113-018-01460-w.

Kempinski, Aharon. 1992. "Middle and Late Bronze Age Fortifications." Pages 127–42 in *The Architecture of Ancient Israel: From the Prehistoric to the Persian Periods*. Edited by Aharon Kempinski and Ronny Reich. Jerusalem: Israel Exploration Society.

Killebrew, Ann E. 2017. "'Out of the Land of Egypt, Out of the House of Slavery…' (Exodus 20:2): Forced Migration, Slavery, and the Emergence of Israel." Pages 151–58 in *Rethinking Israel: Studies in the History and Archaeology of Ancient Israel in Honor of Israel Finkelstein*. Edited by Oded Lipschitz, Yuval Gadot and Matthew Adams. Winona Lake: Eisenbrauns.

Lambdin, Thomas O. 1953. "Egyptian Loan Words in the Old Testament." *JAOS* 73: 145–55.

Levy, Thomas E., Tammi J. Schneider, and William H. C. Propp, eds. 2015. *Israel's Exodus in Transdisciplinary Perspective: Text, Archaeology, Culture, and Geoscience, Quantitative Methods in the Humanities and Social Sciences*. New York: Springer.

Martin, Mario A. S. 2011. *Egyptian-Type Pottery in the Late Bronze Age Southern Levant*. Vienna: Österreichische Akademie der Wissenschaften.

Mazar, Amihai. 2015. "Iron Age I: Northern Coastal Plain, Galilee, Samaria, Jezreel Valley, Judah, and Negev." Pages 5–70 in *The Ancient Pottery of Israel and Its Neighbors from the Iron Age through the Hellenistic Period*. Edited by Seymour Gitin. Jerusalem: Israel Exploration Society.

Morris, Ellen Fowles. 2005. *The Architecture of Imperialism: Military Bases and the Evolution of Foreign Policy in Egypt's New Kingdom*. Leiden: Brill.

———. 2018. *Ancient Egyptian Imperialism*. Hoboken: Wiley Blackwell.

Mullins, Robert A. 2015. "The Emergence of Israel in Retrospect." Pages 517–25 in *Israel's Exodus in Transdisciplinary Perspective: Text, Archaeology, Culture, and Geoscience*. Edited by Thomas E. Levy, Tammi J. Schneider and William H. C. Propp. New York: Springer.

Mullins, Robert A., and Eli Yannai. 2019. "Late Bronze Age I-II." Pages 151–257, 422–33 in *The Ancient Pottery of Israel and Its Neighbors from the Middle Bronze Age through the Late Bronze Age*. Edited by Seymour Gitin. Jerusalem: Israel Exploration Society.

Na'aman, Nadav. 1981. "Economic Aspects of the Egyptian Occupation of Canaan." *IEJ* 31: 172–85.

Noegel, Scott B. 2015. "The Egyptian Origin of the Ark of the Covenant." Pages 223–42 in *Israel's Exodus in Transdisciplinary Perspective: Text, Archaeology, Culture, and Geoscience*. Edited by Thomas E. Levy, Tammi J. Schneider and William H. C. Propp. New York: Springer.

Oren, Eliezer D. 1984. "'Governor's Residences' in Canaan under the New Kingdom: A Case Study of Egyptian Administration." *JSSEA* 14: 37–56.

Panitz-Cohen, Nava. 2006. "'Off the Wall': Wall Brackets and Cypriots in the Iron Age I Israel." Pages 613–36 in *"I Will Speak the Riddles of Ancient Times": Archaeological and Historical Studies in Honor of Amihai Mazar on the Occasion of His Sixtieth Birthday*. Edited by Aren M. Maeir and Pierre de Miroschedji. Winona Lake: Eisenbrauns.

———. 2009. "The Local Canaanite Pottery." Pages 195–433 in *Excavations at Tel Beth-Shean 1989–1996, Volume III: The 13th–11th Century BCE Strata in Areas N and S*. Edited by Nava Panitz-Cohen and Amihai Mazar. Jerusalem: Israel Exploration Society and the Institute of Archaeology, Hebrew University.

———. 2014. "The Southern Levant (Cisjordan) during the Late Bronze Age." Pages 541–60 in *The Oxford Handbook of the Archaeology of the Levant (c. 8000–332 BCE)*. Edited by Margreet L. Steiner and Ann E. Killebrew. Oxford: Oxford University Press.

Rollston, Christopher A. 2019. "The Alphabet Comes of Age: The Social Context of Alphabetic Writing in the First Millennium BCE." Pages 371–90 in *The Social Archaeology of the Levant: From Prehistory to the Present*. Edited by Assaf Yasur-Landau, Eric H. Cline and Yorke M. Rowan. Cambridge: Cambridge University Press.

Schniedewind, William M. 2013. *A Social History of Hebrew: Its Origins through the Rabbinic Period, Anchor Yale Bible Reference Library*. New Haven: Yale University Press.

———. 2019. *The Finger of the Scribe: How Scribes Learned to Write the Bible*. New York: Oxford University Press.

Shuval, Menakhem. 1990. "A Catalogue of Early Iron Stamp Seals from Israel." Pages 67–161 in *Studien zu den Stempelsiegeln aus Palästina/Israel: Die frühe Eisenzeit, ein Workshop*. Edited by Othmar Keel, Menakhem Shuval and Christoph Uehlinger. Göttingen: Vandenhoeck & Ruprecht.

Spalinger, Anthony. 2005. *War in Ancient Egypt: The New Kingdom, Ancient World at War*. Malden: Blackwell.

Stager, Lawrence E. 1998. "Forging an Identity: The Emergence of Ancient Israel." Pages 122–75 in *The Oxford History of the Biblical World*. Edited by Michael D. Coogan. New York: Oxford University Press.

Uziel, Joe, and Yuval Gadot. 2010. "The 'Cup-and-Saucer' Vessel: Function, Chronology, Distribution and Symbolism." *IEJ* 60: 41–57.

Wright, Laura. 2018. "Egyptian Iconography." Pages 159–64 in *Behind the Scenes of the Old Testament: Cultural, Social, and Historical Contexts*. Edited by Jonathan S. Greer, John W. Hilber and John H. Walton,. Grand Rapids: Baker Academic.

Zuckerman, Sharon. 2007. "Anatomy of a Destruction: Crisis Architecture, Termination Rituals and the Fall of Canaanite Hazor." *JMA* 20: 3–32.

35
PHILISTINES AND ISRAELITES/ JUDAHITES
Antagonism and Interaction

Aren M. Maeir

The Philistines are extensively depicted in the biblical texts as one of the major peoples/ cultures with whom the Israelites and Judahites interacted during the Iron Age. While many of the relevant biblical texts describe antagonistic relations with the Philistines, some depict other types of interactions. Nevertheless, the dominant narrative about the Philistines, both in popular traditions and interpretations on the one hand, and contemporary scholarship on the other, is that of seeing the Philistines as one of the primary adversaries of Judah and Israel throughout the Iron Age.

While there is no doubt that the Philistines were, at times, serious adversaries and enemies of Israel and Judah, the complex and multi-faceted character of this relationship is seen not only in the textual sources but also in the archaeological record as well. In the following pages, I will first survey the archaeological evidence from the various stages of the Iron Age that can be used to characterize the relationships between the Philistines and Israel/Judah. Following this, I will suggest how this can enable us to better portray these interconnections, in a more sophisticated and multi-faceted manner.

Early Iron Age (ca. 1200–950 BCE)

The appearance of Philistine culture is part of the complex processes that occurred in the transition between the Late Bronze and Iron Ages (Cline 2014; Maeir and Hitchcock 2017a, 2017b). While in the past this was seen as a rather monolithic migration of peoples of Aegean origin (Dothan 1982; Yasur-Landau 2010), more and more evidence and analyses indicate that this was a much more complex and multi-faceted set of processes, comprised of migrant groups of different origins and character, which combined with local populations, to create an "entangled" culture (Maeir and Hitchcock 2017a, 2017b). The complex nature of the early Philistines and the processes through which they went seem to be reflected in the archaeological evidence of connections between the region of Philistia and the Central Hills area (where the early Israelite/Judahite settlement was concentrated).

In the early stages of the development of the Philistine culture (on the pottery, see, Dothan and Zukerman 2015), that is the Philistine 1 (Mycenaean IIIC) phase (Figure 35.1), there is no evidence of connections between these two regions. Only during the 2nd stage of the Philistine culture (Philistine 2; Bichrome; Figure 35.2) is there evidence of interactions.

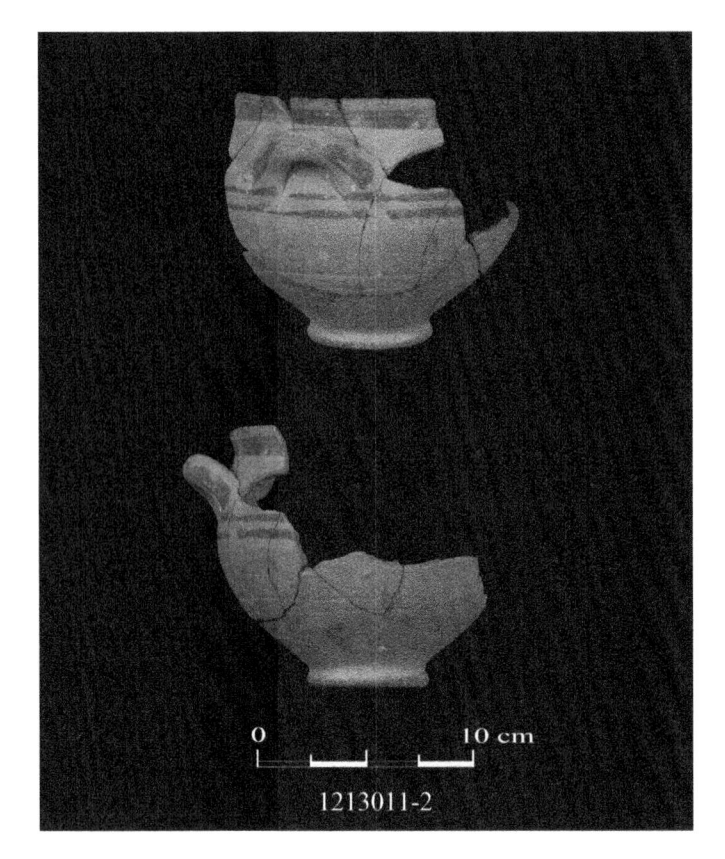

Figure 35.1 Myc IIIC (Philistine 1/Monochrome) Deep Bowl from Tell es-Safi/Gath

Small amounts of Philistine Bichrome pottery were found in the Central Hills (as well as a few other regions in the Southern Levant; Ben-Shlomo and Mommsen 2018; Ben-Shlomo 2019; Keimer 2020; Master 2021). During the later phases of the Iron I, more evidence of connections can be seen. Philistine 3 pottery is found at various sites in the Judean Shephelah, and perhaps in Jerusalem as well. In addition, evidence of the beginning of bi-directional influence can be seen, such as in types of pottery from one region copied and appearing in the other (Ben-Shlomo et al. 2008).

Iron Age IIA (ca. 950–800 BCE)

During the Iron IIA, there is more archaeological evidence of connections between these regions. Late Philistine Decorated Ware (Figure 35.3; formerly termed "Ashdod Ware;" Ben-Shlomo, Shai, and Maeir 2004) is found at sites in Judah, such as Jerusalem (Uziel, Szanton and Cohen-Weinberger 2015; Cohen-Weinberger, Szanton, and Uziel 2017), Motza (Kisilevitz and Lipschits 2020), Tell en-Nasbeh (Keimer 2020: 628) and Khirbet Qeiyafa (Kang and Garfinkel 2009). Figurines reminiscent of figurines from Philistia were found at Moza (Kisilevitz 2015:166–68) and cultic/symbolic objects such as "headcups," were found in the City of David, Jerusalem (Mazar and Karlin 2015; Uziel, Szanton, and Cohen-Weinberger 2015) and at Kh. Dawara north of Jerusalem (Finkelstein 1990; Na'aman 2012). From the

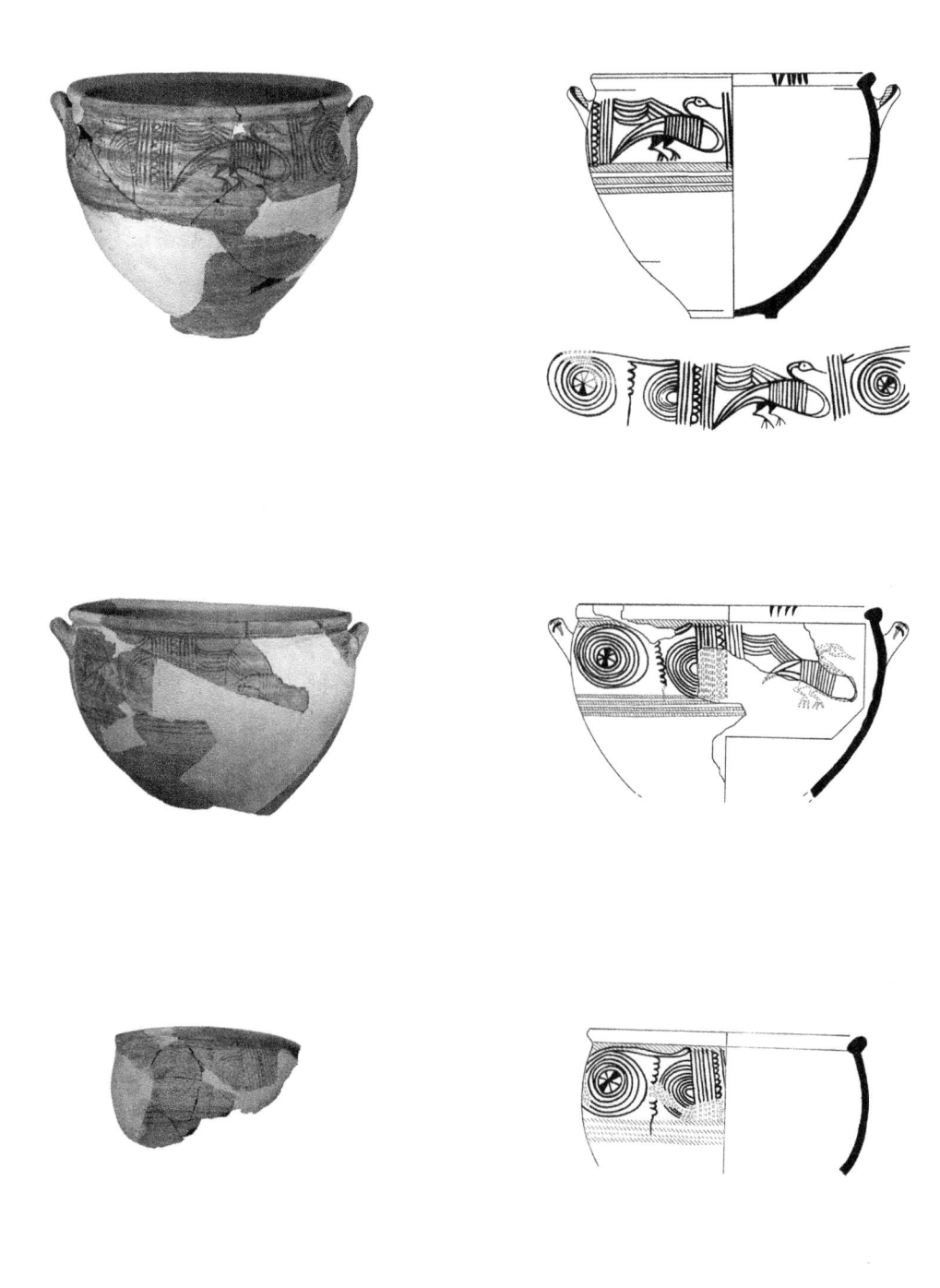

Philistines and Israelites/Judahites: Antagonism and Interaction

Figure 35.2 Bichrome (Philistine 2) Decorated Kraters from Tell es-Safi/Gath

Figure 35.3 Late Philistine Decorated Ware from Tell es-Safi/Gath

other direction, Judahite finds are seen in Philistia, such as a jar with an inscription found in a temple at Tell es-Safi/Gath (Maeir and Eshel 2014).

The bi-directional influence between the regions continues to be seen in the appearance and appropriation of material culture in one region from the other (Figure 35.4), such as in the expansion of the use of "Philistine"-style cooking vessels in Judah and Israel (Figure 35.5; Ben-Shlomo et al. 2008). Additional evidence of connections between Philistia and Judah may be reflected in imported objects such as fish, bulla, and other items that are found in Judah, which may very likely have arrived via Philistia (Maeir 2022). All told, there seems to have been extensive contacts between the regions and cultures.

Iron Age IIB (ca. 800–700 BCE)

The material culture at several Iron IIB sites in Philistia points to interactions between the Philistines and the Israelite/Judahites. This can be seen in various pottery types from one of these cultures that are found in ceramic assemblages of the other (Gitin 2015a: 257–59; Herzog and Singer-Avitz 2015: 214), perhaps indicating cultural influence and trade. In addition, there are sites such as Tel Batash and Tell es-Safi/Gath where changes in material culture during this period hint at shifts in political control and cultural affiliation (Mazar and Panitz-Cohen 2001: 287–88; Chadwick and Maeir 2012). In both cases, close relations between the Philistines and the Israelites/Judahites are reflected through this, and it can be assumed that other aspects suggest this as well. For example, the appearance of the Judahite type of olive presses in Iron IIB–IIC Philistia might be an indication of such influence.

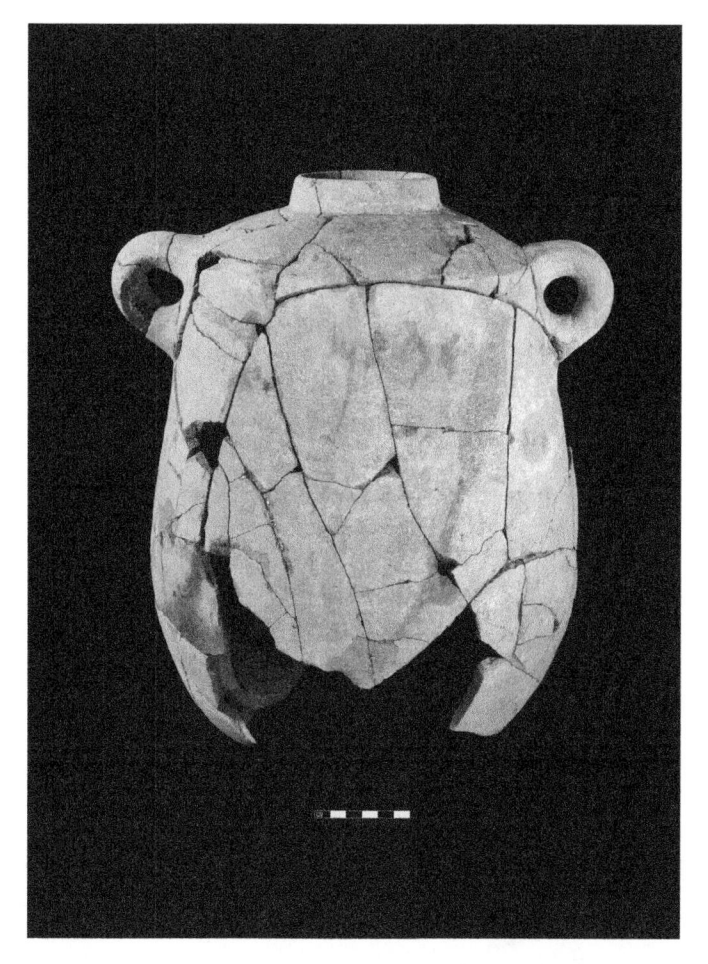

Figure 35.4 Jar from the Jerusalem Area with a Judahite Inscription, found in the Iron IIA temple in Area D West in the lower city of Tell es-Safi/Gath

While it is clear that olive oil was an important product in Iron I–IIA Philistia, other types of olive presses were common in these earlier stages and the "Judahite" type appears only later (Maeir, Welch, and Eniukhina 2021).

Iron Age IIC (ca. 700–600 BCE)

Throughout the Iron Age, the Shephelah was a region where much of the interface between the Philistine culture and the Israelite/Judahite culture occurred. The accepted interpretation of what happened in the Shephelah during the Iron IIC was that following the late 8th century BCE Assyrian campaigns, the Judahite presence in this region was of minimal character (Bunimovitz and Lederman 2017). Recent finds from the eastern part of the site of Tel Beth Shemesh appear to change this view, with substantial evidence of Judahite presence in the eastern Shephelah during the Iron IIC (Haddad, Ben-Ari, and de Groot 2020). Thus, this region most likely continued to be a region of intense interactions between these cultures.

As in the Iron IIB, bi-directional cultural influences are reflected in the Iron IIC pottery assemblages in Philistia and Judah (Gitin 2015b: 345; 384–85), indicating various types of cultural interactions. It was suggested that the discovery of numerous horned altars in Iron IIC Philistia is evidence of Israelite cultic influence, due to Israelite refugees who fled to the region after the fall of the Kingdom of Israel in 722 BCE (Gitin 1993). However, this is difficult to accept since horned altars are already known in Philistia, in Iron IIA Gath (Figure 35.6; Maeir 2012: 54). That said, the possibility of other cultural influences cannot be denied. Archaeological evidence of the close connections between Philistia and Judah can be seen in the archaeobotanical evidence from the 604 BCE destruction level of Ashkelon, where evidence for grain originating from the Judean highlands was found (Weiss and Kislev 2004; Faust and Weiss 2005).[1] This along with various evidence of Judahite pottery in Philistia and pottery from Philistia in Judah, indicate that these two regions closely interacted during this period.

Integrating the Archaeological Data

There is very little reflection in the Hebrew Bible of the actual appearance and development of the Philistine culture during the early Iron Age. While vague hints of an Aegean connection can be found (Amos 9:7; Jer 47:4; Zeph 2:5), there is little evidence that the biblical authors had a detailed picture of the early Philistine culture and how it developed (just as they seem to be oblivious of the Egyptian rule in Late Bronze Age Canaan). While it is clear that many of the biblical narratives that attempt to reflect the early Iron Age were written at later stages, it is possible that a lack of any traditions relating to this early phase of the Philistine culture may reflect limited connections between these cultures during the initial Iron

Figure 35.5 Selection of Iron IB–IIA Philistine Cooking Jugs from Tell es-Safi/Gath

Age, which is supported by the dearth of archaeological evidence for connections between Philistia and the Central Hills.

At a slightly later stage of the early Iron Age, this appears to change. Philistine-style pottery (whether imported or locally made) dating to the mid- to late Iron I (Philistine 1 and Philistine 2), which is found in the Central Hills and the Jezreel Valley (Martin 2017; Ben-Shlomo 2019; Keimer 2020; Master 2021), point to connections between Philistia and Israel/Judah at the time, which might be reflected in the various biblical narratives of connections, often of a war-related character, between the two cultures. While in the past this has been argued that one can posit even a Philistine control of parts of the Central Hills in the late Iron I, Master (2021) has recently argued that a more likely scenario was that this might reflect a situation with ongoing Philistine raids into the region, and not actual control.[2] That said, as I have suggested recently (Maeir 2018; see below), the military might of the Philistines, as reflected in the biblical texts, might be somewhat exaggerated.

What can be said about the character of the relationships between the Philistines and the Israelites and Judahites during the early stages of the Iron IIA, the next phase of the Iron Age? Is it justified to accept biblical traditions that the character of these relations "flipped"

Figure 35.6 Two-horned stone altar found in the Iron IIA temple in Area D West in the lower city of Tell es-Safi/Gath

at this time? Did the "United Monarchy" dominate Philistia? I believe that just as a Philistine domination of the Central Hills in the late Iron I has been questioned, so also a Davidic conquest and subjugation of Philistia is questionable. In the past, it has been suggested that Tel Qasile, Stratum X, was destroyed by a Judahite campaign (perhaps of King David) in the late 11th/early 10th centuries BCE (Mazar 1985). Likewise, Faust (2013, 2015a, 2015b; Faust and Lev-Tov 2011) has repeatedly claimed that a supposed Judahite dominance of Philistia in the 10th century BCE had a profound effect on the development of the Philistine culture. In his view, due to Judahite political and cultural domination, the Philistine culture sheds the supposedly Aegean-influenced material facets, such as decorated pottery and the consumption of pork. In addition, he suggests that at this time the Philistines commenced the practice of circumcision.

This view of the relations between Philistia and the early Judahite monarchy is hard to accept (Maeir, Hitchcock, and Horwitz 2013; Maeir and Hitchcock 2016). Following more than 20 years of excavation, it is clear that Gath was a large and prosperous city, from the early Iron I until its final destruction by Hazael in the Iron IIA (ca. 830 BCE). During the Iron IB and IIA, the site was of extensive size, including an upper and lower city (of ca. 45–50 ha), most likely the largest city in the Levant at the time. There is no evidence of any traumatic events in the history of Philistine Gath, from the early 12th century BCE until the Hazael destruction, nor any major, drastic, or sudden changes in the material culture at the site. The finds at Gath argue quite convincingly that the site was a large and prosperous site throughout the Iron Age I–IIA, most likely the primary polity in the Southern Levant at the time. In fact, if one can speak of dominant kingdoms in the southern Levant during the Iron IIA, the Kingdom of Gath is a much more likely candidate than the early Judahite Kingdom. Possible evidence of this may be seen at Kh. Qeiyafa (Garfinkel, Kreimerman, and Zilberg 2016). Whether one accepts the identification of the site as Judahite or not, the close proximity to Gath (ca. 11 km to the east of Tell es-Safi/Gath) and the fact that the fortified site of Kh. Qeiyafa was destroyed soon after it was built, raises the possibility that the site was destroyed by the Kingdom of Gath, as it was seen as a threat. The large and massively fortified site of Gath, flourishing during the Iron I and Iron IIA, is clearly a large and prosperous kingdom, and there is no evidence at all of Judahite domination.

Similarly, the claim that from the Iron IIA, the Philistine culture loses its unique aspects due to cultural domination is hard to accept. This is seen in various facets, such as the continuation of early motifs in Iron IIA Philistine decorated pottery (Maeir and Shai 2015), the continuation of pork consumption at some Philistine sites (Horwitz et al. 2017), and non-local cultic behaviors (Hitchcock, Maeir, and Dagan 2016). Foreign influences are indeed seen in Philistia in the Iron I and Iron II, and some of the earlier non-local cultural manifestations of the early Philistine culture disappear over an extended period, but this does not occur suddenly in the 10th century BCE. In addition, while Levantine influences are seen in various aspects of daily life, Philistine influences on Judahite material culture are seen as well, such as in cooking vessels, LPDW pottery and Philistine cultic items appearing in Judah (as noted above).

Thus, as opposed to a picture of Judahite domination of Philistia during the Iron IIA, a picture emerges of the Kingdom of Gath being the dominant polity at the time, and the ongoing relations between Philistia in the west and the Shephelah and the Central Hill regions in the east were of a bi-directional nature. If anything, one can assume that the Kingdom of Gath broadcasted power from west to east, and it most probably curtailed the ability (or at least the extent) of the Judahite Kingdom's expansion westwards in the Iron IIA. It should be noted that at this time, the closest Philistine city to Gath, Ekron, was not a large site, while on the coast, Ashdod seems to have been more substantial than Ashkelon at this time (see Maeir 2012: 39–40). Thus, most probably, during the Iron IIA, Gath was the dominant inland Philistine city, while Ashdod may have had this role along the coast.

There are divergent opinions on the dating and context of the biblical narratives relating to the Philistines. Some see them as reflecting the early stages of the Israelite/Judahite monarchies (Singer 2013; Niesiołowski-Spanò 2016; Master 2021; Münnich 2021). On the other hand, there are those who suggest that there is very little historicity and realistic connection between the Philistines depicted in the biblical text and those that actually existed, as the relevant biblical texts, according to such views are post-Iron Age (Davies 1992; Lemche 1993; Thompson 1999; Rodan 2015). Israel Finkelstein (2002) suggested that a large part of what is described in the biblical text regarding the Philistines reflects the very late Iron II, and reflects the strong Greek influence in the Levant during the 8th and 7th centuries BCE.

I believe that the evidence is more complex and multi-layered. There is no substantial evidence of an in-depth knowledge and detailed reflection of Iron I Philistine culture and society in the biblical text. That said, I believe that there is a reflection of some of the socio-political realia of the Iron I (at least of the Iron IB) in Philistia, and its relation to Judah is evident, in the biblical text. For example, the dominant portrayal that the biblical narratives relating to pre- and early monarchical times espouse for the Philistines in general, and the Kingdom of Gath in particular, seems to quite accurately reflect what we know from the archaeological evidence. In particular, the large city of Gath, from the mid-late Iron I (11th century BCE) up until the destruction of the city by Hazael, is eloquent evidence of this. The prominent position of Gath in the biblical text, which is terminated in the late 9th century BCE with the destruction of Hazael, could not have been reflected in the biblical texts if these texts did not retain historical memories of at least the Iron IIA and perhaps even into the later parts of the Iron I. In addition to this, there may be some linguistic hints to early Philistine language, including early names and words, embedded in the biblical narratives (see also discussion of Philistine language above). Finkelstein suggested (2002) that the biblical term for the leaders of the Philistines, is a reflection of the use of the Greek term *tyranos*, dating to the late Iron Age, and in his opinion, indicative of the mainly late Iron Age realia reflected in the biblical description of the Philistines. Contrary to this view, *seren*, may very well reflect the Luwian term *tarwanis* (military leader), known from as early as the 10th century BCE (Giusfredi 2009; Maeir, Davis, and Hitchcock 2016) – and if this is the case, the retention of an early term for the Philistine leaders can be seen as an example of the retention of early Iron Age cultural facets in the biblical narratives regarding the Philistines.

In the past, I suggested that several phallic objects found at Tell es-Safi/Gath in the Iron IIA, 9th century BCE destruction level, might be related to the enigmatic "ophalim" mentioned in the Ark Narrative in I Samuel 4–6 (Figure 35.7; Maeir 2007). This might be an example of early Philistine cultic manifestations, remembered in the biblical text, even if the latter is comprised of significant portions that were compiled and edited at a later phase.

On the other hand, to relate the biblical narratives on the Philistines, and their relations with Israel/Judah in pre- and early monarchical times, in a straightforward, and historically accurate manner, seems unwarranted. An example of this can be seen in the veritable lack of references to the Kingdom of Gath in the 9th century BCE, save for its destruction by Hazael (II Kings 12:17/18). Even though the city was the largest city, and perhaps the most dominant polity, both in Philistia and even the entire southern Levant at the time, there is no explicit mention of its role in 9th-century politics. Even if one assumes that some of the mentions of Gath in the David stories (Na'aman 2002) reflect a 9th century BCE realia, Gath does not figure in any of the biblical depictions of the geopolitical events of the 9th century

Figure 35.7 Phallic-shaped cultic vessels from cultic corners in Iron IIA Area A, in the upper city of Tell es-Safi/Gath

BCE. This indicates that there was a lack of information about Philistia in the Iron IIA, by the time the biblical narratives were compiled.

As noted often in the past (Weitzman 2002; Maeir and Hitchcock 2016; Leonard-Fleckman 2021), the Shephelah, the region between Philistia (the southern Coastal Plain) and the Central Hills, was a major player in the interactions between the Philistine and Israelite/Judahite cultures. Not only are many of the biblical narratives about such interactions placed in this region (the Samson narratives, David and Goliath, David and Achish, etc.), but the archaeological evidence (above) also indicates that in this region there was much cultural interchange and interaction – and even sites that "switched" cultural affiliations during the Iron Age. These complex interactions are seen at sites which are "full-fledged" Philistine sites, such as Tell es-Safi/Gath, as well as sites whose shifting identities are more complex (such as Beth Shemesh and Azekah; Maeir and Hitchcock 2016).

For example, at Tell es-Safi/Gath, there are various examples of the complex interface between cult traditions in Philistia and other regions during the Iron Age. As noted above, while Gitin (1993) asserts that four-horned altars reached Philistia by way of Israelites who escaped from the Assyrian destruction of the Kingdom of Israel in the late 8th century BCE, their appearance in earlier Iron IIA contexts indicates a much more complex and drawn-out interaction (Maeir 2012: 24). Similarly, a jar of Judahite origin, with a Judahite name on it, was found in the Philistine temple at Gath, perhaps evidence that people from Judah participated in cult activities at this same temple (Maeir and Eshel 2014). In other words, bi-, and perhaps multi-directional influences in cultic traditions and praxis existed at the time in Philistia and adjacent regions. This ties in with the evidence noted above, of bi-directional cultural influences seen in Philistia and adjacent regions, in aspects such as pottery, cooking traditions, and cultic objects. It can be perhaps suggested that the intense and multi-directional interactions between Judah and Philistia, as depicted in the biblical Samson cycle (Weitzman 2002; Leonard-Fleckman 2021), might in some way mirror the complex interactions that actually existed in this region during the Iron Age.

When one views the biblical narratives about the Philistines, and in particular their relationship with Israel and Judah during the early Iron Age, a repeating motif is the Philistines' strength and military dominance, something that has been accentuated in ancient and modern biblical interpretations (1 Sam 4:1–10; 13:19–21). Somewhat surprisingly, there is little evidence of this in the archaeological record. After more than a century of excavations in Philistia, there is very little material reflection that can be seen as evidence that the Philistines had an overly martial, and militarily dominant culture. Thus, while no doubt there were cases where the Philistines were the dominant polities (such as Gath was during Iron IB–IIA), it would appear that the biblical image of a mighty and feared enemy was perhaps over accentuated, for ideological reasons, in the Bible and later interpretations (Maeir 2018). Thus, while Philistine Gath was a dominant polity in the Iron IIA, I believe the Philistines' might as depicted in the biblical text is a purposeful exaggeration.

The complex nature of the biblical traditions about the Philistines – and their reflection in the archaeological remains – might be reflected in the biblical traditions connecting the Philistines to giants. I have suggested (Maeir 2020) that the massive remains of the destroyed city of Gath of the Philistines, seen during later phases of the Iron Age – may have served to foster the biblical tradition of Philistine giants. Associated traditions and memories may also have arisen from these monumental remains, including: (a) various traditions in the Davidic cycle in relationship to Gath, even if deeply changed over time, such as the stories of David and Goliath (1 Sam 17), David and Achish (1 Sam 21:10–15), and Solomon and Shimei (1 Kgs 2:36–46); (b) the biblical memory of the destruction of the large city of Gath by Hazael, and the moral lesson to be learned from this (Amos 6:2; Maeir 2004); and (c) King Uzziah of Judah's supposed destruction of the walls of Gath in the early 8th c. BCE (2 Chr 26:6), which, based on the archaeological evidence at the site, is without any factual basis (Maeir 2012: 50, 54). The impressive remains of Gath, easily seen long after its destruction, with massive fortifications and large-scale masonry all located close to the surface (since the lower city of Gath was not resettled after the Hazael destruction), contributed to the creation of myths about the former giant inhabitants of Gath (Figure 35.8). These giants, and their compatriots, were seen as those who built these impressive remains in the early stages of Israelite and Judahite history. This larger-than-life, even frightening, image of the Philistines, among which giant warriors dwelt, dovetails with a general tendency to portray the Philistines as a fierce and powerful enemy, an image that seems to have been emphasized in the biblical texts (McDonagh 2004; Maeir 2018). In turn, this continued to influence the perception and reception of the Philistines, and their role in the ancient Levant, until modern times (Silberman 1998). Considering this, I believe caution is warranted as to how the modern "images" of the Philistines, based on biblical traditions and modern ideological constructs, can affect our understanding of the past, and create misguided reconstructions of the early Iron Age.

Biblical depictions do retain information on certain aspects of the early Iron Age Philistines, but significant parts of these depictions reflect later ideologically driven narratives. Names and terms relating to the Philistines appearing in the biblical texts and epigraphic finds, clearly indicate connections with the early Iron Age (Davis, Maeir, and Hitchcock 2015; Maeir, Davis, and Hitchcock 2016). Similarly, as previously noted, the important status

Figure 35.8 View of Iron IB and Iron IIA fortifications and gate in Area D East in the lower city of Tell es-Safi/Gath

of Gath as portrayed in the biblical texts relating to the period of the early Judahite monarchy fits in well with the archaeological evidence from the excavations at Tell es-Safi/Gath (see Maeir 2012 and additional literature therein). Moreover, the image of the Philistines as a socially, technologically, and even military advanced society (in comparison to the Israelites) is well evidenced by the archaeological finds at the various Philistine sites (Maeir 2012).

However, many of the depictions relating to the Philistines during the early Iron Age clearly include aspects more at home with later parts of the Iron Age, and in some cases, post-Iron Age periods as well. While I do not accept suggestions that all aspects of the David and Goliath story relate to the very late Iron Age (Finkelstein 2002) or post-Iron Age (Gmirkin 2006; Rodan 2015), the mixed nature of Goliath's weaponry (already noted by Galling 1966), and clear evidence of the complex editing of the David and Goliath narrative (Auld and Ho 1992; van der Kooij 1992) indicate that the story reflects early and later aspects mixed together.

A similar insight can be seen from study of the depictions of the Sea Peoples and the Philistines in the Medinet Habu reliefs, which are often seen as straightforward historical depictions of the early Iron Age Philistines. However, despite the fact that some contemporary early Iron Age evidence can be gleaned from these depictions, a facile extrapolation of these depictions to recreate early Iron Age Philistine society and military prowess is hard to accept, as it is clear that these depictions are highly ideologically-colored (Ben-Dor Evian 2015).

Finally, modern perceptions of the Philistines and the Sea Peoples contribute to this image. Silberman (1998) has already noted the very strong influence of Victorian-era worldviews on the early interpretation of the Philistines as invading peoples, and the ongoing influence of these views in modern research. Other aspects of modern ideological underpinnings undoubtedly contribute to this as well.

In summary, throughout most of the Iron Age there were ongoing and intensive interactions between the Philistines and the Israelites. Some were of an antagonistic nature befitting neighboring groups competing for resources, while others were of a more friendly nature, reflecting the daily interactions of people living in adjacent regions. This is mirrored in the biblical texts as well as in the archaeological remains. While modern narratives about the Philistines often stress the former (antagonistic) nature of these relations, both types should be taken into account when understanding the character of these interactions. To summarize, it is clear that if one compares the Philistine culture to that of the early Israelites and Judahites, it does appear that the former had distinct technological, organizational, and most probably military advantages. At the same time, some of the depictions of the Philistines and their culture, in the biblical texts – and their later receptions – may be somewhat overstated. I would suggest that attempts to recreate the social, political, and military characteristics of the Philistines, and their relations with other contemporary cultures should be more cautious in accepting age-old images of who the Philistines were. Instead, a close review of up-to-date historical and archaeological data should be used, which seems to paint a somewhat different picture.

Notes

1 Although one should note the possibility that that the foodstuffs from Judah (and other regions) might have arrived in Ashkelon due to the exceptional situation of preparations for the Babylonian onslaught, and do not represent the regular trade connections in agricultural goods between these regions.
2 But see Keimer 2020 who argues for an actual Philistine presence at Tell en-Nasbeh.

Bibliography

Auld, A. G., and C. Y. S. Ho. 1992. "The Making of David and Goliath." *JSOT* 17: 19–39.
Ben-Dor Evian, S. 2015. "The Battles between Ramesses III and the Sea-Peoples. When, Where and Who? An Iconic Analysis of the Egyptian Reliefs." *ZÄS* (2): 151–68.
Ben-Shlomo, D. 2019. *The Iron Age Pottery of Jerusalem: A Typological and Technological Study*. Ariel: Ariel University Press.
Ben-Shlomo, D., and H. Mommsen. 2018. "Pottery Production in Jerusalem during the Iron Age: A New Compositional Profiling." *Geoarchaeology* 33: 349–63.
Ben-Shlomo, D., I. Shai, and A. M. Maeir. 2004. "Late Philistine Decorated Ware ('Ashdod Ware'): Typology, Chronology and Production Centers." *BASOR* 335: 1–35.
Ben-Shlomo, D., I. Shai, A. Zukerman, and A. M. Maeir. 2008. "Cooking Identities: Aegean-Style and Philistine Cooking Jugs and Cultural Interaction in the Southern Levant during the Iron Age." *AJA* 112: 225–46.
Bunimovitz, S., and Z. Lederman. 2017. "Swinging on the 'Sorek Seesaw': Tel Beth-Shemesh and the Sorek Valley in the Iron Age." Pages 27–43 in *The Shephelah During the Iron Age: Recent Archaeological Studies*. Edited by O. Lipschits and A. M. Maeir. Winona Lake: Eisenbrauns.
Chadwick, J. R., and A. M. Maeir. 2012. "How Households Can Illuminate the Historical Record: The Judahite Houses at Gath of the Philistines (A Case Study in Household Archaeology at Tell es-Safi/Gath, Israel)." Pages 601–18 in *Household Archaeology: New Perspectives from the Near East and Beyond*. Edited by B. Parker and C. Foster. Winona Lake: Eisenbrauns.
Cline, E. H. 2014. *1177 B.C.: The Year Civilization Collapsed*. Princeton: Princeton University Press.

Cohen-Weinberger, A., N. Szanton, and J. Uziel. 2017. "Ethnofabrics: Petrographic Analysis as a Tool for Illuminating Cultural Interactions and Trade Relations between Judah and Philistia During the Iron II." *BASOR* 377: 1–20.

Davies, P. 1992. *The Search for "Ancient Israel."* Sheffield: JSOT Press.

Davis, B., A. M. Maeir, and L. A. Hitchcock. 2015. "Disentangling Entangled Objects: Iron Age Inscriptions from Philistia as a Reflection of Cultural Processes." *IEJ* 65: 140–65.

Dothan, T. 1982. *The Philistines and Their Material Culture.* Jerusalem: Israel Exploration Society.

Dothan, T., and A. Zukerman. 2015. "Chapter 1.2. Iron Age I: Philistia." Pages 71–96 in *The Ancient Pottery of Israel and Its Neighbors from the Iron Age Through the Hellenistic Period, Vol. 1.* Edited by S. Gitin. Jerusalem: Israel Exploration Society.

Faust, A. 2013. "From Regional Power to Peaceful Neighbour: Philistia in the Iron I–II Transition." *IEJ* 63: 154–73.

———. 2015a. "The Bible, Archaeology, and the Practice of Circumcision in Israelite and Philistine Societies." *JBL* 134: 273–90.

———. 2015b. "Pottery and Society in Iron Age Philistia: Feasting, Identity, Economy, and Gender." *BASOR* 373: 167–98.

Faust, A., and J. Lev-Tov. 2011. "The Constitution of Philistine Identity: Ethnic Dynamics in Twelfth to Tenth Century Philistia." *OJA* 30: 13–31.

Faust, A., and E. Weiss. 2005. "Judah, Philistia, and the Mediterranean World: Reconstructing the Economic System of the Seventh Century BCE." *BASOR* 338: 71–92.

Finkelstein, I. 1990. "Excavations at Khirbet Ed-Dawwara: An Iron Age Site Northeast of Jerusalem." *TA* 17: 163–208.

———. 2002. "The Philistines in the Bible: A Late-Monarchic Perspective." *JSOT* 27: 131–67.

Galling, K. 1966. "Goliath und Siene Rüstung." *VT Supplement* 15: 150–69.

Garfinkel, Y., I. Kreimerman, and P. Zilberg. 2016. *Debating Khirbet Qeiyafa: A Fortified City in Judah from the Time of King David.* Jerusalem: Israel Exploration Society.

Gitin, S. 1993. "Seventh Century B.C.E. Cultic Elements at Ekron." Pages 248–58 in *Biblical Archaeology Today, 1990: Proceedings of the Second International Congress on Biblical Archaeology, Jerusalem, June-July 1990.* Jerusalem: Israel Exploration Society.

———. 2015a. "Chapter 2.5. Iron Age IIA–B: Philistia." Pages 257–80 in *The Ancient Pottery of Israel and Its Neighbors from the Iron Age Through the Hellenistic Period, Vol. 1.* Edited by S. Gitin. Jerusalem: Israel Exploration Society.

———. 2015b. "Chapter 3.5. Iron Age IIC: Philistia." Pages 383–418 in *The Ancient Pottery of Israel and Its Neighbors from the Iron Age Through the Hellenistic Period, Vol. 1.* Edited by S. Gitin. Jerusalem: Israel Exploration Society.

Giusfredi, F. 2009. "The Problem of the Luwian Title *Tarwanis*." *AoF* 36: 140–45.

Gmirkin, R. 2006. *Berossus and Genesis, Manetho and Exodus: Hellenistic Histories and the Date of the Pentateuch.* New York: T & T Clark.

Haddad, E., N. Ben-Ari, and A. de Groot. 2020. "A Century Old Enigma: The Seventh-Century BCE Settlement at Tel Beth Shemesh (East)." *IEJ* 70: 173–88.

Herzog, Z., and L. Singer-Avitz. 2015. "Chapter 2.5. Iron Age IIA–B: Judah and the Negev." Pages 213–56 in *The Ancient Pottery of Israel and Its Neighbors from the Iron Age Through the Hellenistic Period, Vol. 1.* Edited by S. Gitin. Jerusalem: Israel Exploration Society.

Hitchcock, L. A., A. M. Maeir, and A. Dagan. 2016. "The Entanglement of Aegean Style Ritual Actions in Philistine Culture." Pages 519–26 in *METAPHYSIS: Ritual, Myth and Symbolism in the Aegean Bronze Age.* Edited by E. Alram-Stern et al. Liège: Université de Liège.

Horwitz, L. K., A. Gardeisen, A. M. Maeir, and L. A. Hitchcock. 2017. "A Brief Contribution to the Iron Age Philistine Pig Debate." Pages 93–116 in *The Wide Lens in Archaeology: Honoring Brian Hesse's Contributions to Anthropological Archaeology.* Edited by J. Lev-Tov, P. Hesse, and A. Gilbert. Atlanta: Lockwood Press.

Kang, H.-G., and Y. Garfinkel. 2009. "Chapter 7: Ashdod Ware I: Middle Philistine Decorated Ware." Pages 151–60 in *Khirbet Qeiyafa Vol. 1. Excavation Report 2007–2008.* Edited by Y. Garfinkel and S. Ganor. Jerusalem: Israel Exploration Society.

Karlin, M., and E. Mazar. 2015. "A Lion-Headed Rhyton from the Ophel." Pages 559–62 in *The Ophel Excavations to the South of the Temple Mount, 2009–2013: Final Reports Volume I.* Edited by E. Mazar. Jerusalem: Shoham Academic Research and Publication.

Keimer, Kyle H. 2020. "Ritual or Military Action? Interpreting Israel's Muster at Mizpah in 1 Sam 7:2–17." *VT* 70: 620–33.

Kisilevitz, S. 2015. "The Iron IIA Judahite Temple at Tel Moza." *TA* 42: 147–64.

Kisilevitz, S., and O. Lipschits. 2020. "Tel Moẓa: An Economic and Cultic Center from the Iron II (First Temple Period)." Pages 295–312 in *The Mega Project at Motza (Moẓa): The Neolithic and Later Occupations up to the 20th Century*. Edited by H. Khalaily, A. Re'em, J. Vardi and I. Milevski. Jerusalem: Israel Antiquities Authority.

Lemche, N. 1993. "The Old Testament: A Hellenistic Book." *SJOT* 7: 163–93.

Leonard-Fleckman, M. 2021. "Binding Samson to Yhwh: From Social Ambiguity to Order in the Samson Cycle." Pages 49–68 in *God and Gods in the Deuteronomistic History*. Edited by C. Carvalho and J. McLaughlin. Washington, DC: Catholic Biblical Association.

Maeir, A. M. 2004. "The Historical Background and Dating of Amos VI 2: An Archaeological Perspective from Tell es-Safi/Gath." *VT* 54: 319–34.

———. 2007. "A New Interpretation of the Term ʿopalim (עפלים) in Light of Recent Archaeological Finds from Philistia." *JSOT* 32: 23–40.

———. 2012. "Chapter 1: The Tell es-Safi/Gath Archaeological Project 1996–2010: Introduction, Overview and Synopsis of Results." Pages 1–88 in *Tell es-Safi/Gath I: Report on the 1996–2005 Seasons*. Edited by A. M. Maeir. Wiesbaden: Harrassowitz.

———. 2018. "The Philistines Be Upon Thee, Samson (Jud. 16:20): Reassessing the Martial Nature of the Philistines – Archaeological Evidence Vs. Ideological Image?" Pages 158–68 in *Change, Continuity and Connectivity: North-Eastern Mediterranean at the Turn of the Bronze Age and in the Early Iron Age*. Edited by L. Niesiołowski-Spanò and M. Węcowski. Wiesbaden: Harrassowitz.

———. 2022. "Jerusalem and the West – Via Philistia: An Early Iron Age Perspective from Tell es-Safi/Gath." Pages 7–21 in *Jerusalem and the Coastal Plain in the Iron Age and Persian Periods: New Studies on Jerusalem's Relations with the Southern Coastal Plain of Israel/Palestine (c. 1200–300 BCE)*. Edited by F. Hagemeyer. Tübingen: Mohr Siebeck.

Maeir, A. M., B. Davis, and L. A. Hitchcock. 2016. "Philistine Names and Terms Once Again: A Recent Perspective." *JEMAHS* 4: 321–40.

Maeir, A. M., and E. Eshel. 2014. "Four Short Alphabetic Inscriptions from Iron Age IIA Tell es-Safi/Gath and their Contribution for Understanding the Process of the Development of Literacy in Iron Age Philistia." Pages 69–88 in *"See, I Will Bring a Scroll Recounting What Befell Me" (Ps 40:8): Epigraphy and Daily Life - From the Bible to the Talmud Dedicated to the Memory of Professor Hanan Eshel*. Edited by E. Eshel and Y. Levin. Göttingen: Vandenhoeck & Ruprecht.

Maeir, A. M., and L. A. Hitchcock. 2016. "'And the Canaanite Was Then in the Land'? A Critical View on the 'Canaanite Enclave' in Iron I Southern Canaan." Pages 209–26 in *Alphabets, Texts and Artefacts in the Ancient Near East: Studies Presented to Benjamin Sass*. Edited by I. Finkelstein, C. Robin, and T. Römer. Paris: Van Dieren.

———. 2017a. "The Appearance, Formation and Transformation of Philistine Culture: New Perspectives and New Finds." Pages 149–62 in *The Sea Peoples Up-To-Date: New Research on the Migration of Peoples in the 12th Century BCE*. Edited by P. Fischer and T. Bürge. Vienna: Austrian Academy of Sciences.

———. 2017b. "Rethinking the Philistines: A 2017 Perspective." Pages 249–67 in *Rethinking Israel: Studies in the History and Archaeology of Ancient Israel in Honor of Israel Finkelstein*. Edited by O. Lipschits, Y. Gadot, and M. J. Adams. Winona Lake: Eisenbrauns.

Maeir, A. M., L. A. Hitchcock, and L. K. Horwitz. 2013. "On the Constitution and Transformation of Philistine Identity." *OJA* 32: 1–38.

Maeir, A. M., and I. Shai. 2015. "The Origins of the 'Late Philistine Decorated Ware': A Note." *TA* 42: 59–66.

Maeir, A. M., E. L. Welch, and M. Eniukhina. 2021. "A Note on Olive Oil Production in Iron Age Philistia: Pressing the Consensus." *PEQ* 153: 129–44.

Martin, M. A. S. 2017. "The Provenance of Philistine Pottery in Northern Canaan, with a Focus on the Jezreel Valley." *TA* 44: 193–321.

Master, D. M. 2021. "The Philistines in the Highlands: A View from Ashkelon." *JJAR* 1: 203–20.

Mazar, A. 1985. *Excavations at Tell Qasile. Part II. The Philistine Sanctuary: Various Finds, the Pottery, Conclusions, Appendixes*. Jerusalem: Institute of Archaeology.

Mazar, A., and N. Panitz-Cohen. 2001. *Timnah (Tel Batash) II: The Finds from the First Millennium BCE*. Jerusalem: Institute of Archaeology.

Mazar, E., and M. Karlin. 2015. "A Fragment of a Lion-Headed Rhyton." Pages 539–40 in *The Summit of the City of David, Excavations 2005–2008. Final Reports Volume 1, Area G*. By E. Mazar. Jerusalem: Shoham Academic Research and Publication.

McDonagh, J. 2004. "The Philistines as Scapegoats: Narratives and Myths in the Invention of Ancient Israel and in Modern Critical Theory." *Holy Land Studies* 3: 93–100.

Münnich, M. M. 2021. "The Sphere of David's Influence During His Service to the Philistines (1 Sam 30:26–31): Between Text and Archaeology." *ZDPV* 137: 29–59.

Na'aman, N. 2002. "In Search of the Reality Behind the Account of David's Wars with Israel's Neighbors." *IEJ* 52: 200–24.

———. 2012. "Ḥirbet Ed-Dawwāra - a Philistine Stronghold on the Benjamin Desert Fringe." *ZDPV* 128: 10–14.

Niesiolowski-Spano, L. 2016. *Goliath's Legacy. Philistines and Hebrews in Biblical Times*. Wiesbaden: Harrassowitz.

Rodan, S. 2015. *Aegean Mercenaries in Light of the Bible: Clash of Cultures in the Story of David and Goliath*. Oxford: Archaeopress.

Silberman, N. 1998. "The Sea Peoples, the Victorians and Us: Modern Social Ideology and Changing Archaeological Interpretations of the Late Bronze Age Collapse." Pages 268–75 in *Mediterranean Peoples in Transition: Thirteenth to Early Tenth Centuries BCE*. Edited by S. Gitin, A. Mazar and E. Stern. Jerusalem: Israel Exploration Society.

Singer, I. 2013. "The Philistines in the Bible: A Short Rejoinder to a New Perspective." Pages 19–27 in *The Philistines and Other "Sea Peoples" in Text and Archaeology*. Edited by A. E. Killebrew and G. Lehmann. Atlanta: SBL.

Thompson, T. L. 1999. *The Mythic Past: Biblical Archaeology and the Myth of Israel*. London: Basic Books.

Uziel, J., N. Szanton, and A. Cohen-Weinberger. 2015. "From Sea to Sea: Cultural Influences and Trade Connections Between Judah and Philistia in the Iron Age II, in Light of Petrographic Study of Late Philistine Decorated Ware from the City of David." *Innovations in the Archaeology of Jerusalem and Its Environs* 9: 74–87.

van der Kooij, A. 1992. "The Story of David and Goliath: The Early History of Its Text." *Ephemerides Theologicae Lovanienses* 68: 118–31.

Weiss, E., and M. Kislev. 2004. "Plant Remains as Indicators for Economic Activities: A Case Study from Iron Age Ashkelon." *JAS* 31: 1–13.

Weitzman, S. 2002. "The Samson Story as Border Fiction." *Biblical Interpretation* 10: 158–74.

Yasur-Landau, A. 2010. *The Philistines and Aegean Migration at the End of the Late Bronze Age*. Cambridge: Cambridge University Press.

36
EARLY INTERACTIONS BETWEEN THE ARAMEANS AND ISRAELITES

Scott W. Booth

Introduction

Israel and Aramean geopolitical events and socioeconomic realities were center stage in southern Canaan from the 9th to mid-8th centuries BCE, particularly in northern Israel. This essay aims to shed light on the preceding 12th–10th centuries using available data from geography, material culture, and texts. As will be seen, such an investigation calls attention to methodological issues and so provides an opportunity to move Israel and Aramean research forward. With minor adjustments to the current model and methods, and the external controls provided by studies of early Arameans in North Syria, much can be said of early Israel and its northern neighbors in the early Iron Age.

Overview of Data

The geography of the Beqaa, Hauran, and Huleh are well understood, and detailed soil, rain, and resource maps are available for each area.[1] The situation regarding the archeological data is a bit more complicated. First, the data is not evenly distributed. Most of the detailed data is found within the borders of modern Israel. The Beqaa, Hauran, and Damascene plain are limited to surveys with only a few excavations (Figure 36.1; e.g., comments in Sader 2010). The second issue is periodization. In addition to ongoing disputes, much of the work in the Beqaa, Damascene plane, and Hauran was done when "Iron I" meant 1200–1000 BCE. These deficits are in part mitigated by two recent works. The first is Assaf Kleiman's dissertation (2019) in which he pulls together all the available archeological data (including some survey work not yet published), and, in places, offers updated analyses. The second is Jérôme Rohmer's recent (2020) survey and review of Iron Age sites in the Hauran. It contains the most up-to-date survey data, as well as an important reanalysis of site occupation.[2]

As for texts, the Hebrew Bible is the only available source for the region and time.[3] It is important to note, however, the numerous challenges the Hebrew Bible presents for the study of Arameans and Northern Israel in the early Iron Age: It is a non-native text that makes use of unknown sources for its own various ideological and theological purposes, written long after the events it describes, and subject to the forces of transmission (redaction, editing, and corruption). But it is equally important to recognize that these challenges are

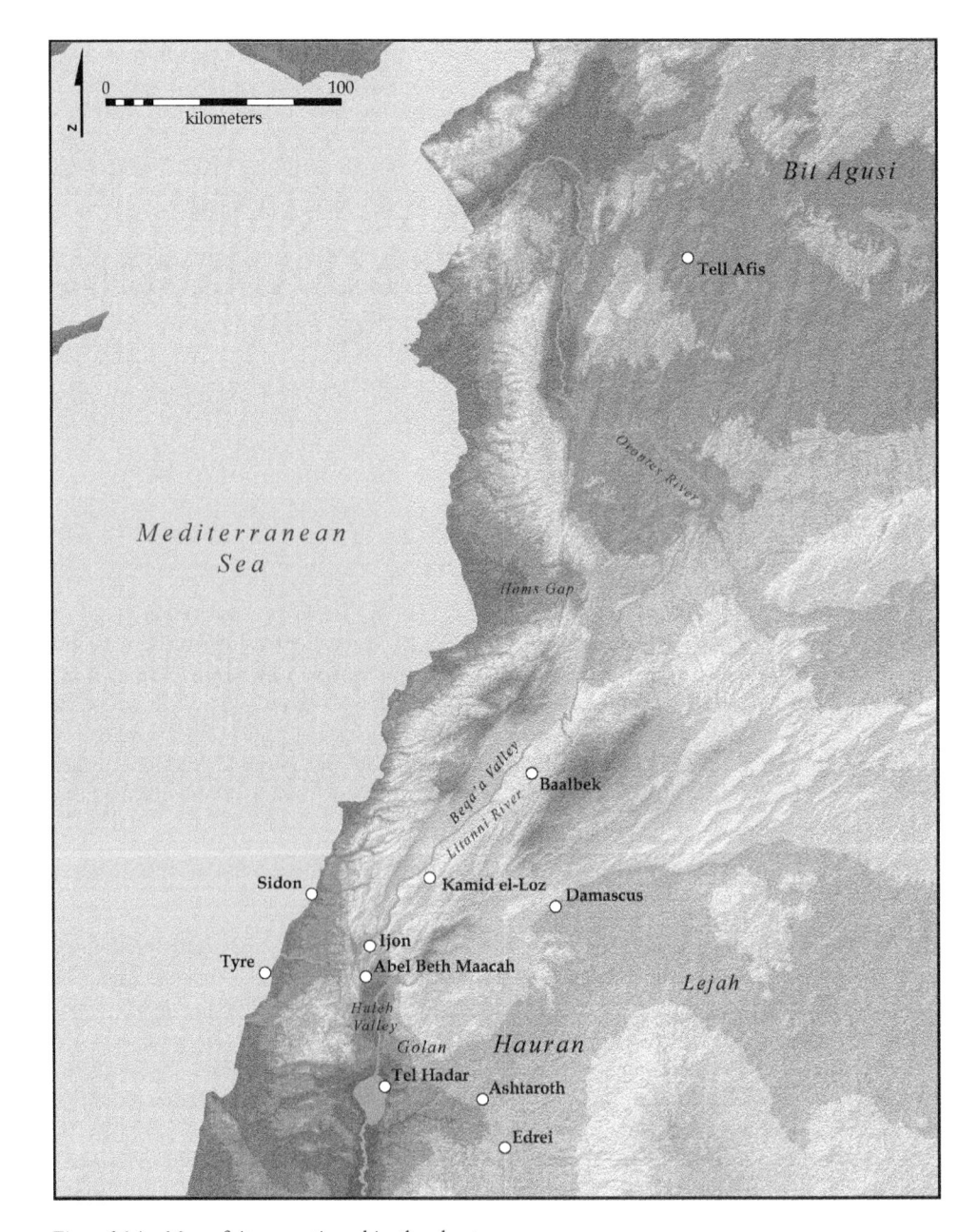

Figure 36.1 Map of sites mentioned in the chapter

regularly encountered by philologists and historians working outside the Hebrew Bible. It is a rather normal situation.

For example, parallel studies of early Arameans in north-central Syria rely on Akkadian and Hieroglyphic Luwian texts that likewise make use of unknown sources, are ideologically driven, and are not written by Arameans themselves. A good case in point is the early Aramean takeover of the East and West banks of the Euphrates near Til Barsip. It is accepted by historians (e.g., Younger 2017: 209; Galil 2013: 164; Lipiński 2000: 163; Tadmor 1975: 38) that the forts of

Mutkīnu and Pitru were built by Tiglath-Pileser I (1114–1076 BCE), were lost when unnamed Arameans drove out the Assyrians during the reign of Aššur-rabi II (1012–972 BCE), then regained by Shalmaneser III (858–824 BCE). Both the loss and subsequent retaking of the forts are only known through the Kurkh Monolith inscription (*RIMA III*, A.0.102.2: ii 35b–38; Yamada 2000: 362–63)—a much later royal inscription of Shalmaneser III known to contain errors (Younger 2016: 202) and written to support the ideologies of – among other things – reestablishing Assyrian presence west of the Euphrates, the campaigns against Arameans, and linking Shalmaneser III with the great Tiglath-Pileser I. Shalmaneser's story makes reasonable sense given the sparse information we have: Namely, Aššurnaṣirpal II's encounter with Bit-Adini in the area (*RIMA II*, A.0.101.1: iii.50b–56; A.0.101.81, 86b, 87; A.0.101.1: iii.56b–57a, 60b–84), the possibility of Aramean names in the Luwian inscriptions of Masuwari (Younger 2016: 42; Bunnens 2006: 86), and archeological data indicating diminishing Assyrian presence at the time (Bunnens 2013: 180). But as for the arrival of Arameans, and the attribution of Assyrian withdrawal to them, we are wholly dependent on the claim of an Assyrian king 150 years after the event.

The point is this: Methodologically speaking the challenges the biblical texts present historians are not categorically distinct from the challenges presented by non-biblical texts. The real challenge is the old problem of a sound model and method for combining data from both text and material culture studies in a manner that does justice to both sets of data. And it is to this problem that I briefly turn, presenting findings and proposals from outside biblical and ancient Near Eastern studies that have the potential to move our understanding of early Aramean-Israelite contact forward.

Method

Space does not permit a review of the long history of the problem of text and artifact in historical studies. But two points are important to note before looking briefly at the current situation. First, history writing was a *text-driven* endeavor for centuries, to the extent that when historians imagined *more data*, they simply imagined *more text* (e.g., Fraser 1842: v–vi). When archeology began cutting its teeth as a discipline, it labored under this "epistemological priority" of text (Moreland 2001: 12; Matthews 2003: 6–7; Andrén 1998: 17). Second, when history as a formal discipline in the academy began in the late nineteenth century, there was a philosophical divide that impacts the current scenario (Iggers 2012). In one camp was the top-down, state-first, *text-driven* approach of the professional historians (Kelley 2006: 25–29; Iggers 1987: 20–22). On the other side, outside the discipline, "there was widespread conviction that the subject matter of history must be expanded and greater space be given to the role of society, the economy, and culture" (Iggers 2012: 31; Burke 2004: 9–10). Thus, when archeology expanded its capability and scope, such that it could tell a story without the aid of texts, its abilities fell naturally within the second, ready-made camp.

For the purposes here, we can fast-forward to 1993, when William Dever (1993: 709) ushered in the New Biblical Archaeology and with it aimed to also begin a "new style of correlating artifactual and textual approaches to history-writing." In his essay, which reviews the move from the so-called new archaeology to Ian Hodder's contextual archaeology, Dever again asks the question (not unlike the one posed in the present study):

> [H]ow shall we write a history of ancient Israel that does justice to all that we can now know of artifacts and texts? Which is better: history written from the top down [read text driven], or from the bottom up [read archeologically driven]?
>
> *(1993: 711)*

Dever has offered his answer on several occasions (2017: 1–44; 2001: 85), which can be boiled down to a few principles. First, both texts and material culture are artifacts and should be recognized as having a parallel character (historical setting, cultural context, intent, etc.). Second, "A text or an archaeological artifact requires an external referent, an independent witness, to corroborate it before it can become valid testimony" (Dever 2001: 107). Given this, the method is quite simple. Both text and artifact "must be interpreted separately and similarly, and then compared" (Dever 2001: 79). The testimony of the sources will either converge or not. When they converge, "a historical datum (or given) may be said to have been established beyond reasonable doubt" (Dever 2001: 108). Third, when text and artifact do not converge, Dever argues that archeology ultimately holds sway (though, see Pioske, this volume). This is because archeology is an independent witness, has not been deliberately edited, is more objective (less enigmatic), and, unlike texts, archeological data is "potentially unlimited" (Dever 2001: 89). There is, of course, subjectivity involved in this process, but this can be combated by engaging with the academic community over time. With some variation, Dever's answer has been widely adopted (e.g., Gilboa and Sharon 2008: 149).

While the "convergence" approach seems reasonable and straightforward enough, Anthony Snodgrass, a classical archeologist, observes that it has failed to produce reliable results in classical studies. For Snodgrass (1985: 194), the root of the problem is "[the assumption] that the kinds of event likely to feature in a conventional historical narrative and the kinds of episode likely to be detectable by the excavation of a site (primarily, a settlement-site) substantially coincide." One effect of this assumption is that it presses scholars to make bad historical decisions. To this, he offers the following modern data and future hypothetical to demonstrate: "On 1 May 1951 the Grand-Theatre de Genève was destroyed by fire. On 4 August 1964 the Bâtiment Electoral, only 250 meters away, suffered a similar fire." Snodgrass then asks us to "consider the plight of the future excavator of Geneva." Since the fires were so close in time and so close to the time of WWII, they would be linked and the conclusion obvious: "Geneva suffered, in the course of the war, a bombardment severe enough to burn two of its main public buildings." Although the documents would show that Switzerland was neutral during the war, the more complete picture now indicates that it eventually took sides. And in this way, "archaeology will ... have fruitfully enlarged on the bare documentary record" (Snodgrass 1985: 197).

Among the concrete examples, Snodgrass provides are those where "convergences" got historians into trouble in terms of logic (1985: 202). The following is one such example:

- Major premise: Selinus was founded in 629/8 B.C., because that is the date that emerges from Thucydides, and he is our best source.
- Minor premise: The earliest Corinthian pottery found at Selinus is of the beginning of the (Early) Ripe Corinthian phase, or just before.
- Ergo: The Ripe Corinthian phase should begin close to 625 B.C.

Problematically, pottery from a much earlier phase was later discovered in the basement of the museum of Polerno (contra the minor premise above). Snodgrass observes that the response to this information was counterintuitive: "Now when a logician discovers that his minor premise is mistaken, one expects him instantly to suspend belief in his conclusion, pending the reexamination of his whole argument" (1985: 202). In this case, fundamental questions such as the following are called for:

> Can we be sure that the word colony (apoikia) in our sources has a constant meaning in terms of material culture? Can we take the presence of Greek pottery in graves, when

the full circumstances of their finding have not been published, to indicate the presence of Greek settlers? Can we even, at a more trivial level, be sure of the provenience of pots found, without full documentation, in museum basements?

(Snodgrass 1985: 203)

But most did not raise these questions. Instead, some proposed a pre-colonial Greek presence, while others "jettisoned their own major premise [that Thucydides was right] in the effort to salvage the conclusion" (1985: 202–03). While it might have been correct that Thucydides was inaccurate (though in this case, it turns out that his testimony stands), the arguments proceeded on the assumption that "the evidence of excavation can be expected to speak in the same clear language as that of the historical event" (1985: 203).

I agree with Snodgrass's observations concerning the reliability of the "convergence" approach. But Harding has persuasively argued that the issue lies not in the type of data, but in the undertheorized temporal model of the Annales School through which we view it.[4] We briefly review that model below before turning to Harding's observations and proposal.

The Annales School is a group of historians loosely organized around a broader paradigm of a bottom-up approach to history (Burke 1990: 107; Burguière 2009). It is history from the facts on the ground, not facts as given in state propaganda (Bintliff 1991: 5–6). A common feature in this approach is time perspectivism, which began with Fernand Braudel's (1995: 1238) "total history, written in three different registers, on three different levels, perhaps best described as three different conceptions of time...." The first of the three timescales is the *longue durée*, "whose passage is almost imperceptible, that of man in his relationship to the environment, a history in which all change is slow, a history of constant repetition, ever recurring cycles." The second level is the "slow but perceptible rhythms... the history of groups and groupings ... [comprised of] ... economic systems, states, societies, civilizations ...." Archeology is particularly well suited to speak to this scale. The third level is where political histories normally reside, it is "on the scale not of man, but of individual men" (Bintliff 1991: 20–21). Textual data is well suited for this third scale.

The time perspectivism model has its benefits. It provides an avenue for archeology to permanently enter into the historical discussion via the long-term perspective it is so keen to provide (Bintliff 1991: 30; Knapp 1992: 10–14). In addition, the data set provided by archaeology can be valued without having to see it as missing and incomplete. However, as many have noted, Braudel fails to link the medium and short-term time scales in an acceptable way (Bintliff 1991:8). He envisioned nesting the fast-moving scales within the slower ones such that material culture "even though initially derived from human actions... [creates] circumstances with which individuals and social groups [have] to cope" (Fletcher 1992: 38; see Braudel 1995: 102). While this may be a useful way to highlight the impact of slower changing cultural phenomena on historical events, it forces one to take a *deterministic* view of the relationship between structure and events (Fletcher 1992: 37–38). This means that social and cultural *processes* are distinct from those at the time scale of the events of history, which take place in them. This, in turn, has a direct and unintended impact on the way history writing is approached. Archeologically driven scholars are justified in considering the material culture as the location of real history because of the structure's deterministic function. Conversely, those who use text as their primary source for history are justified in keeping to events, highlighting structural elements when they are felt to be particularly relevant or impactful because the determined part reveals the whole.

Rather than trying to solve the problem of the relationship of the timescales (as Fletcher has), Harding (2005: 195) argues that time perspectivism *must* fail because "its starting-point is not a theoretically-informed understanding of how time becomes bound into any social system." Following Durkheim's (1995: 441) axiom that "the category of time has the rhythm of social life as its basis," Harding (2005: 89) observes that time perspectivism surely "divorce[s] time from the very social context within which it acquires meaning." He rightly asks,

> What, then, is the point of imposing the analytical scales of time perspectivism without first assessing whether they may have actually existed as recognizable categories to the societies in question, especially since preliterate non-Western communities clearly possess very different conceptions of ideological time?
>
> *(2005: 93)*

To correct this, Harding proposes two shifts, neither of which are difficult but have a significant outcome on method and (likely) outcomes. The first is to shift to a temporal model based on Husserl's observation that *people* experience cognitive time as "both memories of the past and as future anticipations" (Harding 2005: 94). The present is thick, not the knife-edge of a moment; or as Harding put it, "the awareness of the passage of cognitive time is not so much by way of a repetitive sequence of here-and-now's as by a single extended present constantly sliding forward" (2005: 95). The present for *society* is likewise thick, comprised of (1) retention of the past and (2) protention of expected future experiences. An example can be seen in the repetition of rituals, whereby "the past is not only swallowed up in the present day 'sameness' of these events but also projected forward to create the contemporary values which orientate future social activity" (Harding 2005: 90). In this way, whether in rituals, ceramics, buildings, or literature, societies *actively* select what comprises the time of structure using "both memories of the past and … future anticipations" (Harding 2005: 94; similarly Moreland 2001: 96). And because the selections are continuously happening, the time of structure is collapsed onto the time of the event. Structure and event are lived as one thick layer in which "social [production and] reproduction is grounded in the performativity of a group's members" (Harding 2005: 95). Thus, rather than distinct categories, "concepts such as 'event' and 'structure' … are fused together in a complex network of mnemonic and anticipatory relations played-out within present-day existence" (Harding 2005: 194).

For the second shift, Harding observes that the past, like the present, is not a cleanly woven together set of memories and anticipations (Harding 2005: 198). Societies are complex, comprised of different groups with varying degrees of agreement on memories and anticipation. As a society's "thick present" slides forward through time, it contains many elements, some that are static and some that are in the process of changing (slowly, rapidly, or variably). This means that a society's "thick present" is a complex and dynamic dataset in which knowing the status of one element, whether at a particular moment or through time, does not grant that one knows the status of any other. That is, elements in society can behave in unexpected ways relative to other elements. Furthermore, the *meaning* of a change in one element, or lack thereof, is always colored by what other elements in society did, whether that be the same or something else entirely.

Using the model of the "thick present" the question of a reliable method for historians to combine data falls away. The data was always already combined in the thick past, just as it is in the thick present. It is simply a matter of overlaying the findings from the various disciplines in a manner consistent with those findings. Reliable points of historical data are not limited to convergences alone, for there is no more value in convergence than non-convergence. And the historian is no longer in a position to violate or prefer the findings of one discipline over another. This more theoretically informed temporal model shifts the methodological question from the historian, who combines data, to the disciplines that provide it.

Instead, the question posed by the "thick present" is whether one's findings, particularly those that do not "converge" with other findings, are reflective of the complexities of the "thick past" under investigation, or bad interpretation, or bad data. The disciplines already have a way to answer this internally using the hypothesis–theory–law method of the sciences. But the impact of the "thick present" model is that the process is slowed down. Since the model of the "thick past" does not pit the disciplines against each other, but allows all testimony to stand, an incorrect historical view is the result of bad, poorly communicated, or overstated testimony from at least one of the disciplines. This collaborative, rather than competitive model, pressures the disciplines toward care and caution in their findings, so as not to be the cause of failure.

Thus, the way forward in using the Hebrew Bible alongside the material culture is to use the methods and findings of similar studies from surrounding areas as an external control for what can be understood to be ordinary versus extraordinary claims. Ordinary claims can be accepted, extraordinary claims are allowed and entertained, but are held in tension and require further scrutiny by the appropriate disciplines (cf. the questions Snodgrass asked in the example above). In this way, we follow the hermeneutical spiral towards better understanding of data, both the parts and the whole.

Controls

To begin, current data suggests that Aramean tribes have an adaptive strategy for settling into an area (Mazzoni 2016: 299). That is, they seem to assume the existing culture's current trajectory is the stable one; and align with it. So, when it is obvious that Aramaic speaking people are at a site, there are no things that correspond to their arrival (e.g., exclusively Aramean technology, or architecture, or style of pottery).[5] Maeir's (2017: 60) recent review of the data in Israel led him to conclude that while Syrian influence is detectable in Iron I and II (e.g., a cult stand from Tell Reḥov with parallels at Emar), "many of the suggested identifications are insufficiently 'robust' – to enable us to accept this suggestion without hesitation." So, for now, we still need texts to tell us when and where Arameans are, which can happen in one of the following ways:

- The appearance of texts written in Aramaic
- The appearance of Aramaic names (people or deities)
- Use of the label "Aram" or "Aramean," whether someone self-identifies as "Aramean," or that label is put on a group by another.

The following are lessons learned from similar studies involving Arameans in Syria. First, Arameans appear in multicultural and multiethnic environments. One example is Tell Ahmar during the kingdom of Masuwari. Arameans are known to be in the area during the time (RIMA II, *A.0.102.2*: *ii.35b–38*; Yamada 2000: 362–63) and may have been among the rulers of the city (Younger 2016: 42; Bunnens 2006: 86). Moreover, there is religious plurality at the site, something not seen at nearby Karkamish.[6] Indeed, the problem of Masuwari and Bit-Adini itself is evidence of the ability of Arameans to exist within a multiethnic environment (Booth 2018: 468–70; Younger 2016: 137–43). A similar scenario is seen at Zincirli within the Kulamuwa stele:

> Kulamuwa bears a Luwian name, but is son of Hayanu, whose name is Aramaean; he is then represented in the Assyrian gesture of devotion of ubāna tarāṣu ("stretching the

finger") under the symbols of the gods and dressed as an Assyrian ruler, but holding a wilted flower like a Syrian dead king, at the side of his inscription written in Phoenician (KAI 24).

(Mazzoni 2016: 286)

It is also seen at Tell Afis, though more quietly, where the question of "local population" and "Aramean" becomes obviously fuzzy in the 8th century and leaves open the question of when that fuzziness began.

Second, when texts indicate geopolitical shifts involving Arameans, those shifts are often undetectable in the material culture; and conversely, when shifts are suspected by the material culture, they can go unknown in the textual record (both scenarios are present in early Israel and Aram). For example, at Tell Ahmar, neither the political intrigue within the kingdom of Masuwari nor the transition from Masuwari to Bit-Adini (if these two are different) is known in the material culture. Likewise, Tell Afis must have been involved, in some way, with the many political shifts of the 11th–10th centuries. It might be indicated by closely paralleled building activity at ʿAin Dārā and Tell Tayinat, but they are unknown in the textual record (see discussion in Booth 2018: 439–53). The point is that Arameans were already there, and we cannot tell when, or even where, they arrived (Mazzoni 2016: 299).

Lastly, and relatedly, Arameans move. One clear instance of this is the Yaḫānu tribe, which is first encountered in the Assyrian material in the annals of Aššur-dān (934–912 BCE) near the joining of the Tigris and Lower Zab (*RIMA* II A.0.98.1: 23–25a). They are subsequently encountered by Aššurnaṣirpal II (883–859 BCE) north of Aleppo (the group would subsequently be called Bīt-Agūsi; *RIMA* II A.0.101.1: *iii*.77b–78). Younger (2016: 413) understands the movement of the Yaḫānu, along with some of the others, to have been prompted by Assyrian aggression.

With these concepts in mind, I turn to look at northern Israel and Aram.

Review of Textual Data

The Hebrew Bible provides a snapshot of the southern Levant following, or coinciding with, diminishing Egyptian control in the region, and Israel's entry. It indicates a fragmented area comprised of four political entities. In the Beqaa, Num 13:21 mentions a Reḥov, which is near Lebô Ḥamat. This could be taken together with "Bēt-Reḥov" of Judg 18:28 (spelled the same in the LXX) and "Aram Bēt-Reḥov" of 2 Sam 10:6 to indicate the presence of Arameans in the Beqaa very early. But that is not necessarily the case. Several points need to be taken into consideration.

First, the Hebrew Bible is unique in using "Aram" as a compound with other toponyms like "Aram Bēt-Reḥov" (Younger 2016: 96). So, we immediately slip some distance from our control set. Second, it does not apply the term "Aram" as a compound in a consistent way. For example, while "Aram Bēt-Reḥov" is found in 2 Sam 10:6, just two verses later it is simply "Reḥov" (2 Sam 10:8), but in both verses, one finds "Aram Ṣobah." Examples like this abound. Third, though these texts may make use of earlier records, they are a product of a much later political reality. Thus, from a purely philological perspective, the following scenario, which Younger (2016: 215) gave for Maacah, is entirely possible for Reḥov (or Ṣobah):

> ["Reḥov"] may have been originally the personal name of an eponymous ancestor of an early West Semitic tribal group (hence, the usage of the *Bēt*-X formulation), which gave its name to the area that later came under the control of Arameans.

If the Hebrew Bible is claiming Reḥov is Aramean, this would be substantially earlier than what is seen in the north. This is not an impossibility, since Arameans were obviously present before Tiglath-Pileser I encountered them, and given the contextual differences between city-state/West Semitic polities of southern Canaan and the Neo-Hittite states in Syria. But caution is warranted. If, on the other hand, "Aram" is used anachronistically, then an entirely different situation is in view; perhaps akin to Tell Afis following Hittite withdrawal and prior to the expansion of Palistin\Walistin. To sum up, it seems that the text does indicate that Reḥov was in the Beqaa, but it is not clear whether it is claiming the group was Aramean at this time or not.

As for the extent of Reḥov's territory, Num 13:21 has been taken together with Judg 18:28 to indicate that Bēt-Reḥov designates an area from Labwe to the southern end of the Beqaa Valley (Na'aman 2002: 204; Younger 2016: 195). However, caution is warranted. The text here is only intended to provide the northern extent of the spies' journey, using the standard northernmost waypoint Lebô Ḥamat (Num 34:8; Judg 3:3; 1 Kgs 8:65; 2 Kgs 14:25; etc.). It does not indicate the southern extent of Reḥov. Also, the chronology of the text that mentions its southern border, Judges 18, is difficult to establish (discussed below). Since Aramean tribes are known to move, and borders (Aramean and otherwise) are known to shift and fluctuate during the early Iron Age, we should only say Bēt-Reḥov is in the north-central part of the Beqaa at this point and the extent of its borders is not known.

The status of Damascus in the early Iron Age is not indicated in the texts. This does not necessarily indicate Damascus was weak or in decline. It could be the result of maintaining its Amarna period relationships: That is, strong ties with the Beqaa, and poor relations with Ashtaroth. Og controlled the entire Bashan up to Mt. Hermon from Ashtaroth and Edrei (though the phrasing is peculiar here: מֶלֶךְ הַבָּשָׁן אֲשֶׁר־יוֹשֵׁב בְּעַשְׁתָּרֹת בְּאֶדְרֶעִי). His territory extended West to that of Maacah and Geshur. As for their location, Maacah is widely accepted to have been based out of Tell Abil al-Qamḥ/Tel Abel Beth Maacah in the northern Huleh Valley. Geshur is in the area around the Sea of Galilee (see the discussion below). The exact location of relevant place names and geographic terms used in the Hebrew Bible are not settled. Of particular interest is the Golan, which may or may not have been included in the term Bashan (see Moster 2017: 122–30).

As is the case with Bēt-Reḥov, it is unclear whether Maacah and Geshur were Aramean at this time, or whether they were (and/or remained) a local Canaanite population. Maacah is once called "Aram-Maacah" (2 Chr 19:6; see compound name discussion above). Geshur is once identified as "Geshur in Aram," which is clearly a topographic clarifier (Geshur in the north, as opposed to the south [cf 1 Sam 27:8]). Albright (1956: 12; cf. Hendel 2005: 111) first proposed that the name Geshur itself may be Aramaic, consistent with an Old Aramaic spelling of the root *gtr* and reflected in Gen 10:23, where *Gether* is one of the sons of Aram. But as Younger (2016: 204, n.314) has observed, the root also occurs in Akkadian (*gašāru*) and in Ugaritic (*gtr*). Thus, it is not at all certain that the name is Aramaic.

Within the context just discussed, Israel entered the land and Manasseh took control of the Bashan. "Control" should be understood as rather loose, or nominal, as there are also indications that the territory claimed by Manasseh remained to be completely conquered (cf. the story of Jair at Havvoth-Jair and Nobah at Kenath). Maacah and Geshur remained in the land following Israel's entry. It is noteworthy that the text nowhere connects their independence to their military strength or opposition, as neither are listed as involved in the campaigns. The two polities remained independent and maintained their border (Deut 3:14; Josh 12:5; 13:11, 13). Later, during the time of David, the "wise woman" of Maacah makes a statement that may reflect a longstanding political arrangement (and possible religious activity, see below):

> They used to say in former times, "Let them ask in Abel." And thus they settled (it).
> I am peaceable and faithful *in* Israel. You are seeking to destroy a city and mother in Israel. Why would you swallow up the heritage of the LORD?
>
> *(2 Sam 20:18–19)*

This holds true for Maacah until the rise of Ṣobah in the region (2 Samuel 10, discussed below), and Geshur until some time after Solomon, when Geshur joined with Aram to take Havvoth-Jair; 1 Chr 2:23; see Japhet 1993: 80–85).

The Hebrew Bible provides only a few direct comments about this area regarding the years between Israel's arrival in the land and the battles of Saul and David against the Arameans. They are given here in the order they appear. Due to the unique way the book of Judges is composed and arranged, the chronology is largely unknown (see Beldman 2017 and Younger 2021).

In Judg 3:3, among the nations left to "test Israel" in war are the Sidonions and Hivvites on Mt. Lebanon from Mt. Baal-Hermon to Lebo Hamat. Hivvites are likely from Cilicia (Singer 2006: 735; Collins 2007: 201–202; Na'aman 1994: 240; Dinçol et al. 2015: 67). In addition to the noteworthy multiethnic and multicultural environment, this verse may also indicate shifting powers in the area. Hivvites are said to have been previously living "*under* Mt. Hermon" (Josh 11:3), a phrase that is sometimes used for territory included within the Beqaa Valley (Josh 11:17, 13:5). Furthermore, in Judges 18, Bēt-Reḥov's territory is said to have extended beyond the Beqaa to Tel Dan (the city of Laish which would become Dan). Laish is described as "living securely, like the Sidonians," being isolated, and "in a valley that belonged to Bēt-Reḥov" (Judg 18:7, 28; note the use of עמק for "valley," not בקע). This indicates that Bēt-Reḥov both took control of the southern portion of the Beqaa and extended their reach southward. Of further interest is that, even though the עמק belonged to Bēt-Reḥov, Laish's isolation meant that no one would come to their rescue. So, either Bēt-Reḥov's grasp on the עמק was always loose, or their grip on it had already begun to wane. In this regard, it should be noted that Beldman (2017: 127–36) has argued that the events of Judges 17–21 should be situated very early after the death of Joshua. Lastly, while Laish's isolation is a curious situation, given nearby Maacah, it is about as philologically unambiguous as possible.

Judges 3:8 provides a second indication of the volatile nature of the early Iron Age when it mentions that Israel served Cushan-Rishathaim of Aram-Naharaim for eight years and that Othniel was judging in Judah. The location and nature of the oppression, along with the location of the battle are not given (note, judges could travel, e.g., Deborah). However, the text is indicating that a force from the extreme north was able to penetrate into the Israel-held territory from the north (either via Damascus and the Hauran or the Beqaa and Hulah). Such brief, flash-in-the-pan expansions under a charismatic ruler are known from later periods (e.g., Bit-Adini's expansion to the Middle Euphrates), and there is little reason to suspect they could not happen earlier and in this region.

The last direct comment from Judges comes from the introduction to the judgeship of Jephthah, a Gileadite warrior who was exiled to Tov, where he lived among "worthless fellows who went out with him" (Judg 11:3). Jephthah is portrayed as a kind of bandit, which could have implications for how the region is viewed. Of more importance here is that Israel is said to have served, among others, the gods of Aram. It seems likely that this is geographically related, but, again, due to compositional factors, we cannot know for certain whether the claim is that the influence is geographic or chronological, or both. Perhaps related to this is the "wise woman" of Abel Beth Maacah's statement about seeking answers.

At the beginning of the United Monarchy, some tantalizing political information is given. "Aram-Ṣobah" became the major military power in the north. Hadadezer, king of Ṣobah, was king over smaller kingdoms, which included Bēt-Reḥov, Maacah, and Damascus (2 Sam 8:6; 10:19). The relationship between Ṣobah and Reḥov seems to have been different from other areas, implied both by the fact that Hadadezer was a Bēt-Reḥovite and that their military contingents are listed as one (2 Sam 10:6), while Maacah, itself ruled by a "Tovite" (Wee 2005: 195–98; Younger 2016: 216–18), is separate and small. As for Maacah, its Tovite ruler makes one wonder if its borders extended to include Tov at this time, or if no such implication is intended. At any rate, it may be that Ṣobah's dominance began earlier. The northern extent of Saul's military victories is listed as "against the kings of Ṣobah" (1 Sam 14:47). Since, as mentioned above, Lebô Ḥamat is frequently the northernmost waypoint in the Hebrew Bible, these texts may imply that Ṣobah included that city within its territory. Ṣobah was expanding North as well (battling Hamat, and overextending itself toward the Euphrates, 2 Sam 8:3). Indeed, Ṣobah and Israel are quite alike. This understanding of the text comports well with contemporary events elsewhere in the Levant (e.g., Palistin/Walistin's rapid expansion to include Aleppo; Booth 2018: 442–46).

Combining Data

With the textual data evaluated and in hand, it can now be overlayed on top of material culture and geographic data. At some early point following the Egyptian withdrawal from the region, (Bēt-)Reḥov emerged as a power in the Beqaa (whatever that might have meant). Its location and extent are unknown, but it is important to keep in mind that the Beqaa is not a uniform valley. The southern part receives much more rainfall and has more arable soil (Marfoe 1998: 37). Beyond a lake and surrounding marshes are alluvial fans and colluvial-alluvial terraces that extend to the central part of the valley and are well suited for agriculture. This is where the sites of Kamid el-Loz, Tell Qabb Elyās, Tell Rayyāq, Tell Ghassil, and Baalbek are located. The northern end of the valley is predominantly rocky piedmont with karstic springs, around which are clusters of sites. Marfoe (1998: 220–21) has suggested that the northern and central locations may have seen a more gradual abandonment at the end of the Late Bronze (LB) II than in the southern area, which means resettlement may have begun in the north sooner than the south. If the Reḥov of Num 13:21 is Bēt-Reḥov, and if it is to be understood as "near" Lebô Ḥamat, then it may have been part of the early resettlement.

Even if Bēt-Reḥov controlled the entire valley, it was not centered at Kamid el-Loz at this early time. That site was abandoned at the end of the Late Bronze age (Iron Age material is separated from the LB material "by an alluvial and a sedimentary level," Marfoe 1995: 160). When it was resettled (date unknown), the palace was transformed into an ordinary house, indicating a break from the previous tradition. At Tell Ghassil in the central part of the valley, Kleiman has reanalyzed the findings there, arguing that layers previously identified as Iron II (Area I, levels 3–1, and Area III levels 1–2) belong instead to Iron I, with a few intrusions from a poorly preserved Iron II layer (2019: 262). If he is correct, it may have been an important site within the valley during the Iron Age I, which is important for identifying the political center(s) of Rehov (and/or later Ṣobah; Kleiman 2019: 267). Interestingly, the entire valley maintained the decidedly southern orientation of its ceramic tradition, which the Egyptians had been so keen to promote.

Survey data indicates a few trends throughout the Beqaa. There was a slight increase in the number of sites during the Iron Age I (when the valley reached its peak occupation; Marfoe 1998: 218). The type of settlement during this period "seems to have been more dispersed into smaller agglomerations than in the previous period" (Marfoe 1998: 221). Overall, there is strong continuity with LB distribution, which "suggests that the difference between LB II and Iron I settlement lay more in the settlement functions than in land use," with perhaps a larger reliance on pastoralism (Marfoe 1998: 223).[7] Marfoe (1998: 224) suggests all this indicates "the possibility that frequent shifts in settlement may have occurred among different population groups, each vacillating between sedentary and non-sedentary modes." He speculates the lack of "recognisable regional centres may reflect a political landscape of small, relatively autonomous and loosely connected villages and towns" (1998: 220–21). But the size of the settlement does not necessarily positively correlate to the strength of the connection, particularly when in a tribal context. Lastly, there was a greater concentration of sites in the Wadi et-Taym during the Iron Age I. According to Marfoe (1998: 223), this "suggests a preference for the hilly terrain, or an important route through the pass." If the latter is true, then the strong connection between the Beqaa and the south that was initiated by the Egyptians continued (and possibly strengthened) during the Iron I. This may also be reflected in language about the territory of Bēt-Reḥov, which is said to have continued to the עמק south of the Beqaa. Interestingly, many of these sites do not show Iron II occupation, indicating a change in orientation during that period.

In addition to survey data, findings from two excavations are helpful in forming a picture of what happened in the valley. After Kamid el-Loz was resettled, and the palace was transformed into an ordinary house, there were three Iron I building phases, each consisting of two to three subphases (Marfoe 1995: 160–61; 1998: 221–22; Echt 1984: 60 pl. 3). Interestingly, continuity in architecture typically extended through only a few phases at a time, "with breaks in settlement often indicated by burnt or fill layers" (Marfoe 1998: 221–22; Echt 1984: 42–49). There were two Iron I destructions at Kamid el-Loz; the latter is dated to the end of the period (Heinz et al. 2010: 15).[8] At Tell Ghassil, Kleiman (2019: 262) argues that, like Kamid el-Loz, "during this timeframe, the site experienced at least two, if not three, traumatic events." How the building phases and traumatic events correlate to the rise of Reḥov then Ṣobah in the region, or to the battles with external forces (Saul and David [and Toi?]), is unknown.

Damascus is noticeably absent from the texts until David battles with Hadadezer, king of Ṣobah in 2 Samuel 8. Due to a lack of data from Damascus itself, it cannot be known if this is because the city went into a period of decline, or because of the selectivity of the textual data. The data we do have may suggest the latter. First, the defeat of Og did not grant Mannaseh ascendency over Damascus. Second, Damascus and the Beqaa have a strong geographic connection. A cursory glance at maps of the Anti-Lebanon range might make this seem unlikely, but there is a significant break between Mt. Hermon (Jabal el-Shaykh) in the south and Jebel Magdouche and Ra's al Mudawwar in the north. Here, unlike the Lebanon range, "not only [are] winter snows just an occasional hindrance, but the slopes, too, are more amenable to traditional forms of transportation" (Marfoe 1998: 23). This important pass, in combination with the al-Zabadani saddle, links Damascus to each of the alluvial fans in the Beqaa: Namely, the important sites of Baalbek, Tell Ghassil, Tell Rayyāq, Tell Qabb Elyās, and Kamid el-Loz. Third, Hadadezer himself was a Bēt-Reḥovite. Thus, it is entirely possible that the connection between Damascus and Bēt-Reḥov was maintained following Egyptian withdrawal.

The northern Huleh Valley was, like the Beqaa, active in terms of construction and destruction. Tel Abel Beth Maacah was one of three urban centers in the region, alongside Tel Kinrot and Tel Hadar (Susnow et al. 2021: 59). Unlike Hazor, at Abel Beth Maacah "there were no traces of destruction of the Late Bronze Age city or any indication of a prolonged chronological gap" (David, Mullins, and Panitz-Cohen 2016: 8 and 10, n.45). There are five Iron I strata, with the latest covering the entire 10 ha site. Interestingly, each of the first three strata is described by the excavators as "entirely different in character, though all of them contain the same pottery assemblage" (i.e., local Canaanite forms along with Phoenician imports; Yahalom-Mack, Panitz-Cohen, and Mullins 2018: 151). Of particular interest given the comments by the "wise woman" in 2 Samuel 20 (above) are two prominent cultic settings, one of which may indicate divinatory and magico-medical activities at the site (Yahalom-Mack, Panitz-Cohen, and Mullins 2019; Booth et al. Forthcoming). After an 11th-century destruction, there were two more strata, also different from each other, the latter of which was destroyed in the 10th century (Yahalom-Mack, Panitz-Cohen, and Mullins 2018: 151). It is noteworthy that nearby Tel Tannim (a much smaller site, 1.5 km east of modern Kiryat Shemona) also had two Iron I destruction layers (Avshalom-Gorni and Getzov 2008). Maacah did shift political allegiance at the time from Israel to Ṣobah to Israel, but what impact this had on the site, or whether the destructions are tied to those shifts, is unknown.

At nearby Tel Dan, Ilan (2019: 637) suggests that in the early Iron Age I, following Egyptian withdrawal, the site "was an independent entity with a small population having limited, if any, alliances." While this comports well with the description in Judges 18, it seems odd, particularly given the prominence of nearby Maacah, 7 km northwest at Tell Abil al-Qamḥ. The survey data *may* provide a clue. It indicates that during the Iron I the primary (indeed new) connection between the Huleh and the Hauran was via a route toward Ashtaroth. The route connecting Damascus and Tyre seems to have grown in the Iron II (though caution is warranted because detailed data from the northern Hauran is absent). If this is correct, then Maacah in the Iron I would have minimal interest in the direction of Dan, but greater interest in the South and West (borne out by the ceramics). In addition to the Egyptian elements, Aegean objects (including ritual objects) and spatial organization are noteworthy, given the presence of Hivvites in the area (see above). Given all this, it is easier to understand how the site got its reputation for isolation. Lastly, the site saw two Iron I destructions. The first does not seem to have been extensive (Ilan 2019: 19, table 2.2.; 637–38), but was followed by a shift in political and economic development (Statum V, c. 1100–1000 BCE(?). This is around the time Ṣobah was gaining power, but, again, we do not yet know how it correlates.

Farther south, around the Sea of Galilee, the story is somewhat muddy. Tell Kinrot and Tell Hadar experienced growth after a short gap in occupation, followed by what seems to be concomitant building, expansion, and destruction phases (Sergi and Kleiman 2018: 8, table 2). Sergi and Kleiman note (2018: 7) that because of this and because the sites "shared a similar material culture, it is commonly agreed that they formed a single socio-political entity." However, given that external controls restrict our ability to suppose identity between material culture and political affinity (see above), this suggestion is unwarranted. The data indicates that there was a small political entity called Geshur on the east side of the Sea of Galilee. Tell ʿEn Gev *may* be an option (Sergi and Kleiman 2018: 8, table 2, but see Sugimoto 2015), but it also might be better to look for it in the lower Golan at this early stage. There is no reason to suppose that the largest site must be the seat of power, nor that monumental activity must be immediately or approximately dated to the founding of political organization (Keimer and Thomas 2022), or indeed that boundaries apply only to groups with walled cities. Thus, the actual lived borders of Geshur, Naphtali, Manasseh, and Abel Beth Maacah remain unknown without textual indications (though the line of sites on the North side of the Golan that descends from the Bashan is a tempting object for speculation). The borders likely fluctuated, as political affiliation was prone to sometimes rapid movement (perhaps seen in the Tovite in Maacah).

In the Hauran, Rohmer's recent survey work shows a slight decrease in the number of sites when Manasseh took control of the region (from 20 sites during the bronze/Iron Transition to 14 during Iron IB).[9] Rohmer (2020: 575) notes "Nearly all large tells are abandoned, and most sites are either small settlements built in the previous periods and resettled (not necessarily on a permanent basis) or campsites, which provide evidence for mobile pastoral groups." While the picture of the period remains unclear, the current impression is one of decline. Rohmer notes that the area is akin to what Marfoe found in the Beqaa that led him to suggest small, shifting social groups (2020: 575).

The two exceptions were Ashtaroth and Suwaydā' (some 30 miles from Ashtaroth, at the base of Jebel Druze). Ashtaroth, like Edrei, is located near where the Jedur and Nuqra plains meet (c. 45 miles from Damascus). It is the best area for farming in the Hauran because it has the right combination of sufficient rainfall and unbroken, boulder-free plains.[10] Rohmer's work indicates that Ashtaroth (6 ha) was occupied during both the LB/Iron transition and Iron I. Ceramics indicate trade continued with the Cisjordan (Rohmer 2020: 401). Ashtaroth likely experienced at least one destruction during the Iron I (Rohmer 2020: 397). There may have been a period of abandonment, but Rohmer is cautious on this point because the publications are scant; the excavations were interrupted by the Six-Day War, and Iron IB is difficult to dissociate from Iron IIA (Rohmer 2020: 399, 402). Ancient texts are quiet about this area until Damascus begins to exert its influence.

Summary

The geopolitical events and socioeconomic realities of northern Israel and its neighbors remain fuzzy, but a few points emerge. After the withdrawal of the Egyptians, local traditions and connections continued. The orientation was broadly southern Levantine, with regional variation. The earliest Iron Age residents of Tel Dan clung to a Late Bronze Age Egyptian trajectory that was not seen elsewhere. There was periodic upheaval across the area, which preceded change in some areas of society—such as building plans and perhaps political organization—but other parts of society remained largely untouched (e.g., ceramics). The texts indicate new and changing polities and alliances, but most of the details are missing. Damascus may have maintained the orientation toward the Beqaa that it had in the Amarna period. The later part of the Iron Age I saw the formation of regional kingdoms. Ṣobah rose as a regional power at the same time as Saul in Israel, but also could have been earlier. The process of kingdom expansion may have been violent or peaceful, or a combination. Since upheaval can appear locally, the relationship of the regional destructions to the political events (which have been selected and colored for literary purposes) remains unknown. Many questions remain for further research. It is hoped that the model and method espoused here may prove fruitful.

Notes

1. A large collection can be found at https://esdac.jrc.ec.europa.eu
2. Both works are invaluable, and I thank the authors for their assistance and resources.
3. The Amarna letters do provide a helpful backstory, which will be referenced occasionally here (for updated analyses of texts pertinent to this study area, see Vita 2015: 23–47, 59–74). Merneptah's campaign would be helpful, but the location of Yenoam is not secure.
4. For apparent acceptance of the model, see Dever 2017: 12–13, 531–32.
5. Mazzoni has likened finding Aramean identity in material culture to similar attempts to find Phoenician identity and ethno-genesis (2016: 282).

6 Of particular interest are ("Halabean") Tarhunza, Ea, and the "Harranean Moon-god" (see esp. *CHLI I.1*: 228, 232, 240).
7 The evidence is a lack of change of technology, slight increase in density on fans and terraces, and decrease of population in the flood plain.
8 The excavators date this to 1000 BCE (Heinz 2016: 192), but that is not secured by C14.
9 The appearance of one new site in the Nuqra, Tall Kutayba Sud, should be noted (Rohmer 2020: 370–72).
10 Edrei is located at the 250–300mm level. Ashtaroth is within the 300–350mm band (see Rohmer 2020: Fig. 0.3). The Nuqra and Jedur plains are historically divided at the wadi al-Hurayr (Rohmer 2020: 22–24).

Bibliography

Albright, W. F. 1956. "The Biblical Tribe of Massa' and some Congeners. Pages 1–14 in *Studi Orientalistici in Onore di Giorgio Levi Della Vida*. Edited by R. Ciasca. Pubblicazioni dell'Istituto per l'Oriente 52. Rome: Istituto per l'Oriente.

Andrén, Anders. 1998. *Between Artifacts and Texts: Historical Archaeology in Global Perspective*. New York: Plenum Press.

Avshalom-Gorni, Dina, and Nimrod Getzov. 2008. "Tannim, Tel." Pages 24–36 in *NEAEHL* 5.

Beldman, David J. H. 2017. *The Completion of Judges: Strategies of Ending in Judges 17–21*. Winona Lake: Eisenbrauns.

Bintliff, John L. 1991. "The Contribution of the Annaliste/Structural History Approach to Archaeology." Pages 1–33 in *The Annales School and Archaeology*. Edited by John L. Bintliff. Leicester: Leicester University Press.

Booth, Scott W. 2018. "Northwest Syria between the Hittite and Assyrian Empires: Text, Artifact, Geography, and a Way Forward." PhD diss., Trinity Evangelical Divinity School.

Booth, Scott W., Ariel Shatil, Nava Panitz-Cohen, Naama Yahalom-Mack, Carroll Kobs and Robert A. Mullins. forthcoming. "The Buck Stops Here: Deer Antlers in Iron Age I Cultic Contexts at Tel Abel Beth Maacah and Their Implications."

Braudel, Fernand. 1995. *The Mediterranean and the Mediterranean World in the Age of Philip II, Volume* II. Translated by Siân Reynolds. Los Angeles: University of California Press.

Bunnens, Guy. 2006. *A New Luwian Stele and the Cult of the Storm-God at Teil Barsib-Masuwari*. Tel Ahmar 2. Publications de la Mission archéologique de l'Université de Lièege en Syrie. Lueven: Peters.

———. 2013. "Looking for Luwians, Aramaeans and Assyrians in the Tell Ahmar Stratigraphy." Pages 177–97 in *Syrian Archaeology in Perspective: Celebrating Twenty Years of Excavations at Tell Afis; Proceedings of the International Meeting Percorsi di Archeologia Siriana, giornate di studio, Pisa, 27–28, Novembre 2006*. Edited by S. Mazzoni and S. Soldi. Pisa: ETS.

Burguière, André. 2009. *The Annales School: An Intellectual History*. Translated by Jane Marie Todd. Ithaca: Cornell University Press.

Burke, Peter. 1990. *The French Historical Revolution: The Annales School, 1929–1980*. Cambridge: Polity.

———. 2004. *What Is Cultural History?* Second edition. Cambridge: Polity.

Collins, Billie Jean. 2007. *The Hittites and Their World*. Atlanta: SBL.

David, Arlette, Robert A. Mullins, and Nava Panitz-Cohen. 2016. "A *Mnḫprr'* Scarab from Tel Abel Beth Maacah." *JAEI* 9:1–13.

Dever, William G. 1993. "Biblical Archaeology: Death and Rebirth." Pages 706–22 in *Biblical Archaeology Today, 1990. Proceedings of the Second International Congress on Biblical Archaeology. Jerusalem, June–July 1990*. Edited by Avraham Biran and Joseph Aviram. Jerusalem: Israel Exploration Society.

———. 2001. *What Did the Biblical Writers Know and When Did They Know It?: What Archeology Can Tell Us About the Reality of Ancient Israel*. Later Printing edition. Grand Rapids: Eerdmans.

———. 2017. *Beyond the Texts: An Archaeological Portrait of Ancient Israel and Judah*. Atlanta: SBL Press.

Dinçol, Belkıs, Ali Dinçol, J.D. Hawkins, Hasan Peker, Aliye Öztan and Ömer Çelik. 2015. "Two New Inscribed Storm-God Stelae from Arsuz (İskenderun): ARSUZ 1 and 2." *Anatolian Studies* 65: 59–77.

Durkheim, Emile. 1995. *The Elementary Forms of the Religious Life*. Translated by Karen E. Fields. New York: The Free Press.

Echt, Rudolf. 1984. *Kāmid el-Lōz 5: Die Stratigraphie*. Bonn: Dr. Rudolf Habelt GmbH.

Fletcher, R. 1992. "Time Perspectivism, *Annales*, and the Potential of Archaeology." Pages 35–49 in *Archaeology, Annales, and Ethnohistory*. Edited by Bernard Knapp Cambridge: Cambridge University Press.

Fraser, James Baillie. 1842. *Mesopotamia and Assyria, from Their Earliest Ages to the Present Time with Illustrations of Their Natural History*. London: Oliver & Boyd.

Galil, Gershon. 2013. "David, King of Israel, between the Arameans and the Northern and Southern Sea Peoples in Light of New Epigraphic and Archaeological Data." *UF* 44: 159–74.

Gilboa, Ayelet, and Ilan Sharon. 2008. "Between the Carmel and the Sea: Tel Dor's Iron Age Reconsidered." *NEA* 71: 146–70.

Harding, Jan. 2005. "Rethinking the Great Divide: Long-Term Structural History and the Temporality of Event." *Norwegian Archaeological Review* 38: 88–101.

Heinz, Marlies. 2016. *Kamid el-Loz: 4000 Years and More of Rural and Urban Life in the Lebanese Beqa'a Plain*. Beirut: The Lebanese British Friends of the National Museum.

Heinz, Marlies, Elisabeth Wagner, Julia Linke, Alexandra Walther, Antonietta Catanzariti, Jan-MatthiasMüller, Martin Weber. 2010. Kamid el-Loz – Report on the excavations in 2008 and 2009. *BAAL* 14: 9–134.

Hendel, Ronald. 2005. *Remembering Abraham. Culture, Memory, and History in the Hebrew Bible*. Oxford: Oxford University Press.

Iggers, Georg G. 1987. *New Directions in European Historiography*. Revised edition. Middletown: Wesleyan University Press.

———. 2012. *Historiography in the Twentieth Century: From Scientific Objectivity to the Postmodern Challenge*. Middleton: Wesleyan University Press.

Ilan, David. 2019. *Dan IV: The Iron Age I Settlement. The Avraham Biran Excavations (1966–1999)*. Jerusalem: Hebrew Union College-Jewish Institute of Religion.

Japhet, Sara. 1993. *I & II Chronicles. A Commentary*. Old Testament Library. Louisville: Westminster/John Knox Press.

Keimer, Kyle H., and Zachary Thomas. 2020-2021 [2022]. "Etic and Emic Expressions of Power in Ancient Israel: Recalibrating a Discussion." *JEOL* 48: 69–92.

Kelley, Donald R. 2006. *Frontiers of History: Historical Inquiry in the Twentieth Century*. New Haven: Yale University Press.

Kleiman, Assaf. 2019. "The Archaeology of Borderlands between Israel and Aram in the Iron I-II." PhD diss., Tel Aviv University.

Knapp, A. Bernard. 1992. "Archaeology and *Annales*: Time, Space, and Change." Pages 1–22 in *Archaeology, Annales, and Ethnohistory*. Edited by A. Bernard Knapp. Cambridge: Cambridge University Press.

Lipiński, Edward. 2000. *The Aramaeans: Their Ancient History, Culture, Religion*. Leuven: Peeters.

Maeir, Aren. 2017. "Evidence of Aramean Influences in Iron Age Judah and Israel." Pages 53–64 in *Wandering Arameans: Arameans Outside Syria Textual and Archaeological Perspectives*. Edited by Angelika Berlejung, Aren M. Maeir, and Andreas Schüle. Wiesbaden: Harrassowitz.

Matthews, Roger. 2003. *Archaeology of Mesopotamia: Theories and Approaches*. New York: Routledge.

Marfoe, L. 1995. *Kamid el-Loz 13. The Prehistoric and Early Historic Context of the Site: Catalog and Commentary*. Bonn: Habelt.

———. 1998. *Kāmid el-Lōz 14. Settlement History of the Biqā' up to the Iron Age*. Bonn: Habelt.

Mazzoni, Stefania. 2016. "Identity and Multiculturality in the Northern Levant of the 9th–7th Century BCE, with a Case Study on Tell Afis." Pages 281–304 in *In Search for Aram and Israel: Politics, Culture, and Identity*. Edited by Omer Sergi, Manfred Oeming, and Izaak J. de Hulster. Tübingen: Mohr Siebeck.

Moreland, John. 2001. *Archaeology and Text*. London: Duckworth.

Moster, David. 2017. "The Tribe of Manasseh and the Jordan River: Geography, Society, History, and Biblical Memory." PhD diss., Bar-Ilan University.

Na'aman, Nadav. 1994. "The 'Conquest of Canaan' in the Book of Joshua and in History." Pages 218–81 in *From Nomadism to Monarchy. Archaeological and Historical Aspects of Early Israel*. Edited by Israel Finkelstein and Nadav Na'aman. Jerusalem: Israel Exploration Society.

———. 2002. "In Search of Reality behind the Account of David's Wars with Israel's Neighbours." *IEJ* 52: 200–24.

Rohmer, Jérôme. 2020. *Hauran VI: D'Aram à Rome. La Syrie du Sud de l'âge du Fer à l'annexion rommaine (XIIe siècle av. J.-C. - Ier siècle apr. J.-C)*. Beyrouth: Institut français du Proche-Orient.

Sader, Hélène. 2010. "Tell Hizzin: Digging Up New Materials from an Old Excavation." Pages 635–49 in *Proceedings of the 6th International Congress of Archaeology of the Ancient Near East. Volume 2: Excavations, Surveys and Restorations: Reports on the Recent Field Archaeology in the Near East.* Edited by Paolo Matthiae, Frances Pinnock, Lorenzo Nigro, and Nicolo Marchetti. Wiesbaden: Harrassowitz.

Sergi, Omer and Assaf Kleiman. 2018. "The Kingdom of Geshur and the Expansion of Aram-Damascus into the Northern Jordan Valley: Archaeological and Historical Perspectives." *BASOR* 379: 1–18.

Singer, Itamar. 2006. "The Hittites and the Bible Revisited." Pages 723–35 in *"I will speak the riddles of ancient times." Archaeological and Historical Studies in Honor of Amihai Mazar on the Occasion of his Sixtieth Birthday.* Volume 2. Edited by Aren M. Maeir and Pierre de Miroschedji. Winona Lake: Eisenbrauns.

Snodgrass, Anthony M. 1985. "Greek Archaeology and Greek History." *Classical Antiquity* 4: 193–207.

Sugimoto, David T. 2015. "History and Nature of Iron Age Cities in the Northeastern Sea of Galilee Region: A Preliminary Overview." *Orient* 50: 91–108.

Susnow, Matthew, Nimrod Marom, Ariel Shatil, Nava Panitz-Cohen, Robert Mullins, and Naama Yahalom-Mack. 2021. "Contextualizing an Iron Age IIA Hoard of Astragali from Tel Abel Beth Maacah, Israel." *JMA* 34: 58–83.

Tadmor, Hayim. 1975. "Assyria and the West: The Ninth Century and its Aftermath." Pages 26–48 in *Unity and Diversity: Essays in the History, Literature, and Religion of the Ancient Near East.* Edited by Hans Goedicke and J. J. M. Roberts. Baltimore and London: The Johns Hopkins University Press.

Vita, Juan-Pablo. 2015. *Canaanite Scribes in the Amarna Letters.* Ugarit-Verlag: Münster.

Wee, John Zhu-En. 2005. "Maacah and Ish-Tob." *JSOT* 30: 191–99.

Yahalom-Mack, Naama, Nava Panitz-Cohen, and Robert Mullins. 2018. "From a Fortified Canaanite City-State to a "City and a Mother" in Israel: Five Seasons of Excavation at Tel Abel Beth Maacah." *NEA* 81: 145–56.

———. 2019. "An Iron Age I cultic context at Tel Abel Beth-Maacah." Pages 233–50 in *Research on Israel and Aram: Autonomy, Independence and Related Issues.* Edited by A. Berlejung and A. M. Maeir. Tübingen: Mohr Siebeck.

Yamada, Shigeo. 2000. *The Construction of the Assyrian Empire: A Historical Study of the Inscriptions of Shalmaneser III (859–824 B.C.) Relating to His Campaigns in the West.* Boston: Brill.

Younger, K. Lawson Jr. 2016. *A Political History of the Arameans: From Their Origins to the End of Their Polities.* Atlanta: SBL.

———. 2017 "Tiglath-Pileser I and the Initial Conflicts of the Assyrians with the Arameans." Pages 195–228 in *Wandering Arameans: Arameans Outside Syria. Textual and Archaeological Perspectives.* Edited by Angelika Barlejung, Aren M. Maeir, and Andreas Schüle. Wiesbaden: Herrassowitz.

———. 2021. *Judges, Ruth: Revised Edition.* Grand Rapids: Zondervan Academic.

37

PHOENICIANS AND ANCIENT ISRAEL

Ilan Sharon

Phoenicians in the Bible?

There are several reasons for the question-mark in the section title. The first is obvious: "Phoenicians" is a Greek, rather than Hebrew (or Phoenician) term. What did the Israelites call them? Did they consider the inhabitants of Tyre, Sidon, Byblos, and Arwad as some corporate entity? Was that entity limited to the territories of these states, or did it extend (in one historical period or another) beyond them? Is that entity homologous to what the Greeks called φοῖνικεσ (a definition that itself probably changed over the years, van Dongen 2010: 479)? This ties into one of the main concerns of Phoenician studies in recent decades: Did Phoenicians themselves (however we define them) have some sort of unified self-identity? And if so when? (Feldman 2014; Vella 2014; Martin 2017; Quinn 2018; but see López-Ruiz 2021: 15–19).

In Isaiah's prophecy on Tyre (Ch. 23), parallelisms for the latter include Sidon, Kition (in Cyprus), Tarshish, and Canaan. Jeramiah 25:22 groups together Tyre, Sidon, and "the island[s] across the sea." The sailors in Ezekiel's (Ch. 27) Tyrian ship parable are Sidonians, Arwadians, and Byblians, though many other nations (probably standing in for the entire known world) are noted in other roles. In most cases, however, individual towns or kingdoms are just noted by their names (in the story of Elijah and the widow of Zarephat in 1 Kgs 17, the latter is referred to as "Sarepta in the kingdom of Sidon").

If there was a Hebrew or Phoenician term for "Phoenicians," what might it have been? One possibility is that they were all "Sidonians." There is persistent ambivalence in the use of the term by ancient sources (Boyes 2012). In several cases in Phoenician inscriptions, the Bible, Assyrian annals, and classical sources, kings of Tyre are apparently referred to as "Sidonians." While other explanations are possible in each case, the conflation of evidence seems to indicate that "Sidonians" could be used as a metonym for a wider group. Another possibility is "Canaanites." In most cases, the use of this word in the Bible denotes the inhabitants of the Levant in the Bronze Age. But there are several cases where the term is used in a specifically Iron Age context to denote people from Tyre/Sidon or as a synonym for "merchants." Isaiah, in the passage already referred to, does both.

This ties into another major debate in Phoenician studies: To what extent is the Iron Age Phoenician civilization a direct continuation of the Bronze Age Canaanite one? One extreme position is that Phoenicia emerged unscathed from the collapse of the Bronze Age, and that therefore, while other parts of the Levant were settled by new peoples (Israelites, Sea Peoples, Arameans, etc.) unadulterated Canaanites continued to occupy the central Levantine coast (Stern 1991, 2003; Stager 1995; Aubet 2001: 11–13; van Dongen 2010: 477; Elayi 2018; Edrey 2019). In this view, the terms "Canaanite," "Phoenician," and "Punic" are nothing but a modern scholarly convention to arbitrarily divide this continuum at c. 1200 and c. 600 by using the Hebrew, Greek, and Latin names for the same ethnos in three different periods.

The contrasting view (Gilboa 2005, 2022; Sader 2019: 3–4; López-Ruiz 2021: 10; but see the opposite on p. 29) holds that the Iron Age Phoenicians, whether they saw themselves as a corporate entity or not, were just as much an amalgam of different groups of Bronze Age "refugees" as others that were defining themselves into "peoples" in the Near East and around the Mediterranean at about the same time.

Without resorting to the other extreme position, that "Phoenicianism" is entirely a modern scholarly construct (Vella 2014), it must be admitted that identities on the ground were probably considerably murkier than modern perception considers them to be.

A Phoenician Language?

One obvious purported commonality is the Phoenician language. Can we not simply call "a Phoenician" anyone who spoke (or, rather, wrote) Phoenician? Against this, we must weigh that the entire Iron Age Levant was a patchwork of Northwest Semitic dialects, probably mutually comprehensible, written in variants of the same script (see below). There were regional differences within the dialect/script we now call "Phoenician" (Krahmalkov 2000: 10); just as there were within what we now consider "Hebrew" (van Dongen 2010: 473–474). In addition, some of the most comprehensive Phoenician inscriptions of the Iron Age Levant were not found in Phoenicia proper (see below for geographic delineations) but rather in regions identified as Neo-Hittite/Aramean/generically North Syrian. Thus, Phoenician was used as a *lingua franca* outside Phoenicia; and/or linguistic/ethnic identities were in a state of flux and capable of being manipulated for political or other purposes (see, e.g., Brown 2008 with further bibliography).

The same reservation should be applied to the use of Phoenician language in the West. How would a first millennium BCE Iberian, say, communicate with a Sardinian, except in Phoenician or Greek? Indeed, the role of Phoenician as a medium of multi-littoral conversations may well have been instrumental in the development of a unified Phoenician language (as in *koine* Greek). Assuming that Phoenician was a single common language, what was it called by its speakers? Here we must refer to yet another recent debate in Phoenician studies—about the statement by St. Augustine that the local dialect in North Africa in his time was "Chanani." Quinn (2018: 31–32) argues that the context of that statement was a literary polemic on the story of Jesus healing the Canaanite woman's daughter (Matt 15:21–28; Mark 7:24–30), based on a Latin/Punic pun, and should not be understood as an anthropological observation. This may be, but it should not hide the facts that a woman of Tyre was called "Canaanite" in the 1st century CE, that that designation in Matthew was rendered "Syro-Phoenician" in Mark, or that educated readers in the 5th century CE were supposed to know that the Punic language spoken in North Africa at the time was a derivative of Canaanite—or else the pun would have no point.

Where Is Phoenicia?

The same quandary of "who is a Phoenician?" colors the delineation of the borders of Phoenicia. That the Mediterranean coast between Arwad and Tyre is Phoenician is consensual.

But how far does Phoenicia extend inland? Is the Beqaa in Phoenicia or in Syria? If the toponyms accorded to the Phoenician polities in the Assyrian annals are correctly identified (Sader 2019, Figure 3.6), the answer seems to be that the Phoenician polities did not extend beyond the Mt. Lebanon watershed divide, though at least some of them may have expanded their borders eastwards later.

Things get more complicated with the southern border. One often-repeated convention (of unclear derivation) has been that the southern edge of Phoenicia is the point of the Carmel. But the excavators of Dor have argued (Gilboa et al. 2008; Nitschke et al. 2011) that—possibly except for a short Israelite interlude in the mid-Iron Age—Dor is part of the Phoenician sphere. By the early Persian period—according to the Eshmunazar inscription (KAI 14)—Jaffa is Sidonian too; and by the end of this era, in the geographical compendium known as Pseudo-Skylax (Shipley 2011), all the towns along the coast, down to Ashkelon, are labeled as either Tyrian or Sidonian.

Elayi (1982) coined the term "southern Phoenicia" for this expansion of Phoenician territory into present-day Israel in the Persian period. The Dor excavators extended this designation for the liminal (and historically changing) zone between Central Phoenicia, Israel, and Philistia back into the early Iron Age. Note, though, that for the latter period, the claim is only that Dor is Phoenician in material culture and economy (for which see below). What this means in terms of political affiliation, language, or self-ascription is moot.

A similar phenomenon, of a mutable transitional zone, exists also north of Central Phoenicia. Following Sader (2019), we shall call it here Northern Phoenicia. The general division there is between the Phoenician-speaking (or, rather, Phoenician-writing) region and polities with a Luwian-writing elite ruling over an Aramean-reading population. The liminal zone here encompasses the area of the Late Bronze Age kingdoms of Amurru and Ugarit. According to Assyrian annals, it was occupied in the late Iron Age by several small polities. Archaeological excavations in several sites (Ras Ibn Hani, Tell Tweini, Tell Sukas, Tell Sianu, Tell Iris) show Phoenician traits of material culture (Sader 2019: 59–62 with further bibliography there). Moreover, as noted above, the so-called Neo-Hittite kingdoms further north were wont to manipulate their "Phoenicianness" as well when it suited their purpose. When reading Homeric descriptions of φοῖνικεσ plying their wondrous δαιδαλια across the Mediterranean (Morris 1992) one wonders: Did Homer make the same distinctions between Phoenician and Neo-Hittite art (for which, see below) as modern art-historians? Or were all perfidious, trinket-selling, child-snatching Levantines φοῖνικεσ?

More problematic is the case of Cyprus. When the island re-emerges from illiteracy in the Iron Age, three languages are spoken (or rather written): A minority of the inscriptions is in "Eteo-Cypriot" (presumably descendent from the indigenous Bronze Age language) in the Cypro-Syllabic script. Then there are Greek inscriptions written either in Greek script or in Cypro-Syllabic, and Phoenician inscriptions written in Phoenician script. The question now becomes, should we regard Cyprus, as is usually done in traditional scholarship, as a case (perhaps the first case) of Phoenician colonization? Or is it more profitable to think of Cyprus as part of the Phoenician phenomenon *ab-initio*?

Gilboa (most recently 2022) characterizes the formative period of Phoenician civilization—the early Iron Age—with pervasive contacts between the central Levantine coast (from Dor northwards) and the southeastern Cypriot one. In the realm of material culture, this is manifested both by imports from one coast to the other, and emulation of the products of one littoral on the other, but mainly by the mutual manipulation of the same symbolic assets. The Cypriot Bichrome style is not a copy of Phoenician Bichrome, or vice versa; but the decorative syntax is the same. Moreover, this stylistic conversation is durative: the

Phoenician Wavy-Line pithoi of the very beginning of the Iron Age are clear derivatives (but not copies) of Bronze Age Cypriot proto-types; the above-mentioned conjunction of Phoenician and Cypriot Bichrome comes later; and the appearance of red-slip decoration on the mainland at the beginning of the Iron Age II is echoed by the advent of the Black-on-Red style on the island in Cypro-Geometric III (Gilboa 2022 and further references there).

All this is in stark contrast to the general characteristics of the "Dark Age" in the Near East and around the Mediterranean; and in particular to those of Phoenicia's southern neighbor, Philistia. Despite the foreign, "Sea Peoples," origin of Philistine material culture (according to most authorities), subsequent stylistic changes after its initial appearance are not due to overseas influences, but rather evince a gradual "Levantinization" or "Phoenicianization" (Ben-Shlomo et al. 2004).

Gilboa believes that these influences indicate the physical presence of Cypriots on the mainland, and their involvement (along with, perhaps, that of others, e.g., North Syrians) in the development of a distinct Phoenician material culture (see also below). But should not the mirror-image of this process apply to Cyprus, as well? If (mainland) Levantines were present in Cyprus from the end of the Bronze Age and had a hand in the formation of Cypriot material culture of the Iron Age, then perhaps the explanation for the appearance of Phoenician-writing polities on the island is not some overt process of colonization, but rather the *in situ* formation of distinct self-identities on the island.

Phoenician Religion?

On the face of it there is no single Phoenician religion (van Dongen 2010: 478). Each Phoenician polity had [a] patron god[s] of its own: Eshmun for Sidon, Melqart for Tyre, Baalat Gebal for Byblos, etc. And yet, traditional scholarship proceeded—as in the case of other cultural facets—from the assumption of unity (both geographic and temporal, i.e., that observations by Roman writers on the religion of North Africa in the early centuries CE can be applied to the Levant in the second millennium BCE and vice versa). The problem is that if we strip away this assumption, we are left with little but a series of questions. This is much aggravated by the lack of contemporary data. The closest substantial corpus of theological/mythological literature is Late Bronze Age Ugarit, strictly outside the Phoenician orbit on both temporal and geographic parameters. Internal evidence is limited to little but dedicatory inscriptions (numerous but repetitive) and theophoric components in personal names. Secondary evidence comes from the Bible and classical sources but is clearly warped by both naïve and willful misunderstandings.

The logic of polytheism, wherein metaphysical entities can transmute in complex ways, and appear to believers in different manifestations, is notoriously difficult to grasp from a rationalistic/etic perspective. For one thing, there is an inherently ambiguous relationship between a deity's name and title. Baal (lit. Lord) is a case in point. Most extant references are to a generic Baal, but some are specific such as Baal Zaphon or Baal Zebul, or even Baalat Gebal. Ugaritic mythology often conflates Baal with *Hd* (later Hadad, patron of Aram). There are also references to Baals in the plural. Is Baal a single entity? Are there completely different gods who happen to be lords-of-something-or-other? Or, most likely, is the answer somewhere in the middle, varying according to specific place, epoch, and the context in which the question is posed? The Hebrew Bible seems exceptional in relegating this term to a seemingly specific foreign deity, but then the Israelite god is often referred to as "אדני" (Lord), i.e., the analogous term in Hebrew (for all these see Xella 2019 with references to earlier literature).

Another inherent ambiguity is between the deity and its representation[s]. Consider Asherah (Hadley 2000, with copious discussions of earlier literature): In Ugaritic mythology, Athirat is El's consort and "mother of 30 (or else 33) gods." Specifically, she is distinct from Astarte and Anat, who are second-tier deities. In the Bible the term usually refers to a cultic object, specifically a tree (or perhaps just a cut trunk) standing by an altar (e.g., Deut 16: 21), but in some cases (e.g., 1 Kgs 18:19), it refers to a goddess. Meanwhile in the first millennium Athirat/Asherah seems to fade back in Phoenicia proper, while Astarte becomes the principle female deity. A stylized "sacred tree" is one of the common artistic motifs in the first millennium, but whether it represents a deity (or is called an Asherah) is moot.

The male counterpart of the sacred tree is the standing stone (*massebah*). Many artistic representations, as well as actual specimens of such, exist in Phoenician contexts. Classical sources refer to them as "baetyls." This is usually taken to be a transcription of "בית אל" (lit. "house of [the god] El" or "house of [a generic] god"). However, Bethel is also a deity (Baumgarten 1981: 202–203) mentioned in the treaty of Baal of Tyre with Esarhaddon and in later sources (see also Gen 31:13). The semiotic trajectory here seems to be that the divine pair Asherah and El are aniconically represented by a tree and a stone, the stone is then explained away as El's house, and that then takes on an independent deified identity.

A similar trajectory is evidenced in Tanit, the most popular goddess in the Phoenician west (Lipiński 1995: 199–215). Her epithet is פנבעל (lit. "The face of Baal"). This fits her main role as an intermediary between the supplicant and a main god (usually Baal Hamon). First, the face of the deity becomes a metonym for the god himself, and then it takes an independent identity, with its own schematically anthropomorphic sign. For a long time, Tanit was considered a Punic (i.e. western) invention. Since the 1970s, however, both the sign and the name have been increasingly found in the Levant, and it is now clear that both originate there before the western expansion (Arie 2017, with references to earlier studies).

As a final layer of complication, the contact between Phoenicians, Egyptians, and Greeks led to syncretism between their respective pantheons. Melqart was associated with Herakles, Eshmun with Asklepios, Astarte with Aphrodite, etc. Initially, this may have been a mere translation of names, to enable Egyptian/Greek speakers to grasp Phoenician pantheons; but Phoenician dedications in Greek sanctuaries show that Phoenicians accepted this syncretism (if not actually manipulated it, e.g., Martin 2017). This inevitably led to attributes, mythologies, and artistic representations moving from one sphere to the other and back again. And these associations are not constant. For instance: Egyptian Hathor attributes are often identified with Asherah, Astarte, or Anat (Cornelius 2008). Syncretism is also possible between Phoenician gods themselves, leading to double-gods such as TanitAstarte, MlkAstart, or AnatBethel (Xella 2019).

The common second-millennium Canaanite triad of divine representations consists of a seated, robed, bearded male, usually identified as El; A striding, kilted, shaved male, usually identified as Baal; and a naked female, variously identified as Astarte, Anat, or Asherah. The males are often depicted in the round in gilded copper, whereas the females are most often depicted as two-dimensional plaques, or thin metal leaves (Negbi 1976). These give way in the first millennium to a humbler set of representations—usually in clay. They consist of a hollow-modeled, dressed female, often cradling her breasts, pregnant, or holding a baby—which are usually called "fertility figurines;" and solid-modeled males, often mounted, with a variety of facial-hair styles and of headgears. But what do they represent: Deities? And if so which? Unlike their Bronze Age predecessors, they lack recognizable divine attributes. Perhaps they are the worshippers? What is their function? Are they votive—as is suggested, e.g., by figurines apparently tossed in the sea at designated spots (Erlich et al. 2020)? Are they apotropaic? Do they represent household cults? Both the latter could explain the great amounts found in domestic contexts, e.g., in late Iron Age Jerusalem or Persian period Dor. Lastly, if they do not represent deities, what does? Is the lack of cult statues (in contrast to *massebot*, for instance) indicative of a trend toward aniconism (Ornan 2005)?

Phoenician art (see below) is replete with a menagerie of icons such as sphinxes, winged sun disks, "trees of life," Bes figures, Khepri dung-beetles, etc. Do these have any religious significance? Strangely enough, most Phoenicianists have dismissed the possibility. Traditional scholarship took the orientalist view that Phoenician art was a mere mindless copy of Egyptian iconography—stripping the symbols of meaning and retaining shapes only (e.g., Contenau 1926: 118–119; Frankfort 1954). More sophisticated modern scholarship claims that to serve as "daidalia" or as lubricant for diplomacy or trade, "International" art must display emotionally neutral values (Morris 1992; Feldman 2006, and see discussion below). Hence a choice of symbols evoking a sense of exotica and ancientness but lacking a specific theology. This position may have to be rethought. There are plenty of indications that "minor deities" and icons appearing in Phoenician art do have specific religious connotations.

"The number of excavated Phoenician sanctuaries is surprisingly small; even smaller are those dating to the Iron Age" (Stern 2003: 310). On the contrary, I would argue that that number is surprisingly large, given the limited exposures at sites of the relevant period in Lebanon (Sader 2019: 188–203 for a general list—of 14—and references to previous literature and excavation reports). This is in stark contrast to the situation in Israel, where religious architecture (excluding open-air installations and household shrines) is extremely sparse in these periods, despite infinitely larger exposures (Faust 2019).

The simplest and perhaps most common type of cultic structure (if it can even be called a structure) is the household shrine; by which I mean only that cultic implements are found in (or outside) what looks like regular domestic units. Whether these represent worship of household gods or some other cultic activity is another question. I also draw a distinction between a shrine (which has some contextual evidence for cultic activity) and figurines or amulets found in domestic contexts. The recently excavated structure at the "College Site" in Sidon phase B (of the 11th century BCE) seems a *bona fide* domestic shrine, while phases A (Late Bronze Age) and C (Iron Age II) are, to my mind, cases of the latter kind. The cultic installation at Tell el Burak, consisting of a *massebah* with a circle of stones at the corner of a house and dating to the 8th century is another example of such a cult-corner. It is unclear if it is inside a dwelling or in the street. Curiously enough such "cult corners" seem an Iron Age innovation, both in Israel (where they are rather common) and in Lebanon.

The simplest type of proper temple (i.e., a purpose-built cult structure) is exemplified in Sarepta (Pritchard 1978: 134–140). It consists of a single room with benches along three walls and a raised platform by the fourth. This is the traditional design of the so-called "irregular" temples in the Levant since the Late Bronze Age at least. The early phase of this temple was dated by Pritchard to the 7th–6th centuries BCE, and it continues in use into the Persian period. An inscribed ivory plaque in this temple is dedicated to "TanitAstart." The early (7th-century) phase of the temple at Tell Sukas also has the same plan, as do most of the structures in the sequence of temples at Tell Kazel. More elaborate, and even monumental temple structures were not yet found prior to the Persian period. (The temple at Amrit (Dunand and Saliby 1985) and the temple of Eshmun near Sidon (Stucky and Mathys 2000) are prime examples). However, they must have existed, since sanctuaries in colonies abroad, dating to the 8th—6th centuries have clear Levantine antecedents (e.g. at Motya, Nigro 2015: 86-90)

In conclusion, the religions of Phoenicia in the first millennium BCE are best described as a cluster of similar systems, with slightly different pantheons (mainly—each polity has its own patron god), a more-or-less common iconography and a variety of sacral architecture.

The problem is that the same can be said of all other Iron Age polities of the Levant as well. Thus the Arameans substitute Haddad for Baal (this equation already occurs in Ugaritic literature), Ammonites switch Melqart with Milkom. Kemosh is the patron of Moab and Qos of Edom. For students of early Israelite religion, the interesting question is to what extent it, too, is part of the same cluster and when—and under what circumstances—it departed from it.

Child Sacrifice in Phoenicia and Israel?

One of the most contentious debates in modern Phoenician Studies is the Tophet phenomenon. But it is hardly a modern debate, nor are its implications to ancient Israel. The 11th century CE exegetes Shlomo Yitschaki (Rashi) offers this polemic on Jeremiah 7:31 ("And they have built the high places of Topheth which are in the valley of Ben-Hinnom, to burn their sons and daughters with fire"):

> The high places of Topheth: That is Molech, which was of copper, and they would heat it up from underneath it with its hands spread out and heated. And they would place the child on his hands, and he would be burnt and moan, and the priests would beat drums so that the father should not hear his son's voice and take pity. It is called Topheth because of the drum (תוף), Hinnom because of the child's moaning (נהמת).

Apart from the (mistaken) etymologies Rashi is repeating what had become by then an ancient tradition, beginning with Cleitarchus (*Scholia to Plato*; *FGrHist* 137 F 9; ca. 300 BC trans. Mosca 1975: 22):

> There stands in their midst a bronze statue of Kronos, its hands extended over a bronze brazier, the flames of which engulf the child. When the flames fall upon the body, the limbs contract and the open mouth seems almost to be laughing until the contracted body slips quietly into the brazier. Thus it is that the 'grin' is known as 'sardonic laughter,' since they die laughing.

This, or similar stories, are often repeated in Greco-Roman literature (*inter alia* by Q. Curtius Rufus, Diodorus, Plutarch, see Mosca 1975; Xella 2009 for references and discussion).

Direct historical references to such practices in the Bible center around a specific place—called "Tophet" in Gei-Ben-Hinnom near Jerusalem. There, Judeans, and in particular their kings (e.g., Manasseh, 2 Kgs 21:6), "burn their sons and their daughters in the fire" (in the above-quoted passage in Jeremiah). No wonder that in Medieval (and Modern) Hebrew, Tophet came to mean "inferno" and Gehinnom became "hell." An often-repeated related term is *mlk* (Moloch), as in—"pass through fire to [or as] *mlk*" (2 Kgs 23:10)—which can be understood either as the name of a deity (as in Tyrian *Mlqrt* or Ammonite *Mlkom*), or as seems to be the consensus nowadays, the type of sacrifice (see Xella 2012–13: 263–266).

Surprising archaeological confirmation came in the early 1900s, when stelae with Phoenician inscriptions came into the antiquities market in Tunis, and were found to come from a cemetery at Carthage. Several unusual features set this site apart from other cemeteries. First, there was a mix of human and animal (kid and lamb) cremations in the urns. Second, both humans and animals were very young—newborns or babies. Third and most significant, the inscriptions (found on several hundred out of the thousands of stelae) were not funerary but had to do with the fulfilling of vows. The concordance with the above-quoted stories is obvious, and the biblical appellation Tophet stuck. Once found in Carthage, it was quickly realized that similar sites had already been discovered before, and more have been excavated since (see Xella 2012–13: 261 for a comprehensive list).

But should we accept these interpretations at face value? Before the discovery of the Tophet sites, one could (and some did) dismiss the classical sources as anti-Phoenician (or rather anti-Punic) propaganda. The biblical allegations can be differently interpreted, e.g., as symbolic ceremonies or as demonization of cult practices deemed unacceptable by the writers. Much of the discussion on the more modernly excavated cremations centers on aging the skeletal remains and determining cause of death. It must be admitted that, unlike the television show CSI, differentiating between "mature" fetuses, still-borns, and babies in their first months based on burnt bones disinterred after many years, is difficult; and whether death was by immolation or from natural causes well-nigh impossible (compare Hays, this volume). The decisive evidence is still the inscriptions on the stelae, plus the general context (children and animals together, etc.), and these indicate that the Tophets are no ordinary cemeteries (Xella 2012–13). It should perhaps be pointed out that, even if miscarried or stillborn babies were occasionally (or even often) used to sublimate the horrific act of sacrificing one's own children, the latter is still the intent of the practice. We already know that a sublimation in the form of offering an animal instead of a child was a possibility.

Lastly, we should stress that Tophets were thus far found only in the central Mediterranean (North Africa, Sicily, and Sardinia). None are known in the Levant, or in the extreme western Phoenician dominions in Iberia or the Atlantic coast. Excavations, e.g., in Tyre and Achziv, have found evidence of cremation burials, some with stelae (both practices are foreign to the local burial traditions in the second and first millennia BCE), but they are of adults. Perhaps the practice originated in the diaspora? The biblical allegations argue against this, as do the attestations of Quintius Rufus (History of Alexander IV.iii.23) for this practice at Tyre at the time of Alexander's siege; though Rufus' sources are obscure, and he may merely be embellishing his story for popular Roman consumption. Assuming child immolation came with the Phoenicians from their homeland we may argue that it was rare (e.g., practiced only by kings) or that it was not followed by burial of the remains in specialized cemeteries, which would make it archaeologically invisible.

Phoenician Art?

The first discovery of what we now call Phoenician ivories, by Austen Henry Layard at the Assyrian site of Nimrud (Calah), was made on the very second day of his excavation in 1845. Layard (1849: I, 29–30), whose object was the recovery of monumental sculpture, was not impressed. Though he did find more ivories later (1849: II, 8–10) real progress in identifying them was not made till his second expedition, in 1850, when he found a hoard of bronze objects, some of which were decorated in the same style.

> From the Egyptian character of the designs ... it may be inferred that some of them were not Assyrian, but had been brought from a foreign people... The Sidonians ... were the most renowned workers in metal of the ancient world, and their intermediate position between the two great nations ... may have been the cause of the existence of a mixed art amongst them.
>
> *(Layard 1853: I, 192)*

There were other clues he was aware of. Metal bowls decorated in the same style had been found already in tombs in Italy *(ibid, 190)* and in Cyprus *(ibid, 192)*. The "smoking gun" might have been the inscriptions on some of the objects. Layard, however, could not read them. He thought they were "either in the Phoenician or Assyrian cursive character" (1853: I, 188—*the latter is a script that does not exist I.S.*). Alas, now we know that some of these inscriptions were Aramean (e.g. López-Ruiz 2021: 86)

How did Layard know that "The Sidonians ... were the most renowned workers in metal of the ancient world"? He appeals to the authority of the Bible (1 Kgs 7:14) and of Homer (e.g., Il. 23.740–45). The first is the passage that states that the craftsman who made the cultic vessels for Solomon's temple was the son of a Tyrian coppersmith. In and of itself this might or might not be interpreted as Layard understands it. Homer refers to Phoenician craftsmanship in his descriptions of "δαιδαλια." These, in the heroic ethos, are precious objects that the hero receives as gifts, loot in battle, or wins in competitions. While their primary value is probably in the material from which they are wrought and in the quality of their decoration, they accrue prestige by their biography: their great age, exotic origins, and heroes they have been associated with (Morris 1992). The attribution of (some of) these daidalia to Phoenician craftsmen may be due to any of these.

As far as identifying this art, this is where things stood for some 150 years (Vella 2010: 23; Suter 2015: 32). Large collections have been found since: For ivories, these include Samaria, Arslan Tash (an Assyrian administrative center in north Syria), Salamis in Cyprus, and the Mt. Ida cave sanctuary in Crete. The concentrations for engraved metal bowls remain Cyprus and Italy, but many more have been found since. Individual pieces have been found in many other sites, including (but not exclusive to) Phoenician colonies in the western Mediterranean. Important typological work has been done (Winter 1981; Barnett 1982; Markoe 1985; see Suter 2015: 32–41 for summary and critique in the case of ivories) and the assemblage has been divided into styles and sub-styles. Up until the nineties, though, the identification of this art as Phoenician was hardly challenged. This, even though empirical confirmation in Phoenicia failed to appear, and some evidence points in other directions (e.g., Aramean inscriptions on ivories and bowls). Even reasoned critiques, proceeding from the assumption that the courts of various Levantine states of the Iron Age must have had their own artisanal schools (e.g., Winter 1981) accepted the basic premise that the purer (i.e., more Egyptianizing) the style the more Phoenician it must be.

Over the last quarter-century, this paradigm came under increasing attack (Vella 2010, 2014; Feldman 2014; Suter 2015; Martin 2017; but see rebuttal in López-Ruiz 2021: 87–89). To be sure, no one is claiming that such ivories, metal bowls, or other classes of objects decorated in the same style (e.g., ostrich eggs, *tridachna* shells) were *never* made in Tyre or Sidon (among other places), or that Phoenicians did not have a hand in their dispersal around the Mediterranean. The question is whether this appellation is useful, or does it ultimately obscure more than it can reveal? For instance, it is generally conceded (e.g., Suter 2011) that this art is the continuation of the so-called International Style of the Late Bronze Age (Feldman 2006). If we are not calling the predecessor 'Canaanite Art,' why should we ethnicize the successor?

Another example, relevant to the present context, is the classification of the Samaria ivories as Phoenician. Barnett (1982: 46) is able not only to naively associate them with Jezebel (despite there being no contextual evidence to their date), but also to characterize them as foreign and "pagan." He thus not only deprives Israel of art of its own but denies the possibility that the ivories reflect Israelite religion or ideology.

Similar arguments can be made for other media (e.g., terra-cottas, glass, faience) but the above examples suffice for our purpose. We argue that the term "Phoenician" Art covers a loose *koiné* of artisanal production in the Levant and across the Mediterranean, *including* Israel and (perhaps to a lesser degree) Judah.

Phoenician Material Culture?

Similar problems pertain to humbler artifacts. Here we must start with a methodological disclaimer: It is a fact of archaeology that material culture nearly always displays auto-correlation in space and time. By this, I merely mean that if we find a trait of material culture (whether it be pottery type, a production technique, or a food-way) at a site, it is *ipso facto* more likely that we find the same trait in nearby sites of a comparable period (van Dongen 2010: 474–477). Thus it is not enough that a certain material attribute occurs in Judah, for instance, to label it "Judean" (with all the cultural and ideological baggage that this involves). To label a trait with an ethnonym such as "Phoenician" we should require that at least several additional considerations be met: That it be *made* (rather than just found) in Phoenicia. That it be *not made* (though may be found) outside Phoenicia. That it be found (though not necessarily made) *all over* Phoenicia. In the special case of Phoenicia, we should require that it be also found (and perhaps also made) in the Phoenician diaspora.

But are there (many) categories that satisfy all (or even most) the above? Again, we cannot hope to cover all material categories, and will only give several examples of traits that have been hailed as hallmarks of Phoenician material culture.

Decorated Pottery

The earliest pottery style specifically attributed to the Phoenicians is the so-called Phoenician Bichrome. Its early development was studied by Ayelet Gilboa (1999 and see there for a comprehensive definition and further bibliography). Its signature motif, appearing on almost every vessel, is the Enclosed Band: A thick red stripe encircling the vessel (horizontally or, in the case of pilgrim flasks, vertically) with one or two thin black (and sometimes also white) lines symmetrically placed on either side (Figure 37.1). The style appears in the late Iron Age I (c. 1000 BCE) and is found in the Levant and in Cyprus. It develops into the Iron Age II (though gradually superseded by the Phoenician Red Slip, see below) and enjoys a late *floruit* in the Phoenician colonies in the West (Giardino 2017).

Figure 37.1 Phoenician bichrome pottery (courtesy of the Tel Dor Excavation Project)

The technique of painting pottery with two or three colors (red and black, sometimes also white) was well known in the Levant throughout the Late Bronze Age and into the early Iron Age. However, this decoration was almost always linear; i.e. altering band thickness in predefined patterns was not part of the decorative syntax. The initial origins of the latter are in Mycenaean Greece, but the immediate source is Cyprus, where such syntax is common (together with other decorative elements typical to Phoenician Bichrome) from the Late Cypriot IIIB (Gilboa 2022). Indeed, just prior to the appearance of the full-fledged Bichrome style there is, according to Gilboa, an 'experimental stage' where one may find linear two-colored designs *or* the enclosed band syntax in monochrome, but not both on the same vessel. Not randomly, this is also the period where contact between Phoenicia and Cyprus is re-established. Indeed, she hypothesizes that this somewhat-hybrid style was invented to brand whatever was being exported in small containers. According to residue analysis, at least some of them contained distillations of spices from Southeast Asia in wine or oil. Quite soon after the arrival of Bichrome vessels in Cyprus a local Bichrome style develops using the same syntax on typically Cypriot vessels.

Petrographic analysis shows that only about one-third of the Phoenician Bichrome vessels found in Cyprus in the early Iron Age is from the Tyre – Sidon region, another third is from the Carmel Coast (probably Dor) and about one-third is locally made in Cyprus (Gilboa and Goren 2015: 86–87); only a few were from the Akko plain (between the Carmel and the Ladder of Tyre) or from the area from Beirut northwards. Analysis of Phoenician Bichrome vessels from the Southern Levant shows the Carmel Coast as the major supplier, but also that a few were locally made in the Jezreel Valley (probably Megiddo) and the Upper Jordan Valley (Dan; Gilboa and Goren 2015: 79–80). Note that the excavators of Dor consider it to be within the Phoenician orbit at that time, but the latter areas are outside Phoenicia as usually defined. Dan, specifically, is considered by its excavators to be Israelite in the Iron Age I.

During the Iron Age II, Phoenician Bichrome is gradually replaced by the Phoenician Red Slip (PRS) in the medium of high-end tableware. The term refers to bowls (a.k.a. "Samaria Bowls") and jugs (a.k.a. "Achzivian Jugs") with highly burnished red slip (Waiman-Barak 2020). The nicknames echo the sites in which these wares were first identified. Apart from the slip and burnish they are characterized by certain technological traits (e.g., the bowls are extremely thin, made from highly levigated clay and fired at high temperatures) and distinctive shapes (e.g., mushroom or trefoil lips for the jugs). Some of these shapes are also found with Bichrome decoration, forming a link between the two groups. Additional decoration may consist of bands of reserved slip and/or black circles.

PRS was found along the coasts of the Levant (but also inland, particularly in the Kingdom of Israel), in Cyprus, and in Phoenician sites in the western Mediterranean (Fletcher 2006 with bibliography). It should be noted that the shift from painted decoration to red slip (sometimes with black paint) is part of a wider trend. It is found, contemporaneously, also in Israel, Judah, and Philistia—where it is found in the Late Philistine Decorated Ware (Ben-Shlomo et al. 2004), as well as in Northern Syria (Waiman-Barak 2020) and in Cyprus—specifically in the Black-on-Red Ware (Schreiber 2003), and Phoenician colonies in the west (Giardino 2017).

Where was it made? A comparison of PRS bowls from Dor, Hazor, Samaria, and Kition demonstrated that for the latter three about half the bowls came from the Lebanese coast, and the other half was made locally near each site. At Dor, all the PRS bowls were imported from the coast of Lebanon (Sharon 1990, note that the Dor excavators maintain that at that time Dor was under the domination of the Kingdom of Israel). A much wider petrographic provenience study of fine-ware bowls from sites in Israel (Aznar 2005) gave similar results.

The major production centers are the Phoenician coast and Hazor (only two bowls from Samaria were sampled in this study) with Hazor-made bowls predominating at Hazor. Most other sites imported this ware from Phoenicia.

Building Techniques and Architectural Decoration

Historically, the claim, on behalf of the Phoenicians, to fame as builders rests squarely on 1 Kgs 5:31–32 [17–18]; 7:21–22, which recount aspects of the construction of Solomon's temple. Yet, when Iron Age ashlar construction (along with a lily-shaped Proto-Aeolic capital) was first encountered on the ground, at Megiddo in 1906, the excavator had this to say:

> The unstable maze of wall courses of small rubble stones and fieldstones encountered in earlier levels … [was] … here suddenly replaced by the skilled arrangement of large, hewn ashlars. This construction technique was no doubt introduced with the aid of foreign architects—presumably Phoenicians.
> (Schumacher 1908, transl. M. Martin p. 91, see also Figure 178 for the capital)

Similar sentiments are echoed in almost every publication on this subject since then (including several of this writer's, see Sharon 1987 for definitions and an introduction). One dissenting voice was Yigal Shiloh's (1979), who claimed both ashlar construction and the capitals are Israelite in origins (see a similar attribution, to a Judean origin for these features, in Mumcuoglu and Garfinkel 2021). Shiloh argued that there was a 250 year and 350 km gap between the disappearance of ashlar architecture in Syria in the Late Bronze Age (most conspicuously at Ugarit) and its reappearance in the Iron Age in Israel, and not in Phoenicia. While this may have been true for 1979, many instances in Phoenicia are known today. The gap between Sidon c. 1180 BCE and Dor at c. 1100/1050 did not altogether close but is considerably shorter (Sharon 2009).

The case for Proto-Aeolic capitals is somewhat different. Their earliest appearance (in well-dated contexts) is still in Israel, and they are also found in Judah, Amon, Moab, Cyprus (the bulk), and scattered around the Mediterranean (these last being mainly representations on stelae and model shrines rather than actual structural elements; see Franklin, this volume). They are rare, but exist, in heartland Phoenicia both in actual and representational forms (Kahwagi-Janho 2014). Moreover, as the name suggests, they are the precursor of the Aeolic (and eventually Ionic) forms. The agents of this diffusion to the west in the 6th C. BCE could hardly be Israelites, much less Judeans. There is regional variation in the design of Proto-Aeolic capitals. Cypriot capitals are commonly topped with papyrus fluorescence, of which the 'ordinary' volutes form the sepal leaves. The recent find of a cache of architectural elements near Jerusalem (Bilig et. al. 2022) allows for the definition of a "Jerusalem style" of capitals, with certain attributes that do not appear elsewhere (e.g. oculi—concentric circles—between the central triangle and the volutes). Such regionalism belies the notion of Phoenician craftsmen 'imported' into the various courts of Levantine kingdoms for important building projects. Rather, schools of resident craftsmen developed these local characteristics over time.

Conclusion—Material Culture

What, if any, are the commonalities between these different case studies? I refer to the methodological query with which we started this chapter. Almost all material culture usually earmarked as Phoenician was not produced *only* in Phoenicia. Many were not made (or even used) *all over* Phoenicia. Nevertheless, it is Phoenicians (presumably) who are responsible for their diffusion across the Mediterranean.

Moreover, many of these are objects of multi-littoral (or at least inter-regional) *conversations* (e.g., the Cypriot Bichrome style is not a *copy* of Phoenician Bichrome, but a *response* to it). Potters in Cyprus were perfectly capable of producing, and did occasionally make, vessels in the Phoenician Bichrome style which are indistinguishable from the "original" except by chemistry. They *chose* to use the same decorative syntax in a traditional Cypriot ceramic context. Nor is there a clear "core"—which furnishes innovations or "originals"—and a periphery which copies them. Rather, the style develops as a recursive interaction between both littorals. The Phoenician Bichrome that Cypriots were responding to was produced by Levantine potters applying a Canaanite production technique to a Cypriot (and originally Mycenaean) decorative syntax. The same can be shown for the relationship between Phoenician Red Slip and Cypriot Black-on-Red (as well as Late Philistine Decorated Ware, Aegean Black-on-Red, and other red-burnished wares of the Iron Age). Even the relationship between the "Proto-" and the "Aeolic" can perhaps most profitably be seen as such a conversation, wherein the style develops recursively, at different places with contacts to each other.

The Beginning of Phoenician Overseas Ventures

All the above sections go some way to explain why many contemporary Phoenicianists define the Phoenicians not as a polity or an ethnic group, nor their material culture as a distinct "archaeological culture," but rather as defined by a set of activities (namely Levantine trade and colonization over the Mediterranean) and their material correlates (and perhaps less-material aspects, e.g., the alphabet) as objects of multi-littoral conversations as defined above. López-Ruiz (2021) calls this the "orientalizing kit" and Gilboa (2022) talks about a "Phoenicianizing process."

This begs the question "when did these activities begin?" Traditional historical answers were several:

- They were already established in the Bronze Age. This depends on one's reading of the references to Phoenicians in Homer (already discussed above), and the question of to what extent these reflect the situation at the time of the telling of the story or the time in which the narrative is set.
- Closely following the Trojan War (e.g., the foundation of Kition by Teucros, of Utica (in Modern day Tunis "298 years before Carthage," Ps.-Arist. Mir. 134) and Cadiz (on the Atlantic coast of Spain "in the Trojan era," Pomp. Mela 3.46).
- Sometime before Solomon's exploits with Hiram king of Tyre (1 Kgs 9:27, 10:22).
- Sometime before the establishment of the first Greek colonies (8th C. BCE, based, e.g., on Thuc. VI.2).

Archaeological evidence favored the last. The earliest Phoenician wares in the colonies correlated with Iron Age IIB of the Levant (8th century BCE in today's terms).

All this changed in 1998 when a construction company pumping mud out of the Rio Tinto estuary, in order to drive foundation-pilings for a building project in Huelva, on the Atlantic coast of Spain, north of Cadiz unearthed potsherds and other artifacts from levels up to 2.5 m. below the current water table (de Canales et al. 2006). A Phoenician colony at Huelva is documented by classical sources and verified by numerous excavations—both the town and its cemeteries—but none of the finds thus far were earlier than c. 700 BCE in date.

The ceramics from the Plaza de las Monjas construction site correlate with Levantine Iron Age IIA (perhaps even early within it), including PRS, and are accompanied by other typical Phoenician finds such as ivories and even two fragmentary inscriptions, as well as several ^{14}C dates, spanning the 9th C. BCE.

Shortly thereafter a deep probe sunk by the University of Ghent at Carthage found ceramics earlier than any previously known at that site and a sequence of ^{14}C dates establishing the date of the earliest layers of the probe to c. 815 BCE, rather close to the date calculated by Josephus for the establishment of this colony (Docter et al. 2008).

This reliable data on early Phoenician colonization in the western Mediterranean painted a picture different than reconstructions based on dubious historical sources. First, rather than gradual westward expanding cycles of exploration-exploitation-consolidation we see a mighty leap to the very western edge of the known world, followed by the establishment of stations on the way. This happened about a century after Hiram and Solomon (according to the biblical chronology) and about a century before Greek colonization started in earnest.

Such waystations may just as well have been established by the colonists themselves as by the metropoleis in the Levant. It is worthwhile noting that according to their foundation myth, Carthaginians saw themselves as offspring of Tyrian men and women from Kition.

The motivation for the westward leap also becomes clear. The Rio Tinto mines are a major source of silver, as well as gold and copper, active from the Bronze Age to the modern era. Indeed, lead-isotope analysis from silver hoards in the Levant shows that the first introduction of silver from the western Mediterranean (first from Sardinia and later from Iberia) occurs somewhat earlier than this date (Eshel et al. 2019). In addition to metallurgy there

Figure 37.2 Phoenician silver bowl (8th c.; Walters Art Museum)

is evidence, in Huelva and other early Iberian sites, of local production of purple dye (no *in situ* installations but many murex shells), and procurement (as well as local processing) of ivory and ostrich eggs. These last commodities could have been obtained via indirect trading chains from Sub-Saharan Africa, or from animal populations which still existed at the time on the North African coast.

It seems that, as has always been supposed, the main imports from the colonies were raw materials. In return, exports from the Levant would have been finished craft objects, especially ones with high added-value (i.e., high expertise/craftsmanship: raw-material ratio)—Homer's "trinkets." The most visible of these being the silver bowls (Figure 37.2) and ivory-inlaid objects but also, in all probability, high-end textiles (esp. purple-dyed). Another export of which we have recently been made aware, due to modern analytic methods, are spices (cinnamon and probably nutmeg) originating in the Far East, processed (into infusions), and trans-shipped in Phoenicia (Gilboa and Namdar 2015). It was realized quite quickly, though, that exporting expertise (in the form of actual crafts[wo]men or of knowledge) may be more efficient than back-and-forth trans-shipment of materials (sent forth in raw and received back in finished states). Even the earliest colonies bear evidence of local production in Phoenician style. This would have been conducive to the establishment of permanent colonies (rather than transient or semi-transient trade, which seems to be the rule in the Bronze Age), and to the creation of communities of craft "conversing" as it were across the Mediterranean, as our evidence indicate.

What was the impact of all this on the Israelites? They were certainly aware of the economic exploits of their neighbors to the north, as attested by the prophecies on Tyre, with which we opened this essay. Whether kings like Solomon or Jehoshaphat actually participated in such ventures alongside Phoenicians depends on whether the relevant biblical passages are historical or hopeful fancy, a subject this writer is ill-equipped to comment on. In as much as the Spice Route through the Negev was active this early, the kings of Judah and perhaps also Israel were well positioned to benefit from the spice trade; though South Asian spices may have reached the Mediterranean coast via Transjordan (thus benefitting Edom, Moab, and Ammon) or even via the Persian Gulf, up the Euphrates and then down the Orontes rivers. As we have seen, there certainly is evidence that local craft communities, whether under royal tutelage or not, participated in on-going multi-littoral conversations.

Conclusions

Recent scholarship provides two different, though not necessarily contradictory, definitions of the term "Phoenician," as it may pertain to ancient Israel. First, the Phoenicians were the interface between the Levant (or perhaps even the Ancient Near East as a whole) and the newly emerging civilizations of the central and western Mediterranean: the perfidious traders carrying exotic goods mentioned by Homer; the window through which bi-littoral conversations, as defined above, took place. Gilboa's (2022) "Phoenician process" falls into this category. As such, the exact identity of these traders is not determined, though note that by the time the first contacts solidified into colonization, southern Phoenicia was no longer active in them, probably having been incorporated into the Kingdom of Israel. This leaves Tyre and Sidon, and perhaps points north of there, as the initial colonizers, though Cypriots also may have been involved from the very beginning as well.

Second, the term "Phoenician" implies a cultural *koiné*, or a bundle of cultural attributes (language, religion, art, material culture, etc.) all of which are *present* in the central Phoenician polities, but none is *exclusive* to them. If we define the bundle, again, as those facets which make it out of the "window" and into other littorals—López-Ruiz's (2021) "orientalizing kit," then similarities will decrease further away from central Phoenicia. Israel will be more "Phoenician" than Judah, and Judah more than Moab, though some "Phoenician" traits manifest in the latter as well (e.g., ashlar construction, Proto-Aeolic capitals). Thus the "World of the Israelites," in many of its facets, including art, material culture, and perhaps aspects of religion is very much a Phoenician world.

Bibliography

Arie, Eran. 2017. "The Earliest Known 'Sign of Tanit' Revealed in 11th Century BCE Building at Megiddo." *TA* 44: 61–71.

Aznar, Carolina A. *Exchange Networks in the Southern Levant during the Iron Age II: A Study of Pottery Origin and Distribution*. Ph.D. diss., Harvard University, 2005.

Aubet, Maria E. 2001. *The Phoenicians and the West: Politics, Colonies and Trade*. Cambridge: Cambridge University Press.

Barnett, Richard D. 1982. *Ancient Ivories in the Middle East*. Jerusalem: Institute of Archaeology.

Baumgarten, Albert I. 1981. *The Phoenician History of Philo of Byblos: A Commentary*. Leiden: Brill.

Ben-Shlomo, David, Itzhaq Shai, and Aren M. Maeir. 2004. "Late Philistine Decorated Ware ("Ashdod Ware"): Typology, Chronology, and Production Centers." *BASOR* 335: 1–35.

Boyes, P. J. 2012. "'The King of the Sidonians': Phoenician Ideologies and the Myth of the Kingdom of Tyre-Sidon." *BASOR* 365: 33–44.

Brown, B. 2008. "The Kilamuwa Relief: Ethnicity, Class and Power in Iron Age North Syria." Pages 339–55 in *Proceedings of the 5th International Congress on the Archaeology of the Ancient near East Madrid, April 3–8, 2006*. Edited by J. M. Córdoba et al. Madrid: Centro Superior de Estudios sobre el Oriente Próximo y Egipto.

Contenau, G. 1926. *La Civilisation Phénicienne*. Paris: Payot.

Cornelius, Izak. 2008. *The Many Faces of the Goddess: The Iconography of the Syro-Palestinian Goddesses Anat, Astarte, Qedeshet, and Asherah c. 1500–1000 BCE*. Fribourg/Göttingen: Academic Press/Vandenhoeck & Ruprecht.

Dever, William G. 1984. "Asherah, Consort of Yahweh? New Evidence from Kuntillet Ajrud." *BASOR* 255: 21–37.

Docter, R., F. Chelbi, B. Maraoui Telmini, A. Nijboer, J. van der Plicht, W. Van Neer, K. Mansel, and S. Garsallah. 2008. "New Radiocarbon Dates from Carthage: Bridging the Gap between History and Archaeology?" Pages 379–422 in *Beyond the Homeland: Markers in Phoenician Chronology*. Edited by C. Sagona. Louvain: Peeters.

Dunand, Maurice and Nessib Saliby, 1985. *Le Temple d'Amrith dans la Pérée d'Aradus*. Paris: Librairie Orientaliste Paul Geuthner.

Edrey, M. 2019. *Phoenician Identity in Context: Material Cultural Koiné in the Iron Age Levant*. Munster: Ugarit Verlag.

Elayi, Josette. 1982. "Studies in Phoenician Geography during the Persian Period." *JNES* 41: 83–110.

———. 2018. *The History of Phoenicia*. Atlanta: Lockwood.

Erlich, Adi, Assaf Yasur-Landau, and Meir Edrey. 2020. "Shipwreck or Sunken Votives? The Shavei Zion Assemblage Revisited." *IJNA* 49: 249–62.

Eshel, T., Y. Erel, N. Yahalom-Mack, O. Tirosh, and A. Gilboa. 2019. "Lead Isotopes in Silver Reveal Earliest Phoenician Quest for Metals in the West Mediterranean." *PNAS* 116/13: 6007–6012.

Faust, Avraham. 2019. "Israelite Temples: Where was Israelite Cult not Practiced, and Why." *Religions* 10, article 106. Onlione: doi:10.3390/rel10020106

Feldman, Marian H. 2006. *Diplomacy by Design: Luxury Arts and an International Style in the Ancient Near East, 1400–1200 BCE*. Chicago: University of Chicago Press.

———. 2014. *Communities of Style: Portable Luxury Arts, Identity, and Collective Memory in the Iron Age Levant*. Chicago: University of Chicago Press.

Fletcher, Richard. 2006. "The Cultural Biography of a Phoenician Mushroom-Lipped Jug." *OJA* 25: 173–94.

Frankfort, Henri. 1954. *The Art and Architecture of the Ancient Orient*. Harmondsworth: Penguin.

Giardino, Sara. 2017. "Phoenician Ceramic Tableware between East and West: Some Remarks on Open Forms and on Their Absolute Chronology." *Cartagine. Studi e Ricerche* 2: 1–21.

Gilboa, Ayelet. 1999. "The Dynamics of Phoenician Bichrome Pottery: A View from Tel Dor." *BASOR* 316: 1–22.

———. 2005. "Sea Peoples and Phoenicians along the Southern Phoenician Coast–A Reconciliation. An Interpretation of Šikila (Skl) Material Culture." *BASOR* 337: 47–78.

———. 2022. "The Southern Levantine Roots of the Phoenician Mercantile Phenomenon." *BASOR* 387. Online: doi.org/10.1086/718892.

Gilboa, Ayelet and Yuval Goren. 2015. "Early Iron Age Phoenician Networks: An Optical Mineralogy Study of Phoenician Bichrome and Related Wares in Cyprus." *Ancient West & East* 14: 73–110.

Gilboa, Ayelet and Dvori Namdar. 2015. "On the Beginnings of South Asian Spice Trade with the Mediterranean Region: A Review." *Radiocarbon* 57: 265–83.

Gilboa, Ayelet, Ilan Sharon, Ruth Shahack-Gross, Avshalom Karasik, and Uzy Smilansky. 2008. "Between the Carmel and the Sea: Tel Dor's Iron Age Reconsidered." *NEA* 71: 146–70.

Hadley, Judith M. 2000. *The Cult of Asherah in Ancient Israel and Judah: Evidence for a Hebrew Goddess*. Cambridge: University Press.

Kahwagi-Janho, H. 2014. "Les Chapiteaux À Volutes Verticales Du Liban." *Chronos: Revue d'Histoire de l'Université de Balamand* 29: 95–125.

Krahmalkov, C. R. 2000. *Phoenician-Punic Dictionary*. Leuven: Peeters.

Layard, Austin Henry. 1849. *Nineveh and Its Remains: With an Account of a Visit to the Chaldaean Christians of Kurdistan, and the Yezidis, or Devil-Worshippers; and an Enquiry into the Manners and Arts of the Ancient Assyrians*. 2 Vols. London: John Murray.

———. 1853. *Discoveries in the Ruins of Nineveh and Babylon: With Travels in Armenia, Kurdistan and the Desert: Being the Result of a Second Expedition Undertaken for the Trustees of the British Museum*. London: John Murray.

Lipiński, Edward. 1995. *Dieux Et Déesses de L'univers Phénicien et Punique*. Leuven: Peeters.

López-Ruiz, Carolina. 2021. *Phoenicians and the Making of the Mediterranean*. Cambridge: Harvard University Press.

Markoe, Glenn. 1985. *Phoenician Bronze and Silver Bowls from Cyprus and the Mediterranean*. Berkeley: University of California Press.

Martin, S. Rebecca. 2017. *The Art of Contact: Comparative Approaches to Greek and Phoenician Art*. Philadelphia: University of Pennsylvania Press.

Morris, Sarah P. 1992. *Daidalos and the Origins of Greek Art*. Princeton: Princeton University Press.

Mosca, Paul G. *Child Sacrifice in Canaanite and Israelite Religion: A Study in Mulk and Molech*. Ph.D. diss., Harvard University, 1975.

Mumcuoglu, Madeleine and Yosef Garfinkel. 2021. "Royal Architecture in the Iron Age Levant." *JJAR* 1: 450–81.

Negbi, Ora. 1976. *Canaanite Gods in metal. An Archaeological Study of Ancient Syro-Palestinian Figurines* Tel Aviv: Tel Aviv University Institute of Archaeology

Nigro, Lorenzo. 2015. Temples in Motya and Their Levantine Prototypes: Phoenician Religious Architectural Tradition. *BAAL Hors-Série* 10: 83–108.

Nitschke, Jessica L.; S. Rebecca Martin, and Yiftah Shalev. 2011. "Between Carmel and the Sea. Tel Dor: The Later Periods." *NEA* 74: 132–54.

Ornan, Tallay. 2005. *The Triumph of the Symbol, Pictorial Representation of Deities in Mesopotamia and the Biblical Image Ban*. Gottingen: Vandenhoeck and Ruprecht.

Pritchard, James B. 1978. *Recovering Sarepta. A Phoenician City*. Princeton: Princeton University Press.

Quinn, J. C. 2018. *In Search of the Phoenicians*. Princeton: University Press.

Sader, Helene S. 2019. *The History and Archaeology of Phoenicia*. Atlanta: SBL.

Schreiber, Nicola. 2003. *The Cypro-Phoenician Pottery of the Iron Age*. Leiden: Brill.

Sharon, Ilan. 1987. "Phoenician and Greek Ashlar Construction Techniques at Tel Dor, Israel." *BASOR* 267: 21–42.

———. 1990. "Statistical Methods for Interpreting the Results of Provenience Analysis of Ceramics." MA thesis, The Hebrew University of Jerusalem. (Hebrew)

———. 2009. "Ashlar Construction at Dor: Four Comments on the State of Research." *EI* 29: 362–82.

Shiloh, Yigal. 1979. *The Proto-Aeolic Capital and Israelite Ashlar Masonry*. Jerusalem: Institute of Archaeology, Hebrew University of Jerusalem.

Shipley, Graham. 2011. *Pseudo-Skylax's Periplous: The Circumnavigation of the Inhabited World: Text, Translation and Commentary*. Exeter: Bristol Phoenix Press.

Stager, Lawrence E. 1995. "The Impact of the Sea Peoples in Canaan (1185–1050 B.C.E.)." Pages 332–348 in *The Archaeology of Society in the Holy Land*. Edited by T. E. Levy. London: Leicester University Press.

Stern, Ephraim. 1991. "Phoenicians, Sikils and Israelite in the Light of Recent Excavations at Tel Dor." Pages 85–94 in *Studia Phoenicia XI: Phoenicia and the Bible, Orientalia Lovaniensia Analecta*. Edited by E. Lipinski. Louvain: Peeters Press.

———. 2003. "The Phoenician Source of Palestinian Cults at the End of the Iron Age." Pages 309–22 in *Symbiosis, Symbolism, and the Power of the Past: Canaan, Ancient Israel, and Their Neighbors, from the Late Bronze Age through Roman Palaestina*. Edited by W. G. Dever and S. Gitin. Winona Lake: Eisenbrauns.

Stucky, Rolf A., and Mathys, Hans-Peter. 2000. "Le Sanctuaire Sidonien d'Echmoun Aperçu Historique du Site, des Fouilles et des Découvertes Faites a Bostan ech-Cheikh". *BAAL* 4: 123–48.

Suter, Claudia E. 2011. "Images, Tradition, and Meaning: The Samaria and Other Levantine Ivories of the Iron Age" Pages 219–41 in *A Common Cultural Heritage: Studies on Mesopotamia and the Biblical World in Honor of Barry L. Eichler*. Edited by G. Frame, E. Leichty, K. Sonik, J. Tigay, and S. Tinney: Bethesda: CDL Press.

———. 2015. "Classifying Iron Age Levantine Ivories: Impracticalities and a New Approach." *AoF* 42: 31–45.

van Dongen, E. 2010. 'Phoenicia': Naming and Defining a Region in Syria-Palestine. Pages 471–88 in *Interkulturalität in Der Alten Welt: Vorderasien, Hellas, Ägypten Und Die Vielfältigen Ebenen Des Kontakts*, eds. R. Rollinger; B. Gufler; M. Lang; and I. Madreiter. Wiesbaden: Harrassowitz.

Vella, N. C. 2010. "'Phoenician' Metal Bowls: Boundary Objects in the Archaic Period." *Bollettino di Archeologia on line* 1: 22–37.

———. 2014. "The Invention of the Phoenicians: On Object Definition, Decontextualization and Display." Pages 24–41 in *The Punic Mediterranean: Identities and Identification from Phoenician Settlement to Roman Rule*. Edited by J. C. Quinn and N. C. Vella. Cambridge: Cambridge University Press.

Waiman-Barak, Paula. 2020. "Phoenician Iron Age Red Slipped and Burnished Ware." *The Levantine Ceramics Project*. Online: https://www.levantineceramics.org/wares/916-phoenician-iron-age-red-slipped-and-burnished-ware

Winter, Irene J. 1981. "Is There a South Syrian Style of Ivory Carving in the Early First Millennium B.C.?" *Iraq* 43: 101–30.

Xella, Paolo. 2009. "Sacrifici Di Bambini Nel Mondo Fenicio E Punico Nelle Testimonianze in Lingua Greca E Latina – I." *Studi Epigrafici e Linguistici sul Vicino Oriente antico* 26: 59–100.

———. 2012–2013. "'Tophet': An Overall Interpretation." Pages 259–81 in *The Tophet in the Phoenician Mediterranean*. Edited by P. Xella. Verona: Essedue edizioni.

———. 2019. "Religion." Pages 273–92 in *The Oxford Handbook of the Phoenician and Punic Mediterranean*. Edited by C. López-Ruiz and B. R. Doak. Oxford: Oxford University Press.

38
AMMONITES IN THE WORLD OF ISRAEL

Randall W. Younker

Introduction

According to the biblical account (Gen 19:36–38), the Ammonites were the descendants of an incestuous relationship between Lot and his younger daughter. The child was named Ben Ammi. Some scholars have assumed that the name, which means "son of my people," or "son of my paternal father," was a popular etymology that evolved in support of a tradition of a kindred relationship between Ammon and Israel. However, Landes (1956: 4–6) shows from Ugaritic texts that Ben-'ammi was both a genuine clan name and a personal name. Block (1984: 197–212) further shows that *bny 'mwn* (the Hebrew expression for the Ammonite people) cannot be interpreted in the same way as *bny yśr'l* ("sons of Israel"), even though they appear to be analogous. Rather, the initial element *bn* or *bny* was an integral part of the full name, like the well-known Semitic name *Benjamin*. Thus, the proper designation for the land of the Ammonites was not Ammon, but Bene-'ammon. Similarly, the full and proper form of the name for the eponymous ancestor of the Ammonites is Ben-'ammi. Thus, while it is highly unlikely that the existence of Lot's son could be historically established apart from the biblical record, the idea that the Ammonites had an ancestor with such a name is not impossible.

Research on Ammonites

Despite their importance to biblical and Syro-Palestinian history, there have been only a couple of comprehensive studies of the Ammonites, but neither is from a purely archaeological perspective. Landes completed a historical study of the Ammonites in 1956 (which did incorporate the archaeological findings known up to that time) and a literary/historical study has been undertaken by Hübner (1992). Apart from these studies and occasional incidental references, treatments of the Ammonites have generally been limited to either brief surveys or encyclopedia articles (e.g., Glueck 1937; Albright 1953; Landes 1961; Oded 1971, 1979; Horn 1976; Thompson 1982; MacDonald 1994). Macdonald and Younker (1999) and Younker (2003) provided the most compressive review of Ammonite archaeology up to their time. Daviau and Dion (2007: 301–07) have provided a brief overview of Ammon during the Iron Age II with a helpful discussion on ceramics and connections with Assyria. Lipinski provides a summary of the Ammonites in his *On the Skirts of Canaan in the Iron Age* (2006: 295–318). More recently, Tyson has published *The Ammonites: Elites, Empires, and Sociopolitical Change (1000–500 BCE)* (2014) which provides a valuable update to both the archaeology and history of the Ammonites. Tyson includes significant discussion on the biblical texts that refer to the Ammonites as well.

Periodization

There is a debate about the periodization of the Iron Age II for ancient Jordan and Israel. The periodization which I have used (the so-called Modified Conventional Chronology—see Mazar 2005; Frese and Levy 2010; Younker 2017) dates the Iron Age IIA from the early part of the 10th century BCE (ca. 980) down to about the time of Mesha in Jordan (840/830 BCE). The Iron Age IIB covers the late 9th to the late 8th centuries BCE (840/830–732/701 BCE), and the Iron Age IIC is dated from the 7th to the 6th centuries BCE—ca. 732/701–605/586 BCE. Some working in Jordan have added a transitional period at the end of the Iron IIC that we call Iron IIC–Persian which runs about from the end of the 7th century to the end of the 6th century BCE. Regardless of the precise start of the Iron Age II, most scholars agree that from a sociopolitical view, the beginning of that period in the eastern Levant—especially Cis- and Transjordan—witnessed the coalescence of local tribal groups into territorial monarchies (sometimes called "tribal kingdoms or states") that we know as Israel, Ammon, Moab, and Edom (LaBianca and Younker 1995; Tyson 2014; see LaBianca and Hudon this volume).

Material Cultural Overview

Ammonite material culture is characterized by several distinctive features. These include a unique ceramic corpus, architectural styles, Ammonite inscriptions (found at 'Amman, Umm Udhayna, Umayri, Siran, Jalul, and elsewhere), and the appearance of stone and ceramic statues and figurines of males wearing various styles of the Egyptian *atef* crown (Horn 1973; Daviau and Dion 1994). Sites that have been dated to the Iron Age and identified as Ammonite include several tombs found in Amman, Sahab, and Meqabalein. Several *rujms* and *qasrs* (towers and fortified structures) were excavated that date to the Iron II—these served several functions including fortified farmsteads, watch towers, caravanserai, etc. Settlement sites that include most or all of these Ammonite material culture features, include al-Baq'ah Valley, Safut, Amman, Sahab, Tall al-Umayri, Tall Jawa, Hesban, Jalul, and other sites (Figure 38.1). Important pillared domestic structures have been found at Tell Jawa, Umayri, and Jalul—a tripartite building was also found at the later site (Figure 38.2; Gregor 2009). Iron Age casemate walls have been found at Jawa and Umayri and a solid offset wall at Jalul. Excavations have continued intermittently at Hesban and Jalul.

Geographic Range of Ammon

According to Deut 2:26–37, the boundary of Ammon, over which Israel was not to cross, was largely defined by the course of the Jabbok (modern Zerqa) River—"neither the land along the course of the Jabbok nor that around the towns in the hills." This would seem, at first glance, to be a rather straightforward delineation. However, unlike other rivers in Jordan which flow in a true east to west direction, the course of the Jabbok forms an almost complete circle from its head (source) at 'Ain Ghazal near the base of the ancient capital

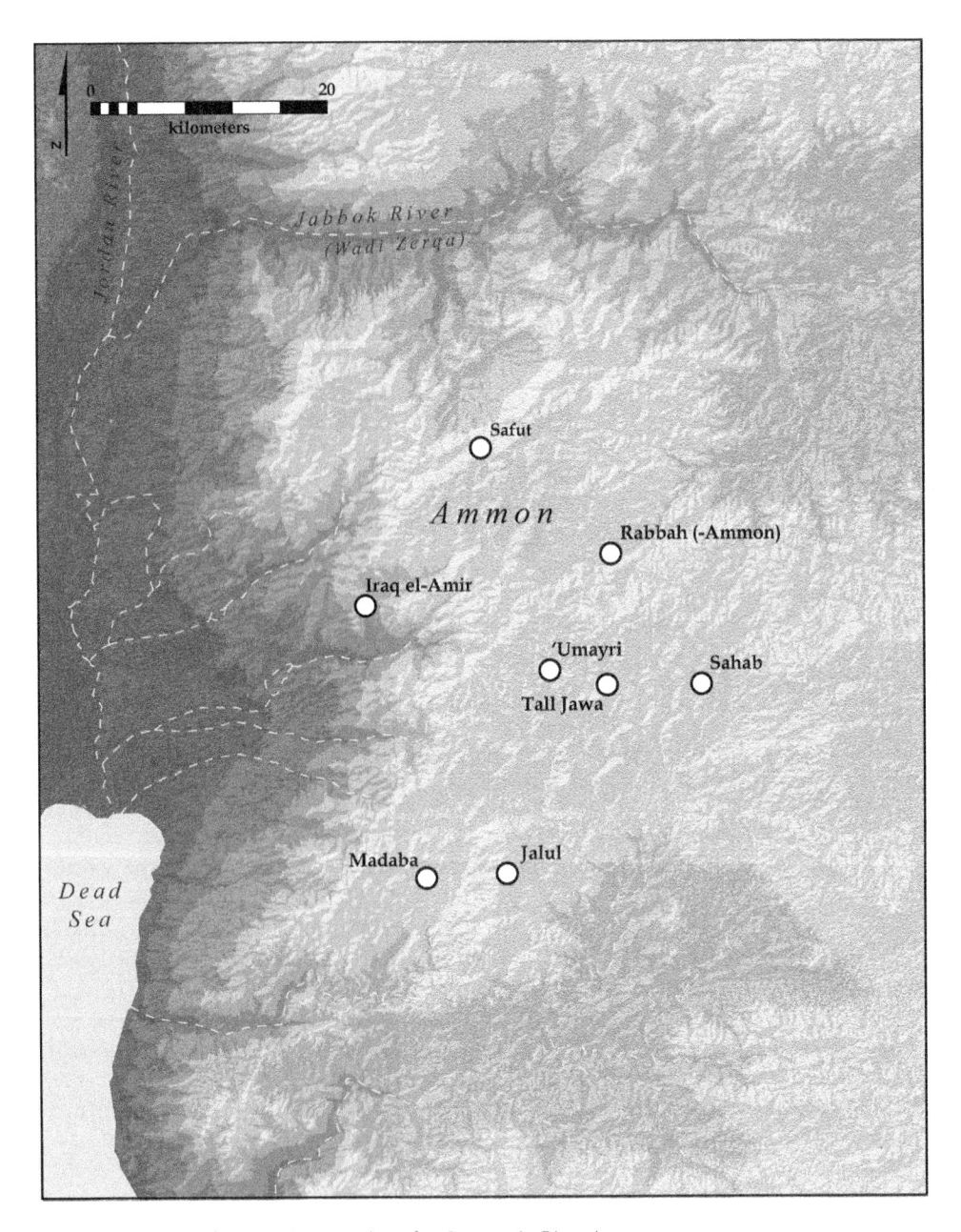

Figure 38.1 Map of sites in Ammon (map by George A. Pierce)

Rabbath-Ammon (modern Amman), from which it sets out in an easterly direction, then makes a broad northward arch until it bends back due west, ultimately emptying into the Jordan River. This has led to much consternation and discussion among biblical geographers who have tended to prefer nice, straight borders and have restricted the use of the Jabbok as a boundary to either its east to west stretch in the north or its south to north stretch in the east (Younker 1994: 61).

Figure 38.2 Tripartite building, Jalul

For example, Landes, following Glueck and others, argues that the biblical text describes only the downstream stretch of the Jabbok beginning northeast of Ammon where the stream flows generally in a south-north direction (Glueck 1939: 246; Landes 1956: 70). This would place the territory of Ammon on the east side of this stretch. Bustenay Oded (1971), on the other hand, interprets the same textual data to argue that the biblical text refers to the east-west stretch of the Jabbok—even more downstream where it flows into the Jordan river. Ammon's territory would then be located to the south of the river.

It is, however, quite possible that the biblical texts do not limit the Jabbok's boundary to either the east-west or the south-north stretches of the river. Although there is a major spring in the wadi (Ras al-Ain, "head of the spring") at the foot of the city of Amman, which certainly serves as a major source for the Jabbok, the wadi itself does not actually begin there. Rather, it can be traced back through several confluences to what is known today as Wadi Hannutiya, near Umm es-Summaq, at least six miles northwest of Amman (Kallai 1986: 298 n. 35). The upper reaches of the wadi (geo-physically a single feature) assume various names as it winds along—names of recent origin, having been assigned by farmsteads or villages located adjacent to the various stretches. However, there is no evidence that this toponymic classification existed in antiquity. Indeed, it seems likely that the ancient Ammonites used a single name for both the principal wadi and its tributaries (Dearman 1989: 58).

Recognizing that the ancient Jabbok included the upper reaches of the wadi and its numerous tributaries and that it can be traced west and north-west of Amman means that the Jabbok essentially formed a complete circle around the ancient kingdom of Ammon (Figure38.3). Its territory would thus include a considerable amount of land to the south, west, and northwest of the old capital city. This is likely what Deut 2:37 is referring to when it describes the "land along the course of the Jabbok" as the territory of Ammon (see also Oded 1971: 854). The hill country of the Ammonites mentioned in this same verse likely refers to the hills adjacent to the Jabbok's tributaries and the range of undulations south of Amman that form a natural geographical barrier between ancient Ammon and the Madaba Plains—traditional Moabite land (that would later become Amorite and then Israelite territory). Indeed, it is within these southern hills that several sites possessing distinctive Ammonite material culture have been excavated, including Tall al-Umayri, Tall Jawa (South),

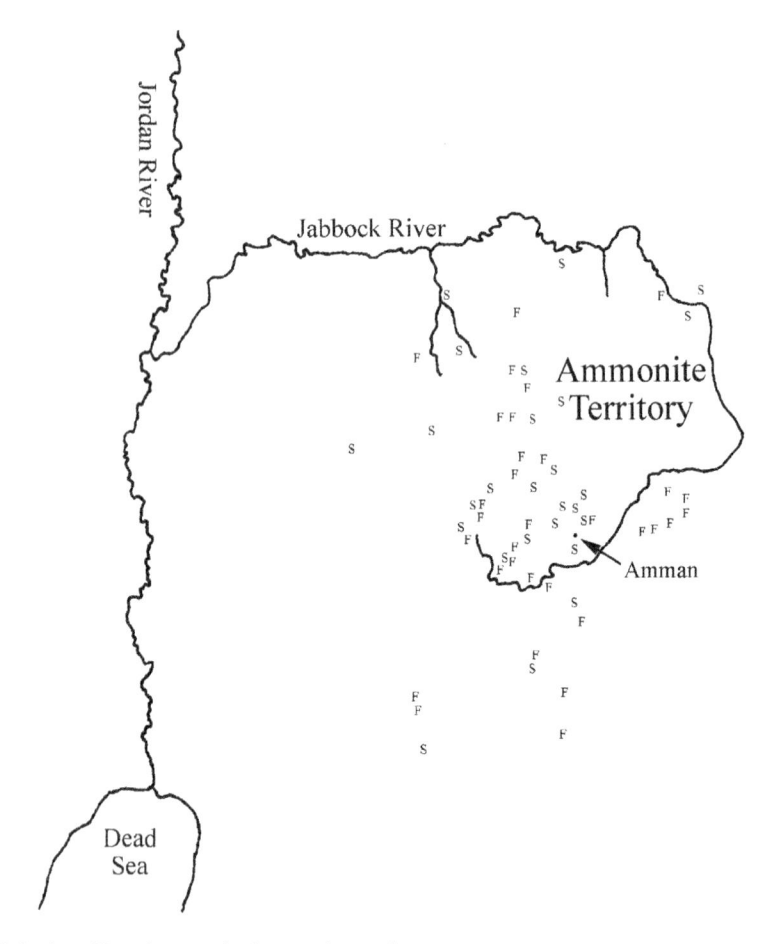

Figure 38.3 Iron II settlements in Ammonite territory

and Tall Sahab—all of which appear to have been continuously occupied from at least the Late Bronze Age (ca. 1400 BCE) through the Iron Age and perhaps into the Persian period.

10th Century BCE (Iron Age IIA)

Biblical Account

As noted in the introduction, the Ammonites are described in the Bible as an indigenous people whose origins can be traced to an incestuous relationship between Lot and one of his daughters. Archaeology does not provide any information on that, nor are there any extra-biblical texts. The Ammonites appear in the Bible during the time of the United Monarchy of Israel, in the 10th century BCE. It is during this period that the first reference to an Ammonite king—Nahash—appears (1 Sam 11 and 1 Chr 19:1–2). Nahash is noted for his conquest of Israelite territories bordering Ammon, especially his invasion across the Jabbok and the siege of Jabesh-Gilead (1 Sam 11:1–14). His abhorrent command to put out the right eye of every Israelite incited the Israelites to rally around their own king, Saul, who led them to victory.

Despite Saul's success against the Ammonites, Nahash retained his throne and eventually obtained a small amount of revenge by providing sanctuary to Saul's antagonist David. In time, David himself became king of Israel, and when Nahash died David sent an envoy to Hanun, the son and successor of his former benefactor, to express sympathy (2 Sam 10:1–2). Hanun's advisors, however, accused David's delegates of spying and unwisely persuaded Hanun to humiliate and return them to David. This outrageous act incited David to immediately initiate a war against the Ammonites. In desperation, the Ammonites hired Aramean mercenaries to assist in their defense but to no avail. Under the leadership of commanders Joab and Abishai (2 Sam 10; 1 Chr 19) the Israelites defeated the Ammonite-led coalition in the field and eventually captured their capital city, Rabbah, as well (2 Sam 11:1; 12:26–31; 1 Chr 20:1–3 (Lawlor 1982: 193–205)). Whether or not Hanun was killed for his impudence is uncertain, but it seems clear that he did not continue in power, for after pillaging the city, David seized the royal crown and placed it upon his own head. The crown sculpted on male busts found in and around Amman may be typical depictions of the Ammonite royal diadem (Horn 1973; below) (Figure 38.4). Although Hanun's fate is unknown, it is of interest that when David was forced to flee from his own son Absalom many years later, he headed to Ammon, where he was ministered to by Shobi, the son of Nahash—probably a brother of Hanun (2 Sam 17:27).

Figure 38.4 Ammonite statue with royal diadem

Interestingly, an expanded account of Israel's encounter with Nahash appears in both Josephus and the Dead Sea Scrolls (Cross 1983; Cross et al. 2005). The passage appears as part of the book of Samuel—but appears in neither the Greek Septuagint nor the Hebrew Masoretic text! Rather it is inserted between 1 Sam 10:27a and 10:27b. It reads:

> [N]ahash, king of Ammonites would put hard pressure on the descendants of Gad and the descendants of Reuben and would gouge everyone's right eye out, but no res(cuer) would be provided for Israel and there was not left anyone among the children of Israel in the Tr(ans Jordan) whose right eye Nahash the king of Ammonites did not gouge out but be(hold) 7000 men (escaped the power of) Ammonites and they arrived at (Ya)besh Gilead. About a month later Nahash the Ammonite went up and besieged Jabesh-Gilead.

This passage provides additional information in that it says that Nahash had conquered the tribal lands of Gad and Reuben, and a portion of the population had fled from him to Jabesh-Gilead, which is why he laid siege to it. The extra material is generally viewed as a "midrash" that was later added to the original text (Cross 1983; Cross et al. 2005; Lipinski 2006: 302).

After David, it is generally assumed that the Ammonites remained under the suzerainty of Israel during Solomon's reign. Ammonite females were among the many foreign women whom Solomon loved (1 Kgs 11:1) and married, and under whose influence the king was persuaded to build a sanctuary to their god Milcom or Molech (1 Kgs 11:7; for discussion see Puech 1977: 117–25). One of these women, Naamah, was the mother of Rehoboam who inherited the throne of Israel (1 Kgs 14:21, 31; 2 Chr 12:13) and whose intransigence led to the division of the Israelite monarchy.

Extra-Biblical Textual Sources

Outside of the biblical references noted above, ancient historical sources for Iron Age IIA Ammon are, unfortunately, lacking. While some scholars are uncertain of the historical veracity of some biblical sources, the references to Ammon are neither confirmed nor contradicted by any known historical sources.

Archaeological Sites

Though there are presently no extra-biblical texts for Ammon during this period, there is some archaeological evidence. Recent excavations are exposing more and more material from this once sparsely represented period. Remains from the 10th century have been found in at least seven important sites so far. Some architectural and ceramic remains from this period have been recovered at the Amman Citadel (Jebal Amman), downtown in modern Amman), Tall Hesban, Tall Jawa (South), Tall Jalul, Tall Sahab, Khirbet Ḥajjar, and Tall al-'Umayri Stratum 9.

The most dramatic find at 'Umayri, on the western slope of the tall, was an Iron Age I casemate wall supported by a rampart and dry moat (Geraty et al. 1990: 59–88). A destruction layer ca. 10 cm thick composed of burned mud bricks, stones, and collapsed wooden roofing beams was found in the debris inside the casemate. Many collared-rim pithoi, typical of the Iron Age I, were also found underneath the collapsed roof debris. Larry Herr, director at 'Umayri, suggests that this destruction could have been caused by King David's campaign against the Ammonites. Although the store jars (or more properly pithoi) possibly date to the earlier part of the Iron Age I period, it is not uncommon for such pithoi to be used for a long period of time (London 1999: 46). Unfortunately, no unequivocal clues as to the identity of the destroyer of the city have yet been found, so the association with David's campaign remains only a suggestion.

Excavations at the Amman Citadel have revealed some materials that can be dated to the 10th century BCE. This would be the period during which David fought against Rabbath-amman and arranged to have his officer, Uriah the Hittite, killed while fighting close against the city wall. Soundings in Area II exposed some defensive walls and a possible gate at the edge of the Citadel. The ceramics pointed to a 10th–9th-century date (Dornemann 1983; Tyson 2014: 20). Also, a torso of a female figurine holding a round stick—likely a tambourine—was found on the surface (Dornemann 1983: 129–31, Figure 89:3). Excavations on the lower terrace of the citadel also uncovered 10th–9th-century ceramics in ashy layers (Zayadine 1973: 30).

Hesban Stratum 18 has been dated by Ray (2001) to 1050–925 BCE based on the pottery finds. The most significant architectural find from this stratum is a reservoir cut into the bedrock with an ashlar wall of good quality constructed in header-stretcher fashion on one side. The reservoir is about 17.5 x 17.5 m square and 7.0 m deep. Sauer dated the reservoir on both ceramic data and the construction technique of the wall to the 10th century BCE. Ray assumes that such a structure was possibly built under "royal auspices" (2001: 99, 107). If this is correct, it is tempting to associate the reservoir with the "pools of Hesban" found in Song of Solomon 7:4. However, such a claim is by no means certain (see Tyson 2014: 22). Besides the reservoir, a subterranean room with a cobbled floor dates to this period. Some 71 artifacts from this stratum were also recovered from dump or fill loci. They included "fifty-five spindle whorls and fragments of whorls, four pottery discs, three stone weights, one muller, one stone bowl, one [stone] door socket, one sling stone, one bead, one [carnelian] ring inset, two [anepigraphic] seals, and one figurine" (Ray 2001: 106).

Tall Jawa Strata X–IX have been dated to the 10th century based on ceramic remains including collared-rim pithoi (Daviau 2003: 468–69). Tall al-'Umayri Stratum 9 has yielded a few pieces of slipped and hand-burnished pottery (Herr 2002:17; Herr and Clark 2007: 126). A floor from the preceding Field H sanctuary seems to have been used during this period (Herr and Clark 2009: 90). Tall Jalul has yielded a 10th-century phase of a pillared building in Field G on the southeast side of the tall. One of the phases of a four-room house in Field C may also date to the 10th century.

Several tombs in the territory of Ammon have also yielded materials from the 10th century. These include Amman Tomb E (Jabal Jofeh ash-Sharqi); the Raghdan Royal Palace Tomb in Amman (Jabal al-Qusur); and Sahab Tombs A and C (Younker 1999; Tyson 2014).

Several Ammonite artifact types which reached their zenith in development during the 9th–6th centuries BCE find their predecessors in the 10th century, although they are not very abundant. These include the earlier figurine forms of a woman holding a tambourine, terra-cotta shrines, and anthropomorphic coffins (Figure 38.5). Most metal objects are made of bronze and include knives, straight toggle pins, arrowheads, spearheads, bracelets, anklets, earrings, finger rings, razors, and armor scales (Dornemann 1983: 149).

9th–8th Centuries BCE (Iron Age IIB)

Biblical and Extra-biblical Texts

According to 2 Chr 26:8; 27:5, which details the time of the Divided Monarchy, the Ammonites were forced to pay tribute to the southern kingdom of Judah—first to king Uzziah and then to king Jotham (2 Chr 26:8; 27:5). Later, when the Assyrian juggernaut rolled through

Figure 38.5 Anthropoid Ammonite coffins

the region, the Ammonites joined other Syro-Palestinian kingdoms in a coalition of resistance. The Ammonite army, led by King Ba'sa, son of Ruhubi, joined the alliance arrayed against Shalmaneser III at Qarqar in 853 BCE.

However, after this battle, the western alliance unraveled, and the Israelites became entangled in a confrontation with the Arameans. With Israel thus distracted, the Ammonites, who may have enjoyed a degree of independence after the division of the Israelite monarchy, joined forces with the Moabites and Meunites in an invasion of Judah—possibly at the instigation of the Arameans (2 Chr 20:1, 10). Judah's king, Jehoshaphat, was able to rally his army to meet this threat, but the Transjordanian coalition unraveled before the Judahite army arrived (de Tarragon 1992: 195)

The occasional subjugation of Transjordanian kingdoms by Cisjordanian kingdoms is supported by some extra-biblical evidence such as the Mesha inscription; thus, many scholars are inclined to think that Ammon's subjection to Judah is plausible (e.g., Barton 2002: 516).

Ammon was later forced to pay tribute to Uzziah, King of Judah (767–740), and his son Jotham (2 Chr 26:8; 27:5). In 734 the Ammonite king Sanipu was a vassal of Tiglath-Pileser III and his successor, Pudu-ilu held the same position under Sennacherib and Esarhaddon.

Archaeological Sites

At least seven sites that can be considered major Ammonite settlements have been excavated so far: (1) the Amman Citadel; (2) Tall Hesban [Heshbon] Stratum 17; (3) Tall Jalul (Bezer); (4) Tall Jawa South Stratum IX-VIII; (5); Tall Safut; (6) Sahab; and (7) Tall al-'Umayri Stratum 8.

Significant architectural finds from these sites include unpublished volute ("proto-aeolic" or "proto-ionic") capitals found at the Amman Citadel, which may date to the 9th century given that they are like the Type A capitals found at Megiddo (Strata VA–IVA) and at Samaria (Strata I–II), which are dated by some to the 9th century BCE (see Franklin this volume).

At Jalul the tripartite building in Field A (Figure 38.2), and one of the four phases of the gate complex in Field B, and a pillared building in Field G also date to the 9th–8th centuries BC. Of special interest was a pottery cache in a small room in the south part of the pillared building. Much of the pottery was Moabite in style and ware—suggesting some sort of Moabite presence or influence at Jalul during the 9th–8th centuries (see Younker 2016; Orellana 2022). If Jalul is indeed Bezer, one is tempted to make a connection to Mesha's reference to the Moabite capture of Bezer from Israel and rebuilding it as recorded in the Mesha Inscription. The dating is based on Iron Age IIB ceramics (see Herr and Bates 2011).

At Tall Jawa, a solid offset-inset wall that surrounded the city was revealed. Also, a retaining wall, passageways, a tower, and a guard room were also exposed. At Tall al-'Umayri, excavations of Stratum 8 revealed three rooms of a house in Field A and a possible sanctuary in Field H that was founded in Iron IIA and apparently continued in use during this period.

In addition to these excavated sites, the Hesban survey documented about 384 sites that date to the Iron Age II. Tyson (2014:29) assumes a significant number of these—especially the larger ones that likely had a longer occupational history—dated to the 9th–8th centuries. A number of Tombs also exhibited remains from these centuries: the Raghdan Royal Palace Tomb; Amman Tombs B and C; Amman Tomb D (on the Amman Citadel); Amman Tomb E (Jabal Jofeh ash-Sharqi); and Sahab Tomb B. Significant finds from the tombs include two clay coffins (Type III) from the Raghdan Royal Tomb; a clay shrine found in Amman Tomb E; and various objects from Sahab Tomb B including a circular decorated limestone palette, shells with blue pigment, metal anklets, fibulae, earrings, arrowheads, a knife handle, some iron points, and a crystal bead.

Imported Materials

The 9th–8th centuries BCE witnessed the importation of items into Amman from adjacent regions. Some of these materials include alabaster from Egypt and Turkey; ivory from African and Syrian elephants, wild boar tusks, and hippopotamus teeth; marine shells used as pendants or beads; and various metal objects of gold, silver, bronze, copper, iron, and lead. Most metal objects–including fibulae, kohl sticks (for applying make-up made of stibnite), tweezers, needles, blades, and arrowheads—were made of bronze or iron, but jewelry (e.g., earrings, finger rings), were typically made of gold and silver (Tyson 2014: 32, 33).

Inscription

One of the earliest distinctively Ammonite inscriptions comes from the 9th century: the Amman Citadel Inscription (Figure 38.6), which was found by Rafik Dajani in 1961. The text consists of thirty-three words carved on a limestone block measuring approximately 26 × 19 cm. Because the inscription is incomplete, it has been interpreted in a variety of ways (e.g., Cross 1969; Horn 1969; Fulco 1978; Shea 1981). Several scholars have seen it as a building inscription, perhaps from a temple or citadel. Others understand it as an oracle from the Ammonite god Milcom, ordering the construction of defensive towers around the perimeter of Rabbah-ammon—the discovery of at least 19 megalithic towers in the area around Amman appears to give credence to this interpretation. A final consensus on

Figure 38.6 Amman Citadel inscription

its meaning remains to be established. Despite its uncertain meaning, the inscription provides important clues about the linguistic and paleographic characteristics of the Ammonite language and writing system.

7th–6th Centuries BCE (Iron Age IIC–Persian Period)

Biblical Text

The 7th–6th centuries continued to witness increased economic and political power for the Ammonites. This success is reflected in Jer 49, where the prophet rebukes the Ammonites for taking advantage of Judah's misfortunes by moving into the territory of Gad. "Why do you boast of your valleys, boast of your valleys so fruitful? O unfaithful daughter, you trust in your riches and say, 'Who will attack me?'" (v. 4 NIV). The Hesban and Madaba Plains projects' surveys have recorded several Iron Age IIC–Persian Period structures throughout the Ammonite hinterland that appear to be part of well-planned agricultural complexes. This interpretation is confirmed by the presence of enclosure walls, cisterns, winepresses, cupholes (for grinding), terraces, smaller field towers, and other associated food-production features found in the immediate vicinity of these structures. Obviously, Ammonite agricultural success provided a firm economic base that in turn led to political confidence which provoked the prophet's rebuke.

It was this same economic and political confidence that undoubtedly led to the events described in Jeremiah 27 and 40, where the prophet accuses an unnamed Ammonite king of leading a rebellion against Babylon. Jeremiah later identifies Baalis as the one responsible for the assassination of the Babylonian-appointed governor, Gedaliah. A seal impression with an Ammonite inscription, discovered at Tall al-'Umayri reads, "Belonging to Milkom-'ur, servant of Ba'al-yasha'" (Figure 38.7). The owner's name contains the theophoric element Milcom, the primary Ammonite deity; the king's name B'lysh', may be identified with Baalis of Jer 40:14 (Herr 1985). The identification of the person on the seal with the Ammonite king is also supported by the date of the script (ca. 600 CE) and by the iconography, which includes the four-winged scarab, formerly used as a royal motif of the western kingdoms of Israel and Judah (Younker 1985). The Ammonite adoption of this symbol is another indication that political power and prestige had gravitated to the Ammonite ruler by the 7th and 6th centuries BCE.

There was no way the Babylonians were going to ignore the blatant murder of their own appointed leader of Judah (Gedaliah), and indeed Josephus (*Ant.* 10:9:3–4) claims that Nebuchadnezzar conducted a punitive campaign against the Ammonites in his 23rd year (582–581 BCE). There is some indication that Josephus' account of Nebuchadnezzar's campaign against the Ammonites is historical. Occupation at several Ammonite sites such as Tall Safut, Tall el-Mazar, Tall Jawa (South), and Tall Hesban may have suffered occupational disruption or was completely terminated at this time (Wimmer 1987a, 1987b; Yassine 1988; Ray 2001; Younker 2014).

While it may be that the Ammonite kingdom ceased to function as an independent or semi-independent polity about this time, the Ammonite people appear to have continued to occupy their land well into Hellenistic times and beyond. This is supported by later literary

Figure 38.7 Baalis seal impression

references to Ammonites and the recent archaeological findings of the Madaba Plains Project, which show continuous occupation in Ammonite territory down into the Persian and perhaps the early Hellenistic periods (below).

Archaeological Sites

Excavations on the Amman Citadel's upper terrace revealed part of a 7th–6th century BCE building, probably a domestic dwelling (Tyson 2014: 34). The exposed section of the building includes an east-west wall 21.3 m long and a north-south wall 6 m long. A section of wall found in another square may continue the north-south wall so that its total length is 19 m. The walls, of irregular stones, survive to a height of 1.2–1.9 m and are 0.7–1.1 m thick. Finds in the building include Iron IIC pottery, an ostracon, two figureheads, beads, spindle whorls, and some shells (Momani et al. 1997: 160–70). Excavations on the lower terrace also exposed walls and buildings dating to the 7th–6th centuries BCE (Zayadine, Humbert, and Najjar 1989: 362; Humbert and Zayadine 1992: 247–60). The most important finds were part of a building with a beaten earth "courtyard" measuring about 10 x 15 m; a stone toilet and drain, and some storage rooms (Humbert and Zayadine 1992: 253–54). Tyson suggests the building is part of an Assyrian open-court style building, dating to ca. 700 BCE (2014: 35). In this same area, double-faced female busts were found.

The Iron Age IIC is represented at Hesban by materials from Stratum 16 dated from 700–500 BCE (Ray 2001: 126–49). The finds from this stratum include several walls, a replastered cistern, some silos, and Iron IIC pottery. The most interesting finds are three seals (Eggler and Keel 2006: Hisban 2, 5, 6), six ostraca, and three inscribed sherds (see Cross 2003 and Tyson 2014).

Tall Jalul yielded a considerable amount of material from the 7th–6th centuries BCE (Younker 1999, 2007: 132–33) Remains from this period include the second phase of the tripartite building in Field A, the later phases of the four-room pillared house (Figure 38.8), a large courtyard building in Field C, the later phases of the Gate complex and approach road in Field B, the courtyard building in Field D, and a pillared building and drainage channel in Field G. Small finds included animal and human figurines, a deity figurine, an inscribed seal from the 7th century, and an ostracon dated to the 6th century. Other seals and a bulla were also found (ibid.; Goulart and Gane 2012).

Tall Jawa (South) Strata VIIB yielded 7th century remains while Strata VIIA yielded 6th century remains. Stratum VIIB consisted of two large buildings, 800 and 700, that exhibit parallels with Neo-Assyrian domestic architecture and support the existence of a rather high-status existence for some occupants of the city (Daviau 2001: 219–23; Tyson 2014: 35). Settlement in the Persian period is indicated by a late Persian period burial—dated by the presence of a fibula with parallels in the 6th–4th centuries BCE (Daviau 2003: 93).

Tall Safut revealed a lower city wall and settlement that expanded outside the city walls (Chesnut 2019). A variety of buildings and parts of buildings were exposed along with food processing equipment (mortars, pestles, grinding stones), some metal objects, a scarab stamp seal with Assyrian iconography, Assyrian type bottles, a Neo-Babylonian seal impression, a horse figurine, and painted figurine heads (Wimmer 1987b: 166–72). Tyson correctly suggests that the Iron Age IIC was the high point of occupation for Safut. Its location along the main route between Amman and the Jabbok River to the north made it a strategic location for monitoring and controlling traffic in the area (ibid.).

Sahab's Iron IIC settlement seems to be smaller but better organized than the Iron I settlement that preceded it. Remains from the Iron IIC include a large orthogonal building

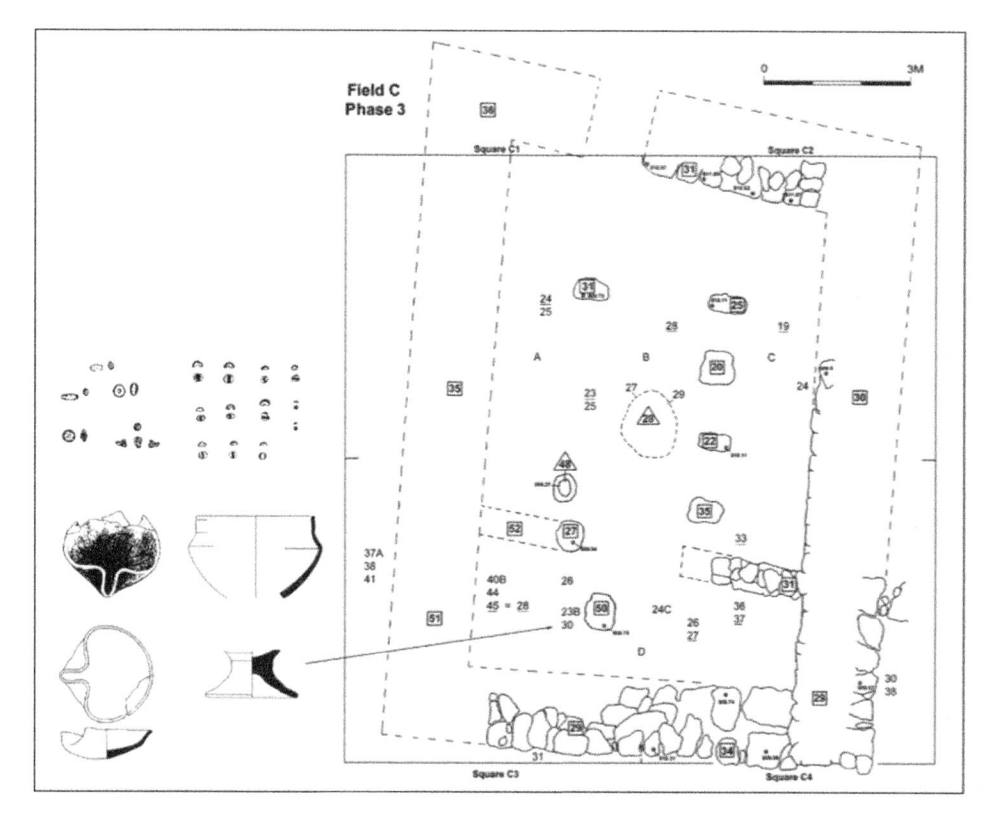

Figure 38.8 Four-room pillared building at Jalul

(19 × 10 m) in Area B (Ibrahim 1975: 71, Figures 1–2). The largest room was supported by four stone pillars. Objects and materials on the floor of the building include grinding stones, a figure-like piece of basalt of uncertain purpose, and seeds. Another room in the complex contained two ceramic alabastra, loom weights, a spindle whorl, a bronze fibula, a miniature stone table, a pottery tripod bowl, and various sone grinding and polishing tools (Ibrahim 1975: 73). The ceramics, which include a black burnished bowl, and the alabastra date to the Iron IIC. Ibrahim suggests an industrial function for the building based on its contents (Ibrahim 1975: 82, 1997: 451–52).

At Tall al-'Umayri a complex of three stone-walled buildings was built within an area of 15 m × 25 m in the 6th century BCE (Strata 7–6). Objects found in this complex include 16 seals and sealings, some of which belong to a high-status individual in the Persian province of Ammon. The seal of an official of king Ba'lyasu' (equated with Baalis mentioned in Jer 40:14) belongs to this stratum although it was found in a surface probe. A pointed bottle, like those found in the Ammon tombs, was found in Building C (Lawlor 1997: 44, Figure 3.15:1). The large number of seals and sealings prompted the excavators to suggest an administrative function for the building. However, the presence of 20 spindle whorls, four loom weights, and six weaving spatulas came from the same complex, raising the question of whether the building can be considered an administrative center (Lawlor 1997: 51; Tyson 2014: 37). Of note, industrial areas—especially if they don't create noxious fumes and smoke—can be found near structures with other functions, such as seen in Kition on Cyprus. In addition to the buildings on the mound, a water system was excavated at the northern base of the tall with ceramic remains going back to the Early Bronze Age but including materials from later periods such as the Iron Age IIC. This testifies to the long use of the water source—not surprising since there is no other source in the immediate vicinity of the tall. The Iron IIC remains at the water system include some walls, a plastered installation, and some cobbled surfaces that probably helped channel water into the system (Fisher 1997: 178–80).

At Rujm al-Kursi, located about 10 km west of the Amman Citadel, the contours of a possible Iron IIC building have been detected. It has been suggested it could possibly be the remains of a temple (Tyson 2014: 37). The outer dimensions of the building are 18.7 m x 12.6 m defined by exterior stone walls 1.5–1.6 m thick. The interior space is divided into a smaller outer chamber and a larger inner chamber evoking the idea of a holy and most holy place. On either side of the entrance, there is a cubical block of smoothed limestone measuring less than 1 m per side. On the front face of each block is a relief depicting a lunar crescent supported by a pillar on top of a table. It has been suggested that the reliefs point to the temple being dedicated to the moon god. Parallel examples suggest a date of the 7th century BCE. If the dating is correct, then the building provides an insight into the development of religion while Ammon was under Neo-Assyrian rule (see Koch, this volume). The adoption of the moon god motif may reflect a local adaption of the worship of Sin of Harran (Hübner 2009: 149–51; Tyson 2014: 39).

The Hesban survey documented 484 sites in its vicinity that likely date to the Iron IIC. This shows the continued growth of rural sites in Ammon during this period.[1] In addition to the smaller sites are several larger significant sites comprised of "towers" (round [*rujm*] and rectangular [*qasr*]) and "fortified" farmsteads—larger compounds often with a perimeter wall and agricultural features such as cisterns, presses, etc.[2] These structures, especially the "towers," are typically constructed of "megaliths"—huge unhewn cherty limestones that gave rise to the belief among later peoples that the builders were ancient giants. Different functions have been ascribed to these structures—military watch towers or defense towers, fortified agricultural complexes near the border areas, etc. They likely served several functions either at the same time or alternately, depending on regional activities and needs (for a more detailed discussion on these structures see Kletter 1991; Younker 1991, 2003; Tyson 2014: 45–52).

Most of the Ammonite tombs from the latter part of the Iron IIB (8th century BCE) continued to be used during the Iron IIC. Twelve tombs dated to this period have been excavated or explored. These include: (1) Amman Tomb A (Jabal Jofeh); (2) Amman Tomb B (Jabal Jofeh); (3) Amman Tomb C (Jabal al-Jedid); (4) Amman Tomb E (Jabal Jofeh ash-Sharqi); (5) Amman Tomb F; (6) the Adoni-nur Tomb in Amman; (7) the Raghdan Royal Place Tomb in Amman; (8) the Abu Nseir Tomb 1; (9) the Abu Nsier Tomb 2; (10) The Khilda Tomb 1; (11) the Khilda Tomb 2; (12) the Meqabalein Tomb; (13) the Sahab Tomb B; and (14) the Umm Adayna Tomb (see MacDonald 1999: 42–46; Younker 1999: 1–23; Tyson 2014: 39–45 for details and references). The tombs have been dated by the various grave goods that were found therein including ceramics—some quite distinctive (bull rhytons, pointed Assyrian bottles, carinated bowls, Attic wares)—clay figures (various animals, horse and rider figurines, male and female figurines), objects of gold, silver, and especially bronze and iron (fibulae, mirrors, kohl sticks, armlets, bracelets, anklets, earrings, finger rings, bells, swords, daggers, arrowheads, knives, and knife handles, nails, metal bowls, juglets, strainers, a caryatid censer ladles), stone objects (alabastra, cosmetic palettes, marble palettes, stamp seals, cylinder seals, Egyptian scarabs), glass (ring inlays, beads,), bone (astragali), ivory (seals), and shells.

5th–4th Centuries BCE – The Persian Period

Biblical Texts and History

There are few literary references to shed light on Ammon during the Persian period. Nehemiah 3:35 mentions Tobiah the Ammonite (who was of Judahite heritage) whose family had long held land in Ammonite territory in the modern Wadi es-Sir (west of Amman). According to the book of Nehemiah (2:10, 19; [MT 4:1]; 6:1, 12, 14; 13:4–8), Tobiah had moved into the Temple compound in Jerusalem and was one of the local leaders who tried to oppose Nehemiah's government-sanctioned building project. Nehemiah, had him ejected.

Some scholars believe that Tobiah may have served as an Ammonite governor. Evidence for the Tobiads in Transjordan has been found in the Wadi es-Sir at Iraq el-Amir, west of Amman. The name *Tobiah* is carved in old Hebrew script on the rock face next to the entrances of two caves on the north side of the wadi. Epigraphers date the inscriptions between the 2nd and 4th centuries CE (Cross 1979: 191 n. 13). A large 2nd-century building known locally as Qasr el-Abd ("the castle of the slave") is believed to be either the fort or the palace of the Tobiads.

Apart from the Tobiah account, there is little written record of Ammon in the Persian period. However, the amount of archaeological material recovered from the Persian period in Ammon has increased in recent years. Dating material remains from the Persian period in Jordan has been greatly facilitated by the refined ceramic chronology of Sauer (1986) and Herr (1997: 244–46). The presence of Attic ware at 'Umayri and Jalul, typical Persian period incense altars at Jalul, along with the discovery of two Persian period "provincial" seals at 'Umayri, have helped in securely dating the Persian period material in Amman. Recognizing the Persian ceramic horizon in Ammon has made it possible to identify Persian period occupation at several sites, including Hesban, Tall al-'Umayri, Tall Jawa, Jalul, Dreijat (a fortified site southwest of 'Umayri), and elsewhere. Thus, thanks to recent excavations and research, the Persian period in Ammon is now being revealed.

Conclusion

The Ammonite people resided on the central Transjordanian plain from at least the Late Bronze Age until the end of the Iron Age, and perhaps beyond. For much of their early existence, the Ammonites were integrated with the political/economic system of the Cisjordanian Kingdoms of Israel and Judah, as reflected in the transformation of their socioeconomic structure from a pastoral mode into one of intensive agriculture. While their initial interaction with and domination by Israel and Judah may have contributed to their socioeconomic development, it was not until they were freed of the dominance of the west that they were truly able to develop. The Ammonites reached the zenith of their power in the 7th and 6th centuries BCE. Sometime during the 6th century, the power they wielded seems to have waned, but their occupation of the land appears to have continued into the following Persian and Hellenistic periods.

Notes

1. For comparison with Cisjordan during the same period, see Pierce, this volume.
2. The tower and fortified farmstead sites include: (1) Jabal al-Akhadar; (2) Ad-Dreijat; (3) Kirbat al-Hajjar; (4) Rujm al-Henu West; (5) Khilda Fortress A; (6) Rujm al Malfuf North; (7) Rujm al-Malfuf South; (8) Rujm al-Mekheizin; (9) Abu Nsier; (10) Khirbat Salameh; (11) and Rujm

Selim. Other sites existed but have been destroyed by modern highway and building construction. Some have been identified east of Amman but have not been documented. These sites are under threat from the eastward growth of modern Amman.

Bibliography

Albright, William F. 1953. "Notes on Ammonite History". Pages 131–36 in *Miscellanea Biblica B. Ubach*. Edited by R. M. Díaz Carbonell. Barcelona: Montisserrat.

Barton, John 2002. *The Biblical World*. Vol. 1. London: Routledge.

Block, Daniel I. 1984. "*Bny 'mwn*: The Sons of Ammon." *AUSS* 22: 197–212.

Chesnut, Owen. 2019. "A Reassessment of the Excavations at Tall Safut." PhD diss., Andrews University.

Cross, Frank M. 1969. "Epigraphic Notes on the 'Ammān Citadel Inscription." *BASOR* 193: 13–19.

———. 1979. "The Development of the Jewish Scripts." Pages 131–202 in *the Bible and the Ancient Near East: Essays in Honor of William Foxwell Albright*. Edited by G. Ernest Wright. Winona Lake: Eisenbrauns.

———. 1983. "The Ammonite Oppression of the Tribes of Gad and Reuben: Missing Verses from 1 Samuel 11 Found in 4QSamuel[a]." Pages 148–58 in *History, Historiography and Interpretation: Studies in Biblical and Cuneiform Literatures*. Edited by H. Tadmor and M. Weinfeld. Jerusalem: Magnes.

———. 2003. "Ammonite Ostraca from Tell Hisban." Pages 70–99 in *Leaves from an Epigrapher's Notebook: Collected Papers in Hebrew and West Semitic Paleography and Epigraphy*. Winona Lake: Eisenbrauns.

Cross, Frank M., Donald W. Parry, Richard J. Saley, and Eugene Ulrich (eds). 2005. *Qumran Cave 4 – XII, 1–2 Samuel*. Oxford: Clarendon Press.

Daviau, P. M. Michèle. 2001. "Assyrian Influence and Changing Technologies at Tall Jawa, Jordan." Pages 214–38 in *The Land that I Will Show You: Essays on the History and Archaeology of the Ancient Near East in Honour of J Maxwell Miller*. Edited by J. A. Dearman and M. P. Graham. Sheffield: Sheffield Academic.

———. 2003. *Excavations at Tall Jawa, Jordan. Vol.1: The Iron Age Town*. Leiden: Brill.

Daviau, P. M. Michèle and P.E. Dion. 1994. "El the God of the Ammonites? The Atef Crowned Head from Tell Jawa, Jordan." *ZDPV* 110: 158–67.

———. 2007. "Independent and Well-Connected: The Ammonites of Central Jordan." Pages 301–07 in *Crossing Jordan: North American Contributions to the Archaeology of Jordan*. Edited by Thomas E. Levy, P.M. Michèle Daviau, Randall W. Younker, and May Shaer. London: Equinox.

Dearman, J. Andrew. 1989. "Levitical Cities of Reuben and Moabite Toponymy." *BASOR* 276: 55–66.

De Tarragon, Jean-Michel. 1992. "Ammon/Ammonite." Pages194–96 in *ABD 1*.

Dornemann, Rudolph. 1983. *The Archaeology of Transjordan in the Bronze and Iron Ages*. Milwaukee: Milwaukee Public Museum.

Eggler, Jürg and Othmar Keel. 2006. *Corpus der Siegel-Amulette aus Jordanien: Vom Neolithikum bis zur Perserzeit*. Fribourg: Academic Press.

Fisher, James. 1997. "Field E: The Water System." Pages 176–87 in *Madaba Plains Project 3: The 1989 Season at Tell el-'Umeiri and Vicinity and Subsequent Studies*. Edited by Larry G. Herr, Lawrence T. Geraty, Øystein S. LaBianca, and Randall W. Younker. Berrien Springs: Andrews University Press.

Frese, Daniel A. and Thomas E. Levy. 2010. "The Four Pillars of the Iron Age Low Chronology." Pages 187–204 in *Historical Biblical Archaeology and the Future: The New Pragmatism*. Edited by Thomas E. Levy. London: Equinox.

Fulco, William J. 1978. "The 'Ammān Citadel Inscription: A New Collation." *BASOR* 230: 39–43.

Geraty Lawrence et al. 1990. "Madaba Plains Project: A Preliminary Report of the 1987 Season at Tell El-'Umeiri and Vicinity." *BASOR, Supplement* 26: 59–88.

Glueck, Nelson. 1937. "Explorations in the Land of Ammon." *BASOR* 68: 13–21.

———. 1939. "Explorations in Eastern Palestine, Part 3." *AASOR* 18–19: 151–251.

Gregor, P. Z. 2009. "A Tripartite Building in Transjordan." *ADAJ* 53: 9–19.

Goulart, Christie J. and Roy E. Gane. 2012. "Three Epigraphic Finds from Tall Jalul, Jordan." *BASOR* 365: 27–32.

Herr, Larry. 1985. "The Servant of Baalis." *BA* 48: 169–72.

———. 1997. "The Pottery." Pages 228–49 in *Madaba Plains Project 3: The 1989 Season at Tall el-'Umeiri and Subsequent Studies.* Edited by L. G. Herr; D. R. Clark; L.

———. 2002. "Excavations and Cumulative Results." Pages 8–22 in *Madaba Plains Project 5: The 1994 Season at Tall Al-'Umayri and Subsequent Studies.* Edited by L. G. Herr, D. R. Clark, L. T Geraty, R W. Younker, and Ø. S. LaBianca. Berrien Springs: Andrews University Press.

Herr, Larry, and Robert Bates. 2011. "The Iron IIB Pottery from a Stratum 8 House at Tall al-'Umayri, Jordan." *EI* 30: 18–31.

Herr, Larry, and Doug Clark. 2007. "Tall al- 'Umayri through the Ages." Pages 121–28 in *Crossing Jordan: North American Contributions to the Archaeology of Jordan.* Edited by Thomas Levy, Michele Daviau, Randall W. Younker and May Shaer. London: Equinox.

———. 2009. "From the Stone Age to the Middle Ages in Jordan: Digging up Tall al-'Umayri." *NEA* 72: 68–97.

Horn, Siegfried H. 1969. "The Ammān Citadel Inscription." *BASOR* 93: 2–13.

———. 1973. "The Crown of the King of the Ammonites." *AUSS* 1: 170–80.

———. 1976. "Heshbon." Pages 410–11 in *The Interpreter's Dictionary of the Bible—Supplementary Volume.* Edited by in K. R. Crim, V. P. Furnish, and L. R. Bailey. Nashville: Abingdon.

Hübner, Ulrich. 1992. *Die Ammoniter: Untersuchungen zur Geschichte, Kultur und Religion eines transjordanischen Volkes im I. Jahrtausend v, Chr.* Wiesbaden: Harrassowitz.

———. 2009. "Der Mondtempel auf Rugm al-Kursi in der Ammonitits." Pages 145–53 in *Israel zwischen den Mächten: Festschrift für Stefan Timm zum 65. Geburtstag.* Edited by B. Sass and C. Uehlinger. Fribourg: University Press Fribourg.

Humbert, Jean-Baptiste and Fawzi Zayadine. 1992. "Trois Campagnes de Fouilles à Ammân (1988–1991): Troisième Terrasse de la Citadelle (Mission Franco-Jordanienne)." *RB* 1992: 214–60.

Ibrahim, Moawiyah M. 1975. "Third Season of Excavations at Sahab, 1975." *ADAJ* 20: 69–82, 169–78.

———. 1997. "Sahab." *OEANE* 1: 105–7.

Kallai, Zecharia. 1986. *Historical Geography of the Bible: The Tribal Territories of Israel.* Jerusalem: The Magness Press.

Kletter, Raz. 1991. "The Rujm el Malfuf Buildings." *BASOR* 284: 33–50.

LaBianca, Øystein S. and Randall W. Younker. 1995. "The Kingdoms of Ammon, Moab and Edom: The Archaeology of Society in the Late Bronze/Iron Age Transjordan (ca. 1400–500 BCE)." Pages 399–415 in *The Archaeology of Society in the Holy Land.* Edited by T. E. Levy. New York: Facts on File.

Landes, George M. 1956. "A History of the Ammonites." PhD diss., Johns Hopkins University.

———. 1961. "The Material Civilization of the Ammonites." *BA* 24: 65–86.

———. 1982. "Theology and Art in the Narrative of the Ammonite War (2 Samuel 10–12)." *GTJ* 3/2: 193–205.

Lawlor, John I. 1997. "Field A: The Ammonite Citadel." Pages 233–43 in *Madaba Plains Project1: The 1984 Season at Tell el- 'Umeiri and Vicinity and Subsequent Studies.* Edited by L. G. Herr, D. R. Clark, L. T. Geraty, R. W. Younker, and Ø. S. LaBianca. Berrien Springs: Andrews University Institute of Archaeology.

Lipinski, Edward. 2006. *On the Skirts of Canaan in the Iron Age: Historical and Topographical Perspectives.* Leuven: Peeters.

London, Gloria. 1999. "Central Jordan Ceramic Traditions." Pages 57–102 in *Ancient Ammon.* Edited by Burton MacDonald and Randall W. Younker. Leiden: Brill.

MacDonald, Burton. 1994. *Ammon, Moab and Edom: Early States/Nations of Jordan in the Biblical Period (End of the 2nd and During the 1st Millennium B. C.).* Amman: Al Kutba.

———.1999. "Ammonite Territory and Sites." Pages 30–56 in *Ancient Ammon.* Edited by Burton MacDonald and Randall W. Younker. Leiden: Brill.

MacDonald, Burton, and R. W. Younker, eds. 1999. *Ancient Ammon.* Leiden: Brill.

Mazar, Amihai. 2005. "The Debate over the Chronology of the Iron Age in the Southern Levant." Pages 15–30 in *The Bible and Radiocarbon Dating: Archaeology, Text and Science.* Edited by Thomas E. Levy and Thomas Higham. London: Equinox.

Momani, A. et al. 1997. "The 1993 Excavations." Pages 157–71 in *The Great Temple of Amman: The Excavations.* Edited by A. Koutsoukou, K. W. Russell, M. Najjar, and A. Momani. Amman: ACOR.

Oded, Bustenay. 1971. "Ammon, Ammonites." Page 854 in *Encyclopedia Judaica* 2. Jerusalem: Keter.

———. 1979. *Mass Deportations and Deportees in the Neo-Assyrian Empire.* Wiesbaden: Reichert.

Orellena, Michael. 2022. *Pottery Horizons of the Jalul Ceramic Assemblage in the Iron Age IIA-C from Square G4 in its Historical and Geographical Context.* Unpublished PhD dissertation. Andrews University, Institute of Archaeology: Berrien Springs.

Puech, Emile. 1977. "Milkom, le dieu ammonite, en Amos I 15." *VT* 27: 117–25.

Ray, Paul. 2001. *Hesban 6: Tell Hesban and Vicinity in the Iron Age.* Berrien Springs: Andrews University Press.

Sauer, James. 1986. "Transjordan in the Bronze and Iron Ages: A Critiques of Glueck's Synthesis." *BASOR* 263: 1–26.

Shea, William H. 1981. "The Amman Citadel Inscription Again." *PEQ* 113: 105–10.

Thompson, Henry O. 1982. "The Biblical Ammonites." *Bible and Spade* 11: 1–14; 47–61.

Tyson, Craig. 2014. *The Ammonites: Elites, Empires, and Sociopolitical Change (1000–500 BCE).* New York: Bloomsbury/T&T Clark.

Wimmer, Donald. 1987a. "The Excavations of Tell Safut." *SHAJ* 3: 279–82.

———. 1987b. "Tell Safut Excavations 1982–1985 Preliminary Report." *ADAJ* 31: 159–74.

Yassine, K. 1988. *The Archaeology of Jordan: Essays and Reports.* Amman: Department of Antiquities, University of Jordan.

Younker, Randall W. 1985. "Israel, Judah, and Ammon and the Motifs on the *Baalis* Seal from Tell el-'Umeiri." *BA* 48: 173–80.

———. 1991. "Architectural Remains from the Hinterland Survey." Pages 335–42 in *Madaba Plains Project 2: the 1987 Season at Tell el-'Umieri and Vicinity and Subsequent Studies.* Edited by L. G. Herr, L. T. Geraty, Ø. S. LaBianca, and R. W. Younker. Berrien Springs: Andrews University Press.

———. 1994. "Hesban: Its Geographical Setting." Pages 55–64 in *Hesban After 25 Years.* Edited by D. Merling and L. T. Geraty. Berrien Springs: Institute of Archaeology/Horn Archaeology Museum.

———. 1999. "Review of Archaeological Research in Ammon." Pages 1–29 in *Ancient Ammon.* Edited by Burton MacDonald and Randall W. Younker. Leiden: Brill.

———. 2003. "The Emergence of Ammon: A View of the Rise of Iron Age Polities from the Other Side of the Jordan." Pages 153–76 in *The Near East in the Southwest: Essays in Honor of William G. Dever.* Edited by B. A. Nakhai. Boston: American Schools of Oriental Research.

———. 2007. "Highlights from the Highlands of Jalul." Pages 129–35 in *Crossing Jordan.* Edited by Thomas Levy, Michele Daviau, Randall W. Younker and May Shaer. London: Equinox.

———. 2014. "Ammon During the Iron Age II Period." Pages 757–69 in *The Oxford Handbook of the Archaeology of the Levant c 8000–332 BCE.* Oxford: Oxford University Press.

———. 2016. "Tall Jalul: Biblical Bezer, a City of Refuge?" Pages 306–22 in *Meeting with God on the Mountains: Essays in Honor of Richard M. Davidson.* Edited by Jiri Moskala. Berrien Springs: Seventh-day Adventist Theological Seminary, Andrews University.

———. 2017. "Israel: The Prosperous Northern Kingdom." Pages 363–89 in *The Old Testament in Archaeology and History.* Edited by Jennie Ebeling, J. Edward Wright, Paul V. M. Flesher. Waco Texas: Baylor University Press.

Zayadine, Fawzi. 1973. "Recent Excavations at the Citadel of Amman." *ADAJ* 18: 17–35.

Zayadine, Fawzi, Jean-Baptiste Humbert, and Mohammad Najjar. 1989. "The 1988 Excavations of the Citadel of Amman, Lower Terrace, Area A." *ADAJ* 33: 357–63.

39
THE INVENTION OF ANCIENT MOAB[1]

Benjamin W. Porter

Over two decades ago, Whitelam's *The Invention of Ancient Israel: The Silencing of Palestinian History* (1995) was published in the midst of a raucous scholarly debate on the historicity of ancient Israel. Biblical scholars and archaeologists alike reacted strongly and often negatively to the book's principal arguments (e.g., Dever 1999; Halpern 1997, to name only a few). Whitelam accused both post-Exilic biblical writers and modern scholars, despite being two millennia apart, of fabricating ancient Israel's United Monarchy to serve both groups' political goals to erase the indigenous populations of Bronze Age Canaan and Ottoman Palestine. Described as 'post-modernist' and 'revisionist' by its critics, the book now holds an important place in the intellectual history of the divisive debates of late-20th-century biblical studies.

Reassessing Whitelam's book more than two decades later, one is struck by how its critics so soundly dismissed the idea that the United Monarchy was an 'invention' that they were blinded to opportunities to appreciate how leaders in Israel, Judah, and indeed throughout the first-millennium BCE Levant carried out hegemonic strategies of statecraft to forge fresh identities, unite people, and create new political organizations. In this fractious political world, where households formed and dissolved alliances through flexible patrimonial kinship systems, these acts were not necessarily easy feats, as textual and archaeological evidence suggests.

This chapter explores the many inventions and reinventions of one of ancient Israel's neighbors, Moab, a culture area and, for a few brief centuries, a political polity located in what is today west-central Jordan, a horizontal slice of the Transjordanian Plateau east of the Dead Sea (Figure 39.1). This space is positioned within a Mediterranean landscape that had already seen desiccation thanks to Neolithic and Bronze Age farming communities (Cordova 2007). In the late second and first millennium BCE, people who lived in this area sustained themselves through subsistence agriculture and animal pastoralism organized across rolling grassy tablelands. Deep canyons such as the Wadi al-Walla, the Wadi al-Mujib (the biblical Arnon), and the Wadi al-Hasa (the biblical Zered) cut through these tablelands, providing fresh water that drained westward into the Jordan Valley (Figure 39.2).[2] It was upon this landscape that Moab was invented and reinvented multiple times in antiquity as a space in a landscape, a political polity, and a textual construct in first-millennium BCE/CE written sources. This chapter traces these early inventions of Moab using the available textual and archaeological evidence and concludes with a parting thought about the toponym's afterlife.[3]

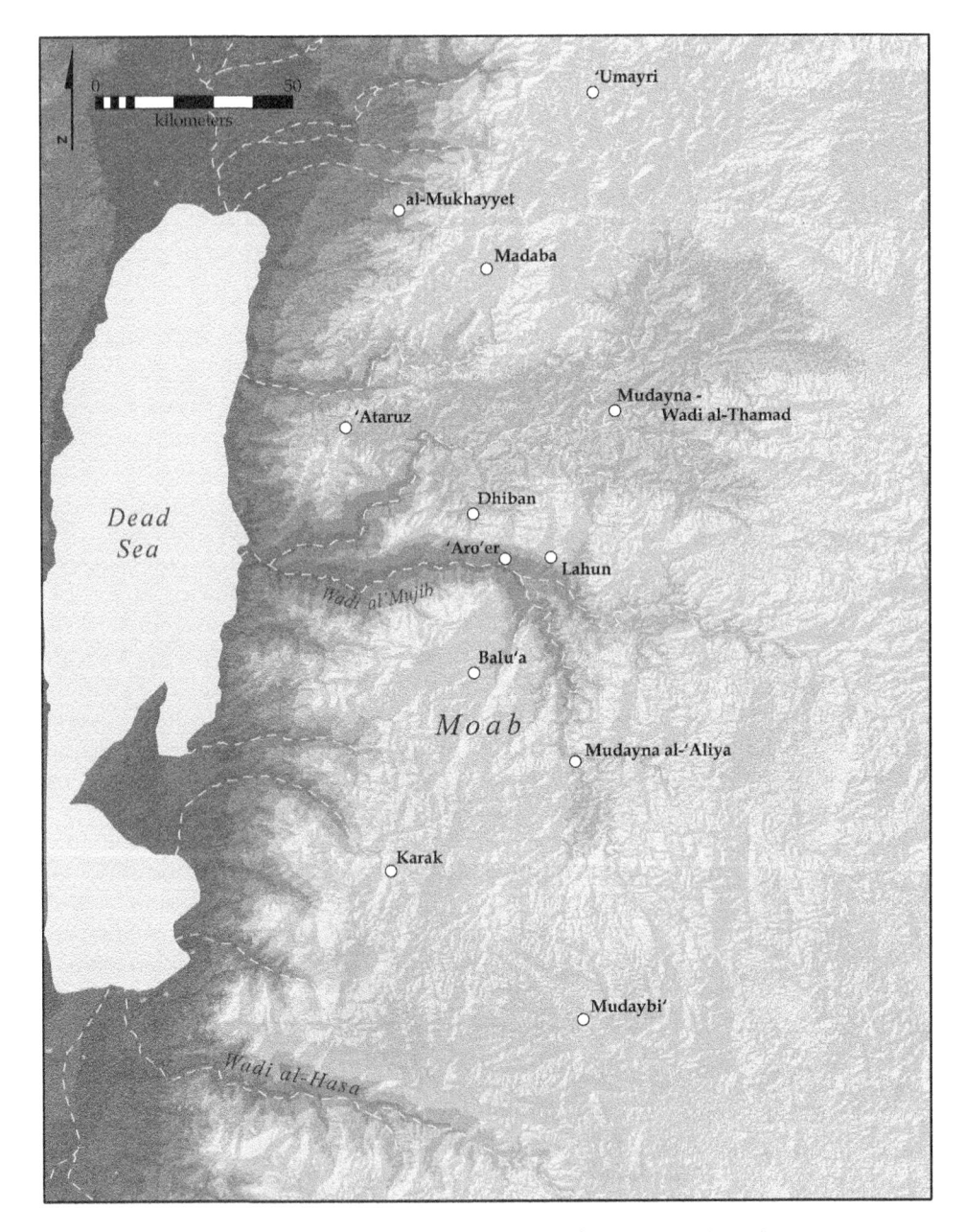

Figure 39.1 Map of settlements in west-central Jordan (map by George A. Pierce)

Searching For Early Moab

The earliest inventions of Moab occurred in the second half of the second millennium BCE, not in western Jordan, but in the minds of Egyptian scribes who imagined a distant territory just beyond the New Kingdom's control. Texts, many of which were inscribed on Egyptian monuments dating to the Eighteenth, Nineteenth, and Twentieth Dynasties, characterized the region as the domain of at least semi-mobile pastoralists—Egyptian *shashu* or, in Amarna

Figure 39.2 The Wadi al-Mujib, known as the Arnon in the Hebrew Bible, looking west from Lahun, as a winter rainstorm approaches (Image: B. Porter, March 2002)

Akkadian, *sutu* or *shutu*—who moved across the landscape and occasionally disrupted Canaanite and Egyptian interests to the west (Kitchen 1992; Redford 1982). Among this scribal activity, the name 'Moab' first appears in a text located on the wall of Ramses II's temple at Luxor. The occasion is the commemoration of the pharaoh's destruction of a town in the 'land of Moab' named *b[w]trt*, a town whose location may be modern Rabba. The inscription lacks a date, but the consensus is the ninth year of Ramses II's rule, ca. 1270 BCE, about a century before the Bronze Age crisis substantially weakened Egypt and its Mediterranean peers (Cline 2014). This passing mention of Moab is the only known instance of the toponym before the mid-9th-century BCE Mesha Inscription (see below). The Luxor inscription also says little about the political organization of west-central Jordan. A likely campaign itinerary from the Eighteenth Dynasty pharaoh Thutmoses III at Karnak, dating some two centuries earlier, suggests sedentary life in western Jordan was sparse, but certainly not devoid of settlements. Settlements 98–101 list the names of four towns, *tipun*, *'ubir*, *yarutu*, and *harkur*, the first of which may be Dhiban and the last, Karak; the locations of the other two towns are unknown (Redford 1982).[4]

The archaeological evidence from the few mid- to late-second-millennium (i.e., the Middle and Late Bronze Ages) settlements that have been documented in west-central Jordan does not offer much insight into the region's political organization. Settlement activity has been detected through the discovery of broken ceramic vessels in archaeological surveys and on the surface of ancient sites in the region. Excavations have also documented Bronze Age objects in later Iron Age, Classical, and Islamic deposits. Although helpful in certifying the presence of earlier communities, the fragmentary evidence offers little useful information.

Tall al-'Umayri, located south of 'Amman and resting just north of the border of the territory scholars usually attribute to Moab, is a rare exception. Excavations here have documented Middle Bronze Age fortifications and a Late Bronze Age building that have been interpreted as either a small temple or palace (Herr, Clark, and Bramlett 2009). However, south of al-'Umayri, fortified settlements like those described in Thutmoses III's campaign itinerary have not been identified after several decades of intensive research. This pattern suggests the region possessed, at best, a low population density that was distributed thinly across the landscape, a pattern expected of nomadic and semi-nomadic pastoralist communities.

A slight intensification in sedentary settlement practices occurred between the late-12th century and mid-10th century BCE, however.[5] This nearly two-century period saw the construction and abandonment, usually after 75 years of use, of small (<1 ha) agro-pastoralist settlements. Several settlements were perched on remote outcrops overlooking the Wadi al-Mujib and its tributaries. Documented examples include Balu'a, Lahun, and Mudayna al-'Aliya, among several others (Figure 39.3; cf. Porter 2013). Despite the relatively short period of habitation, these settlements saw substantial investments in their architecture. Stone-built casemate fortifications encircled rows of domestic residences whose entrances faced large communal courtyards. Some settlements were well defended thanks to tall stone walls and towers, punctuated in places with fortified gates. Archaeological and environmental research have determined that these settlements used the lush riparian zones at the bottom of wadis for growing plants, watering livestock, hunting, and fishing (Farahani et al. 2016; Porter 2014). These ecological zones were essential to these settlements, which were otherwise at the mercy of the semi-arid conditions of the Eastern Karak Plateau.

Upon their discovery, these settlements were interpreted as garrisons protecting the eastern border of a late-second-millennium BCE kingdom of Moab (Glueck 1940: 167–72; van Zyl 1960).[6] This interpretation was inspired by the Hebrew Bible's narrative describing the Israelites' experiences as they passed through western Jordan (see below). However, excavations have since determined these settlements were semi-autonomous agro-pastoralist communities in which no one settlement dominated the others in a ranked settlement hierarchy, a defining characteristic of territorial polities in the Levant (Porter 2013). In fact, a careful consideration of each settlement's history of occupation indicates that many were not inhabited at the same time. While this pattern of shifting settlement practices was symptomatic of the decentralized political and economic conditions throughout the Levant during the final two centuries of the second millennium BCE, somewhere amidst these small settlements the stage was set for the emergence of the kingdom of Moab in the 9th century BCE.

The House that Mesha Built

There is unfortunately little evidence with which to understand how the groups that lived in the disparately arranged settlements described above eventually established the kingdom of Moab. Leaders likely took their first steps to organize a polity in the late-10th or early-9th century BCE in a location south of the Wadi al-Mujib. Karak, ancient Kir-Hareseth, is a good candidate for Moab's earliest capital. First-millennium BCE spolia found in later Crusader and Islamic contexts attest to the presence of an Iron Age settlement that has since been dismantled (e.g., Weber 2017).[7] Chronologically secure historical and archaeological evidence for the kingdom's development only becomes visible in the mid-9th century BCE. An essential text for reconstructing the polity's emergence is the Mesha Stele, a basalt monolith bearing a royal inscription written in 'Moabite,' a variation of a Canaanite-Phoenician alphabetic script. A European Christian missionary documented the stele in 1868 when traveling by Dhiban (ancient

Figure 39.3 Early Iron Age Lahun, looking south (Image: Lehun © Aerial Photographic Archive for Archaeology in the Middle East. APAAME_19980520_DLK-0035. Photograph: David L. Kennedy)

Dibon), one of the kingdom's ancient capitals (Figure 39.4).[8] With only 34 lines extant, the inscription is a first-person narrative in the voice of the Moabite king Mesha that details his revolt against the Kingdom of Israel, an event also mentioned in 2 Kings 1, and his ensuing building program during the mid-9th century BCE. The god Kemosh, Mesha's patron deity, and presumably the patron deity of Moab, inspired and supported this revolt. However, a careful reading of the text reveals a hidden transcript explaining how Mesha and his royal court organized familial segments and territories on either side of the Arnon into a polity that took the preexisting regional name 'Moab' for its title (Routledge 2004: 133–53). Mesha used the flexible patrimonial system that was commonly practiced throughout the second and first millennium BCE that encouraged households to use kinship metaphors to reimagine themselves as members of a broader collective without sacrificing much local autonomy (Schloen 2001).

Figure 39.4 The Mesha Stele. The light gray stone is the original preserved portions. The black stone is a cast reconstructed from a frieze of now-missing portions. Original photo by Élisée Reclus (1830–1905), now in the Louvre (AP 5066)

Mesha expanded Moab's territory through military campaigns against the Kingdom of Israel and, possibly, Judah. According to Mesha's inscription, Israel's Omride Dynasty controlled three territories north of the Arnon—the 'Land of Madaba,' the 'Land of 'Aṭarot,' and 'All of Dibon'-prior to Mesha's revolt. A 'Land of Ḥawronen' is mentioned in the final lines (31–33) of the inscription's preserved text, although its precise location is unknown.[9] Line 31 of the text includes the reconstructed phrase, 'House of David,' an alternative name for Judah, as the territory's ruler at the time, although this interpretation must be accepted cautiously due to the passage's fragmentary state. 'Men of Gad,' presumably members of the Israelite tribe of Gad, and other groups ('Men of Sharon' and 'Men of Maḥarot) were living in the Land of 'Aṭarot and possibly other regions. When Mesha assumed control over these territories, his armies killed many inhabitants and enslaved the survivors that supplied labor for building projects. Mesha also describes how he destroyed temples dedicated to Yahweh and transferred ritual equipment into Kemosh's possession.

The archaeological evidence for Israel's rule over regions north of the Wadi al-Mujib is meager and disputed. Excavations at 'Ataruz (ancient 'Aṭarot) have recently documented a temple complex whose initial construction may have occurred in the late-10th or early-9th century BCE (Ji 2012; 2018) (Figure 39.5).[10] Multiple altars, hearths, standing stones, and ritual equipment were recovered including a four-horned ceramic altar, incense cups, and many ceramic and metal oil lamps. The temple shows signs of a violent destruction, possibly in the mid-9th century, followed by a substantial reconstruction and expansion later in the century (Bean et al. 2018; Ji 2018). If the date of the complex's construction and destruction phases are accurate, it conspicuously aligns with Mesha's claim in his inscription that he attacked an Israelite settlement at 'Ataruz, killed all its inhabitants, and stole its ritual equipment for Kemosh.[11]

Additionally, the settlement design of three towns, 'Ataruz, Mudayna on the Wadi al-Thamad (ancient Yahaṣ), and al-Mukhayyat (ancient Nebo), is notably similar to early-9th-century BCE towns in Israel such as Samaria, Hazor, and Jezreel (Edwards 2019; Finkelstein 2013: 85–103). Settlements were constructed on artificial podia that elevated them above the landscape. Moats and glacis surround the towns with entrances guarded

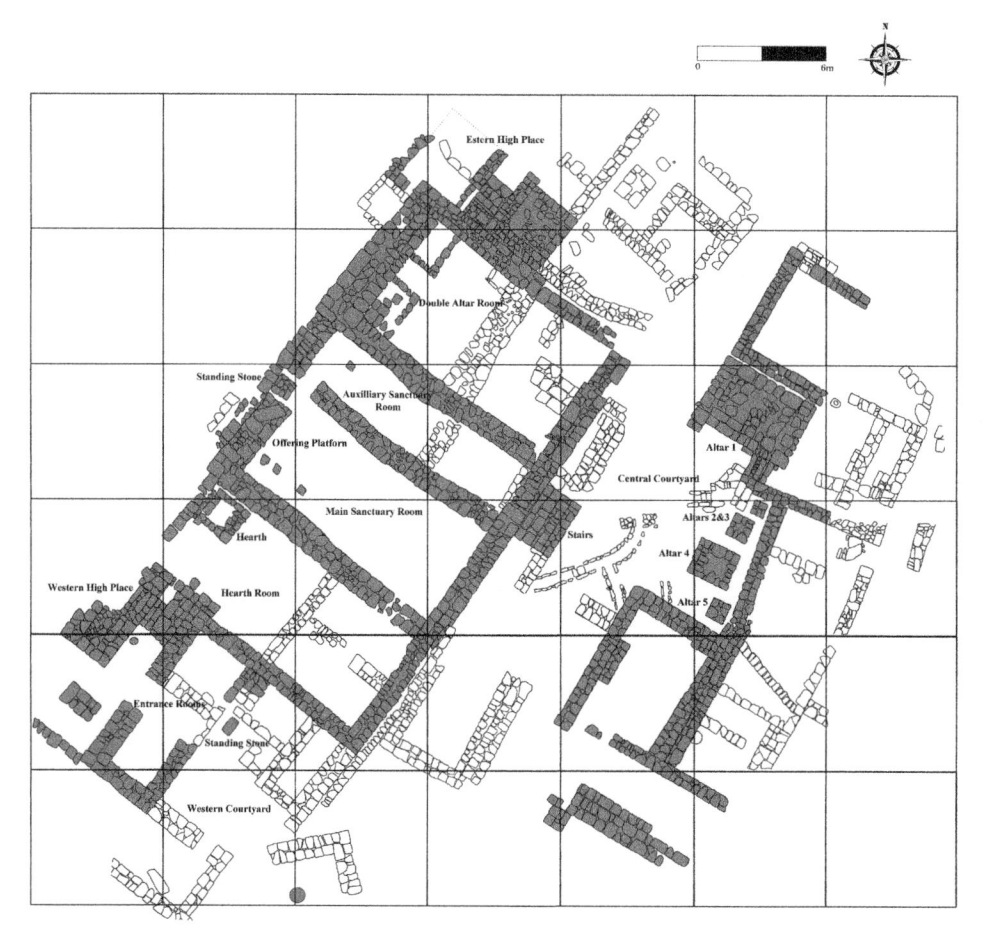

Figure 39.5 The 'Ataruz temple complex with the late-ninth and eighth-century architecture shaded in dark gray (Image courtesy of Chang-Ho C. Ji)

with multi-chambered gates. This repeated construction pattern may be part of a building program carried out during the early decades of Israel's Omride Dynasty.

While a tempting reconstruction, these features have not been sufficiently excavated to assign a hypothetical late-10th- or early-9th-century BCE date of construction. These settlement features were more likely constructed during Mesha's sweeping mid-9th-century BCE building campaign that he carried out following his consolidation of power across the region. Many projects are described in his inscription, including the construction of new settlements, roads, temples, and hydrological infrastructure. Some of these achievements are visible in the archaeological evidence. Excavations at Dhiban, Mesha's capital determined that the town's northwest corner was deliberately enlarged by .75 ha with an artificial fill that was buttressed with a fortification system (Tushingham 1972). Multiple cisterns and reservoirs for capturing rainfall have been documented throughout the site (Routledge 2013: 57). Mesha describes ordering the construction of similar hydrological features in his inscription (Lines 24–25). On the site's highest elevation, a monumental building at least 20 m wide and possibly as long as 43 m was constructed in the mid-9th century BCE and used through the 8th century (Figure 39.6). This building was likely associated with Mesha's and his successors' administration (Routledge 2004:161–73).

Other settlements with substantial 9th- and 8th-century BCE settlements have been documented. The 'Ataruz temple complex was rebuilt and expanded, as described earlier. Fortification systems at Madaba, Mudayna on the Wadi al-Thamad, and Mukhayyat were strengthened.[12] Archaeological surveys on either side of the Wadi al-Mujib have documented dozens of smaller 9th- and 8th-century settlements attesting to the kingdom's three-tier settlement hierarchy. These settlements played an important role in supporting Moab's economy, although the extent to which the royal administration controlled its organization is difficult to determine. Moab's economy was, like most Levantine polities, primarily based on agro-pastoralism that insured a basic level of subsistence for households. Workshops produced ceramic vessels of all sizes from local clays, including ones with burnished bodies that were covered with red slips and decorated

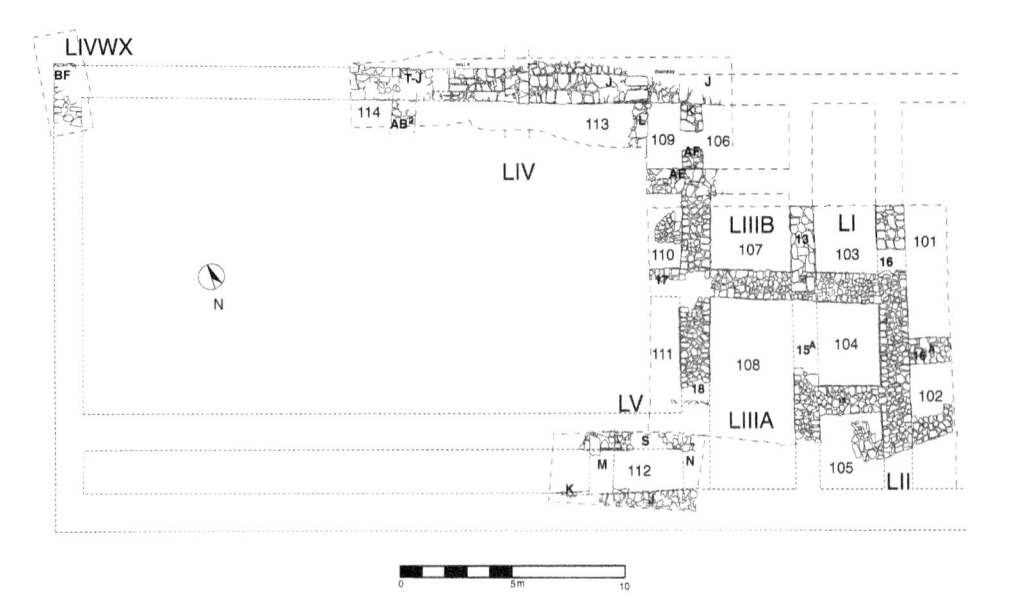

Figure 39.6 The Iron Age monumental Building L at Dhiban (Image courtesy of B. Routledge)

with bands of black, red, and white pigments (Herr 2015). Animal pastoralism supplied enough wool to support textile production. Weaving equipment and loom weights found in residences suggest production was organized at least at the cottage level (Wade and Mattingly 2003). The presence of relief images carved in local stone suggests that some artists had training in orthostat carving, a popular artistic trading in the Levant and Mesopotamia (Weber 2017) (Figure 39.7). The kingdom's economy benefited from the commercial networks that passed through the region, notably the King's Highway that connected the land and maritime commercial routes of Arabia and the Red Sea with destinations to Moab's north, such as Damascus and Karkemish. Caravans of traders moved highly desired luxury items—carved shells, precious gems, spices, and aromatics—along this highway. The kingdom's administration likely collected tariffs from these caravans as they passed through Moab.

The Mesha Inscription makes clear that Moab's royal court promoted the worship of the deity Kemosh to integrate different groups under their polity. Mesha describes how he built a sacred precinct he named Qarḥoh in or near Dhiban that he dedicated to Kemosh. The precise location of Qarḥoh has yet to be determined. However, evidence for ritual practices has been identified in Dhiban's vicinity, although apparently unassociated with Kemosh's cult. A shrine located along a north-south road was identified not far from Mudayna on the Wadi al-Thamad (WT-13; Daviau and Steiner 2017). Among other ritual equipment found were distinctive anthropomorphic ceramic figures. Ritual spaces with equipment, including altars, have also been documented at 'Ataruz (Bean et al. 2018; Ji 2012, 2018) and Mudayna on the Wadi al-Thamad (Daviau and Steiner 2000). These different installations suggest that any attempt by Moab's kings to centralize the worship of a patron deity in a single location failed just as much as their Israelite and Judahite peers to the west.[13]

Figure 39.7 Basalt orthostat with carved relief scene of lion's hindquarters and tail. The orthostat is today displayed at the entrance to the Karak Archaeological Museum in Jordan (Image: B. Porter)

Yahweh's Washbasin: Moab in the Hebrew Bible

The archaeological and textual evidence that describes the steps west-central Jordan's political leaders took to establish and sustain the kingdom of Moab should be distinguished from what was written about Moab and its people in the Hebrew Bible. Biblical writers were certainly aware of Moab, mentioning the region and the polity numerous times and showing basic competency in the names and locations of settlements. The biblical writers used this knowledge to develop literary versions of Moab to support the Hebrew Bible's rhetorical needs. The Moabites make a rather infamous entrance into the biblical narrative in Gen 19:30–38. Following the destruction of Sodom and Gomorrah, Lot and his daughters take shelter in a cave near Zoar in the hills east of the Dead Sea. The daughters, having lost their fiancés in the towns' destruction, take turns having sexual intercourse with their drunken father in order to preserve the family's lineage. The older daughter gives birth to Lot's son who is given the name Moab while Ben-Ammi, the ancestral Ammonite, is born to the younger daughter. The Genesis story presents an incestuous origin story for Israel's neighbors and sometimes adversaries. The story reflects later, likely post-Exilic writers' beliefs about Moab's primordial past that place them in western Jordan before Israel's entrance during the final stages of the Exodus. The Septuagint adds an additional gloss in a clever act of philology to note that Moab's name was based on the Hebrew, מאבי, 'He is from my father' (LXX Gen 19:37), reflecting their incestuous origins.

In Numbers, west-central Jordan is a key theater in the Exodus narrative that is characterized as a region controlled by fully developed territorial polities led by kings. Moab's northern border is conspicuously placed at the Arnon (Num 21:13), north of which resided the territory of the Amorites in a region the biblical writers label the *mishor*. Prior to Israel's arrival, Sihon of Heshbon had won the *mishor* during earlier battles with the Moabites (Num 21:26). Sihon refused the Israelites' request to pass through his territory, leading to a battle in which the Israelites conquered the region, a battle memorialized in the Ballad of Heshbon (Num 21: 27–30). The Moabite king Balak responded to this threat on his northern border by asking Balaam to curse the Israelites in a formal ceremony (Num 22–24). In an extended scene, Balaam, under Yahweh's guidance, defies Balak's request, issuing four oracles that bless Israel, and predicts its success in the coming centuries (esp., Num 24:17–24).

Living in close proximity to Moab brought Israelite men to intermingle with Moabite and Midianite women, leading some men to worship Moabite gods, specifically Baal of Peor. Moses later had all offenders summarily executed (Num 25:1–5). Israel's newly won territory north of the Arnon was granted to two tribes, Gad and Reuben, both of whom are said to have desired the *mishor's* pasture lands for their herds (Numbers 32). Gad received the southern portion, including the towns of Ataroth and Dibon, among others, while Reuben received the northern portion that included Heshbon and Nebo (Num 32:34). Mesha recounts in his inscription, described above, that he conquered the region from Israel in the mid-9th century BCE, notably recognizing Gad's affiliation with the Omride Dynasty.

Scholars have interpreted these encounters between Moab and Israel in various ways. While portions of the text may date to earlier centuries (e.g., the Ballad of Heshbon),[14] most passages about west-central Jordan were set down in the 9th and 8th centuries BCE by scribes working in the Northern Kingdom of Israel and later edited again by the Priestly School after the 6th century (Leveen 2008; Levine 2000: 37–46). The earlier strata reflect the Kingdom of Israel's concerns, and perhaps its anxieties, during the early 9th century BCE when the kingdom controlled the *mishor*. Scribes included these passages in part to justify Israel's control of the region as well as express the fact that the territory was won from the Amorites and not the Moabites, therefore not encroaching on what was considered to be the sovereign territory of 9th- and 8th-century BCE Moab (Levine 2000: 39). The text may have also been composed to justify the tribes of Reuben and Gad's membership in Israel, an opinion that not everyone may have necessarily shared.

Moses delivered his final speech in the closing chapters of Deuteronomy and died on Mount Nebo, a promontory on western Jordan's plateau overlooking the Dead Sea. Thereafter, the Deuteronomistic History's (Joshua through 2 Kings) theater shifted west of the Jordan River to the Central Highlands where the remaining Israelite tribes established themselves amidst conflicts with their Canaanite and Philistine neighbors. Moab plays cameo roles here and there throughout the Deuteronomistic History. One significant scene appears in Judges when Ehud assassinated the Moabite king Eglon in his palace, ending what was reported to have been 18 years of Moabite rule over the Israelites (Judg 3:12–30). 2 Kings 1 and, more substantially, 3 describe Mesha's revolt against the Kingdom of Israel, an event that was reported in the Mesha Inscription. The 2 Kings 3 account, however, describes Jehoram's response, which was to recruit the kings and armies of Judah and Edom to join him in an invasion of Moab from its southern border. Upon running out of water, the kings desperately seek an oracle from Elisha, who not only predicts that pools of water will appear in what was likely the Zered Valley (the modern Wadi al-Hasa), but that the kings would succeed in their campaign. The story concludes with Israel conducting a scorched-earth campaign through the territory that was so destructive that an unnamed king of Moab—probably Mesha—sacrificed his firstborn son on what was likely Kir-Hareseth's walls. The sacrifice paid off as a 'great wrath' came upon Israel, forcing them to retreat to their territory.

The prophetic and literary texts also characterize Moab in adversarial tones. Passages in three psalms disparage Moab alongside Israel's Levantine neighbors. In an often-quoted passage, Ps 60:8//108:9 describe Moab as Yahweh's toilet: "Moab is my washbasin; on Edom I hurl my shoe; over Philistia I shout in triumph." Neither did the prophets spare Moab their critique. Amos (2), Ezekiel (25:8–11), Isaiah (11; 15–16), Jeremiah (9; 25; 48), Micah (6), and Zephaniah (2) all mention Moab, many forecasting the polity's downfall. Exilic and post-Exilic period texts including Daniel (11), Ezra (9), Judith (1, 5, 7), and Nehemiah (13) continue the tradition of disparaging Moab alongside Israel's neighbors.

The Book of Ruth, however, tells a different story about Israel's relationship with Moab. Escaping a famine, an Israelite family moves to Moab where the sons marry Moabite wives, one of whom is Ruth. After the men of the family die, Ruth and her mother-in-law Naomi relocate to Bethlehem, a town in Israelite territory, after the famine had ended. In search of a husband, Ruth endears herself to Boaz, a somewhat distant relative of Naomi's family, yet near enough in lineage to take the role of Ruth's deceased husband. After their marriage, Ruth bears a son, Obed, the grandfather of David, ancient Israel's second king. This story of intermarriage between two distinct ethnic groups as well as the display of hospitality to foreigners suggests that the biblical writers' animosities toward Moab may not have been as common in everyday life as most biblical passages convey. Although the text places the story of Ruth in the late second millennium BCE ("In the days when the judges ruled…," Ruth 1:1), scholars have debated the date of the text's composition. Some assign it a post-Exilic date, believing the text to be a counterargument responding to Ezra and Nehemiah's xenophobic positions on intermarriage. Others date Ruth's composition earlier to the 7th century after Josiah's reign, or perhaps the 6th century, a tumultuous century that saw the destruction of Jerusalem and the deportation of many Levantine communities.[15]

Because many biblical writers presented Moab and its inhabitants as adversarial stock characters in their compositions, one must exercise a great deal of caution when using the biblical text as a historical source for the culture area and kingdom. Of course, the historiography of Moab has been dominated by scholarship that has done just the opposite, uncritically plucking information from biblical texts to support their interpretations of archaeological evidence (see above). Glueck (1940) and van Zyl (1960), following Albright and his students' tendencies to forego the use of source-critical methods, liberally drew on biblical passages to write histories of Moab. It was only in the 1980s and continuing into the 1990s that scholars considered the reliability of the biblical evidence for Jordan's first-millennium history, pointing out the disjunctions between the archaeological evidence and the biblical sources (Bienkowski 1992; Miller 1989, 1992; Sauer 1986, to name only a few). Some scholars (e.g., Finkelstein and Lipschits 2011; Petter 2014) still treat biblical commentaries on Moab as historical records while downplaying or ignoring the literary purposes these passages played in the compositions of Israelite and Judahite scribes.

Navigating Mesopotamian Imperialism

Moab was not immune to the Assyrian Empire's incursions into the Levant that intensified during the mid-8th century.[16] The empire's often violent military campaigns established a network of provinces and vassals throughout the region that lasted into the mid-7th century. Like many of its neighbors, Moab assumed the status of a vassal under the Assyrian king Tiglath-Pileser III likely around 734 BCE. This patron-client relationship was enshrined by Moab's king swearing a loyalty oath to his Assyrian counterpart and making a pledge to send regular tribute payments to the imperial capital. In exchange, Moab preserved a limited degree of political and economic autonomy and, in theory, Assyria's protection. Moab's interactions with Assyria are recorded in at least 14 recovered cuneiform records found in imperial archives.[17] These records add four names to Moab's list of known kings between 732 and 652 BCE, demonstrating that the office continued during the kingdom's vassalship under Assyria. Assyrian records also describe the amount and kinds of tribute (Akkadian *madattu*) and gifts (*tâmartu*) Moab paid to Assyria as part of its vassal obligations. According to one source, court officials (*serani*) representing Moab personally delivered these materials to the Assyrian royal court, likely a strategic move to strengthen the patron-client relationship.[18] *Minas* of silver, gold, tin, and other rare metals are listed among Moab contributions, materials likely acquired from their neighbors along the Levantine coastline that were better connected with Mediterranean commercial networks.

These sources also describe Moab's political relationships with Assyria and its Levantine neighbors. Moab joined its neighbors in a short-lived unsuccessful revolt against Assyria during Sargon II's rule, an event that took place around 713 BCE.[19] Conversely, Moab sat out its neighbors' later 701 BCE revolt against Sennacherib that saw the destruction of Lachish and the threatening of Jerusalem, among other Levantine settlements. Moab's king instead paid tribute to Sennacherib, a symbol of fealty, during his campaign. Moab also carried out Assyria's interests through military actions. Moab is listed among the participating vassals and provinces in Ashurbanipal's invasion of Egypt in c. 667 BCE. Moab also led campaigns on behalf of Assyria. According to Ashurbanipal's accounts, Moab's king Kamās-haltâ captured Ammu-ladīn, a king of the Qedarites, an Arabian tribe likely residing in eastern Jordan that carried out incursions against Assyrian interests. The defeated king was sent to Nineveh in shackles.[20]

Like the written evidence, the archaeological evidence from the late- 8th and 7th centuries suggests Moab seamlessly reinvented itself from an independent kingdom to an imperial vassal. No dramatic destructions of towns by the Assyrian military, like that seen elsewhere in the region (e.g., Lachish), have so far been documented. Many of the settlements established in the 9th and early 8th centuries BCE continued into the late 8th and 7th centuries. The best-documented settlements include Baluʻa; Dhiban; Lahun; Madaba; Mudayna on the Wadi al-Thamad (Figure 39.8); al-Mukhayyat; and Mudaybiʻ (Figure 39.9).[21] Sedentary and semi-sedentary populations were not limited to these larger settlements, however. Nearly 50 isolated farmsteads and similar agricultural centers dating to the 7th century were identified on the semi-arid eastern edge of the Karak Plateau (Routledge 2004: 192–201; Figure 9.4). This expansion into less optimal lands may have been part of the kingdom's efforts to intensify Moab's agrarian economy during a prosperous period attributed to Assyrian economic policies in the Levant.

Moab's history following the Assyrian Empire's withdrawal from the Levant c. 640 BCE is murky. The Egyptian incursion into the Southern Levant between c. 640 and 605 BCE, an expansion that is itself not well understood (Schipper 2011), was largely concentrated along the Levant's Mediterranean coastline. Egypt's influence may have only been tangentially felt east of the Rift Valley. Moab's kings likely prospered with this increased autonomy, although there is no evidence available yet to make a determination. The Babylonian Empire's (very) late-7th and early-6th-century BCE campaigns in the Levant saw the destruction of major Levantine settlements, including Ashkelon (604 BCE) and Jerusalem (c. 586 BCE). A poorly preserved ostracon excavated at Lachish and dating to c. 589 BCE mentions a broken name of a king of Moab, Kemoš[—], suggesting that the polity's office of kingship remained intact into the 6th century (no. 8; Lemaire in Ussishkin 2004: 2106–07). This good fortune likely did not last, however. Josephus records that Nebuchadnezzar campaigned against the Ammonites and Moabites during the 23rd year of his reign, c. 582 BCE (*Ant.* 10.9.7). Likewise, Nabonidus, the

Figure 39.8 Mudayna on the Wadi al-Thamad, looking east. (Khirbat al-Mudayna eth-Thamad © Aerial Photographic Archive for Archaeology in the Middle East. APAAME_20191029_RHB-0053. Photograph: Robert Bewley)

empire's final king, likely campaigned through Moab on his way south to Edom and presumably bound toward the northern Arabian town of Tayma around 550 BCE. The fragmentary cuneiform Nabonidus Chronicle and a cliff-side relief sculpture at Sela', north of the Edomite capital Bozrah (modern Busayra), attest to this campaign (Da Riva 2020).

Settlements associated with Moab show signs of decline, destruction, and abandonment during the late 7th and early 6th centuries BCE. It is difficult, however, to pin these changes to specific causes, such as an Egyptian or Babylonian campaign, or internal economic collapse. The gate and several buildings at Mudayna on the Wadi al-Thamad show signs of burning in the decades on either side of 600 BCE, possibly the result of Babylonian attacks (Figure 39.8). Major settlements such as 'Ataruz, Balu'a, Lahun, and likely Dhiban were abandoned before the mid-6th century.[22] There is evidence that some Moabites, like many of their neighbors, were relocated to Babylon during the 6th century. The names of two individuals, Ka-mu-šú-šarra-uṣu and Ka-mu-šu-i-lu, possess the theophoric element Kemosh in their names. Both individuals are described in 5th-century BCE documents as living in or near Babylon (Zadok 1978: 62).

Written sources about Moab and archaeological evidence in west-central Jordan both fall silent between the remaining decades of the 6th century and the end of the 4th century BCE, the era of the Achaemenid Persian Empire. Western Jordan, now integrated into the larger Eber-Nari, or 'Beyond the River' satrap, was certainly not lacking in population at this time, as settlement activity around the capitals of Ammon and Edom has been documented (Bienkowski 2008). There is so far no evidence suggesting the same in the territory traditionally attributed to Moab. Settlement activity once again intensified in the 3rd

Figure 39.9 Mudaybi'. Some Iron Age features are obscured by later features built during the Middle and Late Islamic Periods. Mudeibi (Miller #435) © Aerial Photographic Archive for Archaeology in the Middle East. APAAME_20191024_DS-0327. Photograph by Dana Salameen

century BCE, when west-central Jordan was absorbed into the Nabataean Kingdom. By that point, however, Moab had lost all political meaning and returned to its role as a space with which later writers and artists used to craft new inventions.

Conclusion: The Afterlife of Moab

If, as Bruce Routledge has argued, "the 'land of Moab' was simultaneously a place and an argument about that place" during the first millennium BCE (Routledge 2004: 41), then one may ask if this argument continued in the millennia following the kingdom's demise. Authors writing in Greek, Latin, Arabic, and Syriac demonstrated an awareness of Moab in their texts, likely due to the availability of biblical manuscripts and related source materials. Josephus, for instance, recounts many of ancient Israel's encounters with Moab in his *Jewish Antiquities* that were described in the Hebrew Bible.[23] Josephus added to Moab's historical record between the late 4th and 1st centuries BCE, when much of west-central Jordan fell under the Nabataean Kingdom (*Ant.* 13.5; 15.4). The Moabites along with the Gileadites are classified as 'Arabians' who paid tribute to Alexander the Great during the Macedonian general's campaign through the Levant in 332 BCE. After the Roman Empire annexed the region in 106 CE, placing it under the province of Arabia Petraea, Moab's name was preserved in the toponyms of two major settlements, Rabbathmoba (modern Rabba), and Karakmoba (modern Karak). Ptolemy mentions both names (*Geography* 5.16.4) and Eusebius mentions Rabbathmoba among other settlements in west-central Jordan (*Onom.* 10.17; 36:20, 25; 122:28; 124:17). The 6th-century Madaba Map mosaic preserves a small fragment of Karakmoba's name in Greek (…χμωβ) (Piccirillo and Alliata 1999). Geographers writing in Arabic, such as al-Yaʻqubi and al-Muqaddasi, also preserve the name *Maāb* in their description of the region, or when naming Rabba or Karak in their list of settlements. Unlike the Mesha Inscription (and, on occasion, the Hebrew Bible), these texts do not make the case for Moab's territorial sovereignty. Collectively, however, they demonstrate that much of west-central Jordan retained the Iron Age kingdom's name well after the polity had receded in the historical imagination.

Moab makes appearances in texts circulating in Europe during the first and second millennia CE, offering itself up for reinvention in ecclesiastical writings and works of art, too many to be named here. Moab makes a brief, but familiar cameo in the opening to *Paradise Lost* (Book One; line 406), when the territory is castigated along with Kemosh and an assortment of settlements (Hesebon, Aroar, Nebo) and toponyms (Arnon) affiliated with Moab, information that Milton likely gleaned from biblical sources. European artists drew frequently on biblical narratives about Moab. Characters such as Balaam, Ruth, and Eglon were frequent subjects in illuminated manuscripts and paintings from the medieval to the modern era. These media preserved an awareness of Moab among European audiences who considered the place within the sacred imaginary of the 'Holy Land.' Arguments about Moab were resuscitated in Europe during the nineteenth and early 20th centuries, assisted by the work of European and, later, North American, explorers who documented the names of ruined settlements preserved by local Arabic speakers and associated them with older toponyms preserved in texts (e.g., Burckhardt 1822; Glueck 1940). The widely publicized discovery of the Mesha Inscription in 1868 reintroduced Moab into the scholarly, theological, and public imagination as a place that could be known and defined through the emerging discipline of archaeology. The inscription's discovery along with other notable Iron Age objects (e.g., the Baluʻa Stele; the Shihan Warrior Stele) found in west-central Jordan raised the possibility that Moab's history, fraught with lacunae in written sources, could finally be pieced together through careful archaeological research. However, the archaeological evidence has not always been recoverable or easily interpretable, as this chapter has demonstrated, making any such history difficult to render.

Despite these frustrations, historical and archaeological research in west-central Jordan has yielded the raw materials with which Moab can be invented and, indeed, reinvented now and into the future. One ongoing use of Moab is its incorporation into the national story of the Hashemite Kingdom of Jordan, a relatively young country that is leveraging the antiquities within its borders to craft a cultural heritage (Corbett 2014). Reaching deep into time for such materials is of course nothing new among Middle Eastern nations founded in the 20th century. The recently built King Hussein Gardens, constructed by Jordan's King Abdullah to commemorate his father, includes the Mesha Inscription along with other monuments from the Bronze and Iron Ages on the Garden's 488-meter Historical Passageway (Figure 39.10). As the monarchy and government draw on their Iron Age past to self-fashion Jordan's antiquity, arguments about Moab, its history, and legacy will no doubt continue in the decades to come.

Figure 39.10 A modern fabrication of the Mesha Inscription installed in King Hussein's Gardens in 'Amman, Jordan (Image courtesy of E. Corbett)

Notes

1. This publication was written during the COVID-19 pandemic. I thank several colleagues who made digital versions of their images and publications available to me for research purposes, including Robert Bewley, Elena D. Corbett, Bruce Routledge, and Jeremy Schipper.
2. See Cordova 2007 and Porter 2014 for an introduction to west-central Jordan's landscape and environment.
3. The extensive literature on Moab and the Moabites cannot be fully described in this brief chapter. Therefore, see Porter 2019 for an annotated bibliography with sources that can guide the reader through different topics.
4. Complicating these identifications is the fact that late second-millennium evidence at Dhiban and Karak was largely obscured by later settlement activity. Ceramic vessels identified in surveys and later deposits attest to the presence of human activities at both settlements during this time (e.g., Miller 1991: 89) although it is impossible to characterize these activities from the evidence.
5. This period is approximate to what most archaeologists working in the Southern Levant call the Iron Age I period. For broader reviews of the region's period, see Porter 2016 and relevant chapters in Steiner and Killebrew 2014. For a review of Jordan, see Herr and Najjar 2008.
6. Finkelstein and Lipschits (2011) have argued in favor of an Early Iron Age kingdom of Moab. While their ideas are worthy of consideration, much of their argument depends on an overinterpretation of the available evidence, and confusion over the date and accuracy of the biblical sources.
7. Some scholars have suggested that Balu'a, located north and west of Karak, as a possible alternative early capital of Moab. The discovery of the Balu'a Stele depicting a royal investiture scene in relief with a still-indecipherable inscription has supported such an interpretation (See Routledge and Routledge 2009 for summary). However, the inscription was found on the site's surface and was likely used as spolia in Balu'a's Middle and Late Islamic settlements. Archaeological evidence for Iron Age settlement activity at Balu'a exists and is largely dated to the 11th and 7th centuries (Worschech 1995). Settlement activity between those centuries is ephemeral, making it difficult to determine if the town played any administrative role in the region. Furthermore, the current size and extent of the town's Iron Age settlement in any century is obscured by later settlement activity in the Classical and Islamic Eras.
8. The Louvre Museum cares for the Mesha Stele today (AO 5066). For a detailed account of the stele's recovery and early study, see Graham 1989. Its discovery was notable at the time because it was among the earliest pieces of evidence to corroborate a historical event described in the Bible (2 Kgs 1:3). Due to the circumstances of its recovery, the text exists today in two parts, the original stone and a plaster frieze made of the inscription upon its discovery. See Dearman 1989 and Routledge 2004 for critical treatments and translations of the stele's inscription.
9. The Land of Ḥawronen was likely located on the southern edge of the Karak Plateau or in the vicinity of the Dead Sea. See Dearman 1989: 188–89 for a discussion of possible locations.
10. See Ji 2012 and 2018 for discussions about the different phases of this important building and how each is dated using ceramic vessel evidence.
11. See lines 10–13 in the Mesha Inscription.
12. See Porter 2019 for a bibliography of technical excavation reports with published evidence.
13. There is unfortunately no space to discuss the evidence for ritual and mortuary practices in west-central Jordan. See Porter 2019 for an annotated bibliography.
14. See Petter 2014: 35–54 for a review of biblical scholarship on the Ballad of Heshbon.
15. See Schipper (2016: esp. 20–22) for a thoughtful commentary of Ruth and a discussion about the date of composition.
16. See Frahm 2017 for introductions and overviews of the Assyrian Empire.
17. Gass 2009: 115–36 has published all known instances with transliterations and (German) translations. See Timm 1989 for a nearly complete listing.
18. A handful of examples exist. Visit http://oracc.org/rinap/Q003705/html and consult line ii 25 for one instance. See Gass 2009 for all known examples.
19. See Nineveh Prism A at http://oracc.org/rinap/Q006563/html, specifically vii 8"b for the full text.
20. Ashurbanipal lauds Kamās-haltâ in different accounts. Visit http://oracc.org/rinap/Q003703/html and consult viii 36 for the fullest account.

21 Space does not permit the citation of published evidence on these settlements. See Gass 2009: 213–306; Porter 2019; Routledge 2004:184–212 for discussion and bibliography.
22 One interpretive challenge is archaeologists' inabilities to distinguish 7th-century from 6th-century ceramic vessel evidence in west-central Jordan. Likewise, radiocarbon dating methods do not provide reliable dates due to the Halstatt Plateau phenomenon.
23 See Schwartz 2016 for a discussion of Josephus's use of sources.

Bibliography

Bean, Adam L., Christopher A. Rollston, P. Kyle McCarter, and Stefan J. Wimmer. 2018. "An Inscribed Altar from the Khirbat Ataruz Moabite Sanctuary." *Levant* 50: 211–36.

Bienkowski, Piotr ed. 1992. *Early Edom and Moab: The Beginning of the Iron Age in Southern Jordan.* Sheffield: J.R. Collis.

———. 2008. "The Persian Period." Pages 335–51 in *Jordan: An Archaeological Reader.* Edited by Russell Adams. Sheffield: Equinox.

Burckhardt, John Lewis. 1822. *Travels in Syria and the Holy Land.* London: John Murray.

Cline, Eric H. 2014. *1177 B.C.: The Year Civilization Collapsed.* Princeton: Princeton University Press.

Corbett, Elena D. 2014. *Competitive Archaeology in Jordan: Narrating Identity from the Ottomans to the Hashemites.* Austin: University of Texas Press.

Cordova, Carlos. 2007. *Millennial Landscape Change in Jordan: Geoarchaeology and Cultural Ecology.* Tucson: University of Arizona.

Da Riva, Rocío. 2020. "The Nabonidus Inscription in Sela (Jordan): Epigraphic Study and Historical Meaning." *ZA* 110: 176–95.

Daviau, P. M. Michèle, and Margreet Steiner. 2000. "A Moabite Sanctuary at Khirbat al-Mudayna." *BASOR* 320: 1–21.

———, eds. 2017. *A Wayside Shrine in Northern Moab: Excavations in the Wadi ath-Thamad.* Oxford: Oxbow Books.

Dearman, Andrew, ed. 1989. *Studies in the Mesha Inscription and Moab.* Atlanta: Scholars Press.

Dever, William. 1999. "Histories and Nonhistories of Ancient Israel." *BASOR* 316: 89–105.

Edwards, Steven. 2019. "Omride Architecture at the Town of Nebo." *ZDPV* 135(2): 143–57.

Farahani, Alan, Benjamin W. Porter, Hanna Huynh, and Bruce Routledge. 2016. "Crop Storage and Animal Husbandry at Early Iron Age Khirbat al-Mudayna al-'Aliya (Jordan): A Paleoethnobotanical Approach." *AASOR* 69: 27–89.

Finkelstein, Israel. 2013. *The Forgotten Kingdom: The Archaeology and History of Northern Israel.* Atlanta: SBL.

Finkelstein, Israel, and Oded Lipschits. 2011. "The Genesis of Moab: A Proposal." *Levant* 43: 139–52.

Frahm, Eckart, ed. 2017. *A Companion to Assyria.* Malden: Wiley Blackwell.

Gass, Erasmus. 2009. *Die Moabiter: Geschichte und Kultur eines Ostjordanischen Volkes im 1. Jahrtausend v. Chr.* Wiesbaden: Harrassowitz.

Glueck, Nelson. 1940. *The Other Side of the Jordan.* New Haven: ASOR.

Graham, M. Patrick. 1989. "The Discovery and Reconstruction of the Mesha Inscription." Pages 41–92 in *Studies in the Mesha Inscription and Moab.* Edited by Andrew Dearman. Atlanta: Scholars Press.

Halpern, Baruch. 1997. "Review of *The Invention of Ancient Israel: The Silencing of Palestinian History.*" *Shofar: An Interdisciplinary Journal of Jewish Studies* 16: 127–30.

Herr, Larry. 2015. "Iron Age IIA–B: Transjordan." Pages 281–99 in *The Ancient Pottery of Israel and Its Neighbors from the Iron Age through the Hellenistic Period, Vol. 1.* Edited by Seymour Gitin. Jerusalem: Israel Exploration Society.

Herr, Larry, and Mohammed Najjar. 2008. "The Iron Age." Pages 311–34 in *Jordan: An Archaeological Reader,* edited by Russel B. Adams. London: Equinox.

Herr, Larry, Douglas Clark, and Kent Bramlett. 2009. "From the Stone Age to the Middle Ages in Jordan: Digging up Tall al-'Umayri." *NEA* 72: 68–97.

Ji, Chang-Ho. 2012. "The Early Iron Age II Temple at Hirbet 'Atarus and Its Architecture and Selected Cultic Objects." Pages 203–21in *Temple Building and Temple Cult: Architecture and Cultic Paraphernalia of Temples in the Levant (2.–1. Mill. B.C.E.).* Edited by Jens Kamlah. Wiesbaden: Harrassowitz Verlag.

———. 2018 "A Moabite Sanctuary at Khirbat Ataruz, Jordan: Stratigraphy, Findings, and Archaeological Implications." *Levant* 50: 173–210.

Kitchen, Kenneth. 1992. "The Egyptian Evidence on Ancient Jordan." Pages 21–34 in *Early Edom and Moab: The Beginning of the Iron Age in Southern Jordan.* Edited by Piotr Bienkowski. Sheffield: J.R. Collis.

Leveen, Adriane. 2008. *Memory and Tradition in the Book of Numbers.* Cambridge: Cambridge University Press.

Levine, Baruch A. 2000. *Numbers 21–36: A New Translation with Introduction and Commentary.* New York: Doubleday.

Miller, J. Maxwell. 1989. "Moab and the Moabites." Pages 1–40 in *Studies in the Mesha Inscription and Moab.* Edited by Andrew Dearman. Atlanta: Scholars Press.

———. 1992. "Early Monarchy in Moab?" Pages 77–92 in *Early Edom and Moab: The Beginning of the Iron Age in Southern Jordan.* Edited by Piotr Bienkowski. Sheffield: J.R. Collis.

———, ed. 1991. *Archaeological Survey of the Kerak Plateau.* Atlanta: Scholars Press.

Petter, Thomas. 2014. *The Land Between the Two Rivers: Early Israelite Identities in Transjordan.* Winona Lake: Eisenbrauns.

Piccirillo, Michele and Eugenio Alliata, eds. 1999. *The Madaba Map Centenary, 1897–1997: Travelling through the Byzantine Umayyad Period.* Jerusalem: Studium Biblicum Franciscanum.

Porter, Benjamin W. 2013. *Complex Communities: The Archaeology of Early Iron Age West-Central Jordan.* Tucson: University of Arizona.

——— 2014. "Toward a Socionatural Reconstruction of the Early Iron Age Settlement System in Jordan's Wadi al-Mujib Canyon." Pages 133–50 in *From Gilead to Edom: Studies in the Archaeology of Jordan in Honor of Denyse Homès-Fredericq.* Edited by Eric Gubel and Ingrid Swinnen. Brussels: Centre Assyriologique Georges Dossin.

———. 2016. "Assembling the Iron Age Levant: The Archaeology of Communities, Polities, and Imperial Peripheries." *JAR* 24: 373–420.

———. 2019. "Archaeology and Material Culture of Moab and the Moabites." *OBBS.* doi: 10.1093/obo/9780195393361-0265.

Redford, Donald B. 1982. "Contact between Egypt and Jordan in the New Kingdom: Some Comments on Sources." Pages 115–20 in *SHAJ I.* Edited by Adnan Hadidi. 'Amman: Jordanian Department of Antiquities.

Routledge, Bruce. 2004. *Moab in the Iron Age: Hegemony, Polity, Archaeology.* Philadelphia: University of Pennsylvania Press.

———. 2013. "On Water Management in the Mesha Inscription and Moab." *JNES* 72: 51–64.

Routledge, Bruce, and Carolyn Routledge. 2009. "The Balu'a Stela Revisited." Pages 71–95 in *Studies on Iron Age Moab and Neighbouring Areas in Honour of Michele Daviau.* Edited by Piotr Bienkowski. Leuven: Peeters.

Sauer, James A. 1986. "Transjordan in the Bronze and Iron Ages: A Critique of Glueck's Synthesis." *BASOR* 263: 1–26.

Schipper, Bernd U. 2011. "Egyptian Imperialism after the New Kingdom: The 26th Dynasty and the Southern Levant." Pages 268–90 in *Egypt, Canaan and Israel: History, Imperialism, Ideology and Literature.* Edited by Shay Bar, Dan'el Kahn, and J. J. Shirley. Leiden: Brill.

Schipper, Jeremy. 2016. *Ruth: A New Translation with Introduction and Commentary.* New Haven: Yale University Press.

Schloen, J. David. 2001. *The House of the Father as Fact and Symbol: Patrimonialism in Ugarit and the Ancient Near East.* Winona Lake: Eisenbrauns.

Schwartz, Daniel R. 2016. "Many Sources but a Single Author: Josephus's *Jewish Antiquities.*" Pages 36–58 in *A Companion to Josephus.* Edited by Honora Howell Chapman and Zuleika Rodgers. New York: Wiley.

Steiner, Margreet L., and Ann E. Killebrew, eds. 2014. *The Oxford Handbook of the Archaeology of the Levant (8000–332 BCE).* Oxford: Oxford University Press.

Timm, Stefan. 1989. *Moab Zwischen den Mèachten: Studien zu Historischen Denkmèalern und Texten.* Wiesbaden: Harrassowitz.

Tushingham, A. Douglas. 1972. *The Excavations at Dibon (Dhiban) in Moab. The Third Campaign 1952–1953.* New Haven: ASOR.

Tyson, Craig W. 2013. Josephus, *Antiquities* 10.180–82, Jeremiah, and Nebuchadnezzar. *JHS* 13: Article 7, 1–16.

Ussishkin, David, ed. 2004. *The Renewed Archaeological Excavations at Lachish (1973–1994).* Tel Aviv: Institute of Archaeology, Tel Aviv University.

van Zyl, Albertus Hermanus. 1960. *The Moabites*. Leiden: Brill.
Wade, John M., and Gerald L. Mattingly. 2003. "Ancient Weavers at Iron Age Mudaybi'." *NEA* 66: 73–75.
Weber, Martin. 2017. "Two(?) Lion Reliefs from Iron Age Moab: Further Evidence for an Architectural and Intellectual Koiné in the Levant." *BASOR* 377: 85–106.
Whitelam, Keith W. 1995. *The Invention of Ancient Israel: The Silencing of Palestinian History*. London: Routledge.
Worschech, Udo. 1995. "City Planning and Architecture at the Iron Age City of al-Balu' in Central Transjordan." Pages 145–50 in *SHAJ V*. Edited by Khairieh 'Amr, Fawzi Zayadine, and Muna Zaghloul. 'Amman: Department of Antiquities of Jordan.
Zadok, Ran. 1978. "Phoenicians, Philistines, and Moabites in Mesopotamia." *BASOR* 230: 57–65.

40

EDOM AND SOUTHERN JORDAN IN THE IRON AGE

Juan Manuel Tebes

Introduction

During the Iron Age, the region of modern southwestern Jordan was known as Edom, a name that appears in biblical and post-biblical literature and in contemporary Egyptian, Assyrian, and Neo-Babylonian sources. (Another name, Seir, was very much related to Edom in biblical and extra-biblical texts, to the extent that some scholars consider them to be synonyms.) Our knowledge about Edom is much more limited than about their central Transjordanian neighbors, Ammon and Moab, owing to the very few Edomite inscriptions found and the problems of interpretation of the local archaeological evidence.

Since the early 19th century southwestern Jordan was visited by European travelers who noted the local topography and documented the still visible archaeological remains. However, it was not until Nelson Glueck carried out three seasons of exploration of local sites in the 1930s, followed by the excavation of the prominent Iron Age site of Tell el-Kheleifeh, that serious knowledge of the region was acquired. Glueck's conclusions regarding the history of settlement during the Iron Age have remained influential until today (Brown and Kutler 2006: 65–90). During the 1960s–1980s, C.-M. Bennett directed excavations at three Edomite sites, Busayra, Tawilan, and Umm al-Biyara, building the skeleton of the chronology of the Edomite settlement (Bennett and Bienkowski 1995; Bienkowski 2002, 2011). Until the 1990s, scholarship studied the history of Edom based to a large extent on the biblical narrative, viewing the relations between Judahites and Edomites as central for the identarian configurations of both peoples (Bartlett 1989). However, during the last 20 years new archaeological research in the region, accompanied by novel interpretations drawing from anthropology and ethnography, have tremendously widened our knowledge about the Edomites, extending their origins to the early Iron Age.

Southwestern Jordan is characterized by different geographical areas and diverse ecological niches, features that influenced the Iron Age inhabitants (MacDonald 2015: 1–5). The region is traversed from north to south by the southernmost portion of the central Jordanian plateau (more than 1700 m above sea level), the only area where precipitation is high enough to allow agriculture and horticulture. To the west, a sharp drop in altitude leads to the Arabah Valley, a hyper-arid region connected with the plateau by only a few wadis. The Wadi Faynan, one of these wadis, is the location of one of the richest sources of copper in the southern Levant (Hauptmann 2007). The central plateau descends abruptly into the Hisma Desert to the south, while in the east it slopes gently into the vast spaces of the Syro-Arabian Desert. Owing to this multiplicity of geographical areas, contacts between zones were difficult, and except for a few periods, southwestern Jordan was never fully controlled by a unified polity (Figure 40.1).

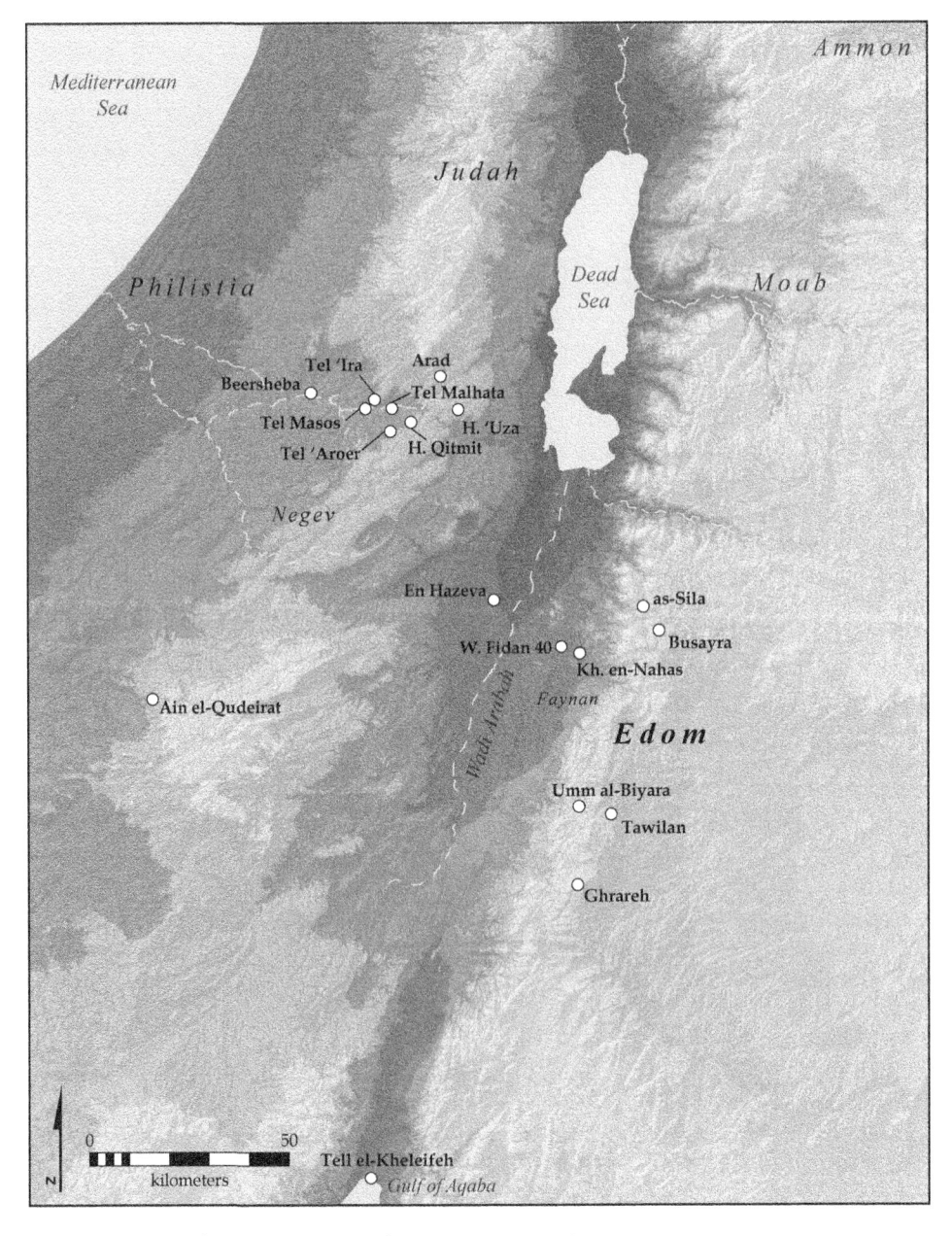

Figure 40.1 Map of sites in Edom (map by George A. Pierce)

Tribalism and Chiefdom Formation in Edom

Early scholarship, beginning with Glueck's publications, saw Edom as a "kingdom" with all those "national" attributes that are commonly ascribed to modern states, including a monarchy, one capital (Busayra), a line of bordering fortresses, one deity (Qos), one script and one ceramic style. Scholarly views started to change in the 1990s when new data began to emerge from surveys in Edomite mountain-top sites that did not accommodate easily into the one-nation model. At the same time, studies drawing from comparative anthropological and ethnographic material suggested that tribalism was the most important social configuration of Edom, as it has been in other periods of the history of southwestern Jordan. Lindner and Knauf (1997) were the first to recognize that the manifest dichotomy between the city of Busayra and the Edomite mountain-top sites reflected an antagonism between the state and local tribes avoiding taxation and military control. Bienkowski and van der Steen (2001) further suggested that Edom was a "tribal kingdom" akin to Ammon and Moab, comprised of tribal groups linked to a supra-tribal "monarchy" located in Busayra. Porter (2004) studied the series of strategies by which the Edomite elite unified and consolidated its power upon a basically "segmentary society." Innovative as these models were, they still recognized in Edom features that are commonly ascribed to state societies.

During most of their history, the most significant social organization of the peoples living in southwestern Jordan was the tribe (Bienkowski and van der Steen 2001; Tebes 2016). Tribal organizations, whether based on location or relations of kinship (or both), provided the framework for the contacts beyond the family, the structure for the economic activities, and the language for the social interactions. For nomadic semi-pastoral tribes, which constituted a large part of the Iron Age Transjordanian populations, tribal organizations procured access to distant pastures and women and assured the safety of the migration routes (Tebes 2013: 31–32). It is possible that the biblical lists of "sons of Esau," "chiefs of the sons of Edom" and "sons of Seir" (Genesis 36: 1–5, 9–30) can be related to actual Edomite clans and families (Knauf-Belleri 1995: 100–107), even though tribal or clan names are completely absent in the few surviving Edomite inscriptions.

The Iron Age tribes of southwestern Jordan were unstable and very much affected by external events, the latter causing changes in the balance of power between the different local social organizations. The genesis of the Iron Age polities should be sought in local tribes gaining leverage from outside factors, such as changes in the trade routes or in the external demand for local commodities. The resulting growth of social hierarchies led to the rise of local chiefdoms that managed to control one or several areas of southwestern Jordan, but because these chiefdoms were still structured on tribal organizations, they were highly vulnerable to changes on the external front.[1] During the Iron Age, southwestern Jordan experienced two successive phases of formation and collapse of complex societies. The first phase occurred during the 10th–9th centuries BCE, with the emergence and downfall of a chiefdom located in the Faynan district. The second phase was characterized by the rise of a chiefdom in Busayra during the late 8th century BCE, which was later conquered by the Babylonians in 553–551 BCE.

Early Edom: The Faynan Chiefdom

The name Edom is first attested in an Egyptian New Kingdom source, a frontier report from Merenptah's reign documenting the permission of pass of some *Shasu* groups of Edom with their livestock into the Delta pastures (*ANET* 259). The name *Shasu* usually refers to nomadic groups with whom the Egyptians were in contact. As is customary in relationships between states and desert nomads, the relationship with these groups was at times peaceful and at times conflictive. Thus, Ramses III boasted to have destroyed and pillaged the tents, people, property, and livestock of the *Shasu* people of Seir, another name related to Edom (*ANET* 262; Kitchen 1992: 27). Egyptian temple lists from the reigns of Ramses II and Ramses III also record five names containing the particle *q-ś*, identified by some scholars as Qos, the name of the most important Edomite deity. While not universally accepted, these names would point to the existence of Edomite clans or tribes during the Late Bronze Age (Oded 1971; Knauf 1999; Lipiński 2006: 364). Even if these sources do not make explicit allusions to southern Transjordan, they probably constitute references to Edomite nomadic groups moving in the Negev and Sinai.

During the 2nd millennium BCE southern Jordan, and to a larger extent the Negev and Sinai, was populated by people living a nomadic way of life, thus leaving few if any archaeological remains. Radiocarbon dates from slag heaps and mines in the Faynan region attest some engagement in copper metallurgy during the mid-second millennium BCE. Copper exploitation increased further during the 13th–12th centuries BCE, as attested by slag heaps and occupation levels at several sites located next to local wadis, particularly at Khirbet en-Nahas. The increased demand for the Faynan copper came from Canaan and especially Egypt, after shipments of copper from Cyprus (their traditional copper supplier) were interrupted at the end of the Late Bronze Age. The peak of copper production occurred in the late-10th–9th centuries BCE, evidenced by the large heaps of slag deposited next to or over buildings excavated at Khirbet en-Nahas and Khirbet al-Jariya (Figure 40.2; Levy *et al.* 2014; Ben-Yosef, Najjar, and Levy 2014: 798–816). Analysis of the copper slag demonstrates that the local metal industry at this time experienced a technological "leap" based on a more efficient control over the copper production and refining process (Ben-Yosef *et al.* 2019).

Excavations at Khirbet en-Nahas (Figure 40.3) by a team directed by Levy have provided evidence of an increased economic specialization and social hierarchization during the Iron Age IIA – the 10th and especially the 9th centuries BCE. A large square fortress with a four-chambered gate was built (Area A), probably for housing and protecting the workforce operating the mining industry (Figure 40.4). Other monumental buildings were erected in the vicinity, where the elite controlling the industrial operation resided (Levy *et al.* 2014).

The publication of the initial finds from Khirbet en-Nahas sparked a fierce debate over the date and function of these buildings. Some scholars, such as Finkelstein, Bienkowski, van der Steen, and Tebes criticized the excavators' overreliance on the radiocarbon dates. Since these dates were presumably taken from mixed fills coming from the industrial production, they were not related to the original dates of deposition. Critics also claimed that the excavators used the statistical (Bayesian) analyses on the radiocarbon dates to accommodate their unusually high dates (van der Steen and Bienkowski 2006; Finkelstein and Piasetzky 2008). Further, Finkelstein and Singer-Avitz (2008) re-dated most of the local pottery types to the Iron Age IIB–C (late 8th to mid-6th centuries BCE), thus contradicting the Iron Age IIA occupation of the site postulated by the excavators. Finkelstein identified the buildings at Khirbet en-Nahas as a Neo-Assyrian fortified complex guarding the access to the copper mines. Much of this criticism is correct, as most of the archaeological deposits excavated at Khirbet en-Nahas consists of mixed fills, while the Iron IIA dating is based on Bayesian analyses incorporating external data to the radiocarbon dates. However, a few intact floors and surfaces with radiocarbon dates were recorded, while the architecture of the fortress presents few features consistent with Neo-Assyrian building projects. Overall, the archaeological evidence suggests that sedentary settlement began in Khirbet en-Nahas around the

Figure 40.2 Bing Map satellite view of Khirbet en-Nahas, with excavation areas. © 2021 Microsoft

10th century BCE and grossly accelerated with the erection of monumental, specialized buildings in the 9th century BCE. It is possible that, after a hiatus of a century, the site was re-occupied in the 7th to early 6th centuries BCE with a smaller, more circumscribed metallurgical operation that caused the mixture of industrial deposits that can be seen today (Tebes 2021).

Figure 40.3 Khirbet en-Nahas, Area M slag mound (now infilled) and building

Figure 40.4 Khirbet en-Nahas, Area A fortress gatehouse looking to the northeast

The archaeological remains excavated at Khirbet en-Nahas witness the development of a chiefdom polity in the lowlands of Edom in the 9th century BCE, with evidence of hierarchical relations of power, as attested by the erection of monumental buildings and defensive structures and the operation of highly specialized economic activities, including the mining and processing of the local copper ores (Tebes 2013: 40–42; Levy, Najjar, and Ben-Yosef 2014: 981–986). The nomadic sector was a main societal component of this polity; the bulk of the population would have lived in tents that have not survived in the archaeological record (Ben-Yosef 2019). The only surviving archaeological traits of this population are the several cemeteries scattered around the region, the most significant of which is a vast 10th century BCE necropolis excavated at Wadi Fidan 40. A total of 245 graves were recorded there, although there is space to contain as many as 1380 graves (Figure 40.5; Beherec, Najjar, and Levy 2014).

By the late 9th or early 8th century BCE, the Faynan chiefdom declined, probably as a consequence of the resumption of copper shipments from Cyprus and the resultant drop in demand for the local copper. During the 8th century BCE, occupation at Khirbet en-Nahas seems to have been minimal or non-existent. The site was probably used as base for a reduced metallurgical industry in the 7th to early 6th centuries BCE, but it never reached the levels of the previous centuries.

Classical Edom: The Busayra Chiefdom

Although the central plateau provides a more hospitable ecological niche for human settlement, evidence of sedentary occupation during the Iron Age I is sparse and unclear for

Figure 40.5 Wadi Fidan 40, Iron Age graves

this region. Some occupation probably existed, as attested by the sporadic finds of pottery types allegedly dating to the Iron Age I, such as "collared rim pithoi" and northern Arabian Qurayyah wares (Finkelstein 1992). However, the date of this pottery is disputed; most of the adduced parallels of the pithoi come from Cisjordan, not Transjordan, and could date to later in the Iron Age (Bienkowski 1992). Also, the temporal range of the use of the Qurayyah pottery is so wide that it cannot be used as a chronological marker for Iron Age Edom.

The Neo-Assyrian inscriptions attest the existence of "kings" of Edom as early as the early 8th century BCE, although it is likely that the history of this polity preceded the earliest attestations (see Millard 1992). Adad-Nirari III campaigned in the west around 796 BCE and recorded a submission of tribute from Edom (*ANET* 281), but it could be a reference to the still existing chiefdom of Faynan. References to actual "kings" begin with Tiglath-Pileser III alluding to tribute from Qausmalak of Edom, between 734 and 732 BCE (*ANET* 282). Following Ashdod's rebellion in 713 BCE, Sargon II claimed submission by Edom (*ANET* 287). During his third campaign in the west (701 BCE), Sennacherib received tribute from Ayarammu of Edom (*ANET* 287). The submission of tribute of Qausgabri of Edom is mentioned in sources from Esarhaddon's (673 BCE) and Assurbanipal's (667 BCE) reigns (*ANET* 291, 294, also 301). Although tributary to Assyria, Assyrian armies probably never occupied Edom. The only time the Assyrians seem to have set foot in Edom is during Assurbanipal's war against the Arabs, when his armies are said to have reached as far south as Edom (*ca.* 650 BCE; *ANET* 298).

Genesis 36:31–39 preserves a list of kings "who ruled in the land of Edom before an Israelite king ruled" (v. 31); this list depicts a line of succession, but each "king" is associated with a distinct place. The list includes the names of Bela of Dinhabah, Jobab from Bozrah, Husham from the land of the Temanites, Hadad of Avith, Samla of Mazrekah, Shaul of Rehoboth-han-nahar, Baal-hanan (no city), and Hadad of Pau. Some of these names are decidedly Aramaean, like Hadad, or Phoenician, like Baal-hanan (Lipiński 2006: 389; Lemaire 2010: 227–228), and some may not have ruled in Edom at all, as several of the placenames were related to Moab rather than Edom (Bartlett 1965). For some scholars, this list confirms the existence of a "kingdom" of Edom in the late 9th–8th centuries BCE (Lipiński 2006: 388–390), but for others, it is a Persian-period list referring to local Arab "sheikhs" (Knauf 1985).

Two of the king names mentioned by the Assyrian sources, Qausmalak and Qausgabri, contain the theophoric name Qos, considered the most important Edomite deity. Little is known about worship of Qos during the Iron Age, a divinity only mentioned by name in a few epigraphic inscriptions from Edom and the Negev and otherwise unknown from the Hebrew Bible. The only relevant inscription from Edom is a bowl sherd found at Busayra and probably used for offerings containing the phrase *[b]rk / qws* ("may Qos be blessed") (Millard 2002: 432–433). A large building excavated in Busayra was identified as a temple (Bienkowski 2002: 478–479), although no inscription of Qos was ever found there. Two Edomite sacred places are probably mentioned in Assurbanipal's account of the war against the Arabs (*ANET* 298). Their names should probably be interpreted as Aramaic or North Arabian composite names: *Az/ṣarilu*, "enclosure/sheepfold of (the) god," and *Ḥiratâqaz/ṣaya*, "cultivated land of Qos" (Tebes 2017: 71–81).

The name Qos has been related to *qaus*, Arabic for "bow," and thus he has been identified as a war or weather divinity holding a "bow" as a divine element (Vriezen 1965). This name was usually used as a theophoric element in Edomite royal and official names, and so it is possible that Qos was the patron deity of the Edomite monarchy (Dearman 1995; Knauf 1999). Some scholars have suggested that Qos and Yahweh had several features in common, were worshipped by the same people, or even were one and the same deity. They take the enigmatic absence of references to Qos in the Hebrew Bible and the several biblical texts suggesting a southern origin of Yahweh as indicative evidence of the common worship of Yahweh and Qos (Rose 1977; Kelley 2009). It is true that both gods probably originated as desert tribal deities in the Late Bronze Age, but extreme precaution should be exercised when assessing Qos' features, given that most of what we know of his cult comes from later Idumaean, Nabataean, and Greek sources long detached from the Edomite cult.

An exact chronology of Iron Age II Edom is difficult to establish. The most important problems are the absence of well-dated Edomite inscriptions and the lack of deep stratigraphies in the excavated Edomite sites. The periodization of the Edomite highland sites can be approximately constructed from two chronological pegs. The first one is the few references to Edomite tribute in the Neo-Assyrian inscriptions, which range from the late 8th to the mid-7th centuries BCE. None of these kings are known by name in the Hebrew Bible. The most important Edomite inscription is a bulla found in Umm el-Biyara containing the name *qwsg[br] mlk 'dm* ("*Qwsgbr* the king of Edom"), most likely the same Qausgabri paying tribute to Esarhaddon and Assurbanipal (van der Veen 2011: 80–81). Unfortunately, its context of discovery is problematic: the bulla was found in a non-stratified context, while Umm el-Biyara is a one-period site which was likely occupied during a short period of time.

Therefore, if this bulla attests that Umm el-Biyara was settled during the first half of the 7th century BCE, this dating should not be extended quite easily to the other settlements in the Edomite highlands.

The second chronological peg is the pottery found in the local archaeological assemblages. Known since Glueck's times as "Edomite" pottery, it was later renamed as "Southern Transjordan-Negev Pottery" (STNP) or "Busayra Painted Ware" to avoid the obvious ethnic connotations that the original label entailed (Tebes 2011a). It is comprised of several pottery types that share a distinctive painted decoration, including shallow bowls, carinated bowls imitating Assyrian "Palace" ware, and plain cooking pots with a distinctive rim. The pottery found at Busayra can be considered the standard corpus of STNP; it contains the complete range of pottery types, with a predominance of delicate, painted forms. Throughout the use of these vessels, the people of Busayra, probably Edom's "capital" and the only real urban site in Edom, consciously imitated the culinary tastes of the contemporary southern Levantine elites. At other sites, painted types are less frequent and forms are more restricted, particularly at mountain-top settlements in the greater Petra area such as Umm al-Biyara, as-Sadeh, Ba'ja III and as-Qseir (Bienkowski 2011: 73–77).

The Edomite highland sites, in general, devoid of deep stratigraphy, offer little in the way of the development of the STNP types. This pottery, however, has also been found in sites located in the northern Negev with a much more developed stratigraphy, such as Tel 'Aroer, Tel 'Ira, 'Ain el-Qudeirat, Tel Arad, Tel Beersheba, Horvat 'Uza, and Tel Masos (Singer-Avitz 2014). Although the STNP forms do not constitute a large proportion of the local ceramic assemblages, their development can be traced through the successive stratigraphic layers. The bulk of the STNP forms in the northern Negev are probably dated to the 7th century BCE, as they are "sandwiched" between the destruction levels of the military campaigns of Sennacherib (701 BCE) and Nebuchadnezzar (587–586 BCE; Tebes 2011a: 81). This dating, however, is not unanimous, as some scholars believe that the evidence of Sennacherib's campaign in the northern Negev is flimsy and prefer to date the bulk of the STNP based on the epigraphic evidence from Edom alone, downdating it to the 6th century BCE (van der Veen 2020: 106–12).

The sites of the Edomite highlands present a clear settlement pattern, with a central site (Busayra) located in the northern region with secondary sites dotting its hinterland. Busayra is the only Edomite site that can be properly called a city, although it was of small dimensions (0.32 ha) even for southern Levantine standards (Figures 40.6 and 40.7). The "official"

Figure 40.6 Bing Map satellite view of Busayra, with excavation areas. © 2021 Microsoft

Figure 40.7 Busayra, archaeological remains. Wikimedia image

quarter was located on an easily defensible hill spur, built over an artificial podium. Remains of monumental buildings were found, two of them identified as a palace (Area C) and a temple (Area A) (Bienkowski 2002: 478–479). Busayra, most likely the biblical Bozrah, can be identified as the capital of the Edomite polity. Its relationship with the Edomite monarchy is confirmed by the several biblical passages that refer to Bozrah as the seat of one of the early Edomite "kings" (Gen 36:33) and it is the only Edomite site (together with Teman, location unknown) focused on in the fierce invectives of the Israelite prophets (Amos 1:12, referring to Bozrah's "palaces"; Isa 34:6; 63:1; Jer 49:13).

Other small-size sites were located in the Edomite highlands; some of them can be categorized as small plateau villages, such as Tawilan (Bennett and Bienkowski 1995) and Ghrareh (Hart 1989). Others were mountain-top sites, such as as-Sila (Da Riva 2019), north of Busayra. They were particularly prevalent in the greater Petra area (Lindner 1992), like Umm al-Biyara (Figure 40.8) (Bienkowski 2002), of restricted accessibility and likely outside the reach of the control of Busayra. A very different kind of site is Tell el-Kheleifeh, close to the Gulf of Aqaba. Located far away from the core of the Edomite settlement, Tell el-Kheleifeh was built as a fortified complex probably aimed at controlling the route of the lucrative trade in southern Arabian incense (Pratico 1993).

Few Edomite epigraphic sources have come to light in southwestern Jordan, most of them consisting of short inscriptions on seals, bullae, and ostraca, attesting the existence of a more or less developed administrative apparatus. These inscriptions contain personal names, including the name of "*Qwsgbr* the king of Edom" in the bulla from Umm el-Biyara (van der Veen 2011: 80–81) and the names of some king's officials, such as a seal found in Busayra inscribed with the name *Mlklb' 'bd hmlk* ("*Mlklb'* the servant of the king") (Millard 2002:

Figure 40.8 Umm el-Biyara, Iron Age domestic structures

430–431) and numerous seal impressions from Tell el-Kheleifeh with the name *Qws'nl 'bd hmlk* ("*Qws'nl* the servant of the king") (Divito 1993: 53–55). Given the fragmentary nature of this epigraphic corpus, it is difficult to identify the linguistic features of the Edomite language, but there is consensus that it should be classified as a Northwest Semitic language of the Canaanite branch (Vanderhooft 1995; Rollston 2014).

The sociopolitical configuration of Edom was very different from that of the other Iron Age southern Levantine societies, including its Transjordanian neighbors. Edom does not present any of the features commonly associated with early states: the Busayra elite did not possess the monopoly of force over the entire territory of Edom, but only over the city's hinterland, while the construction of monumental architecture at Busayra and the redistribution of prestige items to the secondary sites could also have been achieved by a non-state polity. Busayra thus can be better interpreted as a chiefdom whose sovereignty only encompassed the northern part of the Edomite highlands (Tebes 2016). The larger part of the region, especially the Petra area, was probably organized along tribal lines, some of them with little if any administrative contact with the Busayra chiefs. The Busayra chiefs were able to co-opt other tribes of the Edomite highlands and to operate in the interregional political arena of the southern Levant, presenting themselves as "kings" of all the land of Edom.

Busayra owed its paramount position in the Edomite tribal society to its prime geographical location, being strategically located on a promontory overlooking the two main ecological niches of southwestern Jordan: the Edomite plateau and the Faynan lowlands. The Faynan lowlands were accessible via the Wadi Dana, starting south of the site and giving access to the region's rich copper resources. There is archaeological evidence of an Iron

Age IIC mining industry in Faynan, never reaching the levels of the Iron Age IIA, at Rujm Hamra Ifdan and especially at Ras al-Miyah, closer to Busayra and where two fortresses were built (Ben-Yosef, Najjar, and Levy 2014: 816–839; Smith, Najjar, and Levy 2014).

The central plateau provided the little agricultural output that Edom was able to offer. But most importantly, Busayra was located 4 km west of the "King's Highway", across which passed the route of the southern Arabian incense trade. Thus, Busayra enjoyed an excellent location to serve as a point of detour, for shipments going to the west toward the northern Negev, and to the north toward central Transjordan and Syria. Arabian or Arabizing archaeological finds in southwestern Jordan and the northern Negev attest the wide-range commercial contacts with Arabia, including stone stoppers, cuboid limestone altars, and inscriptions in South Arabian, Thamudic, proto-Dedanitic or Minaean scripts, even featuring Arabian names (Tebes 2013: 47–48; van der Veen and Bron 2014).

Assyrian interest in the control of the Arabian trade is evident in the several military campaigns launched against the Arabian tribes in southern Syria. As we have seen, at least one Assyrian king (Assurbanipal) was involved in military operations reaching as far south as Edom (Tebes 2017: 71–81). Starting with Tiglath-Pileser III, the Assyrians also raided the southern coastal region of Philistia and the northwestern Negev, where the western branch of the Arabian trade route ended. Being as it may, the Assyrians never conquered Edom and probably never had reasons to do so. As a peripheral tributary polity located in a remote region, local outsourcing of the control and taxation of the Arabian trade was logistically more convenient and economically more profitable.

Our sources say little about the end of Edom as an independent entity. Contemporary reconstructions include Edom as one of the regions conquered by the Babylonian king Nabonidus in his campaign in the Levant and northern Arabia (553–551 BCE; Crowell 2007; Da Riva 2020). The march of his army is recollected in the fragmentary *Nabonidus Chronicle*, where the king claims to have set up camps "against the land of E]dom" (*Udummu*) and large armies in "the g]ate of RUG*dini*" (read as Rugdini or Šintīni). The latter site has been identified as Rekem (the Semitic name of Petra) or as-Sila (Da Riva 2019: 171). The Babylonian conquest of Edom is confirmed by a badly preserved relief of Nabonidus carved on a cliff overlooking as-Sila, showing the figure of the king standing with the typical Neo-Babylonian royal attire and three divine symbols, facing a barely legible inscription (Da Riva 2020). There are a number of destruction levels at Busayra, Tawilan, and Tell el-Kheleifeh that could be attributed to the Babylonian conquest (Crowell 2007: 83–84), although the chronology of the Edomite sites is too problematic to put the burden on Nabonidus in all cases. The incorporation of Edom into the Babylonian imperial realm gave Nabonidus the control of the northern section of the Arabian trade and opened the way for the conquest of the Hejazi oasis-towns, reaching as far south as Tayma and Dedan.

Neo-Babylonian control of Edom was short-lived as the region soon fell, like the rest of the southern Levant, under the aegis of Persian imperialism. The nature of the settlement in Edom during the Persian period is difficult to establish, as is the question of the relationship with later Nabataean sites. Only one inscription dating from this period is known, a cuneiform tablet found at Tawilan and dated to the accession year of a king Darius, although it is impossible to know with certainty if it refers to Darius I (accession date 521 BCE), Darius II (423 BCE) or Darius III (335 BCE; Dalley 1995). Attic and Hellenistic sherds found in stratified contexts at Busayra attest occupation during the late 4th and late 3rd centuries BCE, if not later, thus showing some continuity in the region with the settlements of the Nabataean period (Bienkowski 2013: 29–30). This evidence has been used to claim that the apparent "dark age" of archaeological remains during the Persian period stems from an incorrect dating of most of the STNP pottery forms, most of which should date to the 6th century BCE (van der Veen 2020: 109). In sum, the transition in Edom between the Iron Age and the Persian period seems to have been one of continuity rather than an abrupt break.

Relationship with the Israelites and Edomites in the Negev

The nature of the relationship between the Edomites and the Israelites is controversial, owing to the problems of dating and interpretation of the relevant biblical texts (Bartlett 1989: 90–93, 103–128; Lemaire 2010). Biblical traditions concerning the exodus (Num 20:14–21) imply the existence of a "king" of Edom, but the reference to the "King's Highway" suggests a redaction in the Assyrian period or later (Bartlett 1989: 92). The Deuteronomistic History recounts a long conflictive history between the Israelites and Edomites starting with king David and extending throughout the 9th and 8th centuries BCE. David is said to have defeated the Edomites in the Valley of Salt and established garrisons in Edom (2 Sam 8:13–14). We are later informed that Hadad, an Edomite of "kingly stock" managed to flee to Egypt only to come back during Solomon's time (1 Kgs 11:14–22). It is possible that in this story we encounter a confusion between the names Edom and Aram (the letters *dalet/resh* are very similar in Hebrew script), and therefore the original reference might be to Hadad of Aram, an otherwise typical Aramaean name (Lemaire 2010: 228–229). We have no other news until the reign of Judaean king Jehoshaphat (870–848 BCE), when "there was no king in Edom; a deputy was king" (1 Kgs 22:47). This statement is contradicted by the account of the expedition of Israelite king Jehoram (852–841 BCE) against Moab, in alliance with the unnamed kings of Judah (the context suggests he is Jehoshaphat) and Edom (2 Kgs 3:9). Only during the reign of Jehoshaphat's son Jehoram (848–841 BCE) were the Edomites able to break Judah's rule, claiming victory at Zair (2 Kgs 8:20–22). Another conflict erupted under Amaziah of Judah (796–781 BCE), who is said to have defeated the Edomites in the Valley of Salt and taken Sela (2 Kgs 14:7), while his son Uzziah (781–740 BCE) recovered and rebuilt Elath (2 Kgs 14:22). The last annalistic report is the reference to the loss of Elath to Edom during Ahaz's reign (736–716 BCE; 2 Kgs 16:6).

One aspect of these annalistic references to Edom that is particularly troubling is that they allude to events occurring in the 10th to 8th centuries BCE, when archaeological evidence of settlement in the Edomite highlands is scarce and at best disputed. Except for the problematic verses referring to Hadad, no Edomite king is mentioned by name in Samuel-Kings. It could be adduced that these events correspond to the Edomite kings listed in Genesis 36 (where incidentally a Hadad is mentioned; Gen 36: 35–36), but as we have seen the historicity of this king-list is suspect.

The location of the battles between the Israelites and Edomites are not easy to identify. The names of two of these places, the Valley of Salt and Zeir (Byzantine Zoara?), suggest a location in the southern end of the Dead Sea, while Sela is traditionally identified as Umm al-Biyara or as-Sila in the Edomite highlands. Intriguingly, Bozrah is never mentioned by name. In the face of the new knowledge we have of Iron Age IIA Edom, it would be tempting to associate the Samuel-Kings references (and Genesis 36) to the chiefdom of Faynan, but the question should be kept open until new evidence is found.

Coinciding with the end of the annalistic references to Edom, archaeological evidence indicates the appearance of Edomite-related cultural traits in the northern Negev during Judah's last century of existence. This evidence includes STNP or "Edomite" pottery and epigraphic and iconographic traits of the worship of the god Qos, although their nature and dating are objects of controversy.

We have already discussed the presence of STNP in the pottery assemblages of several of the Negev sites and how it has been used as a chronological peg for dating the Iron Age settlement in the Edomite plateau. The quantity of STNP found in Negev locations ranges from a few sherds in sites located in the westernmost portion of the northern Negev to a large proportion of the pottery assemblages of eastern sites like Tel Malhata and Horvat Qitmit (Singer-Avitz 2014; Thareani 2010). Pottery types broadly coincide with those found at Busayra, including decorated bowls imitating Assyrian fine vessels, even though most of them were produced in the Negev with local clays. An exception is a specific type of cooking pot that was manufactured with clays from the northern Arabah or southwestern Jordan (Freud 2014). Transported a long way until its final use in the northern Negev, the use of these cooking pots indicates a conscious desire for the preparation and consumption of specific meals and flavors. Far from reflecting the presence of a specific ethnic or social group (the Edomites), the different STNP pottery types found in the Negev were used for diverse purposes, including the cooking of specific meals with characteristic pots, the elite emulation and conspicuous drinking and eating using imitations of fine Assyrian wares, and the performance of religious offerings with specific cultic wares (Tebes 2011a; Danielson 2021).

Three short inscriptions in Edomite script attest the worship of Qos in the northern Negev during the late Iron Age. These comprise formulaic phrases inscribed on ritual objects, including an ostracon from Horvat 'Uza with the blessing formula *whbrktk / lqws* ("I bless you by Qos;" Beit-Arieh 2007: 133–137) and two ceramic fragments from Horvat Qitmit with the dedication phrase *lqws* ("for Qos") (Beit-Arieh 1995: 260–262). The Qos inscriptions found at the open-air shrine of Horvat Qitmit led to its early identification as an "Edomite" sanctuary, although the trove of figurines and cultic vessels unearthed there exhibits an iconography broadly related to the southern Levantine cultic world rather than being specifically Edomite. No clear representation of Qos was found, but a three-horned head of a goddess could be associated with Qos' consort wife (Beck 1995). Cultic vessels with a similar human-like iconography were found buried and smashed in a *favissa* outside the fortress of 'En Hazeva in the northern Arabah (Ben-Arieh 2011). They presumably formed part of a small open-air sanctuary that was later destroyed, although lacking a final excavation report it is impossible to check the accuracy of the excavators' reconstruction of the shrine (Figure 40.9; see Cohen and Yisrael 1995). In sum, the evidence of worship of Qos in the northern Negev is clear, even if the association between his cult, onomastics, and an "Edomite" ethnicity is problematic.

These Edomitizing traits are usually discussed alongside some biblical texts and local epigraphic inscriptions to suggest a takeover of the northern Negev by the Edomites during the dwindling days of Judah's rule in the region. Most of the biblical sources are prophetic or literary texts composed or re-edited long after the fall of Judah in 586 BCE – such as Amos 1:11, Joel 4:19 and Ezek 25:12; 35:5. They condemn Edom of unlawful behavior toward his "brother", reflecting the biblical tradition of the brotherhood between Israel and Edom. Other texts are more explicit, accusing the Edomites of the destruction of Jerusalem (Obad 11; Lam 4:21–22; Ps 137:7), although their graphic imagery and lack of historical details betray the vindictive rhetoric against Edom that was common in the post-monarchical period rather than actual historical events (Tebes 2011b). Hebrew ostraca found at the fortress of Tel Arad referring to the "evil" done by Edom (Arad 40.15) and to the dispatch of reinforcements "lest Edom should come there" (Arad 24.20) have also been adduced as evidence supporting the "Edomite threat" model. However, more prosaic explanations can be offered for these references, such as conflicts over sheep-stealing and grazing rights rather than an Edomite invasion (Guillaume 2013).

Figure 40.9 Reconstruction of the open-air shrine of 'En Hazeva

It is difficult to disentangle the role of Edom in the late Iron Age Negev from the clear-cut evidence of the presence of Edomites in the post-Iron Age Negev. Deprived of their southwestern Jordanian polity, Edomites living west of the Wadi Arabah would go through a profound process of identity transformation whose specifics we barely know, but that will end in the formation of the multi-cultural society that characterized Persian and Hellenistic period Idumaea (Stern 2007).

Note

1 The use given in Levantine archaeology to the terms "tribe" and "chiefdom" is currently stripped of the neo-evolutionary perspective within which they were embedded in anthropological theory. Although tribes and chiefdoms are considered as complex stateless societies with distinct characteristics, scholars no longer see them as prerequisites for the emergence of the state; in fact, both can coexist with state societies and collapse into less-complex societies. See Tebes 2013: 31–36.

Bibliography

Bartlett, John R. 1965. "The Edomite king-list of Genesis XXXVI. 31–9 and I Chron. I. 43–50." *JTS* 16: 301–14.

———. 1989. *Edom and the Edomites*. Sheffield: Sheffield Academic Press.

Beck, Pirhiya. 1995. "Catalogue of Cult Objects and Study of the Iconography." Pages 27–197 in *Horvat Qitmit: An Edomite Shrine in the Biblical Negev*. Edited by Itzhaq Beit-Arieh. Tel Aviv: Institute of Archaeology, Tel Aviv University.

Beherec, Marc A., Mohammad Najjar, and Thomas E. Levy. 2014. "Wadi Fidan 40 and Mortuary Archaeology in the Edom Lowlands." Pages 664–721 in *New Insights into the Iron Age Archaeology of Edom, Southern Jordan: Surveys, Excavations, and Research from the University of California, San Diego & Department of Antiquities of Jordan, Edom Lowlands Regional Archaeology Project (ELRAP)*, Vol. 2. Edited by Thomas E. Levy, Mohammad Najjar, and Erez Ben-Yosef. Los Angeles: Cotsen Institute of Archaeology Press.

Beit-Arieh, Itzhaq. 1995. "Inscriptions." Pages 258–68 in *Ḥorvat Qitmit: An Edomite Shrine in the Biblical Negev*. Edited by Itzhaq Beit-Arieh. Tel Aviv: Institute of Archaeology, Tel Aviv University.

———. 2007. "Epigraphic Finds." Pages 122–87 in *Ḥorvat 'Uza and Ḥorvat Radum: Two Fortresses in the Biblical Negev*. Edited by Itzhaq Beit-Arieh. Tel Aviv: Institute of Archaeology, Tel Aviv University.

Ben-Arieh, Sara. 2011. "Temple Furniture from a Favissa at 'En Ḥazeva." *'Atiqot* 68: 107–75.

Bennett, Crystal.-M, and Piotr Bienkowski, eds 1995. *Excavations at Tawilan in Southern Jordan*. Oxford: British Institute at Amman for Archaeology and History by Oxford University Press.

Ben-Yosef, Erez. 2019. "The Architectural Bias in Current Biblical Archaeology." *VT* 69: 361–87.

Ben-Yosef, Erez, Brady Liss, Omri A. Yagel, Ofir Tirosh, Mohammad Najjar, and Thomas E. Levy. 2019. "Ancient Technology and Punctuated Change: Detecting the Emergence of the Edomite Kingdom in the Southern Levant." *PLoS ONE* 14/9: e0221967.

Ben-Yosef, Erez, Mohammad Najjar, and Thomas E. Levy. 2014. "New Iron Age Excavations at Copper Production Sites, Mines, and Fortresses in Faynan." Pages 766–885 in *New Insights into the Iron Age Archaeology of Edom, Southern Jordan: Surveys, Excavations, and Research from the University of California, San Diego & Department of Antiquities of Jordan, Edom Lowlands Regional Archaeology Project (ELRAP)*, Vol. 2. Edited by Thomas E. Levy, Mohammad Najjar, and Erez Ben-Yosef. Los Angeles: Cotsen Institute of Archaeology Press.

Bienkowski, Piotr. 1992. "The Beginning of the Iron Age in Edom: A Reply to Finkelstein." *Levant* 24: 167–69.

———, ed. 2002. *Busayra Excavations by Crystal-M. Bennett 1971–1980* (British Academy Monographs in Archaeology 13). Oxford: Council for British Research in the Levant by Oxford University Press.

———, ed. 2011. *Umm Al-Biyara. Excavations by Crystal-M. Bennett in Petra 1960–1965*. Oxford: Oxbow.

———. 2013. "The Iron Age in Petra and the Issue of Continuity with Nabataean Occupation." Pages 23–34 in *Men on the Rocks: The Formation of Nabataean Petra. Proceedings of a Conference Held in Berlin 2–4 December 2011*. Edited by Michel Mouton and Stephan G. Schmid. Berlin: Logos Verlag Berlin GmbH.

Bienkowski, Piotr, and Eveline van der Steen. 2001. "Tribes, Trade and Towns: A New Framework for the Late Iron Age in Southern Jordan and the Negev." *BASOR* 323: 21–47.

Brown, Jonathan M., and Laurence Kutler. 2006. *Nelson Glueck. Biblical Archaeologist and President of Hebrew Union College – Jewish Institute of Religion*. Detroit: Hebrew Union College—Jewish Institute of Religion.

Cohen, Rudolph, and Yigal Yisrael. 1995. *On the Road to Edom: Discoveries from 'En Ḥazeva*. Jerusalem: The Israel Museum.

Crowell, Brad L. 2007. "Nabonidus, as-Sila', and the Beginning of the End of Edom." *BASOR* 348: 75–88.

Dalley, Stephanie. 1995. "The Cuneiform Tablet." Pages 67–68 in *Excavations at Tawilan in Southern Jordan*. Edited by Crystal-M. Bennett and Piotr Bienkowski. Oxford: British Institute at Amman for Archaeology and History by Oxford University Press.

Danielson, Andrew J. 2021. "Culinary Traditions in the Borderlands of Judah and Edom during the Late Iron Age." *TA* 48: 87–111.

Da Riva, Rocío. 2019. "The King of the Rock Revisited: The Site of as-Sila (Tafila, Jordan) and the Inscription of Nabonidus of Babylon." Pages 161–74 in *Over the Mountains and Far Away. Studies in Ancient Near Eastern History and Archaeology presented to Mirjo Salvini on the Occasion of His 80th Birthday*. Edited by Pavel S. Avetisyan, Roberto Dan, and Yervand H. Grekyan. Oxford: Archaeopress.

———. 2020. "The Nabonidus Inscription in Sela (Jordan): Epigraphic Study and Historical Meaning." *ZA* 110: 176–95.

Dearman, J. Andrew. 1995. "Edomite Religion: A Survey and an Examination of Some Recent Contributions." Pages 119–36 in *You Shall Not Abhor an Edomite for He Is Your Brother: Edom and Seir in History*. Edited by Diana V. Edelman. Atlanta: Scholars Press.

Divito, Robert. 1993. "Tell el-Kheleifeh Inscriptions." Pages 51–64 in *Nelson Glueck's 1938–1940 Excavations at Tell el-Kheleifeh: A Reappraisal.* Edited by Gary Pratico. Atlanta: Scholars Press.

Finkelstein, Israel. 1992. "Edom in the Iron I." *Levant* 24: 159–66.

Finkelstein, Israel, and Eli Piasetzky. 2008. "Radiocarbon and the History of Copper Production at Khirbet en-Nahas." *TA* 35: 82–95.

Finkelstein, Israel, and Lily Singer-Avitz. 2008. "The Pottery of Edom: A Correction." *AntOr* 6: 13–24.

Freud, Liora. 2014. "Local Production of Edomite Cooking Pots in the Beersheba Valley: Petrographic Analyses from Tel Malhata, Horvat 'Uza and Horvat Qitmit." Pages 283–306 in *Unearthing the Wilderness: Studies on the History and Archaeology of the Negev and Edom in the Iron Age.* Edited by Juan M. Tebes. Leuven: Peeters.

Guillaume, Philippe. 2013. "The Myth of the Edomite Threat: Arad Letters # 24 and 40." *KUSATU* 15: 97–108.

Hart, Stephen. "The Archaeology of the Land of Edom." PhD diss., Macquarie University, 1989.

Hauptmann, Andreas. 2007. *The Archaeometallurgy of Copper: Evidence from Faynan, Jordan.* Berlin: Springer.

Kelley, Justin. 2009. "Toward a New Synthesis of the God of Edom and Yahweh." *AntOr* 7: 255–80.

Kitchen, Kenneth A. 1992. "The Egyptian Evidence on Ancient Jordan." Pages 21–34 *in Early Edom and Moab: The Beginning of the Iron Age in Southern Jordan.* Edited by Piotr Bienkowski. Sheffield: Collis.

Knauf, Ernst A. 1985. "Alter und Herkunft der edomitischen Königliste Gen 36,31–39." *ZDPV* 97: 245–53.

———. 1999. "Qôs." *DDD,* 674–77.

Knauf-Belleri, Ernest A. 1995. "Edom: The Social and Economic History." Pages 93–117 in *You Shall Not Abhor an Edomite for. He Is Your Brother: Edom and Seir in History.* Edited by Diana V. Edelman. Atlanta: Scholars Press.

Lemaire, André. 2010. "Edom and the Edomites." Pages 225–43 in *The Books of Kings. Sources, Composition, Historiography and Reception.* Edited by André Lemaire and Baruch Halpern. Leiden: Brill.

Levy, Thomas E., Mohammad Najjar, Thomas Higham, Yoav Arbel, Adolfo Muniz, Erez Ben-Yosef, Neil G. Smith, Marc Beherec, Aaron Giddin, Ian W. Jones, Daniel Frese, Craig Smitheram, and Mark Robinson. 2014. "Excavations at Khirbat en-Nahas 2002–2009. An Iron Age Copper Production Center in the Lowlands of Edom." Pages 89–245 in *New Insights into the Iron Age Archaeology of Edom, Southern Jordan: Surveys, Excavations, and Research from the University of California, San Diego & Department of Antiquities of Jordan, Edom Lowlands Regional Archaeology Project (ELRAP), Vol. 1.* Edited by Thomas E. Levy, Mohammad Najjar, and Erez Ben-Yosef. Los Angeles: Cotsen Institute of Archaeology Press.

Levy, Thomas E., Mohammad Najjar, and Erez Ben-Yosef. 2014. "Conclusion." Pages 977–1001 in *New Insights into the Iron Age Archaeology of Edom, Southern Jordan: Surveys, Excavations, and Research from the University of California, San Diego & Department of Antiquities of Jordan, Edom Lowlands Regional Archaeology Project (ELRAP), Vol. 2.* Edited by Thomas E. Levy, Mohammad Najjar, and Erez Ben-Yosef. Los Angeles: Cotsen Institute of Archaeology Press.

Lindner, Manfred. 1992. "Edom outside the Famous Excavations: Evidence from Surveys in the greater Petra area." Pages 143–66 in *Early Edom and Moab: The Beginning of the Iron Age in Southern Jordan.* Edited by Piotr Bienkowski. Sheffield: Collis.

Lindner, Manfred, and Ernst A. Knauf. 1997. "Between the Plateau and the Rocks: Edomite Economic and Social Structure." *SHAJ* 6: 261–64.

Lipiński, Edward. 2006. *On the Skirts of Canaan in the Iron Age: Historical and Topographical Researches.* Leuven: Peeters, 2006.

MacDonald, Burton. 2015. *The Southern Transjordan Edomite Plateau and the Dead Sea Rift Valley: The Bronze Age to the Islamic Period (3800/3700 BC–AD 1917).* Oxford: Oxbow.

Millard, Alan. 1992. "Assyrian Involvement in Edom." Pages 35–39 in *Early Edom and Moab: The Beginning of the Iron Age in Southern Jordan* (Sheffield Archaeological Monographs 7). Edited by Piotr Bienkowski. Sheffield: Collis.

———. 2002. "Inscribed Material." Pages 429–39 in *Busayra Excavations by Crystal-M. Bennett 1971–1980.* Edited by ed. P. Bienkowski. Oxford: Oxford University Press.

Oded, Bustenay. 1971. "Egyptian References to the Edomite Deity Qaus." *AUSS* 9: 47–50.

Porter, Benjamin W. 2004. "Authority, Polity, and Tenuous Elites in Iron Age Edom (Jordan)." *OJA* 23: 373–95.

Pratico, Gary. 1993. *Nelson Glueck's 1938–1940 Excavations at Tell el-Kheleifeh: A Reappraisal*. Atlanta: Scholars Press, 1993.

Rollston, Christopher A. 2014. "The Iron Age Edomite Script and Language. Methodological Strictures and Preliminary Statements." Pages 960–75 in *New Insights into the Iron Age Archaeology of Edom, Southern Jordan: Surveys, Excavations, and Research from the University of California, San Diego & Department of Antiquities of Jordan, Edom Lowlands Regional Archaeology Project (ELRAP) Vol. 2*. Edited by Thomas E. Levy, Mohammad Najjar, and Erez Ben-Yosef. Los Angeles: Cotsen Institute of Archaeology Press.

Rose, Martin. 1977. "Yahweh in Israel – Qaus in Edom?" *JSOT* 4: 28–34.

Singer-Avitz, Lily. 2014. "Edomite Pottery in Judah in the Eighth Century BCE." Pages 267–82 in *Unearthing the Wilderness: Studies on the History and Archaeology of the Negev and Edom in the Iron Age*. Edited by Juan M. Tebes. Leuven: Peeters.

Smith, Neil G., Mohammad Najjar, and Thomas E. Levy. 2014. "A Picture of the Early and Late Iron Age II in the Lowlands. Preliminary Soundings at Ruj, Hamra Ifdan." Pages 723–39 in *New Insights into the Iron Age Archaeology of Edom, Southern Jordan: Surveys, Excavations, and Research from the University of California, San Diego & Department of Antiquities of Jordan, Edom Lowlands Regional Archaeology Project (ELRAP) Vol. 2*. Edited by Thomas E. Levy, Mohammad Najjar, and Erez Ben-Yosef. Los Angeles: Cotsen Institute of Archaeology Press.

Stern, Ian. 2007. "The Population of Persian Period Idumea according to the Ostraca: A Study of Ethnic Boundaries and Ethnogenesis." Pages 205–38 in *A Time of Change: Judah and its Neighbors in the Persian and Early Hellenistic Period*. Edited by Yigal Levin. London: Bloomsbury.

Tebes, Juan M. 2011a. "The Potter's Will: Spheres of Production, Distribution and Consumption of the Late Iron Age Southern Transjordan-Negev Pottery." *Strata* 29: 61–101.

———. 2011b. "The Edomite Involvement in the Destruction of the First Temple: A Case of Stab-in-the-Back Tradition?" *JSOT* 36/2: 219–55.

———. 2013 *Nómadas en la encrucijada: Sociedad, ideología y poder en los márgenes áridos del Levante meridional del primer milenio a.C.* Oxford: Archaeopress.

———. 2016. "The Kingdom of Edom? A Critical Reappraisal of the Edomite State Model." Pages 113–22 in *Framing Archaeology in the Near East - The Application of Social Theory to Fieldwork*. Edited by Ianir Milevski and Thomas E. Levy. London: Equinox.

———. 2017. "Desert Place-Names in Numbers 33;34, Assurbanipal's Arabian Wars and the Historical Geography of the Biblical Wilderness Toponymy." *JNSL* 43/2: 65–96.

———. 2021. "A Reassessment of the Chronology of the Iron Age site of Khirbet en-Nahas, Southern Jordan." *PEQ* 154/2: 113–40.

Thareani, Yifat. 2010. "The Spirit of Clay: 'Edomite Pottery' and Social Awareness in the Late Iron Age." *BASOR* 359: 35–55.

Vanderhooft, David. S. 1995. "The Edomite Dialect and Script: A Review of the Evidence." Pages 137–57 in *You Shall Not Abhor an Edomite for. He Is Your Brother: Edom and Seir in History*. Edited by Diana V. Edelman. Atlanta: Scholars Press.

van der Steen, Eveline, and Piotr Bienkowski. 2006. "How Old is the Kingdom of Edom? Review of New Evidence and Recent Discussion." *AntOr* 4: 11–21.

van der Veen, Pieter. 2011. "The Seal Material." Pages 79–84 in *Umm al-Biyara: Excavations by Crystal-M. Bennett in Petra 1960–1965*. Edited by Piotr Bienkowski. Oxford: Oxbow and Council for British Research in the Levant.

———. 2020. *Dating the Iron Age IIB Archaeological Horizon in Israel and Judah. A Reinvestigation of "Neo-Assyrian (Period)" Sigillographic and Ceramic Chronological Markers from the 8th and 7th Centuries B.C.* Münster: Zaphon.

van der Veen, Pieter, and François Bron. 2014. "Arabian and Arabizing Epigraphic Finds from the Iron Age Southern Levant." Pages 203–26 in *Unearthing the Wilderness: Studies on the History and Archaeology of the Negev and Edom in the Iron Age*. Edited by Juan M. Tebes. Leuven: Peeters.

Vriezen, Theodor. C. 1965. "The Edomitic Deity Qaus." *OTS* 14: 330–53.

41

EGYPT AND THE LEVANT IN THE THIRD INTERMEDIATE PERIOD (IRON IB–IIIA)

Fragmentation, Foreignness, and Fungibility

Krystal V. L. Pierce

Prologue: Fragmentation, Foreignness, and Fungibility

The Third Intermediate Period (ca. 1076–656 BCE[1]; Iron Age IB–IIIA) in Egypt was defined by political shifts in fragmentation and unification, alterations in sociocultural concepts of foreignness and familiarity, and movements between the economic spheres of fungibility and intangibility. These undulations consistently impacted and regulated the relationship between Egypt and its Levantine neighbors. The definition of Egypt as a political, social, and economic unit was complicated and flexible throughout the Third Intermediate Period, with multiple dynasts from both native and foreign backgrounds ruling simultaneously across Lower, Middle, and Upper Egypt. These administrative and cultural shifts played a role in the exchange of fungible goods and immaterial services, as well as in the transfer of conceptual ideas, theoretical beliefs, and iconographic motifs.

Egypt was also socially heterogeneous, as reflected in the Egyptian traveler Sinuhe exclaiming to his Levantine host that traveling abroad was like "when a Delta man sees himself in Elephantine," illustrating the perceived contrast between the northern and southern areas of the country (Simpson 2003: 63). During the Third Intermediate Period, a time when the movement and mobility of peoples between Egypt and the Levant were heightened and expanded, the concept of foreignness and indigeneity also fluctuated. What defined an individual or a group as Egyptian or non-Egyptian was influenced by permanence, acculturation, residence, heritage, ethnic stereotypes, social status, hybridity, occupation, and ideology. The overgeneralization of ethnonyms and cultural markers also complicated these definitions, which were sometimes characterized emically within social groupings or reflected more external etic perspectives. Shifts in political fragmentation, sociocultural foreignness, and economic fungibility that defined the Third Intermediate Period established and transformed the relationship and interactions between Egypt and the Levant.

Transition to the Third Intermediate Period (Early Iron Age IB)

Egypt's political fragmentation and the status of the relationship between Egypt and the Levant at the end of the New Kingdom and the beginning of the Third Intermediate Period were described in the Egyptian *Report of Wenamun* (Ritner 2009: 87–99). When the text was first discovered in the 19th century, it was viewed as an official administrative account dating to either the end of the 20th Dynasty or the beginning of the 21st Dynasty, however, the *Report of Wenamun* is now believed to have been a work of historical fiction composed in the 22nd Dynasty (Winland 2011). The story was meant to illustrate the chaos and fragmentation of Egypt during a transitional period, in contrast to the control and unification of Egypt by the Libyan Sheshonq I at the beginning of the 22nd Dynasty (Sass 2002: 253).

In the story, a senior official of the Temple of Amun at Thebes, Wenamun, was dispatched by the High Priest Herihor on a trade mission to Phoenicia to purchase cedar wood for the construction of a ritual barque for Amun. Although Rameses XI was likely still the king of Egypt at this time, Herihor had already assumed control of much of Upper Egypt, and would later give himself a full royal titulary, enclose his name in a cartouche, perform ritual activities reserved for the king, and wear royal accoutrements like the uraeus and double crown (James and Morkot 2010).

However, before Wenamun could leave Egypt, he had to visit the equally powerful ruler Smendes in Tanis in Lower Egypt. Smendes' high position was described as coming from the god Amun, with his power illustrated through providing a ship from his own fleet for Wenamun, as well as sending payment from Egypt to purchase the wood. Like Herihor, Smendes would eventually take on the trappings of kingship as the first king of the 21st Dynasty. The current king, Ramesses XI, was never mentioned by name in the *Tale of Wenamun*, where it was instead implied that the true king of Egypt was the god Amun-Re.[2]

The power struggle in Egypt during this time was not only illustrated by the two compeer rulers in the north and south but also in the reception of Wenamun when he arrived in the Levant. After the ship arrived at Byblos' harbor, Wenamun offloaded his belongings and the ship departed, but the ruler of Byblos, Tjekerbaal, refused to admit the Egyptian official and told him to leave. After a month of waiting in the harbor, Tjekerbaal agreed to see Wenamun and asked for his official dispatch papers from Herihor, but Wenamun had given them to Smendes. The ruler was angry and commented on the Egyptian lack of professionalism and competence, even declaring that Smendes' ship was operated by a non-Egyptian Syrian captain and crew, who were meant to kill Wenamun. Wenamun responded that only Egyptian crews sailed under Smendes, and since the captain's name was clearly Syrian, this statement implied that the sociocultural foreignness of an individual was altered once they worked under the command of an Egyptian ruler.

During this period, Egyptian dependence on foreign sailors and traders, especially Canaanites, Phoenicians, and Syrians, is perceived to have been politically and economically crucial (Monroe 2009: 189–92, 225).[3] Several Egyptian documents attested to the presence of people from these cultural groups in Egypt at the end of the New Kingdom and the beginning of the Third Intermediate Period (Winnicki 2009). The discovery of an Israelite four-room house in Thebes might establish the permanence of some expatriates (Bietak 1992). Many of those designated as Levantine foreigners were labeled with the generalized epithet "Asiatics (*Aamu*)," yet actually bore Egyptian names, which may indicate that they were acculturated descendants of earlier immigrants (Riggs and Baines 2012: 6). Wenamun himself requested that a Phoenician scribe travel with him back to Egypt. The *Tale of Wenamun* also implied that there were Egyptians semi-permanently or permanently residing and working in the Levant, where the ruler of Byblos had employed an Egyptian butler and chantress, with Wenamun interacting with other Egyptian speakers at Dor as well.[4]

After Wenamun requested the timber from Byblos and mentioned how Tjekerbaal's father and grandfather had supplied Egypt before, the ruler noted that Egypt had previously sent six ships filled with goods as payment along with the requests, suggesting that Egypt might not even have the means to purchase the timber because of the current sociopolitical fragmentation. Wenamun assumed that Byblos would present the timber as a gift, not necessarily to Egypt or its current leaders, but to the god Amun, who was the true ruler of the entire created world, including foreigners. When Wenamun realized that he would need payment for the wood, he wrote to Smendes that if he would supply the goods, Herihor would reimburse him. The absence of King Rameses XI in these terms showcases the lack of a central authority and the wealth and power of both men as separate from the palace.

The payment that Smendes sent from Egypt to Byblos comprised both fungible and inestimable commodities, including gold and silver vessels, linen garments, oxhides, ropes, lentils, and fish. Although the intensity of maritime trade between Egypt and the Levant during the early Iron Age has been debated, the presence of foreign cultural material in both lands illustrates that, even though Egypt lacked a unified political center, robust commerce was still occurring between the two areas.[5] Egyptian imports discovered in the Levant during this period include figurines, jewelry, pottery, stone and metal vessels, cosmetic containers, weights, ivory inlays, gameboards, and tools (Mumford 2007: 164–66).

Due to the perishable nature of most of the materials mentioned in the *Tale of Wenamun*, tracing the presence of Egyptian linen, leather, and ropes in the Levant is difficult. However, Egyptian fish and lentils, and the containers used to ship them, have been discovered at several sites in the Levant during this period. Nile perch shipped in baskets or jars were a major import to the northern and southern Levantine coast, where they were then distributed inland (Routledge 2015: 216–18). Lentils were shipped in sacks or jars, for example, a large concentration of lentils was discovered underneath a crushed Egyptian pithos in a destruction context at Tel Dor (Gilboa 2015: 255, note 17). Other large Egyptian commercial jars and jugs have been found at Tell Qasile, 'Atlit, and Achziv (Ben-Dor Evian 2011). Trade in fungible goods was not the only exchange between Egypt and the Levant during the early Iron Age. Egyptian motifs featuring Amun, hunting scenes, lions, lotus flowers, and Nilotic designs appeared on locally-produced Levantine seals, pottery, boxes, inlays, and ivories, especially in Philistia (Ben-Dor Evian 2017: 34).

Evidence of trade in the other direction, from the Levant to Egypt, is also extant for the early Iron Age. The cedar wood that Wenamun brought back to Egypt for a barque for Amun might be connected to a tableau in the Khonsu Temple at Karnak that depicted Herihor with a newly constructed barque for Amun (James and Morkot 2010: 246–47). Levantine juglets, spherical jugs, and pilgrim flasks from this period have been discovered at several sites in Lower, Middle, and Upper Egypt (Gilboa 2015: 254–57; Bennett 2019: 160).

Some of these vessels may have also carried materials needed for Egyptian cultic offerings and rituals. A High Priest of Amun during the reign of Rameses IX noted that imported cedar, malachite, resin, and lapis lazuli were among an essential list of provisions for a Karnak chapel (*ARE* 4: 239–40). The High Priests of Amun were not the only ones able to obtain these materials, as both Smendes and King Psusennes I possessed inscribed lapis lazuli beads, again illustrating the duality and fragmentation of power in this period. The bead of Psusennes bore a cuneiform inscription for the daughter of an Assyrian vizier (Kitchen 2003: 120). During the reign of Psusennes' successor, a Libyan family line was gaining power and control in Lower Egypt, which resulted in the reign of the first pharaoh from the Tribe of the Ma/Meshwesh, Osochor. There was no evidence of a hostile Libyan coup, but instead, the now mostly acculturated family appeared to have been resident in the western Delta for generations, distinguishing their foreignness only by their ancestral names and titles (Bennett 2019: 1).

Mid to Late Dynasty 21 (Late Iron Age IB–Early IIA)

Of the four successors of Psusennes, only Siamun left traces of connections between Egypt and the Levant. However, for the remainder of the 21st Dynasty and throughout the rest of the Third Intermediate Period, several descriptions of interactions between Egypt and the Levant can be found in the biblical text. Although many of these texts may have been recorded in later periods and might belong to the genre of historical fiction, like the *Tale of Wenamun*, they can still provide relevant information that generally reflects contemporary or future perspectives on the historical, political, and social nature of the period.[6]

During the proposed reign of the first king of the Israelite United Monarchy, Saul, who would have been contemporary with the early 21st Dynasty, an Egyptian man, who was the slave of an Amalekite, was found during an expedition to the Negev (1 Sam 30:11–16). It is unclear how the Egyptian became a slave to the nomadic Amalekites, but he was not the only Egyptian listed among groups fighting against Israel, as an Egyptian warrior was recorded as among those killed by a soldier of the next Israelite king, David (2 Sam 23:20–21; 1 Chr 11:22–23). This Egyptian may have been a hired mercenary or retainer of the Moabites, whose warriors were also killed by the soldier (Mumford 2007: 155).

More connections between Egypt and the enemies of Israel from this southern region are reflected in the asylum of a young Edomite prince, Hadad, by an Egyptian pharaoh during the reign of David (1 Kgs 11:14–22). Edomites had previously sought refuge in Egypt in the New Kingdom (Goedicke 1987). While in Egypt, the king not only provided Hadad with a house, land, and food but also allowed him to marry the sister of a queen designated as "Tahpenes."[7]

Hadad and Tahpenes' sister had a son, who was brought up in the palace with the pharaoh's children, a common custom of Canaanite foreign princes during the New Kingdom. Although Hadad grew up in Egypt, where he owned a house and land, married an Egyptian, and raised a son, he desired to return to Edom after hearing of David's death. The pharaoh asked Hadad what Egypt was lacking, to which Hadad replied "nothing," but this still did not deter him from returning to Edom. Was Hadad an Edomite because of his birthplace or an Egyptian because of his residence, marriage, and son? Was Hadad's son an Egyptian because of his birthplace and mother or an Edomite because of his father? The story of Hadad illustrates the complex nature of foreignness, ethnicity, and cultural identity, which are created, maintained, and altered both temporally and spatially as a system of dynamic behaviors, rather than static and hackneyed entities (Pierce 2013: 48–77).

Two more themes from this story, Egyptian foreign asylum and diplomatic marriage, also appeared in the biblical text under the rule of David's successor, Solomon. According to the biblical record, Solomon made an alliance with Egypt and then married the Egyptian king's daughter, for whom he built a palace in Jerusalem (1 Kgs 3:1; 7:8; 9:16, 24; 2 Chr 8:11). While diplomatic marriages between Egyptian and foreign royalty were common in the New Kingdom, along with the construction of palaces for foreign princesses in Egypt, examples from the Third Intermediate Period are rare (Shulman 1979). During the New Kingdom, several Levantine rulers sent their daughters to marry pharaohs to forge alliances, and there was at least one example of an Egyptian queen, Dakhamunzu,[8] who sought a diplomatic marriage with a Hittite prince outside of Egypt (*ANET*, 319).[9]

Due to the fragmented nature of Egypt during the 21st Dynasty, diplomatic marriages in this period focused on uniting the Libyan kings of the north with the High Priests of Amun in the south (Myśliwiec 2000: 33). It has been proposed that these unions between Libyan kings and Theban princesses should be considered examples of foreign diplomatic marriages, suggesting that the foreignness of an individual in Egypt at this time may have more to do with heritage than long-term residence (Kitchen 2003: 119). The king who allowed the diplomatic marriage between his daughter and Solomon also gave her the gift of the city of Gezer, which had been conquered by the pharaoh (1 Kgs 9:16). King Siamun, the penultimate king of the 21st Dynasty, may have campaigned in the Levant, as one of his rare scarabs was discovered at Tell el-Far'ah (S) (Brandl 1982: 383). Additionally, a monumental block from Tanis in northern Egypt showed Siamun smiting an enemy who held a double axe, which has been compared to similar weapons found in early Iron Age Philistia, including Gezer (Lance 1976: 252–93; Kitchen 2003: 118–20).

Siamun's military actions in the Levant were probably quite limited and more for fungible gain rather than imperialistic purposes. If he did indeed give away an important city like Gezer, it may show the continuing weakness of the Tanite kings during this period (Myśliwiec 2000: 33). The biblical text also recorded that Egypt underwent trade with Solomon and the Hittites, specifically mentioning the exchange of horses and chariots, which Egypt had previously traded with the Levant in the New Kingdom (1 Kgs 10:28–29; 2 Chr 1:16–17; Ikeda 1982). During the reign of the final king of the 21st Dynasty, Psusennes II, two men with Egyptian names and Syrian epithets were described as working for the future King Sheshonq (Ritner 2009: 166–72). These men may provide evidence of interactions between Egypt and Syria during this period, likely in terms of mercenaries or merchants, although their Egyptian names possibly illustrate an acculturated long-term or second-generation presence in Egypt.

Early Dynasty 22 (Iron Age IIA)

The first king of the Egyptian 22nd Dynasty, Sheshonq I, was a Libyan ruler from the Tribe of the Ma/Meshwesh in northern Egypt, who subjugated the High Priests of Amun at Thebes, and reunited Upper and Lower Egypt under one pharaoh (Myśliwiec 2000: 41–44). According to the biblical text, Egypt continued to provide a haven for political refugees from the Levant, with "King Shishak" allowing the Israelite prince Jeroboam to reside in Egypt after Solomon attempted to kill him (1 Kgs 11:40; 12:2; 2 Chr 10:2).[10] Sheshonq not only reunited Egypt but also renewed Egyptian imperialism in the Levant through a campaign that focused on the Negev, Philistia, Judah, and Israel. This campaign was depicted and recorded in several reliefs, texts, and a stela at the Karnak Temple (Figures 41.1 and 41.2) and el-Hibeh Temple, a private cartonnage from the Ramesseum, and a royal altar from Heracleopolis (Ritner 2009: 180–86, 193–213, 215–18, 220–27). A stela fragment with the cartouche of Sheshonq from Megiddo may be related to this campaign, as well as destruction levels at sites in the Negev (Herzog and Singer-Avitz 2004; Ritner 2009: 218–19).[11]

Several theories have been suggested regarding the purpose of Sheshonq's Levantine campaign: to gain control over coastal and inland trade routes, to bolster Jeroboam's efforts to rule Israel, or just to heighten the prestige and wealth of a new king with foreign roots (Myśliwiec 2000: 46; Wilson 2005; Schipper 2012: 36). Although Jerusalem was not mentioned by name in the Theban inscriptions, the biblical text recorded that "King Shishak" attacked the city during the reign of Rehoboam and carried off treasures from the temple and palace (1 Kgs 14:25–26; 2 Chr 12:1–9). After Sheshonq returned to Egypt, the presentation of the tribute from his Levantine campaign to Amun-Re was shown in a relief at Karnak, and the king proceeded to use this affluence to construct several monumental structures across Egypt (Bennett 2019: 252–54).

Figure 41.1 Reliefs showing Sheshonq I and the "conquered" cities of Judah, Karnak Temple (photo by George A. Pierce)

Figure 41.2 Detail of the Judahite city names, Karnak Temple (photo by George A. Pierce)

Inscribed statues of Sheshonq I discovered in Byblos, as well as those of royal successors Osorkon I and Osorkon II, show that interactions between Egypt and Phoenicia were renewed at the beginning of the 22nd Dynasty and continued for at least a century (Ritner 2009: 219–20, 233–34, 288). Osorkon I also mentioned a donation of Lebanese cedar to the Khonsu Temple at Thebes, as well as imported lapis lazuli for several divine estates listed at the Atum Temple in Bubastis (Ritner 2009: 252–58). During this period, the biblical text recorded that "Zerah the Kushite (Nubian)" battled against King Asa of Judah at Mareshah but was not victorious (2 Chr 14:9–13). It has been suggested that Zerah may have been a military commander under Osorkon I, who attempted to continue his father Sheshonq's Levantine campaign but failed (Kitchen 2003: 124).

Fungible trade between Egypt and the Levant continued during the first half of the 22nd Dynasty, with Egyptian imports found not only along the coast, but also inland in the Jezreel Valley, Beersheba Valley, Negev, Shephelah, and Yarkon Basin (Ben-Dor Evian 2011: 110). Egyptian and Egyptianized objects at these sites included pottery, luxury containers, jewelry, gameboards, and weights (Mumford 2007: 168). Egyptian fish also continued to be imported to the Levant during the Iron Age II, albeit on a much wider scale than the previous period, with Nilotic fishbones appearing at five coastal and 15 inland sites (Van Neer et al. 2004: 120–24). Locally-produced Egyptianized pottery and seals also began to appear in the Beer-Sheva Valley and the Lowlands early in the 22nd Dynasty (Münger 2005: 398). The nonfungible transfer of Egyptian motifs to the Levant can be seen in the iconographic representations of cultic practices in the Iron Age IIA (Keel and Uehlinger 1998: 122, 138, 178; see also Uehlinger, this volume).

Information regarding the interactions between Osorkon II, his successors in the second half of the 22nd Dynasty, and the Levant can be found in the Assyrian royal records of Shalmaneser III and Adad-nirari III. The western expansion of the Neo-Assyrian Empire led the rulers of Egypt and Israel to develop stronger ties and form an alliance against the ongoing foreign threat. In the Kurkh Monolith Inscription, Shalmaneser III described how he fought against a coalition of 12 kings, including troops from Damascus, Hamath, Israel, Byblos, and Egypt (*Mu-us-ra-a-a*)[12] at the Battle of Qarqar (*COS* 2.113A). Although the ruler of Egypt was not named in the Assyrian text, an alabaster vessel with the cartouches of Osorkon II and a hieroglyphic *hin* measurement discovered in the Israelite palace at Samaria might represent a diplomatic gift of a precious commodity from the Egyptian king to his contemporary King Ahab, whose name does appear on the stela (Reisner et al. 1924: 334). Shalmaneser III recorded on the Black Obelisk from Calah that he later received tribute from Ahab's successor, King Jehu, as well as the Egyptians (*COS* 2.113F).

Late Dynasty 22–Dynasty 23 (Iron Age IIB)

The remainder of the 22nd Dynasty coincided with the reign of Shalmaneser's successor, Adad-nirari III, who recorded in texts from Tell al Rimah and Calah that thousands of linen garments, a well-attested Egyptian export to the Levant, were sent from Mari (*COS* 2.114F–G). While Egypt does not appear to be a vassal of Assyria during this period, the contemporary political fragmentation in the country might provide a context for the tribute sent to the Assyrian kings. During the Tanite reign of Osorkon II midway through the 22nd Dynasty, several local kinglets of foreign origin appeared in Lower and Middle Egypt, with power bases located at Heracleopolis and Hermopolis (Jansen-Winkeln 2006: 234). A further division came through the appearance of a king based in Thebes, Takeloth II, who was not only contemporary with Orsokon's successor in Tanis but also became embroiled in a Theban civil war when another rival king set himself up in opposition to Takeloth (Aston 2009).[13]

These contemporary rival dynasts located in Tanis, Heracleopolis, Hermopolis, and Thebes all vied for power during the 23rd Dynasty, which may provide a context for the varying support of opposing political entities in the Levant. On the one hand, the suggestion from the biblical text that multiple Egyptian "kings" might have sent troops to support the ruler of Israel against Damascus probably reflected the fragmented multi-rulership of Egypt during this period (2 Kgs 7:6). On the other hand, the texts of Tiglath-Pileser III and Sargon II recorded that Egypt continually sent tribute to Assyria in the form of gold, silver, linen garments, and horses (COS 2.117A–E, 2.118E). These contradicting attitudes toward Israel and Assyria may also have been due to the competing dynasties of Egypt during the Iron Age IIB.

Although the biblical and Assyrian texts do not always name the pharaoh involved in these interactions, King Osorkon IV of the Tanite 23rd Dynasty was mentioned specifically during the reigns of Hoshea of Israel and Sargon II of Assyria. Prior to these references, Tiglath-Pileser III recorded in several inscriptions from Nimrud that the fugitive ruler of Gaza, Hanunu, escaped to Egypt, but then quickly returned and paid obeisance to the Assyrian king (COS 2.117C, E, F). It has been suggested that Osorkon IV, or his predecessor Pedubast, repatriated Hanunu to not risk a military conflict with Assyria due to the lack of centralized power in Egypt (Schipper 2012: 37). The Assyrian king then banned Sidon from exporting lumber to Egypt and installed an official at the frontier of Egypt (COS 2.117C–E).

During the reign of Tiglath-Pileser's successor, Shalmaneser V, the biblical text recorded that King Hoshea of Israel had sent olive oil and envoys to "King So of Egypt" and sought help but was ridiculed by the Egyptians (2 Kgs 17:4; Hos 7:11, 16; 12:1). These references are generally accepted as referring to Osorkon IV, who would again not aid the Levantine enemies of Assyria to avoid military action (Kitchen 2003: 126–27).[14] However, by the reign of Sargon II, Osorkon had decided to enter the conflict and sent his commander Re'e to support Hanunu of Gaza against the Assyrian troops (COS 2.118A, E). According to a rock face inscription at Tang-i Var and inscribed slabs and cylinders in Sargon's palace at Khorsabad, Re'e and Hanunu were not successful (COS 2.118E–H, J).

In his Khorsabad Annals and prisms from Nimrud, Sargon II described how he reopened the sealed borders and harbor of Egypt, mingled the Assyrians and Egyptians together, and reinstated trade between the two areas (COS 2.118A, D). There was a general revival in the quantity and diversity of Egyptian and Egyptianized fungible commodities and intangible influence in the Levant during the Iron Age IIB, including objects found in domestic, mortuary, and cultic contexts (Mumford 2007: 168–70). These objects included figurines, jewelry, pottery, gameboards, linen, inscribed weights, fittings, and stone, faience, and ivory cosmetic containers (Van Neer et al. 2004: 124). Trade in the other direction, from the Levant to Egypt, might also have included precious commodities like resins, wine, honey, and olive oil, as referenced above in Hos 12:1, as well as other objects mentioned in the conquest of the later king of Egypt, Piankhy (Maeir 2002: 241, note 13; Bennett 2019: 160). The transfer of nonfungible Levantine decorative elements and iconographic motifs to Egypt can also be recognized on certain vessel types like the relief chalice (Boschloos 2009).

Dynasty 24–Early Dynasty 25 (Late Iron Age IIB–Early IIIA)

While the contemporary kinglets of the 23rd Dynasties were competing for power in Tanis, Hermopolis, Heracleopolis, and Thebes, another ruler appeared in the Lower Egyptian city of Sais and eventually took control of the entire western Delta, becoming the first king of the 24th Dynasty (Kahn 2009: 139). This ruler, Tefnakht, attempted to extend his control south to Heracleopolis and Hermopolis, but was eventually stopped by the Kushite (Nubian) king Piankhy coming from the south. Piankhy had already conquered Upper and Middle Egypt and was able to repel Tefnakht back to the Delta, where the 23rd and 24th Dynasties continued to be in power until the end of Piankhy's reign.

Piankhy became the first king of the 25th Dynasty, ruling Middle and Upper Egypt from the city of Napata in Nubia, where he placed his Victory Stela detailing his conquest of Egypt (Ritner 2009: 465–92; Figure 41.3). In the reliefs and text of the stela, Piankhy

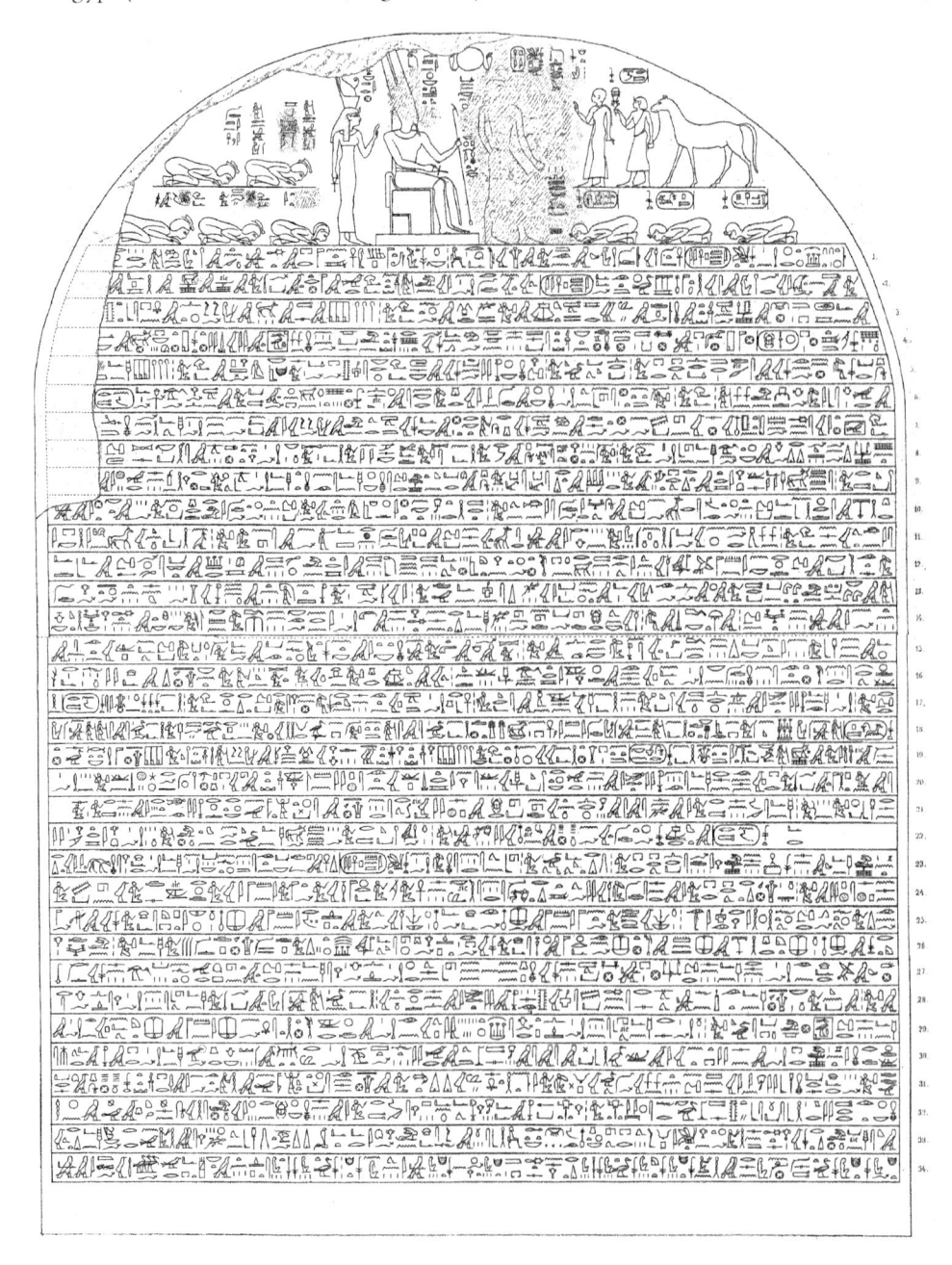

Figure 41.3 Victory Stela of Piankhy, Napata, Nubia

presented himself as a true Egyptian, who was beloved of Amun, celebrated religious festivals, protected temples, and spoke in classical Middle Egyptian, while his Libyan opponents were depicted as uncircumcised foreigners who wore feathers, ate fish, and spoke the common vernacular. After conquering each city on his march north, Piankhy listed the booty and tribute from the subjugated rulers, including imported lapis lazuli, turquoise, copper, oil, and "every product of Syria (*Khar*)." These foreign materials and products are thought to represent trade between Egypt and the Levant during the previous Iron Age IIB period mentioned above, as Piankhy's only other reference to the Levant was that his renown even reached the "Asiatics (*Setyu*)."

The presence of Levantine imports, such as torpedo jars and other vessels, in Kushite tombs dating to the reign of Piankhy has also been attributed to booty or tribute from his conquest of Egypt (Lohwasser 2002: 229). However, another theory posits that these objects were the result of direct contact and trade between Kush and Phoenicia, without the interference of Egypt (Lipiński 2004: 228). Some of these vessels were Egypto-Phoenician hybrids manufactured out of Egyptian materials like calcite-alabaster and faience but exhibiting Phoenician morphology and decoration like bulls and molded palmettes. It has been suggested that these vessels may have been created by Phoenician craftsmen operating in local workshops within Nubia (Bonadies 2020: 1043).

Piankhy was succeeded by Shabatako, whose foreign relations were only hinted at in generalized militaristic images and epithets at Memphis and Thebes (Pope 2014: 116).[15] The almost complete absence of Shabatako's name in the Levant was probably related to his short reign and focus on internal Egyptian affairs, especially establishing control of Lower Egypt after the end of the 24th Dynasty at Sais. In several inscriptions from Nineveh, Khorsabad, and Tang-i Var, Sargon II related how the ruler of Ashdod, Yamani, rebelled against Assyria, sent bribes to "Pharaoh, King of Egypt," and then fled to the border area of Egypt and "Meluhha (Nubia)" after hearing that Sargon was marching his army toward Ashdod (*COS* 2.118A, E–F, J; *ANET*, 287). Sargon continued his report by stating that "Shapataku, King of the Land of Meluhha" then extradited Yamani back to Assyria in iron manacles. The book of Isaiah (20:1–6) also mentioned Sargon's attack on Ashdod and warned against those who rely on or flee to Kush or Egypt for support or protection.

After Shabatako's short reign, his successor, Shabako, took an opposite stance toward Judah and Assyria. According to Sennacherib's Rassam Cylinder, the kings of Egypt and Kush forged an alliance with Judah and sent troops to help defend the city of Ekron against the advancing Assyrian army (*COS* 2.119B). This alliance was also referenced in the biblical record, where Isaiah 18 and 28 mention Kushite and Judahite messengers traveling between the two lands and again warned against dependence on Egypt (Lavik 2019). Sennacherib reported that he defeated the Egyptians and then marched through Judah, where he conquered 46 cities and exacted tribute from King Hezekiah.

The biblical text specified that it was "King Tirhakah of Kush" who came to the aid of Judah, who, contra the Assyrian record, were both able to miraculously defeat the Assyrian army (2 Kgs 19:9, 35–36; Isa 37:9, 36–37). Although Shabako was the king of Egypt and Kush at the time, he sent Prince Taharqo, who would later succeed Shabako and had been given a proleptic title in the biblical account, to command the military in the defense of Judah (Kitchen 2003: 127–28). On a large commemorative scarab from the Levant, Shabako mentioned defeating rebels "in every foreign land," including capturing the "sand-dwellers (*Heryu-Shayu*)," which probably refers to Semitic-speaking Bedouin of the southern Levant and Sinai (Ritner 2009: 496). Whether the Assyrians or Judahites could claim a decisive military victory is debatable, however, there was evidence of a "negotiated settlement" between the three regions (Aubin 2002: 152). The Egyptian involvement in the conflict itself and subsequent diplomatic negotiations may have been deliberately minimized in the biblical and Assyrian accounts, but the former often thereafter presented Kush in positive terms (Lavik 2019; Park 2019).

The interests of all three regions were well-served by the pact, which opened wide-scale commercial access and trade between Egypt and the Levant. This may be the reason that Shabako left a larger Levantine presence than his predecessor, with his name appearing in seal impressions at Megiddo and Nineveh, where it was joined by official Assyrian signets that were possibly attached to diplomatic documents (Ritner 2009: 499). Scarabs of the king from Tell el-Far'ah (S) and Beth-Shean also included the name of a contemporary Egyptian vassal ruler, while a statue from the Levant featured Shabako and a God's Wife of Amun (Mumford 2007: 151–52).

Late Dynasty 25 (Iron Age IIIA)

International relations, fungible trade, and immaterial iconographic exchange between Egypt and the Levant reached new heights during the reign of Shabako's successor, Taharqo. Egyptian and Egyptian-style figurines, jewelry, seal impressions, pottery, cosmetic containers, ivory carvings, sistra, molds, hieratic ostraca, and faience, stone, and metal vessels were discovered across the northern and southern Levant during the Iron Age IIIA (Mumford 2007: 187; Ben-Dor Evian 2017: 37). Other aspects of trade during this period might be gleaned from the biblical record, which emphasized the proposed loss of certain Egyptian fungible industries like fish, flax, and grain that were commonly imported to the Levant through trade centers like Tyre and Sidon (Isa 19:5–10; 23:1–5).

In several inscriptions from Memphis and Thebes in Egypt and Kawa in Nubia, Taharqo and his administrative officials recorded that imported oil, copper, tin, bronze, lapis lazuli, turquoise, cypress seeds, cedar, and juniper were all donated to temples across Egypt and Nubia (Ritner 2009: 512–16, 527–35, 545–64). Some of these materials, including bronze, cedar, and pinewood were also identified as specifically "Asiatic (*Setjet*)," "Lebanese (*Khenty/Khetyu*)," or "Aleppian (*Qedet*)," and were used to construct temple bolts, doors, flagpoles, and divine barques (Ritner 2009: 545–64). While most of these foreign materials probably entered Egypt and Nubia through direct commercial exchange with the Levant, some might have also arrived as booty or tribute from Taharqo's campaigns to these regions (Leclant and Yoyotte 1951: 28–29).

Reliefs and inscriptions on temple walls, stelae, and statues of Taharqo across Egypt and Nubia depicted and described the king as defeating, smiting, and trampling "Asiatics (*Setyu*)" and the people of Shasu, "Phoenicia (*Fenkhu*)," "Syria (*Khar*)," Naharin, Hatti, Arzawa, "Assyria (*Assur*)," Tunip, Kadesh, and "Babylon (*Senger*)" (Ritner 2009: 505–11, 524–27, 539–45; Pope 2014: 121–22). In a stela from Kawa, Taharqo boasted that he was a military leader from a young age, when he was called up to Memphis to support earlier Kushite kings, similar to what was recorded in the abovementioned biblical text mentioning the proleptic royal title (Ritner 2009: 535–39). The pharaoh also mentioned that he brought in horticulturists from the "tribesmen of Asia (*Mentyu-Setjet*)" to take care of the gardens at the Kawa Temple in Nubia (Ritner 2009: 545–52). These men may have been prisoners from a Levantine military campaign, political exiles, or voluntary immigrants seeking asylum or sustenance, as was commonly reported in the biblical text (Yurco 1980: 240, n. 146).

Although many of the reliefs and inscriptions of Taharqo celebrating military victories might have been propagandistic hyperbole, the fact that so many specific toponyms and cultural groups were listed likely shows that robust international relations were occurring between Egypt and the Levant in the first two decades of his reign. If Taharqo did campaign in the Levant, it was probably not with the goals of imperialistic hegemony or sustained garrisoning of troops, but instead more for royal ideology, domestic security, and controlled commercial access (Török 1997: 166–67). For the Kushite pharaohs, the repelling of many foreign enemies from Egypt, along with the ability to obtain luxurious and exotic goods from the Levant, helped sustain political legitimacy for these foreign rulers through conspicuous consumption and redistribution (Pope 2014: 159).

The Kushite peak in Levantine prominence during the reign of Taharqo collapsed with the resumption of direct military conflict between Egypt and Assyria. On the way to Egypt, the Assyrian king Esarhaddon attacked the city of Tyre, whose king had an alliance with Taharqo, thereby affecting the important fungible trade relationship between Kush and the port city (Leichty 2011: 87, 135). According to the Zinjirli Stele, Esarhaddon besieged and destroyed Memphis, shot Taharqo with arrows, extricated his family members, took massive amounts of booty, installed Assyrian officials, enacted a yearly tribute, and "tore out the roots of Kush from Egypt" (Leichty 2011: 182, 185–86). The Assyrian records commonly described and depicted the foreignness of the Kushite rulers, who needed to be removed from Egypt, in contrast to the Kushite perspective of themselves as emically Egyptian. Only one extracted member of Taharqo's family was mentioned by name, "Ushanahuru, his Crown Prince," who was likely the young prisoner wearing the uraeus headdress depicted on two stelae of Esarhaddon from Tell Ahmar and Zinjirli (Leichty 2011: 179, 182, 185–86, 192). In an inscription at the Karnak Temple, Taharqo bemoaned that the "tribute of the land of Syria (*Khar*)" has been diverted away from the god Amun, whom he then entreated to "[protect] my wives and let my children live," possibly referencing the unknown perilous status of his captured family members abroad (Ritner 2009: 509).

During the reign of Esarhaddon's successor, Ashurbanipal, Assyrian troops in Lower Egypt uncovered a plot of local rulers to overthrow the Assyrian occupation through diplomatic correspondences to Taharqo "so no foreigner shall be ruler among us" (*ANET*, 295–97). It appears that by the reign of Taharqo, the people of Egypt had accepted the Kushite dynasty as legitimate Egyptian pharaohs, at least in relation to the Assyrian "foreigners." The presence of foreign troops in Lower Egypt might be connected to a bronze figurine of the demon Pazuzu from Tanis (Moorey 1965). Pazuzu was an apotropaic deity especially associated with the protection of pregnant women and young children, which had facilitated a connection with the Egyptian god Bes. Amulets and figurines of Pazuzu and Bes have been discovered together in several Levantine and Assyrian contexts (Frahm 2018: 284–86; see also Garroway, this volume). If the users of the figurine from Tanis were from the Levant, this object, as well as another similar statuette from Luxor, might be evidence of the presence of Levantine women or children in Egypt during the 25th Dynasty.

After the death of Taharqo, his successor Tanutamani recorded that he had a dream where he was inspired to reconquer all of Egypt (Ritner 2009: 566–73). The king sailed from Napata to Thebes and then on to capture Memphis, with the locals praising and supporting him as the proper Egyptian pharaoh along the way. Tanutamani then commanded the construction of a new Lebanese cedar shrine for Amun in Napata, reminiscent of the cedar sought by Wenamun for a barque for Amun centuries before. Tanutamani's control of Egypt only lasted a year, as Ashurbanipal returned to Egypt, reconquered Memphis and Thebes, and went back to Assyria with Egyptian prisoners and booty (*ANET*, 295). These events may be referenced in the biblical account of Nahum (3:8–10), who mentioned the Assyrian capture of Thebes and imprisonment of Egyptian officials. After Ashurbanipal retook Egypt,

Tanutamani retreated to Nubia, where his death ended the 25th Dynasty and the Third Intermediate Period concluded.

Epilogue: Fragmentation, Foreignness, and Fungibility

The Third Intermediate Period in Egypt began with an inherited late Ramesside fragmented rule that caused complications in trade relations, however, there is evidence for a robust exchange of both fungible goods and intangible ideas between Egypt and the Levant during the 21st Dynasty. Egyptian and biblical texts recorded that foreign sailors, traders, scribes, exiles, diplomats, and officials were residing and working in Egypt during this period, while Egyptian servants, mercenaries, merchants, butlers, and chantresses were employed in the Levant. The early Third Intermediate Period also inherited the New Kingdom conception of foreignness, where foreigners were included as part of the created world under the rule of Egyptian deities, whom they should respect and honor.

The Egyptian royal ideology of keeping order and balance in the world through the constant repelling of foreign enemies was upheld, however, it was now more focused on outside groups as topos rather than mimetic individuals (Schneider 2010: 147). Social status and professional affiliation became more important than ethnicity, which resulted in the diminished use of ethnonyms and an increase in the display of foreign names. There was a graduate shift between the adoption of Egyptian names requiring an additional label of Levantine heritage, like the officials with Egyptian names and Syrian epithets working for Prince Sheshonq, to the open acceptance and exhibition of foreign names, like the sailors with Syrian names working with Wenamun, whom he referred to as Egyptians.

While the subsequent 22nd Dynasty ended the fragmentation of Egypt through reunifying the Delta and Nile Valley, the dynasty also ushered in the commencement of foreign kings ruling Egypt, a characteristic that would continue throughout the rest of the Third Intermediate Period. The Libyan kings embraced their foreign heritage, introducing the idea that ethnicity and ethnic marking was a positive factor in identity formation in Egypt. However, the shifting imperialistic, diplomatic, and economic relations between Egypt and the Levant during this period directly affected the acceptance of foreign exiles, envoys, and merchants in Egypt, as well as fungible commerce between the two areas. While some foreigners were able to seek refuge, like Jeroboam of Israel from the biblical text, others were refused entry, like Hanunu of Gaza from the Assyrian records. Eventually, domestic and international threats in the 22nd Dynasty led to another fragmentation of Egypt, where Libyans, Kushites, and Egyptians were all vying for power and control during the overlapping periods of the 22nd, 23rd, 24th, and 25th Dynasties.

A major shift in the concept of foreignness in Egypt occurred with the advent of the 25th Dynasty and the rule of the Kushite pharaohs. It became extremely important for these new rulers of Egypt to depict and describe themselves as fully Egyptian in terms of appearance, titles, religion, language, writing, feasting, and monument building to legitimize their right to kingship in Egypt. They portrayed the Libyan rulers in the Delta as non-Egyptian outsiders and foreign enemies who must be repelled by the true Egyptian king to create stability and legitimacy in Egypt. At the beginning of the 25th Dynasty, the Kushite kings were not accepted as proper Egyptian rulers, as etically evidenced by the Assyrians and the much later Herodotus, who claimed through an oracle of Amun that "all the land watered by the Nile in its course was Egypt, and all who dwelt lower than the city Elephantine and drank of that river's water were Egyptians," illustrating that while Nubia may have been part of Egypt, the inhabitants were not Egyptian (Book II: Chapter 18).

A zenith in international relations and trade occurred midway through the 25th Dynasty, fostered by the necessity of obtaining luxurious exotic goods to truly depict the wealth and power of an authentic Egyptian king. This foreign policy also impacted the mobility of people between Egypt, Nubia, and the Levant, with political fugitives like Yamani of Ashdod being extradited from Kush to Assyria, while Phoenician craftsmen and Asiatic horticulturists were welcomed to Nubia. The perspective regarding the foreignness of the Kushite rulers was altered by the onslaught of the Assyrians on Egyptian soil. The Assyrians then became the chaotic foreign outsiders who need to be repelled from Egypt, while the Kushite kings were now considered to be true Egyptians. Although the Assyrian campaigns affected commercial fungibility between Egypt and the Levant in the late 25th Dynasty, nonfungible intercultural religious ideas and iconographic motifs, like Pazuzu and Bes, were shared across both areas.

After the Third Intermediate Period, the relationship between Egypt and the Levant continued to be affected by political fragmentation, sociocultural foreignness, and economic fungibility. In the 26th Dynasty (ca. 664–526 BCE), Egypt attempted to fill the vacuum of power left by the Assyrians in the southern Levant through establishing a hegemonic system of vassal states. In the biblical record, the Egyptians battled the Judahite army, exacted tribute, and killed, removed, and replaced their kings several times (e.g., 2 Kgs 12:29–30, 23:29–35, 24:1–7; 2 Chr 35:20–24, 36:1–7; Ezek 17:11–17; 19:3–4; Jer 22:10–12; 37:5–11; 39:1–10; 40:7; 42:15–17; 43:8–13; 46:1–28). The Neo-Babylonian Empire eventually took control of the Levant, whose rulers then attempted to obtain Egyptian assistance without success. Royal and private Egyptian and Egyptianized objects, texts, fortresses, and people in the Levant during the 26th Dynasty illustrate the continuance of exchange between the two areas (Mumford 2007: 152, 161–64).

In Egypt, large foreign enclaves of Asiatics, Phoenicians, Greeks, and Jews appeared in northern and southern border areas with trade depots and military garrisons. These 26th Dynasty groups of foreigners were much more conspicuous than the arbitrary individuals of the Third Intermediate Period, due to the sociocultural mentality of residing together, building foreign-style structures, and communicating and writing in their native languages (Schipper 2012: 39). The book of Jeremiah (24, 26, 42–43, 46) especially related the presence of a large amount of Judahite mercenaries and refugees dwelling in Egypt, particularly after the Babylonian destruction of Jerusalem. Archaeological and textual evidence in Egypt demonstrates that Jewish enclaves were present at several sites in the Delta and at Elephantine (Maeir 2002; Modrzejewski 1995: 21–44).

Some of these foreign enclaves became acculturated and Egyptianized, while others preferred to keep their distinct foreignness and stay independent and segregated from Egyptian culture. For example, the Greek mercenaries who left inscriptions at Abu Simbel in the 26th Dynasty referred to themselves as foreigners, while also suggesting that the nearby Phoenician soldiers were Egyptian (Schmitz 2012: 42). These Asiatic, Phoenician, Greek, and Jewish enclaves and their sociocultural designations reflect a further post-Third Intermediate shift in the concept of foreignness and indigeneity in Egypt, which was always intimately connected to issues of political fragmentation, sociocultural unification, and economic fungibility and intangibility.

Notes

1 For discussions on the contested chronology of the Third Intermediate Period, see Jansen-Winkeln 2006; Aston 2009; and Dodson 2012.

2 The ruler of Byblos mentioned a "Khaemwaset" of Egypt, which could be a reference to Rameses XI, but described him as "just a man" (Dodson 2012:17).
3 These foreign sailors and traders were sometimes referred to using the Semitic loanword *khabar* (Hoch 1994: 240–41).
4 For Egyptians residing and working in the Levant during the New Kingdom, see Pierce 2013 and 2021.
5 For discussions about trade between Egypt and the Levant during this period, see Monroe 2009: 189–92; and Ben-Dor Evian 2017: 31–35.
6 See Schipper 2012: 35–40 for the viewpoint that the biblical texts describing David and Solomon more likely reflect the Levantine historical-political situation of the late 8th–7th centuries BCE.
7 Like the connection between the king as "pharaoh (*per-aa*)," Tahpenes may be the title of the queen as "wife of the king (*ta-h[mt]-pa-nes[u]*)" (Grdseloff 1947: 88–90). Tahpenes may have also been the actual name of the queen, as this and other similar names appear in the Third Intermediate Period (Muchiki 1999: 228–29).
8 Like "Tahpenes," "Dakhamunzu" was probably a foreign phonetic rendering of the Egyptian "wife of the king" (Reeves 2001: 176).
9 Earlier, Amenhotep III claimed that no Egyptian princess had ever gone or been sent to a foreign ruler for marriage (EA4).
10 For the contrasting idea that the "flight into Egypt" motif was a fictional literary device, see Ash 1999: 109–10.
11 See Fantalkin and Finkelstein 2006 for an opposing view regarding the connection between Sheshonq and the Negev destruction levels.
12 While traditionally thought to refer to Egypt, other theories connect this designation with Sumur in Syria (Schipper 1999: 144–49; Lipiński 2006: 132).
13 For the opposing idea that Takeloth II was the Tanite successor of Osorkon II, see Kitchen 2009: 168–91.
14 For other interpretations regarding the identity of "So," see Redford 1992: 346.
15 For a discussion of the historical changes in the numeration of kings in the 25th Dynasty, see Pope, this volume.

Bibliography

Ash, P. 1999. *David, Solomon and Egypt*. Sheffield: Sheffield Academic Press.
Aston, D. 2009. "Takeloth II, a King of the Herakleopolitan/Theban Twenty-Third Dynasty Revisited." Pages 1–28 in *The Libyan Period in Egypt*. Edited by G. Broekman, R. Demarée, and O. Kaper. Leuven: Peeters.
Aubin, Henry. 2002. *The Rescue of Jerusalem*. New York: Soho Press.
Ben-Dor Evian, Shirly. 2011. "Egypt and the Levant in the Iron Age I–IIA: The Pottery Evidence." *TA* 38: 94–119.
———. 2017. "Egypt and Israel: The Never-Ending Story." *NEA* 80: 30–39.
Bennett, James. 2019. *The Archaeology of Egypt in the Third Intermediate Period*. Cambridge: Cambridge University Press.
Bietak, Manfred. 1992. "An Iron Age Four-Room House in Ramesside Egypt." *EI* 23: 10–12.
Bonadies, Luisa. 2020. "Phoenician Trade in the Nile Valley: The Contribution of Some Luxury Items from Sudan." Pages 1035–45 in *A Journey between East and West in the Mediterranean*. Edited by S. Pérez and E. González. Mérida: Instituto de Arqueología.
Boschloos, V. 2009. "L'iconographie des calices en relief égyptiens par rapport aux adaptations phéniciennes." Pages 285–305 in *Syrian and Phoenician Ivories of the Early First Millennium BCE*. Edited by S. Cecchini, S. Mazzoni, and E. Scigliuzzo. Pisa: Edizioni ETS.
Brandl, B. 1982. "The Tel Masos Scarab: A Suggestion for a New Method for the Interpretation of Royal Scarabs." Pages 371–405 in *Egyptological Studies*. Edited by S. Israelit-Groll. Jerusalem: Magness Press.
Dodson, A. 2012. *Afterglow of Empire: Egypt from the Fall of the New Kingdom to the Saite Renaissance*. Cairo: American University in Cairo Press.
Fantalkin, Alexander, and Israel Finkelstein. 2006. "The Sheshonq I Campaign and the 8th Century BCE Earthquake." *TA* 33: 18–42.

Frahm, Eckart. 2018. "A Tale of Two Lands and Two Thousand Years: The Origins of Pazuzu." Pages 272–91 in *Mesopotamian Medicine and Magic*. Edited by S. Panayotov and L. Vacín. Leiden: Brill.

Gilboa, Ayelet. 2015. "Dor and Egypt in the Early Iron Age: An Archaeological Perspective of (Part of) the Wenamun Report." *AeL* 25: 247–74.

Goedicke, Hans. 1987. "Papyrus Anastasi VI 51–61." *SAK* 14: 83–98.

Grdseloff, B. 1947. "Édôm d'après les sources égyptiennes." *Revue de l'Histoire Juive en Égypte* 1: 69–99.

Herzog, Ze'ev, and Lily Singer-Avitz. 2004. "Redefining the Centre: The Emergence of State in Judah." *TA* 31: 209–44.

Hoch, J. 1994. *Semitic Words in Egyptian Texts of the New Kingdom and Third Intermediate Period*. Princeton: Princeton University Press.

Ikeda, Y. 1982. "Solomon's Trade in Horses and Chariots in Its International Setting." Pages 215–38 in *Studies in the Period of David and Solomon and Other Essays*. Edited by T. Ishida. Winona Lake: Eisenbrauns.

James, P., and R. Morkot. 2010. "Herihor's Kingship and the High Priest of Amun." *JEH* 3: 231–60.

Jansen-Winkeln, K. 2006. "The Chronology of the Third Intermediate Period: Dyns. 22–24." Pages 234–65 in *Ancient Egyptian Chronology*. Edited by E. Hornung, R. Krauss, and D. Warburton. Leiden: Brill.

Kahn, D. 2009. "The Transition from Libyan to Nubian Rule in Egypt: Revisiting the Reign of Tefnakht." Pages 139–48 in *The Libyan Period in Egypt*. Edited by G. Broekman, R. Demarée, and O. Kaper. Leuven: Peeters.

Keel, Othmar, and Christophe Uehlinger. 1998. *Gods, Goddesses and Images of God in Ancient Israel*. Minneapolis: Fortress.

Kitchen, Kenneth. 2003. "Egyptian Interventions in the Levant in Iron Age II." Pages 113–32 in *Symbiosis, Symbolism, and the Power of the Past*. Edited by W. Dever and S. Gitin. Winona Lake: Eisenbrauns.

———. 2009. "The Third Intermediate Period in Egypt: An Overview of Fact and Fiction." Pages 161–202 in *The Libyan Period in Egypt*. Edited by G. P. F. Broekman, R. J. Demarée, and O. E. Kaper. Leuven: Peeters.

Lance, H. Darrell. 1976. "Solomon, Siamun, and the Double Axe." Pages 252–93 in *Magnalia Dei, the Mighty Acts of God*. Edited by F. Cross. New York: Doubleday.

Lavik, Marta. 2019. "Are the Kushites Disparaged in Isaiah 18?" Pages 17–43 in *Jerusalem's Survival, Sennacherib's Departure, and the Kushite Role in 701 BCE*. Edited by A. Bellis. Lausanne: Swiss French Institute for Biblical Studies.

Leclant, Jean, and Jean Yoyotte. 1951. *Notes d'histoire et de civilisation éthiopiennes*. Cairo: Institut Français d'Archéologie Orientale.

Leichty, Erle. 2011. *The Royal Inscriptions of Esarhaddon, King of Assyria (680–669 BC)*. Winona Lake: Eisenbrauns.

Lipiński, Edward. 2004. *Itineraria Phoenicia*. Leuven: Peeters.

———. 2006. *On the Skirts of Canaan in the Iron Age*. Leuven: Peeters.

Lohwasser, A. 2002. "Eine phönizische Bronzeschale aus dem Sudan." *AeL* 12: 221–34.

Maeir, Aren M. 2002. "The Relations Between Egypt and the Southern Levant During the Late Iron Age: The Material Evidence from Egypt." *AeL* 12: 235–46.

Modrzejewski, Joseph. 1995. *The Jews of Egypt*. Princeton: Princeton University Press.

Monroe, C. 2009. *Scales of Fate*. Münster: Ugarit Verlag.

Moorey, P. 1965. "A Bronze 'Pazuzu' Statuette from Egypt." *Iraq* 27: 33–41.

Muchiki, Y. 1999. *Egyptian Proper Names and Loanwords in North-West Semitic*. Atlanta: SBL.

Mumford, G. 2007. "Egypto-Levantine Relations During the Iron Age to Early Persian Periods." Pages 225–88 in *Egyptian Stories*. Edited by T. Schneider and K. Szpakowska. Münster: Ugarit-Verlag.

Münger, Stefan. 2005. "Stamp-Seal Amulets and Early Iron Age Chronology." Pages 381–403 in *The Bible and Radiocarbon Dating*. Edited by T. Levy and T. Higham. London: Equinox.

Myśliwiec, Karol. 2000. *The Twilight of Ancient Egypt*. Translated by David Lorton. Ithaca and London: Cornell University Press.

Park, Song-Mi S. 2019. "Egypt or God? Who Saved Judah from the Assyrian Attack in 701?" Pages 45–89 in *Jerusalem's Survival, Sennacherib's Departure, and the Kushite Role in 701 BCE*. Edited by A. Bellis. Lausanne: Swiss French Institute for Biblical Studies.

Pierce, Krystal. 2013. "Living and Dying Abroad: Aspects of Egyptian Cultural Identity in Late Bronze Age and Early Iron Age Canaan." PhD diss., UCLA.

———. 2021 "Living and Dying as an Egyptian Woman in Canaan: A Gendered Cultural Study of Tomb 118 at Deir el-Balah." Pages 25–52 in *Material Culture and Women's Religious Experience*. Edited by M. Ellison, C. Taylor, and C. Osiek. Maryland: Lexington Books.

Pope, Jeremy. 2014. "Beyond the Broken Reed: Kushite Intervention and the Limits of L'Histoire Événementielle." Pages 105–60 in *Sennacherib at the Gates of Jerusalem*. Edited by I. Kalimi and S. Richardson. Leiden: Brill.

Redford, D. 1992. *Egypt, Canaan, and Israel in Ancient Times*. Princeton: Princeton University Press.

Reeves, C. 2001. *Akhenaten, Egypt's False Prophet*. London: Thames and Hudson.

Reisner, George, Clarence Fisher, and David Lyon. 1924. *Harvard Excavations at Samaria, 1908–1910*, vol. 1. Cambridge: Harvard University Press.

Riggs, Christina, and John Baines. 2012. "Ethnicity." *UCLA Encyclopedia of Egyptology*. Edited by E. Frood and W. Wendrich. Online: http://digital2.library.ucla.edu/viewItem.do?ark=21198/zz002bpmfm

Ritner, R. 2009. *The Libyan Anarchy*. Atlanta: SBL.

Routledge, Bruce. 2015. "A Fishy Business: The Inland Trade in Nile Perch (*Lates niloticus*) in the Early Iron Age Levant." Pages 212–33 in *Walls of the Prince*. Edited by T. Harrison, E. Banning, and S. Klassen. Leiden: Brill.

Sass, Benjamin. 2002. "Wenamun and His Levant, 1075 BC or 925 BC?" *AeL* 12: 247–55.

Schipper, Bernd. 1999. *Israel und Ägypten in der Königszeit*. Freiburg: Universitätsverlag.

———. 2012. "Egypt and Israel: The Ways of Cultural Contact in the Late Bronze and Iron Age." *JAEI* 4: 30–47.

Schmitz, Philip. 2012. *The Phoenician Diaspora*. Winona Lake: Eisenbrauns.

Schneider, Thomas. 2010. "Foreigners in Egypt." Pages 143–63 in *Egyptian Archaeology*. Edited by W. Wendrich. Oxford: Wiley-Blackwell.

Shulman, Alan. 1979. "Diplomatic Marriage in the Egyptian New Kingdom." *JNES* 38: 177–93.

Simpson, William. 2003. *The Literature of Ancient Egypt*. New Haven: Yale University Press.

Török, L. 1997. *The Kingdom of Kush*. Leiden: Brill.

Van Neer, W., O. Lernau, R. Friedman, G. Mumford, J. Poblome, and M. Waelkens. 2004. "Fish Remains from Archaeological Sites as Indicators of Former Trade Connections in the Eastern Mediterranean." *Palaeorient* 30/1: 101–48.

Wilson, K. 2005. *The Campaign of Pharaoh Shoshenq I into Palestine*. Tübingen: Mohr Siebeck.

Winland, Jean. 2011. "The Report of Wenamun: A Journey in Ancient Egyptian Literature." Pages 541–59 in *Ramesside Studies in Honour of K. A. Kitchen*. Edited by M. Collier and S. Snape. Boston: Rutherford.

Winnicki, J. 2009. *Late Egypt and Her Neighbors*. Warsaw: Journal of Juristic Papyrology.

Yurco, Frank. 1980. "Sennacherib's Third Campaign and the Coregency of Shabaka and Shebitku." *Serapis* 6: 221–40.

42
RECONSTRUCTING THE KUSHITE ROYAL HOUSE
The Chronology of Egypt's 25th Dynasty and Its Relation to Judah

Jeremy Pope

Introduction

At the close of the 8th century BCE, a text attributed to the prophet Isaiah described "swift messengers" heading west toward the Nile (Isa 18:1–7). The reasons for their mission were predictable, but the results decidedly were not. Faced with the Assyrian threat in the east, the inhabitants of the Levant had been appealing to Egypt for decades, with varying degrees of success. When Tilgath-Pileser III swept down the Mediterranean littoral, Hanunu of Gaza found refuge in the Nile Valley, but after the Assyrian king's death, Hoshea of Samaria received little help from the obscure "So, King of Egypt" (Pope 2014b: 108–11). Iamani of Ashdod fared even worse when he arrived in northeast Africa, as the pharaoh readily extradited him into the hands of Sargon II. Subsequent envoys from Ekron and Judah were somehow able to convince the pharaoh to dispatch his own troops to fight Sennacherib on their behalf. Levantine appeals to Egypt continued after Isaiah's lifetime, with an equally mixed record. When Ba'alu of Tyre sought help against Sennacherib's successor, he turned once again to Egypt, which soon folded against the Assyrian threat (Onasch 1994). Egypt thereafter employed Judahite soldiers (Kahn 2007), but it then invaded the Levant, clashed with Judah's troops, and deposed its king, Jehoahaz (2 Kgs 23:34). Just a few generations later, Egypt was once again in Judah's corner, encouraging Zedekiah's rebellion against Babylonia (Jer 44:30; 2 Kgs 25:1). For Levantine diplomats in the Late Iron Age, Egypt must have seemed a protean enigma.

Egypt's changing policies and fortunes during this era were due in large part to the unprecedented stakes of dynastic turnover: in no other period had the transition between dynasties corresponded to such radical fluctuations in the size of a pharaoh's domain. When a Kushite king asserted his suzerainty over Memphis in the second half of the 8th century BCE, the length of the pharaonic state *doubled*, stretching from the Sahelian steppe to the marshy apex of the Egyptian Delta (Figure 42.1; Pope 2014a). His successors then extended their dynasty's authority to the Sinai border, and the population under their control was now capable of fielding some of the largest armies in Egypt's history. The resulting Double Kingdom of Kush and Egypt was a mosaic of contrasting ecozones and local cultures, each with its own political traditions, styles of warfare, and priorities for international relations (Pope forthcoming). When the Kushite kings based in Upper Nubia became Egypt's 25th

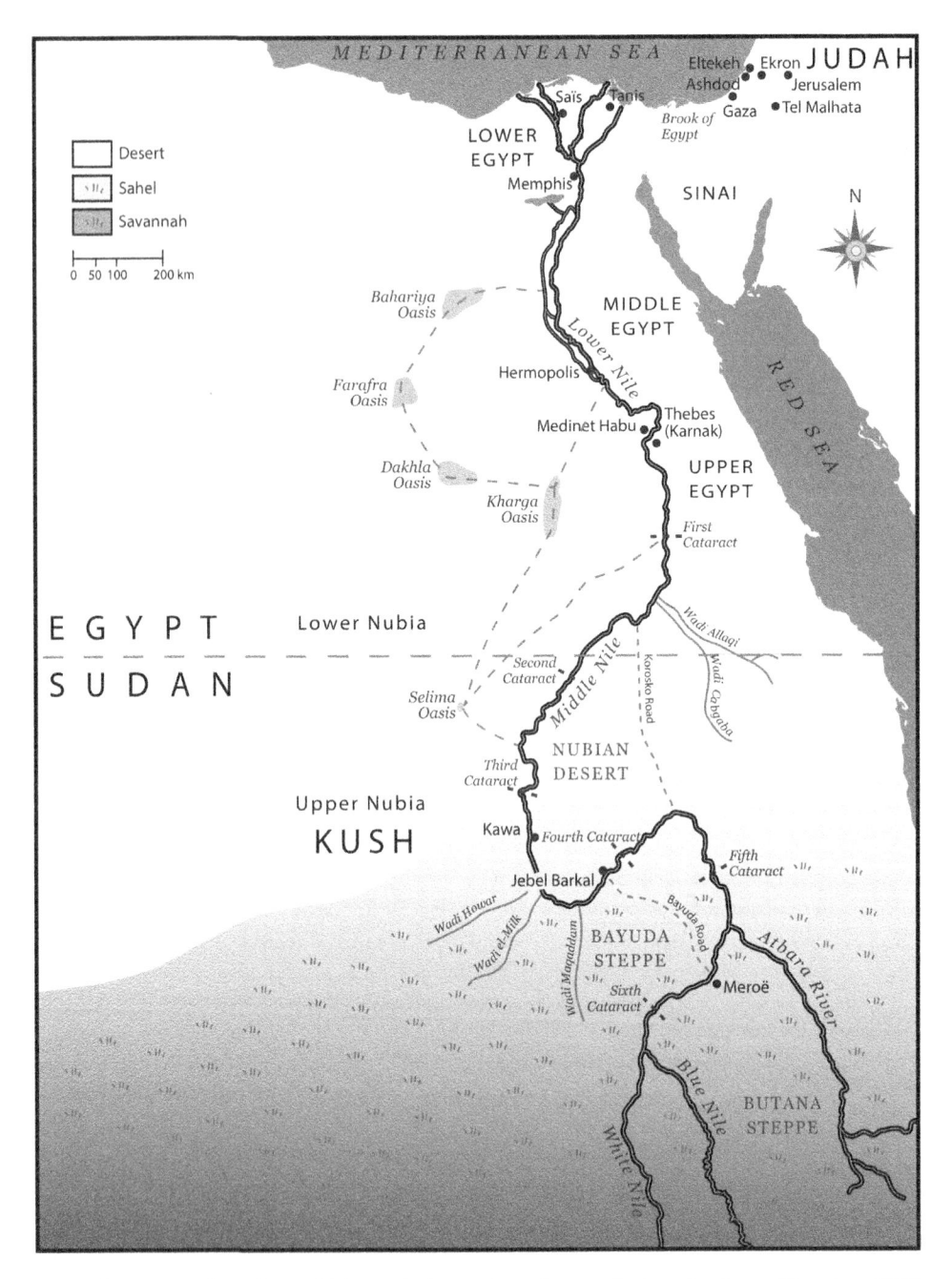

Figure 42.1 Map of northeast Africa and the southern Levant during the first millennium BCE. Courtesy of the University of Wisconsin-Madison Cartography Laboratory

Dynasty, they faced the challenge of amalgamating these disparate polities into a single state.

The new dynasty's sense of territorial ownership and responsibility appears to have evolved in stages. The Kushite king Pi(ankh)y was content to let the petty rulers of the

22nd, 23rd, and 24th Dynasties war among themselves in Lower Egypt, but he objected when they involved Hermopolis in Middle Egypt (Eide et al. 1994: 69). The Kushite royal house initially manifested little interest in political affairs of the Near East (Pope 2014b: 113), and the Assyrian king Sargon II complained of Kush that it was "an inapproachable region" ruled by a dynasty "whose fathers never—from remote days until now—had sent messengers to inquire after the health of my royal forefathers" (Frame 2021: 153). Pi(ankh)y's successors would soon become more possessive of the Delta and more assertive in the Near Eastern theater of war, but their involvement later precipitated an Assyrian reprisal that expelled the Kushite rulers from Egyptian soil (Onasch 1994). In the power vacuum left by the Assyrian conquest, unification of Egypt now proceeded in reverse order—this time, from north to south and eventually into the fortresses of Lower Nubia—under the command of a Lower Egyptian 26th Dynasty increasingly hostile to the retracting Kushite state. The continuity of pharaonic propaganda across the 8th through 6th centuries BCE therefore obscures significant changes in the geographic territory, military capacity, and international priorities that constituted "Egypt" on the world stage.[1]

As a result, scholarship on the 22nd through 26th Dynasties in Egypt has become a very interdisciplinary field—involving not only Egyptologists, but also Nubiologists, even Meroiticists, and many specialists in Libyan studies. While this dialogue has enhanced the accuracy and depth of historical research, it has rendered Egypt of the Late Iron Age less accessible to colleagues in biblical studies, Near Eastern archaeology, and Assyriology. Like the Levantine messengers of antiquity who sought a recognized authority in Egypt only to find that political fissures had divided the country, many scholars today *cherchent le chef* in Egyptology only to find that disciplinary fissures have divided the study of the Third Intermediate Period. Scholars of the ancient Near East have long turned to Redford as one of the Egyptologists most attuned to Levantine and Assyriological connections, because he has published extensively on Egyptian history of the Third Intermediate Period (Redford 2004). However, the Nubiologist Török lamented that "[t]he sweeping summary of Nubian history after the end of the Egyptian rule of the Twenty-Fifth Dynasty by Redford (2004: 139ff.) was written in a surprisingly guileless ignorance of the literature produced on the subject in the last decades" (2009: 359). Scholars relying on the magisterial work of Kitchen will perhaps find fewer critiques from Nubiologists and Libyanists, but they may also be treated to the typographical equivalent of a shouting match.[2] Warning his readers against new interpretations as a matter of principle, Kitchen advises that "it is *always* wisest to look first for the most banal and *un*exciting interpretation possible; and if that is inadequate, only then to look further afield" (2009: 162, emphasis in the original). Faced with such rancorous dismissals, scholars from other disciplines may well infer that ongoing research by other Egyptologists, Nubiologists, and Libyanists must have nothing fundamental to add to the inherited wisdom of 20th-century Egyptology, and thus the non-specialist need not engage with the most recent publications on the Third Intermediate Period.

Such an assumption would be misguided for the 25th Dynasty, because the last eight years have witnessed a fundamental revision in the regnal chronology of the period that has earned widespread acceptance among many of the most recognized authorities in Egyptology, Nubiology, and Libyan studies. The new chronology is considered "a real possibility" by several others—including Kitchen (see Broekman 2017a: 13, n. 4)—and it bears substantial implications for the history of ancient Judah. The chronology of the 25th Dynasty has affected multiple questions of importance to the Levant: Why did Gaza, Samaria, Ashdod, Ekron, Judah, and Tyre seek help from Egypt, and what form of help did they expect to receive? Why did Egypt remain aloof on some occasions but send troops on others? What precipitated Sennacherib's departure from Jerusalem in 701 BCE? Could the Kushite king Taharqo really have been involved in that conflict, as reported in 2 Kings and Isaiah? Did Sennacherib campaign twice against Judah or just once? And what were Judah's relations with Egypt in the decades that followed? At a broader level, the 25th Dynasty is crucial to the interlocking chronologies of the Near East during the 8th and 7th centuries BCE. As Morkot and Quirke have observed, "[t]he 25th Dynasty was (and remains) the earliest fixed date—or the latest uncertain point in 'absolute chronology'" (2001: 353).

Chronologies of the 25th Dynasty

The essay that follows will trace seven major phases of evolution in modern chronological understanding of the 25th Dynasty to demonstrate the ways in which new evidence and assumptions were integrated and sometimes uncritically perpetuated from the early 19th century to the present.[3] The closing section will consider the evidentiary basis for the newest chronology introduced in 2014 and then examine its significance for Judah's relations with northeast Africa during the Late Iron Age.

I. From Manetho to the Monuments: The First Chronologies, ca. 1833–1854

Historiographic discussion of the chronology of the "25th Dynasty" must necessarily begin with the earliest known source to use that moniker: the lost *Aegyptiaca*, as composed in Greek by the Egyptian priest Manetho (3rd century BCE) and then conveyed through the epitomai of Sextus Julius Africanus (3rd century C.E.) and Eusebius of Caesarea (4th century C.E.) to the earliest surviving copies: the Armenian version of Eusebius translated by Jerome (5th century C.E.) and another Greek version of both Africanus's and Eusebius's epitomai recorded by the Byzantine chronicler George Syncellus (9th century C.E.) (Waddell 1964: 166–9). According to Manethonian tradition, Egypt's 25th Dynasty consisted of three "Aithiopian kings" (Αἰθιόπων βασιλέων, loosely "kings of the people with kindled faces") who ruled in the following order: Σαβάκων, then Σεβιχὼς, and then Ταρακός. The epitomai of Africanus and Eusebius both adhered to this sequence but differed in the number of years that they attributed to each king (Table 42.1):

Table 42.1 Manetho's 25th Dynasty according to the epitomai of Africanus and Eusebius

| Royal Names | | Regnal Years | |
Greek	Latin	Africanus	Eusebius
Σαβάκων	Sabacon	8	12
Σεβιχὼς	Sebichos	14	12
Ταρακός	Saracus	18	20
		40	44	Totals

Scholars during the early modern era supplemented this information with the accounts of Herodotus (5th century BCE) and Diodorus Siculus (1st century BCE), but neither of those ancient authors was entirely consonant with Manethonian tradition: Herodotus claimed that Egypt across its long history had been ruled by "18 Aithiopian kings and one queen," but he named only Σαβακῶς and ascribed to him a reign of 50 years (Godley 1946: 386–7, 440–5, 462–3), whereas Diodorus recorded that "Egypt was ruled by Σαβάκων, who was by birth an Aithiopian," while stating in quotations elsewhere that in Egyptian history there had been "four Aithiopian kings, and they did not rule in a single sequence but at separate times," so that, "in total, they ruled slightly less than 36 years" (Karst 1911: 62; Oldfather 1946: 224–5). The Hebrew Bible named the "sons of Kush" as "Seba, Havilah, Sabta, Raamah, and Sabteca" (Gen 10:7; 1 Chr 1:9), but assigned the title of "King of Kush" (מלך־כוש) to only a single named individual: "Tirhaqah" (תרהקה), of 2 Kgs 19:9 and Isa 37:9. Attempts to establish the chronology of the 25th Dynasty solely on the basis of ancient Greek and Hebrew sources were therefore deprived not only of coherent structure but also of sufficient raw material—a task less akin to the biblical challenge of making bricks without straw than to the Sherlockian challenge of making bricks without *clay* (Exod 5:7; Conan Doyle 1892: 298).

Champollion's 1822 decipherment of Egyptian hieroglyphs offered the new possibility of building that chronology upon a foundation of *native* and *contemporaneous* testimony as carved in monumental stone. Inscriptions from the monuments of Egypt's Kushite kings were first translated by the Franco-Tuscan expedition to Egypt in 1828–9 and then interpreted by Rosellini in the 1833 *Monumenti Storici* fascicles of his multi-volume *Monumenti dell'Egitto e della Nubia*. Armed with Champollion's decipherment of the hieroglyphic script, the expedition identified three non-Egyptian royal names that seemed to match those of Manetho's "Aithiopian" 25th Dynasty. The clearest of these was found upon a pylon at Medinet Habu and read ⌈𓇳𓉘⌉ *T3-h-r-q*, which Rosellini readily equated with "the king Tarakus [Ταρακός]... in the list of Manetho" and the "Tirhaqah" of the Hebrew Bible (1833: 105–13, tab. VIII). From the Fourth Pylon at Karnak, Rosellini recorded the name ⌈𓇳𓊽𓏌⌉ *Š3-b3-k3* and noted that it matched hieroglyphic inscriptions upon a statue and two amulets that had already been taken to Europe during the 18th century. Rosellini also encountered a very similar name, ⌈𓇳𓊽𓏌⌉ *Š3-b3-t3-k3*, among reliefs on a chapel by the Sacred Lake at Karnak. Though this name differed from that on the Fourth Pylon by only a single hieroglyphic grapheme ▬ and corresponding phoneme **t3** (in bold font hereafter for clarity), its accompanying royal titulary was distinct on several points. Rosellini therefore proposed that ⌈𓇳𓊽𓏌⌉ *Š3-b3-**t3**-k3* and ⌈𓇳𓊽𓏌⌉ *Š3-b3-k3* had been separate pharaohs, each corresponding to one of the two remaining "Aithiopian" kings recorded in Greek by Manetho.

Less clear was the way Manetho would have transliterated into Greek the names ⌈𓇳𓊽𓏌⌉ *Š3-b3-**t3**-k3* and ⌈𓇳𓊽𓏌⌉ *Š3-b3-k3*. Manetho's Σαβάκων echoed the sequence of sibilant *š*, labial *b*, and velar *k* sounds from both hieroglyphic royal names—but the same was equally true of Manetho's Σεβιχώς. Moreover, neither Σαβάκων nor Σεβιχώς contained any dental phoneme corresponding to the **t3** of *Š3-b3-**t3**-k3*, and neither *Š3-b3-**t3**-k3* nor *Š3-b3-k3* contained any nasal phoneme corresponding to the ν of Σαβάκων. Complicating matters further was the Manethonian tradition's inconsistent transliteration of Egyptian *3* into Greek: in some cases, Manetho (or his epitomists) would render Egyptian *3* with a Greek epsilon (*Mn-k3.w-rʿ* > Μενχέρης) or possibly iota (*B3(?)-k3-rʿ* > βίχερις and *Z3-Imn* >(?) Ψιναχῆς), while in other cases Egyptian *3* was rendered by Manethonian tradition as alpha (*P3-di-Bʿst.t* > Πετουβάστις), omicron (*Bʿk-n-rn=f* > βόχχωρις), or omega (*Š3-š3-n-q* > Σέσωγχις) (Waddell 1964: 46–7, 154–67; Von Beckerath 1999: 54–5). This variability is likely due to the fact that, after the New Kingdom, Egyptian *3* seems to have conveyed "nil or minimal" phonological value of its own in the spoken language (Allen 2020: 45–6). As a result, both Manetho's Σαβάκων and his Σεβιχὼς were plausible Greek transliterations of either (𒀀𒀀𒀀) *Š3-b3-t3-k3* or (𒀀𒀀𒀀) *Š3-b3-k3*.

Despite this ambiguity, Rosellini confidently declared that the (𒀀𒀀𒀀) *Š3-b3-k3* of the monuments (Rosellini's "Sciabak") was equivalent to Manetho's Σαβάκων (Rosellini's "Sabbakon, Sabaco"). By default, the similarly-named (𒀀𒀀𒀀) *Š3-b3-t3-k3* (Rosellini's "Sciabatok") was deemed the equivalent of Manetho's Σεβιχὼς (Rosellini's "Sevechus, Sebichus"). Rosellini did not explain the reasoning behind his conclusion, but three possible influences can be hypothesized. First, the ν of Manetho's Σαβάκων could simply reflect the Greek practice of using -ων as a variant of the -ως ending on masculine personal names (e.g., the spellings μανεθώς and μανέθων used for Manetho himself); Σαβάκων would then be an alternative writing of Σαβακῶς—a form used by Herodotus (II.139.4)—with consonantal skeleton Σ-β-κ. Second, Champollion's "Lettre à M. Dacier" had already equated Egyptian 3 with the Greek alpha (1822), inaugurating the popular but inaccurate convention of rendering that ancient Egyptian phoneme with the letter 'a' in modern European languages. Between Manetho's Σαβάκων and his Σεβιχὼς, only the name Σαβάκων contained Greek alphas, and thus, to modern Western eyes, it could appear an appealing match for *Š3-b3-k3*. By contrast, Σεβιχὼς presented no apparent vocalic match to the hieroglyphic options, just as *Š3-b3-t3-k3* presented an imperfect consonantal match to Manetho's Greek options. So those two inconvenient names were equated with one another and thereby quarantined from the more satisfying equation of Σαβάκων = *Š3-b3-k3*. Third, the growing historical positivism of 19th-century European scholarship may have favored Rosellini's confident identification of one match (Σαβάκων = *Š3-b3-k3*) over the more equivocal identification of two plausible matches for each (Σαβάκων = *Š3-b3-k3* or *Š3-b3-t3-k3*, and Σεβιχὼς = *Š3-b3-k3* or *Š3-b3-t3-k3*). Rosellini was followed in his judgment by the most influential figures of early Egyptology (Hoskins 1835: 296–97; Wilkinson 1837: 138–39; Heeren 1838: 214; Gliddon 1843: 65; Lepsius 1853: 6, 505), even as some of these scholars continued to implicitly acknowledge the orthographic ambiguity by designating the two kings as "Sabaco I"/"Sabaco II" (Wilkinson) or "Sevech I"/"Sevech II" (Lepsius).

The monumental records did not immediately clarify the duration of each king's reign, in part because the various epitomai of Manetho had themselves offered no ancient consensus on the subject. When Rosellini discovered a hieroglyphic inscription referencing the 12th regnal year of *Š3-b3-k3*, he did not then cite the congruity of this figure with the 12 regnal years allotted by Eusebius to Σεβιχὼς, nor did he remark the hieroglyphic inscription's *incongruity* with the figure of only eight regnal years allotted by Africanus to Σαβάκων; instead, Rosellini cited the new hieroglyphic evidence as confirmation of the 12 regnal years allotted by Eusebius to Σαβάκων (1833: 107, tab. VIII). Further attempts to map this relative chronology onto an absolute one varied wildly: Wilkinson posited the accession of *Š3-b3-k3* as early as 778 BCE, and Rosellini and Gliddon both ascribed the same event to 719 BCE, while peer scholars ranged between these two extremes (Layard 1853: 133; cf. Wilkinson 1837: 138–9). All seemed to share Heeren's (1838: 214) assumption that the chronology of the 25th Dynasty was ultimately to be "determined by the Jewish history" as documented in the Hebrew Bible, and most likewise concurred that the "So, King of Egypt" to which Hoshea of Samaria appealed (2 Kgs 17:4) must have been identical to either *Š3-b3-k3* or *Š3-b3-t3-k3* of the Egyptian monuments; yet they did not agree upon the Gregorian calendric year when that appeal had occurred. As a result, the stones of Egypt still resembled wet clay in the hands of Egyptologists for most of the 19th century.

Historical repercussions for the Near East were then illustrated by a fascinating discussion in Layard's 1853 book, *Discoveries among the Ruins of Nineveh and Babylon*. Layard had discovered within Room LXI of Sennacherib's Southwest Palace at Kuyunjik (Nineveh) a trio of clay sealings bearing the cartouche of *Š3-b3-k3*, one of which was also stamped with an Assyrian signet impression. Layard then opined:

> It would seem that a peace having been concluded between the Egyptians and one of the Assyrian monarchs, probably Sennacherib, the royal signets of the two kings, thus found together, were attached to the treaty, which was deposited amongst the archives of the kingdom.
>
> *(1853: 134)*

To situate this Assyrian sealing within Egyptian dynastic chronology, Layard quoted the Egyptologist Birch in a footnote that spanned three pages of Layard's book. Birch's note explained that the discipline of Egyptology now recognized two kings named "Sabaco" who had ruled Egypt consecutively before the accession of "Tirakhah" during the 25th Dynasty. Observing that the Hebrew Bible mentioned "Tirakhah" as a contemporary of Sennacherib, Layard therefore deduced that the *Š3-b3-k3* named on the sealings in Sennacherib's palace would most likely have been "Tirakhah's" immediate predecessor, "the *second* Sabaco the Æthiopian," concluding: "There can be no doubt whatever as to the identity of the cartouche" (1853: 132, emphasis added). By comparing Manethonian tradition and the Egyptian monuments to the newly excavated data from Nineveh, Layard became the first prominent scholar to assert that *Š3-b3-k3* was the *second* "Sabaco": Manetho's Σεβιχώς.

Remarkably, Layard seems not to have noticed that the Egyptologist whom he quoted for support was actually *contradicting* his own judgment: just two pages after Layard's pronouncement, Birch's footnote instead followed the lead of Rosellini and asserted that the *Š3-b3-k3* whose "seal was affixed to some treaty between Assyria and Egypt" was, in fact, Σαβάκων, "the name of the *first* king" in Manetho's chronology (Layard 1853: 134, emphasis added). Neither Birch nor Layard acknowledged the discrepancy between their conclusions, but the stakes were potentially significant. Within the scenario envisioned by Rosellini and then Birch, the diplomacy between Assyria and Egypt could have *preceded* Sennacherib's invasion of Judah; within Layard's scenario, that same diplomacy was more likely to have *followed* the invasion of Judah.

II. The Saqqara Revision, 1855–1883

At the beginning of the 1850s, the absolute chronology of the 25th Dynasty presented a rather pitiful contrast against that of the 26th: while the latter was buttressed by numerous synchronisms with Assyrian, Babylonian, Hebrew, and Greek sources, the former was still an incoherent scatter of data points—the building blocks of a chronology but lacking structure. Without a foundation in external sources, the newly discovered evidence for the 25th Dynasty could provide at best *relative* dates, because nearly all of the monuments of ancient Egypt and Kush had been inscribed with only *regnal* years and therefore consistently restarted their internal chronology with 'year one' at the accession of a new king. Birch's assessment was bleak: "The great difficulty is the dreadful confusion of the period" (Layard 1853: 133).

Even as Birch wrote those words, a solution was beginning to emerge from the rock substratum of Saqqara near Memphis. Just two years prior, Mariette had discovered there a Serapeum—a vast network of underground crypts for sacred Apis bulls, many replete with inscribed stelae enumerating the duration of their lives and the regnal years of their births and deaths. Because some of these bulls outlived the pharaohs who had appointed them for veneration, their stelae were *double*-dated—with a birth ascribed to the regnal year of one king and a death ascribed to the regnal year of his successor. Conveniently, the lifetime of one such Apis bull straddled the end of the 25th Dynasty and the early decades of the 26th: according to his stela, the bull was born in the 26th regnal year of 🔲 *T3-h-r-q* (the Ταρακός who closed Manetho's 25th Dynasty), lived for 21 years, and then died just before the 21st regnal year of 🔲 *P(3)-z(i)-mtk* (the Ψαμμήτιχος of Manetho's 26th Dynasty). When de Rougé published an interpretation of the stela in 1855, he calculated on the basis of later synchronisms that the reign of this "Psammétik" had begun "à l'an 665 avant Jésus-Christ," and thus the Aithiopian "Tahraka" would seem to have ascended the throne no earlier than 691 BCE (de Rougé 1855: 39–42). De Rougé immediately recognized a potential contradiction between this new information and the accepted chronologies of Assyria and Judah: Assyriologists such as Oppert had deduced that Sennacherib campaigned against Judah at the end of the 8th century BCE, but the biblical testimony of 2 Kgs 19:9 and Isa 37:9 claimed that the Assyrian had received a report in Judah that תרהקה מלך־כוש "Tirhaqah, King of Kush," was coming forth to meet him. The attempt of de Rougé to anchor the chronology of the 25th Dynasty into the bedrock of the Saqqara Serapeum thereby cracked open a fault approximately ten years wide between monumental and biblical testimony, one that future scholars would struggle to bridge.

The 1860s then witnessed the discovery and publication of five Kushite royal stelae from the Sudanese site of Jebel Barkal, several of which contained detailed historical narratives set in the 8th through 6th centuries BCE (Mariette 1865). However, these stelae did little to clarify the chronology of Manetho's 25th Dynasty, because not a single one of them so much as mentioned 🔲 *Š3-b3-t3-k3*, 🔲 *Š3-b3-k3*, or 🔲 *T3-h-r-q*—even as two of the stelae attributed a series of actions to kings named 🔲 *P-ʿnḫ-y* and 🔲 *T3-n-w3-ti-'Imn* that were strikingly reminiscent of the exploits that Herodotus had attributed to his Σαβάκως (Török 2014: 78–9). The inadequacy of Greek evidence for Egyptian history was becoming increasingly evident, but scholars continued to lean heavily upon it. Egyptologists consistently echoed Rosellini's proposed equations of *Š3-b3-k3* as Σαβάκων and *Š3-b3-t3-k3* as Σεβιχὼς (e.g., Mariette 1865: 167), thereby using Manetho to sequence the monuments.

III. The Turin Revision, 1884–1940

Published in 1884, Wiedemann's two-volume *Ägyptische Geschichte* was one of the earliest and most influential attempts to use the Manethonian scheme of numbered dynasties as scaffolding for a narrative history of ancient Egypt; yet it was also one of the first studies to prioritize an Egyptian monument *over and against* Manethonian testimony about the 25th Dynasty. Wiedemann drew his readers' attention to a stela in the Turin Museum, published by Pleyte in 1876, that featured a pair of crowned and seated kings on the left with cartouches reading (from the center outwards) *Š3-b3-k3* and *Š3-b3-t3-k3* and facing a male and female pair on the right. Neither of the kings on the left was represented iconographically or textually as a deceased ancestor, and thus Wiedemann logically concluded that *Š3-b3-k3* and *Š3-b3-t3-k3* must have ruled concurrently for a time and the stela must have been commissioned during the overlap between their reigns (1884: 585). No epitome of Manetho's *Aegyptiaca* had ever asserted such coregency for the "Aithiopian" kings. Wiedemann was not the first modern scholar to entertain the possibility of a coregency during the 25th Dynasty, but others had done so only *sotto voce* based on highly ambiguous evidence (Maspero 1868: 332–3; Rawlinson 1881: 455 n. 2). Wiedemann foregrounded a coregency between *Š3-b3-k3* and *Š3-b3-t3-k3* as a "very probable" ("sehr wahrscheinlich") conclusion. It is important to note that Wiedemann did not propose this coregency as a solution to any chronological problem, whether the conflicting reign estimates of Africanus and Eusebius or the seeming anachronism of "Tirhaqah's" appearance as "King of Kush" in 2 Kgs 19:9 and Isa 37:9; for Wiedemann, coregency was presented as simply the most defensible interpretation of the Turin stela. Nevertheless, the historical implications of Wiedemann's proposal were considerable: if any two Kushite kings had ruled Egypt concurrently, this would greatly increase the odds that other members of the same dynasty might have followed an identical practice, so that a variety of chronological problems could be resolved simply by overlapping the estimated reigns of any two consecutive Kushite pharaohs.

Unfortunately, Wiedemann had overlooked a crucial sentence in the Turin Museum's catalog: "Questa stela, pervenuta al Museo per dono, è un lavoro moderno fatto in Egitto" (Fabretti, Rossi, Lanzone 1882: 126). *The stela was a modern fake*, lacking provenance and rife with both errors and unparalleled idiosyncrasies. For instance, the male figure on the right not only bore a feminine title (*dw3t nṯr*) but also the personal name (*Šp-n-Wpt*) of a prominent royal *woman* known to have used that title during the 25th Dynasty (Morkot and Quirke 2001: 350–52). To make matters worse, the male figure's accompanying statement of filiation was garbled, as if it had been copied inexpertly from a genuine artifact. In the top half of the stela, a scarab had been painted in a shape never attested on any other monument, and, as if to underscore the deception, the whole ensemble sat atop a checkered band that was equally without parallel on objects of this type and date. As a foundation for chronologies of the 25th Dynasty, the Turin stela was effectively quicksand.

Two decades after the publication of Wiedemann's *Ägyptische Geschichte*, Petrie recognized that the Turin stela was a fake, yet he chose to retain the coregency theory that Wiedemann had derived from that stela (Petrie 1905: 287–97). After all, a hypothesis based upon spurious evidence was not necessarily false, just unfounded. Rather than advocating for a coregency between *Š3-b3-k3* and *Š3-b3-t3-k3*, Petrie concluded that *Š3-b3-t3-k3* had ruled concurrently with his successor, *T3-h-r-q*, between 701 and 693 BCE, after which the latter ruled alone until 667. The apparent utility of this reconstruction lay precisely in its ability to bridge the aforementioned cleft between monumental and biblical evidence: under Petrie's scenario, the biblical account had accurately described the coregent "Tirhaqah" as "King of Kush" when he advanced against Sennacherib in the late 8th century BCE, because this same *T3-h-r-q* then continued to rule alongside *Š3-b3-t3-k3* for eight years, before governing without *Š3-b3-t3-k3* for 26 more. Petrie was not alone in his adoption of the coregency theory, but his contemporaries used it for different ends. In the analysis of Breasted, it was instead "Taharka" and "Tanutamon" (the *T3-n-w3-ti-Imn* of the Barkal stelae) who had ruled concurrently in 663 BCE (1905: 558). The appearance of "Taharka" in 2 Kings and the Book of Isaiah was instead explained by Breasted as a case of biblical prolepsis: the Hebrew authors had erroneously "suppose(d) him to have already been king in 701" (1905: 554). Two decades after Breasted, Hall decided that it was more likely "Shabaka" who had been "associated with Piankhi [the *P-ʿnḫ-y* of the Barkal stelae] about 715 (?)," and "Tirhaqah" was not "King of Kush" when he faced Sennacherib ca. 700 BCE but instead a mere "turtan" (1925: 277). The fake Turin stela was now disregarded, but scholars continued to repurpose Weidemann's coregency theory as a kind of bivouac that could be pitched at various spots across the timeline whenever circumstances required.

Despite their disagreements about the chronology of the 25th Dynasty, Egyptologists during the first half of the 20th century converged on two larger points of history. First, they held unanimously that *Š3-b3-k3* had ruled before *Š3-b3-t3-k3*. Thus, when a fragmentary inscription discovered at Tanis mentioned that a 20-year-old prince *T3-h-r-q* had been summoned to Egypt by a preceding Kushite king, Breasted inferred that the king must have been *Š3-b3-k3* recruiting *T3-h-r-q* to assist with the suppression of βόχχωρις in Lower Egypt—an event ascribed to Σαβάκων in Manethonian tradition (Breasted 1906: 455). Second, scholars observed that the reigns of *Š3-b3-k3* and *Š3-b3-t3-k3* had been very dissimilar: 15 regnal years were now attested for *Š3-b3-k3*, and his name had circulated in the Near East, not only on the three sealings at Nineveh but also on another recently excavated at Megiddo (Lamon and Shipton 1939: 172, pls. 41, 115). By contrast, his presumed successor *Š3-b3-t3-k3* was, in Hall's words, "totally undistinguished," with only three attested regnal years and no influence in the Near East during the period following Sennacherib's campaign against Judah (1925: 279). The historical trajectory of the 25th Dynasty was now plotted with an initial peak of grand international ambitions followed by a sharp decline toward irrelevance; their involvement in Judah was deemed to be a cause of that decline.

IV. The Aššur Revision, 1941–1948

Just as de Rougé's analysis of a stela from the Serapeum crypt at Saqqara had laid a cornerstone at the low end of the dynasty's chronology (ca. 665 BCE), Weidner's (1941) analysis of a prism from the temple at Aššur would now lay another cornerstone at the high end of the dynasty's chronology. The prism had been discovered in 1910, but it was Weidner who first highlighted within it a passage referencing the 5th regnal year of Sargon II, in which one "Shilkanni, Ruler of Egypt," sought to conciliate the Assyrian by sending a gift of "12 large horses from Egypt." Weidner recognized that the consonantal skeleton of the name *Ši-il-kan-ni* was an identically-sequenced four-point match with that of the Egyptian pharaoh *W3-s3-i-r-k-n*, "Osorkon" (IV) (1941: 44–5), whose name was attested upon the monuments of the Delta and then echoed as Ὀσορχώ and Ὀσορθών in the epitomai recording Manetho's 23rd Dynasty (Waddell 1964: 160–3). Unlike the "Sib'e, turtan of Egypt," with whom Hanunu of Gaza had allied in the Assyrian records, and the "So, King of Egypt," to whom Hoshea of Samaria had appealed in 2 Kgs 17:4, the "Shilkanni" of the Aššur prism could not reasonably be transmuted into the name of one of the kings of the 25th Dynasty. Scholars therefore concluded that the Kushite kings could not have assumed primary rulership of the Egyptian Delta until the 5th regnal year of Sargon II—a date calculated as 716 BCE by Assyriologists using the meticulously documented astronomical phenomena and eponym lists of Mesopotamia (Bickerman 1991: 67, 86–87). According to this understanding, the 15 attested regnal years of *Š3-b3-k3* and the 26 attested regnal years of *T3-h-r-q* both had to be accommodated within the narrow span of just five decades (ca. 716-665 BCE), leaving for *Š3-b3-t3-k3* at most nine years ruling alone between those two reigns. During the 1940s, these new parameters were not yet regarded as particularly troublesome for the chronology of the 25th Dynasty, but they had set strict limits into which all future discoveries would need to be incorporated; even if the structure began to teeter, its foundations could no longer be widened.

V. The Kawa Revision, 1949–1998

The discovery of the Jebel Barkal stelae in the 1860s had provided lengthy historical narratives commissioned in the Egyptian hieroglyphic script by Kushite kings, but it was not until Griffith's excavations at the Sudanese site of Kawa in 1930–1931 that scholars finally gained access to lengthy historical narratives in that same hieroglyphic script referencing the names of *Š3-b3-t3-k3* and *T3-h-r-q*. After Griffith's passing in 1934, his assistant Macadam assumed the responsibility of publishing those excavations—including five stelae commissioned by *T3-h-r-q*, one of which (Kawa IV) mentioned *Š3-b3-t3-k3*. The relevant passage was translated by Macadam as follows:

> Now His Majesty had been in Nubia as a goodly youth, a king's brother, pleasant of love, and he came north to Thebes in the company of goodly youths whom His Majesty King Shebitku had sent to fetch from Nubia, in order that he might be there with him, since he loved him more than all his brethren.
>
> *(1949: 15)*

An accompanying stela (Kawa V) further revealed that *T3-h-r-q* had been 20 years old when he first left his mother in Nubia to travel to Egypt (Macadam 1949: 17, 28). Taken together, Kawa stelae IV and V decisively overturned Breasted's earlier interpretation of the Tanis inscription (Breasted 1906: 455), demonstrating that it had not been *Š3-b3-k3* but rather *Š3-b3-t3-k3* (Macadam's "Shebitku") who had recruited *T3-h-r-q* to come to Egypt at the age of 20; as *Š3-b3-k3* was still held to be the Σαβάκων responsible for the suppression of βόχχωρις in Manethonian tradition, the recruitment of *T3-h-r-q* could no longer be connected to that event. Kawa IV further specified that, during the trip northwards to join *Š3-b3-t3-k3*, prince *T3-h-r-q* became dismayed when he saw a ruined temple at Kawa:

> And His Majesty's heart grew sad at it until His Majesty appeared as King, crowned as King of Upper and Lower Egypt, (and) when the Double Diadem was established upon his head and his name became Horus Lofty-of-Diadems, he called to mind this temple, which he had beheld as a youth in the first year of his reign. Then His Majesty said to his courtiers, "Lo, I desire to rebuild the temple..."
>
> *(Macadam 1949: 15)*

Macadam (1949: 17–20) drew several inferences from this new evidence: (1) *Š3-b3-t3-k3* had summoned *T3-h-r-q* north to Egypt to establish a coregency between the two Kushite kings. (2) That event was later remembered as the first regnal year of *T3-h-r-q*, and thus it occurred ca. 689 BCE. (3) It was during his summons in that year that *T3-h-r-q* first observed the ruined temple at Kawa. (4) The coronation of *T3-h-r-q* as the **sole** king took place five years later, ca. 684 BCE, when he vowed to rebuild the temple. (5) As this scenario would attribute to *T3-h-r-q* only 20 years of age ca. 689 BCE, then "the statement in 2 Kings xix 9 that the enemy of Sennacherib at Altaqu [Eltekeh] in 701 B.C. was Taharqa is manifestly a mistake, since he was then only eight years old" (Macadam 1949: 19–20). Accepting Macadam's interpretations of the Kawa stelae, Albright and other eminent biblicists therefore proposed that the reference in 2 Kings was to a *second* campaign waged by Sennacherib against Judah and its Kushite defender, "Tirhaqah" (תרהקה), several years *after* 701 BCE (Albright 1953: 8–9; Horn 1966: 3–11; Bright 1972: 298 n. 9; Shea 1999).

Unfortunately, the assumption that *T3-h-r-q* was "too young" to be involved in 701 BCE (Arkell 1961: 126) became widely disseminated throughout academe before scholars had yet considered a crucial 1952 intervention: Leclant and Yoyotte observed that the grammatical conventions of the Egyptian language would require instead in Kawa IV that the adverbial phrase "in the first year of his reign" specify the moment when the king "called to mind this temple," *not* when he had first "beheld (it) as a youth" (Leclant and Yoyotte 1952: 20–21). Consequently, several of Macadam's other conclusions dependent upon that one were unnecessary and even unlikely: (1) The "first year of his reign" did *not* need to correspond to the year when prince *T3-h-r-q* was called to Egypt and passed the Kawa temple *en route*, so (2) the summons may have been wholly unrelated to any assumed coregency with *Š3-b3-t3-k3*. (3) If the summons was unrelated to *T3-h-r-q*'s first regnal year, then his age during that summons was in no way tied to his own regnal chronology: he could have reached the age of 20 at any point during the reign of *Š3-b3-t3-k3*. Realizing this, Kitchen would later propose that *Š3-b3-t3-k3* had summoned the 20-year-old *T3-h-r-q* to Egypt in 701 B.C. to send him at the head of the troops that would defend Judah against Sennacherib, thereby producing his appearance as "Tirhaqah" in 2 Kgs 19:9 and Isa 37:9 with the proleptic title, "King of Kush." As Kitchen explained: "If in current speech one says that Queen Elizabeth was born in 1926, this is precisely like saying that king Taharqa was in Palestine in 701 B.C.; only a fool and a pedant would seek to 'correct'" either statement as anachronism (1973: 160). At the end of the 20th century, Shea (1999) revived the theory that Sennacherib had campaigned twice against Judah and encountered "Taharqa" only during his latest attempt, citing a newly discovered stela that, according to Redford, documented the exploits of "Taharqa in Western Asia" (Redford 1994). Yet the stela made no actual mention of "Taharqa," and a subsequent analysis by Revez (2003) has assigned it to a different dynasty altogether. Whatever one thinks of the two-campaign theories still repeated in biblical studies (Sadler 2005: 116–18), they are neither grounded in nor required by Egyptian and Kushite evidence from the 25th Dynasty.

The new evidence from Kawa precipitated two further developments that deserve brief comment here. First, Kawa stelae III, VI, and VII documented the import into Kush of "Asiatic copper," "true cedar of Lebanon," and "good gardeners of the Mentiu of Asia" during the reign of *T3-h-r-q* (Macadam 1949: 9, 35–6, 42). When combined with Kletter's discovery of commercial weights bearing Egyptian hieratic numerals at Tel Malhata, these references suggested a lively trade between the Double Kingdom and the Levant during the first quarter of the 7th century BCE (see K. Pierce, this volume). Many scholars interpreted this commerce as one cause of the Assyrian invasion that would follow roughly 15 years later under Esarhaddon (Spalinger 1974: 301–2; Redford 1992: 356; Kitchen 1995: 117; Picchi 1997: 44), rather than as one result of the Assyrian invasion that had withdrawn from Jerusalem 15 years prior under Sennacherib. Second, Macadam's publication of the Kawa evidence introduced a new, modern spelling of the name *Š3-b3-t3-k3*. Following Griffith's unpublished notes, Macadam inserted into the name a series of vowels borrowed from its presumed Manethonian equivalent, Σεβιχὼς: *Š3-b3-t3-k3* thereby became "Shebitku" (1949: 124). As Griffith was the leading scholar of the Meroitic language spoken in Kush during the 25th Dynasty, Macadam also heeded his advice that the phonemes *-k3* and *-q* at the ends of the names *Š3-b3-k3*, *Š3-b3-t3-k3*, and *T3-h-r-q* were likely all Egyptian transliterations of the demonstrative pronoun *-qo* and copula *-o* that closes many Kushite names later written in the Meroitic script (Pope 2014a: 8, n. 13). Thus, *Š3-b3-t3-k3* soon came to be rendered in the secondary literature as "Shebitqu" (Bakr 1965) and eventually as "Shebitqo" (Wenig 1978)—a modern spelling so close to Manetho's Σεβιχὼς that it could easily be mistaken for proof of their *ancient* equivalence. The basic chronological structure of the 25th Dynasty had now stood for decades, so it seemed prudent to cover the joints with a coat of paint.

VI. The Tang-i Var Revision, 1999–2013

Those joints began to crack after Frame (1999) published an English translation of the Tang-i Var Inscription. Just as scholars had long assumed from the Tanis Inscription that Prince *T3-h-r-q* had been called to Egypt at the age of 20 by (the unnamed) *Š3-b3-k3*, only to be surprised by Kawa stela IV where the ruler in question was actually *Š3-b3-t3-k3*, scholars had long assumed from the Great Display Inscription at Khorsabad that Iamani of Ashdod had been extradited from Egypt by (the unnamed) *Š3-b3-k3*, only to be surprised by the Tang-i Var Inscription where the ruler in question was actually—once again—*Š3-b3-t3-k3*. This new revelation was more destabilizing, however, because it could not be averted by simply detaching the monumental chronology of Egypt from the later, external testimony of the Hebrew Bible; the Tang-i Var Inscription shook the presumed internal chronology of the 25th Dynasty by forcibly realigning it with that of Assyria. Copious Assyrian evidence had already demonstrated that the extradition of Iamani had occurred at some point between 712 and 706 BCE, so the Tang-i Var evidence now required that *Š3-b3-t3-k3* was already ruler during that span. If his predecessor on the throne were indeed *Š3-b3-k3*, then it appeared that the 15 attested regnal years of *Š3-b3-k3* in Egypt now had to be wedged like an oversized voussoir between the reign of Osorkon IV (Shilkanni) ca. 716 BCE and the accession of *Š3-b3-t3-k3* ca. 706 BCE.

Scholars proposed three main ways of salvaging the existing structure. Redford and Dallibor returned to coregency theories not unlike that which Wiedemann had derived from the fake Turin stela, overlapping the reigns of *Š3-b3-k3* and *Š3-b3-t3-k3* by several years (Redford 1999; Dallibor 2005: 20–5). Kitchen, for his part, opined that the *Š3-b3-t3-k3*, "ruler of Meluḫḫa (Kush)," who extradited Iamani could not have been more than the "deputy" in Kush of King *Š3-b3-k3* in Egypt, but he concurred with Redford and Dallibor that the two Kushites must have governed together in some fashion. All three authors speculated that the length of the Double Kingdom might have necessitated a "bifurcation" of the realm, with *Š3-b3-k3* and *Š3-b3-t3-k3* each responsible only for their half, and Kitchen (2009: 163) even offered from his own imagination the words with which *Š3-b3-k3* might have explained such an arrangement to the Assyrian king. By contrast, Kahn (2006) quoted from multiple Kushite royal inscriptions to directly challenge the notion of a 'Divided Kingdom' ruled by coregency: no ancient monuments were double-dated to the reigns of two Kushite kings, and individual Kushite pharaohs had made frequent claims to rule both Egypt and Kush simultaneously, with some stating quite explicitly that they would share the kingdom with no one. Rather than overlapping the reigns of two *Kushite* kings, Kahn therefore proposed to overlap the reigns of one Kushite and one *Egyptian* king, by dislodging Weidner's cornerstone from its position in 716 BCE: Kahn argued that when "Shilkanni (Osorkon IV), Ruler of Egypt," sent tribute from the Delta to Assyria, he must have done so in bold defiance of his Kushite overlord, *Š3-b3-k3*, even though the latter was, according to Kahn, "the *recognized* king of Egypt" even "in the Delta" (Kahn 2001: 9). Despite the ingenious solutions offered by Redford, Dallibor, Kitchen, and Kahn, many specialists now agreed that the chronology of the 25th Dynasty in use for most of the past century no longer appeared sound under the weight of the new evidence from Tang-i Var. As summarized by Brunet (2005: 29): "[t]his carefully crafted reconstruction tumbled down in 1999."

VII. From the Monuments to Manetho: The New Chronology, 2014–Present

His Majesty found it built in mudbrick, a (collapsed) heap thereof having reached its roof. He rebuilt it in stone, as an excellent construction.

—*Taharqo's Kawa stela VI*

(Pope 2014a: 49–51)

In 2014, Nubiologist Lohwasser convened a roundtable to discuss an ostensibly new idea about the chronology of the 25th Dynasty: the possibility that the reign of *Š3-b3-t3-k3* might have *preceded* that of *Š3-b3-k3* (Bányai et al. 2015). This theory was not actually as new as the roundtable participants seem to have supposed, having been first advanced by Layard in 1853. Yet it did contradict the orthodoxy established by Rosellini at the very dawn of Egyptology and subsequently followed by every specialist in the field for the past 161 years of scholarship. The only published voices of dissent across that long span had come from outsiders to Egyptology and Nubiology (Brunet 2005; Bányai 2013). Even though many participants were not convinced by some details of Bányai's own theory (2013), not a single scholar at the roundtable mounted an open refutation of the larger proposal that *Š3-b3-t3-k3* had reigned before *Š3-b3-k3*.[4] After the Münster roundtable, the proposed *Š3-b3-t3-k3* → *Š3-b3-k3* sequence gained further published support from Egyptologists (Payraudeau 2014; Broekman 2015, 2017a, 2017b; Agut-Labordère and Moreno García 2016; Jansen-Winkeln 2017; Jurman 2017; Donker van Heel 2021).

These authors have buttressed the new chronology with a wide variety of evidence from cemeteries, temples, and both hieroglyphic and hieratic texts. Their recent articles and books combine to demonstrate that the *Š3-b3-t3-k3* → *Š3-b3-k3* sequence accords better with: the evolution of Kushite royal tombs and burial equipment; the chronology of temple construction at Karnak and Medinet Habu; the placement of successive Nilometer readings at Karnak's quay; the evolution of private donation stelae in the Delta and of Apis burials in the Saqqara Serapeum; the sequence of archaizing prenomina chosen by the Kushite kings; the limited genealogical data available for the Kushite royal family; the prosopographic chronology of private papyri and inscriptions; and, most pointedly, a Kushite royal statue from the reign of *T3-n-w3-ti-Imn* in Egypt that lists his predecessors as *Š3-b3-k3* and *T3-h-r-q*, while omitting *Š3-b3-t3-k3* altogether (Bányai 2013: 49–50, 76–81, 84–92; Payraudeau 2014: 118–20, 124–6; Bányai et al. 2015: 148–60, 171–3; Broekman 2015: 21–3, 25, 27–8; Jurman 2017: 129–36,

Table 42.2 Absolute chronology of the 25th Dynasty according to Payraudeau 2014: 127

Hieroglyphic Names	Transliterated Names	Years B.C.E.
	Š3-b3-t3-k3	714 – 705
	Š3-b3-k3	705 – 690
	T3-h-r-q	690 – 664

138–45; Donker van Heel 2021: 27–9). According to the interpretations of these scholars, *Š3-b3-t3-k3* was featured in Kawa stela IV, not because he was the direct predecessor or coregent of *T3-h-r-q*, but simply because it was King *Š3-b3-t3-k3* who first summoned a young prince *T3-h-r-q* to serve the Kushite regime in Egypt—precisely as stated in the text. The new chronology would easily accommodate the monumental evidence of 15 attested regnal years for *Š3-b3-k3* between the reigns of *Š3-b3-t3-k3* and *T3-h-r-q*; the absolute dates for those three kings are estimated by Payraudeau (2014) as shown above (Table 42.2):

If Manetho's information about the sequence was accurate, then this new chronology would also require that he rendered the name *Š3-b3-t3-k3* as Σαβάκων and the name *Š3-b3-k3* as Σεβιχώς. As we have seen above, these Greek transliterations are indeed every bit as plausible as Rosellini's alternative.

However, the temptation to build this new chronology upon Manetho misses a crucial point of methodology. As explained by Broekman (2015: 21): "[T]he first-hand data of the monuments should be given greater consideration than Manetho's tradition, composed centuries later, and from which we possess only very late copies of copies, frequently having been manipulated in a tendentious way." Accordingly, scholars in recent years have begun to abandon spellings of the Kushite royal names that were based on presumed Manethonian equivalents, in favor of more neutral transliterations that conform as closely as possible to the consonantal skeletons of their Egyptian hieroglyphic writing, their vocalic transliteration in contemporaneous Assyrian texts, and their underlying Meroitic grammar: Shaba**ta**ko, Shabako, and Taharqo.

In comparison to previous interpretations, the new chronology also suggests a very different history of Egypt's relations with the Levant during the Kushite era. The absence of Shaba**ta**ko's name in the Near East and his decision to extradite Iamani are tied to his new chronological position as the first Kushite king to establish a permanent presence in Lower Egypt and treat its security as his own responsibility. The subsequent extension of Kushite royal alliances to include Ekron and Judah would not have been a *volte face* by Shaba**ta**ko but instead a new position taken by his successor, Shabako. Following Kushite royal custom of delegating actual leadership in combat to a subordinate (Pope fc.), Shabako would then have sent to Judah's defense his kinsman, Taharqo—who could have been anywhere between 25 and 33 years old in 701 BCE. The Hebrew Bible's subsequent description of "Tirhaqah" (תרהקה) as "King of Kush" (מלך־כוש) would be nothing more than prolepsis, exactly as recognized by Breasted (1905: 554) and then explained by Kitchen (1973: 160). Under this historical scenario, circulation of Shabako's name upon objects in the Near East and especially the sealings at Sennacherib's palace—whether affixed to actual state documents or merely trade items—would most likely have *followed* the Assyrian king's withdrawal from Jerusalem, suggesting that the two rulers had reached some diplomatic resolution to their conflict in Judah that was deemed advantageous to both sides (Pope 2019). The long-term advantages for Kush are suggested by Taharqo's receipt of "Asiatic copper," "cedar of Lebanon," and viticulturists from western Asia during the 680s BCE, as well as by the use of Egyptian hieratic numerals upon commercial weights at Tel Malhata in Judah. Viewed as a whole, the shape of this reconstruction shows the Double Kingdom's gradual ascent toward international prominence, peaking in the reign of Taharqo before the devastating reprisals by Esarhaddon and Aššurbanipal. If this new chronology of the 25th Dynasty continues to pass inspection in the years to come, then it should place the history of Egypt's relations with Judah on a more solid foundation.

Notes

1 For Egypt's interactions with the Levant during the Third Intermediate Period, see K. V. L. Pierce, this volume.
2 Kitchen has vociferated against the "mere guesses" and "stupid illusion" of peer scholars in a strident essay whose every page is marked by either triplicate exclamation points, underlined, bold, and italic fonts (sometimes with all three combined), or words printed in all-caps (2009).
3 Between the earliest and most recent attempts, intermediate phases are named for consistency here by either the place of accession for the key evidence (e.g., Turin) or its provenance (Saqqara, Aššur, Kawa, and Tang-i Var). The modern year ranges given correspond to dates of subsequent public dissemination.
4 The only scholar to reject that proposal outright since 2014 has been the Egyptologist Robert Morkot, speculating only that "a more detailed knowledge of the Libyan dynasts and Theban officials" may undermine it in the future (2016: 108).

Bibliography

Agut-Labordère, Damien, and Juan Carlos Moreno García. 2016. *L'Égypte des pharaons*. Paris: Belin.
Albright, William F. 1953. "New Light from Egypt on the Chronology and History of Israel and Judah." *BASOR* 130: 4–11.
Allen, James P. 2020. *Ancient Egyptian Phonology*. Cambridge: Cambridge University Press.
Arkell, A. J. 1961. *A History of the Sudan from the Earliest Times to 1821*. 2nd ed. London: University of London, Athlone Press.
Bakr, Mohammed. 1965. "The Relationship between the C-Group, Kerma, Napatan and Meroitic Cultures." *Kush* 13: 261–4.
Bányai, Michael. 2013. "Ein Vorschlag zur Chronologie der 25. Dynastie in Ägypten." *JEH* 6: 46–129.
Bányai, Michael, et al. 2015. "Die Reihenfolge der kuschitischen Könige." *JEH* 8: 115–80.
Bickerman, Elias J. 1991. *Chronology of the Ancient World*. London: Thames & Hudson.
Breasted, James H. 1905. *History of Egypt*. New York: Scribner.
———. 1906. *Ancient Records of Egypt*. Chicago: University of Chicago Press.
Bright, John. 1972. *A History of Israel*. Philadelphia: Westminster.
Broekman, Gerard P. F. 2015. "The Order of Succession between Shabaka and Shabataka: A Different View on the Chronology of the Twenty-Fifth Dynasty." *GM* 245: 17–31.
———. 2017a. "Genealogical Considerations regarding the Kings of the Twenty-fifth Dynasty in Egypt." *GM* 251: 13–20.
———. 2017b. "Some Consequences of the Reversion of the Order Shabaka-Shabataka." *GM* 253: 25–32.
Brunet, Jean-Frédéric. 2005. "The XXIInd and XXVth Dynasties Apis Burial Conundrum." *JACF* 10: 26–34.
Champollion, Jean-François. 1822. *Lettre à M. Dacier*. Paris: Firmin Didot.
Conan Doyle, Arthur. 1892. *The Adventures of Sherlock Holmes*. London: George Newnes.
Dallibor, Klaus. 2005. *Taharqo - Pharao aus Kusch*. Berlin: Achet.
Donker van Heel, Koenraad. 2021. *The Archive of the Theban Choachyte Petebaste Son of Peteamunip*. Leiden: Brill.
Eide, Tormod, et al., eds. 1994. *Fontes Historiae Nubiorum: Textual Sources for the History of The Middle Nile Region Between the Eighth Century BC and the Sixth Century AD*. Vol. 1: *From the Eighth to the Mid-Fifth Century BC*. Bergen: University of Bergen.
Fabretti, A., F. Rossi, and R. V. Lanzone. 1882. *Regio Museo di Torino: Antichità egizie*. Turin: Museo di Torino.
Frame, Grant. 1999. "Inscription of Sargon II at Tang-i Var," *Or* 68: 31–57, Tab. I–XVIII.
———. 2021. *The Royal Inscriptions of Sargon II, King of Assyria (721–705 BC)*. University Park: Eisenbrauns.
Gliddon, George. 1843. *Ancient Egypt*. New York: Winchester.
Godley, Alfred D. 1946. *Herodotus*. London: Heinemann.
Hall, Henry. 1925. "The Ethiopians and Assyrians in Egypt." Pages 270–88 in *The Assyrian Empire*. Edited by John B. Bury, Stanley A. Cook, Frank E. Adcock. Cambridge: Cambridge University Press.

Heeren, Arnold H. L. 1838. *Historical Researches*. London: Bohn.
Horn, Siegfried H. 1966. "Did Sennacherib Campaign Once or Twice against Hezekiah?" *AUSS* 4: 1–28.
Hoskins, George A. 1835. *Travels in Ethiopia*. London: Longman.
Jansen-Winkeln, Karl. 2017. "Beiträge zur Geschichte der Dritten Zwischenzeit." *JEH* 10: 23–42.
Jurman, Claus. 2017. "The Order of the Kushite Kings According to Sources from the Eastern Desert and Thebes. Or: *Shabataka was here first!*" *JEH* 10: 124–51.
Kahn, Dan'el. 2001. "The Inscription of Sargon II at Tang-I Var and the Chronology of Dynasty 25." *Or* 70: 1–18.
———. 2006. "Divided Kingdom, Co-Regency, or Sole Rule in the Kingdom(s) of Egypt-and-Kush?" *AeL* 16: 275–92.
———. 2007. "Judean Auxiliaries in Egypt's Wars against Kush." *JAOS* 127/4: 507–16.
Karst, Josef. 1911. *Eusebius Werke*. Leipzig: Hinrichs.
Kitchen, Kenneth A. 1973. *The Third Intermediate Period in Egypt (1100–650 BC)*. Warminster: Aris & Phillips.
———. 1995. "Egypt." Pages 108–21 in *BEBP*.
———. 2009. "The Third Intermediate Period in Egypt." Pages 161–202 in *The Libyan Period in Egypt*. Edited by Gerard P. Broekman et al. Leuven: Peeters.
Kletter, Raz. 1998. *Economic Keystones*. Sheffield: Sheffield Academic.
Lamon, R. S., and G. M. Shipton. 1939. *Megiddo I*. Chicago: University of Chicago Press.
Layard, Austen H. 1853. *Discoveries among the Ruins of Nineveh and Babylon*. New York: Harper & Brothers.
Leclant, Jean, and Jean Yoyotte. 1952. "Notes d'histoire et de civilization éthiopiennes." *BIFAO* 51: 1–39.
Lepsius, K. Richard. 1853. *Letters from Egypt, Ethiopia, and the Peninsula of Sinai*. London: Bohn.
Macadam, Miles F. L. 1949. *The Temples of Kawa*. Vol. 1: *The Inscriptions*. London: Oxford University Press.
Mariette, Auguste. 1865. "Quatre pages des archives officielles de l'Éthiopie." *RAr* 12: 161–79.
Maspero, Gaston. 1868. "Essai sur la Stèle du Songe," *RAr* 17: 329–39.
Morkot, Robert. 2016. "The Late-Libyan and Kushite God's Wives: Historical and Art-historical Questions." Pages 107–19 in *Prayer and Power*. Edited by Meike Becker, Anke Ilona Blöbaum, and Angelika Lohwasser. Münster: Ugarit.
Morkot, Robert, and Stephen Quirke. 2001. "Inventing the 25th Dynasty: Turin Stela 1467 and the Construction of History." Pages 349–63 in *Begegnungen: antike Kulturen im Niltal*. Edited by Caris-Beatrice Arnst et al. Leipzig: Wodtke & Stegbauer.
Oldfather, Charles H. *Diodorus of Sicily*. Cambridge, MA: Harvard University Press, 1946.
Onasch, Hans-Ulrich. 1994. *Die assyrischen Eroberungen Ägyptens*. Wiesbaden: Harrassowitz.
Payraudeau, Frédéric. 2014. "Retour sur la succession Shabaqo-Shabataqo." *Nehet* 1 (2014): 115–27.
Petrie, W. M. F. 1905. *A History of Egypt*. London: Methuen.
Picchi, Daniela. 1997. *Il conflitto tra Etiopi ed Assiri nell'Egitto della XXV dinastia*. Bologna: La Mandragora.
Pleyte, Willem. 1876. "Über zwei Darstellungen des Gottes Horus-Seth." *ZÄS* 14: 49–52.
Pope, Jeremy. 2014a. *The Double Kingdom under Taharqo: Studies in the History of Kush and Egypt, c. 690–664 BC*. Leiden: Brill.
———. 2014b. "Beyond the Broken Reed: Kushite Intervention and the Limits of *l'histoire événementielle*." Pages 105–60 in *Sennacherib at the Gates of Jerusalem, 701 BCE: Story, History, and Historiography*. Edited by Isaac Kalimi and Seth F. C. Richardson. Leiden: Brill.
———. 2019. "Sennacherib's Departure and the Principle of Laplace." Pages 91–131 in *Jerusalem's Survival, Sennacherib's Depature, and the Kushite Role in 701 BCE: An Examination of Henry Aubin's Rescue of Jerusalem*. Edited by Alice O. Bellis. *JHS* 19. Online: doi.org/10.5508/jhs29552.
———. "'Like the Coming of the Winds': Warfare during the Twenty-Fifth Dynasty." In *Warfare in Ancient Egypt*. Edited by Anthony Spalinger. Leiden: Brill, forthcoming.
Rawlinson, George. 1881. *History of Ancient Egypt*. Vol. 2. New York: Scribner.
Redford, Donald B. 1992. *Egypt, Canaan, and Israel in Ancient Times*. Princeton: Princeton University Press.
———. 1994. "Taharqa in Western Asia and Libya." *EI* 24: 188–91.
———. 1999. "A Note on the Chronology of Dynasty 25 and the Inscription of Sargon II at Tang-i Var." *Or* 68: 58–60.

———. 2004. *From Slave to Pharaoh: The Black Experience of Ancient Egypt*. Baltimore: Johns Hopkins University Press.
Revez, Jean. 2003. "Une stele inédite de la troisième période intermédiaire à Karnak: une guerre civile en Thébaïde?" *Cahiers de Karnak* 11: 535–65 and pls. I–IV.
Rougé, Emmanuel de. 1855. *Notice de quelques textes hiéroglyphiques récemment publiés par M. Greene*. Paris: Thunot.
Rosellini, I. 1833. *I monumenti dell'Egitto e della Nubia*. Parte I: *Monumenti Storici*. Pisa: Niccolo Capurro.
Sadler, Rodney S. 2005. *Can a Cushite Change His Skin? An Examination of Race, Ethnicity, and Othering in the Hebrew Bible*. New York: T&T Clark.
Shea, William H. 1999. "Jerusalem Under Siege: Did Sennacherib Attack Twice?" *BAR* 25: 36–44, 64.
Spalinger, Anthony J. 1974. "Esarhaddon and Egypt: An Analysis of the First Invasion of Egypt." *Or* 43: 295–326.
Török, László. 2009. *Between Two Worlds: The Frontier Region Between Ancient Nubia and Egypt 3700 BC–500 AD*. Leiden: Brill.
———. 2014. *Herodotus in Nubia*. Leiden: Brill.
Von Beckerath, Jürgen. 1999. *Handbuch der ägyptischen Königsnamen*. Mainz: Philipp von Zabern.
Waddell, William G. 1964. *Manetho*. London: Heinemann.
Weidner, Ernst F. 1941. "Cilkan(he)ni, König von MuÕri, ein Zeitgenosse Sargons II., nach einem neuen Bruchstück der Prisma-Inschrift des assyrischen Königs." *AfO* 14: 40–53.
Wenig, Steffen. 1978. *Africa in Antiquity: The Arts of Ancient Nubia and the Sudan*. Brooklyn: Brooklyn Museum Press.
Wiedemann, Alfred. 1884. *Ägyptische Geschichte*. Gotha: Friedrich Andreas Perthes.
Wilkinson, John Gardner. 1837. *Manners and Customs of the Ancient Egyptians*. London: John Murray.

43

ISRAEL AND ASSYRIA, JUDAH AND ASSYRIA

Ido Koch

Assyria has a special place in the history of ancient Israel, conventionally known as the vanquisher of the Kingdom of Israel and the subjugator of the Kingdom of Judah, initiating an imperial era that would end only with the rise of the Hasmonean state. The rapid and brutal conquest of the southern Levant during the 730s and 720s BCE brought the destruction of the major southern Levantine polities and the eradication of their local social landscape by large-scale atrocities and the deportation of communities. Imperial administrators and soldiers governed the depleted conquered territories. They monitored the subjugated rulers of the remaining polities, who were forcefully integrated into the empire, obliged to send their best belongings as tribute and their best of men as labor or soldiers.

While this image is justified, it is only one, albeit major, aspect of the multifaceted Assyrian–southern Levantine interaction. In the mid-9th century BCE, indirect Assyrian impact is seen in their expansionist policy that forced the Israelite kings to strengthen their military abilities and form alliances with northern peers. By the early 8th century, the main impact of Assyria was the weakening of Damascus, which allowed Israel to become the leading polity in the southern Levant for several decades even though Israelite kings had to pay tribute to Assyria once or twice. Assyria's conquest of the southern Levant during the late 8th century led to the subjugation of the Kingdom of Judah and its neighbors and their integration within the imperial sphere. In this context, the southern Levantine elites were attracted to the empire (but also resisted it) and were exposed to non-local objects and ideas that they appropriated and entangled with their way of living. In the end, a century of Assyrian colonialism completely altered the southern Levant—politically, demographically, and culturally—and nothing looked the same when the empire rapidly collapsed in the late 7th century BCE.

In what follows, I review the impact the Assyrian conquest had on the inhabitants of Israel and Judah and the significance of the encounters between the locals and the Assyrian courts and the latter's agents. I begin with a short historical synopsis followed by four topics: the structure of the Assyrian Empire in the southern Levant, the impact of the deportations on the local social landscape, the Assyrian economic involvement in subjugated polities, and the colonial encounters and the appropriation of Assyrian ideas by the locals.

DOI: 10.4324/9780367815691-49

The Assyrian Period in the Southern Levant: A Short Synopsis

The southern Levantine–Assyrian encounters can be artificially divided into several phases: early encounters, conquest, and the colonial period until the collapse of the empire. The first began in the days of Shalmaneser III (reigned 858–824 BCE), following the establishment of firm Assyrian control over the Jazira up to the Euphrates River (Frahm 2017b: 167–70; Younger 2018: 19–20). Shalmaneser III raided the Levant 19 times and reached the Mediterranean (an idyllic achievement of a Mesopotamian king) and south—somewhere in the Carmel ridge, the northwestern edge of the Kingdom of Israel—as no king before him (Yamada 2000). Shalmaneser III previously led his army across the Euphrates and fought against alliances of Levantine kings who were able to stop him, at least once—in the famous battle of Qarqar (853 BCE) that included the forces of Ahab of Israel. This first mention of Israel in Assyrian sources had a remarkable impact on modern scholarship of the Old Testament, considering that the biblical text is unaware of the great status Ahab had in the Levantine politics, hinting at the limited information the authors of the Book of Kings had about such an early period in the history of Israel (Na'aman 2007: 398).

From this point onwards, Assyrian sources mention Israelite kings from the house of Jehu. The inscriptions of Shalmaneser III record the submission of Jehu, who was called "the son of Omri," legitimizing him as king of Israel (Na'aman 1998; Hasegawa 2012: 46–50). The visualization of Jehu's submission on the famous Black Obelisk is the only recognizable depiction of an Israelite king to date (Uehlinger 2007: 201–10). Following 30 years without encounters (Frahm 2017b: 172–73), the Assyrian army marched against Damascus during the reign of Adad-Nirari III (reigned 810–783 BCE), Shalmaneser III's grandson, and collected tribute given by the local kings, among them Jehoash of Samaria (Hasegawa 2012: 115–22). The Assyrians concentrated their efforts on weakening Damascus during the following decades, with minimal involvement in the southern Levant (Frahm 2017b: 175–76; Younger 2018: 24) that allowed the astute kings of Israel to lead their kingdom to its most prosperous years (Finkelstein 2013: 127–38). Diplomatic relations were formed between Samaria and Nimrud, thus attesting the importance of Israel at that stage; envoys from Israel and Judah, frequently visited the Assyrian court, brought gifts to the kings, and were hosted as welcome guests (Na'aman 2019b).

The next phase in the southern Levantine–Assyrian interaction was triggered by the ambitious expansionist policy of Tiglath-Pileser III (reigned 745–727 BCE) (Frahm 2017b: 176–78; Younger 2018: 25–26). By the end of his first decade as king, Tiglath-Pileser III subdued the Levant, reaching as far south as Gaza—facing northern Sinai, a week-long walk from the minor Egyptian states of the Nile Delta. In several campaigns, he conquered Damascus and turned it into an Assyrian stronghold, and defeated the kingdoms of Israel and Gaza, deporting thousands of their people and wreaking havoc in their lands. All local kings acquiesced and raised tribute, including Ahaz of Judah, the first Judahite king mentioned in Assyrian sources. The next Assyrian king, Shalmaneser V (reigned 727–722 BCE), conquered Israel, and his successor, Sargon II (reigned 722–705 BCE), turned Samaria into an Assyrian center.[1] Sargon's conquest of Samaria, and Ashdod (the central Philistine city at that time[2]) eight years later, marked the beginning of firm Assyrian rule over the southern Levant, the last phase in the southern Levantine–Assyrian relations. Those years are sometimes termed the "Pax Assyriaca" although there was never peace (Faust 2021: Chapter 9).

Sargon II was killed on the battlefield during a disastrous campaign in Anatolia, and his corpse was left unburied, leading to revolts across the empire, the southern Levant included—namely, the revolt of Hezekiah and his allies (Frahm 2017b: 183–84). Once Sennacherib (reigned 705–680 BCE), Sargon II's son, consolidated his rulership in Mesopotamia, he mobilized his army to defeat his enemies in the southwest. Assyrian sources, archaeological excavations, and to some extent also the Hebrew Bible all attest the devastating campaign and its impact on the minds of the survivors (Kalimi and Richardson 2014; Matty 2016). Thousands of people were killed or deported while others became refugees. Cities and towns were destroyed, and the Kingdom of Judah lost its greatest assets precisely at the point when its economy reached an unprecedented zenith (Lipschits 2021: 159). However, Jerusalem was saved, and a new Jerusalem-centered ideology emerged during these decades of recovery (Römer 2015: 184–87).

Revolts brought retaliation by successive Assyrian kings, Esarhaddon (reigned 680–669) and Ashurbanipal (reigned 669–627 BCE), but overall, these decades were a time of prosperity among several subjugated kingdoms. The ultimate example is Ekron, Judah's immediate neighbor to the west, where settlement expanded and included an extensive olive-oil extraction industry and a monumental palace incorporating Assyrian architectural elements (Gitin 2003, 2012). Other examples are the kingdoms of Transjordan that flourished through their integration within the empire and the advancement of the transregional trade connecting the northern Levant and Mesopotamia with the Arabian Peninsula (Tyson 2014; Crowell 2021). At the same time, the rulers of the southern Levant as an integral part of the empire had to send labor for building projects at the new capital of Nineveh and soldiers to fight in the Assyrian campaigns in Egypt.

However, the Assyrian state fell into disorder shortly after the death of Ashurbanipal (Frahm 2017b: 191–93). The Egyptian king Psammetichus I soon exploited the weakness of Assyria in the west to expand his hegemony over the Levant and faced Babylonia, led by Nabopolassar, who had joined forces with Cyaxares king of the Medes to destroy the Assyrian heartland and even conquer Harran, the last Assyrian stronghold. Assyria was gone and was soon followed by the remaining Levantine states. Necho II, the new king of Egypt, and Nebuchadnezzar II, the new king of Babylon, fought over the southern Levant in a fierce struggle that concluded with a Babylonian victory at Carchemish. In the following years, constant Egyptian intervention in the local politics against Babylonian interests led to the destruction of all local polities that survived the Assyrian period. A long transition period began, and the southern Levant looked much different once the Persian empire reestablished stability at the end of the 6th century BCE.

The Assyrian Colonial Network: The Provinces of Megiddo and Samaria as a Case Study

An overview of the Assyrian sources and the material record from the southern Levant attests to the devastating results of the conquest on the local landscape. The aggressive strategy of the Assyrian army led to the deaths of tens of thousands of people by war, famine, and plague; cities and towns were destroyed, havoc was wreaked upon the countryside, and thousands of the survivors were deported (Faust 2015: 768–69, 776–78, 2021; Streit 2021: 265, 269).[3] The ultimate goal was to exploit the conquered polity, extract its people and transport them to the imperial heartland (see further below). However, as stated by Liverani (2017b: 541), "destruction was not the end goal of conquest, merely a necessary preliminary action," and where needed, there was reconstruction to respond to the needs of the empire. Written sources refer to a governor installed at the conquered capital soon after the conquest who was responsible for reorganizing and revitalizing the devastated land according to imperial needs (Younger 2015; Liverani 2017a: 149–56, 179–86). These textual references are corroborated by material remains across the western part of the empire, from provincial centers to their hinterland to fortresses guarding topographic corridors (MacGinnis et al. 2016). Assyrian officials headed rebuilt cities populated by deportees brought from the other reaches of the empire. Supply to the colonial installations was sent from neighboring subjugated kingdoms that had to host visiting imperial officials who were involved in their economies.

Narrowing the discussion to the conquered Kingdom of Israel, the Assyrians based their rule on two centers: Samaria and Megiddo. Beginning with the former, Sargon II followed a known Assyrian practice to turn the capital of a conquered polity into a provincial center. Economically, Samaria had little to offer, but as the symbol of the Israelite kingdom, it became a beacon that spread Assyrian imperialism across the conquered land and sent a clear message to other polities: the empire possessed the former capital of the vanquished (Tappy 2019: 186). Only partial material evidence exists, thus preventing the chronicling of detailed settlement history,[4] yet it is accepted that Samaria was not destroyed during the Assyrian conquest and continued to exist for centuries. Textual sources provide valuable (and unparalleled) information on the destination of the people taken from the city, and the origin of the people brought to repopulate it (Radner 2019). Additional sources reveal a snippet of the character of Assyrian Samaria such as its administrative structure, construction efforts led by imperial officials, and the rights and dues of its inhabitants (Zilberg 2018: 67–70).

Megiddo appears in Assyrian records as an imperial possession beginning in the days of Sargon II (Na'aman 2009: 97–98) and as the seat of the eponym of the year 679 BCE.[5] The thorough excavations at Megiddo showed that the former Israelite stable compound (Stratum IVA) was abandoned, and a temporary settlement was established atop it, which was eventually superimposed by the Assyrian town (Stratum III; Finkelstein and Ussishkin 2000: 597–98, 601–02). This well-planned settlement included several large buildings identified as housing the administrative apparatus of the province, while most of the hill was occupied by smaller domestic units clustered into insulae (Peersmann 2000). Assyrian Magiddu was densely populated, far more so than the many earlier towns that existed at the site. While there is no reference to its population in the sources (in contrast to Samaria), there should be little doubt that its inhabitants were newcomers, considering the deportation of thousands of the previous inhabitants of the northern valleys and the size of the new town. The rationale underlying the investment at Megiddo was its strategic location at the southwestern end of the Jezreel Valley, close to the topographic corridors connecting it to the coastal plain. It was joined by forts and settlements established around it.[6]

The Assyrians revived three additional regions of the fallen Kingdom of Israel:

- The Huleh Valley—Tel Dan (Thareani 2016b, 2018, 2019): a new settlement was built on top of the ruins of Israelite Dan (Stratum IIA). The new town (Stratum I) included public buildings and paved streets, with all available space utilized, and became more populous than ever, with the settlement growing to ca. 20 hectares. Housing reached the top of the ridge surrounding the site, with residential neighborhoods occupying most of the mound.[7]
- The Central Coastal Plain—Tel Dor (Gilboa and Sharon 2016): the last Israelite town at Tel Dor was abandoned, and the site was rebuilt during the Assyrian period. The finding of Assyrian-style vessels and the abundance of Phoenician-style vessels in refuse pits demonstrate the town's role in maritime trade.
- The Yarkon–Ayalon basin: farther inland and southwards, the destroyed Israelite administrative center at Gezer (Stratum VI; see Wolf 2021) was rebuilt as well, and while it is difficult to reconstruct its outline, the new town (Stratum V) was associated with

Assyrian-style artifacts that might attest to its regional importance (Reich and Brandl 1985; Ornan, Ortiz, and Wolff 2013). North of Gezer was Hadid, where large-scale olive-oil production demonstrates the region's importance to the imperial interests, and in both Gezer and Hadid epigraphic remains attest the presence of newcomers from the Northern Levant and Mesopotamia—ostensibly deportees (Na'aman and Zadok 2000; Koch and Brand forthcoming; and see further below). North of Hadid and as far as Aphek, small rural settlements appeared on the spurs of the central highland and the eastern edges of the coastal plain, along the assumed north–south main road, either as part of a planned policy or in response to the Assyrian demands of agricultural commodities (Aster and Faust 2015; Itach 2022).[8]

At the same time, there is no doubt that other devastated regions were left desolate (Faust 2015: 767–764). While those regions had previously been dominated by the Levantine courts and their clients and served their interests, the Assyrian interests differed. Since the main aim was to strengthen the imperial system rather than a local elite, some portions of the fallen Levantine polities were left deserted, while others prospered. This duality in the fate of the conquered lands under Assyrian rule, of massive construction in enclaves surrounded by desolation, is better perceived if one rejects the conventional understanding of ancient states as territories with fixed boundaries and embraces the concept of networks.

Recent scholarship tends to emphasize the structural complexity of ancient states, understanding a polity as having complex, sometimes flexible boundaries that might include several noncontiguous territorial islands bound by reciprocal, familial, religious, and additional relations (see overview in Koch 2018: 368–71 with extensive literature). A polity might expand into an overarching system by solidifying its network by establishing new hubs—such as administrative centers, colonies, trading posts, and ritual centers—and incorporating other networks using force or allegiance. Viewing the Assyrian Empire as a network reconstructs its initial expansion and incorporation of neighboring entities into an "imperial heartland," followed by the conquest of remote regions (such as the southern Levant) and establishing hubs to craft a network of topographical corridors leading to the frontiers.

In the context of the Assyrian Empire in the southern Levant, the conquered lands were reorganized to fit the imperial needs, and it is suggested that the primary need was controlling topographic corridors connecting the northern Levant with the region of Gaza. The Assyrian kings were attracted to this region because of its proximity to Egypt and its location on the Mediterranean endpoint of the desert routes connecting the Levant with the Arabian Peninsula (see detailed overview in Na'aman 2004; Ben-Shlomo 2014). Tiglath-Pileser III, Sargon II, and Esarhaddon led military campaigns to block the Egyptian influence and pacify local resistance in Gaza and its neighbor Arza. At the same time, both Tiglath-Pileser III and Sargon II documented their investment in the region, which included the establishment of trade stations and the elevation of local tribal leaders as imperial agents, while Sargon II settled people in the region that had been dislocated from the Zagros (Na'aman and Zadok 1988). Against this background, scholars attributed the founding of new settlements, erection of forts, and rebuilding of towns to the Assyrians and their proxies (Na'aman 2004; Ben-Shlomo 2014; Thareani 2016a; Fantalkin 2018). Following that, the location of most colonial possessions is telling, suggesting that the strategic and economic importance of the region of Gaza as gleaned from the Assyrian sources might be the reason for building projects and rearranging infrastructure in the lands ruled directly by the empire.

The Assyrian network developed over decades and, remarkably, continued with no apparent interruption when the imperial core crumbled, and Psammetichus I expanded his hegemony over the Levant. The Egyptians faced some resistance, as might be gleaned from the destruction of several sites in the region of Gaza. However, other parts of the southern Levant continued to develop, be they local polities such as Ashkelon (Stager, Master and Schloen 2011) or the colonial centers—an intriguing endurance considering the collapse of Assyria and the difference between the Assyrian and the Egyptian interests. Given that these centers existed as nodes in the broader colonial network, how did they survive the Assyrian collapse? Officials and soldiers may have been called back home or left without orders or supplies. Furthermore, how long could they have kept the colonial network active while Assyria itself was conquered, and what led them to collaborate with the Egyptians?

Regardless of these circumstances, none of the colonial or local centers survived the Babylonian rule. Bothered with the rehabilitation of their homeland devastated during the wars against the Assyrians, the Babylonians did not maintain the colonial system or rebuild towns following the destruction of the local polities (Levavi 2020). The colonial network eventually fragmented; most of its centers were abandoned, and a demographic depletion hit the land that recovered only a century afterward.

Deportations and Their Impact on the Local Landscape

Upon the conquest of the Levant by Tiglath-Pileser III, the Assyrian imperial system that had been developing for centuries began reorienting people and resources following the needs of the empire. Foremost among the colonial means used to achieve this task—as well as to break local resistance—was the forced movement of conquered populations (Oded 1979; Liverani 2017a: 187–94; Radner 2017, 2019; Sano 2020; Valk 2020; Koch 2022). The chief destination was the Assyrian heartland, with its gigantic cities and their vast agricultural hinterland. At the same time, an unknown number of deportees were sent to remote provinces and settled in frontier strongholds to serve as the demographic backbone supporting the imperial apparatus. Overall, a century of Assyrian colonialism in the Levant forced tens of thousands—and even hundreds of thousands—of men, women, and children to leave their homes and to march interminable routes.

The practice of deporting conquered peoples was a fundamental component of Assyrian royal ideology and policy, following a millennium-old Mesopotamian practice of relocating defeated groups into the victorious society (Liverani 2017a: 187–92). By the days of Tiglath-Pileser III and the Sargonid kings, deportations were a common yet catastrophic punishment that removed local resistance and issued an aggressive warning to rival polities (Liverani 2017a: 192, 2017b: 542; Sano 2020; Valk 2020). At the same time, the resettlement strategy stimulated a complex logistic system. The state valued the deportees for their demographic contribution and skills. The deportees were directed to the imperial core and predominantly to the Assyrian heartland, absorbed into the expanding cities, or deployed to develop their hinterland. In this framework, the state orchestrated the deportations and appointed provincial governors who monitored the routes, supported the deportees, and provided shelter, food, and clothing (Radner 2017: 210–11). A more limited number of marches led deportees to the colonial holdings. These include deportees (comprising defeated enemies from conquered polities, and sometimes also rivals from Assyria) sent to maintain urban centers or fortresses that guarded topographic corridors (Frahm 2022) and, farther away, to support forces protecting the frontiers, such as the western Iranian plateau facing mountainous tribes (Radner et al. 2020) or the southern Levant facing Egypt, as detailed below.

Even though the state provided the deportees with food and shelter, they still faced loss and suffering that accompanied the horrifying events of the war, expulsion, and long marches—events that must have contributed to the psychological breakdown of many and the disintegration of social bonds (Battini 2022). Upon arrival at their new locale, the deportees were dislocated. They faced an unfamiliar landscape and language(s) they did not understand. They had to preserve (yet modify) some of their traditional practices while abandoning others, especially those related to the homeland and its landscape, and had to adopt new practices appropriated from the hosting society (Berlejung 2022). These shared components in the experience of suffering deportation materialized based on changing social positions and reactions to encounters with the locals (continuous exposure vs. segregation).

The fate of the Israelite deportees in the imperial heartland is shrouded in obscurity due to the limited information at our disposal. A handful of written sources from the Assyrian heartland refer to individuals labeled "Samarians" or individuals bearing Yahwistic names; these demonstrate the complexity of integration in the Neo-Assyrian Empire and the gap between the royal language of assimilation and the reality of daily affairs. The earlier sources deal with chariot troops integrated into the Assyrian army and artisans participating in the construction of Dur-Sharruken; they thus point to the presence of the first generation of deportees in the Assyrian heartland. Later sources, from Guzana (Tell Halaf) during the days of Esarhaddon and Ashurbanipal, and Dur-Katlimmu (Tell Sheikh Hamad) following the collapse of Assyria, are mainly concerned with economic transactions (Zadok 2015: 163–76; Radner 2019: 113–22; Berlejung 2022). The individuals mentioned in these sources identified themselves or were identified by others as associated with Samaria even though they were third-, fourth-, or even fifth-generation deportees.

Moving to the southern Levant, only Sargon II details explicitly the settlement of conquered people in Samaria (as well as in Ashdod and Gaza). Additional deportations to Samaria might be embedded in the biblical texts, such as Ezra 4:10 on the people brought to Samaria by king Asnapar (Na'aman and Zadok 2000: 178–79; Levin 2022). Nothing is known about the large cities the Assyrians built at Megiddo and Dan that must have had a large population that partly came from afar. The knowledge gap is somewhat completed by material remains, mostly inscribed objects and pottery. However, one should be cautious about using them as indicators of the presence of deportees, as there is a risk of oversimplifying the material record into a Pots-equal-People scenario.

An established point of departure is inscribed objects such as the ones found in Samaria (Horowitz and Oshima 2006: 112–15) that are commonly considered to attest to the presence of people from Mesopotamia. Of these, a bulla stamped by a royal seal, a stele fragment, and a judicial document attest to colonial involvement in the city. Only a single object, a votive cylinder mentioning Babylonian deities and individuals with Babylonian theophoric elements in their names, can be reliably connected to people from Babylonia. However, one question remains: were they deportees or other agents that served the colonial administration?[9]

Another group of inscribed objects includes clay tablets documenting economic transactions unearthed at Tel Gezer, Tel Hadid, and Kh. Kusia.[10] The tablet from Kh. Kusia (Horowitz and Oshima 2006: 100–01) records a land sale with only one preserved name, possibly Elamite; it was stamped by a seal that might have been imported from Babylonia (Ornan 1997: 333 No. 93). Of the two tablets from Hadid (Na'aman and Zadok 2000),[11] one records a land sale deed from 698 or 697 BCE and mentions several names, all Akkadian but one, which may be Aramean. The other tablet documents a debt note with a pledge from 664 or 663 BCE. It mentions a creditor and a debtor, the latter's name is Canaanite–Hebrew, and so are the names of his sister and wife, and four witnesses: two with Akkadian names, one is identified as an Egyptian, and one with a West-Semitic name. A similar mixed community is illustrated in the two tablets from Gezer that document land sales, one from 651 or 650 BCE and the other from 649 or 648 BCE (Horowitz and Oshima 2006: 55–60). The former tablet mentions Akkadian, Aramean, and Egyptian names, while the latter has a similar composition of names alongside another individual—the seller, named Netanyahu.

These mixed communities represent the essence of the Assyrian colonialism in the southern Levant and its complexity. The individuals bearing Canaanite–Hebrew, Akkadian, Aramaic, and Egyptian names might have been locals and newcomers who mingled in their daily activities. The newcomers could have been deportees, officials in the service of the empire, merchants, other agents. The Assyrian network was diversely interrelated and staffed by various kinds of agents since there were constant movements of soldiers and deportees from other parts of the empire, alongside traffic of merchants, immigrants, and other individuals and groups—each with their own personality, past, status, and aim. The multiplicity of options hinders any generalized assumption. Moreover, the situation might have been even more complex, considering the possibility that some of the individuals with local names were members of the newcomer community who, after several decades in their new homes, began to give their children local names—a reflection of their integration into the local landscape.

The tablets from Hadid pose a further complexity. While Gezer features various Assyrian-style seals and high-quality architectural elements, some in Assyrian style, which points to the integration of the settlement within the colonial network, no such remains are documented from Tel Hadid. One of the two tablets from Tel Hadid was found on the floor of a structure built in local techniques according to a local ground plan, among local-style artifacts, such as pottery and stone objects. The question is: had no tablets been found at Hadid, would scholars have even considered its inhabitants to be deportees?

Another category of objects is pottery.[12] Typical of the 7th century BCE in the central highlands, mainly in rural sites located around Shechem, is a deep bowl in a local form that combines a specific surface treatment originating in southern Mesopotamia—wedge-shaped impressions on their interior (Itach, Aster and Ben-Shlomo 2017). Following previous suggestions, the surface treatment might suggest a utilitarian purpose associated with food production. In their words (ibid.: 89), "the wedge impressions are indeed effective in grating vegetables such as onions and other root vegetables, producing a thin paste that could then facilitate food preparation." This bowl type might serve as a vivid example of newcomers' adaptation: there was a need to replace something they used to have that was needed to cook a meal that would remind them of home by taste and aroma. Thus, the adaptation included the appropriation of a local vessel by adding the wedge impression, presumably by a simple request of a newcomer client from a local potter.

Beyond these two sets of sources, evidence is limited to the point of being non-existent. No cuneiform writing or wedged-impressed bowls were found thus far at Megiddo or Dan, where Assyrian-style architecture served the imperial administration—probably due to the usage of Aramaic as the colonial language in the Levant (Zilberg 2018: 76–77 with literature). In this regard, the large assemblages of Mesopotamian-style seals in the provincial capitals and other administrative centers are illuminating. In her seminal study, Ornan pointed to the concentration of imported seals from Mesopotamia at a few significant sites: Samaria, Megiddo, and Gezer (1997: 287, 292). Moreover, only at Samaria have Neo-Babylonian stamp seals been uncovered, indicating the city's continued importance in the days of the

Neo-Babylonian and Achaemenid empires. Alas, it is impossible to determine who the seals' owners were during the Neo-Assyrian period: administrators installed at these centers or deportees who carried their valuable personal belongings with them.

The scarcity of material remains of the deportees might have stemmed from a travel restriction—their limited baggage (Koch 2022). The deportees depicted marching in the Assyrian reliefs are seen with only the very few belongings they could have carried. Some were fortunate enough to use their animal-driven cart, but in either case, they carried small bags, probably holding their most personal belongings. Minor artifacts such as seals could have arrived by such a mechanism (although these might have belonged to officials, as part of their job), but larger objects would have been left behind. In other words, the limited number of remains associated with the deportees might be understood because very few large artifacts traveled with them. Such a situation requires scholars to augment the classification of objects with the study of their function. Given the organized character of the deportations, the forced settlement of deportees while maintaining their social structure, and the common tendency in migrant communities to preserve domestic practices, it is hypothesized that meticulous archaeological analyses of domestic behavioral patterns such as cooking, crafts such as pottery production, and animal exploitation trends would identify the behavioral patterns of migrants and pinpoint their transformation.

As detailed above, the end of the settlement pattern imposed by the Assyrians came decades after the collapse of Assyria, and multiple questions related to these eventful years remain unresolved. In the context of the deportations, questions arise regarding the fate of the deportee communities. Would they mingle with the locals, and would the locals accept them and forget or diminish their previous role as collaborators of the empire (Levin 2013)? Only future inquiries into the archaeology of the 6th century might provide clues to this enigma.[13]

Involvement in Subjugated Polities

As early as the days of Shalmaneser III, tribute was a common demand in the Assyrian interaction with the Levantine kings. Metals, ivory, furniture, and textiles were among the commodities sent to the Assyrian court.[14] Another mechanism that brought the riches of the Levant to Assyria was the looting of conquered cities that brought the treasures of palaces and temples to be displayed, consumed, and hoarded at the court. There is no wonder why the image of a vandal-like empire is still present in scholarship, illustrating the Assyrians as solely interested in collecting tribute while leaving the conquered lands to decline. However, such a view overlooks the investment in the reestablishing of the colonial centers in the provinces of Samaria and Megiddo (as detailed above) and in other conquered polities, such as a large structure built in Assyrian style northeast of Ashdod—most probably after the conquest of the city by Sargon II (Kogan-Zehavi 2018). Moreover, the view of the Assyrians as no more than looters negates textual information in hand directly describing Assyrian economic involvement in the southern Levant as early as the days of Tiglath-Pileser III. But unlike local polities that developed their economies in environmental and social peculiarities, the Assyrian economic policy was motivated by the interests of the empire, which had a different view of the land and its resources. Textual sources even attest to the presence of Assyrian officials in local politics and the intervention of Assyrian officials in the local economies to shift income to Assyrian hands (Yamada 2008; Na'aman 2018b).

No boundary blocked the Assyrian kings and their agents from intervening in local polities' economies. Even though no provinces were established south of Samaria and Ashdod, the Assyrian Empire's involvement was felt far beyond any imagined line supposed to demarcate its provinces. The best example of that is the region of Gaza, as detailed above. All kingdoms in the southern Levant had to comply with the Assyrian demands, and if they did, they were left unharmed (on the Assyrian diplomacy with subjugated polities, see Fales 2009); but the demands imposed by the imperial court that the rulers had to fulfill were enormous, including tributes, *corvée*, and human resources support for military campaigns. Furthermore, the local elites were exposed to imperial practices, and the expansion of interregional trade led to increased consumption of luxury products (see contributions in Tyson and Herrmann 2019). At the same time, new connections with production centers and markets near and far, in addition to the forced migration of artisans and craftsmen, would have exposed the locals to new ideas and technologies (further below). This complex meshwork of interactions resulted in the development of local economies by the rulers and other prominent groups, aimed and increasing their capital (see Sinopoli 2003; Zori 2011: 30–37).

In agricultural-based societies, this process materialized in intensified and specialized crop production and animal exploitation to create surplus needed for obtaining finished products such as metals and luxury commodities. A fine example comes from the Kingdom of Judah. Sometime during the last third of the 8th century BCE, the Jerusalemite court developed a new administrative system based on storage jars containing oil and wine (see detailed discussion in Lipschits 2021: 35–48). The jars were marked by seals declaring their belonging to the king (Hebrew: *lmlk*), featuring an emblem (a beetle or a winged disc) and a place name—probably of a royal estate. Considering the time of its introduction, when Judah was subjugated to Assyria, the new administrative system exemplifies the empire's indirect economic impact. Related to that is the emergence of Ekron as a chief olive-oil producer that was briefly mentioned above. Significant parts of the city were occupied by oil press compounds, featuring sophisticated technology that allowed the large-scale processing of olives brought from the entire region. Indeed, and contrary to the preliminary interpretation of the finds, there is no evidence of Assyrian direct involvement (Faust 2011). Still, it is impossible to understand the rise of Ekron without the empire's impact on the southern Levant: Sennacherib's arrangements following his 701 BCE campaign (the transfer of the Judahite possessions in the Shephelah—the hub of olive horticulture in this part of the southern Levant—to the hands of the Philistine cities), and the new economic opportunities created by the empire (Na'aman 2003).

Another major commodity in the southern Levant was wool. Previous studies (Sapir-Hen, Gadot, and Finkelstein 2014; Sapir-Hen 2017) have shown that animal exploitation during the Iron IIC focused on prime-aged sheep. By examining relative livestock frequencies, Sapir-Hen and colleagues (2014) demonstrated that the dominance of sheep over other livestock prevailed in all southern Levantine sites during Iron IIC, a dominance that emerged in Judah already during the Iron IIB. As the dominance of sheep was not typical of earlier periods, Sapir-Hen and colleagues (2014: 735) attributed it to the imposition of central government control over the economy and the promotion of raising sheep for their wool to be used as tax exported to Assyria (and see also Sapir-Hen 2017: 344–45). The picture of an intensified sheep herding for secondary products during the Iron IIB and IIC is corroborated by the large number of textile production tools found across the southern Levant (Koch and Sapir-Hen 2018). The Assyrian court demanded wool and its final products, especially blue and red-purple wool garments. At the same time, the value of finished wool products also meant that surpluses were traded for the exotic commodities brought to the southern Levant by the desert fringe network, and hence the dense evidence of economic activity that included weaving and trade.

Such economic development alters social structure since redistribution of capital leads to the emergence of new focal points in society, and specifically, it leads to the expansion of the elite. In turn, the elite used some of these surpluses to legitimize their status by commending monumental building projects that conveyed their own ideology (see below regarding the visual language). Moreover, the elite used surpluses to participate in interregional networks that were continuously expanded to supply the demands of luxury commodities (such as spices) by the growing Assyrian state, which dictated the ever-expanding imperial involvement—as exemplified in the region of Gaza. With the subjugation to Assyria, boundaries between kingdoms were removed as they became nodes of an interregional trade network that allowed the acquisition of valuable commodities that the Assyrians sometimes demanded. Enjoying the surpluses gained from the prospering economic initiatives, the southern Levantine elite acquired luxury commodities, sent some as a tribute to the Assyrian court, and kept some for their consumption. These triggered the mind of the southern Levantines, who changed their practices and ideas to accommodate the new way of living. This change is discussed in the following and last section.

Colonial Encounters

The integration of a society into an empire forces its members to encounter non-local people, artifacts, and ideas. Under specific circumstances, mostly of the long colonial experience, the encounters shape the involved parties, both the empire and its subjects (Herrmann 2018; Tyson and Herrmann 2019; Koch 2021: 3–4 and 67–70 with literature). It is, therefore, illuminating to see the immediate impact of the encounters with Assyria and its agents on the local southern Levantine societies, despite the relatively short period of Assyrian rule compared to other colonial periods.[15]

In fact, the encounters might have started long before the conquest of the Levant. One can only imagine what spectacular experience it was for the Israelite messengers visiting the Assyrian court in the early 8th century: the magnitude of Nimrud, the monumentality of its palaces and temples, and the unfamiliar appearance, language, and behavior of its people. Upon their return, they told stories and might have brought with them souvenirs that expressed somewhat of their understanding of Assyria. Back then, Assyria was a faraway place that only a few visited, and still, some Israelite pictorial conventions were possibly borrowed from Assyrian royal imagery (Ornan 2016: 21).

The conquest of the Levant by Tiglath-Pileser III forced the local kings to send their representatives to Assyria (Na'aman 2019b: 13) and by that, the exposure to Assyrian ideology intensified. At the same time, the establishment of colonial holdings at Samaria, Megiddo, and elsewhere placed Assyria in the heart of the southern Levant. Being governed by Assyrian officials and populated by newcomers, these settlements were the hubs from which the Assyrian cultural impact spread to neighboring kingdoms.

Both types of colonial arenas triggered multifaceted encounters that changed the local societies. As described above, one medium of interaction was stamp seals. Imported Assyrian, Babylonian, and north Levantine seals were distributed in and from the colonial centers, where one finds a variety of styles and icons as well as the most substantial evidence for their localization. These artifacts were spread and appropriated within the framework of intense interaction between the many nodes of the Assyrian network. The variability of encounters precludes the formulation of any generalized reconstruction as to why and how a specific artifact was brought to its final deposition and why some icons and scenes were accepted and entangled into the local repertoire, while others were not (Keel and Uehlinger 1998: 286–87; Koch forthcoming).

The most prominent pictorial assemblage spread and localized in the southern Levant beyond the Assyrian provinces involved lunar imagery—specifically, the iconography of the moon deity of Ḥarran (Figure 43.1). The temple at Ḥarran was embraced by Assyrian kings as early as Adad-Nirari III, and its cult was employed in the service of imperial ideology during the days of the Sargonids (Holloway 1995; Groß 2014). Considering the diffusion of Assyrian and Aramean practices in the imperial heartland and the service of Aramean-speaking individuals in the imperial administration, scholars consider the spread of lunar imagery to reflect an intensification of Assyrian activity during the 7th century BCE across the southern Levant. Furthermore, scholarly discussion of the relationships between images depicted on seals/amulets and biblical texts has embraced this specific pictorial assemblage and its imperial association to argue for Assyrian influence on Judahite religion (e.g., Keel 1998: 60–109), yet not without criticism (Cooley 2011: 286–87 with literature). Indeed, when the *context of the finds* typically employed in this discourse is scrutinized (Koch forthcoming), it becomes clear that the many exemplars mentioned in the scholarly literature come primarily from the northern valleys and Transjordan. At the same time, only three items featuring the lunar imagery are known from stratified Iron IIC assemblages in Judah. All other items from Jerusalem and its vicinity were found in mixed, later, or unstratified contexts; thus, the timespan of their use cannot be determined.[16] Such limited evidence should deter scholars from suggesting a widespread Assyrian impact on Judahite religion—at least on this point.

Contrary to that, the Assyrian impact on Judah is visible the most in the royal sphere: the appropriation of imperial textual language manifested in the Hebrew Bible and the pictorial language as attested in the material records. Regarding the former, several passages in the Hebrew Bible attest to the incorporation of Assyrian royal ideology (Van Der Kooij 2012; Aster 2017; Frahm 2017a; Dubovský 2021). Another impact is the appropriation of Assyrian oaths of loyalty embedded in Deuteronomy; the Assyrian kings were preoccupied with the danger of revolts (Radner 2016) and imposed loyalty oaths on members of the state and its subordinates (Frahm 2016: 84). Such oath documents are known from the Assyrian capitals and a 7th-century BCE temple at Tell Tayinat, and it has been suggested that a similar treaty was perhaps accessible to the authors of the early version of the covenant between YHWH and his people (see Edenburg and Müller 2019 with further literature). Lastly, the magnificent Assyrian court and its eventful history inspired scribes in describing their petty kingdoms and their past. Scholars long ago saw the figure of glorious Solomon (or significant components of it) as a composite construct made of accomplishments achieved by Assyrian kings (Na'aman 2019a). A recent study even claimed remarkable accords between the "Succession Narrative" and the events leading to Esarhaddon's accession to the throne (Na'aman 2018a)

Material remains also attest to the appropriation of the Assyrian royal pictorial language by the local courts. The rosette was a meaningful Assyrian icon—a symbol of Ištar that adorned the crowns and clothes of the king and the heir apparent and that also decorated royal monuments (Albenda 2020). Appropriated rosettes are known from two southern Levantine contexts (see discussion in Koch and Lipschits 2021): the Judahite administrative system based on storage jars replaced its icons and adopted the rosette (Figure 43.2), which, although previously known in the Levantine pictorial repertoire, rarely appeared in Levantine stamp seals and is yet to be found on seals from Jerusalem prior to the Iron IIC (Koch forthcoming). The second context is at Ekron, in the palace mentioned above that was influenced by Assyrian architecture. The central room of the complex featured the famous inscription placed by Achish, dedicating the shrine to his patron goddess. The excavators associated a large stone slab from that room engraved with a rosette icon with the city patron goddess and interpreted as reflecting Assyrian influence (Gitin 2012: 233 and pl. 252A).

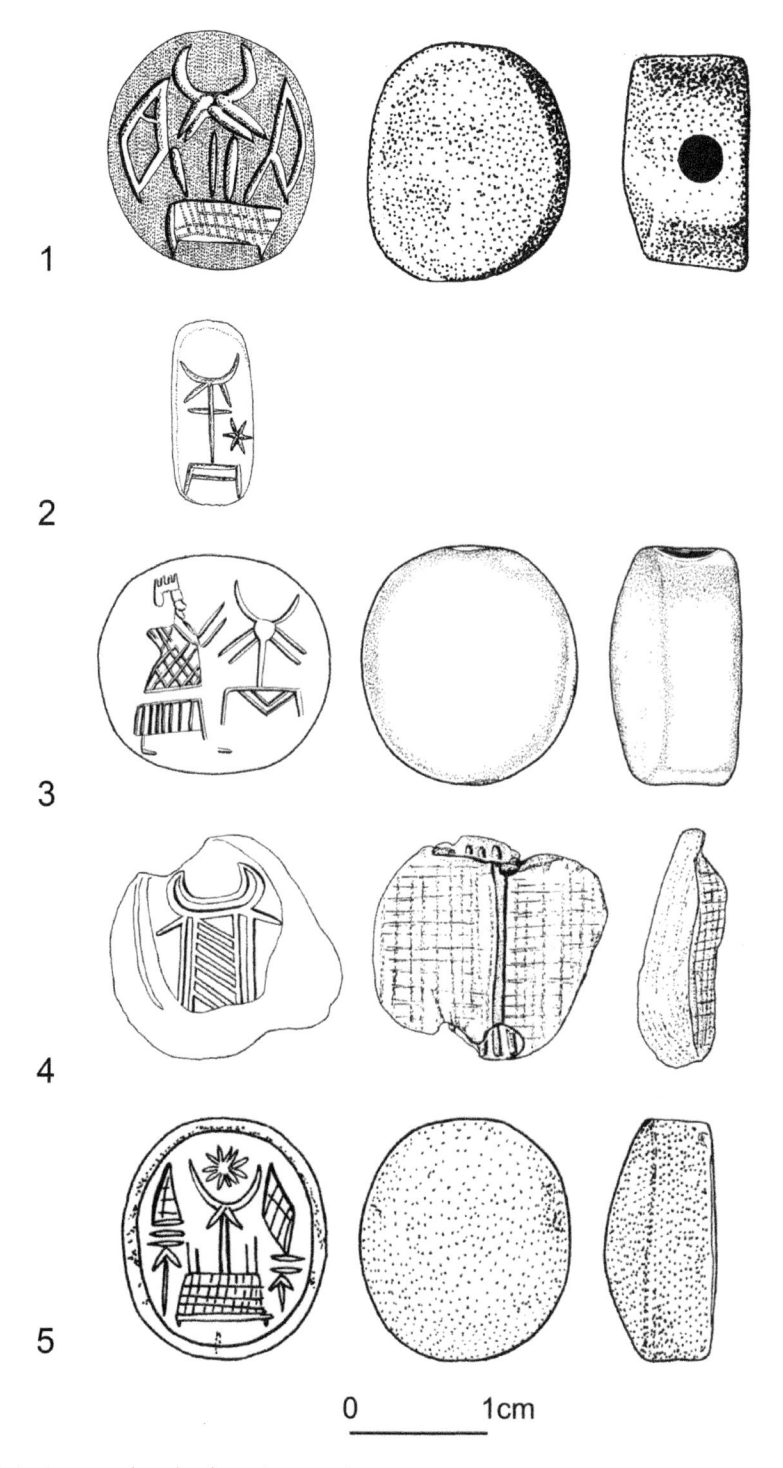

Figure 43.1 Stamp seals and sealings depicting lunar imagery: 1. Tell Keisan (after Keel 2017: 589 No. 14); 2. Tel Gezer (after Keel 2013: 167 No. 3); 3. Tell Jemmeh (after Keel 2013: 23 No. 49); 4. Jerusalem (after Keel 2017: 323 No. 100); 5. Tawilan (after Eggler and Keel 2006: 447 No. 2)

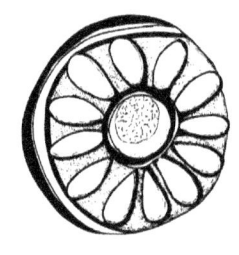

Figure 43.2 Main types of rosette seal impressions on jar handles

These innovations in southern Levantine royal ideology appeared during the zenith of Assyrian power or the chaotic decades of its rapid downfall. It was an act of usurpation—the localization of the ruler's language by the colonized as a means of resistance to colonial domination and its cultural influence. A prime example of such localization is the appropriation of the ruler's language by the colonized, coupled with its manipulation to promote a message, usually subversive, regarding the colonial arena. Looking back at 7th-century BCE Judah, scholars have long ago considered the appropriation of the imperial language by the Jerusalemite court as an act of resistance, in a manner that involved the *removal* of the Assyrian king and his replacement by YHWH.

Epilogue

Assyria collapsed in the late 7th century BCE, replaced by the Babylonians who, shortly afterward, destroyed the remaining southern Levantine polities, Judah included. Remarkably, little of Assyria is remembered in the collective memory of the Judahites in the Persian and the Hellenistic periods—a faded memory of Assyria and the deportations from the Levant, perhaps overshadowed by the trauma of the destruction of Jerusalem (Levin 2022). As for the Assyrian deportations to the Levant, the texts describing the Persian period in the southern Levant provide limited information on the residents of Samaria, restricted to their Babylonian background and their Yahwistic orientation.

Overall, Assyria lost, and therefore its memory was (mis)represented in outside writings: Biblical, Aramaic, and Greek sources. These sources commemorate the aggressiveness of the Assyrian Empire, its great cities, and the many revolts resisting its expansions, yet they differ in the memories of specific events or figures (e.g., Richardson 2014; Rollinger 2017). An illuminating example of a memory of Assyria relates to the conflict between Ashurbanipal and his brother, Šamaš-šumu-ukin (Frahm 2003), which evolved into orientalist narratives of Sardanapalus—a feminine, corrupted, and voluptuous last king of the Assyrian Empire, who decided before the fall of Nineveh to die in a great pyre together with his entourage and treasures. This image continued in Greek, Latin, and eventually, western European literature, fascinated with its connotations of decadence along with the tragic ending of its life. It is only with the discoveries at the ruins of the Assyrian capitals and the deciphering of cuneiform writings that the imagined Sardanapalus and other "Assyrian" figures like Ninus and Semiramis began to fade and the real importance of Assyria in world history has been acknowledged (Frahm 2006).

Notes

1. Much ink has been spilled over the exact order of events leading to the conquest of Samaria in the late 720s. See, most recently, Becking 2019; Fales 2019; Frahm 2019; Kahn 2019; Novotny 2019.
2. On Ashdod during the Assyrian period see Fantalkin 2018: 170–77 and Aster 2021.
3. For a more general overview on the collateral impact of wars on civilians, see Nadali and Vidal 2014.
4. The absence of a stratigraphic sequence and the partial nature of the finds prevent any comprehensive reconstruction of post-Israelite Samaria until the Roman period (Tappy 2019). Having said that, dozens of dateable artifacts permit object-oriented studies of the inhabitants of Samaria and their relations with the empires.
5. Various historical reconstructions attribute the establishment of Megiddo as a colonial center to Tigalth-pileser III, although his inscriptions do not mention the city or the installation of a governor at any Israelite locale.
6. Including the late Iron Age fortress at En-Tut, dominating a corridor connecting the Jezreel Plain with the Coastal Plain just east of Tel Dor (Finkielsztejn and Gorzalczany 2010).
7. See also the building unearthed at Ayyelet HaShahar, east of Tel Hazor (Kletter and Zwickel 2006).
8. And see a fortress at the mouth of Yarkon River that might also be associated with the Assyrian network (Fantalkin and Tal 2015).
9. Horowitz (2018) suggested that the inclusion of individual cuneiform signs on 4th-century BCE coins from Samaria are evidence that the inhabitants of the city during the Late Persian period preserved their Mesopotamian heritage as part of their collective belonging.
10. Another cuneiform tablet from the Assyrian period is known from Tel Keisan (Zilberg 2015), possibly documenting a delivery of grain by the imperial administration (Berlejung 2012: 43).
11. For an updated study of the tablets from Tel Hadid see Zadok forthcoming.
12. One group of pottery vessels is the so-called Assyrian Palace Ware, or Assyrian-style pottery, a stylistic group of serving vessels found throughout the southern Levant and predominantly at Tell Jemmeh and Tel Dor. Several studies consider these vessels to have been produced to supply the needs of Assyrian officials or to reflect the presence of potters deported from northern Mesopotamia, although, as stated by Na'aman, "the problem of the origin of the vessels classified as 'Assyrian-style pottery' is even more complicated, as some of them were discovered in strata that antedated the Assyrian conquest of the kingdom of Israel" (2016: 279). Moreover, Hunt (2015, 2016), who conducted the most detailed study of these vessels thus far, concluded that these vessels reflect the embracement of feasting practices associated with Assyria by local elite members.
13. Archaeologically speaking, the Babylonian period and the early Persian period in the southern Levant are largely unknown, and most studies on this period have been dedicated to the material remains from the central highlands (see most recently Lipschits et al. 2021).
14. As detailed in royal inscriptions and archival notes, and is evident by findings such as bullae used to seal commodities sent from subjugated polities (e.g., Zilberg 2018: Table 3.2)
15. This is the place to underline that scholarship of the previous decade rejected terms employing models of acculturation and favoured more nuanced understanding of attraction (and rejection) to imperial influence (see discussions in Berlejung 2012; Bagg 2013; Koch 2018: 377–81 with literature; Faust 2021: Chapter 8).
16. The various possible scenarios for reconstructing the biography of each artifact should be entertained, just like the possible circumstances that led to their appearance in the southern Levant. After all, even if manufactured in Sargonid Assyria, the continuous Levantine–Mesopotamian interaction that characterizes the post-Assyrian era under the Neo-Babylonian empire and Achaemenid empires provides ample paths for such importation.

References

Albenda, P. 2020. "The Royal Assyrian Rosette." *NABU* 2020 (1): 73–75.
Aster, S. Z. 2017. *Reflections of Empire in Isaiah 1–39: Responses to Assyrian Ideology*. Atlanta: SBL.
———. 2021. "Ashdod in the Assyrian Period: Territorial Extent and Political History." *JNES* 80 (2): 323–40.
Aster, S. Z., and A. Faust. 2015. "Administrative Texts, Royal Inscriptions and Neo-Assyrian Administration in the Southern Levant: The View from the Aphek-Gezer Region." *Or* 84 (3): 292–308.

Bagg, A.M. 2013. "Palestine under Assyrian Rule: A New Look at the Assyrian Imperial Policy in the West." *JAOS* 133 (1): 119–44.

Battini, L. 2022. "During the Displacement: Life, Death, Health and Psychological Conditions of Migrants." *HBAI* 11 (Supplement): 25–55.

Becking, B. 2019. "How to Encounter an Historical Problem? '722–720' BCE as a Case Study." Pages 17–32 in *The Last Days of the Kingdom of Israel*. Edited by S. Hasegawa, C. Levin, and K. Radner. Berlin: de Gruyter.

Ben-Shlomo, D. 2014. "Tell Jemmeh, Philistia and the Neo-Assyrian Empire during the Late Iron Age." *Levant* 46 (1): 58–88.

Berlejung, A. 2012. "The Assyrians in the West: Assyrianization, Colonialism, Indifference, or Development Policy?" Pages 21–60 in *Congress Volume Helsinki 2010*. Edited by M. Nissinen. Leiden: Brill.

———. 2022. "A Sketch of the Life of the Golah in the Countryside of Babylonia: Risks and Options of Unvoluntary Resettlement in the Sixth Century BCE." *HBAI* 11 (Supplement): 148–188.

Cooley, J.L. 2011. "Astral Religion in Ugarit and Ancient Israel." *JNES* 70 (2): 281–87.

Crowell, B.L. 2021. *Edom at the Edge of Empire: A Social and Political History*. Atlanta: SBL Press.

Dubovský, P. 2021. "Inverting Assyrian Propaganda in Isaiah's Historiography: Writing the Hezekiah-Sennacherib Conflict in the Light of the Ashurbanipal-Teumman War." Pages 365–406 in *The History of Isaiah*. Edited by J. Stromberg and J.T. Hibbard. Tübingen: Mohr Seibeck.

Edenburg, C., and R. Müller. 2019. "Perspectives on the Treaty Framework of Deuteronomy." *HBAI* 8 (2): 73–86.

Eggler, J., and O. Keel. 2006. *Corpus der Siegel-Amulette aus Jordanien: vom Neolithikum bis zur Perserzeit*. Fribourg and Göttingen: Academic Press and Vandenhoeck & Ruprecht.

Fales, F. M. 2009. "'To Speak Kindly to him/them' as Item of Assyrian Political Discourse." Pages 27–40 in *Of God(s), Trees, Kings, and Scholars: Neo-Assyrian and Related Studies in Honour of Simo Parpola*. Edited by M. Luuko, S. Svärd, and R. Mattila. Helsinki: Finnish Oriental Society.

———. 2019. "Why Israel? Reflections on Shalmaneser V's and Sargon II's Grand Strategy for the Levant." Pages 87–99 in *The Last Days of the Kingdom of Israel*. Edited by S. Hasegawa, C. Levin, and K. Radner. Berlin: de Gruyter.

Fantalkin, A. 2018. "Neo-Assyrian Involvement in the Southern Coastal Plain of Israel: Old Concepts and New Interpretations." Pages 162–85 in *The Southern Levant under Assyrian Domination*. Edited by S. Z. Aster and A. Faust. University Park: Eisenbrauns.

Fantalkin, A., and O. Tal. 2015. *Tell Qudadi: An Iron Age IIB Fortress on the Central Mediterranean Coast of Israel (with References to Earlier and Later Periods)*. Leuven: Peeters.

Faust, A. 2011. "The Interests of the Assyrian Empire in the West: Olive Oil Production as a Test-Case." *JESHO* 54: 62–86.

———. 2015. "Settlement, Economy, and Demography under Assyrian Rule in the West: The Territories of the Former Kingdom of Israel as a Test Case." *JAOS* 135 (4): 765–89.

———. 2021. *The Neo-Assyrian Empire in the Southwest: Imperial Domination and Its Consequences*. Oxford: Oxford University Press.

Finkelstein, I. 2013. *The Forgotten Kingdom: The Archaeology and History of Northern Israel*. Atlanta: SBL Press.

Finkelstein, I., and D. Ussishkin. 2000. "Archaeological and Historical Conclusions." Pages 576–605 in *Megiddo III: The 1992–1996 Seasons*. Edited by I. Finkelstein, D. Ussishkin, and B. Halpern. Tel Aviv: The Institute of Archaeology, Tel Aviv University.

Finkielsztejn, G., and A. Gorzalczany. 2010. "'En Tut." *HA/ESI* (122). http://www.hadashot-esi.org.il/report_detail_eng.aspx?id=1412&mag_id=117

Frahm, E. 2003. "Images of Ashurbanipal in Later Tradition." *EI* 27: 37*–48*.

———. 2006. "Images of Assyria in Nineteenth- and Twentieth-century Western Scholarship." Pages 74–94 in *Orientalism, Assyriology and the Bible*. Edited by S.W. Holloway. Sheffield: Sheffield Academic Press.

———. 2016. "Revolts in the Assyrian Empire: A Preliminary Discourse Analysis." Pages 76–89 in *Revolt and Resistance in the Ancient Classical World and the Near East*. Edited by J.J. Collins and J.G. Manning. Leiden: Brill.

———. 2017a. "Assyria in the Hebrew Bible." Pages 556–69 in *A Companion to Assyria*. Edited by E. Frahm. Hoboken: Wiley-Blackwell.

———. 2017b. "The Neo-Assyrian Period (ca. 1000–609 BCE)." Pages 162–208 in *A Companion to Assyria*. Edited by E. Frahm. Hoboken: Wiley-Blackwell.

———. 2019. "Samaria, Hamath, and Assyria's Conquests in the Levant in the Late 720s BCE: The Testimony of Sargon II's Inscriptions." Pages 55–86 in *The Last Days of the Kingdom of Israel*. Edited by S. Hasegawa, C. Levin, and K. Radner. Berlin: de Gruyter.

———. 2022. "The Intellectual Background of Assyrian Deportees, Colonists, and Officials in the Levant." *HBAI* 11 (Supplement): 56–82.

Gilboa, A., and I. Sharon. 2016. "The Assyrian kāru at Dor (ancient Du'ru)." Pages 241–52 in *The Provincial Archaeology of the Assyrian Empire*. Edited by J. MacGinnis et al. Cambridge: McDonald Institute for Archaeological Research.

Gitin, S. 2003. "Neo-Assyrian and Egyptian Hegemony over Ekron in the Seventh Century BCE: A Response to Lawrence E. Stager." *EI* 26: 55*–61*.

———. 2012. "Temple Complex 650 at Ekron: The Impact of Multi-Cultural Influences on Philistine Cult in the Late Iron Age." Pages 223–56 in *Temple Building and Temple Cult: Architecture and Cultic Paraphernalia of Temples in the Levant (2.-1. Mill. B.C.E.)*. Edited by Jens Kamlah. Wiesbaden: Harrassowitz.

Groß, M. 2014. "Ḥarrān als kulturelles Zentrum in der altorientalischen Geschichte und sein Weiterleben." Pages 139–54 in *Kulturelle Schnittstelle. Mesopotamien, Anatolien, Kurdistan. Geschichte. Sprachen. Gegenwart*. Edited by L. Müller-Funk, S. Procházka, G.J. Selz, and A. Telič. Vienna: Institut für Orientalistik der Universität Wien.

Hasegawa, S. 2012. *Aram and Israel during the Jehuite Dynasty*. Berlin: de Gruyter.

Herrmann, V.R. 2018. "Cosmopolitan Politics in the Neo-Assyrian Empire: Local Elite Identity at Zincirli-Sam'al." *Semitica* 60: 493–535.

Holloway, S.W. 1995. "Harran: Cultic Geography in the Neo-Assyrian Empire and its Implications for Sennacherib's Letter to Hezekiah in 2 Kings." Pages 276–314 in *The Pitcher Is Broken: Memorial Essays for Gösta Ahlström*. Edited by S.W. Holloway and L.K. Handy. Sheffield: Sheffield Academic Press.

Horowitz, W. 2018. "The Last Days of Cuneiform in Canaan: Speculations on the Coins from Samaria." Pages 236–45 in *The Southern Levant under Assyrian Domination*. Edited by S. Z. Aster and A. Faust. University Park: Eisenbrauns.

Horowitz, W., and T. Oshima. 2006. *Cuneiform in Canaan: Cuneiform Sources from the Land of Israel in Ancient Times*. Jerusalem: Israel Exploration Society.

Hunt, A. 2015. *Palace Ware Across the Neo-Assyrian Imperial Landscape: Social Value and Semiotic Meaning*. Leiden: Brill.

———. 2016. "The Social Value of Semiotic Meaning of Neo-Assyrian Palace Ware." Pages 71–78 in *The Provincial Archaeology of the Assyrian Empire*. Edited by J. MacGinnis et al. Cambridge: McDonald Institute for Archaeological Research.

Itach, G. 2022. The Assyrian Interests in the Western Part of the Province of Samaria: A Case Study from Khallat es-Siḥrij and its Vicinity. *HBAI* 11 (Supplement): 82–112.

Itach, G., S. Z. Aster, and D. Ben-Shlomo. 2017. "The Wedge-Impressed Bowl and the Assyrian Deportation." *TA* 44: 72–97.

Kahn, D. 2019. "The Fall of Samaria: an Analysis of the Biblical Sources." Pages 229–49 in *The Last Days of the Kingdom of Israel*. Edited by S. Hasegawa, C. Levin, and K. Radner. Berlin: de Gruyter.

Kalimi, I., and S. Richardson. 2014. *Sennacherib at the Gates of Jerusalem: Story, History and Historiography*. Leiden: Brill.

Keel, O. 1998. *Goddesses and Trees, New Moon and Yahweh: Ancient Near Eastern Art and the Hebrew Bible*. Sheffield: Sheffield Academic Press.

———. 2013. *Corpus der Stempelsiegel-Amulette aus Palästina/Israel. Von den Anfängen bis zur Perserzeit— Band IV: Von Tel Gamma bis Chirbet Husche*. Fribourg and Göttingen: Academic Press and Vandenhoeck & Ruprecht.

———. 2017. *Corpus der Stempelsiegel-Amulette aus Palästina/Israel. Von den Anfängen bis zur Perserzeit— Band V: Von Tel el-'Band bis Tel Kitan*. Fribourg and Göttingen: Academic Press and Vandenhoeck & Ruprecht.

Keel, O., and C. Uehlinger. 1998. *Gods, Goddesses, and Images of God in Ancient Israel*. Minneapolis: Fortress Press.

Kletter, R., and W. Zwickel. 2006. "The Assyrian Building of 'Ayyelet ha-Šaḥar." *ZDPV* 122 (2): 151–86.

Koch, I. 2018. "Introductory Framework for Assyrian-Levantine Colonial Encounters." *Semitica* 60: 367–96.

———. 2021. *Colonial Encounters in Southwest Canaan during the Late Bronze Age and the Early Iron Age*. Leiden and Boston: Brill.

———. 2022. "A Framework for the Study of Deportations to and from the Levant during the Age of the Empires." *HBAI* 11 (Supplement): 10–24.
———. forthcoming. "A New Look at Late Iron Age Stamp-seals from Judah." *HBAI*.
Koch, I., and E. Brand. forthcoming. *Tel Hadid I: Excavations during the Years 1995–1997*. Tel Aviv and University Park: Emery and Claire Yass Publications in Archaeology and Eisenbrauns.
Koch, I., and O. Lipschits. 2021. "Stamped Jars from Judah: Official Pictorial and Textual Language." *Judaïsm ancien/Ancient Judaism* 9: 287–312.
Koch, I., and L. Sapir-Hen. 2018. "Beersheba-Arad Valley during the Assyrian Period." *Semitica* 60: 427–52.
Kogan-Zehavi, E. 2018. *The Neo-Assyrian Administrative Architecture in the Western Province: Government Buildings in the Land of Israel and Transjordan in the 8th and 7th Centuries BCE, with Emphasis on the Findings of the Excavations North of Tel Ashdod*. Haifa University of Haifa.
Levavi, Y. 2020. "The Neo-Babylonian Empire: The Imperial Periphery as Seen from the Centre." *JANEH* 7 (1): 59–84.
Levin, Y. 2013. "Bi-Directional Forced Deportations in the Neo-Assyrian Empire and the Origins of the Samaritans: Colonialism and Hybridity." *ARC* 28: 217–40.
———. 2022. "Memories of the Assyrian Exile in Persian-Period Yehud: A View from Chronicles and Ezra-Nehemiah." *HBAI* 11 (Supplement): 224–238.
Lipschits, O. 2021. *Age of Empires: The History and Administration of Judah in the 8th-2nd Centuries BCE in Light of the Storage-Jar Stamp Impressions*. University Park: Eisenbrauns.
Lipschits, O., L. Freud, M. Oeming, and Y. Gadot. 2021. *Ramat Raḥel VI: The Renewed Excavations by the Tel Aviv-Heidelberg Expedition (2005–2010): The Babylonian-Persian Pit*. Tel Aviv and University Park: Emery and Claire Yass Publications in Archaeology and Eisenbrauns.
Liverani, M. 2017a. *Assyria: The Imperial Mission*. Winona Lake: Eisenbrauns.
———. 2017b. "Thoughts on the Assyrian Empire and Assyrian Kingship." Pages 534–46 in *A Companion to Assyria*. Edited by E. Frahm. Hoboken: Wiley-Blackwell.
MacGinnis, J., D. Wicke, T. Greenfield, and A. Stone, eds. 2016. *The Provincial Archaeology of the Assyrian Empire*. Cambridge: McDonald Institute for Archaeological Research.
Matty, N. K. 2016. *Sennacherib's Campaign Against Judah and Jerusalem in 701 B. C.: A Historical Reconstruction*. Berlin: de Gruyter.
Na'aman, N. 1998. "Jehu Son of Omri—Legitimizing a Loyal Vassal by His Lord." *IEJ* 48: 236–238.
———. 2003. "Ekron under the Assyrian and Egyptian Empires." *BASOR* 332: 81–91.
———. 2004. "The Boundary System and Political Status of Gaza under the Assyrian Empire." *ZDPV* 120: 55–72.
———. 2007. "The Northern Kingdom in the Late Tenth-Ninth Centuries BCE." Pages 399–418 in *Understanding the History of Israel*. Edited by H. G. M. Wilkinson. Oxford: Oxford University Press.
———. 2009. "Was Dor the Capital of an Assyrian Province." *TA* 36: 95–109.
———. 2016. "Locating the Sites of Assyrian Deportees in Israel and Southern Palestine in Light of the Textual and Archaeological Evidence." Pages 275–82 in *The Provincial Archaeology of the Assyrian Empire*. Edited by J. MacGinnis et al. Cambridge: McDonald Institute for Archaeological Research.
———. 2018a. "Game of Thrones: Solomon's 'Succession Narrative'and Esarhaddon's Accession to the Throne." *TA* 45 (1): 89–113.
———. 2018b. "Qurdi-Aššur-Lamur as Governor in Phoenicia and South Syria." *NABU* 26: 42–45.
———. 2019a. "Hiram of Tyre in the Book of Kings and in the Tyrian Records." *JNES* 78 (1): 75–85.
———. 2019b. "Samaria and Judah in an Early 8th-Century Assyrian Wine List." *TA* 46: 12–20.
Na'aman, N., and R. Zadok. 1988. "Sargon II's Deportations to Israel and Philistia (716–708 BC)." *JCS* 40: 36–46.
———. 2000. "Assyrian Deportation to the Province of Samaria in the Light of Two Tablets from Tel Hadid." *TA* 27: 159–88.
Novotny, J. 2019. "Contextualizing the Last Days of the Kingdom of Israel: What Can Assyrian Official Inscriptions Tell Us?" Pages 36–53 in *The Last Days of the Kingdom of Israel*. Edited by S. Hasegawa, C. Levin, and K. Radner. Berlin: de Gruyter.
Oded, B. 1979. *Mass Deportations and Deportees in the Neo-Assyrian Empire*. Wiesbaden: Reichert.
Ornan, T. 1997. *Mesopotamian Influence on the Glyptic of Israel and Jordan in the First Millennium B.C.* Ph.D. diss., Tel Aviv University.
———. 2016. "Sketches and Final Works of Art: The Drawings and Wall Paintings of Kuntillet 'Ajrud Revisited." *TA* 43: 3–26.

Ornan, T., S. Ortiz, and S. Wolff. 2013. "A Newly Discovered Neo-Assyrian Cylinder Seal from Gezer in Context." *IEJ* 63: 6–25.

Peersmann, J. 2000. "Assyrian Magiddo: The Town Plan of Stratum III." Pages 524–34 in *Megiddo III: The 1992–1996 Seasons*. Edited by I. Finkelstein, D. Ussishkin, and B. Halpern. Tel Aviv: The Institute of Archaeology, Tel Aviv University.

Radner, K. 2016. "Revolts in the Assyrian Empire: Succession Wars, Rebellions Against a False King and Independence Movements." Pages 41–54 in *Revolt and Resistance in the Ancient Classical World and the Near East*. Edited by J.J. Collins and J.G. Manning. Leiden: Brill.

———. 2017. "Economy, Society, and Daily Life in the Neo-Assyrian Period." Pages 209–28 in *A Companion to Assyria*. Edited by E. Frahm. Hoboken: Wiley-Blackwell.

———. 2019. "The 'Lost Tribes of Israel' in the Context of the Resettlement Programme of the Assyrian Empire." Pages 101–23 in *The Last Days of the Kingdom of Israel*. Edited by S. Hasegawa, C. Levin, and K. Radner. Berlin: de Gruyter.

Radner, K., M. Masoumian, H. Karimian, E. Azizi, and K. Omidi. 2020. "Neo-Assyrian Royal Monuments from Lake Zeribar in Western Iran: A Stele of Sargon II and a Rock Relief of Shalmaneser III." *ZA* 110: 84–93.

Reich, R., and B. Brandl. 1985. "Gezer under Assyrian Rule." *PEQ* 117: 41–54.

Richardson, S. 2014. "The First 'World Event': Sennacherib in Jerusalem." Pages 433–505 in *Sennacherib at the Gates of Jerusalem: Story, History and Historiography*. Edited by I. Kalimi and S. Richardson, S. Leiden: Brill.

Rollinger, R. 2017. "Assyria in Classical Sources." Pages 570–82 in *A Companion to Assyria*. Edited by E. Frahm. Hoboken: Wiley-Blackwell.

Römer, T. 2015. *The Invention of God*. Cambridge: Harvard University Press.

Sano, K. 2020. *Die Deportationspraxis in neuassyrischer Zeit*. Münster: Ugarit-Verlag.

Sapir-Hen, L. 2017. "Pax Assyriaca and the Animal Economy in the Southern Levant: Regional and Local-Scale Imperial Contacts." Pages 341–53 in *Rethinking Israel: Studies in the History and Archaeology of Ancient Israel in Honor of Israel Finkelstein*. Edited by O. Lipschits, Y. Gadot, and M.J. Adams. Winona Lake: Eisenbrauns.

Sapir-Hen, L., Y. Gadot, and I. Finkelstein. 2014. "Environmental and Historical Impacts on Long Term Animal Economy: The Southern Levant in the Late Bronze and Iron Ages." *JESHO* 57: 703–44.

Sinopoli, C. M. 2003. *The Political Economy of Craft Production: Crafting Empire in South India, c.1350–1650*. Cambridge: Cambridge University Press.

Stager, L. E., D. M. Master, and J. D. Schloen. 2011. *Ashkelon 3: The Seventh Century B.C.* Winona Lake: Eisenbrauns.

Streit, K. 2021. "After The Storm: Political, Economic And Socio-Demographic Aspects of the Assyrian Defeat of the Southern Levant." Pages 261–86 in *Culture of Defeat*. Edited by K. Streit and M. Grohmann. Piscataway: Gorgias Press. 261–286.

Tappy, R.E. 2019. "The Annals of Sargon II and the Archaeology of Samaria: Rhetorical Claims, Empirical Evidence." Pages 147–87 in *The Last Days of the Kingdom of Israel*. Edited by S. Hasegawa, C. Levin, and K. Radner. Berlin: de Gruyter.

Thareani, Y. 2016a. "The Empire and the 'Upper Sea': Assyrian Control Strategies along the Southern Levantine Coast." *BASOR* 375: 77–102.

———. 2016b. "Imperializing the province: A residence of a Neo-Assyrian city governor at Tel Dan." *Levant* 48: 254–83.

———. 2018. "Revenge of the Conquered: Paths of Resistance in the Assyrian City of Dan." *Semitica* 60: 473–92.

———. 2019. "From Expelled Refugee to Imperial Envoy: Assyria's Deportation Policy in Light of the Archaeological Evidence from Tel Dan." *JAA* 54: 218–34.

Tyson, C. W. 2014. *The Ammonites: Elites, Empires, and Sociopolitical Change (1000–500 BCE)*. London: Bloomsbury.

Tyson, C. W., and V. R. Herrmann. 2019. *Imperial Peripheries in the Neo-Assyrian Period*. Louisville: The University Press of Colorado.

Uehlinger, C. 2007. "Neither Eyewitnesses, Nor Windows the to the Past, but Valuable Testimony in Its Own Right: Remarks on Iconography, Source Criticism and Ancient Data-Processing." Pages 173–228 in *Understanding the History of Israel*. Edited by H. G. M. Wilkinson. Oxford: Oxford University Press.

Valk, J. 2020. "Crime and Punishment: Deportation in the Levant in the Age of Assyrian Hegemony." *BASOR* 384: 77–103.

Van Der Kooij, A. 2012. "'Nimrod, A Mighty Hunter before the Lord!' Assyrian Royal Ideology as Perceived in the Hebrew Bible." *Journal for Semitics* 21: 1–27.

Wolf, S. R. 2021. "The Date of Destruction of Gezer Stratum VI." *TA* 48: 73–86.

Yamada, S. 2000. *The Construction of the Assyrian Empire: A Historical Study of the Inscriptions of Shalmanesar III (859–824 BC) Relating to His Campaigns to the West*. Leiden: Brill.

———. 2008. "Qurdi-Assur-Lamur: His Letters and Career." Pages 296–311 in *Treasures on Camels' Humps: Historical and Literary Studies from the Ancient Near East Presented to Israel Eph'al*. Edited by M. Cogan and D. Kahn. Jerusalem: The Hebrew University Magnes Press.

Younger, K. L. 2015. "The Assyrian Economic Impact on the Southern Levant in the Light of Recent Study." *IEJ* 65: 179–204.

———. 2018. "Assyria's Expansion West of the Euphrates (ca. 870-701 BCE)." Pages 17–33 *Archaeology and History of Eighth-Century Judah*. Edited by Z. I. Farber and J. L. Wright. Atlanta: SBL Press.

Zadok, R. 2015. "Israelites and Judaeans in the Neo-Assyrian Documentation (732-602 BCE): An Overview of the Sources and a Socio-Historical Assessment." *BASOR* 374: 159–89.

———. forthcoming. "Cuneiform Tablets." in *Tel Hadid I: Excavations during the Years 1995–1997*. Edited by I. Koch and E. Brand. Tel Aviv and University Park: Emery and Claire Yass Publications in Archaeology and Eisenbrauns.

Zilberg, P. 2015. "A New Edition of the Tel Keisan Cuneiform Tablet." *IEJ* 65: 90–95.

———. 2018. "The Assyrian Provinces of the Southern Levant: Sources, Administration, and Control." Pages 59–88 in *The Southern Levant under Assyrian Domination*. Edited by S. Z. Aster and A. Faust. University Park: Eisenbrauns.

Zori, C. M. 2011. *Metals for the Inka: Craft Production and Empire in the Quebrada de Tarapaca, Northern Chile*. PhD diss., University of California, Los Angeles.

44
BABYLON AND ISRAEL
Cultural Contact and Cultural Impact

Laurie E. Pearce

Babylon's fame towers over that of any city of ancient Mesopotamia. Its hanging gardens[1] and imposing walls and ziggurat—wonders of the ancient world—have captured the attention and imagination of writers, historians, artists, and musicians from antiquity to the modern era. Modern reception studies address the visual, auditory, and plastic representations and interpretations of the city's glory, as well as its shame, symbolized in the topos of the Whore of Babylon (Verderame and Garcia-Ventura 2020). Among other media, operatic arias and cinematic extravaganzas perpetuate receptions of Babylon's power and fame,[2] particularly in its connections to the history and fate of the kingdoms of Israel and Judah.

Central to the biblical narratives concerned with the history of the Second Temple Period and the development of early Judaism, Nebuchadnezzar's subjugation and deportation of Judah, and Judah's eventual return, has earned it a position of importance, disproportionate to its size and role in the imperial history of which it is part. Babylonian sources provide a more balanced assessment of Babylon's impact on Judah. The present exploration of Babylon's impact on Judah considers the following: (1) Babylon's treatment of peripheral provinces and deportee populations; (2) identification of foreign populations and their social standing; (3) documentary evidence for Babylon's impact in the Levant; (4) locations and contexts of intellectual and cultural contact; and (5) Babylon's impact on the re-formation of Judean identity.

Babylon's Treatment of Provinces and Deportees

Descriptions of Jerusalem's capture (2 Kgs 24: 12–16), successive waves of Judean deportations (Jer 52: 28–30), and Cyrus' edict of return (Ezra 1: 1–3) presented in biblical narratives and in prophetic and psalmodic passages must be read against sources that originate in two Mesopotamian empires, Babylonia and Persia. The corpus of more than 35,000 cuneiform texts from the late 7th to early 5th centuries BCE (625–484 BCE)—termed "the long sixth century" (Jursa 2010: 5)—reflect continuity in social and economic practices and policies that affected deportee life. These texts help identify the differences that existed between Babylonian and Assyrian imperial policy.

Assyrian kings as early as Tukulti-Ninurta I (1244–1208 BCE) recorded their treatment of enemies, defeated populations, and deportees in detailed words and/or images. Assyrian policies were designed to minimize and punish resistance while allocating human resources throughout the empire; some groups were removed from their homelands and settled in disparate locations, among them the Israelites, whence the notion of "the ten lost tribes."

Contrary to Assyrian sources, Babylonian historical records provide no details of their deportation practices. In spite of the strategic importance and geographic scope of Nabopolassar's and Nebuchadnezzar's campaigns to the west, the chronicle reports are characteristically terse, as in the record of the assault on Jerusalem in 597 BCE:

> In the seventh year: In the month Kislev, the king of Akkad mustered his army and marched to Ḫattu. He encamped against the city of Judah and on the second day of the month Adar he captured the city (and) seized (its) king. A king of his own choice, he appointed in the city (and) taking the vast tribute he brought it into Babylon.
> (ABC 5: 102)

Like other chronicles, this laconic report, the only reference to Judah in Babylonian historical sources, offers no evidence of Babylon's resettlement practices. Those must be deduced from administrative records, where onomastic and geographic data provide important clues to Babylonia's unidirectional policy of relocating royal and non-royal deportees.

As Babylonia did not transfer populations to fill demographic vacuums created in the wake of deportations, the scale of human movement never approached that documented for the Assyrian empire. Babylonia characteristically retained the communal integrity of its deportee communities, resettling significant numbers of individuals from a single locale together in new settlements termed *mirror (or twin) towns*, named for the inhabitants' place of origin. Their location at the outskirts or at a distance from urban centers fostered a degree of social cohesion among deportees and may have contributed to the maintenance of some cultural practices from their homelands.

Most mirror towns have been identified due to their role as the place in which a transaction occurred. Attestations of mirror towns are concentrated in texts from the Murašû archive, establishing their proximity to Nippur, where this group of approximately 700 texts was excavated in the late 19th century.[3] These documents, dating to the second half of the 5th century BCE (454–405 BCE), record entrepreneurial activities of Murašû family members who held lands, granted by the crown, encumbered with tax and military service obligations. The military obligations are reflected in the lands' designation as *bīt qašti* ("bow lands"), *bīt sīsê* ("horse land"), and *bīt narkabti* ("chariot land"), and in the articulation of associated responsibilities to provide archers, horses, and chariots, respectively (Alstola 2020: 108–10). These lands were leased to members of communities, *ḫadru*s, organized around their members' professional or geographic background: e.g., [lú]*maṣṣarū bābāti* ("gate guards"), [lú]*Arūmāya* (an Iranian group), [lú]*Ṣūrāya* (Tyrians).

Although not referenced in the Murašû texts, transactions that occurred in and around the mirror town *ālu ša Yāḫūdāya*, "the town of the Judeans," (Joannès and Lemaire 1999; Pearce and Wunsch 2014) are of the same nature as activities attested in the Nippur corpus.[4] These texts establish that the Judeans were settled in this mirror town and participated in the land-for-service sector. *ālu ša Yāḫūdāya* is first attested (CUSAS 28 1) in the 33rd year of the reign of Nebuchadnezzar II (572 BCE), roughly two decades after the initial wave of Judean deportations (2 Kgs 24:12; Jer 52:28), and approximately 130 years prior to the earliest recorded Murašû family transactions. The significance of this text group is clear: It contextualizes the impact of exile on the Judeans (as well as other deportee groups) as a crucial labor source for measures implemented to revitalize agricultural lands decimated in the Assyro-Babylonian wars and establishes continuity of the Judean community from the earliest days in Babylon through the end of the Babylonian archives (Pearce and Wunsch 2014: 4–5; Waerzeggers 2003–04).

Nebuchadnezzar II's extensive re-building program of Babylon's temple(s), walls, and famously, the Ishtar Gate, depended on financing derived from tribute from defeated polities and on taxes collected in Babylon's urban centers. For the reinvigorating empire, settlement of deportees in the lands around Nippur provided alimentary and financial support, through intensified agricultural output and the expansion of the practice of granting parcels of land in exchange for payment of taxes and fulfillment of military service. The persistence, well into the Persian period, of mirror towns in the land-for-service economic sector, reinforces our perception of the stability of the economic environment in which deportees lived. Moreover, these administrative documents offer a perspective on deportees' lives, especially in lower sectors of Babylonian society and economy.

Identification of Foreign Populations and Their Social Standing

Although Babylonian sources do not detail the process of resettling deportee groups, administrative records provide glimpses of Judeans (and others) living among and interacting with residents of Babylon's urban centers and rural regions. Detecting the participation of Judeans and other foreigners depends on identifying them as individuals and groups in the sources. Two linguistic features facilitate this task, namely, the use of gentilics (adjectives that describe a person's place of origin) and the distinctive linguistic background of personal names.

Gentilics are formed in Akkadian by appending the suffix -*āya* to a toponym, e.g., *Ṣūrāya* (Tyrian [Akkadian, *ṣūru*]), *Arbāya* (Arabian), *Miṣirāya* (Egyptian [Akkadian, *miṣru*]), and *Yāḫūdāya* (Judean). Gentilics primarily designate groups of individuals from the marked toponyms and rarely apply to named persons. A notable exception is their use to label individual Egyptian-Carians, which likely reflects a different imperial perception of the social standing of individual members of this group.[5]

Although the gentilic "Judean" does not label any individual person (named or otherwise), the designation applies to a group of persons identified in the Weidner Ration Lists (Weidner 1939). This group of texts excavated in Nebuchadnezzar II's South Palace lists rations provided to individuals—including kings, high officials, and royal family members—grouped and labeled by their places of origin, including, e.g., lú*Yāḫūdāya*, Judean(s). Within geographically defined groups, professional designations are more frequent than personal names: Egyptians (*Miṣirāya*) are marked as guards of the palace administrative area (*bīt qīpūti*) and of the boatyard (*bīt sapīnāti*), boatmen (*malāḫū*), and monkey keeper (*šušān uqūpē*), a position charged with care and training of animals kept for court entertainment. The notable exception to the anonymity of persons listed in the ration lists is the identification by name of the deported Judean king, Jehoiachin. He and his five (unnamed) sons received ration allotments larger than others listed, a fact that aligns with the description in 2 Kgs 25:27–30 of Evil-Merodach (= Babylonian Amēl-Marduk)'s alleged beneficences toward Jehoiachin. However, motivations prompting the composition of each narrative associated with Jehoiachin's detention differ dramatically. Babylon-issued rations to members of deported royal households (including craftsmen who labored for the Babylonian empire) were sufficient, but hardly sumptuous. By creating an impression of concern for the good and welfare of deported rulers, Babylon may have aimed to mitigate antagonism from the captives' homelands and populace. On the other hand, the biblical narrative offers to the exiles a theologically driven message of hope and return.[6]

Evidence for the treatment of defeated and deported rulers also appears in the final section of the Nebuchadnezzar Prism (*Hofkalendar*), which appends to a standard Neo-Babylonian building inscription a list of "palace officials, governors of provinces and tribal areas, and officials in charge of the Babylonian cities." In groupings that represent the three sectors of the Neo-Babylonian imperial administration, the text lists, according to their place of origin, persons assigned to *corvée* work (Da Riva 2013: 197, 204). Whether or not the (now destroyed) eighth face of the prism originally contained a reference to the Judean king or palace officials, the text confirms the obligation of deportee populations to provide equal quantities of mandatory labor.

In addition to toponyms and gentilics, specific components in personal names may support the identification of a person's background. Theophoric elements, integral components of a large percentage of Semitic personal names, can be diagnostic. Associated (nearly) exclusively with Judean and Israelite cultic practice, the divine element Yahweh (represented in cuneiform as *Yāḫû* or *Yāma*) is considered a reliable marker of a person's background. Yahwistic names identified in the earliest publications of the Murašû texts confirmed a presence of Judeans in Babylonia from 454–405 BCE; the texts from Yāḫūdu increases to approximately 280 the total number of Judeans participating in the Babylonian economy from 591–413 BCE (Alstola 2020: 57).

Onomastic Evidence of Acculturation

Names with distinctive and culturally specific components permit tracing patterns both of acculturation and the avoidance of acculturation of individuals under the influence of an imperial power (Bickerman 1978; Golub and Zilberg 2019). The Ariḫ family tree (Figure 44.1) demonstrates the critical role a single distinctive name may play in determining the background of a particular family, and the degree of acculturation that may be evident even in a single family of deportee descendants. Ariḫ's four known grandsons all bear Babylonian names, as does his granddaughter. However, the names of two of his four sons point to the family's Judean origins: Amušeḫ (Hebrew *Hôšēᵃ'*) and Aḫī-Yāma ("Yahweh is my brother"). Aḫī-Yāma was one of two sons designated *tamkār šarri*, "royal merchant" (see below); the other, Basīya, bears a Babylonian name, confirming that all individuals in a single family did not have to adopt outward signs of acculturation in order to participate in economic activities, even in those with support from the crown. Additionally, the divergent linguistic backgrounds of the *tamkār šarri* brothers' names point to a milieu in which foreigners were integrated into the vital imperial economy while allowing for the expression of cultural differences.

Beamtennamen

One pattern of name construction has particular utility in identifying the social status of the individuals who bear them. *Beamtennamen* ("officials' names"), formulated with *šarru(m)*, "king", as the verbal object (e.g., Nabû-šar-uṣur, "O Nabû! Protect the king!"), designate individuals with a connection to the court. The name Yāḫû-šar-uṣur ("O Yahweh! Protect the king!"), which combines the Judean god's name with a wholly Babylonian predicate, appears in two different scenarios demonstrating onomastic accommodation as a marker of acculturation.

First, three texts from the early days of Judean presence in Babylonia preserve instances in which the name Yāḫû-šar-uṣur alternates with the wholly Babylonian name, Bēl-šar-uṣur, designating the same person.[7] The substitution of the name of the Babylonian god Bēl demonstrates that Babylonians (or at least the scribes composing these documents) recognized

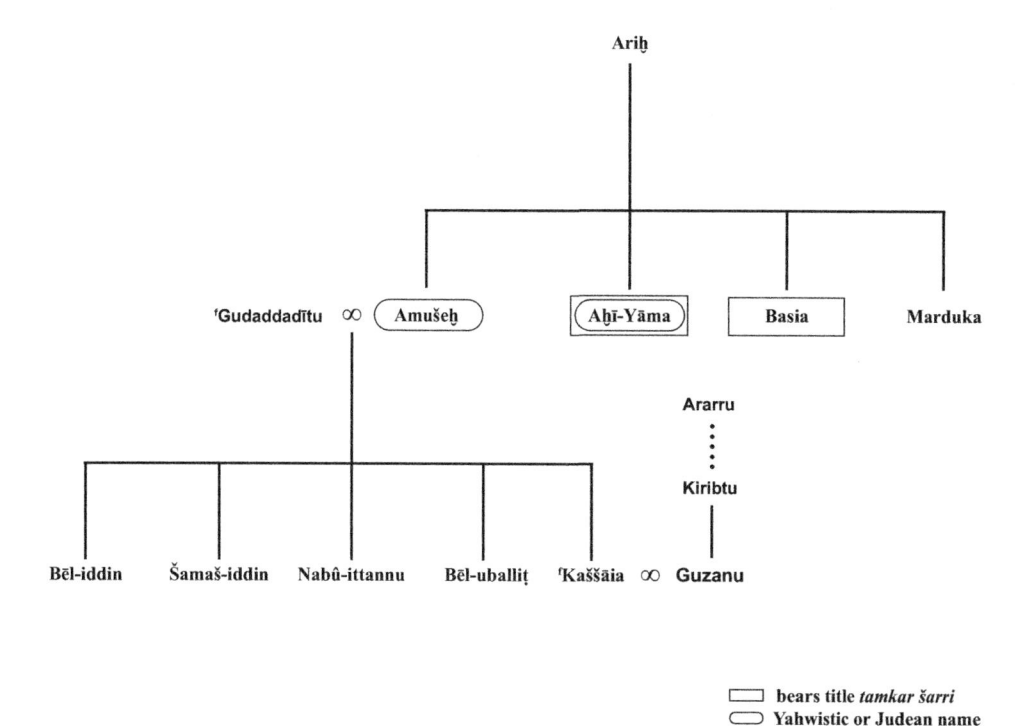

```
                          Ariḫ
                            |
    ┌───────────┬──────────┬──────────┐
'Gudaddadītu ∞ Amušeḫ   Aḫī-Yāma    Basia    Marduka
    |
    |                            Ararru
    |                              ⋮
    |                            Kiribtu
    |                              |
┌───────┬───────────┬──────────┬────────┐
Bēl-iddin Šamaš-iddin Nabû-ittannu Bēl-uballiṭ 'Kaššāia ∞ Guzanu
```

▭ bears title *tamkar šarri*
⌒ Yahwistic or Judean name

Figure 44.1 Ariḫ family tree

that, in the Judean cultic environment, Yahweh occupied a position equivalent to that of Babylon's supreme deity, Bēl (Marduk; Pearce and Wunsch 2014: 101–02). Although Yāḫû-šar-uṣur's role in the administration cannot be determined from the preserved evidence, his use of a *Beamtenname* acknowledges Babylonian receptivity to incorporating members of outside communities into the administrative hierarchy.[8]

Second, in a text from Susa (OECT 10 152), the wholly Babylonian name of the father of the witness named Yāḫû-šar-uṣur suggests that well into the reign of Darius, even as they primed their offspring for administrative careers, Judean families retained an attachment to their cultural heritage.

Royal Service

The biblical books of Nehemiah and Esther narrate the experiences of two Judeans at court. Imperial service was one means of social advancement. Although few could expect to achieve the standing of those two figures, Judeans are attested in positions of authority in Persian period Yehud. Their need and/or desire to collaborate with the state may have incentivized their expansion of administrative centers, such as Ramat Raḥel. This complex, one of the few physical markers of Judah's place in the imperial organization and understood to have been a Persian *paradise*,[9] would have impressed at least the local nobles, and accreted to the local Judean governor(s) social standing appropriate to an agent of the *Pax Persica* (Silverman 2020: 8–10). This physical imprint of the imperial agenda is correlated to the transformation of the iconographic encapsulation of imperial ideology into the performativity of Ezra's presentation of the law to an assembly of Judeans (see below).

The standing of Nehemiah as royal cupbearer, *mashqeh* (משקה; Neh 1:9–2:6) is frequently invoked as evidence that Persian period Judeans had attained high social standing within the court. A title cognate with Hebrew *mashqeh* is unattested in the cuneiform sources. However, in the *Hofkalendar*'s inventory of court officials, the title "chief baker" (*rab nuḫatimmī*) appears among the group of high palace officials. The holder of this title likely bore responsibility for the royal table, and should not be considered a royal title (Da Riva 2013: 202). Nabû-zēr-iddin, the chief baker named in the *Hofkalendar*, is attested in other contemporaneous sources, but rarely outside of Babylon. However, members of his staff appear in sources from other cities, suggesting mobility for lower-level functionaries. If it is reasonable to assume that Nehemiah, as a member of the corps responsible for the royal table, would have enjoyed degrees of mobility and responsibility similar to those of the chief baker, Nehemiah's theologically driven request for leave to return to "Judah, unto the city of my father's sepulchers" (Neh 2:6) in order to rebuild Jerusalem may have been consistent with patterns of activity and movement among various court officials, for which evidence, albeit limited, exists.

Two texts document Judean presence at or in proximity to the court at the Persian capital Susa. Written in consecutive years (494–493 BCE), they provide snapshots of the individuals' social situation, but offer no indication of the process by which Judeans might have gained entrée into such positions. OECT 10 152, written in Susa on 18 Nisan of Darius' 28th year, records a loan of silver to be repaid in Babylon by the debtor, a member of the famous Achaemenid-period entrepreneurial Egibi family[10] to a member of the Ea-ēppeš-ili family. All the witnesses, except one, bear clan names indicating they belonged to the urban elite of Babylonia; the exception is Yāḫû-šar-uṣur son of Šamaš-iddin, mentioned above, whose *Beamtenname* indicates he had achieved sufficient social standing to be included among prominent Babylonians as witnesses to this transaction. VS 6 155, also written in Susa, includes a single Judean witness, Šabbatāya, whose father, Nabû-šar-bulliṭ, bears a *Beamtenname*. In this text, two of the witnesses, descendants of the prominent Šangû-Gula clan, bear official titles: "deputy of the one responsible for the *šušānu*-servicemen," and "the inspector of the Ekitušgina (located in the Babylonian city, Bāṣ) temple." Thus, Šabbatāya's cohort includes individuals with identifiable administrative standing, including oversight of cult installations.

Merchants

Texts from Sippar dating to 546–544 BCE, within the first two generations of exilic life, attest to Judean integration into the Babylonian mercantile sector (Jursa 2008; Bloch 2014: 153f.)—the Ariḫ family members Aḫi-Yāma and his Babylonian-named brother, both bear the title "royal merchant," a designation that is now used to characterize this Judean family (Jursa 2007). The precise standing and duties of royal merchants are not fully known, although it is clear that they enjoyed the support of temple and crown. Their presence at Sippar suggests a social environment that welcomed foreigners, especially skilled deportees, to urban centers where their abilities could be exploited for the benefit of the crown. Sippar's standing as an important urban and economic center can be linked further to the Judean experience in Babylon via the administrative document recording a shipment, in 594 BCE, of gold to Babylon at the order of Nabû-šarrūssu-ukīn, *rab ša rēš āli* (a military designation), present at the assault on Jerusalem (Vanderhooft 1999: 149–52; Jursa 2008, 2011: 164; Jer 39:3). At some point following the Jerusalem assault in 597 BCE, Nabû-šarrūssu-ukīn returned to Babylonia; between 597 and 594 BCE, the date of the dispatch, deported Judean merchants would have passed through or near Sippar, one of the northern-most cities en route from the Euphrates crossings into the Mesopotamian heartland. The Babylonians, recognizing the potential of integrating skilled merchants into the mercantile activities in the urban center, may have encouraged or required the settlement of Judean merchants at Sippar, instead of with their comrades in the Nippur countryside. It is difficult to detect individual gain in available sources, but the possibility must be considered that some deportees profited personally even if their fortunes did not expand to match those of families like the Egibi. Regardless of the Judeans' standing in Babylonia's economic networks, Babylonian vocabulary of mercantile commerce made its way into the prophetic book of Ezekiel, adding to the intellectual dimension of Babylon's impact on Judah (see below).

Farmers

Biblical reports record that Nebuchadnezzar deported all the Judean royalty, upper classes, and skilled craftsmen, leaving only the poorest of the poor in the land:

> And he (Nebuchadnezzar) carried away all Jerusalem, and all the princes, and all the mighty men of valor, even ten thousand captives, and all the craftsmen and the smiths; none remained, save the poorest sort of the people of the land.
>
> *(2 Kgs 24: 12–16)*

Although the Murašû texts post-date Nebuchadnezzar's deportations by some 150 years, their discovery underscored a discrepancy between the social standing of the biblical listing of persons deported and the relatively poor Judean farmers attested there. The Yāḫūdu texts clarify the genesis of Judean participation in the agricultural sector of the economy. CUSAS 28 2 states that the Judean, Ṣidqi-Yāma, held a plot of land termed *bīt azanni*, "quiver land." The etymology of this less common land designation associates it with the military service obligations defining the land-for-service model. Prosopographical evidence places this earliest known Judean involvement in the land-for-service sector toward the end of Nebuchadnezzar's reign (604–562 BCE), even though the year number is not preserved (Waerzeggers 2015: 189). It also stands in close chronological proximity to the earliest dateable attestation of a bow-fief in Nebuchadnezzar's 35th year (569 BCE). While it is impossible to draw a direct line from Ṣidqi-Yāma to Judeans attested in the Murašû documents, this text confirms immediate installation of Judean deportees in rural, agricultural lands of the type the Murašû administered. Additional documents from Yāḫūdu illustrate their participation paralleled the developing system.

In the land-for-service system, populations sharing a common geographic, ethnic, or professional background were constituted into larger administrative units termed *ḫadru*. Although no *ḫadru* is explicitly associated with the Judeans or their town, features typical of *ḫadru* organizations are evident, notably in two rent-obligation lists containing a significant number of individuals bearing Yahwistic names. They are organized into groups of ten persons and listed under the rubric of the nominal debtor, a practice well attested in the administration of *ḫadru*. *Šušānû* ("horse trainer," a designation associated with military service) held the lands from which these rent payments were due. By the reign of Darius I, the term *šušānû* appears in designations of lands cultivated by Judeans. Together with the designation of Judeans as tax collectors (*dēkû*), the integration of the Judean population into administrative roles associated with the agricultural production sector points to imperial organization shaping the trajectory of Judean society in Mesopotamia and paving a way for Judeans to engage with Babylonians (and Persians) of varying social ranks, and to gain a foothold in the cosmopolitan world of those empires.

Documentary Evidence for Babylon's Impact in the Levant

Many details of Babylonian history, including details of its presence in the Levant, are lost to us, as excavations at Babylon have failed to yield state archives in buildings and areas that would be expected to hold them.[11] This stands in marked contrast to the extensive state archives of the Neo-Assyrian empire, with its thousands of letters and documents detailing aspects of provincial administration. Further limiting the corpus of evidence for details of imperial administration in Babylonia is the use of perishable writing materials in the production of texts written with alphabetic script. The limited epigraphic evidence originating in the provinces, including Judah, constrains our assessment of Babylon's and Persia's impact on them.

Cuneiform Sources, Administrative and Otherwise

Cuneiform sources originating from first millennium Levantine contexts are few. No objects inscribed with cuneiform can be reliably assigned to the Neo-Babylonian period; only four objects may belong to it or its successor, the Persian empire. An inscription in Neo-Babylonian cuneiform script on a bronze ringlet from Tel en-Naṣbeh (Mizpah) suggests a Babylonian presence at the site where Nebuchadnezzar installed Gedaliah as Judah's governor following Jerusalem's fall (Horowitz, Oshima, Sanders 2018: 22). However, the nature of the inscription, a private dedication of a son into service of a deity (Vanderhooft and Horowitz 2002: 323; Vanderhooft 2003: 253), offers no evidence for Babylonian administration in Judah.

From the excavations at Mikhmoret comes the solitary Persian period cuneiform administrative tablet from the region (Vanderhooft and Horowitz 2002: 323; Vanderhooft 2003:253). The language of the damaged text of this slave sale, dated to Cambyses' fifth year (525 BCE), follows the standard pattern of the genre. Otherwise unexceptional, it uniquely records the sale price in *pym* (/pi-im/), a Judean unit of weight, and its equivalent in shekels (the standard Babylonian and Persian unit of valuation of silver; 1 shekel =.75 *pym*). The presence of a Babylonian vendor on the coast points to an extension of demographic shifts that began under Assyrian domination (Spar, Paley, and Stieglitz 2018: 183), reflected in the "men of Erech (Uruk)" and Susa (Ezra 4:9–10), descendants of deportees from Assyrian reigns, who continued to populate Samaria generations after Cambyses's reign. The evidence for deportee populations conducting transactions in the imperial idiom while preserving local terminology points to an administration that acknowledged, but did not subsume, local convention. The Mikhmoret text thus provides a frustratingly rare example of ongoing interactions between imperial administrations and the local population.

Monuments as Imperial Markers

To announce its might, Assyria constructed palace reliefs and erected rock carvings and stelae throughout the empire. However, the Babylonian empire produced only the latter two to delineate imperial boundaries and display political ideologies. Rock reliefs and stelae mitigate gaps in our knowledge of imperial ideology and policy resulting from the absence of the elaborate visual and textual records of the palace reliefs that abundantly adorned Neo-Assyrian palaces. Their iconography illuminates the Babylonian imperial agenda program in ways that the terse language of the historiographic chronicles cannot capture. Although none is located in Judah, per se, the propagandistic message surely reverberated throughout the entire Levant.

Naḥr el-Kalb

The strategic locations of reliefs carved into stone walls flanking mountain passes, such as those at Naḥr el-Kalb (the Biqaʻ valley, Lebanon), presented passers-by with explicit and implicit statements of Babylon's power. Once the focus of Assyrian campaigns, by the late 9th century BCE, the Biqaʻ suffered regional decline, until Assyria began to resettle peoples there to offset later incursions of Arab population groups into the region (Da Riva 2012: 13–14). While Babylonian kings did not adopt a resettlement strategy here or in any area in the imperial periphery, the area remained strategically important, as the pass was located at a point from which the Babylonian army would move to enter Egyptian territory. The relief directly, if symbolically, challenged Egyptian power (Da Riva 2015: 617), and passers-by would have absorbed the message of Babylon's power.

Nabonidus' stele at Selaʻ

Free standing stela established at important communication and trade junctures likewise expressed imperial objectives. Nabonidus' still inexplicable 10-year sojourn at Tayma—an absence from Babylon which contributed to his fall to Cyrus (Eichmann et al. 2006: 169)—dominates the historiography of his reign. His assumed route from Babylon to Tayma passed through the fertile crescent, and down into Edom (Ephʻal 1982: 185–88; Dalley and Goguel 1997). At Selaʻ, he commissioned a rock monument, which, although now badly effaced, confirms a Babylonian presence in Edom at a strategic location near the caravan route connecting Gaza, Beersheba, and the southern Dead Sea (Da Riva 2015: 620–21). Two explanations for the setting up of this monument are offered: (a) commemoration of Nabonidus' departure from Babylon for Tayma, or (b) commemoration of military activity, as suggested by the Harran and Tayma stelae records of Nabonidus's travels and the Arabians' taking up of arms against the moon god (Zayadine 1999: 88).

While Babylon's presence in Edom has no immediate bearing on its impact on Judah, this was a region characterized by permeable borders. Edomites were attested in Judah prior to Babylon's rule, and ostraca from Arad attest to Edomite activity in southern Judah prior to Nebuchadnezzar's foray into the region (Pardee 2003: esp. letters 24, 40). Nabonidus' presence in Edom may have prompted the additional movement of some Edomites into southern Judah. The ill-defined territories and the marginal status of Judah in the Mesopotamian empires may have allowed for increased inter-community contact. In the wake of Cambyses' western campaigns (Stern 2007: 235–37), additional deportations of individuals from the southern Levant to Babylonia could account for individuals with Judean and Edomite names co-occurring in a cuneiform source from Yāḫūdu. CUSAS 28 30 (507 BCE, reign of Darius II) records that Bulluṭâ son of Qūs-rahā, an individual with a Babylonian name and Edomite patronymic, entered into an agreement with a Judean (Haggâ son of Yāḫû-azar) regarding the leasing of a cow. The evidence for Edomites in Babylonia is sparse, and their names are notoriously difficult to distinguish from Arabian ones (Zadok 2013: 264, n. 5). Yet this particular document may reflect the outcome of political fluidity in Judah and Edom, with the result that these two populations interacted both in the home as well as in their exilic locales.

Thus, the monuments of Neo-Babylonian kings, from Nebuchadnezzar to Nabonidus, impacted regions proximate to Judah by affirming imperial boundaries and Babylonian presence at important commercial and strategic crossroads.

Laurie E. Pearce

Locations and Contexts of Intellectual and Cultural Contact

Babylon's intellectual impact on Israel and Judah was recognized from the earliest days of Assyriology, notably preserved in the tale of George Smith's dancing on tables in the British Museum's Arch Room upon recognizing close textual parallels between the flood narratives of the Gilgamesh epic and the Bible. The historiography of the study of Judeans in Babylonia is roughly coeval with the trajectory of the exploration of biblical and Assyriological parallels initiated in F. Delitzsch's controversial 1902 "Bibel und Babel" lecture. The first 94 Murašû texts published in 1898 by A.T. Clay and Hermann Hilprecht, Delitzsch's own student, did not figure in the discussion, as activities of poor Judean tenant farmers could hardly have been expected to have impacted the biblical text or to contribute to understanding the exiles' intellectual life. In spite of the fact that cultural influence of Babylon on Judah is evident in their literary outputs, it is much more difficult to identify and contextualize *where* and *how* such contact occurred. However, Ezekiel scholarship, particularly in the last four decades, demonstrates that Babylonian intellectual activity contributed to the shaping of that prophetic book and influenced other aspects of the evolution of the Judean cultural record.

Geographic proximity provided contexts in which intellectual contact between Babylonians and Judeans could occur and evolve. Cuneiform administrative texts attest to the presence of Judean exiles and their descendants in or near several major Babylonian and Persian cities and waterways. The Chebar canal (*Nār Kabara*), the purported locus of Ezekiel's prophetic activity (Ezek 1:1, 3; 3:16, 23; 10:15, 20, 22; 43:3), ran through the rural countryside in the vicinity of Yāḫūdu. In its flow toward Susa, the canal ran near Babylon and Nippur (Waerzeggers 2010: 804; Tolini 2011: 491–98); the suggestion that boats were transferred at the mound of the Nār Kabara points to the canal's strategic location in trade. Reinforcing the notion that the Nār Kabara served as a locus of Babylonian and Judean contact and interaction is the fact that a transaction, dated to the fourth year of Xerxes' reign, occurred at the "town of the Chebar canal", *(āl) Nār Kabari* (Zilberg, Pearce, and Jursa 2019) and references a middle-level administrator, Zababa-šar-uṣur, who had demonstrable, if indirect, connections to the community of Judeans (Joannès and Lemaire 1996; Al-Bayati 2021). As Ezekiel's 20 years of prophetic activity is said to have begun c. 593 BCE, his arrival in Babylon coincides with the early Judean participation in Babylonian commerce in Susa, the destination of the commercial route of which Nār Kabara was a part. In that environment, Ezekiel could have encountered Babylonian merchants and casually acquired the Babylonian vocabulary of commerce that appears in the biblical text. But this would not account for the range and depth of Babylonian learning that marks Ezekiel as the repository of the greatest number of Akkadian loanwords, hapax legomena, and calques in the Hebrew Bible (Winitzer 2014:165–66, Table 1e).

Of several scenarios proposed to identify where and how transmission occurred, the most notable is the suggestion that Ezekiel attended the *edubba* ("the tablet house," the cuneiform scribal school) and mastered its standard curriculum (Stökl 2015: 51, 54f.; Winitzer 2014: 165–66). Scribal training included several stages of learning: (1) production of sign forms and the writing of personal names; (2) standard vocabulary lists, and in the advanced stages, (3) training in literary structures and hermeneutic techniques (Robson 2001:47). While it is unlikely that a 30-year-old Judean would have attended Babylonian scribal school, an Ezekiel-like figure could have recognized the value of sending his children to Babylonian school, initiating the Judean community's exposure to and immersion in the cuneiform scribal curriculum.

Literate members of the Judean community, trained in the scribal and priestly arts in Judah, surely continued training in their tradition (Sweeney 2020: §1). Prior to his return, Ezra the scribe, deemed "skilled in the Torah of Moses" (Ezra 7:6), had lived far from Jerusalem and maintained an identification with Israel and Torah, which presupposed "that the community in Babylon had a Torah scroll and that Ezra (and others) not only read (or recited) it but also made a point of studying it" (Knoppers 2009: 156). Ezra's focus on teaching upon his return from exile, even though the Torah Ezra was teaching did not prioritize pedagogy as Levitical duty, marks a shift in the conception of Judean identity (Knoppers 2009: 160–61). This also underscores the impact of scribal training, including its Babylonian expression, on the development of Judean identity.

Historically, the Judeans were not the only population on which Babylonian schools and their standardized curriculum had an impact. Cuneiform schools were present in the Levant, Anatolia, and North Syria from the Late Bronze Age, at major sites such as Ugarit, Emar, Nuzi, Amarna, and in smaller polities like Hazor, Ashkelon, Megiddo, and Aphek (Horowitz, Oshima, and Sanders 2018). But the recent study demonstrating the integration of features of the cuneiform scribal curriculum into the training of scribes utilizing alphabetic scripts in the first millennium BCE Levant, epitomized in the Kuntillet 'Ajrud corpus (Schniedewind 2019), confirms the impact of Babylonian learning on literacies throughout the region.

Babylonian impact on the composition of the biblical historiographic Chronicles is also widely acknowledged (Liverani 2010: 184). Just as with Ezekiel, it is a challenge to identify scenarios in which contact could have occurred between urban priests, the producers and transmitters of Babylonian chronicle texts, along with members of the urban elite with whom the priests regularly interacted, and the community of Judeans resident in Babylonia. The temples of the Babylonian cities Sippar, Babylon, and Borsippa served as sites of chronicle production and deposition. While Borsippa's temple was the most active chronicle producer, social network analysis suggests that the most likely paths of potential encounters in which Judeans could have been exposed both to the Babylonians responsible for chronicle production and to the texts themselves occurred in Sippar (Waerzeggers 2014: 140). One plausible example of such contact appears in the marriage of a Judean merchant's daughter to a Sippareaen related to an Ebabbar temple scribe who also held priestly offices (Waerzeggers 2014: 140–41). However, a plausible locus for contact does not explain the process or the means of transmission. Notably, Babylonian chronicles, apart from the literary Weidner Chronicle, are not considered part of the scribal school curriculum. Nonetheless, the close formal relationship between the Babylonian chronicles and the biblical book speaks to the Babylonian influence on the Judeans, as well as to the exiles' adaptation to the local intellectual environment.

Babylon and the Re-Formation of Judean Identity

The Judean exilic experience in Babylon catalyzed the process of transforming Judean identity into Jewish identity, a complex process reflected in numerous biblical passages. Two in particular—Nehemiah 8:1–8 and Ezra 9–10—focus on issues that are concerned with perceived distinctions between "us" and "them", and thus may be considered for indications of Babylon's impact on the Judean community following its return to Yehud.

Nehemiah 8:1–8, which records Ezra's ceremonial presentation of the law to the congregation of returned Judeans, is considered a foundational text for the restoration of Israel. A recent study suggests that this passage constitutes a liturgy and echoes the performativity captured in the

Apadana reliefs at Persepolis (Whitters 2017: 65). In this view, while the returnees enjoyed the beneficences of the Persian king, their marginal political status influenced their development of a ceremony that would curry and retain favor with their Persian overlords and with sympathizers in and around Yehud. Ezra faces the assembled congregations in a public location and parades the scroll to the place from which he reads it. He is flanked by attendants in formal pose, blessings are exchanged, the people prostrate themselves in acceptance of the law. This ceremony incorporates the Apadana's ideological message of the ideal empire and transforms it into an expression of Yahweh's hegemony (Whitters 2017). As in the case of the influence of Babylonian chronicles on the biblical books, it is impossible to identify agents or loci of transmission. Nevertheless, the cultural milieu and the contemporaneity of the literary settings render plausible such borrowings as a nuanced expression of how "we" Judeans differed from "them," affirming their identity while subtly signaling acceptance of Persian rule.

Ezra 9–10 confronts identity formation in his response to the foreign wives of the returnees. The vast literature on the topic integrates sociological and anthropological theory (e.g., Eskenazi and Richards 1994; Southwood 2012), and recent work in the study of marriages in the cuneiform world of the Neo-Babylonian and Persian empires promises to inform the ongoing discussion.

Still's ground-breaking study employing social network analysis identifies marriage patterns in the priestly community of Borsippa. More than 70% of marriage alliances attested in Borsippa are hypergamous, joining individuals (typically, the brides) from lower-status priestly families into more prominent priestly families (Still 2019: 239). This arrangement guaranteed an income flow (from bridal dowries) into the upper social strata, and, in doing so, closed Borsippa's priestly families off to outsiders (Waerzeggers 2020: 105). A single marriage between an outsider and a member of Borsippa's priestly culture occurred with the marriage of king Neriglissar's (559–556 BCE) daughter to the high priest of Borsippa, a politically motivated union. The social, economic, and political ramifications of Babylonian marriage practices are evident, and their implications should be considered in ongoing study of Ezra's response to the foreign wives.

Among the hundreds of documents referencing legal and administrative matters related to Babylonian marriage, few marriage contracts survive—fewer still involving Judean partners (Waerzeggers 2020: 102–03). Aspects of hypergamous marriage are reflected in one text set in the social and entrepreneurial milieu of Sippar: it records the marriage of Ariḫ's granddaughter, Kaššaya, to the Babylonian, Gūzānu son of Kiribtu descendant of Ararru, whose family name (meaning "Miller") marks his membership in the upper social stratum (Bloch 2014: 142–52; Abraham 2015: 206–08; Alstola 2017). Kaššaya's marriage contract adheres to the patterns seen in all marriages of foreign wives to Babylonian husbands, including the "iron dagger clause." This clause, combined with the substantial financial divorce penalties to be imposed on the husband in the case of divorce (Waerzeggers 2020: 118), protected not only the husband but also his family from financial ruin and subsequent decrease in social standing. The recent analysis of marriage patterns at Borsippa and Sippar identifies issues of social standing and intermarriage reflected in Ezra's diatribe; further investigation of the marriage concerns in the biblical narrative may reveal the impact of Babylon's social and economic structures on the shaping and expectations of the community of returnees.

Concluding Observations

Babylon's impact on Judah is evident in both biblical and cuneiform records. In focusing on Babylonian texts dating from the start of the exile through the end of the archival documentation of the long 6th century, the impact of Babylonian rule on Judean deportees, from exiled king to tenant farmer, emerges. Babylonian policies, implemented to invigorate the Babylonian economy through relocation of deportee populations, contributed to the preservation of distinct community identity, evident in naming practices of new settlements, professional designations, and culture-specific elements of personal names. Babylonian society offered access to multiple levels of social and economic life in which Judean and other immigrant populations could participate. Hypergamy evident in marriage practices both protected the insularity and social standing among families in the priestly circles and provided an entrée for Judean integration into upper-class families in the host society. Geographic proximity promoted cultural contact, both in rural and urban settings, as evidenced in the numerous Babylonian influences on the vocabulary of Ezekiel and the social setting of the temples as the locus of chronicle production. These scenarios substantiate Babylon's cultural imprint on the returning Judean community, while the continuity of the diaspora community attests to the viability of the mechanisms of social integration.

Notes

1 Pointing to inconsistencies between the classical authors' descriptions of the gardens and the lack of textual or visual reference to them in Babylonian sources, Dalley (1994, 2002) proposes the famed gardens were not located in Babylon, but rather in the Assyrian capital, Nineveh. Although this suggestion has found some support (Foster 2004), it is not universally accepted.
2 For example, "Va, pensiero" (the Hebrew slave chorus) from Verdi's *Nabucco*, as well as the Babylon storyline of D. W. Griffith's 1916 film, *Intolerance*.
3 The majority of the Murašû texts are published in Clay 1904; Clay 1912; Donbaz and Stolper 1997; Stolper 1985.
4 At a point later in Nebuchadnezzar's reign, the settlement's name is shortened to Yāḫūdu, "Judah," and is so referenced here. The change is evident in the date formula in CUSAS 28 2; although the year of Nebuchadnezzar's reign is omitted from the text, prosopographical evidence points to a very late date in his reign (Waerzeggers 2015: 189).
5 Hackl and Jursa 2015 present the documentation and discuss the complex situation of the status of Egyptians and Egyptian-Carians in Babylonia, a topic beyond the scope of this essay.
6 Alstola 2020: 70-78.
7 CUSAS 28 2 (Nbk, year omitted), CUSAS 28 3 (Nbn 4); CUSAS 28 4 (Nbn 6).
8 While it is unprecedented to find substitution of the divine element from one linguistic and cultural context for another in the name formulation for a single person, instances of an individual bearing two names are attested. Apart from nicknames (attested primarily as shortened name forms, such as Zēr-iddin in lieu of Nabû-zēr-iddin), cuneiform sources record individuals who carried two distinct names. In the Hellenistic period, such names were introduced by the expression "whose other name is." The most prominent witness to this practice was in the name formula "Anu-uballiṭ, whose other name was Nikarchos." A building inscription from the reign of Seleucus informs us not only that Anu-uballiṭ was the city's chief administrator, responsible for reconstruction of Uruk's Rēš temple, but that he received his second, Greek, name directly from the king. This calls to mind the passage in Daniel 1:7, in which the chief administrator of Nebuchadnezzar's court assigned Babylonian names to Daniel and his colleagues, all of whom bore good Hebrew names. Daniel's new name, Belteshazzar, is a Hebraicized, abbreviated form of a name such as Marduk-balaṭ-šar-uṣur ("O Marduk! Protect the life of the king!"), itself a *Beamtenname*. Despite the many historical difficulties associated with the book of Daniel, its author was certainly aware of onomastic practices current in Babylonia from the long 6th century BCE onward.
9 For the political, philosophical, and religious symbolism of the *paridaida-* (Greek *paradeisoi*), a fertile garden bringing symmetry and order out of chaos, duplicating the divine paradise on earth, see Fakour (2021).
10 Wunsch (2007) provides a general description of the composition and activities of the Egibi family. Wunsch (2000) presents detailed analysis of the Egibi archive.
11 In Pedersén 2021's synthetic treatment of the excavations of Babylon, he notes the excavation in the Neo-Babylonian period levels of homes of private individuals, which have yielded private archives. See Pedersén (2005: 109–296) for detailed discussion of these archives.

Bibliography

Abraham, Kathleen. 2015. "Negotiating Marriage in Multicultural Babylonia: An Example from the Judean Community in Āl-Yāhūdu." Pages 33–57 in *Exile and Return: The Babylonian Context*. Edited by Jonathan Stökl and Caroline Waerzeggers. Berlin: De Gruyter.

Al-Bayati, Aminah Fadhil. 2021. *The Archive of Zababa-šarru-uṣur. Texts from the Iraq Museum*. Dresden: ISLET.

Alstola, Tero. 2017. "Judean Merchants in Babylonia and Their Participation in Long-Distance Trade." *WdO* 47: 25–51.

———. 2020. *Judeans in Babylonia: A Study of Deportees in the Sixth and Fifth Centuries BCE*. Leiden: Brill.

Bickerman, E. J. 1978. "The Generation of Ezra and Nehemiah." *Proceedings of the American Academy for Jewish Research* 45: 1–28.

Bloch, Yigal. 2014. "Judeans in Sippar and Susa during the First Century of the Babylonian Exile: Assimilation and Perseverance under Neo-Babylonian and Achaemenid Rule." *JANEH* 1: 119–72.

Clay, Albert. 1904. *Business Documents of Murashû Sons of Nippur Dated in the Reign of Darius II (424–404 B.C.)*. Philadelphia: Dept. of Archaeology and Paleontology of the University of Pennsylvania.

———. 1912. *Business Documents of Murashu Sons of Nippur Dated in the Reign of Darius II*. Philadelphia: University Museum.

Dalley, Stephanie. 1994. "Nineveh, Babylon and the Hanging Gardens: Cuneiform and Classical Sources Reconciled." *Iraq* 56: 45–58.

———. 2002. "More about the Hanging Gardens." Pages 67–73 in *Of Pots and Plans: Papers on the Archaeology and History of Mesopotamia and Syria Presented to David Oates in Honour of his 75th Birthday*. Edited by Lamia Al-Gailani Werr. London: NABU.

Dalley, Stephanie, and A. Goguel. 1997. "The Selaʿ Sculpture: A Neo-Babylonian Rock Relief in Southern Jordan." *ADAJ* 41: 169.

Da Riva, Rocío. 2012. *The Twin Inscriptions of Nebuchadnezzar at Brisa (Wadi Esh-Sharbin, Lebanon): A Historical and Philological Study*. Wien: Institut für Orientalistik der Universität Wien.

———. 2013. "Nebuchadnezzar II's Prism (EŞ 7834): A New Edition." *ZA* 103: 196–229.

———. 2015. "Enduring Images of an Ephemeral Empire. Neo-Babylonian Inscriptions and Representations on the Western Periphery." Pages 603–29 in *Mesopotamia in the Ancient World: Impact, Continuities, Parallels. Proceedings of the Seventh Symposium of the Melammu Project Held in Obergurgl, Austria, November 4–8, 2013*. Edited by Robert Rollinger and Erik van Dongen. Münster: Ugarit-Verlag.

Donbaz, Veysel, and Matthew Stolper. 1997. *Istanbul Murašû Texts*. Istanbul: Nederlands Historisch-Archaeologisch Instituut te Istanbul.

Eichmann, Ricardo, Hanspeter Schaudig, and Arnulf Hausleiter. 2006. "Archaeology and Epigraphy at Tayma (Saudi Arabia)." *Arabian Archaeology & Epigraphy* 17: 163–76.

Ephʿal, Israel. 1982. *The Ancient Arabs: Nomads on the Borders of the Fertile Crescent, 9th–5th Centuries B.C.* Jerusalem: Magnes Press.

Eskenazi, Tamara C., and Kent H. Richards, eds. 1994. *Second Temple Studies 2: Temple Community in the Persian Period*. Sheffield: JSOT Press.

Fakour, Mehrdad. 2021. "Garden i. Achaemenid Period." *Encyclopaedia Iranica* X/3: 297–98. https://iranicaonline.org. Accessed August 15, 2021.

Foster, Karen Polinger. 2004. "The Hanging Gardens of Nineveh." *Iraq* 66: 207–20.

Golub, Mitka R., and Peter Zilberg. 2019. "Judean Onomastic Trends from the Beginning of the Babylonian Diaspora." *Journal of Ancient Judaism* 9/3: 312–25.

Grayson, Albert. 2000. *Assyrian and Babylonian Chronicles*. Winona Lake: Eisenbrauns.

Hackl, Johannes, and Michael Jursa. 2015. "Egyptians in Babylonia in the Neo-Babylonian and Achaemenid Periods." Pages 57–70 in *Exile and Return: The Babylonian Context*. Edited by Jonathan Stökl and Caroline Waerzeggers. Berlin: De Gruyter.

Hilprecht, Hermann, and Albert T. Clay. 1898. *Business Documents of Murashû Sons of Nippur Dated in the Reign of Artaxerxes I. (464–424 B.C.)*. Philadelphia: University of Pennsylvania.

Horowitz, Wayne, Takayoshi Oshima, and Seth L. Sanders. 2018. *Cuneiform in Canaan: The Next Generation*. Winona Lake: Eisenbrauns.

Joannès, Francis, and André Lemaire. 1996. "Contrats babyloniens d'époque achéménide du Bît-abî Râm avec une épigraphie araméenne." *RA* 90: 41–60.

———. 1999. "Trois tablettes cunéiformes à l'onomastique ouest-sémitique." *Transeuphratène* 17: 17–34.
Jursa, Michael. 2007. "Eine Familie von Königskaufleuten judäischer Herkunft." *NABU* 2007/22: 23.
———. 2008. "Nabû-šarrūssu-ukīn, *rab ša-rēši*, und 'Nebusarsekim' (Jer. 39:3)." *NABU* 2008/5.
———., ed. 2010. *Aspects of the Economic History of Babylonia in the First Millennium BC: Economic Geography, Economic Mentalities, Agriculture, the Use of Money, and the Problem of Economic Growth*. Münster: Ugarit-Verlag.
———. 2011. "Höflinge (*ša rēši, ša rēš šarri, ustarbaru*) in babylonischen Quellen des ersten Jahrtausends." Pages 159–73 in *Ktesias' Welt = Ctesias' World*. Edited by Josef Wiesehöfer, Robert Rollinger, and Giovanni B. Lanfranchi. Wiesbaden: Harrassowitz.
Knoppers, Gary N. 2009. "Ethnicity, Genealogy, Geography, and Change: The Judean Communities of Babylon and Jerusalem in the Story of Ezra." Pages 147–71 in *Community Identity in Judean Historiography: Biblical and Comparative Perspectives*. Edited by Gary N. Knoppers and Kenneth A. Ristau. Winona Lake: Eisenbrauns.
Liverani, Mario. 2010. "The Book of Kings and Ancient Near Eastern Historiography." Pages 163–84 in *The Books of Kings: Sources, Composition, Historiography and Reception*. Edited by André Lemaire, Baruch Halpern, and Matthew J. Adams. Leiden: Brill.
Pardee, Dennis. 2003. "Arad Ostraca." Pages 81–85 in *The Context of Scripture 3: Archival Documents from the Biblical World*. Edited by William W. Hallo and K. Lawson Younger. Leiden: Brill.
Pearce, Laurie, and Cornelia Wunsch. 2014. *Documents of Judean Exiles and West Semites in Babylonia in the Collection of David Sofer*. Bethesda: CDL Press.
Pedersén, Olaf. 2005. *Archiv und Bibliotheken in Babylon: die Tontafeln der Grabung Robert Koldeweys 1899–1917*. Berlin: Deutsche Orient-Gesellschaft in Kommission bei sdv Saarländische Druckerei und Verlag.
Pedersén, Olaf. 2021. *Babylon. The Great City*. Münster: Zaphon.
Robson, Eleanor. 2001. "The Tablet House: A Scribal School in Old Babylonian Nippur." *RA* 93: 39–66.
Schniedewind, William M. 2019. *The Finger of the Scribe: How Scribes Learned to Write the Bible*. New York: Oxford University Press.
Silverman, Jason M. 2020. *Persian Royal-Judean Elite Engagements in the Early Teispid and Achaemenid Empire. The King's Acolytes*. London: T. &T. Clark.
Southwood, Katherine E. 2012. *Ethnicity and the Mixed Marriage Crisis in Ezra 9–10: An Anthropological Approach*. Oxford: Oxford University Press.
Spar, Ira, Samuel M. Paley, and Robert R. Stieglitz. 2018. "A Cuneiform Contract Fragment from Tel Mikhmoret." *IEJ* 68: 182–91.
Stern, Ian. 2007. "The Population of Persian-Period Idumea According to the Ostraca: A Study of Ethnic Boundaries and Ethnogenesis." Pages 205–38 in *A Time of Change: Judah and Its Neighbours in the Persian and Early Hellenistic Periods*. Edited by Yigal Levin. London: T. & T. Clark.
Still, Bastian. 2019. *The Social World of the Babylonian Priest*. Leiden: Brill.
Stökl, Jonathan. 2015. "Schoolboy Ezekiel: Remarks on the Transmission of Learning." *WdO* 45: 50–61.
Stolper, Matthew W. 1985. *Entrepreneurs and Empire: The Murašû Archive, the Murašû Firm, and Persian Rule in Babylonia*. Leiden: Nederlands Historisch-Archaeologisch Instituut te Istanbul.
Sweeney, Marvin A. 2020. "Ezekiel in Its Historical Context." In *The Oxford Handbook of Ezekiel*. Edited by Corrine L. Carvalho. New York: Oxford University Press. (Online edn, Oxford Academic, 8 Oct. 2020), https://doi.org/10.1093/oxfordhb/9780190634513.013.24, accessed 12 Aug. 2022.
Sweeney, Marvin A., 'Ezekiel in Its Historical Context', in Corrine Carvalho (ed.), The Oxford Handbook of Ezekiel (online edn, Oxford Academic, 8 Oct. 2020), https://doi.org/10.1093/oxfordhb/9780190634513.013.24, accessed 12 Aug. 2022.
Tolini, Gauthier. 2011. "La Babylonie et l'Iran. Les relations d'une province avec le coeur de l'empire Achéménide (539–331 avant nôtre ère)." Ph.D. diss., Université Paris I - Panthéon-Sorbonne.
Vanderhooft, David. 1999. *The Neo-Babylonian Empire and Babylon in the Latter Prophets*. Atlanta: Scholars Press.
———. 2003. "Babylonian Strategies of Imperial Control in the West: Royal Practice and Rhetoric." Pages 235–62 in *Judah and the Judeans in the Neo-Babylonian Period*. Edited by Oded Lipschits and Joseph Blenkinsopp. Winona Lake: Eisenbrauns.
Vanderhooft, David, and Wayne Horowitz. 2002. "The Cuneiform Inscription from Tell En-Naṣbeh: The Demise of an Unknown King." *TA* 29: 318–27.

Verderame, Lorenzo, and Agnès Garcia-Ventura, eds. 2020. *Receptions of the Ancient Near East in Popular Culture and Beyond.* Atlanta: Lockwood Press.

Waerzeggers, Caroline. 2003–04. "The Babylonian Revolts Against Xerxes and the 'End of Archives'." *AfO* 50: 150–73.

———. 2010. "Babylonians in Susa. The Travels of Babylonian 'Businessmen' to Susa Reconsidered." Pages 777–813 in *Der Achämenidenhof = The Achaemenid Court: Akten des 2. internationalen Kolloquiums zum Thema "Vorderasien im Spannungsfeld klassischer und altorientalischer Überlieferungen", Landgut Castelen.* Edited by Bruno Jacobs and Robert Rollinger. Wiesbaden: Harrassowitz.

———. 2014. "Locating Contact in the Babylonian Exile: Some Reflections on Tracing Judean-Babylonian Encounters in Cuneiform Texts." Pages 131–46 in *Encounters by the Rivers of Babylon: Scholarly Conversations Between Jews, Iranians, and Babylonians in Antiquity.* Edited by Uri Gabbay and Shai Secunda. Tübingen: Mohr Siebeck.

———. 2015. "Review of Laurie E. Pearce and Cornelia Wunsch, Documents of Judean Exiles and West Semites in Babylonia in the Collection of David Sofer. Cornell University Studies in Assyriology and Sumerology (CUSAS) 28." *STRATA* 33: 179–94.

———. 2020. "Changing Marriage Practices in Babylonia from the Late Assyrian to the Persian Period." *JANEH* 7: 101–31.

Weidner, Ernst. 1939. "Jojachin, König von Juda, in Babylonischen Keilschrifttexten." Pages 923–35 in *Mélanges Syriens Offerts à M. René Dussaud.* Paris: Paul Geunther.

Whitters, Mark. 2017. "The Persianized Liturgy of Nehemiah 8:1–8." *JBL* 136: 63–84.

Winitzer, Abraham. 2014. "Assyriology and Jewish Studies in Tel Aviv: Ezekiel among the Babylonian Literati." Pages 163–216 in *Encounters by the Rivers of Babylon: Scholarly Conversations Between Jews, Iranians, and Babylonians in Antiquity.* Edited by Uri Gabbay and Shai Secunda. Tübingen: Mohr Siebeck.

Wunsch, Cornelia. 2000. *Das Egibi-Archiv.* Groningen: Styx Publications.

———. 2007. "The Egibi Family." Pages 236–47 in *The Babylonian World.* Edited by Gwendolyn Leick. New York: Routledge.

Zadok, Ran. 2013. "The Onomastics of the Chaldean, Aramean, and Arabian Tribes in Babylonia during the First Millennium." Pages 261–336 in *Arameans, Chaldeans, and Arabs in Babylonia and Palestine in the First Millennium B.C.* Edited by Angelika Berlejung and Michael P. Streck. Wiesbaden: Harrassowitz.

Zayadine, Fawzi. 1999. "Le relief néo-babylonien à Selaʿ près de Tafileh: interprétation historique." *Syria* 76: 83–90.

Zilberg, Peter, Laurie Pearce, and Michael Jursa. 2019. "Zababa-šar-uṣur and the Town on the Kabar Canal." *RA* 113: 165–69.

PART VII

The Legacy and Future of Ancient Israel

45
THE FUTURE OF STUDYING ANCIENT ISRAEL

Insights from the Archaeological Sciences with a Focus on Food and Society

Lidar Sapir-Hen

Introduction

The study of ancient Israel has benefited greatly in the past 20 years from rapid developments in the archaeological sciences at large, and specifically from the growing place of these sciences in the study of the Iron Age (ca. 1200–586 BCE) (reviewed in Finkelstein, Weiner, and Boaretto 2015). Studies that are based on archaeological sciences tackle large questions regarding the material culture, language, society, economy, politics, and religion of past societies. They challenge long-standing assumptions in the research and contribute greatly to the formulation of new archaeological theories.

The term Archaeological Sciences refers to studies where archaeological questions are approached with techniques and knowledge from Natural, Life, and Exact Sciences. This broad definition includes studies that are based on organic[1] and inorganic[2] finds, and studies that employ techniques from natural and exact sciences[3] (see Martinón-Torres 2018). While they are all under the larger umbrella of "Archaeological Sciences," these fields of study use different techniques and are based on varied knowledge, and—most notably—scholars in these fields rely on different archaeological theories and assumptions in their research (and see Martinón-Torres and Killick 2015).

This chapter first provides a general overview of the impact that archaeological sciences have had on the study of ancient Israel in the past few decades. It is followed by a review focusing on the topic of food and identity in ancient Israel, per the research interest of the author. It entails changes in research methodology and the development of specific research questions in zooarchaeology and adjunct archaeological sciences.

Impact of Archaeological Sciences on the Study of Ancient Israel

The significant impact that archaeological sciences has already had on the study of ancient Israel includes changes in excavation and research methodology, the ability to develop new and nuanced research questions, and the refinement of our understanding of various aspects of ancient Israelite society.

Several research fields in archaeological sciences that emerged in the mid-20th century are time-honored and formed the basis of multiple studies (e.g., radiocarbon dating, archaeobotany, zooarchaeology). Still, it is in the past two decades that archaeological research that is based on archaeological sciences gradually became a fundamental aspect of the excavations of historical periods in the southern Levant. Contrary to the previous century, when archaeological sciences were often employed by researchers outside of the field of archaeology, to date, this is clearly no longer the practice. Today, researchers in these fields are an integral part of every excavation team, and often research is carried out on site, during the excavation itself. The researchers influence the excavation strategy and the fieldwork itself, with instructions for the best retrieval of finds, and implementation of methods for artifact processing (e.g., Eliyahu-Behar 2017; Sapir-Hen et al. 2017). One of the consequences is that excavation directors today routinely take into consideration possible future technological developments.

The research methodology includes the collaboration and exchange of knowledge with researchers that employ archaeological science techniques. These include,[4] e.g., palynological studies that aim to reconstruct the past climate (Langgut, Finkelstein, and Litt 2013; Langgut et al. 2015); studies of materials origins (provenance), using petrography (Martin et al. 2013), organic residue analysis of vessels (Gilboa and Namdar 2015), and the ratio of lead isotopes in metals (Eshel et al. 2019; Kiderlen et al. 2016; Yahalom-Mack et al. 2014); dating techniques that provide the chronological anchors for the discussion of changes in these periods (Boaretto et al. 2019; Regev et al. 2020; Toffolo et al. 2020; these are supplemented with new techniques as well (Shaar and Ben-Yosef 2017)); how the local ancient environment and its impact on people's lifeways can be reconstructed by using wood analysis and ancient charcoal (Benzaquen, Finkelstein, and Langgut 2019), as well as animal remains (Sapir-Hen, Gadot, and Finkelstein 2014; Tsahar et al. 2009), and the combination of both (Vermeersch et al. 2021); the development of literacy as examined through image processing and machine learning technologies (Faigenbaum-Golovin et al. 2015); ancient DNA studies of human remains (Agranat-Tamir et al. 2020; Feldman et al. 2019) and non-human animal remains (see below), which shed light on issues of migration and origin; technological change and its relation to societies as examined through the analysis of ancient metals (Ben-Yosef et al. 2019; Eliyahu-Behar et al. 2013); the revelation of settlement patterns through geoarchaeology studies (Shahack-Gross and Finkelstein 2008, 2015), including studies of space use (Regev et al. 2015; Shahack-Gross et al. 2005). Naturally, this quick overview provides only a glimpse and cannot cover every research field and all research questions, as the scope of these studies is ever-expanding.

When looking at the numerous publications and the subjects they tackle, it is clear that their impact on our current understanding of ancient Israel is significant. They enable new insights into the lifeways of past societies and refine our understanding of the environment, politics, and religion, among many other aspects of ancient life. The impact that archaeological sciences have had on the study of the Late Bronze and Iron Ages in the southern Levant should not be attributed only to the scarcity of textual materials and thus to the importance of other finds in these periods, but to the fact that, often, such scientific research helps to illuminate various aspects in the lives of past populations that are invisible with other common archaeological evidence (see Ben-Yosef 2019).

Finally, these developments also pose some opportunities and challenges. With the growing possibilities of networking and globalized information exchange, initiatives for data sharing are emerging, and are promoting better collaboration and communication between researchers, in addition to introducing new opportunities for large regional synchronic and diachronic studies. Inter-disciplinary collaboration and knowledge exchange will promote studies with finer resolution and broader significance.

Archaeological Sciences and the Study of Food and Identity in Ancient Israel

A major topic in the study of ancient Israel is the food habits of ancient populations. Food habits relate to questions of identity and they can illuminate various aspects of society, economy, and religion. The field of zooarchaeology is most suitable to approach such questions as it examines archaeological animal remains, which often originate from food refuse (Davis 1987). The examination of animal remains can shed light on aspects that are otherwise archaeologically (and textually) invisible—past populations' daily lives, rituals, social status, economies, and politics (Crabtree 1990; Twiss 2012).

In early archaeological research, animal remains were not routinely collected in excavations, and when they were, studies focused on bone counts alone (reviewed in Klein and Kruz-Uribe 1984). However, this practice has changed substantially over the past ~50 years. Today, studies of animal remains—including retrieval methods to be employed—begin already in the fieldwork itself, with the incorporation of zooarchaeologists on many excavation teams. Processing techniques have also developed and include taphonomic studies that consider both the anthropogenic factors and the natural factors that shaped the animal bone assemblages (reviewed in Fernandez-Jalvo and Andrews 2016; Lyman 1994). In addition, new techniques for the estimation of animal age and sex now enable a more nuanced understanding of the way animals were raised and exploited and promote a better understanding of human-animal interaction (recently reviewed in Gifford-Gonzalez 2018). The theoretical framework of social archaeology and zooarchaeology (Russell 2012) promotes the realization that these finds go beyond diet and subsistence strategies. But most notably, these advances stimulated the incorporation of this field within archaeological research, posing questions that relate to the identity of ancient populations, specifically that of ancient Israel for the current chapter.

Zooarchaeology, a time-honored archaeological science field that emerged in the 1950s, is increasingly collaborating with state-of-the-art archaeological sciences techniques—ancient DNA and stable isotopes analysis. Ancient DNA studies on animal remains are carried out on mitochondrial or nuclear DNA extracted from bones and teeth. They enable the identification of species and their origins, and thus they can shed light on questions of migration, trade, animal domestication, and more. Stable isotope studies are carried out on animal bone collagen and teeth enamel (Makarewicz 2016; Pilaar-Birch 2013). The isotopic composition values represent a joint influence of dietary intake, drinking behavior, and physiology (Makarewicz and Pederzani 2017), and they provide a wealth of environmental information that can be used in order to reconstruct a herd's behavior—foraging areas of herds, mobility, seasonality, and more.

A combination of these sciences enables researchers to shed new light on the economy and society during the Late Bronze and Iron Ages. Macro-faunal assemblages that are dated to this time frame are dominated by livestock animals (such as sheep, goats, and cattle), supplemented with varied amounts of pigs, donkeys, camels, and game animals (recently reviewed in Sapir-Hen 2019a, 2019b, 2020). Livestock animals were exploited during these periods for both their primary product, meat, and for their secondary products—milk, wool, and work (Wapnish and Hesse 1988, 1991). Birds (recently reviewed in Spiciarich 2020a) and fish (Adler and Lernau 2021) also played a role in the economy. Different factors shaped human decisions of management and consumption: such factors include the local climate (temperature and precipitation, and in turn the vegetation locally available for herding), economic considerations such as the interaction between producers and consumers, political processes that include the outer demand for products, and cultural preference (for the southern Levant in the periods under discussion, see Sapir-Hen, Gadot, and Finkelstein 2014). Identifying wide patterns, such as cultural change (or continuity) over time, local and immigrant behavior, and possible foreign influences is possible with both in-depth studies of specific sites and with the accumulation of data that enables meta-analysis (e.g., Lev-Tov, Porter, and Routledge 2011; Sapir-Hen, Gadot, and Finkelstein 2014; Sasson 2010; Vermeersch et al. 2021).

Animals and Identity

Studying how animals were raised and exploited, how they were prepared for consumption and the way they were consumed, may illuminate questions related to meat consumption habits and food traditions (reviewed in Campana et al. 2010; Crabtree 1990; Gumerman 1997; Mintz and Du Bois 2002; Pearson 2003; Twiss 2012). When discussing ancient Israel, the question of the development of *kosher* rituals, including food taboos and instructions for butchery practices, is tackled with zooarchaeological analysis.

Kosher butchery practices (proper ways to prepare and cook the food) can be examined through a taphonomic study that seeks to identify and categorize cut marks on animal bones. It is expected that the choice of cuts and their preparation will leave distinct marks. *Kosher* butchery practices were first studied by Cope (2004, 2016), who identified cut marks on zooarchaeological assemblages from the Roman period in Gamla and Yodefat. Greenfield and Bouchnick (2010; Bouchnick 2016) explored the two main aspects of *kosher* butchery: *shechita* (religious butchery) and *nikur* (porging, the removal of the sciatic nerve), along with the historical methods employed for such butchery. Thus far, exact parallels between modern *kosher* butchery practices and zooarchaeological remains have been identified only in assemblages from Medieval Europe (Lisowski 2019; Valenzuela-Lamas et al. 2014). Moreover, a comprehensive recent study on zooarchaeological assemblages dated to the Iron Ages and Classical Periods from Jerusalem did not find evidence on the bones from these periods for the intensive modifications associated with medieval and modern *kosher* butchery (Spiciarich 2020b).

Equally important insights on food taboos are also now available. Adler and Lernau (2021) studied fish remains from numerous Iron Age and Persian period Judahite/Judean sites and demonstrated that catfish was consumed at those sites during these periods. These finds contradict the Pentateuchal prohibition against eating finless and scaleless aquatic species, which are considered *non-kosher*.

The most researched animal in regard to food taboo in ancient Israel is the pig, which is also considered a *non-kosher* animal in Judaism today. Pig frequency in Iron Age archaeological assemblages was often considered a prime indicator of the identity of ancient populations of the southern Levant. This view was based on the biblical narrative, on past research that reviewed pig frequencies (Hesse 1990), and on reviews that correlated evidence for pork avoidance with the emergence of early Israel (Faust 2018; Faust and Lev-Tov 2014; Finkelstein 1996). A reassessment of available data, in correlation to chronological and contextual information, had challenged the above notion and now encourages a renewed debate on the identification of ethnic identity using pig frequency (Sapir-Hen et al. 2013). Sapir-Hen et al. (2013)[5] demonstrated that pork consumption or avoidance cannot serve as a cultural marker when attempting to classify the identity of a site's population in the Late Bronze and Iron Ages. Pork was consumed in Philistine urban centers (although it was not the main component of their diet), but pigs were not consumed in the smaller settlements and the rural area of Philistia (Maeir, Hitchcock, and Horwitz 2013; Sapir-Hen et al. 2013). Outside Philistia, pigs were found in very low frequencies or were absent in most Iron I sites, whether they were Canaanite centers, Aramaean, or Phoenician. In the following period, during the Iron IIB, a dichotomy in pork consumption was observed between the Northern Kingdom of Israel (where pigs appear in significant numbers) and the Southern Kingdom of Judah (where pigs are found in lower frequencies, see below).

In addition to the traditional bone counts of pigs that were used in earlier studies on the topic, recent studies also relied on taphonomic data about the animal remains in order to understand the deposition of the bones and the treatment of pigs: were their remains distributed with the rest of the livestock animals? Were they a part of their daily lives? The answer to both questions was yes (Sapir-Hen et al. 2013).

This topic was also illuminated by using ancient DNA analysis. Studies of recent and archaeological mitochondrial DNA demonstrated that pigs were continuously imported into the southern Levant, starting probably around the time that Philistine settlements appear (Meiri et al. 2013, 2017). It was suggested that pig was consumed in the early phases of their settlements (Maeir and Hitchcock 2017) as it was a common and easy-to-transport dietary staple, providing a reliable source of meat for the migrant population (Sapir-Hen, Meiri, and Finkelstein 2015).

A recent study adds to the complicated picture, as a complete skeleton of an articulated pig was found in Jerusalem in an 8th century BCE building that collapsed and caught the pig *in situ*. When considered with evidence from other excavations of the same period, it seems that minor pork consumption, of 1–2% of the consumed animals, took place in Jerusalem and Judah in the 8th century BCE (Sapir-Hen, Uziel, and Chalaf 2021). Recent biblical scholarship (Altman and Angelini 2020) also supports the notion that pork prohibition is late to the Iron Age.

In conclusion, zooarchaeological studies enable exploring questions of identity, and it seems that consumption or avoidance of pork can be related to various factors in these periods (Horwitz et al. 2017; Maeir, Hitchcock, and Horwitz 2013; Sapir-Hen et al. 2014).

Animals and Society

Another aspect of ancient Israelite society that could be illuminated through the study of ancient bones is the emergence and evolution of social complexity. Knowledge about the nature of social organization between and within sites dated to the Late Bronze-Iron Ages has benefited from studies of animal remains. Such studies have explored evidence for food provisioning systems within urban sites and between them and their rural hinterland. Differential access to meat is the most prominent characteristic used to identify social disparity in ancient assemblages based on food (Curet and Pestle 2010; Trusler 2017). Meat value may be related to the animal's taxon, age at death, meat quantity and quality, and the secondary products it produced (e.g., Ervynck et al. 2003; O'Day et al. 2004). Thus, studying the identity of fauna consumed by humans (i.e., which animals?), their strategies of exploitation, and the choice of body parts to be consumed, as well as the methods of cooking, may also help to decipher the modes of economic specialization in early urban societies. This analytical approach should be integrated, naturally, with the knowledge about the contextual origin of the assemblage within the examined site.

A growing volume of publications from recent years, focusing on livestock exploitation, have demonstrated the social complexity within Late Bronze—Iron Age settlements in relation to the variety of animal exploitation styles. Sapir-Hen and others have examined animal remains in various neighborhoods within single sites (Megiddo, Jerusalem, and Timna) and have demonstrated the way specific populations in the given city—namely those residing in higher status neighborhoods—were provisioned with meat through a redistribution mechanism (Sapir-Hen and Ben-Yosef 2014; Sapir-Hen, Gadot, and Finkelstein 2016; Sapir-Hen et al. 2016). Analysis showed that these higher status neighborhoods were provisioned with the best cuts of caprine meat—young, tender (slaughtered at a young age) meat-rich body portions (upper fore and hind limbs)—while the lower status populations were engaged with animal raising and food production. This was also evident in other sites, where only a specific portion of the population was examined (e.g., Lev-Tov 2010; Marom and Zuckerman 2012) as well as in studies on the regional scale (Lev-Tov, Porter and Routledge 2011; Sapir-Hen, Gadot and Finkelstein 2014; Sapir-Hen, Gadot and Finkelstein 2016). These studies have shown that differential access to animals and their products was used as a way to construct and maintain social status in ancient Israel.

Social disparity can be expressed not only through differential access to "good" meat but also to specific animals. Cattle are relatively higher-maintenance animals compared to other livestock animals such as sheep and goats, as they require vast pasture land and a larger amount of food and water (see also in Zeder 1991). They are also of great importance to the sustainability of grain agriculture in the Bronze and Iron Ages as they are often exploited for the plow (Hellwing, Sade, and Kishon 1993; Sasson 2005). Thus, keeping them signifies that their owners have vast lands, and their exploitation also provides these same owners with market opportunities. These circumstances make cattle more expensive, and thus more "luxurious" to consume than other livestock (Sapir-Hen 2019b). In accordance with this notion, cattle are the dominant animals in assemblages of public rituals and feasting events, along with rare exotic wild animals (see Sapir-Hen, Martin, and Finkelstein 2017 and references therein), making them a symbol of wealth and power in historical periods in the Near East. Cattle are followed in symbolic importance by sheep, the dominant animal in sacrificial burials with humans. The importance of sheep is attributed to their economic and symbolic roles (Sapir-Hen, Martin, and Finkelstein 2017).

In conclusion, the above studies demonstrate the contribution of zooarchaeological studies to the understanding of past societies of ancient Israel. These studies have benefited from advanced techniques in zooarchaeology, dating techniques, archaeological contextual data, ancient DNA analysis, and also biblical scholarship. Stable isotope studies that were mentioned above were not carried out yet on assemblages of these periods, but studies on later historic periods (e.g., Hartman et al. 2013) demonstrate their potential contribution to the study of Iron Age assemblages.

Conclusion

The incorporation of archaeological sciences into archaeological study enables a major change in our understanding of past lives and is already resulting in paradigm shifts. With the advance in data collection and analysis techniques, our knowledge of the past is expanding immensely. Still, while archaeological science techniques, theories, and knowledge are rapidly expanding, much is left to be revealed. As with any aspect of archaeology, the more we find, we understand that there is more waiting to be understood.

Notes

1 E.g., animal and human remains, pollen, seeds, charcoal, plant oils and sediments.
2 E.g., metals.

3   E.g., GIS mapping, residue analysis, ancient DNA, stables isotopes analysis, radiocarbon dating, digitalizing and scanning (see also Howland and Levy this volume).
4   This overview includes only studies that focus on the time frame of the chapter.
5   Sapir-Hen 2019a provides updated review with more recent data.

Bibliography

Adler, Yonatan, and Omri Lernau. 2021. "The Pentateuchal Dietary Proscription against Finless and Scaleless Aquatic Species in Light of Ancient Fish Remains." *TA* 48: 5–26.

Agranat-Tamir, Lily, Shamam Waldman, Mario A.S. Martin, David Gokhman, Nadav Mishol, Tzilla Eshel, Olivia Cheronet, Nadin Rohland, Swapan Mallick, and Nicole Adamski. 2020. "The Genomic History of the Bronze Age Southern Levant." *Cell* 181 (5):1146–57.

Altman, Peter, and Anna Angelini. 2020. "Purity, Taboo and Food in Antiquity Theoretical and Methodological Issues." Pages 9–24 in *Food Taboos and Biblical Prohibitions: Reassessing Archaeological and Literary Perspectives*. Edited by Peter Altman, Anna Angelini and Abra Spiciarich. Tubingen, Germany: Mohr Siebek.

Ben-Yosef, Erez. 2019. "Archaeological Science Brightens Mediterranean Dark Age." *PNAS* 116 (13):5843–45.

Ben-Yosef, Erez, Brady Liss, Omri A. Yagel, Ofir Tirosh, Mohammad Najjar, and Thomas E. Levy. 2019. "Ancient Technology and Punctuated Change: Detecting the Emergence of the Edomite Kingdom in the Southern Levant." *PloS One* 14 (9):e0221967.

Benzaquen, Mordechay, Israel Finkelstein, and Dafna Langgut. 2019. "Vegetation History and Human Impact on the Environs of Tel Megiddo in the Bronze and Iron Ages: A Dendroarchaeological Analysis." *TA* 46: 42–64.

Boaretto, Elisabetta, Yotam Asscher, Louise A. Hitchcock, Gunnar Lehmann, Aren M. Maeir, and Steve Weiner. 2019. "The Chronology of the Late Bronze (LB)-Iron Age (IA) Transition in the Southern Levant: A Response to Finkelstein's Critique." *Radiocarbon* 61:1–11.

Bouchnick, Ram. 2016. "Meat Consumption Patterns as an Ethnic Marker in the Late Second Temple Period: Comparing the Jerusalem City Dump and Qumran Assemblages." Pages 303–22 in *Bones and Identity: Zooarchaeological Approaches to Reconstructing Social and Cultural Landscapes in Southwest Asia*. Edited by Nimrod Marom, et al. Oxford: Oxbow Books.

Campana, D., A. Choyke, P. Crabtree, S. D. deFrance, and J. Lev-Tov, eds. 2010. *Anthropological Approaches to Zooarchaeology: Colonialism, Complexity and Animal Transformations*. Oxford: Oxbow Books.

Cope, C. R. 2004. "The Butchering Patterns of Gamla and Yodefat: Beginning the Search for 'Kosher' Practice." Pages 25–33 in *Behaviour Behind Bones*, edited by S. Jones, W. Van Neer, and A. Ervynck. Oxford: Oxbow Books.

Cope, C. R. 2016. "Butchery Patterns." Pages 331–42 in *Gamla III: Shmarya Gutmann Excavations 1976–1989 Finds and Studies, Part 2*. Edited by D. Syon. Jerusalem: IAA Reports.

Crabtree, P. J. 1990. "Zooarchaeology and Complex Societies: Some Uses of Faunal Analysis for the Study of Trade, Social Status, and Ethnicity." *AMT* 2: 155–205.

Curet, L. Antonio, and William J. Pestle. 2010. "Identifying High-Status Foods in the Archeological Record." *JAA* 29: 413–431.

Davis, S.J.M. 1987. *The Archaeology of Animals*. New Haven: Yale University Press.

Eliyahu-Behar, Adi. 2017. "Archaeological Science in the Early Bronze Age Levels." *NEA* 80: 276–78.

Eliyahu-Behar, Adi, Naama Yahalom-Mack, Yuval Gadot, and Israel Finkelstein. 2013. "Iron Smelting and Smithing in Major Urban Centers in Israel during the Iron Age." *JAS* 40 (12): 4319–30.

Ervynck, Anton, Wim Van Neer, Heide Hüster-Plogmann, and Jörg Schibler. 2003. "Beyond Affluence: the Zooarchaeology of Luxury." *WA* 34: 428–41.

Eshel, Tzilla, Yigal Erel, Naama Yahalom-Mack, Ofir Tirosh, and Ayelet Gilboa. 2019. "Lead Isotopes in Silver Reveal Earliest Phoenician Quest for Metals in the West Mediterranean." *PNAS* 116 (13): 6007–12.

Faigenbaum-Golovin, Shira, Arie Shaus, Barak Sober, Israel Finkelstein, David Levin, Murray Moinester, Eli Piasetzky, and Eli Turkel. 2015. "Computerized Paleographic Investigation of Hebrew Iron Age Ostraca." *Radiocarbon* 57 (2): 317–25.

Faust, Avraham. 2018. "Pigs in Space (and Time): Pork Consumption and Identity Negotiations in the Late Bronze and Iron Ages of Ancient Israel." *NEA* 81: 276–299.

Faust, Avraham, and J. Lev-Tov. 2014. "Philistia and the Philistines in the Iron Age I: Interaction, Ethnic Dynamics and Boundary Maintenance." *HIPHIL Novum* 1:1–24.

Feldman, Michal, Daniel M. Master, Raffaela A. Bianco, Marta Burri, Philipp W. Stockhammer, Alissa Mittnik, Adam J. Aja, Choongwon Jeong, and Johannes Krause. 2019. "Ancient DNA Sheds Light on the Genetic Origins of Early Iron Age Philistines." *Science Advances* 5 (7):eaax0061.

Fernandez-Jalvo, Yolanda, and Peter Andrews. 2016. *Atlas of Taphonomic Identifications: 1001+ Images of Fossil and Recent Mammal Bone Modification*: New York: Springer.

Finkelstein, I. 1996. "Ethnicity and Origin of the Iron-I Settlers in the Highlands of Canaan—Can the Real Israel Stand Up." *BA* 59: 198–212.

Finkelstein, Israel, Steve Weiner, and Elisabetta Boaretto. 2015. "Preface—The Iron Age in Israel: The Exact and Life Sciences Perspectives." *Radiocarbon* 57:197–206.

Gifford-Gonzalez, Diane. 2018. *An Introduction to Zooarchaeology*. New York: Springer.

Gilboa, Ayelet, and Dvory Namdar. 2015. "The Beginnings of South Asian Spice Trade with the Mediterranean Region: A Review." *Radiocarbon* 57 (2):265–83.

Greenfield, H.J., and Ram Bouchnick. 2010. "Kashrut and Shechita—The Relationship between Dietary Practices and Ritual Slaughtering of Animals on Jewish Identity." Pages 106–20 in *Identity Crisis: Archaeological Perspectives on Social Identity: Proceedings of the 42nd (2010) Annual Chacmool Archaeology Conference*. Edited by L. Amundsen-Meyer, N. Engel, and S. Pickering. Calgary: University of Calgary.

Gumerman, G. IV. 1997. "Food and Complex Societies." *JAMT* 4: 105–39.

Hartman, Gideon, Guy Bar-Oz, Ram Bouchnick, and Ronny Reich. 2013. "The Pilgrimage Economy of Early Roman Jerusalem (1st Century BCE–70 CE) Reconstructed from the $\delta15N$ and $\delta13C$ Values of Goat and Sheep Remains." *JAS* 40 (12):4369–76.

Hellwing, S., M. Sade, and V. Kishon. 1993. "Faunal Remains." Pages 309–50 in *Shiloh: The Archaeology of a Biblical Site*, edited by I. Finkelstein. Tel Aviv: Tel Aviv University.

Hesse, Brian. 1990. "Pig Lovers and Pig Haters: Patterns of Palestinian Pork Production." *JEth* 10:1 95–225.

Horwitz, Liora Kolska, Armelle Gardeisen, Aren M. Maeir, and Louise A. Hitchcock. 2017. "A Brief Contribution to the Iron Age Philistine Pig Debate." Pages 93–116 in *The Wide Lens in Archaeology: Honoring Brian Hesse's Contributions to Anthropological Archaeology*. Edited by J. Lev-Tov, Paula Hesse and Allan Gilbert. Atlanta: Lockwood Press.

Kiderlen, Moritz, Michael Bode, Andreas Hauptmann, and Yannis Bassiakos. 2016. "Tripod Cauldrons Produced at Olympia Give Evidence for Trade with Copper from Faynan (Jordan) to South West Greece, c. 950–750 BCE." *JASR* 8: 303–13.

Klein, R.G., and K. Kruz-Uribe. 1984. *The Analysis of Animal Bones from Archaeological Sites*. Chicago: University of Chicago Press.

Langgut, Dafna, Israel Finkelstein, and T. Litt. 2013. "Climate and the Late Bronze Collapse: New Evidence from the Southern Levant." *TA* 40 149–75.

Langgut, Dafna, Israel Finkelstein, T. Litt, H.F. Newmann, and M. Stein. 2015. "Vegetation and Climate Changes During the Bronze and Iron Ages (~3600–600 BCE) in the Southern Levant Based on Palynological Records." *Radiocarbon* 57:217–35.

Lev-Tov, Justin. 2010. "A Plebeian Perspective on Empire Economies: Faunal Remains from Tel Miqne-Ekron, Israel." Pages 90–104 in *Anthropological Approaches to Zooarchaeology: Colonialism, Complexity and Animal Transformation*. Edited by D. Campana, et al. Oxford: Oxbow Books.

Lev-Tov, Justin, Benjamin W. Porter, and Bruce E. Routledge. 2011. "Measuring Local Diversity in Early Iron Age Animal Economies: A View from Khirbat al-Mudayna al-'Aliya (Jordan)." *BASOR* 361: 67–93.

Lisowski, M. 2019. "The Identification of Jewish Patterns of Food Preparation and Consumption: A Zooarchaeological Approach to the Medieval and Early Modern Evidence from Central-Eastern Europe." PhD diss., University of Sheffield.

Lyman, R.L. 1994. *Vertebrate Taphonomy*. Cambridge: Cambridge University Press.

Maeir, Aren M., Louise A. Hitchcock, and Liora Kolska Horwitz. 2013. "On the Constitution and Transformation of Philistine Identity." *OJA* 32: 1–38.

Maeir, Aren M., and Louise A. Hitchcock. 2017. "The Appearance, Formation and Transformation of Philistine Culture: new Perspectives and new Finds." Pages 149–62 in *The Sea Peoples Up-To-Date: New Research on the Migration of Peoples in the 12th Century BCE*. Edited by Peter M. Fischer. Vienna: Austrian Academy of Sciences.

Makarewicz, Cheryl A. 2016. "Toward an Integrated Isotope Zooarchaeology." Pages 189–209 in *Isotopic Landscapes in Bioarchaeology*. Edited by Gisela Grupe, George C. McGlynn. Berlin: Springer.

Makarewicz, Cheryl A., and Sarah Pederzani. 2017. "Oxygen (δ 18 O) and Carbon (δ 13 C) Isotopic Distinction in Sequentially Sampled Tooth Enamel of Co-localized Wild and Domesticated Caprines: Complications to Establishing Seasonality and Mobility in Herbivores." *PPP* 485: 1–15

Marom, Nimrod, and Sharon Zuckerman. 2012. "The Zooarchaeology of Exclusion and Expropriation: Looking up from the Lower City in Late Bronze Age Hazor." *JAA* 31: 573–85.

Martin, Mario A.S., Adi Eliyahu-Behar, Michael Anenburg, Yuval Goren, and Israel Finkelstein. 2013. "Iron IIA Slag-Tempered Pottery in the Negev Highlands, Israel." *JAS* 40: 3777–92.

Martinón-Torres, M. 2018. "Archaeological Sciences." In *The Encyclopedia of Archaeological Sciences*, edited by Sandra L. López. Varela: Wiley Online Library.

Martinón-Torres, Marcos, and David Killick. 2015. "Archaeological Theories and Archaeological Sciences." In *The Oxford Handbook of Archaeological Theory*. Edited by Andrew Gardner, Mark Lake, and Ulrike Sommer. Oxford: Oxford University Press. DOI: 10.1093/oxfordhb/9780199567942.013.004

Meiri, Meirav, Dorothée Huchon, Guy Bar-Oz, Elisabetta Boaretto, Liora Kolska Horwitz, Aren M. Maeir, Lidar Sapir-Hen, Greger Larson, Steve Weiner, and Israel Finkelstein. 2013. "Ancient DNA and Population Turnover in Southern Levantine Pigs-Signature of the Sea Peoples Migration?" *SR* 3: 1–8.

Meiri, Meirav, Philipp W. Stockhammer, Nimrod Marom, Guy Bar-Oz, Lidar Sapir-Hen, Peggy Morgenstern, Stella Macheridis, Baruch Rosen, Dorothée Huchon, and Joseph Maran. 2017. "Eastern Mediterranean Mobility in the Bronze and Early Iron Ages: Inferences from Ancient DNA of Pigs and Cattle." *SR* 7: 1–10.

Mintz, S.W., and M. Du Bois. 2002. "The Anthropology of Food and Eating." *ARA* 31: 99–119.

O'Day, Sharyn Jones, Wim Van Neer, and Anton Ervynck, eds. 2004. *Behaviour Behind Bones: The Zooarchaeology of Ritual, Religion, Status and Identity*. Oxford: Oxbow.

Pearson, M.P. 2003. "Food, Identity and Culture: An Introduction and Overview." Pages 1–30 in *Food, Culture and Identity in the Neolithic and Early Bronze*. Edited by M.P. Pearson. Oxford: Archaeopress.

Pilaar-Birch, Suzanne E. 2013. "Stable Isotopes in Zooarchaeology: An Introduction." *AAS* 5: 81–83.

Regev, Johanna, Joe Uziel, Tehillah Lieberman, Avi Solomon, Yuval Gadot, Doron Ben-Ami, Lior Regev, and Elisabetta Boaretto. 2020. "Radiocarbon Dating and Microarchaeology Untangle the History of Jerusalem's Temple Mount: A View from Wilson's Arch." *Plos One* 15 (6):e0233307.

Regev, Lior, Dan Cabanes, Robert Homsher, Assaf Kleiman, Steve Weiner, Israel Finkelstein, and Ruth Shahack-Gross. 2015. "Geoarchaeological Investigation in a Domestic Iron Age Quarter, Tel Megiddo, Israel." *BASOR* 374: 135–57.

Russell, Nerissa. 2012. *Social Zooarchaeology: Humans and Animals in Prehistory*. Cambridge: Cambridge University Press.

Sapir-Hen, Lidar. 2019a. "Food, Pork Consumption and Identity in Ancient Israel." *NEA* 82: 52–59.

———. 2019b. "Late Bronze and Iron Age Livestock of the Southern Levant: Their Economic and Symbolic Roles." *TA* 46: 227–32.

———. 2020. "Human-animal Relationship with Work Animals: Donkeys and Camels during the Bronze and Iron Ages in the Southern Levant." *ZDPV* 136: 83–94.

Sapir-Hen, Lidar, Guy Bar-Oz, Yuval Gadot, and Israel Finkelstein. 2013. "Pig Husbandry in Iron Age Israel and Judah: New Insights regarding the Origin of the 'Taboo'." *ZDPV* 129: 1–20.

Sapir-Hen, Lidar, Guy Bar-Oz, Ilan Sharon, Ayelet Gilboa, and Tamar Dayan. 2014. "Food, Economy and Culture at Tel Dor, Israel: A Diachronic Study of Faunal Remains from Fifteen Centuries of Occupation." *BASOR* 371: 83–101.

Sapir-Hen, Lidar, and Erez Ben-Yosef. 2014. "The Socioeconomic Status of Iron Age Metal Workers: Animal Economy in the 'Slaves' Hill,' Timna, Israel." *Antiquity* 88:775–90.

Sapir-Hen, Lidar, Yuval Gadot, and Israel Finkelstein. 2014. "Environmental and Historical Impacts on Long Term Animal Economy: The southern Levant in the Late Bronze and Iron Ages." *JESHO* 57: 703–44.

———. 2016. "Animal Economy in a Temple City and its Countryside: Iron Age Jerusalem as a Case Study." *BASOR* 375: 103–118.

Sapir-Hen, Lidar, Mario A.S. Martin, and Israel Finkelstein. 2017. "Food Rituals and their Social Significance in the Mid-Second Millennium BC in the Southern Levant: A View from Megiddo." *IJO* 27: 1048–1058.

Sapir-Hen, Lidar, Meirav Meiri, and Israel Finkelstein. 2015. "Iron Age Pigs: New Evidence on Their Origin and Role in Forming Identity Boundaries." *Radiocarbon* 57: 307–15.

Sapir-Hen, Lidar, Aharon Sasson, Assaf Kleiman, and Israel Finkelstein. 2016. "Social Stratification in the Late Bronze and Early Iron Ages: An Intra-site Investigation at Megiddo." *OJA* 35: 744–84.

Sapir-Hen, Lidar, Ilan Sharon, Ayelet Gilboa, and Tamar Dayan. 2017. "Wet Sieving a Complex Tell: Implications for Retrieval Protocols and Studies of Animal Economy in Historical Periods." *JAS* 82: 72–79.

Sapir-Hen, Lidar, Joe Uziel, and Ortal Chalaf. 2021. "Everything but the Oink: On the Discovery of an Articulated Pig in Iron Age Jerusalem and its Meaning to Judahite Consumption Practices." *NEA* 84: 110–19.

Sasson, Aharon. 2005. "Economic Strategies and the Role of Cattle in the Southern Levant in the Bronze and Iron Ages." Pages 208–21 in *Archaeozoology of the Near East VI. Proceedings of the Sixth International Symposium on the Archaeozoology of Southwestern Asia and Adjacent Areas*. Edited by H. Buitenhuis, et al. Groningen: ARC Publications.

———. 2010. *Animal Husbandry in Ancient Israel: A Zooarchaeological Perspective on Livestock Exploitation, Herd Management and Economic Strategies*. London: Equinox.

Shaar, Ron, and Erez Ben-Yosef. 2017. "Paleomagnetic Geochronology of Quaternary Sequences in the Levant." Pages 53–61 in *Quaternary Environments, Climate Change, and Humans in the Levant*. Edited by Yehouda Enzel and Ofer Bar-Yosef. Cambridge: Cambridge University Press.

Shahack-Gross, Ruth, Rosa-Maria Albert, Ayelet Gilboa, Orna Nagar-Hilman, Ilan Sharon, and Steve Weiner. 2005. "Geoarchaeology in an Urban Context: the Uses of Space in a Phoenician Monumental Building at Tel Dor (Israel)." *JAS* 32: 1417–1431.

Shahack-Gross, Ruth, and Israel Finkelstein. 2008. "Subsistence Practices in an Arid Environment: a Geoarchaeological Investigation in an Iron Age Site, the Negev Highlands, Israel." *JAS* 35: 965–82.

———. 2015. "Settlement Oscillations in the Negev Highlands Revisited: The Impact of Microarchaeological Methods." *Radiocarbon* 57:253–64.

Spiciarich, Abra. 2020a. "Birds in Transition: Bird Exploitation in the Southern Levant During the Late Bronze Age, Iron Age I, and Iron Age II." *BASOR* 383: 61–78.

———. 2020b. "Identifying the Biblical Food Prohibitions using Zooarchaeological Methods." Pages 57–72 in *Food Taboos and Biblical Prohibitions: Reassessing Archaeological and Literary Perspective*. Edited by Peter Altman, Anna Angelini and Abra Spiciarich. Tubingen, Germany: Mohr Siebek.

Toffolo, Michael B., Lior Regev, Eugenia Mintz, Ifat Kaplan-Ashiri, Francesco Berna, Stéphan Dubernet, Y. Xin, Johanna Regev, and Elisabetta Boaretto. 2020. "Structural Characterization and Thermal Decomposition of Lime Binders allow Accurate Radiocarbon Age Determinations of Aerial Lime Plaster." *Radiocarbon* 62:633–55.

Trusler, A. Kate. 2017. "Evaluating Socioeconomic Status using *Sus scrofa* Food Utility Indices in Historical Faunal Assemblages." *AAS* 9: 831–41.

Tsahar, E., I. Izhaki, S. Lev-Yadun, and G. Bar-Oz. 2009. "Distribution and Extinction of Ungulates during the Holocene of the Southern Levant." *PLOS One* 4:e5316.

Twiss, K. C. 2012. "The Archaeology of Food and Social Diversity." *JAR* 20: 357–95.

Valenzuela-Lamas, Silvia, Lua Valenzuela-Suau, Oriol Saula, Anna Colet, Oriol Mercadal, Carme Subiranas, and Jordi Nadal. 2014. "Shechita and Kashrut: Identifying Jewish Populations Through Zooarchaeology and Taphonomy. Two Examples from Medieval Catalonia (North-Eastern Spain)." *Quaternary International* 330: 109–17.

Vermeersch, Shyama, Simone Riehl, Britt M Starkovich, and Jens Kamlah. 2021. "Developments in Subsistence during the Early Bronze Age through the Iron Age in the Suthern and Central Levant: Integration of Faunal and Botanical Remains using Multivariate Statistics." *QSR* 253: 106776.

Wapnish, Paula, and Hesse Brian. 1988. "Urbanization and the Organization of Animal Production at Tell Jemmeh in the Middle Bronze Age Levant." *JNES* 47: 81–94.

———. 1991. "Faunal Remains from Tel Dan: Perspectives on Animal Production at a Village, Urban and Ritual Center." *Archaeozoologia* 4 (2):9–86.

Yahalom-Mack, Naama, Ehud Galili, Irina Segal, Adi Eliyahu-Behar, Elisabetta Boaretto, Sana Shilstein, and Israel Finkelstein. 2014. "New insights into Levantine Copper Trade: Analysis of Ingots from the Bronze and Iron Ages in Israel." *JAS* 45: 159–77.

Zeder, Melinda A. 1991. *Feeding Cities: Specialized Animal Economy in the Ancient Near East*. Washington, DC: Smithsonian Institution.

46
CYBER-ARCHAEOLOGY AND THE STUDY OF ANCIENT EDOM AND ISRAEL

Matthew D. Howland and Thomas E. Levy

The practice of archaeology in the southern Levant has a long history, and to the casual observer of an excavation in process, not much has changed. Many of the same sites continue to be excavated over 100 years after they were first subjected to intensive archaeological scrutiny. Indeed, excavators at these sites still use tools that would not have seemed out of place in the late 19th century; a trowel, a spade, and a brush are still the tools of the trade. Typological study of ancient artifacts still primarily relies on experts familiar with the material from long careers bent over tables full of sherds or lithics. These methods, tried and true, are the foundation of most archaeological fieldwork and will continue to be so into the foreseeable future.

What has changed drastically, though, are many of the recording and analytical methods used by the excavators at these sites. The enormous increase in the use of scientific methods to extract new information from even the smallest amount of sediment has opened new vistas in how we study and interpret the past. Digital analysis in archaeology is having its own moment as well. Recent years have seen an enormous expansion of the viability and cost-effectiveness of digital techniques, to the extent that they are now widely applied in archaeological projects. If not an out-and-out revolution of analysis, perhaps these methods represent at least a "subtle revolution" allowing for new ways of learning about the past (Shott 2014). The application of technology to archaeology ranges from straightforward (e.g., using digital cameras for site photographs) to sophisticated and specialized (e.g., developing custom gaming applications for users to experience sites). Some of these advances represent only upgrades in resolution or efficiency, while others truly provide new perspectives. Understanding the ways in which digital approaches to archaeology can advance our understanding of ancient people and society is critical for the future of archaeology in the southern Levant.

Cyber-archaeology

Cyber-archaeology is a seemingly straightforward term with a somewhat complicated definition. The term has undergone a schism with two primary approaches toward conducting cyber-archaeology, exemplified by their respective advocates, Maurizio Forte and Thomas E. Levy. Forte's (2014) approach to cyber-archaeology combines digital datasets collected through field documentation and recording with an interactive digital interface or cyber-environment. By interacting with and experiencing digital datasets in a simulated online environment, Forte argues, archaeologists generate new knowledge and new ways of understanding the past (2011). These experiences then, in turn, contribute to how archaeologists approach the investigation of the past through fieldwork (Forte 2011, 2014). Other researchers have also examined the implications of digital technology for knowledge creation, documentation, and issues of authority (Cameron and Kenderdine 2010).

Levy's approach toward cyber-archaeology, though sharing its origins in digital recording at archaeological sites, is fundamentally different. Levy places a primary emphasis on the use of digital tools to collect data with a combination of methods borrowed from "computer science, engineering, the natural sciences, and archaeology" (2013; Levy and Liss 2020). In Levy's model, natively digital data collected in the field using cutting-edge methods is curated, analyzed, and disseminated as part of a comprehensive cyber-archaeology workflow (2013; Levy and Liss 2020). Thus, rather than emphasizing the interactive experience one can have while interacting with data online, Levy's cyber-archaeology focuses on the collection and use of data to address research questions and ultimately disseminate the results of the analysis. This model was applied to varying degrees of success in a recent University of California multi-campus project focused on "At-Risk World Heritage and the Digital Humanities" (Lercari et al. 2016, 2022). In general, in Levy's model, data is inducted into the cyber-archaeology workflow through data collection (with a "digital toolbox") where it undergoes curation, analysis, and dissemination sequentially (2013).

In this chapter, we will be using Levy's conception of cyber-archaeology as a model for understanding how cyber-archaeology can contribute generally to the study of ancient society through the material culture they leave behind, and specifically to the ancient historical regions of Israel and Edom. As such, discussion of how digital data is collected in the field, analyzed, and disseminated will be the primary focus. This model allows us to provide perspective on how cyber-archaeology is applied in the field today.

Despite the rise of cyber-archaeology, the ideal of an integrated, four-part workflow in which digital data collected at archaeological sites is subject to a comprehensive package of curation, analysis, and dissemination does not always reflect the reality of practice in the field. Archaeologists in the southern Levant have become familiar with the use of cyber-archaeological tools to acquire and curate data, but the potential of digital techniques for analysis and dissemination, to address research questions and publicize results, has not been fully realized (Howland 2018; Magnani et al. 2020). The use of digital methods in archaeology has been criticized for failing to move beyond proof-of-concept uses or recording for documentation, rather than serving as a basis for new analysis (Shott 2014; Magnani et al. 2020). Others have also argued that engaging physically with the archaeological record is still crucial for archaeologists to develop skills, make important finds, and generally increase their familiarity with the archaeological record (Caraher 2016; Kersel 2016). As such, talk of a paradigm shift from analog to digital is overstated, as archaeologists must continue to apply traditional field methods to study the past (Gordon et al. 2016). However, if archaeologists fail to collect data with research purposes in mind, instead of recording for documentation and relying solely on discovering patterns in the data avalanche, we run the risk of transitioning into a Big Data-era of cyber-archaeology in which hypotheses are subjected to data, rather than the reverse (Huggett 2020).

Still, digital field recording can go beyond just adding to the pile of documents; it can provide an important representation of the intentional choices made by archaeologists (Roosevelt et al. 2015) and generate datasets that answer larger research questions when used appropriately (Howland 2018; Jones and Levy 2018). To that end, cyber-archaeologists must move beyond data recording for the purposes of documentation alone and apply the digital data collected for analysis to address research questions (cf. Magnani et al. 2020). Thus, our discussion of cyber-archaeology must consider both technical advances in documentation strategies and novel strategies of analysis and dissemination that truly open new pathways to understanding the ancient world.

Data Acquisition: Recording for Documentation

Data acquisition, in the broadest terms, is necessary for any archaeological study. However, a more nuanced perspective on the ethical obligations of data collection is useful for understanding how data acquired in archaeological fieldwork affects our ability to curate, analyze, and disseminate. Borrowing and adapting from the related field of cultural heritage, digital data acquisition can be understood through the twin concepts of recording and documentation. In the field of cultural heritage, recording and documentation can be treated as before and after, or as activity and product—"today's recording is tomorrow's documentation" (Letellier et al. 2007). Cultural heritage professionals perform heritage recording by collecting information about a monument in the field, which produces records and material that becomes the documentation for that site (Letellier et al. 2007). Archaeologists can borrow this concept. The excavation of a site necessarily implies its destruction, meaning that the recording done during excavation will produce the only documentation of the site's character that will ever exist. Because of this, archaeologists have a pressing responsibility to make sure their records are detailed and comprehensive enough to allow for later reinterpretation.

This responsibility is central to the concept of cyber-archaeology, and there is no doubt that the development of cyber-archaeological methods has dramatically shaped the ways in which excavated sites in Israel and Edom are recorded. Digital recording methods allow for the regular acquisition of extremely comprehensive datasets, to the point that the data collected has been called a "data avalanche" (Levy et al. 2010). This data avalanche is, in its purest form, documentation. When consistently and effectively applied, cyber-archaeology methods have the potential to produce excellent, comprehensive documentation of sites. Moreover, this wealth of documentation has the potential to be produced more efficiently and accurately than using traditional methods (Howland 2018). Indeed, maximizing the efficiency and accuracy of digital methods is a primary concern among archaeologists using the cyber-archaeology toolkit (Gordon et al. 2016). Many of the digital approaches to archaeology applied in the southern Levant appeal to cyber-archaeologists because of their efficiency. These recording techniques also range in their sophistication, from straightforward digital photography to 3D recording using expensive, specialized equipment. It is not possible to discuss the full range of cyber-archaeological techniques in one chapter without giving each approach short shrift. As such, we will focus on the techniques most widely applied in active archaeological excavations: digital photography, GIS, image-based modeling, and digital context recording.

Digital Photography

Of the many techniques applied by cyber-archaeologists, digital photography is the simplest and likely the most widespread. Digital photography is not often thought of as a tool of cyber-archaeology or digital archaeology, and in fact, the use of photography in general has been under-considered as a specifically interpretive process. Indeed, photographs are used as an argument for proving the objectivity of the record when in fact the rise of digital photography and related photo-editing software have further removed the act of taking and publishing a photo from the reality of a scene at a given time (Shanks 1997). In this sense, capturing digital photographs at a site is quite similar to the production of 3D models at a site—an attempt at capturing objective documentation of a site at a moment in time, but thoroughly impacted by the choices made by the photographer and excavators (Garstki 2020). Adopting a careful attitude can ensure that the interpretive power of imaging is cautiously, rather than uncritically, applied.

In general, the growth of digital photography in archaeology provides a clear model for how digital techniques can prove essential for field recording and the production of quality documentation, which is necessary even as it is subjective. Nearly as soon as digital cameras became viable for use on archaeological projects, they were adopted by specialists eager to efficiently capture high-quality digital data rather than wait on a site photographer with a traditional film camera (Wallrodt 2016). Digital cameras also allow photographers, experienced or otherwise, to check the quality of their image immediately rather than waiting significant lengths of time to have their film developed (Morgan 2012; Wallrodt 2016). This instant feedback allows for an easier and more efficient photo-taking progress (Morgan 2012). In addition, the "born-digital" nature of digital photographs substantially eases their integration into photo-editing software. This passage, along with subsequent manipulations simultaneously distance the image from reality and make potential interpretations more explicit and easier, for example by digitally adding scales to artifact photographs (Shanks 1997; Morgan 2016). Ultimately, the relative simplicity of digital photography and the potential to capture images without concern for the misuse of film has allowed archaeologists to reach new heights in field recording for documentation. Its use provides a case study in how digital techniques can influence and improve archaeological fieldwork, even as the new methods bring along theoretical concerns.

Digital Spatial Recording and GIS

The rise of Geographic Information Systems (GIS) has undoubtedly been one of the most significant developments in archaeological field recording and documentation. The use of GIS, in some ways, parallels cyber-archaeology as an integrated workflow. GIS software packages perform five main tasks: data acquisition, spatial data management, database management, spatial data analysis, and spatial data visualization (Connolly and Lake 2006). These categories mirror Levy's (2013) model of cyber-archaeology. For GIS use at active field excavations, data acquisition, spatial data management, and database management are of primary importance.

A key aspect of field recording for documentation is the generation of top plans and architectural diagrams of an active excavation. These illustrations provide spatial context to excavated finds and are essential in understanding the relationships between excavated loci at sites. Producing these diagrams is traditionally the realm of a site architect, a specialty requiring important expertise in geometry and the use of specialized survey equipment such as a surveyor's (or "dumpy") level or theodolite (Dinsmoor 1977). With the rise of GIS software and surveying technology in archaeology, the architect role underwent a shift. Rather than using tape measures and pencil and paper to represent features and finds at the site, these could be recorded using digital technology such as GPS recorders, Total Stations, or even vertical images used as the basis for GIS vectorization (Levy and Smith 2007).

Increasingly, projects have shifted to using digital recording tools with the objective of collecting GIS data, including both surveys and excavations (Levy and Smith 2007;

Tripcevich and Wernke 2010). The shift to GIS-oriented field recording represents about half of the transition to "paperless" field strategies—descriptive context recording, discussed below, makes up the other half (Levy et al. 2001; Ellis 2016; Motz 2016). The advantages in efficiency, accuracy, and precision provided by digital spatial recording all make a strong case for the use of GIS for "digital illustration," without necessarily sacrificing the benefits of physical engagement with the archaeological record (Ellis 2016). Arguably, this approach to field recording of point finds, contexts, and other objects of interest with digital, GIS-based technology has become standard practice in archaeology, likely because of these advantages. However, caution should be taken to ensure digital recorders retain their familiarity with the physical archaeological record (Caraher 2016; Kersel 2016). Overall, the advantages of GIS-based recording can be further improved through combination with 3D methods.

Image-Based Modeling and 3D Recording

Image-based modeling (IBM, also referred to as digital photogrammetry or Structure-from-Motion) is undoubtedly the trendiest application of cyber-archaeology currently. IBM refers to the use of digital photographs to generate 3D models through photogrammetric methods (Olson et al. 2013; Howland 2018). This technique has been widely applied at many archaeological sites in the southern Levant as archaeologists discover the potential of generating 3D models cheaply, efficiently, and accurately. These aspects of IBM have been the primary focus of much of the literature advocating for the use of this technique for archaeological field recording, and many scholars explicitly emphasize its usefulness for producing site documentation (Olson et al. 2013; Howland 2018). IBM is certainly an excellent tool for documenting a site's conditions and the technology is now widely used for the recording of active excavation (Olson et al. 2013; Howland et al. 2014; Roosevelt et al. 2015). During excavation, archaeologists have the greatest responsibility to conduct recording for the sake of producing documentation, as the destructive nature of excavation means that information not recorded is information lost. Given this responsibility, the comprehensiveness and speed of 3D recording with photogrammetry are of major importance for field recording (Magnani et al. 2020). The 3D models produced through these methods provide an entirely new level of sophistication over traditional methods and photography that can aid future researchers working with legacy data (Garstki 2020). As such, the production of 3D documentation of sites is an important and worthwhile goal in and of itself.

Though the widespread production of 3D models in archaeology would seem to be something of a revelation, archaeologists have primarily used IBM to improve the efficiency and accuracy of their traditional field recording. In other words, archaeologists have gotten more use out of the 2D derivatives of 3D models than of the 3D datasets themselves (Garstki 2020). The straightforward integration of IBM-based workflows with GIS has facilitated an overhaul of field recording and site surveying. Even the GIS-based techniques described above have been subject to improvements in the efficiency and accuracy provided by 3D techniques. IBM software packages, most notably Agisoft Metashape (formerly Agisoft Photoscan), easily allow for models to be georeferenced and exported as GIS-compatible datasets such as orthophotographs (vertical images corrected for lens and elevation distortion) and digital elevation models (DEMs; Howland et al. 2014; Agisoft 2020). These datasets are an excellent basis for vectorizing features with a high level of accuracy, producing extremely accurate and detailed top plans and site drawings while reducing human error inherent to measuring and hand-drawing features at a site or even illustrating from uncorrected vertical images (Olson et al. 2013; Howland et al. 2014; Prins et al. 2014; Quartermaine et al.

2014). These increases in accuracy provide a strong incentive for archaeologists to apply these techniques.

An even greater strength of IBM for archaeologists interested in recording features at their site and documenting thier condition is the multiscalar nature of the technology. Cyber-archaeologists can collect data sufficient to produce 3D models at scales ranging from small artifacts to large sites (Olson et al. 2013; Roosevelt et al. 2015). Scholars have taken increasing advantage of IBM's capability of generating high-resolution models at site-wide scales by capturing the digital photographs needed to create 3D models through low-altitude aerial photography (LAAP). The use of LAAP for archaeology has a long history and the resulting digital photographs can be incredibly useful for archaeologists for survey purposes, intra-site mapping, or producing high-quality publication photos (Crawford 1928; Myers and Myers 1992; Bewley 2003; Verhoeven 2009). In the latter category, the stunning photography produced by the Aerial Photographic Archive of the Middle East (APAAME) provides an excellent example from the southern Levant. However, the use of digital aerial photographs for IBM has provided new potential for this old technique and literally provides a new perspective on sites. 3D models created through LAAP and IBM are an excellent basis to produce orthophotos and DEMs at centimeter resolution, providing a combination of resolution and scale not attainable through other methods (Verhoeven et al. 2012; Howland 2018; Magnani et al. 2020). These datasets provide an excellent basis for efficient and accurate GIS-based site mapping (Quartermaine et al. 2014; Hill and Rowan 2017; Liss et al. 2020). There are many methods of capturing low-altitude aerial images, including kites, balloons, and survey poles (Verhoeven 2009). Most of these techniques remained extremely viable, with a choice of approach depending on site conditions and project goals. However, recent developments in the cost-effectiveness, ease-of-use, and image quality from unmanned autonomous vehicles (UAV) platforms have meant that these must be considered the default option, even viable for less-well funded projects (Campana 2017; Hill 2019; Waagen 2019). These methods have been widely applied in the southern Levant to great effect (Smith et al. 2014; Hill and Rowan 2017; Homsher et al. 2017). Overall, UAVs and IBM have become a near-essential part of the archaeological toolkit for archaeologists interested in applying cutting-edge techniques for producing high-resolution documentation.

Digital Context Recording

One additional category of cyber-archaeological tools bears discussion as an important component of a typical cyber-archaeological workflow. The use of context recording software is a prototypical example of a digital method that exclusively aims to improve documentation, rather than provide new forms of analysis. However, advocates of digital context recording have identified two primary advantages of using context recording apps over the paper notebooks they replace: the efficiency of immediate recording of contextual information during the process of excavation and the reduction of manual translation errors. The use of iPads or similar tablets trench side can allow for more data to be recorded and accessed during excavation (Ellis 2016). Data recorded in an online database can also be accessible onsite for immediate consultation, unlike paper records stored in a lab (Gordon et al. 2016). Secondly, recording by paper often necessitates the digitization of these records for storage and eventual publication. This process is time-consuming and is a potential source of human error as data originally recorded in the field is translated to derivatives further from the primary record (Sobotkova et al. 2016; Wallrodt 2016). The collection of born-digital data can avoid this issue entirely.

Regarding the choice of recording application, many custom apps have been developed for context recording at sites, and undoubtedly custom apps meet the needs of individual projects most directly (Vincent et al. 2014; Fee 2016). However, these apps are often impractical in the medium to long term as they lack the institutional support and expertise needed to keep them operational (Sobotkova et al. 2016; McKinny and Shai 2018)—the Oriental Institute's OCHRE platform is one example of a recording system with a longer track record of institutional support (Schloen and Schloen 2012). As such, the refinement and longer technical support timelines of off-the-shelf applications speak strongly in favor of their use, though open-source options are also viable (Ellis 2016; Sobotkova et al. 2016; Garstki 2020). These advantages of off-the-shelf applications for context recording apply to other cyber-archaeology pursuits as well. Overall, digital approaches to context recording seem to offer some technical advantages for the efficient production of documentation while minimizing sources of error. However, archaeologists should approach these applications cautiously with institutional resources and data archiving in mind, a topic discussed in greater detail below.

Data Curation: A Pressing Responsibility

The curation of digital data is the most challenging aspect of cyber-archaeology. Archaeologists can easily be tempted into applying the latest and greatest technology, producing flashy and crowd-pleasing results. However, the unappreciated work of curating that data to ensure the long-term viability of the documentation generated through digital methods may not be as appealing. To some extent, concerns over the vulnerability of digital data being lost to various accidents have been overblown (Ellis 2016). However, born-digital data is undoubtedly at risk of being lost, whether due to file corruption or the physical media of data storage becoming obsolete (Jeffrey 2012). Digital datasets, unlike paper notebooks, cannot be expected to be easily accessible after being left in a dusty closet for 25 years. This creates a unique challenge for field archaeologists. The ethical responsibility to produce rigorous and comprehensive documentation of the sites they excavate inevitably turns into an equal responsibility to ensure this documentation is available to future generations (Sheehan 2015). To a large extent, archaeologists have not necessarily met this challenge, as the amount of data produced by archaeologists exceeds the amount of data that is carefully curated (York et al. 2016; McManamon et al. 2017). Arguably, archaeologists must be forced into appropriately curating their data through funding or publication mechanisms given the extent to which scholars are incentivized to collect new data rather than take care of old data (Opitz and Hermann 2018). However, cyber-archaeologists face similar problems in data curation as they do in context recording—a lack of expertise and resources can hamstring even the best-intentioned efforts (McManamon et al. 2017). The necessity of proper curation means that archaeologists should consider the lifecycle of their data while planning a project rather than wait until the data is already collected (McKeague et al. 2012; Opitz and Hermann 2018), lest they be buried by the "data avalanche."

There are two main solutions for archaeologists to responsibly curate their data. First, archaeologists can benefit from collaborating with institutions, such as university libraries, whose missions encompass the long-term storage and archiving of data (Johnson 2002; Lynch 2003). Large academic libraries may be an ideal partner for this type of data curation, given their resources and expertise in handling large datasets and making them accessible to public audiences. The challenge of curating an ever-increasing stockpile of high-resolution documentation may be cost-prohibitive for some smaller libraries to take on (Lynch 2017; McManamon et al. 2017). However, when available, collaborating with libraries or other similar institutions can be a useful hedge against data being lost to degradation or obsolete technology. In cases where libraries are not suitable, digital data repositories such as the Digital Archaeological Record (tDAR, McManamon et al. 2017) and OpenContext, which archives data with the California Digital Library (Kansa et al. 2014), are available. These services are representative of the most organized attempts at solving what will be a permanent problem for archaeologists.

Data Analysis: Unrealized Potential

Despite the enthusiastic and nearly universal adoption of cyber-archaeological methods by field archaeologists, the digital toolkit has not yet come into its own as a theoretically-grounded practice. Approaches to the use of digital techniques in archaeology have largely focused on their usefulness as improvements to field methodology, whether as demonstrating the use of a particular technology or identifying best practices (Magnani et al. 2020). This holds particularly true for IBM, the proverbial new kid on the block. Many papers discussing photogrammetry focus on its use for data acquisition (Sapirstein and Murray 2017; Magnani et al. 2020). These approaches are important for refining and developing the future of data acquisition, and as discussed above, can truly move the field forward. However, purely treating digital methods as technical improvements, void of theoretical implications is naive (Zubrow 2006). Indeed, critiques of digital approaches to archaeology have emphasized the extent to which digital methods do in fact affect how archaeologists approach and understand the past (Caraher 2016). However, the caution that digital techniques will change the way we study the past need not be seen as a drawback. Rather, it should be considered an opportunity for ambitious cyber-archaeologists to develop new ways to study the past (Huggett 2015, 2016). In general, cyber-archaeology methods do have the potential to address grand questions in new ways that are not possible through other methods, though the full potential of these approaches has not been seen (Howland 2018; Magnani et al. 2020). For archaeologists in the southern Levant to recognize the full potential of cyber-archaeology methods, we must develop an understanding of how these methods can actively contribute to theoretical development through analyses not possible through traditional methods applied to digital data.

GIS Analysis

GIS, having been increasingly applied since the 1990s, has experienced growth and development as a method of inquiry, to the extent that the theoretical advantages and limits of the tool are clear (Zubrow 2006; Fletcher and Winter 2008). One of the greatest strengths of GIS is its ability to factor in many different overlapping datasets, especially environmental data, for analysis (Sharon et al. 2004; Fletcher and Winter 2008)—though archaeologists should take care to avoid environmental determinism (Wheatley and Gillings 2002) and over-reliance on the top-down "God's View" provided by GIS that does not reflect the lived reality of ancient landscapes (Zubrow 2006). In general, theoretical guidelines and critiques of GIS are well-established (e.g., Wheatley and Gillings 2002; Conolly and Lake 2006; Fleming 2006; Llobera 2012), enabling scholars to avoid the pitfalls of inappropriately applied techniques. The full range of GIS analyses is far too vast to discuss in this chapter. However, in Israel and Jordan, scholars have applied GIS analyses to make the most of these environmental datasets for understanding the ways in which people have interacted with their environment or distributed themselves across the landscape (Fletcher and Winter 2008;

Ullah 2011; Horwitz et al. 2018; Edwards 2020). In that avenue, remote sensing is an approach with huge potential (Parcak 2017), though outside of this paper's focus on field data collection and its uses.

GIS analyses at the intra-site level may be the most interesting avenue of current and future research. These may focus on, for example, the reconstruction of ancient hearths (Alperson-Afil 2017), the use of hydrological modeling to understand the impacts of precipitation on site use and development (Howland et al. 2018; Bruins et al. 2019), or the depositional history of a site (Meier et al. 2017). These approaches make full use of the precise and detailed spatial recording, including IBM and its 2D derivatives, that is often part and parcel of the cyber-archaeology workflow. Relatedly, GIS analyses based in remote sensing, aerial survey, or environmental data have the potential to be applied in non-destructive ways by making maximum use of previously recorded data or that which is available from surface analysis. This potential provides opportunities for more ethical research that takes advantage of the "data avalanche" for conducting novel analyses.

IBM Analysis

Despite the ubiquity of IBM, archaeologists have been relatively slow to apply it as an analytical method (Magnani et al. 2020). Many discussions of the use of photogrammetry have emphasized its usefulness or discussed best practices (Sapirstein and Murray 2017), but fewer studies identify novel ways to approach the resulting 3D datasets. In theory, the possibility of volumetric analyses should be an appealing line of inquiry for archaeologists, interested in spatial relationships, but as discussed above, archaeologists have tended to prefer the use of IBM to produce documentation and 2D, GIS-based datasets (cf. Garstki 2020). In some cases, archaeologists have applied volumetric study to models recorded at archaeological sites with great success (Jaklič et al. 2015; Magnani and Schroder 2015; Fulton et al. 2016). However, these analyses are far less commonly applied by archaeologists working in Israel and Jordan, where IBM and LAAP have caught on but primarily in GIS-based contexts. Despite this, archaeologists working in the southern Levant have been able to apply IBM for artifact modeling and analysis (e.g., Zapassky et al. 2006; Karasik and Smilansky 2008; Olson et al. 2013). A full discussion of IBM approaches to artifact modeling is beyond the scope of this paper but nevertheless is an avenue of great potential for extremely precise measurements and automated classification of artifacts.

Data Dissemination: Engaging the Public

If the curation of cyber-archaeological data is predominantly a responsibility and the analysis of that data provides great opportunity, the dissemination of digital data offers both responsibility and opportunity. Though most archaeologists publish regularly in academic journals, our responsibility to share our findings goes beyond our academic peers and extends to the general public (Kintigh 1996). Digital datasets should be predisposed to public archaeology as they are easily shared online. However, archaeologists have not always taken full advantage of the outreach potential of born-digital data. For example, despite the ever-increasing availability of digital spatial data, archaeologists continue to apply spatial technologies primarily for data acquisition or analysis rather than dissemination (Earley-Spadoni 2017). 3D digital datasets, on the other hand, have been more successfully applied for public archaeology. Immersive technologies such as virtual reality (VR), augmented reality (AR), and archaeogaming are excellent tools for presenting 3D datasets to the public in compelling ways (Ellenberger 2017). These approaches have been applied effectively in the Eastern Mediterranean (Malinverni and Pierdicca 2017; Parrinello et al. 2017; Lercari et al 2018), though effective digital outreach projects have not kept pace with the exponential growth of digital data acquisition.

For projects with less technological savvy than needed to develop custom VR/AR/gaming applications, simply sharing digital data online through social data platforms such as Sketchfab can allow the public to experience a greater level of interaction with 3D archaeological datasets (Means 2015; Scopigno et al. 2017). This method of sharing datasets has been readily adopted by museums, including, notably, the British Museum (Garstki 2020; https://sketchfab.com/britishmuseum), and by archaeologists in Israel and Jordan to a lesser extent (e.g. Malinverni and Pierdicca 2017). Archaeologists would also be well-advised to borrow dissemination strategies from the Digital Humanities, who have made effective use of digital spatial history (Earley-Spadoni 2017). In particular, the integration of spatial data, 3D data, and contextual information has great potential for the dissemination of archaeological data. These combined publishing strategies can be tailored to academic audiences, public audiences, or both (Opitz 2018; Howland et al. 2020). The flexibility and dynamic nature of digital platforms can also allow for the implementation of multi-vocal storytelling and potentially the ability to involve local communities in telling their own stories (Richardson 2013). This aspect of a public cyber-archaeology is critical for the future of the field, as archaeologists must engage with the communities in which they work. Overall, the comprehensive and open sharing of datasets is relatively uncommon but is undoubtedly a strong model for how cyber-archaeology can generate new interest in the field and set new, high standards for data dissemination in archaeology.

Conclusions

Cyber-archaeology has enormous potential to change the way field archaeology is done forever. Adoption of digital data acquisition tools has already dramatically changed field recording for the purposes of producing ever-more detailed and accurate documentation of sites, even as excavation techniques remain largely the same. GIS and IBM recording has become *de rigeur* on projects in Israel and Jordan. The wealth of data generated by these techniques provides cyber-archaeology with perhaps its greatest challenge. With born-digital data not having any physical presence beyond the drives they are stored on, the accessibility of data for future generations is in doubt. Archaeologists must responsibly manage datasets and ensure their longevity and accessibility in the future. In the Levant, archaeologists have a good model of responsible data curation and publishing in the OpenContext platform, which has provided a framework for data publishing with curation in mind. For data analysis and dissemination, there is great, largely unrealized, potential in what can be done with digital datasets. The combination of GIS analyses and IBM has been an exciting trend in recent years and can be explored further at an intra-site scale. However, perhaps the greatest opportunities for future cyber-archaeological analysis would take advantage of the enormous advances in 3D recording for true three-dimensional analyses. Since archaeology as a field relies on the study of both horizontal and vertical spatial relationships, analyses that obscure the vertical dimension, as most GIS analyses do, miss the full picture. By taking advantage of the ever-increasing availability of 3D documentation of sites for analytical purposes, including volumetric and contextual analyses, archaeologists will literally open a new dimension for understanding sites and the past. Finally, the dissemination of data truly has the potential to increase the relevancy of our field. Publishing digital datasets can provide the public, including stakeholders and local communities, with ways to engage with archaeological findings and the archaeological process. By increasing the accessibility of archaeology, we make our field relevant and important for the future. Ultimately, the potential of cyber-archaeology is vast. Archaeologists working in the southern Levant need no encouragement to adopt its methods. Undoubtedly, we can anticipate an exciting future in which enthusiasts and critics alike contribute to a greater understanding of how cyber-archaeology can be situated in theoretical frameworks that allow us to develop a deeper understanding of the past.

Note

1   Laws and regulations in Israel and Jordan often affect archaeologists' ability to fly UAVs, in which case other LAAP methods may be preferred.

Bibliography

Agisoft. 2020. Agisoft Metashape User Manual: Professional Edition, Version 1.6.
Alperson-Afil, Nira. 2017. "Spatial Analysis of Fire: Archaeological Approach to Recognizing Early Fire." *Current Anthropology* 58: S258–S266.
Bewley, Robert H. 2003. "Aerial Survey for Archaeology." *The Photogrammetric Record* 18: 273–92.
Bruins, Hendrik J., Hodaya Bithan-Guedj, and Tal Svoray. 2019. "GIS-based Hydrological Modelling to Assess Runoff Yields in Ancient-Agricultural Terraced Wadi Fields (Central Negev Desert)." *Journal of Arid Environments* 166: 91–107.
Cameron, Fiona, and Sarah Kenderdine, eds. 2010. *Theorizing Digital Cultural Heritage - A Critical Discourse.* Cambridge: The MIT Press.
Campana, Stefano. 2017. "Drones in Archaeology. State-Of-The-Art and Future Perspectives." *Archaeological Prospection* 24: 275–96.
Caraher, William. 2016. "Slow Archaeology: Technology, Efficiency, and Archaeological Work." Pages 421–42 in *Mobilizing the Past for a Digital Future: The Potential of Digital Archaeology.* Edited by Erin Walcek Averett et al. Grand Forks: The Digital Press @ The University of North Dakota.
Conolly, James, and Mark Lake. 2006. *Geographical Information Systems in Archaeology.* Cambridge: Cambridge University Press.
Crawford, O.G.S. 1928. "Air Survey and Archaeology." *Ordnance Survey Professional Papers* 7. Southampton.
Dinsmoor, William B. 1977. "The Archaeological Field Staff: The Architect." *JFA* 4: 309–28.
Earley-Spadoni, Tiffany. 2017. "Spatial History, Deep Mapping, and Digital Storytelling: Archaeology's Future Imagined through an Engagement with the Digital Humanities." *JAS* 84: 95–102.
Edwards, S. 2020. "On the Lookout: Directional Visibility Cones and Defense in the Nebo Region, West-Central Jordan." *Open Archaeology* 6: 2–18.
Ellenberger, Kate. 2017. "Virtual and Augmented Reality in Public Archaeology Teaching." *AAP* 5: 305–09.
Ellis, Steven J.R. 2016. "Are We Ready for New (Digital) Ways to Record Archaeological Fieldwork? A Case Study from Pompeii." Pages 51–76 in *Mobilizing the Past for a Digital Future: The Potential of Digital Archaeology.* Edited by Erin Walcek Averett et al. Grand Forks: The Digital Press @ The University of North Dakota.
Fee, Samuel B. 2016. "Reflections on Custom Mobile App Development for Archaeological Data Collection." Pages 221–36 in *Mobilizing the Past for a Digital Future: The Potential of Digital Archaeology.* Edited by Erin Walcek Averett et al. Grand Forks: The Digital Press @ The University of North Dakota.
Fleming, A. 2006. "Post-processual Landscape Archaeology: A Critique." *CAJ* 16: 267–80.
Fletcher, Richard, and Rona Winter. 2008 "Prospects and Problems in Applying GIS to the Study of Chalcolithic Archaeology in Southern Israel." *BASOR* 352: 1–28.
Forte, Maurizio. 2011. "Cyber-archaeology: Notes on the Simulation of the Past." *VAR* 2: 7–18.
———. 2014. "3D Archaeology: New Perspectives and Challenges–The Example of Çatalhöyük." *JEMAHS* 2: 1–29.
Fulton, Carrie, Andrew Viduka, Andrew Hutchison, Joshua Hollick, Andrew Woods, David Sewell, and Sturt Manning. 2016. "Use of Photogrammetry for Non-Disturbance Underwater Survey: An Analysis of In Situ Stone Anchors." *AAP* 4: 17–30.

Garstki, Kevin. 2020. *Digital Innovations in European Archaeology.* Cambridge: Cambridge University Press.

Gordon, Jody Michael, Erin Walcek Averett, and Derek B. Counts. 2016. "Mobile Computing in Archaeology: Exploring and Interpreting Current Practices." Pages 1–32 in *Mobilizing the Past for a Digital Future: The Potential of Digital Archaeology.* Edited by Erin Walcek Averett et al. Grand Forks: The Digital Press @ The University of North Dakota.

Hill, Austin Chad. 2019. "Economical Drone Mapping for Archaeology: Comparisons of Efficiency and Accuracy." *JASR* 24: 80–91.

Hill, Austin Chad, and Yorke Rowan. 2017. "Droning on in the Badia: UAVs and Site Documentation at Wadi al-Qattafi." *NEA* 80: 114–23.

Homsher, R. S., M. Adams, A.B. Prins, R. Gardner-Cook, and Y. Tepper. 2017. "New Directions with Digital Archaeology and Spatial Analysis in the Jezreel Valley." *JLE* 10(3): 154–64.

Horwitz, Liora Kolska, Rona Winter-Livneh, and Aren M. Maeir. 2018. "The Archaeological Picture Went Blank": Historical Archaeology and GIS analysis of the Landscape of the Palestinian Village of Tell eş-Şâfi. *NEA* 81: 85–91.

Howland, Matthew D. 2018. "3D Recording in the Field: Style Without Substance?" Pages 19–33 in *Cyber-Archaeology and Grand Narratives.* Edited by Thomas E. Levy and Ian W.N. Jones. New York: Springer.

Howland, Matthew D., Ian W.N. Jones, Mohammad Najjar, and Thomas E. Levy. 2018. "Quantifying the Effects of Erosion on Archaeological Sites with Low-Altitude Aerial Photography, Structure from Motion, and GIS: A Case Study from Southern Jordan." *JAS* 90: 62–70.

Howland, Matthew D., Falko Kuester, and Thomas E. Levy. 2014. "Structure from Motion: Twenty-first Century Field Recording with 3D Technology." *NEA* 77: 187–91.

Howland, Matthew D., Brady Liss, Thomas E. Levy, and Mohammad Najjar. 2020. "Integrating Digital Datasets into Public Engagement through ArcGIS StoryMaps." *AAP* 8: 351–60.

Huggett, Jeremy. 2015. "A Manifesto for an Introspective Digital Archaeology." *Open Archaeology* 1.

———. 2016. "A Digital Detox for Digital Archaeology?" *Introspective Digital Archaeology* https://introspectivedigitalarchaeology.wordpress.com/2016/04/.

———. 2020. "Is Big Digital Data Different? Towards a New Archaeological Paradigm." *JFA* 45: S1, S8–S17.

Jaklič, Aleš, Miran Erič, Igor Mihajlović, Žiga Stopinšek, and Franc Solina. 2015. "Volumetric Models From 3D Point Clouds: The Case Study of Sarcophagi Cargo from a 2nd/3rd Century AD Roman Shipwreck Near Sutivan on Island Brač, Croatia." *JAS* 62: 143–52.

Jeffrey, S. 2012. "A New Digital Dark Age? Collaborative Web Tools, Social Media, and Long-term Preservation." *WA* 44: 553–70.

Johnson, Richard K. 2002. "Institutional Repositories: Partnering with Faculty to Enhance Scholarly Communication." *D-Lib Magazine* 8 http://www.dlib.org/dlib/november02/johnson/11johnson.html.

Jones, I.W.M. and T.E. Levy. 2018. "Cyber-archaeology and Grand Narratives: Where Do We Currently Stand?" Pages 1–118 in *Cyber-Archaeology and Grand Narratives: Digital Technology and Deep-Time Perspectives on Cultural Change in the Middle East.* Edited by I.W.N Jones and T.E. Levy. New York: Springer.

Kansa, Eric C., Sarah Whitcher Kansa, and Benjamin Arbuckle. 2014. "Publishing and Pushing: Mixing Models for Communicating Research Data in Archaeology." *IJDC* 9: 57–70.

Karasik, Avshalom, and Uzy Smilansky. 2008. "3D Scanning Technology as a Standard Archaeological Tool for Pottery Analysis: Practice and Theory." *JAS* 35: 1148–68.

Katsianis, M., S. Tsipidis, K. Kotsakis, and A. Kousoulakou. 2008. "A 3D Digital Workflow for Archaeological Intra-site Research Using GIS." *JAS* 35: 655–67.

Kersel, Morag M. 2016. "Response: Living a Semi-digital Kinda Life." Pages 475–92 in *Mobilizing the Past for a Digital Future: The Potential of Digital Archaeology.* Edited by Erin Walcek Averett et al. Grand Forks: The Digital Press @ The University of North Dakota.

Kintigh, Keith W. 1996. "SAA Principles of Archaeological Ethics." *SAA Bulletin* 14: 5–17.

Lercari, Nicola, Emmanuel Shiferaw, Maurizio Forte, and Regis Kopper. 2018. "Immersive Visualization and Curation of Archaeological Heritage Data: Çatalhöyük and the Dig@IT App." *JAMT* 25: 368–92.

Lercari, N., J. Shulze, W.Z. Wendrich, B. Porter, and T.E. Levy. 2016. "3-D Digital Preservation of At-Risk Global Cultural Heritage". Pages 123–26 in *EUROGRAPHICS Workshop on Graphics and*

Cultural Heritage, Vol 2016. Edited by C.E. Catalano, and L. De Luca. Eurographics Proceedings: The Eurographics Association.

Lercari, Nicola, Willeke Wendrich, Benjamin W. Porter, Margie M. Burton, and Thomas E. Levy (eds.). 2022. *Preserving Cultural Heritage in the Digital Age: Sending Out an S.O.S*. Sheffield: Equinox.

Letellier, R., W. Schmid, and F. Leblanc. 2007. *Recording, Documentation, and Information Management for the Conservation of Heritage Places: Guiding Principles*. Los Angeles: The Getty Conservation Institute.

Levy, Thomas E. 2013. "Cyber-Archaeology and World Cultural Heritage: Insights from the Holy Land." *Bulletin of the American Academy of Arts & Sciences* LXVI: 26–33.

Levy, Thomas E., J. D. Anderson, M. Waggoner, N. Smith, A. Muniz, and R. B. Adams. 2001. "Interface: Archaeology and Technology – Digital Archaeology 2001: GIS-based Excavation Recording in Jordan." *The SAA Archaeological Record* 1: 23–29.

Levy Thomas E., and Brady Liss. 2020. "Cyber-archaeology." *Encyclopedia of Global Archaeology*. Edited by Claire Smith. New York: Springer.

Levy, Thomas E., and Neil G. Smith. 2007. "On-site Digital Archaeology: GIS-Based Excavation Recording in Southern Jordan." Pages 47–58 in *Crossing Jordan–North American Contributions to the Archaeology of Jordan*. Edited by T. E. Levy, et al. London: Routledge.

Levy, Thomas E., Vid Petrovic, Thomas Wypych, Aaron Gidding, Kyle Knabb, Dávid, Hernández, N. Smith, Jürgen P. Schlulz, Stephen H. Savage, Falko Kuester, Erez Ben-Yosef, Connor Buitenhuys, C. J. Barrett, Mohammad Najjar, and Thomas DeFanti. 2010. "On-site Digital Archaeology 3.0 and Cyber-Archaeology: Into the Future of The Past – New Developments, Delivery and The Creation of a Data Avalanche." Pages 135–53 in *Introduction to Cyber-Archaeology*. Edited by Maurizio Forte. Oxford: Archaeopress.

Liss, Brady, Matthew D. Howland, Brita Lorentzen, Craig Smitheram, Mohammad Najjar, and Thomas E. Levy. 2020. "Up the Wadi: Development of an Iron Age Industrial Landscape in Faynan, Jordan." *JFA* 45: 413–27.

Llobera, M. 2012. "Life on a Pixel: Challenges in the Development of Digital Methods within an "Interpretative" Landscape Archaeology Framework." *JAMT* 19: 495–509.

Lynch, Clifford L. 2003. "Institutional Repositories: Essential Infrastructure for Scholarship in the Digital Age." *Libraries and the Academy* 3: 327–36.

———. 2017. "Updating the Agenda for Academic Libraries and Scholarly Communications. Copyright, Fair Use, Scholarly Communication, etc. 40." Electronic document, http://digitalcommons.unl.edu/scholcom/40, accessed April 20, 2017.

Magnani, Matthew, M. Douglass, W. Schroder, J. Reeves, and D. Braun. 2020. "The Digital Revolution to Come: Photogrammetry in Archaeological Practice." *AA* 85: 737–60.

Magnani, Matthew and Whittaker Schroder. 2015. "New Approaches to Modeling the Volume of Earthen Archaeological Features: A Case-Study from the Hopewell Culture Mounds." *JAS* 64: 12–21.

Malinverni, Eva Savina and Roberto Pierdicca. 2017. "Discovering and Sharing of Secret Architectures: The Hidden Tomb of The Pharaoh of El-Khasneh, Jordan." *ISPRSA* 42: 459–65.

McKeague, P, A. Corns, and R. Shaw. 2012. "Developing a Spatial Data Infrastructure for Archaeological and Built Heritage." *IJSDIR* 7: 38–65.

McKinny, Chris, and Itzhaq Shai. 2018 "Using Tools in Ways in Which They Were Not Intended: A Test Case of the Use of PlanGrid for Field Registration at Tel Burna." Pages 51–66 in *Cyber-Archaeology and Grand Narratives*. Edited by Thomas E. Levy and Ian W.N. Jones. New York: Springer.

McManamon, Francis P., Keith W. Kintigh, Leigh-Anne Ellison, and Adam Brin. 2017. "tDAR: A Cultural Heritage Archive for Twenty-First-Century Public Outreach, Research, and Resource Management." *AAP* 5: 238–49.

Means, Bernard K. 2015. "Promoting a More Interactive Public Archaeology: Archaeological Visualization and Reflexivity through Virtual Artifact Curation." *AAP* 3: 235–48.

Meier, Jacqueline S., A. Nigel Goring-Morris, and Natalie D. Munro. 2017. "Depositional Histories of Faunal Remains from the Neolithic Cultic Site of Kfar HaHoresh, Israel." *JAA* 48: 233–49.

Morgan, Colleen Leah. 2012. "Emancipatory Digital Archaeology." Ph.D. diss., University of California, Berkeley.

———. 2016. "Analog to Digital: Transitions in Theory and Practice in Archaeological Photography at Çatalhöyük." *Internet Archaeology* 42. https://doi.org/10.11141/ia.42.7

Motz, Christopher F. 2016. "Sangro Valley and the Five (Paperless) Seasons: Lessons on Building Effective Digital Recording Workflows for Archaeological Fieldwork." Pages 77–110 in *Mobilizing* the *Past for a Digital Future: The Potential of Digital Archaeology.* Edited by Erin Walcek Averett et al. Grand Forks: The Digital Press @ The University of North Dakota.

Myers, J.W. and E. E. Myers. 1992. *Aerial Atlas of Ancient Crete.* Los Angeles: University of California Press.

Olson, Brandon R., Ryan A. Placchetti, Jamie Quartermaine, and Ann E. Killebrew. 2013. "The Tel Akko Total Archaeology Project (Akko, Israel): Assessing the Suitability of Multi-Scale 3D Field Recording in Archaeology." *JFA* 38: 244–62.

Opitz, Rachel. 2018. "Publishing Archaeological Excavations at the Digital Turn." *JFA* 43: S68–S82.

Opitz, R. and J. Herrmann. 2018. "Recent Trends and Long-standing Problems in Archaeological Remote Sensing. *JCAA* 1: 1–24.

Parcak, Sarah H. 2017. "GIS, Remote Sensing, and Landscape Archaeology." *Oxford Handbooks Online.* New York: Oxford University Press.

Parrinello, Sandro, Monica Bercigli, and Daniele Bursich. 2017. "From Survey to 3D Model and from 3D Model To 'Videogame.' The Virtual Reconstruction of a Roman Camp in Masada, Israel." *Disegnare con* 10: 1–11.

Prins, Adam B., Matthew J. Adams, Robert S. Homsher, and Michael Ashley. 2014. "Digital Archaeological Fieldwork and the Jezreel Valley Regional Project, Israel." *NEA* 77(3): 192–97.

Quartermaine, Jamie, Brandon R. Olson, and Ann E. Killebrew. 2014. "Image-based Modeling Approaches to 2D and 3D Digital Drafting in Archaeology at Tel Akko and Qasrin: Two Case Studies." *JEMAHS* 2, 110–27.

Richardson, Lorna. 2013. "A Digital Public Archaeology?" *Papers from the Institute of Archaeology* 23: 1–12.

Roosevelt, Christopher H., Peter Cobb, Emanuel Moss, Brandon R. Olson, and Sinan Ünlüsoy. 2015. "Excavation is Destruction Digitization: Advances in Archaeological Practice." *JFA* 40: 325–46.

Sapirstein, Philip and Sarah Murray. 2017. "Establishing Best Practices for Photogrammetric Recording During Archaeological Fieldwork." *JFA* 42: 337–50.

Schloen, J. David, and Sandra R. Schloen. 2012 *OCHRE: An Online Cultural and Historical Research Environment.* Winona Lake: Eisenbrauns.

Scopigno, Roberto, Marco Callieri, Matteo Dellepiane, Federico Ponchio, and Marco Potenziani. 2017. "Delivering and Using 3D Models on the Web: Are We Ready?" *VAR* 8: 1–9.

Shanks, Michael. 1997. "Photography and archaeology." Pages 73–107 in *The Cultural Life of Images: Visual Representation in Archaeology.* Edited by Brian Leigh Molyneaux. London: Routledge.

Sharon, Ilan, Yehuda Dagan, and Gilah Tzionit. 2004. "The [Awful?] Truth about GIS and Archaeology." *BSAS* 11: 151–62.

Sheehan, B. 2015. "Comparing Digital Archaeological Repositories: tDAR Versus Open Context." *Behavioral & Social Sciences Librarian* 34: 173–213.

Shott, Michael. 2014. "Digitizing Archaeology: A Subtle Revolution in Analysis." *WA* 46: 1–9.

Smith, N.G., L. Passone, S. Al-Said, M. Al-Farhan, and T.E. Levy. 2014. "Drones in Archaeology: Integrated Data Capture, Processing, and Dissemination in the al-Ula Valley, Saudi Arabia." *NEA* 77: 176–81.

Sobotkova, Adela, Shawn A. Ross, Brian Ballsun-Stanton, Andrew Fairbairn, Jessica Thompson, and Parker VanValkenburgh. 2016. "Measure Twice, Cut Once: Cooperative Deployment of a Generalized, Archaeology-Specific Field Data Collection System." Pages 337–72 in *Mobilizing the Past for a Digital Future: The Potential of Digital Archaeology.* Edited by Erin Walcek Averett et al. Grand Forks: The Digital Press @ The University of North Dakota.

Tripcevich, Nicholas and Steven A. Wernke. 2010. "On-site Recording of Excavation Data Using Mobile GIS." *JFA* 35: 380–97.

Ullah, Isaac I.T. 2011. "A GIS Method For Assessing the Zone of Human-Environmental Impact around Archaeological Sites: A Test Case from the Late Neolithic of Wadi Ziqlâb, Jordan." *JAS* 38: 623–32.

Verhoeven, Geert J.J. 2009. "Providing an Archaeological Bird's-Eye View–An Overall Picture of Ground-Based Means to Execute Low-Altitude Aerial Photography (LAAP) in Archaeology." *Archaeological Prospection* 16: 233–49.

Verhoeven, Geert, Michael Doneus, Ch Briese, and Frank Vermeulen. 2012. "Mapping by Matching: A Computer Vision-Based Approach to Fast and Accurate Georeferencing of Archaeological Aerial Photographs." *JAS* 39(7): 2060–70.

Vincent, M. L., F. Kuester, and T. E Levy. 2014. "OpenDig: Digital Field Archeology, Curation, Publication, and Dissemination." *NEA* 77: 204–08.

Waagen, Jitte. 2019. "New Technology and Archaeological Practice. Improving the Primary Archaeological Recording Process in Excavation by means of UAS Photogrammetry." *JAS* 101: 11–20.

Wallrodt, John. 2016. "Why Paperless: Technology and Changes in Archaeological Practice, 1996–2016." Pages 33–50 in *Mobilizing the Past for a Digital Future: The Potential of Digital Archaeology*. Edited by Erin Walcek Averett et al. Grand Forks: The Digital Press @ The University of North Dakota.

Wheatley, D. and M. Gillings. 2002. *Spatial Technology and Archaeology: The Archaeological Applications of GIS*. New York: CRC Press.

York, Jeremy, Myron Gutmann, and Francine Berman. 2016. "What Do We Know about the Stewardship Gap?" Ann Arbor: University of Michigan Library. http://hdl.handle.net/2027.42/122726.

Zapassky, Elena, Israel Finkelstein, and Itzhak Benenson. 2006. "Ancient Standards of Volume: Negevite Iron Age Pottery (Israel) as a Case Study in 3D Modeling." *JAS* 33: 1734–43.

Zubrow, Ezra B.W. 2006. "Digital archaeology: A Historical Context." Pages 10–32 in *Digital Archaeology: Bridging method and theory*. Edited by Thomas L. Evans and Patrick Daly. London: Routledge.

47

ISRAEL, ANCIENT AND MODERN

Representations and Misrepresentations of the Past in Dialogue with the Present

Rachel Hallote

This chapter will examine how the ancient past of the land of Israel is perceived and misperceived when put in dialogue with the present. Worldwide, ancient history and archaeology are often taken out of context to make arguments about current conflicts. This is true on both sides of the Arab-Israeli conflict. To understand how the past both informs and misinforms the current political discourse about Israel, this article will review several topics that are not usually understood as interconnected. These include the origins of western interest in Ottoman Palestine, the 19th-century birth of Jewish nationalism known as Zionism, the birth of biblical archaeology, and the forming of the borders of modern Israel in contradistinction to those of ancient Israel. We will also examine various trends in archaeological thought and theory that exist in opposition to a strong public thirst for understanding topics in biblical archaeology. The way these various strands of thought interact with each other contributes to the politization of the archaeology of ancient Israel. The unusual breadth of topics to be addressed necessitates a streamlined presentation. Each point could be the subject of deeper, specialized analyses, and most have already been studied in far greater depth than is possible here.

Background–Ancient Judahite, Israelite, and Jewish history

Jewish history is long and varied, as is the Jewish connection to the land of Israel.[1] One important point to remember is that "Jews" and the religion of "Judaism" did not exist in the period of the Hebrew Bible. Rather, there were "Israelites" and "Judahites" who practiced Israelite and Judahite religion—out of which normative Judaism developed. In the Iron Age II, "Israel" was a polity with the capital city of Samaria, near modern Nablus, while "Judah" was a polity centered in the southern part of the central hill country with Jerusalem as its capital.[2] Israel and Judah were conquered and subsumed by the Assyrian and Babylonian empires, respectively, in the 8th and 6th centuries BCE. The many other polities in the region had similar fates, and as their peoples were absorbed by the conquering empires, they lost their cultural identities. This includes the Israelites.[3]

Only one people remembered their cultural origins—the Judahites. When the Babylonians conquered Judah in 586 BCE, they destroyed much of Jerusalem, including the Temple of the Judahite deity Yahweh. They also deported many of the people to Babylon. Those who survived the journey gradually integrated into Babylonian society but still remembered their origins and identity and were always known as "the people from Judah"—the Jews, who practiced the religion of Judah, i.e., Judaism.[4]

These Jews of the Babylonian diaspora had to find a way to practice a religion that was previously centered on one site—the Temple to Yahweh in Jerusalem—without access to that site. Not only had their Temple been destroyed, but they were also living far away from where it had been located. This is how and when the Jewish religion developed. Without the Temple, the three daily sacrifices could no longer be performed. To compensate, the religion changed significantly. Prayer services and study replaced animal sacrifice, and a new religion, Judaism, was born (Marx 2013; Reif 1995). The concept of Yahweh as the sole, universal god, i.e., the concept of monotheism, which had not been accepted by all Judahites prior to exile, was now solidified for the Jews. So too was the idea of nationhood—that is, the Jews still thought of themselves as a group tied to the territory from which they originated, through their relationship with their god. This link between nation, land, and religion became influential and later informed western and Jewish thinkers regarding nationalism.

The names for the land changed over time, from Judah or Yehud in the Persian period, to Judea, and finally to Palestine. This latter term was used by the Romans, who adapted the regional term "Philistia" that previously referred only to the southwestern part of the country where the Philistines, ancient enemies of biblical Israel, had once lived. Throughout these changes of names and administration, and onwards into the Middle Ages and beyond, Jews always lived in the land as a minority population.

The nineteenth century: Millenarism, Zionism, and archaeology

While Palestine always retained its minority population of Jews, by the Roman Period, the Jewish diaspora had spread from Babylon, Egypt, and Persia to Greece, Rome, and ultimately to the rest of the Roman Empire including the emerging European countries. In fact, by the early Middle Ages, the Church largely viewed Jews through the lens of supercessionist Augustine doctrine, as a people divorced from their land, wandering the earth as exiles to bear witness to the truth of Christianity (Hood 2019). The fact that there were still some Jews in Palestine was not important.

In the 19th century CE, an aspect of Christian thought regarding Jews coalesced into a religious movement known as Millenarism.[5] This is the belief that all Jews need to be restored to their ancient homeland before the Second Coming of Jesus will take place. This theology was based on passages within Romans 11 regarding the salvation of the Jews, which since the Reformation, had gradually integrated into English Protestant thought (Cohen 2005: 259–62; Matar 1985: 115). Millenarists actively encouraged Jews living all over the world to leave their current diasporic countries and return to the Holy Land, now Ottoman Palestine. Millenarist beliefs were influential in many countries but were particularly formative in England where they spurred on interest in Jews in general and Palestine in particular.

Besides this religious interest, England also had a political interest in Palestine, as a land bridge to its imperial holdings in India and Africa. To that end, it established a consular office in Jerusalem in 1838. However, Ottoman Palestine was unstable politically. At the very end of the previous century, in 1799, Napoleon's troops had entered the land leading to a year of warfare. Then came the period of Muhammed Ali, who briefly conquered and held both Egypt and Palestine during the 1830s. He and his son Ibrahim Pasha instigated comprehensive reforms that raised the status of non-Muslims in Palestine, but these also caused significant unrest on the part of the majority Muslim population (Scholch 1992: 40–41).

Looking to restore calm, the British helped oust Muhammed Ali's dynasty and restored Ottoman rule.

In this atmosphere of unrest, Britain found itself in competition with the French as well as the Russian Empire for a foothold in the land. The French presence could be traced back to the Crusades when the Latin Church was firmly established in the region. France claimed sovereignty over various Christian holy places because of that history. Meanwhile, Russia claimed control over Christian holy places as the protector of the Eastern Orthodox Christians. The dominance of these other European powers led Britain to want to entrench itself even further in the region, which it did via a Millenarist agenda. In 1841, Foreign Secretary Palmerston, deeply influenced by the Millenarist beliefs of his son-in-law Lord Ashley Cooper, the seventh Earl of Shaftsbury and a member of Parliament, declared that Britain would be the protector of the Jews of Palestine (see Green 2008: 177–80; Verete 1970: 317–26). British "protection" of the Jews manifested itself over the next 60 years through the sending of missionaries and the founding of schools.

Like Millenarism, Zionism advocated a return of Jews to their Holy Land, yet Zionism's evolution was unrelated to Millenarism.[6] Originally denoting a particular hill within the city, the term "Zion" refers to the holy city of Jerusalem. For Jews living in diaspora communities, the yearning for Zion/Jerusalem was a concept expressed within Jewish prayers, but only in the abstract. While individual Jews had "returned to Zion" as pilgrims over the centuries, for most Jews, the idea was unattainable and unthinkable, except in the eschatological sense.

In fact, many Jews actively rejected any ties to their ancient homeland. During the 19th century, Jews were finally being granted citizenship in some European countries, yet still were not emancipated in others. The leaders of the new Reform movement of Judaism that had begun in Germany were concerned about accusations of dual loyalty: should Jews be perceived as yearning for a country far away, they were in danger of having their new rights of citizenship revoked at home. Therefore, all mentions of Zion were expunged from Reform prayer books.[7]

Thus, it is not surprising that Zionism was not born in western Europe but in Russia. The Russian czars of the 18th and 19th centuries had oppressed their Jewish communities with multiple restrictions and violent persecutions, until the reign of Czar Alexander II (r. 1855–81), who was known for his reforms. Under his rule, the Jews of the Russian Empire were allowed to move around freely, could live in the major cities of the Empire, and attend schools and universities for the first time. These freedoms ended with Alexander's assassination in 1881, for which the Jews were blamed.

The assassination led to violet anti-Jewish riots throughout Russia. Jews began to flee the country in large numbers and continued to leave for the next 40 years. Ninety percent of these Jewish refugees went to the United States for economic opportunities, but small numbers fled to other places such as South America and Western Europe while a very small percentage of them headed for Ottoman Palestine because of newly forming Zionist ideals.

Zionism is a secular movement, whose roots go back to intellectual developments of the 1850s and 1860s, during the time of Czar Alexander II when Jews studying in universities for the first time became interested in reviving Hebrew as a spoken language. For most of Jewish history, Hebrew was only used for prayer and study and was not spoken. Secular, educated Russian Jews began experimenting with writing literature in Hebrew and even publishing Hebrew newspapers.

This revival of the language of ancient Israel might have remained an intellectual exercise if not for the assassination of the czar and the ensuing attacks on Jews throughout Russia.

This wave of violence forced European Jews to realize that even in the post-Enlightenment world, they were not guaranteed safety in any country in which they lived. Within months of the assassination, in 1882, a Jewish physician from Odessa named Leon Pinsker published a pamphlet titled "Autoemancipation." Pinsker's main argument was that Jews would never be secure, even in countries where they had been emancipated, because nations can only make peace with other nations, not with a disparate ethnic grouping (Pinsker 1976). In other words, Pinsker believed that the Jews needed their own homeland to be secure because only then they would be considered an equal partner.[8]

The term "Zionism" as applied to this national idea came into use in the early 1880s by the Austrian Jewish writer Nathan Birnbaum. The Viennese journalist Theodor Herzl brought the concept to the Jews of western Europe, creating a larger Zionist movement. Thanks to Herzl's writings and the international congresses he organized, western European Jews started to financially support the Zionist movement by funding the new settlements populated by eastern European emigrants to Ottoman Palestine.

The settlers themselves were part of a youth culture in Eastern Europe, often members of youth groups, who were idealistic and largely university educated. Some were influenced by socialism, and most were immersed in the movement to revive the Hebrew language. Few were religious, as this was a secular movement. Within their concept of Zionism was the desire to work the land that had been the homeland of the Jews of antiquity—the ancient Israelites and Judahites—as farmers.

But these young pioneers could not afford to buy land in Ottoman Palestine, even when it was available. The Musha system of land tenure meant that most of the Empire belonged to the Sultan or to absentee private landowners, who usually lived far from the land they owned, often outside of Palestine (Kark and Grossman 2003). When land was available, it was purchased for the new settlers by western European Jews such as Baron Edmund de Rothschild and Baron Maurice de Hirsch as well as many small "holding companies."

Statistics vary but approximately 12,500 Jews lived in 50 small farming settlements on the eve of World War I (Ben Artzi 1990: 145). Some of these immigrant Jews also lived in villages and founded new neighborhoods on the outskirts of cities. Jewish communities grew from there. While these young Jewish immigrants to Ottoman Palestine valued the biblical connection of Jews to the land of Israel, and trained themselves to speak in Hebrew, they were completely secular in their interests, lifestyles, and intentions. This was vastly different from the Millenarist equating of ancient and modern Jews, yet both Millenarist Christians and Zionists were eager to see Jews move to Ottoman Palestine—the modern incarnation of their ancient homeland.

The archaeology of Palestine in the late 19th century

The Millenarist interest in revitalizing the Jewish connection to their ancient land spurred interest in the land itself—specifically in the remains of its ancient Jewish past. Since the 1840s, archaeological excavations had taken place in the "Bible land" of Iraq. Biblical Nineveh and other Assyrian cities had been uncovered, meaning that the history of the conquerors of ancient Israel was now known in a brand-new way (Hallote 2017). It took until the 1870s for scholars to become interested in the primary land of the Bible, ancient Israel. The reason for the delay was that Ottoman Palestine had a poor reputation among westerners as being desolate and dirty, with unsafe roads and violent clashes between Bedouin tribes. This reputation derived from numerous travelers' accounts, including that of Edward Clarke, James Silk Buckingham, Ulrich van Seetzen, John Lewis Burckhardt, and more. For westerners, a disconnect had developed between desolate Ottoman Palestine and the ancient, fertile "land of milk and honey" of the Bible.

This is where the religious interests of Millenarists, missionaries, and clergy in general intersect with the story of archaeology. Clergy, not explorers, were interested in approaching desolate Palestine for religious reasons, which soon led to serious scientific investigation. The first serious academic approach was made by the American minister and professor Edward Robinson who journeyed to Palestine in 1838 and 1852, identifying the location of multiple sites mentioned in the Bible by noting the transformation of Hebrew place names into Greek and Arabic ones (Robinson and Smith 1856; see also McKinny, this volume).

For Britain, the birth of biblical archaeology was directly connected to missionary activity. In the early 1860s, British missionaries in Jerusalem had encountered poor sanitary conditions and realized that the water system of the city was spreading cholera. This led to the founding of an organization to mitigate the water problem. In 1865, this organization paid for an engineering survey of the water systems of Jerusalem by Charles Wilson of the Royal Corps of Engineers (Moscrop 2000), with the goal of identifying all springs, aquifers, and cisterns to clean them. The decision to undertake this survey underscores the intersection of religious beliefs with government personnel and resources (Hallote 2006: 48–49).

As he surveyed, Wilson sent reports back to London, which included mentions of the ancient ruins that were still visible on the ground. Ultimately, the excitement over uncovering parts of ancient Jerusalem took precedence over the water issues, and a new organization was founded in London, the Palestine Exploration Fund, which went on to do a comprehensive survey of all of Palestine during the 1870s and 1880s, an effort that aided the imperial goal of mapping all portions of the British Empire (see Conder and Kitchener 1880; Gavish 2005: 3–17).

The Fund then undertook the very first professional archaeological excavation in the country in 1890, at the mound of Tell el-Hesi, a site that was incorrectly thought to be the important biblical city of Lachish. Nearly all the subsequent early excavation sites were of places that were well-known from the Hebrew Bible as archaeology of the late 19th and early 20th centuries was unapologetically seen to explore, illuminate, and ultimately confirm the world of the Bible. After the Tell el-Hesi excavations concluded, the British went on to work in Jerusalem, then biblical Azekah, Gath, Taanach, and Gezer, and later at Beth Shemesh. The Germans then excavated at biblical Megiddo, the Austrians at biblical Jericho, and later Shechem, the Americans at biblical Samaria. These projects uncovered archaeological remains from well before and after the Iron Age "biblical" period, and these were recorded properly and preserved according to the developing standards of the day; however, the motive for choosing where to excavate was always biblical/religious in nature.

The biblical framework continued deep into the 20th century. The scholarship of American archaeologist William F. Albright, often called the father of biblical archaeology, was oriented toward the Bible, as was that of his student G. Ernest Wright. This generation of archaeologists came largely from Protestant clerical backgrounds, and while their field approaches were objective, they did not reject that heritage in their choice of sites or their synthetic analyses. Albright's first important excavation was at Tell el-Ful, which he identified as Saul's capital city of Gibeah, and the excavation that he is best remembered for, Tell Beit Mirsim, was then identified as Debir/Kiryat Sepher of Joshua and Judges. Wright in turn worked at Tell Balata, biblical Shechem. Similarly, the rapidly growing cadre of Jewish archaeologists in early 20th-century Palestine, who were almost all secular Zionists, were also drawn to biblical questions.

The trend of exploring biblical sites even continued into the 1950s, when Kathleen Kenyon worked at Jericho.[9] By the time Kenyon began her excavations, the site had been excavated by several previous teams, and it was clear that there were no significant Iron Age remains to be found as the site had already been abandoned at the time when biblical Joshua was supposed to have besieged it. For all of Kenyon's careful reassessing of the stratigraphy of the site, it was this chronological problem that drove her and others' interest. In other words, the Bible could not be left out of archaeological discussions even though the site had limited early Iron Age remains.[10] Similarly, other biblically oriented issues persisted in the field, as the style of fortification architecture found at sites that the Bible associated with King Solomon (1 Kgs 9:15) was labeled as "Solomonic" architecture.

The birth of the conflict between Arabs and Jews in reference to the land of Palestine

To understand how this biblically oriented archaeology became entwined with the politics of the region, we need to quickly review the years leading up to the founding of the modern State of Israel in 1948. When the first excavations in Palestine took place, the region was still part of the Ottoman Empire, which collapsed at the end of World War I. The earlier British involvement in the region now became international policy, as Britain was granted the Mandate on Palestine, and a civil government was formed. The Mandate, which called on Britain to develop the country for the benefit of its inhabitants, lasted from 1920 until 1948.

British political control in Palestine exacerbated some growing tensions between Jews, more of whom were arriving as immigrants, and the Muslim Arabs. The British refocused their original Millenarist-inspired protection of the Jews of Palestine into a more solid statement in the Balfour Declaration of 1917, which stated that Britain would support the establishment of a "national home for the Jewish people" within Palestine.

At the same time, the British made contradictory secret promises to the Hashemite Arab leader Hussein of Mecca, regarding a future Arab state in the region.[11] In this way, the British soon found themselves enmeshed in, and in large part causing, a growing rift between the Muslim Arabs of Palestine and Jews of Palestine (the Christians were quiescent).

Neither of these groups were fully native to the land. We have seen that the Jewish population was a mix of indigenous local Jews and recent arrivals. There were also many new arrivals among the Arabs, a population that had been shifting and evolving for several centuries. Most of the local Arabs were descendants of local Jews and Christians who had converted to Islam centuries earlier, or else descendants of Arab migrants who had entered the region after the Islamic conquest in the 7th century CE. More arrived as part of the many forced migrations that took place during the regimes of various Muslim empires. During the 19th century alone, various Ottoman-appointed pashas had forcibly moved Muslim population groups from other parts of the Empire into Palestine as part of larger political initiatives, or as punishments. These included migrations from Egypt, Algeria, Yemen, and other locations. Population movements continued into the first half of the British Mandate when approximately 60,000 Arabs from other countries voluntarily immigrated to Palestine, which was growing economically more than any other country in the region.[12]

As neither all the Jews nor all the Arabs were fully indigenous to Palestine (perhaps because of that), tensions grew between the two groups. Arab peasants felt threatened by Jewish land purchases and a new, export-driven agricultural economy, while Arab elites felt threatened by the fact that under Britain, Jews who had always been second-class citizens, were no longer in that position. Incidents such as the 1920 Arab assault on the Jewish settlement of

Tel Hai (Zerubavel 1991) and clashes in Jerusalem instigated by the Grand Mufti of Jerusalem Amin al- Husseini exacerbated social tensions that had been rising in some Arab villages since the late Ottoman period when the first Jewish farming settlements were established. [13] Arab peasants who farmed but did not own land (called *fellahin*), feared having the land they worked sold out from under them by the absentee Arab landlords. Strong Husseini influence in the villages throughout the countryside as well as in the cities spurred these anxieties, leading to further riots in Jerusalem and Hebron in 1928 and 1929.[14]

The birth of the modern State of Israel, and its borders in relation to the borders of ancient Israel and Judah

The British saw the growing tension between the groups they governed and tried to find solutions. In 1922 they divided the land of their Mandate in two, giving all the territory east of the Jordan River (Trans-Jordan) to the Hashemite family of Arabia to govern as an emirate. In 1930, they restricted Jewish immigration to Palestine to maintain Arab dominance, but neither of these actions resolved the tensions. The Arab population rebelled in 1936 against British rule in an uprising, and the British pushed back using overwhelming force. Following this Arab rebellion, the British issued another edict to further limit Jewish immigration to the region, to appease the Arab population and garner Arab support during World War II.[15] This 1939 white paper limited immigration exactly when the Jews of Europe were attempting to flee and find safe haven from Hitler.[16]

There was not another attempt to solve the problem of Palestine until after the end of World War II. At this point, the British resolved to end their Mandate and to turn the issue of Palestine over to the newly formed United Nations. The United Nations decided that the best solution would be to partition the land. The Partition Plan was brought to a vote of the General Assembly in 1947, and it passed by a two-thirds majority. And this brings us to the crux of the issues—the borders of the modern State of Israel, and their relationship to the borders of ancient Israel and Judah.

When Jewish immigrants came to Ottoman Palestine during the first wave of immigration in the 19th century, some settled on the outskirts of existing cities like Jaffa (forming the city of Tel Aviv) or in the "new city" of Jerusalem to the west of the old walled city, but others established small agricultural communities. These various settlements clustered in the following regions: the northern Jordan Valley, north and west of the Sea of Galilee, a northern coastal area approximately stretching from Haifa to Hadera, and a southern coastal area stretching from Jaffa down to the area inland from Ashdod (see Aaronsohn 1990: 149; Ben-Bassat 2009: 45). While a few other settlements formed in the Jerusalem and Hebron areas, the main part of the central hills had none. Even though the central hills had been the heartland of biblical Israel and Judah, they were of little interest to early Zionists who wanted land with agricultural potential (see Stein 1984).

The borders established by the 1947 Partition Plan reflected the areas where Jewish settlements were densest, reserving those areas for a Jewish state, while the places with fewer or no Jewish settlements were reserved for an Arab state. As stated in Chapter 4, Section 6 of the official report to the United Nations General Assembly, "The greater part of Palestine would be divided into an Arab province and a Jewish province, the latter including almost the entire area on which Jews had already settled, together with a considerable area between and around the settlements," (United Nations General Assembly 1947; see Figure 47.1). This minimized potential population transfers for both groups.[17]

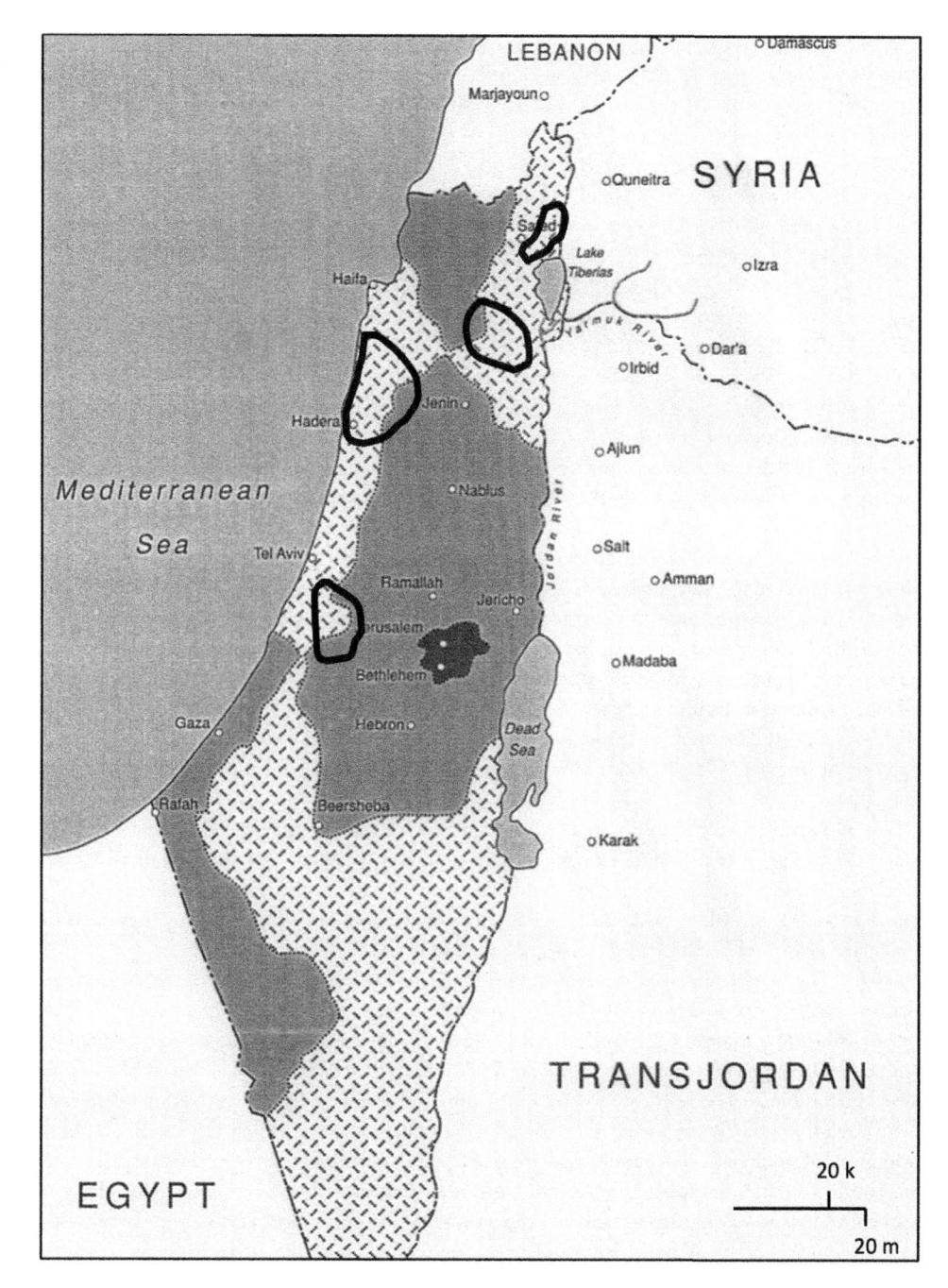

Figure 47.1 Proposed borders of 1947 Partition Plan as reflecting densest areas of early 19th century Jewish settlements (following Ben-Bassat 2009: 45). Hatched gray: area designated for a Jewish state; dark gray: area designated for Arab state; circles: densest Jewish settlement areas

It is very important to note that these borders reflected the situation on the ground, and in no way reflected the borders of the ancient polities of Israel and Judah. In fact, the central hill country, the main area of ancient Israel and Judah, was almost entirely designated for the potential Arab state (see Figure 47.2).

When the British withdrew in May 1948, the Jews declared statehood on their portion of the land and chose the name "Israel" although other names, including Judea, were considered (see Kramer 2020). The new country was immediately attacked by five Arab countries which had not supported the Partition Plan. This war lasted until March 1949. Besides the violence and death that marked it, two major changes happened during these months. First was a movement of people as hundreds of thousands of Arabs left their villages in the land designated for the new Jewish state, some fleeing, as they had been doing since the approval of the Partition Plan, and some being forced out by the advancing Israeli army. Those who moved or fled from the coastal plain headed into the hill country, to the area designated (but not claimed) as an Arab state—that is, the land currently referred to by the geographic term the West Bank, or else to neighboring countries like Jordan, with promises by these neighbors that once the war was won, they would be able to return home. Statistics vary widely, but 1948 British estimates say that between 550,000 and 600,000 Arabs left (Karsh 2011).[18]

The second change was one of territory. By the war's end, the borders originally designated by the United Nations had evolved, as the Israeli army pushed back its attackers on several fronts, meaning that the cease-fire lines of 1949 left less territory for the Arab state than originally proposed, moving Israel's borders east toward the hill country, south toward Gaza in the Negev, and closed a gap in the north. However, these 1949 borders of Israel still did not include the bulk of what had been ancient Israel and ancient Judah, according to generally accepted borders of those ancient kingdoms' potential extent. That territory was largely within in the West Bank, which Jordan immediately occupied and held between 1949 and 1967.

The next time the borders changed significantly was after the June 1967 conflict between Israel and Egypt, Jordan, and Syria, known as the Six-Day War.[19] By the end of that war, Israel had gained territory, much of which was later given back through peace treaties.[20] The part that Israel still administrates today includes parts of the West Bank—other parts of which are governed by the Palestinian authority, founded in 1994.

Today, the West Bank has two discrete populations living in it. One is the Arab population, and the other is a Jewish "settler" population that has been there since 1967. The settlers are largely Haredi ("ultra-Orthodox") Jews.[21] These religious Zionist settlers believe that the land is theirs because it was the land of ancient Israel and Judah of the Bible, as can be seen from Figure 47.3. Therefore, settler groups and those that support them use different terminology for the West Bank, referring to it as Judea-Samaria, which reflects the biblical kingdoms of ancient Judah, and Israel (whose capital city was Samaria). Historically and geographically, this territorial equivalency is largely accurate, however, the terminology is political in intent—equating territory taken in war by the contemporary State of Israel with territory controlled by ancient "Jewish" states, as a way of claiming the legitimacy of Israel's current hold on the land. This will be returned to below.

Archaeology of the West Bank

After 1967, Israeli archaeologists had access to the West Bank for the first time, and exploration got underway quickly.[22] Several surveys were led by Israeli scholars including Moshe Kochavi, Adam Zertal, and Israel Finkelstein (Greenberg and Keinan 2009: 11). These

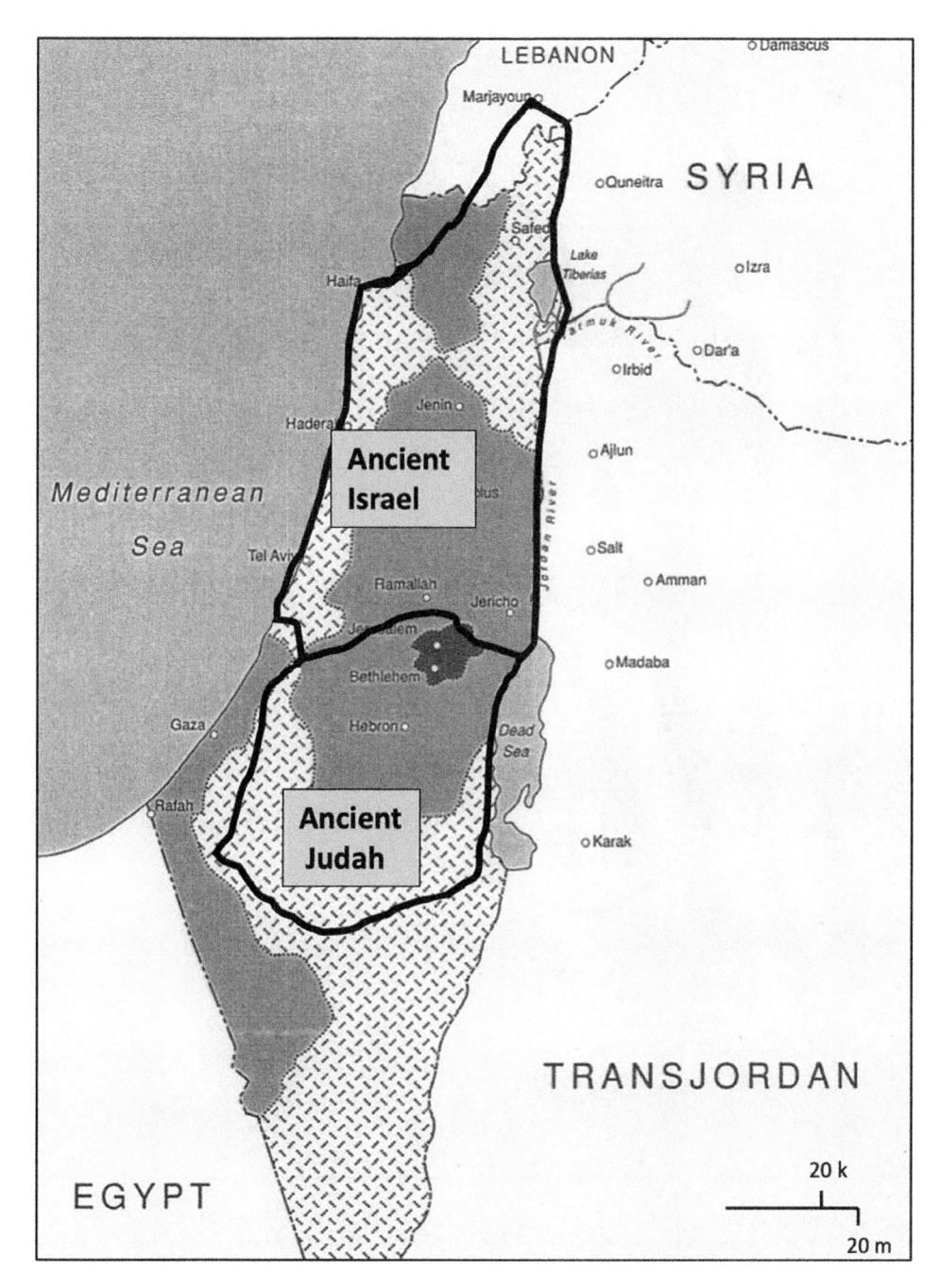

Figure 47.2 Map of the 1947 Partition Plan with "biblical" borders of Iron Age Israel and Judah overlaid on top. Note that the potential Arab state's borders—dark gray—included the main areas of the ancient kingdoms

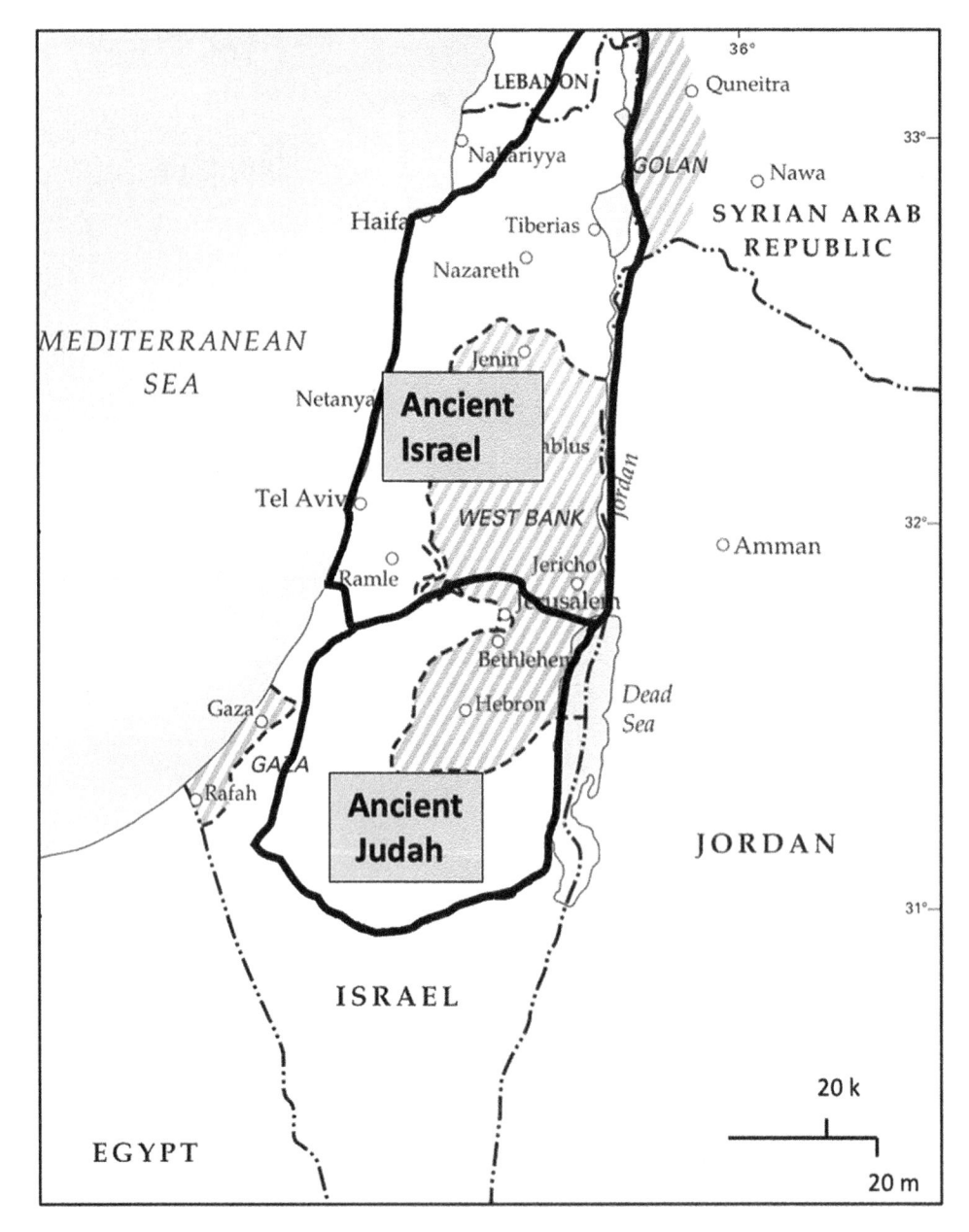

Figure 47.3 Map showing the West Bank with "biblical" borders of Iron Age kingdoms of Israel and Judah overlaid on top. Note that all the land of the West Bank falls within the territories of the ancient kingdoms

surveys led to multiple excavation projects, and so, during the 1970s and 1980s, an "archaeology of Israelite settlement" developed.

These excavations and surveys in the West Bank revealed a semi-consistent style of a domestic structure known as the 4-room house. These structures seemed to define a new ethnic grouping in the hill country. Other elements also associated with these sites included silos, terraces, and the general settlement pattern itself, centered within the hill country (Faust 2017; Faust and Bunimovitz 2003). The scholars researching these sites were not looking for biblical associations, as they were of a younger generation for whom the Bible was not the primary focus, and yet, what they uncovered made clear that a new group of people had settled in the hill country around 1200 BCE. While this new ethnic grouping can confidently be identified with the Israelites, their material culture was closely connected to that of Bronze Age Canaan. This led to non-biblical approaches to the origins of the Israelites, ones that favored a local development, not an outside conquest as described in the Bible (Gottwald 1979; Mendenhall 1962).

The 1960s and 1970s: two conflicting trends in archaeology

While the Israeli archaeological exploration of the West Bank was taking place, there was a major shift in the discipline of archaeology as a whole. By the 1960s and 1970s, archaeologists who worked in the Middle East were beginning to embrace the new approach of processual archaeology.

Sometimes called the New Archaeology, processual archaeology was a New World development often associated with the American archaeologist Lewis Binford, the British archaeologist Colin Renfrew, as well as others.[23] Processual archaeology borrowed methodologies from the hard sciences and was associated with anthropology departments where New World archaeologists were situated, rather than departments of Near Eastern studies, Classical studies, Art History, and religious studies, the homes of biblical archaeologists. With theoretical frameworks such as systems theory adapted from biology, statistical analyses took precedence.

Processual archaeology became popular in Near Eastern archaeological circles and began to influence biblical archaeologists. In fact, the very name of the discipline changed at this point. The term "biblical archaeology" had from the beginning implied a religious orientation for the field, not a scientific one. It also implied an exclusive interest in the biblical periods—largely the Iron Age—as opposed to the plethora of earlier and later material.

To include all time periods from prehistory forward, while at the same time shedding the religious image, and acknowledging cultural influences across borders, some American scholars argued for the term "Syro-Palestinian archaeology," or sometimes the "archaeology of the southern and northern Levant." These seemingly neutral geographic terms were intended to situate the erstwhile "biblical archaeology" both within the larger Near East and also within world archaeology. But it is important to note here that the "archaeology of Palestine," or "Palestinian archaeology" were also phrases that had been used interchangeably with "biblical archaeology" since the 19th century, as the geographic area in question was Ottoman and later British Mandatory Palestine as we have seen.[24]

Yet the terminological change immediately became a problem for the discipline, albeit an unacknowledged one: for interested lay people, these terms obfuscated what the field was about, that is, the land of the Bible. Most non-scholars are not familiar with the term Levant, and when the name Palestine is used nowadays, it has a different, political meaning, referring to a future Palestinian state to be located in the West Bank.

Even after processualism had ebbed, many scholars continued to disassociate themselves from the Bible and "biblical" archaeology.[25] In 1998 the important scholarly organization the American Schools of Oriental Research changed the name of one of its main journals from *The Biblical Archaeologist* to *Near Eastern Archaeology*, to reflect how archaeologists of the region now thought of themselves, and in 2020 this organization voted to change its name from the "American Schools of Oriental Research" to the "American Society of Overseas Research." This was done to get away from 19th-century Orientalist implications, but in so doing, the identity of the organization and the field has been compromised.

Contra the trend of scholars actively "secularizing" the profession, the public wanted more of the traditional narratives. Popular interest in archaeology has increased tremendously in recent decades. This can be seen across the board, with the proliferation of archaeology programming on cable television channels such as the Discovery Channel, the Learning Channel, the National Geographic Channel, and especially the History Channel, as well as on PBS, not to mention movies and video games.[26]

Most formative for public interest was the 1975 founding of a popular magazine called *Biblical Archaeology Review*, founded and edited by a lawyer named Hershel Shanks. Exposed to biblical archaeology in mid-life, Shanks wanted to bring the many discoveries coming out of Israel and Jordan into the public eye, as professionals within the discipline were not interested in doing so. He capitalized on a public that was still deeply interested in exploring the archaeology of this region as the land of the Bible. In an uncredited editorial note in the first issue, Shanks explained that "the aim of *The Biblical Archaeology Review* is to make available in understandable language the current insights of professional archaeology as they relate to the Bible" (anonymous 1975: 2).[27]

The magazine quickly evolved from a newsletter format to a glossy, quality publication with engaging color photographs, and a large lay readership of well over 100,000 subscribers. Promoting the actual ideas (as well as artifacts) of biblical archaeology to the public had not been done properly before, and beyond the magazine, the Biblical Archaeology Society publishes books on specific topics, to satisfy the large public appetite.[28]

This public appetite continues to grow, as is clear from the high level of interest and funding for the new Museum of the Bible in Washington DC, founded in 2017 and situated close to the Mall. Controversies have swirled since its founding, but this publicity has only increased public interest in it.[29] Even more problematic from a scientific point of view, but equally popular within the public sphere is the "Ark Encounter," a creationist-oriented theme park which opened in Kentucky in 2016, and which has been successful to date. These two examples show how the American public continues to be deeply interested in knowing more about the biblical world, even as the field becomes more specialized and less accessible to that public.

This divide between what the public is interested in versus how academics have reshaped their own views is problematic, as the expectations of one group are vastly different from those of the other. Ironically, it is the public sphere that allows academic research to continue, through financial contributions, both direct and indirect via taxpayer-funded agencies. Most archaeological projects in the field require private funding to run, and even when a university contributes funding, it often comes to the academic department through private donations. Additionally, funding for research from public sources like the National Endowment for the Humanities and the National Science Foundation is affected by how politicians—who are not archaeologists—perceive and understand archaeology and archaeologists, demonstrating the need for more accurate depictions of the profession within popular culture (see Moshenska 2017: 155).[30]

Misrepresentations of Ancient History and Archaeology in the Politics of Israel and the Palestinian Territories

The fact that archaeologists do not control their own narrative allows for easy misunderstanding of facts and conclusions by laypeople, and intentional distortions by politicians.

The stakes are particularly high in the context of the Arab-Israeli conflict, where the attention given to archaeology has been uniquely distorting as well as destructive. Palestinian and allied scholars describe the totality of Israeli archaeology as being oriented toward validating the antiquity of Jews, (i.e., the ancient Israelites and Judahites), to legitimize the modern State of Israel. We have seen how for many decades the discipline had an oversized interest in the Iron Age, but we have also seen how the profession changed its orientation dramatically since the 1960s and 1970s.

The archaeology of Jerusalem is a perfect example of how archaeology is misrepresented for political gain. The many excavations that have been carried out in Jerusalem over the last century and a half demonstrate that Jerusalem was inhabited continuously from prehistory through the present day, with no significant gaps in settlement. The so-called "biblical period," that is, the period of the height of the kingdom of Judah in the Iron Age, is well represented in the area known as the "City of David" just south of the Old City. Archaeologists have excavated and fully analyzed domestic as well as public structures and artifacts that date from the 8th century through to the 6th century BCE (Shiloh 1984).

The one area of Jerusalem that has never been excavated is the Temple Mount/Haram esh-Sharif itself. This spot that lies at the heart of the biblical tradition remains unexamined due to the Islamic religious structures constructed on its summit in the 7th century CE, structures that are still in use today. This area is on the top of the high platform built by Herod in the 1st century BCE, when he famously refurbished the Jewish Second Temple that had been built in the Persian period. That Temple in turn was built over the remains of the First Temple, destroyed by the Babylonians in 586 BCE, and built centuries before that—the Bible attributes its building to Solomon. If there is a single locus in which the biblical tradition and all that flows from it could be confirmed, it is there.

Because of the impossibility of excavating on the Temple Mount/Haram esh-Sharif, a restriction imposed by local Muslim authorities and respected by Israeli archaeological authorities, there is little direct archaeological evidence for either the First Temple or the Second Temple besides the Herodian enclosure walls themselves. Only scattered finds and those excavated from the immediate vicinity indicate the existence of the Temples. This paucity of archaeological evidence has led to some outrageous political claims. In 2002, the first president of the Palestinian Authority, Yassir Arafat was quoted in the London-based Arab newspaper *al-Hayyat* (October 5, 2002) as saying, "[The Israelis] have dug tunnels [around the Temple Mount]...they found not a single stone proving that the Temple of Solomon was there because historically the Temple was not in Palestine [at all]." Similarly, in 2001 the Grand Mufti of Jerusalem Ekrima Said Sabri was interviewed by the German magazine the German magazine *Die Welt* (January 17, 2001) saying,

> There is not the smallest indication of the existence of a Jewish Temple on this place in the past. In the whole city, there is not even a single stone indicating Jewish history...It is the art of the Jews to deceive the world...Besides, they have already dug everywhere. All they could find were remnants of buildings of the Omayyad Period. Everything they excavated was related to Arabs and Muslims.

In 2000, Mahmoud Abbas, who later succeeded Arafat as president of the Palestinian Authority, stated in the Israeli-Arab newspaper stated in the Israeli-Arab newspaper *Kul al-Arab* (August 25, 2000) that "[The Israelis} claim that 2000 years ago they had a Temple [on the Haram esh-Sharif]. I challenge the claim that this is so." Other examples abound (Reiter 2008). These misrepresentations of archaeology are made specifically to strengthen Palestinian political claims on the area, and to weaken Israeli ones. They stand in contrast to the view of local Muslim authorities in the 1920s and 1930s when the presence of the Jewish Temples was freely acknowledged in publications (Supreme Muslim Council 1925).

Another worrisome trend within scholarship that gives fuel to these misrepresentations is the trend toward biblical minimalism (also known as revisionism) which peaked in the 1990s and early 2000s but continues in various forms. Minimalist scholarship states that the biblical texts were composed long after the Iron Age and effectively invented the kingdoms of Israel and Judah. Some minimalist scholars state that ancient Israel was merely a construct created in the Persian period, or even later. Their arguments further suggest that the archaeological evidence indicates that Iron Age populations were "Canaanite" or even "Palestinian" and that that Christian fundamentalist scholars and Israeli archaeologists have systematically skewed or omitted data to create a sense of continuity and justification for modern Israel. By extension, Judaism is regarded as a late product of the Persian or Hellenistic period that created a historical tradition that "silenced" "Palestinian" narratives of the 2nd and 1st millennia BCE. Among the scholars who argue toward this are Niels Peter Lemche (1998), Thomas Thompson (1999), Philip Davies (1992) and Keith Whitelam (1996).

The radical skepticism of minimalism has been refuted and essentially discredited by archaeological scholars, vocally led by William G. Dever, and by biblicists such as Lester Grabbe who have documented the ways in which minimalist scholars misinterpret the archaeological evidence (Dever 2003: 137ff; Grabbe 2017), and yet this school of thought sustains the political statements quoted above. In this context, minimalist ideas easily descend into anti-Zionism and anti-Semitism. The misconceptions they perpetuate—that there was no ancient Israel, that the entire idea of an ancient Israel was just a later Jewish construct—can and does mislead people into thinking that the Jews are illegitimate latecomers, who fooled the rest of the world into thinking they have an ancient claim on the land of Israel. This is a case of ancient history being far from irrelevant, but rather being misused and abused to foment current political discord.

However, there is another side of the coin-this one based on proper interpretations of archaeology that are inappropriately used for political arguments. As mentioned above, the "City of David" area has a large amount of evidence for the ancient Judahites of the Bible, and there is similar evidence all over the city—including from the Temple Mount/Haram esh-Sharif, even without any proper scientific excavation there. The Temple Mount/Haram esh-Sharif evidence comes via the results of a salvage project that followed a Palestinian unpermitted construction project of a wider access point and new mosque undertaken between 1996 and 1999. During this project, bulldozers dug up and then dumped many thousands of cubic meters of material from the interior of the Temple Mount/Haram esh-Sharif. In 2004, Israeli archaeologists began a project to sift through the bulldozed dump piles. While all stratigraphic connections were lost, they found ceramic remains (sherds) from almost all historical periods, including a full 42% from the Iron Age II "First Temple" Period and the Hellenistic and Roman "Second Temple" Periods combined (Barkay and Dvira 2006: 224).

Other excavations, conducted under problematic conditions, have also demonstrated Iron Age occupation of the area. Several religiously oriented and politically conservative Israeli organizations use the indisputable archaeological evidence of the ancient Judahite/Jewish presence on the Temple Mount to potentially strengthen their political positions. The main one is the Ir David (City of David) Foundation. This NGO was founded in 1986, with the goals of increasing Jewish tourism to the City of David archaeological area and establishing a greater Jewish presence there and in the Arab neighborhood of Silwan adjacent to the archaeological area.

Problems specifically arose, however, when Hebrew University archaeologist Eilat Mazar began her excavations of a large, previously unexcavated public building within the City of David in 2005, excavations that were funded in part by the Ir David Foundation. While she published her results in the usual peer-reviewed professional journals, she garnered considerable media attention because the building she was excavating was touted as King David's palace. The biblical associations distracted from the scientific rigor of her excavation methodology. For instance, she penned an article for the aforementioned popular magazine *Biblical Archaeology Review* provocatively titled "Did I Find King David's Palace?" (Mazar 2006).

While it is entirely possible that Mazar's large 10th-century BCE public structure was built by the incoming Israelites, it could just as easily be a late Canaanite administrative building. But press reports ignored or downplayed that possibility. The biblical associations also pleased Mazar's funders at the Ir David Foundation, as it advanced their goal of strengthening the ancient Jewish connection to Jerusalem through archaeology—a legitimate connection, but now exploited to make political inroads.[31] In these ways, legitimate archaeological research, conducted scientifically and objectively, is quickly subsumed by politics and polemics.

Conclusions and Toward the Future

This article has discussed the ways in which the archaeology of ancient Israel connects to early 20th-century political situations that in turn connect to current political situations within the modern State of Israel and the West Bank. These connections have been underexplored to date. While Jews have always lived in the land of Israel, a new influx of secular Jewish immigrants arrived in the late 19th century, spurred on by the new ideas regarding "Zion" as a safe haven. This movement was supported by contemporary Christian Millenarist religious beliefs about the need for the Jews to return to their land. The new Jewish arrivals joined a local Jewish minority population as well as an Arab peasant majority, which included groups that had arrived over the last several centuries due to the policies of various Ottoman-appointed pashas. It was in this atmosphere that archaeologists began exploring sites in Ottoman Palestine. These archaeologists did not separate the Bible from archaeology, rather they focused on sites of biblical importance, forming a loop with Millenarist beliefs.

This paper has also highlighted the fact that the land purchased by Jewish immigrant settlers in Ottoman Palestine was mainly *outside* the heartland of ancient Israel/Judah (Figures 47.1–47.3). The locations of those Jewish settlements became the borders of the State of Israel, modified slightly by acquisitions during the 1948 war, while the heart of ancient Israel and Judah—the modern West Bank—only came under Israeli sovereignty at the conclusion of the 1967 war. This very territory is the land that will likely become a future state for the Palestinians, despite the protestations of some religious Jewish settlers who currently reside there.

We also saw how the disciple of biblical archaeology remade itself in the second half of the 20th century, rejecting and deemphasizing religious and biblical connections, and thereby abandoning the 19th century easy connection between ancient and modern Jews. The minimalism of the 1990s went even farther, questioning the very existence of ancient Israelites and Judahites, through an incomplete understanding of the archaeological data and a radical skepticism about the Bible itself—led by textual scholars. These developments were in defiance of the growing public appetite for learning more about the archaeology of the biblical world.

All these contradictory strands come together as the land and thus the archaeology of ancient Israel and Judah is inevitably politicized. While much of the Jewish population of Israel is secular, a minority of extremely religious Israelis have lived within the West Bank since 1967. These religious settlers legitimate their claim to the West Bank by using terminology (Judea/Samaria) that references the fact that this land belonged to their ancient ancestors. Similarly, Palestinian leadership has drawn false conclusions based on archaeology. They attempt to delegitimize the Israeli presence in Jerusalem (and sometimes in any of the territory that used to be part of Ottoman Palestine) by referencing the lack of archaeological excavations of the Temple Mount/Haram esh-Sharif (excavations that have always been forbidden) and deemphasizing if not outright denying the existence of archaeological finds from the kingdom of Judah. This denial benefits from the minimalist trend in scholarship.

The last question to take up has to do with the future: how will the entanglements between the Bible, ancient Jews, modern Jewish and non-Jewish Israelis, archaeologists, and West Bank Palestinians play out in the future? We can speculate about a future Palestinian state being created in the West Bank. Such a state would likely entail the dismantling of at least some of the Jewish settlements there—something that Israel has done in the past with settlements in Sinai and Gaza. In politicized archaeo-religious terms, this might mean that modern Jews would be completely removed from the land of the ancient Judahites and Israelites. It would also mean that modern Palestinians, whose roots as a cohesive people in Ottoman Palestine go back at least several centuries, would govern themselves for the first time. Their relationship to their past as articulated by archaeology is still underexplored. But archaeologists like to work from physical evidence, rather than speculate about a yet unwritten future. All that can be said for certain is that archaeology of the land of Israel, despite the protests of archaeologists themselves, will never be disentangled from the Bible.

Notes

1 There are multiple names for the land in question. In this paper, several of these names will be explained and used when chronologically appropriate, but as a default semi-neutral term I will use the phrase "the land of Israel."
2 Early narratives in the biblical books of Joshua, Judges, and 1-2 Samuel imply that there was a period when the two polities were politically united, and the term "Israel" is commonly used for this "United Monarchy."
3 The Samaritans still exist as a small religious and ethnic grouping today—still located near Samaria. The Samaritans are not direct descendants of the ancient Israelites, most of whom were deported by the Assyrians and scattered throughout that vast empire. A few, however remained, and were joined by deportees from other lands conquered by the Assyrians, becoming a mixed grouping. This grouping kept many of the religious rituals of the ancient Israelites, and still practice them today. Samaritan religion is quite different from Judaism.
4 This is clear from Jewish sources like the Babylonian Talmud, as well as from the Murashu Archive, a 4th century BCE set of documents from Nippur in Babylonia.
5 Sometimes Millenarism is referred to as Millenialism or Millenarianism
6 But see Shalom Goldman (2009) who has engaged in a detailed study of the relationship between Christian Millenarism and early Zionism.
7 The Reform Movement would not officially embrace Zionism until the Columbus Platform of 1937.
8 For a recent view of Pinsker's "Autoemancipation" as not being as major a change in thought as it is generally thought, see Shumsky 2011.
9 John Garstang had previously excavated Jericho between 1907-1911.
10 But see Nigro 2020 on the recent Jericho excavations including Late Bronze and Iron II remains.
11 These promises were written in a series of letters between the British High Commissioner Lt. Col. Henry McMahon and the Sharif of Mecca, Hussein ibn Ali, that have come to be known as the McMahon-Hussein correspondence. See for instance Friedman 2000. It should also be noted

that a clause within the Balfour Declaration expressed protection for the non-Jewish population of Palestine.

12 See for instance Seker 2013: 3-6; Yazbak 2013: 717; Gottheil 1973: 319. It is worth noting that this movement of populations to Palestine goes back at least to goes back at least to the late eighteenth century. Under both Dahir Pasha and Jazzar Pasha, Jews had been relocated from other parts of the Ottoman Empire to Palestine. See for instance Yazbak 2013: 716 and more generally Sharon 2001: 305.

13 The Husseini clan's radical approach overshadowed the more moderate Nashashibi clan's willingness to accept Jewish settlements (Morris 1987: 7-23).

14 For a good account of this moment in history see Cohen 2015.

15 Prior to issuing the 1939 White Paper, the British had suggested partitioning Palestine between the Arabs and the Jews in 1937, a plan that appealed to the leadership of the Jewish side but was rejected by the Arabs. The plan was eventually abandoned. See Bartal 2017: 1.

16 Meanwhile, the Grand Mufti of Jerusalem had formed friendships with some of the leading members of the Nazi party, including Heinrich Himmler.

17 While 43% of the territory was allotted to the Arab state and 56% to the Jewish state (Beinin and Hajjar 2014), these numbers are slightly deceptive, because much of the acreage of the Jewish territory was in the sparsely occupied and hard to farm Negev desert.

18 But when international funds for refugees became available, over 960,000 Arabs claimed refugee status. In addition to the Arabs who fled to the West Bank, those who lived in the north fled to Lebanon and Syria, while those from the south moved into the Egyptian controlled Gaza Strip.

19 There was also a war in 1956 between Israel and Egypt, resulting from Egypt's first attempt to nationalize the Suez Canal. Israel captured the Sinai Peninsula during the fighting, but under American pressure retreated to its original boundary line.

20 Israel annexed the Golan Heights, taken from Syria, but returned the Sinai to Egypt in 1982 in accordance with the American brokered Camp David treaty. Israel continues to hold East Jerusalem but withdrew unilaterally from Gaza in 2005. The Palestinian Authority's hold over the latter was short-lived, as the terrorist group Hamas took Gaza in 2007.

21 Over 40% of Israeli Jews identify as completely secular, while the remainder fall into various levels of observance (Levy, Levinsohn, and Katz 2002: 5). The settler population comes from the most observant strata of Jewish Israelis, largely identifying as "Haredi." Haredim, while very visible and active politically, make up only about 8% of the population of Israel.

22 Archaeological surveys and excavations were carried out in the Sinai and the Golan as well.

23 See Binford 1962, Binford 1965, Renfrew 1979, and Trigger 2006: 394-480

24 The scholar William Dever is often associated with this renaming of the discipline (Dever 1974). Dever was one of the directors of the major excavations of the site of Gezer in the 1960's and 1970's, a site that had already been excavated several times for its biblical connections. Although a "biblical" site, the Gezer excavations became known for its field methods and recording system which were based on processual ideas and standards.

25 There was a backlash to processual archaeology by the 1980s (cf. Hodder 1986). "Post-processual" archaeology emphasizes subjectivity without abandoning the scientific methodologies that came to be standard. Despite the backlash against processualism, the scientific approaches that began in the 1960s are still very much part of archaeology today. As chemical analysis techniques for dating become more accurate, and as more viable scanning methodologies evolve, mere field archaeology is often neglected or relegated to a lower status among up-and-coming scholars in the field.

26 For a full treatment of this topic see Moshenska 2017. Examples of programming include *National Geographic Explorer* (begun in 1985), NBC's *Lost Civilizations* (1995), PBS's *Secrets of the Dead* (begun in 2000), the History Channel's *Digging for the Truth* (2005–2007), and *Ancient Aliens* (2009-present) Nova's 2-hour, 13-part series *The Bible's Buried Secrets* (2008), as well as *Expedition Unknown* (2015–2017) on the Travel Channel (2018–present on the Discovery Channel).

27 The statement currently on the Magazine's website reads, "BAR is the only magazine that connects the academic study of archaeology to a broad general audience eager to understand the world of the Bible." https://www.biblicalarchaeology.org/about-the-biblical-archaeology-society/.

28 The professional organization of archaeologists of the southern Levant, the American Schools of Oriental Research had begun a semi-popular newsletter in 1938, but it soon evolved into a professional, peer-reviewed journal. But since 2013 the organization has been publishing a successful online newsletter geared towards lay and undergraduate audiences, called *The Ancient Near East Today*.

29 The controversies include the fact that some of the Dead Sea Scroll fragments it purchased turned out to be forgeries, the purchase of thousands of looted antiquities, and the conservative political orientation of the Green family that founded it (see Moss and Baden 2017).
30 A few archaeologists are beginning to recognize and address this divide. See Eric Cline's 2019 plenary address to ASOR, https://www.asor.org/am/plenary-address-2019/.
31 Another such funding organization called Foundation Stone, which associated itself with Jewish religious approaches to the Hebrew Bible, partially supported some archaeological excavations in the early 2000s, also leading to sensationalized correlations between biblical materials and archaeology touted by the press.

Bibliography

Aaronsohn, Ran. 1990. "Cultural Landscape of Pre-Zionist Settlements." Pages 147–63 in *The Land that Became Israel: Studies in Historical Geography*. Edited by Ruth Kark. New Haven: Yale University Press.

anonymous. 1975. "Introducing…the BAR." *BAR* 1: 2, 16.

Anti-Defamation League. 2003. "Arab Leaders Deny Jewish History on The Temple Mount." *Anti-Defamation League*, August 6, 2003. http://www.adl.org/Anti_semitism/arab/temple_denial.asp, accessed October 23, 2011.

Barkay, Gabriel and Zachi Dvira. 2006. "The Temple Mount Sifting Project: First Preliminary Report." Pages 213–37 in *New Studies on Jerusalem: Proceedings of the Eleventh Conference*. Edited by E. Baruch, Zvi Greenhut, and Avraham Faust. Ramat Gan: The Ingeborg Rennert Center for Jerusalem Studies Publications.

Bartal, Shaul. 2017. "The Peel Commission Report of 1937 and the Origins of the Partition Concept." *Jewish Political Studies Review* 28: 51–70.

Beinin, Joel and Lisa Hajjar. 2014. *Palestine, Israel and the Arab-Israeli Conflict: A Primer*. Washington, DC: Middle East Research and Information Project. https://merip.org/palestine-israel-primer/

Ben-Artzi, Yossi. 1990. "Traditional and Modern Rural Settlement Types in Eretz-Israel in the Modern Era." Pages 133–46 in *The Land that Became Israel: Studies in Historical Geography*. Edited by Ruth Kark. New Haven: Yale University Press.

Ben-Bassat. 2009. "Proto-Zionist-Arab Encounters in Late Nineteenth-Century Palestine: Socioregional Dimensions." *Journal of Palestine Studies* 38: 42–63.

Ben-Yehuda, Nachman. 1995. *The Masada Myth: Collective Memory and Mythmaking in Israel*. Madison: University of Wisconsin Press.

Binford, Lewis. 1962. "Archaeology as Anthropology." *AA* 28: 217–25.

———. 1965. "Archaeological Systematics and the Study of Culture Process." *AA* 31: 203–10.

Cohen, Hillel. 2015. *Year Zero of the Arab-Israeli Conflict*. Waltham: Brandeis University Press.

Cohen, Jeremy. 2005. "The Mystery of Israel's Salvation: Romans 11:25–26 in Patristic and Medieval Exegesis." *HTR* 98: 247–81.

Conder, Claude Reignier and Horatio H. Kitchener. 1880. *Map of Western Palestine in 26 Sheets from Surveys Conducted for the Committee of the Palestine Exploration Fund*. London: Palestine Exploration Fund.

Davies, Philip R. 1992. *In Search of "Ancient Israel."* London: Bloomsbury.

Dever, William G. 1974. *Archaeology and Biblical Studies: Retrospects and Prospects*. Evanston: Seabury-Western.

———. 2003. *Who Were the Early Israelites and Where Did They Come From?* Grand Rapids: Eerdmans.

Faust, Avraham. 2017. "An All-Israelite Identity: Historical Reality or Biblical Myth." Pages 169–90 in *The Wide Lens in Archaeology: Honoring Brian Hesse's Contributions to Anthropological Archaeology*. Edited by Justin Lev-Tov, Paula Wapnish Hesse, and Allan Gilbert. Columbus: Lockwood Press.

Faust, Avraham and Shlomo Bunimovitz. 2003. "The 4-Room House: Embodying Israelite Iron Age Society." *NEA* 66: 22–31.

Friedman, Isaiah. 2000. *Palestine: A Twice-Promised Land? Volume 1: The British, the Arabs, and Zionism*. New Brunswick: Transaction Publishers.

Gavish, Dov. 2005. *The Survey of Palestine Under the British Mandate, 1920–1948*. London: Routledge.

Goldman, Shalom. 2009. *Zeal for Zion: Christians, Jews, & the Idea of the Promised Land*. Chapel Hill: University of North Carolina Press.

Gottheil, Fred M. 1973. "Arab Immigration into Pre-State Israel: 1922–1931." *Middle Eastern Studies* 9: 315–24.

Gottwald, Norman. 1979. *The Tribes of Yahweh: A Sociology of the Religion of Liberated Israel*. Maryknoll: Orbis.

Grabbe, Lester L. 2017. *Ancient Israel: What Do We Know and How Do We Know It?* London: Bloomsbury.

Green, Abigail. 2008. "The British Empire and the Jews: An Imperialism of Human Rights?" *Past and Present* 199: 175–205.

Greenberg, Raphael and Adi Keinan. 2009. *Israeli Archaeological Activity in the West Bank 1967–2007: A Sourcebook*. Bar-Lev Industrial Park: Rahas Press.

Hallote, Rachel. 2006. *Bible, Map and Spade: The American Palestine Exploration Society, Frederick Jones Bliss and the Forgotten Story of Early American Biblical Archaeology*. Piscataway: Gorgias Press.

———. 2017. "The Development of 'Bible Lands Archaeology' and 'Biblical Archaeology' in the Nineteenth and Early Twentieth Centuries." Pages 111–40 in *The Old Testament in Archaeology and History*. Edited by J. Ebeling. et al. Waco: Baylor University Press.

Hodder, Ian. 1986. *Reading the Past: Current Approaches to Interpretation in Archaeology*. Cambridge: Cambridge University Press.

Hood, J. Y. B. 2019. "Did Augustine Abandon His Doctrine of Jewish Witness in Aduersus Iudaeos?" *Augustinian Studies* 50: 171–95.

Kark, Ruth, and David Grossman. 2003. "The Communal (Musha') Village of the Middle East and North Africa." Pages 223–36 in *Policies and Strategies in Marginal Regions*. Edited by W. Leimgruber, R. Majoral, and C-W. Lee. Aldershot: Ashgate.

Karsh, Efraim. 2011. "How Many Palestinian Arab Refugees Were There?" *Israel Affairs* 17: 224–46.

Kramer, Martin. 2020. "1948: Why the Name Israel?" MartinKramer.org, 2020, April 27. https://martinkramer.org/2020/04/27/1948-why-the-name-israel/ accessed July 12, 2021.

Lemche, Niels Peter. 1998. *The Israelites in History and Tradition*. Louisville: Westminster John Knox Press.

Levy, Shlomit, Hanna Levinsohn, and Elihu Katz. 2002. *Beliefs, Observances and Values among Israeli Jews: Highlights from an In-Depth Study Conducted by the Guttman Center of the Israel Democracy Institute for the AVI CHAI Foundation*. Jerusalem: The Israel Democracy Institute and The AVI CHAI Foundation.

Marx, Dahlia. 2013. "The Missing Temple: The Status of the Temple in Jewish Culture Following its Destruction." *European Judaism* 46: 61–78.

Matar, Nabil I. 1985. "The Idea of the Restoration of the Jewish in English Protestant Thought, 1661–1701." *HTR* 78: 115–48.

Mazar, Eilat. 2006. "Did I Find King David's Palace?" *BAR* 32: 16–27.

Mendenhall, George. 1962. "The Hebrew Conquest of Palestine." *BA* 25: 66–87.

Morris, Benny. 1987. *The Birth of the Palestinian Refugee Problem, 1947–1949*. Cambridge: Cambridge University Press.

———. 2008. *1948: A History of the First Arab-Israeli War*. New Haven: Yale University Press.

Moscrop, John. 2000. *Measuring Jerusalem: The Palestine Exploration Fund and British Interests in the Holy Land*. London: Leicester University Press.

Moshenska, Gabriel. 2017. "Archaeologists in Popular Culture." Pages 151–65 in *Key Concepts in Public Archaeology*. Edited by Gabriel Moshenska. London: University College of London Press.

Moss, Candida R. and Joel S. Baden 2017. *Bible Nation: The United States of Hobby Lobby*. Princeton: Princeton University Press.

Nigro, Lorenzo. 2020. "The Italian-Palestinian Expedition to Tell es-Sultan, Ancient Jericho (1997–2015): Archaeology and Valorisation of Material and Immaterial Heritage." Pages 175–214 in *Digging Up Jericho: Past, Present and Future*. Edited by R. Sparks, et al. Oxford: Archaeopress.

Pinsker, Leon. 1976. *Autoemancipation*. London: Federation of Zionist Youth.

Reif, Stefan. 1995. *Judaism and Hebrew Prayer: New Perspectives on Jewish Liturgical History*. Cambridge: Cambridge University Press.

Reiter, Yitzhak. 2008. *Jerusalem and its Role in Islamic Solidarity*. New York: Palgrave Macmillan.

Renfrew, Colin. 1979. *Problems in European Prehistory*. Cambridge: Cambridge University Press.

Robinson, E. and E. Smith. 1856. *Later Biblical Researches in Palestine, and in the Adjacent Regions: A Journal of Travels in the Year 1838*. Boston: Crocker and Brewster.

Scholch, Alexander. 1992. "Britain in Palestine, 1838–1882: The Roots of the Balfour Policy." *Journal of Palestine Studies* 22: 39–56.

Seker, Nesim. 2013. "Forced Population Movements in the Ottoman Empire and the Early Turkish Republic: An Attempt at Reassessment through Demographic Engineering." *European Journal of Turkish Studies* 16: 1–16.

Sharon, Moshe. 2001. "Palestine under the Mameluks and the Ottoman Empire (1291–1918)." Pages 272–322 in *A History of Israel and the Holy Land*. Edited by Michael Avi-Yonah. New York: Continuum.

Shiloh, Yigal. 1984. *Excavations at the City of David I, 1987–1982: Interim Report of the First Five Seasons*. Jerusalem: Institute of Archaeology, The Hebrew University of Jerusalem.

Shumsky, Dimitry. 2011. "Leon Pinsker and 'Autoemancipation!': A Reevaluation." *Jewish Social Studies: History, Culture, Society* 18: 33–62.

Stein, Kenneth W. 1984. *The Land Question in Palestine, 1917–1939*. Chapel Hill: The University of North Carolina Press.

Supreme Muslim Council. 1925. *A Brief Guide to Al-Haram Al-Sharif*. Jerusalem.

Thompson, Thomas L. 1999. *The Mythic Past: Biblical Archaeology and the Myth of History*. London: Basic Books.

Trigger, Bruce. 2006. *A History of Archaeological Thought*. Cambridge: Cambridge University Press.

United Nations General Assembly. 1947. "Report to the General Assembly, Vol. 1." *Official Records of the Second Session of the General Assembly, Supplement No. 11*. United Nations Special Committee on Palestine. Lake Success, New York. https://unispal.un.org/DPA/DPR/unispal.nsf/5ba47a5c6cef541b802563e000493b8c/07175de9fa2de563852568d3006e10f3?OpenDocument

Vereté, Mayir. 1970. "Why Was a British Consulate Established in Jerusalem?" *English Historical Review* 85: 316–45.

Whitelam, Keith W. 1996. *The Invention of Ancient Israel: The Silencing of Palestinian History*. London: Routledge.

Yazbak, Mahmoud. 2013. "The Politics of Trade and Power: Dahir al-'Umar and the Making of Early Modern Palestine." *JESHO* 56: 696–736.

Zerubavel, Yael. 1991. "The Politics of Interpretation: Tel Hai in Israeli Collective Memory." *AJSR* 16: 133–60.

INDEX

Abdi-heba 55, 58–61
Abdon 46, 413
Abdullah 634
abecedary 52, 250, 337, 343, 344, 378, 382, 394
Abel Beth Maacah (Tell Abil al-Qamh) 38, 281, 573, 574, 576, 577
Abel Meholah 392, 504
Abiathar 243
Abigal 24
Abihu 483, 484, 492
Abijah 42
Abimelech 46, 145, 281, 413
Abishai 605
Abner 323
Abram/Abraham 3, 34, 39, 87, 264, 295, 481, 509
Absalom 240, 324, 605
Achaemenid 632, 701, 718
Achan 326
Achish 15, 24, 558, 559, 704
Achziv 589, 660
Adadah 18, 19, 21, 22
Adad-nirari III 40, 646, 664, 694, 704
Adam 34, 292
Adapa 406
Adar 40, 714
Admah 525
Adoniram 243, 244
Adonizedek 59
Afghanistan 213, 214, 217
afterlife 185, 429, 505–9, 511, 513–19, 619, 633
Agisoft 745, 751
agriculture 34, 44, 111, 136, 137, 196, 229, 241, 263, 269, 437, 529, 575, 615, 619, 639, 727, 736
Ahab 40, 42, 45, 324, 391, 475, 498, 664, 694
Ahaz 40, 42, 500, 510, 694

Ahaziah 42, 509
Ahijah 343, 497, 499, 503
Ahilud 243
Ahimaaz 244
Ahiqam 344, 346
Ahiram 338, 506
Ahithophel 24
Akkad 296, 714
Akkadian 194, 240, 249, 335, 524, 540, 541, 566, 573, 621, 630, 699, 700, 715, 722
Akko 205, 366, 592, 754
Aleppo 531, 536, 572, 575
alliance(s) 51, 211–14, 218, 222, 227, 249, 329, 388, 498, 503, 526, 543, 544, 577, 578, 608, 619, 661, 667, 669, 689, 693, 694, 724
alphabet 336, 338, 341, 345–47, 380, 382, 383, 386, 402, 547, 594
alphabetic 52, 60, 336–39, 341, 345–47, 352, 361, 363, 364, 379, 380, 382, 541, 547, 563, 622, 720
altar(s) 29, 146, 148, 150, 158, 159, 168, 170, 283, 309, 378, 382, 422, 426, 469–72, 477, 478, 481–85, 489, 492, 504, 532, 555, 586, 625, 636, 662
Amalekite(s) 15, 16, 20, 24, 25, 27, 325, 490, 661
Amarna 38, 47, 58, 60, 61, 65, 66, 82, 114, 193, 205, 240, 318, 330, 504, 524, 525, 540, 573, 578, 581, 620, 723
Amenhotep 240, 295, 318, 672
Aminadab 244
Amiran 6, 10, 174, 466, 477
Amman 167, 601–3, 605–10, 612, 614–18, 622, 634, 637, 638, 655
Amorite(s) 9, 10, 30, 523–35, 538–40, 546, 603, 628, 629
amphictyony 221, 239, 247

Index

amulet(s) 43, 52, 283, 300, 340, 366, 423, 424, 427–29, 431, 432, 442, 459, 508, 509, 543, 587, 669, 673, 679
Amun-re 659, 662
Anatolia 1, 36, 37, 155, 229, 360, 530, 534, 694, 723
aniconic 434, 435, 448, 461, 475, 533
aniconism 463, 543, 587
annals 36, 38, 52, 318, 320, 407, 413, 572, 582, 584, 665, 711
Aphek 38, 39, 538, 546, 697, 723
apiary 366, 379, 392, 402, 471
Arabah 33, 49, 50, 149, 247, 442, 639, 653, 654
Arabia 70, 73, 220, 259, 260, 347, 627, 633, 651, 726, 754, 762
Arad 16–21, 25–32, 149, 150, 246, 247, 340, 342, 376, 377, 394, 395, 399, 426, 431, 440, 449, 465, 469, 470, 472–75, 477, 478, 531, 532, 534, 647, 653, 656, 721, 727
archaeomagnetism 10, 52
archaeometallurgy 656
archaeometry 261
archaeozoology 740
Aroer 16, 18, 19, 21, 22, 27–29, 31, 33, 647
Ashdod 39, 150, 177, 188, 550, 557, 561, 562, 667, 671, 675, 677, 687, 694, 699, 707, 710, 762
Asherah 281, 283, 292, 446, 450, 454, 459, 460, 462, 498, 508, 586, 597, 598
Ashkelon 16, 177, 178, 195, 205, 229, 383, 448, 506, 518, 554, 557, 561, 563, 564, 584, 631, 698, 711, 723
ashlar 121, 149, 159, 174, 593, 597, 598, 607
Ashurbanipal 36, 40, 322, 526, 531, 635, 647, 651, 669, 689, 695, 699, 706, 708
Aššurnaṣirpal 567, 572
Astarte 158, 159, 450, 586, 597
astragali 581, 614
Ataruz 378, 382, 470, 473, 477, 478, 625–27, 632, 636
Athaliah 42, 281, 391, 475
atonement 484, 485, 491
Atrahasis 294
Azekah 39, 558, 760

Babylon 3, 35, 36, 94, 321, 412, 418, 500–502, 598, 611, 632, 655, 668, 680, 691, 695, 713–15, 717–23, 725–28, 756, 757
Babylonia 68, 74, 276, 302, 433, 499, 675, 695, 699, 708, 713, 714, 716, 718, 720–23, 725–28, 772
Baden 187, 293, 303, 316, 404, 406, 408, 410, 412, 414, 416, 418, 462, 728, 774, 775
Balaam 340, 628, 633
Balfour 761, 773, 775
Barkay 60, 61, 63, 64, 77, 80, 90, 95, 427–29, 431, 509, 517, 770, 774

Bar-Rakib 396–98
Batash, Tell/Timnah 87, 95, 110, 112, 113, 128, 179, 187, 188, 552, 564
bead(s) 256, 259, 423, 424, 429, 459, 607, 609, 612, 614, 660
Becking 40, 49, 65, 275, 707, 708
bedouin 216, 219, 229, 233, 234, 275, 667, 759
beekeeping 267, 275, 402, 442
Beersheba 3, 4, 16, 18–21, 25–30, 96, 107, 116, 150, 179, 181, 302, 451, 471, 472, 475, 647, 656, 664, 721
Beit-Arieh 21, 26, 31, 653–55
Belnap 476, 480, 482, 484, 486, 488–90, 492, 493
Belteshazzar 725
Ben-Dor 560, 561, 660, 664, 668, 672
Bennett 639, 649, 655–57, 660, 662, 665, 672
Ben-Shlomo 27, 31, 60, 65, 108, 109, 115, 117, 256, 260, 550, 552, 561, 585, 597, 697, 700, 708, 709
Ben-Tor 6, 10, 70, 80, 95, 174, 184, 188, 546
Ben-Yosef 17, 21, 26, 31, 43, 44, 48, 49, 73, 80–82, 167, 173, 238, 247, 642, 645, 651, 655–57, 732, 736, 737, 739, 740, 753
Berlejung 400, 461, 580, 581, 699, 707, 708, 728
Bernick-Greenberg 59, 60, 64
Bethel 3, 16, 18–20, 22, 25, 27–29, 148, 150, 155, 251, 327, 415, 469, 475, 476, 478, 481, 498, 499, 512, 586
Bethlehem 23, 24, 268, 491, 629
Bethsaida 183, 438, 441
Beth-Shean 51, 59, 116, 117, 187, 337, 345, 366, 392, 445, 462, 478, 504, 538, 547, 668
Beth-Shemesh 95, 181, 184, 276, 337, 346, 561
bichrome 107, 114, 256, 549–51, 584, 585, 591, 592, 594, 598
Bienkowski 95, 97, 224, 230, 232, 630, 632, 636, 637, 639, 641, 642, 646, 647, 649, 651, 655–57
Bietak 36, 49, 72, 80, 535, 659, 672
Bilgin 172, 247, 248
Binford 767, 773, 774
Bintliff 569, 579
Biran 22, 31, 148, 153, 164, 172, 220, 303, 439, 461, 579, 580
Blakely 181, 183, 243, 248, 381, 382, 431
Blenkinsopp 185, 222, 516, 517, 727
Bloch-Smith 63, 64, 70, 72, 80, 274, 427, 431, 507, 508, 510, 517, 519, 532, 535
Blum 339, 345, 406, 415, 418, 430, 431
Boaretto 26, 31, 48, 49, 187, 274, 536, 731, 732, 737–40
bone(s) 148, 173, 191, 264, 284, 300, 357, 424, 429, 443, 444, 455, 457, 459, 469, 508, 509, 512, 514, 536, 589, 614, 733–35, 737–39
Borowski 30, 31, 279, 288, 431
Borsippa 35, 723, 724

Index

Bourdieu 209, 220
Bozrah 632, 646, 649, 652
bracelets 459, 607, 614
Brady 655, 737, 752, 753
Braemer 121, 123, 126, 128, 129, 132, 140
Brandl 163, 172, 543, 545, 662, 672, 697, 711
Braudel 225, 229, 233, 569, 579
bread 66, 71, 132, 138, 141, 249, 264, 265, 268–70, 272, 274, 275, 282, 288, 289, 308, 314, 432, 481, 491, 499, 511
Brichto 516, 518
Brody 119, 131, 140, 251, 252, 254, 256–62, 432
Broekman 672, 673, 677, 688–91
Broshi 219, 220
Buchholz 156, 169, 172
Buckingham 759
Buckley 275
Budde 511, 518
Budin 278, 279, 283, 285, 288, 289
bulla(e) 238, 242, 245, 248, 284, 339, 345, 380–82, 391, 457, 458, 501, 504, 541, 552, 612, 647, 649, 707
Bunimovitz 48, 51, 56, 63–65, 70, 74, 75, 77, 80, 103, 104, 115, 126, 128, 133–35, 140, 142, 154, 181, 184, 209, 215, 220, 337, 346, 518, 553, 561, 767, 774
Burckhardt 82, 633, 636, 759
bureaucracy 154, 230, 231, 248, 251
Burke 193, 204, 386, 387, 396, 400, 523, 524, 526, 528–40, 542–46, 548, 567, 569, 579
Burna, Tel 27, 39, 262, 753
Busayra 229, 632, 639, 641, 645–51, 653, 655, 656
Byblos 193, 336–38, 346, 506, 582, 585, 597, 659, 660, 664
Byrne 295, 302, 336, 345, 365, 379, 380, 382, 386, 400
Byzantine 6, 21–23, 27, 30, 31, 203, 254, 637, 652, 678

Cahill 59–61, 64, 148, 153, 357, 361
cannabis 426, 431, 465, 477
centralization 32, 42, 50, 221, 261, 309, 310, 315, 399, 430, 517
Chadwick 27, 28, 31, 141, 205, 218, 220, 432, 552, 561
chalcolithic 21, 22, 26, 197, 264–66, 275, 751
Chaldean(s) 500, 598, 728
Chapman 226, 233, 299, 302, 423, 431, 637
chariots 226, 227, 329, 662, 673, 714
Charpin 178, 184
Cherethites 15, 16, 24, 25, 30, 242
Chesnut 612, 616
Chesson 218, 220
chiefdom(s) 212, 215, 641, 645, 646, 650, 652, 654
Cifarelli 288, 289

clan(s) 25, 134, 144, 152, 210, 214, 218, 219, 222, 230, 231, 236, 238–42, 244, 247, 249, 266, 306, 308, 310, 393, 464, 467, 476, 525, 600, 641, 642, 718
Classen 422, 432
Cohen-weinberger 115, 550, 562, 564
colonialism 455, 535, 693, 698, 700, 708, 710, 737, 738
conflict 4, 45, 177, 180, 183, 186, 239, 258, 476, 489, 516, 537, 540, 652, 665, 668, 669, 678, 689, 706, 708, 756, 761, 764, 769, 774
Cooley 203, 204, 215, 220, 704, 708
copper 20, 33, 43, 49, 50, 73, 82, 256, 381, 586, 588, 595, 609, 639, 642, 645, 650, 655, 656, 667, 668, 686, 689, 738, 740
correspondence 58, 240, 243, 249, 330, 336, 341, 772
corvee 138
corvée 241, 243, 244, 497, 702, 716
covenant 144, 146, 148, 152, 154, 239, 243, 294, 306, 307, 316, 324, 325, 331, 407, 416, 428, 429, 489, 512, 543, 547, 704
craft 9, 103, 105, 108, 115, 117, 136, 190, 191, 241, 259, 357, 364, 371, 541, 596, 633, 634, 697, 711, 712
craftsmen 92, 385, 435, 442, 455, 590, 593, 667, 671, 702, 715, 719
Crawford 140, 184, 188, 192, 204, 746, 751
Crowell 651, 655, 695, 708
Crowfoot 162, 163, 169, 172, 203, 204, 542, 546
cuneiform 36, 60, 65, 66, 193, 306, 308, 311, 312, 336, 341, 381, 386, 387, 540, 546, 616, 630, 632, 655, 660, 700, 706, 707, 709, 712, 713, 716, 718, 720–28
customs 92, 101, 108, 219, 272, 506, 509, 511, 519, 529, 530, 537, 541, 545, 692
cyber-archaeology 741–45, 747–53, 755
cylinder seal(s) 40, 295, 455, 461, 542, 614, 667, 699, 711
cypro-archaic 156, 169
cypro-geometric 585
cypro-phoenician 598
cypro-syllabic 584
Cyprus 36, 168, 174, 546, 582, 584, 585, 589–94, 598, 613, 642, 645
Cyrus 713, 721
Cytryn-Silverman 65

Dagan 17, 31, 32, 146, 295, 432, 556, 562, 754
Damascus 37, 40, 42, 185, 412, 438, 573–78, 627, 664, 665, 693, 694
Daniels 226, 233, 394, 401
Danielson 546, 653, 655
Darby 285, 288, 449, 461, 508, 518
Darius 651, 717–19, 721, 726
Debir 16, 25, 221
Deleuze 55, 57, 58, 63, 64

demography 49, 134, 141, 184, 205, 220, 708
deportation(s) 2, 40, 41, 187, 188, 310, 538, 539, 617, 629, 693, 698, 699, 701, 706, 710–14, 719
deuteronomic 310–12, 503, 512, 515, 524
deuteronomistic 44, 48, 68, 252, 309, 312–15, 404, 412, 413, 459, 496, 497, 499, 503, 514, 515, 517, 535, 563, 629, 652
Dewrell 300, 302, 513, 518
diaspora 315, 589, 591, 674, 725, 726, 757, 758
Dibon/Dhiban 229, 388, 390, 621–23, 626–28, 631, 632, 635, 637
diet 87, 91, 263–67, 275, 282, 296, 733, 734
disease 133, 191, 264, 268, 269, 273, 300, 510
distribution 24, 31, 87, 103–8, 115, 117, 128, 177, 187, 191, 246, 251, 253, 258, 261, 264, 266, 341, 345–47, 382, 400, 423, 438, 455, 475, 576, 597, 657, 740
domination 50, 154, 213, 214, 218, 228, 229, 262, 516, 556, 592, 615, 706, 708, 709, 712, 720
Dornemann 607, 616
Dothan 102, 115, 117, 141, 174, 196, 202–5, 215, 217, 218, 220, 222, 328, 438, 440, 472, 545, 549, 562
Dozeman 64, 65, 418
Driessen 175, 177, 183–86, 546
drought 129, 264, 268, 269, 273, 539, 546
Duistermaat 105–7, 114, 115
Dunand 587, 597
Dutcher-Walls 141, 210, 211, 220, 431
dwelling(s) 76, 80, 82, 119, 120, 125, 126, 132, 135–37, 141, 190, 191, 194, 196, 222, 242, 358, 378, 421–23, 425, 429, 430, 587, 612, 671

ecology 103, 116, 191, 203, 223, 234, 262, 474, 478, 636
Edelman 84, 96, 431, 535, 655–57
education 86, 138, 298, 306, 346, 349, 364, 365, 379, 381, 383, 390, 399, 400
Egyptianizing 38, 442, 454, 457, 458, 537, 540, 542, 590
Egyptology 519, 674, 677, 680, 681, 688
Ekron/Tel Miqne 39, 87, 140, 145, 184, 188, 361, 475, 543, 556, 562, 667, 675, 677, 689, 695, 702, 704, 709, 710
elders 16, 23, 211, 213, 214, 218, 229, 231, 239–41, 292, 342, 516
el-Hesi, Tell 148, 153, 302, 760
Elijah 281, 328, 497–99, 503, 582
en-Nahas, Kh. 642–45, 656, 657
Eph'al 184, 712, 721
epigraphy 50, 51, 80, 95, 140, 141, 209, 335, 345, 346, 361, 365, 378, 382, 384, 402, 430, 432, 563, 616, 726
Esarhaddon 40, 309, 321–23, 330, 458, 586, 608, 647, 669, 673, 686, 692, 695, 697, 699

Eshel 21, 23, 29, 32, 48, 49, 117, 344, 345, 353–55, 360, 382, 391, 400, 552, 558, 563, 595, 597, 732, 737
Ešnunna 188, 312, 316
ethnoarchaeology 115, 116, 118, 141
ethnogenesis 77, 79, 80, 96, 204, 220, 248, 504, 546, 657, 727
ethnography 80, 115, 276, 289, 304, 639
etiology 416
Euphrates 3, 53, 566, 567, 574, 575, 596, 694, 712, 718
Eusebius 15, 17, 21, 29, 30, 33, 633, 678, 680, 683, 691
Evil-merodach 715
exchange 38, 51, 107, 117, 192, 222, 249, 252, 256, 258–62, 324, 352, 379, 393, 466, 546, 597, 630, 658, 660, 662, 668, 671, 715, 732
execration texts 187, 319, 494, 503
exile 2, 11, 39, 68, 77, 178, 269, 286, 315, 335, 347, 413, 430, 494, 495, 497, 499, 501, 503, 710, 714, 723, 724, 726, 728, 757

faience 296, 424, 590, 665, 667, 668
Fantalkin 81, 205, 218, 221, 672, 697, 707, 708
Farahani 622, 636
Farber 53, 269, 274, 517, 712
farming 138, 193, 228, 293, 578, 619, 759, 762
favissa 107, 437, 445, 469, 471, 653, 655
Faynan, Wadi 43, 81, 639, 641, 642, 645, 646, 650–52, 655, 656, 738
feasting 107, 263, 265, 267–75, 421, 486, 487, 491, 507, 511, 536, 562, 670, 707, 736
feasts 136, 241, 263, 266, 268–72, 274–76, 478
Federico 155, 362, 403, 754
Federov 202, 204
Feinman 117, 221, 258, 261
Feldman 403, 415, 418, 492, 493, 542, 546, 582, 587, 590, 597, 732, 738
feminism 278, 289, 290, 302
feminist 278, 279, 285, 290
fertility 270–72, 285, 292, 445, 449, 464, 586
festival(s) 35, 269, 274, 309, 310, 312, 314–16, 426, 477, 511, 518
Finkielsztejn 707, 708
fish 61, 66, 266, 274, 276, 366, 552, 660, 664, 667, 668, 674, 733, 734, 737
flax 541, 668
foreigners 87, 94, 318, 330, 629, 659, 660, 667, 670, 671, 674, 715, 716, 718
fortification(s) 23, 60, 62, 63, 81, 128, 135, 140, 147, 180, 191, 194, 203, 204, 215, 217–19, 221, 252, 325, 387, 531, 540, 545, 547, 559, 560, 622, 626, 761
four-room house 26, 73, 77, 80, 95, 126, 140–42, 205, 219, 258, 260, 282, 423, 607, 612, 613, 659, 672

Index

Frahm 635, 636, 669, 673, 694, 695, 698, 704, 706–11
Frick 194, 204, 228, 233
Fried 179, 180, 185, 219, 221
Friedman 66, 256, 261, 274, 276, 537, 542, 543, 546, 674, 772, 774
furniture 125, 126, 179, 427, 442, 454, 481, 542, 655, 701

Gadot 39, 43, 50, 65, 104, 116, 140, 166, 172, 173, 186, 215, 221, 249, 259, 262, 347, 426, 431, 538, 541, 546–48, 563, 702, 710, 711, 732, 734, 736, 737, 739
Galil 35, 40–42, 48, 50, 73, 81, 176, 185, 346, 566, 580
Galilee 37, 38, 40, 120, 145, 187, 203, 205, 206, 233, 239, 264, 275, 477, 547, 573, 577, 581, 762
gameboards 660, 664, 665
Gamla 734, 737
Ganor 17, 32, 48, 51, 73, 81, 115, 154, 186, 222, 242, 248, 249, 345, 347, 401, 562
Garfinkel 6, 10, 17, 27, 32, 44, 48, 50, 51, 73, 81, 115, 154, 176, 178, 181, 185, 186, 222, 242, 248, 249, 337, 345, 347, 387, 401, 445, 461, 545, 550, 556, 562, 593, 598
Garfinkle 153, 154, 247, 248
garment(s) 282, 308, 355, 356, 358, 362, 438, 511, 660, 664, 665, 702
Garr 389, 401, 511, 518
Garraty 251, 258, 261, 262
garrison(s) 39, 51, 60, 191, 241, 253, 366, 395, 538, 540, 622, 652, 671
Garroway 119, 286, 289, 291–302, 304, 424, 431, 669
Gath *see* es-Safi, Tell
Gaza 16, 38, 60, 448, 455, 463, 525, 665, 670, 675, 677, 684, 694, 697–99, 702, 703, 710, 721, 764, 772, 773
gender 75, 86, 101, 104–6, 138, 141, 209, 277–81, 283, 285–90, 298, 299, 302, 303, 312, 422, 432, 518, 562
genealogy/ies 36, 44, 66, 211–13, 230, 406, 414, 415, 525, 727
genre 34, 45, 66, 184, 361, 363, 379, 405–7, 410, 411, 414, 437, 445, 531, 661, 720
geoarchaeology 141, 205, 561, 636, 732, 740
geochemical 261
geochronology 740
Geoghegan 270, 274
geography 3, 15, 17, 19, 21, 23–25, 27–29, 31–33, 51, 81, 154, 185, 204, 237, 247–49, 401, 433, 526, 544, 565, 579, 580, 597, 617, 633, 657, 709, 727, 774
Gerar 15, 16, 25, 302, 525
Geraty 606, 616–18
Gerizim 164, 171, 173, 174

Geshur 573, 574, 577, 581
Gezer 39, 41, 43, 60, 61, 82, 87, 95, 147, 148, 150, 151, 163, 188, 271, 302, 355, 387, 388, 402, 406, 445, 472, 662, 696, 697, 699, 700, 705, 711, 712, 760, 773
giants 515, 534, 535, 559, 614
giardino 591, 592, 597
Gibeah 16, 18, 19, 23, 24, 27, 28, 30, 487, 760
Gibeath-elohim 496
Gibeon 23, 30, 32, 150, 218, 396, 456, 526
Giddens 209, 221
Gilboa 73, 81, 107, 116, 141, 163, 174, 187, 260, 261, 568, 580, 583–85, 591, 592, 594, 596–98, 660, 673, 696, 709, 732, 737–40
Gilead 194, 231, 238, 637
Gilgamesh 293, 303, 345, 415, 512, 722
Gilibert 391, 401
Gilmour 45, 50, 460, 462, 466, 478
Giloh 30, 146, 153, 197, 205, 469, 478
Gitin 89, 96, 109, 114, 116, 117, 140, 155, 184, 187, 188, 204, 223, 250, 261, 273, 289, 430, 432, 433, 545, 547, 552, 554, 558, 562, 564, 599, 636, 673, 695, 704, 709
glass 65, 66, 256, 259, 429, 590, 614
Glueck 167, 172, 439, 600, 603, 616, 622, 630, 633, 636, 639, 655
Gmirkin 560, 562
Goedicke 581, 661, 673
Golan 32, 438, 573, 577, 773
Goliath 242, 558–62, 564
Golub 248, 345, 716, 726
Gomorrah 525, 628
Gonen 533, 535, 538, 540, 545, 546
Gonzales 73, 81
Gophna 27, 31, 32
Gordon 115, 173, 177, 185, 345, 742, 743, 746, 752
Goren 64, 65, 107, 114, 336, 345, 354, 362, 431, 517, 592, 598, 739
Gottwald 210, 212, 219, 221, 261, 767, 775
government 35, 136, 144, 213, 214, 217, 219, 220, 222, 226, 229, 254, 337, 634, 710, 760, 761
governor(s) 106, 145, 321, 322, 366, 611, 615, 695, 698, 710, 711, 716, 720
Grabbe 65, 97, 275, 770, 775
graffiti 78, 341, 342, 452, 472
grave(s) 57, 215, 271, 272, 291, 300, 397, 444, 507–9, 514, 517, 536, 568, 614, 645
Greece 172, 187, 214, 218, 219, 222, 223, 229, 402, 592, 738, 757
Greek 16, 30, 33, 65, 82, 172, 174, 222, 239, 245, 246, 248, 341, 402, 525, 557, 568, 569, 581–84, 586, 594, 595, 598, 606, 633, 647, 671, 678–82, 689, 706, 725, 760
Greenberg 153, 164, 172, 180, 182, 183, 185, 764, 775

781

Greene 339, 363, 364, 366, 368, 370, 372, 374, 376, 378, 380–82, 692
Greenfield 64, 710, 734, 738
Greenhut 150, 154, 774
Greenspahn 362, 403
Greenwood 97, 223
Greer 234, 249, 269, 272–74, 476, 478, 479, 548
Guattari 57, 58, 63, 64
Gudme 358, 361, 422, 423, 431
Guillaume 357, 361, 653, 656
Gunkel 417, 418
Güterbock 178, 185
Gutiérrez 183
Gutmann 737, 755

Hackett 345–47
hacksilber 32, 259
Hadad 181, 185, 438, 507, 585, 646, 652, 661
Hadadezer 575, 576
Hadar 148, 153, 576, 577
Hadid, Tel 697, 699, 700, 707, 710, 712
Hadley 586, 598
Halbertsma 438, 442, 462, 465–67, 478
Halif, Tel 28, 30, 31, 140, 141, 181, 184, 185, 299, 303, 426, 431
Hallote 756, 758–60, 762, 764, 766, 768, 770, 772, 774–76
hallucinogens 425, 426
Halpern 30, 32, 50, 63, 65, 72, 73, 81, 114, 170, 172, 184, 211, 221, 262, 310, 316, 619, 636, 656, 708, 711, 727
Hamilakis 75, 81, 430, 432
Hamilton 338, 345, 349, 360
Hammurabi 292, 305, 306, 316, 531, 536
Haran 302, 356, 361, 406, 415, 417, 418, 425, 432
Hardin 119, 128, 129, 131, 134, 137, 140, 141, 181, 183, 185, 243, 248, 299, 303, 381, 382
Harding 569, 570, 580
Harmanşah 169, 171, 172, 179, 180, 185
Harran 458, 614, 695, 709, 721
Harrison 42, 48, 50, 153, 154, 176, 185, 674
Hasegawa 38, 50, 52, 694, 708–11
Hasel 17, 27, 32, 38, 39, 44, 50, 73, 81, 91, 115, 154, 180, 185, 248
Hatti 319, 506, 514, 534, 668
Hauran 438, 565, 574, 577, 578, 580
Hawkins 70, 72, 81, 153, 154, 230, 233, 467, 469, 478, 579
Hayden 219, 221, 265, 269, 274
Hayes 24, 33
Hays 44, 50, 291, 301, 303, 329, 330, 505, 506, 508, 510, 512, 514, 516–19, 589
Hazael 40, 42, 44, 49, 52, 390, 401, 403, 531, 556, 557, 559
Hazor 30, 38, 43, 59, 68, 80, 147, 148, 150, 151, 163, 167, 169, 172–74, 176–78, 182, 183, 188, 203, 231, 261, 443, 471, 473, 532, 533, 540, 548, 576, 592, 593, 625, 707, 723, 739
Headdress(es) 356, 357, 448, 460, 542, 669
Hebron 16, 18, 19, 22–25, 27, 28, 30, 31, 33, 46, 150, 218, 220, 231, 245, 246, 259, 526, 762
hegemonic 74, 229, 230, 278, 286, 287, 359, 619, 671
hegemony 68, 202, 223, 234, 290, 361, 393–95, 402, 637, 669, 695, 698, 709, 712, 724
heirloom(s) 144, 203, 449
Heracleopolis 662, 664, 665
hermeneutics 53, 155, 309, 316
Hermopolis 664, 665, 677
Hernández 753
Herodotus 670, 679, 680, 682, 690, 692
Herzog 6, 10, 21, 26, 27, 29, 32, 71, 81, 84, 94, 96, 136, 140, 150, 151, 154, 181, 185, 470, 478, 552, 562, 662, 673
Hes(h)ban 233, 526, 601, 606–12, 614, 615, 617, 618, 635
Hesse 266, 267, 273–75, 562, 733, 734, 738, 740, 774
Hezekiah 40, 42, 53, 150, 246, 249, 250, 284, 324, 330, 394, 397, 398, 401, 475, 492, 500, 510, 667, 691, 694, 709
hierarchy 42, 190, 194, 196, 212, 213, 217, 231, 252, 362, 399, 488, 510, 622, 626, 717
hieratic 337, 338, 341, 344, 347, 371, 383, 541, 668, 686, 688
Higginbotham 542, 546
Higham 10, 403, 617, 656, 673
Hiram 73, 324, 594, 595, 710
Hirschfeld 121, 132, 133, 141
historiography 35, 48, 50–52, 58, 84, 185, 330, 436, 485, 580, 616, 656, 708, 711, 721, 722, 727
Hitchcock 179, 185, 209, 221, 549, 556–59, 562, 563, 734, 735, 737, 738
Hittite(s) 25, 36, 37, 82, 93, 155, 174, 179, 184, 187, 248, 295, 305, 319, 320, 327, 329, 336, 495, 506, 524–27, 534, 536, 540, 542, 573, 579, 581, 607, 661, 662
Hodder 75, 81, 95, 96, 104, 108, 116, 226, 233, 385, 401, 773, 775
Hoffman 104, 115
Hoffmeier 45, 50, 330, 400, 537, 546
Höflmayer 36, 37, 49, 50, 538, 546
Hogue 95, 143, 144, 154, 339, 355, 361, 384, 386, 388–92, 394, 396, 398, 400–402
holiness 289, 315, 316, 408, 418, 432, 477, 492, 493, 512, 515
Holladay 43, 50, 77, 81, 121, 126, 128, 129, 131–35, 137, 141, 211, 221, 252, 260, 261, 382, 429, 432, 466, 478
Homsher 173, 739, 746, 752, 754
honey 191, 261, 267, 275, 276, 392, 489, 526, 665, 760

Index

Horowitz 65, 540, 546, 699, 700, 707, 709, 720, 723, 726, 727
horse(s) 226, 227, 318, 329, 423, 424, 440, 446, 612, 614, 662, 665, 673, 714, 719
horticulture 529, 639, 702
Hübner 62, 65, 168, 173, 463, 600, 614, 617
Hudon 224, 226, 228, 230, 232, 234, 601
Huelva 81, 594, 596
husbandry 192, 228, 262, 275, 437, 636, 739, 740
Hyksos 318, 535, 538

Iberia 260, 262, 589, 595
iconography 39, 51, 81, 120, 149, 285, 299, 434, 435, 438, 442, 445, 455, 459–62, 472, 475, 476, 536, 541–43, 548, 587, 597, 611, 612, 653, 654, 704, 711, 720
immigrant(s) 112, 310, 659, 668, 700, 724, 725, 734, 759, 761, 762, 771
immigration 396, 475, 762, 774
imperialism 51, 403, 543, 547, 630, 637, 651, 662, 696, 775
incense 220, 256, 259, 283, 423, 425, 426, 431, 432, 469, 470, 472, 481, 483–85, 492, 493, 504, 615, 625, 649, 651
industry/ial 33, 49, 81, 105, 107, 109–12, 176, 246, 274, 442, 613, 642, 643, 645, 651, 695, 753, 775
infant(s) 85, 283, 293, 295–300, 302, 303, 430, 432
inheritance 33, 137, 211, 213, 293, 301, 302, 310, 422, 427
Iran 1, 40, 141, 275, 304, 711
Iraq 188, 304, 330, 599, 615, 673, 726, 759
Isaiah 219, 281, 284, 306, 398, 409, 413, 418, 430, 477, 499–502, 504, 508, 514, 516, 518, 582, 629, 667, 673, 675, 678, 683, 707, 708, 774
Išbaʻal 248, 337, 345
Ish-bosheth 45, 46
Ishida 239, 248, 526, 535, 673
Ishtar 292, 715
Ivory/ies 150, 166, 204, 259, 429, 442–44, 449, 450, 454, 455, 457, 461, 462, 542, 587, 596, 599, 609, 614, 660, 665, 668, 672, 701

Jaʼazaniah 254, 255
Jabbok 601–4, 612
Jabesh-Gilead 240, 487, 604, 606
Jabin 46, 231
Jaffa 38, 195, 205, 534, 538, 546, 762
Jamieson-Drake 379, 380, 382
Jansen-Winkeln 664, 673, 688, 691
Janssen 295, 303
Janzen 47, 50, 52, 511, 518
Japhet 362, 574, 580
Jebus 80
Jebusite(s) 30, 59, 62, 66, 240, 524–26, 534

Jehoahaz 42
Jehoash 40, 42, 694
Jehoiachin 42, 715
Jehoiakim 42
Jehoram 42, 510, 652
Jehoshaphat 498, 596, 608, 652
Jehu 40, 42, 153, 286, 287, 475, 664, 694, 710
Jemmeh, Tell 16, 705, 707, 708, 740
Jephthah 45, 46, 53, 413, 574
Jerahmeelites 15, 16, 18, 19, 24–28
Jericho 30, 182, 185, 302, 326, 329, 456, 760, 761, 772, 775
Jericke 29, 30, 32
Jeroboam 41, 42, 151, 266, 345, 393, 394, 396, 401, 457, 475, 476, 498, 499, 662, 670
Jerome 33, 678
Jesus 583, 757
jewelry 256, 259, 358, 423, 427, 429, 432, 442, 449, 507, 508, 609, 660, 664, 665, 668
Jezebel 281, 324, 391, 475, 498, 590
Jezreel 38, 50, 107, 147, 151, 155, 281, 547, 555, 563, 592, 625, 664, 696, 707, 752, 754
Joab 242, 323, 605
Josephus 15, 36, 39, 595, 611, 631, 633, 637
Josiah 41, 42, 249, 309, 475, 509, 511, 515, 516
Jursa 713, 718, 722, 725–28
J/Yarmuth 18, 19, 30, 526

Kalimi 38, 51, 52, 330, 674, 691, 695, 709, 711
Kallai 22, 23, 30, 32, 238, 245, 248, 603, 617
Kamlah 174, 183, 185, 462, 478, 636, 709, 740
Kaniewski 539, 546
Kaplan 144, 151, 154, 159, 173
Karageorghis 174
Karak 167, 171, 173, 621, 622, 627, 631, 633, 635
Karasik 103, 110, 111, 116, 598, 749, 752
Karnak 42, 538, 621, 660, 662, 663, 669, 679, 688, 692
Kassite 295
Keel 55, 59, 61, 65, 76, 81, 300, 303, 434, 441, 443, 447, 451, 455, 458, 461, 462, 547, 612, 616, 664, 673, 703–5, 708, 709
Keisan, Tell 38, 705, 707, 712
Kemosh 45, 588, 623, 625, 627, 632, 633
Kempinski 26, 32, 82, 96, 140, 141, 153–55, 535, 540, 547
kenite(s) 15, 16, 18–20, 24–28, 30, 32, 230, 249
Kenyon 9, 10, 66, 162, 163, 165, 169, 172, 173, 203, 204, 527, 535, 761
Kersel 275, 742, 745, 752
Khorsabad 161, 173, 463, 526, 665, 667, 687
Kilamuwa 597
Killebrew 38, 51, 64, 85, 91, 94–96, 116, 153, 527, 535, 543, 547, 564, 635, 637, 754
kin 125, 133, 134, 138, 204, 213, 217, 232, 244, 245, 259, 293, 294, 301, 302, 429, 431, 513, 516–18, 540

Kinrot 183, 187, 576, 577
kinship 103, 107, 134, 137, 191, 203, 209–19, 221–23, 237, 239, 247, 271, 303, 425, 533, 539, 619, 623, 641
Kisilevitz 439, 462, 470, 478, 532, 536, 550, 563
Kitchener 23, 31, 760, 774
Kleiman 79, 81, 110, 116, 159, 170, 171, 173, 176, 183, 186, 575–77, 580, 581, 739, 740
Kletter 23, 32, 88, 94–96, 116, 161, 173, 176, 186, 259, 261, 507, 518, 614, 617, 691, 707, 709
Klingbeil 17, 32, 81, 248, 481, 492, 493
Knapp 240, 248, 390, 401, 569, 580
Knauf 65, 168, 172, 176, 186, 463, 641, 642, 646, 656
Koch 176, 186, 192, 246–49, 357, 361, 438, 455, 457, 458, 462, 614, 693, 694, 696–98, 700–704, 706–10, 712
Kochavi 22–24, 32, 215, 221, 764
Kramer 107, 114, 116, 131–33, 141, 764, 775
Kreimerman 27, 32, 81, 175–80, 182, 184–86, 188, 242, 248, 556, 562
Kush 260, 667–69, 671, 674, 675, 677, 679, 681–83, 686, 687, 689–91

Laato 36, 40–42, 44, 46, 48, 51
LaBianca 224, 226–28, 230–35, 601, 616–18
labor 118, 125, 136, 144, 170, 209, 241, 243, 244, 264, 265, 268, 270, 271, 273, 282, 288, 294, 306, 385, 393, 399, 423, 425, 430, 435, 624, 693, 695, 714, 716
Lahav 140, 184, 185, 303
Lahun 621–23, 631, 632
Laish 327, 574
Lambdin 542, 547
Lamon 157–59, 161, 169, 170, 173, 176, 186, 684, 691
Layard 589, 590, 598, 680, 681, 688, 691
Lebanon 4, 34, 150, 164, 167, 259, 574, 576, 584, 587, 592, 686, 689, 721, 726, 773
Lebo-Hamath 3, 325
Lederman 48, 51, 56, 65, 181, 184, 189, 204, 346, 553, 561
Lehmann 38, 51, 96, 104, 116, 119, 132, 134, 191, 192, 205, 209–12, 214, 216–18, 220, 222, 338, 343, 346, 564, 737
Lehner 247, 248
Lemaire 20, 32, 44, 45, 50, 51, 66, 141, 247, 248, 262, 336, 337, 339, 343, 346, 366, 383, 389, 392, 402, 631, 646, 652, 656, 714, 722, 726, 727
Lemche 69, 81, 84, 97, 210, 212–14, 216, 222, 528, 536, 557, 563, 770, 775
Leonard-Fleckman 559, 563
Lernau 66, 266, 275, 276, 391, 402, 674, 733, 734, 737
Leuchter 362, 383

Levenson 270, 275, 403, 513, 514, 518
Levin 23, 29, 32, 38, 48–50, 52, 345, 382, 534, 535, 563, 657, 699, 701, 706, 708–11, 727, 737
Levine 301, 303, 628, 629, 637
Levinsohn 773, 775
Levinson 309, 316
Levi-Strauss 464
Levite(s) 342, 493, 542, 543
Lev-Tov 96, 264, 275, 532, 536, 556, 562, 734, 736–38, 774
Levy 10, 47, 50–52, 64, 72, 73, 80–82, 221, 223, 233, 261, 403, 537, 546, 547, 599, 601, 616–18, 642, 645, 651, 655–57, 673, 737, 741–46, 748, 750, 752–54, 773, 775
Lewis 76, 82, 155, 180, 186, 271, 275, 427, 428, 432, 459, 460, 462, 517, 519, 636, 759, 767, 774
Libation(s) 299, 472
liberation 35, 45, 231, 314
Libnah 27
library/ies 55, 403, 526, 531, 547, 580, 739, 747, 748, 753, 755
Libya 691
Libyan 659–62, 667, 670, 672–74, 677, 690, 691
Lion(s) 267, 439, 444–46, 452, 455, 457, 460, 533, 638, 660
Lipiński 566, 580, 586, 598, 642, 646, 656, 667, 672, 673
Lipschits 74, 82, 164, 166, 169, 171–73, 176, 182, 185, 186, 230, 233, 245–49, 357, 361, 439, 462, 470, 478, 550, 561, 563, 630, 635, 636, 695, 702, 704, 707, 710, 711, 727
Lipschitz 402, 547
literacy 43, 243, 245, 249, 335, 337, 339–50, 352, 355, 360–62, 365, 378, 380–83, 399, 402, 403, 563, 732
liturgy 183, 185, 410, 723, 728
Liverani 528, 536, 695, 698, 710, 723, 727
lmlk 107, 109–11, 113, 137, 242, 245–47, 249, 253, 259, 457, 458, 542, 702
López-Ruiz 582, 583, 590, 594, 598, 599
Lundberg 347, 383, 431, 432
Luwian 557, 562, 566, 567, 571, 579

Macdonald 95, 97, 173, 175, 177, 184, 241, 249, 266, 275, 356, 360, 361, 426, 432, 600, 614, 617, 618, 639, 656
Macginnis 696, 709, 710
Machinist 39, 51, 501, 504
Malamat 182, 187
Malena 363, 365, 378–81, 383
Mandell 143, 155, 348, 350, 352–56, 358, 360–62, 365, 383, 397, 399, 401, 403, 430, 432
Manetho 36, 562, 678–82, 684, 686, 688, 689, 692
Marduk 35, 458, 717, 725
Mareshah 16, 27, 29, 501, 664

Marfoe 216, 222, 575, 576, 578, 580
Mari 184, 188, 300, 302, 524, 525, 528, 529, 531, 534, 535, 664
Marx 212, 222, 226, 227, 234, 347, 757, 775
maryannu 542
masonry 121, 149, 158, 159, 174, 559, 598
mazzoni 531, 536, 571, 572, 578–80, 672
Mccarter 16, 23–25, 32, 48, 51, 52, 243, 250, 337, 346, 382, 636
Mcgeough 532, 536
Mckinny 15, 16, 18, 20–24, 26, 28–30, 32, 39, 51, 154, 245, 246, 249, 262, 432, 747, 753, 760
Mcnutt 210, 214, 219, 222
meals 264, 268, 271, 273, 283, 299, 422–27, 429, 444, 469, 485, 493, 653, 700
melammu 186, 726
Melqart 585, 586, 588
Meluḫḫa 667, 687
Melville 320, 330
mercenary/ies 246, 330, 538, 540, 564, 605, 661–62, 670, 671
merchant(s) 92, 329, 385, 392, 540, 582, 662, 670, 700, 716, 718, 719, 722, 726
metallurgy 81, 442, 541, 595, 642
metaphor(s) 136, 213, 380, 457, 461, 623
Michalowski 34, 51, 178, 182, 187, 188
migration(s) 38, 53, 102, 109, 185, 189, 191, 216, 229, 244, 543, 546, 547, 549, 563, 564, 641, 702, 732, 738, 739, 761
Milcom 606, 609, 611
Milevski 563, 657
Millard 337, 341, 346, 378, 383, 387, 402, 646, 649, 656
millenarism 757, 758, 772
mines 43, 73, 256, 595, 642, 655
mishpaha/ot 210–15, 217, 218
Mitanni 36, 524
Mizpah 221, 252, 261, 563, 720
mizrāq 272, 274
Moabite(s) 93, 171, 224, 233, 326, 339, 346, 347, 378, 382, 384, 388–90, 392, 402, 470, 473, 478, 507, 531, 603, 608–9, 616, 622, 623, 628, 629, 631–33, 635–38, 661
monotheism 475, 476, 513, 757
Monson 203, 205, 222
monumentality 50, 142–44, 146, 152, 153, 155, 183, 355, 361, 362, 401, 403, 467, 703
Moore 63, 65, 95, 97, 115, 302, 345–47, 478
Moran 60, 65, 205, 318, 330, 503, 504
Moreland 63, 65, 567, 570, 580
Moreno 688, 690
Moresheth-gath 29, 33
motza 147, 149, 150, 154, 439, 462, 470, 472–75, 531, 532, 536, 550, 563
Mudaybi 173, 631, 632, 638
Mudayna 622, 625–27, 631, 632

mudbrick 121, 125, 159, 168, 169, 171, 180, 186, 471, 688
Mullins 38, 53, 261, 432, 541, 544, 547, 576, 577, 579, 581
multimodal 349–51, 357, 359, 361
multimodality 348–62
Mumcuoglu 186, 445, 461, 593, 598
Mumford 66, 276, 660, 661, 664, 665, 668, 671, 673, 674
Münger 43, 52, 183, 187, 457, 462, 664, 673
myth(s) 50, 80, 81, 86, 94, 96, 97, 214, 223, 294, 383, 406, 528, 559, 562, 564, 595, 597, 656, 774, 776

Nabataean 633, 647, 651, 655
Nabonidus 511, 631, 632, 636, 651, 655, 721
Nabopolassar 302, 695, 714
Naboth 231, 281, 498
Nadab 42, 483, 484, 492
Najjar 73, 81, 82, 167, 173, 612, 617, 618, 635, 636, 642, 645, 651, 655–57, 737, 752, 753
Nakhai 80, 116, 274, 279–81, 283–86, 288, 289, 422–24, 430–33, 478, 618
Namdar 73, 81, 108, 116, 260, 261, 426, 431, 465, 477, 596, 598, 732, 738
Naṣbeh, Tell en- 128, 147, 150, 218, 221, 251–54, 256, 258–62, 302, 472, 550, 561
Naveh 20, 25, 31, 341, 346, 365, 381, 383, 387, 389, 402
Nebo 625, 628, 629, 633, 636, 751
Nebuchadnezzar 40, 41, 175, 182, 611, 631, 637, 647, 695, 713–16, 719–21, 725, 726
Necho 42, 695
netzer 77, 82, 121, 123, 125, 126, 128, 131, 132, 141
niditch 64, 66, 80, 222, 249, 276, 433, 535
Nigro 49, 184, 581, 587, 598, 772, 775
Nihan 357–59, 362, 493, 516, 518
Nile 61, 538, 660, 670, 672, 674, 675, 690, 694
Nimrod 579, 581, 712, 737, 739
Nimrud 40, 286, 330, 589, 665, 694, 703
Nimshi/ide 392
Nineveh 40, 55, 135, 286, 448, 526, 598, 630, 635, 667, 668, 680, 681, 684, 691, 695, 706, 725, 726, 759
Nippur 714, 715, 719, 722, 726, 727, 772
Nissinen 322, 330, 342, 346, 536, 708
Nitschke 584, 598
nomad(s) 28, 49, 92, 187, 215, 221, 234, 238, 249, 318, 642, 726
nomadic 17, 20, 21, 26, 43, 44, 49, 64, 128, 175, 210, 215, 216, 222, 227, 233, 234, 238, 239, 244, 247, 545, 622, 641, 642, 645, 661
nomadism 215, 216, 220, 221, 238, 545, 580
Notley 15, 16, 20, 21, 23–25, 29, 30, 33, 230, 231, 234, 503, 504
Novotny 707, 710

Index

Nubia 36, 152, 538, 666–68, 670, 671, 676, 679, 685, 692

Olyan 80, 188, 271, 275, 430, 432, 433, 510, 511, 518, 535
Omri 35, 42–45, 66, 155, 275, 276, 402, 509, 655, 694, 737
Omride 43, 70, 153, 154, 162, 163, 391, 518, 531, 624, 626, 628, 636
Ophel 60, 65, 66, 73, 92, 155, 173, 249, 337, 339, 501, 504, 562
orthostat(s) 164, 167–69, 171, 172, 627
Ortiz 387, 402, 697, 711
Osborne 143, 152, 155, 385, 402
Osorkon 664, 665, 672, 684, 687
ostraca/ostracon 17–20, 31, 91, 95, 150, 244–47, 249, 266, 275, 276, 280, 284, 340, 342, 344, 377, 393, 394, 399, 612, 616, 649, 653, 657, 668, 721, 727, 737
ottoman 28, 80, 230, 528, 535, 619, 756–62, 767, 771–73, 775, 776
oven(s) 121, 124, 126, 131, 132, 137, 138, 163, 191, 192, 282, 283, 289, 424

paleography 254, 340, 363, 380, 394, 616
paleo-hebrew 335, 346, 428
paleolithic 95
paleomagnetic 740
Panitz-cohen 29, 33, 38, 53, 101, 102, 104, 106–12, 114–18, 177, 187, 267, 274, 275, 345, 462, 478, 504, 539–41, 545, 547, 552, 564, 576, 577, 579, 581
Pardee 343, 346, 387, 402, 507, 518, 533, 536, 721, 727
Parker 76, 82, 140, 171, 291, 296, 298, 302, 303, 365, 366, 369–72, 375, 380, 381, 383, 391, 402, 536, 561, 754
Parpola 172, 499, 504
passover 146, 150, 269, 270, 274, 275, 299–301, 303, 326, 465
pastoral 61, 194, 216, 238, 258–60, 263, 270, 272, 545, 578, 615
pastoralism 222, 234, 263, 528, 529, 534, 536, 545, 576, 619, 627
pastoralist(s) 92, 112, 136, 268, 270, 528, 529, 622
patriarchs 39, 48, 68, 69, 71, 79, 220, 241, 316, 528, 533
patrimonial 33, 87, 210, 214, 223, 237, 241, 242, 244, 247, 250–52, 623
patrimonialism 66, 141, 143, 154, 155, 205, 223, 238, 247–49, 637
Pauketat 143, 151, 155, 179, 187
Pearce 713–18, 720, 722, 724, 726–28
Pentateuch 48, 309, 315, 316, 362, 383, 404, 405, 407, 414, 416–18, 493, 496, 562
Petra 647, 649–51, 655–57

Petrie 683, 691
petrography 103, 117, 732
Petter 230, 234, 247, 249, 630, 635, 637
phoenicia 32, 43, 95, 96, 116, 117, 256, 259, 260, 272, 391, 582–84, 586–88, 590–94, 596–99, 659, 664, 667, 668, 673, 710
photogrammetry 745, 748, 749, 751, 753, 755
Piasetzky 50, 79, 81, 178, 184, 401, 403, 504, 642, 656, 737
Pioske 47, 52, 54–56, 58, 60–64, 66, 92, 97, 237, 378, 379, 382, 477, 568
Pratico 203, 204, 215, 220, 649, 656, 657
Pritchard 101, 118, 587, 598
Propp 47, 51, 72, 82, 184, 357, 362, 537, 546, 547
Proverbs 282, 315, 404, 417, 431, 526
Psalm(s) 81, 266, 272, 308, 404–8, 410–12, 417, 418, 482, 492, 508, 513, 515, 629
Psammetichus 695, 697
Puech 339, 341, 346, 606, 618
Punic 583, 586, 599

Qarqar 40, 608, 664, 694
Qasile, Tell 39, 73, 87, 95, 104, 128, 148, 475, 556, 563, 660
Qeiyafa 10, 31, 32, 48, 51, 96, 115, 147, 148, 153, 154, 185, 218, 221, 242, 248, 249, 337, 345, 346, 378, 386–89, 401, 402, 441, 445, 471–74, 550, 556, 562
Queen(s) 272, 273, 275, 281, 283, 301, 318, 324, 391, 401, 661, 672, 679, 686
Qumran 403, 616, 737

Rabba(h) 25, 275, 605, 621, 633
Rabbath-ammon 229, 602
Rabbinic 39, 272, 347, 362, 403, 547
radiocarbon 10, 31, 37, 39, 44, 49–52, 81, 92, 103, 118, 261, 275, 382, 401–3, 538, 597, 598, 617, 636, 642, 656, 673, 732, 737–40
Radner 38, 50, 52, 531, 536, 696, 698, 699, 704, 708–11
Rainey 9, 15, 16, 20, 21, 23–25, 27, 29, 31, 33, 63, 66, 230, 231, 234, 240, 247, 249, 383, 503, 504, 524, 536
Rame(s)ses 50, 51, 330, 561, 659, 660, 672
Ramesside 39, 60, 292, 330, 538, 546, 670, 672, 674
redaction 2, 306, 307, 309, 408, 409, 413–15, 417, 478, 565, 652
Redford 318, 319, 330, 534, 536, 621, 637, 672, 674, 677, 686, 687, 691
redistribution 241, 243, 650, 669, 703, 736
refugee(s) 188, 396, 400, 544, 546, 554, 583, 662, 671, 695, 711, 758, 773, 775
Reich 82, 121, 123, 140, 141, 144, 145, 154, 155, 218, 266, 275, 391, 402, 535, 536, 547, 697, 711, 738

remembering 535, 580
remembrance 146, 152, 361, 536
Rendsburg 362, 397, 402, 403
Renfrew 75, 82, 102, 117, 189, 204, 205, 467, 478, 767, 773, 775
resettlement 55, 192, 220, 310, 544, 575, 708, 711, 714, 721
resistance 50, 80, 96, 180, 204, 220, 226, 229, 390, 502, 504, 538, 542–46, 697, 698, 706, 708, 711, 713
revolt(s) 24, 246, 386, 623, 624, 629, 630, 694, 695, 704, 708, 711, 727
Richard 65, 66, 97, 155, 172, 221, 232, 303, 304, 382, 402, 431, 535, 536, 546, 597, 616, 618, 691, 751, 752
Richards 76, 82, 724, 726
Richardson 52, 276, 330, 674, 691, 695, 706, 709, 711, 750, 754
Richelle 48, 52, 63, 66, 249, 335–40, 342, 344, 346, 378, 383
Richey 348, 362, 365, 378, 380, 381, 383
Ricoeur 56, 58, 63, 66
Roberts 65, 213, 217, 222, 345, 581
Robinson 17, 20, 23, 24, 33, 656, 760, 775
Rollston 48, 52, 60, 66, 243, 245, 248, 249, 336, 337, 339–41, 344, 346–48, 362, 365, 366, 371, 375–83, 387, 391, 398, 399, 402, 541, 547, 636, 650, 657
Rosellini 679–81, 688, 692
Rosen 221, 274, 426, 431, 465, 477, 739
Rosenberg 259, 261
rosette(s) 186, 248, 357, 361, 704, 706, 707
Roth 250, 292, 295, 303, 531, 536
Rothenberg 82
Rothschild 759

sabbath 87, 314, 315
Sader 114, 117, 183, 185, 565, 581, 583, 584, 587, 598
es-safi, Tell/Gath 23, 32, 39, 44, 48, 186, 472, 477, 550–58, 560, 561, 563
Safut, Tell 601, 608, 611, 612, 616, 618
Sagan 224, 234
Saggs 180, 188, 322, 330
Sahlins 210, 212, 223, 227, 234
Sam'al 401, 507
Samaritan(s) 48, 94, 164, 173, 335, 710, 772
Sanders 49, 336, 347, 348, 362, 378–80, 383, 385, 389–91, 402, 404, 406, 417, 418, 540, 546, 720, 723, 726
Sandhaus 182, 188
Sapir-Hen 73, 80, 82, 95, 97, 259, 262, 702, 710, 711, 731–40
Sapirstein 748, 749, 754
Saqqara 681, 682, 684, 688, 690
Sardinia 589, 595
Sarepta/Zarephat 582, 587

Sargon 37, 40, 52, 176, 321, 322, 448, 630, 646, 665, 667, 675, 677, 684, 690, 691, 694–97, 699, 701, 708–11
Sass 336, 337, 339, 340, 345, 347, 365, 371, 380, 382, 383, 389, 391, 393, 395, 396, 400, 402, 563, 617, 659, 674
Sasson 66, 251, 259, 262–64, 268, 275, 734, 736, 740
Sauer 65, 607, 615, 618, 630, 637
scales 569, 570, 607, 673, 744, 746
scarab 26, 49, 245, 366, 455–57, 545, 579, 611, 612, 614, 662, 667, 668, 672, 683
Schade 402, 470, 478
Schäfer-Lichtenberg 223
Schiffer 104, 105, 111, 115, 117, 118, 142, 155, 175, 186, 188
Schiffman 117
Schipper 631, 635, 637, 662, 665, 671, 672, 674
Schloen 63, 66, 126, 128, 131–33, 135–37, 140, 141, 143, 153, 155, 184, 192, 205, 217–19, 223, 237, 239, 241, 242, 245, 247, 249, 545, 623, 637, 698, 711, 747, 754
Schmid 405, 418, 655, 753
Schmidt 48, 50, 81, 271, 276, 346, 383, 513, 517, 519
Schmitt 80, 183, 185, 219, 422, 423, 429–34, 437, 461, 462, 466, 477
Schmitz 671, 674
Schneider 47, 51, 72, 82, 301, 303, 537, 546, 547, 670, 673, 674
Schniedewind 2, 10, 245, 249, 337, 338, 341, 344, 347, 348, 353, 355, 362, 386, 387, 389–94, 396, 397, 400, 402, 403, 417, 418, 538, 541, 547, 723, 727
Schreiber 592, 598
Schroer 434, 451, 461, 462
Schulman 318, 330
Schumacher 156, 158, 174, 593
Schwartz 80, 389, 403, 418, 636, 637
Schwengel 187
Scott 302, 547, 565, 566, 568, 570, 572, 574, 576, 578–80
Scurlock 295, 303, 517, 519
Scythians 323
Segal 361, 391, 402, 740
Segev 179, 182, 186
segmentary 227, 233, 234, 236, 260, 641
Seleucid(s) 35, 36, 48, 52
Sennacherib 37, 51, 52, 175, 176, 289, 330, 448, 608, 630, 646, 647, 667, 674, 675, 678, 681–83, 685, 686, 691, 692, 694, 709, 711
Septuagint 33, 36, 48, 410, 606, 628
Sergi 44, 49, 61, 66, 95, 97, 186, 187, 246, 247, 249, 363, 383, 577, 580, 581
Shalmaneser 2, 37, 40, 176, 286, 498, 526, 534, 567, 581, 608, 664, 665, 694, 701, 708
Shanahan 381, 382

Shanks 81, 96, 744, 754, 768
Shasu 72, 318, 319, 641, 642, 668
Shebna 284, 398–400, 508
Shechem 25, 60, 61, 132, 146, 151, 152, 155, 164, 185, 196, 202, 206, 215, 217, 218, 220, 232, 240, 423, 457, 475, 700, 760
Sheehan 747, 754
shekel 87, 88, 257, 720
Shephelah 15, 20, 23, 30, 31, 33, 38, 39, 96, 145, 184, 195, 218, 222, 246, 259–61, 336, 337, 342, 457, 550, 553, 556, 558, 561, 664
Sherden 538, 542
Sherlock 346, 690
Sherratt 106, 109, 117
Sherwood 285, 289, 290
Sheshonq 659, 662–64, 670, 672
Shiloh 55, 59, 61, 64–66, 73, 77, 82, 89, 128, 136, 141, 144, 159, 161, 163, 165, 166, 170, 171, 174, 469, 478, 497, 593, 598, 738, 769, 776
Shipton 157–59, 161, 169, 170, 173, 176, 186, 684, 691
Shryock 226, 227, 234
Shukron 266, 275, 391, 402
Siamun 661, 662, 673
Sidon 229, 324, 507, 524, 525, 534, 577, 582, 585, 587, 590, 592, 593, 596, 665, 668
siege 38, 42, 184–86, 188, 231, 299, 328, 500, 545, 589, 604, 606, 692, 714
Sihon 47, 326, 526, 628
Silberman 6, 11, 65, 70, 72, 75, 78, 79, 81, 394, 396, 401, 560, 564
Siloam 339, 340, 396–99, 402
Silverman 717, 727
Silwan 147, 149, 150, 284, 508, 770
Sinai 39, 307, 309, 312, 313, 315, 316, 324, 340, 347, 393, 452, 474, 531, 546, 642, 667, 675, 691, 694, 772, 773
Singer-avitz 6, 10, 21, 26, 32, 185, 259, 262, 552, 562, 642, 647, 653, 656, 657, 662, 673
Sinopoli 101, 105, 117, 702, 711
Sinuhe 658
Siphmoth 16, 18, 19, 22, 28, 29, 32
Sippar 161, 718, 719, 723, 724, 726
Sisera 264, 281
slave(s) 61, 82, 92, 93, 134, 227, 270, 296, 306, 307, 309, 316, 322, 615, 661, 692, 720, 725, 739
Smilansky 103, 111, 116, 598, 749, 752
Smoak 143, 155, 299, 348, 352, 361, 362, 365, 383, 397, 399, 401, 403, 421, 422, 424, 426, 428–30, 432, 433, 442, 466, 509, 519, 534
Snodgrass 218, 223, 568, 569, 571, 581
Sobotkova 746, 747, 754
Socoh 245, 246, 259
Söderström 303
Sodom 525, 628

Sommer 225, 234, 409, 418, 503, 504, 739
sovereignty 231, 237, 314, 389, 391, 402, 495, 633, 650, 758, 771
Spalinger 51, 538, 542, 547, 686, 691, 692
Sparks 84, 89, 94, 95, 97, 336, 347, 775
specialization 9, 103, 105, 106, 108, 110, 114, 115, 190, 191, 195, 642, 735
sphinx(es) 444, 446, 457, 542, 587
spice(s) 81, 259, 261, 510, 592, 596, 598, 627, 703, 738
Spiciarich 266, 267, 274, 733, 734, 737, 740
Spieckermann 65, 82
spies 146, 319, 323, 325, 326, 330, 573
Stager 39, 52, 81, 94, 97, 121, 123, 126, 128, 129, 132–36, 138, 140, 141, 145, 155, 184, 205, 209, 217, 218, 223, 231, 234, 236, 237, 242–44, 248, 250, 279, 287, 289, 544, 545, 548, 583, 599, 698, 709, 711
statue(s) 38, 229, 282, 358, 434, 445, 448, 506, 587, 588, 601, 605, 664, 668, 679, 688
Stavrakopoulou 271, 276, 421–23, 433, 437, 461, 508, 519
Steadman 76, 82, 262
Steiner 52, 59–61, 66, 116, 260, 262, 547, 627, 635–37
Steitler 73, 82
Stern 117, 164, 174, 179, 182, 188, 534, 564, 583, 587, 599, 654, 657, 721, 727
Stökl 722, 726, 727
Stolper 725–27
Stoltz 76, 82
Sugimoto 577, 581
Sukenik 162, 163, 169, 172, 203, 204
Sumerian 34, 35, 48, 52, 154, 185, 187, 240, 292, 406
Summeily, Kh. 248, 381, 382
Suriano 44, 52, 148, 155, 247, 250, 266, 271, 272, 276, 390, 400, 403, 427, 433, 507, 508, 512, 517, 519
Surplus(es) 105, 240, 245, 259, 702, 703
Susa 717, 718, 720, 722, 726, 728
symbolism 47, 140, 204, 223, 250, 273, 289, 433, 438, 443, 457, 458, 517, 543, 546, 548, 562, 599, 673, 725
symbols 81, 104, 143, 154, 182, 203, 284, 330, 360, 436, 449, 452, 455, 458, 493, 542, 572, 587, 651
synagogue(s) 22, 23, 33, 343
synchronisms 35, 36, 40, 41, 49, 681, 682
Syro-hittite 172, 174, 401, 507
Syro-Palestinian 64, 303, 361, 515, 597, 598, 600, 608, 767
Szanton 59–62, 66, 550, 562, 564

Taanach 38, 197, 441, 442, 445, 447, 472, 760
tabernacle 144, 146, 150, 355–61, 415, 464, 480–84, 543

Index

taboo(s) 80, 734, 737, 739, 740
Tadmor 566, 581, 616
Talmud 49, 345, 382, 526, 534, 563, 772
Tamassos 156, 158, 159, 163–69, 172–74
Tanis 659, 662, 664, 665, 669, 684, 685, 687
Tappy 38, 48, 52, 178, 188, 243, 250, 696, 707, 711
Tavger 30, 148, 155, 469, 475, 478
Tawilan 639, 649, 651, 655, 705
taxation 106, 111, 137, 243, 245, 254, 259, 497, 641, 651
taxes 78, 107, 178, 231, 242, 246, 262, 457, 715
Tayinat 531, 572, 704
Tekoa 23, 281
Teman 345, 362, 402, 454, 459, 461, 462, 649
textile 259, 261, 282, 283, 438, 541, 596, 627, 701, 702
Thareani 22, 33, 176, 178, 188, 653, 657, 696, 697, 711
Thebes 319, 659, 662, 664, 665, 667–69, 685, 691
Thebez 146, 281, 282
Thiele 41, 42, 45, 52
throne 145, 172, 193, 231, 438, 506, 507, 605, 606, 682, 687, 704, 710
Thutmose(s) 319, 494, 503, 538, 621, 622
Tiglath-pileser 37, 40, 448, 525, 567, 573, 581, 608, 630, 646, 651, 665, 675, 694, 697, 698, 701, 703, 707
Timber(s) 121, 123, 125, 324, 659, 660
Timna 43, 49, 73, 80, 82, 87, 381, 735, 739
Timnah 16, 18, 19, 23, 24, 27–29, 187, 564
tirhaqah 667, 679, 682, 683, 685, 686, 689
Tirzah 151, 202, 423, 431, 463
Tithe(s) 107, 243, 244, 247, 262, 271
tophet 300, 588, 589, 599
topography 31, 55, 125, 227, 470, 477, 639
toponyms 16, 17, 23, 27–30, 572, 584, 633, 668, 715, 716
toponymy 28, 616, 657
Torah 289, 305, 306, 312, 315, 316, 342, 415, 418, 496, 509, 723
treaty 321, 379, 586, 681, 704, 708, 773
tribalism 213, 224, 226–28, 230–33, 528, 529, 641
tribute 40, 61, 65, 106, 259, 261, 286, 462, 500, 607, 608, 630, 633, 646, 647, 662, 664, 665, 667–69, 671, 687, 693, 694, 701, 703, 714, 715
Trimm 93, 178, 188, 317–20, 322, 324, 326, 328–30
Tsumura 16, 33
Tufnell 181, 188, 424, 433
Tukulti-ninurta 713
Tyre 74, 229, 321, 324, 338, 412, 475, 534, 582, 583, 585, 586, 589, 590, 592, 594, 596, 668, 669, 675, 677, 710
Tyson 168, 174, 601, 607, 609, 612–14, 618, 637, 695, 702, 703, 711

Uehlinger 300, 303, 316, 434, 436, 438, 440, 442–44, 446–48, 450–52, 454–56, 458, 460, 462, 463, 475, 547, 664, 673, 694, 703, 709, 711
Umayri 128, 140, 601, 606, 615, 617
Ussishkin 38, 52, 79, 82, 114, 159, 161, 170, 172–74, 176, 178, 180, 181, 184, 185, 188, 247, 250, 471, 472, 479, 631, 637, 696, 708, 711
Uza, H. 25, 29, 31, 340, 342, 344, 346, 471, 647, 653, 655, 656
Uziel 43, 50, 51, 59–62, 65, 66, 186, 218, 243, 250, 432, 506, 519, 541, 548, 550, 562, 564, 735, 739, 740
Uzziah 41, 42, 394–96, 510, 559, 607, 608, 652

Vanderhooft 223, 339, 340, 347, 650, 657, 718, 720, 727
vassal(s) 36, 38, 58, 61, 240, 287, 318, 321, 329, 339, 394, 396, 500, 608, 630, 664, 668, 671, 710
Vaughn 64, 153, 246, 247, 250, 431
Vermeule 63, 66
vineyards 22, 227, 250, 265, 266, 269, 272, 430, 433
violence 179, 187, 188, 305, 308, 313, 330, 535, 539, 544, 759, 764
viticulture 192, 529
volute(s) 149, 156–74, 446, 593, 598, 609
votive(s) 168, 170, 357, 361, 362, 449, 513, 597, 699

Wachtel 274
Waerzeggers 35, 53, 715, 722–27
Walton 234, 331, 477, 479, 548
Wampler 253, 262
Wapnish 266, 267, 274, 733, 740, 774
warfare 176, 179, 185–88, 191, 232, 259, 285, 287, 317, 319, 321, 323, 325, 327, 329–31, 539, 540, 675, 691, 757
warlord(s) 43, 53, 155, 218, 229, 382
weapons 227, 323, 331, 427, 442, 662
weaving 129, 132, 137, 138, 191, 282, 283, 424, 442, 536, 613, 627, 702
Weber 237, 250, 580, 622, 627, 638
weights 57, 87, 88, 91, 137, 259, 282, 283, 288, 607, 613, 627, 660, 664, 665, 686, 689
Weiner 116, 141, 187, 731, 737–40
Weinfeld 185, 616
Weingart 40, 41, 48, 53, 210, 223
Weippert 65, 216, 223, 463
Weissbein 183, 188
Weitzman 55, 66, 558, 559, 564
Wellhausen 48, 417, 418
Wenamun 381, 659–61, 669, 670, 673, 674
Wendrich 674, 752
Westbrook 186, 213, 223, 305, 316, 536
Whitelam 84, 97, 619, 638, 770, 776

Wilkinson 192, 205, 680, 692, 710, 712
Williamson 151, 155, 383, 402
Wilson 63, 66, 119, 131, 141, 662, 674, 760
Wimmer 371, 382, 383, 611, 612, 618, 636
wisdom 138, 293, 306, 307, 324, 404, 464, 513, 536, 677
wool 260, 263, 267, 268, 270, 627, 702, 733
Woolley 532, 536

Xenophon 55
Xerxes 722

Ya'ama 284
yad 150
Yah 508
Yaḫānu 572
Yahaṣa 625
Yahdun-lim 531
Yāḫû-azar 721
Yāḫūdu 716, 719, 722
Yāḫû-šar-uṣur 716–18
Yahwism(s) 3, 87, 461, 464–67, 469, 471, 473, 475–77, 479, 516
Yahwist(s) 86, 459, 527, 532
Yāma 716
Yamani 667, 671
Yarkon 664, 696
Yarmûk 18, 19
yarutu 621
Ya'ush 342
Yavneh 107, 437, 472
Yehud 3, 94, 717, 723, 724, 757
Yemen 214, 217, 220, 222, 223, 336, 346, 761
Yeroham 25
yhw (theophoric element) 394, 396
YHW/YHWH 2, 3, 35, 45, 53, 144, 146, 237, 239, 243, 292, 308–11, 313–15, 323–29, 331, 354–57, 359, 402, 403, 461, 466, 474, 476, 483, 485, 495, 497, 498, 500, 508, 509, 513, 516, 535, 563, 704, 706
Yobana 396
Yodefat 734
yogurt 264
Yoqneam 38

young—newborns 588
youth 61, 430, 444, 457, 685, 759, 775
yrḥw 387
ywbnh 396
ywkn 396
yw (theophoric element) 354, 391, 396
yyn 375

Zababa-šar-uṣur 722
Zabdi 22
Zadok 243
Zagros 697
Zair 652
Zeboiim 525
zebu 440
Zechariah 42
Zedekiah 42, 498, 500–502
Zemarites 525
Zephaniah 629
Zephath 26
zeqenim 218
Zerah 664
Zered 619, 629
Zerî 320
zeribar 711
Zerqa 601
ziggurat 713
Ziklag 15, 16
Zilpah 295
Zimri 42
Zimri-lim 300
zinc 507
Zincirli-Sam'al 169, 401, 518, 571, 669, 709
Zionism 84, 756–59, 772, 774
Zion (Jerusalem) 62, 63, 457, 474, 758
Zion (Jewish homeland) 771
Ziph (Tell Zîf) 16, 18, 19, 23, 24, 27, 28, 245, 246, 259, 327, 328
Ziqlâb 754
Zoar 628
Zoara 652
zooarchaeology 731–33, 736–40
zoomorphic 423, 424, 472, 475
Zorah 469

For Product Safety Concerns and Information please contact our EU representative GPSR@taylorandfrancis.com Taylor & Francis Verlag GmbH, Kaufingerstraße 24, 80331 München, Germany

Printed and bound by CPI Group (UK) Ltd, Croydon, CR0 4YY
20/05/2025
01877228-0001